THE SLA
LANGUAGES

Routledge Language Family Descriptions

In this series:

The Celtic Languages
Edited by Martin Ball

The Dravidian Languages
Edited by Sanford B. Steever

The Germanic Languages
Edited by Ekkehard König and Johan Van Der Auwera

The Indo-European Languages
Edited by Paolo Ramat and Anna Giacalone Ramat

The Romance Languages
Edited by Martin Harris and Nigel Vincent

The Semitic Languages
Edited by Robert Hetzron

The Slavonic Languages
Edited by Bernard Comrie and Greville G. Corbett

The Turkic Languages
Edited by Lars Johanson and Éva Ágnes Csató

The Uralic Languages
Edited by Daniel Abondolo

Also available in paperback:

The Germanic Languages
Edited by Ekkehard König and Johan Van Der Auwera

The Celtic Languages
Edited by Martin Ball

The Slavonic Languages
Edited by Bernard Comrie and Greville G. Corbett

THE SLAVONIC LANGUAGES

EDITED BY
Bernard Comrie
and
Greville G. Corbett

Routledge
Taylor & Francis Group

LONDON AND NEW YORK

First published in 1993
by Routledge
2 Park Square, Milton Park, Abingdon, Oxon, OX14 4RN

Simultaneously published in the USA and Canada
by Routledge
a division of Routledge, Chapman and Hall, Inc.
270 Madison Ave, New York, NY 10016

Reprinted 2001, 2006

First published in paperback 2002

Transferred to Digital Printing 2008

Routledge is an imprint of the Taylor & Francis Group, an informa business

Selection and editorial matter © 1993, 2002 Bernard Comrie and Greville G. Corbett

British Library Cataloguing in Publication Data

A catalogue record for this book is available from the British Library.

Library of Congress Cataloging in Publication Data

A catalog record for this book is available on request.

ISBN 10: 0-415-04755-2 (Hbk)
ISBN 10: 0-415-28078-8 (Pbk)
ISBN 13: 978-0-415-04755-5 (Hbk)
ISBN 13: 978-0-415-28078-5 (Pbk)

Contents

WEST SLAVONIC LANGUAGES

EAST SLAVONIC LANGUAGES

Acknowledgements

We wish to thank Veronica Du Feu for her invaluable assistance in the early stages of preparation of this volume. The Max-Planck-Institut für Psycholinguistik provided support to Bernard Comrie in the summer of 1990, which made possible an editorial meeting between the two editors that greatly facilitated the writing of chapter 1. We are grateful to the editorial staff at Routledge for their continuing willingness to consult with us on all details of the preparation of this volume; particular thanks are due to Jonathan Price, Shân Millie, Alex Clark, Jenny Potts, Meg Davies and Robert Potts.

Chapter 13, Cassubian: Gerald Stone would like to thank Professor E. Breza and Dr J. Treder, both of the University of Gdańsk, and Professor H. Popowska-Taborska, of the Polish Academy of Sciences, for their valuable comments on a draft of this chapter. The important contribution of many other colleagues is recorded at the end of the relevant chapters.

Abbreviations

ABL	ablative
ACC	accusative
ACT	active
AN	animate
AOR	aorist
AUX	auxiliary
Bel.	Belorussian
Bg.	Bulgarian
Cass.	Cassubian
COLL	collective
COND	conditional
Cz.	Czech
DAT	dative
DEF	definite
DET	determinate
DIMIN	diminutive
DISTR	distributive
DU	dual
EMPH	emphatic
EPSl.	Early Proto-Slavonic
F	feminine
FREQ	frequentative
FUT	future
GEN	genitive
GER	gerund

HON	honorific
HUM	human
IMP	imperative
IMPF	imperfect
IMPFV	imperfective
INAN	inanimate
IND(EF)	indefinite
INDET	indeterminate
INF	infinitive
INST	instrumental
INT	interrogative, question
INTNS	intensifier
IPA	International Phonetic Association
ITR	intransitive
LOC	locative
LPIE	Late Proto-Indo-European
LPSl.	Late Proto-Slavonic
LSo.	Lower Sorbian
M	masculine
Mac.	Macedonian
N	neuter
NEG	negative
NOM	nominative
O(BJ)	object (personal verb affix)
OCS	Old Church Slavonic
OPT	optative
PART	participle
PASS	passive
PAST	past
PERS	personal
PIE	Proto-Indo-European
PL	plural
Po.	Polish
Polab.	Polabian
PRF	perfect
PRFV	perfective
PRS	present
PRT	preterite

PSl.	Proto-Slavonic
PTL	particle
PTT	partitive
REFL	reflexive
REL	relative
RSLT	resultative
Ru.	Russian
S(BJ)	subject
SCr.	Serbo-Croat
SG	singular
Slk	Slovak
Sln.	Slovene
Slovinc.	Slovincian
SUP	superlative
TR	transitive
Ukr.	Ukrainian
USo.	Upper Sorbian
VOC	vocative
1	first person
2	second person
3	third person

Note on symbols

Ø   zero (see chapter 1, section 2.1)

*   in historical linguistics, the sign for a reconstructed (not attested) form; in descriptive linguistics, the sign for an unacceptable form

ˈ   indication of the stressed vowel

Transliteration from Cyrillic

Language	Letter	Transliteration
	а	a
	б	b
	в	v
Bg. Mac. Ru. SCr.	г	g
Bel. Ukr.	г	h
Ukr.	ґ	g
	д	d
SCr.	ђ	đ
Mac.	ѓ	ǵ
	е	e
Bel. Ru.	ё	ë
Ukr.	є	je
	ж	ž
Mac.	ѕ	dz
	з	z
Bg. Mac. Ru. SCr.	и	i
Ukr.	и	y
Bel. Ukr.	і	i
Ukr.	ї	ji
Mac. SCr.	ј	j
Bel. Bg. Ru. Ukr.	й	j
	к	k
	л	l
Mac. SCr.	љ	lj
	м	m
	н	n
Mac. SCr.	њ	nj
	о	o
	п	p
	р	r

	с	s
	т	t
SCr.	ħ	ć
Mac.	ќ	ḱ
	у	u
Bel.	ў	ŭ
	ф	f
Bel. Bg. Ru. Ukr.	х	x
Mac. SCr.	х	h
	ц	c
	ч	č
Mac. SCr.	џ	dž
	ш	š
Ru. Ukr.	щ	šč
Bg.	щ	št
Ru.	ъ	"
Bg.	ъ	ă
Bel. Ru.	ы	y
Bel. Bg. Ru. Ukr.	ь	'
Bel. Ru.	э	è
Bel. Bg. Ru. Ukr.	ю	ju
Bel. Bg. Ru. Ukr.	я	ja

Notes:

1 When the language column is blank, the Cyrillic character is found in the alphabets of all the languages in question – those of Belorussian (Bel.), Bulgarian (Bg.), Macedonian (Mac.), Russian (Ru.), Serbo-Croat (SCr.) and Ukrainian (Ukr.).

2 For languages which normally use the Cyrillic script, examples in the text are given in that script, followed by an oblique stroke and then the transliteration into the Latin script, according to the table above. Examples from languages for which the Latin script is generally used, are given in that script (and languages without a standard orthography, such as Polabian, are given in transcription). Serbo-Croat uses both scripts (see chapter 2, part A, sections 3.2, 4.2.3 and 9, and chapter 7, sections 1 and 2.1); examples are given in Latin script, followed by an oblique, followed by the corresponding Cyrillic form. For the transliteration of Old Church Slavonic, from Glagolitic and from Cyrillic, see chapter 2, table 2.2.

1 Introduction

Bernard Comrie and Greville G. Corbett

The Slavonic languages (usually called the Slavic languages in the United States) are the major languages spoken over most of eastern and much of central Europe, as indicated in map 1.1 on page 2. The Slavonic language with the greatest number of speakers, Russian, has spread, as a result of gradual expansion, from its original heartland in eastern Europe across most of northern Asia to the Pacific coast. The parts of eastern and central Europe where Slavonic languages are spoken are areas of great current political interest, with the emergence of new experiments in democracy, economic organization and artistic expression in societies whose recent history has been primarily one of tight centralized control.

The Slavonic languages form a genetic unit, that is they are all descendants of a single ancestor language, conventionally called Proto-Slavonic, whose characteristics can be reconstructed by comparing the various attested Slavonic languages. Going further, the Slavonic languages in turn form a branch of the Indo-European family, the family of languages that covers most of Europe and large parts of south-western Asia and South Asia and which includes English: the ultimate genetic relatedness of English and Russian, while perhaps not apparent at first glance, can still be seen in such similar items as Russian три/tri, English *three*, Russian сын/syn, English *son*, Russian свинья/svin'já 'pig', English *swine*.

1 The structure and scope of the book

In this book, a separate chapter is devoted to each of the following languages: Bulgarian, Macedonian, Serbo-Croat, Slovene, Czech, Slovak, Upper and Lower Sorbian (one chapter devoted to these two closely related languages), Polish, Russian, Belorussian, Ukrainian. For the present geographical location of these languages, reference should be made to map 1.1. These are the generally recognized contemporary standard literary Slavonic languages, each of which is either the (at least *de facto*) official language of an independent country or countries (Belorussian, Bulgarian, Czech, Macedonian, Polish, Russian, Serbo-Croat, Slovak,

Map 1.1   Approximate present-day distribution of Slavonic languages in Europe

Source: Adapted from Jakobson, 1955

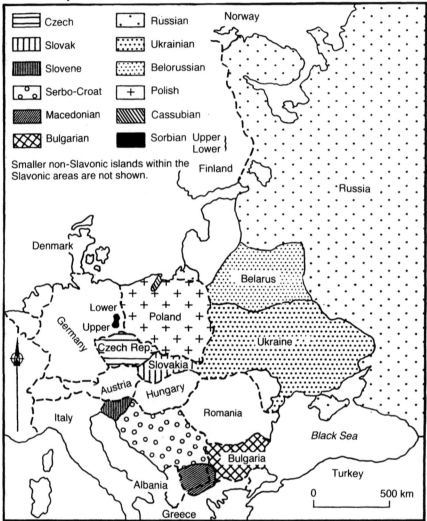

More detail can be found on the maps in the individual chapters; this is particularly relevant for the area of the former Yugoslavia.

Slovene, Ukrainian) or is used locally for some official purposes (Upper Sorbian, Lower Sorbian) – this reflects the political situation in early 1993. Although the official status of Cassubian is as a dialect of Polish rather than as a separate language, the distinctiveness of this variety in comparison to the bulk of Polish dialects has led us, following the practice of many other

Slavists, to treat it as a separate language. In addition, two extinct languages have been included: Old Church Slavonic, as the language of the oldest attested writings in a Slavonic language, of great importance for our understanding of the early history of Slavonic languages, and Polabian, which is structurally clearly to be considered a distinct Slavonic language. A further chapter has been devoted to Proto-Slavonic, the reconstructed ancestor of the Slavonic languages, which provides the necessary bridge between the Indo-European family and its Slavonic branch. Finally, two chapters do not deal with individual languages: that on alphabets and transliteration (chapter 2) discusses material particularly important in the case of Slavonic because of the variety of alphabets, orthographic conventions and scientific and non-scientific transliterations of non-Roman alphabets that are current for Slavonic languages, while the chapter on the Slavonic languages in emigration (chapter 18) emphasizes that many Slavonic languages are spoken in lands far beyond the Slavonic heartland in eastern and central Europe and shows the importance of these far-flung communities for socio-linguistic research.

This volume differs from previous surveys of the Slavonic family in several significant respects. First, each chapter is written by an acknowledged specialist in the particular language. The expansion of work in the field means that it is now impossible for an individual to cover the whole family with the necessary level of expertise. Second, the chapters are highly structured, with each author providing detailed information on the same important topics. Thus the reader interested in a specific topic, whether it be verbal aspect, clitics or numerals, can easily find comparable information on each of the Slavonic languages. And the comparison is further facilitated by treating the languages as of equal linguistic interest; the relative standing of the different languages in terms of number of speakers and political importance does not influence the attention accorded to each. Third, within the descriptions syntax is given its due place. Modern linguistics has put syntax in the centre of the stage; this means that much more is known about the syntax of the Slavonic languages than was the case even a few years ago. Fourth, the book is accessible to a wide readership. To assist non-Slavists, all the examples from languages which use the Cyrillic alphabet are given in transliteration (as well as in the Cyrillic form; see Transliteration from Cyrillic and notes there; pages xii–xiii). Terms which are likely to be less widely known are explained. Thus, besides providing an up-to-date survey of current knowledge for Slavists, the volume is also a source of reference for all others with an interest in the Slavonic family; indications of further sources in English and other widely read languages are provided where possible in the bibliographies. Given the major input from Slavists into mainstream linguistics in the past (see section 2) and from linguistics into Slavonic studies, it is natural to seek to maintain this relationship.

As was mentioned above, each of the individual-language chapters is written according to a single general plan. The structure of each chapter is as follows. An introductory section 1 provides a brief account of the current status of the language and of its historical development in social terms (including the development of the literary standard). The section on phonology (section 2) deals with the sounds of the language in question and relations among them, in particular the inventory of phonemes (section 2.1), that is which sounds can be used in the language to distinguish words (in the way that the phonemic opposition between /p/ and /b/ in English enables one to distinguish between *pin* and *bin*); the subsections on morphophonemics (sections 2.2 and 2.3) deal with the ways in which the phonemic shape of an item can change in different morphological forms, as in the way that the English morpheme (minimal grammatical unit) *wife* appears in phonemically different shapes in the words *wife* /waif/ and *wives* /waivz/, that is, /waif/ versus /waiv/. The section on morphology (section 3) deals with the details of how morphemes are combined into words, such as how the English morphemes *pen* and *-s* (the plural suffix) combine to give *pens* or, to take a more complex example, how the morpheme *sing* combines with the morpheme for past tense to give the word *sang*. Morphology can be further divided into inflectional morphology (sections 3.1 and 3.2), which deals with relations among different forms of a single lexical item, such as the relations among *walk*, *walks* and *walked* as different forms of the lexical item WALK in English, and derivational morphology (section 3.3), which deals with the relations among distinct but formally related lexical items, such as among English *observe, observer, observation* and *observational.* Within inflectional morphology, Slavonic languages, like most Indo-European languages, make a clear distinction between nominal morphology (section 3.1) and verbal morphology (section 3.2); linguistic terminology is not entirely standardized in this area, so readers are asked to take particular care in noting the senses in which we use the following terms, especially *nominal* and *noun*: *nominal* is a cover term subsuming nouns (see below), adjectives, pronouns and numerals; *noun* refers to nouns in their narrow sense, the traditional 'name of a person, place or thing'; *adjective, pronoun* and *numeral* are used in their usual senses, as is *verb.* In general, the same paradigm items are given for each language to make comparison easier. Section 4 of each chapter deals with syntax, the various patterns of combining words into phrases and sentences. Section 5 of each chapter deals briefly with the lexis (vocabulary) of that language, including in particular the relative weight of lexical items inherited from Proto-Slavonic (or created using morphemes of Proto-Slavonic origin) and those borrowed from other languages; for comparative purposes, lexical items are given from three well-defined lexical fields that have been important in recent linguistic and anthropological studies of lexis, namely colour terms (following Berlin and Kay 1969), body parts and kinship terms. Finally, section 6 discusses the most salient characteristics of the main dialects of the language.

Our emphasis on the innovative nature of the present volume should not be interpreted as a lack of gratitude towards the pioneering work of our predecessors, which has indeed made this book possible. The scientific study of the Slavonic language family has a history of well over a century, the initial work generally being considered Miklosich (1852–75), a detailed and compendious comparison of the individual Slavonic languages and of Slavonic with other Indo-European languages; the inclusion of a volume on syntax set an example that only too many successors have failed to heed. The next major landmark is Vondrák (1906–8); it is chastening to see how many of the problems that remain at the forefront of Slavonic linguistics are already treated in these early works, such as the positioning of clitic pronouns and the use of different cases after the copula. The intervening years have seen the appearance of the detailed comparative grammar of the Slavonic languages by Vaillant (1950–77), in addition to the first two volumes of the more concise work by Bräuer (1961–). Scholarly (as opposed to pedagogical) introductions to the Slavonic language family are available in various Slavonic languages, such as Бернштейн/Bernštejn (1961) in Russian, Horálek (1962) in Czech, Lehr-Spławiński, Kuraszkiewicz and Sławski (1954) in Polish and Nahtigal (1952) in Slovene (also available in a Russian translation). In Continental Western European languages there is van Wijk (1956) in French, in addition to the German translation of Nahtigal (1952) and most recently Panzer (1991). In English such works range from the concise introduction of Jakobson (1955) via the medium-sized Entwistle and Morison (1949) to the detailed survey of the individual Slavonic languages of De Bray (1951). Finally, important recent contributions to the social and cultural development of the Slavonic languages have appeared in the publications of the Yale Concilium on International and Area Studies: Schenker and Stankiewicz (1980) and Picchio and Goldblatt (1984), and in Stone and Worth (1985).

In many ways the Slavonic languages form a homogeneous group within Indo-European. They are therefore an ideal area for comparative and typological work. A very positive aspect of this research has been the concern to consider data from each of the Slavonic languages, rather than just from the most easily accessible. This concern to give the comprehensive picture was initiated by Rudolf Růžička: see, for example, his account of reflexives (1973).

The perceived strategic importance of Russian from the 1950s on meant that American work on machine translation concentrated on translation from Russian to English, as in the Georgetown GAT system and the well-known SYSTRAN work (Hutchins 1986: 70–8, 209–18). There has also been a good deal of research in the former Soviet Union. While machine translation has had a chequered history, the linking of interest in Slavonic languages with computer technology has had several spin-offs. The Slavonic family is probably uniquely well provided with research tools in the form of morphological dictionaries (whether giving roots and derived forms or concentrating on inflectional information), frequency dictionaries and reverse dictionaries. Russian is particularly well covered, but researchers working on certain other Slavonic languages also have useful grammatical and lexicological reference works at their disposal.

2   Some salient characteristics of Slavonic languages

In this section, we list some of the most important typological character-istics of the Slavonic languages, in particular those that have provided important material for the development of general linguistic theory (sections 2.1–2.4).

In phonology, one of the most distinctive features of Slavonic languages is the presence of a substantial number of palatal and palatalized con-sonants, in many Slavonic languages forming pairs of palatalized (soft) and non-palatalized (hard) consonants; perhaps the extreme case is Russian, where almost every consonant participates in this palatalization opposition. Another characteristic of Slavonic languages is the presence of an extensive set of morphophonemic alternations within inflectional and, especially, derivational morphology, as in the $k:č$ alternation in Russian крик/krik 'shout' versus кричáть/kričát' 'to shout'; see further section 2.1.

All Slavonic languages have a rich morphology, including a rich inflec-tional morphology, and in this respect can be characterized as conservative Indo-European languages. While some languages have lost some of the inflectional categories found in Proto-Slavonic (perhaps most strikingly the near-complete loss of case in Bulgarian and Macedonian), all Slavonic languages retain a rich set of morphological categories; often there are even a few innovations relative to Proto-Slavonic. Typologically, Slavonic morphology is primarily fusional, that is a given affix frequently combines the expression of a number of grammatical categories, for example in Russian столý/stolú 'table' (DAT SG), the inflection -u encodes simul-taneously dative case (compare NOM SG стол/stol) and singular number (compare DAT PL столáм/stolám). Morphologically, verbs and, especially, nouns fall into a number of distinct conjugational/declensional classes, so that while Russian стол/stol 'table' has its dative singular in -u, женá/žená 'wife' has женé/žené with the affix -e, and кость/kost' 'bone' has кóст-и/kóst-i with the affix -i. Most of the morphological categories found in Slavonic languages are those familiar from other Indo-European languages, but one verbal category that is particularly richly developed in Slavonic languages is aspect (section 2.2).

Perhaps the most salient syntactic characteristic of Slavonic languages is their so-called free word order, whereby the order of major constituents is determined not so much by syntactic factors (grammatical relations, such as subject, object) as by pragmatic factors (such as topic, focus; see further section 2.3); this makes it hard to characterize individual Slavonic languages in terms of such typologies as Subject–Verb–Object versus Subject–Object–Verb. This freedom of word order is particularly clear in the case of the major constituents of the clause (such as subject, verb/predicate, direct object, indirect object), while the order within individual constituents tends to be more fixed (though by no means always absolutely so): thus genitives usually follow their head noun, while demonstratives, numerals and adjectives usually precede; all Slavonic languages make extensive use of prepositions, with postpositions having at best marginal status.

Slavonic languages have extensive agreement systems, for instance between adjectives and their noun or between verbs and their subject, and the intersection of agreement with the rich morphology already alluded to gives rise to a number of complications with theoretically interesting resolutions (see further section 2.4). The fact that finite verbs usually encode the person–number of their subject leads to the possibility of omitting unstressed subject pronouns, although the extent to which such omission is favoured differs from language to language: in Serbo-Croat, for instance, it is normal to omit unstressed subject pronouns, while in Russian their inclusion is usual.

Subordination in Slavonic languages in general follows patterns familiar in other European languages, with a strong preference for finite subordinate clauses with clause-initial conjunctions and, in most languages (the exceptions are Bulgarian, Macedonian and the eastern variant of Serbo-Croat), an infinitive used in certain constructions where its understood subject can be retrieved from the syntactic context. The written Slavonic languages also make extensive use of other non-finite constructions, such as participles substituting for relative clauses and gerunds (verbal adverbs) substituting for adverbial clauses, although such non-finite constructions are not characteristic of the spoken languages.

2.1 Morphophonemics (Morphophonology)

One characteristic of all Slavonic languages is a rich set of morphophonemic (morphophonological, morphological) alternations. Indeed, it is perhaps not surprising that much of the fundamental work in morphophonemics, including generative phonology, has been done by linguists who worked largely with Slavonic material: Jan Baudouin de Courtenay, Nikolaj Trubeckoj (Trubetzkoy), Roman Jakobson and Morris Halle; see, for instance, Anderson (1985: 56–139, 318–22), Jakobson (1948) and Halle (1959).

By a morphophonemic alternation we understand a situation where a given morpheme (minimal grammatical unit) has more than one phonemic representation in different words into which that morpheme enters. In English, for instance, the alternation between /ei/ and /ou/ in *break* /breik/ versus *broken* /broukən/ is an instance of morphophonemic alternation involving the two allomorphs (/breik/, /brouk/) of the morpheme *break*.

A few of the morphophonemic alternations found in Slavonic languages continue alternations found in Proto-Indo-European: for instance, the vowel alternation found in Russian теку́/teкú 'I flow' versus ток/tok 'current' is a direct reflex of the Indo-European ablaut alternations that also show up in, for example, English *break* versus *broken*. For the most part, however, the morphophonemic alternations of Slavonic languages represent either Proto-Slavonic innovations or the innovations of individual Slavonic languages, since a propensity for generating new morphophonemic alternations seems to be a characteristic of Slavonic languages.

In the Proto-Slavonic period, for instance, major new morphophonemic alternations arose as the result of the various palatalizations (see further sections 2.9–2.10 of chapter 3). Thus, the alternation that shows up in Russian пеку́/pekú 'I bake' versus печёшь/pečёš´ 'you bake' derives from the first palatalization of k to $č$ before a front vowel (in this case, Proto-Slavonic e). Another set of morphophonemic alternations that arose in the Proto-Slavonic period was that between back and front vowels, depending on whether the preceding consonant was hard (non-palatalized) or soft (palatalized), as the result of a sound change whereby vowels were fronted after soft consonants. Thus the ending of the nominative–vocative–accusative singular of o-stem neuter nouns remained -o after hard consonants, but became -e after soft consonants, as can still be seen in Russian ме́сто/mésto 'place' versus по́ле/póle 'field'.

In the late Proto-Slavonic period, new morphophonemic alternations between a vowel and zero arose; the sign for zero is Ø. These alternations came about through the loss of the reduced vowels (symbolized ъ and ь deriving from Proto-Indo-European u and i, respectively), which are known as *jers*. *Jers* in strong positions developed into full vowels (the actual vowels are different in different Slavonic languages) while those in weak positions were lost, thus producing alternations like Russian рот/rot 'mouth', GEN SG рта/rta (that is, *rot-* alternates with *rØt-*), for Old Russian ръть/гъть, GEN SG ръта/гъта. (See further section 2.25 of chapter 3.) Vowels that alternate with zero in this way are known as 'mobile', 'fugitive' or 'fleeting' vowels.

The phenomenon of akan´e in Russian (see chapter 15, sections 2.2 and 6), whereby unstressed a and o became ʌ or ə in unstressed syllables, provides an example of a language-specific sound change that has given rise to morphophonemic alternations, as can be seen from comparing the

vowels in the different inflectional forms of Russian голова/golová 'head':
NOM SG голова/golová [gəlʌvá], NOM PL го́ловы/gólovy [góləvɨ], GEN
PL голо́в/golóv [gʌlóf], where the shifting stress gives rise to alternations
between *o* on the one hand (under stress) and ʌ or ə on the other (no
stress). Note that we mark stress by ' on the stressed vowel; this symbol is
chosen to avoid confusion with other diacritics.

The existence of morphophonemic alternations led linguists investigating Slavonic languages to posit a level of morphophonemic representation at which a given morpheme would be given a constant
representation; one convention for indicating that a representation is
morphophonemic is to enclose it in braces, that is { }. Thus, the stem of the
Russian word for 'head' would be {golov-}, which would then be related, by
the operation of rules, to more phonetic representations such as those given
above for individual inflectional forms. Because of different morphophonemic behaviour, segments that are phonetically and phonemically
identical may receive different morphophonemic representations. Thus the
vowels of the first syllable of Russian сова/sová [sʌvá] 'owl' and страна/
straná [strʌná] 'country' are phonetically identical, but are differentiated in
other inflectional forms of the words when the first syllable is stressed, as in
nominative plural со́вы/sóvy [sóvɨ], стра́ны/strány [stránɨ], that is, the
morphophonemic representations of these stems would be {sov-} and
{stran-}, respectively. In describing the morphology of Old Church
Slavonic, it is necessary to distinguish morphophonemically between two
kinds of *y*, since {y₁} shows up after soft consonants as *i*, while {y₂} shows up
as ę after soft consonants; compare the following forms of the masculine
o-stem nouns *rabъ* 'slave' and *mǫžь* 'man': INST PL *raby* (morphophonemically {raby₁}), *mǫži*, ACC PL *raby* (morphophonemically {raby₂}),
mǫžę. In this, one can see the origin of abstract levels of phonological
representation in generative phonology. The precise degree of abstractness
that should be allowed in morphophonemic alternations has proved to be
controversial; while probably most linguists would be happy with the
morphophonemic representations proposed in the preceding paragraph,
many would be less happy with Jakobson's attempt to account for the alternation found in Russian examples like жать/žat' 'to press', first person
singular present tense жму/žmu, by positing a morphophonemic representation {žm-} and a rule that drops the nasal and inserts *a* in the infinitive
stem; instead, this latter example would probably be treated most simply as
a morphological irregularity.

Although morphophonemic alternations typically arise as the result of
conditioned sound changes, there is a tendency, well reflected in Slavonic
languages, for the original phonological conditioning to be lost, that is for
morphophonemic alternations to become increasingly morphologized. In
Proto-Slavonic, the difference in endings selected by hard- and soft-stem
nouns was transparently phonological, so that in Old Russian, for instance,

we find the ending for hard stems -ъ in genitive plural рабъ/rabъ 'slave' and the corresponding ending for soft stems -ь in дъждь/dъždь 'rain'. In Modern Russian, however, the relevant forms are рабо́в/rabóv and дожде́й/doždéj, where the suffixes -ov and -ej are morphological, rather than morphophonemic, alternants; the expected correspondent of -ov for soft stems, namely -ev, occurs only with nouns ending in j, for example геро́ев/geróev from геро́й/gerój 'hero'. Finally, in every Slavonic language at least some instances of some inherited morphophonemic alternations have been lost by analogy. In Old Russian, for instance, the dative–locative singular of рука/ruka 'hand' was руцѣ/rucě, with c as a result of the second palatalization; in Modern Russian, however, we have simply NOM SG рука́/ruká, DAT-LOC SG руке́/ruké. In Proto-Slavonic, and still in Old Church Slavonic, the morphophonemic opposition of hard versus soft consonants corresponds exactly to the phonetic opposition of non-palatalized versus palatalized consonants. During the history of several individual Slavonic languages, however, some of these consonants have become phonetically non-palatalized but none the less retain their earlier morphophonemic behaviour. In such languages, the morphophonemic class of soft consonants thus no longer corresponds exactly to the phonetic class of palatalized consonants, as when Russian masculine nouns ending in (synchronically non-palatalized) ž require the genitive plural ending -ej characteristic of soft stems, rather than -ov as with hard stems, as in ежей/ežéj, genitive plural of ёж/ёž 'hedgehog'.

2.2 Aspect

One of the major contributions of Slavonic linguistics to general linguistic theory has been the notion of verbal aspect; indeed the very term 'aspect' in this sense is a direct translation of Russian вид/vid (compare ви́деть/ vídet´ 'to see'). In every Slavonic language, with Russian used here as an illustration, most verbs occur as a pair, one member of the pair being of the imperfective aspect (such as писа́ть/pisát´ 'to write'), the other being of the perfective aspect (such as написа́ть/napisát´). Like tense, aspect is concerned with the general notion of time, but whereas tense is concerned with locating the situation described by the clause in time, relative to other time points (most commonly the present moment), aspect is concerned with the internal temporal structure of situations. The essential content of the perfective/imperfective opposition is that between bounded and unbounded situations, or rather between the presentation of situations as bounded or unbounded, respectively. In a sentence like Ко́ля написа́л (PRFV) письмо́/Kólja napisál (PRFV) pis´mó 'Kolja wrote a letter', Kolja's writing of the letter is presented as a bounded event, that is as an event that is complete – from which we can deduce that Kolja did indeed finish writing the letter. By contrast, Ко́ля писа́л (IMPFV) письмо́/Kólja pisál (IMPFV) pis´mó 'Kolja was writing the letter', makes no explicit reference to the boundedness or completion of the writing; indeed, it is quite possible that Kolja gave up writing the letter before completing it. As this example illustrates, the distinction sometimes corresponds to that between simple and progressive verb forms in English, namely with dynamic verbs referring to a single action, but this is not a general equation. Stative verbs are typically in the simple form in English, for example *the book lay on the table*, whereas in Russian they are typically in the imperfective, since a state is by definition unbounded (to begin or to end a state is an action, not part of the state), whence Russian книга лежала (IMPFV) на столе/kniga ležala (IMPFV) na stolé. In English, habitual situations are usually in the simple form, for example *Kolja wrote a letter every day*, whereas Russian uses the imperfective, since the habit (as opposed to any individual act of letter writing) is not bounded, that is Коля писал (IMPFV) письмо каждый день/Kolja pisàl (IMPFV) pis'mó kàždyj den'.

Aspect is particularly salient in the Slavonic languages because the perfective/imperfective opposition characterizes virtually all verb forms, usually covering all moods and tenses (though the present/future opposition is typically neutralized in the perfective) and both finite and non-finite forms. The pervasiveness of aspectual oppositions in Slavonic languages is, no doubt, one reason for the extent to which aspectology has leant on the Slavonic opposition; see, for instance, Comrie (1976).

Although the perfective/imperfective opposition is the basic opposition in all Slavonic languages, most Slavonic languages also have some other, typically more restricted, aspectual oppositions (called sub-aspects). Most Slavonic languages, for instance, have an opposition, restricted to verbs of motion, between a determinate sub-aspect (essentially, motion in a single direction) and an indeterminate sub-aspect (motion in various directions). Russian contrasts determinate идти/idti with indeterminate ходить/xodit' 'to go', for example он идёт в школу/on idёt v školu 'he is going to school' versus он ходит по полю/on xodit po polju 'he is walking about the field'; both are imperfective – the perfective is пойти/pojti 'to go, set out', as in он пошёл в школу/on pošёl v školu 'he has gone to (set out for) school'.

It is worth noting briefly the basic principles of the formation of imperfective–perfective verb pairs in Slavonic languages, using Russian examples. In general, simple unprefixed verbs are imperfective (such as писать/pisat' 'to write'), with only a handful of exceptions being perfective (like дать/dat' 'to give'). Perfective verbs are formed from simple unprefixed imperfective verbs primarily by prefixation. Prefixation also normally changes the lexical meaning, so that, for instance, the perfective verb описать/opisat' means 'to describe', though for a given simple unprefixed imperfective verb there is typically one (lexically determined) prefix that is most neutral; in the case of писать/pisat' this is на-/na-, so that написать/napisat' can be glossed simply as 'to write' (PRFV) –

whether such prefixes are ever truly lexically neutral is one of the controversies in current Slavonic aspectology. Less commonly, perfectives are formed by suffixation, as in Russian исчéзнуть/isčéznut′ 'to disappear', the perfective of исчезáть/isčezát′. Prefixed perfectives (in particular, those where the prefix carries a difference in lexical meaning), and also simple unprefixed perfectives, form corresponding imperfectives by suffixation: the imperfective of описáть/opisát′ 'to describe' is опи́сывать/opísyvat′, that of дать/dat′ 'to give' is давáть/davát′. In addition, most languages have some idiosyncratic pairs, including suppletive pairs, for example, Russian брать/brat′ (IMPFV) versus взять/vzjat′ (PRFV) 'to take'.

2.3   Functional Sentence Perspective

In English, word order plays an important role in carrying the basis syntactic relations within a sentence. In *John saw Mary*, for instance, only this particular order of words is possible, and any change in the order of words either changes the meaning (as in *Mary saw John*) or leads to a nonsentence (for example, *John Mary saw, saw Mary John*). In Slavonic languages, however, the word order is not tied to the expression of syntactic relations in this way. In Russian, for instance, any of the six logically possible word-order permutations of the sentence Кóля (NOM) ви́дел Тáню (ACC)/Kólja (NOM) vídel Tánju (ACC) 'Kolja saw Tanja' is grammatical and has the same basic meaning, that is refers to a situation in which Kolja saw Tanja; thus Тáню (ACC) ви́дел Кóля (NOM)/Tánju (ACC) vídel Kólja (NOM) still means 'Kolja saw Tanja', and not, for instance, 'Tanja saw Kolja'. This freedom of word order goes hand in hand with the richer morphology of Slavonic languages. In the Russian example just cited, the prime indication of who did the seeing is the nominative case of the noun phrase Кóля/Kólja, while the prime indication of who was seen is the accusative case of the noun phrase Тáню/Tánju, thus freeing word order to express other distinctions.

Just what does order express in Slavonic languages? There is no uniformity of terminology, and even some disparity of conceptual basis, in answering this question, but the following represents something approaching a consensus. Word order in Slavonic languages is determined primarily by the arrangement of given and new information, more specifically placing towards the beginning of the sentence information that is given (that is, already shared by speaker and hearer) and placing towards the end of the sentence information that is new (that is, the new information that the speaker wants to convey to the hearer). If one interlocutor asks 'Who did Kolja see?', then the fact of Kolja's seeing is given information and will come first in the answer in a Slavonic language, while the fact that the one seen is Tanja is new information, so that this will come last, giving, for instance, the version Кóля (NOM) ви́дел Тáню (ACC)/Kólja (NOM) vídel

Tánju (ACC) in Russian. Conversely, if the question is 'Who saw Tanja?', then the fact of Tanja's being seen is given information, while the identification of the one who did the seeing as Kolja is new information, giving, for instance, the Russian version Та́ню (ACC) ви́дел Ко́ля (NOM)/Tánju (ACC) vídel Kólja (NOM) as an appropriate answer. The new information is also referred to as the focus of the sentence.

Sometimes, the structure of the discourse will force or suggest a particular constituent of the sentence as what that sentence is about. For instance, if someone asks 'What about Tanja?', then an appropriate reply must be about Tanja. The item that the sentence is about is called its topic (or theme), the rest of the sentence is the comment (or rheme). In Slavonic languages, the topic usually occurs at the beginning of the sentence. Imagine the following conversation between A and B:

A: Vanja saw Vera.
B: What about Kolja? Who(m) did he see?
A: Kolja saw Tanja.

In the last turn of the conversation, Kolja has been established as topic, and the rest of the sentence is the comment. Furthermore, the fact that the person seen is Tanja is the new information or focus, so we have: topic *Kolja*, comment *saw Tanja*, focus *Tanja*, giving in Russian the word order Ко́ля (NOM) ви́дел Та́ню (ACC)/Kólja (NOM) vídel Tánju (ACC). Thus, in a sense the basic word order in most Slavonic languages can be said to be Topic–X–Focus, where X represents material other than the topic and focus (non-focus comment material); deviations from this order serve primarily to indicate emotional expressiveness in spoken registers.

These major differences between the function of word order in English and in Slavonic languages were first studied in detail by linguists of the Prague School, such as Vilém Mathesius (Mathesius 1939 and, more generally, 1947), who were interested in comparing and contrasting English and Czech syntax. The general area of study that covers such notions as topic, comment, focus, is referred to variously as functional sentence perspective, communicative dynamism, topic–comment (theme–rheme) structure; the Prague School used the Czech term *aktuální členění.* They noticed another distinction that ties in closely with those already mentioned (freedom of word order, richness of morphology). English has a number of productive syntactic processes that enable one to change grammatical relations (such as which noun phrase is subject of a sentence); the most evident is the passive, which enables one to rephrase *Kolja saw Tanja* as *Tanja was seen by Kolja.* One function of such syntactic processes in English is to bring a noun phrase to sentence-initial position, thus marking it overtly as topic of the sentence. While passives are possible in Slavonic languages, they tend not to be particularly idiomatic, especially in spoken registers, and are usually much more heavily restricted than in English, with, for instance, no possibility of a literal translation of *Kolja was given a book by Tanja*. In functional terms, the equivalent of English *Tanja was seen by Kolja* in a Slavonic language is not a passive, but rather an active sentence with the object preposed, such as Russian Та́ню (ACC) ви́дел Ко́ля (NOM)/Tánju (ACC) vídel Kólja (NOM). To a large extent, the functional equivalent of English rules that change grammatical relations is the possibility of word-order permutations in Slavonic languages.

While it is reasonably clear that for English the basic word order is Subject–Verb–Object (SVO), the question of the basic word order in Slavonic languages is not so clear in syntactic terms (though one can say that the basic order is Topic–X–Focus). For some languages, such as Russian, there is consensus that the basic order is SVO, for instance on the basis of the greater textual frequency of SVO over other word orders and on the basis of the preferred interpretation of potentially ambiguous sentences like мать лю́бит дочь/mat' ljúbit doč' 'the mother loves the daughter' (rather than 'the daughter loves the mother'), where both nouns happen not to distinguish nominative from accusative. The grammatical traditions of some other Slavonic languages, however, either suggest other basic orders or no basic order in syntactic terms, and this is reflected in the chapters on individual Slavonic languages.

2.4   Agreement and agreement categories
Slavonic languages preserve a rich inflectional morphology and have made innovations in the categories involved in agreement; these two facts result in complex agreement systems, which have attracted considerable interest. Typically, we find agreement within the noun phrase in case, number and gender. In Russian интере́сн-ая кни́га/interésn-aja kníga 'interesting book', the adjective интере́сн-ая/interésn-aja stands in the nominative singular feminine form, these features matching those of the head noun. Finite verbs typically agree with their subject in person and number; Russian мы пи́ш-ем/my píš-em 'we write' as opposed to, say, они́ пи́ш-ут/oni píš-ut 'they write'. Past tenses are frequently formed with the so-called *l*-participle, which creates a more interesting situation, as in Serbo-Croat Snèžana je dòšla/Снѐжана је до̀шла 'Snežana came (literally: Snežana is come)'. Here the auxiliary verb je/je 'is' shows agreement in person and number (third person singular), while the participle shows agreement in number and gender (singular and feminine). Some Slavonic languages, such as Russian, use a null form for the verb 'be' in the present tense, so that we find: Та́ня пришла́/Tánja prišlá 'Tanja came'. The former participle is the sole form in the past tense, so it may be said that Russian verbs agree in person and number in the present, but in number and gender in the past. Various types of pronoun also show agreement with their antecedents, in number and gender. The description given so far

covers a large proportion of the instances of agreement in Slavonic. There are, however, many examples where additional factors are involved, which require elaboration of our account. We will consider these first in terms of the constructions where complications occur, and then by looking at the agreement categories affected.

There are several constructions where more than one agreement form may be found. Consider this example of agreement with conjoined noun phrases in Russian: преподавалась математика и физика/ prepodaválas′ matemátika i fizika 'was taught mathematics and physics', that is, 'mathematics and physics were taught'. We find agreement (feminine singular) with just the nearer conjunct математика/ matemátika. But the plural form преподавались/prepodavális′ is also possible, showing agreement with both conjuncts. A similar option occurs in comitative constructions (such as Иван с братом/Iván s brátom 'Ivan with brother', that is 'Ivan and his brother'). Quantified expressions too are a complex area: given a phrase like пять девушек/pjat′ dévušek 'five girls' we may find plural agreement, but alternatively also neuter singular agreement. Subject–verb agreement in Slavonic is normally controlled by a noun phrase in the nominative case. Here, however, the part of the phrase which is in the nominative case, пять/pjat′ 'five', lacks gender and number features, while девушек/dévušek 'girls' is in the genitive plural; one possibility, therefore, is that agreement fails, and so the verb takes the default form, the neuter singular. Alternatively, the plural may be used, given that the quantified expression, though not formally nominative plural, nevertheless denotes a plurality. This gives rise to variants пришло (SG) пять девушек/prišló (SG) pjat′ dévušek and пришли (PL) пять девушек/prišli (PL) pjat′ dévušek 'five girls came'. The constructions discussed have in common a choice between agreement determined by the form, 'syntactic agreement', or by the meaning, 'semantic agreement'. Several factors bear on the choice in individual instances. Let us look at the problem from the viewpoint of the item which determines the agreement, the 'agreement controller' (for instance, the conjoined noun phrases in our first example). We find that controllers which precede the agreeing element and controllers which denote animates are more likely to give rise to semantic agreement (plural in this case) than those which do not. If we start from the agreeing element or 'target' we find that predicates are more likely to show semantic agreement than are attributive modifiers, relative pronouns more so than predicates, and personal pronouns more so than relative pronouns. This is the Agreement Hierarchy (attributive < predicate < relative pronoun < personal pronoun). Further patterns have been established, in addition to the interaction of these two major types of factor, so that the picture is indeed complex; see, for instance, Corbett (1983) for further details.

Let us now move on to consider the agreement system in terms of the categories involved. Person is perhaps the least controversial since Slavonic has the three persons found widely within and beyond Indo-European. It is worth noting, however, that Polish uses third-person forms for polite address. Number is more complex; Slavonic inherited a three-number system, singular/dual/plural, but the dual has been lost in almost all the modern Slavonic languages. However, this loss has caused considerable complications in agreement within numeral phrases involving the number 'two', and often 'three' and 'four' as well.

Slavonic languages are particularly helpful for coming to a clearer understanding of the category of gender (for a general survey see Corbett 1991). The standard languages preserve three genders, masculine, feminine and neuter, though the neuter is under pressure in several languages and is being lost in some dialects. In addition to the three main genders, a new subgender of animacy has arisen. In the accusative case, animates take different agreements from inanimates, for example Serbo-Croat òvāj prózor/òвāj прóзор 'this window' (inanimate) as opposed to òvog sȉna/ òвог сȕна 'this son' (animate). There are no separate accusative forms involved, but always syncretism with the genitive; thus òvog sȉna/òвог сȕна 'this son' is also a genitive case form. There is considerable variation of two sorts, first in the forms affected. In the south-west, as in the case of Serbo-Croat, only the masculine gender is subdivided into animate and inanimate, and that in the singular only. Russian, in the north-east, is at the other end of the spectrum since animacy affects the masculine singular and all genders in the plural. The other type of variation is in the categories of nouns treated as animate. First male humans of certain types were included, and then the boundary spread 'downwards'. The animate sub-gender is still much more firmly based on semantic classifications than are the three older genders, but in some languages various inanimates may be treated as animate and the semantic basis is becoming less clear.

In addition to this elaboration of the gender system, some West Slavonic languages have further introduced special agreements for nouns denoting male persons (thus a subset of the masculine animate subgender). In Polish, for example, we have in the plural an opposition between predicate agreement forms such as *byli* 'were', for subjects denoting male persons, and *były* 'were' for all other plural subjects. Here again, the assignment of nouns to the masculine personal category is much more clearly based on semantics than are the traditional genders.

Finally, we look at case (though recognizing that the matching of case forms need not necessarily be treated as agreement). Most of the Slavonic languages preserve a vital case system, with minor weakenings (several have lost the vocative, for example). However, Bulgarian and Macedonian have dramatically reduced the inherited case system. For the languages which retain a substantial case system, a particularly interesting problem of case agreement is the question of whether nominal complements of copular verbs agree in case with their subject or not: in the equivalent of sentences like 'he was a fine poet', the complement may be nominative or instrumental, depending on the language, with both possibilities acceptable in some languages.

3   Suggestions for using this book

The book has been designed to meet the differing requirements of a variety of readers. Some need a straightforward reference work, and for them information on particular languages can be found through the contents page, while more specific data on particular topics is to be located through the index. Then there are linguists of various types, who may require a general introduction to the Slavonic family. Such readers might start by working on any one of the chapters devoted to a contemporary Slavonic language, and then by branching out from there. Typologists can begin from a particular problem, whether in phonology, morphology, syntax or lexis, and move from language to language concentrating on the relevant section. Historical linguists with a grounding in Indo-European philology will no doubt prefer to start with the chapters on Proto-Slavonic, Old Church Slavonic and the alphabets and transliteration, and then progress to the modern languages. Sociolinguists should begin at the end, with the chapter on the Slavonic languages in exile, and then refer particularly to the introductory and dialect sections of the chapters on the modern languages.

Slavists too can approach the book in various ways. The Slavist could look first at the Slavonic language he or she knows best, since this will make it clear how the familiar information is organized. Alternatively, it makes sense to explore the family either by looking at a new Slavonic language which is closely related to a familiar one, or to take the opposite view and to look at a language which is as different as possible from the language or languages already known. After looking at one or more of the contemporary languages, the Slavist might then take in the chapter on alphabets and transliteration, followed by the historical perspective in the chapters on Proto-Slavonic and Old Church Slavonic, and also the chapter on the Slavonic languages in exile.

References

Anderson, Stephen R. (1985) *Phonology in the Twentieth Century: Theories of Rules and Theories of Representations*, Chicago and London: University of Chicago Press.

Berlin, Brent and Kay, Paul (1969) *Basic Color Terms: their Universality and Evolution*, Berkeley: University of California Press.

Bräuer, Herbert (1961–) *Slavische Sprachwissenschaft*, Berlin: Walter de Gruyter.

Comrie, Bernard (1976) *Aspect*, Cambridge: Cambridge University Press.

Corbett, Greville G. (1983) *Hierarchies, Targets and Controllers: Agreement Patterns in Slavonic*, London: Croom Helm.
—— (1991) *Gender*, Cambridge: Cambridge University Press.
De Bray, R.G.A. (1951) *Guide to the Slavonic Languages*, London: Dent. (Third edition 1980 in three volumes: *Guide to the South Slavonic Languages*; *Guide to the West Slavonic Languages*; *Guide to the East Slavonic Languages*, Columbus, Oh.: Slavica.)
Entwistle, W.J. and Morison, W.A. (1949) *Russian and the Slavonic Languages*, London: Faber & Faber.
Halle, Morris (1959) *The Sound Pattern of Russian*, The Hague: Mouton.
Horálek, Karel (1962) *Úvod do studia slovanských jazyků*, 2nd edn, Prague: Nakladatelství Československé akademie věd.
Hutchins, W.J. (1986) *Machine Translation: Past, Present, Future*, Chichester: Ellis Horwood, and New York: John Wiley.
Jakobson, Roman (1948) 'Russian conjugation', *Word* 4: 155–67. Reprinted 1984 in Roman Jakobson, *Russian and Slavic Grammar: Studies 1931–1981*, Berlin: Mouton, 15–26.
—— (1955) *Slavic Languages: a Condensed Survey*, New York: King's Crown Press.
Lehr-Spławiński, Tadeusz, Kuraszkiewicz, Władysław and Sławski, Franciszek (1954) *Przegląd i charakterystyka języków słowiańskich*, Warsaw: Państwowe wydawnictwo naukowe.
Mathesius, Vilém (1939) 'O tak zvaném aktuálním členění věty', *Slovo a slovesnost* 5: 171–4.
—— (1947) *Čeština a obecný jazykozpyt: soubor statí*, Prague: Melantrich.
Miklosich, Franz (1862–75) *Vergleichende Grammatik der slavischen Sprachen*, vol. I *Lautlehre*, vol. II *Stammbildungslehre*, vol. III *Formenlehre*, vol. IV *Syntax*, Vienna: Wilhelm Braumüller.
Nahtigal, Rajko (1952) *Slovanski jeziki*, Ljubljana: Univerza v Ljubljani, Filozofska fakulteta. (German translation 1961: *Die slavischen Sprachen, Abriß der vergleichenden Grammatik*, Wiesbaden: Harrassowitz; Russian translation 1963: Славянские языки, Москва: Издательство иностранной литературы.)
Panzer, Baldur (1991) *Die slavischen Sprachen in Gegenwart und Geschichte: Sprachstrukturen und Verwandtschaft* (Heidelberger Publikationen zur Slavistik. A: Linguistische Reihe, 3). Frankfurt am Main: Peter Lang.
Picchio, Riccardo and Goldblatt, Harvey (eds) (1984) *Aspects of the Slavic Language Question*, vol. I *Church Slavonic – South Slavic – West Slavic*, vol. II *East Slavic*, New Haven, Conn.: Yale Concilium on International and Area Studies.
Růžička, Rudolf (1973) 'Reflexive versus nonreflexive pronominalization in Modern Russian and other Slavic languages', in F. Kiefer and N. Ruwet (eds) *Generative Grammar in Europe* (Foundations of Language Supplementary Series 13), Dordrecht-Holland: Reidel, 445–81.
Schenker, Alexander M. and Stankiewicz, Edward (eds) (1980) *The Slavic Literary Languages: Formation and Development*, New Haven, Conn.: Yale Concilium on International and Area Studies.
Stone, Gerald and Worth, Dean (eds) (1985) *The Formation of the Slavonic Literary Languages* (UCLA Slavic Studies 11), Columbus, Oh.: Slavica.
Vaillant, André (1950–77) *Grammaire comparée des langues slaves*, 5 vols, Paris: IAC (vols I–II), Klincksieck (vols III–V).
van Wijk, Nicolaas (1956) *Les Langues slaves. De l'unité à la pluralité*, 2nd edn, The Hague: Mouton. (First edition 1937 in *Le Monde slave*.)

Vondrák, Václav (1906–8) *Vergleichende slavische Grammatik*, vol. I *Lautlehre und Stammbildungslehre*, vol. II *Formenlehre und Syntax*, Göttingen: Vandenhoeck & Ruprecht. (Second edition 1924–28.)

Бернштейн, С.Б. (1961) *Очерк сравнительной грамматики славянских языков*, Москва: АН СССР.

2 Alphabets and Transliteration

Paul Cubberley

ALPHABETS

Many alphabets have been used at one time or another to represent the Slavonic languages. The most commonly used, to be looked at in detail, are Glagolitic, Cyrillic and Latin (which we will hereafter call by the Slavonic name 'Latinica', for lack of a useful parallel English term like 'Latinic'); sporadically also the Greek, Arabic and even Hebrew alphabets have been used, and we will also deal briefly with these.

The distribution by location and period is roughly as follows:

Glagolitic: Moravia ninth century; Macedonia ninth to eleventh centuries; Bulgaria ninth to twelfth centuries; Croatia tenth to sixteenth centuries, then in Church usage until the nineteenth century, and sporadically into the twentieth century; Slovenia fifteenth to sixteenth centuries; Bohemia and Poland fourteenth to sixteenth centuries;

Cyrillic: Bulgaria ninth century to present; all the East Slavonic area (Russia, Ukraine, Belorussia/Belarus), Macedonia and Serbia (also Bosnia, Montenegro) tenth century to present;

Latinica: the West Slavonic area in general tenth century to present; Croatia and Slovenia tenth century to present; Serbia (but always secondary to Cyrillic), also Bosnia, the same period; Belorussia (and part of Ukraine) sixteenth to twentieth centuries;

Greek: Macedonia (especially Aegean) fifteenth to nineteenth centuries;

Arabic: Belorussia sixteenth to eighteenth centuries; Bosnia fifteenth to twentieth centuries;

Hebrew: Belorussia (fragmentary) sixteenth to eighteenth centuries.

Generally, there has always been a close correlation between alphabet and religion, though not necessarily one of cause and effect. The main correlations are shown in Table 2.1.

In the following we shall consider the early period as a whole, to indicate the establishment of the three main alphabets, and then follow the development of each separately. For the later periods only major reforms will be dealt with, and the details of reforms in each language should be sought in the relevant chapter.

Table 2.1: Slavs: alphabet and religion

Poland: Cath. – Lat.	Belarus: Orth. – Cyr. (Lat.) (Cath. – Lat.) (Musl. – Arab.) (Jud. – Hebr.)	Russia: Orth. – Cyr.
Lusatia (Sorbs): Cath. (Prot.) – Lat. Bohemia/Moravia: Cath. – Lat.	Slovakia: Cath. – Lat.	Ukraine: Orth. – Cyr. (Cath. – Lat.)
Slovenia: Cath. (Prot.) – Lat.	Croatia: Cath. – Lat. (Glag.)	Serbia: Orth. – Cyr. (Glag./Lat.)
Bosnia: Musl. – Lat. (Arab.) Orth. – Cyr. Cath. – Lat.	Macedonia: Orth. – Cyr. (Glag./Greek.)	Bulgaria: Orth. – Cyr. (Glag.)

Note: Parentheses indicate former or coexisting situations; layout is roughly geographical. Abbreviations used: Cath. Catholic, Orth. Orthodox, Prot. Protestant, Musl. Muslim, Jud. Judaic, Lat. Latinica, Cyr. Cyrillic, Glag. Glagolitic, Arab. Arabic, Hebr. Hebrew.

1 Early history

Traditionally, the start of Slavonic writing is credited to Constantine (also known as Cyril, the name he took on becoming a monk), who with his brother Methodius led a mission from Byzantium to the Moravian Slavs in the early 860s, in preparation reputedly having created an alphabet in which to write Slavonic speech.

1.1 Pre-Constantine period

The question of the extent to which any Slavonic language was written before the time of Constantine and Methodius remains unanswered, but of course not without hypotheses. The fact is that there are few facts! There is no hard evidence of any such written form for that period. In a general way, one can hypothesize that there must have been some cases of a written Slavonic language if only because the Slavs were active on many fronts well before 860: in the west, they lived next to, and usually, but not always, under the domination of, various Germanic peoples; in the south they had been fighting and living next to Greeks since the sixth century; in the east, they had been trading with the Greeks and the Scandinavians since at least the early ninth century. All of these peoples already had a writing system, whether Latinica or Greek, and it would be logically surprising if no attempt was ever made to use these alphabets to write some Slavonic language, if only for trade or treaty purposes. Would a victorious side be content to see a treaty supposedly favouring them written only in the language of the conquered side? At best only if many of the victors' leaders were fluent in the language of the losers.

The fact remains, however, that there are no concrete examples of such writing, but only elusive pieces of a suggestive sort, the most famous being that occurring in the work of the monk Chrabr in his *O pismenech* (On the Letters) – believed to have been written in the 890s, or possibly even earlier and by Constantine himself – in which he enigmatically describes the pre-Constantine Slavs as having used *čerty i rězy* 'lines and cuts' with which to count and predict (*čьtaaxǫ i gadaaxǫ*). Speculation on the meaning of this has, not surprisingly, been wide, the most popular view being that the lines and cuts are no more than just that – counting signs, and not an alphabet; another, once common, view was that they might have been a runic alphabet, borrowed presumably from the Scandinavians.

A similar enigma surrounds the mention in the *Pannonian Life of Constantine* that during a mission to the Crimea in 860 he was shown a Gospel and Psalter written in *rousskymi pismeny*, on the face of it meaning 'in Russian letters' (or rather Rus´-ian, since the adjective would at that time have referred to the ethnonym 'Rus´', thus to all the East Slavs and not just the north-eastern branch later referred to as 'Russians'); were these indeed some local Slavonic version of, say, a Greek alphabet (whether uncial or minuscule)? The only other hint is that Constantine is reported not to have seen these before, but to have learnt to read them surprisingly quickly. Does this suggest that he recognized the language beneath them and simply not the letters? Or that, as the legend implies, he was simply brilliant at learning a whole new language? The most popular view has been that the name of the letters has been corrupted, and originally read *sourskymi pismeny*, that is Syriac, the only problem being that Constantine is elsewhere credited with already knowing, or at least being familiar with Syriac, so that his effort at learning these 'new' letters is somewhat diminished. In the circumstances of the eulogic way in which his character is built up in this 'Life', the 'Syriac' explanation is unsatisfactory. By the same token, there is no other explanation for this phrase which fits either: the letters could not be Greek, Hebrew or Armenian since Constantine would likewise have recognized these; it remains possible that what he saw were corrupted forms of one of these alphabets, and that his 'feat' was to decipher the corrupted letters and reconstruct their original Greek (or whatever) form. Given that the document was allegedly a Gospel, he would already know the content, and thus be able to give the impression of understanding the new language. This interpretation is tempting also in that it could suggest the origin, at least in principle, of the alphabet which Constantine is credited with creating a few years later, and it brings us to the central question of the appearance of an entirely new alphabet applied to a Slavonic language. (Another view places the creation earlier, in the mid 850s; see below.)

1.2   Constantine

While there is taken to be no doubt that Constantine was the prime mover in the 'creation' of a Slavonic alphabet, there is an immense amount of doubt about every detail of this business, especially on the formal questions like: did he 'create' an alphabet, in the sense that he dreamt up the forms from scratch? If so, which alphabet did he 'create'? Did he 'create' two alphabets, or was one 'created' by someone else? Did he adapt some existing alphabet to Slavonic needs? If he adapted some other one, which was it? And so on.

Questions of principle (Why? Who for?) are less crucial, but merit a brief review before we take up the formal ones. The traditional view is that the alphabet (whichever it might have been) was created specifically in response to the Moravian request to Byzantium for a mission. Scepticism about this has centred around the speed with which everything was done, apparently no more than a year having passed between the request and the mission, a short time for the creation of an excellent alphabet plus the translation into a Slavonic language, using this new alphabet, of at least the Gospels. The only response has been that Constantine's philological interest might have led him to 'play' with an alphabet before this.

Two further points have been made: (1) only a native Slav, and not even a Greek philologist, would be likely to engage so seriously in the alphabet creation, which was hardly 'play'; (2) the translation of the Gospels into a vernacular was dubious, only the three 'sacred' languages being fully acceptable, and it is doubtful that a highly placed Greek would lightly consider it. (True, there were precedents in the Eastern Church in the Coptic and Armenian rites.) A recent work (Hoffer Edle and Margaritoff 1989) takes this further; assuming on the basis of the above that Constantine was Slav, the claim is made that he was in fact ethnically a Bulgarian, though born in Byzantium (Salonica), and this heritage led him to be interested in the cultural freeing of Bulgaria from Byzantine influence, complementing its political and military independence. The later return of the missionaries to Bulgaria and not Constantinople is taken to support this. In sum, it is claimed that the alphabet was created (as early as 855) as the first step in allowing Bulgaria to develop its own culture. The general idea that Constantine was Slav, and had been working on an alphabet for the Slavs, has been common amongst Bulgarian historians.

The most persuasive aspect of this view is that it offers an answer to the awkward question of the acceptability of the vernacular at this date: while the use of the vernacular was fine for missionary activity in general, its use in translating the Church books was quite another matter; the subsequent

Table 2.2: Old Slavonic alphabets

Cyrillic (OCS)	Glagolitic (OCS)	Name (in transliteration)	Transcription (transliteration, if different)	Modern Cyrillic
а	ⴀ	azъ	a	a
Б	ⴁ	buky	b	б
в	ⴂ	vědi/vědě	v	в
г	ⴃ	glagoli/glagolь	g	г
д	ⴄ	dobro	d	д
є	ⴅ	jestь/estъ	e	e
ж	ⴆ	živěte	ž′ (ž)	ж
ѕ ꙃ	ⴇ	(d)zělo	dz′ (dz)	Mac. s
ꙁ	ⴈ	zemlja	z	з
и	ⴈ	i, ižei	i	и
ї	ⴉ ⴡ	iže	i	Ukr. i
ћ	ⴐ	g′ervь/d′ervь	g′/j (ǵ/j)	SCr. ħ
к	ⴌ	kako	k	к
л	ⴊ	ljudьje/ljudije	l	л
м	ⴋ	myslite/myslěte	m	м
н	ⴍ	našь	n	н
о	ⴑ	onъ	o	о
п	ⴒ	pokoi	p	п
р	ⴓ	rьci	r	р
с	ⴔ	slovo	s	с
т	ⴕ	tvrdo/tverdo	t	т
оу ꙋ	ⴖ	ukъ/ikъ	u	у
ф	ⴼ	frtъ	f	ф
х	ⴗ	xěrъ/xerъ	x	х
ѡ	ⴘ	otъ	o	(о)
ц	ⴜ	ci	c′ (c)	ц
ч	ⴝ	črvь	č′ (č)	ч
ш	ⴈ	ša	š′ (š)	ш
щ	ⴉ	št′a	št′ (št)	щ
ъ	ⴟ	jerъ	ŭ/ə (ъ)	ъ
ꙑ ꙃи	ⴟⴎ ⴡⴟ	jery	y	ы
ь	ⴠ	jerь	ĭ (ь)	ь
ѣ	ⴡ	ětь/jatь	ä (ě)	(e)
ю	ⴀ	ju	ju	ю
ꙗ	–	ja	ja	я
ѥ	–	je	je	e
ѧ	ⴕ	jusъ malyj	ę	(я)
ѩ	ⴖ	jusъ malyj jotirovannyj	ę/ję	(я)
ѫ	ⴗ	jusъ bolьšij	ǫ	(у)
ѭ	ⴘ	jusъ bolьšij jotirovannyj	jǫ	(ю)
ѯ	–	ksi	ks	(кс)
ѱ	–	psi	ps	(пс)
ѳ	ⴛ	thita/fita	f	(ф)
ѵ	ⴞ	ižica	i/v	(и/в)

Note: Double forms in columns 1 and 2 are free variants. Variant names in column 3 (separated by /) reflect local differences. The transliteration is given in parentheses in column 4 only where different from the transcription, and corresponds to that used throughout this book. Transcription and transliteration are discussed later in this chapter. Column 5 gives in parentheses the most frequent equivalents where the actual form no longer occurs anywhere.

trouble in Moravia was clearly centred on that problem, the Slavonic liturgy being seen as heretical. Of course, practical Church (and state) politics could and did bend the rules, as is apparently the case in the Byzantine acceptance in 863 of Constantine's alphabet and translations (with some precedents as noted above), and in the Roman acceptance in 869 (with no precedents), but it is interesting to contemplate the notion that Constantine – who was as yet only a scholar and official, and not religious, becoming a monk only in 869 – might have *secretly and unofficially* applied his existing alphabet and (effectively illegal) translations to the Moravian business, though they were intended to be used for non-religious purposes in Bulgaria. This would not necessarily conflict with the early historical records of what happened, as these could easily (prefer to) recognize the later official acceptance as having preceded the unofficial use, even if they were aware of this unofficial use. General awareness of the problem at the time is seen in the report in the *Life of Constantine* of the debate in which Constantine became engaged in Venice (while on the way to Rome) precisely on this matter; or in Chrabr's *On the Letters*, equally clearly a defence of the use of a Slavonic alphabet and language for liturgical purposes.

The formal problems are many, and they all centre round the one fact, that there are *two* alphabets both clearly 'created' to fit Slavonic needs: Glagolitic and Cyrillic. If only Cyrillic existed, there would have been little trouble: it is clearly based on uncial (capital) Greek, and the problems would have been reduced to determining the origin of the letters which could not have come from Greek, like those representing the sounds /ž, š, č, c/, which Greek did not have. It should be said, incidentally, that even determining the origin of these letters would not have been as simple as it looks, as their origins in either alphabet are by no means unequivocally proved, and this is especially the case if one tries to omit Glagolitic from the equation. We shall return to this question after some discussion of Glagolitic. Table 2.2 gives a parallel list of forms and values. The letter-names are included partly out of simple interest, but mainly because some letters will be referred to by name later in the text. Discussion of the origin and development of the names may be found in Cubberley (1988).

The search for the formal origins of Glagolitic has occupied Slavists for well over a century, and remains unsolved. There are still attempts at new solutions (the present author being guilty of one in 1982), and still no fully accepted view. One very popular view is that Glagolitic is a *totally individual creation* 'from scratch', the corollary, of course, being that the creator was Constantine; the advantage of this view is that it appears to obviate the need to find a formal model in some other alphabet – I say 'appears' because I, amongst many others, find it difficult to believe that any normal person with no ulterior motive would rather work from scratch than adapt some existing system; and even if there is an ulterior motive, say the need to disguise the source or the application, it is still more natural to work from a real base. Moreover, it is said that as Constantine was a philologist this approach would have appealed to him, but it is precisely as a philologist that he would have had access to many existing systems to use as, at least, a notional base. Thus the 'genuine creation' theory seems to me formally somewhat unsatisfactory.

Most popular is the view that Glagolitic is based on Greek cursive forms. This view has been around since the last century and, while there is much uncertainty about many of the derivations, the general principle seems provable, that is most Glagolitic letters can be derived from Greek cursive forms in a way that is formally satisfying. Moreover, there is the circumstantial evidence that such a use of Greek forms is logical, first because Constantine was either Greek or bilingual in Greek, second, if the Slavs in closest contact with the Greeks were writing their languages, it would logically be in Greek letters, and finally, we have the enigmatic 'Russian letters' mentioned above, possibly suggesting that Constantine observed some such use of Greek letters and noted it as a model. In this view Constantine's role is mainly that of formalizer: he would have settled on formal variants for each sound needed; his creative contribution would have been in the addition of letters needed for non-Greek sounds, especially the palatals. This scenario also answers the protest that Constantine would not have used *cursive* Greek for the Gospels, as this was unacceptable Greek usage (in that for Church books they used either the uncial or the minuscule forms): he was formalizing an *existing* usage, and not establishing his own. Indeed, it is when one turns to an explanation of the appearance of *Cyrillic* that this argument becomes pertinent, and may even be used to support the above scenario: if Constantine's disciples were to start thinking in terms of the *dignity* of Church books rather than the more philological question of a Slavonic alphabet, and if they *knew* that Glagolitic was based on cursive forms, then they would logically have opted for a 'new' form based on the 'more dignified' uncial forms. Of course, as indicated above, any argument of dignity or acceptability militates against the whole idea of using a Slavonic vernacular or alphabet in the Church books anyway, but at least by the time of the Bulgarian period some official recognition had been given by Rome, albeit fleetingly.

Many other 'sources' have been suggested for Glagolitic, in fact just about any other alphabet which was around at the time (for a list see Истрин/Istrin 1963: 65); however, none of these has been as generally accepted as the cursive Greek theory. The most interesting variation is that the source for Glagolitic was Cyrillic. This found many important supporters earlier this century, the most notable being Karskij (Карский 1928/1979: 249–50), and more recently has been put by Istrin (1963: 147; 1988). It is generally now rejected on various grounds, both formal and logical: (1) while one can see Cyrillic as only indirectly derived from Glagolitic, in that the model here was basically the existing Greek uncial variant, the opposite derivation of converting to a cursive form is not acceptable, so one is stuck with a formal derivation, which requires considerable inventiveness on the part of the interpreter, and implies the same inventiveness on the part of the creator; and (2) what could be the motivation for rejecting Cyrillic in favour of a much less 'dignified' script? The only answer which makes any sense here is 'as a code': holders of this view (including Karskij and Istrin) argue that this was deemed necessary in Moravia after the proscription of the Slavonic liturgy (after the death of Methodius in 885), where the new script would have served to disguise the Slavonic content. However, it does not seem likely that the marauding German clergy would be fooled for long by a script that no one had seen before; what else could they think it was? And how many of the underground Slavonic brethren could have learnt to use this script in the circumstances? Altogether, this seems an unlikely sequence of events, and one is left with the conclusion that Cyrillic cannot have predated Glagolitic.

Other circumstantial arguments put forward to support the Glagolitic before Cyrillic order include: the existence of palimpsests (reused manuscripts) with Cyrillic superimposed on Glagolitic, but none in the other direction; the identification of local features which unite the Macedonian area with Glagolitic (for example no Turkisms) and the Bulgarian area with Cyrillic (Turkisms); and the (supposed) superiority of Glagolitic as representative of the early Slavonic (Macedonian) phonological system. None of these features is really of any clear significance, and all have been challenged even factually.

Let us assume, then, that the order of events is: Glagolitic is formed by the adaptation of cursive Greek by some Slavs during the preceding couple of centuries (Istrin accepts the possibility of such a 'Proto-Glagolitic', which at best would have helped in the conversion of Cyrillic to Glagolitic – 1963: 147); it is formalized by Constantine, who also adds letters for the non-Greek sounds; Constantine's disciples in Bulgaria perceive Glagolitic as unsuitable for Church books and make a new Slavonic alphabet based on uncial Greek. The only remaining formal questions are then: where did the added letters come from? And can we satisfactorily relate the Glagolitic and Cyrillic versions of these (that is, can we derive the Cyrillic ones from the Glagolitic)?

Of the many Slavonic sounds not existing in Greek, the most obvious are the palatals – /š, ž, č/ – but also /c/ and /b/, and of course many vowels, especially the nasals, *jers* (mid-high reduced) and *jat'* (low front) (see table 2.2 for names and symbols). Very little attempt has been made at finding sources for the vowel letters; most attempts at finding sources for the palatals and /c/ offer multiple sources, for example Coptic for /ž/ and Hebrew for /š/, /č/ and /c/. In the belief, mentioned above, that Constantine, as a philologist, would have used some consistency in his choice of sources, and as far as possible seek a single source for all of these sounds, I have argued elsewhere for Armenian as such a source for the consonants, and Greek variants for the vowels. The details may be found in Cubberley (1982), and here I mention only the three main issues relating to Armenian: (1) Constantine would almost certainly have known at least the Armenian alphabet (if not some of the language), there being many highly educated Armenians living in Constantinople, possibly including some of his colleagues at the 'university', where he taught philosophy, like John the Grammarian and Leo the Philosopher, who was also head of the institution, and at least one recent emperor having been Armenian (see Charanis 1961: 211); (2) Armenian had a wealth of palatal sounds, more than Slavonic, with letters to represent them all; (3) it is possible to make formal associations between these and the corresponding Glagolitic letters (except for one – /š/, for which one must argue via some confusion over the letter representing the reflex of PS1. *tj*, resulting in the later formation, in Cyrillic, of the form ш, which was then borrowed back into Glagolitic (discussion in Cubberley 1982: 299–302)).

As to the Cyrillic versions of these Slavonic sounds, it is not too difficult to see enough similarities to manage a derivation from Glagolitic. Of course, one could argue in either direction, but for the reasons listed above we are now assuming Glagolitic primacy. Thus for example we can derive Cyrillic ж,ү,ц from Glagolitic ⰶ,ⱛ,ⰲ respectively; ш is the same in both; for the vowels we derive з,ь,ѫ,ѧ from ⰸ,ⰵ,ⱘ,ⰵ respectively, while the symbol originally used for /ě/ (Cyrillic ѣ, Glagolitic ⰻ) has been confused through the many changes and local reflexes of this Proto-Slavonic sound (see Cubberley 1984: 284–5).

1.3 End of the ninth century

I thus favour the view that at the end of the ninth century Constantine's disciples, many of them nameable, such as Kliment Oxridskij, Naum Preslavskij, Konstantin Preslavskij, 'created' the alphabet now known as Cyrillic on the basis of the (more dignified) Greek uncial script, using Glagolitic as the model for the Slavonic-only sounds, to some extent giving them a 'square' look to match the uncial style of the rest. This period was that of the First Bulgarian Empire, with the strong Car' Symeon in charge, and a generally pro-Greek attitude, at least in matters cultural.

The question of the naming of the two alphabets is really a minor one, and is probably most simply explained by a confusion in the reporting of the creation of 'the alphabet', since no early source talks of two alphabets; both are referred to, if at all, as 'bukvica', 'azbuka', etc., with no further qualification. Only much later did either name, whether that of Cyril (*kirillica*), from Constantine's adopted monastic name, or Glagolitic (*glagolica*), from *glagol-* ('word, say'), become attached to one or the other alphabet. The name *glagolica* appears to have developed in the Croatian area – probably in the fourteenth century – from the name *glagolity*, applied to adherents of the Slavonic liturgy. In the South Slavonic area in general, but especially where Glagolitic remained active, there arose in the seventeenth century the legend that Glagolitic had been created by St Jerome (Hieronymus), and the two alphabets are typically listed side by side as the alphabets of St Hieronymus and St Cyril. This may well be the start of the association of Cyril with Cyrillic, which then spread to the East Slavonic area. The names *glagolica* and *kirillica* are attested there only in the nineteenth century.

1.4 Tenth–eleventh centuries
In the First Bulgarian Empire, which lasted until 1018, when it was militarily defeated by the Byzantine Empire, Cyrillic and Glagolitic must both have flourished, though we have, in fact, no original documents from that period; the number of later copies, however, testifies to the strong tradition which was established there. There is also some epigraphical evidence for both (see Велчева/Velčeva 1989). This tradition spread first into Serbia, possibly during the tenth century, or perhaps only in the next – the eleventh-century Glagolitic *Codex Marianus* is thought to be of Serbian origin (Ивић/Ivić 1986: 111), and a recently found pottery inscription from Kosovo is claimed to be from the tenth century (*Borba* 6.3.90); also into Bosnia, where a Glagolitic tradition lasting into the thirteenth century has been claimed (Kuna 1977) and even Croatia, where the two coexisted until the Reformation (Jurančič 1977); and then, more importantly for its subsequent fate, to Rus', officially in 988, when Prince Vladimir formally adopted Orthodox Christianity as the state religion (though there were certainly conversions before that date, for example Princess Ol'ga, daughter of Igor', is supposed to have been baptized around 957). For Rus', the eleventh century was one of intense 'literary' activity, in the sense of large-scale copying of the Bulgarian books (as well as some original translation from Greek). *Ostromir's Gospel* (dated 1056) is one of the earliest and finest examples of what might already be called Russian (Rus'-ian) Church Slavonic, using a classic square uncial Cyrillic (see figure 2.2(a) on page 34).

On Old Church Slavonic as such, see chapter 4 of this book; on local versions and the role played by Church Slavonic in various areas, see the collections by Schenker and Stankiewicz (1980) and Stone and Worth (1985). For our purposes, I would like only to mention that all three major alphabets were used even for early Old Church Slavonic documents, for example the following, none of which is later than the eleventh century:

Glagolitic: *Codex Zographensis* (Bulgaria), *Kiev Fragments* (Moravia)
Cyrillic: *Ostromir's Gospel* (Rus'), *Savvina Kniga* (Macedonia)
Latinica: *Freising Fragments* (Slovenia)

2   Glagolitic: later history

After the initial period, what one might call the Constantinian period (to the end of the ninth century), there is some evidence (mainly epigraphic) of the continued existence of Glagolitic, alongside Cyrillic, in the Bulgarian/Macedonian area, around the centres of Preslav and Ohrid, until the beginning of the thirteenth century (Велчева/Velčeva 1989: 21). However, Cyrillic steadily became dominant throughout the twelfth century. As noted above, Glagolitic also survived briefly in Serbia, probably into the twelfth century, and in Bosnia possibly into the thirteenth. Its subsequent history, however, belongs almost exclusively to the Croatian area.

2.1   Rus'

In Rus' there are a few early (eleventh-century) examples of Glagolitic graffiti in Novgorod (Vajs 1937; Медынцева/Medynceva 1969), indicating only that it was known there, but apparently not much used; possibly it travelled north with some of the Bulgarians who were brought, especially by Jaroslav the Wise in the eleventh century, as we know from the *Laurentian Chronicle*, to undertake translation and teaching activity, but another view is that the source was Bohemia (Štefanić 1963: 29). It may have been used or passed on in Rus' as a curiosity or even as a cipher.

2.2   Bohemia

Glagolitic may have arrived in Bohemia even before the death of Methodius, and probably continued to be used till the late eleventh century (Štefanić 1963: 28); later, there was a period of Glagolitic activity at the Emmaus Monastery from the fourteenth to the early seventeenth century, the active period lasting only till the mid-fifteenth century (Mareš 1971: 187–90). The source of this was Croatian in any case; that is, it was a secondary development of Croatian Glagolitic. However, it did produce important texts like the *Reims Evangelistary* and the *Czech Bible* of the fifteenth century, and served to convey the views of the Hussites back to the Croatian area (Hamm 1974: 41–2).

2.3 Poland

From Bohemia, Glagolitic was taken to one monastery in Poland (Kraków) at the end of the fourteenth century and may have survived there too till the sixteenth century; however, only fragments remain as evidence of this sojourn (Hamm 1974: 41–2).

2.4 Slovenia

Slovenia too had a flirtation with Glagolitic, probably likewise of a secondary nature, through Croatian influence, in the fifteenth–sixteenth centuries (Kolarič 1970); some believe that Glagolitic remained known in this area from the original (ninth century) Pannonian period, and is thus not a secondary product (Zor 1977).

2.5 Croatia, Dalmatia

Croatia and Dalmatia were the areas in which Glagolitic not only survived, but flourished for many centuries, having arrived in Croatia probably by the tenth century (Štefanić 1963: 31), though others have dated the arrival later (Велчева/Velčeva 1989: 18). The apparent reasons are somewhat paradoxical, in that these were the areas dominated from early on by the Roman Church (especially after the Schism of 1054, when contact with Byzantium became more restricted), so that one would expect Latinica to have been *de rigueur*. In fact, Glagolitic became the symbol of (partial or nominal) independence from Rome; it was tolerated by Rome as a small concession permitting its continued influence where it mattered (in this case in the otherwise Byzantine-dominated Balkans), and finally made official in the mid-thirteenth century.

Formally, there was a gradual but marked change in the letter shapes: from the original round style, there was a shift first to a slightly more square shape, and finally the typical Croatian very square shape. (See figure 2.1 (a/b/c) for examples.)

Glagolitic continued to be used in Croatia until the early nineteenth century, especially on the Adriatic islands, during that time having acquired a cursive form, as it was used in administrative functions also (see figure 2.1 (d)), and having been printed in several major centres, like Venice, Tübingen and Rome (the earliest is a Missal of 1483 (place unknown), and other important examples are a Primer of 1527 (Venecija), a Testament of 1562 (Tübingen) and a Missal of 1631 (Rome)). As late as 1893 a Missal was printed in Rome, and Glagolitic was still used within the Church until the 1920s (Ивић/Ivić 1986: 117 places the end point at 1927, when a Latinica edition of the Glagolitic Missal was produced). However, Glagolitic ceased to be very active outside the church from the seventeenth century.

Figure 2.1

a. Round Glagolitic: eleventh century, Bulgaria

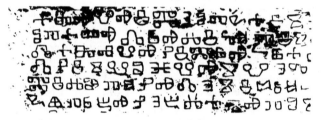

b. Transitional Glagolitic: twelfth century, Croatia

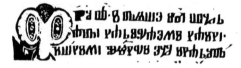

c. Square Glagolitic: thirteenth century, Croatia

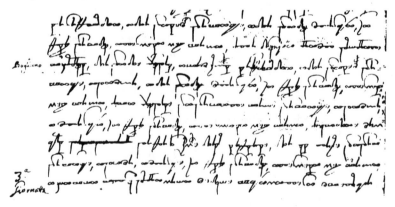

d. Cursive Glagolitic: sixteenth century, Croatia

3 Cyrillic: later history

Cyrillic remained ensconced in the three basic areas in which it first developed: Rus', Bulgaria and Serbia. Its further development is of a marginal nature – partly related to local phonological changes and partly to purely graphic ones. Only in the case of its application to non-Slavonic languages were there any major changes in its form. After looking at the main Slavonic developments in the three basic areas, we shall briefly consider the non-Slavonic situation. In each case, at issue are both stylistic developments, affecting the alphabet as a whole, and purely formal ones, related to graphic and orthographic reforms (whether official or spontaneous), that is the exclusion of letters or introduction of new ones and changes to shapes.

3.1 Style

In all areas, the initial square *uncial* style (Ru./Bg./SCr. устав/ustav), as seen in *Ostromir's Gospel*, gave way by the fourteenth century to a less square and slightly more irregular style referred to as *semi-uncial* (полуустав/poluustav), at first in less religious contexts, but eventually even in fully religious ones. (See figure 2.2 for examples.)

As more and more completely non-religious works came to be written, notably administrative documents of one sort or another, we observe a steady 'corruption' of the letter shapes: a new *cursive* form gradually takes shape. The period of development of this form relates directly to the status of the administration in given areas, thus it is earlier in the Grand Duchy of Lithuania (where Belorussian was used in this role) and the Kingdom of Serbia (both from the fourteenth century), but later in the Russian and Bulgarian areas. The Bulgarian area is the one in which the cursive forms never really developed, as their language was rarely used in the administrative role during the Byzantine and Turkish periods; it is only in the nineteenth century that we find large numbers of examples. In the Russian area, it is not until the fifteenth century that we can identify such a style (Ru. скоропись/skoropis'). For the East Slavonic area it may be thought somewhat paradoxical that it was in the non-Russian area of the Grand Duchy of Lithuania that this cursive style was first developed, but the reason is that the use of Belorussian and its alphabet as the administrative language was not tied in the same way to the more serious, religious applications of Cyrillic, as was the case in Muscovite Rus', as well as the fact that the latter's administration itself was developing more slowly. At any rate by the end of the fifteenth century we have a more or less united cursive throughout the East Slavonic and Serbian areas, with only one or two local features, such as flourishes on particular letters. This similarity should not surprise us, as both the starting point and the motivation for change were the same in all areas (see figure 2.3).

Apart from the Bulgarian area, where, as mentioned, the cursive forms

Figure 2.2

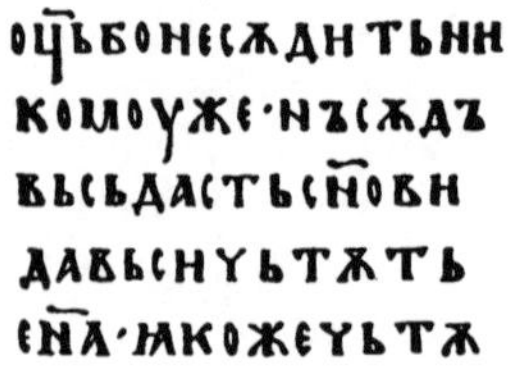

ОЦЬБОНЕСѦДНТЬНН
КОШОУЖЕ·НѢСѦДЪ
ВЬСЬДАСТЬСНОБН
ДАВЬСНУЬТѦТЬ
ЕНА·ІАКОЖЕУЬТѦ

a. Ustav: eleventh century, Rus´

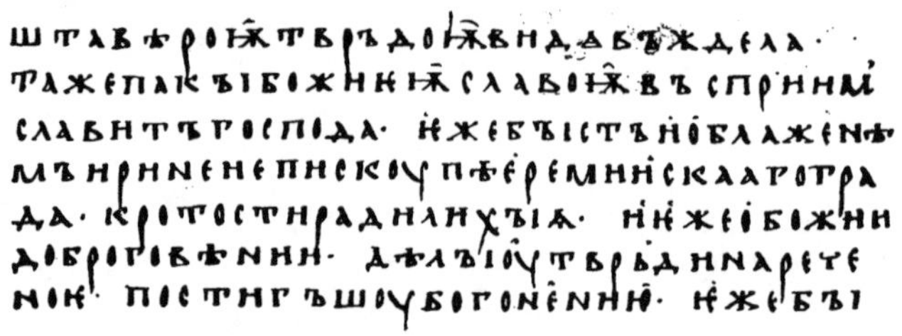

ШТЛВѣ ОНѪТ ВЬ ДОНѪ ВНД ДВѢЖДЕЛА ·
ТАЖЕПЛКЪ ВІ БОЖ НН НѪ СЛАВОНѪ ВЪ СПРНН
СЛАВНТ ТР ГСПДА · НЖЕБЫСТ НОБЛАЖЕНѢ
МЪ НРНН ЕНЕ ПНСКОУ ПѣЕРЕМНН СКЛ АРОТРА
ДА · КРНТОСТНРАДНАНХЪІА · ННЖЕІ БІЖНН
ДІ БРІ ГІ ВѣННН · ДѢЛЪІ ОУ ТВРЬД ННА РЕЧЕ
НІН · ПІС ТНГ ъ ШІ ОУ БОГОНЕННН · НѢ ЖЕ БЫ

b. Ustav: eleventh century, Bulgaria

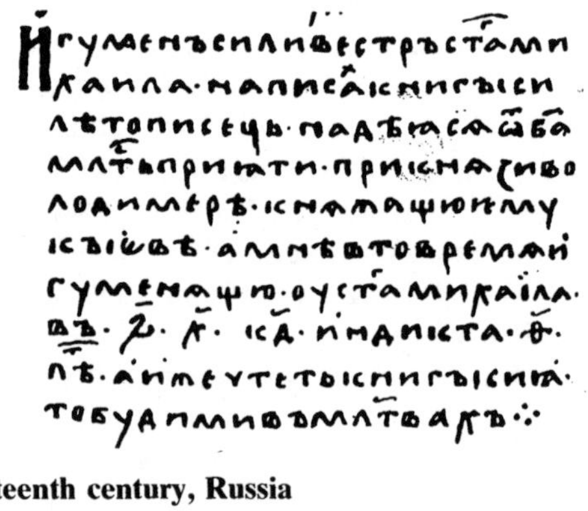

Ηгумснъ спл нвесстръ стамн
хаплл · маппсакнигъісн
лѣтопнссць · надбѫса біба
мллѣ прнмтн · прнсна гнво
лоднмѣрѣ · кнамащнонму
кзівсѣ · амнѣотоврѣман
гумснацн оустамнхаıла
въ · ç · ẍ · ка нмапнста · Ꝋ
пѣ · анмеутетъіснигъіснм̈
тобуапмнвомлтваръ ·:·

c. Poluustav: fourteenth century, Russia

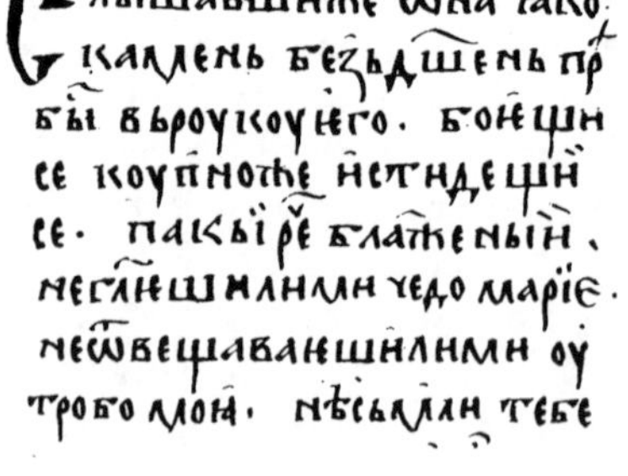

 Слъішавшнѣѣе шна ıако.
ккаленъ безѣдашенъ пр̈
бъі вброукоунго. боіцн
се коупмотѣ нстндещн
се · плкъі рѣ блатенъıн ,
несãнш млнлн чедо марıе·
нешбещлванншнлнмн оу
тробо лон · нѣсьлан тебе

d. Poluustav: fourteenth century, Bulgaria

Figure 2.3

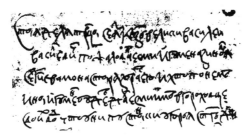

a. Cursive Cyrillic: fifteenth century, Belorussian

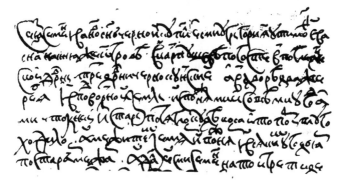

b. Cursive Cyrillic: sixteenth century, Russia

c. Cursive Cyrillic: sixteenth century, Dubrovnik

d. Cursive Cyrillic: sixteenth–seventeenth century, Bulgaria

did not have a chance to develop in any formal way (though at many levels of written interaction the same process must have occurred – see Figure 2.3 (d)), there is one area where the administration adhered to a much more formal semi-uncial style – Bosnia. This peculiar style, which, however, is very similar to the early printing style which was developed in Belorussia by such as Francišak Skaryna, is referred to as *bosančica* (see figure 2.4 (a/b)).

Cursive style is by definition handwritten and rather idiosyncratic, in spite of the degree of normativization which still occurs at the levels of teaching and formal application, and so it was not appropriate for printing when this arrived. For this more formal shapes were necessary, and as most of the early printing was religious in application, a version of the most formal *ustav* was the first norm in all areas. It was only when administrative printing became common that a simpler form, based on the *poluustav*, arose. The leader in the Cyrillic area was Peter the Great with his *graždanskij šrift* 'civil script' (or, rather, 'typeface'), of 1710. This in turn was exported to Serbia in the eighteenth century and to Bulgaria and Macedonia in the nineteenth (see figure 2.4 (c)).

3.2   Form

Changes in the application of letters (as opposed to purely formal changes and overall styles) are usually the result of phonological changes which cause either redundancies or inadequacies in the symbolic representation of the sounds. Thus, for example, when the nasal vowels of Proto-Slavonic ceased to be nasals and fused with other, existing vowels (as was the case in all Cyrillic areas), the problem arose of what to do with the now redundant 'nasal' symbols. Three solutions were possible: (1) retain the old symbols as phonetically redundant, but etymologically informative, symbols; (2) delete the old symbols, replacing them with the ones used for the sounds with which they have fused (e.g. ѫ > y (u), ѧ > ꙗ/я (ja); (3) apply the old symbols to some new function for which a new need has arisen (for this there will usually need to be some association between the old and new functions).

All of these approaches were applied at some stage in the various reforms of Cyrillic in every area. For all areas the following principal phonological changes caused such problems: for vowels, denasalization, the loss of the *jers* and the development of /ě/; for consonants, the development of the palatals, especially the complex ones, like the reflexes of Proto-Slavonic **tj/dj*, and /j/ itself.

Another general cause of trouble, of course, is the inheritance of an alphabet that was created for another language system, as was the case for Cyrillic in general (and to a lesser extent Glagolitic), with the rather serious problems of the multiple vowel symbols brought in from the Greek system (where they were by medieval times equally redundant!): the three letters

Figure 2.4

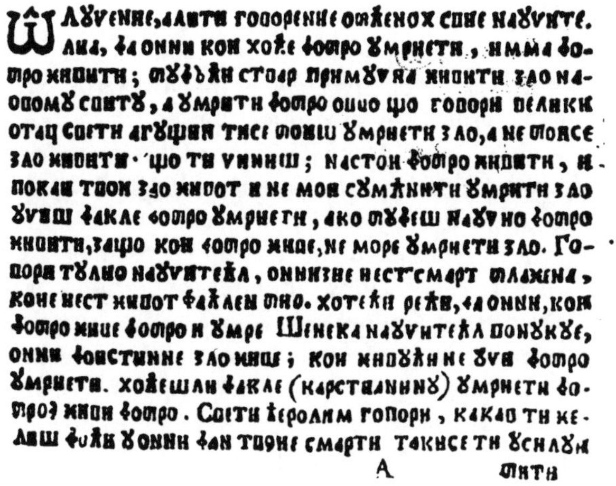

a. Bosnian Cyrillic (Bosančica), seventeenth century

b. Printed Cyrillic: religious, sixteenth century, Belorussia

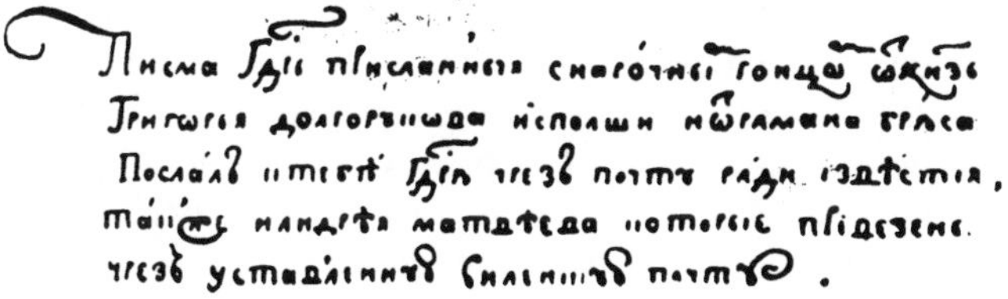

c. Printed Cyrillic: civil, eighteenth century, Russia

for /i/, the two for /o/ and the variants for /u/. There were similar problems with the Greek consonantal letters, with two each for /z/ and /f/ (see table 2.2).

For all areas the solution to all these problems was a very long time coming: the earliest solution by far was that of Serbia (or rather of the whole area where Cyrillic was subsequently used for Serbo-Croat), namely that of Vuk Karadžić in 1814 and 1818; for Ukrainian the final (modern) version arrived only in 1917; for Russian in 1918; Bulgarian in 1925 and 1945; Belorussian in 1933; Macedonian in 1944. Up to the eighteenth century there was very little in the way of 'conscious' reform. One can identify only isolated conscious attempts at rationalization at earlier periods, but even the 'grammarians' of those periods, for example Konstantin Kostenečki (a Bulgarian living and writing in Serbia) in the fifteenth century or Maksim Grek (a Greek living and writing in Russia) in the sixteenth (both of whose 'grammars' were well known throughout the Cyrillic Slavonic world), in principle accepted problems like redundant letters as normal, based as much on the sacredness of the written form as on what might have been seen as important etymological information. It is rather in the practice of religious copyists and then secular clerks that we find rationalizations like the separation of ѩ and ѧ by phonetic context: ѩ initially and post-vocalic (= [ja]), ѧ post-consonantal (= [a] after soft consonant).

The first real attempt in Russia to come to grips with these problems was Peter the Great's 'civil script' (Ru. гражданский шрифт/graždanskij šrift) of 1708/10: not only did this settle on simpler forms of all letters for use in administrative printing, but it also made a start on deleting redundant letters which were marked as 'Church' variants, and also introduced some new forms, notably э and я. Э was to serve the needs of foreign words, where the sound [e] occurred initially without any prothetic [j], and was done by employing a little-used variant of e, which some regard as the Glagolitic letter э; however, no Glagolitic form would be known at this stage in Russia; the variant involved had in fact been used for some time in the southern (Ukrainian) area, and before that in the fourteenth century for Greek words; the shape of я had arisen in the seventeenth-century cursive style, especially for ѧ, but also for ѩ, and was probably seen as a useful unified form of these two letters, which by now represented effectively the same vowel sound ([a]), though varying by position, as indicated above. At the same time, by no means all the redundancies were removed in this reform: double symbols continued to exist for /i/, /f/, /z/; also this system was by no means a universally accepted one, tied as it was at first to administrative usage. The debate about shapes and variants was to be conducted fairly freely until 1918, basically because in Russia, as elsewhere, there was as yet no mechanism for the enforcing of a norm.

The Russian Academy of Sciences, founded in 1725, offered potentially such a mechanism, and indeed had such a role in view for itself, but its attempts at reform were few and not particularly effective, especially in the sense that individual writers, whether as theorists or creative writers, went their own way, not recognizing the dictates of the Academy. The 'final' formal reform came only in 1918, when the new regime included ortho-graphy in its range of general reforms: only then were redundant letters like i, v, ѣ, and ѳ completely removed, and ъ in its redundant final position.

This Russian scenario is typical of the whole Cyrillic area, in that ortho-graphic reform really relied on the acceptance of a literary norm for the whole language, and generally the latter was worked out only during the nineteenth century. This was certainly the pattern also for Ukrainian, Belorussian, Bulgarian and Macedonian.

For Ukrainian and Belorussian the main differences from Russian reflect the different behaviour of the vowel /i/ and its variants: since Ukrainian early fused the back and front variants [y] and [i], it had no need for two letters for those, and they became written both with и; however, it then developed a new high front phoneme /i/, and used for this the 'redundant' і rather than recast everything in the Russian style (ideologically not a serious option). For Belorussian the phonemic situation is the same as Russian; however, they opted for the і letter rather than и for the front [i]. Examples are the words for 'son', 'blue', and 'hay':

	'son'	'blue'	'hay'
Russian	сын [sy-]	синий [s′i-]	сено [s′e-]
Ukrainian	син [sy-]	синій [sy-]	сіно [s′i-]
Belorussian	сын [sy-]	сіні [s′i-]	сена [s′e-]

A second area of difference lies in the presence in both Ukrainian and Belorussian, but not Russian, of the semi-vowel [u̯]: in both it is a positional variant of either /v/, /l/ or /u/. While Ukrainian makes use of the existing letters for those sounds, Belorussian shows the innovation of the letter ў; to some extent this reflects Belorussian's different attitude towards orthographic principles (see below, section 8); for details refer to the relevant language chapters.

For Bulgarian one of the central issues of the orthography debate has been the phoneme /ă/: etymologically, it comes from Proto-Slavonic *ъ, *ǫ and even *ь, so that all of the three Old Church Slavonic letters ѧ, ѫ or ь have at some time been used for it, and not always etymologically either. In the early nineteenth century the letter ă was used for this sound from whatever source, then ѫ became the popular letter, though ъ was still in contention. From the middle of the century the etymological principle was applied, with ѫ for etymological *ǫ and ъ for etymological *ъ/ь, and this usage survived effectively until 1945. In addition ъ and ь were still written in final position, as in pre-1918 Russian, though they no longer had any phonetic value. Only in 1945 was ѫ removed entirely, ъ written for /ă/ when internal, and value-less final ъ dropped; the last problem, that of final /ă/, was then handled by the use of a in that position. Examples are, of Proto-Slavonic, pre-1945 and post-1945 Bulgarian:

	'hand'	*'sleep'*	*'I can'*
Proto-Slavonic	*rǫka	*sъpъ	*mogǫ
Pre-1945 Bulgarian	ръка	сънъ	могѫ
Post-1945 Bulgarian	ръка	сън	мога

(See Мирчев/Mirčev 1963: 25–33.)

Another issue of some difficulty has been the use of ѣ in its etymological place in competition with the dialectal reflexes (sometimes /a/, sometimes /e/, both by position and by dialect). The 1945 reform removed ѣ and settled for я/е as they occur in the new standard.

Macedonian had fewer problems of this sort, its only real phonetic peculiarity being the reflexes of Proto-Slavonic *tj and *dj, namely /ḱ/ and /ǵ/ respectively. The nineteenth-century efforts at sorting out the orthography were influenced greatly by Vuk Karadžić's reforms (see below), and it was only the larger problem of the codification of the language which slowed things up, so that it was not until 1903 that a system virtually that of Vuk was made as formal as the situation allowed (that is, not very), through the efforts of writer and publicist Krste Misirkov. The main differences from Vuk's system lay in the use of the apostrophe to indicate palatal consonants rather than a ligature with ь, thus н', л', к', г'; he also used i rather than j for /j/. Misirkov's system was not widely known or applied, but its principles were the ones used in the orthography officially adopted as part of the new standard language in 1945; at this point, the Serbian ligatures њ and љ were adopted, as well as j, and the acute rather than the apostrophe in ќ and ѓ (see Koneski 1983: 111–15).

The case of the Serbian–Croatian area was different, probably, in that the question of orthography was actually at the forefront of the larger business of literary norms, and this was because of the parallel existence of at least two alphabets – Cyrillic and Latinica, but indeed even of three, since Glagolitic was still functioning in the Croatian area. It was Vuk Karadžić who led and carried out the crucial reforms of the Cyrillic alphabet. These reforms, described and put into practice in his grammar of 1814 (*Писменица сербскога језика/Pismenica serbskoga jezika*) and, especially, in his dictionary of 1818 (*Српски рјечник/Srpski rječnik*), were mainly concerned with the writing of the 'new' palatals /č' /, /dž' /

(from PS1. **tj*, **dj*) and /dž/ (foreign, from Turkish), and also of /j/ itself. For the first Vuk used a form which had been around for a long time in Serbian Cyrillic – ħ (see table 2.2, th letter called *g′ervь*, originally representing Greek /g′/ or /j/, then Serbian /j/). He used the recently invented longer-tailed variant ħ to mark the voiced equivalent and the form џ (inverted ħ or a variant of ц?) for the foreign sound (Младеновић/ Mladenović 1989: 156–7). The letter for /j/ – j – was, not surprisingly, taken from Latinica in its Croatian usage. Most subsequent discussion of orthography in the Serbian–Croatian area centred around the relationship between the two major alphabets and their application to the literary language, whose variants were the main point of issue in the establishment of norms. We will have some more to say on this in the discussion of Latinica developments in the area.

3.3 Non-Slavonic use of Cyrillic

While this book deals with the Slavonic languages, it may also be of interest to note that some non-Slavonic areas have used or still use Cyrillic, through Slavonic influence in the religious, cultural or political domains:

1 Rumania for all its early literary history used not only Cyrillic, but the entire Old Church Slavonic language, like the use of Latin in western Europe. The first examples of written Rumanian date from the sixteenth century, but the alphabet remains Cyrillic. It was only around 1860 that Cyrillic was replaced by Latinica in non-religious writing, and in the Church only in 1890.

2 Of the sixty-two non-Slavonic written languages of the former Soviet Union listed by Gilyarevsky and Grivnin (1970: 9), fifty-five use Cyrillic; many of the fifty-five have additional letters in their alphabet, sometimes from Latinica, often variations of Cyrillic, and often by the use of diacritics. The Turkic languages were written first in Latinica during the early Soviet period (many having previously used Arabic), but converted to Cyrillic in the late 1930s.

3 Mongolian has been written in Cyrillic in the Mongolian People's Republic since 1941 (though Mongolian in Inner Mongolia (in China) still uses the traditional Old Mongolian vertical script).

4 Latinica

4.1 Early history

If Glagolitic and Cyrillic, both based on Greek, had problems of redundancy, they nevertheless represented fairly early alphabets dedicated to representing Slavonic speech, and especially through the early creation of extra symbols for specifically Slavonic sounds, they both ended up being rather good in this function. Latinica, on the other hand, in the early stages at least, had no one attempting to make it fit a Slavonic system; in all the Slavonic areas in which it became established early, there was no early attempt at writing the given Slavonic language, it being assumed that written documents, even secular ones, used Latin (language and therefore alphabet). When we do find examples of Slavonic words written in Latinica at this stage, the specifically Slavonic sounds clearly present an insurmountable problem, or at least one which no one attempted to surmount! By way of example, the earliest list of Slavonic letter names, dating from the twelfth century (known as the 'Paris Alphabet' or 'Abecenarium Bulgaricum'), has names like: 'iſe, giuete, naſ, ſaraue' (for iže, živěte, našь, čьrvь – see table 2.2), indicating no attempt, or at any rate complete failure, to come to grips with the Slavonic sounds [š], [ž], [č]. Another problem is that even in the writing of Latin, there were already local variations in the use of letters, but only one 'new' letter – the 'long' ſ – used at some stages in the early Middle Ages as a contextual variant of s like the σ/ς of Greek. By the late Middle Ages it would appear that this usage was confused, and in most cases the two forms s and ſ seem to be free variants. Certainly, in the early Slavonic examples there is no evidence of this symbol being used for a particular sound. In the Paris Alphabet, in addition to the above examples, where ſ represents all three palatals, it occurs also in 'aſ' (= azъ) and 'hieft' (= estь). The only innovation that we find at this stage (thirteenth century) is the (inconsistent) use of digraphs, like ss, zz, to indicate non-Latin sounds, specifically [š], [ž]. The different local varieties of Latin are reflected in the Latinica forms which became used for Slavonic languages when this usage was established in each area; thus, for example, the German (Gothic) tradition operated in Bohemia and Moravia, the Italian or Hungarian in Slovenia and Croatia; in Poland (as in Hungary) the use of digraphs remained particularly active.

4.2   Later history

The above situation continued up to the fifteenth century. There was still not very much written in Slavonic vernaculars till then, except in Bohemia, where the fourteenth century, especially under Charles IV, saw a considerable amount of local writing (for example, Chronicle of Dalimil, Legend of St Catherine). The early Polish hymn known as 'Bogurodzica' (thirteenth century) is isolated, but does indicate the use of digraphs. Let us now follow what happens in the various areas.

4.2.1   Czech and Slovak (Bohemia, Moravia, Slovakia)

In the fifteenth century we find the first serious attempt to go beyond the digraph system and make Latinica fit Slavonic in a more direct way: this is the system reputedly devised by Jan Hus and described in his *De Orthographia Bohemica* (of 1406?; see Schröpfer 1968), and it has been improved on only in minor details. Its simple power is derived from the use of diacritics: Hus himself used dots over consonants for the palatals (e.g. ś, ż), and the acute for long vowels (for example é, í), while the modern Czech hook (the *háček* – the 'inverted circumflex', as in š, ž) appeared in the late sixteenth century. This system is so elegant and efficient that it is, in addition to being the standard orthography of Czech, Slovak, Slovene and Croatian, also the transcription system used by Slavonic linguists. (See below on transcription.)

Other general problems included the writing of /j/: the early tradition was to use g before front vowels and y before back, and this survived until the mid-nineteenth century, when j was established in this role (by Pavel Šafařík, a Slovak). At the same time the form v was fixed for /v/ in place of w. Phonological changes like the fusion of former variants [i] and [y] produced the usual problem of how far to retain etymological information as opposed to phonetic. Czech made the etymological decision early (eighteenth century) and has not retracted from it, retaining the letters i and y in spite of their phonetic identity (and it was followed in this by Slovak), while all other languages with the same fusion (Bulgarian, Ukrainian, Serbo-Croat, Slovene) have opted for phonetic spelling of this /i/. A parallel case of etymological spelling is the distinction between the two sources of [ū]: original /ū/ is rendered by ú, original /ō/ by ů. Thus the final Czech system was in place by the second half of the nineteenth century.

Slovak has not deviated far from the Czech system, having been able basically simply to drop unnecessary Czech letters like ě, ř, ů; its only innovation has been the vowel symbol ô, used to represent the diphthong [uo] (etymological [ō]). The etymological principle was accepted here too, by 1852, though only after proposals for phonetic spelling by notable names like Anton Bernolák and L'udovít Štúr (de Bray 1980, II: 132–3).

4.2.2   Polish and Sorbian (Poland, Lusatia)

The only Latinica Slavonic area not to adopt this diacritic system is the Polish one, apparently partly from initial resistance on religious grounds to borrowing the Hus system, but mainly perhaps because of its phonological system: while it has the usual collection of (old) palatals (/š/, /ž/, /č/), all now phonetically hard, it also has a new set of soft ones (from the soft dentals), and it may be that it could not come to terms with two (or worse, three) sets of diacritics. Thus Polish uses the acute to indicate the new soft palatals (ś, ź, ć), a usage established in the early sixteenth century, but digraphs for most of the old, namely sz, cz, rz (the latter an etymological spelling for phonetic [ž] from /r'/ and /rj/); for old /ž/ it retains the dot as in Hus's system – ż; and for both old and new /nj/ (now identical) it uses the acute – ń (see chapter 12 for details on the current situation). The sixteenth-century digraph system still included **tz** or **cz** for /c/, and /š/ also appeared as **ss** (de Bray 1980, II: 231). While there were objections to the digraph system already in the fifteenth century, no doubt through the influence of the Hus system, Polish has not replaced its digraphs with the Czech *háček* symbols, and at this stage the problem is that of any language with an established literature behind it. English users are hardly in a position to be critical of the Polish spelling system in this respect, and the Polish system is as efficient as any other Slavonic language in terms of the correlation between sound and symbol.

As for the vowels, the nasals are the most typical feature of the Polish system, and their spelling by the symbols ą and ę is (morpho-)phonological, the surface realization being accessible by fairly consistent rules. These symbols date from the same period (early sixteenth century). So too does the one case of etymological spelling: the letter ó, which represents a former long /ō/, with the acute used as in Czech, but a modern short [u]. While long vowels were still around, in the fifteenth century, writing them double was a usage predating that of the acute, and perhaps matching the digraph consonant system.

For Sorbian, as for Slovak, the nineteenth century was the time for sorting out the orthography, though like Serbian and Croatian, there were major problems with the competing literary variants, not only Upper and Lower Sorbian, but also the Protestant and Catholic versions of Upper Sorbian. These major questions found their modern resolutions only in this century. The modern spelling system of both variants is diacritic, using both the Czech hook (for the old palatals) and the Polish acute (for the new palatals), and was developed by the mid-nineteenth century, being referred to then as the 'analogical' system (de Bray 1980, II: 342).

4.2.3   Croatian (and Serbian), Slovene (Croatia, Dalmatia, Serbia, Slovenia)

Apart from a few details of the application of certain Latin letters, these areas share the same tradition, originally that of Italian Latin. Thus, for example, /j/ was early represented by **g** or **i**; /č/ by **c** or **ch**, /š/ by **sc**, /c/ by **z**, etc. Local variations developed over the late Middle Ages in the representation particularly of the palatals. For /č/ northern Croatian (influenced by Hungarian) used **cs** or **ch**, southern Croatian used simply **c** and Slovene used **zh**; for /š/ northern Croatian used **ſ/s**, southern Croatian **sc** and Slovene used **ſh/sh**; for /ž/, which did not occur in Italian, a new model was set up only in the Dubrovnik area: **sg** or **x**, while else-where there was the usual vague usage, northern Croatian again **ſ/s**, south-ern (Zadar) simply **s** or **z**, Slovene **sh** (see below on the use made of the 'long' s (ſ) as a visual differentiator in Slovene); for /c/ Croatian used **z** and (especially northern) **cz**, Slovene **c**. In so far as Latinica was used in

Serbia (mainly in the north), the only special usage was **x** for /ž/, though this was used, less consistently at first, in southern Croatia too, where it became common from the seventeenth century (however, Vuk Karadžić, in a comparative list of alphabets (*Srpski rječnik* 1818: lxix), lists **x** for /ž/ in the column headed 'Serb. Lat.', but for Croatian only **s** in this role, with **sz** for /s/, as in Hungarian; he also lists only **ch** for /č/ under 'Croatian').

The first area to start formalizing the language was Slovenia, where the late sixteenth century marked the appearance of a series of grammars, starting with that of Adam Bohorič in 1584. As far as spelling is concerned, these grammars fixed the tradition in use at that point. They did not embark on discussions of problems or suggest any changes. Some earlier non-grammatical works are of interest too in listing the letters before their text – usually biblical, for example Sebastian Krelj's *Otrozhia Biblia* of 1566. In these the items of interest are:

digraphs using **h**: **sh** for [ž] and [š], **zh** for [č], **ch** for [šč];
sh for [ž], but **fh** for [š];
s (low) is in fact commonly used for voiced [z] as opposed to **f** for [s], while **z** is used for [c], but so also is **c**.

Thus, overall, there was still a great amount of confusion in these about the use of Latin letters. This situation did not change much in published grammars for a long time: Marko Pohlin in 1768 and 1783 was still using the same system (known as 'bohoričica'), and so were Jernej Kopitar in 1808 and Pavao Solarič in 1814. None of these seems concerned about the orthography, and it was only in the 1820s that the debate hotted up into a 'war' between new systems proposed by Peter Dajnko ('dajnčica') and Franc Metelko ('metelčica'), the former proposing ŋ, ɣ (!) and ч for /nj/, /š/, /č/ respectively, and the latter a whole series of Cyrillic letters, some directly, notably ш, ч for /š/, /č/, also щ, ф, others in adapted form, notably **L** and **N** with hooks for /lj/ and /nj/ – modelled on Vuk's Cyrillic (see Jurančič 1977: 143–5). But it was, in fact, in Croatia that the orthography of both languages was sorted out: following Vuk's reform of Cyrillic (see above) in the early nineteenth century, Ljudevit Gaj in the 1830s performed the same operation on Latinica, using the Czech system and producing a one-to-one symbol correlation between Cyrillic and Latinica as applied to the Serbian and Croatian parallel systems. In turn, Gaj's system ('gajica') was adopted in Slovene in the 1840s, especially through the efforts of the editor Janez Bleiweis (see de Bray 1980, I: 235, 312). The modern systems date from this time.

4.2.4   Other Slavonic – Belorussian
After the Polish–Lithuanian Union of Lublin (1569) and the religious Union of Brest (1596), Belorussian came under direct Polish influence, at

the expense of the freedom it had had under Lithuania alone. At the level of orthography this led to the extensive use of Latinica to write Belorussian. By definition, the graphic system used was that of Polish, and this usage survived until early this century, when the Czech *háček* letters began to be substituted for **cz**, **sz** and **ż**, and **v** for **w**. Many publications at this time were printed in both alphabets. After the Revolution, the use of Latinica was virtually eliminated, though it survived in the western areas until the Second World War (see Mayo 1977: 29–31).

5   Greek

The consistent use of the Greek alphabet to write a Slavonic language is limited to the Macedonian area. It starts from the Turkish conquest in the late fourteenth century and continues through the later Greek domination in the nineteenth century, and, to the extent that any Macedonian is still written in Aegean Macedonia, which would be in private correspondence only, continues until now. In fact, however, since the First World War Greece has effectively not recognized any Slavonic Macedonian minority, and so there is no recognized need for the writing of their language. During the nineteenth century especially there was a large body of Macedonian literature written in Greek script; indeed the first book printed in Macedonian, in 1794, used the Greek alphabet (see Koneski 1983: 112–15).

The problem is the same as with Latinica: the Greek alphabet does not contain sufficient letters to cope with the extra Slavonic sounds, and so there is great vagueness in the application of Greek letters to these. This problem may be seen very early in the alphabet names reported by Banduri (in 1711), and supposed to date from the thirteenth century, though possibly Banduri's source was not in Greek. Here we find, for example, /š/ written as σ/ς ('σαα', 'vας' for 'ša', 'našь'), /ž/ as ζ ('ηζε', 'ζηβητ' for 'iže', 'živite'), and /č/ as τζ ('τζερβη' for 'čьrvь'). The same problem is still around in the eighteenth century, for example the *Lexicon Tetraglosson* (see Kristophson 1974) also has τζ for /č/ (e.g. 'ρετζε' for 'reče'). This document does use the iota subscript on **a** to represent [ă] (e.g. 'ταρβα' for 'd(ă)rva'). Otherwise there appears to be no evidence of any innovation in the form or application of Greek letters to Macedonian.

6   Arabic

The use of Arabic script for a Slavonic language applies to Belorussia, starting from the arrival of the Tatars in the thirteenth-fourteenth centuries, and to Bosnia from the arrival of the Turks in the fourteenth century. For Belorussia we have many examples of such material from the mid-sixteenth to the twentieth centuries (see the collection by Антонович/Antonovič 1968). For Bosnia there exists an Islamic literature for a similar period, including some forty printed books from the nineteenth and twentieth centuries (Janković 1989: 36). Ивић/Ivić (1986: 155) dates such a Bosnian literature from the early seventeenth to the nineteenth centuries. In theory, Arabic – at least in its classical form – would have presented similar problems to Latinica or Greek, since Arabic is also short on symbols for palatals and affricates; further, it would certainly have had problems also in the representation of the vowels; however, it did have extra symbols for 'emphatic' and fricative consonants, as well as the possibility of varying the number of dots on a given symbol. These resources had already been utilized in the application of Arabic script to Turkish, and it was this adapted script which was used by the Slavs, with some innovations of their own; thus, for example – according to the list given by Супрун, Калюта/Suprun, Kaljuta for Belorussian usage (1981: 11–14), the letter *za* was used for /dz/, *tha* for /s'/, *ta* for /t/ and *ta* for /t'/; /c/ is written with *sad* but with three dots added, and the same three dots replace the one of *jim* for /č/, the one of *za* for /ž/ and the one of *ba* for /p/. For the vowels: /o/ is represented by the superscript **a** (') written over *waw*, that is, the classical Arabic diphthong [au] collapsed; however, so also is /u/ written thus (classical Arabic superscript **u** (') followed by *waw*), that is, the superscript difference appears not to have been retained; /e/ is written by what appears to be the superscript **a** (') enlarged to letter size.

A similar description of late Bosnian Arabic script is given by Janković (1989: 32–3), indicating the additional influence of the Vuk/Gaj system of diacritics. Thus, the same three-dot versions as above are used for /č/, /ž/ and /p/; however, a two-dot version of *jim* is used for /c/ and a version of the latter with a circumflex instead of the dots for /č'/; /dž'/ and /dž/ are both simply the original (one-dot) *jim*; a circumflex is also used over *nun* for /n'/ and a *háček* over *lam* for /l'/(!); similarly /o/ is represented by *waw* with a circumflex and /u/ by *waw* with a *háček*; /e/ is simply the classical letter *ha*.

7   Hebrew

Some scant evidence exists of the use of Hebrew script by Belorussian Jews, but it was apparently never used for more than personal writing or place names (Wexler 1973: 47).

8   Orthographic principles (Cyrillic and Latinica)

Apart from odd proposals of a phonetic principle, the clear track in most areas has always been to work on the 'morphological' principle in orthography, that is to retain visible morphological relations in spite of surface phonetic facts. While this would seem to be natural, or at least a 'good idea', for languages like Russian (and English), where surface phonetic changes can be major, theorists do not always see it that way: thus Belorussian has gone for a phonetic representation of the vowels, though, inconsistently, not of the consonants. Thus, while the common lexeme /solod/ 'malt' is realized (in the nominative singular) in both languages with a final [t], Russian spells it солод/solod, Belorussian солад/solad, both on the principle that in all the other forms of this word the /d/ is realized as [d], and so the root morpheme is {solod}. Languages with simpler surface realizations of the morphology do not have the same problems; thus, for example, Serbo-Croat, and to a lesser extent Ukrainian, can boast of having a 'phonetic spelling system' – they simply do not have the linguistic problems of languages like Russian; hence the above word in Ukrainian is realized as [solod], and thus may be spelt 'phonetically' солод/solod; the cognate Serbo-Croat /slad/ is realized as [slad] and spelt slad/слад.

Apart from Serbo-Croat and Ukrainian, all Slavonic languages devoice final obstruents, but none indicate this in the spelling. Ukrainian is odd in respect also of the (regressive) assimilation of obstruents in groups: it does not allow devoicing to occur, but does allow voicing, while all the other languages, including Serbo-Croat, allow assimilation of both sorts. Most languages are inconsistent in their attitude towards the spelling of this assimilation; however, Serbo-Croat maintains its 'phonetic' spelling by writing the surface value of the obstruent, for example sladak/сладак masculine 'sweet', feminine slatka/слатка.

As for the spelling of the vowels, only Belorussian attempts to spell them phonetically, as indicated above (солад/solad = [sòlat]); thus those other languages which show surface changes related to stress position do not represent these in the spelling, for example Russian (солод/solod = [sòlət]); in many cases the vowel changes occur only in certain variants of the standard languages, for example the raising of Bulgarian pre-tonic /o/ to [u], so that no single spelling would be phonetic for the whole standard, not to mention the non-standard variations.

All of the above applies equally to the Cyrillic and Latinica users; in fact, no Latinica user follows the Belorussian model for vowels, that is all follow the morphological principle, but the Latinica version of Serbo-Croat, of course, follows the Cyrillic one in spelling the voice assimilation (*sladak*, but *slatka*).

Finally, in many systems extra diacritics may be used in particular circumstances, for example to indicate suprasegmental features, or to aid disambiguation; examples of the first are:

1   stress position may be indicated by an acute accent in East Slav and Bulgarian dictionaries and textbooks for pedagogical purposes;
2   length and tone may be indicated in Serbo-Croat (with four accent marks) and Slovene's conservative variant (with three accent marks);

3   length (and also quality) of some vowels (*e, o*) may be indicated in the modern variant of Slovene (with the same three accent marks);
4   length may be indicated in post-tonic syllables in Serbo-Croat (by a macron).

Examples of the disambiguation function are:

1   Russian usually marks the word *čto* with an acute to indicate the object pronoun ('what') as opposed to the conjunction ('that');
2   Bulgarian marks the pronoun *i* ('to her') with a grave accent as opposed to the conjunction *i* ('and');
3   Russian has available the letter ё – phonetically representing stressed [o] after a soft consonant – which is used both in pedagogical functions and for disambiguation, as for example to distinguish все/vsë (/vs'o/ 'all', neuter singular) from все/vse (/vs'e/ 'all' plural).

The regular orthographic use of diacritics to indicate suprasegmental features is limited to Czech and Slovak, which use the acute to indicate vowel length.

9   Summary

The modern situation is thus:

Glagolitic is no longer used anywhere (but is still recognized in Croatian Church usage, even if not decipherable by many – for example, Zagreb Cathedral bears a prominent Glagolitic inscription of recent provenance on its interior back wall);

Cyrillic is used throughout the East Slavonic area (Russian, Ukrainian, Belorussian); in the south in Bulgaria, Macedonia and Serbia, and also in Bosnia and Montenegro, thus in the whole of the east and south of the Balkan Slavonic region;

Latinica is used throughout the West Slavonic area (Czech, Slovak, Polish, Sorbian); in the south in Slovenia, Croatia, Bosnia and Dalmatia; also in Serbia, where it exists alongside Cyrillic, though the latter is dominant in most parts.

For details on the modern systems, see the relevant chapters of this book.

TRANSCRIPTION AND TRANSLITERATION

1 Definitions

Most of what is included under both of the terms *transcription* and *trans-literation* can be generalized as 'conversion of scripts' (see Wellisch 1978), in the sense that almost all this activity centres around the business of making one alphabet (or, more generally, a 'script', or writing system) accessible to users of a different system. The one area which is not sub-sumable under this general description is the representation of *phonetic* elements (sounds) in a written form for use not only by users of different phonetic systems, but also by learners of native systems.

Of the two terms, the second – transliteration – is the easier to relate to its application: as its name suggests, it involves the transference (con-version) of *letters*. It is concerned with the conversion of one writing system – and specifically an alphabetic one – to another, and is not necessarily concerned with sounds at all. Transcription, on the other hand, in spite of the root 'script', is applied to the representation of either a writing system *or* a sound system in a written form which will allow users of other systems in particular to appreciate the *sounds* of the source system. While it may use the symbols of a particular target language's orthography, this is not essential, and any symbolic system may be used, depending only on the requirements of the target audience.

2 Target audiences

Who needs conversion of a writing system? It is the huge variety of answers to this question that produces the likewise huge variety of conversion systems. A few of the major customers are: librarians, who want to provide access via their catalogues to material written in scripts other than their own; editors of journals or newspapers, which have to refer at least to names of people, places and other journals in their discussion of foreign sources and events; and linguists, who want to describe languages at various levels of detail to other linguists who may not need (or desire) to access the source script.

While it is probably true to say that linguists are the easiest target audience, in that they are usually by definition well-informed in the busi-ness of scripts and sounds, even they may be subdivided into a variety of groupings related to the reasons why they want a conversion. There may, for example, be linguists reading this book who are unfamiliar with any Slavonic language, let alone the Cyrillic script, and whose needs in terms of conversion are limited to the minimum which will give them access to information about higher levels of the languages, say the morphology or syntax. For these – assuming they are users of a Latinica script – a basic transliteration will suffice, and they may not need any comment at all on those languages which already use a Latinica script. Others will be interested in the sound systems themselves, and will want to know much more than can be got from simple transliteration: at the 'top' end, they will want a highly sophisticated transcription system which will give them minute details about the sounds of the source language.

Other customers for conversion are usually much more diverse in their needs, as also in their degree of sophistication in the general use of scripts. For example, librarians need not be concerned at all about the sounds underlying the foreign symbols, as their primary concern is that material can be accessed in the alphabetic order of their native system, and then its issue and return controlled by staff who do not know the foreign system. If staff or users need to say aloud names or titles, the roughest of approximations is quite satisfactory. On the other hand, radio commentators have to say aloud such foreign names all the time, and so are forced to make decisions about how best to approach this, that is how far they should go in imitating the source pronunciation, if indeed they have any idea of this. The practical situation which clearly occurs typically is that the foreign forms are first written, that is transliterated, by journalists or editors, using whatever degree of approximation suits their minimal written needs, and then the radio journalist, say a news reader, is required to read the form aloud, guided at best by formal recommendation (based, it is hoped, on informed sources), and at worst by uninformed common journalistic usage.

This last case, of the radio announcer's problem, is, of course, not limited to the situation of transliterated source scripts: that of other systems based on the same script as the target is just as great a problem, indeed potentially greater, as the expectation that the system is different is diminished by the apparent familiarity of the script. Two aspects of this are: (1) the different values of the same symbol in different systems, for example the sound value of **ch** in English, French and German; and (2) the use of diacritic signs which tend not to be transferred, and whose function cannot thus be carried over, for example the French vowel accents, whose omission does not produce serious problems, or the Czech consonant hooks, whose omission does produce potentially serious ones.

Ultimately, so long as we are dealing with proper names, as is usually the case in journalism, any approximation will do, so long as it is said often enough to be identifiable in a given form. However, much of this approximation is unsatisfactory even to non-linguists, if only in that it causes much puzzlement and confusion. English-speaking non-Russianists are frequently puzzled by the fact that a name spelt in transliteration with an **e** can be pronounced with an [o], as in 'Gorbach*e*v'; the problem is, of course, that transliteration and imitation have been mixed, in that the Russian letter is indeed the one transliterated as **e**, while the sound is indeed [o]; writing **e** is fine until the name has to be said, just as saying [o] is fine until the written form interferes. This particular problem is reconcilable only by an editorial decision to temper the transliteration with phonetic information – in other words, to go rather for (or towards) a transcription; in the case in question the name would be better written 'Gorbachov' (as in the usual German version 'Gorbatschow').

Just as much confusion is caused by Latinica source names like the Czech names 'Dvorak' (for Dvořák) or 'Mecir' (for Mečíř) – in which the Czech letter ř represents a vibrant palatal fricative sounding somewhat like the sequence 'rzh', and moreover devoiced ('rsh') in final position, as in the second name. As they stand, without their diacritic marks, they can be used as satisfactory visual references to the people in question, but as soon as someone tries to say them (and in the case of a top tennis player, like the latter, this will happen rather often), problems arise: the uninformed, that is the vast majority, are highly puzzled by the addition of a spurious [ž] after r in the first name, and by the pronunciation of c as [č] and r as [š] in the second – always assuming that this is what is indeed said. A Polish name like 'Walesa' (for 'Wałęsa', where w represents [v], ł [w] and ę a front nasal vowel) presents similar problems.

Since the idea of transliteration is perceived as impossible within versions of the same script, we are left with the paradoxical situation that transliterated names, say from Cyrillic, are more likely to be pronounced accurately than names in other Latinica alphabets. It would be nice if everyone moved to a transcription system for all names, whether for print or sound-media use. However, against this stands the inertial force of tradition: once a particular form of a proper name has been used often or long enough, it becomes 'the' form of that name, and in all approximative uses will resist any attempt to make it 'more accurate'. Thus Russian names ending in [-skij] are happily written '-sky', this not conforming to any formal transliteration scheme (though often used in the style of individual journals), but providing a reasonable approximation; 'Dvorak' is generally pronounced (more or less) correctly with the 'extra' [ž], in spite of no clue to this being offered in its form; by now 'Gorbachev' is such an accepted form. A parallel situation is the use of established foreign versions of place names which are not transliterations of the modern native names, but usually represent old variants: for example, Moscow, Vienna, Copenhagen, China, or French 'Londres'. Only occasionally does tradition change, as in the recent conversion of Peking to Beijing in English usage.

Before passing to looking at the major transcription and transliteration systems which are (or have been) in use, we must first sort out a bit of terminological confusion: Wellisch, amongst others, refers to the script as 'Roman', and the alphabet as 'Latin'; it is probably useful to use 'alphabet' in the language-specific sense and 'script' in the general, and I adhere to this usage in general, but I do not regard it as crucial, since the context always makes the meaning clear; however, to many, 'Roman' – or at least 'roman' – refers to a type-style, opposed to 'bold', 'italic' and so on; furthermore, the term 'romanization', as applied to situations like Chinese and Japanese, is used in the sense of an alternative usable script for natives, rather than a transliteration for specific purposes or for foreigners. I therefore use only 'Latinica' for both purposes, and never the term 'Roman' in any form.

The assumption in this book is that we are concerned with conversion *into Latinica*. All other scripts have exactly the same problems, simply viewed from a different perspective; they all perform conversion into their own systems. Earlier in this chapter we considered examples like the representation of Slavonic sounds in the Greek or Arabic alphabets. The common problem is that languages have scripts which, at least by tradition, if not by consistency, represent their own sound system, which is different from others' sound systems; and since even native scripts are only rarely accurate representers of the sounds, it is hardly surprising that trying to apply a different script to a given sound system should create problems.

3   Transcription systems

As transcription is concerned with the transmission of the *sounds* of the source language, the two basic variants needed are: one for specialist linguists, and one for 'approximations' usable for the like of radio journalists.

In the first case, there are two subdivisions: one for the phonologist and one for the phonetician. The phonologist is interested primarily in the phonemes of the source language, and not in the fine details of pronunciation; for this purpose we need what is called a 'phonemic' or 'broad' transcription; thus, for example, 'Gorbachev' could be transcribed as /gorbačóv/. The phonetician is in addition interested in the details, including the effect of stress, and requires a 'phonetic' or 'narrow' transcription; the same name could be transcribed as [gərbʌʧɔf]. (In each case I say 'could' be transcribed, because the given versions are only two of many possible transcription systems or degrees of detail, some of which we will take up below.)

The ideal 'narrow' transcription will allow the (ideal) phonetician to produce a native-like version of any sound or sequence of sounds from any language. The only condition is that the describer and the interpreter are using exactly the same system, that is the interpreter must know the exact (intended) value of every symbol used; for this reason it is necessary to establish widely recognized and accepted systems, indeed preferably only one such system, as transcription would then know no boundaries. This last situation is unfortunately not quite the case, although at least amongst professional phoneticians there is now one such system, known as the International Phonetic Alphabet, whose symbols are used in the above phonetic transcription. Amongst local language pedagogues, especially those using scripts other than Latinica, there is much less acceptance of this alphabet, and more use of variants based on the native alphabet; thus descriptions of Russian intended for internal use prefer a Cyrillic-based system. It is notable, however, that recourse to IPA symbols is frequent in the transcription of details.

For most linguistic purposes, a broad transcription is sufficient, and this presents fewer problems, as the number of symbols required is much smaller. Again, most systems are based on the native alphabet, which means that Latinica is certainly the most popular, but not the only one; again, Russian sources use Cyrillic exclusively for phonemic descriptions. Further, there are variants in the Latinica usage also, depending on the typical sorts of phonemes in particular language groups; it has been common for descriptions of western European languages to use IPA symbols also for broad transcription, thus 'Gorbachev' could be transcribed phonemically as /gorbatʃov/ (the symbol /tʃ/ being the IPA one for the voiceless palatal affricate). Amongst Slavists, however, the tradition has for some time been to use, rather, the symbols existing in the Czech alphabet for this purpose. Thus, for example, palatal consonants are transcribed by the Czech 'hook' letters (š, ž, č); softness of consonants is indicated by an acute (s′, z′). This system has proved very efficient in describing all the Slavonic languages, including their older stages, and also the reconstructed forms of Proto-Slavonic.

One further advantage of this system is that it is easily used also for general transliteration purposes, as it does not use the 'odd' shapes of many IPA symbols, but only regular Latinica letters with diacritics. This is a major advantage, as it reduces the overall number of systems which any reader has to deal with. We will treat this usage below.

Finally, a word about the 'approximative' transcription: while the users of such transcriptions are normally not linguists, and need have no real interest in a 'good' pronunciation of a name, they must still produce something recognizable, and if they consider themselves professionals, they owe it to their public to make a serious stab at correctness. In this case, it is true that using any symbols which do not occur in the native alphabet is a waste of time: no non-linguist can be expected to know the significance of č or tʃ. Provided the sound concerned exists in the target language, there is little problem: here, English would use (its normal) **ch**; but with a foreign sound, there must inevitably be problems: some of these are insurmountable in the sense that given sounds will simply not be imitated, for example Czech /ř/; others are amenable to analogical transcription, like the writing of /ž/ in English as **zh** or of /x/ as **kh**, etc.

At this point the border between transcription and transliteration becomes blurred: such users are both transliterators and transcribers, and the importance of the sound media has made the latter function much more important than previously. It is no longer good enough for a name to be simply transliterated: someone will soon have to say it aloud, and will get it badly wrong if transcription has not been considered, as in the case of the last vowel of 'Gorbachev', or the initial sound of 'Evtushenko' – an effective transliteration/transcription will allow for the pronunciation and produce rather 'Gorbachov' and 'Yevtushenko'. The marking of stress position is also highly desirable.

4 Transliteration systems

I have argued that some of the above instances of transliteration are negative in that what is required in such cases is at least some consideration of sound values, and thus of transcription. For 'pure' transliteration to be justified, the sound must be completely unimportant and irrelevant. Only then can one be 'scientific', that is consistent, in the activity. Consistency here means that a given letter (syllable, ideogram, etc.) of one language is *always* represented by the same *distinct* letter etc. of the target language, without any regard to the behaviour of the underlying sound. In this way 'reversibility' is assured. Potential users of such systems are such as librarians and cartographers; amongst the users of libraries and maps are those who are familiar with the source script, and they want to be able to reconstruct precisely the source form; in any case it must still be assumed that the transliterated forms are for *reading only*; as soon as the question of *speaking* them arises, as in, say, an oral request for a foreign title, or in the teaching of geography, some guidance on the source sounds is desirable to say the least. This is, of course, a linguist's view of the world, and while I would expect to find plenty of support among the readers of this book, it is certainly not a view held by the non-linguistically minded majority.

And so to the systems in use. Not surprisingly, it is the librarians who have done the most work in this area, with the major libraries of the world devising such scientific systems as mentioned above, in the first place for their own direct users, but indirectly also for smaller libraries and many others who adopt their systems. The two major English-language systems are those of the Library of Congress and the British (Museum) Library; both of these are based on the use of the Latinica letters without diacritics, though the Library of Congress system does use the ligature ( ) and breve (˘). Both of these systems date from early this century (1905 and 1917 respectively), and have thus built up a tradition as difficult to replace as a standard orthography.

For the great majority of letters there is no problem, since the basic sounds are the same in all the languages involved and both systems use the 'simple' letters 'a', 'b', 'd', etc. From those that do cause problems, examples of these two systems applied to Russian Cyrillic are as follows:

Russian	Library of Congress	British (Museum) Library
ж	zh	zh
х	kh	kh
ц	ts	ts
щ	shch	shch
й	ĭ	i
ы	y	ui
ъ	″	(omit)
ь	′	′
я	ia	ya

Clearly, the two are very close, but they are nevertheless different enough to cause some confusion, and certainly some aggravation amongst library staff when the wrong one is used! A practical problem with the Library of Congress system is that the diacritics must be done by hand, undesirable in the mechanical age. However, this has been seen as a problem with any foreign diacritics, and in this age of computerised typography need no longer be insurmountable.

Alongside these two English-based systems there have existed others in various European countries, the most important and 'scientific' being the German *Preussische Instruktionen*; the system used in the French *Bibliothèque Nationale* catalogue is somewhat less 'scientific' (Wellisch 1978: 250). Most other countries likewise have used more or less local versions. The problems inherent in such diversity led to the desire for some uniformity, and to the production by the International Organization for Standardization (ISO) of its first transliteration standard (ISO/R9, published in 1954), which was, in fact, for transliteration of Cyrillic. It opted for the Czech/Croat-style use of diacritics, and the above sample letters were transcribed thus:

Russian	ISO
ж	ž
х	h
ц	c
щ	šč
й	j
ы	y
ъ	″
ь	′
я	ja

Adherents of the two English-based systems were not impressed, and stuck to their own systems (compare the 1958 British Standards Institution (BSI) system, virtually the same as the British Library, except 'ȳ' for ы and 'ŭ' for ъ; and the 1976 American Standards Association – now American National Standards Institute (ANSI) – system). The second edition of ISO/R9, in 1968, conceded defeat in acknowledging the British/American system as an acceptable alternative, but the 'double standard' involved clearly defeated the whole purpose, and was reported by Wellisch (1978: 258) as about to be rejected in the third edition ('probably in 1977'), which was to revert to the system of the first edition. (In fact, there was apparently considerable disputation over this edition, and it was finally published only in 1986, as the first 'proper' edition (called ISO 9), as opposed to the previous 'recommendations'.)

Wellisch gives a useful comparative table of the many systems (1978: 260–2), as part of the history of Cyrillic transliteration (pp. 256–64). This includes the draft changes of the ISO third edition.

All of these systems were set up in principle by and for cataloguers. But others were using them too, and in our context most importantly the editors of scholarly journals and books. Inevitably, the confusion of the cataloguers has continued here, and the same variety of systems is apparent throughout the Slavist academic world. Moreover, not only are there different systems in different countries, but even internally in different disciplines. For English-language journals, the BSI or ANSI systems are normal, but now only for non-linguistic material: Slavist linguists have, not surprisingly, opted for the ISO system, based as it is on the Czech model, which thus conveniently serves both purposes of phonemic transcription and transliteration.

One final point must be made about the non-ISO systems: they are more than simply transliteration systems since they, somewhat surprisingly, take into consideration the phonemic system of the particular language involved; for example, in the BL and LC catalogues, the letter **x** is transliterated as 'kh' for all but Serbo-Croat and Macedonian, when it is 'h'; similarly for these two languages the Croat (= Czech) Latinica letters are used for **ж, ц, ч, ш** (see the *British Library Reader Guide no. 3 – Transliteration of Cyrillic*). This usage is based, presumably, on the parallel use of Latinica in Serbo-Croat, expanded to include Macedonian as another Yugoslav alphabet. Likewise, **щ** is transliterated as 'shch' for Russian, but 'sht' for Bulgarian. The example of **г** transliterated as 'g' for most, but as 'h' for Ukrainian and Belorussian, may be defended by the previous existence of the second letters **ґ** (Ukrainian) and **г'** (Belorussian), inconsistently, and no longer, used for [g] as opposed to [h] (Ukrainian) or [ɣ] (Belorussian).

Overall, one would think that a strict transliteration system should be 'language-neutral'. However, as linguists, we can have no objection to the inclusion of language-specific information of this sort, especially as it draws transcription and transliteration closer together. It is this principle which lies behind the system used in this book.

5   The system used in this book

This then being a book on Slavonic linguistics, for the joint purposes of phonemic transcription and graphic transliteration we use the system which has become standard in Slavonic linguistics. This is based on the ISO system, with some relevant phonemic information being allowed as in the above cataloguing practices. These cases are few, and are as follows (the justification given in parentheses):

Letter	Language	Transcription/transliteration
г	Bg. Mac. OCS Ru. SCr.	g
	Bel. Ukr.	h (phonemic/phonetic)
и	Bg. Mac. OCS Ru. SCr.	i
	Ukr.	y (with i for і)
х	Bel. Bg. OCS Ru. Ukr.	x
	Mac. SCr.	h (to match SCr. usage in Latinica)
щ	Ru. Ukr.	šč
	Bg. (OCS Ш)	št (phonemic/phonetic)
ъ	Ru.	″
	Bg.	ă (phonemic/phonetic)
	OCS	ъ (phonemic)
ь	Bel. Ru. Ukr.	′
	OCS	ь (phonemic)

Further, certain local situations will call for some variation between the transcription and transliteration details (for example, in the rendering of soft consonants in Russian). These will be treated in the relevant chapters. Note too that we use the acute rather than the apostrophe for **ь** to avoid confusion.

Finally, where *phonetic* transcription is necessary, the IPA symbols are used, written in square brackets; phonemic transcription is written in oblique brackets. The full transliteration table is given on pp. xii–xiii.

References

Charanis, P. (1961) 'The Armenians in the Byzantine Empire', *Byzantinoslavica* 22: 196–240.
Cubberley, P. (1982) 'Glagolitic's Armenian connection', *Wiener Slawistischer Almanach* 9: 291–304.
—— (1984) 'The formation of Cyrillic and problems of the early Slav alphabets', *Wiener Slawistischer Almanach* 14: 283–302.
—— (1988) 'On the origin and development of the Slavonic letter-names', *Australian Slavonic and East European Studies* 2, 1: 29–54.
de Bray, R.G.A. (1980) *Guide to the Slavonic Languages*, 3 vols, 3rd edn, Columbus, Oh.: Slavica.
Gilyarevsky, R. and Grivnin, V. (1970) *Languages Identification Guide*, Moscow: Nauka.
Hamm, J. (1974) *Staroslavenska gramatika*, Zagreb: Školska knjiga.
Hoffer Edle von Sulmthal, A., and Margaritoff, M. (1989) *За Кирил и Методий*, София: Изд. на Отечествения фронт (Text in Bulgarian, German, Russian and English; English pp. 255–324, 332–3).
Istrin, V. (1988) *1100 Years of the Slavonic Alphabet*, Moscow: Nauka (translation of Истрин 1963).
Janković, S. (1989) 'Ortografsko usavršavanje naše arabice u štampanim

tekstovima. Uticaj ideja Vuka Karadžića', *Prilozi za orijentalnu filologiju* 38: 31–8.

Jurančič, J. (1977) 'Problem cirilice na severozahodu južnoslovanskega etničnega ozemlja', in F. Jakopin (ed.) *Slovansko jezikoslovje. Nahtigalov zbornik*, Ljubljana: Univerza, 135–52.

Kolarič, R. (1970) 'Slovenci in glagolica', *Зборник за филологију и лингвистику* 13, 1: 77–83.

Koneski, B. (1983) *Historical Phonology of Macedonian*, Heidelberg: Carl Winter.

Kristophson, J. (ed.) (1974) 'Das Lexikon Tetraglosson des Daniil Moschopolitis', *Zeitschrift für Balkanologie* 10, 1.

Kuna, H. (1977) 'Neke grafijske osobine bosanskih srjednjovekovnih kodeksa u odnosu prema staroslavenskoj glagoljskoj grafijskoj tradiciji', in F. Jakopin (ed.) *Slovansko jezikoslovje. Nahtigalov zbornik*, Ljubljana: Univerza, 153–66.

Mareš, F. (1971) 'Hlaholice na Moravě a v Čechach', *Slovo* 21: 133–99.

Mayo, P. (1977) 'The alphabet and orthography of Byelorussian in the twentieth century', *The Journal of Byelorussian Studies*, 4, 1: 28–47.

Schenker, A., Stankiewicz, E. (eds.) (1980) *The Slavic Literary Languages: Formation and Development*, New Haven, Conn.: Yale Concilium on International and Area Studies.

Schröpfer, J. (1968) *Hussens Traktat 'Orthographia Bohemica'*, Wiesbaden: Harrassowitz.

Stone, G., Worth, D. (eds.) (1985) *The Formation of the Slavonic Literary Languages*, Columbus, Oh.: Slavica.

Štefanić, V. (1963) *Tisuću i sto godina od moravske misije Ćirila i Metodija* (*Slovo*, Posebni otisak iz br. 13), Zagreb: Staroslavenski institut.

Vajs, J. (1937) 'Hlaholica na Rusi – Novgorodské sgrafity', *Byzantinoslavica* 7: 184–8.

Wellisch, H. (1978) *The Conversion of Scripts – its Nature, History, and Utilization*, New York: Wiley.

Wexler, P. (1973) 'Jewish, Tatar and Karaite communal dialects and their importance for Byelorussian historical linguistics', *The Journal of Byelorussian Studies* 3, 1: 41–54.

Zor, J. (1977) 'Glagolica na Slovenskem', in *Slovansko jezikoslovje. Nahtigalov zbornik*, Ljubljana: Univerza, 483–95.

Антонович, А.К. (1968) *Белорусские тексты, писанные арабским письмом, и их графико-орфографическая система*, Вильнюс.

Велчева, Б.А. (1989) *Глаголица на Балканите до началото на XIII век*, София: БАН (Автореферат).

Ивић, П. (1986) *Српски народ и његов језик*, Београд: Српска књижевна задруга.

Истрин, В.А. (1963) *1100 лет славянской азбуки*, Москва: ИАН.

Карский, Е.Ф, (1928) *Славянская кирилловская палеография*, Ленинград (Reprint 1979, Москва: Наука).

Медынцева, А.А. (1969) 'Глаголические надписи из Софии новгородской', *Советская археология*, 1.

Мирчев, К. (1963) *Историческа граматика на българския език*, София: Наука и изкуство.

Младеновић, А. (1989) 'Око Лукијановог (Вуковог) слова «Ђ»', *Српска Академија Наука и Уметности. Балканолошки институт*. Посебна издања 38: 155–8.

Супрун, А.Е., Калюта, А.М. (1981) *Введение в славянскую филологию*, Минск: Выш. школа.

3 Proto-Slavonic

Alexander M. Schenker

1 Introduction

Proto-Slavonic was the parent language of the thirteen living and two extinct Slavonic speech communities. Most of these speech communities are accorded the status of autonomous languages. However, the distinction between dialect and language being blurred, there can be no unanimity on this issue in all instances, notably that of Slovincian as separate from Cassubian and, indeed, of Cassubian as separate from Polish (see further chapter 13, section 1).

Traditionally, Slavonic is classified into three basic branches, East, West

Table 3.1 Classification of the Slavonic languages

	South	Eastern	[Old Church Slavonic] Bulgarian Macedonian
		Western	Serbo-Croat Slovene
		Czecho-Slovak	Czech Slovak
Proto-Slavonic	West	Sorbian	Upper Sorbian Lower Sorbian
		Lechitic	Polish Cassubian [Polabian]
	East		Russian Ukrainian Belorussian

and South, and subdivided further according to the similarities and distinctions within these branches. This classification is given in table 3.1 (the extinct languages are placed in square brackets).

In addition, it is convenient to group the East and West branches into North Slavonic and the East and South branches into East/South Slavonic. A survey of Late Proto-Slavonic dialects is provided in section 6.

Unlike Latin, the parent language of the Romance languages, Proto-Slavonic was not recorded, and its forms must be reconstructed. Such a reconstruction is accomplished by comparing the forms of all the Slavonic languages and of the languages which, together with Slavonic, constitute the large **Indo-European family of languages** of south-western Asia and Europe. In addition to Slavonic, this family includes Indic (Vedic and classical Sanskrit and many languages of modern India), Iranian (Avestan, Persian and the northern Iranian languages of the Eurasian steppe), Tocharian, Anatolian (Hittite and the lesser languages of Asia Minor), Armenian, Greek, Albanian, Italic (including classical and popular Latin which gave rise to the Romance languages), Celtic, Germanic (the medieval languages with which the Slavs came into contact were Gothic, Old and Middle High German and Old Norse) and Baltic (Lithuanian, Latvian, Old Prussian). As is the case with Slavonic, the genetic relationship of the Indo-European languages is attributed to their descent from a common ancestor, the Proto-Indo-European language, which must also be reconstructed. It is a common practice in historical linguistics to provide reconstructions with asterisks. In this survey, however, language labels will be relied upon to differentiate between attested and reconstructed forms, and asterisks will not be used except to avoid ambiguity.

It is useful to subdivide the period, perhaps four millennia long, separating the disintegration of the Indo-European linguistic unity and the formation of individual Slavonic languages or language groups (about the ninth century AD). While there is no agreement on the criteria for such a subdivision and, hence, on the number of **Proto-Slavonic subperiods**, the least arbitrary formula appears to be one based on the differences in the extent of linguistic change. Thus, the period encompassing the beginning of dialect differentiation within Slavonic is called Late Proto-Slavonic, the period during which changes affected all of Slavonic and only Slavonic is termed Early Proto-Slavonic, and the period characterized by changes affecting Slavonic and Baltic is called Balto-Slavonic. Analogously, it is convenient to subdivide Proto-Indo-European into dialectally diversified Late Proto-Indo-European and dialectally uniform Early Proto-Indo-European. Some scholars use the term 'Common Slavonic' and apply it either to all of 'Proto-Slavonic' or to the last phase of Slavonic linguistic unity (approximating 'Late Proto-Slavonic' of this survey).

The similarities between **Baltic** and **Slavonic** have long been noted. In phonology one could mention the common treatment of the Proto-Indo-

European vocalic sonants (see 2.1) and the development of phonemic pitch (see 2.16); in morphology – the tendency of consonantal stem nouns to acquire -*ĭ*- stem endings (see 3.1.2, note 5), the rise of the category of definiteness in the adjective (see 3.1.4), the development of a two-stem conjugational system (see 3.2), the extension of the participial suffixes -*nt*- and -*ŭs*- by the suffix -*ĭ*- (see 3.2.2(f)); in syntax – the use of the instrumental in the predicate and of the genitive as object of negated verbs (see 4). There are also many coincidences in Baltic and Slavonic lexicon (see 5). Some scholars, from August Schleicher and Karl Brugmann in the nineteenth century to Jerzy Kuryłowicz and André Vaillant more recently, attributed these similarities to a period of shared history and postulated the existence of Balto-Slavonic as an autonomous, post-Proto-Indo-European linguistic entity. Others, like Jan Baudouin de Courtenay, Antoine Meillet, Alfred Senn and Christian Stang, claimed that the features common to Baltic and Slavonic are, in so far as they are not inherited from Proto-Indo-European, a product of separate, though parallel, development, enhanced by territorial contiguity of the two speech communities and by their social and linguistic interaction. This disagreement appears to be largely terminological in nature and the two points of view need not be viewed as contradictory. Since Baltic and Slavonic were at the tail end of the process of the disintegration of the Indo-European speech community, what is termed 'Balto-Slavonic' is, in fact, the very latest stage of Late Proto-Indo-European. Once separated from each other, Baltic and Slavonic (or, at least, some of their dialects) continued to exist side by side and underwent a period of parallel developments and of outright linguistic borrowing.

The Slavs were the last Indo-Europeans to appear in the annals of history. Slavonic texts were not recorded till the middle of the ninth century and the first definite reference to the Slavs' arrival on the frontiers of the civilized world dates from the sixth century AD, when the Slavs struck out upon their conquest of central and south-eastern Europe. Before that time the Slavs dwelled in the obscurity of their **ancestral home**, out of the eye-reach of ancient historians. Their early fates are veiled by the silence of their neighbours, by their own unrevealing oral tradition and by the ambiguity of such non-verbal sources of information as archaeology, anthropology or palaeobotany. It is generally agreed that the search for the ancestral home of the Slavs should be limited to the region bordered by the Oder, the Baltic, the Dnieper, and the Danube, that is, to the approximate area of current Slavonic settlement, excepting the lands which are known to have been colonized in historical times. However, a more precise location of the Slavonic homeland within that region is still a matter of scholarly controversy. Of the several theories proposed, the one which has gained the most adherents would place the prehistoric Slavs in the basin of the middle Dnieper, that is, in what is today north-central and western Ukraine and south-eastern Belarus (Belorussia).

2 Phonology

The reconstructed system of Proto-Indo-European phonemes is so remote from our own linguistic experience and so little susceptible to verification that it is still a subject of scholarly debate. Among the most controversial issues are the role of the laryngeals and of the vowel ə (shwa) in the formation of the Proto-Indo-European vowel system and the number and nature of phonemically relevant features in the system of the Late Proto-Indo-European stops. In order to describe the complex interrelated changes within the phonological system, we shall number the salient points within this section (2.1–2.35) to facilitate reference forward and back.

2.1

With the above caveats in mind, we will assume that the **Late Proto-Indo-European phonemic system** consisted of five short and five long vowels, $\bar{\imath}\ \bar{u}\ \bar{e}\ \bar{o}\ \bar{a}$, and that the consonants included the spirant *s*, three unaspirated tense (unvoiced) stops, *p t k*, three unaspirated lax (voiced) stops, *b d g*, and three aspirated stops which were neutral as to tenseness or laxness and which in this presentation will be transcribed in the traditional way as *bh dh gh*. The three plain velar stops, *k g gh*, contrasted with the palatalized *k′ g′ g′h* and labialized $k^w\ g^w\ g^wh$. In addition, four sonants (or sonorants), *m n r l*, were consonantal when preceded or followed by a vowel but vocalic or syllabic in a non-vocalic environment. In their vocalic function (indicated by a subscript circle), these sonants were short or long. One should also mention the laryngeal sonants ($H_1\ H_2\ H_3$), partly evidenced by Hittite and credited with the transformation of the univocalic system of Early Proto-Indo-European into the multivocalic system of Late Proto-Indo-European.

The mid and low vowels entered into tautosyllabic combinations with high vowels and sonants. In such combinations or diphthongs, the high vowels became semi-vowels, that is they acquired a non-syllabic or consonantal function. There are several ways of marking isolated semi-vowels (in diphthongs, the environment indicates unambiguously the non-syllabic function of semi-vowels). Contrary to the English practice of transcribing non-syllabic *i* and *u* as *y* and *w*, Slavonic linguistic writings favour *i̯* and *u̯* or *j* and *v*. In this survey, *j* and *v* are used for Late Proto-Slavonic reconstructions, with *i̯* and *u̯* reserved for the earlier periods (see 2.33).

Thus, late Proto-Indo-European had a potential for thirty-six short and long diphthongs:

ei̯	eu̯	em	en	er	el
oi̯	ou̯	om	on	or	ol
ai̯	au̯	am	an	ar	al

In addition, during the Balto-Slavonic period, the four syllabic sonants developed epenthetic high vowels, providing a potential for another sixteen diphthongs:

PIE   m̥̄   n̥̄   r̥̄   l̥̄   >   BSl.   ĭm/ŭm   ĭn/ŭn   ĭr/ŭr   ĭl/ŭl

2.2

Comparative evidence suggests the existence of a Proto-Indo-European system of grammaticalized vowel alternations, best known by the German term '**ablaut**' (the terms 'apophony' and 'vowel gradation' are also used). It represents a system of morphophonemic relationships whereby the unmarked vowel *e* entered into a number of marked qualitative and quantitative alternations, depending on the grammatical function of the form. In the qualitative ablaut, the vowel *e* (*e*-grade) alternated with the vowel *o* (*o*-grade). The *e*-grade characterized non-derived verbal roots; the *o*-grade was typical of derived nominal roots. In the quantitative ablaut, a short vowel (normal grade) alternated with a long vowel (long grade) or the absence of a vowel (zero grade). The zero grade of diphthongs consisted in the loss of the vowel and the transfer of its syllabic function to the semi-vowel, sonant or laryngeal, leading to their vocalization: *i̯ u̯ m n r l H* became *i u m n̥ r̥ l̥ ə*. The zero grade of diphthongs extended by a laryngeal yielded long vocalic sonants: *m̥̄ n̥̄ r̥̄ l̥̄*.

The basic *e ~ o* ablaut is represented in Slavonic by many roots, for example OCS *vezǫ* 'I transport' ~ *vozъ* 'cart', *grebǫ* 'I dig' ~ *grobъ* 'grave', *vedǫ* 'I lead' ~ *voždь* 'leader', *rekǫ* 'I say' ~ *rokъ* 'fixed time'. The *e ~ o ~ Ø* ablaut may be exemplified by roots containing semi-vowels or sonants. In the Old Church Slavonic examples below, the Proto-Indo-European diphthongs are no longer perceivable as such because of their monophthongization (see 2.13, 2.21, 2.22):

e-*grade*	o-*grade*	zero grade
-cvisti (i < ĕi̯) 'to bloom'	cvĕtъ (ĕ < ŏi̯) 'flower'	-cvьtǫ (ь < ĭ) 'I bloom'
bl'usti ('u < ĕu̯) 'to watch'	buditi (u < ŏu̯) 'to awaken'	bъdĕti (ъ < ŭ) 'to be awake'
-čęti (ę < ĕn) 'to begin'	konьcь (on < ŏn) 'end'	-čьnǫ (ьn < n̥) 'I begin'
berǫ (er < ĕr) 'I take'	sъborъ (or < ŏr) 'synod'	bьrati (ьr < r̥) 'to take'

These alternations suggest that in Early Proto-Indo-European the vowel *e* was basic, *a* was marginal, *o* arose as an ablaut variant of *e*, and *i* and *u* were ablaut variants of diphthongs.

2.3

The dissolution of Proto-Indo-European linguistic unity was attended by several sound changes which affected clusters of language families.

(a) One such change, the **merger of the aspirated stops with the unaspirated lax stops**, connected Slavonic with Baltic, Iranian, Albanian and Celtic. In other Indo-European languages (like Latin) the aspirated and unaspirated lax stops did not fall together:

LPIE	Balto-Slavonic	OCS	Latin
bh	b	berǫ 'I take'	ferō 'I carry'
b		bolje 'more'	dē-bilis 'weak'
dh	d	dymъ 'smoke'	fūmus 'smoke'
d		dati 'to give'	dare 'to give'
gh	g	gostь 'stranger'	hostis 'enemy'
g		ǫgъlъ 'corner'	angulus 'corner'

(b) Another change produced an important dialect isogloss by dividing the Proto-Indo-European area into the south-central **satem** languages (Slavonic, Baltic, Indic, Iranian, Armenian and Albanian) and the peripheral **centum** languages (Tocharian, Anatolian, Greek, Italic, Celtic and Germanic). In the centum languages, the palatalized velar stops merged with the plain ones, while the labialized velar stops remained distinct; by contrast, in the satem languages, it was the labialized velars which merged with plain velars, while the palatalized velars retained their identity by undergoing spirantization (k' g' > $š$ $ž$). The satem hushing $š$ $ž$ were retained in Lithuanian, but changed in other Baltic languages and in Slavonic into the hissing s z:

LPIE	Balto-Slavonic	Lithuanian	OCS	Latin
k^w	k	kàs 'who'	kъto 'who'	quod 'what'
k	k	kraũjas 'blood'	krъvь 'blood'	cruor 'blood'
k'	š	dĕšimt 'ten'	desętь 'ten'	decem 'ten'
g^w	g	gývas 'living'	živъ (< *g^wīu̯-) 'alive'	vīvus 'alive'
g	g	jùngas 'yoke'	[j]ьgo 'yoke'	iugum 'yoke'
g'	ž	žinaũ 'I know'	znajǫ 'I know'	co-gnoscō 'I know'
g^wh	g	gariù 'I burn'	gorĕti 'to burn'	formus 'hot'
gh	g	gar̃das 'enclosure'	gradъ 'town'	hortus 'garden'
$g'h$	ž	vežù 'I transport'	vezǫ 'I transport'	vehō 'I carry'

(c) In the eastern group of the Indo-European languages, after $i/i̯$, $u/u̯$, r or k, the LPIE s, not followed by a stop, became retroflex. This change proceeded in two stages. The **first stage, s to $š$,** connected Slavonic with Indic, Iranian and Baltic (however, in Latvian and Old Prussian $š$ reverted to s):

PIE	OCS	
nŏk'-ĕi̯-sĭ	nosiši	'you carry' (PRS)
ōu̯s-ī	uši	'ears'
pĕr-sĭd-l-ā	prĕšьla	'passed' (RSLT PART F)
rēk-s-ņt (> rēk-s-int)	rĕšę	'they said' (AOR)

In the solely Slavonic **second stage, š to x** before a back vowel or sonant (alternatively, s > š > x, unless followed by a stop, and x > š by the first palatalization of velars, see 2.9):

PIE	OCS	
ŏrbh-ŏ-i̯-sŭ	rabĕxъ	'servants' (LOC PL)
ōu̯s-ŏ-s	uxo	'ear'
pĕr-sŏd-ī-tēi̯	prĕxoditi	'to pass'
rēk-s-ŏ-m	rĕxъ	'I said' (AOR)

The retroflexion of s did not involve the s issued from the spirantization of k', which suggests that the retroflexion occurred before the satem change of š ž to s z – an example of relative dating of linguistic change.

(d) With these consonantal changes, the period of Balto-Slavonic may be said to have ended. Among the vowels, the dividing line between Balto-Slavonic and Early Proto-Slavonic is provided by the **merger of LPIE ŏ and ă:** ŏ ă merged as ă still in Balto-Slavonic, while ō ā merged as ā in Slavonic, but remained distinct in Baltic.

PIE	Latin	Lithuanian	OCS
ŏu̯ĭ-	ovis 'sheep'	avìs 'sheep'	ovьca 'sheep'
sálĭ-	sāl, sălis 'salt'	saldùs 'sweet'	solь 'salt'
dō-	dōnō 'I present'	dúoti 'to give'	dati 'to give'
mātĕr-	māter 'mother'	mótė 'wife'	mati 'mother'

Similar changes occurred in other Indo-European languages: in Germanic the vowels ŏ ă merged as a and ō ā merged as o, in Indo-Iranian ĕ ŏ ă merged as ă.

2.4

Thus, in the **inventory of Early Proto-Slavonic phonemes**, one may assume a balanced system of four short and four long vowels, in which the 'mid' feature was no longer distinctive (with a corresponding reduction among the diphthongs):

	Front	Back
High	ĭ̄	ŭ̄
Low	ĕ̄	ă̄

Since Balto-Slavonic *ă* eventually yielded Slavonic *ŏ* (see 2.27(a)), questions arise about its quality in Early Proto-Slavonic. The assumption of an *ă* is supported by the Baltic *ă*, by the fact that quantity was a distinctive feature in the Slavonic vocalic system (*ă* to *ā* as *ĕ* to *ē*) and by loans from and into Slavonic (Vaillant 1950: 107). There are also questions about the phonetic value of *ē*, which in some positions yielded an *ā*. It is for these reasons that, instead of the symbols *ĕ* and *ă* used in this survey, some scholars write *ǣ* and *å*.

Among the consonants and sonants, the palatal *š* and the velar *x* were in complementary distribution:

	Labial		Dental		Palatal		Velar	
	Voiceless	*Voiced*	*Voiceless*	*Voiced*	*Voiceless*	*Voiced*	*Voiceless*	*Voiced*
Stop	p	b	t	d			k	g
Spirant			s	z	š		x	
Nasal	m		n					
Liquid			r	l				

2.5

The Proto-Slavonic sound system, throughout its long history, was affected by two fundamental tendencies in the structure of the syllable. One was the **tendency for intrasyllabic harmony**, that is for a back to front (plain to soft or flat to sharp) accommodation within the same syllable. This tendency manifested itself in the palatalization of consonants before front vowels (see 2.9, 2.19), the yodization (see 2.10) and the fronting of back vowels after palatal consonants and after *i̯* (see 2.12).

The other was the **tendency for rising sonority** or a tendency for an intrasyllabic arrangement of phonemes proceeding from lower to higher sonority (the phonemes with the lowest sonority are voiceless spirants, those with the highest are low vowels). The most signal consequences of this tendency were the elimination of closed syllables, otherwise known as the **law of open syllables**, and the rise of prothetic semi-vowels (see 2.8). The former led, in turn, to the loss of final consonants (see 2.6), changes in syllable-initial consonant clusters (see 2.7), and the elimination of diphthongs (see 2.13, 2.21, 2.22).

2.6

The tendency for rising sonority called for the **elimination of all inherited word-final consonants**:

Balto-Slavonic	*OCS*	*Compare Sanskrit*
sūnŭs	synъ 'son'	sūnús 'son'
pādĕs	pade 'you fell'	ábharas 'you carried'
pādĕt	pade 'he fell'	ábharat 'he carried'
u̯ĭlkād	vlьka 'wolf' (GEN SG)	vṛkād 'wolf' (ABL SG)

2.7

Similarly, all **syllable-initial clusters** which were not in accord with the tendency for rising sonority had to be **simplified or modified**:

Balto-Slavonic	OCS	Compare OCS
pŏktŏs	potъ 'sweat'	pekǫ 'I bake'
dādmĭ	damь 'I will give'	dadętъ 'they will give'
sŭpnŏs	sъnъ 'sleep'	sъpati 'to sleep'
grĕbtēį	greti 'to bury'	grebetъ 'he buries'
māzslŏ	maslo 'oil'	mazati 'to spread'
ŏbuīdētēį	obiděti 'to offend'	viděti 'to see'
nŏktĭs	noštь 'night' (see 2.23)	Latin nox, noctis 'night'
ptrūįŏs	Church Slavonic stryi 'paternal uncle'	pater 'father'

When the juxtaposition of a morpheme final and a morpheme initial did not create an impermissible consonant cluster, syllables were opened by a mere shifting of syllable boundaries. Thus, the Old Church Slavonic syllabification *kъ-nje-mu* 'to him', *vъ-zda-ti* 'to give back' derived from the morphemic division *kъn-j-emu, *vъz-da-ti.

2.8

The tendency for rising sonority favoured **prothesis** in syllable-initial vowels. Before *ū*, there developed a prothetic *u*, while before front vowels and, in most dialects, before *ā*, a prothetic *į* arose: *ūdrā* › *uūdrā* › ORu. *vydra* 'otter', *įdōm* › *įidǫ* › OCS *idǫ* [*jьdǫ*] 'I go', *ĕsmĭ* › *įesmĭ* › OCS [*j*]*esmь* 'I am'. The short *ă* remained without prothesis: *ătĭkŏs* › OCS *otьcь* 'father'.

2.9

The principle of intrasyllabic harmony led to the affrication or palatalization of Balto-Slavonic velars before front vowels: *k* to *č* and *g* to *ʒ́* to *ž*. Since this change was followed by two younger palatalizations (see 2.19), it is referred to as the **first palatalization of velars**.

	Balto-Slavonic	OCS		Balto-Slavonic	OCS	
NOM SG	uĭlk-ŏ-s	vlъkъ	VOC	uĭlk-ē	vlьče	'wolf'
	băg-ŏ-s	bogъ		băg-ē	bože	'god'

The new palatal consonants *č* and *ž* were in complementary distribution with *k* and *g* respectively, paralleling the status of *š* and *x* (see 2.3(c)):

	LPIE	OCS		LPIE	OCS	
NOM SG	dŏus-ŏ-s	duxъ	VOC	dŏus-ē	duše	'ghost'

2.10

Sequences of a consonant or sonant followed by the front semi-vowel *į* yielded palatal sounds. This change has come to be known as the **yodization** (from *yod,* the Hebrew name of *į*).

(a) The velar stops developed analogously to the first palatalization of velars, *k* to *č* and *g* to *ǯ* to *ž*:

Balto-Slavonic	OCS		Compare OCS	
plāk-į-ō-m	plačǫ	'I cry'	plakati	'to cry'
lūg-į-ō-m	lьžǫ	'I lie'	lьgati	'to lie'

Forms like OCS *duša* (< PIE *dhŏųs-į-ā*) 'soul', *dušǫ* (< PIE *dhŏus-į-ō-m*) 'I blow' are usually considered instances of the yodization of the velar *x* (compare OCS *duxъ* 'breath', *duxati* 'to blow'), and are listed together with examples of the yodization of *k* and *g*. However, the derivation of *duša, dušǫ* does not require an assumption of the intervening stage **dŏųx-į-ā,* *dŏųx-į-ō-m (compare 2.3(c) and 2.10(b)).

(b) The hissing sibilants yielded hushing ones, *s* to *š*, *z* to *ž*:

Balto-Slavonic	OCS	Compare OCS
dŏųs-į-ō-m (s < s)	dušǫ 'I blow'	duxati 'to blow'
pěįs-į-ō-m (s < k´)	pišǫ 'I write'	pьsati 'to write'
māz-į-ō-m (z < g´)	mažǫ 'I smear'	mazati 'to smear'

As a result of the yodization of *k g s z*, the sounds *č ž š*, previously positional variants of *k g x*, became independent phonemes as shown by such Early Proto-Slavonic minimal pairs as:

lŏųkā 'garlic' (GEN SG)		lŏųčā 'ray' (GEN SG)
nŏgā 'leg' (NOM SG)	versus	nŏžā 'knife' (GEN SG)
dŏųxā 'spirit' (GEN SG)		dŏųšā 'soul' (NOM SG)

(c) The labials developed an epenthetic *l* (labial + *į* > labial + *l* + *į*), which was lost in West Slavonic and Bulgarian/Macedonian in non-initial syllables due to paradigmatic levelling:

Balto-Slavonic	OCS	Compare OCS
sŭp-į-ō-m	sъpljǫ 'I sleep'	sъpati 'to sleep'
gūb-į-ō-m	gybljǫ 'I perish'	gybati 'to perish'
zěm-į-ā	zemlja 'earth'	zemьnъ 'earthly'

The yodization of *ų* was probably a Late Proto-Slavonic change. It contributed to the consonantization of the back semi-vowel (*ų > v*): OCS *loviti, lovljǫ* 'hunt' (see 2.34).

(d) The dental stops *t d* produced different reflexes in different dialect areas. Their discussion, therefore, belongs properly to the Late Proto-

Slavonic period. To avoid this chronological disjunction and to preserve typological symmetry, some scholars assume that *ti̯ di̯* became *t′ d′* in Early Proto-Slavonic, with further developments in Late Proto-Slavonic. This solution is adopted in the present survey, even though there is nothing in the structure of Slavonic to militate against a continued existence of *ti̯ di̯* sequences until their ultimate replacement by palatal consonants (see 2.23).

(e) A similar problem is posed by the yodization of the sonants *n r l*, which, in the name of uniformity of treatment, are transcribed as *n′ r′ l′*.

2.11

Thus, except for the results of the second and third palatalizations of velars, that is, the addition of the palatal *c ʒ* and, dialectally, of *s′* (see 2.19), from the end of Early Proto-Slavonic down to the end of Late Proto-Slavonic the following **consonant system** may be posited:

	Labial		Dental		Palatal		Velar	
	Voiceless	Voiced	Voiceless	Voiced	Voiceless	Voiced	Voiceless	Voiced
Stop	p	b	t	d	t′	d′	k	g
Spirant			s	z	š	ž	x	
Affricate					č			
Nasal		m		n		n′		
Liquid			r	l		r′ l′		

The labial semi-vowel *u̯* and palatal semi-vowel *i̯* were in complementary distribution with the vowels *u* and *i* respectively. The palatal consonants and sonants and the semi-vowel *i̯* are conveniently grouped as 'soft', in opposition to the non-palatal 'hard' sounds.

2.12

In a process which operated throughout the Proto-Slavonic period, **back vowels were fronted** after soft consonants, that is, they were replaced by their front counterparts: *ă* to *ě* and *ŭ* to *ĭ*. When not counteracted by analogy, this change created 'hard' versus 'soft' alternations, frequently referred to by the German term 'umlaut'. The fronting of back vowels may be exemplified by the Old Church Slavonic pairs: *nes-otъ* 'carried' versus *zna[j]-etъ* 'known', *lьv-ovъ* 'leonine' versus *zmi[j]evъ* 'serpentine', *myti* 'to wash' versus *šiti* 'to sew' and so on (for the Late Proto-Slavonic changes in vowel quality, see 2.27). It is also responsible for the alternating 'hard' and 'soft' endings in the inflection of such stems as OCS *sel-o* 'village' versus *polj-e* 'field' (see 3.1.2):

GEN SG	sel-a (‹ *-ā)	polj-ě (‹ *-ē, dialectally)
LOC SG	sel-ě (‹ *-ai̯)	polj-i (‹ *-ei̯, see 2.13)
INST SG	sel-omь (‹ *-āmĭ)	polj-emь (‹ *-ēmĭ)
GEN PL	sel-ъ (‹ *-ŭ)	polj-ь (‹ *-ĭ)
INST PL	sel-y (‹ *-ū)	polj-i (‹ *-ī)

2.13

Complying with the law of open syllables, the many closed-syllable diphthongs were replaced by long vowels. Chronologically, first was the **monophthongization of the diphthongs in i̯ and u̯**. The resultant vowels are often marked with a subscript $_2$: $ăi̯ > ē_2$, $ĕi̯ > ī_2$, $ău̯ > ū_2$, $ĕu̯ > i̯ū_2$.

Balto-Slavonic	*EPSl.*	*OCS*	*Compare Greek*
běrŏi̯tĕ	běrē$_2$tĕ	berěte 'take!'	phéroite 'bring'
stĕig-	stī$_2$g-nōm	stignǫ 'I'll reach'	steíkhō 'I walk'
lŏu̯ki̯ŏs	lū$_2$čĭ	lučь 'light'	loûsson 'white wood'
běu̯d-	bi̯ū$_2$d-ōm	bljudǫ 'I keep'	peúthomai 'I ask'

The instances of $ī_2$ occurring for the expected $ē_2$ (NOM PL of the masculine -ŏ- stems, 2 SG IMP) are probably analogical to the umlauted forms (see 3.1.2 note 6 and 3.2.2(d)). Some scholars, however, formulate phonological rules to account for this replacement.

2.14

In a departure from the tendency for intrasyllabic harmony, $ē$ **became** $ā$ **after soft consonants**. This change is best presented in three stages:

	'to shout'	*'to hear'*	*'to hold'*	*'to stand'*	*Compare 'to see'*
Stage 1	*krīkētei̯	*slūšētei̯	*dĭrgētei̯	*stăi̯ētei̯	*u̯ĕi̯dētei̯
Stage 2	*krīčētei̯	*slūšētei̯	*dĭržētei̯	*stăi̯ētei̯	*u̯ĕi̯dētei̯
Stage 3	*krīčātei̯	*slūšātei̯	*dĭržātei̯	*stăi̯ātei̯	*u̯ĕi̯dētei̯

Slavonic languages show the final stage of this change, except for the Old Church Slavonic texts of Macedonian provenience which, faithful to the tendency for intrasyllabic harmony, retained stage 2:

Old Russian	kričati	slyšati	dьržati	stojati	viděti
Dialectal OCS	kričěti	slyšěti	drьžěti	sto[j]ěti	viděti

The sequences of a prothetic i̯ and root-initial $ē$ were sometimes retained by analogy to the sequences in which a prefix prevented the development of prothesis. Thus, the expected *i̯-ād- from *ēd- 'eat' was replaced in some Slavonic languages by the analogical *i̯-ēd- under the influence of *sŭn-ēd- 'eat up'; compare Old Church Slavonic jasti and sъněsti with Old Russian [j]ěsti and sъněsti.

2.15

The Early Proto-Slavonic back vowels were redundantly and, hence, weakly labialized. However, the introduction of a fully labialized $\bar{u}$ ‹ $\bar{u}_2$, endowed labialization with a phonemic status and contributed to a complete **delabialization of $\bar{u}_1$ to $\bar{y}$**, for example Old Church Slavonic *tu* 'here' (‹ *tŏu̯) versus *ty* 'thou' (‹ *tū).

2.16

The monophthongization of diphthongs led to the development of **phonemic distinctions in pitch** (intonation). Before the monophthongization, long vowels and long diphthongs were rising in pitch, while short vowels and short diphthongs were non-rising (falling). These differences in pitch were automatic, hence phonemically non-distinctive. When, after the monophthongization, Proto-Slavonic obtained non-rising long vowels from originally short diphthongs or two contracting short vowels (see 2.32), the formerly redundant distinctions in pitch became phonemic. Consequently, the long *ī ē ȳ ū ā* could be either rising or non-rising, while the short *ĭ ŭ ĕ ă* were inherently non-rising, contrasting with the corresponding long non-rising vowels. It is customary to refer to the Proto-Slavonic rising and non-rising intonations as 'acute' and 'circumflex' respectively and to transcribe them with an acute (´) and circumflex (˜) accent marks. This practice will be followed in the present survey.

Note: The acute accent mark has multiple values as a vowel diacritic in different Slavonic languages. It denotes the following: (a) the acute in Proto-Slavonic; (b) long rising pitch in Serbo-Croat and Slovene; (c) vowel length in Czech and Slovak; (d) place of stress in East Slavonic, Bulgarian and Macedonian (but recall that in this volume we use '); (e) *u*-like pronunciation of *o* (originally *ō*) in Polish and Sorbian.

2.17

Thus, by the end of the Early Proto-Slavonic period, the **vocalic system** consisted of five long acute vowels, five long circumflex vowels and four short vowels:

	Acute			Circumflex				
	Front	Back		Front	Back		Front	Back
		Unrounded	Rounded		Unrounded	Rounded		
High	í	ý	ú	ĩ	ỹ	ũ	ĭ	ŭ
Low	é		á	ẽ		ã	ĕ	ă

The vowels *ȳ* and *ā*, though typically acute, could be circumflex when their length was not inherited from Balto-Slavonic but was due to Late Proto-Slavonic developments, such as the contraction of circumflex vowels (see 2.32).

2.18

The introduction of pitch distinctions marks the end of the uniform Early Proto-Slavonic period. During the **Late Proto-Slavonic** period, linguistic developments were dialect specific, leading up to the eventual disintegration of Proto-Slavonic. While it is virtually impossible to establish an absolute chronology of change within Early Proto-Slavonic, the task of dating particular Late Proto-Slavonic changes is somewhat easier. One may surmise that they began with the breakup of the territorial integrity of Slavonic around the end of the sixth century AD, when the Slavs began their push into the Balkans and central Europe. It is even possible to assign certain changes to the beginning or the end of Late Proto-Slavonic by assuming that greater dialectal variation implies a more recent event.

2.19

Two new palatalizations of velars (compare 2.9) and the treatment of the *tl dl* clusters are responsible for a major isogloss, separating West Slavonic from East and South Slavonic. In the **second and third palatalizations of velars**, the velar stops developed identically throughout the Slavonic territory: *k* to *c* and *g* to $\jmath$ (simplified to *z'* in most Slavonic languages). However, the palatalization of the velar spirant *x* yielded *š* in West and *s'* in East and South Slavonic. The second palatalization was caused by the new front vowel $\bar{e}_2$ ($< \bar{a}\underline{i}$) acting on the preceding velar. The third palatalization was caused by a high front vowel, with or without an intervening nasal, acting on the following velar. The few Old Church Slavonic examples of *k* becoming *c* after *ĭr* appear to be analogical (Shevelov 1965: 341). The third palatalization started as a phonological development before *ā*, but soon became grammaticalized. Its extent in the individual Slavonic languages is due to various morphological factors.

Second palatalization of velars				Third palatalization of velars			
EPSl.	LPSl.			EPSl.	LPSl.		
	East and South	West			East and South	West	
kåįnā	cē₂nā		'price'	åuįkā	åuįcā		'sheep'
gåįl-	ʒē₂lå		'very'	lėįkå	līcė		'face'
xåįr-	s'ē₂r-	šē₂r-	'grey'	kŭning-	kŭninʒ-		'ruler'
				uįx-	uįs'-	uįš-	'all'

Thus the reflexes of the two palatalizations of *k* and *g* are the same throughout Slavonic: OCS *cěna, ʒělo*; *ovьca, lice, kъnęʒь*; Old Czech *ciena, zielo*; *ovcie, líce, kniez*. However, the East and South Slavonic reflexes of palatalized *x* do not agree with the West Slavonic ones: Old Russian *sěrъ*; OCS *vьsь* versus Old Czech *šierý*; *veš*.

Additional dialect differentiation was provided by the simplification of the affricate $\jmath$ to *z'*, which occurred throughout the Slavonic territory except in Lechitic and the oldest Old Church Slavonic texts, and by the fact that the sequences *ku̯* and *gu̯* underwent the second palatalization in South Slavonic and parts of East Slavonic, but not in West Slavonic:

EPSl.	East and South	West		
ku̯ȁi̯t-	cu̯ē₂t-	ku̯ē₂t-	'flower'
gu̯ȁi̯zdā	ʒu̯ē₂zdā	gu̯ē₂zdā	'star'

These differences may be exemplified by Russian *cvet, zvezdá*; SCr. *cvȉjet, zvijèzda* versus Czech *květ, hvězda*; Polish *kwiat gwiazda*.

2.20
The **clusters tl dl** were permitted only in West Slavonic. Elsewhere, they were simplified to *l* or, as in some Slavonic dialects, replaced by *kl gl*:

EPSl.	East and South	West	
mětlā	mēlā	mětlā	'swept' (RSLT PART F)
sādlā	sālā	sādlā	'fat'

Compare Russian *melá, sálo*; SCr. *mèla, sàlo* with Czech *metla, sádlo*; Polish *miotła, sadło*.

2.21
The monophthongization of diphthongs (see 2.13) affected also the **diphthongs in nasal sonants** (*N*), resulting in the creation of two nasal vowels, a front one derived from *ěN* and a back one derived from *ăN*. As for the diphthongs *ĭN ŭN*, it appears that those derived from the Proto-Indo-European vocalic sonants *n̥ m̥* were denasalized, while those resulting from later borrowings fell together with the vocalic reflexes of *ěN ăN* respectively. Nasal vowels were retained in Lechitic and some Bulgarian and Slovene dialects and denasalized elsewhere. In either case, their reflexes differ so widely as to suggest that their phonetic value in Late Proto-Slavonic was not uniform (see 2.27(c)).

2.22
Early Proto-Slavonic inherited from Balto-Slavonic two types of **diphthongs in liquid sonants** (*R*), differentiated by the height of their vocalic nuclei: the high-vowel diphthongs, *ĭR ŭR*, derived from Proto-Indo-European vocalic liquids and the low-vowel diphthongs *ěR ăR*, derived from *ěR ŏR ăR*. These diphthongs occurred word-initially (*#VRC*) or word-internally (*CVRC*); we use *C* to denote a consonant, and *V* a vowel. In either position the law of open syllables demanded their elimination. There was little dialectal differentiation in the resolution of the *#VRC* diphthongs, testifying to the antiquity of this change. More variegated and, therefore, more recent was the resolution of the *CVRC* diphthongs. There is, in fact, evidence to suggest that this change was still operative in the

ninth century. Its results subdivide the Slavonic territory into four dialect areas: (1) South Slavonic, Czech, and Slovak; (2) East Slavonic; (3) Polish and Sorbian; (4) Cassubian (including Slovincian) and Polabian.

(a) The $\# \breve{a}RC$ sequences (the only examples of the $\# VRC$ formula) were resolved by metathesis, that is, reversal of positions of the vowel and sonant. However, in North Slavonic the distinction between long and short vowels was preserved, while in South Slavonic (and central Slovak dialects), the short diphthongs were lengthened and merged with the long ones, transferring the difference in vowel quantity to that of pitch. As expected (see 2.16), Early Proto-Slavonic long diphthongs yielded acute vowels, while short diphthongs yielded circumflex vowels.

EPSl.	Russian	Polish	Czech	OCS	Serbo-Croat
ărŭĭn- 'even'	róvnyj	równy	rovný	ravьnъ	rávan
ălkŭt- 'elbow'	lòkot´	łokieć	loket	lakъtь	làkat
ārdlă 'plough'	rálo	radło	rádlo	ralo	ràlo
ālkăm- 'greedy'	làkomyj	łakomy	lakomý	lakomъ	làkom

(b) The $C\breve{\imath}RC$ $C\breve{u}RC$ sequences developed in two stages. In the Early Proto-Slavonic stage, common to all the Slavonic languages, the vowel was lost and the vocalic function was transferred to the sonant, which, depending on the quality of the vowel, was either soft, $r´$ $l´$ ($< C\breve{\imath}RC$), or hard, r l ($< C\breve{u}RC$). Vocalic length was replaced by rising pitch.

In Late Proto-Slavonic, vocalic sonants remained syllabic in area 1, with $r´$ becoming r, while $l´$ retained its distinctiveness in Polish, Sorbian and partly Czech, merging elsewhere with l. In other areas, the sonant was preceded by a homorganic vowel, leading to the sequences of the $CVRC$ type. Such a contravention of the law of open syllables suggests that the development of the syllabic sonants outside area 1 belongs to the histories of the individual languages.

(c) The resolution of the $C\breve{e}RC$ $C\breve{a}RC$ sequences was one of the last changes of Late Proto-Slavonic. The $C\breve{e}lC$ sequences fell together with $C\breve{a}lC$ in areas 2 and 4. In area 1 the liquid diphthongs were resolved through metathesis, with the short diphthongs lengthened. The Late Proto-Slavonic pitch distinctions were continued in Serbo-Croat and Slovene, but reinterpreted as place of stress in Bulgarian and Macedonian and as quantity in Czech and Slovak.

In other areas, the short and long diphthongs were resolved by the introduction of an epenthetic vowel creating disyllabic sequences of the CV_1RV_2C type. In area 2, V_1 was the vowel of the original diphthong and V_2 an epenthetic short high vowel, homorganic with V_1. These epenthetic vowels were the later front or back jers, which in this position were always 'strong' (see 2.25). The resultant disyllable is known under its Russian name as '*polnoglasie*' (or, less frequently, 'pleophony'). The Late Proto-Slavonic pitch distinctions were replaced by distinctions in place of stress. The polnoglasie sequences derived from acute diphthongs stressed V_2, while those going back to circumflex diphthongs did not.

In areas 3 and 4, except in Polabian, V_1 was an epenthetic short high vowel, while V_2 continued the vowel of the diphthong. The epenthetic vowels were treated as 'weak' *jers* (see 2.25) and were lost. Their reconstruction is prompted by circumstantial evidence from Polish and Lower Sorbian. Later Proto-Slavonic pitch distinctions were replaced in area 3 by distinctions in vowel quantity. However, only Upper Sorbian has preserved reflexes of quantity distinctions resulting from the acute versus circumflex opposition.

The Polabian facts are difficult to interpret because of the paucity and unreliability of the written records. The *CĕrC* sequences seem to have developed similarly to those in area 3, *CărC* fell together with *CȓC*, and *CălC* yielded *ClŭC*.

EPSl.	Russian	Polish	Czech	Upper Sorbian	Serbo-Croat	Bulgarian
bĕrg- 'bank'	bėreg	brzeg	břeh	brjoh	brȉjeg	breg-ъt
bērzā 'birch'	berëza	brzoza	bříza	brěza	brȅza	brėza
bărnā 'harrow'	boronà	brona	brana	bróna	brána	branà
u̯ārnā 'crow'	voronà	wrona	vrána	wróna	vrȁna	vràna

In Late Proto-Slavonic reconstructions, the diphthongs in liquid sonants will be cited in their *VR* form, in bold face, for example **berg-** 'bank'.

2.23

The **development of t′ d′** (see 2.10(d)) was also characterized by dialectal fragmentation, testifying to the lateness of this change. The reflexes of *t′ d′* fall into five groups: (1) *št žd* in Old Church Slavonic and Bulgarian; (2) *ć ȝ́*, spelled *ć* and *dj/đ* in Serbo-Croat; (3) *k′ g′* in standard Macedonian; (4) *č ȝ̌* in Slovene and East Slavonic, with *ȝ̌* becoming *j* in Slovene and *ȝ̌* becoming *ž* in Russian and, partly, in Ukrainian and Belorussian; (5) *c ȝ* in West Slavonic, with *ȝ* becoming *z* in Czech and Sorbian.

The palatal *t′* had two sources: *ti̯* and *kt* + front vowel. The latter sequence presupposes the lenition of *kt* to *i̯t* and its metathesis to *ti̯* in accordance with the tendency for rising sonority within a syllable.

EPSl.	OCS	Serbo-Croat	Russian	Polish
su̯ē₂t′ā (‹ su̯ăi̯t-i̯-ā) 'candle'	svěšta	svijèća	svečà	świeca
năt′ī (‹ năkt-ī-s) 'night'	noštь	nôć	noč′	noc
mĕd′ā (‹ mĕd-i̯-ā) 'boundary'	mežda	mèđa	mežà	miedza

2.24
Comparative evidence indicates that, except for a small number of enclitics, Late Proto-Slavonic developed distinctive **word stress**. However, the task of reconstructing it and of tracing the evolution of the Slavonic accentual system is rendered difficult by the tensions between phonological principles and morphological patterning. It is for this reason that the formulations given below are to be understood as tendencies, nullified often by morphological factors.

(a) In words whose roots contained an acute vowel, word stress coincided with that vowel and, unless overridden by morphological patterns, was fixed. This can be seen in such Russian word families as *véra véry* 'faith', *vérnyj* 'faithful', *uvérennyj* 'confident', *vérju* 'I believe', *Véročka* 'Verochka' (< *$*u\bar{e}_1r$-* 'believe'); *berëza berëzy berëzu* 'birch', *berëzina* 'birchwood', *berëzka* 'small birch', *beréznik* 'birch grove', *berëzovyj* 'birchen' (< *$*b\bar{e}_1rz$-* 'birch').

(b) In words whose roots contained a circumflex vowel, word stress was movable. If no acute vowel followed, the onset of stress was on the first syllable of the phonological word; when an acute vowel followed the circumflex vowel, the onset of stress was on the acute vowel. This principle, which is known as the law of Saussure/Fortunatov, may be exemplified by such Russian word families as *béreg, bérega* 'shore', *ná bereg* 'to the shore', *náberežnaja* 'embankment' versus *beregá* 'shores', *na beregú* 'on the shore' (< *$*b\breve{e}rg$-* 'elevation'); *vólok* 'portage', *óblako* 'cloud', *návoločka* 'pillowcase' versus *volokú* 'I drag', *oblaká* 'clouds' (< *$*u\breve{e}lk$-* 'drag'); *úmer* 'he died' *versus umerlá* 'she died' (< *$*mr\breve{}$-* 'die').

(c) Fixed oxytonic (that is, word-final) stress was typical of suffixal derivatives and borrowings, as in the following Russian examples: *moloták, molotká* 'mallet' versus *mólot* 'hammer' (< *$*m\breve{a}lt$-* 'mallet'); *kolesó, kolesá, kolesóm* 'wheel' versus *ókolo* 'around' (< *$*k\breve{a}l$-* 'wheel'); *vorotník, vorotniká* 'collar' versus *vórot* 'large collar', *závorot* 'twisting' (< *$*u\breve{a}rt$-* 'turn'); *koról', koroljá, korolëm* 'king' (< *$*k\breve{a}rl$-i-* 'king' < Old High German *Karl*); *molokó, moloká, molokóm* 'milk' (< Germanic *$*meluk$-* 'milk'); *topór, toporá, toporóm* 'axe' (< Avestan *$*tapara$-* 'axe').

2.25
The short high vowels, *ĭ* and *ŭ*, are also referred to as the **jers**, in anticipation of the name given to their reflexes, ь and ъ, in Old Church Slavonic. In word-final position, these vowels were further reduced in length, giving rise to shortened or weak variants of the *jers*. In accordance with Havlík's law, the occurrence of these variants was regulated by an alternating pattern of weak and strong positions counting from the end of the phono-

logical word. The *jers* were weak in word-final position, strong before a weak *jer*, and weak before a strong *jer* or any other vowel. Since the distribution of strong and weak *jers* was automatic, there is no need for special symbols to distinguish between them. When the difference has to be emphasized, strong *ĭ ŭ* (*ь ъ*) will be shown in bold face: NOM SG **dĭnĭ* (*дьнь*) 'day', **sŭnŭ* (*сънъ*) 'sleep'; INST SG **dĭnĭmĭ* (*дьньмь*), *sŭnŭmĭ* (*сънъмь*). This shortening process culminated in the elimination of the weak *jers*, thus ending the era of open syllables and, at the same time, of the Proto-Slavonic period.

2.26
The weakening of *jers* led to a shift of word stress from the weak *jers* to the preceding syllable. Since all pre-tonic vowels were automatically rising, this shift of stress created a new rising pitch, called **neoacute** and transcribed with a superscript tilde (˜).

The appearance of the neoacute disturbed the old pitch distinctions. In the initial syllable of disyllabic words, the acute (**párgŭ* 'doorsill') and the neoacute (**kãrl-i̯-ĭ* 'king') contrasted with the circumflex (**gârdŭ* 'town'). The former binary opposition (acute versus non-acute) was restored when the old acute ceased to function as a phonemically distinct entity throughout Slavonic. The varied modes of its elimination mark off four dialect areas, suggesting a post-Proto-Slavonic development.

(a) In Serbo-Croat, the acute versus circumflex opposition was reinterpreted as a distinction of quantity, with the acute yielding a short fall (ˋ) and the circumflex a long fall (ˆ). The long neoacute remained as a long rise (´). In the Čakavian dialect of Serbo-Croat, the three nouns listed above appear as *präg králj grâd.*

(b) In Czech, Upper Sorbian and Slovene the acute fell together with the neoacute. In Czech and Upper Sorbian it yielded vowel length, which contrasted with vowel shortness generated by the circumflex: Czech *práh král* versus *hrad.* Slovene continues the opposition as one between a long rise and a long fall: *prág králj* versus *grâd.*

(c) In Slovak, Polish and Lower Sorbian, the acute fell together with the circumflex yielding vowel shortness which contrasted with vowel length generated by the neoacute: Slovak *prah hrad* versus *král.*

(d) In Bulgarian, Macedonian and East Slavonic, where the original situation must have resembled that of Czech and Upper Sorbian, quantity distinctions were eventually lost. Instead, vowel length under the acute and neoacute, contrasting with the brevity under the circumflex, was reinterpreted in Bulgarian and Macedonian as an opposition between a stressed and an unstressed vowel and in the East Slavonic *polnoglasie* sequences (see 2.22(c)), as an opposition between a stressed and unstressed V_2; for example, Bulgarian *prág-ът králj-at* versus *grad-ът* (-*ът*/-*at* are postpositive definite articles); Russian *poróg koról'* versus *górod* or *prigorod* 'suburb' (compare 2.24(b)).

2.27
As was seen in the preceding section, the introduction of the neoacute resulted in the shortening of some Early Proto-Slavonic long vowels: the acute long vowels in Serbo-Croat and Slovene, the circumflex long vowels in Czech, Upper Sorbian, East Slavonic, Bulgarian and Macedonian, and both the acute and circumflex long vowels in Slovak, Polish and Lower Sorbian. This shortening led in turn to the phonemicization of previously non-distinctive **differences in vowel quality** which characterized Early Proto-Slavonic (Stankiewicz 1986: 26).

(a) Early Proto-Slavonic **short vowels** were more central (mid-high and mid-low) than their long counterparts. These differences in quality became distinctive as the high short vowels *ĭ ŭ* yielded ь ъ (the so-called front and back *jers*) and the low short vowels *ĕ ă* yielded *e o*. The *jers* had strong and weak variants (see 2.25).

(b) Of the Early Proto-Slavonic **long vowels**, the back vowels $\bar{y}$ (< $\bar{u}_1$) $\bar{u}_2$ $\bar{a}$ remained as *y u a*. The front vowels $\bar{\imath}_1$ and $\bar{\imath}_2$ fell together in *i*, while $\bar{e}_1$ and $\bar{e}_2$ merged in *ě*. The vowel *ě* (the so-called *jat'* of Old Church Slavonic) was a low-front vowel. The testimony of many modern Slavonic languages and of the oldest Old Church Slavonic texts suggests that its phonetic value was that of a fronted *a* [æ]. However, its position in the system was unstable and, depending on other developments, it was either pushed higher (as in East Slavonic, after the denasalization of nasal vowels) or back (as in Lechitic and Bulgarian, after the phonemicization of consonant palatalizations). The vowel *ě*, because of its dual origin (*ě* < $\bar{e}_1$ < $\bar{e}$ and *ě* < $\bar{e}_2$ < *ăi̯*), exhibits different morphophonemic properties: *ě* from $\bar{e}_2$ alternates with *i* (< $\bar{\imath}_2$ < *ěi̯*), while *ě* from $\bar{e}_1$ does not (see 2.12 and 2.13); *ě* from $\bar{e}_2$ also affects preceding velars differently than does *ě* from $\bar{e}_1$ (see 2.9 and 2.19). Since these differences prove important in morphological statements, it is convenient to distinguish between $ě_1$ (< $\bar{e}_1$) and $ě_2$ (< $\bar{e}_2$).

(c) The two **nasal vowels** were opposed to each other as front versus back. Since these features were sufficient to secure their distinctiveness, the nasal vowels displayed considerable latitude in the selection of the non-distinctive features of vocalic height and quantity. The South Slavonic standard languages agreed on the reflex of the front nasal as *ę* (< *ě*), but disagreed on the back nasal: Serbo-Croat *u*, Bulgarian ъ, Old Church

Slavonic and Slovene ọ, Macedonian ạ. The North Slavonic languages favoured a diagonal opposition between a low-front nasal ę [æ] (< ẹ̄) and a high back nasal ụ. Thus, the traditional transcription of Late Proto-Slavonic nasals as ę and ọ is an emblematic rather than a phonetic representation.

EPSl.	LPSl.	Bulgarian	SCr.	Slovene	Slovak	Czech	USo.	Polish	Polabian	Russian
mēnsā 'meat'	męso	mesó	mêso	mesô	mäso	maso	mjaso	mięso	mąsü	mjàso
rānkā 'hand'	rǫka	rъká	rúka	róka	ruka	ruka	ruka	ręka	rǫkä	rukà

2.28
A number of Late Proto-Slavonic changes contributed to the **rise of new quantity oppositions**. Some long vowels (going back to Early Proto-Slavonic long vowels and monophthongized diphthongs) were shortened (see 2.26, 2.29); others were preserved (see 2.26, 2.30). In addition, new lengths arose due to compensatory lengthening (see 2.31) and vowel contraction (see 2.32).

2.29
The fact that Late Proto-Slavonic pitch oppositions were distinctive only on long vowels in word-initial syllables contributed to the **shortening of long vowels in word-final position**. This development, affecting all of Slavonic, is discernible in the languages which have or had ways of indicating phonemic length, such as Serbo-Croat, Slovene, Czech, Slovak and Old Polish. Thus, *sěstrā (NOM SG), *sěstrȳ (GEN SG), *sěstrǭ (ACC SG) 'sister' yielded Czech sestra, sestry, sestru, contrasting with ostrá (NOM SG F), ostrý (NOM SG M), ostrú (ACC SG F) 'sharp', whose length (indicated in Czech with the acute accent) is due to vowel contractions (see 2.32).

2.30
In a development which was typologically linked with the rise of the neo-acute (see 2.26), **long vowels** were **preserved in pre-tonic syllables in disyllabic words**:

LPSl.	Čakavian Serbo-Croat	Štokavian Serbo-Croat	Czech	Polish
travá 'grass'	trāvà	tráva	tráva	trowa (dialectal, Old Polish ā̃)
mǫká 'flour'	mūkà	múka	mouka	mąka (Old Polish ā̃)
barzdá 'furrow'	brāzdà	brázda	brázda	bruzda (Old Polish ō)
svět'á 'candle'	svīćà	svijèća	svíce	świca (dialectal, Old Polish ē)
tręstí 'to shake'	trēstì	trésti	třásti	trząść (Old Polish ā̃)

2.31

The reduction and loss of the weak *jers* led to **compensatory lengthening** of the short vowels in syllables immediately preceding the weak *jers*. Although this was a late change whose extent differed from one dialect area to another, it clearly began in the Late Proto-Slavonic period. However, details of its realization belong properly to the histories of the individual languages. Most examples of compensatory lengthening are found in the central group of the North Slavonic languages.

2.32

Towards the end of Late Proto-Slavonic, there developed a tendency for the elision of intervocalic *j* (< *i̯*, see 2.34) and for the contraction of the two vowels in hiatus, resulting in the creation of new vocalic lengths. The most important consequence of **vowel contraction** was the reintroduction of long vowels in word-final position (compare 2.29).

Vowel contractions were more pervasive in South and West Slavonic than in East Slavonic, with Czech/Slovak and Russian at the two poles of the opposing tendencies. The following examples show the extent and sources of the contracted *ā* in several Slavonic languages:

LPSl.	Czech	Old Polish	Serbo-Croat	Russian	
aja	nová	nowā	nòvā	nóvaja	'new' (NOM SG F)
aje	zná	znā	znâ	znà[j]et	'he knows'
oja	pás	pās	pâs	pójas	'belt'
ěja	smáti se	śmiāć się	smèjati se	smejàt´sja	'to laugh'
ija	přítel (í < á)	przyjaciel	prìjatelj	prijàtel´	'friend'

2.33

The sequences *ьjV* and *ъjV* fell together with the sequences *ijV* and *yjV* in what is known as **tense jers** (transcribed *ь̄ ъ̄*). In Old Church Slavonic tense *jers* were written either as *i* and *y* or as *ь* and *ъ*. In other Slavonic languages tense *jers* behaved like regular *jers*, contracting to *i* and *y* in the strong position (that is, *ь̂jь* > *i*, *ъ̂jь* > *y*) and being lost in the weak position. Since Russian did not have contractions across the *j* (see 2.32), its treatment of strong tense *jers* coincided with that of other *jers*.

LPSl.	OCS	Czech	Serbo-Croat	Russian	
prost-ъ̂-j-ь	prostyi/prostъi	prostý	pròstī	prostój	'plain'
pit-ь̂j-e	pitie/pitьe	pití	píće	pit´ё	'drink'

2.34

The Indo-European and Early Proto-Slavonic semi-vowels *i̯* and *u̯* were pre- or post-vocalic variants of the vowels *i* and *u*. When the monoph-thongization of diphthongs limited the semi-vowels to the pre-vocalic position, the **status of *i̯* and *u̯*** changed since they now occupied the position of consonants (C) in the *CV* syllabic formula. Morphological patterning also pointed to the consonantization of *i̯* and *u̯* because structurally there was no difference between such forms as *moi̯-ъ, moi̯-a, moi̯-e* 'my' and *naš-ъ, naš-a, naš-e* 'our' or *nou̯-ъ, nou̯-a, nou̯-o* 'new' and *star-ъ, star-a, star-o* 'old'.

In addition, the tendency for rising syllabic sonority must have enhanced the consonantal status of *u̯* and hastened its change into *v*. Thus, the process of yodization produced the unacceptable syllable initial *u̯li̯* (see 2.10(c)), which, in order to conform to the syllabic laws of Slavonic, had to change to *vli̯* (> *vl'*). Similarly, in South Slavonic, Czech and Slovak, the monophthongization of liquid diphthongs produced the unacceptable syllable initials of the *u̯R* type (see 2.22(c)) which had to become *vR* in agreement with the regular Slavonic *CR* type.

These considerations make it possible to assume that in Late Proto-Slavonic *u̯* became *v*, and that the latter had the status of an independent phoneme. On the other hand, there are no compelling reasons to consider *i̯* phonemically independent of *i*. However, the traditional practice of using the symbol *j* in Late Proto-Slavonic reconstructions is adopted in this presentation.

2.35
The **phonemic inventory of Late Proto-Slavonic** included seven short and seven long non-*jer* oral vowels, two short *jers*, two short and two long nasal vowels, twenty-six consonants and the glide *j* (see 2.34). Among the consonants, the hushing *š ž č* are classified as alveolar, contrasting with the palatal *s' z'* and the dental *c*:

	Front	Back		Front	Back		Front	Back
		Unrounded	Rounded					
High	ī	ȳ	ū	ь	ъ		ę̄	ǭ
Mid	ē	ō						
Low	ě	ā						

	Labial	Dental	Alveolar	Palatal	Velar
Stop	p b	t d		t' d'	k g
Spirant	v	s z	š ž	s' z'	x
Affricate		c ʒ	č		
Nasal	m	n		n'	
Liquid		r l		r' l'	

The affricates, alveolars, palatals and *j* are considered 'soft'. Of these, *t' d'* developed differently in five dialect areas (see 2.23), *z'* and *ʒ* were dialect variants, and *s'* occurred in East and South Slavonic only (see 2.19).

3 Morphology

Words which are morphemically unanalysable are called simple; those which are analysable into two or more discrete morphemes, the etymological root accompanied by derivational and/or inflectional morphemes, are called complex. Except for some conjunctions and particles which were simple, Proto-Slavonic words were complex. Of these, adverbs showed no inflectional morphemes, that is, they were uninflected, while other complex words were inflected. Inflected words belonged to two large classes which expressed different grammatical meanings or categories: (a) nominals (including nouns, pronouns, adjectives and numerals) and (b) verbs. Accordingly, Proto-Slavonic distinguished between nominal and verbal inflections.

Inflected words consisted of stems and endings. Endings included an obligatory inflectional ending which marked such inflectional categories as case, number, gender, person, infinitive and supine. Verbs and adjectives could also have a pre-final desinential suffix which marked such inflectional categories as aspect, tense or mood (for example, -ěa-, the imperfect formant). Some inflectional categories were expressed with the help of an otherwise independent word (for example, sę in the reflexive or an auxiliary verb in the compound tenses or the conditional).

Stems consisted of roots, either alone or accompanied by one or more affixes, which, depending on whether they preceded or followed the root, are called prefixes or suffixes. Affixes showed varying blends of lexical and grammatical meaning. Some could be exclusively or predominantly lexical; such was the negative prefix (for example, OCS ne-plody 'barren woman', ne-vidimъ 'invisible'), the prefixes in many imperfective verbs (for example, OCS vъ-kušati 'taste', pri-běgati 'take refuge'), diminutive or agentive suffixes (for example, OCS dъšt-ic-a 'small board', uči-telj-ь 'teacher'). Others could be exclusively or predominantly grammatical, such as the suffixes switching one part of speech to another (for example, the suffix -ьn- forming adjectives from nouns).

Suffixes which assigned a stem to a particular inflectional pattern are called thematic. Most thematic suffixes of Proto-Indo-European lost their identity in Proto-Slavonic. Such were the thematic vowels of the Proto-Indo-European noun inflection which in Proto-Slavonic blended in with the inflectional endings. Their original morphemic independence is evident from such forms as OCS INST SG grad-omь 'town', syn-ъmь 'son', pǫt-ьmь 'road', whose endings were derived from the sequences of the Proto-Indo-European thematic vowels -ŏ-, -ŭ-, -ĭ- and the inflectional ending -mĭ (compare 3.1.2).

Proto-Slavonic did not use infixation as a grammatical device. It retained, however, traces of the Indo-European present-tense infix -n- in a handful of forms: for example OCS 3 SG AOR sědě, leža vs. 3 SG PRS sędetъ, ležetъ from the roots *sēd-/sē-n-d- 'sit', *lěg-/lě-n-g- 'lie'.

3.1   Nominal morphology

From the standpoint of their derivational structure, Proto-Indo-European nominal stems may be classified into derived and underived or simple.

Derived stems which ended in a thematic vowel are called **thematic (vocalic)**. They included stems in -ŏ- (M and N), -ā- (F and M), -ĭ- (F and M) and -ŭ- (M). Stems in which the thematic vowels -ŏ- and -ā- were preceded by i̯ (typically, the derivational suffix -i̯-) are referred to as the -i̯-ŏ- and -i̯-ā- stems. As expected, back vowels after i̯ were fronted (see 2.12). The -i̯-ī- stems (F and M) were a subclass of the -i̯-ā- stems, differing from them in the nominative singular only. All the thematic stems were represented among the nouns; however, only the -ŏ-/-i̯-ŏ-, -ā-/-i̯-ā- and -ĭ- (F) stems were productive (for examples, see 3.1.2). Of these, the first two characterized the indefinite adjectives, -ŏ-/-i̯-ŏ- (M and N) and -ā-/-i̯-ā- (F). The Late Proto-Slavonic numerals *jedin*- '1' (singular and plural only) and *dъv*- '2' (dual only) belonged to the -ŏ- and -ă- classes, while *tr-ь*- '3' (plural only), *pęt-ь*- '5' (singular only) and higher belonged to the -ĭ- class.

Stems without a thematic vowel are called **athematic (consonantal)**. Of the derived athematic stems, Proto-Slavonic retained stems in the suffixes -ōn-/-ĕn- (M), -ŏs-/-ĕs- (N), -tēr-/-tĕr- and -ū-/-ŭu̯- (F), which showed nominative singular versus non-nominative singular ablaut variants, and stems in -mēn-/-mĕn- and -ēnt-/-ĕnt- (N), where the nominative singular length developed probably within Slavonic (Meillet 1934: 426). In the -tēr-/-tĕr- stems, the NOM SG -tēr- was replaced by -tī- by analogy with the -i̯-ī- stems. Except for the -ēnt-/-ĕnt- stems, the Late Proto-Slavonic athematic stems were unproductive. They included a small number of nouns (see 3.1.2, the numeral *četyr*- '4' and some forms of *desęt*- '10'.

In addition, athematic endings occurred with the plural (that is, second) stems of the masculine personal nouns in -tĕl-i̯-/-tel-, -ār-i̯-/-ār-, -(ān)-īn-/-(ān)- as in OCS NOM PL and GEN PL *žitele žitelь*, *rybare rybarъ*, *graždane graždanъ*, from *žitelj-/žitel-* 'inhabitant', *rybarj-/rybar-* 'fisherman', *graždanin-/graždan-* 'town dweller', as well as with the nominative singular and the nominative plural masculine of the present active and past active participles (see 3.2.2(f)).

Simple athematic nominal stems were either lost in Proto-Slavonic or transferred to a thematic class, with or without a derivational suffix, for example *dĕnt-s* 'tooth' (compare Latin *dēns, dentis*) was lost and replaced by *g'ŏmbh-ŏ-s* 'stake' (compare OCS *zǫbъ* 'tooth'), *k'r̥d-* 'heart' (Latin *cor, cordis*) was replaced by *k'r̥d-ĭk-ŏ-m* (OCS *srьdьce* 'heart'), *(s)nŏigʷh-s* 'snow' (Latin *nix, nivis*) was replaced by *(s)nŏigʷh-ŏ-s* (OCS *sněgъ* 'snow'), *mūs-s* 'mouse' (Latin *mūs*) was replaced by *mūs-ĭ-s* (OCS *myšь* 'mouse').

The shape of inflectional endings allows us to assign Proto-Indo-European and Proto-Slavonic nominals to two inflectional subtypes, one for nouns and numerals and the other for pronouns. The inflection of Proto-Indo-European adjectives did not differ from that of nouns. In Proto-Slavonic, however, only the indefinite adjectives declined like nouns, while the newly created definite adjectives declined like pronouns.

3.1.1   Nominal categories

Among the Slavonic nominals, the adjectives were obligatorily marked for case, number and gender and, in most instances, for gradation and specificity. The nouns were inflected for case and number, and were inherently specified for gender. The gendered pronouns distinguished case, number and gender, while the non-gendered ones and the cardinal numerals '5' and higher were inflected for case only.

Characteristically nominal was the grammatical category of **case**. Late Proto-Indo-European had a seven-case system: nominative, accusative, genitive, dative, instrumental, locative and ablative. The vocative was a case-like address form used with singular personal nouns. Balto-Slavonic lost the distinction between the genitive and ablative (the Proto-Indo-European ablative was not a distinct case except in the singular of the -ŏ-stems), and the new six-case system, with the genitive representing the syncretized cases, was handed down to Proto-Slavonic. Case syncretism was also important in the dual (which distinguished three case forms only: the nominative/accusative, genitive/locative and dative/instrumental), and in the formation of Proto-Slavonic subgenders (see below). The dative and instrumental endings contained the phoneme m, an Indo-European dialect feature connecting Balto-Slavonic and Germanic and opposing them to the other Indo-European languages where the reflexes of bh are found.

Of the three Proto-Indo-European **numbers**, singular, dual and plural, the dual has proved to be least stable. It was still a regular category in Old Church Slavonic, its vestiges are found in all the Slavonic languages but, as a grammatical category, it survives in Slovene and Upper and Lower Sorbian only.

Like most early Indo-European languages Proto-Slavonic distinguished three **genders**: masculine, feminine and neuter. In addition, Proto-Slavonic developed a distinction between two masculine **subgenders**: personal and non-personal, principally among the -ŏ-/-ĭ-ŏ- stems. The former was expressed by the syncretism of the accusative and genitive, the latter by an absence of such a syncretism. This distinction was later extended to oppose the animate and inanimate subgenders.

Proto-Slavonic qualitative adjectives continued the Proto-Indo-European distinctions of **gradation** with positive, comparative and superlative degrees. In addition, Proto-Slavonic non-possessive adjectives developed the distinction of **specificity**, whereby the definite (also known as pronominal or compound) adjectives were opposed to the indefinite adjectives.

3.1.2   Noun morphology

Proto-Indo-European and Proto-Slavonic nouns may be assigned to declensions according to their stem-class (see 3.1), gender, and phonetic developments at the juncture of the stem and the inflectional ending. One athematic and four thematic declensions were distinguished.

The athematic (consonantal) declension had several subtypes, depending on the form of the stem suffix:

	PIE	LPSl.	
-ŏs-/-ĕs- (N)	nĕbh-ŏs-/nĕbh-ĕs-	nebo, nebese	'sky'
-ū-/-ŭu̯- (F)	lĕu̯bh-ū-/lĕu̯bh-ŭu̯-	l'uby, l'ubъve	'love'
-tēr-/-tĕr- (F)	mā-tēr-/mā-tĕr-	mati, matere	'mother'
-ŏn-/-ĕn- (M)	kām-ŏn-/kām-ĕn-	kamy, kamene	'stone'
-mēn-/-mĕn- (M)	pŏl-mēn-/pŏl-mĕn-	polmę, polmene	'flame'
-mēn-/-mĕn- (N)	sē-mēn-/sē-mĕn-	sěmę, sěmene	'seed'
-ēnt-/-ĕnt- (N)	āgn-ēnt-/āgn-ĕnt-	(j)agnę, (j)agnęte	'lamb'

The thematic declensions distinguished four basic subtypes: $-\ŭ-$, $-\ĭ-$, $-\ŏ-/$ $-i̯-ŏ-$ and $-ā-/-i̯-ā-/-i̯-ī-$:

		PIE	LPSl.	OCS	
-ŭ-	(M)	sūn-ŭ-s	synъ	synъ	'son'
-ĭ-	(F)	kŏst-ĭ-s	kostь	kostь	'bone'
	(M)	pŏnt-ĭ-s	pǫtь	pǫtь	'road'
-ŏ-	(M)	ŏrbh-ŏ-s	orbъ	rabъ	'slave'
	(N)	g'r̥n-ŏ-m	zŗ'no	zrьno	'grain'
-i̯-ŏ-(M)		dŭzd-i̯-ŏ-s	dъžd'ь	dъždь	'rain'
	(N)	lŏg-i̯-ŏ-m	lože	lože	'bed'
-ā-	(F)	gʷĕn-ā	žena	žena	'woman'
	(M)	u̯ŏldūk-ā	voldyka	vladyka	'leader'
-i̯-ā-(F)		u̯ŏl-i̯-ā	vol'a	volja	'will'
	(M)	i̯ŏu̯n-ŏs-i̯-ā	junoša	junoša	'youth'
-i̯-ī	(F)	bhăg-ūn-i̯-ī	bogyn'i	bogynji	'goddess'
	(M)	săn-dhī-i̯-ī	sǫdiị̄	sǫdii	'judge'

While the Proto-Indo-European endings of the $-i̯-ŏ-$ and $-i̯-ā-$ stems did not differ from those of the $-ŏ-$ and $-ā-$ stems respectively, in Proto-Slavonic, due to the fronting of back vowels (see 2.12), there arose a distinction between the hard ($-ŏ-$ and $-ā-$) and soft ($-i̯-ŏ-$ and $-i̯-ā-$) stem endings, which manifested itself by the alternations $-ъ \sim -ь$, $-o \sim -e$, $-ě_2 \sim -i_2$, $-y \sim -i$, $-y_2 \sim -ě_2/-ę-$ (see note 2a below). The Late Proto-Slavonic hard stem endings are listed in table 3.2. These Late Proto-Slavonic endings are correlated with the Proto-Indo-European endings listed in table 3.3.

Table 3.2 Noun endings of Late Proto-Slavonic

		Athematic	-ŭ-	-ĭ-	-ŏ-	-ā-
	VOC	= NOM	-u	-i	-e/-u	-o
SG	NOM	(-y, -o, -i, ę)	-ъ	-ь	M -ъ, N -o	-a
	ACC	-ь (-o, -ę)	-ъ	-ь	M -ъ, N -o	-ǫ
	GEN	-e	-u	-i	-a	-y₂
	DAT	-i	-ovi	-i	-u	-ě₂
	INST	M/N -ьmь	-ъmь	M -ьmь	-omь	-ojǫ
		F -ьjǫ		F -ьjǫ	-ъmь	
	LOC	-e	-u	-i	-ě₂	-ě₂
DU	NOM/ACC	M/F -i, N -ě	-y	-i	M -a, F/N -ě₂	-ě₂
	GEN/LOC	-u	-ovu	-ьju	-u	-u
	DAT/INST	-ьma	-ъma	-ьma	-oma	-ama
PL	NOM	M -e, F -i, N -a	-ove	M -ьje, F -i	-i₂	-y₂
	ACC	M/F -i, N -a	-y	-i	-y₂	-y₂
	GEN	-ъ	-ovъ	-ьjь	-ъ	-ъ
	DAT	-ьmъ	-ъmъ	-ьmъ	-omъ	-amъ
	INST	M/F -ьmi, N -y	-ъmi	-ьmi	-y	-ami
	LOC	-ьхъ	-ъхъ	-ьхъ	-ě₂хъ	-ахъ

Table 3.3 Noun endings of Proto-Indo-European

		Athematic	-ŭ-	-ĭ-	-ŏ-	-ā-
	VOC	-∅	-ŏu̯-∅	-ĕi̯-∅	-ĕ-∅	-ă-∅
SG	NOM	-s, -∅	-ŭ-s	-ĭ-s	-ŏ-s	-ā-∅
	ACC	-m̥	-ŭ-m	-ĭ-m	-ŏ-m	-ā-m
	GEN/ABL	-ĕs	-ŏu̯-s	-ĕi̯-s	-ŏ-ăd › -ād	-ās
	DAT	-ĕi̯	-ŏu̯-ĕi̯	-ĕi̯-ĕi̯	-ŏ-ēī › -ōi̯	-ā-ĕi̯ › -āi̯
	INST	-mĭ	-ŭ-mĭ	-ĭ-mĭ	-ŏ-mĭ	-ā-m
	LOC	-ĭ	-ŏu̯-∅	-ĕi̯-∅	-ŏ-i̯	-ā-i̯
DU	NOM/ACC	-ĕ, -ĭ	-ŭ-ĕ › -ū	-ĭ-ĕ › -ī	-ŏ-ĕ › -ō	-ā-i̯
	GEN/LOC	-ŏu̯s	-ŏu̯-ŏu̯s	-ĕi̯-ŏu̯s	-ŏ-ŏu̯s › -ōu̯s	-ā-ŏu̯s › -āu̯s
	DAT/INST	-mō	-ŭ-mō	-ĭ-mō	-ŏ-mō	-ā-mō
PL	NOM	-ĕs	-ŏu̯-ĕs	-ĕi̯-ĕs	-ŏ-es › -ōs, -ŏi̯	-ā-ĕs › -ās
	ACC	-n̥s	-ŭ-ns	-ĭ-ns	-ŏ-ns	-ā-ns
	GEN	-ŏm/-ōm	-ŏu̯-ŏm	-ĕi̯-ŏm	-ŏ-ŏm › -ōm	-ā-ŏm › -ām
	DAT	-mŭs	-ŭ-mŭs	-ĭ-mŭs	-ŏ-mŭs	-ā-mŭs
	INST	-mīs	-ŭ-mīs	-ĭ-mīs	-ŏ-ŏi̯s › -ōi̯s	-ā-mīs
	LOC	-sŭ	-ŭ-sŭ	-ĭ-sŭ	-ŏi̯-sŭ	-ā-sŭ

Notes to tables 3.2 and 3.3

1   The loss of final consonants (see 2.6) and the monophthongization of diphthongs (see 2.13) caused the Proto-Indo-European thematic

vowels and endings to blend into Proto-Slavonic monomorphemic endings; for example, Proto-Indo-European NOM SG *sŭn-ŭ-s*, GEN SG *sūn-ŏu̯-s*, DAT SG *sūn-ŏu̯-ĕi̯* 'son' › *syn-ъ, syn-u, syn-ovi*. The differences in the shape of the thematic vowel are due to ablaut variations, for example NOM SG *-ŏ-s*, *-āØ* versus VOC *-ĕ-Ø, -ă-Ø*, NOM SG *-ŭ-s, -ĭ-s* versus GEN SG *-ŏu̯-s -ĕi̯-s*. In the nominative/accusative singular of the athematic stems, the Proto-Indo-European stem suffixes were reinterpreted as Late Proto-Slavonic inflectional endings (listed in parentheses).

2   Some Proto-Slavonic endings which cannot be derived from the postulated Proto-Indo-European forms by the application of general phonetic laws, may be explained by developments restricted to particular grammatical endings:

(a) In *-Vn(t)s*, *n* was lost and the preceding vowels, if short, underwent compensatory lengthening, and the low back vowels were, as a rule, raised to *ū*; for example NOM SG **kām-ōn-s* 'stone' › **kām-ū* › *kamy*; ACC PL **sūn-ŭ-ns* 'son' › **sūn-ū* › *syn-y*, **kŏst-ĭ-ns* 'bone' › **kŏst-ī* › *kost-i*, **ŏrbh-ŏ-ns* 'slave' › **ŏrb-ū* › *orb-y*, **gʷĕn-ā-ns* 'woman' › **gĕn-ū* › *žen-y*. In the sequence **Cn̥s*, *n̥* was lengthened yielding *i*: ACC PL **kām-en-n̥s* › *kameni*. The sequences *-ĕ-ns*, *-ē-ns* of the *-i̯-ŏ-*, *-i̯-ā-* stems (‹ *-i̯-ŏ-ns*, *-i̯-ā-ns*, by 2.12) yielded the expected *-ē* in North Slavonic (referred to as *-ĕ₃*), while in South Slavonic *n* was retained, yielding *-ę*; for example ACC PL **măng-i̯-ŏ-ns* 'man', **kŏz-i̯-ā-ns* 'goatskin' › North Slavonic *mǫž-ĕ, kož-ĕ* versus South Slavonic *mǫž-ę, kož-ę*. The accusative plural ending of the *-a-/-i̯-ā-* stems spread analogically to the genitive singular and the nominative plural on the model of the *-ĭ-* stems. The alternation *-y ~ -ĕ/-ę* is symbolized by *-y₂*.

(b) Long vowels combined with word-final *m* to form nasal vowels: ACC SG **gʷĕn-ā-m* 'woman' › *žen-ǫ*; however, short vowels in that position were denasalized, and *ŏ* was raised to *ŭ*; ACC SG **sūn-ŭ-m* 'son' › *syn-ъ*, **kŏst-ĭ-m* 'bone' › **kost-ь*, **ŏrbh-ŏ-m* 'slave' › *orb-ъ*. Slavonic is alone among the Indo-European languages to derive the genitive plural of the athematic stems from **-ŏm* rather than **-ōm*: **sēmĕn-ŏm* 'seed' › *sĕmen-ъ*. The athematic genitive plural ending *-ъ* was analogically extended to the *-ŏ-* and *-ā-* stems.

3   All neuter stems syncretized the nominative and accusative. In the athematic stems the nominative/accusative singular was generalized from the nominative singular (**nĕbh-ŏs-Ø* 'sky' › *neb-o*, **sēmēn-Ø* 'seed' › *sĕmę*), while in the *-ŏ-* stems, the nominative/accusative singular ending *-o* was extended analogically from the pronoun *to* 'that' (‹ **tŏd*), replacing the expected *-ъ* (‹ PIE *-ŏ-m*); for example

zŕ'n-o 'grain' (‹ **g'ŕn-ŏ-m*). In the nominative/accusative plural all neuter stems had *-a* (‹ PIE *-ā*), for example *nebes-a, sěmen-a, zŕ'n-a.*

4 The NOM SG *-ъ* of the *-ŏ-* stems and the VOC *-u* of the *-i-ŏ-* stems were taken over from the *-ŭ-* stem declension. In the post-Proto-Slavonic period the *-ŭ-* stem declension, though unproductive as a whole, provided individual endings of several cases of the *-ŏ-* stems. The most ancient instance of these analogical developments is the North Slavonic replacement of the *-ŏ-* stem INST SG *-omь* by the *-ŭ-* stem *-ъmь.*

5 The masculine and feminine athematic and *-ĭ-* stems influenced each other. The INST SG *-ьmь* and *-ьjǫ*, NOM/ACC DU *-i*, DAT/INST DU *-ьma*, LOC PL *-ьхь*, DAT PL *-ьmъ* and INST PL *-ьmi* of the *-ĭ-* stems spread to the athematic stems. By contrast, the DAT SG *-i* of the athematic stems was taken over by the *-ĭ-* stems.

6 The NOM PL *-i₂* of the *-ŏ-* stems was derived from the pronominal ending *-ŏi̯* which replaced the nominal ending *-ŏs*. The expected *-ě₂* was probably displaced by *-i* (‹ *-ĕi̯*) of the *-i-ŏ-* stems. The nominative plural of all the feminine nouns was analogical to the accusative plural.

7 The INST SG *-ojǫ/-ejǫ* of the *-ā-/-i-ā-* stems was taken over from the pronominal type and then spread into the feminine athematic and *-ĭ-* stems as *-ьjǫ.*

8 The LOC PL *-ě₂хъ* (‹ *-ŏi̯-sŭ*) of the *-ŏ-* stems is pronominal in origin. The ending *-aхъ* of the *-ā-* stems for the expected *-asъ* (recorded in Old Czech) was modelled on the phonetically regular locative plural endings of the other thematic declensions.

9 Lacking a satisfactory explanation are LOC SG *-e* of the athematic stems, DAT SG *-u* and INST PL *-y* of the *-ŏ-* stems.

3.1.3 Pronominal morphology

In accordance with their ability to distinguish gender, Proto-Slavonic **pronouns** may be classified into gendered and non-gendered. Gendered pronouns were thematic. They included two *-ĭ-* stems, the demonstrative *sь, si, se* 'this here' (‹ **k'-*) and the anaphoric *jь* 'that which is known'; and various *-ŏ-/-ŏi̯-* and *-ā-/-āi̯-* stems such as the demonstratives *tъ* 'this', *ovъ* 'that', *onъ* 'that yonder'; the interrogatives *kъjь* 'which' (‹ **kʷŭi-*), *kotorъ* 'which of a number'; the possessives *mojь* 'my', *tvojь* 'thy', *svojь* 'one's own', *čьjь* 'whose' (‹ **kʷĭ-i̯-*), *našь* 'our' (‹ **nās-i̯-*), *vašь* 'your' (‹ **u̯ās-i̯-*); the qualitative *sicь* 'like this here' (‹ **k'ī-k-*), *jakъ* 'like that which is known', *takъ* 'like this', *kakъ* 'like what' (‹ **kʷ-āk-*); the quantitative *mъnogъ* 'many', *vьsь* 'all' (‹ **u̯ĭs-*), *selikъ* 'to this degree', *tolikъ* 'to that degree', *jelikъ* 'to the known degree', *kolikъ* 'to what degree'. The anaphoric *j-* and the demonstrative *t-* or *on-* (depending on the dialect) combined to form the suppletive paradigm of the third-person pronoun, with *t-/on-* in the nominative and *j-* in the oblique cases.

The non-gendered pronouns included the *-ŏ-* stem interrogative *kъ-to* 'who' (‹ $*k^w$-ŏ-), the -ĭ- stem interrogative čь-to 'what' (‹ $*k^w$-ĭ-), as well as several athematic pronouns, the reflexive s- 'oneself'; first person (with suppletive stems): SG azъ/m (‹ $*ēg'$-/m-), DU vě/n-, PL my/n-; second person: SG t-, DU/PL v-.

The inflectional endings of the gendered pronouns and of the interrogative non-gendered pronouns are given in table 3.4.

Table 3.4   Pronoun endings of Late Proto-Slavonic

	SG			DU			PL		
	M	N	F	M	N	F	M	N	F
NOM	-ъ	-o	-a	-a		-ě$_2$	-i$_2$	-a	-y$_2$
ACC		-ǫ					-y$_2$		
GEN	-o-go		-oj-y$_2$		-oj-u		-ě$_2$-xъ		
DAT	-o-mu		-oj-i		-ě$_2$-ma		-ě$_2$-mъ		
INST	-ě$_2$-mь		-oj-ǫ				-ě$_2$-mi		
LOC	-o-mь		-oj-i		-oj-u		-ě$_2$-xъ		

Notes

1   The pronominal formants -ŏį̣- (M/N) and -āį̣- (F) were monophthongized to -ě$_2$ before consonants.

2   The fronting of back vowels after soft consonants (see 2.12) caused the expected vowel alternations; -y$_2$ is written as a shorthand term for the y ~ ě/ę alternation (see 3.1.2, note 2(a)).

3   The GEN M/N -ogo represents the Proto-Indo-European ablative -ŏd extended by the particle -go (Arumaa 1985: 175).

4   The non-gendered pronouns kъ-to 'who' and čь-to 'what' were inflected according to the masculine singular paradigm. Their nominative was extended by the particle -to, derived from the demonstrative pronoun. The genitive ending of čь-to was -eso/-ьso reflecting the Proto-Indo-European ending -ěs(į̇)ŏ.

Table 3.5   Paradigm of the anaphoric pronoun j-

	SG			DU			PL		
	M	N	F	M	N	F	M	N	F
NOM	-jь	je	ja	ja	ji		ji	ja	jě/ję
ACC		jǫ						jě/ję	
GEN	jego		jejě/		jeju		jixъ		
			jeję						
DAT	jemu		jeji		jima		jimъ		
INST	jimь		jejǫ				jimi		
LOC	jemь		jeji		jeju		jixъ		

For the inflection of personal pronouns, see section 3.1.3 of chapter 4, Old Church Slavonic.

3.1.4   Adjectival morphology

In addition to their obligatory categories of case, number and gender, most Proto-Slavonic adjectives were either definite or indefinite. Indefinite adjectives were inflected according to the nominal -ŏ- (M/N) and -ā- (F) types. Definite adjectives were formed by adding the anaphoric pronoun *j*- (see table 3.5) to the forms of the indefinite adjective. The coalescence of these forms yielded the definite or pronominal inflection of the adjective.

In some instances the composition was mechanical:

			LPSl.	*OCS*
NOM SG	M	starъ + jь	› starъjь	staryi/starъi [starъjь]
	N	staro + je	› staroje	staro[j]e
	F	stara + ja	› staraja	staraja
ACC SG	F	starǫ + jǫ	› starǫjǫ	starǫjǫ
GEN SG	M/N	stara + jego	› starajego	stara[j]ego
				staraago (with assimilation)
				starago (with contraction)

A sequence of two syllables beginning with *j* was reduced by haplology to one syllable:

LOC SG   F   starě + jeji › LPSl. starěji   OCS starě[j]i

The definite INST SG F -ǫjǫ was derived from the original nominal -ǫ (‹ -ā-m) rather than from the analogical pronominal ending -ojǫ (see 3.1.2, note 7). Thus:

INST SG   F   starǫ + jejǫ › LPSl. starǫjǫ   OCS starǫjǫ

Disyllabic nominal endings were replaced by -y, extended analogically from the GEN PL star-ъ + jixь › staryjixъ (see 2.32) and INST PL M/N star-y + jimi › staryjimi:

	LPSl.	*OCS*
INST PL F	star-ami + jimi › staryjimi	stary[j]imi
LOC PL F	star-axъ + jixъ › staryjixъ	stary[j]ixъ

3.1.5   Numeral morphology

The Proto-Slavonic cardinal numerals '1' to '10' may be subdivided into two groups. The first group included *jedinъ, -a, -o* '1' (‹ *ĕd-īn-ŏ-s*); *dъva* (M), *dъvě* (F/N) '2' (‹ *dŭu̯ō, -ŏi̯*); *trьje* (M), *tri* (F/N) '3' (‹ *tr-ĕi̯-ĕs, *tr-ĭns*); and *četyre* (M), *četyri* (F/N) '4' (‹ *kʷĕtūr-ĕs, -ĭns*). The numerals

'1' and '2' were of pronominal origin and followed the pronominal inflec-tion (*tъ*). 'One' could still be used as an indefinite pronoun meaning 'certain, some' and have the singular and plural, while '2' was restricted to the dual; '3' was inflected like the plural -*ĭ*- stem, while '4' was an athe-matic stem. All four of them were adjectival, that is, they distinguished gender ('2', '3', '4' in the nominative only) and modified the noun counted.

The numerals '5' to '10' were nominal abstract derivatives in -*ĭ*- from the Proto-Indo-European ordinal numerals. They were *pętь* '5' (< **pĕnk^w-t-*), *šestь* '6' (< **ksĕks-t-*), *sedmь* '7' (< **sĕbdm-*), *ostь* '8' (< **ŏk'tm-*), *devętь* '9' (< **nĕuņ-t-*, with the initial *d* by analogy to '10'), and *desętь* '10' (< **dĕ-k' m-t-*). They governed the noun counted and did not distinguish gender. The numerals '5' to '9' were -*ĭ*- stems, while '10' transferred from an athematic stem to the -*ĭ*- stem inflection.

The teens were compounds of the base numeral followed by the pre-position *na* with the athematic locative singular of '10', for example, *dъva na desęte* '12'. The tens were formed with the base numeral followed by the appropriate case form of '10', for example *dъva desęti* '20', *trьje desęte* '30', *pętь desętъ* '50'. The root **kŏm/k' m* of the numeral '10', extended by the suffix -*t*-, appeared also in the numerals *sъto* '100' and *tysęt'a/tysǫt'a* '1,000'. The former was a neuter -*ŏ*- stem (< **k' m-t-ŏ-*); the latter was a feminine -*ĭ-ā*- stem modified by **tū*- 'fat, thick' (< **tū-k' m-t-i-ā*). The hundreds were formed analogously to the tens with the appropriate case form of '100', for example *dъvě sъtě* '200', *tri sъta* '300', *pętь sъtъ* '500'.

3.2 Verbal morphology

Most Proto-Slavonic verbs did not add person and number endings directly to the root, but to the verbal stem, that is, to the root extended by a verb-forming suffix with or without a present-tense suffix. Such verbs are called thematic; those which added person and number endings directly to the root, are called athematic.

There were four **athematic verbs**: 3 SG PRES *jestъ* 'he is' (< **ĕs-tĭ*), *jastъ* 'he eats' (< **ēd-tĭ*), *věstъ* 'he knows' (< **uŏid-tĭ*), *dastъ* 'he will give' (< **dād-tĭ*). Except for *jasti* 'to eat' (< **ēd-tēi̯*), the athematic verbs had dif-ferent stems in the infinitive and the present tense: *byti* 'to be', *věděti* 'to know', *dati* 'to give'. The verb 'to be' had a suppletive infinitive stem *by*-derived from PIE **bhū*- (compare Sanskrit *bhavati* 'he is', Latin *fūi* 'I was'). The verb 'to know' had the infinitive stem *věd-ě*- derived from first person singular middle perfect-tense form **uŏid-ăi̯*. The verb 'to give' had a reduplicated present-tense stem **dā-d-*, while the infinitive stem was the unreduplicated **dā*- (compare Latin *dare* 'to give').

In most **thematic verbs** the verb-forming suffix occurred in two variants, one in the present-tense and related forms and one in the infinitive and related forms. Because of this variation, it is customary to distinguish between the present-tense and infinitive verbal stems. Since the correspondence between the two variants is generally predictable, it is possible to select one of them as basic and use it in classifying verbal stems. The seven regular verb classes thus obtained are listed below, with the present-tense variant (quoted in third singular present) shown first and separated by an oblique from the infinitive variant. The variant used to label a class is given in bold face. Examples transcribed morphophonemically are enclosed in braces.

(a) -*0*--*0*- verbs were unproductive and included three subclasses: **consonantic**, for example *nesetь* {*nes-0-e-tь*}, *nesti* {*nes-0-ti*} 'carry' *rečetь* {*rek-0-e-tь*}, *ret'i* {*rek-0-ti*} 'say'; **sonantic**, for example *pьnetь* {*pьn-0-e-tь*}, *pęti* {*pen-0-ti*} 'stretch', *jьm-0-e-tь*, *jęti* {*jem-0-ti*} 'seize', *mretь* {*mьr-0-e-tь*}, *merti* {*mer-0-ti*} 'die', where the sequences *ьn ьm ьr* developed from the syllabic sonants *n̥ m̥ r̥* before vowels; **semivocalic**, for example *bijetь* {*bij-0-e-tь*}, *biti* {*bij-0-ti*} 'beat', *pojetь* {*poj-0-e-tь*}, *pěti* {*poj-0-ti*} 'sing', with the semivowel *j* lost before consonants through the resolution of syllable-initial clusters (see 2.7) and monophthongization (see 2.13).

(b) -*n*-/-*nǫ*- verbs were productive and included two subclasses: **vocalic** (*V-nǫ*-), for example *minetь*, *minǫti* 'pass'; *slynetь*, *slynǫti* 'be known' and **consonantic** (*C-nǫ*-), with typical omission of the verb-forming suffix in aorist and past participial formations, for example *dvignetь* {*dvig-n-e-tь*}, *dvignǫti* {*dvig-nǫ-ti*} 'move' but *dvigoxъ* (1 SG AOR), *dvigъ* (NOM SG M PAST ACT PART INDEF), *dviženъ* (NOM SG M PAST PASS PART INDEF).

(c) -*j*- (< *i̯*)/-*a*- verbs, for example *kažetь* (< *kāz-i̯*-), *kazati* 'show'; *plačetь* (< *plāk-i̯*-), *plakati* 'weep', were unproductive. This large class was one of two in which the verb-forming suffix -*j*- alternated with -*a*- (compare (d) below).

(d) -*u-j*-/-*ov-a*- (-*ev-a*- after soft consonants, see 2.14) verbs, for example *věrujetь*, *věrovati* 'believe'; *vojujetь*, *vojevati* 'make war', were productive. They differed from the preceding class by the presence of the suffix -*ǒu̯*- which monophthongized to *u₂* in a closed syllable (see 2.13).

(e) -*a-j*- (< *-ā-i̯*-)/-*a*- and -*ě-j*- (< *ē-i̯*-)/-*ě*- verbs, for example *dělajetь*, *dělati* 'do'; *umějetь*, *uměti* 'know how', were productive.

(f) -*i*- (< *-ěi̯*-)/-*i*- (< *-ī*-) verbs, for example *nositь* {*nos-i-0-tь*}, *nositi* 'carry'; *modlitь* {*modl-i-0-tь*}, *modliti* 'beg' were productive. The shape of the present-tense suffix (-*ō*-/-*0*-) and the difference in origin of the verb-forming suffix in the -*i*- and -*ě*- verbs (see below) are discussed in 3.2.2.

(g) -*i*-/-*ě*- (< *-ē*-) verbs, for example *mьnitь*, *mьněti* 'think'; *viditь*, *viděti* 'see' were unproductive. In stems in soft consonants *ē* goes to *ā* (see 2.14), for example *kričitь*, *kričati* {*krič-ě-ti*} 'shout'; *stojitь*, *stojati* {*stoj-ě-ti*} 'stand'. These stems will be listed in their morphophonemic form.

3.2.1   Verbal categories

Among the verbs, Proto-Indo-European distinguished two diatheses, the active (or non-middle) and middle, the latter marked as a category which placed special emphasis on the grammatical subject, leading to the neutralization of the opposition between the agent and the patient (compare the English active *mother washed the baby* or *mother opened the door* with the 'middle' *mother washed* or *the door opened*). The active versus middle opposition was expressed by special sets of inflectional endings. Proto-Slavonic lost these formal distinctions but retained the semantic opposition between the active and the middle, expressing it with a newly developed contrast between two **genera**, the non-reflexive and reflexive, the latter formally distinguished by the particle *sę*. It also added a new **voice** opposition in which the active contrasted with the passive, the latter marked as the category specifying the patient of an action. The active versus passive opposition was formally expressed in the participle only. Genus, by contrast, was an obligatory category of the verb.

Of the four verbal **moods** reconstructed for Proto-Indo-European (indicative, subjunctive, optative and imperative), Proto-Slavonic retained the indicative. The subjunctive (or conjunctive), known from Vedic Sanskrit, Greek, Latin and Celtic, expressed probability or expectation. Therefore, it was frequently reinterpreted as the future tense. In Proto-Slavonic it was replaced by the conditional, in which the resultative (or the -*l*-) participle combined with the auxiliary verb 'to be' to produce an analytical grammatical form. The optative, which occurred in Sanskrit, Greek, Latin and Germanic, expressed desire or potentiality. In Proto-Slavonic it replaced the original Proto-Indo-European imperative.

The oldest system of Proto-Indo-European **tenses**, which included the present, aorist and perfect, appeared to have less to do with temporal relations than with the manner of performance or other characteristics of an action. The present referred to an action which at the moment of speech was not completed. The aorist viewed the action statically, as completed and, therefore, past. The perfect stressed the result of an action, that is, it dwelled on the dynamics of a situation, linking the past and the moment of speech. The future was originally expressed through the modalities of the subjunctive or optative. Specific future-tense formations seem to be Late Proto-Indo-European dialectal innovations. So were the imperfect, which emphasized non-completion of a past action, and the pluperfect, which referred to an action prior to the narrated event.

Aspectual meanings, inherent in the Proto-Indo-European tenses, developed into a new grammatical opposition of two **aspects**, the perfective, specifying a completed action, and the unmarked imperfective;

they became an obligatory category of the Slavonic verb. This development led in turn to the rise of an intricate interplay between the aspects and tenses. The perfective present assumed the function of the future, leaving the imperfective present as the sole indicator of contemporaneity with the moment of speech. Consequently, since the Proto-Slavonic present-tense forms referred either to the present or the future, they may be viewed as non-past and are often so termed. Among the preterite tenses, the opposition between the perfective and imperfective aspects coincided largely with the old opposition between the aorist and the imperfect, leading to a gradual disappearance or reinterpretation of these tenses in the individual Slavonic languages. Proto-Slavonic developed its own perfect and pluperfect, formed analytically with the resultative participle and, respectively, the present or imperfect of the auxiliary verb 'to be'. A Proto-Slavonic innovation was the imperfective future expressed by the infinitive plus the present-tense forms of one of the auxiliary verbs: 'to be', 'to have', 'to want' or 'to begin'.

The three **persons** of the Proto-Indo-European verb remained in Proto-Slavonic. Along with the finite verbal forms, that is, forms inflected for person, Proto-Slavonic had non-finite forms. The **infinitive** and the **supine** were derived from case forms of Proto-Indo-European deverbal nouns, while **participles** and **verbal nouns** combined the functions of verbs with those of adjectives and nouns respectively.

3.2.2 Conjugation

The Proto-Indo-European conjugational system distinguished several sets of personal endings. In the indicative the endings characterizing the active voice were opposed to the endings of the middle voice, and the endings of the present tense, or the so-called primary endings, were opposed to the endings of the preterite tenses, or the secondary endings. Furthermore, some personal endings of the thematic conjugations were different from those of the athematic one. The degree of ending differentiation varied. Thus, in the active voice, the first and second singular admitted three distinct endings, the third singular and plural distinguished two endings, while other persons and numbers displayed one ending only. In Table 3.6 only the most differentiated forms are shown.

Proto-Slavonic, like the ancient varieties of Sanskrit and Greek, exhibited a conjugational system rich in grammatical oppositions. Verbs were inherently specified for government (they were either transitive or intransitive) and, as obligatory categories, they distinguished aspect and genus (they were either perfective or imperfective and reflexive or non-reflexive). Finite verb forms were inflected for person and number, and either tense or mood. Compound finite forms (perfect, pluperfect, conditional) distinguished gender as well. The only form displaying a clearly middle ending was the isolated *vědě* 'I know' found in Old Church Slavonic

Table 3.6   Active personal endings of Proto-Indo-European

	A thematic	*Primary* Thematic	*Secondary*
1 SG	-mĭ	-ō	-m
2 SG	-sĭ	-ĕi̯ (?)	-s
3 SG		-tĭ	-t
3 PL		-ntĭ	-nt

(Codex Suprasliensis), Old Russian, Old Slovene (Freising Fragments) and Old Czech. The ending goes back to the Proto-Indo-European middle -ǎ-i̯ (compare Greek *loúomai* 'I wash myself'). Since *vědě* is related to the root *vid-* 'see' (‹ *u̯ěi̯d-*), its meaning probably developed from 'I have seen for myself' to 'I know'.

Depending on the aspect of the verbal stem, the Proto-Slavonic **present** referred either to an action contemporaneous with the moment of speech (imperfective) or subsequent to it (perfective). Its person and number endings were derived from Proto-Indo-European primary endings. In the thematic verbs, they were added to stems extended by the present-tense suffix. In the verb classes -∅-, -nǫ-, -a-, -ov-a-, and -a-j-, the present-tense suffix was -ŏH₂- in first singular, -ŏ- in third plural and -ě- elsewhere. The present forms of these classes are said to belong to conjugation I. The present forms of verb classes -i- and -ě- belong to conjugation II. Their present-tense suffix was -ŏH₂- in the first singular and -∅- elsewhere. Hence, these presents are sometimes referred to as semi-thematic (Kuryłowicz 1964: 79–80) or semi-athematic (Vaillant 1966: 439).

Table 3.7   Present-tense paradigms of the verbs *ěd-* 'eat', *nes-* 'carry', *kaz-a-* 'explain', *děl-a-j-* 'do' and *modl-i-* 'ask' in Late Proto-Slavonic

		A thematic	*Conjugation I*		*Conjugation II*	
SG	1	jamь (‹ *ēd-mĭ)	nesǫ	kažǫ	dělajǫ	modl'ǫ
	2	jasi (‹ *ēd-sěi̯[?])	neseši	kažeši	dělaješi	modliši
	3	jastь (‹ *ēd-tĭ)	nesetь	kažetь	dělajetь	modlitь
DU	1	javě (‹ *ēd-vē)	nesevě	kaževě	dělajevě	modlivě
	2	jasta (‹ *ēd-tā)	neseta	kaževě?	dělajeta?	...
	2	jasta (‹ *ēd-tā)	neseta	kaževě	...	...
DU	2	jasta (‹ *ēd-tā)	neseta	kažeta	dělajeta	modlita
	3	jaste (‹ *ēd-tě)	nesete	kažete	dělajete	modlite
PL	1	jamъ (‹ *ēd-mǒn)	nesemъ	kažemъ	dělajemъ	modlimъ
	2	jaste (‹ *ēd-tě)	nesete	kažete	dělajete	modlite
	3	jadętь (‹ *ēd-ņtĭ)	nesǫtь	kažǫtь	dělajǫtь	modlętь

Notes

1   The verb-forming suffix *-i-* in the present tense of the *-i-* and *-ě-* class verbs (conjugation II) is different in origin from the verb-forming suffix *-i-* in the infinitive of the *-i-* class verbs. Since the infinitive *-i-* is acute and the present-tense *-i-* is not, it is assumed that the former goes back to a long vowel ($-\bar{\imath}-$), while the latter is derived from a short diphthong (*-ěi̯-*; see 2.16). Hence their dissimilar treatment in those modern Slavonic languages which retain reflexes of Proto-Slavonic intonational distinctions, for example SCr. *mȍli* 'he asks' but *móliti* 'to ask', Russian *mòlit* 'he implores' but *molit'* 'to implore'.

2   The first singular athematic *-mь* continues the Proto-Indo-European athematic *-mĭ* (OCS *esmь*, Greek *eimi* 'I am'). The ending *-ǫ* goes back to the Proto-Indo-European thematic *-ŏH₂* › *ō* (Greek *phérō*, Latin *ferō* 'I carry') extended by the secondary first-singular *-m*. In conjugation II the sequence *-i-ō-m* › *-i̯-ǫ-*, without the expected fronting of the vowel (*-i̯-ē-m* › *i̯-ę*; see 2.12) because of the analogical influence of the ending *-ǫ* of conjugation I.

3   The second-singular endings were the athematic *-si* and thematic *-ši*, as in OCS *esi* 'you are' or *neseši* 'you carry'. The consonant *š* arose regularly in conjugation II as a result of the retroflexion of *s* after *i* (see 2.3(c)) and spread analogically to conjugation I. The final *i* (for the expected *ь*) could have been derived from the Proto-Indo-European second-singular thematic *-ěi̯*, which some scholars (Meillet 1934: 253–4, Szemerényi 1989: 250–1) see also in the Greek 2 SG *-eis*, for example *phéreis* 'you carry'. In this explanation, in Greek the primary thematic ending *-ěi̯* was extended by the secondary ending *-s*, while in Proto-Slavonic the ending *-s* was extended by *-ěi̯*.

4   In the third singular and plural, Proto-Indo-European *-tĭ* should yield Proto-Slavonic *-tь* and such reflexes do occur in parts of East Slavonic. However, in Old Church Slavonic as well as in some north Russian dialects (including standard Russian), we find *tъ* instead. It is likely that the 3 SG *-tъ* developed under the influence of the demonstrative pronoun *tъ* 'this', which functioned also as the third-person pronoun 'he'. From there *tъ* could have spread analogically to the third plural. In West Slavonic and West South Slavonic the ending *-tь/-tъ* has been lost altogether. In other Slavonic languages it shows varying degrees of staying power (see section 6).

5   The 1 DU *-vě*, instead of the expected *-ve* (‹ *-u̯ěs*), is probably analogical to the pronoun *vě* 'we two' (‹ *u̯ēs*).

6   The 1 PL *-mъ* seems to be a reflex of *-mŏn* (compare Attic Greek *-men*, as in *phéromen* 'we carry'). The ending *-mo*, which appears in some Slavonic languages (see section 6), is probably derived from *-mŏs*, which is the more common variant of this ending in Proto-Indo-European (compare Latin *-mus* from *-mŏs* as in *ferimus* 'we carry').

7   The third plural ending of the athematic conjugation was *-ętъ* (‹ *-ǫtĭ*). The ending *-ǫtъ* (‹ *-ŏ-ntĭ*) of the *-∅-* and *-nǫ-* classes spread analogically to the *-a-*, *-ov-a-* and *-a-j-* classes replacing the expected *-ętъ* (‹ *-ı̯-ě-ntĭ* ‹ *-ı̯-ŏ-ntĭ*). The conjugation II ending *-ętъ* could be attributed to the influence of the athematic conjugation or it could represent a regular phonetic development of *-ěı̯-ntĭ*.

The **aorist** designated a completed action, without affirming either its duration or resultative value. As such, it served as the narrative preterite tense. Aorist endings were derived from Proto-Indo-European secondary endings and were added to the infinitive stem. Proto-Slavonic had three different aorist formations. Two of them, the root (or simple) and sigmatic aorists, were relics inherited from Proto-Indo-European. The third type appeared alongside and eventually replaced the two older types, thus becoming the only productive aorist formation in Slavonic.

The **root aorist** combined the forms of the Proto-Indo-European thematic aorist and imperfect (compare Vedic Sanskrit *bháram*, Homeric Greek *phéron* 'I carried'). Its endings were preceded by a thematic vowel which was added directly to the verbal root (in other words, the suffix *-nǫ-* in the *-nǫ-* class verbs was omitted). Before *-t* and *-s* the thematic vowel was *-ě-*; elsewhere it was *-ŏ-*.

The root aorist survived in the *-∅-* and *-nǫ-* class verbs. We know, however, from Old Church Slavonic that only in the second and third singular was it used regularly with all the verbs of these classes. In other persons it was used sporadically with about a dozen stems, such as *jьd-* 'go', *lěz-* 'climb', *mog-* 'be able'.

The **sigmatic aorist** was found with verbs of the *-i-* class and with sonantic and about twenty consonantic verbs of the *-∅-* class, for example *greb-* 'bury', *męt-* 'stir', *tek-* 'run'. The endings of the sigmatic aorist were preceded by the formant *-s-* (hence the name 'sigmatic'), followed in the first person of all numbers by the thematic vowel *-ŏ-*. The root vowel of the *-∅-* verbs was lengthened: *i ě ŏ* became *ī ē ō*.

Table 3.8   Root aorist paradigms of *pad-* 'fall' and *dvig-(nǫ-)* 'move'

SG	1	padъ	dvigъ	(‹ -ŏ-m, see 3.1.2, note 1b)
	2	pade	dviže	(‹ -ě-s)
	3	pade	dviže	(‹ -ě-t)
DU	1	padově	dvigově	
	2	padeta	dvižeta	
	3	padete	dvižete	
PL	1	padomъ	dvigomъ	
	2	padete	dvižete	
	3	padǫ	dvigǫ	(‹ -ŏ-nt)

Table 3.9 Sigmatic aorist paradigms of the verbs *bod-* 'pierce' and *nos-i-* 'carry', and partial paradigms of *čьt-* 'read', *pьn-/pę-* 'stretch', *mьr-/mer-* 'die', *rek-* 'say' in Late Proto-Slavonic

SG	1	basъ (‹ *bōd-s-ŏ-m)	nosixъ (‹ *nŏs-ī-s-ŏ-m)
	2	bode (root aorist)	nosi (‹ *nŏs-ī-s-s)
	3	bode (root aorist)	nosi (‹ *nŏs-ī-s-t)
DU	1	basově	nosixově
	2	basta (‹ *bōd-s-tā)	nosista (‹ *nŏs-ī-s-tā)
	3	baste	nosiste
PL	1	basomъ	nosixomъ
	2	baste (‹ *bōd-s-tě)	nosiste
	3	basę (‹ *bōd-s-nt)	nosišę (‹ *nŏs-ī-s-nt)

1	SG	čisъ (‹ *kīt-s-ŏ-m)	pęsъ (‹ *pēn-s-ŏ-m)
2	PL	čiste (‹ *kit-s-tě)	pęste (‹ *pēn-s-tě)
3	PL	čisę (‹ *kīt-s-nt)	pęsę (‹ *pēn-s-nt)

1	SG	merxъ (‹ *mēr-s-ŏ-m)	rěxъ (‹ *rēk-s-ŏ-m)
2	PL	merste (‹ *mēr-s-tě)	rěste (‹ *rēk-s-tě)
3	PL	meršę (‹ *mēr-s-nt)	rěšę (‹ *rēk-s-nt)

Notes

1 Forms corresponding to the Proto-Slavonic sigmatic aorist occur in some but not all Indo-European languages (compare the Greek aorist *édeiksa* 'I showed', Latin perfect *dīxī* 'I said'). Of the immediate neighbours of Proto-Slavonic, this aorist does not occur in either Baltic or Germanic.

2 It is often claimed that the lengthening of the root vowel in the *-∅-* class verbs was the result of compensatory lengthening following the simplification of consonant clusters. However, such a lengthening is not observed in analogous situations elsewhere, for example, **ŏpsā* › *osa* 'wasp'. It is more probable, therefore, that it was morphophonemic in nature.

3 There were no second and third singular sigmatic aorist forms with the consonantic verbs of the *-∅-* class; root-aorist forms were used instead.

4 In Old Church Slavonic the second and third singular of the sonantic verbs were extended by the suffix *-tъ*, for example, *pę(tъ)*, *mrě(tъ)*. This suffix appears to have spread there by analogy from the third singular present.

The **productive aorist** arose within Proto-Slavonic as an analogical extension of the sigmatic aorist of the *-i-* class verbs. In the vocalic verbs (that is, all verbs other than those of the *-∅-* class and the consonantic verbs of the *-nǫ-* class) the impulse for this analogical development must have been

provided by the forms in which -s- was pre-consonantal, that is, by the
environments in which all the vocalic class verbs (including -i-) developed
similarly. Compare the following forms of nos-i- 'carry' and děl-a-j- 'do':

2 SG	nosi (‹ *nŏs-ī-s-s)	děla (‹ *dēl-ā-s-s)
3 SG	nosi (‹ *nŏs-ī-s-t)	děla (‹ *dēl-ā-s-t)
2 PL	nosiste (‹ *nŏs-ī-s-tě)	dělaste (‹ *dēl-ā-s-tě)

These similarities were analogically extended to the forms in which -s-
was pre-vocalic, that is, to an environment where the phonological
development of the -i- class verbs was different from that of the other
vocalic verbs. Thus, such phonologically regular forms as

1 SG	nosixъ (‹ *nŏs-ī-s-ŏ-m)
1 PL	nosixomъ (‹ *nŏs-ī-s-ŏ-mŏn)
3 PL	nosišę (‹ *nŏs-ī-s-n̥t)

led to the creation of analogical forms as in kaz-a- 'explain', věr-ov-a-
'believe', děl-a-j-'do'; vid-ě- 'see':

1 SG	kazaxъ	věrovaxъ	dělaxь	viděxь
1 PL	kazaxomъ	věrovaxomъ	dělaxomъ	viděxomъ
3 PL	kazašę	věrovašę	dělašę	viděšę

In the consonantic verbs, that is, verbs whose infinitive (aorist) stem did
not end in a vowel (-∅- and most -nǫ- verbs), the starting point of the
analogy must have been the non-lengthened root-aorist forms of the
second and third singular which, like the corresponding sigmatic aorist
forms of the -i- class verbs, ended in a vowel; compare from ved- 'lead' and
nos-i- 'carry':

	Root	*Sigmatic*
2 SG	vede (‹ *ued-ě-s)	nosi (‹ *nŏs-ī-s-s)
3 SG	vede (‹ *ued-ě-t)	nosi (‹ nŏs-ī-s-t)

Such forms led to the creation of productive aorist forms in which the
abstracted endings of the -i- class verbs were added to the non-lengthened
roots of the consonantal verbs. The thematic vowel was -e- in West
Slavonic and -o- elsewhere.

	West Slavonic	*South/East Slavonic*
1 SG	vedexъ	vedoxъ
1 PL	vedexomъ	vedoxomъ
3 PL	vedexǫ (-xǫ, from the imperfect)	vedošę

The productive aorist occurred with all the consonantal verbs except for the stems in *r*, which had sigmatic forms only. In some verbs the productive aorist competed with one of the unproductive types (see table 3.10).

Table 3.10   Different aorist formations in Old Church Slavonic

	Root		Sigmatic		Productive	
	1 SG	3 PL	1 SG	3 PL	1 SG	3 PL
mьr-/mrě- 'die'			mrěxъ	mrěšę		
[j]i-/[j]ьd- 'go'	idъ	idǫ			idoxъ	idošę
mog- 'be able'	mogъ	mogǫ			mogoxъ	mogošę
dvig-nǫ- 'move'	dvigъ	dvigǫ			dvigoxъ	dvigošę
čьt- 'read'			čisъ	čisę	čьtoxъ	čьtošę
[j]ьm-/[j]ę- 'take'			ęsъ	ęsę	ęxъ	ęšę
rek- 'say'			rěxъ	rěšę	rekoxъ	rekošę

The **imperfect** arose as a Slavonic innovation following the reinterpretation of the Proto-Indo-European imperfect as the Proto-Slavonic root aorist. It indicated non-completion of a past action and stressed the action's duration or repetition. Because of such a semantic specification, the imperfect was restricted almost exclusively to imperfective verbs. The formant of the imperfect was complex and consisted of the suffix *-ěa-* or *-aa-* followed by the suffix *-x-*. The endings were those of the root aorist.

Table 3.11   Paradigms of the imperfect of *nes-* 'carry', *mog-* 'be able', *děl-a-j-* 'do', *vid-ě-* 'see' and *nos-i-* 'carry' in Late Proto-Slavonic

SG	1	nesěaxъ	možaaxъ	dělaaxъ	viděaxъ	nošaaxъ
	2	nesěaše	možaaše	dělaaše	viděaše	nošaaše
	3	nesěaše	možaaše	dělaaše	viděaše	nošaaše
DU	1	nesěaxově	možaaxově	dělaaxově	viděaxově	nošaaxově
	2	nesěašeta	možaašeta	dělaašeta	viděašeta	nošaašeta
	3	nesěašete	možaašete	dělaašete	viděašete	nošaašete
PL	1	nesěaxomъ	možaaxomъ	dělaaxomъ	viděaxomъ	nošaaxomъ
	2	nesěašete	možaašete	dělaašete	viděašete	nošaašete
	3	nesěaxǫ	možaaxǫ	dělaaxǫ	viděaxǫ	nošaaxǫ

Notes

1   The *-a-*, *-ov-a-* and *-ě-* verbs formed the imperfect on the infinitive stem, while the *-nǫ-* and some irregular verbs based it on the present-tense stem. The imperfect of other verb classes could be interpreted as being based on either stem. It appears, however, that the oldest imperfects were built on the present-tense stem. After the loss of the inter-

vocalic yod in the -*a-j*- class (see note 4, below), the present-tense stem was reinterpreted as the infinitive stem, thus providing a model for the other classes.

2   The endings of the imperfect were taken over from the root aorist which, as shown above, consisted of the Proto-Indo-European secondary endings preceded by a thematic vowel.

3   The suffix -*x*- appears to have been introduced into the imperfect from the productive aorist.

4   There is no agreement on the origin of the suffixes -*ĕa*- and -*aa*-. It is likely that the suffix was abstracted from the combination of a stem vowel and a Proto-Indo-European stative suffix -*ē*- (LPSl. -*ĕ*-). This suffix appeared in the stative verbs of the -*ĕ*- class, for example, *sĕdĕti* 'to be sitting' (compare Latin *sedēre* 'to be sitting'), in the infinitive *jьmĕti* 'to have', contrasted with the present *jьmatь* 'I have' (compare Old High German *habēn* 'to have') and in *bĕ*-, the imperfective aorist stem of the verb *byti* 'to be' (see note 6, below). It was also present in the Latin imperfect, for example *legēbam* 'I was reading', *agēbam* 'I was acting'.

For the verbs of the -*a*-, -*ov-a*-, -*a-j*- and -*ĕ*- classes, the phonetic development could be viewed in two ways. The stative suffix -*ē*- could have been added to the yod of the present-tense stem of the -*a-j*- class verbs and changed to *ā* after it (see 2.14). After the intervocalic yod was lost, the present-tense stem was reinterpreted as the infinitive stem and this formation spread by analogy to the other verb classes. Alternatively, the stative suffix was added to the final vowel of the infinitive stem and a prothetic yod developed between the two vowels causing the change of *ē* to *ā*. In either case, the loss of the intervocalic yod could lead to the contraction of the two vowels in hiatus. Thus, *āē* > *āi̯ē* > *āi̯ā* > *aa* (with a possible contraction to *a*) and *ēē* > *ēi̯ē* > *ēi̯ā* > *ĕa* (with a possible contraction to *ĕ* or *ä* [æ]).

With the verbs of the -*∅*-, -*nǫ*- and -*i*- classes, the addition of the stative suffix -*ē*- should yield *nesĕxъ*, *možaxъ* (< *mŏg-ē-x-ŏ-m*), *dvignĕxъ*, *nošaxъ* (< *nŏs-i̯-ē-x-ŏ-m*), and such forms do in fact occur. However, under the influence of the imperfects of the other verb classes, these forms were extended by the vowel *a*, yielding *nesĕaxъ*, *možaaxъ*, *dvignĕaxъ*, *nošaaxъ*.

5   Therefore, such imperfect forms as *nesĕxъ*, *možaxъ*, *nošaxъ*, *bijaxъ*, *živĕxъ*, *idĕxъ* could represent the older state of the language, before their extension by the vowel *a*. On the other hand, one cannot exclude the possibility that these forms were derived from the younger forms *nesĕaxъ*, *možaaxъ*, *nošaaxъ*, *bijaaxъ*, *živĕaxъ*, *idĕaxъ*, with a contraction of the sequences *ĕa* or *aa*, paralleling the development of such clearly contracted forms as *dĕlaxъ*, *dĕlaše* from *dĕlaaxъ*, *dĕlaaše*.

6   A special case was that of the verb 'to be', whose forms with the stative

suffix -ē- took the endings of the productive aorist and were interpreted as the imperfective aorist, while the younger forms, which
occurred in the third person only, were interpreted as the imperfect
and were so inflected. Here are the third-person forms of the two
paradigms:

	Imperfective Aorist	Imperfect
3 SG	bě	běaše
3 DU	běste	běašete
3 PL	běšę	běaxǫ

Proto-Slavonic was alone among the Indo-European languages to derive its
imperative from the Proto-Indo-European optative mood. In the athematic
verbs the Proto-Indo-European optative took secondary personal endings
preceded by the optative suffix -i̯ē- (SG)/ -ī- (DU and PL); in the thematic
ones, the optative suffix was -ŏ-ī-.

This distinction was retained in the Proto-Slavonic imperative, but with
a number of analogical levellings. In the thematic conjugation, the Proto-
Indo-European sequence -ŏ-ī- yielded the diphthong -ōi̯-, whose length
may be inferred from its subsequent development into an acute monoph-
thong. After i̯ (that is, in the -a-, -ov-a, -a-j- classes) the diphthong ōi̯- was
fronted to -ēi̯- and monophthongized to -ī, for example, zna-i̯- 'know'
formed 2 SG zna-j-i from *znā-i̯-ēi̯-s from *znā-i̯-ōi̯-s and 2 PL zna-j-i-te
from *znā-i̯-ēi̯-tě from *znā-i̯-ōi̯-tě. In the athematic conjugation, the suffix
-i̯ē- (SG) was replaced by -ū̯-, which was either derived from -i̯-ŏ-i̯-, with
the expected fronting of ŏ, or was analogical to -ī- (DU and PL), for
example, dād-/dā- 'give' formed 2 SG dad'i from *dād-i̯-ī-s (OCS daždi,
shortened eventually to daždь), 2 PL dadite from *dād-ī-tě.

This development made of -i- the favourite formant of the imperative,
leading to its spread to other imperative formations. Thus, in the singular
of the -∅- and -nǫ- classes, -ě₂-, issued from the monophthongization of
-ōi̯-, was analogically replaced by -i-, for example, OCS 2 SG beri 'take!',
rьci 'say!', dvigni 'move!' (versus OCS 2 PL berěte, rьcěte, dvigněte). The
Old Church Slavonic forms rьci (of rek- 'say') or moʒi (of mog- 'be able')
show that the analogical replacement of -ě₂- by -i- took place after the
second palatalization of velars. The suffix -i- occurred also with all the
imperative forms of conjugation II verbs: for example 2 SG nosi (‹ *nŏs-ī-s),
nosite 'carry!', mьni (‹ *min-ī-s), mьnite 'think!'.

Morphologically least marked verbal forms were the **infinitive** and **supine**.
Like all the non-finite forms, they were not inflected for person, tense or
mood. In fact, they distinguished only aspect and genus, the two obligatory
categories of the verb. The infinitive and supine endings, -ti and -tъ, were
originally case forms of Proto-Indo-European deverbal nouns in the suffix
-t- inflected as the -i- and -ŭ- stems respectively. The form of the supine

and its function (specification of goal or purpose with verbs of motion) point to the accusative singular in *-ŭm* as its Proto-Indo-European source. The specific case from which the infinitive was derived is more difficult to establish. Its semantic affinity is with the dative; however, the *i* of the infinitive ending is acute, implying that it was derived from the long diphthong *ēi̯*, which characterizes the ending of the locative singular (see 3.1.2). The infinitive tended to displace the functionally more restricted supine and, unlike the latter, remained in most Slavonic languages. It also influenced the phonetic development of the supine in the velar stems of the *-∅-* class verbs. Thus, the Old Church Slavonic supine of *pek-* 'bake' was *peštь* from PSl. *pěk-t-ŭ-m* by analogy to the infinitive *pešti* from PSl. *pěk-t-ēi̯* (see 2.23). Because of its semantic and formal simplicity, the infinitive is traditionally used as the citation ('dictionary') form of the Slavonic verb.

Some Proto-Slavonic forms combined the functions of verbs with those of adjectives or nouns. The former are known as **participles**, the latter as **verbal nouns**.

Participles were inflected for the adjectival categories of case, number, gender and specificity and for the verbal categories of aspect, genus and tense. However, participial tense distinctions were defined in relative rather than absolute terms: actions contemporaneous with the tense of the main verb were expressed by present participles, while the actions anterior to it, were expressed by past participles. In addition, transitive verbs showed distinctions of voice (active versus passive), and past active participles were either resultative or non-resultative. These distinctions yielded five participles: present active, present passive, past active non-resultative, past active resultative and past passive.

The **present active participle** was marked by the Proto-Indo-European suffix *-nt-* (compare Latin *amāns, amantis* 'loving') added to the present-tense stem and, except in the nominative singular masculine/neuter, extended by the suffix *-i̯-*. The present-tense suffix was *-ŏ-/-i̯-ŏ-* in conjugation I verbs, with *-i̯-ŏ-* fronted to *-i̯-ě-* in the nominative singular masculine/neuter, but retained by analogy in the other cases (compare 3.2.2, note 7), and *-ěi̯-* in conjugation II verbs. In the athematic verbs, the original formant of the present active participle must have been *-ęt-* from *-n̥t-*. However, its only trace is the rare OCS *vědę* 'knowing'; more recent forms show an analogical thematic *-ǫt-* from *-ŏ-nt-*.

The declension of the present active participle followed the Proto-Indo-European athematic type in the NOM SG M (*-s*), NOM SG N (*-∅*), NOM SG F (*-ī-∅*), NOM PL M (*-ěs*), and the thematic *-i̯-ŏ-* (M/N) and *-i̯-ā-* (F) types in the other cases. The vowel *ŏ* in the NOM SG M *-ŏ-nt-s* and NOM SG N *-ŏ-nt-∅* is expected to be lengthened and raised to *ū₁* › *y* (see 3.1.2, note 2a). This is how it develops in South Slavonic but not in East Slavonic and Czech/

Slovak where instead of -*y* we find -*a*. Since -*a* occurred also sporadically in Old Polish (next to -*ę*), one could posit an Early Proto-Slavonic dialect isogloss separating the South Slavonic -$\bar{u}_1$ (with vowel raising) from the North Slavonic $\bar{o}$ (without vowel raising or nasalization). Alternatively, this discrepancy may be explained as a late East Slavonic and Czech/Slovak analogical accommodation to the nominative singular masculine/neuter of other verb classes in which -*ä* derived from -*ę*; compare *nosä from *nosę of *nos-i-* 'carry'. In this explanation the Old Polish -*a* forms would be considered a borrowing from Old Czech.

The **present passive participle** was formed from the present-tense stem of transitive, mostly imperfective verbs by the addition of the suffix -*m*-. In the -*i*- presents of conjugation I the thematic suffix -*ŏ*- was fronted to -*ě*-; the -*ěi̯*- of conjugation II verbs was monophthongized to -*i*-. Athematic verbs showed an analogical -*ŏ*-. The declension was that of the -*ŏ*- (M/N) and -*ā*- (F) stems.

The following are various Late Proto-Slavonic nominative singular masculine present passive participle forms: *nes*- 'carry': *nesomъ*, *děl-a-j*- 'do': *dělajemъ*, *vid-ě*- 'see': *vidimъ*, *věd*- 'know': *vědomъ*.

The **past active participle** was derived from the Proto-Indo-European suffix -*ŭs*-/-*u̯ĕs*-/-*u̯ŏs*-. In Slavonic this suffix was simplified to -*ŭs*-/-*u̯ŭs*- and extended by -*i*- in forms other than the nominative singular masculine/neuter (similarly to the present active participle), yielding EPSl. -*ŭš*-/-*u̯ŭš*- › *ъš*-/-*vъš*- (see 2.10(b)). It was added to the infinitive stem. The suffix -*ъš*- occurred with the verbs of the -*Ø*- and -*i*- classes and with the consonantic verbs of the -*nǫ*- class; the suffix -*vъš*- occurred elsewhere. In the -*i*- class the stem final *i* › *i̯* before a vowel, causing the expected yodization

Table 3.12   Present active participle forms of *mog*- 'be able', *děl-a-j*- 'do', *nos-i-* 'carry' in Late Proto-Slavonic

NOM SG M/N	mogy/moga	dělaję	nosę
NOM SG F	mogǫt´i	dělajǫt´i	nosęt´i
NOM PL M	mogǫt´e	dělajǫt´e	nosęt´e
GEN SG M/N	mogǫt´a	dělajǫt´a	nosęt´a

Table 3.13   Past active participle forms of *ved*- 'lead', *dvig*-(*nǫ*-) 'move', *pros-i-* 'ask', *děl-a-j*- 'do', *vid-ě*- 'see' in Late Proto-Slavonic

NOM SG M/N	vedъ	dvigъ	prošь	dělavъ	viděvъ
NOM SG F	vedъši	dvigъši	prošьši	dělavъši	viděvъši
NOM PL M	vedъše	dvigъše	prošьše	dělavъše	viděvъše
GEN SG M/N	vedъša	dvigъša	prošьša	dělavъša	viděvъša

Table 3.14   Selected nominative singular masculine past passive participle forms in Late Proto-Slavonic

pьn-/pę- 'climb'	pętъ (‹ pn̥-)	pьr-/per- 'push'	pŗ'tъ
jьm-/ję- 'seize'	jętъ (‹ m̥-)	tьr-/ter- 'rub'	tŗ'tъ
u-kaz-a- 'indicate'	ukazanъ	dar-ov-a 'donate'	darovanъ
sъ-děl-a-j- 'make'	sъdělanъ	u-vidě- 'see'	uviděnъ
pri-ved- 'bring'	privedenъ	nos-i- 'carry'	nošenъ
dvig-(nǫ-) 'move'	dviženъ	rod-i- 'give birth'	rod'enъ
	dvignovenъ		

changes (see 2.10). As in the present active participle, the declension was athematic in the nominative singular of all genders and in the nominative plural masculine; in other cases it followed the thematic -i-$ŏ$- (M/N) and -i-$ā$- (F) types.

The **resultative participle** indicated the result of a completed action. It was formed with the suffix -l- added to the infinitive stem. The declension was that of the -$ŏ$- (M/N) and -$ā$- (F) stems. The resultative participle was regularly used in **compound verbal categories** (perfect, conditional), where it was accompanied by a finite form of the verb 'to be': *jesmь neslъ* 'I have carried', *bimь/byxъ neslъ* 'I would carry'.

The following are various Late Proto-Slavonic nominative singular masculine resultative participle forms: *pek-* 'bake': *peklъ*, *vęd-(nǫ-)* 'fade': *vędlъ*, *zьr-ě-j-* 'mature': *zьrělъ*, *gor-ě-* 'burn': *gorělъ*.

The **past passive participle** was formed with the suffixes -t- or -n- added to the infinitive stem. The declension was that of the -$ŏ$- (M/N) and -$ā$- (F) stems. The suffix -t- occurred with the sonantic and most semivocalic verbs of the -$\emptyset$- class; the root diphthong in these stems was in the zero ablaut grade. The suffix -n- occurred elsewhere. In the consonantic -$\emptyset$- and in the -$nǫ$- and -i- classes, -n- was linked to the stem by the thematic vowel -$ě$- before which the stem final -i- became -i- with the expected yodization changes in the preceding consonant (see 2.10 and table 3.14).

The **verbal noun** was a -i-$ŏ$- stem neuter noun formed from the stem of the past passive participle by the addition of the suffix -$ьi$- › -$ьj$-. Unlike the past passive participle, which was typically formed from transitive verbs only, the verbal noun was formed from both transitive and intransitive verbs. Like all nouns, the verbal noun was inflected for case and number in addition to being marked for aspect and genus, the obligatory categories of the verb.

The following are various Late Proto-Slavonic verbal nouns: *pri-nes-* 'bring': *prinesenьje* 'the bringing', *dvig-(nǫ-)* 'move': *dviženьje* 'movement', *děl-a-j-* 'do': *dělanьje* 'the doing', *mьn-ě-* 'consider': *mьněnьje* 'consideration', *nos-i-* 'carry': *nošenьje* 'the carrying', *jьm-/ję-* 'seize': *jętьje* 'seizure'.

4 Syntax

Syntactic relationships deal with the interdependence of words in sentences or in segments of sentences (syntactic constructions). These relationships may be purely semantic (for example, agent, patient, beneficiary) or they may represent different levels of linguistic structure: syntagmatic (subject, direct or indirect object, predicate, complement) or paradigmatic (case, gender, person). The latter enter into larger classes of morphosyntactic relationships, known as grammatical categories (compare 3.1.1 and 3.2.1). Research on Proto-Slavonic syntax has concentrated on the reconstruction of grammatical categories and of the rules governing their occurrence in sentences, and it is with these topics that the following cursory survey will be concerned.

Some syntactic relationships were expressed by a system of **government**, whereby a verb, a noun or a preposition required a particular form of a noun – its **case**. Features of government distinguished also between **transitive** and **intransitive verbs**, the latter specifying an obligatory absence of the direct object. Distinctions of government were an inherent feature of the verb.

Case distinctions expressed the opposition between the grammatical terms 'subject' and 'direct object', the subject being indicated by the nominative, and the direct object by the accusative or genitive (see below). By contrast, the semantic terms 'agent' and 'patient' were not so specified. This distinction was involved in the contrast between the **reflexive** and **passive constructions**. While the subject-oriented reflexive constructions indicated the centrality of the subject in the action or state expressed by the verb and neutralized the opposition between the agent and the patient (compare 3.2.1), the patient-oriented passive constructions contained an obligatory patient, expressed by the nominative of the subject, and an optional agent expressed by an oblique case or a prepositional phrase. Thus, the subject could designate the agent in active constructions: *mojь synъ sъpase ženǫ* 'my son saved a woman'; the patient in passive constructions: *žena sъpasena bystь* 'the woman was saved'; or either of these terms in reflexive constructions: *žena sę sъpase* 'the woman saved herself' or 'the woman was saved'.

In addition to personal constructions (active, passive and reflexive), Proto-Slavonic had **impersonal** (or subjectless) **constructions** which neutralized the categories of person/number/gender, expressing them by the third person singular (neuter), the least marked finite form of the verbal paradigm. Impersonal verbs were either intransitive or reflexive. They occurred in predications indicating involuntary or natural phenomena: *ne* *xъťetь sę* 'one does not feel like it', *mьnitь sę* 'it seems', *grьmitь* 'there is thunder', *smŗ́ditь* 'there is a bad smell'.

In personal constructions, the category of person contained in the inflectional endings of the first- and second-person forms allowed the **omission of the subject pronoun**: *věmь* 'I know', *věsi* 'thou knowest'. Overt expression of the subject was reserved for emphasis: *azъ věmь* '**I** know', *ty věsi* '**thou** knowest'.

The main uses of cases were as follows:

The **nominative** was the case of the subject and of the predicative complement: *ta žena bě neplody* 'this woman was barren';

The **accusative** was a typical case of the direct object: *ova žena rodi dъťerь* 'that woman gave birth to a daughter'. It also denoted extent with temporal and spatial expressions: *ona sę jestь trudila vьsь dьnь* 'she has worked all day';

The **genitive** expressed subordination in a sequence of two nouns or of a numeral and a noun (possessive and partitive functions): *nožь otьca* 'father's knife', *pętь synovъ* 'five sons'. In certain marked environments, the genitive replaced the accusative as the case of the direct object. One such situation was when the falling together of the nominative and accusative singular endings of the masculine *-ŏ-* and *-ŭ-* stems (see 3.1.2, notes 2b and 4) created a potential confusion between the subject and direct object. To preserve this distinction, the accusative *-ъ* was replaced by the genitive *-a* in nouns denoting male persons: *mojь bratrъ sъrěte pǫtьnika* 'my brother met a traveller'. The resulting accusative/genitive syncretism led to the creation of a masculine personal subgender, also known as virile. This process continued in the histories of individual Slavonic languages, culminating in the creation of the (masculine) animate subgender. In addition, the genitive denoted quantification as a direct object of verbs: *nalija vody* 'he poured some water'. This usage included the direct object of negated verbs: *ne dastь vody* 'he did not give any water', as well as of verbal substantives and supines: *lovľenьje rybь* 'the catching of fish', *pride lovitъ rybъ* 'he came to catch fish';

The **dative** was a directional case and, as such, served as the case of the indirect object: *ne dastь jemu vody* 'he did not give him any water'. It also indicated the agent/beneficiary in impersonal constructions and functioned as the subject of the infinitive in the 'dative with infinitive' constructions: *jemu sę ne xъťetь* 'he does not feel like it', *tomu ne byti* 'this will not happen';

The **locative** denoted localization in time or space: *zimě* 'in wintertime', *gorě* 'above';

The **instrumental** was a case of an accessory to the performance of an action; it denoted an instrument, means or manner of performance: *rězati nožemь* 'to cut with a knife', *pomajati rǫkǫ* 'to wave with one's hand', *jedinojǫ* 'once'.

Except for the nominative, different cases occurred in **prepositional phrases**, with particular prepositions governing particular cases; for example *u* + genitive 'near', *pro* + accusative 'through', *kъ* + dative 'to', *o* + locative 'about', *sъ* + instrumental 'with' (as accompaniment). The meaning of some prepositional phrases depended on the case of the dependent noun or pronoun, for example *vъ* 'in' or *na* 'on' denoted direction with the accusative but location with the locative.

Attributive relationships between modifiers (adjectives, gendered pronouns, numerals from '1' to '4', participles) and their heads (typically, nouns) were expressed by **agreement** in case, number and gender: *Sь dobrъjь učenikъ* 'this good (male) pupil', *si dobraja učenica* 'this good (female) pupil'.

5   Lexis

5.1   General composition of the word-stock

The Proto-Slavonic lexical stock, as reconstructed through a comparison of the vocabularies of all the Slavonic languages, belonged to the sphere of man's physical environment and emotional concerns, personal attributes, family and community ties, occupations, basic needs and desires, feelings and sensations. Many Proto-Slavonic words had cognates in other Indo-European languages and may, therefore, be considered a Proto-Indo-European inheritance. Others were particular to Balto-Slavonic or Proto-Slavonic, representing local innovations or borrowings from the languages with which the Slavs came into contact. The different origins of Proto-Slavonic words may be gleaned through an examination of several primitive semantic categories and through a survey of lexical borrowings. In the lists below, Slavonic reconstructions are given in their Late Proto-Slavonic form.

5.2   Patterns of borrowing

The lexical stock of Proto-Slavonic includes a number of loan-words from the languages of various tribes and nations who were neighbours of the early Slavs. The earliest lexical or semantic borrowings were from the north Iranian languages of the Scythian, Sarmatian and Alanic tribes. Many of these borrowings had religious connotations and included such terms as *bogъ* 'god', *divъ* 'demon', *gatati* 'to divine', *rajь* 'paradise', *svętъ* 'holy', as well as the name of the supreme Slavonic pagan deity, *Svarogъ*. However, such non-religious terms as *jaščerъ* 'serpent', *patriti* 'to look after', *radi* 'for the purpose of', *sobaka* 'dog', *toporъ* 'axe', *xata* 'house', *xvala* 'glory' are also of Iranian origin.

A few words may have originated in Celtic: for example *bagno* 'bog', *jama* 'cave', *korsta* 'canker', *sěta* 'grief', *sluga* 'servant', *tragъ* 'foot(step)'.

The more numerous loans from Germanic testify to the duration and intensity of contacts between the Slavonic and Germanic tribes. Before the Great Migrations these borrowings were taken from Proto-Germanic and Gothic; later, at the time of the Slavonic colonization of Central Europe, the main source of Germanic borrowings were Old High German dialects. Here are some examples of early Germanic loan-words: *duma* 'thought', *gotoviti* 'to prepare', *kupiti* 'to buy', *kusiti* 'to try', *lěkъ* 'medication', *lixva* 'usury', *lьstь* 'cunning', *měčь* 'sword', *pļkъ* 'host', *stьklo* 'glass', *šelmъ* 'helmet', *t'ud'ь* 'foreign', *tynъ* 'fence', *xǫdogъ* 'wise', *xlěbъ* 'bread', *xlěvъ* 'stall', *xļmъ* 'hill', *xyzъ* 'house'. The later loans were often dialect specific: *bl'udo* 'dish', *buky* 'writing', *gobьʒiti* 'to be fruitful', *gonoziti* 'to rescue', *istъba* 'house', *myto* 'tax', *smoky* 'fig', *useręgъ* 'earring', *vŗ togordъ* 'orchard', *opica* 'monkey', *penęʒь* 'coin', *plugъ* 'plough', *stodola* 'barn', and *korľ ь* 'king', perhaps the most celebrated Germanic loan-word in Slavonic, derived from the name of Charlemagne (Old High German *Kar(a)l*). Germanic also served as a transmitting channel for many Latin and, occasionally, Greek words entering Proto-Slavonic: *cěsar'ь* (Latin *Caesar*) 'emperor', *cŗ'ky* (Greek *kyrikón*) 'church', *čeršn'a* (Popular Latin *ceresia*) 'cherry', *dъska* (Latin *discus*) 'board', *kotъ* (Popular Latin *cattus*) 'cat', *kotьlъ* (Popular Latin *catillus*) 'kettle', *ocьtъ* (Latin *acetum*) 'vinegar', *osьlъ* (Latin *asinus*) 'ass', *raka* (Latin *arca*) 'casket', *velьbǫdъ* (Greek *eléphas, -antos* 'elephant') 'camel'.

Some Greek and especially Latin words seem to have entered Slavonic without Germanic mediation; for example, *kadь* 'pail', *korab'ь* 'boat', *polata* 'abode' – from Greek; *konop'a* 'flax', *lęt'a* 'lentil', *lot'ika* 'lettuce', *(na)gorditi* 'to replace', *poganъ* 'peasant', *port'a* 'lot, work', *skǫdělь* 'tile, crockery', *vino* 'wine' – from Latin. At the end of Slavonic linguistic unity, Greek and Latin provided models for the nascent Slavonic Christian terminology, the choice of the language reflecting the division of Slavdom into Byzantine and Roman ecclesiastic domains; for example, *adъ* 'hell', *dijavoľъ* 'devil', *idoľъ* 'idol', *popъ* 'priest', *psaľъmъ* 'psalm', *sǫbota* 'Sabbath', *xrizma* 'consecrated ointment' – from Greek; *kolęda* 'calendae', *komъkati* 'to communicate', *križь* 'cross', *mьša* 'mass', *oľъtar'ь* 'altar', *papežь* 'pope', *židъ* 'Jew' – from Latin.

The relations of the Slavs with various Turkic tribes (chiefly Bulgars, Khazars and Pechenegs) were reflected in such local borrowings as *bagъrъ* 'purple', *bisьrъ* 'pearls', *bogatyr'ь* 'hero', *bol' arinъ* 'nobleman', *karъ* 'black', *kolpakъ/klobukъ* 'hat', *kovъčegъ* 'box', *kъn'iga* 'book', *sanъ* 'dignity', *sapogъ* 'boot', *sokačijь* 'cook, butcher', *suje* 'in vain', *tļmačь* 'interpreter', *tьma* 'myriad', *xъmeľь* 'hops'.

5.3   Incorporation of borrowings
The mechanism of the incorporation of borrowings into Slavonic allows us to distinguish between productive and unproductive morphological classes, the former admitting loan-words, the latter not. Borrowed nouns are found in the following productive stem types: *-ŏ-/-ĭ-ŏ-* (*plugъ* 'plough' from Old High German *pfluog*, *korľь* 'king' from Old High German *Kar(a)l*, that is Charlemagne), *-ā-/-ĭ-ā-* (*stodola* 'barn' from Old High German *stadal* 'sty', *konopʹa* 'flax' from Popular Latin *canapis*), *-ĭ-* (*kadь* 'pail' from Byzantine Greek *kádion*), and *-ū-/-ŭu̯* (*buky* 'letter' from Gothic *bōka*). Borrowed verbs made their way into the following productive classes: *-nǫ-* (*goneznǫti* 'to be rescued' from Gothic *ganisan* 'to recover'), *-ov-a-* (*kupovati* 'to buy' from Gothic *kaupōn* 'to trade'), *-a-j-* (*komъkati* 'to communicate' from Latin *commūnicāre*), and *-i-* (*kusiti* 'to try' from Gothic *kausjan* 'to test').

As for the gender of borrowed nouns, one notes a very low incidence of neuter. Thus, Germanic masculine and feminine nouns retained, as a rule, their gender in Slavonic (for example, *xļmъ* 'hill' from Germanic masculine **hulmaz*, *lьstь* 'cunning' from Gothic feminine *lists*). On the other hand, Germanic neuter nouns switched to the masculine gender in Slavonic (for example, *xlěvъ* 'sty' from Germanic neuter **hlaiwan* 'grave, hole').

5.4   Lexical fields

5.4.1   Colour terms
Most Proto-Slavonic colour terms have Proto-Indo-European etymologies.

The term for 'white' was *běl-*: PIE *bhāi̯-l-*, a variant of PIE *bha-l-* 'shining'; compare OCS *bělъ*, Lithuanian *báltas*, Sanskrit *bhālas* 'shine', Greek *phalós* 'shining'.

There were two terms for 'black': *čŗ́n-* which was basic and *vornъ*, used to describe an animal's colouring. The former was derived from PIE *kŗsn-*; compare OCS *črьnъ*, Old Prussian *kirsnan*, Sanskrit *kŗṣṇás*; the latter was BSl. *u̯ărn-*: compare OCS *vranъ* 'black', Lithuanian *vařnas* 'raven'.

Proto-Slavonic used two Proto-Indo-European roots in its terms for 'red'. The basic term was derived from *čŗ́mь*: PIE *kŗm-ĭ-* 'worm, vermin' (compare Lithuanian *kirmìs*, Sanskrit *kŗ́mis*), a type of scale insect (*dactylopius coccus*) from which cochineal, a red dye, was produced; it yielded an adjectival derivative, *čŗ́mьnъ* 'red'. From its variant *čŗ́vь* 'worm', the verb *čŗ́viti* 'to dye red' was derived, with its past passive participle *čŗ́vľenъ* 'dyed red', hence 'red'. The terms for '(brownish) red' were derived from the roots *rud-/rus-/ryď-*, ablaut variants of PIE *rĕu̯dh-*; compare Czech *rudý*, Lithuanian *raũdas* 'bay', Sanskrit *róhitas*, Latin *rūfus*, Greek *ereúthō* 'I blush'; OCS *rumĕnъ* (‹ **rŏu̯dh-mēn-*); ChSl. *rusъ*,

Lithuanian *raũsvas,* Latin *russus* (‹ **rŏu̯dh-s-*); ChSl. *ryždь* 'yellow red', Lithuanian *rūdìs* 'rust' (‹ **rūdh-ĭ-*).

The terms for 'green' and 'yellow' were derived from two Proto-Indo-European root variants, *g' hĕl-/g' hŏl-/g' hl̥-* and *ghĕl-/ghŏl-/ghl̥.* The former yielded PSl. *zĕl-/zŏl-/zl̥-;* compare OCS *zelenъ* 'green', *zlato* 'gold', *zlьčь* 'bile' and Lithuanian *žélti* 'overgrow', *žéltas* 'golden', *žãlias* 'green'. The latter gave PSl. *žl̥'t-* 'yellow'; compare Church Slavonic *žlьtъ* and Lithuanian *geltas* 'yellow', Latin *helvus* 'yellow', Greek *khólos, kholḗ* 'bile, gall'.

There were no general Indo-European terms for 'blue' or 'grey'. Proto-Slavonic used three roots in several derivatives to denote a wide range of blue-grey hues. (1) PSl. *si-* from PIE *k'ī-;* compare *sinъ/sinьjь* 'livid, dark blue', *sivъ* 'silver, grey', East Slavonic *sizъ* 'grey', Lithuanian *šẽmas* 'bluish grey', *šývas* 'grey', *šéžis* 'blackbird', Sanskrit *śyāmás* 'dark grey, black'; (2) EPSl. *xŏi̯-;* compare ChSl. *sĕrъ* 'grey', OCS *sĕdъ* 'grey-haired'; (3) PSl. *polv-* from PIE *pĕl-/pŏl-,* in Slavonic extended by *-u̯-;* compare OCS *plavъ,* with meanings ranging from 'pale' (hence, 'fallow, blond') to 'grey' (hence, 'blue'), Greek *peliós* 'pale, dark-grey', Latin *pallidus* 'pale'.

Proto-Slavonic had no term for 'brown' proper. It did, however, have adjectives denoting a swarthy complexion and brown hair colour: *smĕdъ/ snĕdъ* (for people) and *gnĕdъ* (for animals). Neither term has a reliable Indo-European etymology.

The term *bagъrъ* 'purple' and its derivatives appear in South and East Slavonic only. It was borrowed from Turkic.

5.4.2 Body parts
Many Proto-Slavonic terms for body parts have reliable Indo-European etymologies:

oko, očese 'eye' from PIE *ŏk*ʷ*-;* compare OCS *oko, očese,* Lithuanian *akìs,* Sanskrit NOM DU *akṣī́,* Greek *óps,* Latin *oculus.*

uxo, ušese 'ear' from PIE *ōu̯s-;* compare OCS *uxo, ušese,* Lithuanian *ausìs,* Greek *oûs,* Latin *auris.*

nosъ 'nose' from PIE *năs-/nās-;* compare Old Russian *nosъ,* Lithuanian *nósis,* Sanskrit *nā́sā,* Latin *nāris.*

usta 'mouth' from PIE *ău̯s-/ōs-;* compare OCS *usta,* Lithuanian *úostas* 'mouth of a river', Sanskrit *óṣṭhas* 'lip', Latin *austium, ōstium* 'mouth of a river'.

bry, brъve 'brow' from PIE *bhrū-;* compare OCS *brъvь, brъve,* Lithuanian *bruvìs,* Sanskrit *bhrūs,* Greek *ophrŷs,* Old High German *brāwa.*

kry, krъve 'blood' from PIE *krĕu̯-/krū-;* compare Old Russian *kry, krъve,* Lithuanian *kraũjas,* Sanskrit *kravís* 'raw meat', Greek *kréas* 'raw meat', Latin *cruor.*

sr̥'dъce 'heart' from PIE *k'r̥d-;* compare OCS *srъdьce,* Lithuanian *širdìs,*

Greek *kềr* and *kardía*, Latin *cor, cordis*, Gothic *hairtō*.

volsъ 'hair' from PIE *u̯ȯls-*; compare OCS *vlasъ*, Lithuanian *valaī* 'horse-hair', Avestan *varasa-*, Greek *oûlos* 'curly'.

nogъtь '(finger)nail' from PIE *nȯgh-*; compare OCS *nogъtь*, Lithuanian *nagùtis*, Greek *ónyks, ónykhos*, Latin *unguis*, Old High German *nagal* (compare *noga* below).

(*v*)*ǫtroba* 'entrails' from PIE *ȯ/ĕnt(ĕ)r-*; compare OCS *ǫtroba* 'womb' (in other Slavonic languages also 'liver' or 'heart'), Sanskrit *antrám*, Greek *énteron*, Latin *interior* 'inner'.

Some terms are Balto-Slavonic in origin:

golva 'head' from BSl. *gălu̯ā̃*; compare OCS *glava*, Lithuanian *galvà*.

gr̥dlo 'throat' from BSl. *gŭrdl-*; compare Old Russian *gъrlo*, Lithuanian *gurklỹs*.

rǫka 'hand, arm' from BSl. *rănkā̃*; compare OCS *rǫka*, Lithuanian *rankà*.

noga 'leg, foot' from BSl *năgā̃*; compare OCS *noga*, Lithuanian *nagà* 'hoof' (see *nogъtь* above).

pr̥'stъ 'finger' from BSl. *pĭrst-*; compare OCS *prьstъ*, Lithuanian *pirštas* (also Sanskrit *pr̥ṣṭhám* 'peak').

5.4.3   Kinship terms

Kinship terms belong to the oldest layer of Proto-Slavonic vocabulary. Several of them are part of the Proto-Indo-European heritage, while those which are specifically Balto-Slavonic or Proto-Slavonic have identifiable Indo-European roots and suffixes.

PSl. *mati, -ere* 'mother'; *dъťi, -ere* 'daughter'; *bratrъ* 'brother' came from athematic stems in the suffix *-tēr/-tōr/-tr*: PIE *mā-tēr, dhŭghǝ-tēr, bhrā-tēr*. In Balto-Slavonic the former two retained some features of the athematic declension; compare OCS *mati, -ere, dъšti, -ere, brat(r)ъ, -a*; Lithuanian *mótė, -eřs* 'woman', *duktė̃, -eřs, brólis* (< *broter-ėlis, a diminutive formation); Sanskrit *mātā́, duhitā́, bhrā́tā*; Greek *mḗtēr, thygátēr, phrā́tēr*; Old High German *muoter, tohter, bruodor*.

PSl. *sestra* 'sister' (with an epenthetic *t*) was derived from PIE *s(u̯)esȯr*, an athematic *-r-* stem which transferred in Slavonic to the *-ā-* stems; compare OCS *sestra*, Lithuanian *sesuõ, -eřs*, Sanskrit *svásā*, Latin *soror*, Gothic *swistar*.

PIE *pa-tēr* and *ăt-* both denoted 'father'. The former, in its zero grade, was the probable source of PSl. *strъjь* 'paternal uncle'. The latter, extended by the suffix *-ĭk-*, gave PSl. *otьcь* 'father'; compare Greek, Latin and Gothic *atta* 'father', with expressive gemination.

PSl. *svekry* 'husband's mother' from PIE *su̯ĕk'rūs*, an *-ū-* stem which in Slavonic shows a plain velar; compare OCS *svekry*, Sanskrit *śvaśrū́s*,

Greek *hekyrá* 'stepmother', Latin *socrus* 'mother-in-law'.

PSl. *synъ* 'son' from PIE *sūnŭs*; compare OCS *synъ*, Lithuanian *sūnùs*, Sanskrit *sūnus*, Greek *hyiós*.

PSl. *zętь* 'a male kinsman' was probably derived from PIE *g'ĕn-* 'give birth'; compare OCS *zętь* 'bridegroom', Russian *zjat'* 'son-in-law' or 'brother-in-law', Lithuanian *žéntas* 'son-in-law', Sanskrit *jnātis*, Greek *gnōtós* 'relative'.

PSl. *zъly, -ъve* 'sister-in-law' was an *-ū-* stem related to Greek *gáloōs*, Latin *glōs, glōris* 'sister-in-law'.

PSl. *žena* 'woman, wife' from PIE *gʷĕnā*; compare OCS *žena*, Sanskrit *jánis*, Greek *gynḗ*, Gothic *qinō* 'woman'.

PSl. *mǫžь* 'man, husband' from PIE *măn-g-i̯-ŏ-s*; compare OCS *mǫžь*, Sanskrit *mánus*, Gothic *manna* 'man'.

6 Dialects

It is highly probable that the process of dialect differentiation marking the end of the Early Proto-Slavonic period, began soon after the sixth century AD, when the Slavs spread throughout central and south-eastern Europe. It is more difficult to determine when these dialect distinctions became so pronounced as to justify the assumption of the dissolution of Proto-Slavonic linguistic unity and of the rise of separate Slavonic languages. The commonly accepted dating of this process into the ninth-tenth century is based primarily on the political events of the period, such as the attainment of statehood by Bulgaria, Carantania, Croatia, Serbia, Moravia, Pannonia, Bohemia, Poland and Kievan Rus' (see maps 3.2 and 3.4). There is little doubt, however, that by the ninth century there emerged at least three distinct dialects, South Slavonic, East Slavonic and West Slavonic, the latter two grouped as North Slavonic (see map 3.1).

Note: In the following list of isoglosses, only the features not mentioned in the earlier sections of this survey are provided with examples. Features mentioned before are cross-referenced appropriately but no examples are cited.

Some of the features which distinguished South Slavonic (S) from North Slavonic (N) were as follows:

1   PSl. *# ăRC* ‖ S *# RāC* versus N *# RăC* (see 2.22(a)).
2   PSl. *ę* ‖ S *ę* versus N *ě* [ä] (see 2.27(c)).
3   Accusative plural of the *-i-ŏ-* and *-i-ā-* stems ‖ S *-ę* versus N *-ě₃* (see 3.1.2).
4   Instrumental singular of the *-ŏ-* stems ‖ S *-otь* versus N *-ъtь*, for example OCS *godotь* 'year' versus Old Russian *godъtь* (see 3.1.2).
5   Nominative singular masculine present active participle ‖ S *-y* versus N *-a* (see 3.2.2).

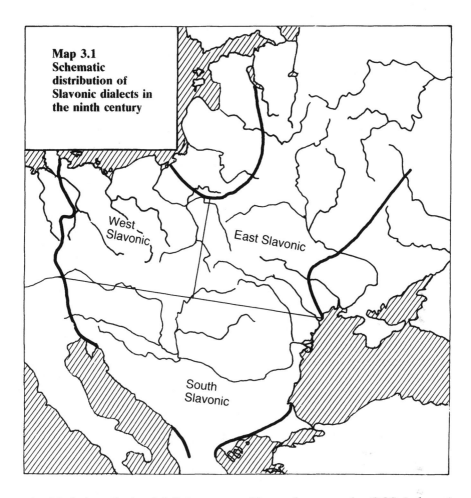

**Map 3.1
Schematic
distribution of
Slavonic dialects in
the ninth century**

West
Slavonic

East Slavonic

South
Slavonic

6   Verbal prefix 'out' ‖ S *jьz-* versus N *vy-*, for example, OCS *iz-bьrati*
     'to elect' versus Old Russian *vy-bьrati.*

The most important features which distinguished West Slavonic (W) from
both South Slavonic and East Slavonic (S/E) were as follows:

1   EPSl. *xē₂ skē₂ ku̯ē₂ gu̯ē₂* ‖ W *šě ščě kvě gvě* versus S/E *s'ě scě cvě ʒvě.*
     These are some of the reflexes of the second and third palatalizations
     of velars (see 2.19); compare LOC SG EPSl. *u̯ăsk-ē₂* 'wax': Old Czech
     voščě, OCS *voscě.*
2   PSl. *tl dl* ‖ W *tl dl* versus S/E *l* (see 2.20). Note that many Slovene
     dialects have *tl dl,* while some Western Russian dialects have *kl gl.*
3   First singular and third plural productive aorist ‖ W *-exъ -exǫ* versus
     S/E *-oxъ -ošę* (see 3.2.2, p. 100).

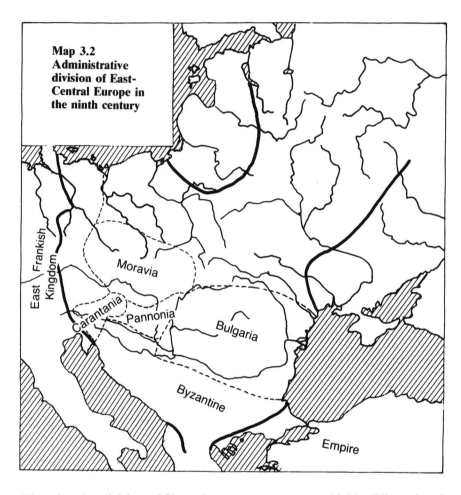

Map 3.2
Administrative
division of East-
Central Europe in
the ninth century

East Frankish Kingdom

Moravia

Carantania

Pannonia

Bulgaria

Byzantine

Empire

The tripartite division of Slavonic soon gave way to a highly differentiated dialect picture (see map 3.3). South Slavonic split into a Western and an Eastern dialect, the former consisting of pre-literary Slovene and Serbo-Croat, the latter of Bulgarian and Macedonian. Practically all extant texts of canonical Old Church Slavonic may be considered examples of literary Eastern South Slavonic. West Slavonic distinguished three dialect groups. The largest was Lechitic, the common ancestor of Polish, Cassubian, Slovincian and Polabian and of the extinct Slavonic Pomeranian dialects attested to by the many surviving place names and a few personal names mentioned in medieval chronicles. The two smaller ones were Sorbian, from which modern Lower and Upper Sorbian are derived, and Czech/Slovak consisting of Czech and Slovak. East Slavonic split first into South-Western and North-Eastern (Russian) variants, the former being the forerunner of Ukrainian and Belorussian.

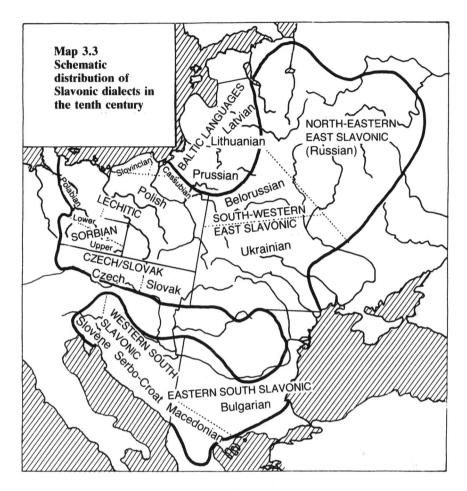

Map 3.3 Schematic distribution of Slavonic dialects in the tenth century

Western South Slavonic (WS) differed from both Eastern South Slavonic and North Slavonic (ES/N) by the following features:

1   Phonemic pitch was retained in WS but lost in ES/N, for example Serbo-Croat NOM SG *rúka* 'hand', ACC SG *rûku* versus Polish *ręka, rękę*.
2   The Proto-Slavonic circumflex (see 2.26) yielded vocalic length in WS but brevity in ES/N.
3   Proto-Slavonic front vowels did not palatalize the preceding consonant in WS but did palatalize them in ES/N, for example, Serbo-Croat *tĭ* 'for you', *dĕset* '10' versus Polish *ci, dziesięć*.

In Western South Slavonic and West Slavonic the Proto-Slavonic strong *jers* fell together, while in Eastern South Slavonic and East Slavonic they

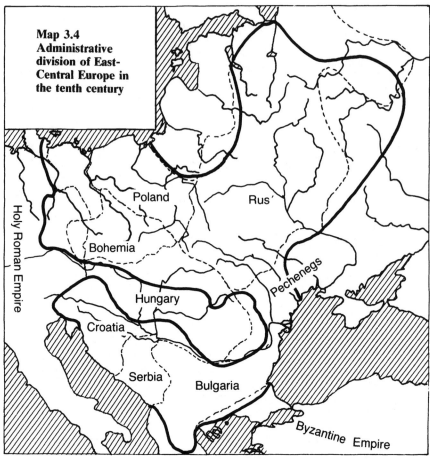

**Map 3.4
Administrative
division of East-
Central Europe in
the tenth century**

Based on map 19 in Konrad Jażdżewski (1949) *Atlas do pradziejów Słowian*, Łódź: ŁTN.

did not; for example, PSl. *dьnь* 'day', *sъnъ* 'sleep': Serbo-Croat *dân, sàn*, Czech *den, sen* versus OCS *dьnь, sъnъ*, Russian *den', son*.

In Eastern South Slavonic and West Slavonic the epenthetic *l* derived from the Proto-Slavonic sequences of a labial (*P*) + *j*, across a morphemic boundary, was lost yielding *P'*, while in Western South Slavonic and East Slavonic it is retained as *Pl'* (see 2.10(c)).

In Czech/Slovak and South Slavonic the syllabic function of Proto-Slavonic syllabic liquids was retained yielding *CRC*, while in East Slavonic, Lechitic and Sorbian it was transferred to a vowel yielding *CVRC* (see 2.22(b)).

Proto-Slavonic soft *r̨′* hardened in Czech/Slovak and South Slavonic and was retained in East Slavonic; in Lechitic and Sorbian it hardened before hard dentals and was retained in other positions, for example, PSl. *tvr̨′dĕjь* 'hard', *tvr̨′diti* 'to affirm': Czech *tvrdý, tvrditi* versus Russian *tvĕrdyj, tverdít′* versus Polish *twardy, twierdzić.*

The reflexes of PSl. *CĕRC CăRC* are threefold (see 2.22(c)); in South Slavonic and Czech/Slovak *CRēC CRāC*, in East Slavonic *CĕRəC CăRəC*, in Lechitic and Sorbian *CəRĕC CəRăC* (note, however, the following point on groups involving an *l*).

Sorbian, Polish, Czech/Slovak and South Slavonic retained a distinction between PSl. *CĕlC* and *CălC*, while Western Lechitic (that is, Cassubian – including Slovincian — and Polabian) and East Slavonic merged them as *CălC* (see 2.22(b)).

Sorbian, Polish and Czech distinguished between PSl. *Cļ′ C* and *CļC*, while in Slovak, Western Lechitic and South and East Slavonic *Cļ′ C* merged with *CļC* (see 2.22(b)).

PSl. *ě* yielded the low vowel [æ] in Lechitic and Bulgarian, while in other Slavonic languages it tended to have high reflexes, *e* or *i* (see 2.27(b)).

PSl. *ǫ* tended to be rounded (*u* or *ọ*) in North Slavonic and Western South Slavonic and unrounded (*ъ* or *ą*) in Eastern South Slavonic (see 2.27(c)).

Lechitic and some Slovene and Bulgarian dialects retained the nasal resonance of Proto-Slavonic nasal vowels which elsewhere were denasalized (see 2.21).

PSl. *ě* and *ę* merged with *a* and *ǫ* respectively before hard dentals in Lechitic, for example, PSl. *lěsъ* 'forest', *sněgъ* 'snow': Polish *las, śnieg* versus Russian *les, sneg*; PSl. *pętьjь* 'fifth', *pętь* '5': Polabian *p′ǫtĕ, pǫt* versus Serbo-Croat *pêti, pêt.*

PSl. *g* was spirantized to [ɣ] or *h* in Southern East Slavonic, Czech/Slovak, Upper Sorbian and West Slovene, for example, Russian *gólos*, Serbo-Croat *glâs* versus Ukrainian *hólos*, Czech *hlas* 'voice'.

The reflexes of PSl. *t′, d′* were fivefold (see 2.23), in West Slavonic *c, ʒ*, in East Slavonic and Slovene *č, ǯ* (in standard Slovene *ǯ* became *j*), in Serbo-Croat *ć, ʒ́*, in standard Macedonian *k′ g′*, in Old Church Slavonic and Bulgarian *št, žd.*

The Proto-Slavonic third singular and plural present-tense suffix is reconstructed as -tь (SG)/ -tь (PL). However, West Slavonic and Western South Slavonic have -∅/-∅, Eastern South Slavonic has -∅/-t, South-Western East Slavonic and some North-Eastern East Slavonic dialects have -∅/-t' in conjugation I and -t'/-t' in conjugation II, and most of North-Eastern East Slavonic has -t/-t (see 3.2.2, p. 97, note 4).

The Proto-Slavonic first plural (see 3.2.2 p. 97, note 6) was -mъ in Old Church Slavonic and North-Eastern East Slavonic, -mo in Western South Slavonic and South-Western East Slavonic, -me in Eastern South Slavonic and Czech/Slovak, -my in Lechitic and Sorbian.

References

Arumaa, Peeter (1964, 1976, 1985) *Urslavische Grammatik: Einführung in das vergleichende Studium der slavischen Sprachen*, 3 vols, Heidelberg: Carl Winter.

Bidwell, Charles E. (1963) *Slavic Historical Phonology in Tabular Form*, The Hague: Mouton.

Birnbaum, Henrik (1979) *Common Slavic: Progress and Problems in its Reconstruction*, Columbus, Oh.: Slavica. (Russian translation (1987) Праславянский язык: Достижения и проблемы в его реконструкции, Москва: Прогресс.)

Birnbaum, Henrik and Peter T. Merrill (1983) *Recent Advances in the Reconstruction of Common Slavic (1971–1982)*, Columbus, Oh.: Slavica. (Russian translation in entry above.)

Bräuer, Herbert (1961, 1969) *Slavische Sprachwissenschaft*, 2 vols, Berlin: de Gruyter.

Carlton, Terence R. (1991) *Introduction to the Phonological History of the Slavic Languages*, Columbus, Ohio: Slavica.

Entwistle, W.J. and Morison, W.A. (1964) *Russian and the Slavonic Languages*, London: Faber & Faber.

Furdal, Antoni (1961) *Rozpad języka prasłowiańskiego w świetle rozwoju głosowego*, Wrocław: Ossolineum.

Horálek, Karel (1962) *Úvod do studia slovanských jazyků*, 2nd edn, Prague: Československá Akademie věd.

Ivšić, Stjepan (1970) *Slavenska poredbena gramatika*, Zagreb: Školska Knjiga.

Jakobson, Roman (1955) *Slavic Languages: a Condensed Survey*, 2nd edn, New York: King's Crown Press.

Kuryłowicz, Jerzy, (1964) *The Inflectional Categories of Indo-European*, Heidelberg: Carl Winter.

Lamprecht, Arnošt (1987) *Praslovanština*, Brno: Univerzita J.E. Purkyně.

Liewehr, Ferdinand (1955) *Slawische Sprachwissenschaft in Einzeldarstellungen*, Vienna: Rudolf M. Rohrer.

Mareš, František V. (1965) *Die Entstehung des slavischen phonologischen Systems und seine Entwicklung bis zum Ende der Periode der slavischen Spracheinheit*, Munich: Sagner. (English translation (1965) *The Origin of the Slavic Phonological System and its Development up to the End of Slavic Language Unity*, Ann Arbor: Department of Slavic Languages and Literatures, University of Michigan.)

Meillet, Antoine (1934) *Le slave commun*, 2nd edn revised by André Vaillant,

Paris: Librairie Champion. (Russian translation (1951) *Общеславянский язык*, Москва: Издательство иностранной литературы.)

Mikkola, J.J. (1913, 1942, 1950) *Urslavische Grammatik: Einführung in das vergleichende Studium der slavischen Sprachen*, 3 vols, Heidelberg: Carl Winter.

Nahtigal, Rajko (1952) *Slovanski jeziki*, 2nd edn, Ljubljana: Jože Moškrič. (German translation 1961) *Die slavische Sprachen: Abriß der vergleichenden Grammatik*, Wiesbaden: Harrassowitz. (Russian translation (1963) *Славянские языки*, Москва: Издательство иностранной литературы.)

Rozwadowski, Jan (1959, 1961, 1960) *Wybór pism*, 3 vols, Warsaw: PWN.

Shevelov, George Y. (1965) *A Prehistory of Slavic: the Historical Phonology of Common Slavic*, New York: Columbia University Press.

Stankiewicz, Edward (1986) *The Slavic Languages: Unity in Diversity*, Berlin, New York, Amsterdam: Mouton de Gruyter.

Stieber, Zdzisław (1979) *Zarys gramatyki porównawczej języków słowiańskich*, Warsaw: PWN.

Szemerényi, Oswald (1989) *Einführung in die vergleichende Sprachwissenschaft*, 3rd edn, Darmstadt: Wissenschaftliche Buchgesellschaft. (Russian translation (1980) *Введение в сравнительное языкознание*, Москва: Прогресс.)

Vaillant, André (1950, 1958, 1966, 1974, 1977) *Grammaire comparée des langues slaves*, vols I–II, Lyon, Paris: IAC; vols III–V, Paris: Klincksieck.

Velcheva, Boryana (1989) *Proto-Slavic and Old Bulgarian Sound Changes*, translated and edited by Ernest A. Scatton, Columbus, Ohio: Slavica.

Vondrák, Wenzel (1924, 1928) *Vergleichende slavische Grammatik*, vols I–II, Göttingen: Vandenhoeck & Ruprecht.

Wijk, Nicolas van (1956) *Les langues slaves: de l'unité à la pluralité*, The Hague: Mouton.

Бернштейн, Самуил Б. (1961, 1974) *Очерк сравнительной грамматики славянских языков*, vol. I, Москва: Издательство Академии наук СССР, vol. II, Москва: Наука.

Булаховський, Леонід А. (1975, 1976, 1977, 1980, 1983) *Вибрані праці в п'яти томах*, 5 vols, Київ: Наукова Думка.

Кузнецов, Петр С. (1961) *Очерки по морфологии праславянского языка*, Москва: Издательство Академии наук СССР.

Савченко, Алексей Н. (1974) *Сравнительная грамматика индоевропейских языков*, Москва: Высшая школа.

Трубачев, Олег Н., ред., (1974–) *Этимологический словарь славянских языков: Праславянский лексический фонд*, Москва: Наука.

SOUTH SLAVONIC LANGUAGES

4 Old Church Slavonic

David Huntley

1 Introduction

Old Church Slavonic is the language extrapolated from a small corpus of probably late tenth-century copies, mainly of translations made about a century earlier of Greek ecclesiastical texts. These Slavonic texts, containing mainly Balkan dialectal features, have an admixture of Moravianisms, since the first translations were used for missionary activity in Greater Moravia, where further translations and copies were made, beginning from about 863. The earliest texts were written in Glagolitic, a script devised by Constantine and Methodius, whereas the misnamed Cyrillic script was devised in the Balkans after the expulsion of the Moravian mission in about 885 (see chapter 2). In this chapter examples will be cited from the following major texts:

Gospel lectionaries (books of lessons from the Gospels to be read at church services):
   Codex Assemanianus (*Evangeliarium Assemani*) (edited by J. Kurz, Prague, 1955), Glagolitic, 158 folia;
   Savvina kniga (edited by V. Ščepkin, St Petersburg, 1903), Cyrillic, 129 folia;
Tetraevangelia (texts of the four Gospels):
   Codex Zographensis (edited by V. Jagić, Berlin, 1879), Glagolitic, 288 folia with lacunae, and including some folia in a younger hand;
   Codex Marianus (edited by V. Jagić, Berlin, 1883), Glagolitic, 174 folia, with fewer lacunae than *Zographensis*;
Psalter (book of psalms):
   Psalterium Sinaiticum (*Sinajskaja psaltyr'*, edited by S. Sever'janov, Petrograd, 1922), Glagolitic, 177 folia, containing Psalms 1–137;
Euchologion (prayer book):
   Euchologium Sinaiticum (edited by R. Nahtigal, Ljubljana, 1942), Glagolitic, 109 folia.
Menologion for the month of May (lives of saints and sermons arranged by day):
   Codex Suprasliensis (*Suprasălski ili retkov sbornik*, edited by J. Zaimov

and M. Capaldo, 2 volumes, Sofia, 1982–3), Cyrillic, 570 folia;
Homiliary (collection of sermons):
  Glagolita Clozianus (*Clozianus*, edited by A. Dostál, Prague, 1959),
  Glagolitic, 14 folia.

No data will be cited here from shorter texts, or from the later recensions, which together with Old Church Slavonic are known as 'Church Slavonic', comprising later copies of texts, copies of texts not extant earlier and new translations of various kinds in copies of Bulgarian, Macedonian, East Slavonic, Serbian, Croatian and Czech–Slovak provenance.

Examples from the texts will be cited in italics, without any normalization in the direction of our reconstruction of the phonemic system of Old Church Slavonic. Phonemic and phonetic reconstructions (of both older and younger forms) will be cited in slanted and square brackets respectively. Unless specified otherwise, these reconstructions will cite infinitives for verbs and nominative singular for nominals, with the masculine cited for nominals inflected for gender. Forms in tables, cited without brackets, are phonemic. The Gospel texts are those of the first witness cited.

2 Phonology

2.1 Segmental phoneme inventory
Tables 4.1 and 4.2 show the segmental phonemes of Old Church Slavonic. In addition, the orthography indicates the following in Greek words: /ü/, /oː/, /ǵ/, /f/, /θ/. For the relation between phonemes and Glagolitic and Cyrillic graphemes, reference should be made to chapter 2.

The symbols ь and ъ represent reduced vowels, phonetically mid. In Eastern (Bulgarian) dialects, these reduced vowels had high allophones contiguous with /j/, that is /ьjь/ is [iji], /ъj/ is [ўj]. Western (Macedonian) dialects did not have this variation, but here, unlike in the

Table 4.1   Old Church Slavonic vowels

Front unrounded		Back unrounded	Back rounded	
Oral	*Nasal*	*Oral*	*Oral*	*Nasal*
i		y	u	
ь		ъ		
e	ę		o	ǫ
ě		a		

Note: In Western dialects, ъ was rounded.

Table 4.2   Old Church Slavonic consonants

	Labial		Dental		Palatal		Velar	
Plosive	p	b	t	d			k	g
Affricate			c	dz	č			
Fricative		v	s	z	š	ž	x	
Nasal		m		n		ń		
Lateral				l		ĺ		
Trill				r		ŕ		
Semi-vowel						j		

east, /ъ/ was phonetically labialized. Glagolitic orthography provides evidence for fronted allophones of the phonemically labialized /u/, /ǫ/. Nasalized and oral vowels are contrasted in word-final position: /duše/ 'soul (VOC SG)', /dušę/ (GEN SG), /ženǫ/ 'woman (ACC SG)', /ženo/ (VOC SG).

The dental affricates /c/, /dz/, post-alveolar /š/, /ž/, /č/, /ŕ/, pre-palatal /ĺ/, /ń/, /j/, and stops in the sequences /št/, /žd/ were pho-netically palatalized. In Eastern dialects, labials, and dentals other than /c/, /dz/ were palatalized phonetically only before front vowels, whereas no such allophonic variation occurred in Western dialects. Younger spell-ings, as in *prědame i* (Matthew 26.15; *Marianus*) 'I will betray him' are evidence for a morpheme /j/. Such spellings arose after the loss of the reduced vowels in the tenth century, and can be explained only as a Western reflex of /prědamь jь/ as /prědame j/, proving that /j/ must have been the stem of the third-person pronoun. The sonorants /l/, /r/ could form syllabic nuclei. Orthographically, and in transliteration in this chapter, the syllabic sonorants are not distinguished from sequences of sonorant followed by reduced vowel. In phonemic and phonetic repre-sentation, the sequences will be shown by writing the *jers*, the reduced vowel letters, on the line, and the syllabic sonorants with the jer above the line.

With respect to constraints on phoneme distribution, only the most conservative system, prior to the loss of the reduced vowels, will be discussed here. The consonant clusters described in table 4.3 do not include sequences containing syllabic sonorants. Apart from the constraint evident from table 4.3, namely that two adjacent consonants tend not to share identical features of manner of articulation, no syllable ends in a consonant, an obstruent other than /v/ agrees in voicing with an immedi-ately following obstruent, velars do not occur before front vowels, and phonetically palatalized consonants do not occur before certain back vowels. Constraints on sequences of consonant and vowel are summarized in table 4.4. The back vowels /y/, /ъ/, and front vowels other than /i/ did

Table 4.3   Old Church Slavonic consonant clusters

Initials	Finals															
	p	b	t	d	k	g	m	n	v	l	r	x	ń	ĺ	ŕ	c
s	+		+		+		+	+	+	+	+	J				J
z		J		I		I	+	+	+	+	+					
g				(I)				+	+	+	+	(I)				
d							(I)		+	+	+					
t, k, x									+	+	+					
p, b									(J)	+	+			+		
ž				I						+	+		+			
m, v										+	+			J		
č										+	+					
š		+									+		J	J		
c, dz									+							
n											+					
sp										J	J					
st										I	J	+				
sk										+	+	+				
sm, sv												+				
sx, zg										J	J	J				
zb, zm											J	J				
zd										J		J				
zv										J	J					
št										J					J	
žd															J	
tv											J					

Note: + no constraints; I word-medial and at morpheme boundary only; J at morpheme boundary only; ( ) restricted to one or a few lexical items.

not occur initially, where the two back vowels took prothetic /v/, and the front vowels prothetic /j/. A vowel sequence is attested in only one native lexical morpheme, namely the root of /paǫčina/ 'spider's web', and in the suffixes /aa/, /ěa/ of the imperfect tense. At morpheme boundaries, the following vowel sequences occur: /ai/, /au/, /ao/, /oi/, /ou/, /oo/, /ěi/, /ěo/.

Most of the variant spellings resulted from changes occurring between the time of the translations and the actual extant copies, while a few variants are the result of prehistoric changes.

Nasal vowels are regular prehistoric reflexes, with a vowel–nasal sequence before a consonant or a long vowel–nasal sequence word-finally giving rise to the nasal vowels /ǫ/ and /ę/. There are attested a few examples of younger reflexes of these nasal vowels, arising probably from historical denasalizations, with /ǫ/ giving /u/ or /o/ and /ę/ giving /e/ or /ě/. In Glagolitic, spellings with o for ǫ and e for ę could have arisen as the result of the omission of the second element of the digraphs for the

Table 4.4 Constraints on consonant–vowel sequences

	y	ъ	o	ǫ	u	a	ě	ę	e	ь	i
Velar	+	+	+	+	+	+	–	–	–	–	–
j	–	–	–	+	+	C	G	+	+	+	+
š, ž, č	–	–	–	+	+	+	–	+	+	+	+
ń, l, f	–	–	–	+	+	S	+	+	+	+	+
c, dz	–	–	–	+	+	+	+	+	+	+	+

Note: + no constraints; C Cyrillic; G Glagolitic; S Suprasliensis. There are no constraints for labials or for dentals other than /c/, /dz/. *š, ž, č* + *ě* are attested in spellings that are possibly Moravian.

nasal vowels. In other contexts there was dialectal sporadic nasalization of a vowel in contact with a nasal consonant giving rise to doublets such as /gnusiti sę/, /gnǫsiti sę/ 'be disgusted', arising probably prehistorically.

Scribal inconsistency indicates that the reduced vowels were lost in Balkan dialects by the end of the tenth century in weak position (/sъna/ › /sna/ 'sleep (GEN SG)', /dьne/ › /dne/ 'day (GEN SG)'), but were transformed in strong position (nominative singular /sъnъ/ › Western /son/, elsewhere /sən/, /dьnь/ › /den/, /dən/). The reduced vowels were in weak position when not immediately followed by a syllable containing another reduced vowel in weak position, but were in strong position when immediately followed by such a syllable. Thus all utterance-final reduced vowels were weak, but a word-final reduced vowel could be in strong position when followed by an enclitic, as in /prědamь jь/, later /prědame j/ 'I will betray him' cited above or in /dьnь sь/, later /dnes/, 'day this (ACC SG)', 'today'.

In dialects with high allophones of the reduced vowels contiguous with /j/, strong reduced vowels in such a context had high-vowel reflexes, instead of the mid-vowel reflexes occurring in other contexts, as in *sъtvorьi* (*Zographensis, Savvina kniga*), *sъtvorii* (*Marianus*), *sъtvorei* (*Assemanianus*) (Luke 10.37) 'do (PAST ACT PART NOM SG M DEF)'. The variants all represent reflexes of /sъtvoŕьjь/. *Zographensis* and *Savvina kniga* represent either this form or a younger /stvorəj/ in a dialect without the high allophones, whereas *Marianus* represents either the older form with high allophones [sъtvoriji] or its reflex /stvorij/. Only *Assemanianus* is unambiguous, representing a Western reflex /stvorej/. All four witnesses typically write the *jer* in the first syllable, even though the vowel had disappeared in this context.

Prehistorically there were back syllabic sonorants and front syllabic sonorants followed by a back and front vocalic glide, respectively. Although this etymological distinction will be observed in phonological representations in this study, the distinction is not observed in the orthography, so that the front and back syllabic sonorants may have merged prehistorically, as in *črъvь* (*Zographensis*), *črъvь* (*Marianus*) (Mark 9.44) 'worm (NOM SG)'. From the palatal initial consonant one may reconstruct etymological /črᵇvь/. The *jer* letters used to indicate syllabic sonorants are never replaced by *e* or *o* letters, whereas such younger spellings are attested for the sonorants followed by a phonemic reduced vowel, as in *skrъžьštetъ* (*Zographensis, Marianus, Assemanianus*; Mark 9.18), *skrežьštetъ* (*Euchologium Sinaiticum* 88a.10) 'gnash (3 SG PRS)'. In this example, a velar, /k/, precedes the sequence of /r/ plus front reduced vowel, whereas a velar could not precede any front segment, including a front syllabic sonorant.

Similarly, the shift of /ъ/ to /o/ is attested in prepositions immediately followed by a syllable containing a sequence /r/ plus reduced vowel in weak position, but such a shift is not attested when the syllable contains a syllabic sonorant; thus *vo krъvi* (*Psalterium Sinaiticum* 57.11) 'in blood (LOC SG)' represents the reflex of an older /vъ krъve/.

Low vowels followed by /r/ or /l/ plus a consonant prehistorically metathesized and lengthened, as is attested by some alternations in the manuscripts: *borę sę* (*Suprasliensis* 56.22) 'fight (PRS ACT PART NOM SG M INDEF)', *sę brati* (*Suprasliensis* 73.9) 'fight (INF)', *meljaaše* (*Suprasliensis* 565.10) 'grind (3 SG IMPF)' (for /melaaše/), *mьlětъ* (*Suprasliensis* 565.4) 'grind (SUPINE)' (for /mlětъ/). Here, /a/ and /ě/ are metathesized reflexes of /o/ and /e/, respectively. There is attested one example which is possibly evidence for a dialect in which this metathesis had not taken place: *zolъta* (*Psalterium Sinaiticum* 71.15) 'gold (GEN SG)'; the normal spelling is *zlata*.

Word-initially, the absence of the metathesis seems more widespread, since there are attested for two roots a number of examples with or without the metathesis, as in *ladii* (*Marianus*), *aldii* (*Zographensis*) (Mark 1.19) 'boat (LOC SG)', *lačǫšta* (*Zographensis*), *alčǫšta* (*Marianus, Assemanianus*), *alъčǫšta* (*Savvina kniga*) (Matthew 25.37) 'hunger (PRS ACT PART ACC SG M)'. One root and one prefix are attested with initial *ra* and *ro*: *rabъ* (*Suprasliensis* 106.1), *robъ* (*Suprasliensis* 106.5) 'slave', *razboinici* (*Suprasliensis* 557.24) 'robber (NOM PL)', *rozboinikъ* (*Suprasliensis* 558.9) (NOM SG). Most likely, the forms with *a* are Balkan, and those with *o* Moravian.

Whereas the dental sonorants followed by front vowels may be preceded by dental obstruents, the palatal sonorants are preceded by palatal obstruents, and therefore must have been articulated further back than were the dentals: *blaznitъ* (*Zographensis*; John 6.61) 'offend (3 SG PRS)', *blažněaxǫ sę* (*Zographensis*; Matthew 13.57) 'be offended (3 PL IMPF)', *myslite* (*Zographensis*; Matthew 9.4) 'think (2 PL PRS)', *myšlěaše* (*Zographensis*; Luke 12.17) (3 SG IMPF). The palatal alternants /ž/, /š/ are attested regularly when immediately preceding the sonorants /ń/, /ĺ/. The sonorant

/f/, or its reflex, is attested with immediately preceding dentals as well as palatals: *sъmotriši* (*Suprasliensis* 241.16) 'observe (2 SG PRES)', *sъmoštraaxǫ* (*Suprasliensis* 184.8) (3 PL IMPF), *sъmotraaše* (*Suprasliensis* 92.17) (3 SG IMPF) (for /sъmoštŕaaše/); *mǫdriši sę* (*Suprasliensis* 49.15) 'dispute (2 SG PRS)', *prěmǫždrati sę* (*Suprasliensis* 21.24) 'philosophize (INF)', *umǫdrěję* (*Psalterium Sinaiticum* 18.8) 'make wise (PRS ACT PART NOM SG N)' (for /umǫždŕaję/). The first member of each triple of examples has the dental stop /t/ or /d/ because the immediately following sonorant is also dental, whereas the second example has the palatal alternant /št/ or /žd/ before the reflexes of palatal /f/. In the third example of each triple, not only has the palatal sonorant merged with dental /r/, but also the dental:palatal alternation has been suppressed analogically. There is attested further orthographical evidence to show that /ń/, /ĺ/ behave more conservatively than /f/. In the most conservative spellings, the palatal sonorants are indicated by a diacritic on the consonant letter, by the use of the letters for the front allophones of /u/, /ǫ/ and by indicating /a/ by the letter *ě* after the palatal sonorants in both Glagolitic and Cyrillic. The diacritic is attested at all regularly only in the Glagolitic *Zographensis* and the Cyrillic *Suprasliensis*. In *Zographensis* the diacritic is used much more consistently for /ĺ/ and /ń/ than for /f/. In *Suprasliensis* the diacritic is used for /ĺ/ and /ń/ even more consistently than in *Zographensis*, but the diacritic is almost never used for /f/. Indeed, in *Suprasliensis* etymological /f/ is frequently not indicated by the following vowel letter, as for instance in *ra* for /fa/ in the examples just cited. The reason for this is that /f/ merged with /r/ when /ĺ/ and /ń/ were still distinct from the dentals. Whereas on typological grounds it is most likely that /ń/ and /ĺ/ were pre-palatal, articulated in the position of /j/, a palatalized vibrant cannot be articulated in this position, so that /f/ must have been post-alveolar, articulated in the position of /ž/, and therefore phonetically closer to the dentals than were /ń/ and /ĺ/.

In some Eastern dialects, labials and dentals were phonetically pala-talized before front vowels. When the reduced vowels were lost in weak position, palatalized labials and dentals became distinct from their non-palatalized counterparts, for instance: [kap′ь] › /kap′/ 'image', versus /popъ/ › /pop/ 'priest', [dan′ь] › /dan′/ 'tribute', versus /danъ/ › /dan/ 'give (PAST PASS PART)'. There is some indication that in some dialects palatal /ĺ/ and /ń/ remained distinct from the dentals after the loss of the reduced vowels, as in *dъnesьńěago* (*Suprasliensis* 35.4), *dnešьńěgo* (*Suprasliensis* 53.10) (for /dnešńago/ from /dъnьsьńajego/) 'today's [date] (GEN SG N)'. For such dialects one may also posit, for instance, /końь/ › /koń/, but since Balkan Slavic dialects which retain the palatal /ĺ/, /ń/ do not have palatalized labials and dentals, it cannot be shown that a ternary opposition of laterals and nasals, such as /n/, /n′/, /ń/, arose anywhere in the Balkans.

Within a morpheme, sequences of a labial and palatal /ĺ/ are attested regularly, without any textual variants, apart from the presence or absence of the diacritic: plьvati (*Zographensis*), plьvati (*Marianus*) (Mark 14.65) 'spit (INF)', sъbljude (*Marianus*) (John 12.7) 'preserve (3 SG AOR)', sъbljudetъ (*Zographensis, Savvina kniga*), sъbljudet (*Assemanianus*) (3 SG PRS). At the end of a morpheme, there are attested forms with and without the lateral before /i/ and /ь/: zemli (*Zographensis*), zemi (*Marianus, Assemanianus, Savvina kniga*) (Matthew 6.10) 'earth (LOC SG)', korablь (*Zographensis*), korabь (*Marianus*), korabъ (*Assemanianus, Savvina kniga*) (Matthew 8.23) 'boat (ACC SG)'. In *Assemanianus, Savvina kniga, Psalterium Sinaiticum, Euchologium Sinaiticum* and *Suprasliensis* the lateral is often omitted before other vowels, often with a *jer* written after the labial: zemlě (*Suprasliensis* 97.2), zemьja (*Suprasliensis* 322.10) 'earth (NOM SG)'. The second of these spellings may denote a shift of /ĺ/ to /j/.

Loss of intervocalic /j/, sometimes with vowel assimilation and sometimes further with vowel contraction, is frequently attested for high vowels, low vowels and /ǫ/: ništiimъ (*Marianus, Savvina kniga*), ništiim (*Assemanianus*) (for /ništijimъ/ or /ništiimъ/), ništimъ (*Zographensis*) (John 12.5) 'poor (DAT PL DEF)'; malyixъ (*Assemanianus*) (for /malyjixъ/ or /malyixъ/), malyxъ (*Zographensis*) (Matthew 5.19) 'small (GEN PL DEF)'; sěěxъ (*Zographensis*) (for /sějaxъ/), sěaxъ (*Marianus*), sěxъ (*Savvina kniga*) (Matthew 25.26) 'sow (1 SG AOR)'; blagaja (*Savvina kniga* 123r), blagaa (*Savvina kniga* 67r), blaga (*Marianus*) (Luke 11.13) 'good (ACC PL N DEF)'; drugǫjǫ (*Marianus*) (Matthew 5.39), drugǫǫ (*Suprasliensis* 120.14), 'other (ACC SG F)'. When the first vowel is /a/, /u/ or /ě/, and the second is /e/, the assimilation of the second vowel to the first is attested after the drop of /j/, while still younger forms show contraction: novaego (*Zographensis*) (for /novajego/ or /novaego/), novaago (*Marianus, Assemanianus*), novago (*Savvina kniga*) (Matthew 26.28) 'new (GEN SG M DEF)'; slěpuemu (*Zographensis*), slěpumu (*Assemanianus*) (John 11.37) 'blind (DAT SG M DEF)'; novuumu (*Marianus*; Luke 5.39) 'new (DAT SG M DEF)'; věčьněemь (*Marianus*), věčněamь (*Assemanianus*), věčьnětь (*Zographensis*), věčьněěm (*Suprasliensis* 367.4) (John 6.27) 'eternal (LOC SG M)'. After a vowel letter, Glagolitic ě corresponds to etymological /ja/ and /jě/, whereas the corresponding letter in Cyrillic never denotes /j/ plus low vowel, hence the spelling difference between *Assemanianus* and *Suprasliensis* in the last example.

Similar contractions, and in Cyrillic an assimilation, are attested in the suffix of the imperfect tense, where no /j/ is involved: xoždaaše (*Zographensis, Assemanianus*), xoždaše (*Marianus, Savvina kniga*) (Matthew 14.29) 'walk (3 SG IMPF)'; iděaše (*Zographensis, Marianus, Assemanianus*), iděše (*Savvina kniga*) (Luke 7.6) 'go (3 SG IMPF)'; běaše, běěše (*Suprasliensis* 46.30) 'be (3 SG IMPF)'.

The affricate /dz/ merged with /z/, both forms being attested in Glagolitic, whereas Cyrillic has only /z/.

For the etymological sequences /jě/, /ja/, Glagolitic has ě and Cyrillic has *ja*. Word-initial etymological /ja/, but not /ě/, is attested with these spellings and also, in both Glagolitic and Cyrillic, *a*: *ěvlenie* (*Marianus*, *Assemanianus*), *javenie* (*Savviņa kniga*), *avlenьe* (*Zographensis*) (Luke 8.17) 'revelation (NOM SG)', *avlenijemъ* (*Suprasliensis* 186.24) (INST SG). Similar variants are attested for /ju/, /u/ 'already' and /jutro/, /utro/ 'morning'.

There are attested a few examples of *i* written for *y*. This could be evidence for a genuine sound shift, but might also result from the omission of the first part of the digraph ъı /y/.

2.2 Morphophonemic alternations

As a result of the second (and third) and first palatalizations, velars alternate with dentals and palatals, respectively, as shown in table 4.5.

Table 4.5 Consonant alternations resulting from the Proto-Slavonic palatalizations

Velar	k	g	x	sk	zg	sx
Dental	c	dz	s	sc/st	zd	sc
Palatal	č	ž	š	št	žd	š

There are also alternations of /c/ with /č/ and of /dz/ with /ž/ in some forms which lack a velar correspondent. The dental alternants occur regularly before /ě/ and /i/ both in declension and in the imperative, and less regularly in various forms after /i/, /ę/, /ь/ and /rь/. The palatal alternants occur before front vowels in environments other than those in which the dental alternants occur, and in various places in inflection and in word formation described in section 3.

Owing to the influence of an etymological following /j/, dentals alternate with palatals in various places in inflection and in word formation, as shown in table 4.6. Occurring in the same places as the dental alternations, labials have the alternants /bĺ/, /pĺ/, /mĺ/, /vĺ/.

As a result of earlier alternations between long and short vowels in roots, and of the fronting of vowels after palatalized consonants in both roots and inflections, the following vowel alternations are found: /ь/:/i/; /ъ/:/y/:/u/; /e/:/ě/:/i/; /o/:/a/; /o/:/e/; /ě/:/a/; /ъ/:/ь/; /y/:/i/; /ě/:/i/; /y/:/ę/.

No vowel: Ø alternations occurred in the language of the original translators, but as a result of the loss of the reduced vowels there arose the following alternations: Western /e/:Ø, /o/:Ø, and in other dialects either /e/:Ø and /ə/:Ø, or a single alternation /ə/:Ø.

Table 4.6 Consonant alternations resulting from Proto-Slavonic *j

Dental	d	zd	t	st	z	s	r	tr	dr	n	sn	zn	l	sl
Palatal	žd	žd	št	št	ž	š	ŕ	štŕ	ždŕ	ń	šń	žń	l	šl

3 Morphology

3.1 Nominal morphology

3.1.1 Nominal categories

The distinction between singular, dual and plural is strictly preserved, except for twelve examples of the noun /roditelь/ 'parent', 20 per cent of the attested total, which have plural forms instead of dual. Nouns referring to groups of people tend to have attributes agreeing syntactically in the singular, but non-attributive forms agreeing semantically, and therefore plural:

vьsь (SG) *že narodъ* (SG) *sъbravъ* (SG) *sę stojaxǫ* (PL) *pozorujǫšte* (PL) (*Suprasliensis* 117.14)
'and all (SG) the crowd (SG), having gathered (SG), were standing (PL) watching (PL).'

Four feminine singular collective personal nouns tend to take feminine singular attributes agreeing syntactically, but non-attributive forms tend to agree semantically, being plural, and masculine if distinct for gender:

vьlězъ kъ sǫštii (F SG) *tu bratii* (F SG) *cělova ję* (M ACC PL) *oni* (M NOM PL) *že umyvše* (M NOM PL) *jemu nozě* (*Suprasliensis* 523.21)
'having gone in to the brothers (F SG) who were (literally: being (F SG)) there, he greeted them (M ACC PL), and they (M NOM PL), having washed his feet ...'

Old Church Slavonic has the following cases: nominative, vocative, accusative, genitive, dative, instrumental, locative. While the nominative, accusative, genitive, dative, instrumental and locative have the major meanings that one might expect, each has a number of uses to which it would be arbitrary to attach an invariant meaning, as may be illustrated by the forms in the dative and genitive in the following passage:

nikomuže (DAT) *sego* (GEN) *ně slyšati tъčьjǫ mъně* (DAT) *jednomu* (DAT) *pověždъ* ... *semu* (DAT) *otьca* (ACC) *pokaži mi* (DAT) (*Suprasliensis* 241.1)
'There is no one (DAT) to hear this (GEN). Tell only me (DAT) alone (DAT) ... show the father (ACC) of this person (DAT) to me (DAT).'

Of the five dative forms in this example, the first is the subject of an infinitive, the second, third and fifth are indirect objects, while the fourth is in the adnominal dative rather than the genitive because its accusative head noun is homonymous with the genitive. The form *sego* is in the genitive, rather than the accusative, because the existential verb is negated.

In the singular, nouns and short masculine adjectives have vocative forms. There is attested one neuter noun in the vocative, *osile* (*Suprasliensis* 313.17) 'trap'. For masculine and feminine singular nouns, including inanimates, there are attested only two types of exception to the use of the vocative for address. In one example (*Suprasliensis* 146.18), *gospodi vojevoda* 'Lord general', the first noun is vocative, the second nominative. In *Suprasliensis*, /bratьja/ 'brothers' has five examples of the vocative, but fifteen examples of the nominative for the vocative, probably because this grammatically singular noun refers semantically to a group of persons.

While most nouns have consistent gender agreement, either masculine, neuter or feminine, some nouns show variance of gender agreement, having attributive forms with syntactic agreement, and non-attributive forms with semantic agreement. Unlike the collective nouns such as /bratьja/ 'brothers' exemplified above, the nouns in question here show variance only for gender, not for number. For the general relationship of declension and gender, see below.

The noun /děti/ 'children', paradigmatically feminine plural, is attested twice with attributes, which are both feminine, but is attested four times with non-attributive forms, all of which are masculine.

The nouns /čędo/ 'child', /ištędьje/ 'offspring' and /mladętьce/ 'infant' are attested with twenty-two examples of neuter attributes, but with eleven non-attributive masculine forms versus only one neuter form, whereas /otročę/ 'child', belonging to a different declension, is attested only with neuter agreement.

Nouns with the nominative singular inflection -/a/ or -/i/ have exclusively feminine agreement when referring to females, animals and inanimates. Male personal nouns in this declension are attested only with masculine agreement in the singular, but in the dual and plural tend to take feminine attributes, whereas non-attributive forms tend to be masculine:

va oba (NOM DU M) *sluzě* (NOM DU) *sotonině* (ADJECTIVE NOM DU F) (*Suprasliensis* 75.1)
'you both (NOM DU M) are servants (NOM DU) of Satan.'

In the dual, there are attested one feminine attribute and three masculine non-attributive forms, whereas in the plural there is attested a hierarchical opposition with twenty-eight feminine attributes and two masculine, but with ten non-attributive feminine forms and seventeen masculine, apparently showing a stronger tendency for syntactic agreement in attributes than for semantic agreement in non-attributive forms. The hierarchical nature of the opposition is exemplified in the following:

sokačiję čistěišę (NOM PL F) *vasъ sǫtъ iže* (NOM PL M) *sǫtъ rabi člověčьsti* (*Suprasliensis* 116.2)
'Cooks who (NOM PL M) are servants of men are cleaner (NOM PL F) than you.'

In this example, a feminine adjective is the predicate of a noun which is the antecedent to a masculine relative pronoun.

zъlomъ (DAT PL M) *sokačijamъ otъdano* (*Suprasliensis* 437.3)
'Handed over to evil (DAT PL M) cooks.'

The noun 'cooks' here has a masculine adjectival attribute.

slugy věděaxǫ počrъpъšei (NOM PL M) (*Zographensis, Marianus*)/ *počrъpъšęję* (NOM PL F) (*Assemanianus*) *vodǫ* (John 2.9)
'The servants who had drawn (literally: having drawn) the water knew.'

In this example, the participle agreeing with the noun is masculine in two witnesses, but feminine in a third.

Of the few attested examples of epicene nouns (that is, nouns that can be of either gender depending on the sex of the referent) in this declension, one example has a feminine attribute which does not refer to a female person:

gospodь moi (M) *i bogъ moi ǫžika moja* (F) *i tvorьcь moi* (*Suprasliensis* 509.11)
'My Lord and my God, my kinsman and my creator.'

The accusative singular of masculine nouns is homonymous either with the nominative singular, or with the genitive singular. Table 4.7 shows a hierarchical attestation of both types of accusative. Although one may conclude from the table that position on the hierarchy is governed largely by the lexical features Personal, Mature, other types of feature, grammatical, syntactic and referential, are also involved.

Proper and common personal nouns at the head of the hierarchy belong to the major masculine declension with genitive singular in -/a/, whereas the common personal nouns *gospodь* 'lord' and *synъ* 'son' did not originally belong to this declension, but acquired the inflection -/a/ as a means of expressing the accusative singular. One other grammatical feature is involved, namely the relationship between the noun and the adjectives formed from the noun stem. If the stem forms an adjective referring exclusively to an individual person, then the noun will occupy a high position on the accusative hierarchy. Such adjectives are formed from all proper personal noun stems, but not from all common personal nouns. Of the

Table 4.7   Attestation of nominative–accusative (NA) and genitive–accusative (GA) of masculine animate nouns

			G	PS	ES	C	S	Total	%
1	Proper	NA	1	–	–	2	–	3	0.4
	personal	GA	507	31	22	10	220	790	99.6
2	Common	NA	17	–	1	2	7	27	2.4
	personal	GA	478	47	75	25	484	1109	97.6
3	gospodь	NA	1	–	–	2	2	5	2.8
	'lord'	GA	60	65	6	4	38	173	97.2
4	rabъ	NA	13	–	2	–	–	15	13.4
	'slave'	GA	30	8	42	–	17	97	86.6
5	synъ	NA	27	–	1	–	2	30	20.8
	'(mature) son'	GA	86	5	7	2	14	114	79.2
6	anǵelъ	NA	8	–	–	–	–	8	57.1
	'angel'	GA	2	–	–	–	4	6	42.9
7	Animals	NA	32	4	6	1	9	52	70.3
		GA	3	3	1	–	15	22	29.7
8	synъ	NA	20	–	–	–	2	22	78.6
	'(infant) son'	GA	4	–	–	–	2	6	21.4
9	běsъ	NA	28	–	–	–	7	35	87.5
	'demon'	GA	1	–	–	–	4	5	12.5
10	Infants	NA	12	1	1	–	5	19	90.5
		GA	–	–	–	–	2	2	9.5
11	duxъ	NA	76	7	18	–	9	110	90.9
	'spirit'	GA	1	–	4	–	6	11	9.1
12	Inanimates	NA	1227	320	203	64	743	2557	96.3
		GA	49	5	–	3	40	97	3.7

Note: *G Gospels*; *PS Psalterium Sinaiticum*; *ES Euchologium Sinaiticum*; *C Clozianus*; *S Suprasliensis*.

twenty-seven examples of common personal nouns attested in the nominative–accusative singular, twenty-one do not have individual personal adjectives. The common personal stem *gospod-*, which does form such an adjective, is higher on the hierarchy than the common personal *syn-*, which has no such adjective. The stem *rab-* 'slave' does have such an adjective, but its position on the hierarchy may be determined by the fact that a slave was low in the real-world hierarchy of persons. None of the nouns in categories 6 to 12 in table 4.7 has an individual personal adjective. In possessive constructions where the head noun controls a single item, the individual personal adjectives are used, instead of the genitive singular, almost without exception, whereas nouns with no individual adjective tend to use the genitive singular of the noun for reference to a definite possessed entity, but an adjective for an indefinite possessed entity. Similarly, there is a strong tendency for the genitive–accusative to refer to a definite object, and for the nominative–accusative to refer to an indefinite object: for instance, of the twenty-seven examples of common personal attestations, seventeen have indefinite reference and only ten have definite reference.

There is also a tendency for the nominative–accusative to occur as object of a preposition, rather than as direct object of a verb. For inanimates, the last group to embrace the genitive–accusative, ninety-one of the attested examples of the genitive–accusative are direct objects, whereas only six examples are objects of prepositions. Returning to the common personal attestations, one notices that six of the examples of the nominative–accusative with definite reference occur as objects of prepositions, leaving only four examples referring to definite objects. Thus the features controlling the accusative singular hierarchy were lexical, the features Personal, Mature and Proper; grammatical, declensional membership and the presence or absence of an individual personal adjective; syntactic, direct object versus prepositional object; and referential, definite versus indefinite reference.

3.1.2   Noun morphology

There are five noun declensions, which can be distinguished by the inflection of the genitive singular. In the singular and plural, six cases are distinguished, but in the dual there are only three sets of forms: nominative/accusative, genitive/locative and dative/instrumental.

The inflectional suffixes for nouns with the genitive singular in -/a/, given in table 4.8, have alternants for phonetically palatalized (soft) and non-palatalized (hard) stem-final consonants. Velar stems undergo alternation before front-vowel inflections, as in table 4.10. In this declension, nouns denoting mature male persons and animals are masculine, while some nouns denoting children and inanimates are masculine, but others are neuter. The noun /podružьje/ 'spouse', not attested with agreeing forms, is morphologically neuter. Typical examples of this declension are: /gradъ/ 'city' (M, hard), /mǫžь/ 'man, husband' (M, soft), /město/ 'place' (N, hard), /srᵇdьce/ 'heart' (N, soft).

The inflectional suffixes for nouns with the genitive singular in -/y/ (hard) or -/ę/ (soft) are given in table 4.9; again, there are hard and soft alternants, and velar stems undergo alternation before front-vowel inflections (table 4.10). Nouns denoting female persons, animals (irrespective of sex) and inanimates are feminine. Nouns denoting male persons have inflectional suffixes identical with the feminine, are attested with masculine agreement in the singular, but with optional masculine or feminine agreement in the dual and plural (see section 3.1.1). Four collective personal nouns, declined only in the singular, have variable number and gender agreement (see section 3.1.1). Stems ending in -/yń/- and some in -/ьj/- have nominative singular -/i/; others have -/a/. Typical

Table 4.8   Inflectional suffixes of nouns with genitive singular in -/a/

| | Masculine | | Neuter | |
	Hard 'slave'	Soft 'man'	Hard 'place'	Soft 'heart'
Singular				
VOC	rabe	mǫžu		
NOM	rabъ	mǫžь	město	sr^{b}dьce
ACC	= NOM/GEN	= NOM/GEN	město	sr^{b}dьce
GEN	raba	mǫža	města	sr^{b}dьca
DAT	rabu	mǫžu	městu	sr^{b}dьcu
INST	rabomь	mǫžemь	městomь	sr^{b}dьcemь
LOC	rabě	mǫži	městě	sr^{b}dьci
Dual				
NOM	raba	mǫža	městě	sr^{b}dьci
ACC	raba	mǫža	městě	sr^{b}dьci
GEN	rabu	mǫžu	městu	sr^{b}dьcu
DAT	raboma	mǫžema	městoma	sr^{b}dьcema
INST	raboma	mǫžema	městoma	sr^{b}dьcema
LOC	rabu	mǫžu	městu	sr^{b}dьcu
Plural				
NOM	rabi	mǫži	města	sr^{b}dьca
ACC	raby	mǫžę	města	sr^{b}dьca
GEN	rabъ	mǫžь	městъ	sr^{b}dьcь
DAT	rabomъ	mǫžemъ	městomъ	sr^{b}dьcemъ
INST	raby	mǫži	městy	sr^{b}dьci
LOC	raběxъ	mǫžixъ	městěxъ	sr^{b}dьcixъ

examples of this declension are: /žena/ 'woman, wife' (F, hard), /sluga/ 'servant' (M, hard), /duša/ 'soul' (F, soft), /rabyńi/ 'slave-woman' (F, soft).

In addition to the velar stem alternants for nouns with genitive singular in -/a/ or -/y/ listed in table 4.10, one noun, /vl^{ъ}xvъ/ 'wizard', has the alternants /vl^{ъ}svi/ (NOM PL), vl^{ъ}šve (VOC SG) even though the velar is not stem-final. For velar clusters a few examples of dental alternants are attested: /drezdě/ 'forest (LOC SG F)' (one example only), /dъska/ 'board', /dъscě/, /dъstě/ (LOC SG), /pasxa/ 'Passover', /pascě/ (LOC SG).

Of nouns with the genitive singular in -/i/ (table 4.11), stems denoting animals and male persons are masculine, inanimates are either masculine or feminine. Declined only in the plural are /ĺudьje/ 'people', and the morphologically feminine /děti/ 'children' (for agreement, see section 3.1.1). Gender is distinguished inflectionally only in the instrumental singular and the nominative plural. Typical examples are: /kostь/ 'bone' (F), /pǫtь/ 'way' (M).

For nouns with the genitive singular in -/u/, there are attested one male

Table 4.9 Inflectional suffixes of nouns with genitive singular in -/y/ (hard), -/ę/ (soft)

	SG Hard	SG Soft	DU Hard	DU Soft	PL Hard	PL Soft
VOC	ženo 'woman'	duše 'soul'				
NOM	žena	duša	ženě	duši	ženy	dušę
ACC	ženǫ	dušǫ	ženě	duši	ženy	dušę
GEN	ženy	dušę	ženu	dušu	ženъ	dušь
DAT	ženě	duši	ženama	dušama	ženamъ	dušamъ
INST	ženojǫ	dušejǫ	ženama	dušama	ženami	dušami
LOC	ženě	duši	ženu	dušu	ženaxъ	dušaxъ

Note: Nouns such as /rabyńi/ 'slave woman' decline like /duša/ except for the nominative singular in -/i/.

personal noun /synъ/ 'son', one animal noun /volъ/ 'ox' and six inanimate nouns, all masculine. The most conservative of the attested inflections are given in table 4.12.

Of nouns with genitive singular in -/e/, masculines include inanimates and one animal, feminines include inanimates and female persons, neuters include inanimates and the young of animals. Table 4.13 lists the singular, including stem alternations in the neuter and feminine. Table 4.14 lists dual and plural inflections. Corresponding to the genitive singular /kamene/ 'stone' (M), the form /kamenь/ is attested as nominative/accusative singular, and in *Suprasliensis* the form /kamy/ is also used for nominative and accusative. Corresponding to nominative/accusative /korenь/ 'root'

Table 4.10 Velar stem alternants in noun inflection

Genitive in -/a/, masculine and neuter

	bogъ 'god'	prorokъ 'prophet'	duxъ 'spirit'
LOC SG	bodzě	prorocě	dusě
NOM PL	bodzi	proroci	dusi
LOC PL	bodzěxъ	prorocěxъ	dusěxъ
VOC SG	bože	proroče	duše

Genitive in -/a/, neuter

	věko 'eyelid'
NOM/ACC DU	věcě

Genitive in -/y/

	noga 'leg'	rǫka 'hand'	muxa 'fly'
DAT/LOC SG, NOM/ACC DU	nodzě	rǫcě	musě

Table 4.11   Inflectional suffixes of nouns with genitive singular in -/i/

	Singular		Dual		Plural	
	M	F	M	F	M	F
VOC	pǫti 'path'	kosti 'bone'				
NOM	pǫtь	kostь	pǫti	kosti	pǫtьje	kosti
ACC	pǫtь	kostь	pǫti	kosti	pǫti	kosti
GEN	pǫti	kosti	pǫtьju	kostьju	pǫtьjь	kostьjь
DAT	pǫti	kosti	pǫtьma	kostьma	pǫtьmъ	kostьmъ
INST	pǫtьmь	kostьjǫ	pǫtьma	kostьma	pǫtьmi	kostьmi
LOC	pǫti	kosti	pǫtьju	kostьju	pǫtьxъ	kostьxъ

Suprasliensis 399.14 has a scribal error *tvorę* for an otherwise unattested nominative singular masculine */korę/. Masculine nouns with the suffixes -/an/-, -/teĺ/-, -/aŕ/- are attested with forms of both the -/a/ and -/e/ types in the plural, but with only forms of the -/a/ type in the singular and dual. Stems with -/an/- and some with -/aŕ/- follow these suffixes with a further suffix -/in/- in the singular and dual.

The loss of the reduced vowels occasioned some later changes in declension. Inflectional suffixes containing a reduced vowel in weak position were shortened by one syllable. In nouns with a reduced vowel in the last syllable of the stem, such as /dьnь/ 'day' (M), genitive singular /dьne/, there arose vowel:zero alternations (see section 2.2). With stem-final /j/, /učenьje/ 'teaching' (N), genitive plural /učenьjь/, for instance, gave Western /učenje/, /učenej/, while elsewhere [učenije], [učeniji] gave /učenje/, /učenij/.

In the dative and locative plural of types with -/i/ and -/e/ genitives, there arose younger -/em/, -/ex/, or -/əm/, -/əx/. In dialects without palatalization of labials before front vowels, the instrumental singular masculine became identical with the dative plural, but in other dialects these two forms came to be distinguished by the presence or absence of

Table 4.12   Inflectional suffixes of nouns with genitive singular in -/u/

	SG	DU	PL
VOC	synu 'son'		
NOM	synъ	syny	synove
ACC	synъ	syny	syny
GEN	synu	synovu	synovъ
DAT	synovi	synъma	synomъ
INST	synomь	synъma	synъmi
LOC	synu	synovu	synoxъ

Table 4.13   Singular of nouns with genitive singular in -/e/

	'day' (M)	'seed' (N)	'lamb' (N)	'word' (N)	'mother' (F)	'church' (F)
NOM	dьnь	sěmę	agnę	slovo	mati	crᵇky
ACC	dьnь	sěmę	agnę	slovo	materь	crᵇkъvь
GEN	dьne	sěmene	agnęte	slovese	matere	crᵇkъve
DAT	dьni	sěmeni	agnęti	slovesi	materi	crᵇkъvi
INST	dьnьmь	sěmenьmь	agnětьmь	slovesьmь	materьjǫ	crᵇkъvьjǫ
LOC	dьne	sěmene	agnęte	slovese	matere	crᵇkъve

palatalization of the final labial. The phonetic reflex of the genitive plural -/ьjь/ was Western /ej/, but elsewhere either regularly /ij/ or else /ej/ by analogy with the dative and locative.

A number of analogical changes in noun declension are attested. The dative plural in -/omъ/ of -/u/ genitives probably arose prehistorically by analogy with -/a/ genitives and with genitive -/ovъ/ of the -/u/ genitive type genitive plural. Then the -/u/ genitive type locative plural -/oxъ/ could have arisen prehistorically by analogy with the dative. In Western dialects younger locative and dative -/ox/, -/om/ could have arisen phonetically from the inflections that can be reconstructed as -/ъxъ/, -/ъmъ/. While the -/u/ genitive type instrumental singular -/omь/ may also be analogical with the -/a/ genitive type inflection, an occasionally attested instrumental singular -ъmь for -/a/ genitive type nouns may be a

Table 4.14   Dual and plural suffixes of nouns with genitive singular in -/e/

	Dual		Plural		
	M	N	M	F	N
NOM	dьni	sěmeně	dьne	materi	sěmena
ACC	dьni	sěmeně	dьni	materi	sěmena
GEN	dьnu	*sěmenu	dьnъ	materъ	sěmenъ
DAT	dьnьma	sěmenьma	dьnьmъ	materьmъ	sěmenьmъ
INST	dьnьma	sěmenьma	dьnьmi	materьmi	sěmeny
LOC	dьnu	*sěmenu	dьnьxъ	*materьxъ	sěmenьxъ

Note: In the neuter nominative–accusative dual, the ending /-i/ is also attested. The feminine dual is not attested, likewise the locative plural of the type /mati/ 'mother' and the genitive–locative dual of the /sěmę/ type (but compare /tělesu/ 'body', of the /slovo/ type). Feminines with nominative singular in -/y/ have in the plural dative -/amъ/, instrumental -/ami/, locative -/axъ/, as in /crᵇkъvamъ/, /crᵇkъvami/, /crᵇkъvaxъ/ 'church'.

Moravian feature. There are also attested a few examples of genitive plural masculine -*ovъ* for -/a/ genitive type nouns by analogy with the -/u/ genitive type form.

Neuter -/e/ genitive type nouns with nominative singular in -/o/ are attested with -/a/ genitive type inflections based on the old nominative/ accusative stem, such as younger /slova/ 'word (GEN SG)' for older /slovese/. Also in the singular -/e/ genitive type nouns have younger genitive/locative in -/i/ by analogy with the dative and with the -/i/ genitive type. In the plural masculine nouns of this declension have in the nominative -/ьje/ and in the genitive -/ьjь/ by analogy with the -/i/ genitive type.

The neuter nouns /oko/ 'eye' and /uxo/ 'ear' in the singular and plural are attested with -/a/ genitive type suffixes, and with stems /očes-/, /ušes-/ with -/e/ genitive type suffixes. Dual forms are irregular: NOM–ACC /oči/, /uši/, GEN–LOC /očьju/, /ušьju/, DAT–INST /očima/, /ušima/. In the dual these nouns may take indefinite adjectives in the feminine as well as in the neuter.

3.1.3 Pronominal morphology

First- and second-person and reflexive pronoun forms are given in table 4.15. Dative clitic pronouns are not used phrase-initially or after a preposition. Accusative clitic pronouns are used after a preposition, but are only rarely attested as phrase-initial, where the full form is usually used. Phrase-internally, without a preposition, both full and clitic forms are attested for dative and accusative, the full form being apparently more emphatic. The full accusative form after a preposition is an innovation resulting from increasing productivity of the genitive–accusative.

As indicated in table 4.16, the inflectional suffixes of other pronouns have vowel alternations for hard and soft stems. In the dual and plural, genders are distinct only in the nominative and accusative. Typical examples of these pronouns are /tъ/ 'this, that' (unmarked demonstrative) (hard) and /našь/ 'our' (soft). The personal masculine accusative singular, with a few exceptions after prepositions, is homonymous with the genitive, apart from /jь/ which is accusative singular masculine regardless of animacy conditions, except as object of a nominative singular masculine definite active participle, as attested, for instance, in /prědajęjь jego/ (*Marianus, Assemanianus, Suprasliensis*) (Matthew 26.25) 'the one betraying him' with the present participle, and /prědavъjь jego/ (*Zographensis*) 'the one who betrayed him' with the past participle. In this construction, object /jego/ is distinguished from subject /jь/. Later, genitive–accusative /jego/ spreads into other contexts.

The pronouns /sicь/ 'such' and /vьsь/ 'all' have hard suffixes where the first segment of the suffix is /ě/, for instance /sicěmь/, /vьsěmь/ (INST SG M/N), but otherwise have soft suffixes. The pronoun /sь/ 'this'

Table 4.15   First- and second-person and reflexive pronouns

	1st person		2nd person		Reflexive	
	Full	*Clitic*	*Full*	*Clitic*	*Full*	*Clitic*
Singular						
NOM	azъ		ty			
ACC	mene	mę	tebe	tę	sebe	sę
GEN	mene		tebe		sebe	
DAT	mьně	mi	tebě	ti	sebě	si
INST	mъnojǫ		tobojǫ		sobojǫ	
LOC	mьně		tebě		sebě	
Dual						
NOM	vě		va/vy			
ACC	na	ny	va	vy		
GEN	naju		vaju			
DAT	nama		vama			
INST	nama		vama			
LOC	naju		vaju			
Plural						
NOM	my		vy			
ACC	nasъ	ny	vasъ	vy		
GEN	nasъ		vasъ			
DAT	namъ	ny	vamъ	vy		
INST	nami		vami			
LOC	nasъ		vasъ			

Table 4.16   Pronominal declension

	Singular			Dual			Plural		
	M	N	F	M	N	F	M	N	F
Hard 'that'									
NOM	tъ	to	ta	ta	tě	tě	ti	ta	ty
ACC	= NOM/GEN	to	tǫ	ta	tě	tě	ty	ta	ty
GEN	togo		toję		toju			těxъ	
DAT	tomu		toji		těma			těmъ	
INST	těmь		tojǫ		těma			těmi	
LOC	tomь		toji		toju			těxъ	
Soft 'our'									
NOM	našь	naše	naša	naša	naši	naši	naši	naša	našę
ACC	= NOM/GEN	naše	našǫ	naša	naši	naši	našę	naša	našę
GEN	našego		našeję		našeju			našixъ	
DAT	našemu		našeji		našima			našimъ	
INST	našimь		našejǫ		našima			našimi	
LOC	našemь		našeji		našeju			našixъ	

Table 4.17 Irregular forms of the pronoun /sь/

	Singular			Dual			Plural		
	M	N	F	M	N	F	M	N	F
NOM	sь/sьjь	se	si	sьja	si	si	sьji	si	sьję
ACC	= NOM/GEN	se	sьjǫ	sьja	si	si	sьję	si	sьję

has soft suffixes, including some irregular ones listed in table 4.17.

The interrogative–indefinite pronouns /kъto/ 'who', /čьto/ 'what', which as indefinites are random 'anybody', 'anything', the negative pronouns /nikъtože/ 'nobody', /ničьtože/ 'nothing', and the non-random indefinite pronouns /někъto/ 'someone', /něčьto/ 'something' have the suffix -/to/ only in the nominative and, in the neuter, in the accusative; see table 4.18 for the forms. Prepositions are embedded in negative and indefinite pronouns, for example /ni o komьže/ 'about nobody', /ně o komь/ 'about somebody'.

3.1.4 Adjectival morphology
Positive adjectives and passive participles with the suffixes of tables 4.8 and 4.9, also active participles and comparative adjectives (for nominative and accusative, see table 4.19) have short forms with indefinite reference (as in 'a new city'), long forms with definite reference (as in 'the new city'). For the long forms, see table 4.20. With the exception of the nominative singular masculine and neuter of active participles and comparative adjectives and of the accusative singular masculine and neuter of comparative adjectives, the short forms have the same stem as the nominative singular feminine and are declined like nouns with genitive in -/a/ (masculine and neuter) or in -/y/ (soft -/ę/) (feminine). Active participles and comparative adjectives have the nominative singular feminine in -/i/ and the nominative plural masculine in -/e/.

Table 4.18 Interrogative and indefinite pronouns

	'who'	'what'
NOM	kъto	čьto
ACC	kogo	čьto
GEN	kogo	česo, česogo, čьso
DAT	komu	česomu, čьsomu, čemu
INST	cěmь	čimь
LOC	komь	čemь, česomь

Table 4.19   Nominative and accusative singular and plural of present and past participles /nesy/, /nesъ/ 'carry' and of comparative adjective /novějь/ 'newer'

SG	NOM	M	nesy	nesъ	novějь
		N	nesy	nesъ	novĕje
		F	nesǫšti	nesъši	novĕjьši
	ACC	M	nesǫštь	nesъšь	novĕjь
		N	nesǫšte	nesъše	novĕje
		F	nesǫštǫ	nesъšǫ	novĕjьšǫ
PL	NOM	M	nesǫšte	nesъše	novĕjьše

Comparison of short and long forms shows that some of the long-form adjectival suffixes are formed directly from the noun inflections of tables 4.8 and 4.9 followed by -/j/- and the soft inflections of table 4.16. Other forms, genitive, dative/locative singular feminine and genitive/locative dual have dropped a syllable -/je/-, while the instrumental singular and the soft locative singular masculine/neuter, the dative/instrumental dual and the genitive/locative and dative plural have been influenced analogically by the instrumental plural masculine/neuter, leaving no gender distinctions in the dual and plural apart from the nominative and accusative.

In the nominative singular masculine, younger forms of the definite adjectives arose as a result of the loss of the reduced vowels: Western /novъjь/ 'new' gave /novoj/, elsewhere [novЎjï] gave /novyj/ then /novy/, Western /ništьjь/ 'poor' gave /ništej/, elsewhere [ništïjï] /ništij/ then /ništi/.

Whereas short active participles do not distinguish masculine from neuter in the nominative singular, long forms have masculine nominative /nesyjь/ (PRS), /nesъjь/ (PAST) and neuter nominative/accusative /nesǫšteje/ (PRS), /nesъšeje/ (PAST).

For the long nominative plural masculine active participle /nesǫšteji/, there is attested younger /nesǫštiji/ by analogy with oblique cases and with adjectives. Conversely, there are attested younger oblique plural forms and instrumental and locative singular such as /nesǫštejixъ/ (LOC PL) for older /nesǫštijixъ/ by analogy with the old nominative plural, differentiating participial long inflections from adjectives, rather than merging them. Spellings of the long accusative singular masculine may be identical with the various nominative plural masculine forms, Western /nesǫštьjь/ giving /nesǫstej/, spelt *nesǫstei*; elsewhere both older and younger [nesǫštiji] gave /nesǫštij/, which may be spelt *nesǫštii*.

Short participles have younger indeclinable /nesǫšte/. For younger adjectival forms arising from the loss of intervocalic /j/ and subsequent vowel assimilation and contraction, see section 2.1.

Table 4.20 Inflectional suffixes of long-form adjectives

	Hard M	N	F	Soft M	N	F
Singular						
NOM	novъjь 'new'	novoje	novaja	vyšьńьjь 'most high'	vyšьńeje	vyšьńaja
ACC	= NOM/GEN	novoje	novǫjǫ	= NOM/GEN	vyšьńeje	vyšьńǫjǫ
GEN		novajego	novyję		vyšьńajego	vyšьńęję
DAT		novujemu	novĕji		vyšьńujemu	vyšьńiji
INST		novyjimь	novǫjǫ		vyšьńijimь	vyšьńǫjǫ
LOC		novĕjemь	novĕji		vyšьńijimь	vyšьńiji
Dual						
NOM	novaja	novĕji	novĕji	vyšьńaja	vyšьńiji	vyšьńiji
ACC	novaja	novĕji	novĕji	vyšьńaja	vyšьńiji	vyšьńiji
GEN		novuju			vyšьńuju	
DAT		novyjima			vyšьńijima	
INST		novyjima			vyšьńijima	
LOC		novuju			vyšьńuju	
Plural						
NOM	noviji	novaja	novyję	vyšьńiji	vyšьńaja	vyšьńęję
ACC	novyję	novaja	novyję	vyšьńęję	vyšьńaja	vyšьńęję
GEN		novyjixъ			vyšьńijixъ	
DAT		novyjimъ			vyšьńijimъ	
INST		novyjimi			vyšьńijimi	
LOC		novyjixъ			vyšьńijixъ	

Table 4.21   Irregular comparative adjectives

Positive	Comparative	
a. grǫbъ	grǫbľьjь	'coarse'
dragъ	dražьjь	'dear'
lixъ	lišьjь	'superfluous'
ľutъ	ľuštьjь	'fierce'
xudъ	xuždьjь	'poor in quality'
b. krěpъkъ	krěpľьjь	'strong, firm'
sladъkъ	slaždьjь	'sweet'
tęžьkъ	tęžьjь	'heavy'
vysokъ	vyšьjь	'high'
glǫbokъ	glǫbľьjь	'deep'
širokъ	šiřьjь	'wide'
c. velikъ, velьjь	bolьjь	'big'
and	vęštьjь	'bigger, more numerous'
malъ	mьńьjь	'small'
blagъ, dobrъ	lučьjь, uńьjь, sulьjь, sulějь	'good'
zъľъ	gořьjь	'bad'

Comparative adjectives, other than those listed in table 4.21, are formed as indicated in table 4.19 by the suffix -/ěj/-, to which inflectional suffixes are added. The forms in table 4.21 are nominative/accusative singular masculine long and short. The nominative/accusative neuter singular short form has the suffix -/e/, as in /bole/ 'bigger'; all other forms replace the nominative/accusative singular masculine suffix -/jь/ by the suffix -/š/- to which the inflectional suffixes are added, for instance /bolьšeje/ (NOM/-ACC N LONG). The superlative is usually not distinct from the comparative, but is occasionally attested with a prefix /najь/-.

Comparative adverbs have either the form of the nominative/accusative neuter short form adjective, as in /dobrěje/ 'better', or else have the instrumental plural suffix, as in /mьnьšьmi/ 'less'.

3.1.5   Numeral morphology
/jedinъ/ 'one' takes singular and plural and /dъva/ 'two' dual pronominal suffixes of table 4.16; /oba/ 'both' is declined like /dъva/. /trьje/ 'three' is an -/i/ genitive plural noun, and /četyre/ 'four' an -/e/ genitive plural noun. All four of these numerals are inflected for gender. /pętь/ 'five', /šestь/ 'six', /sedmь/ 'seven', /osmь/ 'eight', /devętь/ 'nine' are -/i/ genitive type feminine nouns. /desętь/ 'ten' has -/i/ genitive type forms in the genitive and instrumental singular, but -/e/ genitive type masculine forms in all other cases and numbers. /jedinъ na desęte/ 'eleven' to /devętь na desęte/ 'nineteen' are formed with a digit and the preposition /na/ governing /desętь/ in the locative singular. /dъva na desęte/ 'twelve' is distinct from /oba na desęte/ 'the twelve', the latter with /oba/

'both'. Other numerals are occasionally attested with definite forms: /desętьjь/ 'the ten', /jedinъjь na desęte/ 'the eleven'. The digits in compound numerals are inflected for case. The digits take /desętь/ in the dual for /dъva desęti/ 'twenty', the plural for /trьje desęte/ 'thirty', /četyre desęte/ 'forty', and in the genitive plural for /pętь desętъ/ 'fifty' to /devętь desętъ/ 'ninety'. From /dъva desęti/ to /četyre desęte/ both elements are inflected for case, but for the higher numerals, only the first element. /sъto/ 'hundred' is a neuter -/a/ genitive inflected for all cases and numbers. /tysǫšti/, /tysęšti/ 'thousand' is an -/ę/ genitive feminine and /tьma/ 'ten thousand' a feminine -/y/ genitive.

The ordinal numerals are definite adjectives declined in all cases, numbers and genders: /prьvъjь/ 'first', /vъtorъjь/ 'second', /tretьjь/ 'third', /četvrьtъjь/ 'fourth', /pętъjь/ 'fifth', /šestъjь/ 'sixth', /sedmъjь/ 'seventh', /osmъjь/ 'eighth', /devętъjь/ 'ninth', /desętъjь/ 'tenth'. There are various types for higher numerals, all poorly attested: /jedinъjь na desęte/ 'eleventh', /vъtorъjь na desęte/ 'twelfth', /tretьjь na desęte/ 'thirteenth', /osmonadesętъjь/ 'eighteenth', /devętьnadesętъjь/ 'nine-teenth', /dvadesętьnъjь/ or /dъvodesętьnъjь/ 'twentieth', /sъtьnъjь/ 'hundredth', /pętьsъtьnъjь/ 'five hundredth', /tysǫštьnъjь/ 'thousandth'.

/oboje/ 'both' and /dъvoje/ 'two' are neuter pronouns expressing contrastive entities, as in the following example, where the choice is one of two different objects:

jedno otъ dvojego prědъložimъ vamъ (*Suprasliensis* 73.23)
'We offer you one of two options.'

/dъvoji/ 'two', which declines like a plural noun, agrees with a collective noun or with a plural noun. Three numerals are attested with various kinds of reference: /četvero/ 'four' refers to contrasted entities, /sedmoro/ 'seven' has multiplicational reference ('seven times'), while /desętoro/ 'ten' is attested governing a genitive singular collective noun.

/polъ/ 'half' is either an -/u/ genitive noun or else is indeclinable. /desętina/ 'tenth (part)' is an -/y/ genitive feminine noun.

3.2   Verbal morphology

3.2.1   Verbal categories

Finite verbs distinguish three persons in all numbers, but the younger third person dual has merged with the second person dual. Finite forms and participles distinguish singular, dual and plural. Perfect participles have short nominative forms in all three genders, while other types of participle distinguish gender of long and short forms in all cases and numbers. Younger short indeclinable active participles are attested. Younger finite dual forms distinguish masculine from non-masculine third person.

All verbal categories can occur in the perfective aspect, which explicitly characterizes the event as occurring in its entirety, and in the imperfective aspect, which does not explicitly characterize the event in this way.

In the present tense, in the following example the imperfective present characterizes an event which is contemporaneous with the speech event, as being actually in progress, and therefore not as occurring in its entirety:

kto jestъ jegože vedǫtъ (IMPFV PRS) (*Suprasliensis* 146.16)
'Who is it whom they are leading?'

The perfective present in the next example characterizes an event which is contemporaneous with the speech event, as occurring in its entirety:

nynja ti otъnьmǫ (PRFV PRS) *glavǫ* (*Suprasliensis* 512.20)
'Now I take your head off.'

In the next example, the perfective present explicitly characterizes a future event as occurring in its entirety, whereas the imperfective present does not imply that there will be any limit to the event:

pridetъ (PRFV PRS) *godina egda kъ tomu vъ pritъčaxъ ne glagoljǫ* (IMPFV PRS) *vamъ* (*Marianus, Zographensis, Assemanianus, Savvina kniga*; John 16.25)
'There will come (PRFV PRS) a time when I shall no longer be speaking (IMPFV PRS) to you in parables.'

The distinction between the two present forms in the following example is purely aspectual, not lexical:

ne otъběžitъ (PRFV PRS) *grěšьnoju dlanьju našeju ne otъběgajetъ* (IMPFV PRS) *otъ sǫždenyixъ prъstъ našixъ* (*Suprasliensis* 506.21)
'He does not avoid (PRFV PRS) our sinful palms, he does not escape (IMPFV PRS) from our condemned fingers.'

In this statement of general validity, the perfective present expresses the entirety of a change of state, whereas the imperfective present expresses the continuity of that state. In the historic present in the next example, the imperfective present characterizes the event as an ongoing state, whereas the perfective present in the following example characterizes two events as occurring in their entirety, one after the other:

ležitъ (IMPFV PRS) *vъznakъ* (*Suprasliensis* 456.5)
'He was lying on his back.'

i abьje tomužde avitъ (PRFV PRS) *sę episkopu i glasъ uslyšitъ* (PRFV PRS) *pritranъ* (*Suprasliensis* 530.10)
'And immediately he appeared to this same bishop, who heard a clear voice ...'

The aorist and the imperfect, both past tenses, are unmarked for relativity. The imperfect characterizes a past event as being a state or process; the aorist is unmarked for this feature. In the following example, the event characterized by the perfective aorist as occurring in its entirety impinges upon the events characterized by the imperfective imperfect as being ongoing processes:

i ta besědovaašete (IMPFV IMPF) *kъ sebě o vsěxъ sixъ ... i samъ isusъ približi* (PRFV AOR) *sę i iděaše* (IMPFV IMPF) *sъ ńima* (*Zographensis*; Luke 24.14)
'And they were conversing (IMPFV IMPF) with one another about all these things ... and Jesus approached (PRFV AOR) and was going along (IMPFV IMPF) with them.'

Like the forms in this example, the imperfective aorist and the perfective imperfect may refer to an event carried out on one occasion, as in:

aky kъ člověku bo besědova (IMPFV AOR) *i vъzira* (IMPFV AOR) *na ńь* (*Suprasliensis* 122.30)
'for he conversed (IMPFV AOR) with him and looked (IMPFV AOR) at him as if he were a man'

In this example, the imperfective aorists state only that the events occurred, without saying anything about the entirety of their occurrence. In the perfective imperfect in the next example, the perfective component expresses the immediacy of the reaction, whereas the imperfect component presents the event as an ongoing process:

i ěviše (PRFV AOR) *sę prědъ ńimi ěko bledi glagoli ixъ i ne iměaxǫ* (PRFV IMPF) *imъ věry* (*Zographensis, Marianus*; Luke 24.11)
'And their words appeared (PRFV AOR) to them to be nonsense and they would not believe (PRFV IMPF) them.'

Both the aorist and the imperfect may refer to a repeated event:

kotygǫ sьvlěkъ sъ sebe daděaše (PRFV IMPF) *ništuumu tako že tvoraaše* (IMPFV IMPF) *vъsa lěta žitija svojego ... ino že mnogo poučaję ne prěsta* (PRFV AOR) *ni umlъknǫ* (PRFV AOR) *otъ dobra* (*Suprasliensis* 207.14–208.1)
'Taking off his coat, he would give (PRFV IMPF) it to a beggar. For thus would he do (IMPFV IMPF) all the years of his life.... Teaching many other things, he neither ceased (PRFV AOR) from, nor kept silent (PRFV AOR) concerning the good.'

In this example, the imperfect component of the perfective imperfect expresses a habitual state of behaviour consisting of a set of repeated acts each of which is characterized by the perfective component as having occurred in its entirety, whereas the imperfective imperfect expresses such acts as constituting an ongoing state, without saying anything about the entirety of the process. The perfective aorists sum up two sets of repeated acts as events which occurred in their entirety. Indeed, both perfective and imperfective aorists may refer to repeated events:

jednojǫ i dvašdi i mnogašdi rekoxъ (PRFV AOR) *ti* (*Suprasliensis* 165.11)
'I told (PRFV AOR) you once, twice and many times.'

mnogašdi glagolaxъ (IMPFV AOR) (*Suprasliensis* 446.16)
'I said (IMPFV AOR) many times.'

The perfect relates a preceding event to the speech event, or to an event expressed by the present tense; the pluperfect relates a preceding event to an event expressed by either the aorist or the imperfect.

The perfect consists of the present tense of the verb /byti/ 'be' as an auxiliary, in either aspect, plus the perfect participle of the lexical verb in either aspect. In the following example, an event occurring in its entirety precedes the speech event:

prišelъ (PRFV) *jestъ* (IMPFV) *vasilisikъ* (*Suprasliensis* 20.2)
'Basiliscus has (IMPFV) come (PRFV).'

In the next example, the preceding event expressed by an imperfective auxiliary and by an imperfective perfect participle, which says nothing about the entirety of the event, is related to an event expressed by the imperfective present in a statement of general validity:

radujǫtъ (IMPFV PRS) *sę zělo jako u svoixъ sǫtъ* (IMPFV) *si doma ležali* (IMPFV) (*Suprasliensis* 267.17)
'They rejoice (IMPFV PRS) greatly, because they have (IMPFV) been lying (IMPFV) at home with their people.'

In the following example, the perfective auxiliary expresses the eventual result of an event which the imperfective perfect participle expresses as an ongoing process in the past whose limit is not specified, within a statement of general validity:

ašte na to sъtvorimъ (PRFV PRS) *vladyky podražali* (IMPFV) *bǫdemъ* (PRFV) (*Suprasliensis* 379.10)
'If we do (PRFV PRS) it for that purpose, we will have (PRFV) been imitating (IMPFV) the Lord.'

The next example occurs at the end of a long passage in which events of general validity are expressed in both the imperfective and perfective present. The events in the example are all characterized as occurring in their entirety; the perfective auxiliary is coordinated with two perfective present forms, while the perfective perfect participle, unlike the participle in the preceding example, expresses an event which has reached its final limit:

prěklonitъ (PRFV PRS) *sę i padetъ* (PRFV PRS) *egda udoblělъ* (PRFV) *bǫdetъ* (PRFV)
ubogyimъ (*Psalterium Sinaiticum* 9.31)
'He will bend (PRFV PRS) and fall down (PRFV PRS) on his knees when he has (PRFV)
overcome (PRFV) the poor.'

The pluperfect consists of one of the two different types of the imperfective past of /byti/ plus the perfect participle in either aspect:

juže bo sę běaxǫ (AUX) *sъložili* (PRFV) *ijudei* (*Zographensis, Marianus, Assemanianus*; John 9.22)
'for the Jews had (AUX) already agreed (PRFV)'

iže i běaxǫ (AUX) *viděli* (IMPFV) *prěžde* (*Zographensis, Marianus, Assemanianus*;
John 9.8)
'those who had (AUX) seen (IMPFV) him previously'

se bo bě (AUX) *znamenьe dalъ* (PRFV) (*Zographensis, Marianus*; Luke 22.47)
'for he had (AUX) given (PRFV) this sign'

ideže bě (AUX) *ležalo* (IMPFV) *tělo isusovo* (*Marianus, Assemanianus*; John 20.12)
'where the body of Jesus had (AUX) been lying (IMPFV)'

Although the auxiliary in the first two examples is formally an imperfect,
which happens to be attested only in third-person forms, while the auxiliary
in the last two examples is formally an aorist, attested in all persons, there
is no discoverable semantic distinction between the two types of auxiliary.

Not including doubtful examples, or scribal errors, there are attested
about eighty examples of the perfect participle without an auxiliary. None
of these is attested in either the Gospels or the Psalter, most of them being
found in a few sermons in *Suprasliensis*.

ješa i ne sъbrali (PRFV) *sъbora ješa i sice ne besědovali* (IMPFV) *jaru tu grěxovьněi
zъlobi prěstalъ* (PRFV) *konьcъ nъ sъbrašę* (AOR) *sъborъ i glagolaaxǫ* (IMPF) *čto
sъtvorimъ* (*Suprasliensis* 386.6)
'Would indeed they had not convened (PRFV) the council! Would indeed they had
not conversed (IMPFV) thus! Would that at this point an end had been put (PRFV) to
sinful malice! But they did convene (AOR) the council, and were saying (IMPF):
What shall we do?'

Whereas the aorist and imperfect in this example give a purely objective
account of the event, the perfect participles express the narrator's attitude
towards those events. Unlike the perfect and pluperfect, the perfect participle without an auxiliary is unmarked for relativity, but is opposed to the
aorist and imperfect in expressing the narrator's attitude to the event (the
category of status): this form emphasizes that the event is of some special
significance for the narrator, including regret, as in the above example,
rejoicing, and in general adds a rhetorical tone, especially when used in
questions.

Table 4.22   Imperfective correspondents of primary perfective verbs

Perfective		Imperfective		
INF	3 PL PRS	INF	3 PL PRS	
/dati/	/dadętъ/	/dajati/	/dajǫtъ/	'give'
/jęti/	/jьmǫtъ/	/jьmati/	/jemlǫtъ/	'take'
/variti/	/varętъ/	/vařati/	/vařajǫtъ/	'go ahead'

There are three periphrastic futures, each distinct from the perfective and imperfective present used to express a future event (see above).

The relative future is expressed with the auxiliary *xotěti* or *xъtěti* 'wish' in all its forms, finite and non-finite, plus an infinitive in either aspect:

vlъny že vъlivaaxǫ sę vъ ladijǫ ěko uže pogręznǫti (PRFV INF) *xotěaše* (IMPFV) (*Zographensis, Marianus*; Mark 4.37)
'And the waves were pouring into the boat, so that it was already about to sink.'

The auxiliary *iměti* 'have', used only in the present tense with an infinitive of either aspect, expresses the narrator's attitude to the event, and is thus marked for status:

ne ištěte čьto imate ěsti (PRFV INF) *i čьto piti* (*Zographensis*; Luke 12.29)
'Do not consider what you will eat or what you will drink.'

This example expresses the narrator's suggestion that the addressee should avoid asking some important 'matter of life and death' questions. More usually, this auxiliary expresses emphasis that the event is inevitable or inescapable, as in the example from Mark 9.1 below. There are attested eleven examples of the present tense of the probably synonymous perfective verbs *načęti, vъčęti* 'begin' used as auxiliaries only with an imperfective infinitive. These examples seem to have no invariant meaning other than that of introducing perfectivity when no other means are available:

povelě dъrati želězny nogъty doideže črěva načъnǫtъ (PRFV PRS) *xъtěti* (INF) *izvaliti* (INF) *sę na zemьjǫ* (*Suprasliensis* 113.29)
'He ordered them to be flogged with iron nails until their intestines were about to pour out onto the ground.'

The conjunction *doideže* is punctual 'until' only with a perfective verb, but durative 'while' with an imperfective verb. Thus the imperfective relative infinitive auxiliary is governed by a perfective auxiliary in order to specify the appropriate meaning of the conjunction.

The formal relation between imperfective and perfective forms of verbs requires comment. The small number of primary perfective forms have

Table 4.23   Aspect of verbs with lexical prefixes

Imperfective		Perfective	Imperfective	
/tvoriti/	'do, make'	/zatvoriti/	/zatvaŕati/	'lock up'
/zьrěti/	'look'	/vъzьrěti/	/vъzirati/	'look at'

corresponding imperfective forms by addition of a suffix which changes the conjugational class, as in the examples in table 4.22. For such verbs, prefixes change lexical meaning, but not aspect, for example /vъzdati/ (PRFV), /vъzdajati/ (IMPFV) 'give in exchange', /vъzęti/ (PRFV), /vъzьmati/, /vъzimati/ (IMPFV) 'take up'. When the primary verb is imperfective, prefixes usually change both lexical meaning and aspect, while the prefixed item has imperfective forms with suffixation, change of conjugational class and sometimes with alternation of root vowel, as in the examples in table 4.23. A number of primary and prefixed forms are distinct only in aspect, the prefixed item being perfective, as in /tvoriti/ (IMPFV), /sъtvoriti/ (PRFV) 'do', /nenaviděti/ (IMPFV), /vъznenaviděti/ (PRFV) 'hate', /slyšati/, /uslyšati/ 'hear'. Unambiguous evidence for bi-aspectuality is attested very rarely:

ne imǫtь vъkusiti sъmrьti donьdeže vidětь (*Zographensis, Marianus, Savvina kniga*, PRFV)/ *uzrętь* (*Assemanianus*, PRFV) *cěsarьstvie božie* (Mark 9.1)
'They will not taste death until they see the kingdom of God.'

In this example, *Assemanianus* has a form whose tokens are always perfective, while three of the witnesses have a verb which is frequently attested as an imperfective, but which must be perfective in this example because the conjunction is required to be punctual, not durative.

Six pairs of verbs of motion (table 4.24) are attested with imperfective examples for each member of the pair. One set of members states explicitly that the referent of the subject of the verb ends up in a new location, while the other set is unmarked for this feature. Each of these verbs may refer to single events and to repeated events. The unmarked forms may even refer to a change of location carried out on one occasion, in the imperfect and in the present participle, provided that the change of location is expressed explicitly in the context.

Among the moods, the imperative and subjunctive are semantically marked with respect to the indicative.

Forms of the imperative are attested regularly only for the second person in all numbers and for the first person in the dual and plural, and occasionally for the third person singular. For other person–number combinations, /da/ plus the present tense is preferred. However, the

Table 4.24   Paired verbs of motion

Marked	Unmarked	
/iti/	/xoditi/	'go'
/vesti/	/voditi/	'lead'
/vlěsti/	/vlačiti/	'drag'
/gъnati/	/goniti/	'drive'
/nesti/	/nositi/	'carry'
/běžati/	/běgati/	'flee'

following forms are also attested: first person singular *otъraděmъ* (*Psalterium Sinaiticum* 7.5) 'fall off', third person dual *bǫděte* (*Psalterium Sinaiticum* 129.2) 'be', and third person plural *bǫdǫ* (*Zographensis, Marianus, Assemanianus, Savvinakniga*; Luke 12.35) 'be'.

The subjunctive is expressed by the perfect participle plus an auxiliary. The forms of the auxiliary are given in table 4.25. The leftmost forms are older. Younger forms are those of the perfective aorist of /byti/ 'be', except for the second and third persons singular. The plural has compromise forms as well as the older and younger type. In the dual only the first-person younger form is attested. The subjunctive expresses both condition and result in non-factual conditional sentences, in wishes and, with the conjunction /da/, potentiality. The subjunctive of /byti/ may be expressed by the auxiliary alone. The auxiliary is used with the infinitive to express the desiderative.

The passive is expressed by forms of /byti/ 'be', and for frequentative and historical present /byvati/ 'become', with the passive participle, past or present, in either aspect, or by forms of the verb with the enclitic accusative reflexive pronoun /sę/, there being no apparent difference in function between the two formations.

Non-finite forms are the infinitive, supine (with the inflection -/ъ/, for example, /pomolitъ sę/ 'pray') and participles. After verbs of motion, the supine, governing the patient in the genitive case, may be used instead of the infinitive, but is replaced by the infinitive in younger constructions.

Present and past, active and passive participles are attested in both

Table 4.25   Subjunctive auxiliary

	Singular		Dual	Plural		
1	bimь	byxъ	byxově	bimъ	bixomъ	byxomъ
2	bi	by		biste		byste
3	bi	by		bǫ	bišę	byšę

aspects in short and long forms. The aspects are clearly distinct, for instance, in the following examples of the definite past passive participle:

mnogašdi naměńjanaja (IMPFV) *slavъnaja mǫža . . . vъ naměńenĕi* (PRFV) *crъkъvi* (*Suprasliensis* 203.10–208.19)
'the frequently above mentioned eminent men . . . in the above mentioned church'

Although reference to a repeated event is not an invariant feature of the imperfective aspect, the imperfective participle in this example presents a set of events as an ongoing process in the past, whereas the perfective participle expresses a single event in its entirety, there being no lexical distinction between the forms.

Indefinite present active participles may be used with finite forms of /byti/ for explicit expression of simultaneity of one event with another:

bĕ bo umirajǫ (*Marianus, Zographensis, Assemanianus*; John 4.47)
'for he was dying'

For further information on participles, see sections 3.1.1, 3.1.4 and 4.5.

3.2.2 Conjugation
Regular verbs may be divided into two main classes, according to the non-terminal suffixes of the present tense. In the first person singular, there is no non-terminal suffix, but only the terminal suffix -/ǫ/ for both classes. One class (hereafter, -/ǫ/- verbs) has the non-terminal suffix -/ǫ/ for the third person plural and /e/ for other persons; the other (hereafter, -/ę/- verbs) has -/ę/- for the third person plural and -/i/ for other persons. The -/ǫ/- verbs are divided into the following subclasses: consonant stems, -/nǫ/- stems, -/j/- stems and -/a/ stems. In addition to the two main classes, there are also athematic verbs and the anomalous verb /xotĕti/, /xъtĕti/ 'wish'.

Table 4.26 Consonant stem verbal forms of stem /nes/- 'carry'

		Present	Aorist	Imperfect	Imperative
SG	1	nesǫ	nĕsъ, nesoxъ	nesĕaxъ	
	2	neseši	nese	nesĕaše	nesi
	3	nesetъ	nese	nesĕaše	nesi
DU	1	nesevĕ	nĕsovĕ, nesoxovĕ	nesĕaxovĕ	nesĕvĕ
	2	neseta	nĕsta, nesosta	nesĕašeta	nesĕta
	3	nesete	nĕste, nesoste	nesĕašete	
PL	1	nesemъ	nĕsomъ, nesoxomъ	nesĕaxomъ	nesĕmъ
	2	nesete	nĕste, nesoste	nesĕašete	nesĕte
	3	nesǫtъ	nĕsę, nesošę	nesĕaxǫ	

Finite and non-finite forms of consonant stems, using /nes/- as illustration, are set out in table 4.26. Other conjugational types will be described by comparison with the forms in table 4.26. In the infinitive and supine, labial stems, such as /greb/- 'row, bury' have a zero-alternant of the stem-final consonant, as in infinitive /greti/. Dental stem-final stops, as in /ved-/ 'lead', alternate with /s/ in the infinitive and supine (infinitive /vesti/) and with zero in the perfect participle (/velъ/). Velar stem-final consonants alternate with -/š/- in the infinitive (after which the supine inflection is -/ь/): /rek/- 'say', infinitive /rešti/, /obleg-/ 'dine with', supine /obleštь/.

Nasal stems have zero alternation of consonant and nasalization of vowel before consonantal suffixes: /jьm/- 'take', /načьn/- 'begin', infinitives /jęti/, /načęti/. -/r/- stems have -/rě/- before an obstruent suffix, as in the infinitive /umrěti/ 'die', -/r^b/- before a consonantal sonorant suffix, as in the perfect participle /umr^blъ/, and -/ьr/- before a vocalic suffix, as in first person singular present /umьrǫ/; an exception to this distribution is the past passive participle /prostr^btъ/ 'stretch'.

In the third person dual finite forms, younger forms merge with the second person dual in -/ta/. For feminine and neuter there is a younger suffix -/tě/ by analogy with nominal nominative forms.

Of the aorist form variants in table 4.26, older forms are on the left, younger forms on the right. Some stems have the older aorist as in table 4.27. Velar stems of this type have palatal alternants before -/e/ and -/e/-: first person singular /mogъ/, second/third person singular /može/, second person dual /moketa/ 'be able'. There are younger forms: first person singular /idoxъ/, first person plural /idoxomъ/, second person plural /idoste/, as in table 4.26. The younger forms are based on a new vocalic stem with the alternation /s/:/x/:/š/ found in vowel-stem aorists and in velar and -/r/- stems as in table 4.28. Nasal stems have earlier first person singular /jęsъ/, second/third person singular /jętъ/, younger /jęxъ/, /ję/ 'take'. Final /-tъ/ in the second and third person singular is found in nasal stems, -/r/- stems and certain vowel stems; these also have the past passive participle suffix -/t/-. As well as the root alternation -/e/-:-/ě/- as in tables 4.26 and 4.28, there are /o/:/a/ and /ь/:/i/ alternations. For active participles, see table 4.19. Passive participles past /nesenъ/, /načętъ/, present /nesomъ/ are declined as adjectives.

Table 4.27   Asigmatic aorist of stem /id/- 'go'

	Singular	Dual	Plural
1	idъ	idově	idomъ
2	ide	ideta	idete
3	ide	idete	idǫ

**Table 4.28   Aorist of velar stem /rek/- 'say' and -/r/-stem /umrě/-
'die'**

	Singular		Dual		Plural	
1	rěxъ	umrěxъ	rěxově	umrěxově	rěxomъ	umrěxomъ
2	reče	umrětъ	rěsta	umrěsta	rěste	umrěste
3	reče	umrětъ	rěste	umrěste	rěšę	umrěšę

For the younger imperfect forms with vowel contraction and, in Cyrillic,
assimilation, see page 132. There are younger second and third person dual
and second person plural suffixes by analogy with the aorist, such as
/nesěsta/. Velar stems have the palatal alternant in the imperfect, as in
/možaaše/ from /mog/- 'be able'.

In the imperative, velar stems have the vowel alternation /e/:/ь/ in the
root together with the stem-final dental alternant, as in second person
singular /rьci/, second person plural /rьcěte/ from /rek/- 'say'.

Several verbs have vowel alternations between infinitive and present
stem, some with the infinitive stem ending in -/a/-. The following list gives
infinitive and third person plural present forms: /čisti/, /čьtǫtъ/ 'read,
count, honour', /sъsati/, /sъsǫtъ/ 'suck', /zъvati/, /zovǫtъ/ 'call',
/bьrati/, /berǫtъ/ 'gather', /gъnati/, /ženǫtъ/ 'drive', /stati/, /stanǫtъ/
'stop', /lešti/, /lęgǫtъ/ 'lie down', /sěsti/, /sędǫtъ/ 'sit down', /obrěsti/
(stem /obrět/-), /obręštǫtъ/ 'find', /pluti/, /plovǫtъ/ 'sail', /iti/,
/idǫtъ/ (past active participle /šьdъ/) 'go'. There are poorly attested data
for a suppletive stem /jěd/-, /jěxa/- 'go by transport'.

-/nǫ/- stems include the verbs with infinitives /dvignǫti/ 'move',
/minǫti/ 'pass by'. The present-stem forms /dvignǫtъ/ (3 PL PRS),
/dvigněte/ (2 PL IMP) and rarely attested /podvigněaše/ (3 SG IMPF)
parallel forms of /nes/-. Verbs with a root-final vowel have aorist
/minǫxъ/ (1 SG), /minǫ/ (2/3 SG), like /rek/- except in the second/third
person singular. Verbs with a root-final stop, and some with fricatives, do
not have the suffix -/nǫ/- in the aorist, which is formed like /idъ/:
/dvigъ/ (1 SG), /dviže/ (2/3 SG). Two types of younger aorist are
attested: /dvignǫxъ/ (1 SG), /dvignǫ/ (3 SG) and /dvigoxъ/, /dviže/.
Rarely attested present participles are active /dvigny/ and passive
neistrьgnomo (Suprasliensis 560.25) 'ineradicable'; past participles are
active /dvigъ/, /minǫvъ/, passive /dviženъ/, /otъrinovenъ/ 'pushed
aside'; the perfect-participle formation is as in /dviglъ/, /minǫlъ/.

In -/j/- stems, except in the imperfect of stems with a low root vowel,
-/j/- before a vowel alternates with Ø elsewhere: infinitive /dělati/ 'work',
/uměti/ 'know', perfect participle /dělalъ/, /umělъ/; present /dělajǫtъ/,
/umějǫtъ/ (3 PL); aorist /dělaxъ/ (1 SG), /děla/ (2/3 SG). This type and
all regular verbs listed below have only one type of aorist, with which the

older types merged analogically. The imperfect of low root vowel verbs is as in /dĕlaaxъ/, /umĕaxъ/, that of high root vowel verbs as in /čujaaxъ/ 'perceive', /bьjaaxъ/ 'beat'. Imperative forms are /dĕlaji/ (2 SG), /dĕlajite/ (2 PL). The participles are: present active /dĕlaję/, /dĕlajǫšti/, present passive /dĕlajemъ/, past active /dĕlavъ/, past passive /dĕlanъ/. The following verbs have unpredictable root-vowel alternations, the cited forms being infinitive, first person singular aorist, third person plural present and first person singular imperfect: /pĕti/, /pĕxъ/ (2/3 SG /pĕtъ/), /pojǫtъ/, /pojaaxъ/ 'sing'; /brati/, /braxъ/, /boŕǫtъ/, /boŕaaxъ/ 'fight'; /mlĕti/, /mlĕxъ/, /melǫtъ/, /melaaše/ 'grind'; /biti/, /bixъ/, /bьjǫtъ/, /bьjaaxъ/ 'beat'.

In -/a/- stems, except in the imperfect, -/a/- has the alternant Ø before a vocalic suffix, with the palatal alternant of the last consonant of the stem. Verbs in -/ova/- have the alternant -/uj/- before a vowel suffix. Examples are: infinitive /kazati/ 'point', /darovati/ 'grant', perfect participle /kazalъ/, /darovalъ/; present /kažǫtъ/, /darujǫtъ/ (3 PL); aorist /kazaxъ/ (1 SG), /kaza/ (2/3 SG), /darovaxъ/, /darova/; imperfect /kazaaxъ/, /darovaaxъ/ (rare younger form /darujaxъ/); imperative /kaži/ (2 SG), /kažite/ (2 PL), /daruji/, /darujite/ (with attestation of younger forms, such as *glagolĕte* 'say', *sъvęžate* 'tie' (2 PL), by analogy with /nesĕte/); participles: present active /kažę/, /kažǫšti/, /daruję/, /darujǫšti/, present passive /kažemъ/, /darujemъ/, past active /kazavъ/, /darovavъ/, past passive /kazanъ/, /darovanъ/. Verbs with -/j/ as last consonant of the stem, such as /sĕjati/ 'sow', have spellings such as supine *sĕatъ*, perfect participle *sĕlъ* showing loss of intervocalic -/j/- and vowel contraction. /pьsati/ 'write' and /jьmati/ 'take' have alternation in the present stem: /pišǫtъ/, /jemlǫtъ/ (3 PL).

Stems of -/ę/- verbs end either in -/i/-, such as /xodi/- 'go', or in -/ĕ/-, with the alternant -/a/- after a palatal, such as /velĕ/- 'order', /slyša/- 'hear'. The stem-final vowel alternates with Ø before a vowel suffix. Examples are: infinitive /xoditi/, /velĕti/, /slyšati/, perfect participle /xodilъ/, /velĕlъ/, /slyšalъ/; present (with the palatal alternant in the first person singular only) /xoždǫ/ (1 SG), /xodiši/ (2 SG), /xodętъ/ (3 PL); aorist /xodixъ/, /velĕxъ/, /slyšaxъ/ (1 SG), /xodi/, /velĕ/, /slyša/ (2/3 SG); imperfect (with the palatal alternant in -/i/- stems only) /xoždaaxъ/, /velĕaxъ/ (1 SG), /xoždaaše/, /velĕaše/ (2/3 SG); imperative /xodi/ (2 SG), /xodite/ (2 PL); participles: present active /xodę/, /xodęšti/, present passive /molimъ/ 'pray', past (with palatal alternant in -/i/ stems only) active /xoždь/, /velĕvъ/ (with younger analogical /xodivъ/ for -/i/ stems), passive /molenъ/, velĕnъ/. The verb /sъpati/, though having a stem in a hard consonant plus /a/, belongs to this subclass: aorist /sъpaxъ/, imperfect /sъpaaxъ/, past active participle /sъparvъ/; present /sъplǫ (1 SG), /sъpiši/ (2 SG), /sъpętъ/ (3 PL).

The athematic verbs are five verbs, of which three are -/d/- stems, one is an -/s/- stem in the imperfective present, and one has an -/a/- stem in the present tense. They are characterized by first person singular -/mь/, third person plural -/ę/- or -/ǫ/-, but no vowel suffixes in other persons of the present.

The athematic -/d/- stems are: infinitive /jěsti/ 'eat', /věděti/ 'know', /dati/ 'give', perfect participle /jělъ/, /vědělъ/, /dalъ/; present singular /jěmь/, /jěsi/, /jěstъ/, dual /jěvě/, /jěsta/, /jěste/, plural /jěmъ/, /jěste/, /jědętъ/ (first person singular /věmь/ has an exceptional alternant /vědě/); aorist /jěsъ/, /jěxъ/ (both older and younger forms, in second/third person singular /jěstъ/, but *izě* (*Suprasliensis* 138.27) 'eat from'), /věděxъ/ (productive forms only), /daxъ/ (productive forms only, other than second/third person singular /dastъ/, /da/); imperfect /jěděaxъ/; imperative /jěždь/, /jědite/; participles: present active /jědy/, /jědǫšti/, present passive /jědomъ/, past active /jědъ/, /věděvъ/, /davъ/, present passive /jědenъ/, /věděnъ/, /danъ/.

The athematic verb /byti/ 'be' has an imperfective present -/s/- stem. Forms are: perfect participle /bylъ/; imperfective present singular /jesmь/, /jesi/, /jestъ/, dual /jesvě/, /jesta/, /jeste/, plural /jesmъ/, /jeste/, /sǫtъ/ (with contraction in the negative, other than the third person plural, as in /něsmь/; the perfective present is a regular consonant-stem verb /bǫd/-); aorist /běxъ/, /bě/, probably imperfective, alongside perfective aorist /byxъ/, /bystъ/ (younger /by/) 'become, happen'; /běaše/, attested only in third-person forms and morphologically an imperfect; imperative /bǫdi/ (2/3 SG), /bǫděte/ (2 PL); participles: present /sy/, /sǫšti/, past /byvъ/, past passive in the derivative /zabъvenъ/ 'forget'.

The athematic verb /iměti/ 'have' has an -/a/- stem present tense. Forms are: perfect participle /imělъ/; present singular /imamь/, /imaši/, /imatъ/, dual /imavě/, /imata/, /imate/, plural /imamъ/, /imate/, /imǫtъ/ (younger /imějǫtъ/; aorist /iměxъ/; imperfect /iměaxъ/; imperative /iměji/, /imějite/; participles: present /imy/, /iměje/, definite nominative singular masculine only /imějęjь/, oblique cases older /imǫšti/, younger /imějǫšti/, past /iměvъ/.

The anomalous verb /xotěti/, /xъtěti/ 'wish' is conjugated as follows: perfect participle /xotělъ/; present singular /xoštǫ/, /xošteši/, /xоštеtъ/, dual /xoštevě/, /xošteta/, /xoštete/, plural /xoštemъ/, /xoštete/ (these present forms as for an -/a/- stem -/ǫ/- verb), /xotętъ/ (as for an -/ę/- verb); aorist /xotěxъ/; imperfect /xotěaxъ/; participles: present /xotę/, /xotęšti/ (as for an -/ę/- verb), past /xotěvъ/. For the imperative, third person singular /vъsxošti/ is attested. In *Suprasliensis*, the root variant /xъt/- is probably younger.

For all verbs, younger forms without -/tъ/ (3 SG, 3 PL) or -/stъ/ (3 SG) are attested, such as third person singular /je/ 'be', negative /ně/, third person plural /načьnǫ/ 'begin'.

3.3   Derivational morphology

3.3.1   Major patterns of noun derivation

A few noun stems are verb roots with no added nominal suffix. Noun stems formed from verb roots with no added nominal suffix occur with or without prefixes: /prixodъ/ 'arrival', /prinosъ/ 'contribution', /xodъ/ 'movement'. Many nouns have noun, adjective or verb stems with an additional nominal suffix.

The following are examples of noun suffixes. -/ьj/- forms neuter nouns from noun stems /(kamenьje/ 'stones (collective)'), adjective stems (/veselьje/ 'gaiety'), verb stems (/znanьje/ 'knowledge') or prepositional phrases (/bezdъždьje/ 'lack of rain', compare /bez/ 'without', /dъždь/ 'rain'), in addition to one feminine collective noun, /bratrьja/ 'brothers, brethren'. -/ost/- forms feminine -/i/ genitives from adjective stems (/radostь/ 'joy'). -/ьstv/ forms neuter -/a/ genitives from noun stems (/cěsarьstvo/ 'kingdom'), verb stems (/roždьstvo/ 'birth'), adjective stems (/mọdrьstvo/ 'wisdom') and prepositional phrases (/bezoчьstvo/ 'importunity', compare /oko/ 'eye'). The suffix -/ьstvьj/- is probably Moravian.

-/in/- forms -/y/ genitives, from adjective stems (/tišina/ 'quiet'), noun stems (/družina/ 'company (collective)') and comparative adjective stems (/starějьšina/ 'senior, elder, leader'). -tel′/- derives agentive nouns from verb stems (/učitelь/ 'teacher'), while -/aŕ/- derives them from noun stems (/mytaŕь/ 'tax-gatherer').

-/ьc/- derives nouns of all three genders from all types of stem: masculine: /tvorьcь/ 'creator', /starьcь/ 'old man', /bliznьcь/ 'twin', /gradьcь/ 'small town'; feminine: /ovьca/ 'sheep', /dvьrьca/ 'small door'; epicene (masculine or feminine): /jědьca/ 'glutton'; neuter: /čędьce/ 'small child'. -/ik/- derives masculine -/a/ genitives from past passive participle stems (/učenikъ/ 'disciple, pupil', /mọčenikъ/ 'martyr'). -/ic/- derives -/ę/ genitive feminines (/proročica/ 'prophetess', /rybica/ 'small fish') and epicenes (/pьjanica/ 'drunkard'). Both -/ik/ and -/ic/ form derivatives from adjective stems with the suffix -/ьn/-: (grěšьnikъ/ (M), /grěšьnica/ (F) 'sinner', /tьmьnica/ 'jail', /tьmьničьnikъ/ 'jailer' (compare /tьma/ 'darkness', /tьmьnъ/ 'dark').

3.3.2   Major patterns of adjective derivation

Of the more than thirty suffixes, there are listed below only those attached to noun stems and referring to individuals and qualities.

The suffixes -/ьn/- (attached only to non-human stems) and -/ьsk/- (attached to human and non-human stems) form adjectives referring to qualities, individuals and groups. Examples with -/ьn/- are: qualities: *vьse zakonьnoje* (*Suprasliensis* 416.17) 'everything legal'; individuals and groups: *slovesy proročьskyimi i zakonъnyimi* (*Suprasliensis* 346.17) 'in the words of the prophets and of the law', *stražije tьmničьnii* (*Suprasliensis* 184.26) 'the prison guards', *slьzъnyi darъ* (*Suprasliensis* 285.20) 'the gift of tears', *zvěrьпиити našьstviju* (*Suprasliensis* 558.20) 'the onrush of the beast', *soprogъ* (GEN PL) *volovьnyixъ* (Luke 14.19) 'a yoke of oxen'. Examples with -/ьsk/- are: /morьskъ/ 'nautical, of the sea, of the seas', /ženьskъ/ 'female, womanly, of a woman, of women'; with this suffix, older forms have only short forms with no distinction for definite and indefinite, while long forms are younger.

Suffixes which refer only to individuals occur mainly, but not exclusively, with human stems. For human stems other than those with the nominal suffix -/ik/-, -/ic/-, -/ьc/-, these suffixes refer exclusively to individuals, not to groups of persons: -/ov/-: /ženixovъ/ 'bridegroom's', /tektonovъ/ 'carpenter's', /isusovъ/ 'Jesus's'; -/ьj/-: /božьjь/ 'God's', /vražьjь/ 'enemy's', /rabьjь/ 'slave's'; -/in/- (for stems forming nouns with nominative singular in -/a/): /sotoninъ/ 'Satan's', /marijinъ/ 'Mary's'; -/ьň/-: /gospodьňь/ 'Lord's'; palatal alternant of stem-final consonant: /proročь/ 'prophet's' (from /prorok/-), /kъnęžь/ 'ruler's' (from /kъnędz/-), /dijavolь/ 'devil's' (from /dijavol/-), /grěšьničь/ 'sinner's' (from /grěšьnik/-), /otьčь/ 'father's' (from /otьc/-), /mateŕь/ 'mother's' (from /mater/-), /děvičь/ 'maiden's' (from /děvic/-). Such is the productivity of these suffixes that they are attested with both native stems, such as /bog/- 'God', /vrag/- 'enemy', /prorok/- 'prophet', and non-native stems, such as /tekton/- 'carpenter', /isus/- 'Jesus', /dijavol/- 'devil'. Adjectives from stems in -/ik/-, -/ic/- and -/ьc/- may refer to groups of persons as well as to individuals. Adjectives from other types of stems have purely individual reference. For this type of stem, a personal adjective, such as /proročь/, has individual reference, whereas the adjective /proročьskъ/ 'of the prophets, prophetic' refers either to a quality or to a group of individuals.

3.3.3   Major patterns of verb derivation

Verb derivation involves mainly aspect formation by suffixation, and aspect and lexical formation by prefixation, as described briefly in section 3.2.1. The opposition transitive:intransitive is expressed by suffixation for a few roots: /cěliti/ (INF), /cělętъ/ (3 PL PRS) 'cure', /cělěti/, /cělějotъ/ 'recover', or by root vowel alternation: /tešti/, /tekotъ/ 'run, flow', /točiti/, /točetъ/ 'drive, pour', but such morphological contrasts do not express any invariant lexical oppositions, since, for example, /vesti/, /voditi/ 'lead' are both transitive paired verbs of motion.

4 Syntax

4.1 Element order in declarative sentences

Word order in Old Church Slavonic texts in general follows that of the
Greek original. All possible orders of subject and verb in intransitive
clauses and of (subject,) verb and object in transitive clauses are found,
except that a noun object never immediately precedes a noun subject,
suggesting that Old Church Slavonic had free word order, though the imitation of Greek word order makes it impossible to be more precise
concerning the factors governing this freedom:

slěpii prozirajǫtъ (*Zographensis, Marianus*; Matthew 11.5) (Subject–Verb)
'The blind regain sight.'

iscělěetъ otrokъ moi (*Marianus, Zographensis, Assemanianus*; Matthew 8.8)
(Verb–Subject)
'My servant will recover.'

mъzdǫ proročǫ priemletъ (*Marianus, Zographensis, Assemanianus, Savvina
kniga*; Matthew 10.41) (Object–Verb)
'He receives the reward of a prophet.'

nesi darъ (*Zographensis, Marianus*; Matthew 8.4) (Verb–Object)
'Take the gift.'

bogъ vъzljubi mira (*Marianus*; John 3.16) (Subject–Verb–Object)
'God loved the world.'

drěvo dobro plody dobry tvoritъ (*Marianus*; Matthew 7.17) (Subject–Object–Verb)
'The good tree makes good fruit.'

eže ubo bogъ sъčetalъ estъ (*Marianus, Zographensis*; Mark 10.9) (Object–
Subject–Verb)
'for what God has joined ...'

vlastь imatъ synъ člověčьsky (*Marianus, Zographensis, Savvina kniga*; Matthew
9.6) (Object–Verb–Subject)
'The son of man has power.'

prědastъ že bratrъ bratra (*Marianus*; Matthew 10.21) (Verb–Subject–Object)
'for brother will betray brother'

viděvъše i učenici (*Zographensis, Marianus*; Matthew 14.26) (Verb–Object–
Subject)
'The disciples having seen him ...'

Orders for the perfect participle and auxiliary and for clitic pronouns are
the only two items for which there is reliable evidence for the indigenous
word order.

Phrase-initially, the perfect participle precedes the positive auxiliary (which is thus shown to be enclitic), but follows the negative auxiliary:

varila estъ (*Zographensis, Marianus*; Mark 14.8)
'She has gone ahead.'

něstъ umrьla (*Zographensis, Marianus, Assemanianus*; Luke 8.52)
'She has not died.'

Phrase-internally, word order is free, and for negation both the negative auxiliary and the negated participle are attested:

jako varilъ jestъ (*Suprasliensis* 204.29)
'that he has gone ahead'

jakože jestъ obyklъ (*Suprasliensis* 382.24)
'as he has become accustomed'

ideže něsi sělъ (*Marianus, Zographensis, Assemanianus, Savvina kniga*; Matthew 25.24)
'where you have not sown'

nikoliže ne dalъ esi (*Zographensis, Marianus, Assemanianus, Savvina kniga*; Luke 15.29)
'You have never given.'

Enclitic pronouns precede the auxiliary:

vъskǫjǫ mę esi ostavilъ (*Marianus, Assemanianus*; Matthew 27.46)
'Why have you abandoned me?'

dalъ ti bi vodǫ živǫ (*Zographensis, Marianus, Assemanianus*; John 4.10)
'He would have given you living water.'

The enclitic reflexive pronoun, with another pronoun, immediately precedes or follows the verb:

čьto vamъ sę avlěetъ (*Zographensis, Marianus*; Mark 14.64)
'How does it appear to you?'

si vьsě priložetъ sę vamъ (*Marianus, Zographensis*; Luke 12.31)
'All these things will be added to you.'

čьto sę mьnitъ vamъ (*Zographensis, Marianus*; John 11.56)
'What do you think?'

Examples of adjacent clitic pronouns other than with reflexives are not attested. Following the verb, the particle /bo/ 'for' may precede the enclitic reflexive pronoun:

boěaxъ bo sę tebe (*Marianus, Zographensis*; Luke 19.21)
'for I was afraid of you'

4.2   Non-declarative sentence types

Questions requiring the answer 'yes' or 'no', when not marked for a contradictory answer, have the verb or some other emphasized element obligatorily preposed and followed by the particle /li/:

damъ li ili ne damъ (*Zographensis*; Mark 12.14)
'Shall we give or shall we not give?'

ne dobro li sěmę sělъ esi (*Marianus, Zographensis*; Matthew 13.27)
'Did you not sow good seed?'

ne iže li estъ sъtvorilъ (*Zographensis, Marianus*; Luke 11.40)
'Is it not he who has made ...?'

In the sequence predicate + copula + subject pronoun, /li/ may optionally be omitted:

prorokъ esi ty (*Zographensis*)/ *prorokъ li ubo esi ty* (*Assemanianus*; John 1.21)
'(For) are you a prophet?'

The particle /li/ is not used with interrogative pronouns, which occur in clause-initial position, but may be preceded by a personal pronoun:

ty kъto esi ... čьto ubo ty esi ... kъto esi (*Zographensis, Assemanianus*; John 1.19 ... 21 ... 22)
'Who are you? ... Now what are you? ... Who are you?'

For eliciting a contradictory answer the particle /jeda/ precedes the questioned word:

eda kamenь podastъ emu (*Marianus*; Matthew 7.9)
'He won't give him a stone, will he?'

Questions requiring a positive or negative response may be answered by /ei/ 'yes' or /ni/ 'no':

bǫdi že slovo vaše ei ei i ni ni lixoe bo seju otъ neprięzni estъ (*Zographensis, Marianus*; Matthew 5.37)
'Let your word be: yes, yes, or; no, no. Anything extra to this is from the Evil One.'

Direct and indirect questions are marked by /li/ in exactly the same way, but /jeda/ in a subordinate clause marks negative purpose, 'lest'.

Commands are expressed by the imperative, in either aspect. The negated imperative of /mošti/ 'be able' is used for pleading:

ne mozi mene ostaviti (*Suprasliensis* 539.8)
'Do not leave me.'

4.3 Copular sentences

The copula is /byti/ 'be', or non-actual /byvati/, or, for emphasis, zero; for instance, the copula is often omitted in exclamations:

azъ glasъ vъpijǫštago vъ pustyńi (*Zographensis*; John 1.23)
'I am the voice of the one crying in the wilderness.'

The copula is often omitted in the Greek, but included in the Old Church Slavonic in non-exclamatory statements:

i svĕtitъ vьsĕmъ iže vъ xraminĕ sǫtъ (*Zographensis*; Matthew 5.15)
'and it shines for all those who are in the house'

The noun predicate is in the nominative, except when the instrumental is used with /byti/ to refer to an anomalous temporary change of state:

ovogda turomъ (INST) *byvъ* (*Suprasliensis* 7.24)
'sometimes having become a bull'

ne bǫdi niktože ijudojǫ (INST) *tu* (*Suprasliensis* 420.10)
'Let no one there become a Judas.'

For a normal, permanent or beneficial change of state the nominative is used:

byšę krьstijani (NOM) (*Suprasliensis* 4.3)
'They became Christians.'

While reliable examples of long-form adjectival predicates do not happen to be attested, there are a number of examples where a short adjective contrasts with a long participle:

bĕaxǫ vidĕli prĕžde ĕko slĕpъ (SHORT) *bĕ glagolaaxǫ ne sь li estъ sĕdęi* (LONG)
(*Marianus*; John 9.8)
'They had previously seen that he was blind (SHORT), they were saying: Is not this the one sitting (LONG) ...?'

4.4 Coordination and comitativity

Two coordinated or comitative singular subjects take a dual verb:

otecъ tvoi i azъ skrьbęšta (DU) *iskaaxovĕ* (DU) *tebe* (*Marianus, Zographensis, Assemanianus*; Luke 2.48)
'Your father and I, grieving (DU), were looking (DU) for you.'

i ěvi (SG) *sę imъ iliě sъ moseemъ i běašete* (DU) *glagoljǫšta* (DU) (*Marianus, Zographensis*; Mark 9.4)
'And Elijah appeared to them with Moses and they were speaking ...'

If one subject is collective, verbs are plural, not dual:

mati tvoě (F SG) *i bratriě tvoě* (F SG) *vьně stojętъ* (3 PL) *xotęšte* (M PL) *glagolati kъ tebě* (*Zographensis, Marianus*; Matthew 12.47)
'Your mother (F SG) and your brothers (F SG) are standing (3 PL) outside wanting (M PL) to talk to you.'

4.5   Subordination

A few examples are given below of subordinate clauses and of participial and infinitive phrases synonymous with such clauses.

/jegda/ 'when, after' expresses a limit with the perfective, but specifies no limit with the imperfective:

egda svoję ovьcę iždenetъ (PRFV) *prědъ ńimi xoditъ* (IMPFV) (*Zographensis, Marianus, Assemanianus*; John 10.4)
'After he drives (PRFV) his sheep out, he goes (IMPFV) in front of them.'

egda že vodętъ (IMPFV) *vy prědajǫšte ne pьcěte se prěžde čto vъzglagolete* (*Marianus*; Mark 13.11)
'When they lead (IMPFV) you, handing you over, do not trouble yourself beforehand what you will say.'

/dońьdeže/ 'while' expresses no limit with the imperfective:

donьdeže dьnь estъ (IMPFV) (*Zographensis, Marianus, Assemanianus*; John 9.4)
'While it is day ...'

Examples of /dońьdeže/ with the perfective, expressing a limit, are:

povelě dъrati želězny nogъty doideže črěva načъnǫtъ (PRFV) *xъtěti izvaliti sę na zemьjǫ* (*Suprasliensis* 113.29)
'He ordered them to be flogged with iron nails until their intestines were about to pour out onto the ground.'

ne imǫtъ vъkusiti sъmrъti donьdeže uzьrętъ (PRFV) *cěsarьstvie božie* (*Assemanianus*; Mark 9.1)
'They will not taste death until they see the kingdom of God.'

/jako/ has temporal meanings similar to the above, but may also introduce a clause of reason or of result:

izidi otъ mene ěko mǫžь grěšьnъ estь (*Zographensis, Marianus, Assemanianus*; Luke 5.8)
'Go away from me because I am a sinful man.'

učaše ję na sъnьmištixъ ixъ ěko divlěaxǫ sę emu (*Zographensis, Marianus*;
Matthew 13.54)
'He taught them in their synagogues, so that they marvelled at him.'

Conditional sentences have the subjunctive for unreal conditions, but
the indicative for real conditions:

ašte bi bylъ sьde ne bi moi bratъ umrъlъ (*Zographensis, Marianus,
Assemanianus*; John 11.32)
'If you had been here, my brother would not have died.'

ašte li umьretъ mъnogъ plodъ sъtvoritъ (*Marianus, Zographensis, Assemanianus*;
John 12.24)
'If it dies, it will bear much fruit.'

Similarly, /da/ 'so that' with the indicative implies fulfilment of purpose,
but with the subjunctive does not necessarily do so:

iděmъ i my da umьretъ sъ ńimь (*Zographensis, Marianus, Assemanianus*; John
11.16)
'Let us go too, so that we may die with him.'

molěaxǫ i da bi prěbylъ u ńixъ (*Zographensis, Marianus, Assemanianus*; John
4.40)
'They begged him to stay with them.'

Long-form participles are synonymous with headless relative clauses:

věrujei (LONG ACT PART) *vъ syna imatъ životъ věčьny a iže* (REL) *ne věruetъ* (PRS)
vъ syna ne uzьritъ života (*Zographensis, Marianus*; John 3.36)
'Whoever believes in the Son has eternal life, but whoever does not believe in the
Son will not see life.'

Short-form participles in both aspects are synonymous with various types
of subordinate clause:

vъzъpivъ (PAST ACT PART PRFV) *glasomь velьemь glagola* (*Zographensis,
Marianus*; Mark 5.7)
'Having cried out with a loud voice, he said ...'

The perfective past participle in this example characterizes the event as
occurring in its entirety immediately before the event expressed by the
main verb.

baliěmъ izdaěvъši (PAST ACT PART IMPFV) *vьse iměnie ni otъ edinogo že ne može
iscěleti* (*Marianus, Zographensis*; Luke 8.43)
'Having given away all her property to the doctors, she could not be cured by any
one of them.'

The imperfective past participle in this example characterizes the event as an ongoing process not necessarily immediately preceding the event expressed by the main verb.

xodę (PRS ACT PART IMPFV) *že pri mori galilěiscěmь vidě dъva bratra* (*Zographensis, Assemanianus, Savvina kniga*; Matthew 4.18)
'Going by the Sea of Galilee, he saw two brothers.'

The imperfective present participle here characterizes the event as being simultaneous with the event expressed by the main verb.

ašte vidiši člověka dijavola sъtvorьša (PAST ACT PART PRFV) *sę i pridǫšta* (PRS ACT PART PRFV) *kъ tebě* (*Suprasliensis* 381.15)
'If you see a man who has become a devil approaching you ...'

In this example, the perfective past participle characterizes the event as having occurred in its entirety before the event expressed by the perfective present participle, which in turn characterizes the event as one which is about to occur in its entirety.

Participial phrases containing a direct object may occur, instead of a clause containing a finite verb, as objects of verbs of thinking or knowing:

mьněaxǫ duxъ vidęšte (PRS ACT PART) (*Marianus, Assemanianus*; Luke 24.37)
'They thought they were seeing a spirit.'

věděše čto xotę (PRS ACT PART) *sъtvoriti* (*Marianus*; John 6.6)
'He knew what he was about to do.'

Participles may also be synonymous with finite verbs in relative clauses:

vъzemleši ideže (REL) *ne položь* (PAST ACT PART) *i žьneši egože* (REL) *ne sěavъ* (PAST ACT PART) (*Zographensis*; Luke 19.21)
'You take up where you have not put down, and reap what you have not sown.'

The participle and its subject are in the dative, the so-called dative-absolute construction, when the following clause has a main verb with a different subject:

vъlězъšema (DAT) *ima* (DAT) *vъ korabь prěsta větrъ* (*Zographensis, Marianus, Assemanianus*; Matthew 14.32)
'After they had got into the boat, the wind stopped.'

The perfective participle in this example presents the event as having occurred in its entirety before the onset of the event expressed by the main verb.

sicěmi slovesy glagolavъšu (DAT) *otьcu* (DAT) *ne posluša bratъ* (*Suprasliensis* 290.29)
'After the father had been speaking with such words, the brother did not heed him.'

The imperfective past participle in this example expresses an ongoing process preceding the event expressed by the main verb.

vъ crьkъ ve xodęštju (DAT) *emu* (DAT) *pridǫ kъ nemu* (*Marianus*; Mark 11.27)
'While he was walking to the temple, they came up to him.'

Here, the imperfective present participle expresses an event which is simultaneous with the event expressed by the main verb.

zьri da ne paky vъzidǫštu (DAT) *mi* (DAT) *sъ plьtijǫ ty nevěrьnyje rěči vъzъmъ rečeši* (*Suprasliensis* 506.4)
'Take care lest, when I rise up again in the flesh, adopting words of disbelief you say ...'

The perfective present participle of this example expresses an event which will occur in its entirety in the future, which is one of the contextual meanings of the perfective present in general.

The participial phrase may be in the dative when followed by a subordinate clause with a different subject, even though the main clause has the same subject as the participial phrase:

obrǫčeně (DAT) *že byvъši* (DAT) *materi* (DAT) *ego marii* (DAT) *iosifovi prěžde daže ne sъnęste sę obrěte sę impšti vъ črěvě otъ duxa svęta* (*Savvina kniga, Assemanianus*; Matthew 1.18)
'For after his mother Mary had become engaged to Joseph, before they were married, she was found to be pregnant by the Holy Spirit.'

The dative is also attested even when the subject is identical with that of the main verb:

približivъšu (DAT) *že sę svętuumu* (DAT) *i sъtvorivъ* (NOM) *xristosovo znamenije na čelě svojemъ vьnide* (AOR) *vъ crьkъ ve* (*Suprasliensis* 229.3)
'But the holy man, having approached and having made the sign of the cross on his forehead, went into the temple.'

This use of the dative absolute may imitate a similar use of the genitive absolute in the Greek text.

The dative and infinitive are found as complements of /bystъ/ 'it happened':

bystъ že umrěti (INF) *ništjumu* (DAT) (*Zographensis, Marianus, Assemanianus, Savvina kniga*; Luke 16.22)
'The beggar happened to die.'

Other prominent uses of the dative and infinitive, illustrated below, are, respectively, modal, resultative and existential:

počto mi (DAT) *gněviti* (INF) *językъ starcu* (*Suprasliensis* 239.26)
'Why should I (DAT) provoke (INF) the old man's tongue?'

ěko narodu (DAT) *diviti* (INF) *sę* (*Zographensis, Marianus*; Matthew 15.31)
'... so that the crowd marvelled ...'

nikomuže (DAT) *sego ně slyšati* (*Suprasliensis* 241.1)
'There is no one to hear this.'

4.6 Negation
Verbal negation is expressed by the particles /ne/ or /ni/ immediately preceding the main verb. The basic rule is for the direct object of a negated verb to stand in the genitive; both this and various special instances with the accusative are illustrated below. A single verb is negated with /ne/; when there is more than one verb, /ne/ negates the more prominent, /ni/ the less prominent, but only /ni/ is used when the verbs are of equal prominence:

ne sějǫtъ ni žьńǫtъ ni sъbirajǫtъ (*Zographensis, Marianus, Assemanianus*; Matthew 6.26)
'They do not sow, neither do they reap, nor do they gather.'

ni ženętъ sę ni posagajǫtъ (*Zographensis, Marianus*; Mark 12.25)
'Neither do men marry, nor do women marry.'

When a constituent is negated, /ne/ or /ni/ immediately precedes this constituent. If the subject is negated, the object is in the accusative:

ne mosi li dastъ vamъ zakonъ (ACC) *(Zographensis, Marianus*; John 7.19)
'Did not Moses give you the law?'

A negated pronominal object is in the genitive:

ni li sego (GEN) *este čьli* (*Zographensis, Marianus, Assemanianus*; Luke 6.3)
'Have you neither read this?'

/ne/ and /nъ/ contrast negated and non-negated constituents respectively:

ne otъ kvasa xlěbъnaago nъ otъ učeně fariseiska i sadueiska (*Zographensis, Marianus*; Matthew 16.12)
'... not from yeast, but from the teachings of the Pharisees and Saducees.'

More than one negative element is allowed in the same phrase:

ne bě nikъtože nikogdaže položenъ (Luke 23.53)
'Nobody was ever put (literally: Nobody was never not put).'

A negative adverb or pronoun may occur without negating the verb:

nikъtože otъ vasъ tvoritъ zakona (GEN) (*Zographensis, Marianus*; John 7.19)
'No one of you keeps the law.'

In negative clauses, the direct object is expressed either by the genitive or by the accusative, under various conditions some of which have been exemplified above. When the subject is a negative pronoun, or when the verb is negated, the direct object is in the genitive:

ne ostavętъ kamene (GEN) *na kameni* (*Zographensis, Marianus*; Luke 19.44)
'They will not leave stone on stone.'

Similarly with a negative adverb, with no negation of the verb:

nikoliže znaxъ vasъ (GEN) (*Zographensis, Marianus*; Matthew 7.23)
'I never knew you.'

Even if the infinitive is not negated, the direct object of an infinitive dependent on a negated verb is in the genitive:

ne možeši otъvaliti (INF) *kamyka* (GEN) (*Suprasliensis* 316.21)
'You cannot roll away the stone.'

otъpustiti (INF) *ixъ* (GEN) *ne xoštǫ ne ědъšь* (GEN) (*Zographensis*; Matthew 15.32)
'I do not wish to let them go without their having eaten.'

The direct object is also in the genitive when the infinitive is dependent on an adjective with a negated copula:

něsmь dostoinъ poklońь sę razdrěšiti (INF) *remene* (GEN) *sapogu ego*
(*Zographensis, Marianus, Assemanianus, Savvina kniga*; Mark 1.7)
'I am not worthy, having bent down, to untie the strap of his sandals.'

When just the direct object itself is negated, it stands in the accusative:

dělaite ne brašъno (ACC) *gybljǫštee* (ACC) *nъ brašъno prěbyvajǫštee* (*Marianus, Assemanianus*; John 6.27)
'Make not the food that perishes, but the food that remains.'

When a negated verb has an object con·isting of an adverb of place and an infinitive with a direct object, this direct object is in the genitive:

ne imatъ kde glavy (GEN) *podъkloniti* (INF) (*Zographensis, Marianus, Assemanianus, Suprasliensis*; Matthew 8.20)
'He has nowhere to put his head down.'

A noun complement of a negated existential copula is in the genitive, regardless of the tense of the copula:

něstъ istiny (GEN) *vъ ńemь* (*Zographensis, Marianus, Assemanianus*; John 8.44)
'There is no truth in him.'

ne bǫdetъ grěšьnika (GEN) (*Psalterium Sinaiticum* 36.10)
'There will be no sinner.'

ne bě ima města (GEN) (*Zographensis, Marianus, Assemanianus, Savvina kniga*; Luke 2.7)
'There was no place for them.'

When the copula is not existential, the noun complement is in the nominative:

ne bě tъ světъ (NOM) (*Zographensis, Assemanianus*; John 1.8)
'He was not the light.'

něstъ bo člověkъ (NOM) *tvoręi* (NOM) ... *пъ raspęty* (NOM) *za ny xristosъ* (NOM) (*Clozianus* 8a.14)
'It is not a man who is making [this] ... but the Christ who was crucified for us.'

An existential relative pronoun complement is in the nominative:

ne bǫdi emu zastǫpьnika (GEN) *ni bǫdi ižé* (NOM) *pomiluetъ* (*Psalterium Sinaiticum* 108.12)
'Let there be no intercessor for him, nor anyone who shows him mercy.'

When the complement is the pronoun /kъto/ 'someone' as the subject of a participle, both pronoun and participle are nominative:

něstъ kto (NOM) *miluję* (NOM) *i něstъ kto* (NOM) *milosrъduję* (NOM) (*Suprasliensis* 57.9)
'There is no one showing mercy and there is no one showing pity.'

When the complement is the negative pronoun in the genitive case, /nikogože/ 'no one', but the verb is not negated, the participle is also in the genitive:

nikogože (GEN) *bě kažǫšta* (GEN) (*Suprasliensis* 415.4)
'There was no one instructing.'

When the copula is negated, the participle is in the nominative, but the negative pronoun and any object of the participle are in the genitive:

ně sьde nikogože (GEN) *seję* (GEN) *besědy* (GEN) *slyšę* (NOM) (*Suprasliensis* 240.29)
'There is no one (GEN) here hearing (NOM) this conversation (GEN).'

A dative and infinitive may be the complement of a negated copula, so that the subject of the infinitive remains in the dative, but the direct object of the infinitive is in the genitive:

něstъ mьně (DAT) *sego* (GEN) *dati* (INF) (*Marianus, Zographensis* (younger); Matthew 20.23)
'It is not for me (DAT) to grant this (GEN).'

nikomuže (DAT) *sego* (GEN) *ně slyšati* (INF) (*Suprasliensis* 241.1)
'There is no one (DAT) to hear this (GEN).'

glagoljǫtъ ne byti (INF) *vъskrěsenьju* (DAT) (*Zographensis, Marianus*; Mark 12.18)
'They say there is no resurrection.'

4.7   Anaphora and pronouns
Both Old Church Slavonic and Greek encode the person and number of the subject in the verb and allow subject pronouns to be omitted. The presence or absence of pronouns in Old Church Slavonic simply follows the Greek source. Otherwise, third-person reference is made by the demonstratives, /tъ/ unmarked or 'the former', /onъ/ distant or 'the former', with /jь/ in the oblique cases. The proximate demonstrative /sь/ is used for 'the latter'.

4.8   Reflexives and reciprocals
Reflexivity is expressed, for all persons and numbers, by the pronoun /sę/ 'oneself'). There are various ways of distinguishing the reflexive from the passive, for instance, by the conjunction /i/, by the emphatic /samъ/ in the nominative, or by using the full form /sebe/:

da sъpasetъ i sę (*Zographensis, Marianus, Assemanianus, Savvina kniga*; Luke 23.35)
'Let him save himself too.'

sъpasi sę samъ (*Zographensis, Marianus, Assemanianus, Savvina kniga*; Luke 23.37)
'Save yourself.'

sъpasi sebe (*Zographensis, Marianus*)/ *sę* (*Assemanianus, Savvina kniga*) (Matthew 27.40)
'Save yourself.'

The antecedent of a reflexive pronoun in a participial phrase may be the subject of a verb in some other phrase, rather than the subject of the participle:

vidě isusa grędǫšta kъ sebě (*Marianus*; John 1.29)
'He saw Jesus coming towards him.'

The reflexive pronoun, governed by the preposition /meždu/ 'between',
is occasionally used to express reciprocity:

mirъ iměite meždju sobojǫ (*Zographensis, Marianus*; Mark 9.50)
'Have peace one with another.'

More usually, reciprocity is expressed by /drugъ/, in the nominative
singular, followed by the same word in the appropriate singular case,
regardless of the grammatical number of the antecedent:

kъždo (SG) *že tъkaše drugъ druga* (ACC) (*Suprasliensis* 38.13)
'Each was pushing the other.'

poklonista (DU) *sę drugъ drugu* (DAT SG) (*Suprasliensis* 298.21)
'They bowed to one another.'

drugъ druga (ACC SG) *bijaxǫ* (PL) (*Suprasliensis* 74.10)
'They were beating one another.'

The masculine form of /drug/- is used with a neuter antecedent:

čjuvъstvič (N PL) ... *ne zastǫpajǫšta* (N PL) *drugъ* (NOM SG M) *druga* (ACC SG M)
(*Euchologium Sinaiticum* 7b.8)
'Feelings ... not obstructing one another.'

With a feminine antecedent, both components of the reciprocal are
feminine singular:

dъ věma prědъležęštema veštьma (F DU) *i kotorajǫštema sę ima druga* (NOM SG F)
kъ druzě (DAT SG F) (*Suprasliensis* 59.12)
'from two available things contradicting one another'

4.9 Possession
English 'have' is normally translated by the transitive verb /iměti/ 'have'.
Within the noun phrase, first and second persons have the possessive
pronouns /mojь/ 'my', /tvojь/ 'your', /našь/ 'our', /vašь/ 'your' for
singular and plural possessors respectively. For the third person in all
numbers, and for first and second persons in the dual, the genitive of the
personal pronoun is used. The reflexive possessive /svojь/ 'one's own'
refers to persons of any number, and may refer back to a constituent other
than the subject of the main verb:

vъzvrati nožь svoi vъ svoe město (*Zographensis, Marianus, Savvina kniga*;
Matthew 26.52)
'Put your knife back in its own place.'

Grammatical possession of various semantic types is expressed by the dative or genitive of a noun, or by a denominal adjective agreeing in case, number and gender with a head noun:

prědanъ imatъ byti synъ člověčъsky (ADJECTIVE, NOM SG M) *vъ rǫcě člověkomъ* (NOUN, DAT PL) (*Marianus*)/ *vъ rǫcě grěšъnikъ* (NOUN, GEN PL) (*Savvina kniga*) (Matthew 17.22)
'The son of man will be betrayed into the hands of men/into the hands of sinners.'

prědanъ bǫdetъ vъ rǫcě člověčъscě (ADJECTIVE, ACC DU F) (*Zographensis, Marianus, Savvina kniga*)/ *vъ rǫcě člověkomъ* (NOUN, DAT PL) (*Assemanianus*) (Mark 9.31)
'He will be betrayed into the hands of men.'

The adnominal genitive or dative is used much more freely for plural than for singular possessors. In the singular, when the head noun is modified by a single word, the adjective is especially highly preferred for human stems whose adjectives refer exclusively to individual persons. There are strong constraints against the adjective when the head noun is modified by more than one word, in which context the head noun is almost always modified by an adnominal dative or genitive with an accompanying attribute:

tvoręi voljǫ otьca (NOUN, GEN SG) *mojego* (GEN SG) (*Zographensis, Marianus*; Matthew 7.21)
'The one doing the will of my father.'

This pattern is infringed in only one example, with the reflexive dative singular pronoun *si* modifying 'father', expressed in the accusative singular feminine adjective modifying 'will':

da sъtvorǫ volǫ otьčǫ si (*Suprasliensis* 349.27)
'That I should do the will of my father.'

A denominative adjective may be only very exceptionally modified by another denominative adjective. There are attested only two examples, in both of which an adjective with the suffix -/ьn/- is modified by a denominative adjective with a personal stem:

otъ uzdy (GEN SG F) *konьnyję* (ADJECTIVE, GEN SG F) *cěsarę* (ADJECTIVE, GEN SG F) (*Suprasliensis* 193.9)
'from the bridle of the horse of the Emperor'

obrazomъ (INST SG M) *krestъnyimъ* (ADJECTIVE, INST SG M) *xristosovomъ* (ADJECTIVE, INST SG M) (*Suprasliensis* 5.19)
'with the sign of the cross of Christ'

In the one example where a personal adjective appears to have an adjectival attribute, the two adjectives are, in fact, in apposition:

vъspojǫ imeni (DAT SG N) *gospodnju* (ADJECTIVE, DAT SG N) *vyšьnjumu* (ADJECTIVE, DAT SG M) (*Euchologium Sinaiticum* 74a.9)
'I will sing to the name of the Lord, the highest.'

A personal adjective may be in apposition with an adnominal genitive singular noun, when this noun itself has an attribute that is either another personal adjective or a possessive pronoun:

ioanna žena xuzaně (ADJECTIVE) *pristavьnika* (NOUN, GEN) *irodova* (ADJECTIVE, GEN) (*Marianus*; Luke 8.3)
'Joanna, the wife of Chuza, the steward of Herod'

vъ domu davydově (ADJECTIVE) *otroka* (NOUN, GEN) *svoego* (ADJECTIVE, GEN) (*Zographensis*; Luke 1.69)
'in the house of David, his servant'

Denominal adjectives may be conjoined with other types of possessive constructions:

vъ slavě svoei i otьči (ADJECTIVE) *i svętyxъ angelъ* (GEN) (*Zographensis, Marianus, Assemanianus, Savvina kniga*; Luke 9.26)
'in his and the father's and the holy angels' glory'

Denominal adjectives may be antecedents to the subject implicit in the inflection of a finite verb, to relative pronouns, personal pronouns and participles:

privrъgǫ ję kъ nogama isusovama i icěli ję (*Zographensis, Marianus*; Matthew 15.30)
'They put them down at Jesus's feet and he cured them.'

In this example, the adjective *isusovama*, whose stem refers to a male person, is antecedent to the implicit subject of the verb *icěli*.

iakovъ že rodi iosifa mǫža mariina iz nejęže rodi sę isusъ (*Assemanianus, Savvina kniga*; Matthew 1.16)
'And Jacob fathered Joseph, the husband of Mary, from whom Jesus was born.'

Here, the adjective *mariina*, whose stem refers to a female person, is antecedent to the feminine singular relative pronoun *nejęže*.

glagola mati isusova kъ ńemu (*Zographensis, Marianus, Assemanianus*; John 2.3)
'Jesus's mother said to him ...'

In this example, the adjective *isusova*, whose stem refers to a male person, is antecedent to the masculine personal pronoun *ńemu*. A noun with a denominal adjectival attribute may govern a participle either in the genitive or in the dative:

pomoštь naša vъ imę gospodьńe sъtvorьšaago (GEN) *nebo i zemьjǫ* (*Suprasliensis* 80.6, *Psalterium Sinaiticum* 123.9)
'Our help is in the name of the Lord,who created heaven and earth.'

In this example, the stem of the adjective *gospodьńe* invariably refers to a male individual, whence the masculine singular participle *sъtvorьšaago*.

aggelьskъ glasъ slyšanъ bystъ pojǫštemъ (DAT) *i slavoslovęštemъ* (DAT) *boga* (*Suprasliensis* 110.23)
'The voice of angels was heard singing and glorifying God.'

Since the adjective *aggelьskъ* is antecedent to masculine participles that are in the plural, *pojǫštemъ* and *slavoslovęštemъ*, the reference can be neither 'angelic' nor 'of an angel', but only 'of angels' (the noun stem /angel/- 'angel' is male personal and thus forms a masculine noun).

po božiju že popušteniju nakazajǫštuumu prisno na polьzъnoje (*Suprasliensis* 191.14)
'Through God's permission, who instructs always to good purpose . . .'

Grammatically, the participle *nakazajǫštuumu* in this example could be neuter in agreement with the dative noun *popušteniju* 'permission', but for semantic reasons, since an animate subject is required, the participle must be masculine and its antecedent the dative adjective *božiju*, whose stem forms a masculine singular noun. But since participant roles may thus be assigned by purely semantic features, it is possible to break the agreement and government rules and have both adjective and participle agreeing in case, number and gender with the head noun:

promyslomъ (INST SG) *božijemъ* (INST SG) *xotęštiimъ* (INST SG) *člověčьskyi rodъ sъpasti* (*Suprasliensis* 539.30)
'Through the providence of God, who wishes to save the human race.'

The use of the denominal adjective instead of an unmodified genitive or dative singular noun is strongest for personal stems whose adjectives refer exclusively to individuals. For other types of stem, including personal stems with adjectives with the suffix -/ьsk/-, there is a strong tendency for adjectives to be used for indefinite reference, whereas nouns are used for definite reference:

dijavolъ prěměni sę vъ mǫžeskъ (ADJECTIVE) *obrazъ* (*Suprasliensis* 78.24)
'The Devil changed himself into the form of a man.'

vъlězъ vъ lono mǫža (GEN) *mǫčaaše* (*Suprasliensis* 567.6)
'Getting into the man's chest, it was torturing him.'

4.10   Quantification

/malo/ 'few' as a neuter quantifier governs the genitive case and is the subject of a singular verb:

gospodi ašte malo estъ (3 SG) *sъpasajǫštiixъ* (PRS ACT PART GEN PL LONG) *sę*
(*Zographensis, Marianus, Assemanianus, Savvina kniga*; Luke 13.23)
'Lord, are there [only] a few who are saved?'

A relative pronoun relating to an item governed by /malo/ will agree in number with that item:

malo ixъ (GEN PL) *estъ* (SG) *iže* (NOM PL) *i obrětajǫtъ* (3 PL) (*Marianus, Zographensis, Assemanianus*; Matthew 7.14)
'There are few of them who find it.'

/mъnogъ/ 'many' is inflected for case, number and gender in agreement with its expressed or implied head noun:

mъnodzi (NOM PL M) *bo sǫtъ* (3 PL) *zъvanii* (NOM PL M LONG) *malo že izbъranyixъ* (GEN PL LONG) (*Marianus, Assemanianus, Zographensis* (younger); Matthew 20.16)
'for many are called, but few are chosen'

/jedinъ/ is a pronoun agreeing in case, number and gender with a head noun, and as subject takes a singular verb. Forms agreeing with /dъva/ (M), /dъvě/ (N, F) 'two' are dual, and with /trьje/ (M), /tri/ (N, F) 'three' and /četyre/ (M), /četyri/ (N, F) 'four' are plural. The numerals /pętь/ 'five', /šestь/ 'six', /sedmь/ 'seven', /osmь/ 'eight', /devętь/ 'nine', which are feminine -/i/ genitive nouns taking feminine attributes, and /desętь/ 'ten', which has either masculine or feminine agreement, govern the genitive plural (or genitive singular of a collective noun) and as subjects take either plural or singular verbs:

vьsě (NOM SG F) *sedmь umъrěšę* (3 PL) *ne ostavlьše* (NOM PL M) *čędъ* (*Marianus, Zographensis*; Luke 20.31)
'All seven died without leaving children.'

sedmь ubo bratriję (GEN SG) *bě* (3 SG) (*Marianus, Zographensis*; Luke 20.29)
'For there were seven brothers ...'

nadъ desętьjǫ (INST SG) *gradъ* (GEN PL) ... *nadъ pętijǫ* (INST SG) *gradъ* (GEN PL)
(*Marianus, Zographensis, Assemanianus*; Luke 19.17–19)
'Over ten cities ... over five cities.'

sъrĕte (3 SG) *i desętь prokaženъ* (GEN PL) *mǫžъ* (GEN PL) *iže* (NOM PL M) *stasę* (3 PL) *izdaleče*... *ne desętь li ištistišę* (3 PL) *sę* (*Marianus, Zographensis*; Luke 17.12–17)
'There met him ten leprous men who stood a long way off.... Were not ten healed?'

There are attested only two examples of /jedinъ na desęte/ 'eleven' in the nominative with a noun. In the first example below, *ediny* 'one' is the long form, and *učenikъ* could be either nominative singular or the homographic genitive plural. In the second example, the attribute and nouns are in the nominative plural and in both examples the verb is in the plural:

ediny že na desęte učenikъ idǫ (*Marianus, Assemanianus, Zographensis, Savvina kniga*; Matthew 28.16)
'But the eleven disciples went ...'

sii jedin na desęte strastotrъpьci i dobropobĕdьnii mǫčenici trudišę sę (*Suprasliensis* 271.8)
'For these eleven sufferers and triumphant martyrs strove ...'

Only one example is attested with this numeral and a noun in an oblique case:

jednĕmi (INST PL) *bo na desęte zvĕzdъ* (GEN PL) (*Suprasliensis* 389.24)
'for with eleven stars ...'

/dъva na desęte/, /oba na desęte/ 'twelve' take either, as an older pattern, a dual noun agreeing with the first element of the numeral in case and gender, or else, as a younger pattern, the numeral governs the genitive plural:

privesti dъva na desęte malomošti (ACC DU) ... *prizъva dъva na desęte* (ACC) *mǫžь* (GEN PL) *ništъ* (GEN PL) (*Suprasliensis* 121.9–12)
'To bring in twelve cripples ... he invited twelve poor men.'

Within the same clause, 'twelve' governs a dual verb, but a verb in a separate clause may be plural:

pristǫplьša (PAST ACT PART NOM DU M) *že oba na desęte rĕste* (3 DU) (*Zographensis, Marianus*; Luke 9.12)
'Having come up then, the twelve said ...'

sъtvori dъva na desęte da bǫdǫtъ (3 PL) *sъ nimь* (*Marianus, Zographensis*; Mark 3.14)
'He appointed twelve, so that they would be with him.'

The existential copula is attested in the singular:

dъva na desęte ixъ (GEN PL) *jestъ* (3 SG) (*Suprasliensis* 121.20)
'There are twelve of them.'

Attributes of 'twelve' may be dual or plural, while non-attributive pronouns are plural:

prizъvavъ oba na desęte učenika (DU) *svoě* (DU) *dastъ imъ* (PL) *vlastь ... siję* (PL) (*Zographensis, Marianus*)/ *siě* (DU) (*Assemanianus*)/ *si* (!) (*Savvina kniga*) *oba* (DU) *na desęte posъla isusъ zapovědavъ imъ* (PL) (Matthew 10.1–5)
'Having summoned his twelve disciples, he gave them power.... These twelve Jesus sent, having ordered them ...'

/trьje na desęte/ 'thirteen' and /četyre na desęte/ 'fourteen' have plural agreement for all types of form in all of the few attested examples. The equally poorly attested numerals /pętь na desęte/ 'fifteen' to /devętь na desęte/ 'nineteen' show government of the genitive plural, and take plural pronouns:

pętь na desęte stadii (GEN PL) (*Marianus, Zographensis, Assemanianus*; John 11.18)
'fifteen leagues'

oni (NOM PL) *osmь na desęte na ńeže* (NOM PL) *pade stľъpъ* (*Zographensis, Marianus*; Luke 13.4)
'Those eighteen on whom there fell a pillar ...'

/dъva desęti/ 'twenty' to /devętь desętъ/ 'ninety' are formed with the element 'ten' in the required number, dual ('twenty'), plural ('thirty', 'forty') or genitive plural ('fifty' to 'ninety'). Any following unit number is conjoined by /i/ 'and':

sъkonьčašę (3 PL) *že sę svętii* (PL) *četyre desęte* (PL) *i dъva mǫčenika* (DU) (*Suprasliensis* 65.1)
'There met their end the holy forty-two martyrs ...'

In this example, the verb and attributive adjective are plural, but the conjoined /dъva/ requires a dual noun.

A noun preceded by a conjoined numeral requiring the genitive plural is either governed in the genitive plural or else agrees in case with the numeral:

o devęti desętъ i o devęti (LOC) *pravьdьnikъ* (GEN PL) (*Zographensis*)/ *o devęti desętъ i devęti* (LOC) *pravedъnicěxъ* (LOC PL) (*Marianus*) (Luke 15.7)
'concerning ninety-nine just men'

Similarly, when there is no conjoined numeral, the noun is either in the genitive plural or else agrees in case:

četyrьmi desęty (INST PL) *dьnii* (GEN PL) ... *četyrьmi desęty dьnьmi* (INST PL) (*Suprasliensis* 92.7–9)
'With forty days ... with forty days.'

Of the other plural forms agreeing with these numerals, attributes may be genitive plural:

ěvi gospodь i iněxъ (GEN PL) *sedmь* (ACC) *desętъ i posъla ję* (ACC PL) (*Marianus, Zographensis*; Luke 10.1)
'The Lord appointed yet another seventy and sent them ...'

vъzvratišę (3 PL) *že sę sedmь* (NOM) *desętii* (NOM PL LONG) (*Marianus, Zographensis, Assemanianus*; Luke 10.17)
'The seventy returned ...'

As in this example, the rarely attested long form /desętiji/ 'ten' is in the nominative plural in the compound numerals.
/sъto/ 'hundred' governs the genitive plural:

sъtomь (INST SG) *měrь* (GEN PL) (*Marianus, Zographensis*; Luke 16.6)
'with a hundred measures'

In /dъvě sъtě/ 'two hundred' to /devętь sъtъ/ 'nine hundred' the unit numeral, in the nominative and accusative, has the normal patterns of agreement. In the oblique cases, both elements of the numeral are in the required case, while a noun collocated with these numerals is either genitive plural or else agrees in case and number with the numeral:

dъvěma sъtoma (DAT DU) *penędzъ* (GEN PL) (*Marianus, Zographensis, Assemanianus*; John 6.7)
'two hundred pence'

trьmь sъtomъ (DAT PL) *sьcěni dinaremъ* (DAT PL) (*Suprasliensis* 425.24)
'He valued it at three hundred dinars.'

/tysǫšti/, /tysęšti/ 'thousand' is governed by other numerals either in the genitive plural or else agrees in number and case:

sъ desętijǫ (INST SG) *tysǫštъ* (GEN PL) (*Marianus*)/*sъ desętijǫ* (INST SG) *tysęštǫ* (for /tysęštejǫ/ INST SG) (*Zographensis*) ... *sъ dъvěma desętьma* (INST DU) *tysǫštama* (INST DU) (Luke 14.31)
'With ten thousand ... with twenty thousand.'

A verb may be either singular or plural:

vъzleže (3 SG) *ubo mǫžь čislomь ěko pętь tysǫštь* (*Zographensis, Marianus, Assemanianus*; John 6.10)
'for there dined men in number of about five thousand'

napitani (PL) *byšę* (3 PL) *pętь tysǫštъ* (*Suprasliensis* 428.25)
'There were fed five thousand.'

/tъma/ 'ten thousand' governs the genitive plural:

tъmojǫ (INST SG) *talantъ* (GEN PL) (*Marianus*; Matthew 18.24)
'ten thousand talents'

From the data attested of quantifiers with collective nouns, the following
are of special interest:

sъ inĕmi (INST PL) *šestijǫ* (INST) *bratiję* (GEN SG) (*Suprasliensis* 145.30)
'with six other brothers'

množьstvu (DAT SG) *že bratьję* (GEN SG F) *otъ vĕštavъšemъ* (PAST ACT PART DAT PL
M SHORT) (*Suprasliensis* 113.22)
'After many of the brethren had answered ...'

This last example is a dative-absolute construction.

5 Lexis

5.1 General composition of the word-stock
There are very few borrowings, apart from many proper nouns: a few
common nouns, and very few verbs taken over directly from the Greek
sources or calqued on them.

5.2 Patterns of borrowings
Apart from Greek words and calques resulting from the actual translating
of the Greek sources there are a few older borrowings from Greek, such as
/korablь/ 'boat' and /kucija/ 'sweetmeat'. Germanic accounts for the
largest group of borrowings, about forty in number, for instance
/kъnędzь/ 'ruler, prince', /xlĕbъ/ 'bread'. Next come Romance, for
instance /kotъka/ 'anchor', /krabьjь/ 'box', and Turkic, for instance
/bolarinъ/ 'nobleman', /synъ/, genitive /syna/ 'tower'; for each of these
two sources about twenty examples are attested. There are also a few loans
from Iranian.

5.3 Incorporation of borrowings
Not only borrowed nouns, but also nouns taken from the Greek sources,
are declined and may have adjectives derived from their stems. Thus one
finds /kъnędzь/ 'ruler, prince', genitive /kъnędza/, adjective /kъnęžь/,
/xlĕbъ/ 'bread', genitive /xlĕba/, adjective /xlĕbьnъ/, and also /isusъ/
'Jesus', genitive /isusa/, dative /isusu/ and /isusovi/, adjective /isusovъ/.
Very few nouns are indeclinable, and then only optionally, for instance

/pasxa/ 'Passover' is attested not only as indeclinable, but also as a feminine noun (genitive /pasxy/). Borrowed verbs are usually conjugated in both aspects, for instance perfective /kupiti/, imperfective /kupovati/ 'buy', from Gothic. Verbs taken from Greek sources are conjugated, but are usually bi-aspectual, and may have more than one type of suffix or spelling, for instance /vlasvimisati/, /vlasvimĺati/, /vlasfymĺati/ 'blaspheme'.

5.4 Lexical fields

5.4.1 Colour terms
/bělъ/ 'white', /črьnъ/ 'black', /črьmьnъ/, /črьvĺenъ/ 'red', /zelenъ/ 'green', /plavъ/ 'yellow', /praprǫdьnъ/ 'purple', /sěrъ/ 'grey'.

5.4.2 Body parts
/glava/ 'head', /oko/ 'eye', /nozdri/ 'nostrils' ('nose' is not attested), /uxo/ 'ear', /usta/ 'mouth' (N PL), /vlasъ/ 'hair', /šija/ 'neck', /rǫka/ 'arm, hand', /prьstъ/ 'finger', /noga/ 'leg, foot', /nožьnъ prьstъ/ 'toe', /prьsi/ 'chest' (F PL), /srьdьce/ 'heart', /zaždь/ 'anus'.

5.4.3 Kinship terms
/mati/ 'mother', /otьcь/ 'father', /sestra/ 'sister', /bratrъ/ 'brother' (as plural, the feminine singular collective /bratrьja/ is used), /žena/ 'wife' (also 'woman'), /mǫžь/ 'husband' (also 'man') /dъšti/ 'daughter', /synъ/ 'son'. The term for 'aunt' is attested only once, used figuratively and pejoratively in the diminutive, /tetъka/ (*Suprasliensis* 133.11).

6 Variation within Old Church Slavonic

As indicated at several points in this chapter, there is both chronological and geographic variation within Old Church Slavonic, and for details reference should be made to the preceding sections, especially sections 2 and 3. Chronological variation can be seen in that certain forms and constructions can be characterized as older or younger than others. Old Church Slavonic is basically a Balkan Slavonic language, though even within this characterization there is geographical variation between Eastern (Bulgarian) and Western (Macedonian) forms; the use of the language for missionary activity in Great Moravia shows up in the occurrence of some West Slavonic features, even in the major canonical texts. Other local and later features characterize the later recensions of Church Slavonic (see section 1) but do not form part of Old Church Slavonic.

References

Arnim, B. von (1930) *Studien zum altbulgarischen Psalterium Sinaiticum* (*Veröffentlichungen des Slavischen Instituts an der Friedrich-Wilhelms-Universität Berlin*, vol. 3), Berlin (reprinted 1960, Nendeln: Kraus).

Birnbaum, Henrik (1958) *Untersuchungen zu den Zukunftsumschreibungen mit dem Infinitiv im Altkirchenslavischen* (*Acta Universitatis Stockholmiensis, Etudes de philologie slave*, 6), Stockholm: Almqvist & Wiksell.

Brodowksa-Honowska, Maria (1960) *Słowotwórstwo przymiotnika w języku staro-cerkiewno-słowiańskim*, Cracow: Ossolineum.

Diels, Paul (1963) *Altkirchenslavische Grammatik*, 2nd edn, Heidelberg: Carl Winter.

Dobrovsky, Josef (1822) *Institutiones linguae slavicae dialecti veteris*, 2nd edn, Vienna: Schmid.

Flier, Michael S. (1974) *Aspects of Nominal Determination in Old Church Slavic*, The Hague: Mouton.

Hermelin, E. (1935) *Über den Gebrauch der Präsens-Partizipien von perfektiven Verben im Altkirchenslavischen*, Uppsala: Almqvist & Wiksell.

Horálek, Karel (1954) *Evangeliáře a čtveroevangelia*, Prague: SPN.

Huntley, David (1989) 'Grammatical and lexical features in number and gender agreement in Old Bulgarian', *Palaeobulgarica* (*Старобългаристика*) 13, 4: 21–32.

Jagić, Vatroslav (1913) *Entstehungsgeschichte der kirchenslavischen Sprache*, Berlin: Weidmann.

—— (1919, 1922) *Zum altkirchenslavischen Apostolus*, 3 vols (*Akademie der Wissenschaften in Wien. Philosophisch-historische Klasse. Sitzungsberichte*, 191.2, 193.1, 197.2), Vienna: Alfred Hölder.

Kurz, Josef (ed.) (1958–) *Slovník jazyka staroslověnského*, Prague: ČAV.

Leskien, August (1969) *Handbuch der altbulgarischen (altkirchenslavischen) Sprache*, 9th edn, Heidelberg: Carl Winter.

Lunt, Horace G. (1974) *Old Church Slavonic Grammar*, 6th edn, The Hague: Mouton.

—— (1977) 'Limitations of Old Church Slavonic in representing Greek', in Bruce M. Metzger (ed.), *The Early Versions of the New Testament*, Oxford: Clarendon Press, 431–42.

Meillet, Antoine (1897) *Recherches sur l'emploi du génitif-accusatif en vieux-slave* (*Bibliothèque de l'Ecole des Hautes Etudes. Sciences philologiques et historiques*, 115), Paris: Bouillon.

—— (1902, 1905) *Etudes sur l'étymologie et le vocabulaire du vieux slave*, 2 vols (*Bibliothèque de l'Ecole des Hautes Etudes. Sciences philologiques et historiques*, 139), Paris: Bouillon. (Part 2 reprinted 1961, Paris: Champion.)

Metzger, Bruce M. (1977) 'The Old Church Slavonic version', in Bruce M. Metzger (ed.), *The Early Versions of the New Testament*, Oxford: Clarendon Press, 394–431.

Moszyński, L. (1975) *Język Kodeksu Zografskiego*, vol. 1, Wrocław: Ossolineum.

Růžička, Rudolf (1963) *Das syntaktische System der altkirchenslavischen Partizipien und sein Verhältnis zum Griechischen* (*Veröffentlichungen des Instituts für Slawistik* 27), Berlin: Deutsche Akademie der Wissenschaften in Berlin.

Sadnik, L. and Aizetmüller, R. (1955) *Handwörterbuch zu den altkirchenslavischen Texten*, Heidelberg: Carl Winter.

Stanislav, J. (1933) 'Datív absolutný v starej cirkevnej slovančine', *Byzantoslavica* 5: 1–112.

Trubetzkoy, Nikolai S. *Altkirchenslavische Grammatik*, 2nd edn, Graz: Böhlau.
Vaillant, André (1964) *Manuel du vieux slave*, 2nd edn, Paris: Institut d'Etudes Slaves.
van Wijk, Nicolaas (1931) *Geschichte der altkirchenslavischen Sprache*, Berlin: de Gruyter.
Večerka, Radoslav (1989) *Altkirchenslavische (altbulgarische) Syntax*, vol. I: *Die lineare Satzorganisation* (Monumenta Linguae Slavicae Dialecti Veteris. Fontes et Dissertationes, 27), Freiburg i. Br.: U.W. Weiher.

Бунина, И.К. (1959) *Система времен старославянского глагола*, Москва: АН СССР.
Курц, Й. и др. (ред.) (1958) *Исследования по синтаксису старославянского языка*, Prague: ČAV.
Львов, А.С. (1966) *Очерки по лексике памятников старославянской письменности*, Москва: Наука.
Селищев, А.М. (1951, 1952) *Старославянский язык*, Москва: Учпедгиз.

5 Bulgarian

Ernest A. Scatton

1 Introduction

Bulgarian is the national language of the Republic of Bulgaria – the native language of its ethnic Slavonic majority. The estimated population of Bulgaria in 1986 was close to 9 million, nearly 85 per cent of whom were recorded as ethnic Bulgarians. Modern Bulgarian directly continues the Slavonic dialects spoken in the eastern Balkan Peninsula from the time of the arrival of Slavs in the middle of the first millennium AD. It is first recorded in the earliest Slavonic, that is Old Church Slavonic (Old Bulgarian), manuscripts.

Four periods are customarily distinguished in the history of Bulgarian: (1) the **prehistoric period** (essentially Proto-Slavonic), from the time of the Slavonic invasion of the eastern Balkans to the Cyrillo-Methodian mission to Moravia in the ninth century; (2) **Old Bulgarian** – the ninth to the eleventh centuries, reflected in Old Church Slavonic manuscripts; (3) **Middle Bulgarian** – from the end of the eleventh to the beginning of the fifteenth century, a time of rich literary activity and major structural innovation; (4) **Modern Bulgarian** – from the end of Middle Bulgarian to the present, including the years of Ottoman domination (early fifteenth century to 1878).

While the early stages of a number of major innovations are perhaps attested in Old Church Slavonic texts, the most significant changes in the evolution of Modern Bulgarian appear to have begun in the Middle and early Modern periods. Details of these changes are not reflected systematically in written records. The penetration of vernacular features into the written language was impeded for a number of reasons, most importantly conservative scribal attitudes and various **orthographic** reforms which artificially normalized scribal practices during Middle Bulgarian.

Written records from the first two centuries of Modern Bulgarian are quite limited owing to the Ottoman conquest, which severely curtailed the rich literary activity of earlier years. After approximately 1600 – the time of the beginning of the Bulgarian Възраждане/Văzráždane 'Renaissance' – increasingly numerous vernacular intrusions into popular texts suggest that the major changes differentiating Modern Bulgarian from its predecessor were essentially complete. In so far as continuing conservative orthographic conventions make textual evidence problematical, we can only reconstruct the general lines of the actual processes of these changes.

The form of the modern Bulgarian **literary** language began to take shape only towards the middle of the nineteenth century. Earlier, within the prolific literary activity that developed from the beginning of the nineteenth century, three different orthographic positions competed with one another: (1) **conservative**, advocating a modern literary language based on the Russian/Serbian recension of Church Slavonic used in the Bulgarian Orthodox Church at that time; (2) **progressive**, calling for a literary language based on the speech of one or the other of the most influential regions of nineteenth-century Bulgaria; (3) **intermediate**, advocating use of those features shared by *all* regional dialects plus Church Slavonic features whenever the dialects differed. The emergence of north-eastern Bulgaria in the middle of the nineteenth century as the nation's cultural, economic and political centre led to wide acceptance of north-eastern dialects as the basis for the literary language. Of these dialects, that of Tărnovo, one of north-eastern Bulgaria's most important cities and the country's first modern capital, was taken as the model for the emerging literary language. On 5 February 1899, the Bulgarian Ministry of Education officially codified the modern literary language with the adoption of the first orthographic system sanctioned for the entire nation. Reformed to any significant extent only once, in February 1945, this system remains in use today.

Despite the fact that the modern Bulgarian literary language reflects the north-eastern dialect of Tărnovo, it incorporates a number of non-eastern, western features (the major dialect division of Bulgarian is east versus west; see section 6). Originally, 'westernisms' were due to adoption of a number of Church Slavonic features coincidentally identical to features of western Bulgarian. However, with the shift of the Bulgarian capital from Tărnovo to Sofia (in the centre of western Bulgaria) in 1879 and the latter's rapid growth into the nation's single most influential urban centre, literary Bulgarian began a gradual process of accommodation to the native dialect of the new capital. As a result, the official literary language – described in standard reference works (Георгиева, Станков/Georgieva, Stankov 1983; Тилков, Бояджиев/Tilkov, Bojadžiev 1981; Граматика/ Gramatika 1982–3; Пашов, Първев/Pašov, Părvev 1979; Romanski/ Романски 1955–9; Чолакова/Čolakova 1977–90) – represents no naturally occurring regional dialect. Rather, it is an artificial hybrid, learned to a greater or lesser extent by all Bulgarians in the course of their schooling.

Prescriptively correct Bulgarian is **spoken** only under the most formal circumstances and only by speakers particularly concerned with proper usage. In less formal circumstances, non-literary features characteristic of speakers' regional dialects frequently occur. The speech of many educated

Bulgarians represents a continuum, with the colloquial, non-literary speech of their native regions at one end and the learned, literary standard at the other. In actual usage, speakers move back and forth between these two poles, incorporating, to various degrees, non-literary features into their formal speech and vice versa. Since the Second World War, owing to the rapid growth of the population and cultural prestige of Sofia, the westernized conversational speech of educated natives of the city has gained increasing prestige and has come to be regarded by some linguists as a (if not the) standard spoken variant of the literary language.

2 Phonology

2.1 Segmental phoneme inventory

Table 5.1 Vowel phonemes

	Front	Central	Back
High	i		u
Mid	e	ă	o
Low		a	

/i e u o/ are relatively lax. /ă/ is tenser and higher than [a], but lower than Russian [ɨ]. Word-initial vowels are preceded by a glottal stop.

Unstressed vowels are shorter and weaker than their stressed counterparts, and approach one another pair-wise, /i‹›e ă‹›a u‹›o/, without merging completely – at least not in careful literary speech (Граматика/ Gramatika 1: 132). Unstressed word-final vowels are often voiceless.

Vowels are **nasalized** before nasal consonants followed by fricatives; often the nasal consonant is lost: óнзи/ónzi [ǫ́nzi] ~ [ǫ́zi] 'that (M SG)'.

In native Bulgarian words vowel sequences occur only across morpheme boundaries: знáеш/znáeš /znà-e-š/ 'know-PRS-2 SG'. In borrowings they are common: теáтър/teàtăr 'theatre'.

/t d s z c l/ are **alveo-dental**, /n r/ **alveolar**. The acute accent (´) marks **palatalization** in labials and alveolars. Alveo-palatal obstruents are weakly palatalized. Palatalized labials are pronounced by many Bulgarians as sequences of [Cj]; palatalized alveo-dentals, especially /n' l' r'/, may shift towards alveo-palatals.

/n/ has a **velar** allophone, [ŋ], before velars: гáтанка/gàtanka [gàtaŋka] 'riddle'.

/l/ is markedly **velarized** except before front vowels.

/c/ and /x/ have voiced allophones [ʒ] and [ɣ] before voiced obstru-

Table 5.2   Consonant phonemes

	Bilabial	Labio-dental	Alveo-dental	Alveo-palatal	Palatal	Velar
Stops	p p′		t t′		k′	k
	b b′		d d′		g′	g
Fricatives		f f′	s s′	š		x
		v v′	z z′	ž		
Affricates			c c′	č		
				ǯ		
Nasals	m m′		n n′			
Laterals			l l′			
Trills			r r′			
Glide				j		

ents (except /v v′/; see below). /x/ has a palatal allophone [x′] before front vowels (see below).

Some inventories of Bulgarian phonemes include /x′ ʒ ʒ′/. However, /x′ ʒ′/ occur only in foreign proper nouns, for example, Хюм/Xjùm /x′ùm/ from English *Hume*, Ядзя/Jàdzja /jàʒ′a/ from Polish *Jadzia*. Besides foreign proper nouns, /ʒ/ occurs in a small number of non-literary, dialectal words which, if used in the literary language, regularly replace /ʒ/ by /z/: дзифт/dzift ~ зифт/zift 'tar'.

Obstruents contrast **voice** before sonorants and /v v′/: боб/bòb /bòp/ 'bean' versus поп/pòp /pòp/ 'priest', твой/tvòj /tvòj/ 'your-SG (M SG)' versus двор/dvòr /dvòr/ 'yard'. Otherwise they are voiceless word-finally or before voiceless obstruents, and voiced before voiced obstruents.

Palatalized and **non-palatalized** consonants contrast only before non-front vowels. Moreover, in native words they contrast before /ă u o/ only across morpheme boundaries: ходя/xòdja /xòd′-ă/ '(I) walk' (= 'walk-1 SG') versus хода/xòda /xòd-ă/ 'the course' (= 'course-the'), бял/bjàl /b′àl/ 'white (M SG)' versus бал/bàl /bàl/ 'ball (= dance)'. Otherwise – word-finally, before consonants or before front vowels – they are non-palatalized.

Palatals and **velars** contrast before non-front vowels; palatals occur here only in words of foreign origin: гол/gòl /gòl/ 'naked (M SG)' versus гьол/ gjòl /g′òl/ 'puddle' (from Turkish). Otherwise palatals are regular before front vowels, velars elsewhere.

After vowels /j/ occurs at the end of words or before consonants (мой/ mòj 'my (M SG)', дайте/dàjte '(you-PL) give!'); before non-front vowels it occurs word-initially or *after* vowels (язва/jàzva 'ulcer', моя/mòja 'my (F SG)'). It neither follows consonants, nor precedes front vowels – except word-initially in a few borrowings (йезуит/jezuìt 'Jesuit').

Geminate consonants occur only across morpheme boundaries: отдел/

otdèl /od-dèl/ 'department, section' (= 'of-part'). Consonant clusters are subject to other constraints (Граматика/Gramatika 1: 135ff.).

The letters of the Bulgarian alphabet and their standard transliteration according to the Bulgarian Academy of Sciences are shown in table 5.3.

Table 5.3   Bulgarian alphabet

а	a	к	k	ф	f
б	b	л	l	х	h [here transliterated x]
в	v	м	m	ц	c
г	g	н	n	ч	č
д	d	о	o	ш	š
е	e	п	p	щ	št
ж	ž	р	r	ъ	â [here transliterated ă]
з	z	с	s	ь	j [here transliterated ′; occurs only in ьо/′о]
и	i	т	t	ю	ju
й	j	у	u	я	ja

Except for the details that follow, orthographic spellings give a close approximation of phonemic representations (tables 5.1 and 5.2). However:

1   щ denotes /št/. /ʒ/ is written дж/dž. To the extent that it occurs at all, /ʒ/ is written дз/dz.
2   Spellings show the **underlying** (morphophonemic) voicing of obstruents; compare 'alive' M SG жив/živ /žíf/ versus F SG жива/živa /žíva/.
3   **Palatal** and **palatalized** consonants before non-front vowels are indicated by я (for /a/ *and* /ă/), ю (/u/), ьо (/o/). Two of these symbols, я and ю, also indicate /j/ followed by /a ă/ and /u/, respectively (see examples above). Otherwise, /j/ is written й: мой/ мòj 'my (M SG)'.
4   The letter я is ambiguous. Most frequently it represents /a/ after palatals, palatalized consonants or /j/. It is also used in two morphological categories for /ă/ after palatalized consonants or /j/: (a) **masculine singular definite article**, for example, денят/denjàt /den′àt/ 'the day (SBJ)'; (b) **first person singular/third person plural present tense forms of first-/second-conjugation verbs**: хòдя/xòdja /xòd′ă/ 'I walk', броят/brojàt /brojàt/ 'they count'.
5   Similarly, a is ambiguous; in two categories it marks /ă/, not /a/: (a) **objective** (not subjective) **masculine singular definite article of nouns**: градà/gradà /gradắ/ 'the city (M SG OBJ)'; (b) **first person singular/ third person plural present forms of first-/second-conjugation verbs**: пекàт/pekàt /pekăt/ 'they bake'.

/ă/ is the regular Bulgarian reflex of PSl. *ǫ and 'strong' *ъ: *pǫtь пѫт/ pǎt 'road', *zъlъ зъл/zǎl 'evil (M SG)'. Later in the history of Bulgarian, /ă/ was inserted to break up stem-final consonant clusters terminating in liquids or nasals ('epenthetic ǎ'): *dobrъ добър/dobǎr 'good (M SG)' (compare F SG добра́/dobrá). /e/ is the regular reflex of PSl. *ę and strong *ь: *pętь пе́т/pét 'five', *dьnь де́н/dén 'day'. Weak *ъ/ь were generally lost: *zъla зла́/zlá 'evil (F SG)', *dьni дни́/dni 'days'. However, weak *ъ/ь remained in a number of monosyllabic roots (Velcheva 1988: 146–8): дъно/dǎno 'bottom' from *dъno, пе́сове/pésove 'dogs' plural of пе́с/pés from *pьsъ. There is a small number of examples in which PSl. *ь, weak or strong, gives /ă/ ('Umlaut of jers', Velcheva 1988: 136–9): *pьnь gives пъ́н/pǎn 'stump', *tьma gives тъма́/tǎmá 'darkness'.

Bulgarian has lengthened and metathesized reflexes for Proto-Slavonic liquid diphthongs with *o/e:

*gordъ	гра́д/grǎd 'city'
*bolto	бла́то/blǎto 'swamp'
*bergъ	бря́г/brjǎg 'shore'
*melko	мля́ко/mljǎko 'milk'

Proto-Slavonic liquid diphthongs with *ъ/ь + l/r merged with sequences of *l/r + ъ/ь with loss of the distinction between ъ and ь. Subsequently /ă/ developed in all instances, before or after the liquid depending on the following consonantal environment: liquid–vowel before two consonants, vowel–liquid before consonant–vowel. This is the origin of the **metathesis** alternation described in section 2.3 (see examples there).

PSl. *tj (and *kt + front vowel), *dj gave /št žd/:

*světjь	свещ/svešt 'candle'
*noktь	но́щ/nóšt 'night'
*medja	межда́/meždá 'boundary'

Bulgarian **word stress** is **dynamic**: stressed syllables are louder and longer and have a higher fundamental frequency than unstressed syllables. Stress is **free**: it may fall on any syllable of a polysyllabic word. It is **mobile**: its position may vary in inflection and derivation. Compare:

'city'   SG гра́д/grǎd : SG DEF градъ́т/gradǎt : PL градове́/gradové
'bridge' SG мо́ст/móst : SG DEF мо́стът/móstǎt : PL мосто́ве/mostóve

Stress is **distinctive**: въ́лна/vǎlna 'wool' versus вълна́/vǎlná 'wave'. For stress patterns of major lexical categories see section 3.

Simple Bulgarian words have a single stressed syllable. **Compound** words may carry a **secondary** stress, or even two stresses of equal prominence; for example, на́й-добъ́р/nǎj-dobǎr 'best' (= 'most-good'), сѝлнотóков/sìlnotókov 'high-tension (M SG ADJ)'.

Bulgarian distinguishes three small classes of inherently stressless **clitics**: **proclitics**, **enclitics** and **variable clitics** (either enclitic or proclitic depending on syntactic conditions). See 4.1 for details.

2.2 Morphophonemic alternations inherited from Proto-Slavonic

1 **Velar ~ alveo-palatal**: /k g x sk zg/ ~ /č ž š št žd/ – reflexes of the Proto-Slavonic first regressive palatalization of velars before front vowels and *j*. Extremely common in Modern Bulgarian, the alternation is no longer conditioned solely by phonological factors. In inflection, it is limited to three categories: (1) a few masculine **vocatives in /-e/**: 'god' SG бóг/bóg, VOC бóже/bóže; (2) certain types of **first-conjugation verbs**: 'weep' 1 SG PRS плáча/pláča, 1 SG AOR плáках/plákax; (3) two anomalous **neuter plurals**: 'eye' SG окó/okó, PL очѝ/očì and 'ear' SG ухó/uxó, PL ушѝ/ušì. In derivation, it occurs in diverse nominal and verbal formations; for example, млякó/mljàko 'milk' : млéчен/mléčen 'milky, of milk (M SG)', глýх/glùx 'deaf (M SG)' : глушéя/glušéja '(I) grow deaf'.

2 **Velar ~ dental**: /k g x/ ~ /c z s/ – reflexes of the Proto-Slavonic second and third palatalizations of velars. The alternation is regular (though with exceptions) in the plural of masculine nouns with polysyllabic stems, for example, 'language, tongue' SG езѝк/ezìk, PL езѝци/ezìci. It occurs in the plural of two common feminine nouns, 'hand, arm' SG ръкá/răkà, PL ръцѐ/răcè and 'foot, leg' (dialectal) SG ногá/nogà, PL нозѐ/nozè. In derivation it is uncommon; for example, мáлко/málko 'little, few': малцинствó/malcinstvó 'minority'.

The interaction of the two preceding alternations creates a small number of alternations of /c z/ with /č ž/; for example, 'old man' SG стáрец/stárec : VOC стáрче/stárče.

3 **Jotation** reflects the influence of PSl. *j* on preceding dentals and labials (velars above):

labials: /p b v m/ ~ /pl′ bl′ vl′ ml′/
dentals: /t d st s z n l r/ ~ /št žd št š ž n′ l′ r′/

Though once widespread in Old Bulgarian, these alternations are now extremely limited. In inflection, only the alternations /s z l r/ ~ /š ž l′ r′/ are preserved in the paradigms of certain first-conjugation verbs: 'write' 1 SG PRS пѝша/piša, 1 SG AOR пѝсах/pisax. In derivation, all of the alternations occur in isolated, unproductive formations. All examples of alternating labials, most of alternating /s z/ and many of /t d st/ are in borrowings from Russian or Russian Church Slavonic: 'send' 1 SG AOR PRFV прáтих/prátix, 1 SG AOR IMPFV прáщах/práštax; дáвя/dávja '(I) drown (ITR)', давле́ние/davlénie 'pressure (from Russian or Russian Church Slavonic)'; коза́/kozá 'goat', ко́жа/kóža 'skin'.

Rare examples of PSl. *kt/gt before front vowels, which develop like *tj, are included here; for example, мо́га/móga '(I) can', мо́щ/mòšt 'power'.

This set of alternations was radically reshaped by two historical developments: (a) the simplification of sequences of labial and /l'/ to palatalized labials (the loss of 'epenthetic l' originally arising in Proto-Slavonic from labial + j) and (b) the substitution of /t' d' s' z'/ for /št žd š ž/, respectively. The result is the alternation of homorganic palatalized and nonpalatalized   consonants,   /p b f v m t d s z/   ~   /p' b' f' v' m' t' d' s' z'/, in place of the earlier alternations. The newer alternations are common in paradigms of certain first- and second-conjugation verbs; for example, 'drip' 1 SG PRS ка́пя/kápja, 1 SG AOR ка́пах/kápax; 'walk' 1 SG PRS хо́дя/xódja, 1 SG AOR хо́дих/xódix. They are also common in verbal derivation; for example, 'turn' 1 SG PRS PRFV извъртя́/izvärtjá, 1 SG PRS IMPFV извъртя́вам/izvärtjávam.

4 **о ~ е**: This alternation is a vestige of the Proto-Slavonic change of back vowels to front vowels after alveo-palatal consonants or the reflexes of the third palatalization of velars. Compare: градове́/gradové 'cities', but бро́еве/bróeve 'numbers' (SG бро́й/brój). The alternation is nonproductive and lexically limited, and allows numerous alternatives; for example, змѐйове/zméjove ~ змѐеве/zméeve 'dragons'.

5 **Consonant truncation**: Consonants are deleted before other consonants or at the end of a word. This alternation comprises a number of special cases. (a) /j/ is deleted in the inflection of first-conjugation verbs which show stem-final /j/ in the present tense; truncation here is regular and productive, though morphologically conditioned: 'drink' 1 SG PRS пия́/pija, 1 SG AOR пих/pix (but compare 2 PL IMP пийте/pijte). (b) Stem-final /t d/ are regularly deleted before /l/ in the aorist participle of first-conjugation verbs: 'read' 1 SG PRS чета́/četá, M SG AOR PART чел/čel. (c) /n s t/ alternate with Ø in singular and plural forms of some neuter nouns: 'time' SG вре́ме/vréme, PL времена́/vremená; 'taxi' SG такси́/taksi, PL такси́та/taksita. The alternations occur sporadically elsewhere in inflection and derivation: зна́я/znája '(I) know', зна́к/znák 'sign'.

6 **Vowel truncation**: Stem-final vowels alternate with Ø in verbal inflection (the relevant stem elements are italicized in the following transliterated examples): 'walk' 1 SG PRS хо́дя/*xódj*a, 1 SG AOR хо́дих/*xódix*; 'write' 1 SG PRS пи́ша/*pi*š*a, 1 SG AOR пи́сах/*pisax*.

7 **/t/ ~ /s/**: This alternation is limited to a few derivationally related items, such as стра́дам/strádam '(I) suffer', стра́ст/strást 'passion'.

8 **Ablaut**: Vestiges of Proto-Slavonic ablaut are preserved in derivation, particularly aspectual derivation; for example, бера́/berá '(I) gather', и́збор/ízbor 'selection'; 'die' 1 SG PRS PRFV умра́/umrá, 1 SG PRS IMPFV уми́рам/umíram. A few examples occur in verbal inflection: 'gather' 1 SG PRS бера́/berá, 1 SG AOR бра́х/bráx.

2.3 Morphophonemic alternations resulting from changes after Proto-Slavonic

Here three types are distinguished with respect to the conditions of their application.

1 General, phonologically conditioned, optional alternations. In casual speech these apply across word boundaries as well as within words.

(a) **CC ~ C**: Geminate consonants, which arise principally across morpheme boundaries (see above), alternate with their single counterparts: отту́к/ottúk /ottúk ~ otúk/ 'from here'.

(b) **alveo-dental ~ alveo-palatal**: /t d s z c/ ~ /č ǯ š ž č/, respectively, before /č ǯ š ž/: безжи́знен/bezžíznen /bezžíznen ~ bežžíznen/, and with reduction of geminate /žž/ /bežíznen/ 'lifeless (M SG)'.

(c) **ST ~ S**: /s z š ž/ before a word boundary or other consonant, /st zd št žd/ otherwise; for example, мо́щ/móšt /móšt ~ móš/ 'power', 'powerful' M SG мо́щен/móšten /móšten/ and F SG мо́щна/móštna /móštna ~ móšna/.

(d) **E ~ J**: unstressed /e/ and /i/ contiguous to a lower, usually stressed, vowel become /j/; thus, материа́л/materiál /materiál ~ materjál/ 'material', баща́ и́/baštá ì /baštái ~ baštáj/ 'her father' (= 'father her-DAT'). Similarly, /u o/ become [w]: воа́л/voál [voáł ~ vwáł] 'veil'. Sequences of consonant and [j]/[w] of this source are often pronounced as palatalized or labialized consonants: [mater'ál], [vwał].

2 General, phonologically conditioned, but obligatory alternations.

(a) **Word-final devoicing**: Word-final voiceless obstruents alternate with voiced obstruents before non-obstruents. Compare 'city' M SG гра́д/grád /grát/ and PL градове́/gradové /gradové/. While obstruents devoice before enclitics (*except* the **definite article**), they do not devoice at the end of prepositions; compare: гра́д ли/grád li /grátli/ 'a city?' (compare града́т/gradát/gradát/ 'the city') and под липи́те/pod lipíte /podlipíte/ 'under the lindens'.

(b) **Voicing assimilation in clusters**: A voiced obstruent alternates with a voiceless obstruent before a voiceless obstruent; a voiceless obstruent alternates with a voiced obstruent before a voiced obstruent. For

example, 'sweet' M SG сладък/slådăk /slådäk/ ~ F SG сладка/
slådka /slåtka/, сват/svåt /svåt/ 'matchmaker' ~ сватба/svåtba
/svådba/ 'wedding'. The same alternation occurs between fully
stressed words and clitics, and in colloquial speech between fully
stressed words as well: от баба/ot båba /odbåba/ 'from grandmother', без това/bez tovå /bestovå/ 'without this (N SG)'. The alternation applies allophonically to /c x/; for example, четох ги/čétox gi
/čétoɣg'i/ '(I) read (AOR) them'. Presumably inherited from Proto-
Slavonic, the alternation became much more frequent with the loss of
weak *ъ/ь.

/v v'/ followed by sonorants do not cause preceding voiceless
obstruents to become voiced: сват/svåt /svåt/ 'matchmaker'; but от
вдовицата/ot vdovicata /odvdovicata/ 'from the widow'. Between a
voiceless obstruent and a sonorant /v v'/ are optionally voiceless:
/svåt ~ sfåt/.

(c) **Velar ~ palatal**: /k' g'/ before front vowels ~ /k g/ elsewhere (the
rule applies allophonically to /x/); for instance, 'book' F SG книга/
kniga /kniga/ ~ PL книги/knigi /knig'i/. It occurs across word
boundaries in casual speech. The alternation arose after the change of
PSl. *y to i, well after the velar palatalizations of Proto-Slavonic.

(d) **C' ~ C**: Palatalized consonants before non-front vowels alternate with
non-palatalized consonants elsewhere. This alternation is the result of
relatively recent changes which eliminated palatalized consonants
before front vowels, consonants, and word boundaries, as in 'land' F SG
земя/zemjå : PL земи/zemi : земна/zémna 'earthly, earthen (F SG)' :
земляк/zemljåk 'countryman'; 'blue' F SG синя/sinja : N SG синьо/
sin'o : M SG син/sin : PL сини/sini 'blue'.

(e) **/i/ ~ Ø**: /j/ before back vowels, consonants or word boundaries alternates with Ø before front vowels; for example, M SG 'my' мой/mój
versus PL мои/mói. This alternation is perhaps optional (Маслов/
Maslov 1981: 51).

(f) **/j/ ~ C'/**: Root-initial /j/ alternates with palatalization of prefix-final
consonant; thus, ям/jåm '(I) eat' but обядвам/objådvam
/ob'ådvam/ '(I) dine'.

(g) **/s/ ~ Ø**: /s/ alternates with Ø between /št st č š ž/ and /k/. This
alternation occurs only in adjectives with the derivational suffix /-sk-/;
for example, чешки/čéški 'Czech (M SG)' from the noun /čex-/ +
/-sk-/ with /x/ to /š/ (see 2.2).

3 Lexically restricted alternations, conditioned by phonological factors, morphological factors or a combination. All have exceptions.

(a) **C'á ~ Ce**: Stressed /a/ preceded by a palatalized consonant alternates with /e/ (stressed or unstressed) preceded by a non-palatalized

consonant. The alternation is lexically limited to approximately 90–100 stems and several affixes (Scatton 1984, appendices 1 and 2). Otherwise it is conditioned by phonological factors: /C'á/ if the alternating syllable is stressed *and not* followed by (1) a palatalized or alveopalatal consonant; (2) a consonant cluster containing such a consonant; or (3) a syllable containing a front vowel; otherwise /Cé/ or /Ce/. Thus: 'blind' M SG сляп/sljáp : PL слéпи/slépi : слéпчо/ slépčo 'blind man' : заслепя́/zaslepjá '(I) blind'. Exceptions are common: for instance, 'place', N SG мя́сто/mjásto and PL местá/ mestá, but related adjective мéстна/méstna 'local (F SG)'. The alternation is the result of the characteristic north-eastern Bulgarian treatment of PSl. *ĕ *jat'*.

(b) **Metathesis**: As a result of the development of Proto-Slavonic liquid diphthongs with *ъ/ь (section 2.1), the position of the consonants /r l/ with respect to /ă/ varies as a function of the following environment: /ră/ and /lă/ before two consonants, /ăr/ and /ăl/ before a consonant followed by a vowel. Lexically limited, the alternation is common in derivation, but infrequent in inflection; for example, върбá/vărbá 'willow tree' : Врѣбница/Vrábnica 'Palm Sunday'. In monosyllabic forms with more than one consonant after the liquid–vowel sequence, /ă/ always follows the liquid: крѣст/krăst 'cross'. In other monosyllabic forms, both orders occur: грѣм/grăm 'thunder' versus вѣлк/vălk 'wolf'. Exceptions are numerous: смѣртна/ smártna 'fatal (F SG)'. See Scatton (1984, appendix 3) for details.

(c) **Vowel ~ Ø**: In the inflectional and derivational patterns of many nominal and verbal forms, /ă/ and /e/ alternate with Ø. The alternation is the idiosyncratic property of many roots and affixes. For example, 'day' M SG дéн/dén : PL дни́/dni; 'silver (ADJECTIVE)' M SG срéбърен/srébăren : F SG срéбърна/srébărna : срéбърник/ srébărnik 'silver coin' : сребрó/srebró 'silver (N)'. The alternation is the result of the evolution of the PSl. *ъ/ь plus the apparent epenthesis of /ă/ in word-final clusters of consonant plus liquid (see section 2.1).

3 Morphology

3.1 Nominal morphology

3.1.1 Nominal categories
Bulgarian nominal morphology includes the following categories:

1   **Number, singular versus plural**; masculine nouns use a separate **count**

form (Bulgarian бро́йна фо́рма/brójna fórma) with cardinal numerals.
2 **Definiteness**, expressed by a **definite article**, postposed to the first nominal constituent of definite noun phrases.
3 **Case** (extremely limited): Two classes of nouns and masculine singular adjectives have singular **vocative** forms (non-productive and limited). The masculine singular definite article contrasts **subjective** and **objective** forms (a distinction not strictly observed in colloquial Bulgarian). Personal pronouns and the masculine personal interrogative pronoun кóй/kój 'who' (and other pronouns derived from it) have **nominative**, **accusative** and **dative** forms; non-clitic dative forms, however, are replaced by prepositional phrases (see 3.1.3).

Other case forms were common in the literary language in the past, particularly for masculine personal nouns; for example, NOM Влади́мир/Vladimír, DAT Влади́миру/Vladimíru, ACC Влади́мира/Vladimíra. They are now found only in regional, non-literary dialects (see section 6). For case vestiges in adverbial formations, see section 3.1.4.
4 **Grammatical gender: masculine, feminine, neuter**, reflected in the **number** suffixes (singular/plural) of nouns. In addition, gender and number are the basis for agreement of verbal and other nominal forms with nouns. Gender is **natural** only to the extent that certain nouns denoting humans, regardless of their inflectional patterns, are **masculine** or **feminine** for agreement purposes depending on their meaning; for example, although inflected like a feminine noun in /-a/, слугá/slugá '(male) servant' shows masculine agreement; likewise чи́чо/čičo 'uncle', although it is inflected like a neuter noun in /-o/. In addition, a small number of nouns with singulars in /-a/ which denote men or women show masculine or feminine agreement depending on the sex of their referents; for instance, пия́ница/pijánica 'drunkard'.

3.1.2   Noun morphology

The most important inflectional patterns of nouns are as follows:

1 Masculine singular /-∅/

		SG INDEF	SG VOC	PL INDEF	PL COUNT
Monosyllabic	'son'	си́н	си́не	синове́	си́на
		sín	sine	sinové	sína
	'city'	гра́д	гра́де	градове́	гра́да
		grád	gráde	gradové	gráda
Polysyllabic	'teacher'	учи́тел	учи́телю	учи́тели	учи́теля
		učitel	učitelju	učiteli	učitelja

Vowel–zero alternations are common in this class: the vowel occurs in all singular forms and the count plural, zero in other plural forms: 'fool' SG глупе́ц/glupéc, VOC глупе́цо/glupéco – PL глупци́/glupcí.

Vocative suffixes are /-e/, /-u/ (see above), or /-o/ ('man, husband' мъ̀ж/mắž – мъ̀жо/mắžo; 'citizen' гра́жданин/gráždanin – гра́жданино/gráždanino). Their distribution depends on the stem-final consonant (Scatton 1984: 140–2).

/-ove/ is the regular plural suffix for monosyllabic stems. After /j/, it is sometimes replaced by /-eve/: 'tea' ча́й/čáj – ча́еве/čáeve. Often /-i/ replaces /-ove/, especially in borrowings: 'day' де́н/dén – дни́/dní, 'fact' фа́кт/fákt – фа́кти/fákti (borrowed from Latin).

Several common monosyllabic nouns take other plural suffixes: /-išta/: 'path, road' пъ̀т/pắt – пъ̀тища/pắtišta; /-a/: 'brother' бра́т/brát – бра́тя/brátja (with irregular palatalization of /t/); 'foot' кра́к/krak – крака́/kraká; /-ė/: 'man, husband' мъ̀ж/mắž – мъже́/mằžé.

/-i/ is the regular plural suffix for polysyllabic stems; here stem-final velars generally become dentals: 'pupil' учени́к/učeník – учени́ци/učeníci. Exceptions are common, especially in borrowings: 'dinner jacket' (from English via Russian) смо́кинг/smóking – смо́кинги/smókingi. The suffix /-in-/ is lost in the plural: 'citizen' гра́жданин/gráždanin – гра́ждани/gráždani. Rarely, /-ove/ occurs for expected /-i/: 'fire' о́гън/ógăn – огньо́ве/ogn'óve.

Alternative plural forms are common: 'sign' зна́к/znák – зна́ци/znáci ~ зна́кове/znákove.

The suffix of the plural count form is /-a/ – never stressed.

In vocative and count forms, stress falls on the same stem-syllable as in the singular. Monosyllabic stems show three possibilities in the plural:

Stem	'sign'	зна́к/znák	зна́кове/znákove
Suffix initial	'chair'	сто́л/stól	столо́ве/stolóve
Suffix final	'city'	гра́д/grád	градове́/gradové

The first pattern is by far the most common. For polysyllabic stems, stress is fixed on the stem: 'pupil' учени́к/učeník – учени́ци/učeníci; an *apparent* shift to the plural suffix occurs with the loss of stressed suffixal vowels: 'fool' глупе́ц/glupéc – глупци́/glupcí.

2 Neuter nouns with SG /-o/ (/-e/), PL /-a/

	SG INDEF	PL INDEF
'place'	мя́сто/mjásto	места́/mestá
'heart'	съ́рце́/sărcé	сърца́/sărcá
'doctrine'	уче́ние/učénie	уче́ния/učénija

The singular suffix /-o/ may be /-e/ after stems terminating in palatalized, palatal or, rarely, other consonants. Other suffixes are rare: /-i/ (two examples): 'eye' око́/okȯ – очи́/oči, 'ear' ухо́/uxȯ – уши́/uši (both with velar to alveo-palatal); /-é/ (three examples): 'wing' крило́/krilȯ – криле́/krilė (~ крила́/krilȧ), 'knee' коля́но/koljȧno – колене́/kolenė (~ колена́/kolenȧ), 'shoulder' ра́мо/rȧmo – рамене́/ramenė (~ рамена́/ramenȧ).

Stress is usually fixed on the stem ('doctrine' above) or the suffix ('heart'). Some nouns shift stress from stem to plural suffix, for instance 'place'.

A number of kinship terms and names for men have singulars in /-o/; they use the plural suffix /-ovci/; stress is fixed: 'grandfather' дя́до/djȧdo – дя́довци/djȧdovci.

3 Neuter nouns with SG /-e/, PL /-eCa/

	SG INDEF	PL INDEF
'lamb'	а́гне/ȧgne	а́гнета/ȧgneta
'stool'	сто́лче/stȯlče	сто́лчета/stȯlčeta

This formation is regular for neuter nouns with the common diminutive suffix /-e/ or any of its variants, like /-če/. Stress is fixed. The suffix /-ta/ is productive for foreign borrowings terminating in /-i/ or /-u/ (unknown as singular suffixes in native nouns): 'taxi' такси́/taksi – такси́та/taksȧta.

Seven nouns take stressed /-nȧ/ instead of /-ta/: 'seed' се́ме/sėme – семена́/semenȧ; also вре́ме/vrėme 'time', и́ме/ime 'name'.

Stressed /-sȧ/ occurs with two neuters in /-o/ or /-e/: 'sky, heaven' небе́/nebė (archaic не́бо ~ небо́/nėbo ~ небо́) – небеса́/nebesȧ, 'miracle' чу́до/čȧdo – чудеса́/čudesȧ. A few other plurals of this type are archaic alternatives to regular formations; thus, 'speech' сло́во/slȯvo – слова́/slovȧ and archaic словеса́/slovesȧ.

4 Feminine nouns with SG /-a/

	SG INDEF	SG VOC	PL INDEF
'woman, wife'	жена́	же́но	жени́
	ženȧ	žėno	ženi
'land'	земя́	зе́мьо	земи́
	zemjȧ	zėm'o	zemi

The vocative is regularly formed with /-o/ (see above) or /-e/ ('tsarina' цари́ца/carica – цари́це/carice) (Scatton 1984: 140–2 for rules and exceptions). Stress in the vocative is always on the stem. The plural suffix is /-i/, before which velars *do not* become alveo-palatals. Two nouns take /-e/ with shift of velar to dental: 'arm, hand' ръка́/rŭkȧ – ръце́/rŭcė and 'leg, foot' (dialectal) нога́/nogȧ – нозе́/nozė.

This pattern also includes some masculine personal nouns: '(male) servant' SG слуга́/slugá, VOC слу́го/slúgo, PL слуги́/slugí. Vocative forms aside, the stress of nouns in /-a/ is fixed.

5 Feminine nouns with SG /-∅/

	SG INDEF	PL INDEF
'song'	пе́сен/pésen	пе́сни/pésni
'bone'	ко́ст/kóst	ко́сти/kósti

The plural suffix is /-i/. Vowel–zero alternations occur (section 2.3). Stress is fixed (except with the definite article: see below).

Many Bulgarian noun types are defective with respect to number. Some (**singularia tantum**) occur only in the singular: уравновесе́ност/uravnovesénost 'equilibrium'; others (**pluralia tantum**) occur only in the plural: очила́/očilá 'eye glasses'.

As the first constituent of a definite noun phrase, nouns carry the **postposed definite article**:

Singular:
>   masculine -∅: -ът ~ -a (-ят ~ я)/-ăt ~ -a (-jat ~ at) (учи́телят/ učíteljat 'the teacher', глупе́цът/glupécăt 'the fool')
>   feminine/masculine /-a/: -та/-ta (жена́та/ženáta 'the woman, wife')
>   feminine -∅: -та́/-tá (песента́/pesentá 'the song')
>   masculine /-o/, all neuter: -то/-to (мя́стото/mjástoto 'the place')
> Plural:
>   /-a/: -та/-ta (места́та/mestáta 'the places')
>   /-i/ or /-e/: -те/-te (жени́те/ženíte 'the women, wives')

Notes:
1   Masculine singular forms distinguish case: forms in /t/ – nominative, forms without /t/ – objective: то́й е профе́сорът/tój e profésorăt 'he is the professor' versus ста́ята на профе́сора/stájata na profésora 'the room of the professor'. In spoken usage, depending on regional dialect or idiolect, one of the two forms is generalized. With some monosyllabic masculine nouns the stress unpredictably shifts to the article: града́т/gradắt 'the city'. See section 2.1 for spelling.
2   With feminine singular nouns in -∅, stress is always on the article, which, additionally, is often pronounced [-tá]: [pesentá] ~ [pesentá].

Noun morphology has changed dramatically in the history of Bulgarian. Except for masculine and feminine vocative forms, all case forms were lost. The Proto-Slavonic nominative–accusative dual of *o*-stem masculine nouns was the source of masculine count forms. Otherwise, the dual was lost (except for vestiges: some feminine and neuter plurals in /-e/, some masculine plurals in /-a/, the plurals of 'eye' and 'ear' (examples above)). The definite article developed from the demonstrative pronoun PSl. *t-.

The declensional types of Modern Bulgarian continue the major patterns of Late Proto-Slavonic. Masculine and neuter stems with singulars in /-∅/ and /-o/, respectively, are descendants of o-stem masculines and neuters. The plural suffix of monosyllabic masculines, /-ove/, preserves the nominative plural of u-stem masculines, otherwise absorbed by o-stems. The rare masculine plural suffix /-e/, as in мъжѐ/mắžė, reflects nominative plural -ье of masculine i-stems, otherwise absorbed by o-stem masculines. Feminine nouns in /-a/ continue Proto-Slavonic feminine ā-stems, feminine nouns in /-∅/ – i-stems. Masculine personal nouns with singular in /-o/ are an innovation.

Vestiges of Proto-Slavonic 'hard' versus 'soft' inflectional patterns for o- and ā-stems are found in the vocative (though with redistribution of suffixes, including the extension of /-o/ to masculines), in the masculine plural suffix /-eve/ (for /-ove/), and in the neuter singular suffix /-e/ (for /-o/).

With one major exception, all minor classes of Proto-Slavonic nouns were either absorbed by major patterns or became non-productive and limited in number. As mentioned, u-stem and i-stem masculines merged with o-stem masculines. Most feminine ū-stems, developing singular forms in /-va/, merged with ā-stem feminines (цъ̀рква/cắrkva 'church'); a few became feminines in /-∅/ (кръв/krắv 'blood'). Feminine ī-stems became feminines in /-a/ (рабѝня/rabìnja 'slave'). Masculine n-stems generally merged with masculines in /-∅/ – with or without a change of suffix (пла̀мък/plắmăk 'flame' versus дѐн/dèn 'day'). The original suffix of 'stone' was more or less preserved in the plural while being replaced in the singular: ка̀мък/kắmăk – ка̀мъни/kắmăni.

Neuter s-stems became neuters in /-o/ ('speech' сло̀во/slòvo – слова̀/slovà); likewise for several neuter n-stems ('letter' писмо̀/pismò from OCS pismę). Several n-stems retain the old plural ('seed' сѐме/sème – семена̀/semenà). Neuter nt-stems, preserved with plurals in /-ta/, are very common due to the productivity of diminutive suffixes in /-e/ and the use of /-ta/ with borrowings. Finally, two feminine r-stems, OCS mati 'mother' and dъšti 'daughter', became feminine nouns in /-a/: ма̀йка/mắjka and дъщеря̀/dắšterjà (the latter with the vocative дъ̀ще/dắšte).

3.1.3 Pronominal morphology

The **personal pronouns** of Bulgarian are shown in table 5.4. Ний/nìj and вий/vìj are normal in spoken Bulgarian. With decreasing consistency, second person **plural** forms are used for polite address of second person **singular** interlocutors. The clitic feminine dative singular is written with a grave accent to distinguish it from и/i 'and'.

Table 5.4 Personal pronouns

(a)

	NOM	ACC		DAT		
		Stressed	*Clitic*	*Stressed*	*Clitic*	
1 SG	а́з	ме́не	ме	(ме́не)	ми	'I'
2 SG	ти́	те́бе	те	(те́бе)	ти	'you (SG)'
3 SG M	то́й	не́го	го	(не́му)	му	'he/it'
N	то́	не́го	го	(не́му)	му	'it'
F	тя́	не́я	я	(не́й)	й	'she/it'
1 PL	ни́е (ни́й)	на́с	ни	(на́м)	ни	'we'
2 PL	ви́е (ви́й)	ва́с	ви	(ва́м)	ви	'you (PL)'
3 PL	те́	тя́х	ги	(тя́м)	им	'they'
REFL	—	се́бе си	се	(се́бе си)	си	'-self'

(b)

	NOM	ACC		DAT		
		Stressed	*Clitic*	*Stressed*	*Clitic*	
1 SG	àz	mène	me	(mène)	mi	'I'
2 SG	ti	tèbe	te	(tèbe)	ti	'you (SG)'
3 SG M	tòj	nègo	go	(nèmu)	mu	'he/it'
N	tò	nègo	go	(nèmu)	mu	'it'
F	tjà	nèja	ja	(nèj)	ì	'she/it'
1 PL	nìe (nìj)	nàs	ni	(nàm)	ni	'we'
2 PL	vìe (vìj)	vàs	vi	(vàm)	vi	'you (PL)'
3 PL	tè	tjàx	gi	(tjàm)	im	'they'
REFL	—	sèbe si	se	(sèbe si)	si	'-self'

Stressed dative forms, now archaic, are replaced by prepositional phrases of на/na + stressed accusatives. Stressed accusative forms serve as objects of prepositions and, with logical stress, as direct objects of transitive verbs. Clitic forms are normal as unmarked verbal complements, accusative as direct object, dative as indirect object:

Да́дох не́го на не́я./Dàdox nègo na nèja.
'(I) gave *it* to *her*.'
Да́дох й го./Dàdox ì go.
'(I) gave it to her.'

Enclitic datives are the customary expression of possession (see section 4.9). 'Ethical' (modal) dative forms, usually clitics, are common in colloquial Bulgarian: то́й си пи́йва/tòj si pìjva 'he likes to take a drop' (= 'he self-DAT drinks-SEMELFACTIVE').

Personal pronouns are matched by **personal possessive pronouns**, inflected for gender and number like adjectives (see table 5.5). Like adjectives, possessive pronouns may carry the definite article (section 3.1.4). However, in first person singular, second person singular and reflexive

Table 5.5 Personal possessive pronouns

	M SG	F SG	N SG	PL	
(a)					
1 SG	мóй	мóя	мóе	мóи	'my'
2 SG	твóй	твóя	твóе	твóи	'your-SG'
3 SG M/N	нéгов	нéгова	нéгово	нéгови	'his/its'
F	нéин	нéйна	нéйно	нéйни	'her/its'
1 PL	нáш	нáша	нáше	нáши	'our'
2 PL	вáш	вáша	вáше	вáши	'your-PL'
3 PL	тéхен	тя́хна	тя́хно	тéхни	'their'
REFL	свóй	свóя	свóе	свóи	'-own'
(b)					
1 SG	mój	mója	móe	mói	'my'
2 SG	tvój	tvója	tvóe	tvói	'your-SG'
3 SG M/N	négov	négova	négovo	négovi	'his/its'
F	néin	néjna	néjno	néjni	'her'
1 PL	náš	náša	náše	náši	'our'
2 PL	váš	váša	váše	váši	'your-PL'
3 PL	téxen	tjáxna	tjáxno	téxni	'their'
REFL	svój	svója	svóe	svói	'-own'

forms, /-ij-/ is not added before the masculine singular article: 'my' M SG DEF мóят/mójat versus 'their' M SG DEF тéхният/téxnijat.

Other pronominal forms, also inflected for gender and number, are **demonstrative** (table 5.6) and **interrogative** (table 5.7).

The masculine singular form of 'who' and all pronominal forms derived from it (below) have an oblique form, когó/kogó, used as direct object and object of prepositions. In colloquial Bulgarian it is often replaced by кóй/kój. The archaic dative комý/komú is replaced by PREP на/na + когó/kogó.

With the exception of 'everyone, ...' (below), other pronominal forms are derived from interrogatives.

Relative pronouns add the suffix -то/-to: кóйто/kójto 'who, which, that (M SG)', какъ́вто/kakǎvto 'which sort (M SG)'.

Negative pronouns add stressed ни́-/ní-: ни́кой/níkoj 'no one (M SG)', ни́чий/níčij 'no one's (M SG)', ни́какъв/níkakǎv 'no sort of (M SG)', ни́що/ništo 'nothing (N SG)'.

Indefinite pronouns:

1 'some, a certain': stressed ня́-/njǎ- + interrogative; here /ǎ/ ~ with /é/; ня́кой/njǎkoj 'someone (M SG)', ня́какъв/njǎkakǎv 'some sort

Table 5.6   Demonstrative pronouns

	M SG	F SG	N SG	PL
(a)				
'this'	то́зи/то́я	та́зи/та́я	това́/ту́й	те́зи/ти́я
'that'	о́нзи/о́ня	она́зи/она́я	онова́/ону́й	оне́зи/они́я
'such a'	такъ́в	така́ва	тако́ва	таки́ва
(b)				
'this'	tózi/tója	tázi/tája	tová/túj	tézi/tija
'that'	ónzi/ónja	onázi/onája	onová/onúj	onézi/onija
'such a'	takǎv	takáva	takóva	takiva

of (M SG)', не́чий/néčij 'someone's (M SG)', не́що/néšto 'something
(N SG)'.

2   'someone, so-and-so, such-and-such': ѐди-/èdi- + interrogative си/si,
written as two words with secondary stress on the first constituent;
ѐди-ко́й си/èdi-kój si 'so-and-so, a certain one (M SG)', ѐди-какъ̀в
си/èdi-kakǎv si 'such-and-such a, a certain (M SG)'.

3   'whoever, whatever, somebody or other, something or other, whatever
sort of': interrogative + да è/da è, three words with secondary stress
on the last; for example, ко́й да è/kój da è 'someone or other, anyone
(M SG)', какво́ да è/kakvó da è 'whatever (N SG)'. Alternative forms
replace the interrogative with a relative pronoun and add и/i: ко́йто и
да è/kójto i da è.

Table 5.7   Interrogative pronouns

	M SG	F SG	N SG	PL
(a)				
'who, which'	ко́й	коя́	кое́	кои́
'what'			какво́/що́	
'what sort of'	какъ́в	каква́	какво́	какви́
'whose'	чи́й	чия́	чие́	чии́
(b)				
'who, which'	kój	kojá	koé	koi
'what'			kakvó/štó	
'what sort of'	kakǎv	kakvá	kakvó	kakvi
'whose'	čij	čijá	čié	čii

4 'everyone, every single, each' M SG все́ки/vséki, F SG вся́ка/vsjáka, N
SG вся́ко/vsjáko, PL вси́чки/vsíčki. Referring to persons, the masculine singular form of 'everyone …' has accusative forms все́киго/
vsékigo, вся́кого/vsjákogo; they are obsolescent in the colloquial
language.
'everything' N SG вси́чко/vsíčko
'every sort of' M SG вся́какъв/vsjákakǎv, F SG вся́каква/vsjákakva, N
SG вся́какво/vsjákakvo, PL вся́какви/vsjákakvi
'all (of)' M SG вси́чкият/vsíčkijat, F SG вси́чката/vsíčkata N SG
вси́чкото/vsíčkoto, PL вси́чки(те)/vsíčki(te)

See section 4, especially 4.7–4.9 for pronominal usage.

3.1.4 Adjectival morphology
Adjectives are inflected for number and, in the singular, gender; there is a
masculine singular vocative form:

	'new'	'goat's'	'fraternal'
M SG	но́в/nóv	ко́зи/kózi	бра́тски/brátski
M SG VOC	но́ви/nóvi	ко́зи/kózi	бра́тски/brátski
F SG	но́ва/nóva	ко́зя/kózja	бра́тска/brátska
N SG	но́во/nóvo	ко́зе/kóze	бра́тско/brátsko
PL	но́ви/nóvi	ко́зи/kózi	бра́тски/brátski

The usual masculine singular suffix is /-Ø/. The suffix /-i/ is limited to
adjectives in /-sk-/, a small number of possessive adjectives, and a few
Russian loans in /-ov-/ (брегови́/bregoví 'shore (ADJECTIVE)'). Stems
with vowel–zero alternations have a vowel in the masculine singular before
/-Ø/, otherwise zero: 'good' M SG добъ́р/dobǎr – F SG добра́/dobrá.
The regular neuter suffix /-o/ may be /-e/, as in ко́зе/kóze (see
section 2.2).
Most adjectives are stem-stressed. End-stress is limited to Russian
borrowings with /-ov-/ (see above) and two native stems: 'good' (above),
'alone' M SG са́м/sám (F SG сама́/samá).
A few colloquial adjectives borrowed from Turkish and, more recently,
other languages are not inflected: сербе́з чове́к/serbéz čovék 'bold man',
сербе́з жени́/serbéz žení 'bold women' (see section 5.3).
Masculine singular forms in /-i/ continue definite Proto-Slavonic forms;
others continue indefinite forms. All earlier non-nominative case forms,
the dual and, in the plural, gender were lost. Except for irregular neuter
singular forms in /-e/, all trace of the soft adjectival paradigms of Proto-
Slavonic was lost. The number of adjectives with palatalized stem-final
consonants is limited to a few possessive adjectives (ко́зя/kózja 'goat's (F
SG)'), and one non-derived adjective 'blue' M SG си́н/sin, F SG си́ня/sínja,
N SG си́ньо/sin′o, PL си́ни/sini.

Table 5.8   Cardinal numerals

(a)

'1' едѝн	'11' единàдесет		
'2' двà	'12' дванàдесет	'20' двàдесет	'200' двѐста
'3' трѝ	'13' тринàдесет	'30' трѝдесет	'300' трѝста
'4' чèтири	'14' четиринàдесет	'40' четѝридесет	'400' чèтиристòтин
'5' пèт	'15' петнàдесет	'50' петдесèт	'500' пèтстòтин
'6' шèст	'16' шестнàдесет	'60' шестдесèт	'600' шèстстòтин
'7' сèдем	'17' седемнàдесет	'70' седемдесèт	'700' сèдемстòтин
'8' òсем	'18' осемнàдесет	'80' осемдесèт	'800' òсемстòтин
'9' дèвет	'19' деветнàдесет	'90' деветдесèт	'900' дèветстòтин
'10' дèсет		'100' стò	'1,000' хилỳда
	'million' милиòн	'thousand million' милиàрд	

(b)

'1' edìn	'11' edinàdeset		
'2' dvà	'12' dvanàdeset	'20' dvàdeset	'200' dvèsta
'3' trì	'13' trinàdeset	'30' trideset	'300' trista
'4' četiri	'14' četirinàdeset	'40' četirideset	'400' čètiristòtin
'5' pèt	'15' petnàdeset	'50' petdesèt	'500' pètstòtin
'6' šèst	'16' šestnàdeset	'60' šestdesèt	'600' šèststòtin
'7' sèdem	'17' sedemnàdeset	'70' sedemdesèt	'700' sèdemstòtin
'8' òsem	'18' osemnàdeset	'80' osemdesèt	'800' òsemstòtin
'9' dèvet	'19' devetnàdeset	'90' devetdesèt	'900' dèvetstòtin
'10' dèset		'100' stò	'1,000' xiljàda
	'million' miliòn	'thousand million' miliàrd	

Comparative adjectives are formed with preposed **stressed** пò-/pò-: M SG пò-нòв/pò-nòv 'newer'. **Superlatives** use нàй-/nàj-: M SG нàй-нòв/ nàj-nòv 'newest'. Note the regular 'double' stress in both formations.

The synthetic comparative forms of Proto-Slavonic were lost – with vestiges in вѝсш/visš 'higher, superior', нѝзш(и)/nizš(i) 'lower, inferior', стàрши/stàrši 'elder, senior', млàдши/mlàdši 'junior'.

As the first constituent of definite noun phrases, adjectives carry the definite article: M SG /-ă(t)/, F SG /-ta/, N SG /-to/, PL /-te/. Before the masculine singular definite article, the adjectival **stem** is extended with /ij/: 'the new' M SG нòвия(т)/nòvija(t), F SG нòвата/nòvata, N SG нòвото/ nòvoto, PL нòвите/nòvite. See section 2.1 for spelling of masculine singular forms. Forms with /t/ are subjective, those without it are objective (section 3.1.2). Stress remains unchanged with the definite article.

Certain adjectival forms function productively as **adverbs**: (1) masculine singular (or plural) forms of adjectives in /-sk-/ (брàтски/bràtski 'fraternal' and adverb 'fraternally'); (2) neuter singular forms of qualitative adjectives with masculine singular in /-∅/ (хỳбаво/xùbavo 'nice' and adverb 'nicely');

(3) colloquially, definite feminine singular forms (здра́вата/zdrávata 'healthy-the' and adverb 'soundly'). The comparison of adverbs follows rules for the comparison of adjectives: по́-ху́баво/pó-xúbavo 'more nicely'.

Non-productive, lexicalized adverbial formations – from noun and adjectival bases – often preserve old case distinctions; thus, locative до́лу/dólu 'downward'; instrumental ти́хом/tíxom 'quietly'. Similarly in frozen prepositional phrases: сно́щи/snóšti 'last night' (preposition с/s 'from' and genitive singular of но́щ/nóšt 'night').

3.1.5 Numeral morphology

Cardinal numerals (see table 5.8): spoken and sometimes written Bulgarian use /-nájset/ for /-nádeset/ ('11' едина́йсет/edinájset), and in '20', '30', '40', '60' /-jset/ for /-deset/ ('20' два́йсет/dvájset).

Other cardinals are made up of the forms in table 5.8. Here 'thousand' has the plural хи́ляди/xíljadi (with shifted accent), and 'million' and 'thousand million' have the count forms милио́на/milióna, and милиа́рда/miliárda. For example, '36,620,105' три́ста и ше́ст милио́на, ше́стсто̀тин и два́десет хи́ляди, сто́ и пе́т/trísta i šést milióna, šéststòtin i dvádeset xíljadi, stó i pét. Note the regular use of и/i 'and' in each compound term.

'1' is inflected like an adjective: една́ кни́га/edná kníga 'one book'. Its plural is used with pluralia tantum: едни́ кле́щи/ední kléšti 'one (set of) pliers'. Increasingly '1' functions as an indefinite article 'a(n), some': еди́н чове́к/edín čovék 'a person'.

'2' два́/dvá is used with masculine nouns, две́/dvé with neuters and feminines: два́ гра́да/dvá gráda 'two cities', две́ жени́/dvé žení 'two women (F)', две́ места́/dvé mestá 'two places (N)'.

There are special forms of '2'–'6' for masculine personal nouns (and groups of male and female persons):

'2' два́ма/dváma
'3' три́ма/tríma
'4' четири́ма/četiríma ~ чети́рма/četírma
'5' пети́ма/petíma
'6' шести́ма/šestíma

For example, два́ма учени́ци/dváma učeníci 'two pupils'.

Cardinal numerals may be **definite**. In this respect '1' is adjectival: 'the one' M SG еди́ният/edínijat, F SG една́та/ednáta. 'Million', 'thousand million' and all cardinals in /-a/ follow rules for nouns: 'the million' милио́нът/miliónăt, 'the two (M)' два́та/dváta. Remaining cardinals use /-te/, always stressed except with '2 (F/N)' and '3': 'the two (F/N)' две́те/dvéte, 'the 700' седемсто̀тинте́/sedemstòtinté.

Ordinal numerals are adjectives formed from cardinals with characteristic adjectival gender/number suffixes. Masculine singular ordinals up to and including '90' use /-i/, those from '100' on use /-Ø/; пе́ти/péti '5th' (M SG)', сто́тен/stóten '100th (M SG)'. Note:

1   Suppletive forms for:
     '1st' пъ́рви/párvi (~ пръ́в/práv)
     '2nd' вто́ри/vtóri
     '3rd' тре́ти/tréti
     '4th' четвъ́рти/četvárti
2   '100th' is /stóten/; /e/ alternates with Ø and /o/ is stressed: деветсто́тно/devetstótno '900th (N SG)'.
3   'Thousandth', 'millionth' and 'thousand-millionth' use the adjectival suffix /-en-/; /e/ alternates with Ø: хи́ляден/xíljaden 'thousandth (M SG)'.
4   Accent shifts take place in the formation of '9th', '10th', '40th': деве́ти/devéti, десе́ти/deséti, четиридесе́ти/četirideséti.
5   Stem final vowels are lost in '7th' се́дми/sédmi and '8th' о́сми/ósmi.

In compound phrases only the final elements are ordinals: три́ста петдесе́т и *вто́ри*/trista petdesét i *vtóri* '152nd (M SG)'.
Definite ordinal numerals are formed as definite adjectives: вто́рият/vtórijat 'the second (M SG)', сто́тната/stótnata 'the hundredth (F SG)'.

3.2   Verbal morphology

3.2.1   Verbal categories
Finite Bulgarian verbal forms are **simple** or **compound**. Simple forms convey **person** – first, second, third – and **number** – singular, plural. In addition, compound forms using participles show **gender** in the singular: masculine, feminine, neuter.
There are three **tenses** in the **indicative** mood – present, past, future – which, combined with other categories, occur in nine formations:

1 **Present**, temporally unmarked, a simple form made up of verbal stem plus complex suffix – /e/ or /i/ (both Ø in first person singular and third person plural) or /a/, plus person/number marker:

	Singular	*Plural*
First person	/-ă ~ -m/	/-m ~ -me/
Second person	/-š/	/-te/
Third person	/-Ø/	/-ăt/

2 **Past imperfect**, a simple form, expressing actions contemporaneous with

or subordinate to other past actions; made up of the present-tense stem plus a complex suffix consisting of a vowel /e ~ à/ followed by:

	Singular	Plural
First person	/-x/	/-xme/
Second person	/-še/	/-xte/
Third person	/-še/	/-xa/

3 **Past aorist**, a simple form, relating a temporally independent, concrete past action; the **aorist** stem plus:

	Singular	Plural
First person	/-x/	/-xme/
Second person	/-Ø/	/-xte/
Third person	/-Ø/	/-xa/

4 **Future**, a compound form:

invariant proclitic auxiliary ще/šte + present tense

Negated future forms, and other forms involving the future (see below), use the neuter third person singular auxiliary няма да/njáma da ('has-not to'); note the colloquial alternative не ще/ne štė.

5 **Present perfect**, a compound form expressing an action completed in the past but relevant for or related to the present:

present tense 'be' + aorist past active participle

6 **Past perfect**, a compound form expressing an action completed in the past relative to another past action:

past tense 'be' + aorist past active participle

7 **Future perfect**, a compound form expressing an action to be completed in the future prior to another future action:

future tense 'be' + aorist past active participle

8 **Past future**, a compound form expressing an action to be completed in the past but future with respect to another past action; commonly used in conditional constructions (see section 4.5):

imperfect past of щя/štjà '(I) will, want' + да/da + present tense

9 **Past future perfect**, a compound form conveying a past action which is

Table 5.9 Indicative forms

| | Non-perfect | | Perfect | |
	Non-future	*Future*	*Non-future*	*Future*
(a)				
Non-past	пиша	ще пиша	писал съм	ще съм писал
Past		щях да пиша	бях писал	щях да съм писал
Aorist	писах			
Imperfect	пишех			
(b)				
Non-past	piša	šte piša	pisal sǎm	šte sǎm pisal
Past		štjǎx da piša	bjǎx pisal	štjǎx da sǎm pisal
Aorist	pisax			
Imperfect	pišex			

future with respect to a past action, which itself is prior to another past action; rare, commonly replaced by the past future:

past future of щя/štjǎ '(I) will, want' + aorist past active participle

Thus 'write (3 SG M IMPFV)' has the paradigm shown in table 5.9.

Bulgarian verbs also express **aspect**: perfective verbs mark the completion of the action of the verb, imperfective verbs are unmarked. Most Bulgarian verbs have perfective–imperfective pairs: 1 SG PRS IMPFV пиша/ piša '(I) write' – PRFV напиша/napiša '(I) write down, complete writing'. 'Bi-aspectual' verbs – verbs with one stem for both aspects – are common; most are borrowings: тренирам/treniram '(I) train (IMPFV/PRFV)' (from English) (see section 5.3).

Morphological processes related to the creation of aspectual pairs begin with **non-prefixed imperfective** verbs (see section 3.3.3), from which **perfective** stems are formed by **suffixation** or **prefixation**. Besides changing the aspect, perfectivizing prefixes often add their own meaning: допиша/ dopiša '(I) finish writing (PRFV)' versus подпиша/podpiša '(I) sign' (for lists and definitions of prefixes see Граматика/Gramatika 2: 217ff.). The single perfectivizing suffix /-n-/ imparts **semelfactive** meaning to the base: падна/pádna '(I) fall (PRFV SEMELFACTIVE)' (‹ падам/pádam '(I) fall (IMPFV)').

'**Secondary**' imperfectives, all third conjugation (see below), are formed from perfectives by **suffixation**. While this process allows many alternative forms and shows random consonantal and vocalic alternations, there are only two imperfectivizing suffixes. The **non-productive** suffix /-a-/ occurs with a limited number of stems; 'speak' 1 SG PRS IMPFV говоря/govórja › 'converse' 1 SG PRS PRFV разговоря/razgovórja › 1 SG PRS IMPFV разговарям/razgovárjam. The **productive** suffix is /-(a)va-/ (unstressed initial /a/ is deleted): 1 SG PRS IMPFV 'count' броя/brojá › 'enumerate' 1 SG PRS PRFV изброя/izbrojá › 1 SG PRS IMPFV изброявам/izbrojávam; 'write' 1 SG PRS IMPFV пиша/píša › 'copy' 1 SG PRS PRFV препиша/ prepíša › 1 SG PRS IMPFV преписвам/prepísvam. See Scatton (1984: 285–310) for details.

The Proto-Slavonic aspectual distinction between determinate and indeterminate verbs of motion is entirely lost in Bulgarian.

Aspect is subject to some constraints. Only imperfective verbs have present active participles, gerunds, verbal nouns in /-ne/ and negative imperatives. Only imperfective verbs can be complements of verbs meaning 'begin', 'continue' or 'end'. Present perfective verbs are rare in independent clauses. Imperfect forms are most frequently imperfective aspect, and aorists perfective. **Perfective** imperfects and **imperfective** aorists are possible: perfective imperfects for usually repeated series of completed actions presented as subordinate ('backgrounded') with respect to other, 'major' past actions; imperfective aorists for 'major' past events the completion of which is not relevant for the narration. For discussion and examples see Scatton (1984: 318–32) and Lindstedt (1985).

Imperatives are simple or compound. Simple forms are second person singular or plural; there are compound forms for all persons and numbers. Simple forms use the suffixes SG /-i/ and PL /-ete/; the suffix-initial vowel is /j/ with third-conjugation verbs and with verbs of other conjugations whose present stems terminate in /j/; compare 'write' 2 SG пиши/piši, 2 PL пишете/pišéte; 'look' 2 SG гледай/glédaj, 2 PL гледайте/glédajte. The vowel is lost unpredictably in a few other verbs: влез/vléz 'enter (2 SG)'. See section 4.2 for compound imperatives.

The **conditional** is a compound form using the aorist past tense of the stem /bi-/ 'be' (used only here) plus aorist past active participle: 'write' 1 SG M бих писал/bix pisal '(I) could/should/would write/have written'. See section 4.5 for conditionals using the indicative.

There are several **passive** formations:

1 Any tense of 'be' + past passive participle of transitive verbs: писмото беше написано/pismóto béše napisano 'the letter was written'.
2 Finite forms of transitive verbs with the accusative reflexive pronoun ce/se: писмото се пише/pismóto se píše 'the letter is (being) written'.
3 'Impersonal' (subjectless) third person plural finite forms of transitive verbs: там продават мляко/tám prodávat mljáko 'milk is sold there' (= 'there sell-3 PL milk').

These formations have slightly different semantic and grammatical nuances (Граматика/Gramatika 2: 245ff.). A rare 'impersonal passive' uses 'be' and neuter singular past passive participles of transitive *and* intransitive verbs: по травата е ходено/po travàta e xòdeno 'someone (or something) has walked on the grass' (= 'on grass-the is walked'; Граматика/ Gramatika 2: 381).

Reflexive verbs, which carry the clitic accusative reflexive pronoun, have various functions:

1 Many common intransitive verbs are reflexive. Some occur only reflexively: смея се/sméja se '(I) laugh'; others are derived from non-reflexive transitive verbs: бия/bìja '(I) beat (TR)' > бия се/bìja se '(I) fight (ITR)'.
2 Reflexive verbs derived from non-reflexive transitive verbs occur in **passive** constructions (see above).
3 Reflexive forms of transitive *and* intransitive verbs are used in third person singular 'impersonal' constructions: (a) to express desire, спи ми ce/spì mi se 'I want to sleep' (= 'sleep-3 SG me-DAT self-ACC'); (b) to express permission, тук не се пуши/tùk ne sè pùši 'no smoking here' (= 'here not self-ACC smoke-3 SG').

For reciprocal and genuinely reflexive uses of reflexive verbs see section 4.8.

Indicative forms relate events personally witnessed or otherwise assumed to be true by speakers. For events not witnessed or known only through hearsay, Bulgarian uses so-called 'renarrated' forms (Chvany 1988). Every indicative form has a renarrated form; however, each renarrated tense, except one, corresponds to *two* indicative tenses:

Indicative	*Renarrated*	
present/imperfect	present	present 'be' + imperfect past participle
aorist	aorist	present 'be' + aorist past participle
present/past perfect	perfect	perfect 'be' + aorist past participle
(past) future	future	perfect 'will, want' + /da/ + present
(past) future perfect	future perfect	perfect 'will, want' + /da/ + perfect

In addition, the present auxiliary 'be' is deleted in all **third-person** forms. Thus, the renarrated paradigm for 'write (3 SG M IMPFV)' shown in table 5.10. Compare **indicative** той написа писмото/tòj napìsa pismòto 'he wrote the letter (and I saw him do it)' versus **renarrated** той написал писмото/tòj napìsal pismòto '(it is said that) he wrote the letter'.

First-person renarrated forms are uncommon; they convey a sense of surprise or denial: пишел съм роман/pìšel sằm romàn 'I'm writing a novel!?' (= 'it's claimed that I'm writing a novel'). **Emphatic** present, aorist, future and future perfect renarrated forms replace the present-tense auxiliary 'be' with its present perfect form, while dropping the third-person

Table 5.10 Renarrated forms

	Non-perfect		Perfect	
	Non-future	*Future*	*Non-future*	*Future*
(a)				
Non-past	пи́шел	щя́л да пи́ша	би́л пи́сал	щя́л да е пи́сал
Aorist	пи́сал			
(b)				
Non-past	pi̍šel	štjȁl da piša	bil pisal	štjȁl da e pisal
Aorist	pisal			

present auxiliary: **renarrated** пи́шел/pi̍šel – **emphatic renarrated** би́л пи́шел/bil pi̍šel '(he) writes' (Граматика/Gramatika 2: 361).

Some grammars describe another renarrated form, one which relates facts not personally witnessed by speakers, but **presumed** by them to be true. **Presumptive** forms use the present tense of 'be' plus a past participle, either aorist *or* imperfect (only aorist participles are used in indicative forms): то́й е пи́шел писмо́то/tój e pi̍šel pismóto 'he (presumably) wrote the letter'. Largely identical to other indicative or renarrated forms, this category is controversial (Scatton 1984: 332–3).

Non-finite verbal forms are the following:

The late Proto-Slavonic **infinitive** and **supine** have been replaced by phrases with да/da + present tense: и́скам да пи́ша/ískam da piša '(I) want to write'. A vestigial **infinitive** of very limited use is identical to the second–third person singular aorist (see section 4.5).

Bulgarian lost the present active, present passive and the 'first', non-resultative past participles of Proto-Slavonic. On the other hand, it preserved two other participles and innovated two more.

A **present active participle** is formed from imperfective present stems with the suffixes /-ašt- ~ -ešt-/: M SG пи́шещ/pi̍šešt 'writing'. A strictly literary form devised in the late nineteenth century on Russian and Church Slavonic models, it is only used attributively.

The **imperfect past active participle** is formed from imperfect present stems with /-el- ~ -al-/: M SG пи́шел/pi̍šel 'wrote'. Used only in renarrated forms, it is a Bulgarian innovation.

The **aorist past active participle** is formed from aorist stems with the suffix /-l-/: M SG пи́сал/pisal 'wrote'. The direct descendant of the 'second', resultative past active participle of Proto-Slavonic, it is used in compound verbal forms and, occasionally, attributively.

The **past passive participle** is formed from aorist stems with the suffixes /-(e)n- ~ -t-/: M SG писан/pisan 'written'. Continuing the past passive participle of Proto-Slavonic, it is used predicatively in passive formations and attributively.

Based on western Bulgarian forms which continue the Proto-Slavonic present active participle, the Bulgarian **gerund** (verbal adverb) is formed from imperfective present stems with the suffix -(e)jki: пишейки/pišejki '(while) writing'. It relates an action contemporaneous with, but subordinate to, the main verb. It is a strictly literary form. For more on participles and gerunds see section 4.5.

A neuter singular **noun**, denoting the action of the verb, is formed with /-(e)ne/ from imperfective stems: писане/pisane 'writing'.

3.2.2   Conjugation

Traditional grammars distinguish three conjugations on the basis of the initial vowels of present-tense suffixes:

First conjugation	/e/	пиш-е-ш/piš-e-š	'(you-SG) write'
Second conjugation	/i/	ход-и-ш/xód-i-š	'(you-SG) go, walk'
Third conjugation	/a/	им-а-ш/im-a-š	'(you-SG) have'

Various subclasses of the first and second conjugations reflect the relationship between the stems of the **aorist past** and **present** tenses. For example, the first subclass of the first conjugation makes its aorist stem by adding /e/ (2/3 SG) or /o/ (elsewhere) to the present stem. Table 5.11 gives examples of major subclasses and their characteristic alternations. Double stresses indicate alternative pronunciations. See Пашов/Pašov (1966) and Граматика/Gramatika (2: 304ff.) for exhaustive lists.

Other verbal forms belong to one or the other of two 'systems', depending on which of the two stems is the basis for their formation:

Present system	*Aorist system*
present tense	aorist past tense
imperfect past tense	aorist past participle
imperative	past passive participle
present active participle	infinitive (vestigial)
imperfect past participle	verbal noun
gerund	

The first and second conjugations continue thematic patterns of Late Proto-Slavonic – with characteristic Bulgarian changes: loss of dual, loss of

Table 5.11   Bulgarian conjugational patterns

Old Church Slavonic		Modern Bulgarian				
Class 1 SG PRES INF		*Class* 1 SG PRES	3 SG PRES	1 SG AOR		

(a)

I

		Ia				
nesǫ	nesti		до-неса́	до-несе́	до-не́сох	'bring' (= 'carry to')
vedǫ	vesti		до-веда́	до-веде́	до-ве́дох	'bring' (= 'lead')
čьtǫ	čisti		чета́	чете́	че́тох	'read'
idǫ	iti		йда	йде	йдох	'go'
rekǫ	rešti		река́	рече́	ре́кох	'say'
grebǫ	greti		ги́на	ги́не	ги́нах	'perish'
živǫ	žiti		ми́на	ми́не	ми́нах	'go'
na-čьnǫ	na-čęti		за-че́на / по́-чна	за-че́не / по́-чне	за-че́нах / по́-чнах	'conceive' / 'begin'
mьrǫ	mrěti		греба́	гребе́	гре́бах	'row'
stanǫ	stati		ста́на	ста́не	ста́нах	'become'
kovǫ	kovati		кова́	кове́	кова́х	'forge'
zovǫ	zъvati		зова́	зове́	зова́х	'call'
berǫ	bьrati		бера́	бере́	бра́х	'gather'

II

gybnǫ	gybati
minǫ	minati

III

		Ic				
kažǫ	kazati		ка́жа	ка́же	ка́зах	'say'
pišǫ	pьsati		пи́ша	пи́ше	пи́сах	'write'

		Id				
			мра́	мре́	мря́х	'die'

		Ie				
znajǫ	znati		зна́я	зна́е	зна́ях	'know'

		If				
čujǫ	čuti		чу́я	чу́е	чух	'hear'
kryjǫ	kryti		кри́я	кри́е	крих	'hide'
bijǫ	biti		би́я	би́е	бих	'beat'
pojǫ	pěti		пе́я	пе́е	пях	'sing'
umějǫ	uměti		уме́я	уме́е	умя́х	'be able'
dělajǫ	dělati		живе́я	живе́е	живя́х	'live'

		other				
			се́я	се́е	ся́х (се́ях)	'sow'
meljo	mlěti		ме́ля	ме́ле	мля́х	'grind'
darujǫ	darovati					
sějǫ	sějati					

IV

		IIa				
moljǫ	moliti		мо́ля	мо́ли	мо́лих	'beg'
xoždǫ	xoditi		хо́дя	хо́ди	хо́дих	'walk'

		IIb				
tьrpljǫ	tьrpěti		търпя́	търпи́	търпя́х	'tolerate'
ležǫ	ležati		лежа́	лежи́	лежа́х	'recline'

		other				
sъpljǫ	sъpati		спя́	спи́	спа́х	'sleep'

V

		III				
imamь	imati		и́мам	и́ма	и́мах	'have'
			дя́лам	дя́ла	дя́лах/дела́х	'carve'
			дару́вам	дару́ва	дарува́х	'present gifts'

Table 5.11   *continued*

Old Church Slavonic		Modern Bulgarian		
Class 1 SG PRES	INF	*Class* 1 SG PRES	3 SG PRES	1 SG AOR

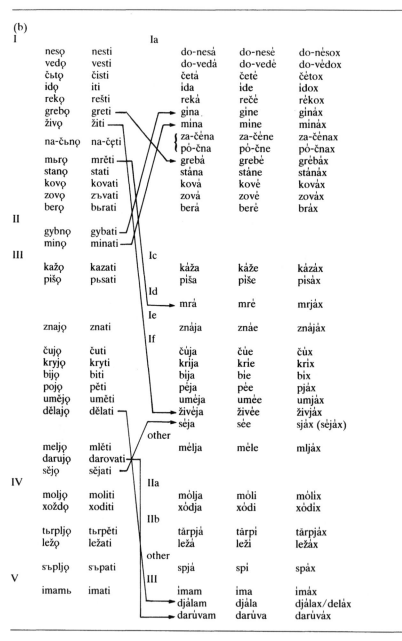

(b)

I

Ia

neso	nesti	do-nesá	do-nesé	do-nésox
vedo	vesti	do-vedá	do-vedé	do-védox
čьto	čisti	četá	četé	četox
ido	iti	ida	ide	idox
reko	rešti	reká	rečé	rékox
grebo	greti	gina	gine	gináx
živo	žiti	mina	mine	mináx
na-čьno	na-čęti	za-čéna	za-čéne	za-čénax
		pó-čna	pó-čne	pó-čnax
mьro	mrěti	grebá	grebé	grébáx
stano	stati	stána	stáne	stánáx
kovo	kovati	ková	kové	kováx
zovo	zъvati	zová	zové	zováx
bero	bьrati	berá	beré	bráx

II

| gybno | gybati | | | |
| mino | minati | | | |

III

Ic

| kažo | kazati | káža | káže | kázáx |
| pišo | pьsati | pìša | pìše | pisáx |

Id

| | | mrá | mré | mrjáx |

Ie

| znajo | znati | znája | znáe | znájáx |

If

čujo	čuti	čúja	čúe	čúx
kryjo	kryti	krìja	krìe	krix
bijo	biti	bìja	bìe	bìx
pojo	pěti	péja	pée	pjáx
umějo	uměti	uméja	umée	umjáx
dělajo	dělati	živéja	živée	živjáx
		séja	sée	sjáx (séjáx)

other

meljo	mlěti	mélja	méle	mljáx
darujo	darovati			
sějo	sějati			

IV

IIa

| moljo | moliti | mólja | móli | mólix |
| xoždo | xoditi | xódja | xódi | xódix |

IIb

| tьrpljo | tьrpěti | tărpjá | tărpi | tărpjáx |
| ležo | ležati | ležá | leži | ležáx |

other

| sъpljo | sъpati | spjá | spi | spáx |

V

III

imamь	imati	imam	ima	imáx
		djálam	djála	djálax/deláx
		darúvam	darúva	darúváx

infinitive and supine, loss of present active, present passive and non-resultative past active participles, simplification of the simple imperative, generalization of a single aorist formation, restructuring of imperfect forms on the present stem, elimination of the results of dental and labial assimilations to *j (see section 2.2), and changes in individual suffixes. The third conjugation, a Bulgarian innovation, was accomplished by extending the unproductive Proto-Slavonic athematic type Old Church Slavonic 'have' PRS 1 SG *imatь* to many first-conjugation verbs with present theme *-je-* (table 5.11). This conjugation, by far the largest, is productive for derivation of secondary imperfectives and the assimilation of borrowed verbs. Otherwise, vestiges of athematic forms are limited: first person singulars дам/dám '(I) give (PRFV)' (otherwise /dad-/: дадеш/dadéš '(you-SG) give') and ям/jám '(I) eat (IMPFV)' (otherwise /jad-/: ядеш/jadéš); imperatives яж(те)/jáž(te) 'eat (2 SG (PL))', виж(те)/víž(te) 'see (2 SG (PL))'.

The following paradigms illustrate the first subtype of each conjugation; those of other subtypes follow from the examples in table 5.11.

Conjugation Ia 'read'

	Present	Imperfect	Imperative	Aorist
1 SG	чета/četá	четях/četjáx		чётох/čétox
2 SG	четеш/četéš	четеше/četéše	чети/četí	чёте/čéte
3 SG	чете/četé	четеше/četéše		чёте/čéte
1 PL	четем/četém	четяхме/četjáxme		чётохме/čétoxme
2 PL	четете/četéte	четяхте/četjáxte	четете/četéte	чётохте/čétoxte
3 PL	четат/četát	четяха/četjáxa		чётоха/čétoxa

Stem-final /t/ or /d/ is lost before /l/ of the aorist participle: M SG чёл/ čél. Otherwise, the consonant is retained with vowel–zero alternation: 'bake' M SG пёкъл/pékäl – F SG пёкла/pékla. Retraction of stress to the root is regular in aorist forms.

Conjugation IIa 'go, walk'

	Present	Imperfect	Imperative	Aorist
1 SG	ходя/xódja	ходех/xódex		ходих/xódix
2 SG	ходиш/xódiš	ходеше/xódeše	ходи/xodí	ходи/xódi
3 SG	ходи/xódi	ходеше/xódeše		ходи/xódi
1 PL	ходим/xódim	ходехме/xódexme		ходихме/xódixme
2 PL	ходите/xódite	ходехте/xódexte	ходете/xodéte	ходихте/xódixte
3 PL	ходят/xódjat	ходеха/xódexa		ходиха/xódixa

This is the only conjugational type that regularly contrasts two stress patterns; compare 'pay' PRS 1 SG платя/platjá, AOR 1 SG платих/platíx.

Conjugation III 'have'

	Present	Imperfect	Imperative	Aorist
1 SG	имам/imam	имах/imax		имах/imax
2 SG	имаш/imaš	имаше/imaše	имай/imaj	има/ima
3 SG	има/ima	имаше/imaše		има/ima
1 PL	имаме/imame	имахме/imaxme		имахме/imaxme
2 PL	имате/imate	имахте/imaxte	имайте/imajte	имахте/imaxte
3 PL	имат/imat	имаха/imaxa		имаха/imaxa

The negated form of 'have' is suppletive: 1 SG PRS нямам/njamam, 1 SG
AOR нямах/njamax and немах/nemax.

The **optional** shift of stress from the root in the present to the suffix
vowel in the aorist occurs in other aorist forms as well: M SG AOR PART
ходил/xodil, имал/imal. Reflecting variation in usage, reference works
do not agree on which stems allow shifted forms. In any case, verbs of
foreign origin are least likely to shift: 'telephone' 1 SG PRS телефонирам/
telefoniram and 1 SG AOR телефонирах/telefonirax.

The conjugational pattern of 'be' is suppletive:

	Present	Imperfect/aorist	Imperative
1 SG	съм/sǎm	бях/bjax	
2 SG	си/si	бе(ше)/be(še)	бъди/bǎdi
3 SG	е/e	бе(ше)/be(še)	
1 PL	сме/sme	бяхме/bjaxme	
2 PL	сте/ste	бяхте/bjaxte	бъдете/bǎdete
3 PL	са/sa	бяха/bjaxa	

Imperfect/aorist participle: M SG бил/bil, F SG била/bila,
                              N SG било/bilo, PL били/bili

Present forms are clitics. Alternative present forms, based on the stem of
the imperative, 1 SG бъда/bǎda, 2 SG бъдеш/bǎdeš, often replace regular
present forms in future constructions and infinitival *da*-constructions.

Preserving a Proto-Slavonic anomaly, the aorist past participle of /id-/
(-jd-) 'go' is suppletive: M SG -шъл/-šǎl and -шел/-šel, F SG -шла/-šla,
N SG -шло/-šlo, PL -шли/-šli; for example 'arrive' 1 SG PRS дойда/dojda,
M SG AOR PART дошъл/došǎl.

3.3 Derivational morphology

3.3.1 Major patterns of noun derivation
Noun derivation is **suffixal** or **compound**. Suffixal formations are **emotive**
or **non-emotive**. Productive emotive formations are (1) **augmentative** and/
or **pejorative**: женище/ženište 'large woman' (< жена/žena 'woman'),
дебелан/debelan 'obese person' (< дебел/debel 'fat (M SG ADJECTIVE)');
or (2) **diminutive** and/or **endearing**: столче/stolče 'stool' (< стол/stol
'chair'), бебенце/bebence '(dear) baby' (< бебе/bebe 'baby').

Typical productive non-emotive formations are:

1   /-ák-/: always stressed, masculine personal nouns: простáк/prosták 'simpleton' (< прóст/próst 'simple (M SG)').
2   /-áč-/: masculine personal agent nouns from verbal bases: водáч/ vodáč 'leader' (< 1 SG PRS вóдя/vódja '(I) lead').
3   /-(e)c-/: masculine personal nouns: лъжéц/lážéc 'liar' (< 1 SG PRS лъжá/lážá '(I) lie').
4   /-ic-/: feminine nouns, often counterparts to masculine nouns in /-(e)c-/: вдовúца/vdovíca 'widower' (< вдовéц/vdovéc 'widower').
5   /-k-/: diverse feminine nouns, including counterparts to masculine personal nouns: водáчка/vodáčka 'leader (F)', простáчка/ prostáčka 'simpleton (F)'.
6   /-ost-/: abstract de-adjectival feminine nouns: вярност/vjárnost 'fidelity' (< вéрен/véren 'faithful, true (M SG)').

There are two types of **compounding**: (1) **with 'linking' vowel /-o-/ (/-e-/)**: хлебопекáр/xlebopekár 'bread-baker' < хляб/xljáb 'bread' + пек-/pek- 'bake'; (2) **simple concatenation**: кандидáт-члéн/kandidát-člén 'non-voting member' < 'candidate' + 'member'.

Bulgarian adjectives are regularly used as nouns: нóвото/nóvoto 'the new one/thing (N)'. Several forms of this origin are used only in this way: 'insect' N SG насекóмо/nasekómo – PL насекóми/nasekómi (as adjective).

3.3.2   Major patterns of adjective derivation
Adjectives are formed by **suffixation** and **compounding**. Productive suffixal formations include:

1   /-(e)n-/: qualitative and relational adjectives: 'successful' M SG успéшен/uspéšen, F SG успéшна/uspéšna (< успéх/uspéx 'success').
2   /-in-/: possessive relational adjectives from animate feminine and masculine nouns with singulars in /-a/: сéстрин/séstrin 'sister's (M SG)' (< сестрá/sestrá 'sister').
3   /-ov-/: possessive relational adjectives from masculine personal nouns: брáтов/brátov 'brother's (M SG)' (< брáт/brát 'brother').

Compound formations use (1) **linking with /-o-/ (/e/)**, злочéст/ zločést 'unfortunate (M SG)' < зъл/zál 'evil (M SG)' + чест/čest 'fate', or (2) **simple concatenation**, полỳграмóтен/polùgramóten 'semi-literate (M SG)' < полу-/polu- 'semi' + грамóтен/gramóten 'literate (M SG)'.

See section 3.1.4 for comparative and superlative adjectives. Two other **stressed** prefixes affect the **degree** of adjectives: (1) въз-/váz- **attenuates** the adjective: въззелéн/vázzelén 'greenish (M SG)'; (2) прé-/pré-

heightens it: пре́доб҄ър/prédobăr 'too good, overly good (M SG)'.

3.3.3   Major patterns of verb derivation
A small number of Bulgarian **non-prefixed imperfective** stems are non-derived, such as пек-/pek- 'bake'. Most are formed with a limited number of **verbalizing suffixes**, which appear in the present and/or aorist stems; for example:

1   present stem in /-∅/ ~ aorist stem /-a-/: 'write' 1 SG PRS пи́ша/píša, 1 SG AOR пи́сах/písax (‹ пис-/pis- 'write');
2   present stem /-ėj-/ ~ aorist stem /-à-/: 'live' 1 SG PRS живе́я/živėja, 1 SG AOR живя́х/živjàx (‹ жи́в/živ 'alive (M SG)');
3   present stem in /-∅/ ~ aorist stem /-i-/: 'go, walk' 1 SG PRS хо́дя/ xódja, 1 SG AOR хо́дих/xódix (‹ хо́д/xód 'course, movement').

In the process of deriving perfective stems from non-prefixed imperfectives the meaning of the verbal base may be augmented (1) by the meaning of the perfectivizing prefix or (2) by the semelfactive meaning of the perfectivizing suffix /-n-/. For examples see section 3.2.1.

4   Syntax

4.1   Element order in declarative sentences
The **unmarked** order of main constituents in simple declarative sentences is **Subject–Verb–Object**: Ива́н отво́ри врата́та/Ivàn otvóri vratàta 'Ivan opened the door'. Other orders change the logical stress or other stylistic nuances: врата́та отво́ри Ива́н/vratàta otvóri Ivàn '*Ivan* opened the door' (Rudin 1986: 14ff.; Пенчев/Penčev 1984: 89ff.).

Adverbial modifiers in verb phrases normally come at the end of the sentence: Ива́н ще до́йде ту́к ра́но у́тре/Ivàn šte dójde tùk ràno ùtre 'Ivan will come here early tomorrow'.

Subjectless sentences are common. Some result from the omission of subject pronouns (see section 4.7). Others – with neuter third person singular verbs – seem to be genuinely **impersonal**; these include (1) verbs denoting natural phenomena (вали́/vali 'precipitates'), (2) the copula 'be' plus adjectives (горе́що е/gorėšto e '(it) is hot'), (3) reflexivized verbs in constructions denoting desire/lack of desire, permission or prohibition (see section 3.2.1), (4) modal verbs (such as би́ва/bíva 'ought', тря́бва/ trjàbva 'needs, must'), (5) certain copular verbs (such as стру́ва се/strùva se 'seems', изгле́жда/izglėžda 'appears').

Bulgarian has many **clitics** – phonologically unstressed words – whose positions with respect to other constituents are fixed. **Proclitics** include (1) prepositions (из на́шата страна́/iz nàšata stranà 'throughout our country'), (2) the negative particle не/ne 'not' (see section 4.6), (3) the future auxiliary ще/šte (section 3.2.1), (4) the infinitival complementizer да/da (искам да пиша/iskam da piša '(I) want to write'), (5) the conjunctions и/i 'and', но/no 'but', а/a 'and/but' and the complementizer че/če 'that' (и мене/i mene 'me too' (= 'and me')).

Enclitics include (1) the definite article (see section 3.1.1), (2) the interrogative particle ли/li (section 4.2), (3) 'short' dative personal pronouns denoting possession (section 4.9).

Two groups of verbal clitics – (1) non-emphatic dative and accusative personal pronouns (as indirect and direct objects, respectively) and (2) present forms of 'be' – are **variable**: when the verb phrase is the **initial** constituent of the sentence, they are **enclitics** on its first stressed constituent; otherwise they are **proclitics**. In addition, dative pronominal clitics precede accusatives; third person singular 'be' follows pronominal clitics while other persons and numbers precede them:

Дал си му ги./Dàl si mu gi.
gave-M SG be-2 SG-PRS him-DAT
        them-ACC
'(You-SG) have given them to him.'

Ти си му ги дал./Tì si mu gi dàl.
you-SG be-2 SG-PRS him-DAT them-ACC
        gave-M SG
'You-SG have given them to him.'

Дала му ги е./Dàla mu gi e.
gave-F SG him-DAT them-ACC
       be-3 SG-PRS
'(She) has given them to him.'

Тя му ги е дала./Tjà mu gi e dàla.
she him-DAT them-ACC be-3 SG-PRS
        gave-F SG
'She has given them to him.'

For details on the interaction among various rules of clitic placement see Hauge (1976) and Ewen (1979).

The order of constituents within simple **noun phrases** is:

demonstrative + possessive + quantifier + adjectival + noun + prepositional
pronoun   pronoun   phrase(s)   phrase

The minimal noun phrase is a single noun; the maximal noun phrase contains all of the above elements: тези мои две много скъпи нови книги от Германия/tèzi mòi dvè mnògo skǎpi nòvi knìgi ot Germànija 'these my two very expensive new books from Germany'.

Quantifiers include cardinal numerals and other quantifying words, such as малко/màlko 'few, little' and много/mnògo 'many, much' (see section 4.10). Only cardinal numerals co-occur with pronouns; *тези мои много книги/tèzi mòi mnògo knìgi 'these my many books' is impossible.

The definite article and demonstrative pronouns do not co-occur: тези книги/tèzi knìgi 'these books' or книгите/knìgite 'the books'.

Adjectival phrases contain any number of adjectives. Adjectives are modified by adverbs of quantity or degree, which regularly precede them: много интересен човек/mnògo interesèn čovèk 'a very interesting person'. Adverbs of this type also modify predicate adverbials (above): мно́го ху́баво/mnógo xúbavo 'very nicely'.

Adjectives and other inflected noun-phrase attributes may follow their heads. Very rhetorical, this usage is common in poetry, both literary and folk: векове́ це́ли/ра́зум и съвест с не́я се бо́рят .../vekové céli/ rázum i sávest s néja se bórjat ... 'entire centuries/reason and conscience struggle with it ...' (= 'centuries entire'; Xristo Botev, cited Граматика/ Gramatika 3: 286).

4.2 Non-declarative sentence types
There are two types of **interrogative** sentences.

1 **Yes–no** questions use several **question-markers**; much less frequently, they are formally identical to declarative sentences but carry a final rising intonation (rather than a falling, declarative intonation).

Neutral yes–no questions use the particle ли/li. The particle follows the first stressed constituent of the verb phrase, if the scope of interrogation is the entire sentence; otherwise it follows the interrogated constituent. In either case, the constituent to which the particle is attached begins the question:

Йскат ли раки́я?/Ískat li rakija?
'Do (they) want brandy?'
Раки́я ли и́скат?/Rakija li ískat?
'Is it brandy (they) want?'

Rarely, the questioned constituent is not initial: мо́жеш да плу́ваш ли?/ móžeš da plúvaš li? and да плу́ваш ли мо́жеш?/da plúvaš li móžeš? 'can (you-SG) *swim*?' (Граматика/Gramatika 3: 53).

In neutral questions an overt subject may follow or precede the interrogated verb phrase. The latter construction, which topicalizes the subject, is marked by a sharp intonational rise over the subject followed by a slight pause before the predicate: ще до́йде ли Ива́н?/šte dójde li Ivan? ~ Ива́н ¦ ще до́йде ли?/Ivan ¦ šte dójde li? 'will Ivan come?'.

Дали́/dali introduces a strongly rhetorical question or one which the speaker regards as difficult to answer in some sense: дали́ ще ни прие́мат?/dali šte ni priémat? 'will (they or won't they) accept us?' (Граматика/Gramatika 3: 54).

Нали́/nali introduces a question anticipating a positive answer: нали́ сте бо́лен?/nali ste bólen? '(you-M SG POLITE) are sick(, aren't you)?'. It is also the universal tag question after declarative sentences: то́й е бо́лен, нали́?/tój e bólen, nali? 'he's sick, isn't he?'.

Нима́/nima forms questions anticipating negative answers, often with a sense of surprise, shock or doubt: нима́ то́й ме е видя́л?/nima tój me e vidjál? 'did he see me?' (= could he possibly have seen me?).

A positive simple question is answered да/dá 'yes' or нé/né 'no' to express the hearer's assertion of the truth or falseness of the corresponding statement:

Ивáн, изпрáти ли писмóто?/Ivàn, izpràti li pismóto?
'Did Ivan send the letter?'
True: Дá, (изпрáти го)./Dà, (izpràti go).
'Yes, ((he) sent it).'
False: Нé, (не гó изпрáти)./Né, (ne gó izpràti).
'No, ((he) didn't send it).'

Simple negative questions, formed with the negative particle не/ne, are answered on the basis of the hearer's assertion of the truth or falseness of the corresponding positive statement:

Не изпрáти ли Ивáн писмóто?/Ne izpràti li Ivàn pismóto?
'Didn't Ivan send the letter?'
He *did not* send it: Нé, (не гó изпрáти)./Né, (ne gó izpràti).
'No, ((he) didn't send it).'
He *did* send it: Дá, изпрáти го./Dà, izpràti go.
'Yes, (he) sent it.'

As an answer to a negative question, да/dá alone is unacceptable. See Лакова/Lakova (1978; examples hers).

2 **Constituent questions** are formed with interrogative pronouns (see section 3.1.3) and interrogative adverbs such as кáк/kàk 'how', къдé/kădé 'where', когá/kogà 'when' and защó/zaštó 'why'. Such wh words generally begin questions: каквó вѝждаш?/kakvó vìždaš? 'what do (you-SG) see?'. Prepositions always precede the wh words they govern: с когó рабóтиш?/s kogó rabótiš? 'with whom are (you-SG) working?'. Multiple wh words normally occur in the beginning of the sentence: кóй каквó когá кáзва?/kój kakvó kogà kàzva? 'who says what when?' (= 'who what when says'). Questions with non-initial wh words are interpreted as echo questions: тѝ си видя́л когó?/tì si vidjàl kogó? 'you-SG saw whom?' (Rudin 1986: 82).

wh words and ли/li co-occur in two ways. (1) ли/li after an initial wh word makes a strongly rhetorical question: и каквá ли слáдост намѝрат в нéго?/i kakvà li slàdost namìrat v négo? 'and what sweetness do (they) find in it?'. (2) Sentence-final ли/li makes an echo question: каквó ще я́м ли?/kakvó šte jàm li? 'what will (I) eat?', as an echo to каквó ще ядéш?/kakvó šte jadéš? 'what will (you-SG) eat?' (Граматика/Gramatika 3: 61).

Simple questions with далѝ/dalì or, less commonly, ли/li and questions with wh words may be embedded in diverse syntactic positions:

Не зная дали е там./Ne znája dali e tám. ~ Не зная там ли е./Ne znája tám li e.
'(I) don't know whether (he/she/it) is there.'

(Дали/dali is more common in indirect questions than ли/li; Rudin 1986: 63.)

Питаха ме, кой те е търсил./Pítaxa me, kój te e tårsil.
'(They) asked me who was looking for you-SG.'

Commands are expressed with **simple** or **compound** imperatives. Simple imperatives are limited to second person singular and plural (see section 3.2). Negative simple imperatives use (1) the negated simple imperative or (2) недей(те) да/nedéj(te) da + second person present tense: не пиши!/ne piší! ~ недей да пишеш!/nedéj da píšeš! 'don't write (you-SG)!'. Rarely, недей(те)/nedéj(te) is followed by the vestigial infinitive (section 3.2): недей писа!/nedéj pisa! Only simple imperfective imperatives can be negated. Positive imperatives are possible for both imperfective and perfective verbs; imperfectives carry a sense of urgency lacking in perfectives.

Compound imperatives use да/da or нека (да)/néka (da) + present tense:

Нека аз (да) пиша!/Néka áz (da) píša!
'Let me write!'
Да знаеш какво става!/Da znáeš kakvó stáva!
'(You-SG) should/ought to know what's happening!/May (you-SG) know what's happening!'

Second-person formations with да/da are more categorical than simple imperatives. Forms with нека/néka carry an element of exhortation; they are uncommon in the second person (Граматика/Gramatika 3: 69ff.).

Present- and future-tense forms spoken with the intonational pattern of simple imperatives commonly serve as imperatives: ще пишеш и ти!/šte píšeš i ti! 'and you-SG too will write!'.

4.3 Copular sentences
Copular sentences use 'be' or one of a small number of other verbs, notably бивам/bivam '(I) happen (to be)', оставам/ostávam '(I) remain', ставам/stávam '(I) become'. Predicate adjectives, including participles, agree in number and gender with the subject: Мама изглежда болна/Máma izgléžda bólna 'Mother looks sick-F SG'. With second person plural personal pronouns referring to singular addressees for politeness (see section 3.2), participles in compound verbal forms and predicative adjectives are **singular** and masculine or feminine as appropriate; simple verbal forms are plural: вие сте била много добра/vie ste bilá mnógo dobrá

'you (= F SG) have been very kind' (= 'you-PL are-2 PL be-F SG-PAST PART very kind-F SG'). In formal writing and speech adjectives and participles in these constructions are often plural.

Perceived qualities or states are commonly expressed by impersonal sentences using neuter adjectives, 'be' and optional prepositional phrases with на/na or clitic dative personal pronouns:

Студе́но ми е./Studéno mi e.
'I feel cold.' (= cold-N SG me-DAT is')
На Ива́н му е мно́го ску́чно./Na Iván mu e mnógo skúčno.
'Ivan is very bored.' (= 'to Ivan him-DAT is very boring-N SG'; for duplicated pronoun see 4.7)

A similar construction with a small number of nouns, like стра́х/strax 'fear', сра́м/sram 'shame', uses an **accusative** pronoun: сра́м го е/sram go e 'he is ashamed' (= 'shame him-ACC is') (Грама́тика/Gramatika 3: 95).

4.4   Coordination and comitativity
The **coordination** of all types of phrasal constituents is possible with the conjunction и/i 'and' preceding the last coordinated constituent: ку́пих си ри́за, чадъ́р и ша́пка/kúpix si ríza, čadăr i šápka '(I) bought myself a shirt, an umbrella and a hat'. Repetition of the conjunction before all conjoined elements stresses their parallelism: и Пе́тър и Ива́н оти́доха на ма́ч/i Pétăr i Iván otídoxa na máč 'both Peter and Ivan went to the game'.

Complete sentences are conjoined with и/i: дъ́жд вали́ и вя́тър ду́ха/dăžd vali i vjátăr dúxa 'rain is falling and wind blowing'. Here repetition or deletion of the coordinating conjunction adds a stylized, literary flavour:

И слъ́нцето се въртѐше, и врѐмето летѐше и изти́чаше като́ ста́до, като́ река́, като́ о́блак./I slănceto se vărtѐše, i vrѐmeto letѐše i iztíčaše kató stádo, kató reká, kató óblak.
'And the sun was revolving, and time was flying and running out like a flock, like a river, like a cloud.' (A. Donček, cited in Грама́тика/Gramatika 3: 294)

Coordinated subjects generally show plural verbal concord (examples above). Singular agreement is also possible, for example (1) with paired subjects construed as a unit: в кола́та ѐкна смя́х и ки́кот/v kolάta ѐkna smjάx i kίkot 'in the car (there) resounded-3 SG laughter and giggling'; or (2) with coordinated series: ни́е не щѐ ка́жем ни́що дру́го осве́н това́ че все́ки чове́к и все́ки наро́д те́гли от ума́ си/níe ne štѐ kάžem nίšto drúgo osvѐn tová če vsѐki čovѐk i vsѐki naród tѐgli ot umá si 'we shall say nothing except that every person and every nation is responsible for itself'. For additional details on singular agreement with plural subjects see Граматика/Gramatika 3: 146–54 (preceding examples there).

Comitative constructions use a prepositional phrase with c/s 'with': ма́йка с дете́ ча́каше на опа́шката/májka s deté čákaše na opáškata 'a mother (together) with a child waited (SG) in the line'. Pronominal heads of comitative constructions, regardless of their actual number, are plural, as are related verbs: ни́е с баща́ ми оти́дохме на ки́но/níe s baštá mi otídoxme na kino 'I went to the movies with my father/my father and I went to the movies' (= 'we with father me-DAT ...'). Comitative constructions are possible as direct and indirect objects:

Аресту́ваха ги с баща́ му./Arestúvaxa gi s baštá mu.
'(They) arrested him and his father.' (= '... them-ACC with father him-DAT')
На на́с със жена́ ми ни изпра́тиха пода́рък./Na nás săs žená mi ni izprátixa podárăk.
'(They) sent me and my wife a gift.' (= 'to us-ACC with wife me-DAT us-DAT ...')

Other types of coordination utilize other conjunctions: или́/iĺi 'or', или́ ... или́/iĺi ... iĺi 'either ... or', a/a 'and, but' (contrasting opposition), но/no 'but, however' (strong contrast, contradiction), оба́че/obáče 'however' (stronger, more literary form of но/no):

Аз и́мам чадъ́р, а тя́ ня́ма./Az imam čadắr, a tjá njáma.
'I have an umbrella, but she doesn't.'
Пие́сата и́ма голя́м успе́х, но въпреки́ това́ па́дна./Piésata íma goljám uspéx, no văpreki tová pádna.
'The play had great success, but nevertheless closed (literally 'fell').'

4.5   Subordination

Headed relative clauses, postposed to noun phrases, are marked by initial relative pronouns (see section 3.1.3), preceded by prepositions governing them. The number and gender of relative pronouns agree with their antecedents; case is determined by the function of the pronouns in the relative clauses: изпра́тих паке́т на студе́нта, с кого́то се запозна́хме ми́налата годи́на в Со́фия/izprátix pakét na studénta, s kogóto se zapoznáxme minalata gódina v Sófija '(I) sent a package to the student, with whom I got acquainted (= with whom-ACC self-ACC acquainted-1 PL) last year in Sofia'. Relative clauses using relativizers formed from interrogative adverbs modify prepositional and adverbial phrases: наме́рих кни́гата та́м, къде́то я бях оста́вил/namérix knigata tám, kădéto ja bjáx ostávil '(I) found the book there, where (I) had left it'.

Relative pronouns with noun phrase antecedents have alternative formations with the invariant relative pronoun де́то/déto 'that'. Most frequent in dialects, this construction is colloquial in literary Bulgarian: това́ е кни́гата де́то (~ коя́то) бе́ше на ма́сата/tová e knigata déto (~ kojáto) béše na másata 'that is the book that (which) was on the table'.

If дѐто/dèto is *not* the subject of its clause, the clause *may* contain a clitic personal pronoun 'echoing' the grammatical categories of the antecedent; in relativization from a prepositional phrase a full, stressed personal pronoun is necessary as the object of the preposition:

Товà е кнѝгата дѐто (я) кỳпих./Tovà e knigata dèto (ja) kùpix.
'This is the book that (it) (I) bought.'
Товà е кнѝгата дѐто говòрехме за нѐя./Tovà e knigata dèto govòrexme za nèja.
'This is the book that (we) spoke about (it).'

See Rudin (1986: 129–30) for discussion; the examples are hers.
Free (headless) relatives are possible:

Вземѝ каквòто ѝскаш!/Vzemi kakvòto iskaš!
'(You-SG) take whatever (you-SG) want!'
Кòйто не внимàва, тòй прàви грѐшки./Kòjto ne vnimàva, tòj pràvi grèški.
'Whoever doesn't pay attention, makes mistakes.'

In multiple free rlatives all WH words are clause initial: кòйто къдѐто е свѝкнал, тàм си живѐе/kòjto kădèto e sviknal, tàm si živèe 'everyone lives where he's accustomed' (= 'whoever wherever is became-accustomed-M SG, there self-DAT lives'; Rudin 1986: 167).

The complementizer че/če 'that' introduces subordinate clauses as complements of verbs of saying or believing, as complements of nouns and as sentential subjects:

Мѝсля че скòро ще завалѝ дъжд./Mislja če skòro šte zavali dàžd.
'(I) think that soon (it) will rain.'
Имам чỳвство че ще дòйдат./Imam čùvstvo če šte dòjdat.
'(I) have a feeling that (they) will come.'
Сѝгурно е че нѝма да дòйдат./Sigurno e če njàma da dòjdat.
'(It) is certain that (they) won't come.'

In place of an **infinitive**, Bulgarian uses a subordinate clause consisting of да/da plus a present-tense verbal form which agrees in person and number with its implicit subject. Infinitive-like '*da*-clauses' are used as complements of many modal verbs (for example, трѝбва/trjàbva '(it) is necessary', ѝскам/iskam '(I) want', мòга/mòga '(I) can'), as complements of verbs of motion or being, as nominal complements, as sentential subjects and in indefinite constructions with 'have' and 'have not':

Ѝскам да отѝда на мàч./Iskam da otida na màč.
'(I) want-1 SG to go-1 SG to a game.'
Дошлѝ сме да слỳшаме мỳзика./Došli sme da slùšame mùzika.
'(We) have come to listen-1 PL to music.'
Нѝмам намерѐние да се напрѝгам./Njàmam namerènie da se naprjàgam.
'(I) don't have (the) intention to exert-1 SG myself.'

Ѝмам с когó да говóря./Ìmam s kogó da govórja.
'(I) have someone to talk to.' (= 'have-1 SG with whom-ACC to talk-1 SG')

The subject of a main clause may differ from that of a *da*-clause: дошлѝ сме да ни разкáжете за пътýването си в Бългáрия/došlì sme da ni razkážete za pătúvaneto si v Bălgárija '(we) have come for (you-PL) to tell us about your (own) trip to Bulgaria'. See Rudin (1986) for discussion of Bulgarian complementizers and relative clauses.

The vestigial **infinitive** (see section 3.2.1) occurs rarely in the literary language as the complement of мóга/móga '(I) can' and смѐя/smèja '(I) dare', and in negative imperatives (section 4.2): не мóга пѝса/ne móga pìsa '(I) can't write'. *Da*-clauses are normal here: не мóга да пѝша/ne móga da pìša '(I) can't write'.

Diverse subordinate clauses expressing circumstances related to the actions of main clauses are formed with subordinating conjunctions.

1 **Conditional** clauses use the conjunction áко/áko 'if' (or its colloquial, poetic variant да/da). **Real** conditionals use indicative verbal forms in both condition and result clauses: áко дóйдат, ще ги вѝдим/áko dójdat, šte gi vìdim 'if (they) come, (we) will see them'. **Contrary-to-fact** conditionals normally use imperfect or past perfect indicative forms in the condition clause and subjunctive or past future indicative forms in the result clause; these tense distinctions apparently entail no semantic differences: бѝх я поздравѝл (щях да я поздравя́), áко бях тáм/bìx ja pozdravìl (štjáx da ja pozdravjá), áko bjáx tám '(I) would greet/would have greeted her, if (I) were/had been there'.

2 Other subordinate clauses function as predicate **adverbials** of time, place, manner, reason and so on:

Говóриш, *без да* знáеш каквó стáва./Govóriš, *bez da* znáeš kakvó stáva.
'(You-SG) speak *without* knowing (= without to know-2 SG) what is happening.'
Докóлкото ми е извéстно, ня́ма да дóйдат./*Dokólkoto* mi e izvéstno, njáma da dójdat.
'*As far as* (it) is known to me, (they) will not come.'

In written and formal spoken Bulgarian **participial phrases** often replace relative clauses. An active participle – either present or aorist – replaces a **subject** relative pronoun and its verb. The participle is present tense if the action of the verb in the relative clause is **contemporaneous** with that of the main verb; it is aorist if the action of the verb of the relative clause **precedes** that of the main verb:

Познáвах протестѝращите хóра./Poznávax protestiraštite (PRS ACT PART) xóra.
'(I) knew the protesting people.'

Намѐрихме пристѝгналия влѐк./Namѐrixme pristignalija (AOR ACT PART) vlɑ̀k. '(We) found the arrived train.'

A past passive participle replaces a transitive verb and direct object relative pronoun: намѐрих загу̀бената кнѝга/namѐrix zagùbenata (PAST PASS PART) kniga '(I) found the lost book'.

The sense of a present passive participle (otherwise lacking) is expressed by an imperfective past passive participle: нòсена от слɑ̀бия у̀тринен вя̀тър, [отрòвна мъглɑ̀] запълзя̀ .../nòsena (IMPFV PAST PASS PART) ot slɑ̀bija ùtrinen vjɑ̀tăr, [otròvna măglɑ̀] zapălzjɑ̀ ... 'carried by the weak morning wind, [a poisonous fog] drifted ...' (Маслов/Maslov 1981: 262).

Participial phrases regularly allow diverse predicative elements: мнòго са желɑ̀ещите да почѝват ту̀к/mnògo sa želɑ̀eštite (PRS ACT PART) da počivat tùk 'many are those wishing (literally 'wishing-the') to vacation here' (*Narodna mladež*, 1 December 1989). While usually preposed to their heads (see above), participial phrases may also be postposed: ... след кардинɑ̀лните промѐни, настъ̀пили в БКП/... sled kardinɑ̀lnite promèni, nastɑ̀pili (AOR ACT PART) v BKP '... after the fundamental changes, which have taken place in the BCP (= Bulgarian Communist Party)' (*Narodna mladež*, 1 December 1989).

An adverbial subordinate clause may be replaced by a **gerundive** phrase if (1) the subjects of both clauses are the same and (2) the action of the subordinate clause is contemporaneous with that of the main clause: четѐйки нòвия му ромɑ̀н, намѐрих .../četèjki nòvija mu romɑ̀n, namèrix ... '[while] reading his new novel, (I) found ...'. Postposed active participles occasionally function as gerunds: машѝната тѐглеше лѐко и плɑ̀вно, не усѐщаща товɑ̀ра/mašinata tègleše lèko i plɑ̀vno, ne usèštaša (PRS ACT PART) tovɑ̀ra 'the car drew away easily and smoothly, not feeling the load' (Маслов/Maslov 1981: 282–3).

Gerundive phrases are limited to formal writing and speech, and even there they are avoided. A study of a corpus of 15,000 words of a modern Russian novel and its Bulgarian translation found that of 107 gerunds in the Russian original, only fifteen (14 per cent) were translated as Bulgarian gerunds; the rest were replaced by subordinate clauses (Дончева/Dončeva 1975).

The extraction of interrogative and relative pronouns from various types of embedded clauses has been studied by Rudin (1986). The following summarizes her major findings.

Questions cannot be formed by extraction from indirect (embedded) questions: *когò се чу̀диш кòй е видя̀л?/kogò se čùdiš kòj e vidjɑ̀l? 'whom do (you-SG) wonder who saw?'. However, interrogation and extraction are possible over the complementizer че/če 'that': когò мѝслиш че е видя̀л?/kogò misliš če e vidjɑ̀l? 'whom do you think that he saw?' (examples from Rudin 1986: 105f.).

Relative-clause formation can move relative pronouns an indefinite distance: кни́гата, коя́то ти́ ми ка́за че Ива́н ми́сли че Пе́тър и́ска да ку́пи .../knigata kojàto ti mi kàza če Ivàn misli če Pètăr iska da kùpi ... 'the book which you-SG told me that Ivan thinks that Peter wants to buy ...'. Similarly, the relativizer де́то/dèto 'that' is interpreted over an unbounded domain: кни́гата де́то ти́ ми ка́за че Ива́н ми́сли че Пе́тър и́ска да (я) ку́пи .../knigata dèto ti mi kàza če Ivàn misli če Pètăr iska da (ja) kùpi ... 'the book that you-SG told me that Ivan thinks that Peter wants to buy (it) ...'.

The formation of WH relative clauses is blocked in two instances:

1   The determiner of a noun phrase cannot be relativized: *това́ е момче́то (на) кое́то тря́бва да наме́рим (не́говата) ма́йка/ *tovà e momčèto (na) koèto trjàbva da namèrim (nègovata) màjka 'this is the boy (of) whom (we) must find (his) mother'.

2   Relativization out of a noun phrase containing a head noun and a modifying clause is impossible: *това́ е момче́то на кое́то мисълта́ че (му) да́дохме бонбо́ни ядо́сва ле́каря/*tovà e momčèto na koèto misăltà če (mu) dàdoxme bonbòni jadòsva lèkarja 'this is the boy to whom the thought that (we) gave him candies angers the doctor'.

Relativization with де́то/dèto is grammatical in both cases. See Rudin (1986: 140–3) for additional discussion (examples hers).

The complementizer че/če 'that' cannot in general be deleted, including cases with movement across the complementizer:

Ми́сля че си видя́л чове́ка./Mislja če si vidjàl čovèka.
'(I) think that (you-SG) saw the man.'
Not *Ми́сля си видя́л .../*Mislja si vidjàl ...
'(I) think you saw ...'
Позна́вам чове́ка кого́то ми́сля че си видя́л./Poznàvam čovèka kogòto mislja če si vidjàl.
'(I) know the man whom (I) think that you saw.'

Infrequent examples with deletion of the complementizer are reported in direct speech (or thought): ми́сля си, ти́ си видя́л чове́ка/mislja si, ti si vidjàl čovèka '(I) think (to myself): you-SG saw the man' (Грама́тика/ Gramatika 3: 344).

4.6   Negation

A sentence or any of its constituents can be negated. If the scope of negation is the entire sentence, the negative particle не/ne attaches to the verb: то́й не рабо́ти/tòj ne ràboti 'he doesn't work'. Otherwise, не/ne precedes the negated constituent, which generally begins the sentence: не на Иван дадох книгата/ne na Ivàn dàdox knigata 'it wasn't Ivan I gave the book to' (= 'not to Ivan gave-1 SG book-the').

Negative sentences are conjoined with ни(то)/ni(to) 'neither, nor', repeated before each conjoined constituent: нито Иван, нито Валя, нито Димчо не знаят, къде живея/nito Ivàn, nito Vàlja, nito Dimčo ne znàjat, kàdè živèja 'neither Ivan, nor Valja, nor Dimčo know where I live'.

Negative constituent questions (see section 4.2) use negative pronouns and other negative pro-forms (section 3.1.3); here не/ne accompanies the verb as well:

На никого не казах новината./Na nikogo ne kàzax novinàta.
'(I) told no one the news.' (= to no-one-ACC not told-1 SG news-the')
Никога не слушат./Nikoga ne slùšat.
'(They) never listen.'

4.7 Anaphora and pronouns
The principal **anaphoric pronouns** of Bulgarian include:

1   third-person personal pronouns: той/tòj 'he, it'
2   personal possessive pronouns: негов/nègov 'his, its'
3   demonstrative pronouns: този/tòzi 'this (M SG)'
     онзи/ònzi 'that (M SG)'
     такъв/takàv 'such (M SG)'

Forms in /on-/ are marked as distanced from the speaker; forms in /t-/ are unmarked.

4   relative pronouns: който/kòjto 'who, which, that (M SG)'
     какъвто/kakàvto 'which sort (M SG)'
5   reflexive pronouns: себе си/sèbe si '-self'

(See section 3.1.3 for full paradigms; for relative, reflexive and personal possessive pronouns see also sections 4.5, 4.9 and 4.10.) For example:

Speaker A: Тя пише нова граматика./Tjà piše nòva gramàtika.
           'She's writing a new grammar.'
Speaker B: Тази граматика не ме интересува/Tàzi gramàtika ne mè
           interesùva
           'This grammar doesn't interest me.'
or B: Това не ме интересува./Tovà ne mè interesùva.
           'This doesn't interest me.'

Anaphoric adverbs are formed from the demonstrative root /t-/ 'this'; for example, там/tàm 'there', тука/tùka 'here', тогава/togàva 'then':

Откриха нов магазин. Там продават всичко./Otkríxa nóv magazín. Tám prodávat vsíčko '(They) found a new store. There (they) sell everything.'

The omission of pronominal subjects, including first and second person, is extremely common. In a comparison of a Russian novel and its Bulgarian translation, Дончева/Dončeva (1975) found that Bulgarian omitted 58 per cent of possible personal pronominal subjects (Russian only 42 per cent). Omission is naturally facilitated by verb and adjective concord with the subject: болен е/bólen e '(he) is sick-м SG'. Often, however, omission leaves the subject ambiguous within its clause: в момента пише/v moménta píše 'at the moment (he/she/it) writes'. In such cases the larger context provides the appropriate interpretation of the intended subject.

The presence or absence of overt personal pronominal subjects may be affected by discourse factors. According to Маслов/Maslov (1981: 356), the pronominal subject is omitted when topic, but retained when focus (where it generally identifies the actual agent among a number of possibilities); compare: днес отивам на кино/dnés otívam na kíno 'today (I) am going to the movies' versus днес аз отивам на кино/dnés áz otívam na kíno 'today *I* (as opposed to someone else) am going to the movies'.

'This' and 'that' used alone as subjects of copular verbs are invariably neuter singular, and verbal concord is with the predicate: това са моите нови дрехи/tová sa móite nóvi dréxi 'these (= this-N SG) are my new clothes'.

The **definite article** marks the presupposition that the referent of the noun phrase is known to the participants in the speech or narrated event: книгата е интересна/knígata e interésna 'the book is interesting'. See Mayer (1988) for details.

'The former' and 'the latter' are expressed by the definite ordinal numerals първият/pắrvijat 'the first (M SG)' and вторият/vtórijat 'the second (M SG)', inflected to agree with their antecedents: първият [пример] показва ..., а вторият .../pắrvijat [primer] pokázva ..., a vtórijat ... 'the former [example-м SG] shows ..., while the latter ...'. Longer series use successive ordinal numerals beyond 'second'.

In colloquial Bulgarian, and to some extent in more formal styles, nouns or full, stressed personal pronouns as direct or indirect objects are often 'echoed' by appropriately inflected clitic personal pronouns (Граматика/Gramatika 3: 186–8, 191). While clitic doubling is generally optional, it is subject to discourse factors: an emphasized noun phrase is apt to occur first in the sentence – the position of focus – and if the noun is the direct or indirect object the clitic pronoun is apt to appear (Rudin 1986: 139). Compare:

Neutral: Казах новините на Иван./Kázax novínite na Iván.
'(I) told the news to Ivan.'

Focus on Ivan: На Иван му казах новините./Na Ivan mu kazax novinite.
'(I) told the news *to Ivan*.' (= 'to Ivan him-DAT told-1 SG news-the')
Focus on news: Новините ги казах на Иван./Novinite gi kazax na Ivan.
'(I) told *the news* to Ivan.' (= 'news-the them-ACC told-1 SG to Ivan')

The pronoun is obligatory if the subject and direct object are ambiguous: майката я гледа детето/majkata ja gleda deteto 'the child takes care of the mother' (= 'mother-the-F SG her-ACC takes-care-of child-the-N SG') versus детето го гледа майката/deteto go gleda majkata 'the mother takes care of the child' (= 'child-the-N SG it-ACC takes-care-of mother-the-F SG').

Echoed clitics are not possible in WH-relative clauses: *човека, който Борис го видя/čoveka, kojto Boris go vidja 'the person, whom Boris saw' (= 'man-the who Boris him-ACC saw-3 SG') (Rudin 1986: 126, for discussion; example hers). On the other hand, echoed clitics with дето/deto-relatives are optional or obligatory depending on the syntactic function of the relative pronoun (see section 4.5 for examples and references).

Bulgarian grammars describe stressed personal pronouns as 'echoes' of subject nouns. Here, however, the nouns are in apposition to the personal pronouns: тя, бедната дама, започна да плаче/tja, bednata dama, započna da plača 'she, the poor lady, began to cry' (Граматика/Gramatika 3: 123; also Пенчев/Penčev 1984: 83).

4.8 Reflexives and reciprocals

Reflexive personal pronouns (see section 3.1.3) replace non-subject personal pronouns whose antecedents are the **subject** of the clause in which they occur: мия се/mija se '(I) wash myself'. Stressed forms – in the case of the dative a prepositional phrase with на/na + accusative – are used for emphasis: себе си мия/sebe si mija '(I) wash *myself*'. In other, non-dative prepositional phrases only stressed accusative forms are possible: той мисли само за себе си/toj misli samo za sebe si 'he thinks only about himself'.

In colloquial Bulgarian first- and second-person non-reflexive forms may replace reflexives in prepositional phrases: вземи ме с тебе!/vzemi me s tebe! ~ ... със себе си!/... săs sebe si! 'take me with you/yourself!'. Although considered non-standard, this usage is gaining ground. Substitution for direct or indirect objects is ungrammatical: only купи си нови дрехи!/kupi si novi drexi!, not *купи ти ~ *на тебе...!/*kupi ti ~ *na tebe ...! 'Buy-2 SG yourself new clothes!'.

Substitution of personal for reflexive pronoun in the third person regularly changes the pronominal reference: той го мие/toj go mie 'he washes him (= someone else)'.

The reflexive pronoun always refers to the subject of the verb of the clause in which it occurs. Through the subject, even if deleted, it may refer to earlier nouns and pronouns:

Ива́н и́ска да си ку́пи но́ва ри́за./Iván iska da si kúpi nóva ríza.
'Ivan wants to buy-3 SG himself a new shirt.'

Possessive expressions (see section 4.9) in predicates use reflexive personal pronouns and possessive adjectives in much the same way: а́з взе́х кни́гата си/áz vzéx knígata si 'I took my (own) book'. The dative enclitic reflexive is regularly replaced by the reflexive possessive adjective for emphasis: а́з взе́х сво́ята кни́га/áz vzéx svójata kníga 'I took *my own* book'. In the first and second person, non-reflexive possessives are possible for greater emphasis: взе́х мо́ята кни́га/vzéx mójata kníga 'it was *my* book that I took' (= 'took 1-SG my book'). Here dative non-reflexive forms are ungrammatical or questionable:

*Взе́х кни́гата ми./Vzéx knígata mi.
'(I) took my book.'
?Да́дох му кни́гата ми./Dádox mu knígata mi.
'(I) gave him my book.'

(Маслов/Maslov 1981: 302)

Reflexive possessives cannot be subjects or predicative nominatives: *ну́жна ми е сво́ята ста́я/*núžna mi e svójata stája 'I need my own room' (= 'necessary-F SG me-DAT is own-F SG room-F SG').

With plural subjects and verbs of appropriate meanings, **reciprocal** constructions are formed with enclitic reflexive pronouns, dative and accusative and/or the expression еди́н дру́г/edin drúg 'one another'. Enclitic pronouns are customary for direct and indirect objects: те́ се целу́ват/té se celúvat 'they kiss (one another)'. Еди́н дру́г/edin drúg is added for emphasis: те́ се целу́ват еди́н дру́г/té se celúvat edin drúg 'they kiss one another'. Еди́н дру́г/edin drúg is the unmarked form of this expression; feminine and neuter forms are used only with subjects that are all feminine or all neuter, respectively.

In other, non-dative prepositional phrases reciprocity is expressed only by еди́н дру́г/edin drúg: те́ нами́рат интере́сни неща́ еди́н в дру́г/té namírat interésni neštá edin v drúg 'they find interesting things in one another'.

Reciprocal sentences with enclitic reflexive pronouns may be ambiguous with respect to number: те́ си пи́шат/té si píšat may mean 'they-two write to one another' or 'they-more-than-two write among themselves'. The ambiguity is eliminated with еди́н дру́г/edin drúg. Compare те́ нами́рат интере́сни неща́ едни́ в дру́ги/té namírat interésni neštá edni (PL) v drúgi (PL) 'they (more than two) find interesting things in one another'.

In so far as they use the same pronouns, reflexive and reciprocal constructions are formally identical. The meaning of the verb often makes one or the other interpretation the more likely. Compare:

Мият се/Mijat se.
'(They) wash themselves.' (not '(They) wash each other.')
Бият се./Bijat se.
'(They) hit one another.' (not '(They) hit themselves.')

Alternative readings are forced and ambiguities avoided with céбе си/ sébe si '-self' and едѝн дрýг/edin drúg 'one another':

Мият се едѝн дрýг./Mijat se edin drúg.
'(They-two) wash one another.'
Céбе си бият./Sébe si bijat.
'(They) beat themselves.'

4.9 Possession

Possession is expressed verbally with ѝмам/imam '(I) have' and its negative counterpart нямам/njámam '(I) don't have': Ивáн ѝма мнóго приятели/Iván ima mnógo prijáteli 'Ivan has many friends'. Possession in noun phrases is expressed in several ways:

1   Clitic dative personal pronouns (see section 3.1.3): товá са кнѝгите ми/tová sa knigite mi 'these are my books' (= 'this-N SG are books-the me-DAT').
2   Prepositional phrases with на/na: товá е домъ́т на брáт ми/tová e domát na brát mi 'this is the home of my brother'.
3   Possessive personal pronouns (section 3.1.3): товá са мóите кнѝги/ tová sa móite knigi 'these are my books'.
4   Possessive adjectives derived from personal nouns (section 3.3.2): товá е брáтовият дóм/tová e brátovijat dóm 'this is (my) brother's home'. Adjectives of this sort are colloquial.

4.10 Quantification

The principal quantifiers of Bulgarian include cardinal numerals (see section 3.1.5), pronominal quantifiers (like кóлко/kólko 'how many, much') and мнóго/mnógo 'many, much', мáлко/málko 'few, little', немнóго/nemnógo 'not many, much'.

Two cardinal numerals are inflected for gender: '1' is masculine, feminine or neuter, depending on the gender of its head; '2' contrasts masculine and feminine/neuter forms. (See section 3.1.5 for forms and examples.)

Used alone, '1' governs a singular noun: еднá кнѝга/ednà kniga 'one book'. In compounds '1' is regularly singular and the noun plural or, less commonly, singular: трѝдесет и еднá кнѝги (кнѝга)/trideset i ednà (F SG) knigi (PL) (kniga (SG)) '31 books' (Граматика/Gramatika 2: 183).

With all other quantifiers, feminine and neuter nouns are plural: мнóго кнѝги/mnógo knigi 'many books (F)', двáдесет и двé писмá/dvàdeset i dvé pismá '22 letters (N)'. Masculine nouns with quantifiers make use of both normal and count plurals (see section 3.1.2):

1   All masculine nouns use the normal plural with 'many', 'few' and 'not many' or with 'how many' in exclamations: мнóго студéнти/mnógo studènti 'many students', кóлко студéнти!/kólko studènti! 'how many students!'.

2   Masculine personal nouns use the normal plural after cardinal numerals '2'–'6' in -(и)ма/-(i)ma: двáма студéнти/dvàma studènti 'two students'; otherwise they use the ordinary plural or count plural (with a clear preference for the former): пéт ученѝци/pét učenici ~ пéт ученѝка/pét učenika 'five pupils (PL ~ COUNT PL)'.

3   Otherwise, masculine non-personal nouns use the count plural: трѝ грáда/tri gràda 'three cities (COUNT PL)'.

'Incorrect' usage with masculine nouns is common; see Граматика/ Gramatika (2: 183) and Scatton (1984: 312–13).

Verbs with cardinal numerals as subjects are singular if the numeral is '1' alone; otherwise they are plural:

Еднá женá дойдé./Ednà ženà dojdè.
'One woman came.'
Двé женѝ дойдóха./Dvé ženi dojdóxa.
'Two women came.'

Personal pronouns are quantified with cardinal numerals. The pronoun occupies the first position; the numeral, generally definite, follows. Cardinals in -(и)ма/-(i)ma ('2'–'6') are used with groups of men or men and women: нѝе двáмата ще дóйдем/nie dvàmata šte dójdem 'we two (= two males or a male and a female) will come-1 PL'.

Quantification is also expressed by nouns denoting measurements (лѝтър/litàr 'litre'), containers (чáша/čàša 'cup, glass'), collections of elements (стáдо/stàdo 'herd'), parts (пóрция/pòrcija 'portion') and others. The quantifier precedes the noun, which is singular or plural as appropriate: лѝтър млякó/litàr mljàko 'a litre of milk', чѝфт вóлове/ čift vólove 'a pair of oxen'. In these constructions verbal concord is usually with the quantifier: чáшата вѝно е билá на мáсата/čàšata vino e bilà na màsata 'the glass-F SG of wine-N SG was-F 3 SG on the table'. However, groups show two types of concord: **singular**, focusing on the group as a unit, or **plural**, focusing on the latter as a collection of individuals:

Накрая група байловчани излезе на сцената./Nakrája grúpa bajlovčáni izléze na scénata.
'Finally a group of inhabitants-of-Bajlovo came-3 SG on stage.'
Група младежи от Русе заминали за Съветския съюз./Grúpa mladéži ot Rúse zaminali za Sâvétskija sâjúz.
'A group of young-people from Ruse left-3 PL for the Soviet Union.'

(Граматика/Gramatika 3: 151–2)

These quantifiers may themselves be quantified as ordinary nouns: две чаши вода/dvé čáši vodá 'two glasses of water'.

'Existential-be' is има/ima 'has'; its negative counterpart is няма/njáma 'hasn't'. They are invariably neuter third person singular and, as the syntax of pronominal forms shows, they take direct object complements:

Нямаше яйца./Njámaše jajcá.
'(There) weren't-3 SG eggs-PL.'
Има ги вкъщи./Íma gi vkâšti.
'They are at home.' (= 'has-3 SG them-ACC at-home')

5 Lexis

5.1 General composition of the word-stock

The standard 'Academy' dictionary of Bulgarian (Романски/Romanski 1955–9) contains over 63,000 entries, of which 25 per cent are foreign borrowings or words derived from them (Бояджиев/Bojadžiev 1970). Of native lexical items, perhaps as many as 2,000 are directly inherited from Proto-Slavonic through Old and Middle Bulgarian (Русинов/Rusinov 1980: 76). Inherited words represent diverse lexical domains and include much of the most common, basic vocabulary of the language. The number of words derived from them is perhaps 15–20 times greater, in the order of 30–40,000.

The relative weight of inherited Proto-Slavonic material can be estimated from Николова/Nikolova (1987) – a study of a 100,000-word corpus of conversational Bulgarian. Of the 806 items occurring there more than ten times, approximately 50 per cent may be direct reflexes of Proto-Slavonic forms; nearly 30 per cent are later Bulgarian formations and 17 per cent are foreign borrowings or words derived from them. (The remaining items are problematical; figures mine, EAS.)

Russian is the only Slavonic language that has had any significant influence on Bulgarian. Large numbers of native Russian and Russian Church Slavonic words are common throughout the language (examples below). Until recently, Russian has been the principal intermediary source for much of Bulgarian's international vocabulary.

5.2   Patterns of borrowing

Of approximately 16,200 foreign words in Романски/Romanski (1955–9), a single original source can be found for about 14,500. Of these, 96 per cent are attributable to only eight languages, each accounting for at least 1 per cent or more:

1	Latin	25.5%	(3,700)
2	Greek	23.0%	(3,350)
3	French	15.0%	(2,150)
4	Turkish*	13.5%	(1,900)
5	Russian	10.0%	(1,500)
6–7	Italian	3.5%	(500)
6–7	German	3.5%	(500)
8	English	2.0%	(300)

*including Arabic and Persian. Figures based on Бояджиев/Bojadžiev 1970.

The vast majority of **Latin** borrowings – mostly international terms in the areas of politics, civil administration, scholarship, law, medicine and others – entered the modern language through Russian or other, western languages: администра́ция/administrácija 'administration', секрета́р/sekretár 'secretary'. (The material here is based on Русинов/Rusinov 1980: 76–94, and works cited there.) A few date from Old and Middle Bulgarian.

Greek lexical material first entered Bulgarian during the Old Bulgarian period, mostly in the areas of religion and civil and military administration: ико́на/ikóna 'icon', деспо́т/despót. During the Ottoman period, strong Greek political and cultural influence facilitated borrowings not only of literary, but also common, popular lexical material: пиро́н/pirón 'nail', е́втин/évtin 'inexpensive'. During the Bulgarian Renaissance (eighteenth and nineteenth centuries), international vocabulary of Greek origin entered Bulgarian through Russian or other languages: грама́тика/gramátika 'grammar', демокра́ция/demokrácija 'democracy'.

French borrowings appear from the beginning of the nineteenth century, first from Russian, later directly from French. They are concentrated in social and political life, military affairs, cooking, dress and the arts: аташе́/ataše 'attaché', бюфе́т/bjufét 'buffet', такси́/taksi 'taxi'.

Bulgarian borrowings from **Turkish** (and through Turkish, Persian and Arabic) were extremely numerous during the time of the Ottoman domination. One of the major features of the history of the modern Bulgarian literary language – particularly after 1878 – was the systematic replacement of Turkish borrowings with Bulgarian neologisms or borrowings from Russian or western European languages. Романски/Romanski (1955–9) now lists only about 2,000 Turkish borrowings, of which about 800 (household items, occupations, items of clothing, foods, plants, animals) are stylistically neutral: чора́п/čoráp 'sock', ча́нта/čánta 'purse'. The remainder are archaic, dialectal, non-standard and/or pejorative, and generally have neutral native synonyms: кютук/kjutŭk (from Turkish) versus пън/pǎn '(tree) stump' (Лакова/Lakova 1972).

In so far as they do not take into account Russian Church Slavonic forms (often indistinguishable from native Bulgarian forms) or the intermediary role of Russian in the transmission of international terminology, the figures above substantially underestimate the impact of Russian on the Bulgarian lexicon. In early Modern Bulgarian, the influence of Russian was through Church Slavonic. By the end of the eighteenth and beginning of the nineteenth centuries, literary Russian was the predominant foreign lexical influence on Bulgarian, and remained so until recently. Russian and Russian Church Slavonic lexical items are found in virtually every area of Bulgarian vocabulary: вселена/vselena 'universe', вероятен/verojaten 'probable', старая се/staraja se '(I) try', обаче/obače 'however'.

The source of several important formations is indeterminate: Old/Middle Bulgarian literary sources and/or early printed Church books from Russia; for example, agent nouns in /-tel/ (учител/učitel 'teacher'), abstract nouns in /-ost/ (нежност/nežnost 'tenderness'), deverbative nouns in /-ie/ (предложение/predloženie 'proposal'), the present active participle (see section 3.2.1).

German borrowings (mostly military and technical) and **Italian** borrowings (concentrated in art, music, business and food) date from the nineteenth and twentieth centuries.

Prior to 1878 **English** borrowings were extremely limited; their numbers did not increase substantially until after the Second World War. Since then, and especially in the last twenty years, English has become the greatest foreign lexical influence on Bulgarian, and this influence is now far greater than the above figures (based on work more than thirty years old) suggest. The impact of English is particularly strong in technology, tourism, sports, dress, the arts and music and popular culture: транзистор/tranzistor 'transistor', мотел/motel, джинси/džinsi 'jeans', танк/tank.

5.3 Incorporation of borrowings

Borrowings are generally adapted to the phonological and morphological systems of Bulgarian. Phonological adaptation is limited to eliminating segments not found in the Bulgarian phonemic system or to correcting violations of sequential constraints. For example, geminate consonants are regularly replaced by single phonemes: Russian грамматика/grammatika becomes Bulgarian граматика/gramatika 'grammar'. Front round vowels are replaced by sequences of palatalized or palatal consonants plus back vowels: French *bureau* gives бюро/bjuro 'office'. Russian palatalized consonants are eliminated where they do not occur in Bulgarian: Russian пятилетка/pjatiletka /p'it'il'etka/ gives Bulgarian петилетка/petiletka /petiletka/ 'five-year plan'.

The last example illustrates an accommodation characteristic of borrowings from Russian and Russian Church Slavonic: the replacement of Russian morphological components with their Bulgarian counterparts, in this case Bulgarian пѐт/pĕt for Russian пя́ть/pjȧt' 'five'.

While showing some anomalies (below), borrowings are generally adapted morphologically. Nouns are assigned to one of the major gender classes, generally on the basis of their final segments. Nouns terminating in consonants are **masculine** (English *ketchup* – кѐтчъп/kĕtčăp); those terminating in /a/ are **feminine** (Rumanian *masă* – мȧса/mȧsa 'table'). Nouns terminating in /o e u i/ are **neuter** if **non-personal** (French *bureau* – бюрѐ/bjurȯ 'office') or **masculine** if **personal** (French *attaché* – аташѐ/atašė 'attaché').

Other, more complex types of adaptation also occur. For example, French feminine nouns ending in 'mute *e*' are regularly borrowed as feminine nouns in /-a/: *allée* – алѐя/alȇja 'avenue, lane'. Greek and Latin borrowings show complex suffix alterations and shifts among inflectional classes (Първев/Părvev 1979).

The inflectional behaviour of borrowed nouns may be anomalous. A fairly large number of the monosyllabic masculine nouns that take the plural suffix /-i/ (instead of /-ove/) are foreign (see section 3.1.2). Similarly, the velar–dental alternation accompanying the masculine plural marker /-i/ is often absent (sections 2.2, 3.1.2).

Borrowed adjectives are altered in order to agree with the shape of **derived** native adjectives. This entails little change in already derived Russian adjectives: Russian кольхо́зный/kol'xȯznyj – Bulgarian колхо́зен/kolxȯzen 'collective-farm (M SG)'. Otherwise, a Bulgarian suffix is commonly added to the foreign adjective: English *loyal* – лоя́лен/lojȧlen.

Borrowed adjectives are generally inflected like native adjectives. However, in the past, many adjectives borrowed from Turkish without the addition of a derivational suffix had a single unchanging form; the few that remain continue to do so (see section 3.1.4). Unmodified, uninflected adjectives from other sources are still possible, particularly in the colloquial language. Many are ephemeral, and even those that survive show syntactic idiosyncrasies (Първев/Părvev 1979: 233f.). For example, гро́ги/grȯgi (from English *groggy*) is used only predicatively: то́й е гро́ги/tȯj e grȯgi 'he is groggy'.

Borrowed verbs are most commonly assimilated into the third conjugation with the suffix /-ira-/ (of German origin): English *train* – трени́рам/treniram '(I) train'. Most verbs of this type are bi-aspectual (see section 3.2.1). There is a tendency in colloquial Bulgarian to integrate them into the aspectual system by creating aspectual mates for them with perfectivizing prefixes or the imperfectivizing suffix /-va-/ (Граматика/Gramatika 2: 268).

The third-conjugation suffix /-uva-/ is used to assimilate Russian verbs in /-ovat´/: арестова́ть/arestovát´ – аресту́вам/arestúvam '(I) arrest (IMPFV and PRFV)'. Many of these verbs are bi-aspectual.

5.4   Lexical fields

5.4.1   Colour terms
Basic colour terms are given in bold; examples are masculine singular.

'white'	**бял/bjál**
'black'	**че́рен/čéren**
'red'	**червѐн/červén**; also а́лен/álen 'scarlet'
'green'	**зелѐн/zelén**
'yellow'	**жъ́лт/žǎlt**; also ру́с/rús 'blond (of hair)'
'blue'	**си́н/sín**; also лазу́рен/lazúren 'azure, sky-blue (poetic)' and електри́к/elektrík 'electric blue (indeclinable)'
'brown'	**кафя́в/kafjáv** (< кафѐ/kafé 'coffee'); also кестеня́в/kestenjáv 'auburn, chestnut (of eyes, hair, horses)' (< кѐстен/késten 'chestnut'), бѐжов/béžov 'beige'
'purple'	**мо́рав/mórav**; also виоле́тов/violétov 'violet', пу́рпурен/púrpuren 'crimson (literary, poetic)'
'pink'	**ро́зов/rózov** (< ро́за/róza 'rose'); also пембя́н/pembján ~ пембѐн/pembén 'hot pink'
'orange'	**ора́нжев/oránžev**
'grey'	**си́в/sív**

5.4.2   Body parts
'head'	глава́/glavá
'eye'	око́/okó (anomalous plural: 3.1.2)
'nose'	но́с/nós
'ear'	ухо́/uxó (anomalous plural: 3.1.2)
'mouth'	уста́/ustá; note related 'lip' у́стна/ústna
'hair'	ко́съм/kósăm 'single hair'; коса́/kosá 'head of hair'
'neck'	вра́т/vrát, ши́я/šíja
'arm, hand'	ръка́/răká (anomalous plural: 3.1.2); also дла́н/dlán 'palm'
'finger'	пръ́ст/prǎst
'leg, foot'	кра́к/krák (anomalous plural крака́/kraká: 3.1.2); also '(sole of) foot' стъпа́ло/stăpálo, ходи́ло/xodílo
'toe'	пръ́ст/prǎst (with на крака́/na kraká 'of the foot' to distinguish 'toe' from 'finger')
'chest'	гърди́/gărdí (plural of гръ́д/grǎd 'breast' (F)') and гръ́ден ко́ш/grǎden kóš (literally 'breast basket')
'heart'	сърцѐ/sărcé

5.4.3   Kinship terms

'mother'   ма́йка/májka, and for one's own mother ма́ма/máma
'father'   бащá/baštá, and for one's own father та́тко/tátko
'sister'   сестрá/sestrá; also ка́ка/káka 'older sister'
'brother'   бра́т/brát (anomalous plural бра́тя/brátja); also ба́тко/
                bátko 'older brother'
'aunt'   ле́ля/lélja 'sister of father or mother', ву́йна/vújna 'wife
                of mother's brother', стри́на/strina 'wife of father's
                brother'; also dialectal те́тка/tétka 'sister of mother'
'uncle'   чи́чо/čičo 'brother of father' and ву́йчо/vújčo 'brother
                of mother'; also dialectal сва́ко/sváko, тети́н/tetin,
                лели́н/lelin 'husband of mother's sister'. Ле́ля/lélja
                'aunt' and чи́чо/čičo 'uncle' are used when the more
                precise relationship is unknown and also to address adults
                in general.
'niece'   пле́менница/plémennica; also dialectal сестрини́ца/
                sestrinica 'daughter of sister' and брата́ница/bratánica
                'daughter of brother'
'nephew'   пле́менник/plémennik; also dialectal се́стриник/
                séstrinik 'son of sister' and брата́нец/bratánec 'son of
                brother'
'cousin'   female   братовче́дка/bratovčédka   and   male
                брадовче́д/bratovčéd
'grandmother'   ба́ба/bába; also used to address elderly women
'grandfather'   дя́до/djádo; also used to address elderly men
'wife'   женá/žená (also 'woman'), съпру́га/săprúga ('spouse-F')
'husband'   мъ̀ж/măž (also 'man'; anomalous plural: 3.1.2),
                съпру́г/săprúg ('spouse-M')
'daughter'   дъщеря́/dăšterjá (anomalous vocative: 3.1.2)
'son'   си́н/sin

6   Dialects

Bulgarian dialects are usually divided into **west** and **east** with respect to the development of late Proto-Slavonic *ě jat'*. West of a line running north–south between A and B on map 5.1, *ě* became /e/: 'big' M SG /golém/, PL /golémi/, 'milk' /mléko/, 'milkman' /mlekár/. East of the line, stressed *ě* in some (if not all) environments either becomes /á/ (as in the literary language; see section 2.3) or retains what may have been one of its late Proto-Slavonic vocalizations, /ä̀/; unstressed /e/ (reduced phonetically to [i], see below) is general: /gol′ám gol′ém′i ml′áko ml′ekár/ (Сто́йков/ Stojkov 1968: 54–5 for details).

While not coinciding exactly with the *jat'* boundary, other important isoglosses generally reinforce the east–west division:

1 Late Proto-Slavonic *a after alveo-palatal consonants (including *j*) gives *ě* in the east, but /a/ in the west (as in the literary language): 'frog' east F SG /žába/ – PL /žéb'i/ versus west /žába/ – /žábi/.

2 Strong reduction of unstressed /a/ to [ă], /o/ to [U], /e/ to [I] is typical in the east, especially north-east; in the west it is lacking altogether or limited to /a/ › [ă] (as in the literary language; see section 2.1).

3 Late Proto-Slavonic *ǫ and *ъ give /ă/ in the east (as in the literary language; section 2.1); in the west both /ă/ and /a/ are common.

4 East Bulgarian commonly has palatalized labial and dental consonants before front vowels and at the ends of words (where they contrast with non-palatalized consonants): /z'ét'/ 'son-in-law'. In the west only /l' n' t' d'/ are common, with /l' t' d'/ often replaced by /j' k' g'/; otherwise consonants are non-palatalized (as in the literary language; section 2.1).

5 Proto-Slavonic *tj and *dj are /št/ and /žd/ in the east (the literary treatment; section 2.1); besides these also /č ӡ/, /k' g'/, and /šč žӡ/ in the west.

6 Word-internal alternations of /ră ~ ăr/, /lă ~ ăl/ (see section 2.3) are characteristic of eastern dialects; in the west one finds syllabic liquids, non-alternating sequences of vowel–liquid or liquid–vowel, or in the case of /l/, replacement by /ă/ or /u/.

7 In the east present-tense verb forms are as in the literary language (see section 3.2). In the west, palatalization is often lost in the first person singular and third-person plural: /xódă/ '(I) go'. Alternatively, the first person singular may be formed with /-m/: /xódim/. In the west /-me/ commonly marks the first person plural in *all* conjugations: /xódime/ '(we) go'.

8 The imperfect past active participle (see section 3.2.1) is typically eastern. Clearly, a number of these features bring western dialects closer to Serbo-Croat and Macedonian.

The most archaic Bulgarian dialects are found in south-eastern Bulgaria, in the Rhodope mountains. Important features (Стойков/Stojkov 1968: 87–91) include:

1 /ä/ as the reflex of *ě and of *a after alveo-palatals: /gol'äm/, /gol'äm'i/, /žäba/;

2 a single reflex /ȧ/, /à/, /ó/ or /ɔ/ for stressed PSl. *ǫ, ъ, ę, ь, with palatalized labials and dentals before the reflexes of *ę and ь: *ǫ – /rǎka/ 'hand, arm', *ъ – /dǎš/ 'rain', *ę – /m'ǎso/ 'meat', *ь – /l'ǎsno/ 'easily';

3 'triple' definite article: unmarked /-t-/, /-s-/ for proximity to the speaker, /-n-/ for distance from the speaker (compare Macedonian);

4 numerous case vestiges in nouns, adjectives and definite articles.

Map 5.1 Bulgarian dialects

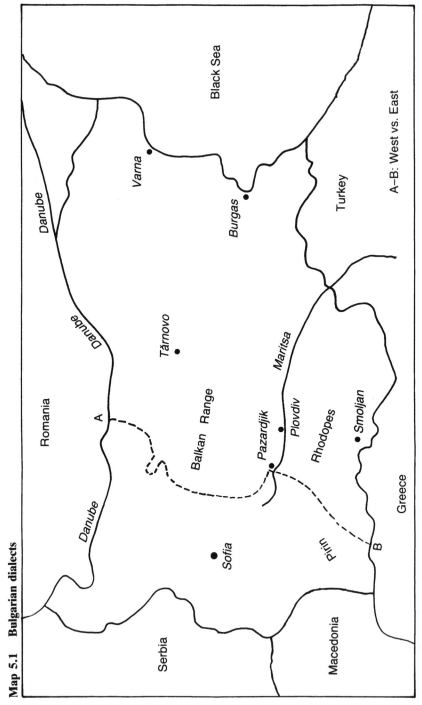

Source: Стойков/Stojkov 1968: 63

This dialect picture is largely **historical**, reflecting the speech of informants at least 50–60 years of age when the data of the major dialectological works of the past 30–40 years were collected (Стойков/Stojkov 1964–81). With the passing of this generation, the spread of literacy, the growth of the mass media and the rapid urbanization of the last twenty years, the older picture has given way to a much different one mixing traditional features and the standard language.

The geographical extent of Bulgarian dialects is controversial. On the level of local dialects there is no sharp boundary between the speech of western Bulgaria and that of eastern Serbia, former Yugoslav Macedonia and areas of Greece and Turkey contiguous to Bulgaria in which Slavonic dialects are still spoken. The official Bulgarian position, with respect to dialects and earlier historical periods, has been that eastern Serbian dialects, all Macedonian dialects in former Yugoslavia and Slavonic dialects in Turkey and Greece are dialects of Bulgarian.

Acknowledgement

I wish to acknowledge the many suggestions, stylistic and substantive, of Borjana Velčeva and Linda Scatton. Special thanks are due to Vladimir Filipov, my Bulgarian-language consultant, whose assistance went far beyond that of a native informant.

References

Aronson, Howard I. (1967) 'The grammatical categories of the indicative in the contemporary Bulgarian literary language', in *To Honor Roman Jakobson*, vol. I, The Hague: Mouton, 82–98.

—— (1968) *Bulgarian Inflectional Morphophonology*, The Hague: Mouton.

Chvany, Catherine V. (1988) '*Distance, deixis* and *discreteness* in Bulgarian and English verb morphology', in Alexander M. Schenker (ed.) *American Contributions to the Tenth International Congress of Slavists, Sofia, September 1988, Linguistics*, Columbus, Oh.: Slavica, 69–90.

Ewen, Robert C. (1979) 'A grammar of Bulgarian clitics', Ph.D. dissertation, Seattle: University of Washington. (Available from Ann Arbor: University Microfilms International.)

Hauge, Kjetil Rå (1976) *The Word Order of Predicate Clitics in Bulgarian* (Meddelelser, 10), Oslo: Slavic–Baltic Institute, Oslo University.

Lindstedt, Jouko (1985) *On the Semantics of Tense and Aspect in Bulgarian*, Helsinki: University of Helsinki.

Mayer, Gerald L. (1988) *The Definite Article in Contemporary Standard Bulgarian*, Wiesbaden: Harrassowitz.

Rudin, Catherine (1986) *Aspects of Bulgarian Syntax: Complementizers and WH Constructions*, Columbus, Oh.: Slavica.

Scatton, Ernest A. (1975) *Bulgarian Phonology*, Cambridge, Ma.: Slavica. (Reprinted. Columbus, Oh.: Slavica, 1983.)

—— (1984) *A Reference Grammar of Modern Bulgarian*, Columbus, Oh.: Slavica.

Velcheva, Boryana (1988) *Proto-Slavic and Old Bulgarian Sound Changes*, Columbus, Oh.: Slavica.

Бояджиев, Симеон (1970) 'За лексиката от чужд произход в книжовния български език', *Известия на Института за български език* 19: 403–7.

Дончева, Лиляна (1975) 'Наблюдения върху квантитативния аспект на номинативните лични местоимения в руски и в български език', *Бъглгарски език* 25, кн. 1: 9–20.

Георгиева, Ел. и Станков, В., отговорни редактори (1983) *Правописен речник на съвременния български книжовен език*, София: Българска академия на науките.

Граматика на съвременния български книжовен език (1982–3) Т. I: *Фонетика*, Димитър Тилков, редактор, Т. II: *Морфология*, Стоян Стоянов, редактор, Т. III: *Синтаксис*, Константин Попов, редактор, София: Българска академия на науките.

Лакова, Мери (1972) 'Турцизмите в „Речник на съвременния български книжовен език" от стилистична гледна точка', *Български език* 22, кн. 1–2: 61–72.

—— (1978) 'Въпросно-отговорни единства в съвременния български книжовен синтаксис', *Български език* 28, кн. 5: 418–34.

Маслов, Ю. С. (1981) *Грамматика болгарского языка*, Москва: Высшая школа.

Николова, Цветанка (1987) *Честотен речник на българската разговорна реч*, София: Наука и изкуство.

Пашов, Петър (1966) *Българският глагол*, София: Наука и изкуство.

Пашов, Петър и Първев, Христо (1979) *Правоговорен речник на българския език*, София: Наука и изкуство.

Пенчев, Йордан (1984) *Строеж на българското изречение*, София: Наука и изкуство.

Първев, Христо (1979) *Помагало по българска лексикология*, София: Наука и изкуство.

Романски, Стоян, главен редактор (1955–9) *Речник на съвременния български книжовен език*, 3 тома, София: Българска академия на науките.

Русинов, Русин (1980) *Речниковото богатство на българския книжовен език*, София: Народна просвета.

Стойков, Стойко, редактор (1964–81) *Български диалектен атлас*, 4 тома, София: Българска академия на науките.

—— (1968) *Българска диалектология*, София: Наука и изкуство.

Тилков, Димитър и Бояджиев, Тодор (1981) *Българска фонетика*, София: Наука и изкуство.

Чолакова, Кристалина, главен редактор (1977–90) *Речник на българския език*, 6 тома [а – й], София: Българска академия на науките. In progress.

6 Macedonian

Victor A. Friedman

1 Introduction

Macedonia has been the name of a Balkan region since ancient times, when it was bounded by Epirus, Thessaly and Thrace on the south-west, south and east. At present, Macedonia is best defined as the region comprising the Republic of Macedonia, the Blagoevgrad District in south-western Bulgaria (Pirin Macedonia) and the Province of Makedonia in northern Greece (Aegean Macedonia). Some adjacent portions of eastern Albania can also be included (compare Vidoeski in Koneski 1983: 117). A map is provided on page 300.

Ancient Macedonian, an independent Indo-European language of uncertain affiliation, was spoken in at least part of Macedonia in the fifth and fourth centuries BC and presumably both earlier and later. This gave way to Greek, which was in turn supplanted by Slavonic when the Slavs invaded and settled in the Balkans in the sixth and seventh centuries AD. For our purposes, Macedonian can be defined as the Slavonic dialects spoken in the territory of Macedonia.

Literary Macedonian is the official language of the Republic of Macedonia and is recognized as such by all countries except Bulgaria, where it is officially viewed as a 'regional norm' of Bulgarian, and Greece, where Macedonian is claimed not to exist – except in proclamations banning its use – or it is claimed that the term 'Macedonian' can only be used to refer to the Greek dialects of Macedonia or to Ancient Macedonian. None the less, there are citizens of and emigrants from both Bulgaria and Greece who identify their native (Slavonic) language as Macedonian. It is also spoken in about fifty to seventy-five villages in eastern Albania, where it is used as a language of instruction in elementary schools up to grade 4. Based on Yugoslav census figures for 1981 and other estimates, the total number of speakers with Macedonian as their first language is probably somewhere between 2 million and 2.5 million, many of whom have emigrated to Australia, Canada and the United States (Friedman 1985).

The Ottoman conquest of the Balkan peninsula in the fourteenth and fifteenth centuries brought about a disruption of cultural continuity with regard to Slavonic literacy in that region. The history of Modern Literary Macedonian begins in the latter part of the eighteenth century with the birth of South Slavonic nationalism. This history can be divided into five periods.

Circa 1794–circa 1840: the first publications using Macedonian dialects

The major figures of this period published ecclesiastical and didactic works in language based in many respects on their local dialects. Their concern was with establishing a vernacular-based Slavonic literary language in opposition to both the archaizing influence of those who would have based the Slavonic literary language on Church Slavonic and the Hellenizing attempts of the Greek Orthodox Church, to which the majority of Macedonians and Bulgarians belonged. The authors of this period in both Macedonia and Bulgaria called their vernacular language 'Bulgarian'.

Circa 1840–70: the rise of secular works using Macedonian dialects

The struggle over the dialectal base of the emerging vernacular literary language became manifest. Two principal literary centres arose on Macedo-Bulgarian territory: one in north-eastern Bulgaria and the other in south-western Macedonia. Macedonian intellectuals envisioned a Bulgarian literary language based on Macedonian dialects or a Macedo-Bulgarian dialectal compromise. Bulgarians, however, insisted that their Eastern standard be adopted without compromise.

1870–1912: the rise of Macedonianism

The establishment of the Bulgarian Exarchate, that is of an autocephalous Bulgarian church, in 1870 marked the definitive victory over Hellenism. It is from this period that we have the first published statements insisting on Macedonian as a language separate from both Serbian and Bulgarian, although these ideas were expressed during the preceding period in private correspondence and similar documentation. In his book *За македонцките работи/Za makedonckite raboti* 'On Macedonian matters' (Sofia, 1903), Krste Misirkov outlined the principles of a Macedonian literary language based on the Prilep-Bitola dialect group, that is, precisely the dialects which later served as the basis of Literary Macedonian. Most copies of Misirkov's book were destroyed, but it documents a coherent formulation of a Macedonian literary language and nationality from the beginning of this century, thus belying the claim that Literary Macedonian was created *ex nihilo* by Yugoslav fiat at the end of the Second World War.

1912–44: the Balkan Wars to the Second World War

On 18 October 1912 the Kingdoms of Bulgaria, Greece and Serbia united against Turkey in the First Balkan War. Less than a year later Macedonia was partitioned among these three allies, essentially marking the end of the development of Literary Macedonian outside the borders of Yugoslavia except for the period 1946–8, during which the Macedonians of Pirin Macedonia were recognized as a national minority in Bulgaria with their own schools and publications in Literary Macedonian. In Yugoslavia, Macedonian was treated as a South Serbian dialect, but the Yugoslav government permitted Macedonian literature to develop on a limited basis as a dialect literature. It was during this inter-war period that linguists from outside the Balkans published studies in which they emphasized the distinctness of Macedonian from both Serbo-Croat and Bulgarian (Vaillant 1938).

1944: the establishment of Literary Macedonian
During the Second World War, Tito's Communists won jurisdiction over Macedonia, and on 2 August 1944, Macedonian was formally declared the official language of the Republic of Macedonia. The standardization of Literary Macedonian proceeded rapidly after its official recognition, in part because an inter-dialectal koine was already functioning. The West Central region (see map 6.1 on page 300), which was the largest in both area and population, supplied a dialectal base to which speakers from other areas could adjust their speech most easily. In many respects these dialects are also maximally differentiated from both Serbo-Croat and Bulgarian, but differentiation was not an absolute principle in codification. A major problem now for Literary Macedonian is the fact that Skopje – the capital and principal cultural and population centre – is outside the West Central dialect area and the republic as a whole is subject to considerable Serbo-Croat influence (see Минова-Ѓуркова/Minova-Ǵurkova 1987). For more details see Friedman (1985), Hill (1982) and Lunt (1986).

2 Phonology
The Macedonian alphabet follows the phonemic principle of Serbian Cyrillic. With certain exceptions, each letter corresponds to a single phoneme and words are pronounced as they are spelled. It was officially established on 3 May 1945 and is given here with its codified Latin transliteration equivalent.

Аа	a	Ее	e	Кк	k	Оо	o	Уу	u
Бб	b	Жж	ž	Лл	l	Пп	p	Фф	f
Вв	v	Зз	z	Љљ	lj	Рр	r	Хх	h
Гг	g	Ss	dz	Мм	m	Сс	s	Цц	c
Дд	d	Ии	i	Нн	n	Тт	t	Чч	č
Ѓѓ	ǵ	Јј	j	Њњ	nj	Ќќ	ḱ	Џџ	dž
								Шш	š

2.1   Segmental phoneme inventory

Table 6.1   Vowels

	Front	Central	Back
High	i		u
Mid	e	(ə)	o
Low		a	

Unrounded	*Rounded*

There is considerable variation among speakers in the realization of the mid vowels /e/ and /o/ from [ɛ] and [o] to [ę] and [ǫ]. The higher variants are particularly characteristic of the Western dialects and also of modern educated Skopje speech, especially among women of the younger generation.

Unstressed vowels are not reduced, although they are slightly laxer and shorter, especially post-tonically and can be devoiced word or phrase finally in informal speech.

Although schwa is phonemic in many dialects, where its realization varies in its closeness to [ʌ] or [ɨ], its status in the literary language is marginal. According to the norm, it is limited to three environments: (1) before syllabic /r/ in absolute initial position and when preceded by a morpheme ending in a vowel (see below); (2) for dialectal effect in words of Slavonic or Turkish origin as in [səza] for /solza/ 'tear', [kəsmet] for /kasmet/ (Turkish *kısmet*) 'fate'; (3) in spelling, each consonant is followed by schwa: *Friedman* [fə-rə-i-e-də-mə-a-nə]. Schwa is spelled with an apostrophe, which is not part of the alphabet.

The consonant /r/ can normally be viewed as having a vocalic (syllabic) realization between consonants and between a word or morpheme boundary and a consonant. It is possible to have minimal or near minimal pairs with vocalic /r/ between a vowel and consonant when the vowel preceding vocalic /r/ is at a morpheme boundary: зарче/zarče 'Muslim veil (DIMIN)' – за'рчев/zaarčev 'begin to snore (1-SG IMPF)'. However, the realization of vocalic /r/ can be [ər] (see above).

Vocalic /r/ occurs in final position only in a few foreign and onomato-poetic words: обр/obr 'cry used to turn horses', жанр/žanr 'genre'.

/i/ is non-syllablic in final position after a vowel colloquially, but can contrast with /j/ in careful speech: одаи/odai 'Turkish style room (PL)' – одај/odaj 'betray (IMP)'.

Sequences of two identical vowels are permitted: таа/taa 'she'. Literary pronunciation has two syllable peaks, some speakers have one long vowel. A third vowel is usually separated from the second by /j/ according to orthographic rule: беа/bea 'be (3 PL IMPF)', живееја/živeeja 'live (3 PL

IMPF)', but наии/naii 'nahija (PL)' (Ottoman administrative unit; the variant нахии/nahii is preferred).

The developments of Proto-Slavonic vowels and liquids reflect the West Central dialects except in isolated lexical items, usually the result of inter-dialectal borrowing.

Front and back nasal vowels generally give /e/ and /a/, respectively: *rǫka › рака/raka 'hand', *pętь › пет/pet 'five'. Initial front and back nasals give /ja/: *ǫže › jаже/jaže 'rope', *[j]ęzykъ › jазик/jazik 'tongue'. Individual lexical items show the Northern (and Serbo-Croat) reflex /u/ instead of /a/ from original *ǫ as in гуска/guska 'goose'. Some of these northern reflexes represent widespread loan-words that date from the medieval period, but an /u/ may reflect an original doublet in Proto-Slavonic: *nǫd-/nud- 'need' › понада/ponada 'gift of food brought to a sick person', понуда/ponuda 'offering'.

Original strong front and back *jer* (that is, reflexes of Proto-Slavonic *ĭ and *ŭ in positions where they were not lost) normally give /o/ and /e/ respectively: *sъpъ › сон/son 'dream', *dьnь › ден/den 'day'. There are four types of exceptions:

1 Tense *jer* (that is one followed by /j/; see chapter 3, section 2.33) gives /i/: *рьji › пиj/pij 'drink (IMP)', *mъji › миj/mij 'wash (IMP)'.

2 Secondary *jer* (one inserted to break up a consonant cluster arising from the loss of a primary *jer*) was generally ъ, which gave o: *reklъ › рекол/rekol 'said (AOR M L-FORM)'. When the secondary *jer* was followed by /m/, the final result was /u/, presumably via /o/ as in седум/sedum 'seven' (compare редум/redum 'in order' from original /-om/). Before final /-r/, the West Central dialects developed /a/: добар/dobar 'good', but other dialects have reflexes of a back or front strong *jer*: добор/dobor, добер/dober. (But ветер/veter 'wind' is now the preferred alternative in Literary Macedonian.) Proto-Slavonic *ognь 'fire' gives оган/ogan, огин/ogin, оген/ogen, огон/ogon in various dialects. The first two are given in Тошев/Tošev (1970), with оган/ogan being preferred.

3 A weak front or back *jer* next to a sonorant whose loss would have resulted in an inadmissible cluster gives the same reflex as *ǫ: *mьgla › магла/magla 'fog', *lьžica › лажица/lažica 'spoon'. Although танок/tanok (‹ *tьnъkъ) is permitted, тенок/tenok, from those dialects where the masculine was influenced by the strong *jer* in the other forms, is now preferred by some younger speakers.

4 Original *v plus front or back *jer* gives *u* in цути/cuti 'bloom' (‹ *cvьt-), суни/dzuni 'ring' (‹ *ʒvъn-).

Jat' gives /e/: лево/levo 'left' (N)'. Original /y/ merges completely with /i/: *synъ 'son' and *sinь 'blue' both give син/sin.

Syllabic /r/ remains syllabic: први/prvi 'first', грло/grlo 'throat'; also крв/krv 'blood', крст/krst 'cross'. *CorC, *orC give CraC, raC: град/ grad 'town', брег/breg 'shore', блато/blato 'mud', млеко/mleko 'milk', раз-/raz- (pre-verb), рало/ralo 'pair, plough', лакот/lakot 'elbow', лаком/lakom 'greedy'. Initial *čr-, *čr̥- give cr: црево/crevo 'gut', црпи/crpi 'extract'.

Syllabic *ļ gives /ol/ in the West Central dialects and most items in Literary Macedonian: волк/volk 'wolf', солза/solza 'tear', јаболко/ jabolko 'apple', жолт/žolt 'yellow'. The East Central reflex, schwa, is only acceptable for dialectal effect. The Northern reflex, /u/, is prescribed for чун/čun 'skiff', Бугарија/Bugarija 'Bulgaria' and their derivatives. Also *ļ gives /o/ in сонце/sonce 'sun' and its derivatives.

Proto-Slavonic pitch and length distinctions have been completely lost. Literary Macedonian has fixed antepenultimate stress (see Franks 1987): воденичар/vodéničar 'miller (SG)', воденичари/vodeníčari (PL), воденичарите/vodeníčárite (PL DEF). Exceptions are lexical, usually unadapted loan-words or suffixes, and phrasal, usually from an expanded word boundary, that is antepenultimate stress within a phrasal (accentual) unit.

Lexical exceptions only permit penultimate and final stress. Some are idiosyncratic: ептен/eptén 'completely'. Others result from contraction: сабајле/sabájle from Turkish sabah ile 'in the morning'. Due to lexical exceptions, stress can be distinctive: кравата/kravàta 'necktie' but кравата/kràvata 'cow (DEF)'.

Phrasal exceptions can have stress more than three syllables from the end of the unit: носејки_му_го/nosèjḱi_mu_go 'while carrying it to him'. Many accentual units prescribed in normative grammars are now considered localisms or dialectisms by educated Macedonians, especially in the younger generations. This is due to the influence of the Skopje dialect (and Serbo-Croat) on the literary language combined with apparent resistance on the part of speakers from outside the Western area to adopt these specifically Western types of pronunciation. Thus, prescribed pronunciations such as еве ти го/evè_ti_go (as opposed to еве ти го/ éve_ti_go) 'here he/it is for you' are now considered Western regionalisms rather than literary pronunciations. Even in those areas where accentual units are native, it seems that the educated younger generation tends to avoid them. Certain shifts occur regularly, however, especially with negated and interrogated mono- and disyllabic verbs: не_знам/nè_ znam 'I don't know', што_сакаш/štò_sakaš? 'What do you want?' Shifts onto monosyllabic prepositions with pronouns are also regular: со_ мене/sò_mene 'with me'.

The phoneme /ʒ/ is usually represented orthographically by ѕ and is transliterated by dz; /ɫ/ is represented by л/l, /l/ by љ/lj, /ʒ/ by џ/dž, /ń/ by њ/nj and /x/ by x/h.

Table 6.2   Consonants: Voiceless precedes Voiced

Place Type	Bilabial	Labio- dental	Dental	Alveolar	Alveo- palatal	Palatal	Velar
Stop	p, b		t, d			ќ, ѓ	k, g
Fricative		f, v	s, z		š, ž		x
Affricate			c, ʒ		č, ǯ		
Glide						j	
Lateral			ł	l			
Nasal	m		n			ń	
Trill				r			

Stops are not aspirated. /r/ is trilled not flapped. /n/ is velarized to [ŋ] before /k, g/: банка/banka = [baŋka] 'bank', мангал/mangal = [maŋgal] 'brazier'. /k, g, x/ may be slightly fronted before front vowels, but the norm separates pairs such as кука/kuka 'hook', plural куки/kuki from куќа/kuḱa 'house', plural куќи/kuḱi and лага/laga 'lie', plural лаги/lagi from лаѓа/laѓa 'boat', plural лаѓи/laѓi (*pace* de Bray 1980: 147).

The palatal stops /ќ, ѓ/ vary considerably both in their position and manner of articulation, although the variation for any individual speaker is quite narrow (Lunt 1952: 13). The prescribed norm is that they are dorso-palatal stops, and this is native for some speakers (Minissi, Kitanovski and Cingue 1982: 22, 30, 34). Possible realizations vary from [t′, d′] to [ć, ʒ́], to complete merger with /č, ǯ/.

There is considerable difference between the prescribed norm and actual pronunciation of л = [ł] or [l] and љ = [l]. According to the norm л is pronounced [ł] in all positions except before front vowels and *j*, where it is pronounced [l] while љ is always pronounced [l] but is spelled only before back vowels, consonants and word finally: љубов/ljubov 'love', биљбиљ/biljbilj 'nightingale', but биљбили/biljbili 'nightingales'. An example of a minimal pair is бела/bela [beła] 'white (F)' – беља/belja [bela] 'trouble'. In actual pronunciation, however, there is a tendency to pronounce љ/lj like the Serbo-Croat palatal [l′] due to the influence of that language and of the local Skopje dialect, which also has palatal /l′/. There is also a tendency among some speakers of the youngest generation to pronounce л as [ł] in all positions.

Geminate /t, d, s, z, l, m, j/ are permitted at some morpheme boundaries, but not if the result would be more than two consonants: пролет/ prolet 'spring', definite form пролетта/proletta, but радост/radost 'joy', definite form радоста/radosta. Geminates are sometimes eliminated where they could be permitted: рассали/rassali 'render [fat]', but расече/raseče 'chop up'. There are also some doublets: одаде/odade and оддаде/oddade 'give up'. Geminate /n/ is avoided: каменен/kamenen '[made of] stone', feminine камена/kamena. Other geminate sonorants are permitted: најјак/najjak 'strongest', каллив/kalliv 'muddy', осуммина/osummina 'eight (M HUM)', also титоввелешки/titovveleški '[pertaining to] Titov Veles (M/PL)'. Gemination can be distinctive: пролета/proleta 'fly by', пролетта/proletta 'spring (DEF)'.

Distinctively voiced consonants /b, v, d, z, ʒ, ž, ǯ, g, ǵ/ are devoiced in final position and before a voiceless consonant: зоб/zob [zop] 'oats', зобта/zobta [zopta] 'oats (DEF)', зобник/zobnik [zobnik] 'oat-sack'. Underlying /ʒ/ does not occur word finally. Non-distinctively voiced consonants may be finally devoiced especially in informal speech. Voiceless consonants are voiced before distinctively voiced consonants: сретне/sretne [sretne] 'meet (PRFV)', средба/sredba [sredba] 'meeting (NOUN)'.

Colloquially, consonant clusters are simplified word finally: радост/radost = [rados] 'joy'. There is some regressive assimilation of voicing across word boundaries within a phrase: jac да си одам/jas da si odam = [jaz da si odam] 'let me go'. Cyrillic в is pronounced [f] in the first person plural aorist/imperfect marker, for example бевме/bevme [befme] 'were (1 PL IMPF)', by analogy with the first singular and second plural as in бев/bev [bef] 'was (1 SG IMPF)' and бевте/bevte [befte] 'were (2 PL IMPF)'. After /s/, /v/ can be pronounced [f]: своj/svoj [sfoj] 'one's own (M SG)', but твоj/tvoj [tfoj] 'your (M SG)' is non-standard, and /v/ is always pronounced [v] in words like квасец/kvasec 'yeast' and жетва/žetva 'harvest'. There is considerable dialectal variation in this regard, and /v/ remains [v] even after /s/ in the younger generation.

Palatal /ń/ does not occur initially except in a few loans such as Њутн/Njutn 'Newton' (note also the final vocalic /n/, which is not otherwise permitted).

The prefixes без-/bez-, из-/iz-, раз-/raz- are spelled бес-/bes-, ис-/is-, рас-/ras- before č/š and are pronounced [beš-, iš-, raš-]. Prefixal /s, z/ becomes /š, ž/ before /č, ǯ, š, ž/ (if the result would be /šš, žž/, this is simplified to /š, ž/): расчисти/rasčisti [raščisti] 'clean up', изживее/izživee [iživee] 'live through'.

Proto-Slavonic *tj/*kt + *ĭ, *dj became /ḱ, ǵ/ in the north but /št, žd/ or /šč, žǯ/ in the south. The two types of reflex met on Central territory, where they competed. In general, the /ḱ, ǵ/ reflexes predominated and this is reflected in the literary language: плаќа/plaḱa 'pay', ноќ/noḱ 'night', para/raǵa 'give birth'. As in the Central dialects, so also in Literary Macedonian, some words have /št, žd/ (or /š, ž/ from /št, žd/), sometimes with both types of reflexes in the same root: гаќи/gaḱi 'breeches, underpants' – гашник/gašnik (‹ *gaštnik) 'belt for holding up breeches'. The evidence of toponymy and medieval manuscripts indicates that /št, žd/ extended much further north in earlier centuries, but individual lexical items with /ќ, ѓ/ such as куќа/kuḱa 'house' have been recorded in southern Aegean Macedonia.

The Proto-Slavonic palatal sonorants /l′, ń, ŕ/ were either hardened or lost in the Central dialects on which Literary Macedonian is based: плука/ pluka 'spit', земја/zemja 'earth', него/nego 'him (ACC)', море/more 'sea'. The Literary Macedonian and Western forms коњ/konj 'horse' and бања/banja 'bath' are borrowed from Northern dialects, which preserved /ń/. Secondary /ń/, for example in verbal nouns such as носење/nosenje 'carrying', is preserved in some Western dialects and the literary language, although in most dialects there is a tendency to eliminate it.

Proto-Slavonic /x/ is lost in most of West and part of East Macedonian. In general it was eliminated initially as in леб/leb 'bread', убав/ubav 'beautiful', and intervocalically as in снаа/snaa 'daughter-in-law/sister-in-law', but it is preserved as /v/ after /u/ or original vocalic /l/: мува/ muva 'fly', болва/bolva 'flea'. Also /v/ (or [f]) occurs before consonants and word finally: тивка/tivka 'quiet (F)' (whence masculine тивок/tivok instead of expected *tiok), грав/grav 'beans'. Initial /xv/ became /f/: фати/fati 'grab'. The phoneme /x/ has been introduced or retained in Literary Macedonian under the following circumstances: (1) new foreign words: хотел/hotel 'hotel'; (2) toponyms: Охрид/Ohrid; (3) Church Slavonicisms: дух/duh 'spirit'; (4) new literary words: доход/dohod 'income'; (5) disambiguation: храна/hrana 'food', рана/rana 'injury'.

In general, original /ʒ/ and /ž/ from the second and first palatalizations, respectively, were levelled to /z/ and /ž/. New /ʒ/ arose from /z/ next to a sonorant or /v/ as in ѕвер/dzver 'beast', in certain lexical items such as ѕирне/dzirne 'take a peek', and was borrowed in loan-words like ѕевгар/dzevgar 'yoke of oxen'. In the case of ѕвезда/dzvezda 'star' and its derivatives, the textual evidence indicates that original /ʒ/ was preserved all along. It is more widespread in the dialects than in the literary language. New /ǯ/ occurs in the following contexts: (1) loans: џуџе/ džudže 'dwarf', буџет/budžet 'budget'; (2) assimilation of voicing to /č/: лиџба/lidžba 'beauty' derived from личи/liči 'suit'; (3) affrication of original /ž/, generally before a consonant: џвака/džvaka 'chew'.

The chief exception to the one-to-one correspondence between letters and phonemes noted at the beginning of this section is in the lateral liquids, where Cyrillic л represents /l/ before front vowels and /j/ but /ł/ elsewhere while љ is used for /l/ before back vowels, consonants and finally. Cyrillic j is always written between и and a. Final devoicing of distinctively voiced consonants is never spelled, while regressive assimilation of voicing or voicelessness is spelled in the results of some suffixal and other morphological processes, but not in others: Cyrillic в is never altered, т in numerals is not altered, д and г are retained before certain voiceless suffixes, the feminine definite article -та does not alter the spelling of a final voiced consonant. Although the devoicing of /z/ in the prefixes /raz-, iz-, bez-/ is spelled, the shift to a palatal articulation before a palatal is not. The grave accent is used to distinguish the following homonyms: cè/sè 'everything' – ce/se 'are, self'; нè/nè 'us (ACC)' – не/ne 'not'; ѝ/ì 'her (DAT)' – и/i 'and'.

2.2 Morphophonemic alternations inherited from Proto-Slavonic

The reflexes of the first palatalization are k › $č$, g › $ž$, x (and also v from earlier x) › $š$. They are productive in some nominal derivation: грев/grev 'sin', грешка/greška 'mistake', граматика/gramatika 'grammar', граматички/gramatički 'grammatical'. They also occur in the vocative: бог/bog 'god', vocative боже/bože, Влав/Vlav 'Vlah (Arumanian)', vocative Влаше/Vlaše. Two plurals also show the alternation: око/oko 'eye', plural очи/oči, уво/uvo 'ear', plural уши/uši. In verbs, the alternation is reflected in both conjugation and derivation but is not productive: потстрижи/potstriži 'trim', потстригов/potstrigov (1 SG AOR), извлече/izvleče 'drag (PRFV)', извлекува/izvlekuva (IMPFV).

The reflexes of the second palatalization are k › c, g › z, x › s. In nouns, the morphophonemic alternation is productive in the masculine plural: паркинг/parking 'parking space', паркинзи/parkinzi (PL), успех/uspeh 'success', успеси/uspesi (PL). Nouns ending in /-a/ do not have the alternation, except владика/vladika 'bishop', владици/vladici (PL). This alternation applies to /v/ (from original /x/) only in two items: Влав/Vlav 'Vlah (Arumanian)', Власи/Vlasi (PL) and сиромав/siromav 'pauper', сиромаси/siromasi (PL) as opposed to the normal орев/orev 'walnut', ореви/orevi (PL). There are also two feminine plurals (etymologically duals) with the alternation: рака/raka 'hand', раце/race (PL), нога/noga 'leg', нозе/noze (PL). In verbs, the alternation has been eliminated in conjugation: речи/reči 'say (IMPFV)', but two stems, namely /-lez-/ 'go' and /molz-/ 'milk', show /g/ in the aorist stem: влезе/vleze 'enter', влегов/vlegov (1 SG AOR), молзе/molze 'milk', [из]молгов/[iz]molgov (1 SG AOR). Younger speakers now have [из]молзев/[iz]molzev.

Sequences of consonant plus /j/ give the following results: /t, k/ become /ќ/; /d, g/ become /ѓ/; /ł, n/ become /l, ń/; /st/ becomes /št/ (verbs) or /sj/ (nouns). In verbal derivation, the imperfectivizing suffixes /-(j)a/ and /-(j)ava/ are limited to a few lexical items. Only /-uva/, which entails no alternations, is productive. Many verbs originally prescribed or at least accepted with /-(j)ava/ have been replaced by corresponding forms with /-uva/ in educated practice: фати/fati (PRFV), фаќа/faќa (IMPFV) 'grab, get'; роди/rodi (PRFV), раѓа/raѓa (IMPFV) 'give birth'; гости/gosti (bi-aspectual), гоштава/goštava (IMPFV) 'treat' (now archaic, replaced by [на]гостува/[na]gostuva); мени/meni (PRFV), мењава/menjava (IMPFV) 'exchange' (now replaced by менува/menuva). The collective suffixes /-je/ and /-ja/ cause alternation (/t, d, ł, n, st, zd/ become /ќ, ѓ, l, ń, s, z/, respectively): работа/rabota 'work', рабоќе/raboќe

(COLL); ливада/livada 'meadow', ливаѓе/livaǵe (COLL); година/godina 'year', годиње/godinje (COLL); лист/list 'leaf', лисје/lisje (COLL); грозд/grozd 'grape', грозје/grozje (COLL). Alternations of dental with dorso-palatal stops are facultative in monosyllabics: прат/prat 'twig', пратје/pratje ~ праќе/praḱe (COLL). Note that the specific collective forms produced by these suffixes differ among themselves in use and meaning, but this is irrelevant to morphophonemic alternations.

Vowel–zero alternation, which results from the loss of a jer in weak position and its retention in strong position, gives zero in masculine definite and all non-masculine adjectives, in plural nouns and in verbal conjugation (aorist stem, non-masculine verbal *l*-form) and derivation (perfective). The most common adjectival suffixes involved are /-en/ and /-ok/ (the unspecified citation form for adjectives is the masculine). Other phonotactic and orthographic rules also apply: низок/nizok 'low', feminine ниска/niska; местен/mesten 'local', neuter месно/mesno; достоен/dostoen 'worthy', masculine definite достојниот/dostojniot. The relevant noun suffixes are /-en/, /-el/, /-ol/, /-ot/, /-ok/: камен/kamen 'stone', plural камни/kamni (but now replaced by collective камења/kamenja); јазел/jazel 'knot', plural јазли/jazli; сокол/sokol, plural сокли/sokli (also соколи/sokoli) 'falcon', нокот/nokot '(finger/toe)nail', plural нокти/nokti; предок/predok 'ancestor', plural предци/predci. Note fleeting vowels in lexical items such as ден/den 'day', plural дни/dni. The alternation is highly limited in verbs: бере/bere 'gather', -бра/-bra (2 SG AOR); рекол/rekol (AOR M L-FORM) 'said', рекла/rekla (F); умре/umre (PRFV) 'die', умира/umira (IMPFV).

Remnants of old length alternations occur in the derivation of imperfective verbs: роди/rodi (PRFV) 'give birth', паѓа/raǵa (IMPFV); собере/sobere (PRFV) 'gather', собира/sobira (IMPFV); but затвори/zatvori (PRFV) 'close', затвора/zatvora (IMPFV).

2.3   Morphophonemic alternations resulting from changes after Proto-Slavonic

Simplifications of clusters of the type fricative plus stop plus consonant to fricative plus consonant occur in certain feminine definite nouns, collective plurals, masculine definite and (in the same lexical items) all non-masculine adjectives, and rarely in the aorist stem of verbs: /radost + ta/ gives радоста/radosta 'joy (DEF)', /list + je/ gives лисје/lisje 'leaves (COLL)', /mest + na/ gives месна/mesna 'local (F)', постеле/postele 'spread' has third person singular aorist посла/posla.

The addition of the diminutive suffix /-če/ causes a dissimilation peculiar to Macedonian: /g, s, z, š, ž, st, sk, šk, zd/ (in principle also /zg, žg/ but the few such nouns take different diminutive suffixes) all become /v/, pronounced [f], before /-če/, for example воз/voz 'train' and вошка/voška 'louse' both give diminutive вовче/vovče. Other consonants simply drop, although /j/ can also be retained as /i/ or, by analogy, it can also be replaced by /v/: шамија/šamija 'scarf', diminutive шамиче/šamiče is prescribed but шамивче/šamivče and шамииче/ šamiiče also occur.

There are also some isolated consonantal alternations: дете/dete 'child', plural деца/deca (also DIMIN PL дечиња/dečinja); Турчин/ Turčin 'Turk', plural Турци/Turci; пес/pes 'dog', plural пци/pci.

3 Morphology

3.1 Nominal morphology

3.1.1 Nominal categories
Macedonian has lost the dual and most of the Proto-Slavonic cases. The maximum possible differentiation in the noun is nominative/oblique/ vocative. There is a tendency to eliminate non-nominative forms, which are always optional. Some masculine adjectives have a facultative vocative that is identical to the indefinite plural. In the pronoun, the maximum possible differentiation is nominative/accusative/dative. All the other cases have been replaced by prepositional or other syntactic constructions: чаша вода/čaša voda 'glass [of] water', тој работел папуџија/toj rabotel papudžija 'he worked [as a] slipper-maker'. After prepositions pronouns are accusative, all other nominals are nominative except the few nouns with facultative oblique forms, which can occur here (see section 3.1.2). The preposition на/na can have local and motional meanings 'on, to, at' but also marks the indirect object (dative) and possession (genitive). Likewise од/od and со/so retain their literal meanings of 'from' and 'with', but од/ od can also mark possession (especially in the West) and agentive 'by' in passives, while со/so marks instrumental 'by': му реков на брат ми дека молбата била потпишана со молив од таткото на ученикот/mu rekov na brat mi deka molbata bila potpišana od tatkoto na učenikot so moliv 'I said to my brother that the request had been signed with a pencil by the father of the pupil'.

The singular gender opposition masculine–feminine–neuter is neutral- ized in the plural, except for a highly restricted distinction in quantified plurals (see section 3.1.5). Neuter gender can refer to animate beings: личното момче дошло/ličnoto momče došlo 'the handsome lad has come', убавото девојче дошло/ubavoto devojče došlo 'the beautiful girl has come'. Feminine nouns can be used expressively to refer to males: брадата/bradata 'the beard' as the nickname of a man: и кога оваа идеше во Вепрчани/i koga ovaa ideše vo Veprčani 'and when he (liter- ally 'this one (F)') came to Veprčani'. Masculine nouns (kinship terms, hypocorisms, pejoratives or recent loans) can end in any vowel, in which case they are animate, usually human: слуга/sluga 'servant', татко/tatko 'father', аташе/ataše 'attaché', денди/dendi 'dandy', гуру/guru 'guru'. The names of the months that end in /-i/ are masculine: јуни/juni 'June'. Most nouns ending in a consonant are masculine, a few are feminine and some vacillate. All other nouns in a vowel are feminine if they are in /-a/ or refer to a female being, otherwise they are neuter. Some recent loans such as виски/viski 'whiskey' show hesitation between masculine and neuter, although prescriptively they are neuter. Since animacy is distinguished by the use of special quantifiers for some male humans and mixed groups (see section 3.1.5) virile or animate gender distinctions exist.

Definiteness is marked by means of the definite article (see also sections 4.4 and 4.7). Macedonian is the only Slavonic literary language with a tripartite distinction mirroring the same distinction in demonstratives, namely unmarked /-t-/, proximate /-v-/, distal /-n-/. Tradition treats the articles as affixes, but they are sometimes analysed as clitics. The article attaches to the end of the first nominal of the noun phrase, that is nouns, adjectives, pronouns, numerals, but not adverbs: не многу постари*те* деца/ne mnogu postari*te* deca 'the not much older children' but една од многу*те* наши задачи/edna od mnogu*te* naši zadači 'one of our many problems'. A noun phrase modified by a demonstrative does not take a definite article according to the norm, but does so in non-standard speech: овие деца*ва*/ovie deca*va* 'these here children'. The numeral еден/eden 'one' functions as an indefinite article denoting specificity and can even trigger object reduplication, especially colloquially (see section 4.7 and Naylor 1989).

3.1.2 Noun morphology

Because the vocative and oblique forms are marginal, facultative phenomena, it is misleading to present them together with plural formation as a reduced declensional paradigm.

Macedonian has restructured plural formation, which is now based on a combination of form and gender (see table 6.3). The vowel of the singular drops before the ending of the plural unless it is stressed. The majority of masculine and feminine nouns take /-i/, most neuters take /-a/, but most monosyllabic masculines, including new loan-words, take /-ovi/ (sometimes /-evi/ after /j/ and palatals), with about ten exceptions and ten more that vacillate; masculines in unstressed /-o, -e/ add /-vci/: татко/tatko 'father', plural татковци/tatkovci; neuters in unstressed /-e/ not preceded by /-c, -št, -i, -j/ take /-inja/. This same suffix pluralizes nouns in /-ce/ with a diminutive meaning (but diminutives in /-ence/ have plural /-enca/). Some neuter loans in stressed /-ė/ take /-inja/, in which case the stress becomes antepenultimate. Other loans in stressed /-ė/ normally add /-a/, but the use of /-inja/ is spreading. Occasionally, plural formation is influenced by the collective: пат/pat means both 'road' and

Table 6.3 Examples of plural formation

(a)

Masculines

град	син	маж	робин[к]а	пат	ден	корен	пријател	граѓанин	слуга
градови	синови	мажи	робин[к]и	пати/патишта	дни/денови	корени	пријатели	граѓани	слуги
town	son	man	slave	time/way	day	root	friend	citizen	servant

Feminines

жена	душа		вест	коска	мајка	црква		
жени	души		вести	коски	мајки	цркви		
woman	soul		news item	bone	mother	church		

Neuters

место	слово	срце	учење	семе	јагне			
места	слова	срца	учења	семиња	јагниња			
place	speech	heart	study	seed	lamb			

(b)

Masculines

grad	sin	maž	robin[k]a	pat	den	koren	prijatel	graǵanin	sluga
gradovi	sinovi	maži	robin[k]i	pati/patišta	dni/denovi	koreni	prijateli	graǵani	slugi
town	son	man	slave	time/way	day	root	friend	citizen	servant

Feminines

žena	duša		vest	koska	majka	crkva		
ženi	duši		vesti	koski	majki	crkvi		
woman	soul		news item	bone	mother	church		

Neuters

mesto	slovo	srce	učenje	seme	jagne			
mesta	slova	srca	učenja	seminja	jagninja			
place	speech	heart	study	seed	lamb			

'time' but the regular пати/pati means 'times' while the collective патишта/patišta is the normal plural meaning 'roads'. Exceptions involving morphophonemic alternation were covered in sections 2.2 and 2.3. The chief remaining exceptions are the following: ветер/veter 'wind', plural ветрови/vetrov; оган/ogan 'fire', plural огнови/ognovi, шура/šura 'wife's brother'; plural шуреви/šurevi; брат/brat 'brother', plural браќa/braќa; човек/čovek 'person', plural луѓе/luǵe 'people'; животно/životno 'animal', plural животни/životni; рамо/ramo 'shoulder', plural рамена/ramena; небо/nebo 'sky', plural небеса/ nebesa; домаќин/domaќin 'master of the house', plural домаќини/ domaќini.

Nouns of all genders can form collective plurals in /-je/, although these forms are fairly restricted in Literary Macedonian usage (see section 2.2 on morphophonemic alternations). At one time these collectives could form a plural in /-ja/, but this is now merely a competing variant (Конески/ Koneski 1967: 224, *pace* Lunt 1952: 31, de Bray 1980: 170–1). Some nouns form collective plurals with /-išta/, which is homonymous with the plural of the augmentative/pejorative suffix (see section 3.3.1). Non-personal masculine nouns (and a few personal ones) also have a quantitative plural: /-a/. This suffix does not cause loss of mobile vowels: ден/den 'day', plural дни/dni and денови/denovi, два дена/dva dena 'two days' (see section 4.10).

The oblique form is a Westernism accepted into Literary Macedonian. It is always facultative and is limited to masculine proper and family names, kinship terms ending in a consonant or /-i, -o, -e/, and the nouns човек/ čovek 'person', бог/bog 'god', ѓавол/ǵavol 'devil' and господ/gospod 'lord'. Oblique forms for nouns denoting domestic animals are now dialectal. Nouns in a consonant, /-o/ or /-i/ take /-a/, nouns in /-e/ add /-ta/: брат/brat 'brother', oblique брата/brata; татко/tatko 'father', oblique татка/tatka; Ѓорѓи/Ǵorǵi 'George', oblique Ѓорѓија/Ǵorǵija; Блаже/Blaže 'Blaže', oblique Блажета/Blažeta. These forms can occur wherever an oblique pronoun would occur: му реков на Ивана пред Блажета/mu rekov na Ivana pred Blažeta 'I said to Ivan in front of Blaže', ене го Ѓорѓија/ene go Ǵorǵija 'there's George!'

The vocative is limited to the masculine and feminine singular. The following have no vocative form: masculine nouns in /-c, -o, -e/, masculine proper names in /-a, -i, -k, -g/, feminine nouns in a consonant and hypocorisms in /-e, -i/. Nouns in /-džija/ drop the /-ja/ (see section 3.3.1). Feminines in /-ka/ and /-ica/ take /-e/ while according to the norm other feminines take /-o/: Станка/Stanka 'Stanka', vocative Станке/Stanke; жена/žena 'woman', vocative жено/ženo. The normative generalization for masculines is that monosyllabics take /-u/ and polysyllabics take /-e/, although there are exceptions and vacillations. The vocative is facultative, and there is an increasing tendency to avoid it

Table 6.4   Definite singulars and plurals

town	news item	woman	place	seed	father	taxi
(a)						
градот	веста	жената	местото	семето	таткото	таксито
градовите	вестите	жените	местата	семињата	татковците	таксијата
(b)						
gradot	vesta	ženata	mestoto	semeto	tatkoto	taksito
gradovite	vestite	ženite	mestata	seminjata	tatkovcite	taksijata

because it is felt to be rude, humorous or dialectal; this is especially true of the vocative marker /-o/. To the extent that the vocative is preserved, the tendency is to generalize /-u/ for masculines and /-e/, which has hypocoristic overtones, for feminines. See section 2.2 on morphophonemic alternations in the vocative.

The shape of the definite article is based primarily on form, with some regard for gender and number. In the singular, masculines in a consonant take /-ot/, feminines in a consonant and all nouns in /-a/ take /-ta/ (a resulting /-tt-/ simplifies to /-t/ if preceded by a consonant), all remaining singulars (and collectives, including луѓе/luǵe 'people') take /-to/. In the plural, nouns in /-a/ take /-ta/, and all other plurals take /-te/. The addition of a definite article does not trigger fleeting vowels, as seen in the following paradigm of 'old man': старец/starec (SG), старецот/starecot (DEF SG), старци/starci (PL), старците/starcite (DEF PL). Table 6.4, based on table 6.3 and its exposition, illustrates the forms.

3.1.3   Pronominal morphology

The personal pronouns are given in table 6.5. Short forms are clitics and are used for the objects of verbs and the possessive and ethical dative (see section 4.1). Long forms are used as the objects of prepositions. The two forms are used together for emphasis and in connection with object reduplication (see sections 4.5 and 4.7). Illustrative possessive pronominals are given in table 6.6. твој/tvoj 'your', and свој/svoj 'reflexive possessive' inflect like мој/moj. ваш/vaš 'your (PL)' inflects like наш/naš. нејзин/nejzin 'her' inflects like негов/negov. нивни/nivni 'their' (нивниот/nivniot, нивната/nivnata and so on) has a remnant of the long adjective in its masculine indefinite form (see section 2.2).

The third-person pronoun тој/toj also functions as the unmarked demonstrative. The proximate demonstratives are овој/ovoj (M), оваа/ovaa (F), ова/ova (N), овие/ovie (PL) 'this'. The distal demonstratives substitute /-n-/ for /-v-/.

Koj/koj is both the animate interrogative pronoun 'who?' (ACC кого/

Table 6.5   Personal pronouns

Case	NOM	ACC-*long*	DAT-*long*[1]	ACC-*short*	DAT-*short*
(a)					
1 SG	jac	мене	мене	ме	ми
2 SG	ти	тебе	тебе	те	ти
REFL	—	себе[си][2]	себе[си]	се	си
1 PL	ние	нас	нам	нѐ	ни
2 PL	вие	вас	вам	ве	ви
3 SG M[3]	тоj	него	нему	го	му
3 SG N	тоа	него	нему	го	му
3 SG F	таа	неа	неjзе	ja	й
3 PL	тие	нив	ним	ги	им
(b)					
1 SG	jas	mene	mene	me	mi
2 SG	ti	tebe	tebe	te	ti
REFL	—	sebe[si]	sebe[si]	se	si
1 PL	nie	nas	nam	nѐ	ni
2 PL	vie	vas	vam	ve	vi
3 SG M	toj	nego	nemu	go	mu
3 SG N	toa	nego	nemu	go	mu
3 SG F	taa	nea	nejze	ja	ì
3 PL	tie	niv	nim	gi	im

Notes: 1 All distinct dative long forms can be replaced by the preposition на/na plus the accusative.
2 The form себеси/sebesi is a variant of себе/sebe.
3 The nominative third person forms он/on (M), оно/ono (N), она/ona (F) and они/oni (PL), which are characteristic of the North and East, are officially permitted in the literary language and seem to be on the increase in Skopje.

kogo, DAT кому/komu) and the interrogative adjective 'which?' (коja/ koja (F), кое/koe (N), кои/koi (PL)). The inanimate interrogative pronoun is што/što 'what'. Pronominal adjectives are чиj/čij, чиja/čija, чие/čie, чии/čii 'whose', каков/kakov, каква/kakva, 'what kind', ко́лка́в/kólkáv, ко́лка́ва/kólkáva 'what size, how big'. Similarly ваков/ vakov 'this kind', таков/takov 'of such a kind', онаков/onakov 'that kind', инаков/inakov 'another kind', о́лка́в/ólkáv 'this big', то́лка́в/ tólkáv 'so big', о́нолка́в/ónolkáv 'that big'. The interrogative pronouns, adjectives and adverbs can all be relativizers (see section 4.5) and can be prefixed with /ni-/ 'no', /se-/ 'every' and /ne-/ 'some' (specific): никоj/ nikoj 'nobody', секоj/sekoj 'everybody, each', некоj/nekoj 'somebody'. Non-specific indefinites are formed from interrogatives according to the following models, given in order of relative frequency: коj било/koj bilo, коj [и] да е/koj [i] da e, коj-годе/koj-gode 'anybody, whoever (non-specific)'. The first two are roughly equivalent, although some speakers

Table 6.6   Possessive pronominal adjectives 'my', 'our', 'his'

	INDEF	DEF	INDEF	DEF	INDEF	DEF
(a)						
M	мој	мојот	наш	нашиот	негов	неговиот
F	моја	мојата	наша	нашата	негова	неговата
N	мое	моето	наше	нашето	негово	неговото
PL	мои	моите	наши	нашите	негови	неговите
(b)						
M	moj	mojot	naš	našiot	negov	negoviot
F	moja	mojata	naša	našata	negova	negovata
N	moe	moeto	naše	našeto	negovo	negovoto
PL	moi	moite	naši	našite	negovi	negovite

judge the first as more literary and the second as more colloquial, while the last is significantly less common and is not used by some speakers.

The word сиот/siot (M), сета/seta (F), сето/seto (N), сите/site (PL) 'all' is always definite except the neuter це/se 'everything', 'constantly', 'even', 'all the more'.

3.1.4   Adjectival morphology

There is no opposition between long and short adjectives. Traces of the long forms survive in the /-i/ that appears when the article is added to inflecting adjectives ending in a consonant (нов/nov gives новиот/noviot), a few vocatives (драги мој/dragi moj 'my dear!'), certain types of derived adjectives (see table 6.7), some toponyms and anthroponyms and lexicalized expressions such as Долни Сарај/Dolni Saraj 'Lower Saraj' (a neighbourhood in Ohrid) and a few ordinal numerals (see section 3.1.5).

The vast majority of adjectives (including син/sin 'blue') are hard. Even the small group of possessive adjectives in /-ji/ are mostly inflected as кравји/kravji. Adjectives that inflect only for number or not at all are of Turkish or more recent foreign origin. For the definite article, masculine adjectives add /-ot/ (/-iot/ if the adjective ends in a consonant), feminines add /-ta/, neuters /-to/, plurals /-te/.

Comparison is entirely analytic. The comparative marker is /po-/, the superlative /naj-/ written unseparated from the adjective: понов/ponov 'newer (M)', најнов/najnov 'newest'. The only irregular comparative is многу/mnogu 'much, many', повеќе/poveḱe 'more', најмногу/najmnogu (најповеќе/najpoveḱe is no longer literary) 'most'. The comparative and superlative markers can also be added to nouns, verbs and adverbial phrases: пријател/prijatel 'friend', попријател/poprijatel 'more of a friend'; на север/na sever 'to/in the north', понасевер/ponasever 'more northerly'; не сака/ne saka 'dislike', најнесака/

Table 6.7 Adjectives

Type Meaning	Hard new/Macedonian	'Soft' cow's/bird's	Number only lucky	Uninflecting wonderful/fresh
(a)				
M	нов/македонски	кравји/птичји	касметлија	супер/тазе
F	нова	кравја/птичја	касметлија	супер/тазе
N	ново	кравјо/птичје	касметлија	супер/тазе
PL	нови	кравји/птичји	касметлии	супер/тазе
(b)				
M	nov/makedonski	kravji/ptičji	kasmetlija	super/taze
F	nova	kravja/ptičja	kasmetlija	super/taze
N	novo	kravjo/ptičje	kasmetlija	super/taze
PL	novi	kravji/ptičji	kasmetlii	super/taze

najnesaka 'dislike the most'. If there are proclitic object pronouns attached to such a verb, however, then each morpheme is spelled as a separate word: нај не го сака/naj ne go saka 'he dislikes him the most'.

Neuter indefinite adjectives also function as adverbs, unless the masculine indefinite ends in a vowel, in which case that is the adverb. See section 3.2.2 for the discussion of participles.

3.1.5 Numeral morphology

Cardinal non-virile

Virile (male human and mixed groups)

1	еден/една/едно/ едни	eden/edna/edno/ edni		
2	два/две	dva(M)/dve(N&F)	двајца	dvajca
3	три	tri	тројца	trojca
4	четири	četiri	четворица	četvorica
5	пет	pet	петмина	petmina
6	шест	šest	шестмина	šestmina
7	седум	sedum	седуммина	sedummina
8	осум	osum	осуммина	osummina
9	девет	devet	деветмина	devetmina
10	десет	deset	десетмина	desetmina
11	единаесет	edinaeset		
12	дванаесет	dvanaeset		
13	тринаесет	trinaeset		
14	четиринаесет	četirinaeset		
15	петнаесет	petnaeset		
16	шеснаесет	šesnaeset		
17	седумнаесет	sedumnaeset		
18	осумнаесет	osumnaeset		
19	деветнаесет	devetnaeset		
20	дваесет	dvaeset		

23	дваесет и три	dvaeset i tri		
30	триесет	trieset		
40	четириесет	četirieset		
50	педесет	pedeset		
60	шеесет	šeeset		
70	седумдесет	sedumdeset		
80	осумдесет	osumdeset		
90	деведесет	devedeset		
100	сто	sto	стомина	stomina
200	двесте	dveste		
300	триста	trista		
400	четиристотини	četiristotini		
500	петстотини	petstotini		
600	шестотини	šestotini		
700	седумстотини	sedumstotini		
800	осумстотини	osumstotini		
900	деветстотини	devetstotini		
1,000	илјада	iljada	илјадамина	iljadamina
2,000	две илјади	dve iljadi		
million	милион	milion		
billion	милијарда	milijarda		

Definiteness: 'One' is an adjective: едниот/edniot, едната/ednata, едното/ednoto, едните/ednite. It can function as an indefinite article, and in the plural it means 'some'. All non-virile cardinals ending in /-a/ and virile cardinals ending in /-ca/ have the definite article /-ta/, all others add /-te/ immediately after the numeral itself: двата/dvata, двајцата/dvajcata, петтемина/pettemina. Милион/milion is a noun, hence милионот/milionot.

Ordinals: The first eight masculine ordinals are formed as follows: прв(и)/prv(i), втор/vtor, трет/tret, четврти/četvrti, петти/petti, шести/šesti, седми/sedmi, осми/osmi. The remaining non-compound numerals up to 100 add /-ti/ to the cardinal. Other genders add /-a, -o, -i/ like other adjectives. The numerals 100–400 have two possible bases: /-stoten, -stotna/ and /-stoti, -stota/. The remaining hundreds use only /-stoten/. The ordinals for 'thousand', 'million' and 'billion' are the following: илјаден/iljaden, илјадна/iljadna (F), двеилјаден/dveiljaden 'two thousandth', милионски/milionski, милијардски/milijardski (Тошев/Tošev 1970:351). Note that quantifiers also have virile forms: мнозина/mnozina 'many', неколкумина/nekolkumina 'a few' and so on.

3.2 Verbal morphology

3.2.1 Verbal categories

Conjugation expresses person (first, second, third), number (singular, plural) and gender (masculine, feminine, neuter). Person and number are expressed in the synthetic paradigms (present, imperfect, aorist) and by the conjugated auxiliary verbs сум/sum 'be' and има/ima 'have' which form paradigmatic sets with the verbal *l*-form, which inflects for gender and number (*sum* series), and the neuter verbal adjective (*ima* series), respectively. Joseph (1983: 24, 110–13) gives morphological and syntactic arguments for treating imperatives as non-finite: lack of person oppositions (it is always second) and clitic placement (see section 4.1). The widespread use of the second person plural as a polite singular form is a relatively recent, urban phenomenon copied from other languages (Lunt 1952: 371; Конески/Koneski 1967: 332), resulting in uncertainty in its application and variation in the agreement of adjectives (singular or plural): вие сте изморен – изморена – изморени/vie ste izmoren – izmorena – izmoreni 'you are tired (M SG, F SG, PL)'. The singular is prescribed, but plurals are frequently heard.

Macedonian maintains the imperfective/perfective aspectual distinction. Aspect can be inherent in the stem or derived (see 3.3.3). There are no special aspectual distinctions in the verbs of motion. Unlike Bulgarian, the Macedonian perfective present and imperfect cannot occur independently but only in subordination to a class of eight modal markers (*pace* de Bray 1980: 200):

1	ќе/ḱe	expectative marker (future, conditional)
2	нека/neka	optative marker (first/third persons only)
3	да/da	subjunctive marker
4	ако/ako	'if'
5	додека (да, не)/dodeka (da, ne)	'while, until'
6	дури (да, не)/duri (da, ne)	'while, until'
7	доколку/dokolku	'in so far as' (frequent, but rejected by some speakers as journalistic jargon)
8	ли/li	interrogative marker when used to mean 'if' (marginal: archaic or dialectal for many speakers)

The perfective present can occur in negative interrogative sentences colloquially: што не седнеш?/što ne sedneš? 'why don't you sit down?' but not in ordinary affirmative or interrogative sentences (Kramer 1986: 163).

Many verbs in /-ira/ are bi-aspectual (Минова-Ѓуркова/Minova-Ǵurkova 1966), and Теунисен/Teunisen (1986) gives a list of forty-two simple bi-aspectuals. Imperfective verbs can occur independently in the present and imperfect, or subordinated to phasal verbs like почна/počna 'begin'. Perfective verbs can occur with откако/otkako 'since', откога/otkoga 'after', штом/štom 'as soon as' or subordinated to успее/uspee (PRFV), успева/uspeva (IMPFV) 'succeed'. Bi-aspectuals can do both.

The aorist/imperfect opposition is prescribed for both perfective and imperfective verbs, and occasional examples of imperfective aorists occur in literature into the first half of the twentieth century (Конески/Koneski 1967: 423; Lunt 1952: 90). Today, however, imperfective aorists are virtually obsolete, unlike in Bulgarian. In the tables and rules, imperfective aorist forms are given with a preceding hyphen to indicate that they now occur only as perfectives.

Most linguists agree that the imperfect is marked, either for duration in time (Конески/Koneski 1967: 427; Усикова/Usikova 1985: 97) or coordination with other events (Lunt 1952: 87). A few hold that the aorist is marked (Elson 1989) or that the marking is equipollent. Friedman (1977: 30–3) argues in favour of the durative viewpoint on the basis of examples in which imperfects are used to describe acts with duration in time that are in sequence with, rather than coordinated with, events described by aorists, but with the death of the imperfective aorist, it could be argued that the aorist is becoming marked.

Macedonian has preserved the Proto-Slavonic perfect in the *sum* series and has created a new series of perfects: the *ima* series. The new perfect is characteristic of Western Macedonian and is marked for present stative resultativity. The *sum* series has lost its marking for resultativity in connection with the rise of the category of **status** (see below in this section). Speakers from Eastern Macedonia use the *ima* perfect less than speakers from Western Macedonia or not at all, and consequently the *sum* series in their speech and writing has a broader range. In the south-west, the *sum* series has become limited to the expression of status. In the rest of Western Macedonia, the *sum* series retains some of its perfect uses as well as entering into status oppositions.

The major tense opposition is present/past. The imperfective present can describe past and future as well as present events: доаѓам утре/ doaǵam utre 'I am coming tomorrow', доаѓа кобна 1912 година/doaǵa kobna 1912 godina 'the fatal year 1912 comes'. The perfective present is limited to occurrence after the eight subordinators listed above. The invariant verbal particle ќе/ḱe (‹ *xъtjetъ* 'want') added to the perfective or imperfective present expresses future or habitual actions. When negated, ќе/ḱe is usually replaced by invariant нема да/nema da. Negative не ќе/ ne ḱe and positive има да/ima da also mark futurity, but carry nuances of volition and obligation, respectively. When ќе/ḱe is added to the imperfect (negative не ќе/ne ḱe + imperfect or немаше да/nemaše da + present), it forms the future-in-the-past (anterior future), the expectative unfulfillable (irreal) conditional or the past iterative: ќе дојдеше/ḱe dojdeše can be translated 'he will have come', 'he would have come' or 'he would come'.

The *beše* pluperfect normally uses the perfective aorist stem. The *imaše* pluperfect and *imal* perfect are distinguished on the basis of the category of status discussed below. The *beše* pluperfect specifies one past event as anterior to another, whereas the *imaše* pluperfect specifies a past result of an anterior event. The difference is illustrated by these sentences: тој ми ја покажа, но јас веќе ја бев видел/toj mi ja pokaža, no jas veḱe ja bev videl 'he pointed her out to me, but I had already seen her' implies I spotted her before he did, whereas тој ми ја покажа, но јас веќе ја имав видено/toj mi ja pokaža, no jas veḱe ja imav videno 'he pointed her out to me, but I had already seen her' could only be used if I had seen her on some previous occasion (Friedman 1977: 105).

The imperative is used for commands (see section 4.2). Both perfective and imperfective imperatives are also used in reference to all three persons where other Slavonic languages can use the independent perfective present for repeated past acts and habitual acts without reference to time: јас речи, тој стори/jas reči, toj stori 'he does whatever I say' or 'he will do whatever I say'; тие бркај нас, ние криј се во дупката/tie brkaj nas, nie krij se vo dupkata 'they chase us, we hide in the hole' (Конески/Koneski 1967: 418–20).

There are two types of conditional: the hypothetical (potential) formed with би/bi plus verbal l-form, and the expectative (real and irreal) formed with ќе/ḱe plus present (real, or fulfillable) and imperfect (irreal, or unfulfillable). Kramer (1986) points out that hypothetical conditions can also be fulfillable or unfulfillable. The following sentences illustrate the four possibilities: (1) fulfillable–expectative: ако ми се јавите, ќе дојдам/ako mi se javite, ḱe dojdam 'if you call me, I will come'; (2) fulfillable–hypothetical: ако ми се јавите, би дошол/ako mi se javite, bi došol 'if you called/were to call me, I would come'; (3) unfulfillable–expectative: ако ми се јавевте, ќе дојдев/ako mi se javevte, ḱe dojdev 'if you had called me, I would have come'; (4) unfulfillable–hypothetical: да може бебето да прозборува, би ти рекло/da može bebeto da prozboruva, bi ti reklo (Lunt 1952: 85) 'if the baby could talk he would say to you ...' The hypothetical conditional also occurs in the protasis of conditional sentences with ако/ako 'if' and кога/koga 'if' (literally 'when'), although its use with ако/ako is not standard. In the protasis of unfulfillable–expectative conditional sentences the imperfect is used after ако/ako 'if' or да/da 'if', as in sentence (3) above. Although ќе/ḱe is still preferred for all expectatives and би/bi for all hypotheticals, би/bi is expanding into the unfulfillable–expectative at the expense of ќе/ḱe in educated formal style (under the influence of Serbo-Croat) while ќе/ḱe is encroaching on би/bi in unfulfillable–hypotheticals in educated colloquial style.

The particles да/da and нека/neka in simple independent clauses express directives, that is permission, tolerance, concession, request, exhortation, wish: нека дојде!/neka dojde! 'let him come!'; да дојдам!/da dojdam! 'let me come!' Ordinarily, нека/neka occurs with the third person present. Some speakers can also use it with the first person, but others reject this. On the rare occasions when нека/neka is used with a past tense form (imperfect, sum imperfect), it expresses an unfulfillable directive.

Да/da occurs with all persons and all finite verb forms (assuming the imperative to be non-finite), although some of these collocations are highly restricted, marginal or dialectal. A traditional cover term for да/da is the marker of the subjunctive. See sections 4.2 and 4.5 for more details.

Macedonian has developed a distinction often described as based on the opposition witnessed/reported (so-called '**renarration**'). Friedman (1977: 7) opts for the term '**status**' meaning the speaker's qualification of the validity of the event. Friedman (1977: 52–81) argues that synthetic pasts are marked for confirmativity while Lunt (1952: 91–4) describes the *sum* aorist/imperfect as marked for distance in time or reality, that is resultative or non-confirmative (see also Усикова/Usikova 1985: 94–106). For example, тој беше во Скопје/toj beše vo Skopje means 'he was in Skopje (I vouch for it)' while тој бил во Скопје/toj bil vo Skopje means either 'he has been in Skopje' or 'he is/was in Skopje (apparently)/(much to my surprise)/(supposedly)'.

The *beše* pluperfect does not enter into this opposition. In the *ima* series, the *imal* perfect is limited to non-confirmed, usually non-witnessed (but also deduced) events. The *imaše* pluperfect is limited to witnessed events. The expectative marker ќе/ḱe with the *sum* imperfect (marginally also the *sum* aorist) is always non-confirmative, usually reported, and is the non-confirmative equivalent of ќе/ḱe plus imperfect or present. The negated realization is немало да/nemalo da and the conjugated present tense. Using ќе/ḱe with the *beše* pluperfect is marginal and is not semantically differentiated from ќе/ḱe plus *sum* imperfect in its past and modal meanings (Конески/Koneski 1967: 498). Similarly, ќе/ḱe plus *ima* series is a marginal south-westernism (Friedman 1977: 19–20, 190). The examples I have found or elicited indicate that ќе/ḱe plus *ima* perfect is suppositional (*pace* Lunt's (1952: 99) elicited future anterior example), ќе/ḱe plus *imaše* pluperfect is unfulfillable–expectative, and ќе/ḱe plus *imal* perfect would be the reported or non-confirmative equivalent of the other two.

The category of transitivity may be inherent in the stem or marked by ce/se: заспие/zaspie 'fall asleep (ITR)' се надева/se nadeva 'hope (ITR)'. In some verbs, ce/se is used as an intransitivizer: разбуди/razbudi 'wake up (TR)' се разбуди/se razbudi 'wake up (ITR)'. Lexical intransitives can also be used as causative transitives with definite objects: го заспав/go zaspav 'I put him to sleep'. For transitive verbs, 'be' plus verbal adjective is one way of forming the passive. For intransitive verbs (including some objectless transitives), 'be' plus verbal adjective is a type of perfect. The construction generally occurs with verbs of motion and in a few colloquial expressions: дојден сум вчера/dojden sum včera 'I came yesterday', веќе сум јаден/veḱe sum jaden 'I've already eaten'.

The passive is formed either with ce/se or with 'be' plus verbal adjective:

Старите треба да се слушаат./Starite treba da se slušaat.
'The old folks should be obeyed.'

Тој нареди да биде разбуден во два саатот./Toj naredi da bide razbuden vo
  dva saatot.
'He ordered that he be awakened at two o'clock.'

The agent in a passive construction is usually expressed with the preposition од/od:

Тој беше разбуден од слугата./Toj beše razbuden od slugata.
'He was awakened by the servant.'

The meaning of ce/se is 'intransitive', including impersonals, reflexives, reciprocals:

се гледа дека/se gleda deka
'it can be seen that'
Еднаш се живее./Ednaš se živee.
'One only lives once.'
Не ми се работи./Ne mi se raboti.
'I don't feel like working.'
Тој се гледа во огледалото./Toj se gleda vo ogledaloto.
'He looks at himself in the mirror.'
Ќе се стрижам на бербер./Ḱe se strižam na berber.
'I'll have my hair cut at the barber's.'
Се гледаат како мачори./Se gledaat kako mačori.
'They look at one another like cats.'

The infinitive and supine are completely lost in Macedonian. Infinitival clauses in other Slavonic languages correspond to constructions with да/da plus finite verb (*da*-clauses) or constructions with the verbal noun (see sections 4.2 and 4.5). The participles have all been lost or transformed. The present active participle survives as the verbal adverb. The past passive participle survives as the verbal adjective. The resultative participle survives as the verbal *l*-form, which is limited to the *sum* series, the *imal* perfect and the hypothetical conditional. Joseph (1983: 113–14) classes it as finite on the basis of clitic placement. The present passive and past active participles survive only as a few lexical items. The verbal noun survives.

The verb сум/sum 'be' is the only verb whose dictionary citation form is first person singular present; all others are third person singular. Сум/sum occurs in the present, imperfect (1 SG бев/bev), a rare (marginal) third person singular aorist (ви/bi) and *l*-form (м бил/bil), which can be used to form a *sum* perfect and a *beše* pluperfect. The regular perfective verb биде/bide supplies the perfective present, imperative and verbal adjective (whose use is limited to the extreme south-west, as is the verbal adjective of има/ima 'have'). The verbal adverb from биде/bide, бидејќи/bidejḱi, has been lexicalized as a conjunction meaning 'because'. The verbal noun can be supplied by суштествува/suštestvuva 'exist'.

Table 6.8   Synthetic endings

	Present	Imperfect	Aorist	Present of 'be' (сум)
(a)				
1 SG	-ам	-в	-в	сум
2 SG	-ш	-ше	-∅	си
3 SG	-∅	-ше	-∅	е
1 PL	-ме	-вме	-вме	сме
2 PL	-те	-вте	-вте	сте
3 PL	-ат	-а	-а	се
(b)				
1 SG	-am	-v	-v	sum
2 SG	-š	-še	-∅	si
3 SG	-∅	-še	-∅	e
1 PL	-me	-vme	-vme	sme
2 PL	-te	-vte	-vte	ste
3 PL	-at	-a	-a	se

Note: The principal exceptions to the rules given above occur in the aorist and the forms based on it and are illustrated in table 6.9.

3.2.2 Conjugation
The following criteria are used here to distinguish analytic paradigms from syntactic constructions:

1   Analytic constructions with inflecting auxiliaries must require that they precede the main verb. This distinguishes the *sum* and *ima* series from constructions with 'be' plus verbal adjective agreeing with the subject, which permit both orders.
2   Analytic constructions with uninflecting clitics must require that they be bound exclusively to a single type of verb form. This distinguishes the hypothetical conditional – би/bi plus verbal *l*-form – from analytic constructions with ќе/ḱe, да/da and нека/neka, which are clitics but occur with more than one type of verb form.

Most verb forms can be predicted from the third person singular present. Those which cannot can be predicted from the first person singular aorist, which preserves some of the alternations characteristic of the infinitive stem in other Slavonic languages. The remaining anomalies are few.

Synthetic paradigms are formed by adding the person/number markers of table 6.8 to the stem. The third person singular present ends in /-a/, /-i/ or /-e/, and is identical to the present stem. In the imperfect, /-i/

Table 6.9   Main morphological verb classes

(a)

		1	2a	2b	2c	3a	3b
3 SG	PRS	чита	моли	оздрави	брои	пише	плаче
1 SG	IMPF	читав	молев	оздравев	броев	пишев	плачев
1 SG	AOR	-читав	-молив	оздравев	-бројав	пишав	-плакав
2,3 SG	AOR	-чита	-моли	оздраве	-броја	пиша	-плаче
Gloss		read	beg	get well	count	write	weep

		3c	3d	3e	3f	3g	3h
3 SG	PRES	бере	умре	тресе	даде	рече	бие
1 SG	IMPF	берев	умрев	тресев	дадев	речев	биев
1 SG	AOR	-брав	умрев	тресов	дадов	реков	-бив
2,3 SG	AOR	-бра	умре	тресе	даде	рече	-би
Gloss		gather	die	shake	give	say	beat

(b)

		1	2a	2b	2c	3a	3b
3 SG	PRES	čita	moli	ozdravi	broi	piše	plače
1 SG	IMPF	čitav	molev	ozdravev	broev	pišev	plačev
1 SG	AOR	-čitav	-moliv	ozdravev	-brojav	pišav	-plakav
2,3 SG	AOR	-čita	-moli	ozdrave	-broja	piša	-plače
Gloss		read	beg	get well	count	write	weep

		3c	3d	3e	3f	3g	3h
3 SG	PRES	bere	umre	trese	dade	reče	bie
1 SG	IMPF	berev	umrev	tresev	dadev	rečev	biev
1 SG	AOR	-brav	umrev	tresov	dadov	rekov	-biv
2,3 SG	AOR	-bra	umre	trese	dade	reče	-bi
Gloss		gather	die	shake	give	say	beat

Note:

1 = *a*-stem   3 = *e*-stem
2 = *i*-stem   a = *a*-AOR
a = *i*-AOR   b = *a*-AOR + velar alternation
b = *e*-AOR   c = *a*-AOR + V ~ Ø alternation
c = *a*-AOR   d = *e*-AOR
                   e = *o*-AOR
                   f = *o*-AOR + C (= dental) › Ø/AOR *l*-form
                   g = *o*-AOR + velar alternation
                   h = Ø-AOR

becomes /-e/. In the aorist, /-e/ becomes /-a/. The aorist and imperfect stems are obtained by dropping the first person singular /-v/.

All stem vowels truncate before the first person singular /-am/. The stem vowels /-i-/ and /-e-/ truncate before the third person plural /-at/. Aside from 1 SG знам/znam 'know' (3 SG знае/znae), which has effectively replaced the regular знаам/znaam (Тошев/Tošev 1970), and the verb сум/sum 'be', there are no irregularities or alternations in the present tense. According to the norm, even prefixed forms of знае/znae do not permit variation, although it occurs. Note the following irregularities:

1　When /-st-/ and /-l-/ are separated by a fleeting vowel, the resulting cluster simplifies to /-sl-/ when the vowel drops: постеле/postele 'spread', послав/poslav (1 SG AOR; type 3c).

2　види/vidi 'see' and -седи/-sedi 'sit' have type 3e *o*-aorists. Some *i*-stem verbs have facultative *o*-aorists: -вади/-vadi 'extract', -врти/-vrti 'turn'.

3　спие/spie 'sleep', -спав/-spav (1 SG AOR).

4　меле/mele 'grind', -млев/-mlev (1 SG AOR).

5　земе/zeme 'take', зедов/zedov (1 SG AOR), зеде/zede (2, 3 SG AOR).

There is a strong tendency to regularize verbs. Two of the four verbs cited in Lunt (1952: 77) as following type 3e are cited in Тошев/Tošev (1970) as following type 3a, although some middle-aged speakers would still treat them as 3e in 1990. The two that vacillate are везе/veze 'embroider' and гризе/grize 'gnaw'; the other two are пасе/pase 'pasture' and тресе/trese 'shake'. Similarly, there is no morphophonemic alternation of the type *ž* ~ *z* in prefixed forms of каже/kaže 'tell' (*pace* Lunt 1952: 74).

　　For the **verbal *l*-form** /-l/ (M SG), /-la/ (F SG), /-lo/ (N SG), /-le/ (PL) is added to the imperfect and aorist stems. The *l*-form agrees in gender and number with the subject. The following alternations and irregularities occur in the formation of *l*-forms:

1　The /-o-/ of the aorist stem (types 3e, f, g) drops when there is a vowel in the following syllable: тресол/tresol, тресла/tresla.

2　Verbs in class 3f lose both the /-o-/ and the preceding consonant in the *l*-form: дал/dal, дала/dala.

3　Some verbs vacillate between 3e and 3f: донесе/donese 'carry' has aorist *l*-form донесол/donesol (M), донесла/donesla (F) or донел/donel (M), донела/donela (F) (Тошев/Tošev 1970). The former is more common and is preferred (Корубин/Korubin 1969: 86).

4　The verb земе/zeme 'take' patterns with type 3f in this respect: aorist *l*-form зел/zel (M), зела/zela (F).

5　Verbs based on иде/ide 'come' have suppletion in the aorist *l*-form: the root consonant /-d-/ is replaced with /-š-/. If the prefix ends in a vowel, /i/ becomes /j/ except in the *l*-forms, where it disappears: отиде/otide 'leave', отидов/otidov (1 SG AOR), aorist *l*-form отишол/otišol (M), отишла/otišla (F) 'leave'; најде/najde 'find', најдов/najdov (1 SG AOR), aorist *l*-form нашол/našol (M), нашла/ našla (F).

6 For *i*-stem verbs with an *o*-aorist such as види/vidi the aorist stem is based on the second/third person singular: aorist *l*-form видел/videl (M), видела/videla (F). Verbs that vacillate in the formation of the aorist such as -врти/-vrti 'turn', may also vacillate between -*e*- and -*i*- in the aorist *l*-form.

7 If the loss of a fleeting -*o*- would create a cluster of the type -*stl*-, it simplifies to -*sl*-; расте/raste 'grow', растов/rastov (1 SG AOR), aorist *l*-form растол/rastol (M), расла/rasla (F) (Тошев/Tošev 1970). According to younger educated speakers, however, the aorist *l*- form is now растел/rastel, by analogy with the type видов/vidov, видел/videl.

Table 6.10 lists verbs according to Proto-Slavonic verb classes for comparative purposes. The third person singular present and first person singular aorist are given for all verbs. The third singular aorist and/or masculine singular *l*-form are given only when they show other alternations. The classification from table 6.9 is given on the far left.

The **verbal adjective** is based on the aorist stem if that stem ends in /-a/, otherwise the imperfect stem is used, then /-t/ is added to stems where the vowel is preceded by /-n/ or /-nj/, otherwise /-n/ is added: покани/pokani 'invite' gives поканет/pokanet 'invited', дојде/dojde 'come' gives дојден/dojden 'arrived'. Verbs with ce/se drop it. There are three types of verbs that can use both aorist and imperfect stems: (1) *i*-verbs with an *a*-stem aorist (type 2c): -бројан/-brojan and броен/broen; (2) regular *e*-verbs (type 3a) in which the stem vowel is preceded by another vowel: пее/pee 'sing' > -пеан/-pean and пеен/peen; (3) *e*-verbs that lose their root vowel in the aorist (type 3c): -бран/-bran and берен/ beren. Тошев/Tošev (1970) also permits both stems for some other *e*-verbs: црпан/crpan and црпен/crpen 'haul' (type 3a), плакан/plakan and плачен/plačen (type 3b), стриган/strigan and стрижен/strižen 'trim' (type 3g) but Конески/Koneski (1967) and Усикова/Usikova (1985) indicate only the aorist stem for these classes of verbs. Note that the norm has changed considerably since Lunt (1952: 75): поште/pošte 'search for lice' belongs to type 3d, пцуе/pcue 'curse' (type 3h) and дреме/dreme 'doze' (type 3a) no longer permit variation according to Тошев/Tošev (1970), and ниже/niže 'string' (type 2c) and пее/pee 'sing' (type 3a) are regular within their classes. In verbs that permit both stems the literary norm is to generalize the aorist stem when the verb is perfectivized by prefixation. This is strongly prescribed for class 3c and members of 3a with the root vowel -*e*-, weakly for the others (Конески/ Koneski 1967: 434).

The **verbal adverb** is formed from the imperfect stem by adding the

Table 6.10 Conjugational patterns

Theme in -e/-o

3e/f	донесе/donese	донесов/donesov, донесол/donesol, донел/donel	bring, carry
3f	доведе/dovede	доведов/dovedov, довел/dovel	bring, lead
1a	чита/čita	-читав/-čitav	read
3f/anomalous	иде/ide	-идов/-idov, -ишол/-išol	come
1a	jава/java	-javaв/-javav	ride
3a	гребе/grebe	-гребав/-grebav	scratch
3a	живее/živee	-живеав/-živeav	live
3g	рече/reče	реков/rekov, рече/reče, рекол/rekol	say
3a	начне/načne	начна/načna	begin
3d	умре/umre	умрев/umrev	die
3a	стане/stane	станав/stanav	become
3h	ткае/tkae	-ткав/-tkav	weave
3c	зове/zove	-звав/-zvav	call
	(poetic/dialectal, now felt as a Serbism; literary вика/vika)		
3c	бере/bere	-брав/-brav	gather

Theme in -ne

3a	стигне/stigne	стигнав/stignav	arrive
3a	мине/mine	минав/minav	pass

Theme in -je

3h	чуе/čue	чув/čuv	hear
3a	пее/pee	-пеав/-peav	sing
3h	крие/krie	-крив/-kriv	hide
3h	бие/bie	-бив/-biv	beat
3d/anomalous	меле/mele	-млев/-mlev	grind
1a	слуша/sluša	-слушав/-slušav	listen
3a	умее/umee	-умеав/-umeav	be able
3a	каже/kaže	кажав/kažav	tell
3a	пише/piše	пишав/pišav	write
3d	[от]ме/[ot]me	[от]мев/[ot]mev	seize
	(occurs only prefixed; IMPFV = отима/otima; now felt as a Serbism)		
3f/anomalous	земе/zeme (‹ vъzę-ti/ vъz-ьmǫ)	зедов/zedov, зел/zel	take
1a	дарува/daruva	-дарував/-daruvav	donate
3a	сее/see	-сеав/-seav	sow

Theme in -i

2a	моли/moli	-молив/-moliv	request
2a	оди/odi	-одив/-odiv	go
2a	вели/veli	-велив/-veliv	say
2a	служи/služi	-служив/-služiv	serve
3c	спие/spie	-спав/-spav	sleep

Athematic

anomalous	сум/sum (1 SG)	би/bi, бил/bil	be
3f	јаде/jade	јадов/jadov, јал/jal	eat
3f	даде/dade	дадов/dadov, дал/dal	give
1a	има/ima	имав/imav (IMPF)	have
	(NEG нема/nema)		

Irregular

not a verb	ќе/ḱe		will

(This reflex of **хътеть* 'want' is now an invariant modal word. The conjugated verb meaning 'want' is now the regular сака/saka. There is a negated reflex of the old verb which still conjugates and serves as a variant of не сака/ne saka)

3d	нејќе/nejḱe	нејќев/nejḱev (IMPF)	not want

invariant suffix /-jḱi/. This suffix always entails penultimate stress. (Historically, the /-j-/ comes from an earlier **-e-*, hence the unusual stress pattern.) The verbal adverb is formed only from imperfective verbs with the lexicalized exception of бидејќи/bidejḱi 'because'.

The **verbal noun** is formed by adding /-nje/ to the imperfective imperfect stem: носи/nosi 'carry', носење/nosenje 'carrying'. The perfective verb венча/venča 'wed' has a lexicalized verbal noun: венчање/venčanje 'wedding'.

The **imperative** is based on the present stem. The stem vowel /-i/ or /-e/ is dropped, the stem vowel /-a/ is retained. When the result ends in a vowel, /-j/ is added for the singular, /-jte/ for the plural. When the result ends in a consonant, /-i/ is added for the singular, /-ete/ for the plural:

гледа/gleda 'look' › гледај/gledaj, гледајте/gledajte
носи/nosi 'carry' › носи/nosi, носете/nosete
пие/pie 'drink' › пиј/pij, пијте/pijte
земе/zeme 'take' › земи/zemi, земете/zemete
пее/pee 'sing' › пеј/pej, пејте/pejte

Exceptions:

даде/dade 'give' › дај/daj, дајте/dajte (also for prefixed forms)
кладе/klade 'put' › клај/klaj, клајте /klajte

Verbs in /-uva/ have alternative imperatives in /-uj[te]/.

3.3 Derivational morphology

3.3.1 Major patterns of noun derivation
The suffix /-nje/ derives concrete deverbal nouns from imperfectives (but see section 3.2.2); /-nie/ derives abstract deverbal nouns from perfective

Table 6.11   Paradigm of the verb моли/moli 'request, beg'

(a)

Synthetic series

Present		Aorist		Imperfect	
молам	молиме	-молив	-моливме	молев	молевме
молиш	молите	-моли	-моливте	молеше	молевте
моли	молат	-моли	-молија	молеше	молеа

Analytic series

SUM SERIES

sum aorist		sum imperfect	
сум -молил	сме -молиле	сум молел	сме молеле
си -молил	сте -молиле	си молел	сте молеле
-молил	-молиле	молел	молеле

beše pluperfect

beše aorist		beše imperfect	
бев -молил	бевме -молиле	бев молел	бевме молеле
беше -молил	бевте -молиле	беше молел	бевте молеле
беше -молил	беа -молиле	беше молел	беа молеле

IMA SERIES

ima perfect		imaše pluperfect	
имам молено	имаме молено	имав молено	имавме молено
имаш молено	имате молено	имаше молено	имавте молено
има молено	имаат молено	имаше молено	имаа молено

imal perfect

сум имал молено	сме имале молено
си имал молено	сте имале молено
имал молено	имале молено

HYPOTHETICAL CONDITIONAL

би молел, би молела, би молело, би молеле

Non-finite series

imperative

моли   молете

verbal adverb

молејќи

verbal noun

молење

verbal adjective

молен, молена, молено, молени

(b)

Synthetic series

Present		Aorist		Imperfect	
molam	molime	-moliv	-molivme	molev	molevme
moliš	molite	-moli	-molivte	moleše	molevte
moli	molat	-moli	-molija	moleše	molea

Analytic series
SUM SERIES

sum aorist		*sum imperfect*	
sum -molil	sme -molile	sum molel	sme molele
si -molil	ste -molile	si molel	ste molele
-molil	-molile	molel	molele

beše pluperfect

beše aorist		*beše imperfect*	
bev -molil	bevme -molile	bev molel	bevme molele
beše -molil	bevte -molile	beše molel	bevte molele
beše -molil	bea -molile	beše molel	bea molele

IMA SERIES

ima perfect		*imaše pluperfect*	
imam moleno	imame moleno	imav moleno	imavme moleno
imaš moleno	imate moleno	imaše moleno	imavte moleno
ima moleno	imaat moleno	imaše moleno	imaa moleno

imal perfect

sum imal moleno	sme imale moleno
si imal moleno	ste imale moleno
imal moleno	imale moleno

HYPOTHETICAL CONDITIONAL
bi molel, bi molela, bi molelo, bi molele

Non-finite series

imperative
moli   molete

verbal adverb
molejḱi

verbal noun
molenje

verbal adjective
molen, molena, moleno, moleni

---

verbs; /-ba/ is permitted with either aspect and either meaning: самоопределување/samoopreduvanje 'an act of self-determining', самоопределба/samoopredelba 'self-determination', решавање/rešavanje 'an act of deciding', решение/rešenie 'decision'. The relative productivity of these suffixes can be seen in Миличиќ/Miličiḱ (1967): approximately 8,500 entries with /-nje/, 220 with /-ba/ and 150 with /-nie/. Other suffixes for deverbal nouns are -∅ or /-a/, /-ačka/ (about 275 total including both abstract nouns and feminine actors), /-ež/ (about 75), /-ka/, /-stvo/.

The masculine agentive suffixes /-ar/, /-ač/ and /-tel/ all add /-ka/ to form the feminine, whereas /-ec/ and /-nik/ have the feminine form /-(n)ica/. The suffixes /-ec/, /-ka/, /-ica/ are sometimes extended by

/-al-/ or /-av-/. The verb вража/vraža 'perform sorcery, tell fortunes' provides examples of many of these suffixes in Конески/Koneski (1961–6), according to which they are synonymous in the case of this particular verbal base, all meaning 'sorcerer' and 'sorceress': вражар/vražar, вражач/vražač, вражалец/vražalec, вражарка/vražarka, вражачка/vražačka, вражалка/vražalka, вражалица/vražalica. Inanimates also have the suffix /-lo/: лепи/lepi 'stick', лепило/lepilo 'glue'.

For de-adjectival nouns, the main suffixes are /-ec/, /-ica/, /-(n)ik/, /-(j)ak/, /-(j)ačka/, /-ina/, /-stvo/, /-ost/, /-ež/: убавец/ubavec 'handsome one', убавица/ubavica 'beautiful one', убавина/ubavina 'beauty'. Many of these same deverbal and de-adjectival suffixes can derive nouns from other nouns: свиња/svinja 'swine', свињар(ка)/svinjar(ka) 'swineherd' (M (F)), свињарник/svinjarnik or свињарница/svinjarnica 'pigsty', свињарство/svinjarstvo 'hog raising', свинштина/svinština 'swinishness'.

Diminutives apply to all three genders: брат/brat 'brother', diminutive брате/brate, братле/bratle, братче/bratče, братенце/bratence, братец/bratec, братуле/bratule, браток/bratok (see also section 2.3). The augmentative suffix is -иште/-ište and is neuter: му свикало жеништето/mu svikalo ženišteto 'his shrewish wife yelled at him'. The chief pejorative suffixes are all neuter in appearance but agree with real gender if they refer to animate beings: /-ko/, /-(a)lo/, /-le/: моч/moč 'urine', мочко/močko and мочло/močlo 'little squirt', мочало/močalo 'organ of urination (colloquial)'.

There are also three derivational suffixes of Turkish origin that are still productive with nouns: /-džija/ (F /-džika/; /dž/ gives /č/ after voiceless consonants due to Turkish rules for voicing assimilation) meaning 'someone who does something regularly' (about 250 items), /-lak/ for abstract nouns (about 200 items) and /-àna/ for nouns of location (about fifty items). These suffixes are used in common words of Turkish origin: јабанџија/jabandžija 'foreigner', јавашлак/javašlak 'slowness (pejorative)', меана/meana 'tavern (archaic)'. They are productive with Slavonic roots: ловџија/lovdžija 'hunter', војниклак/vojniklak 'army service (colloquial)', пилана/pilana 'saw-mill'. They remain productive in recent loan-words, although frequently with pejorative or ironic overtones: фудбалџија/fudbaldžija '(inept) soccer-player', асистентлак/asistentlak 'assistantship (ironic)', хидроелектрана/hidroelektrana 'hydroelectric power station (colloquial but neutral)'. There are also a few derivational affixes of more recent foreign origin: /-ist/ '-ist', /-izam/ '-ism'.

Compounding with the linking vowel /-o-/ is still productive: минофрлач/minofrlač 'mine-thrower'. The Turkish type of compound lacks a linking vowel: тутунќесе/tutunḱese 'tobacco pouch'. There are also native formations without linking vowels, although these generally use disparate parts of speech: зајдисонце/zajdisonce 'sunset'.

Noun prefixation is limited and marginal. The border between suffixation and compounding is clear (suffixes do not possess independent lexical meaning and never stand alone), but the border between prefixation and compounding is hazy. Many items functioning prefixally also function as independent words: само-/samo- 'self-' as in самопридонес/ samopridones 'voluntary contribution' also functions as an independent adjective сам(о)/sam(o) 'oneself'. Other prefixal items are capable of standing alone: /anti-/ 'anti-' can be used predicatively to mean 'against' or 'opposed'. Some prefixes such as /pra-/ 'proto-, great-' are capable of being repeated: прапрадедо/prapradedo 'great-great-grandfather'.

Acronyms also occur, but are not as important as the various processes already discussed thus far.

3.3.2   Major patterns of adjective derivation

There are three suffixes used to derive possessives: (1) /-in/ for nouns in /-a, -e/: мечкин/mečkin 'bear's'; (2) /-ov, -ev/ for nouns in a consonant or /-o/ (masculine and neuter): дабов/dabov 'of oak'; (3) /-ji, -ki, -i/ for people and animals: жабји/žabji 'frog's'.

Adjectives of quality can be formed with /-est/, /-at/, /-[ov]it/, /-(l)iv/ (highly productive): трнлив/trnliv 'thorny'. Another highly productive suffix is /-ski/, /-ški/, which shows reflexes of the first palatalization (and regressive assimilation of voicing) if the stem ends in an underlying velar: бензински/benzinski 'gasoline', филолошки/filološki 'philological'.

The following suffixes are most common for deverbal adjectives: /-en/, /-liv/, /-čki/, /-telen/ (bookish), /-kav/: реши/reši 'decide (PRFV)' gives решен, решлив, решителен/rešen, rešliv, rešitelen 'decided, soluble, decisive (person)'.

The suffixes /-(š)en/ and /-ski/ derive adjectives from adverbs: сегашен/segašen 'present', лански/lanski 'last year's'.

Adjectives can be rendered expressive by a variety of suffixes, some of which are illustrated here with the adjective црн/crn 'black': црникав/ crnikav, црничок/crničok, црнкавест/crnkavest, црнулав/crnulav, црнулест/crnulest.

Two of the most productive suffixes are /-av/ and /-en/, which can also be added to many loans to create doublets: ал/al or ален/alen 'scarlet', ќор/ḱor or ќорав/ḱorav 'blind, one-eyed'. The Turkish suffix /-lija/ (all genders, PL /-lii/) is used to form about 250 adjectives and nouns from all types of nouns – Turkish, Slavonic and international: касметлија/ kasmetlija 'lucky', свездаллија/dzvezdallija 'kind', пубертетлија/ pubertetlija 'teenager (ironic)'.

Compound adjectives can be formed with or without the linking vowel -o- and with or without a suffix: гологлав/gologlav 'bareheaded'.

3.3.3   Major pattern of verb derivation

Taking unprefixed imperfectives as basic, perfectives are derived by pre-fixation and suffixation. The following pre-verbs are used: /v-, vo-, do-, za-, iz-, na-, nad-, o-, ob-, od-, po-, pod-, pre-, pred-, pri-, pro(z)-, raz-, s-, so-, u-, (o)bez-, (s)protiv-, su-/. Pre-verbs can also be added to one another: тепа/tepa 'beat (IMPFV)' поизнатепа/poiznatepa 'beat to a pulp (PRFV)' (see Угринова-Скаловска/Ugrinova-Skalovska 1960 for detailed discussion). The suffix /-ne/ usually forms perfective verbs: седи/sedi 'sit', седне/sedne 'sit down', although a few verbs in -не/-ne are imperfective or bi-aspectual: кисне/kisne 'become sour (IMPFV)', гасне/gasne 'quench, extinguish (bi-aspectual)'. Imperfectives are derived productively from perfectives by means of the suffix /-uva/: седнува/sednuva 'keep sitting down'. Other suffixes such as /-(j)a(va)/ are unproductive or obsolete (see section 2.2).

The suffix /-uva/ is also productive in forming verbs from other parts of speech: збор/zbor 'word', зборува/zboruva 'speak', старт/start 'kick-off (NOUN)' стартува/startuva (VERB). Two other productive suffixes are the Greek /-sa/ (Greco-Turkish /-disa/) and the West European (from Latin through French to German to Slavonic) /-ira/. Verbs in /-sa/ are often perfective and form imperfectives by means of /-uva/ with pre-fixation deriving new perfectives: калај/kalaj 'tin', perfective калаиса/kalaisa 'plate with tin', imperfective калаисува/kalaisuva, прекалаиса/prekalaisa 're-tin (PRFV)'. Verbs in /-ira/ are often bi-aspectual, but show a tendency to be treated as imperfective, with per-fectives being derived by means of prefixation (see section 3.2.1): интерес/interes 'interest', imperfective интересира/interesira 'interest', perfective заинтересира/zainteresira. In some cases, the suffixes con-tribute to semantic differentiation: критика/kritika 'criticism', критикува/kritikuva 'to critique', критизира/kritizira 'to criticize'. While some new loans permit formation freely with more than one of these suffixes, others do not: флерт/flert 'flirt' permits the formation of the verb флертува/flertuva but not флертира/flertira (see Минова-Ѓуркова/ Minova-Ǵurkova 1966).

The suffixes /-ka/ and /-oti/ are diminutive and augmentative, respec-tively: копа/kopa 'dig', копка/kopka 'scratch the surface'; тропа/tropa 'knock', тропоти/tropoti 'pound'. The suffix /-i/ can form verbs from nouns and adjectives, and some of the de-adjectival causatives in /-i/ form intransitives in /-ee/: црн/crn 'black', црни/crni 'blacken', црнее/crnee 'become black'. Verbs are also derived by compounding: обелоденува/ obelodenuva 'reveal' from бел ден/bel den 'broad daylight' (literally 'white day').

4   Syntax

4.1   Element order in declarative sentences

The unmarked order of main constituents is subject–verb–object (if the object is definite, a reduplicative object pronoun must precede the verb): кучето ја каса мачката/kučeto ja kasa mačkata 'the dog bites the cat' (literally: dog (N DEF) it (F ACC) bites cat (F DEF)). In unmarked order, the subject is topic and no constituent bears special sentential emphasis (focus). Topicalization and focus are rendered by a combination of word order and intonation within the context of the discourse. In general, given the appropriate intonation, the position immediately before the verb phrase is that of the topic. If the verb phrase is initial, it is the focus of the sentence, and the topic will depend on intonation. Inversion of subject and object will topicalize the object without focusing on it, while placing both constituents before the verb will focus on the topic. The following examples illustrate the possibilities:

Мачката ја каса кучето./Mačkata ja kasa kučeto.
'The dog bites the cat (topic).'
Кучето мачката ја каса./Kučeto mačkata ja kasa.
'The dog bites the cat (topic/focus).'
Мачката кучето ја каса./Mačkata kučeto ja kasa.
'The dog (topic/focus) bites the cat.'
Ја каса кучето мачката./Ja kasa kučeto mačkata.
'The dog bites (focus) the cat.'
Ја каса мачката кучето./Ja kasa mačkata kučeto.
'The dog bites (focus) the cat.'

There are four possible positions for an adverb, illustrated by the numbers in square brackets: [I] кучето [II] ја каса [III] мачката [IV]/ [I] kučeto [II] ja kasa [III] mačkata [IV] '[I]the dog [II] bites [III] the cat [IV]'. The neutral position for the adverb is usually [I] or [IV]. The position of focus is usually [II] or [IV]. Position [IV] is more likely to be neutral with time adverbs but focus with manner adverbs, but judgments vary from speaker to speaker. Position [III] is acceptable but more likely if the subject is omitted.

Clitics precede finite verb forms. The order is subjunctive – negator – mood marker – auxiliary – ethical dative – dative object – accusative object – verb: да не ќе сум си му го дал/da ne ḱe sum si mu go dal '(they didn't say) that I won't have given it to him (did they)?'. The subjunctive marker follows the expectative in colloquial suppositions: па ќе да има кај четириесет/pa ḱe da ima kaj četirieset 'well, he must be around forty'. The hypothetical marker does not occur after the subjunctive except in old-fashioned curses and blessings, in which case clitic order can be violated: да би волци те јале/da bi volci te jale 'may wolves eat you'.

Clitic pronouns occur on either side of the auxiliary in the *beše* pluperfect: се беше заборчил ~ беше се заборчил/se beše zaborčil ~ beše se zaborčil 'he had got into debt'. The sense of past resultativity is stronger when the auxiliary is closer to the verb (Конески/Koneski 1967: 482–3). Clitics precede the forms of има/ima in the *ima* series, and non-clitic words may come between има/ima and the neuter verbal adjective: не ги има наполнето/ne gi ima napolneto 'he has not filled them'; ги немам видено/gi nemam videno 'I have not seen them'; го имаше сам направено/go imaše sam napraveno 'he has done it himself'. The negative equivalents of ќе/ḱe using нема да/nema da have clitics attaching to the main verb: нема да ги видам/nema da gi vidam 'I will not see them'. The interrogative clitic ли/li normally comes after the first stressed word in the clause or after the verb (see section 4.2).

Present-tense forms of сум/sum 'be' that function as auxiliaries – the first two persons – have auxiliary–clitic order even when functioning as the copula. Other forms of 'be' behave as full verbs when functioning as the copula and are preceded by clitic elements: Jac сум му пријател/jas sum mu prijatel 'I am his friend'; тој ми е пријател/toj mi e prijatel 'he is my friend'; jac му бев пријател/jas mu bev prijatel 'I was his friend'.

Clitics follow non-finite verb forms (including the imperative) донесете ми ја книгата/donesete mi ja knigata 'bring me the book'; донесувајќи му ја книгата/donesuvajḱi mu ja knigata 'bringing him the book'.

Macedonian permits both head–genitive and genitive–head order in prepositional possessive constructions. A dative possessive clitic – limited to a few kinship terms – must follow the kinship term: мајка му на царот/majka mu na carot (literally: mother to-him of the-king) or на царот мајка му/na carot majka mu (more colloquial) 'the mother of the king/the king's mother'. In attributive noun phrases, the clitic comes after the first element. Note that attributes normally precede but can also follow the nouns they modify: мајка му стара/majka mu stara, старата му мајка/starata mu majka 'his old mother'.

The normal order within the noun phrase is determiner – adjective – noun: сите овие три бедни мачки/site ovie tri bedni mački 'all three of these poor cats'. A possessive adjective normally precedes a numeral as in English: моите три пријатели/moite tri prijateli 'my three friends'. However, the numeral precedes if the quantity is not the totality: еден мој пријател/eden moj prijatel 'a friend of mine (one of my friends)'.

4.2   Non-declarative sentence types

Interrogatives are marked by a rising intonation on the verb or the focus of the question: ќе одиш во Битола?/ḱe odiš vo Bitola? 'are you going to Bitola?' Focus on the topic can also be achieved by inversion: во Битола ќе одиш?/vo Bitola ḱe odiš? 'are you going *to Bitola*?' The interrogative particle ли/li is used less in Macedonian than in Bulgarian. In Englund's

(1977: 137–43) corpus of yes–no questions, 60.4 per cent of the Bulgarian questions used ли/li as opposed to 30 per cent in Macedonian, and 44.1 per cent of her Macedonian questions had no lexical interrogative marker but only 19.9 per cent in Bulgarian. Another difference between Macedonian and Bulgarian is that ли/li is more strictly bound to follow the first stressed element in the clause of the verb in Macedonian. Thus if the focus is anywhere but on the verb, that element must be at the beginning of the clause: ќе одиш ли во Битола?/ḱe odiš li vo Bitola? 'will you go to Bitola?'; во Битола ли ќе одиш?/vo Bitola li ḱe odiš? 'is it to Bitola you will be going?'; во Битола ќе одиш ли?/vo Bitola ḱe odiš li? 'are you going to go to Bitola?' but not *ќе одиш во Битола ли?/*ḱe odiš vo Bitola li? Englund's corpus contains six exceptions to these generalizations, but I found that speakers rejected such sentences, indicating that this aspect of the norm has become more stable. A conceptual entity is treated as one stressed unit: Нова Македонија ли му ја донесе?/Nova Makedonija li mu ja donese? 'was it (the newspaper) Nova Makedonija that you brought him?'

Other interrogative particles for yes–no questions:

дали/dali 'request for information': дали знаеш/dali znaeš 'do you know?' зар/zar 'surprise': зар знаеш/zar znaeš 'you mean, you know?!' зар не знаеш/zar ne znaeš 'don't you know?!'

да не/da ne 'tag question': да не си нешто болен/da ne si nešto bolen 'you're not sick, are you?' (Unlike Bulgarian, Macedonian rarely uses да/da by itself for a yes–no question.)

али/ali is a colloquial variant of дали/dali. Зер/zer is a dialectal and зарем/zarem a less preferred variant of зар/zar. Нели/neli can both introduce a negative interrogative and follow as a tag meaning 'isn't that so?' A/a normally occurs at the end of a question, after a pause.

Macedonian can also introduce a question with the following WH words:

кој	како	колку	каков	колкав	што	каде/кај	кога	зошто	чиј
koj	kako	kolku	kakov	kolkav	što	kade/kaj	koga	zošto	čij
who, which	how	how much, many	what kind	how big, much	what, why	where	when	why	whose

Indirect questions can be introduced by a WH word or the interrogative marker дали/dali: тој ме праша/toj me praša 'he asked me' колку години имам/kolku godini imam 'how old I was' дали ќе дојдам/dali ḱe dojdam 'whether I would come'.

An interrogative can be answered with да/da 'yes', не/ne 'no' or with a repetition of the focus of the question, which in itself can constitute affirmation. Typical responses to a negative interrogative such as зар не сакаш да дојдеш?/zar ne sakaš da dojdeš? 'don't you want to come?' are како не/kako ne 'of course', да/da 'yes', сакам/sakam 'I want to', or не/ne 'no', па нејќам/pa nejḱam or не сакам/ne sakam 'I don't want to', јок!/jok! 'no way!'

The normal form of a command is the perfective imperative (all examples are given in the singular, the plural can also be a polite singular): дојди/dojdi 'come!' A *da*-clause with the perfective present expresses a wish and can function as a more polite command or request: да ми го напишеш/da mi go napišeš 'write it down for me'. Negative commands are normally formed with the corresponding imperfective: не доаѓај/ne doaǵaj, да не доаѓаш/da ne doaǵaš 'don't come'. The expression немој/ nemoj (plural немојте/nemojte) 'don't!' can be used by itself or with a perfective *da*-clause to form a negative imperative with other verbs: немој да дојдеш/nemoj da dojdeš 'don't come'. A negative *da*-clause with a perfective verb constitutes a warning: да не дојдеш/da ne dojdeš 'you'd better not come'. A negated perfective imperative is a challenging threat commanding the addressee to perform the action: не дојди/ne dojdi 'just don't you come (and see what happens)!' A *da*-clause with an imperfect can function as a request: да ми ја донесеше книгата/da mi ja doneseše knigata 'bring me the book, would you please'. The second person future (ќе/ḱe + present) can also be used as an imperative either peremptorily or in giving directions: ќе одиш право, па десно/ḱe odiš pravo, pa desno 'go straight, then (take a) right'. Indirect commands are expressed with *da*-clauses: кажи му да оди/kaži mu da odi 'tell him to go'.

4.3 Copular sentences

The usual copula is the verb сум/sum 'be' and is not omitted (see section 4.1). There is no nominative/instrumental contrast in Macedonian since there is no instrumental. There is no long/short adjective distinction, although morphological traces of the masculine long form survive (see section 3.1.4).

4.4 Coordination and comitativity

Coordination is normally marked between the last two elements (orthographically, a comma is never used in this position): семинар за македонски јазик, литература и култура/seminar za makedonski jazik, literatura i kultura 'seminar for Macedonian language, literature and culture'. An и/i 'and' before each element gives the meaning 'both ... and ...'. Prepositions can be conjoined: состојбата во македонија во и непосредно по првата светска војна/sostojbata vo Makedonija vo i neposredno po prvata svetska vojna 'the situation in Macedonia during and immediately after the First World War'. Coordinated singular adjectives modifying the same noun but denoting different entities are both definite and have a singular noun but plural verb agreement, while coordinated adjectives modifying a single entity will take one article and singular agreement: нашата и вашата екипа беа таму/našata i vašata ekipa bea tamu 'your team and our team were there' versus нашата и ваша екипа беше таму/našata i vaša ekipa beše tamu 'your team and ours was there' (see section 3.1.1). Non-pronominal adjectives modifying conjoined nouns of different genders can be plural: љубезни Елена и Виктор/ljubezni Elena i Viktor 'kind Elena and Victor', but *овие маж и жена/*ovie maž i žena *'these man and woman'. Conjoined subject nouns govern a plural verb regardless of word order (but see the end of section 4.10).

Comitative constructions with a coordinative meaning occur colloquially: ние со Јола одевме крај него/nie so Jola odevme kraj nego 'Jola and I (literally: 'we with Jola') walked alongside him'. There is significant variation in the treatment of agreement; considerations of style, region and generation all appear to be relevant: тој со Виктор отиде/ отидоа/toj so Viktor otide/otidoa (3 SG/3 PL) 'he left with Victor' or 'Victor and he left'. The use of singular agreement is favoured by the younger generation of Skopje speakers and is considered correct by strict normativists; the use of plural agreement is favoured by some older speakers, who consider it more literary, and in the south-west.

4.5 Subordination

All the WH words given in section 4.2 except зошто/zošto 'why' can function as relativizers. Except for што/što 'which, that, who' and – according to the modern norm – кога/koga 'when', the relativizing function can be indicated by adding што/što, written without any space after кој/koj and чиј/čij (hence, којшто/kojšto), and written as a separate word after all others. Корубин/Korubin (1969) suggests that што/ što be used for restrictive clauses and кој(што)/koj(što) for the non-restrictive but practice varies. In general, кој(што)/koj(što) is preferred after a preposition: детето што го сретнавме/deteto što go sretnavme 'the child whom we met', човекот со кого(што) се шеташе вчера/čovekot so kogo(što) se šetaše včera 'the person with whom he walked yesterday'. A specific indefinite referent triggers pronoun reduplication: во одајата влезе еден човек кого го видов порано на улица/vo odajata vleze eden čovek kogo go vidov porano na ulica 'into the room came a person whom I had seen (him) earlier on the street' (Topolińska 1981: 114). Relativizers can occur without any overt antecedent: кој вино пие, без невеста спие/koj vino pie, bez nevesta spie 'he who drinks wine sleeps without a bride'. Subjects and objects can both be extracted out of subordinate clauses: човекот за кого(што) мислам дека (ти) си го видел/čovekot za kogo(što) mislam deka (ti) si go videl 'the person that I think you saw'; човекот кој(што) мислам дека (тој) те видел тебе/čovekot koj(što) mislam deka (toj) te videl tebe 'the person that I think saw you'.

The chief phrase subordinators are the indicative дека/deka, оти/oti, што/što and the subjunctive да/da (see also sections 3.2.1 and 4.2): им реков да дојдат/im rekov da dojdat 'I told them to come'; им реков дека/оти ќе дојде/im rekov deka/oti ḱe dojde 'I told them that he will come'; добро е што ги гледаш/dobro e što gi gledaš 'it is good that you are watching them'; добро е да ги гледаш/dobro e da gi gledaš 'it is good (for you) to watch them'.

The verbal adverb normally denotes an action performed by the subject simultaneously with the action of the main verb: одејќи по патот, тој си најде едно ќесе пари/odejḱi po patot, toj si najde edno ḱese pari 'while going along the road, he found a bag of money'. Occasionally the verbal adverb does not refer to the grammatical subject of the main verb or the action is not simultaneous with it: одејќи по патот, ми падна чантата/ odejḱi po patot, mi padna čantata 'while walking along the road, my hand-bag fell'; затворајќи ја вратата, се упатив кај Виктор/zatvorajḱi ja vratata, se upativ kaj Viktor 'having closed the door, I set out for Victor's'. Such usage is rejected by strict normativists.

The most common equivalent of the infinitive is a *da*-clause: сакам ти да ми кажеш/sakam ti da mi kažeš 'I want you to tell me'. As Čašule (1988) points out, the verbal noun can also serve this function: тој има желба за правење штета/toj ima želba za pravenje šteta 'he likes to cause damage'.

4.6 Negation

Sentence negation is expressed by placing не/ne before the verb: Томислав не дојде вчера/Tomislav ne dojde včera 'Tomislav didn't come yesterday'. Constituents can also be negated by не/ne: него го најдов а не неа/nego go najdov a ne nea 'I found him, but not her'; Нина дојде не вчера туку завчера/Nina dojde ne včera tuku zavčera 'Nina came not yesterday but the day before yesterday'; со куче а не со пиле/so kuče a ne so pile 'with a dog and/but not with a chicken'. The position of не/ne with relation to да/da affects meaning: јас дојдов не да те спасам, ами да те убијам!/jas dojdov ne da te spasam, ami da te ubijam! 'I have not come to save you but to kill you!' versus да не те спасам/da ne te spasam 'let me not save you'. A sentence can have more than one negative element, and if a negative pronoun is used the verb must also be negated: никој никому/на никого ништо не рече/nikoj nikomu/na nikogo ništo ne reče 'no one said anything to anyone (West, literary/East, Skopje)'; нема ни месо/nema ni meso 'there isn't even any meat/there isn't any meat, either'.

Since the accusative/genitive distinction does not exist, there can be no such contrast for the direct object. Absence is signalled by the impersonal нема/nema 'it is not' (literally: 'it does not have'): нема никакви директори тука/nema nikakvi direktori tuka 'there aren't any directors here'. If the entity is definite, the verb takes an accusative reduplicative pronoun: директорот го нема/direktorot go nema 'the director isn't here'. The verb 'be' cannot be used in this way: *директорот (го) не бил/било/*direktorot (go) ne bil/bilo.

4.7 Anaphora and pronouns

Macedonian has pronominal anaphora and anaphora without an overt lexical marker (zero anaphora). It also omits unstressed subject pronouns, which normally occur only for emphasis, contrast, disambiguation or formality. Definite and sometimes specific direct objects and all indirect objects trigger reduplicative clitic pronouns within the verb phrase agreeing in gender, number and case with the object.

Subject nominals can have zero anaphora subject marking on the finite verb: човекот влегуваше во собата и се сопна/čovekot vleguvaše vo sobata i se sopna 'the person entered the room and (he) tripped'. A subject nominal eligible for anaphora is replaced by a personal pronoun for emphasis, contrast or disambiguation: ги чекав Кирил и Лиле. Тој дојде, а таа не/gi čekav Kiril i Lile. Toj dojde, a taa ne 'I was waiting for Kiril and Lile. He came, but she didn't'. Otherwise, the presence of a subject pronoun is normally interpreted as non-anaphoric: го видовме Владо, кога Ø/тој влезе/go vidovme Vlado, koga Ø/toj vleze 'we saw Vlado when he (Vlado/someone else) entered'. However, if this were part of a sentence that began: 'we were expecting Peter, but ...', then the subject pronoun could be interpreted as coreferential with Vlado.

Direct-object nominals are eligible for zero anaphora only when they are non-specific indefinite: барав една марка но не најдов/barav edna marka no ne najdov 'I was looking for a stamp but didn't find one'. If there is an anaphoric pronoun, the indefinite object nominal is interpreted as specific (note that ja/ja is the third-person accusative clitic pronoun): барав една марка но не ja најдов/barav edna marka no ne ja najdov 'I was looking for a stamp but didn't find it'. Although not in the norm, it is also possible to mark an indefinite object as specific by means of a reduplicated object pronoun within the verb phrase, in which case the anaphoric pronoun is required: ja барав една марка но не *Ø/ja најдов/ja barav edna marka no ne *Ø/ja najdov 'I was looking for a stamp but didn't find it'. If the direct object is definite, both reduplicated and anaphoric pronouns are required: ja/*Ø барав марката и не *Ø/ja најдов /ja/*Ø barav markata i ne *Ø/ja najdov 'I was looking for the stamp and didn't find it.'

Anaphora with other nominals is by means of pronouns. Macedonian also has anaphoric expressions such as гореспоменатиот/gorespomenatiot 'the above-mentioned' and претходниот/prethodniot 'the preceding'.

4.8   Reflexives and reciprocals

Reflexivity is expressed by reflexive personal pronouns (ce/se, си/si, себе/sebe, себеси/sebesi), the reflexive pronominal adjective (свој/svoj), the emphatic pronominal adjective (сам/sam), the adjective сопствен/sopstven 'one's own' (also 'characteristic') and the verbal prefix само-/samo-. For details on the uses of ce/se see section 3.2.1. On the possessive use of си/si see section 4.9. The prefix само-/samo- and the pronoun себе(си)/sebe(si) refer unambiguously to the subject as both the source and the goal of the action, whereas the intransitive marker ce/se has additional uses and interpretations: залаже ce/zalaže se 'be deceived' or 'deceive oneself', but самозалаже ce/samozalaže se = залаже себеси/zalaže sebesi 'deceive oneself'. The emphatic pronominal adjective сам/sam is normally definite when it means 'self' and indefinite when it means 'alone' (Topolińska 1981: 94–5): Петре дојде самиот/Petre dojde samiot 'Peter came himself'; Петре дојде сам/Petre dojde sam 'Peter came alone'; самиот Петре дојде/samiot Petre dojde 'Peter himself came'; *сам Петре дојде/*sam Petre dojde. With marked intransitives, however, the indefinite can have a reflexive meaning: сам кога ќе се удри човек .../sam koga ќe se udri čovek ... 'When a person hits himself' (Lunt 1952: 39).

A non-reflexive preceding a subject noun phrase is interpreted as referring to someone other than the subject: кај него/кај себеси Коста ги најде потребните пари/kaj nego/kaj sebesi Kosta gi najde potrebnite pari 'Kosta found the necessary money on him (someone else/himself)'. If the pronoun follows, however, it is possible for the regular third person to have a reflexive interpretation: Коста си ги нашол парите кај него/себеси/Kosta si gi našol parite kaj nego/sebesi 'Kosta found the necessary money on him (someone else or himself)/himself'. Unlike other Slavonic languages, the pronominal adjective свој/svoj is becoming like the English emphatic 'one's own', as in the following example: директорот дојде со неговата/својата сопруга/direktorot dojde so negovata/svojata sopruga 'the director came with his/his-own spouse'. Although normal usage would have no possessive pronominal adjective and 'spouse' would simply be definite, the use of неговата/negovata 'his' is unremarkable and would not be interpreted as referring to someone else's wife. Rather, the use of својата/svojata 'his own' would be taken to imply that it was unusual for him to come with his own wife rather than someone else's.

Reflexives normatively have subject-nominative antecedents, and although the following examples show dative object referents, they are unusual or marginal. The following sentence was uttered in a formal speech, but a strict normativist informant rejected it when it was submitted for testing: пожелувајќи ви среќно враќање во својата средина/poželuvajќi vi sreќno vraќanje vo svojata sredina 'wishing you a happy return to your surroundings'. Only some speakers accepted the following invented sentence: својата слика ѝ се покажа на неа/svojata slika ì se pokaža na nea 'her own picture appeared to her'. Reflexives are normally bound to the clauses in which they occur, but the following example shows a reflexive referring outside its clause: Рада ме замоли да купам една кутија цигари за ќерка ѝ и една за себеси/Rada me zamoli da kupam edna kutija cigari za ḱerka ì i edna za sebesi 'Rada asked me to buy a package of cigarettes for her daughter and one for herself'. Although this translation was spontaneously supplied by an educated speaker with excellent English, on later reflection he noted that according to the norm only 'myself' could be used.

The following expressions render reciprocity: еден (на) друг/eden (na) drug 'one another' (other prepositions can also be used); меѓу себе/ meǵu sebe 'among our-, your-, them- selves'; меѓусебно/meǵusebno 'mutually'; ce/se (see section 3.2.1). The following sentences illustrate various possibilities of order and scope: тие си даваат пари еден на друг/tie si davaat pari eden na drug 'they give money to one another'; еден на друг си даваат пари/eden na drug si davaat pari 'to one another they give money'; тие сакаат да си помогнат еден на друг/ tie sakaat da si pomognat eden na drug 'they want to help one another'; тие сакаат еден на друг да си помогнат/tie sakaat eden na drug da si pomognat (acceptable, but not as good); јас би сакал тие да си помогнат еден на друг/jas bi sakal tie da si pomognat eden na drug 'I would like them to help one another'; еден на друг да си помогнат тие, тоа е мојата желба/eden na drug da si pomognat tie, taa e mojata želba 'that they help one another is my desire' (acceptable if the referent of 'they' is already known); ти ги ставаш чиниите една врз друга/ti gi stavaš činiite edna vrz druga 'you put the plates one on another'.

4.9   Possession

The verb има/ima 'have' is the normal clausal expression of possession. The prepositions на/na, од/od 'of' mark nominal possession: книгата на/од Блажета/knigata na/od Blažeta 'Blaže's book'. The use of од/od in this meaning is a Westernism. The normal order is head–prepositional phrase, but the order prepositional phrase–head also occurs, especially colloquially: дај ми ја од Конески граматиката/daj mi ja od Koneski gramatikata 'give me Koneski's grammar' (see section 4.1).

Unlike Bulgarian, Macedonian clitic dative pronouns are not used with noun phrases to indicate possession, except with kinship terms and similar expressions (see section 4.1). Such constructions no longer take the definite article, but, as with body parts, the definite form by itself can be understood to refer to the possessor. Terms denoting close relationships can add a possessive pronominal adjective (without the definite article) for emphasis: татко ми мој/tatko mi moj 'my father'. The reflexive dative clitic си/ si can be used in a verb phrase with the definite form of a noun that does not normally take the possessive dative clitic to indicate possession: земи си го палтото/zemi si go paltoto 'take your coat!'

Possessive adjectives, both pronominal (see section 3.1.3) and those derived from proper nouns and kinship terms (see section 3.3.2), normally precede the head, but can also follow, especially colloquially and vocatively. The first item in a phrase involving a possessive adjective normally takes the definite article except some kinship terms and the vocative: нејзиниот сопруг/nejziniot soprug, сопругот нејзин/ soprugot nejzin 'her spouse'.

4.10 Quantification

Quantifiers do not enter into the few existing case oppositions and normally take the plural. Singular agreement is prescribed for numerals ending in '1', but in practice only the nearest item or noun phrase will be singular. Thus 'thirty-one beautiful girls were dancing' is prescribed as триесет и едно убаво девојче играше/trieset i edno ubavo devojče igraše, but most speakers use a plural verb играа/igraa and some even use a plural noun девојчиња/devojčinja. A verb preceding such a numeral is plural. See sections 3.1.2 and 3.1.5 on the morphology of quantitative plurals and virile numerals. The quantitative plural is obligatory only after два/dva 'two' and неколку/nekolku 'a few'. It is especially common with certain frequently counted nouns such as ден/den 'day'. The most likely environments for the quantitative plural are unmodified monosyllabic nouns of Slavonic origin quantified by numerals under '11'. Although, according to Topolińska (1981: 71), adjectives block the quantitative plural as in пет тома/pet toma 'five volumes' but пет дебели томови/ pet debeli tomovi 'five thick volumes', one can also encounter examples such as два лични дохода/dva lični dohoda 'two incomes'. Virile numerals, used for masculine persons or groups of mixed gender (двајцата родители/dvajcata roditeli 'both parents'), are not used with absolute consistency: два човека/dva čoveka 'two persons' as opposed to двајца луѓе/dvajce luǵe 'two people'.

Collective nouns are not quantified, except by indefinite quantifiers: изминале многу години/izminale mnogu godinje 'many years passed'. The neuter numerical adjective едно/edno '1' can be used to collectivize, quantify or approximate other numerals, except '2', which is rendered approximate by being postposed, an option not open to other numerals: едно осум години/edno osum godini 'about eight years'; година две/ godina dve 'a year or two'; *години осум/*godini osum, *едно две години/*edno dve godini. Approximation can also be rendered by juxta-posing two adjacent numerals: две-три, два-триесет/dve-tri, dva-trieset 'two or three, twenty or thirty'. Partitive quantification is done without any preposition: чаша вода/čaša voda 'a cup of water'. With definite quanti-fied entities, од/od can mean 'some of', 'any of': дај ми од млекото/daj mi od mlekoto 'give me some of the milk'; имате ли од тие мали сливи/imate li od tie mali slivi 'do you have any of those little plums?'

Since quantification does not involve the case complications found in most other Slavonic languages, neither does verb agreement. It is now the norm for collectives to take plural agreement, although singular agreement also occurs. Collective entities that are not morphologically collective take singular agreement: јавноста знае/javnosta znae 'the public knows (SG)'. Expressions such as народот дојдоа/narodot dojdoa 'the people came (PL)' are now considered dialectal but occur colloquially. Quantifiers that take the plural can be used with singulars in an expressive collective meaning: кај се најде толку скакулец?!/kaj se najde tolku skakulec?! 'where did all these grasshoppers come from?!' One problem is when a singular noun quantifies a plural which is followed by a verb: 'a group of journalists came'. The singular quantifier meaning 'group' should determine the number of the verb, but in practice the proximity of the plural quantified entity often causes plural verb agreement as in the following translations: група новинари дојде/grupa novinari dojde (SG), група новинари дојдоа/grupa novinari dojdoa (PL). Some Macedonians faced with this stylistic problem solve it by moving the verb: дојде една група новинари/dojde edna grupa novinari.

5 Lexicon

5.1 General composition of the word-stock

In the absence of an etymological dictionary, it is not practical to attempt an estimate of the proportion of inherited or borrowed items. The standard dictionary (Конески/Koneski 1961–6) contains 64,522 main entries, but the literary language has a much larger vocabulary. Various studies give about 1,000 words each from Greek and Bulgarian, between 4,000 and 5,000 Turkisms and over 100 Germanisms. English and French are also important non-Slavonic, recent sources.

5.2 Patterns of borrowing

Конески/Koneski (1967: 81–3) prescribed the following hierarchy of Slavonic sources for Literary Macedonian: Macedonian dialects; devices such as semantic extension, calquing and neologisms; Church Slavonicisms; Bulgarian and Serbo-Croat; and Russian. Bulgarian and Russian influences were stronger before 1912, Serbo-Croat since 1944. The remaining sources of Macedonian vocabulary can be divided into two groups: the Balkans, that is Turkish, Greek, Albanian and Arumanian (as well as the ancestors of these last two, Thracian and/or Illyrian and Balkan Latin, respectively), and the west, namely Italian, French, German, English and the so-called international lexicon (words of Greco-Latin origin used

Table 6.12   Patterns of borrowing from other Slavonic languages

English	Macedonian	Serbo-Croat	Bulgarian	Russian
(a)				
hero	**xepoj**	xèpōj	герóй	герóй
journal	**списание**	чȁсопӣс	списáние	журнáл
class	**класа**	клȁса	клáса	класс
autonomy	**автономија**	аутонòмија	автонóмия	автонóмия
aristocracy	**аристокра ∣ тија**	-тија/-ција	-ция	-тия
guarantee	**гаран ∣ ција**	-ција/-tija	-ция	-тия
(b)				
hero	**heroj**	hèrōj	gerój	gerój
journal	**spisanie**	čȁsopīs	spisánie	žurnàl
class	**klasa**	klȁsa	klàsa	klass
autonomy	**avtonomija**	autonòmija	avtonómija	avtonómija
aristocracy	**aristokra ∣ tija**	-tija/-cija	-cija	-tija
guarantee	**garan ∣ cija**	-cija/-tija	-cija	-tija

in many languages for modern or western concepts). Many international words entered through the intermediary of other Slavonic languages. The diversity of correspondence can be seen in table 6.12, in which the forms corresponding to Macedonian are in bold type. Literary Macedonian shows a preponderance of the type illustrated by 'hero', whereas some writers in the nineteenth century were even closer to Russian than is Literary Bulgarian.

Arumanian and Albanian loan-words are relatively rare in Literary Macedonian and are more common dialectally, colloquially and in so-called secret languages, that is trade jargons (see Јашар-Настева/Jašar-Nasteva 1970). Greek was the principal language in southern Macedonia at the time of the Slavonic invasions and remained the dominant language of Christian culture and a major contact language on the every-day level throughout the Ottoman period. Most Hellenic ecclesiastical vocabulary and some ordinary words have been retained, but many other Hellenisms are now dialectal or colloquial due to their localness. Unlike Turkish influence, which was spread more or less uniformly all over Macedonia, Greek influence decreases in the north.

Turkish was the most important source of Macedonian vocabulary during the five centuries of Ottoman occupation (1389–1912). Turkish lexical items entered all levels of vocabulary, all the traditional parts of speech and every semantic field, and they have been an issue from the beginning of codification. There was one current of thought maintaining that Turkisms should be encouraged and preserved because they were characteristic of folk speech and also emphasized Macedonian's difference from the other Slavonic languages. The predominant current, however, encouraged Slavonic, Western and 'international' replacements for Turkisms. Some Turkisms remain standard for a concrete meaning while a replacement is used for abstractions: Turkish таван/tavan '(physical) ceiling', but French плафон/plafon '(price) ceiling'. Many Turkisms have been retained for specific stylistic nuances: old-fashioned, folksy, ironic or colloquial. The sociopolitical changes since 1989 have seen a new rise in the use of Turkisms.

Macedonian's first western contact language was Italian, particularly Venetian. French and German words entered in the nineteenth century. German terms are especially evident in vocabulary relating to technology introduced before 1944. In recent decades, the number of English loanwords has increased at all levels. Some are shifted semantically from their English sources: барел/barel 'measure of petroleum'. Anglicisms are often used with irony in the popular press, or are associated with student slang, but many expressions have entered general colloquial use.

5.3 Incorporation of borrowings

Researchers' attention has been directed at sources and types of foreign borrowings rather than at the mechanisms of adaptation. The main issues are stress, inflection of nouns and adjectives, and verbal aspect.

As indicated in section 2.1, many foreign borrowings do not conform to the fixed antepenultimate **stress** pattern. One tendency is in the direction of making more words antepenultimate, the other is to use post-antepenultimate stress even in words where the codified norm requires antepenultimate stress. Конески/Koneski (1967: 156) noted these problems in the early 1950s, but they are still current. Western speakers never allow the stress to move further back than the antepenultimate, and this is the norm.

Borrowed **nouns** tend to be adapted: паркинг – паркинзи/parking – parkinzi 'parking place (SG – PL)'; фри-шоп – фри-шопови/fri-šop – fri-šopovi 'hard currency store (SG – PL)'. Nouns in /-i, -u/ are no longer usually adapted: Turkish *rakı* gives ракија/rakija 'brandy', *gürültü* gives ѓурултија/ǵurultija 'uproar' versus modern такси/taksi 'taxi', интервју/intervju 'interview'; but комбе/kombe 'minibus, van' (from English *comby*, Serbo-Croat *kombi*) represents a modern adaptation to a native desinence (shift of /-i/ to /-e/).

Both older and newer borrowed **adjectives** may be inflected or uninflected. Adapted adjectives may or may not have a derivational suffix added: for example, Turkish *kör* 'blind' gives the inflected adjectives ќор/ќor and ќорав/ќorav, but Turkish *taze* 'fresh' gives only the non-inflecting тазе/taze; recent *normal* gives inflecting нормален/normalen, while супер/super 'terrific' is uninflecting (see section 3.1.4).

Although the **perfective/imperfective opposition** is still sharply distinguished, a relatively large number of common native verbs are bi-aspectual. Borrowed verbs are often bi-aspectual, and prefixation has assumed an increasing role in marking perfectivity. For discussion of the main suffixes used for borrowed verbs – native /-uva/, Greek and Greco-Turkish /-sa/ and /-disa/ and western /-ira/ – see sections 3.2.1 and 3.3.3.

5.4   Lexical fields

5.4.1   Colour terms

white	бел/bel
black	црн/crn
red	црвен/crven
green	зелен/zelen
yellow	жолт/žolt
blue	син/sin (literary), плав/plav (colloquial or dialectal)
brown	кафеава боја/kafeava boja
purple	виолетова боја/violetova boja
pink	каранфил/karanfil, розова боја/rozova boja, румен/rumen, ален/alen, пембе/pembe
orange	портокалова боја/portokalova boja, оранж/oranž (colloquial)
grey	сив/siv

The native basic colour terms are black, white, red, green, yellow, grey and blue. Brown, purple and orange are 'coffee colour', 'violet colour' and 'orange colour', respectively, but are still perceived as basic. Pink is seen as a shade of red. The terms ален/alen (also ал/al, алов/alov) and пембе/pembe are from Turkish, каранфил/karanfil is from Greek and like розова/rozova means 'rose'. The only native term, румен/rumen is synonymous with ален/alen; пембе/pembe is a lighter or brighter shade. For 'blue', the literary син/sin has the broadest reference and should thus be considered basic; модар/modar is used for the darker, more purplish, end of the blue spectrum.

5.4.2   Body parts

head	глава/glava
eye	око/oko, plural очи/oči
nose	нос/nos
ear	уво/uvo, plural уши/uši
mouth	уста/usta
hair	коса/kosa
neck	врат/vrat
hand/arm	рака/raka, plural раце/race
finger	прст/prst
foot/leg	нога/noga, plural нозе/noze

toe   прст на нога/prst na noga
chest   гради/gradi, граден кош/graden koš
heart   срце/srce

5.4.3   Kinship terms

mother	мајка/majka
father	татко/tatko
sister	сестра/sestra
sister (elder)	цеца/ceca
brother	брат/brat
brother (elder)	батко/batko
aunt (parent's sister)	тетка/tetka
aunt (paternal uncle's wife)	стрина/strina
aunt (maternal uncle's wife)	вујна/vujna
uncle (paternal)	стрико/striko, чичко/čičko
uncle (maternal)	вујко/vujko
uncle (aunt's husband)	тетин/tetin
niece, granddaughter	внучка/vnučka
nephew, grandson	внук/vnuk
cousin (female)	братучетка/bratučetka
cousin (male)	братучед/bratučed
grandmother	баба/baba
grandfather	дедо/dedo
wife	жена/žena
husband	маж/maž
daughter	ќерка/ḱerka
son	син/sin

Traditional patriarchal family structure is still very much alive in Macedonia. Extended families are relatively common, especially in rural areas, and affinal kinship terms are maintained.

6   Dialects

A major bundle of isoglosses running roughly from Skopska Crna Gora along the rivers Vardar and Crna divides Macedonian territory into Eastern and Western regions (see Vidoeski in Koneski 1983 and Видоески/Vidoeski 1986). Map 6.1 shows the main dialect regions.

The **vocalic inventories** of the West Central dialects are characterized by a five-vowel system, /a, e, i, o, u/. With the exception of Mala Reka, Reka, Drimkol-Golobrdo, Radožda-Vevčani, Nestram, Korča and parts of Lower Prespa, all the remaining dialects also have phonemic /ə/. Phonemic /ǻ/ or /ɔ/ is found in all of these latter schwa-less dialects except Mala Reka and Korča. Phonemic /ä/ occurs in Radožda-Vevčani, Suho and Visoka and Korča. Vocalic /ḷ/ occurs in Mala Reka. Vocalic /ṛ/

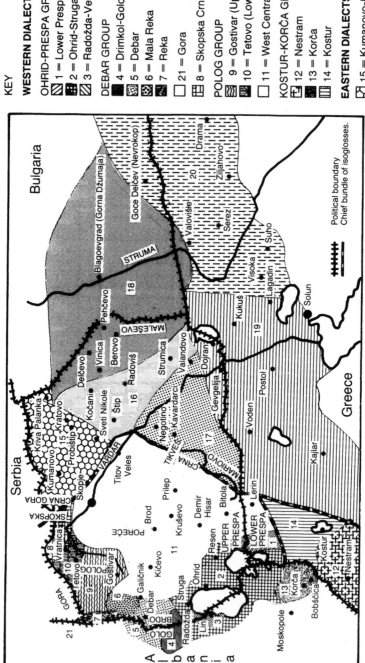

KEY

WESTERN DIALECTS

OHRID-PRESPA GROUP
1 = Lower Prespa
2 = Ohrid-Struga
3 = Radožda-Vevčani

DEBAR GROUP
4 = Drimkol-Golobrdo
5 = Debar
6 = Mala Reka
7 = Reka
21 = Gora
8 = Skopska Crna Gora

POLOG GROUP
9 = Gostivar (Upper Polog)
10 = Tetovo (Lower Polog)
11 = West Central

KOSTUR-KORČA GROUP
12 = Nestram
13 = Korča
14 = Kostur

EASTERN DIALECTS
15 = Kumanovo-Kriva Palanka
16 = Štip-Strumica
17 = Tikveš-Mariovo
18 = Maleševo-Pirin
19 = Lower Vardar
20 = Seres-Nevrokop

++++ Political boundary
━━━ Chief bundle of isoglosses.

Map 6.1   The Republic of Macedonia and adjacent territory

is absent from those dialects that decompose original *r̥, except Radožda-Vevčani. Korča also has phonemic /ü/.

The dialects of the Western region all tend to fixed **stress**, antepenultimate in the Republic of Macedonia, penultimate in Greece and Albania. The Eastern region has various non-fixed stress systems. In Lower Vardar and Seres-Nevrokop unstressed /a, e, o/ are reduced (raised) to /ə, i, u/.

Most dialects have /e/ from original *ě, but the Eastern region is characterized by the development of *ě to /a/ after /c/: Eastern *cal*, Western *cel* 'whole'. In easternmost Aegean and Pirin Macedonia *ě gives /a/ or /ä/ under stress, in the Aegean dialects regardless of the environment, in the Pirin dialects /a/ if there is a back vowel in the following syllable, /e/ if there is a front vowel, as can be seen in 'white' (F – PL): Seres-Drama *b'ala – b'ali*, Suho and Visoka *b'äla – b'äli*, Nevrokop *b'ala – beli*. In Korča, *ě gives /i̯ä/ under stress.

The modern reflexes of the Proto-Slavonic reduced vowels (jers), vocalic sonorants and the back nasal (*ǫ) can be used to separate the dialects into six groups: (1) North (Tetovo, Skopska Crna Gora, Kumanovo-Kriva Palanka), (2) Peripheral (Gostivar, Ohrid-Prespa, Kostur-Korča, Lower Vardar), (3) West Central, (4) East Central (Tikveš-Mariovo, Štip-Strumica, Maleševo-Pirin), (5) Debar and (6) Seres-Nevrokop. Table 6.13 gives illustrative examples.

Table 6.13 Diagnostic reflexes of Proto-Slavonic phonemes

Phoneme	ŭ	ĭ	r̥	l̥	ǫ
North	sən	dən	krv	vuk	put
Central (east)	son	den	krv	vək	pat
Central (west)	son	den	krv	volk	pat
Debar[1]	son	den	korv	volk	pot
Peripheral[2]	son	den	kərv	vəlk	pət
Seres/Nevrokop	sən	den	kərv	vəlk	pət[3]
Gloss	dream	day	blood	wolf	road

Notes: 1 Debar itself has the Peripheral reflexes. Those given in the table represent Reka, Drimkol and Golobrdo, where /o/ stands for /o/, /ɔ/ or /å/. Mala Reka has /krv, vlk, pot/. Gora has /krv, vuk, pət/ but *l̥ generally gives /lə, əl, əv, ov, oy/, depending on village and lexical item.
2 For /ə/ Nestram has /å/, Korča and the northernmost villages of Kostur have /a/. Kostur-Korča has vowel plus nasal sonorant from Proto-Slavonic nasal vowels before some stops: Kostur /zəmb/, Nestram /zåmb/, Korča /zamb/ 'tooth'. Radožda-Vevčani has /påt, kärv, volk/ (but /kälk/ 'thigh'), historically /å/ after bilabials, /ä/ elsewhere; both only under stress. Lower Prespa has /påt, krv, våk/ (but /pålno/ 'full').
3 pənt' in Suho and Visoka (north-east of Salonika).

Table 6.14   Morphological and syntactic features

West	*East*
M DEF /-o/	M DEF /-ot/
Deictic definite articles /-v/, /n-/	No deictic definite articles
Synthetic dative pronouns (/nam/)	Analytic dative pronouns (/na nas/)
3 SG M NOM /toj/ (also Seres-Drama/ Nevrokop)	/on/ (also North-west)
3 SG F ACC /je/ (Tetovo and Gora /ga/)	/ja/ (up to Titov Veles–Prilep–Bitola)
3 SG F DAT /je/	/i/
3 PL ACC /i/	/gi/ (also North-west)
Monosyllabic M PL /-ovi/, /-oj/ (also Tikveš-Mariovo)	Monosyllabic M PL /-ove/
Oblique forms of personal nouns (also North-east)	No oblique noun forms
Quantitative plural not used consistently	Quantitative plural used consistently (also North-west)
3 SG PRES /-t/	3 SG PRES -∅ (also North-west)
/se/ 'they are'	/sa/ (also North-west)
No 3 SG/PL AUX with *l*-form	3 SG/PL AUX with *l*-form
ima series	No *ima* series
Imperfective aorist obsolete	Imperfective aorist used
Perfective present always subordinated	Perfective present occurs independently
Sentence-initial clitics	Clitics never sentence-initial

For **consonantal** features, the entire Western region is distinguished from the East by loss of /x/ (except Tetovo, Gora and Korča) and loss of /v/ in intervocalic position (except Mala Reka and parts of Kostur-Korča): /glava/ 'head' = [glā], /glavi/ = [glaj] 'heads'. The Eastern region preserves /x/ (except Tikveš-Mariovo and Kumanovo-Kriva Palanka) and intervocalic /v/. The East is also characterized by the development of prothetic /v/ before original *ǫ where the West has prothetic /j/: Eastern /vaglen/ 'coal' but Western /jaglen/. As indicated in section 2.2, diphonemic developments of *tj, *kt + *ĭ, *dj ranging from [št/žd] to [šč/ žǯ] or [š′č′/ž′ǯ′] once extended north and west of their current territory. The diphonemic reflexes are most characteristic of the Pirin and Aegean dialects, Kostur-Korča and Ohrid-Prespa. The Seres-Nevrokop dialects have a series of phonemically palatalized consonants.

The dialectal **morphological and syntactic** features of the greatest relevance to the codification of literary Macedonian are given in table 6.14. Occasionally Kumanovo-Kriva Palanka goes with the West, and sometimes Gora, Tetovo and Skopska Crna Gora go with the East. This is indicated in table 6.14 using the terms North-east and North-west for the respective regions. See Elson (1983) for details on verbal morphology.

No reliable population figures are available for the Macedonian dialects of Bulgaria, Greece or Albania nor for those Macedonians living abroad. The Albanian census of 1989 officially registered about 5,000 Macedonians, but sources in Macedonia insist the number is twenty to thirty times greater. The number of Macedonians living in Bulgaria has been estimated at 250,000 (*Nova Makedonija* 16 May 1991). According to the 1981 census there were 1,281,195 declared Macedonians in Yugoslav Macedonia. Based on the census by district (*opština*) the following breakdown gives a general idea of regional population. As a result of massive urban immigration since the Second World War, the population of Skopje is so dialectally mixed that the figures for it cannot be broken down nor do they indicate the actual number of Skopje dialect speakers.

Skopje	321,413
West	478,256
East	481,526

Acknowledgements

I wish to thank the American Council of Learned Societies for a grant for East European Studies, financed in part by the National Endowment for the Humanities and the Ford Foundation. I also wish to thank the Commission for Information of the Republic of Macedonia, the Institute for Macedonian Language, the Macedonian Academy of Arts and Sciences, the Seminar for Macedonian Language of the University of Skopje and the Ministry of Information of the Republic of Macedonia for their generous help. Liljana Minova-Ǵurkova read versions of the manuscript and provided examples, judgments and suggestions at all stages. Blaže Koneski, Božidar Vidoeski, Ilija Čašule, Nina Dimitrova, Tomislav Trenevski, Evica Konečni, Zuzana Topolińska, Ronelle Alexander and Patricia Marsh-Stefanovska read the manuscript and provided many helpful comments, suggestions, judgments and examples. Vera Stoječevska-Antiḱ, Emilija Crvenkovska, Vlado Cvetkovski, Maxim Karanfilovski, Olga Mišeska-Tomiḱ, Kosta Peev, Elena Petroska, Ljudmil Spasov, Zdravko Stamatoski, Goran Stefanovski, Ljupčo Stefanovski and many other friends and colleagues also supplied judgments and examples. I am deeply grateful to all. Responsibility for errors is mine.

References

de Bray, Reginald G.A. (1980) 'Macedonian', *Guide to the South Slavonic Languages* (*Guide to the Slavonic Languages*, 3rd edn, revised and expanded, Part 1), Columbus, Ohio: Slavica, 137–308.
Čašule, Ilija (1988) 'The development of the Macedonian verbal noun in the context of the loss of the infinitive', *International Journal of Slavic Linguistics and Poetics* 37: 61–71.

Elson, Mark J. (1983) 'On the evolution of the present tense in Macedonian dialects', *Die Welt der Slaven* 28, 1: 131–40.

—— (1989) *Macedonian Verbal Morphology: a Structural Analysis*, Columbus, Ohio: Slavica.

Englund, Birgitta (1977) *Yes/no-questions in Bulgarian and Macedonian*, Stockholm: Almqvist & Wiksell.

Franks, Steven L. (1987) 'Regular and irregular stress in Macedonian', *International Journal of Slavic Linguistics and Poetics* 35/6: 93–142.

Friedman, Victor A. (1977) *The Grammatical Categories of the Macedonian Indicative*, Columbus, Ohio: Slavica.

—— (1985) 'The sociolinguistics of Literary Macedonian', *International Journal of the Sociology of Language* 52: 31–57.

Hill, Peter (1982) 'Different codifications of a language', in Wolfgang Girke (ed.) *Slavistische Linguistik 1981, Referate des VII Konstanzer Slavistischen Arbeitstreffens* (Slavistische Beiträge 160), Munich: Sagner, 48–63.

Joseph, Brian (1983) *The Synchrony and Diachrony of the Balkan Infinitive*, Cambridge: Cambridge University Press.

Koneski, Blaže (1983) *Macedonian Historical Phonology*, with a survey of Macedonian dialects and a map by Božidar Vidoeski, translated by Victor A. Friedman (Historical Phonology of the Slavic Languages, 12; series editor George Shevelov), Heidelberg: Carl Winter.

Kramer, Christina (1986) *Analytic Modality in Macedonian*, Munich: Sagner.

Lunt, Horace (1952) *A Grammar of the Macedonian Literary Language*, Skopje: Državno knigoizdatelstvo.

—— (1986) 'On Macedonian language and nationalism', *Slavic Review* 45, 4: 729–34.

Minissi, Nullo, Kitanovski, N. and Cingue, U. (1982) *The Phonetics of Macedonian*, Naples: Bibliopolis.

Naylor, Kenneth E. (1989) 'On the form of the Macedonian article', *Makedonski jazik* 40.

Topolińska, Zuzana (1981) *Remarks on the Slavic Noun Phrase*, Wrocław: Ossolineum.

Vaillant, André (1938) 'Le Problème du slave macédonien', *Bulletin de la Société Linguistique de Paris* 39: 194–210.

Видоески, Божидар (1986) 'Горанскиот говор', *Прилози, Македонска Академија на Науките и Уметностите, Одделение за лингвистика и литературна наука*, 11, 2: 45–76.

Јашар-Настева, Оливера (1970) 'За македонските тајни јазици', *Годишен зборник на филозофскиот факултет на Универзитетот во Скопје*, 22: 553–69.

Конески, Блаже (ed.) (1961–6) *Речник на македонскиот литературен јазик I; II; III*, Скопје: Институт за Македонски Јазик. (Photoreprinted as a single volume in 1986.)

—— (1967) *Граматика на македонскиот литературен јазик, I дел; II дел*, Скопје: Култура. (Combines Part 1 (revised) 1957 and Part 2 1954.)

Корубин, Благоја (1969) *Јазикот наш денешен*, Скопје: Наша книга.

Миличиќ, Владимир (1967) *Обратен речник на македонскиот јазик*, Скопје: Институт за Македонски Јазик.

Минова-Ѓуркова, Лилјана (1966) 'Некои карактеристики на глаголите на -(из)ира во македонскиот литературен јазик', *Македонски јазик* 17: 117–26.

—— (1987) 'Нормата и девијантните појави', *Лик* 2, 6: 3.

Теунисен, Маргарита (1986) 'Македонските двовидски глаголи од словенско потекло', *Македонски јазик* 36/7: 335–40.

Тошев, Крум (ed.) (1970) *Правопис на македонскиот литературен јазик,* Скопје: Институт за Македонски Јазик.

Угринова-Скаловска, Радмила (1960) *Значењата на глаголските префикси во македонскиот јазик,* Скопје: Институт за Македонски Јазик.

Усикова, Рина (1985) *Македонский Язык,* Скопје: Македонска книга.

7 Serbo-Croat

Wayles Browne

1 Introduction

Serbo-Croat(ian) is one of the languages of Yugoslavia. (Even this statement is disputed; see the end of this section.) It is used in four of the
country's six republics: Croatia, Serbia, Montenegro (Cŕnā Gòra/Цŕнā
Гòра) and Bosnia-Hercegovina, and by four of its 'nations' (národi/
нáроди): the Croat(ian)s (approximately 4.5 million), Serbs (8 million),
Montenegrins (600 thousand) and Yugoslav Muslims (2 million).
(Republics and nations coincide only in part. Serbia, predominantly
inhabited by Serbs, incorporates a multilingual northern province
Vojvodina with many Croats, Hungarians, Slovaks, Rumanians and
Rusyns, and a southern province Kosovo having an Albanian majority.
Croatia is about four-fifths Croats, but much of the remaining fifth
comprises Serbs. Montenegro is nearly all Montenegrins. Bosnia-
Hercegovina, home of the Serbo-Croat-speaking Muslims, is a mixture of
all four nations. Slovenes and Macedonians have their own republics and
languages.) Citizens (1.2 million in 1981) who assign themselves to no
national group ('Yugoslav' or 'Undecided' on censuses) mostly also speak
Serbo-Croat. Yugoslavia has no single official language, but Serbo-Croat
often functions for inter-ethnic communication.

Yugoslavia was never a political unit until the break-up of Austria–
Hungary following the First World War. The two largest nations went
through language standardization separately.

Serbia, after Ottoman Turk invaders defeated its culturally advanced
medieval state (the most famous of many battles was at Kosovo Polje,
1389), experienced a period of stagnation. Only the Orthodox Church kept
literacy and learning alive. The Church's language and Cyrillic-alphabet
orthography (first the Serbian recension of Church Slavonic, later the
Russian recension) heavily influenced what secular writing was done in
Turkish-ruled Serbia and in Vojvodina, which was under Austria–Hungary
from about 1700. The resulting 'Slaveno-Serbian', used for literary
purposes from the late 1700s, was less of an amorphous mixture than its
critics claimed; nevertheless, it varied from writer to writer and was easily

intelligible only to those schooled in the Church language.

Meanwhile the Croats, linked administratively and by their Catholic religion with European countries to the north and west, cultivated literature in neighbouring languages and in their own. Writers on the Adriatic coast employed Latin and Italian, as well as the local language of Dubrovnik (Štokavian dialect; section 6) and Split (Čakavian dialect); those in northern Croatia used German, Hungarian, Latin and their own local (Kajkavian) varieties. Orthography was mainly Latin, rendering non-Latin sounds by Hungarian or Italian-like graphic conventions. Since Croatia manifests the greatest dialect differentiation of all the Serbo-Croat territory, considerable differences existed between writing done in Zagreb or Varaždin in the north and works emanating from the coast. However, books and manuscripts circulated: thus Belostenec's dictionary (compiled 1670, published 1740) notes words from diverse locations.

Croats also had a Church Slavonic tradition. Coastal and island regions, often rather against the hierarchy's wishes, held Catholic services with Glagolitic-alphabet Slavonic texts, a practice lasting into this century on the island of Krk. Glagolitic (see chapter 2) served secular writings too; special Croatian square inscriptional characters and cursive script developed.

In the early 1800s Vuk Karadžić, a largely self-taught writer and folklorist, encouraged by Slavist and enlightened Austrian official Bartholomäus (Jernej) Kopitar, proposed a reformed Serbian literary language based on Štokavian folk usage without Church Slavonic phonological and morphological features. He advocated (i)jekavian Štokavian with neo-Štokavian shifted accentuation and newer declensions (merging plural dative, instrumental and locative cases); see sections 2 and 6. His 1818 dictionary showed how to write his new Serbian in a modified Cyrillic remedying the over- and under-differentiating Church orthography. Offensive to some were his dropping the *jer* letters (ь, ъ) and his consonant letter *j*; the last was even called a Latin threat to Orthodoxy. After fifty years of polemics conducted by Karadžić and his disciple Đuro Daničić, the newly independent kingdom of Serbia adopted his language and alphabet, though his (i)jekavian reflex of *jat'* (section 2.1) yielded to ekavian, typical of Eastern Serbo-Croat.

In Zagreb, the cultural centre of Croatia since the late 1700s, the Illyrian Movement sought unity of all South Slavs in the 1820s–1830s, and hence shifted in writing and publishing from local Kajkavian to the more widespread Štokavian. The writer–editor Ljudevit Gaj introduced Latin letters with diacritical marks (č, š, ž, from Czech, ć from Polish) and digraphs (*lj, nj, dž,* originally also *gj* or *dj* for *đ*). Discussion continued throughout the century about which sort of Štokavian to adopt. Several literary figures made a 'Literary Agreement' with Serbian counterparts in 1850 to standardize on Vuk's (i)jekavian Štokavian, but only when Tomo Maretić based a grammar (1899) on a corpus of Vuk's and Daničić's writings did this become established in Croat practice, eliminating ikavian *jat'* reflexes and the older differentiated dative, locative and instrumental plural endings. Puristic tendencies led to maintenance or reintroduction of many words from older literature, and to newly coined domestic terms (section 5.2). These terminological differences, some grammatical preferences and virtually exclusive use of Latin orthography lend Croatia's (i)jekavian standard a somewhat different aspect from that of Serbia (ekavian, Cyrillic and Latin alphabets), Montenegro (ijekavian, mostly Cyrillic) and Bosnia–Hercegovina (ijekavian, more Latin than Cyrillic). The name 'Croatian literary language' is favoured for it within Croatia (as in the 1974 Constitution of the Republic of Croatia), and it is often termed a separate language, although this position is equally often rejected in the press and political circles.

[The above was written in 1991. Since then the destructiveness of the war has led to international recognition of Croatia and Bosnia–Hercegovina as independent within their pre-existing boundaries. Serbia and Montenegro have formed a new non-socialist Yugoslavia against which the United Nations has imposed sanctions. Any observer must regret the war damages to civilian and military persons, economic potentials and cultural heritages. The linguist can expect broken contacts to lead to divergence in the language's standards. Mass expulsions and evacuations of refugees will make the dialect landscape much less differentiated and coherent than that shown in map 7.1 (page 383).]

2   Phonology

2.1   Segmental phoneme inventory
The five vowels *i, e, a, o, u* may occur in any position in a word: initial, medial, final. Each can be long or short (see Prosodic phenomena below). In addition, *r* can act as a vowel (long or short): cȑn/ц̣рн 'black', vȓt/вр̣т 'garden'. 'Vocalic' ('syllabic') *r* (phonetically [r̩]) is not specially marked in normal writing. The pronunciation [r̩] is almost predictable, the rule being *r* → r̩ when not next to a vowel (and in a few other exceptional environments).

Reflexes of *ě*, often called *jat'* (chapter 3, section 2.27) vary geographically, a fact on which one well-known dialect classification is based. Most Eastern Štokavian dialects are ekavian, having *e* from *jat'*: *rěka › *réka* 'river', *věra › *vèra* 'faith' (dialect forms are in Latin transcription throughout) except that *i* usually appears before *j*: *nov-ěj-ьjь › *nòvijī* 'newer'; this holds for the ekavian standard. Some north-central and coastal dialects, termed ikavian, have consistent *i* for *jat'*: *rika, vìra, nòvijī*. An area in western Serbia has a distinct reflex, closed *ę* (between *i* and *e*) (Реметић/ Remetić 1981), as do some settlers in non-Serbo-Croat surroundings.

Other central and southern-coastal Štokavian dialects have a reflex customarily described as *ije* in long syllables, *je* in short: *rijeka* (long), *vjera* (short); the terms ijekavian and jekavian are both used for such dialects. (They typically have *ĕ* › *i* both before *j*: *nòvijī* and before *o* which is an alternant of *l*: *dĕlъ › *dȉo* 'part', but *dijel-* in the rest of the paradigm.) It is this understanding of the (i)jekavian reflex which has led to the traditional spelling and accentuation marking of the standard Serbo-Croat of Croatia, Montenegro and Bosnia-Hercegovina: vjèra/вjȅра in a short syllable, rijèka/риjȅка in a long. It has, however, been demonstrated (Brozović 1973) that the standard language's long-syllable *jat'* reflex does not really consist of two syllables each with a short vowel. Contrasting alleged Nijèmac/Ниjȅмац ‹ *nĕmьсь 'German' with the sequence of short syllables seen in nijèdan/ниjȅдан ‹ *ni jedьnъ 'not one' shows that *ije* in 'German' is optionally one or two syllables but in either case begins with a brief *i* followed by long *e* [ĭē]; thus we here adopt Brozović's rijéka/риjéка, Nijémac/Ниjéмац. Similarly in examples with falling accent: traditional nȉjem/нȉjем, Brozović and here nijêm/ниjêм [nĭēm] 'mute'.

A further (i)jekavian complication is that the short-syllable reflex is *e*, not *je*, after consonant + *r* when all three sounds are in the same morpheme: *xrĕnъ › hrèn/хрȅн 'horseradish'. Compare **rĕš-* › rješávati/ pješáвати 'to solve' with no preceding consonant, and raz+rješávati/ раз+pješáвати 'to release' with intervening morpheme boundary.

The Čakavian dialects are ekavian, ikavian and ikavian/ekavian (having *e* before Proto-Slavonic dental consonant + back vowel, *i* otherwise). Thus from *mĕra 'a measure', *mĕriti 'to measure', *lĕpo 'beautifully', *dvĕ 'two' the first type has *mȅra mȅrit lȇpo dvȇ*, the second *mȉra mȉrit lȉpo dvȉ* and the last *mȅra mȉrit lȉpo dvȉ*. Kajkavian dialects show varied vowel systems, usually with *ĕ* › [ẹ] or [e].

Of other Proto-Slavonic vowels missing in present-day Serbo-Croat, the front and back nasals (chapter 3, section 2.27) have merged with *e* and *u* respectively: *pętь › pêt/пȇт 'five', *rǫka › rúka/рýка 'hand, arm'.

Both jers have developed to *a* in strong position (see chapter 3, section 2.25): *pьsъ › pàs/пȁс 'dog', *sъnъ › sàn/сȁн 'sleep, dream'. In most instances *jers* drop in weak position, yielding *a* ~ Ø alternations: genitives *pьsa › psà/псȁ, *sъna › snà/снȁ. Even when weak they develop into *a* if any of certain obstruent–sonorant clusters would arise: *mьgla › màgla/ мȁгла 'fog'.

Syllabic liquids arose in older Serbo-Croat from merger of liquid–jer and jer–liquid groups in interconsonantal position (without distinction of strong and weak *jers*): *ьr, ъr, rь, rъ* all become *r̩*; *ьl, ъl, lь, lъ* all become *l̩*. Thus *pьrv-ъjь › **pr̩v-*, *tъrg-ъ › **tr̩g*, *grъm-ĕti › **gr̩m-*, *krъvь › **kr̩v*, *vъlk-ъ › **vl̩k*, *sъlnьce › **sl̩nce*, *slьza › **sl̩za*, *glъt-ati › **gl̩tati*. Modern Serbo-Croat preserves *r̩*, and the standard language (like most dialects) has *u* from *l̩*: pȓvī/пȓвӣ 'first', tȓg/тȓг 'town square', gȑm(j)eti/

гр̏м(j)ети 'to thunder', кр̏в/кр̑в 'blood', ву̑к/ву̑к 'wolf', су̏нце/су̑нце 'sun', су̏за/су̑за 'a tear', гу̏тати/гу̏тати 'to swallow'.

Serbo-Croat shows normal South Slavonic reflexes of other Proto-Slavonic interconsonantal vowel–liquid groups, namely metathesis with vowel lengthening: *er* › *rě*, *or* › *ra*, *el* › *lě*, *ol* › *la*. The *ě* develops according to the rules for individual dialects. Examples: *u-mer-ti › ijekavian у̏мријети/у̀мријети, ekavian у̏мрети/у̀мр̄ети 'to die'; *gordъ › гра̏д/гра̏д 'town'; *melko › ijekavian mlijéko/млијéко, ekavian mléko/млéко 'milk'; *molt-iti › mlátiti/млáтити 'to thresh, beat'.

The consonants of Serbo-Croat are shown in table 7.1.

The symbols used here are those of the Latin-alphabet orthography. They largely correspond to the transcription used among Slavists; note specially *h* [x ~ h], *c* [t‿s], *đ* [d‿ʑ], *ć* [t‿ɕ], *dž* [d‿ž], *nj* [ɲ = ñ], *lj* [ʎ].

The Latin alphabetical order is a b c č ć d dž đ e f g h i j k l lj m n nj o p r s š t u v z ž. Each letter with a differentiator follows its counterpart without; the digraphs *dž lj nj* behave as units (filling one square of a crossword puzzle, for example) and follow *d l n* respectively. The corresponding Cyrillic letters are а б ц ч ћ д џ ђ е ф г х и ј к л љ м н њ о п р с ш т у в з ж. Cyrillic alphabetical order differs somewhat: а б в г д ђ е ж з и ј к л љ м н њ о п р с т ћ у ф х ц ч џ ш.

The only exceptions to one-to-one correspondence between Latin and Cyrillic writing are instances where Latin *dž* and *nj* notate a sequence rather than a single sound. This occurs when *d* is the final consonant of a prefix and *ž* is part of a root, as *nad+žív(j)eti* 'to outlive', and when *n* is

Table 7.1 Serbo-Croat consonants

	Bilabial	Labio-dental	Dental	Alveo-palatal	Palatal	Velar
Obstruents						
Stops						
Voiceless	p		t			k
Voiced	b		d			g
Fricatives						
Voiceless		f	s	š		h
Voiced		v	z	ž		
Affricates						
Voiceless			c	č	ć	
Voiced				dž	đ	
Sonorants						
Nasals	m		n		nj	
Liquids						
Laterals			l		lj	
Vibrant			r			
Glide					j	

part of an abbreviation or foreign prefix coming before a root with *j*: *kon+jugácija* 'conjugation'. Cyrillic spellings are then наджи́в(j)ети, конјугáција.

V and *f* are bilabial fricatives, hence obstruents, although *v* is less strident than *f*. However, *v* behaves as a sonorant in never undergoing or causing devoicing. Thus there is no assimilation in óvca/óвца 'sheep' and tvôj/твôj 'your'.

Prosodic phenomena: accent and vowel length. Some words are proclitic or enclitic, thus having no accented syllable of their own (proclitics: certain conjunctions, most prepositions; enclitics: certain pronoun and verb forms, certain particles; see section 4.1). Apart from these, every word form has one accented syllable (some compound words have one on each element). We say accent, not stress, because pitch and length are involved rather than intensity. Accent can alternate in placement or contour within the paradigm of a word. Accented syllables are termed either rising or falling, and contain a long or a short vowel. Traditional notation in grammars and dictionaries combines these two features, using four accent marks: short falling *ä*, long falling *â*, short rising *à*, long rising *á*. The falling accents occur almost exclusively on first syllables of words, and can occur on monosyllables: gòvōr/гôвōр 'speech', lòš/лôш 'bad'; prâvdati/прâвдати 'to justify', grâd/грâд 'city'. The rising accents occur on any syllable but the last, hence not on monosyllables: dòlaziti/дòлазити 'to come', govòriti/говòрити 'to speak', veličìna/величѝна 'size'; glúmiti/глу́мити 'to act', garáža/гарáжа 'garage', gravitírati/гравити́рати 'to gravitate'.

Long and short vowels are distinguished under accent or in later syllables in the word. Thus grâd/грâд 'city', grȁd/грȁд 'hail'; váljati/вáљати 'to roll', vàljati/вàљати 'to be good'. Post-accentual length is notated *ā*: gòdīnā/гòдīнā 'years (GEN PL)'; prâvdā/прâвдā 'he/she justifies', prâvda/прâвда 'justice'; veličìnē/величѝнē 'size (GEN SG)', veličìne/величѝне 'sizes (NOM/ACC PL)'. Many post-accentual lengths are associated with specific suffixes or grammatical forms (as genitive plural of nouns). One can construct examples with multiple lengths like rázbōjnīštāvā/рázбōjнīштāвā, genitive plural of rázbōjnīštvo/рázбōjнī-штво 'banditry', but few people will pronounce all five vowels long; practically every region shortens post-accentual lengths in some positions (P. Ivić 1958 finds a clear hierarchy of dialectal shortenings).

The names of the accents suggest a pitch change on a given syllable. Pitch does ascend within long rising accented vowels, and drops during long fallings. However, short accented vowels have no such obvious pitch rise or fall. Measurements (Lehiste and Ivić 1986) suggest that the only consistent difference between short accents is the relationship with the following syllable: the syllable after a short rising begins equal to or higher in pitch than the accented syllable itself, then declines, whereas the syllable after a short falling begins distinctly lower. The same relationship (equal to or higher versus lower) holds in the syllables following long rising and long falling, and is hence the factor common to all accentual distinctions, though regional variations in accent contour have led to disagreements among scholars.

An analysis attributing phonemic value to the pitch of the post-accentual syllable, rather than to the 'rising' accented syllable itself, was first proposed by Masing and elaborated by Browne and McCawley (1965). It rationalizes the distributional limitations: 'rising' cannot occur on final syllables because the next syllable must be there to bear the distinctive high pitch. This pitch can thus be on any of the syllables; if it is on the second, speakers perceive a rising on the first syllable, if on the third, they hear rising on the second, and so forth. Distinctive high pitch on the initial syllable yields falling accent. Why do Serbo-Croat speakers perceive the accent in the place where they do? This syllable undergoes lengthening by a factor of 1.5 (a long vowel, whose length is about 1.5 that of a short vowel, becomes $1.5 \times 1.5 = 2.25$ times the length of an unaccented short vowel), and the extra length gives it auditory prominence (Lehiste and Ivić 1986). The accented syllable is the one which bears ictus in verse and carries most sentence intonations.

Falling accents can 'jump' onto proclitics (prepositions, the negation *ne* before verbs, sometimes coordinating conjunctions). This is what we expect if the proclitic forms one phonological word with its host word: a falling accent on the initial syllable of brȁt/брȁт 'brother' would find itself on a non-initial syllable in the group od brȁta/од брȁта 'from the brother', violating the distribution rule for falling accents. In many dialects and the more traditional norm for the standard language, the accentuation rules can apply to the entire group, resulting in accent on the proclitic: ȍd brata/ ȍд брата.

Another type of 'jumping' is seen in dialects and in conservative standard Serbo-Croat with such a host word as grȃd/грȃд 'city': u grȃd/у грȃд 'to the city' can yield ȕ grād/ȳ грȃд. The difference between *brȁt-* and *grād-* is that the second has no inherent high pitch; a rule, surviving from Proto-Slavonic, provides an accent to the first syllable of any word (or group) which, at that point in the phonological derivation, has no high pitch marked on any of its syllables.

2.2 Morphophonemic alternations inherited from Proto-Slavonic

The first palatalization of velars, which in Proto-Slavonic changed *k, g, x* to *č, ǯ* (later *ž*) and *š* respectively when a front vowel followed, survives in Serbo-Croat as a family of *k, g, h → č, ž, š* alternations in inflection (before *e*) and word formation (before *j, i, e,* movable *a* and other segments). The conditioning is partly morphological (and lexical), because not every instance of these segments triggers the change. In masculine nouns the

vocative singular ending -e/-e causes it: ǔčenīk/у̀ченйк 'pupil' →
ǔčenīče/у̀ченйче, Bôg/Бôг 'God' → Bôže/Бôже, siròmah/сирòмах
'poor man' → siròmaše/сирòмаше. The accusative plural ending -e/-e
does not: ǔčenīke/у̀ченйке, siròmahe/сирòмахе, bùbrege/бу̀бреге
(from bùbreg/бу̀брег 'kidney'). The -e-/-e- in verb present tenses
invariably causes it: pèći/пèћи 'to bake', stem pèk-/пèк-, present pèčēm/
пèчēм, but third person plural pèkū/пèкӯ, where there is no -e-/-e-.

Diminutive endings such as -ica/-ица commonly trigger the alternation
in question, thus rúka/ру́ка 'hand, arm' → diminutive rùčica/ру̀чица
'small hand/arm'. But in certain instances a differentiation arises: rùčica/
ру̀чица meaning 'handle' invariably has č, but emotional speech, as of or
to a baby, may have unchanged k in diminutive rùkica/ру̀кица 'hand/
arm'. In some instances the alternation has spread to suffixes having no j or
front vowel: nòga/нòга 'leg, foot' has augmentative nòž-ūrda/нòж-ӯрда
'big ugly foot', compare gláva/гла́ва 'head' → glàv-ūrda/гла̀в-ӯрда without j.

Alternation without overt triggering segment characterizes the formation
of adjectives with -skī/-скӣ and its morphophonemic alternants:
Amèrika/Амèрика, amèričkī/амèричкӣ 'American'. In Proto-Slavonic
this suffix began with a front vowel, -ьsk-; but Serbo-Croat has no vowel
here.

The third palatalization of velars (see below) produced c and z from
earlier Proto-Slavonic k, g. In Serbo-Croat, almost all c, and those
instances of z which arose from the third palatalization, alternate with č and
ž respectively. The conditions can be described as 'same as for k, plus
others': inherited stric/стриц 'father's brother' and borrowed prînc/
прȋнц 'prince' have vocative singular striče/стри́че and prînče/прȋнче,
but they also show alternation before ov/ов and ev/ев of the 'long plural'
(section 3.1.2): plural stríčevi/стри́чеви, prînčevi/прȋнчеви, unlike
nouns in k: vûk/вȳк 'wolf', plural vùkovi/ву̀кови. Similarly knêz/кнêз
'prince', vocative knêže/кнêже, plural knêževi/кнêжеви, since this word
had Proto-Slavonic g (*kъnęzь ‹ *kŭnĭngas); but vôz/вôз 'train, cart',
which never underwent the third palatalization, has vocative vôze/вôзе
and plural vózovi/во́зови.

The second palatalization of velars produced c, z (via ʒ) and s from
Proto-Slavonic k, g and x respectively (chapter 3, section 2.19). Serbo-
Croat has three alternations, all of the form k, g, h → c, z, s before i, but
with different conditioning.

First, in verbs with stem-final k, g and one rare verb with h: rèći/pèћи
'to say', stem rek-/рек-, imperative singular rèci/рèци; pòmoći/пòмоћи
'to help', stem pomòg-/помòг-, imperative pomòzi/помòзи; vŕći/вŕћи
'to thresh', stem vŕh-/вŕх-, imperative vŕsi/вŕси. Here it is stable but not
productive, since no new stems can be added.

Further, in two places in noun morphology. Before -i/-и in masculine nominative plurals, the alternation is almost exceptionless: ùčenīci/ у̀ченйци; agnòstik/агно̀стик 'agnostic', agnòstici/агно̀стици; bùbrezi/ бу̀брези; siròmasi/сиро̀маси; ȁlmanah/а̏лманах 'almanac', ȁlmanasi/ а̏лманаси. A few recent words escape it, like kȍk/ко̏к 'coccus bacterium', kȍki/ко̏ки. It is equally regular before the -ima/-има dative– locative–instrumental plural ending: ùčenīcima/у̀ченйцима, agnòsticima/ агно̀стицима, bùbrezima/бу̀брезима.

In the dative–locative singular of the -a declension, the change is common: rúka/ру́ка, rúci/ру́ци (or rūci/рӯци); nòga/но̀га 'foot, leg', nòzi/но̀зи; svȑha/свр̏ха 'purpose', svȑsi/свр̏си; but it is restricted by phonological, morphological and lexical factors, whose hierarchy is only partially investigated. Some stem-final consonant clusters disfavour it: mȁčka/ма̏чка 'cat', mȁčki/ма̏чки, compare d(j)èvōjka/д(j)èво̄jка 'girl', d(j)èvōjci/д(j)èво̄jци. Personal names and hypocoristics avoid it: Mîlka/ Мйлка, Milki/Мйлки; báka/ба́ка 'Granny', báki/ба́ки. This avoidance is stronger than the tendency for words in -ika/-ика to undergo the change: lògika/ло̀гика 'logic', lògici/ло̀гици; Àfrika/Àфрика, Àfrici/ Àфрици; but číka/чи́ка 'Uncle (addressing an older man)', číki/чи́ки. Of the three consonants, k most readily alternates, then g, with h least susceptible.

The third palatalization of velars (c, z, s from earlier Proto-Slavonic k, g, x) survives as a rare alternation in word formation: knêz/кнêз 'prince' but knèginja/кнèгиња 'princess'. Only in the formation of imperfective verbs from perfectives can a pattern (dating to early South Slavonic) be discerned, as ìzreći/ѝзрећи 'to utter', stem ìz-rek-/ѝз-рек-, imperfective izrícati/изри́цати; pòdići/по̀дићи 'to pick up', stem pò-dig-/по̀-диг-, imperfective pòdizati/по̀дизати; udàhnuti/уда̀хнути 'to inhale', stem u-dàh-nu-/у-да̀х-ну-, imperfective ùdisati/у̀дисати.

Proto-Slavonic had a series of alternations in consonant + j groups, termed 'jotations' or 'yodizations' (chapter 3, section 2.10). They appeared *inter alia* in past passive participles of verb stems in -i and in comparatives of some adjectives: *nosi-ti 'to carry', participle *nošenъ 'carried'; *vysokъ 'high', *vyš- 'higher'. Common to all Slavonic languages are the results š, ž from jotation of s, z and the results č, ž, š (= first palatalization of velars) from jotation of k, g, x. The Serbo-Croat 'old jotation' resulting from the Proto-Slavonic jotation is: (1) labials add lj, thus p-plj, b-blj, m-mlj, v-vlj; the newer sound f also becomes flj; (2) s, z alternate with š, ž; (3) t, d alternate with ć, đ; (4) k, g, h alternate with č, ž, š; as in the first palatalization's reflex, c has also come to alternate with č; (5) l, n alternate with lj, nj; (6) r and other consonants (palatals of various sorts, also the group št) are unaffected. Points 2 and 4 are identical throughout Slavonic; the palatals of 5 are presumed to have existed in all but have been eliminated in most. 1 is absent in two areas: West Slavonic and Modern Bulgarian and Macedonian. 3 presents diverse reflexes; Štokavian Serbo-

Croat developments of *tj* (from older *tj* and from *kt* before front vowel) and *dj* are **nokt-i-*, **medja* > nôć/ноћ 'night', mèđa/мèђa 'boundary'. Examples of alternations (passive participles of verbs, masculine singular indefinite): ljúbiti/љу́бити 'to kiss, to love', ljûbljen/љу̑бљен; zašaráfiti/зашара́фити 'to tighten (a screw)', zašàrāfljen/зашàра̄фљен; nòsiti/нòсити 'to carry', nȍšen/нȍшен; vrátiti/вра́тити 'to return', vrâćen/вра̑ћен; báciti/ба́цити 'to throw', bâčen/ба̑чен (there are no verbs in -kiti/-кити, -giti/-гити, -hiti/-хити, except for the baby-talk kákiti/ка́кити 'defecate'); hváliti/хва́лити 'to praise', hvâljen/хва̑љен; izgovòriti/изговòрити 'to pronounce', izgòvoren/изгòворен; túžiti/ту́жити 'to accuse', tûžen/ту̑жен; pòništiti/пòништити 'to cancel', pòništen/пòништен. The inherited jotation yields *št* and *žd* from *st* and *zd*, but these results now compete with *šć*, *žđ* (which come from changing the two consonants separately): iskòristiti/искòристити 'to use', iskòrišten/искòриштен and iskòrišćen/искòришћен. *Šć* is the only possibility in adjective comparison: gûst/гу̑ст 'thick', comparative gȕšćī/гу̏шћӣ.

The groups *sk*, *zg* before front vowel or *j* (first or second palatalization of velars) and *stj*, *zdj* merge, presumably through a stage *šć*, *žđ*, to yield *št*, *žd* in standard Serbo-Croat (compare the later version of the *j* alternation, section 2.3).

Vowel alternations. Proto-Slavonic fronted certain vowels following a palatal consonant (see chapter 3, section 2.25). The fronting led to the existence of parallel sets of nominal endings in morphology. Serbo-Croat eliminated such parallelism in endings in favour of the **fronted** set (as did Slovene); only the *o–e* change survives as an alternation. Thus neuter *o*-declension nouns (section 3.1.2) have -o/-о in m(j)ȅsto/м(j)ȅсто 'place', -e/-е in sȑce/сȑце 'heart' and ùčēnje/у̀чēње 'teaching, learning'.

The Serbo-Croat rule is now: *o* → *e* after palatal consonants and their descendants (*č, dž, š, ž, ć, đ, j, lj, nj, c, št, žd*, sometimes *r* and *z*). It acts in nominal declensions and in word formation. A morphological limitation is that it scarcely applies in feminine declensions (only in the vocative singular of most nouns suffixed with -ica/-ица, as profesòrica/професòрица, vocative profesòrice/професòрице). Feminine adjectives and feminine pronouns are unaffected. The alternation in -om/-ом endings of the masculine and neuter is widespread, but factors hindering it (section 3.1.2) include vowel dissimilation and foreignness of the noun. The *o–e* alternation has spread to a new Serbo-Croat morpheme, the ov/ов and ev/ев of masculine noun 'long plurals' (section 3.1.2); thus grȁd*ov*i/грȁд*ов*и 'cities' but mȕž*ev*i/му̏ж*ев*и 'husbands'.

The main vowel-zero alternation in present-day Serbo-Croat is *a* ~ Ø. As mentioned in 2.1, the Proto-Slavonic *jer* vowels ь, ъ developed into *a* or dropped out, depending on position in the word. This leads to *a* appearing in word forms with zero ending, but not in related forms with a vowel ending. Examples are nominative singular masculine of nouns and indefinite adjectives, masculine singular *l*-participles of verbs; respectively, tȓgovac/тȓговац 'merchant' and genitive tȓgōvca/тȓгōвца; túžan/тýжан 'sad' and feminine túžna/тýжна; ìšao/ѝшао 'went' (from ìći/ѝћи) and feminine singular ìšla/ѝшла. The *a* also appears before certain suffixes, as tȓgovac/тȓговац + skī/скӣ → tȓgovačkī/тȓговачкӣ 'commercial'.

The alternation has been extended to various stem-final consonant clusters (generally containing at least one sonorant) where it had no historical basis. This is termed 'inserted *a*' or 'secondary jer'. Compare Pȅtar/ Пȅтар 'Peter', genitive Pȅtra/Пȅтра (*Petrъ); dȍbar/дȍбар 'good', feminine dȍbra/дȍбра (*dobrъ); the masculine *l*-participle of verbs whose stem ends in an obstruent, as rȅkao/рȅкао 'said' (from rȅkal ‹ *reklъ). Inserted *a* in nominative singulars is frequent in loan-words: kȉlometar/кȉлометар, genitive kȉlometra/кȉлометра; sùbjekat/ сỳбјекат or sùbjekt/сỳбјект, genitive sùbjekta/сỳбјекта.

The Serbo-Croat -ā/-ā genitive plural ending also triggers insertion of *a*, 'breaking' a preceding cluster: tȓgovácā/тȓговáцā, kȉlometārā/ кȉлометāрā, sùbjekātā/сỳбјекāтā, jȕtārā/јȳтāрā from jȕtro/јȳтро 'morning', sestárā/сестáрā from sèstra/сèстра 'sister'. (Only a few clusters such as *st, zd, št, žd, šć, žđ*, consonant–*j* are 'unbreakable'; cȅsta/ цȅста 'road', genitive plural cêstā/цêстā, ráskršće/páскршће 'crossroads', genitive plural ráskȓšćā/páскȓшћā, sázv(ij)ēžđe/cáзв(иј)ēжђe 'constellation', genitive plural sázv(ij)ēžđā/cáзв(иј)ēжђā, nár(j)ečje/ нáр(ј)ечје 'dialect', genitive plural nár(j)ēčjā/нáр(ј)ēчјā.) The inserted -*a*- then undergoes the other notable effect of this ending, namely vowel lengthening in the syllable preceding. A hierarchy exists: insertion in genitive plural can occur without insertion in nominative singular, but not the reverse.

2.3   Morphophonemic alternations resulting from changes after Proto-Slavonic

Upon the dropping of *jer* vowels in weak position, groups of consonant–*jer–j* (the *jer* was apparently always front) became consonant–*j*. Ensuing changes ('new jotation') led to a new set of alternations (it is debatable whether we should seek to collapse the two sets in a description). Points 1, 3 and 5 are as in section 2.2, thus in collective nouns (Proto-Slavonic -ъje): grȍb/грȍб 'grave', grȍblje/грȍбље 'cemetery'; cv(ij)êt/цв(иј)êт 'flower', cv(ij)êće/цв(иj)êће 'flowers'; grána/грáна 'branch', grânje/грâње 'branches' (and verbal nouns like ùčēnje/ỳчēње). *S* and *z* remain unchanged, as does *j*: klâs/клâс 'ear of grain', klâsje/клâсје 'ears'. The *j* remains also after *č, š, ž* from 4 and 6: nòga/нòга 'leg, foot', pòdnōžje/ пòднōжје 'base, foundation', and after *r*: mȍre/мȍре 'sea', prìmōrje/ прȉмōрје 'littoral'. Only after palatals proper (*č, đ, lj, nj, j*) does *j* disappear: mèđa/мèђa 'border', rázmeđe/páзмеђе 'division', *St, zd* yield only *šć*, *žđ*: list/лйст 'leaf', lišće/лйшће 'leaves'; grȍzd/грȍзд 'bunch of grapes', grȍžđe/грȍжђе 'grapes'.

The newest jotation affects a consonant coming before the *je* reflex of short *jat'*. In standard jekavian it makes *l* and *n* into the corresponding palatals: Proto-Slavonic **lěto*, **něga* › *ljěto* 'summer', *njěga* 'care'; as Cyrillic writing makes clear, no separate *j* remains: љȇто, њȇга. (The presence of long or short vowel thus leads to alternation of dental and palatal consonant: Nijémac/Нијémaц 'a German', but adjective njèmačkī/ њèмачкӣ.) In many dialects this type is more extensive, affecting *t*, *d*; in some, also labials and *s*, *z* (Brozović and Ivić 1988: 13 and 56–77). Such progressions may be of general-phonetic interest.

Partly inherited from Proto-Slavonic, where consonant clusters like *st*, *zd* but not 'sd' 'zt' existed, but greatly extended after the fall of the jers is consonant assimilation in voicing. In any cluster of obstruents, the voiced or voiceless quality of the last member controls that of the others. (Recall that *v* is not an obstruent in behaviour, section 2.1). This is both a phonotactic phenomenon, in that clusters like 'sd' 'bč' 'šg' are still impossible, and a morphophonemic one, since alternations occur in final consonants of prefixes: s/c in *s*lȍžiti/*c*лȍжити 'to assemble' but z/з in *z*gàziti/*з*гȁзити 'to trample'; before suffixes, as ù*dž*benīk/ȳ*џ*бенӣк 'textbook' from ù*či*ti/ ỳ*чи*ти 'to teach, learn'; and when *a* alternates with zero, as rédak/péдак 'a line', genitive singular ré*t*ka/pé*т*ка. Voicing assimilation is almost invariably reflected in writing. Only *d* keeps its spelling before *s* and *š*: grâd/грȃд 'city', grȁdskī/грȁдскӣ 'urban'; štèta/штȅта 'damage', ȍdšteta/ȍдштета 'compensation'.

Assimilation to a voiceless final member and assimilation to a voiced final member might seem part of the same rule, but they interact differently with 'cluster-breaking' in noun genitive plurals: a consonant devoiced in a cluster regains its voicing (svȅska/свȅска 'notebook', from svézati/ свéзати 'to bind', genitive plural svȅzākā/свȅзȃкā), whereas one which has become voiced remains so (prìm(j)edba/прѝм(j)едба 'comment', from prim(ij)étiti/прим(иj)éтити 'to remark', genitive plural prìm(j)e*d*ābā/прѝм(j)еɡȃбā).

Assimilation in palatality affects *s* and *z*, which are pronounced and written *š*, *ž* before *č*, *dž*, *ć*, *đ* and *lj*, *nj* (though not root-initial *lj*, *nj*, nor *lj*, *nj* resulting from the newest (jekavian) jotation): ràščistiti/pàшчистити 'to clear up', from prefix raz-/раз- and čìstiti/чйстити 'to clean'; vòžnja/ вȏжња 'driving', from vòziti/вȏзити 'to drive' and suffix -nja/-ња; but not in razljútiti/разљýтити 'to anger' from ljût/љŷт 'angry, sharp', nor in jekavian snjèžan/cњèжан 'snowy' (ekavian snȇžan/cнȇжан).

Serbo-Croat spelling, further, shows changes in consonant clusters. Double consonants simplify: bȅ*z*načājan/бȅзначȃjaн 'insignificant' from bez/бeз 'without' and znàčāj/знȁчȃj 'significance'. Dental stops drop before affricates, as in case forms of òtac/òтaц 'father': genitive òca/òца (from *otca*), nominative plural òčevi/òчеви (from *otčevi*). *T* and *d* are also lost between *s*, *z*, *š*, *ž* and *n*, *l* or various other consonants (ìzra*s*lina/ѝзра*с*лина 'a growth' from the verb stem rást/páст – 'grow'; the adjective ràdostan/pàдостан 'joyful' has feminine ràdo*s*na/pàдос*н*а, from ràdôst/pàдôст 'joy'). They remain at prefix-root boundary: ì*st*lačiti/ѝ*ст*лачити 'to oppress', from iz-/из- 'out' and tlàčiti/тлàчити 'to press'. Such changes, like *a*-insertion, give Serbo-Croat a high relative frequency of vowels as compared to consonants.

A further vowel-enhancing change is that of the consonant *l* to *o*, which occurred when the *l* was pre-consonantal or word-final. The alternation that results is exceptionless in verb *l*-participles: masculine singular dào/дào 'gave', but feminine dála/дáла. In adjectives and nouns it is widespread though lexicalized: masculine singular nominative mìo/мйо 'nice', feminine mìla/мйла, but òhol/òхол 'haughty' – òhola/òхола.

If the *l–o* change yields a sequence *oo*, this contracts to long *ō*: thus the masculine singular *l*-participle of ubòsti/убòсти (stem ubòd/убòд-) 'to stab' is ùbō/ỳбō.

A-insertion and *l–o* are linked. If a word-final cluster of consonant–*l* is split, the *l* almost always becomes *o*. Apart from *l*-participles like rèk-l/pèк-л → rèkao/pèкао 'said', there are nouns like mìsl-/мйсл- → mìsao/мйсао 'thought' and adjectives like tòpl-/тòпл- → tòpao/тòпао 'warm' (tòpal/тòпал is rare). If *a*-insertion fails, as it does in a few loanwords, final *l* becomes syllabic, not changing to *o*: bicìkļ/бицѝкл̥ 'bicycle'.

3 Morphology

3.1 Nominal morphology
All pronouns, almost all nouns, most adjectives and some numerals decline.

3.1.1 Nominal categories
The grammatical categories shown by declension are number, case, gender and animacy. All these participate in agreement within the noun phrase and outside. Further, adjective forms show definiteness–indefiniteness and comparison.

The numbers are singular and plural. Nouns, adjectives and adjectival pronouns also have a form without case distinction, used accompanying the numerals '2', 'both', '3' and '4' (a remnant of the Proto-Slavonic dual). It has had various names; we cite it as the '234 form' (section 4.10).

There are seven cases: nominative, vocative, accusative, genitive, dative, instrumental, locative. Dative and locative have merged; only certain inanimate monosyllabic nouns distinguish them accentually in the singular.

In the plural, nominative and vocative are practically identical, and dative, instrumental and locative are also the same apart from enclitic pronouns which are dative only; hence we write NOM–VOC on one line and DAT–LOC–INST on another in plural paradigms.

Serbo-Croat distinguishes masculine, neuter and feminine genders in singular and plural; the 234 form opposes masculine–neuter to feminine.

Within the masculine singular, the animacy category is important for choosing the accusative of masculine *o*-stem nouns and of pronouns (apart from personal pronouns; section 3.1.3), adjectives and numerals which agree with masculine nouns of any sort. The rule is: like genitive for animates (mǔža/мужа 'husband', lǎva/лава 'lion'), like nominative for inanimates (grȁd/грȁд 'city').

3.1.2   Noun morphology

There are three main declension types. One has -o/-o, -e/-e or zero in the nominative singular and -a/-a in the genitive singular; it arose from Proto-Slavonic *o*-stems. It includes most masculine and all neuter nouns. A second has nominative singular -a/-a, genitive -ē/-ē, continuing Proto-Slavonic *a*-stems. It contains most feminine nouns and small classes of masculines. The third type, from Proto-Slavonic *i*-stems, ends in zero in nominative singular, -i/-и in genitive. It includes all feminines apart from *a*-stems.

The basic *o*-stem endings are those of prózor/прȯзор (table 7.2). Grȁd/грȁд, like most monosyllables and some disyllables, has the 'long

Table 7.2   Masculine *o*-stems

	'city'	'husband'	'window'
Singular			
NOM	grȁd/грȁд	mûž/мûж	prózor/прȯзор
VOC	grȁde/грȁде	mûžu/мûжу	prózore/прȯзоре
ACC	grȁd/грȁд	mǔža/мûжа	prózor/прȯзор
GEN	grȁda/грȁда	mǔža/мûжа	prózora/прȯзора
DAT	grȁdu/грȁду	mûžu/мûжу	prózoru/прȯзору
INST	grȁdom/грȁдом	mûžem/мûжем	prózorom/прȯзором
LOC	grádu/грȃду	mûžu/мûжу	prózoru/прȯзору
234	grȁda/грȁда	mǔža/мûжа	prózora/прȯзора
Plural			
NOM–VOC	grȁdovi/грȁдови	mǔževi/мȕжеви	prózori/прȯзори
ACC	grȁdove/грȁдове	mǔževe/мȕжеве	prózore/прȯзоре
GEN	grȁdōvā/грȁдōвā	mǔžēvā/мȕжēвā	prózōrā/прȯзȯрā
DAT–LOC–INST	grȁdovima/ грȁдовима	mǔževima/ мȕжевима	prózorima/прȯзорима

plural', adding ov/ов before plural endings (ev/ев after palatals and *c*; section 2.2).

Nominative plural -i/-и and dative–locative–instrumental -ima/-има cause consonant alternation (section 2.2).

The genitive plural has -ā/-ā, with an additional -ā inserted to separate most stem-final consonant clusters (section 2.2). A few nouns lacking the long plural take genitive plural -ī/-й (often units of measure, as sát-ī/cát-й 'hour') or -ijū/-ијȳ (gòst-ijū/гȍст-ијȳ 'guest').

A subtype of Proto-Slavonic *o*-stems, the *jo*-stems, had endings preceded by a palatal consonant (originally, by *j*). The descendant of this subtype is the 'soft stems', exemplified by mûž/мȳж. These may end in any palatal or alveo-palatal; words in -*ar*, -*ir* optionally come here as well. Soft stems take vocative singular -u/-y where others have -e/-e, and they cause *o–e* as in instrumental singular -em/-ем for -om/-ом (section 2.2); but -u/-y vocatives and -em/-ем instrumentals do not coincide in scope. -u/-y has spread to some nouns in velars: strȁh/стрȁх 'fear', vocative strȁhu/стрȁху. Instrumental -em/-ем is normal with stems in -*c*, where vocative has -e/-e and the first-palatalization alternation, as òtac/òтац 'father', vocative òče/òче. -om/-ом tends to be kept in foreign words and names (Kȉš-om/Кȉш-ом) and in words with *e* in the preceding syllable: pádež-om/пáдеж-ом 'case'. For fuller treatment of Serbo-Croat declension see P. Ivić/П. Ивич (1972), whom we follow closely here.

Proto-Slavonic masculine *i*-stem, *u*-stem and consonant-stem nouns have joined the *o*-stem declension. *Pǫtь has become pût/пȳт 'way, road, journey, time(s)', genitive púta/пýта. None of this word's forms continue *i*-declension endings. *Synъ is now sîn/сȋн 'son', genitive sîna/сȋна. *Dьnь, *kamy and *korę yield regular *o*-stems dân/дȃн 'day' (genitive dâna/дȃна), kàmēn/кȁмēн 'stone' and kòr(ij)ēn/кȍр(иј)ēн 'root'. Words suffixed with *-*an*- have -anin/-анин as singular stem: grȁđanin/грȁђанин 'city-dweller, citizen', genitive grȁđanina/грȁђанина; and -an/-ан as plural stem: grȁđāni/грȁђāни, genitive grȁđānā/грȁђāнā. Words in *-*telj*- are soft stems without peculiarities: ùčitelj/ỳчитељ 'teacher', genitive ùčitelja/ỳчитеља, plural ùčitelji/ỳчитељи.

The modern locative singular -u/-y comes from the *u*-declension, and the ov/ов of the 'long plural' has been generalized from the *u*-stem plural nominative *-*ove* and genitive *-*ovъ*.

The neuter endings (table 7.3) differ from the masculine only in the nominative, vocative and accusative. These three cases are always the same, having -o/-o or -e/-e for the singular and -a/-a for the plural.

Words of the type s(j)ȅme/c(j)ȅме 'seed' (Proto-Slavonic *n*-stems) have a stem in -*men*- taking *o*-stem endings outside the nominative–vocative–accusative singular: genitive s(j)ȅmena/c(j)ȅмена.

Neuters like jȁ(g)nje/jȁ(г)ње 'lamb' (Proto-Slavonic *nt*-stems) have a stem in -*et*- taking *o*-stem endings in the oblique singular cases, as genitive

Table 7.3   Neuter *o*-stems

	'place'	'heart'	'study'
Singular			
NOM–VOC–ACC	m(j)èsto/м(j)ѐсто	sȑce/cȑце	ùčēnje/ỳчēње
GEN	m(j)èsta/м(j)ѐста	sȑca/cȑца	ùčēnja/ỳчēња
DAT–LOC	m(j)èstu/м(j)ѐсту	sȑcu/cȑцу	ùčēnju/ỳчēњу
INST	m(j)èstom/ м(j)ѐстом	sȑcem/cȑцем	ùčēnjem/ỳчēњем
234	m(j)èsta/м(j)ѐста	sȑca/cȑца	ùčēnja/ỳчēња
Plural			
NOM–VOC–ACC	m(j)èsta/м(j)ѐста	sȑca/cȑца	ùčēnja/ỳчēња
GEN	m(j)ēstā/м(j)ѐстā	sȑcā/cȑцā	ùčēnjā/ỳчēњā
DAT–LOC–INST	m(j)èstima/ м(j)ѐстима	sȑcima/cȑцима	ùčēnjima/ỳчēњима

jȁ(g)njeta/jȁ(г)њета. Their plural stems are usually suppletive: jȁgānjci/ jȁгāњци or jȁgnjići/jȁгњићи masculine plural, or jȁ(g)njād/jȁ(г)њāд *i*-stem feminine.

Traces of Proto-Slavonic *s*-stems (the**slovo* type) are seen in alternative plural stems for nèbo/нѐбо 'heaven', t(ij)èlo/т(иj)ѐло 'body', čȕdo/чȕдо 'miracle': nebèsa/небѐса, t(j)elèsa/т(j)елѐса, čudèsa/чудѐса.

Many masculine names, derivatives and loan-words resemble neuters in having nominative singular in -o/-о or -e/-е: Mȃrko/Мȃрко 'Mark', Pȃvle/Пȃвле 'Paul', nestáško/нестáшко 'brat', rȁdio/рȁдио 'radio', finále/финáле 'finale'. The stems are seen in genitive Mȃrka/Мȃрка, Pȃvla/Пȃвла, nestáška/нестáшка, rȁdija/рȁдиja, finála/финáла. Some names have -*et*- stems: Mȋle/Мȋле, genitive–accusative Mȋleta/Мȋлета.

Most *a*-stems are feminine (table 7.4). Words denoting men (as slúga/ слȳга, koléga/колѐга 'colleague') and certain animals (gorìla/горѝла 'gorilla') are masculine, but even these can take feminine agreement in the plural, as tê kolége/тê колѐге 'these colleagues'. Many masculine names (Àleksa/Àлекса) and hypocoristics (Jóca/Jóца 'Joe') are *a*-stems; other hypocoristics have nominative -o/-о but other cases like *a*-stems (Ìvo/ Ѝво, genitive Ívē/Ѝвē from Ìvan/Ѝван 'John').

The old distinction of hard *a*-stems and soft *ja*-stems is gone: endings from the soft paradigm have been generalized (genitive -ē/-ē is from *-ę not *-y; dative–locative -i/-и from *-i not *-ě). Vocative -o/-о has spread from the hard variant; only certain nouns in -ica/-ица take -e/-е (section 2.2).

Non-hypocoristic names have nominative replacing vocative: Màrija/ Мàриjа! Àleksa/Àлекса!

The dative-locative singular ending causes consonant alternation in

Table 7.4 Feminine (and masculine) *a*-stems

	'woman, wife'	'manservant'	'soul'
Singular			
NOM	žèna/жѐна	slúga/слу́га	dúša/ду́ша
VOC	žȅno/жѐно	slȗgo/слу̑го	dȕso/ду́шо
ACC	žènu/жѐну	slúgu/слу́гу	dȕšu/ду́шу
GEN	žènē/жѐнē	slúgē/слу́гē	dúšē/ду́шē
DAT-LOC	žèni/жѐни	slúzi/слу́зи	dúši/ду́ши
INST	žènōm/жѐнōм	slúgōm/слу́гōм	dúšōm/ду́шōм
234	žène/жѐне	slȗge/слу̑ге	dȕše/ду́ше
Plural			
NOM-ACC	žène/жѐне	slȗge/слу̑ге	dȕše/ду́ше
VOC	žȅne, žène/жѐне, жѐне	slȗge/слу̑ге	dȕše/ду́ше
GEN	žénā/же́нā	slȕgū, slúgā/слу̀гȳ, слу́гā	dúšā/ду́шā
DAT-LOC-INST	žènama/жѐнама	slúgama/слу́гама	dúšama/ду́шама

many *a*-stems (second palatalization of velars, section 2.2).

Nouns with stem-final consonant clusters have lexically conditioned genitive plurals, -ā/-ā (with cluster-breaking *ā*; section 2.2) or -ī/-ӣ: d(j)èvōjka/д(j)ѐвōјка 'girl', d(j)èvojākā/д(j)ѐвојāкā; mâjka/ма̑јка 'mother', mâjkī/ма̑јкӣ.

Proto-Slavonic *i*-nominative nouns now have -*a*: *rabynji › ròbinja/ро̀биња 'slave woman', *sǫdiji › sùdija/су̀дија 'judge'.

Feminine *i*-stems (table 7.5) are a closed class except for those with the productive suffixes -ōst/-ōст '-ness', -ād/-āд 'collective noun, especially suppletive plural of neuter -*et* stem'. The instrumental singular is usually in -ju/-jy (Proto-Slavonic *-*ьjǫ*), causing 'new jotation' (section 2.3): kȍšću/ко̏шћу, ljúbav/љу́бав 'love' ljúbavlju/љу́бављу; but some items permit or require -i/-и: ćûd/ћу̑д 'mood', ćûdi/ћу̑ди.

The *i*-declension continues Proto-Slavonic *i*-stems. Proto-Slavonic *r*-stems yield mȁti/ма̏ти 'mother', genitive mȁterē/ма̏терē (like *a*-stems except accusative mȁtēr/ма̏тēр, vocative mȁti/ма̏ти) and kćî/кћи̑ 'daughter', genitive kćȅri/кће̏ри (like *i*-stems). More frequent now are *a*-stems (from diminutives) mâjka/ма̑јка, (k)ćérka/(к)ће́рка. Proto-Slavonic long *u-stems mostly become *a*-stems in -va/-ва: *cьrky › cȓkva/цȓква 'church', *svekry › svȅkrva/свȅкрва 'mother-in-law'; but two are *i*-stems: *ljuby › ljúbav/љу́бав, *kry › kȓv/кȓв 'blood'.

Besides the declension types given, Serbo-Croat has nouns declining as adjectives. Two noteworthy sets are masculine surnames in -skī/-скӣ, as Bugàrskī/Буга̀рскӣ, genitive Bugàrskōg(a)/Буга̀рскōг(а), and country

Table 7.5   Feminine *i*-stems

'bone'

Singular	
NOM	kôst/кôст
VOC	kȍsti/кȍсти
ACC	kôst/кôст·
GEN	kȍsti/кȍсти
DAT	kȍsti/кȍсти
INST	kȍsti, kȍšću/кȍсти, кȍшћу
LOC	kòsti/кòсти
234	kòsti/кòсти
Plural	
NOM-VOC-ACC	kȍsti/кȍсти
GEN	kòstī, kòstijū/кòстӣ, кòстијӯ
DAT-LOC-INST	kòstima/кòстима

names in -skā/-скā, like Fràncūskā/Фрàнцӯскā 'France', dative–locative Fràncūskōj/Фрàнцӯскōj.

3.1.3   Pronominal morphology

The personal and reflexive pronouns oppose full (accented) and clitic (unaccented; section 4.1) forms in genitive, dative and accusative (table 7.6).

Genitive–accusative syncretism is complete (except njê/њê versus njù/ њу̏ and the lack of a genitive reflexive clitic). There is much additional variation. Instrumental singulars used without a preposition are frequently mnóme/мнóме, njíme/њи̑ме, njóme/њóме. Oblique singulars may have accent -ě- instead of -è-. Si/си is absent in central Štokavian dialects, but found in some Croatian standard codifications. Archaic and literary usage may have accusatives me/ме, te/те, nj/њ, se/се with prepositions, as prȅdā se/прȅдā се 'in front of oneself' = pred sèbe/пред сèбе.

Demonstrative, possessive and other pronouns share a set of endings that may be termed pronominal, again with many alternative forms (table 7.7).

The close and distant demonstratives òvāj/òвāj 'this', ònāj/òнāj 'that' decline like tâj/тâj. The 'movable vowels' (*a*), (*e*), (*u*) tend somewhat to appear in phrase-final position, otherwise not: o tȍme/о тȍме 'about that', o tôm psȕ/о тôм псȳ 'about that dog'. Nȁš/нȁш and vȁš/вȁш 'your (PL)' are 'soft' stems, typified by *o–e* in masculine and neuter endings. Also soft are môj/мôj 'my', tvôj/твôj 'your (SG)', svôj/свôj (reflexive possessive: section 4.8) and kòjī/кòjӣ (stem kòj-/кòj-) 'which'. These, additionally, may contract *oje* to *ō*, yielding five possibilities for

Table 7.6 Personal and reflexive pronouns

	1	2	3 masculine	3 neuter	3 feminine
Singular					
NOM	jȃ/jȃ	tȋ/тȋ	ȏn/ȏн	ȍno/ȍно	ȍna/ȍна
ACC	mène/мѐне	tèbe/тѐбе	njèga/њѐга	njèga/њѐга	njȗ/њȗ
Enclitic	me/ме	te/те	ga/га	ga/га	je/je, ju/jу
GEN	mène/мѐне	tèbe/тѐбе	njèga/њѐга	njèga/њѐга	njȇ/њȇ
Enclitic	me/ме	te/те	ga/га	ga/га	je/je
DAT	mèni/мѐни	tèbi/тѐби	njèmu/њѐму	njèmu/њѐму	njȏj/њȏj
Enclitic	mi/ми	ti/ти	mu/му	mu/му	jȏj/jȏj
INST	mnȏm/мнȏм	tȍbōm/тȍбȏм	njȋm/њȋм	njȋm/њȋм	njȏm/њȏм
LOC	mèni/мѐни	tèbi/тѐби	njèmu/њѐму	njèmu/њѐму	njȏj/њȏj
Plural					
NOM	mȋ/мȋ	vȋ/вȋ	ȍni/ȍни	ȍna/ȍна	ȍne/ȍне
ACC–GEN	nȃs/нȃс	vȃs/вȃс	njȋh/њȋх	njȋh/њȋх	njȋh/њȋх
Enclitic	nas/нас	vas/вас	ih/их	ih/их	ih/их
DAT	nȃma/нȃма	vȃma/вȃма	njȋma/њȋма	njȋma/њȋма	njȋma/њȋма
Enclitic	nam/нам	vam/вам	im/им	im/им	im/им
INST–LOC	nȃma/нȃма	vȃma/вȃма	njȋma/њȋма	njȋma/њȋма	njȋma/њȋма

	Reflexive
Singular/plural	
NOM	—
ACC	sèbe/cèбe
Enclitic	se/ce
GEN	sèbe/cèбe
DAT	sèbi/cèби
Enclitic	(si/си)
INST	sȍbōm/cȍбȏм
LOC	sèbi/cèби

Table 7.7 Demonstrative and possessive pronouns

	'this, that' Masculine	Neuter	Feminine
Singular			
NOM	tâj/тâj	tô/тô	tâ/тâ
ACC	NOM or GEN	tô/тô	tû/тŷ
GEN	t̀òg(a)/т̀òг(a)	t̀òg(a)/т̀òг(a)	tê/тê
DAT-LOC	tòm(e, u)/ тòм(e, y)	tòm(e, u)/ тòм(e, y)	tôj/тôj
INST	tîm, tíme/ тŷм, тŷме	tîm, tíme/ тŷм, тŷме	tôm/тôм
234	tâ/тâ	tâ/тâ	tê/тê
Plural			
NOM	tî/тŷ	tâ/тâ	tê/тê
ACC	tê/тê	tâ/тâ	tê/тê
GEN	tîh/тŷх	tîh/тŷх	tîh/тŷх
DAT-LOC-INST	tîm, tîma/ тŷм, тŷма	tîm, tîma/ тŷм, тŷма	tîm, tîma/ тŷм, тŷма
	'our(s)'		
Singular			
NOM	nàš/нàш	nàše/нàше	nàša/нàша
ACC	NOM or GEN	nàše/нàше	nàšu/нàшy
GEN	nàšeg(a)/ нàшег(a)	nàšeg(a)/ нàшег(a)	nàšē/нàшē
DAT-LOC	nàšem(u)/ нàшем(y)	nàšem(u)/ нàшем(y)	nàšôj/нàшôj
INST	nàšīm/нàшŷм	nàšīm/нàшŷм	nàšōm/нàшōм
234	nàša/нàша	nàša/нàша	nàše/нàше
Plural			
NOM	nàši/нàши	nàša/нàша	nàše/нàше
ACC	nàše/нàше	nàša/нàша	nàše/нàше
GEN	nàšīh/нàшŷх	nàšīh/нàшŷх	nàšīh/нàшŷх
DAT-LOC-INST	nàšīm(a)/ нàшŷм(a)	nàšīm(a)/ нàшŷм(a)	nàšīm(a)/нàшŷм(a)

masculine and neuter dative–locative singular: mòjem/мòjем, mòjemu/ мòjему, môm/мôм, môme/мôме, mômu/мôму. The third-person possessives njègov/њèгов 'his, its', njên/њêн or njézin/њéзин 'her', njȉhov/њȉхов 'their' are treated under short-form adjectives (section 3.1.4).

The pronoun *sь has been lost. *Vьsь 'all' has undergone consonant metathesis vs › sv but still behaves as a soft stem (table 7.8).

Svò/свò for neuter singular svè/свè is non-standard but frequent in modifier position.

The interrogative pronouns have stems k-/к-, č-/ч- with singular

Table 7.8   Declension of sȁv/сȁв 'all'

	Masculine	Neuter	Feminine
Singular			
NOM	sȁv/сȁв	svȅ/свȅ	svȁ/свȁ
ACC	NOM or GEN	svȅ/свȅ	svȕ/свȳ
GEN	svèga/свèга	svèga/свèга	svȇ/свȇ
DAT-LOC	svèmu/свèму	svèmu/свèму	svôj/свôj
INST	svȋm/свȋм	svȋm/свȋм	svôm/свôм
234	svȁ/свȁ	svȁ/свȁ	svȅ/свȅ
Plural			
NOM	svȋ/свȋ	svȁ/свȁ	svȅ/свȅ
ACC	svȅ/свȅ	svȁ/свȁ	svȅ/свȅ
GEN	svȋh/свȋх,	svȋh/свȋх,	svȋh/свȋх,
	svìjū/свìjȳ	svìjū/свìjȳ	svìjū/свìjȳ
DAT-LOC-INST	svȋm/свȋм,	svȋm/свȋм,	svȋm/свȋм,
	svìma/свȋма	svìma/свȋма	svìma/свȋма

pronominal endings (table 7.9). The Croat standard codifies the older forms *tkȍ, štȍ*. Other interrogatives are part of a larger pattern of demonstrative roots and classifying suffixes, thus kàkav/кàкав 'of what sort', ovàkav/овàкав 'of this sort'.

Table 7.9   Declension of 'who' and 'what'

	'who' *masculine*	'what' *neuter*
NOM	(t)kȍ/(т)кȍ	štȍ, štȁ/штȍ, штȁ
ACC	kòga/кòга	štȍ, štȁ/штȍ, штȁ
GEN	kòga/кòга	čèga/чèга
DAT-LOC	kòmu, kòme/кòму, кòме	čèmu/чèму
INST	kȋm, kíme/кȋм, кúме	čȋm, číme/чȋм, чúме

Interrogatives add prefixes or suffixes to give indefinites: nȅ(t)ko/ нȅ(т)ко 'someone', nȅšto/нȅшто 'something', nȅkakav/нȅкакав 'of some sort'. I-/и- means 'any' (negative polarity; section 4.6), ni-/ни- 'no', koje-/кoje- 'one and another' (as kojèšta/кojèшта 'various things; nonsense'), svȁ-/свȁ- (svȅ-/свȅ-, svȕ-/свȳ-) 'every' (svȁ(t)ko/свȁ(т)ко 'everyone', svȕgd(j)e/свȳгд(j)e ('everywhere'). Bȋlo/бȋло..., ma/мa..., ... gȍd/гȍд mean '... ever' (thus bȋlo gd(j)e/бȋло гд(j)e, ma gd(j)ȅ/мa гд(j)ȅ or gd(j)e gȍd/гд(j)e гȍд 'wherever'). The nȅ-/нȅ- type may be used both with and without existence presuppositions:

Nȅšto se dogòdilo!/Нȅшто се догòдило!
'Something has happened!'

Àko se nèšto dògodī, rèci mi!/Ако се нѐшто дòгодӣ, рѐци ми!
'If anything happens, tell me!'

In the second usage bare interrogatives also occur: Àko se štȍ dògodī/
Ако се штȍ дòгодӣ ...

3.1.4   Adjectival morphology

Serbo-Croat preserves the distinction of long- and short-form adjectives
(table 7.10). The citation form of an adjective is the nominative singular
masculine short form (long form if short is lacking).

The long endings are those of the pronominal declension, but with
length on the first vowel and with nominative masculine singular -ī/-ӣ. The
short endings differ in the forms italicized in table 7.10 and in the shortness
of single-vowel endings (nòvo/нȍво versus long nȍvō/нȍвō). Nȍv/нȍв
and some other adjectives distinguish short-long accentually as well
(though much inter-speaker variation exists). Short genitives and dative-
locatives like nòva/нȍва, nòvu/нȍву are most widespread in the Croat
standard. The short genitive ending -a/-a is especially frequent in the
qualifying genitive: čòv(j)ek dòbra sȑca/чȍв(j)ек дòбра сȑца 'a man of
good heart'.

Soft stems differ from hard only in nominative–accusative neuter singular long lȍšē/лȍшē, short lȍše/лȍше 'bad', masculine–neuter genitive
lȍšēg(a)/лȍшēг(a), dative–locative lȍšēm(u)/лȍшēм(у).

Short and long contrast semantically in modifier position: nȍv grâd/нȍв
грâд 'a new city', nȍvī grâd/нȍвӣ грâд 'the new city'. Since Vuk Karadžić
they have been explained as answering the questions kàkav/кàкав? 'of
what sort?' and kòjī/кòjӣ? 'which one?' respectively. Set-phrases regularly
have long forms; thus b(ij)êlī lùk/б(иj)êлӣ лȳк 'white onion' means
'garlic'. Predicate position requires short forms (section 4.3): òvāj grâd je
nȍv/òвāj грâд je нȍв 'this city is new'.

Possessive adjectives (sections 3.3.2, 4.9), including njègov/њȅгов 'his,
its', njên, njézin/њȇн, њȅзин 'her', njȉhov/њȉхов 'their', have only short
endings: Màrijin grâd/Мàриjин грâд 'Marija's city', njên grâd/њȇн грâд
'her city', Ìvanov grâd/Ѝванов грâд 'Ivan's city'. The same is true for the
demonstrative-interrogatives in -àkav/àкав, suiting their meaning. Adjectives having exclusively long forms include mȃlī/мȃли 'small', l(ij)êvī/
л(иj)êви, dȅsnī/дȅснӣ 'left, right', ordinal numerals like drȕgī/дрȳгӣ
'second, other' and most adjectives derived from nouns, adverbs and verbs
(section 3.3.2).

Participles have short and long forms: pȍzvān/пȍзвāн, pȍzvānī/
пȍзвāнӣ 'called; called upon'. The present adverb and the l-participle of
verbs can be adjectivalized, and then take long forms: ìdūćī/ѝдȳħӣ
'coming, next', mínulī/мѝнули 'bygone', pȁlī/пȁлӣ 'fallen'.

Comparatives and superlatives (the comparative prefixed with nâj-/нâj-

Table 7.10   Long and short adjective declension

'new' long	Masculine	Neuter	Feminine
Singular			
NOM	nòvī/нòвӣ	nòvō/нòвō	nòvā/нòвā
ACC	NOM or GEN	nòvō/нòвō	nòvū/нòвӯ
GEN	nòvōg(a)/ нòвōг(a)	nòvōg(a)/ нòвōг(a)	nòvē/нòвē
DAT–LOC	nòvōm(e, u)/ нòвōм(e, y)	nòvōm(e, u)/ нòвōм(e, y)	nòvōj/нòвōj
INST	nòvīm/нòвӣм	nòvīm/нòвӣм	nòvōm/нòвōм
234	nòvā/нòвā	nòvā/нòвā	nòvē/нòвē
Plural			
NOM	nòvī/нòвӣ	nòvā/нòвā	nòvē/нòвē
ACC	nòvē/нòвē	nòvā/нòвā	nòvē/нòвē
GEN	nòvīh/нòвӣх	nòvīh/нòвӣх	nòvīh/нòвӣх
DAT–LOC–INST	nòvīm(a)/ нòвӣм(a)	nòvīm(a)/ нòвӣм(a)	nòvīm(a)/нòвӣм(a)
'new' short			
Singular			
NOM	*nȍv/нȍв*	nòvo/нòво	nòva/нòва
ACC	NOM or GEN	nòvo/нòво	nòvu/нòву
GEN	nòvōg(a)/ нòвōг(a), *nòva/нòва*	nòvōg(a)/ нòвōг(a), *nòva/нòва*	nòvē/нòвē
DAT–LOC	nòvōm(e, u)/ нòвōм(e, y), *nòvu/нòву*	nòvōm(e, u)/ нòвōм(e, y), *nòvu/нòву*	nòvōj/нòвōj
INST	nòvīm/нòвӣм	nòvīm/нòвӣм	nòvōm/нòвōм
234	nòva/нòва	nòva/нòва	nòve/нòве
Plural			
NOM	nòvi/нòви	nòva/нòва	nòve/нòве
ACC	nòve/нòве	nòva/нòва	nòve/нòве
GEN	nòvīh/нòвӣх	nòvīh/нòвӣх	nòvīh/нòвӣх
DAT–LOC–INST	nòvīm(a)/ нòвӣм(a)	nòvīm(a)/ нòвӣм(a)	nòvīm(a)/нòвӣм(a)

yields the superlative) decline precisely like soft-stem long adjectives. Most are formed by adding -ij-ī/-иj-ӣ to adjective stems: lòš/лȍш 'bad', lòšijī/ лòшиjӣ (lòšijē/лòшиjē, lòšijā/лòшиjā ...) 'worse'; múdar/мýдар 'wise', mùdrijī/мỳдриjӣ; pòzvān/пȍзвāн 'called upon', pozvànijī/позвàниjӣ; plemènit/племèнит 'noble', plemenìtijī/племенѝтиjӣ. A smaller set add bare endings with old jotation (section 2.3). These are mostly (1) monosyllables containing long vowel: gûst/гŷст 'thick', gȕšć-ī/гȕшћ-ӣ; skûp/ скŷп 'expensive', skȕplj-ī/скȳпљ-ӣ; (2) disyllables which lose the second syllable: šìrok/шѝрок 'wide', šȋr-ī/шȋр-ӣ; slàdak/слàдак 'sweet', slȃđ-ī/слȃђ-ӣ. Three adjectives have š/ш comparatives: lȁk/лȁк 'light, easy', lȁkšī/лȁкшӣ; mȅk/мȅк 'soft', mȅkšī/мȅкшӣ; l(ij)ȅp/л(иj)ȅп 'beautiful', l(j)ȅpšī/лȅпшӣ (љȅпшӣ). Suppletive comparatives are dòbar/дòбар 'good', bòljī/бòљӣ; lòš/лòш or r̀đav/р̀ђав or zào/зào (stem zl/зл-) 'bad', gòrī/гòрӣ 'worse'; vȅlik/вȅлик 'large', vȅćī/вȅћӣ; mȃlī/мȃлӣ or màlen/мàлен, mȁnjī/мȁњӣ; dȕg/дȕг 'long', dȕžī/дȕжӣ or dùljī/дȕљӣ. See section 5.3 for periphrastic comparison of indeclinables.

Derived adverbs take -o/-o or -e/-e like neuter nominative–accusative singular short adjectives: nòvo/нòво 'newly', lòše/лòше 'badly', mùdro/мȕдро 'wisely'. The accent may differ from the neuter. Their comparatives are formed like those of adjectives: lòšije/лòшиjе, mùdrije/мȕдриjе, lȁkše/лȁкше 'more easily'. However, adverbs from adjectives in -skī/-скӣ (-škī/-шкӣ, -čkī/-чкӣ) end in short -i/-и: ljȕdski/љȕдски 'humanly', gr̀čki/гр̀чки 'in Greek fashion/language'.

3.1.5 Numeral morphology
The cardinal numeral '1' is declined in all genders in singular and (for pluralia tantum) plural. Its nominative masculine singular is jèdan/jèдан and its stem for the remaining forms jèdn/jèдн-; endings are those of tȃj/тȃj (section 3.1.3), but final vowels are short.

'2, both, 3, 4' can be declined (table 7.11). Oblique case forms are rare (and show much accentual and other variation), particularly for '3, 4' and all masculine–neuter forms. Most commonly, the nominative forms are used undeclined (section 4.10).

Higher numerals up to '99' are indeclinable. Stò/стò '100' is indeclinable; there is also stòtina/стòтина, which behaves as a feminine noun, but mostly appears as a fixed accusative stòtinu/стòтину. '1,000' shows the

Table 7.11 Declension of '2, both, 3, 4'

	'2' Masculine–neuter	Feminine	'3'
NOM–ACC–VOC	dvȃ/двȃ	dvȉje, dvê/двѝjе, двȇ	trȋ/трȋ
GEN	dvàjū/двàjӯ	dvȉjū, dvéjū/двѝjӯ, двéjӯ	trìjū/трѝjӯ
DAT–LOC–INST	dváma/двáма	dv(j)èma/дв(j)èма	trìma/трѝма
	'both'		'4'
NOM–ACC–VOC	òba/òба	òb(j)e/òб(j)е	čètiri/чèтири
GEN	obáju/обájу	obíjū, obéjū/обѝjӯ, обéjӯ	četirìjū/четирѝjӯ
DAT–LOC–INST	ob(j)èma/об(j)èма	ob(j)èma/об(j)èма	čètirma/чèтирма

same behaviour, both tȉsuća/тȋсућа (Croat standard) and hȉljada/ хȕљада. For further numerical forms see section 4.10.

3.2 Verbal morphology

3.2.1 Categories expressed

Serbo-Croat finite forms agree with subjects in person and number. Compound tenses containing the *l*-participle also express gender and the 234 form.

The simple tenses are present, aorist and imperfect. The present-tense markers are -m/-м for first person singular (only two verbs maintain -u/-y ‹ *ǫ, namely hòću, ću/хòћу, ћу 'I will' and mògu/мòгу 'I can'); second person singular -š/-ш; and third person singular -∅; first person plural -mo/-мо; second person plural -te/-те; -∅ for third person plural following a changed stem vowel -u-/-y- or -e-/-е-. Although aorist and, particularly, imperfect are not found in all dialects, the literary standards retain them as optional past tenses. Their meanings are much discussed. Briefly, the aorist, formed mostly from perfective verbs, serves to narrate events and express surprising perceived events; the imperfect, (almost) exclusively from imperfectives, describes background situations. Both can be supplanted by the perfect.

The compound tenses are as follows:

1 *Future*: auxiliary clitic ću/ћу or full form hòću/хòћу (section 4.1 and below), with (imperfective or perfective) infinitive or (especially Eastern) da/да₂ + present clause (section 4.5).

Slȃvko će vȉd(j)eti Màriju./Слȃвко ће вȕд(j)ети Màрију.
Slȃvko će da vȉdī Màriju./Слȃвко ће да вȕдȋ Màрију.
'Slavko will see Marija.'

If the infinitive precedes the clitic, the final -ti/-ти of the infinitive is lost and the spelling is *vȉdjet ću* 'I will see' (Croat standard), vȉd(j)eću/ вȕд(j)ећу (elsewhere). Infinitives in -ći/-ћи preserve this marker: dóći ću/ дóћи ћу 'I will come'.

2 *Perfect*: auxiliary clitic sam/сам or full form jèsam/jèсам, with *l*-participle of the verb. This is the all-purpose past tense.

Mȋ smo vȉd(j)eli Màriju./Мȋ смо вȕд(j)ели Màрију.
'We saw (have seen) Marija.'
Jèsmo li vȉd(j)eli Màriju?/Jèсмо ли вȕд(j)ели Màрију?
'Have we seen (Did we see) Marija?'

3 *Pluperfect*: perfect or (rarely) imperfect of 'to be' as auxiliary, with *l*-participle.

Mi smo bíli vȉd(j)eli Màriju./Мȕ смо бȉли вȉд(j)ели Мàриjу.
Mi bȉjāsmo (bȅjāsmo) vȉd(j)eli Màriju./Ми бȕjāсмо (бȅjāсмо) вȉд(j)ели Мàриjу.
'We had seen Marija.'

4 *Future II*: auxiliary bȕdēm/бȳдȇм (extra present of 'to be'; table 7.16 below) with *l*-participle.

Kȁd (ȁko) bȕdēmo govòrili s Màrijōm, svȇ će bȉti jȁsno./Кȁд (ȁко) бȳдȇмо говòрили с Мàриjōм, свȇ ħе бȕти jȁсно.
'When (if) we speak with Marija (in the future), everything will be clear.'

The future II is usually from imperfectives, since a perfective present tense is usable in kȁd/кȁд or ȁko/ȁко clauses for future time: kȁd (ȁko) nádēmo Màriju/кȁд (ȁко) нáħēмо Мàриjу ... 'When/if we find Marija (in the future) ...'.

5 *The conditionals*: see under moods below.

Aspect affects a lexical item's whole paradigm; a verb is either perfective (napísati/напȕсати 'to write' and all its forms) or imperfective (písati/пȕсати 'to write' with its forms). However, many verbs are bi-aspectual, including some of the commonest: ȉći/ȕħи 'to go', bȉti/бȕти 'to be', razùm(j)eti/разȳм(j)ети 'to understand', kázati/кázати 'to say', vȉd(j)eti/вȉд(j)ети 'to see', čȕti/чȳти 'to hear', rúčati/рȳчати 'to have lunch'.
Most non-prefixed verbs are imperfective. Prefixing a verb yields a perfective: písati/пȕсати imperfective 'to write' → napísati/напȕсати perfective 'to write', písati/пȕсати → upísati/упȕсати perfective 'to write in, register'. The first example keeps its lexical meaning; but there is no prefix which invariably perfectivizes without changing lexical meaning. A suffix yielding perfectives is -nuti/-нути, added mostly to imperfective -ati/-ати verbs: gúrati/гȳрати 'to push', gȕrnuti/гȳрнути 'to push once'.
Perfective (especially prefixed perfective) verbs can be imperfectivized by adding suffixes, commonly -ati/-ати, -ívati/-ȕвати (present -ujēm/-yjȇm) and -ávati/-áвати (-āvām/-āвāм). Consonant-stem verbs with -e-/-е- themes usually take -ati/-ати with present in -ām/-āм: is-trés-ti/истрéс-ти 'to shake out', imperfective istrés-ati/истрéс-ати, ȉstrēsām/ȕстрȇсāм. Velar stems, however, prefer -ati/-ати with third-palatalization reflex of the velar and -jēm/-jȇм present: ȉzreći/ȕзреħи (stem ȉz-rek-/ȕз-рек-) 'to express', imperfective izríc-ati/изрȕц-ати with present ȉzrīčēm/ȕзрȕчȇм. An additional mark of imperfectivizing consonant stems is stem-internal -i-/-и- or other vowel change, as pòčēti/пòчȇти, pòčnēm/пòчнȇм 'to begin', imperfective pòčinjati/пòчињати pòčinjēm/пòчињȇм; ùmr(ij)ēti/ỳмр(иj)ȇти ȕmrēm/ỳмрȇм 'to die',

imperfective ùmirati/ỳмирати ùmirēm/ỳмирēм.

-iti/-ити verbs imperfectivize with -ati/-ати (-ām/-ām) (causing internal *o*–*a* alternation: otvòriti/отвòрити 'to open', otvárati/отвáрати), or with the more productive -ívati/-ѝвати or -ávati/-áвати. All three generally cause old jotation (section 2.2): òs(j)etiti/òс(j)етити 'to feel', òs(j)ećati/òс(j)еħати; izgráditi/изгрáдити 'to construct', izgradívati/изграħѝвати; ràniti/рàнити 'to wound', ranjávati/рањáвати. Verb types in -ati/-ати imperfectivize with -ívati/-ѝвати or -ávati/-áвати, mostly without jotation: iskázati/искáзати 'to state', iskazívati/исказѝвати; izòrati/изòрати 'to plough up', izorávati/изорáвати.

The remaining verb types (-nuti/-нути, -(j)eti/-(j)ети) may use any of a number of methods of imperfectivization. A very few -ovati/-овати and -evati/-евати verbs imperfectivize, taking -ívati/-ѝвати (present optionally in -īvām/-ӣвām): daròvati/дарòвати 'to donate', imperfective darívati/дарѝвати dàrīvām/дàрӣвām or dàrujēm/дàруjēm.

There are also suppletive pairs: dóći/дòħи perfective, dòlaziti/дòлазити imperfective 'to come'.

The present of a perfective verb does not mean future, except in 'when/ if' clauses; it forms an 'infinitive substitute' with da/да₂ (section 4.5), and in main clauses it expresses 'typical action' if something in the context indicates generalization, as čêsto/чêсто 'often':

Stvâri čêsto ìspadnū (perfective present) drugàčije nêgo što očèkujēmo./
Ствȁри чêсто ѝспаднȳ (perfective present) другàчије нêго што очèкујēмо.
'Things often turn out different from what we expect.'

Verbs of motion lack determinate–indeterminate distinctions, thus ìći/ ѝħи – hòditi/хòдити are not a pair. The first means 'to go (in one or several directions, on foot or by vehicle)', the second 'to walk'. In several instances the old determinate stem appears only prefixed, with the indeterminate stem serving to imperfectivize it, as nòsiti/нòсити imperfective 'to carry', dòn(ij)eti/дòн(иј)ēти, stem donès-/донèс- perfective 'to bring' → donòsiti/донòсити imperfective. Certain motion verbs derive explicit multidirectionals: nósati/нóсати 'to carry about'. A few verbs make iteratives: vȉd(j)eti/вȉд(ј)ети → víđati/вѝħати 'to see now and then'.

Moods, besides indicative, include imperative (section 4.2), with second person singular and plural (-te/-те) and first person plural (-mo/-мо) forms: Rèci/рèци! Rècite/рèците! Rècimo/рèцимо! 'Say!'; and the conditional, made with auxiliary bih/бих 'would' (section 4.1) and *l*-participle:

Kȁd biste me pítali, rȅkao bih/Kȁд бисте ме пѝтали, рȅкао бих.
'If you (plural) asked me, I would tell.'

The conditional is used in both clauses of hypothetical *if*–*then* sentences.

The same form can express past *if–then* relations, but a past conditional is also possible with the *l*-participle of 'to be':

Kȁd biste me bȉli pítali, bȉo bih rȅkao./Кȁд бисте ме бȉли пи́тали, бȉо бих рȅкао.
'If you had asked me, I would have told.'

An alternative to kȁd bih/кȁд бих 'if' in the protasis is dȁ/дȁ with indicative tense:

dȁ me pītāte/дȁ ме пӣта̄те
'if you asked me (now)'
dȁ ste me pítali/дȁ сте ме пи́тали
'if you had asked me'

A further use of the conditional is in purpose clauses, alternative to da/да$_2$:

Pīšēm da Vas pītām/пӣшēм да Вас пи́та̄м ...
'I write to ask you ...'
Pīšēm da bih Vas pítao/пӣшēм да бих Вас пи́тао ...
'I write in order to ask you ...'

Active and passive voice are distinguished. The passive (section 4.5) consists of a passive participle and a tense of 'to be' as auxiliary:

Knjȉga je nàpīsana./Књȉга je нàпӣсана.
'The book has been written.'
Knjȉga je bíla nàpīsana./Књȉга je би́ла нàпӣсана.
'The book was written.'
Knjȉga će bȉti nàpīsana./Књȉга ће бȉти нàпӣсана.
'The book will be written.'

The clitic se/ce indicating unspecified human subject can be used to form a quasi-passive (always without agent-phrase):

Knjȉga se pīšē./Књȉга се пӣшē.
'The book (NOM) is being written.'

Some Western dialects and recent Croatian codifications can keep the underlying object in the accusative ('impersonal passive'): knjȉgu se pīšē/ књȉгу се пӣшē.

The non-finite forms (for uses see section 4.5) are infinitive (na)písati/ (на)пи́сати 'to write'; passive participle pȉsan, nàpīsan/пӣсан, нàпӣсан 'written'; verbal noun písānje/пи́са̄ње 'writing (of ...)'; two verbal adverbs ('gerunds'), present pīšūći/пӣшӯћи and past napísāvši/напи́са̄- вши; and the *l*-participle (table 7.12), used in compound tenses (perfect, pluperfect, future II) and conditionals.

Table 7.12   *L*-participle

	Masculine	Neuter	Feminine
Singular	(na)písao/(на)пѝсао	(na)písalo/(на)пѝсало	(na)písala/(на)пѝсала
234	(na)písala/(на)пѝсала	as plural	as plural
Plural	(na)písali/(на)пѝсали	(na)písala/(на)пѝсала	(na)písale/(на)пѝсале

3.2.2   Conjugation

One can classify Slavonic verbs by the formants of their present stems, by their infinitive(-aorist) stems or by the relationship between the two (constructing Jakobsonian underlying stems). This treatment is based on present stems: themes in -e-/-e-, in -ne-/-не-, in -je-/-je-, in -i-/-и-. Within each, we show infinitive stem shapes.

Themes in -e-/-e-. The largest subtype has infinitive stem in consonant. Our example (table 7.13) is trés-/трéс- 'to shake', since *nes- has become irregular and occurs only prefixed.

Do-nès-/до-нѐс- 'bring' has corresponding forms from the present stem: donèsēm/донѐсēм. Its infinitive-stem forms are dò-n(ij)ē-ti/дòн(иj)ē-ти, dònio/дòнио (dòneo/дòнео) dòn(ij)ēla/дòн(иj)ēла, donè-soh/донѐсох, dònese/дòнесе or dòn(ij)ēh/дòн(иj)ēх, dòn(ij)ē/дòн(иj)ē, donèsen/донѐсен or dòn(ij)ēt/дòн(иj)ēт, dòn(ij)ēvši/дòн(иj)ēвши.

T and *d* stems: do-vèd-ēm/до-вѐд-ēм 'lead in', infinitive dòvesti/дòвести, dòveo/дòвео, dòvela/дòвела (*tl, dl* become *l*). Ìd-ēm/ѝд-ēm 'go' has infinitive ìći/ѝħи, *l*-participle ìšao/ѝшао ìšla/ѝшла, ìdoh/ѝдох. Prefixed forms have *đ* (‹ *jd): nádēm/нáħēм 'find', infinitive náći/нáħи, nàšao/нàшао nàšla/нàшла, nádoh/нáħох nàđe/нàħe, nàđen/нàħен, nàšāvši/нàшāвши. *Čьt- is lost ('to read' is čìtati/чѝтати čìtām/чѝтāм, of the -a-je-/-a-je- type). *Jad- is lost ('to ride' is jàhati/jàхати, jàšēm/jàшēм).

P and *b* stems: grèb-ēm/грѐб-ēм 'scratch', grèpsti/грѐпсти, grèbao/грѐбао, grèbla/грѐбла. (*Živ- 'to live' now has the shape žìv(j)eti/жѝв(j)ети, žívīm/жѝвūm.)

K and *g* stems: rèk-/pèк- 'say' has present rèčēm/pèчēм, rèčēš/pèчēш ... rèkū/pèкȳ or, like other perfective consonant stems, joins the ne/не type: rèk-n-ēm/pèк-н-ēм, rèk-n-ēš/pèк-н-ēш ... rèk-n-ū/pèк-н-ȳ. The imperative is rèci/pèци. Infinitive rèći/pèħи, aorist rèkoh/pèкох rèče/pèче, *l*-participle rèkao/pèкао, rèkla/pèкла, participle rèčen/pèчен. One rare verb, 'to thresh', is an *h*-stem: vŕšēm/вŕшēм, vŕšēš/вŕшēш ... vŕhū/вŕхȳ, vŕći/вŕħи or vr(ij)éći/вp(иj)éħи, vŕhoh/

Table 7.13   Conjugation of an -e/e- verb

	Singular	*Plural*

Forms made from present stem
Present

1	trésēm/трéсēм	trésēmo/трéсēмо
2	trésēš/трéсēш	trésēte/трéсēте
3	trésē/трéсē	trésū/трéсȳ

Present adverb trésūći/трéсȳħи
Imperative trési/трéси
Imperfect

1	trésijāh/трéсијāх	trésijāsmo/трéсијāсмо
2	trésijāše/трéсијāше	trésijāste/трéсијāсте
3	trésijāše/трéсијāше	trésijāhu/трéсијāху

Forms made from infinitive stem
Infinitive trésti/трéсти
Aorist

1	trésoh/трéсох	trésosmo/трéсосмо
2	trèse/трȅце	trésoste/трéсосте
3	trèse/трȅце	trésoše/трéсоше

L-participle masculine singular trȇsao/трȇсао, feminine singular trésla/трéсла
(further see table 7.12).
Passive participle trésen/трéсен
Past adverb (po)trésāvši/(по)трéсāвши

вр̀хох, vȑše/вр̀ше, vȑhao/вр̀хао vȑhla/вр̀хла, vȑšen/вр̀шен. (Vȑšiti/
вр̀шити, vȑšīm/вр̀шūм 'to perform; thresh' is much more frequent.)

N and m stems have infinitive stem in -ē-: pȍ-čn-ēm/пȍ-чн-ēм 'to begin', pòčēti/пòчēти, participle pȍčēt/пȍчēт. Stàn-ēm/стȁн-ēм 'to stand, step, stop' has stàti/стȁти, stàh/стȁх, stà/стȁ, stȁo/стȁо stàla/стȁла.

R stems: ȕ-mr-ēm/ȳ-мр-ēм 'die', ùmr(ij)ēti/ȳмр(иј)ēти, l-participle ȕmro/ȳмро ȕmȓla/ȳмȓла.

A few -ra- stems have infinitive -a- alongside present -e-, like bȅr-ēm/бȅр-ēм 'pluck', bràti/брȁти; also zòv-ēm/зȍв-ēm 'call', zvàti/звȁти. (*Sъsa- 'suck' is now sȉsati/сȉсати, sȉšēm/сȉшēм or sȉsām/сȉсāм.)

Themes in -ne-/-не-. These have infinitive stem in -nu-/-ну-, usually identifiable as a suffix. An example is dȉgn-ēm/дȉгн-ēм 'raise' (< *dvig-), imperative dȉgni/дȉгни, infinitive dȉgnuti/дȉгнути, dȉgnuh/дȉгнух, dȉgnu/дȉгну, dȉgnuo/дȉгнуо dȉgnula/дȉгнула, dȉgnut/дȉгнут, dȉgnūvši/дȉгнȳвши. This, like many consonant -nu-/-ну- verbs, has alternative forms lacking -nu-/-ну-: dȉći/дȉħи (infinitive like stems in k, *g*), dȉgoh/дӥгох, dȉže/дӥже, dȉgao/дӥгао, dȉgla/дӥгла, dȉgāvši/ дӥгāвши. No alternatives exist for -nu-/-ну- preceded by vowel: minēm/ мӥнēм 'pass', mínuti/мӥнути, mínuh/мӥнух, minū/мӥнӯ, mínuo/ мӥнуо, mínula/мӥнула, mínūvši/мӥнӯвши. The few imperfective verbs can make an imperfect: tòn-ēm/тȍн-ēм 'sink', tònuti/тȍнути, tònjāh/ тȍњāх.

Themes in -je-/-je-. The *-j-* appears on the surface (after a vowel: table 7.14) or causes old jotation (after a consonant: section 2.2). Imperative -i/ -и is dropped after surface *-j.*

Like čȕ-ti/чӯ̀-ти čȕ-jēm/чӯ̀-jēm 'to hear' are krȉ-ti/крӥ-ти, krȉ-jēm/ крӥ-jēm (‹ **kryti*) 'to hide', bȉ-ti/бӥ-ти, bȉ-jēm/бӥ-jēm 'to beat' and others. Passive participles take -t/-т, -ven/-вен or -jen/-jен: krȉt/крӥт or s-krȉven/с-крӥвен, bȉjen/бӥjен. ('To sing' is now p(j)èva-ti/ п(j)èва-ти p(j)èvām/п(j)èвāм.) Two -je-/-je- present verbs involve metathesis in the infinitive stem: klȁ-ti/клȁ-ти (‹ **kol-ti*) kòljēm/кȍљēм 'to slaughter', ml(j)ȅ-ti/мљȅ-ти or млȅ-ти (‹ **mel-ti*) mèljēm/мȅљēм 'to grind'. (**Bor-* is now bòriti se/бȍрити се, bòrīm se/бȍрӣм се 'to struggle'.)

The largest subset (Matešić 1965–7 shows over 5,000 items) of vowel- je-/-je- presents are those with a/a. Thanks to the contraction of *-aje-* into *-ā-*, their present tenses, for instance the rarely used verb d(j)èla-ti/ д(j)èла-ти 'to act', go d(j)èlām/д(j)èлāм d(j)èlāš/д(j)èлāш d(j)èlā/ д(j)èлā, but third person plural d(j)èlajū/д(j)èлаjӯ.

A similar but tiny type is ùm(j)eti/ӯ̀м(j)ети 'to know how to', present stem **umě-je-* › ekavian contracted ùmēm/ӯ̀мēм, ùmēš/ӯ̀мēш ... ùmejū/

Table 7.14   Conjugation of a -je-/-je- verb

Forms made from present stem
Present čȕjēm/чӯ̀jēm (like trésēm/трéсēм)
Present adverb čȕjūći/чӯ̀jӯħи
Imperative čȕj/чӯ̀j
Imperfect čȕjāh/чӯ̀jāх (like trésijāh/трéсиjāх)

Forms made from infinitive stem
Infinitive čȕti/чӯ̀ти
Aorist

	Singular		Plural
1	čȕh/чӯ̀х		čȕsmo/чӯ̀смо
2	čȕ/чӯ̀		čȕste/чӯ̀сте
3	čȕ/чӯ̀		čȕše/чӯ̀ше

L-participle čȕo/чӯ̀о, čȕla/чӯ̀ла (as table 7.12)
Passive participle čȕ-v-en/чӯ̀-в-ен
Past adverb čȕvši/чӯ̀вши

ỳmejȳ, ijekavian ùmijēm/ỳмиjēм, ùmijēš/ỳмиjēш ... ùmijū/ỳмиjȳ; the imperative is ùmēj/ỳмēj, ùmīj/ỳмиj. *L*-participles are ekavian ùmeo/ ỳмео, ùmela/ỳмела, ijekavian ùmio/ỳмио, ùmjela/ỳмjела.

Consonant -je-/-je- presents all have -*a*- in the infinitive stem, which is lost in the present. Consonants undergo jotation: infinitive kázati/кáз-а-ти 'to say', present *kaz-je-m → kâžēm/кâжēм. The accent change, widespread in this subtype, lends credence to a description with synchronic truncation of the *a*. The type may be termed productive, to the extent that the suffix -isa-/-иса- used for adapting loan verbs (section 5.3) has present -išē-/-ишē-. Vowel alternations between infinitive and present have been lost (*pьsa- yields písati/пи́сати, pišēm/пи́шēм 'to write'; *jьma- has become ùzimati/ỳзимати, ùzimām/ỳзимāм or ùzimljēm/ỳзимљēм 'to take', the imperfective of ùzēti/ỳзēти, ȕzmēm/ỳзмēм). However, one new alternation has arisen: *sьla- is now slȁ-ti/слȁ-ти, šȁljēm/ шȁљēм 'to send'.

Presents from -va-/-ва- infinitives, however, almost never show jotation; rather, there is alternation with -ujē-/-yjē-. Some 1,000 infinitive stems in -ova-ti/-ова-ти like daròva-ti/дарòва-ти 'to donate' and a dozen in -eva-ti/-ева-ти like mačèvati se/мачèвати се 'to fence' have presents dàrujēm/дàруjēм, -ujēš/-yjēш ... -ujū/-yjȳ. Almost 2,000 derived imperfectives in -íva-ti/-и́ва-ти, a Serbo-Croat innovation, also have -ujē-/-yjē-: kazívati/казѝвати, kàzujēm/кàзуjēм ... -ujū/-yjȳ 'to tell'. Serbo-Croat has regularized *-ьvati verbs into -ùvati/-ỳвати with the same alternation: pljùvati/пљ̀ỳвати, pljȕjēm/пљ̀ȳjēм ... pljȕjū/пљ̀ȳjȳ 'to spit'.

A similar alternation -áva-/-áва- ~ -ājē-/-ājē- (without contraction to -*ā*-) occurs in dávati/дáвати imperfective 'to give', dâjem/дâjēм ... dâju/ дâjȳ; similarly poznávati/познáвати 'to be acquainted with' and other imperfectives of prefixed forms of znàti/знàти 'to know'.

Stems like sȉjati/сȉjати, ekavian sèjati/сèjати 'to sow' have presents without double *jj*; ijekavian sȉjēm/сȉjēм ... sȉjū/сȉjȳ, ekavian sèjēm/ сèjēм ... sèjū/сèjȳ.

Themes in -i-/-и-. The infinitives may have -i-ti/-и-ти: mòliti/мòлити 'to ask, pray' (table 7.15), -(j)e-ti/-(j)е-ти: vȉd(j)eti/вȉд(j)ети 'to see' or (after a palatal) -a-ti/-а-ти: dȑžati/дȑжати 'to hold'. The first subtype is large (over 6,000) and productive. The other two are smaller, a few hundred stems, even though Serbo-Croat has shifted the de-adjectival type *zelen-ě-ti, *zelen-ě-je- here: zelèn(j)eti/зелèнети or зелèњети, zelènīm/зелèнӣм 'to turn green'.

The -(j)e-/-(j)e and palatal -a-/-a subtypes have imperfects vȉđāh/ вȉђāх, dȑžāh/дȑжāх, aorists vȉd(j)eh/вȉд(j)ех, dȑžah/дȑжах, *l*-participles ijekavian vȉdio/вȉдио, vȉdjela/вȉдjела, ekavian vȉdeo/ вȉдео, vȉdela/вȉдела, dȑžao/дȑжао, dȑžāla/дȑжāла, passive participles

Table 7.15   Conjugation of an -i-/-и- verb

Singular	*Plural*

Forms made from present stem
Present
1	mòlīm/мо̀лӣм	mòlīmo/мо̀лӣмо
2	mòlīš/мо̀лӣш	mòlīte/мо̀лӣте
3	mòlī/мо̀лӣ	mòlē/мо̀ле̄

Present adverb mòlēći/мо̀ле̄ħи
Imperative mòli/мо̀ли
Imperfect mòljāh/мо̀љāх (like trésijāh/тре́сиjāх)

Forms made from infinitive stem
Infinitive mòliti/мо̀лити
Aorist
1	mòlih/мо̀лих	mòlismo/мо̀лисмо
2	mòlī/мо̀лӣ	mòliste/мо̀листе
3	mòlī/мо̀лӣ	mòliše/мо̀лише

L-participle mòlio/мо̀лио, mòlila/мо̀лила
Passive participle mòlj-en/мо̀љ-ен
Past adverb (za)mòlīvši/(за)мо̀лӣвши

---

vìđen/вѝħен, dȑžān/дȑжāн, past adverbs vìd(j)ēvši/вѝд(j)ēвши, dȑžāvši/дȑжāвши. The spread of old jotation (like *d* → *đ*: section 2.2) to imperfects and passive participles of the -(j)e/-(j)e subtype is a Serbo-Croat innovation.

Hòditi/хо̀дити 'to walk' is like mòliti/мо̀лити: hòdīm/хо̀дӣм ... hòdē/хо̀де̄, imperfect hòdāh/хо̀дāх, participle pòhođen/по̀хоħен 'visited'. *Vel-ě-* is defective, found only in the present: vèlīm/вѐлӣм ... vèlē/вѐле̄ 'say'. *Slyša-* has become an *-ā-* present: slìšati/слѝшати, slìšām/слѝшāм 'to quiz'. 'To sleep' is now spávati/спа́вати, spávām/спа́вāм, but prefixed zàspati/за̀спати 'to fall asleep' has the -i-/-и- present zàspīm/за̀спӣм.

Athematic presents. Apart from bīti/бӣти 'to be', none remain in Serbo-Croat.

'To be' is noteworthy for having an extra present tense (table 7.16). Jèsam/jѐсам, clitic sam/сам is imperfective, whereas bùdēm/бу̀дēм is perfective and imperfective: it can denote 'typical action', but otherwise occurs only in kȁd/кȁд or ȁko/ȁко clauses, da/да₂ clauses and as an auxiliary for the future II. The imperative is bùdi/бу̀ди, the present adverb bùdūći/бу̀дӯħи, from the 'extra' stem. The imperfect is ijekavian bìjāh/бѝjāх or bjèh/бjȅх, ekavian bèjāh/бѐjāх, bȅh/бȅх. Other forms are regular from the stem bí-/би́-.

'To eat' is a regular -e-/-e- present, jèdēm/jѐдēм, infinitive jèsti/jѐсти.

Table 7.16   Presents of bȉti/бити

	Full	Clitic	Negated	'Extra'
Singular				
1	jèsam/jècaм	sam/caм	nísam/нйcaм	bȕdēm/бȳдēм
2	jèsi/jècи	si/cи	nísi/нйcи	bȕdēš/бȳдēш
3	jȅst(e)/jȅcт(e)	je/je	nìje/нйje	bȕdē/бȳдē
Plural				
1	jèsmo/jècмo	smo/cмo	nísmo/нйcмo	bȕdēmo/бȳдēмo
2	jèste/jècтe	ste/cтe	níste/нйcтe	bȕdēte/бȳдēтe
3	jèsu/jècy	su/cy	nísu/нйcy	bȕdū/бȳдȳ

'To give' is a regular -je-/-je- present, dȁti/дȁти, dâm/дâм ... dàjū/дàjȳ, though an alternative present exists with -d-e-/-д-е-: dádēm/дáдēм, -ēš/ -ēш ... dádū/дáдȳ. Similarly regular but with parallel -d-e-/-д-е- present forms are: znȁti/знȁти 'to know (persons or information)' znâm/знâм ... znȁjū/знȁjȳ or znádēm/знáдēм ... znádū/знáдȳ, ìmati/ѝмати 'to have' ìmâm/ѝмâм ... ìmajū/ѝмajȳ or imádēm/имáдēм ... imádū/имáдȳ (but negated present nêmâm/нêмâм ... némajū/нéмajȳ). *Vĕdĕti, *vĕmь 'know' is lost.

A verb with suppletive stems is 'want, will'. The infinitive is ht(j)èti/ xт(j)èти, with matching aorist and *l*-participle (ijekavian htȉo/xтȉo, htjèla/xтjèла). The presents are as in table 7.17; considerable accentual variation exists in practice.

Table 7.17   Presents of ht(j)èti/xт(j)èти

	Full	Clitic	Negated
Singular			
1	hòću/xòħy	ću/ħy	néću/нéħy
2	hòćeš/xòħeш	ćeš/ħeш	néćeš/нéħeш
3	hòće/xòħe	će/ħe	néće/нéħe
Plural			
1	hòćemo/xòħeмo	ćemo/ħeмo	néćemo/нéħeмo
2	hòćete/xòħeтe	ćete/ħeтe	néćete/нéħeтe
3	hòćē/xòħē	ćē/ħē	néćē/нéħē

3.3   Derivational morphology
The most thorough treatment, including productivity information, is Babić (1986), relied on throughout this chapter.

3.3.1   Major patterns of noun derivation
These are suffixal; there is also compounding and prefixation. Character-

istic for Serbo-Croat are zero-suffixed nouns from verb roots: nápad/ нáпад 'attack' (nàpasti/нàпасти, nàpad-n-ēm/нàпад-н-ēм 'to attack'). The verbal noun in -(ē)nje/-(ē)ње, -će/-ħe is highly productive from imperfective verbs in the meaning of an action. As a concrete act or product it is derived from some perfectives (and a few imperfectives) and has accent -ánje/-áње, -énje/-éње, -V́će/-V́ħe: izdánje/издáње 'edition' (versus izdávānje/издáвāње from imperfective, 'publishing'). Further typical deverbal nouns are in -(é)tak/-(é)так (a ~ Ø alternation): počétak/ почé ħак 'beginning' (pòčēti/пòчēти 'to begin'), -nja/-ња: šétnja/ шéтња 'stroll' from šétati (se)/шéтати (се) 'to stroll' and -āj/-āj: dògađāj/дòгаħāj 'event' from dogáđati se/догáħати се 'to occur'.

In de-adjectival abstracts, -ōst/-ōст '-ness' is most productive: naívnōst/наúвнōст 'naïveté'. -oća/-oħa partly replaces -ota/-ота: pun-òća/пун-òħa 'fullness'.

Abstracts of many sorts and sources are made with -stvo/-ство: sús(j)ed-stvo/сýс(j)ед-ство 'neighbour-hood', piján-stvo/пијáн-ство 'drunken-ness', zakon-o-dáv-stvo/закон-о-дáв-ство 'law-giving, legislation' (zákon/зáкон 'law').

Productive person noun suffixes are -lac/-лац and -telj/-тељ, which compete somewhat: slùšalac/слỳшалац, slùšatelj/слỳшатељ 'listener'; further, -āč/-āч and -ār/-āр, both particularly from -ati/-ати verbs: predávāč/предàвāч 'lecturer', vlàdār/влàдāр 'ruler' (predávati/ предáвати 'to lecture', vládati/влáдати 'to rule'). Foreign -ik normally becomes -ičār/-ичāр: krìtičār/крùтичāр. -ār/-āр, -ist(a)/-ист(a), -āš/ -āш and -ac/-ац are frequent denominals: zlàtār/злàтāр 'goldsmith' (zlâto/злâто 'gold'), flàut-ist(a)/флàут-ист(a), folklòrāš/фолклòрāш 'folkdancer', tekstílac/текстúлац 'textile worker'. The Turkish suffix -džija/-џија is somewhat productive: tramvàjdžija/трамвàjџија 'tram-driver'.

Inhabitant name suffixes include -(j)anin/-(j)анин, -čanin/-чанин, both of which lose -in/-ин in the plural (see page 320), -ac/-ац: Kanàda/ Канàда, Kanàđanin/Канàħанин; Ljubljàna/Љубљàна, Ljubljánčanin/ Љубљáнчанин; Ìndija/Ѝндија, Indíjac/Индúјац. A few names have Turkish -lija/-лија: Saràjlija/Сарàjлија 'Sarajevo resident'.

Feminine formation is typically with -ica/-ица: učitèlj-ica/учитèљ-ица 'teacher'; šêf/шêф 'chief', šèfica/шèфица. -ka/-ка occurs bound to particular suffixes: vlàdārka/влàдāрка, Ljubljánčānka/Љубљáнчāнка. -inja/-иња attaches to velars: bòg-inja/бòг-иња 'goddess', Ùzbek-inja/ Ỳзбек-иња; and -kinja/-киња often to final t: kandìdāt-kinja/ кандùдāт-киња 'candidate', feminìstkinja/феминùсткиња 'feminist'.

Diminutives of masculine o-stems take -ić/-иħ or -čić/-чиħ: brôd/ брôд 'ship', bròdić/брòдиħ; sîn/сûн 'son', sìnčić/сùнчиħ. Feminines in -a/-a get -ica/-ица: vòda/вòда, vòdica/вòдица. Neuters take -ce/-це or various extended versions: písmo/пúсмо 'letter', pisámce/писáмце;

gŕlo/гр̏ло 'throat', gŕl-ašce/гр̏л-ашце. Masculines and feminines add neuter -če/-че (stem -čet/-чет-) in the meaning 'young ...': čòbanin/чо̀банин 'shepherd', čòbānče/чо̀ба̄нче 'shepherd boy'; gȕska/гу̏ска 'goose', gȕšče/гу̏шче 'gosling'. Hypocoristics shorten names to (consonant-) vowel–consonant and add -o/-о, -e/-е or -a/-а: Ívo/И́во or Íve/И́ве from ÌvanÌван, Mára/Ма́ра, Máre/Ма́ре or Mája/Ма́ja from Màrija/Ма̀рија. Augmentatives take -ina/-ина and extensions: bròd-ina/бро̀д-ина 'big boat', sob-ètina/соб-ѐтина 'big room'.

First members of compounds can be nouns (often with object interpretation), adjectives or combining forms: brod-o-grádnja/брод-о-гра́дња 'ship-building = building of ships', nov-o-grádnja/нов-о-гра́дња 'new construction', vȅle-mājstor/вȅле-ма̄јстор 'grand master'.

3.3.2   Major patterns of adjective derivation

These involve suffixation. Descriptive adjectives can be predicated and compared. They distinguish long and short declension, and their citation form is short, as míran/ми́ран 'peaceful'. Relational adjectives do not distinguish long/short. Their citation form is long (mìrōvnī/мѝро̄внӣ 'peace ...') except for certain possessives (-ov/-ов, -ev/-ев, -in/-ин). Relational adjectives are often replaceable by modifying phrases: mìrōvnī ȕgovōr/мѝро̄внӣ ȳгово̄р or ȕgovōr о míru/ȳгово̄р о ми́ру 'treaty of peace'.

The most widespread descriptive adjective suffix is -an/-ан ($a \sim \emptyset$ alternation: sections 2.1 and 2.2), as in míran/ми́ран above, with variants -en/-ен, -ven/-вен. Clearly deverbal is prȋvlāčan/прȋвлачан 'attractive' from privláčiti/привла́чити 'to attract'. Other descriptive suffixes have more specific semantics, as -(lj)iv/-(љ)ив '-able, given to ...': plȁkati/пла̏кати 'to cry', plȁčljiv/пла̏чљив 'tearful'. Compounds are formed with -an/-ан or (particularly with body-part nouns in second place) without suffix: kratk-ò-trāj-an/кратк-о̀-тра̄ј-ан 'short-lasting', kratk-ò-rep/кратк-о̀-реп 'short-tailed'.

The most general relational-adjective suffix is -nī/-нӣ, with extended forms -enī/-енӣ, -anī/-анӣ, -ovnī/-овнӣ and others: drúštvo/дру́штво 'society', drùštvenī sȅktor/дру̀штвенӣ сȅктор 'the public sector'. A deverbal example is prodúžiti/проду́жити 'to extend': pròdužnī gàjtan/про̀дужнӣ га̀јтан 'extension cord'; a dephrasal is star-o-záv(j)et-nī/стар-о-за́в(ј)ет-нӣ 'Old Testament' from stárī/ста̄рӣ 'old', záv(j)et/за́в(ј)ет 'testament'.

-Skī/-скӣ, its allomorphs (s/с, z/з + skī/скӣ = -skī/-скӣ, š/ш, ž/ж, h/х, g/г + skī/скӣ = -škī/-шкӣ, с/ц, č/ч, k/к + skī/скӣ = čkī/-чкӣ, ć/ħ + skī/скӣ = -ćkī/-ħкӣ) and extended forms (-ačkī/-ачкӣ, -inskī/-инскӣ, -ovskī/-овскӣ ...) form ethnic and geographical adjectives: Amèrika/Амѐрика, amèričkī/амѐричкӣ; and are also the relational suffix for most personal nouns: stùdentskī žìvot/сту̀дентскӣ жи̏вот 'student life'. The -skī/-ски set encroaches onto the general relational territory of -nī/-ни, being predictable on stems in -ij/-иj, -ija/-иjа, -ika/ -ика, -n/-н, -ar/-ар and other finals: filozòfija/филозòфија, filòzofskī/ филòзофски; bètōn/бèтōн 'concrete', bètōnskī/бèтōнски.

Animal names typically take -jī/-jи (-ijī/-иjи): mȉš/мȉш 'mouse', mȉšjī/мȉшjи (mȉšjā rùpa/мȉшjā рỳпа 'mousehole'). There is overlap with other types: d(j)èca/д(j)èца 'children' has d(j)èčjī/д(j)èчjи; orangùtan/орангỳтан, orangùtanskī/орангỳтански 'orangutan'.

Possessive adjectives from nouns referring to definite singular possessors (section 4.9) take -ov/-ов for *o*-stem nouns, -ev/-ев for soft *o*-stems and -in/-ин for *a*-stems: stùdentov/стỳдентов 'student's', mûžev/мûжев 'husband's', žènin/жènин 'wife's', Tȇslin/Тȇслин 'Tesla's'. Nouns in -*v* take -ljev/-љев: Jȁkov/Jȁков 'Jacob', Jȁkovljev/Jȁковљев.

Plant names of all declensions favour -ov/-ов: lȋpa/лȋпа 'linden', lȋpov čȁj/лȋпов чȁj 'linden tea'.

Adverbs of place and time form adjectives with -njī/-њи, -šnjī/-шњи, -ašnjī/-ашњи: jȕtro/jȕтро 'morning', jȕtārnjī/jȕтāрњи; jùčē(r)/jỳчē(р) 'yesterday', jučèrašnjī/jучèрашњи.

Relationals from verbs (or from verbal nouns) can be in -aćī/-аћи: pìsaćī stȏ(l)/пѝсаћи стȏ(л) 'writing table' from písati/пѝсати 'to write' or písānje/пѝсāње 'writing'.

3.3.3   Major patterns of verb derivation

These are suffixation and prefixation. Suffixes forming verbs from nouns include -ati/-ати (present -ām/-āм), -iti/-ити, -írati/-ѝрати (bi-aspectual, from foreign bases), -ovati/-овати (alternant -evati/-евати: domestic and foreign, often bi-aspectual): kârtati se/кȁртати се 'to play cards, gamble with cards', bòjiti/бȍjити 'to paint, colour with paint/dye (bòja/бȍja)', torpedírati/торпедѝрати 'to torpedo', gostòvati/гостò-вати 'to be a guest', mačèvati se/мачèвати се 'to fence, fight with swords (mȁč/мȁч)'.

More rarely, denominals arise by prefixation–suffixation: po-latín-iti/ по-латѝн-ити 'to Latinize', obèšumiti/обèшумити 'to deforest' (o-bez-šum-iti/о-без-шум-ити, šȕma/шȕма 'forest').

Verbs from (descriptive) adjectives mean (1) 'to become ...', (2) 'to make something ...'. Of productive suffixes, -(j)eti/-(j)ети (present -īm/ -ӣм, section 3.2.2) has only the first meaning: gládn(j)eti/гла́днети or гла́дњети 'to become hungry (gládan/гла́дан)'. -iti/-ити yields both transitive kȉseliti/кȉселити 'to make sour (kȉseo/кȉсео)', with intransitive kȉseliti se/кȉселити се 'to become sour', and intransitive ćòraviti/ ћȍравити 'to become blind (ćòrav/ћȍрав)'. -ati/-ати (present -ām/-āм), with both meanings, often attaches to comparatives: jàčati/jàчати '(1) to become stronger; (2) to strengthen something' from jȁčī/ jȁчи 'stronger' (jȁk/jȁк 'strong'). Prefixation–suffixation is widespread:

o-sposòb-iti/о-спосо̀б-ити 'to make something/someone capable' from spòsoban/спо̀собан 'capable', o-bes-hrábr-iti/о-бес-хра́бр-ити 'to discourage' from hrábar/хра́бар 'brave'.

Verbs are made from verbs by prefixation, suffixation or use of the 'reflexive' particle se/ce. Se/ce can intransitivize a verb, as držati/д𝑟жати 'to hold', držati se/д𝑟жати ce with genitive 'to hold to'; dropping a basic verb's se/ce can transitivize it, as priblížiti se/приближити ce 'to come nearer', priblížiti/приближити 'to bring nearer'.

Prefixation yields a perfective verb which may or may not coincide semantically or syntactically with the input verb (section 3.2.1). U-/у- may represent old *u- 'away', as uklòniti/укло̀нити 'to eliminate', but usually means 'in', as ùt(j)erati/ у̀т(j)ерати 'to drive in'.

Apart from aspect changes, suffixation of verbs may also yield iteratives (section 3.2.1) and diminutives, for which the suffixes mostly involve k/к, c/ц and r/p: gȕr-kati/гу̑р-кати 'to push a little': p(j)ev-ùckati/п(j)е-ву̀цкати 'to hum' from p(j)èvati/п(j)е̏вати 'to sing'; šet-kàrati/шет-ка̀рати 'to stroll a little (somewhat pejorative)' from šétati/ше́тати.

Verb compounds are scanty; compare kriv-o-tvòr-iti/крив-о-тво̀р-ити 'to counterfeit'.

4 Syntax

4.1 Element order in declarative sentences

Element order is determined largely by topic–comment structure. The topic in unmarked order precedes the comment. The simplest situation, a frequent one, is subject = topic, verb + object = comment. If subject and object are both known to the participants in conversation and the verb has unsurprising meaning, the order is SVO.

Slȃvko vȋdī Ȍlgu./Слȃвко вȋдӣ О̏лгу.
'Slavko sees Olga.'

If arguments and predicate are all new in the discourse, the order is again SVO.

Jèdan stùdent vȍdī pìtomu óvcu./Jèдан сту̀дент во̏дӣ пѝтому о́вцу.
'A student is leading a tame sheep.'

An element can be made the information focus by placing it sentence-finally:

Slȃvko Ȍlgu *prèzirē.*/Слȃвко О̏лгу *прѐзирē̄.*
'Slavko *despises* Olga.'

Focused subjects, such as answers to questions, can be final as well.

Q: (T)kȍ dònosī šūnku?/(T)кȍ дòносӣ шŷнку?
   'Who is bringing the ham?'
A: Šūnku dònosī *Slâvko.*/Шŷнку дòносӣ *Слȃвко.*
   '*Slavko* is bringing the ham.'

Serbo-Croat has a constraint against separating post-verbal subjects from verbs, so we would not normally find ?dònosī šūnku Slȃvko/ дòносӣ шŷнку Слȃвко. A topicalized element is put first, as 'Olga' in the second sentence:

Slâvko vȉdī Ȍlgu. *Ȍlgu* vȉdīmo i mî./Слȃвко вȉдӣ Ȍлгу. *Ȍлгу* вȉдӣмо и мȋ.
'Slavko sees Olga. We too see *Olga*.'

Certain lexical elements (like nȅšto/нȅшто 'something', tô/тô 'this, that', čòv(j)ek/чòв(j)ек in the meaning 'one') have inherent low prominence (contributions to Filipović 1975: 97–104), and are sentence-final only under emphasis. They normally display SOV order:

?Slȃvko vȉdī nȅšto. Slȃvko nȅšto vȉdī. (or: Slȃvko vȉdī *nȅšto.*)/
?Слȃвко вȉдӣ нȅшто. Слȃвко нȅшто вȉдӣ. (or: Слȃвко вȉдӣ *нȅшто.*)
'Slavko sees something.'

Departures from topic–comment order yield special effects, such as extra emphasis on a preposed comment:

vȉdī Slȃvko./ВЍДӢ Слȃвко.
'Slavko DOES see.'

Adverbs modifying a verb tend to precede it, whereas adverbials of other sorts follow:

Slȃvko jȁsno vȉdī Ȍlgu./Слȃвко jȁсно вȉдӣ Ȍлгу.
'Slavko sees Olga clearly.'
Slȃvko vȉdī Ȍlgu kroz dîm./Слȃвко вȉдӣ Ȍлгу кроз дȋм.
'Slavko sees Olga through the smoke.'

Without an object, unmarked order of subject and verb is still SV:

Slȃvko spâvā./Слȃвко спȃвā.
'Slavko is sleeping.'

However, subjects are frequently put after the verb. One grammaticalized instance is the existential or presentative, announcing the existence or availability of the subject. Here the order is optional time or place frame– verb–subject:

Na stòlu lèžï knjīga./На столу лежй књйга.
'On the table lies (is) a book.'

A suppletive present tense of 'to be' for existentials is ìmā/ѝмā 'there is' (negative nêmā/нêма 'there is not'). It and other tenses of bìti/бйти with a genitive (singular or plural) subject mean 'there is/are some ..., there isn't/aren't any ...':

U friždéru ìmā šūnkē (mȁslīnā)./У фрижидéру ѝмā шȳнкē (мȁслйнā).
'In the refrigerator there is some ham (there are some olives).'

Some speakers use ìmā/ѝмā with nominative singular subjects, while others (particularly in the Croat standard) require je/je:

Na stòlu ìmā (or: je) knjīga./На стòлу ѝмā (or je) књйга.
'On the table there is a book.'

Clitic-placement rules operate within a simple sentence. Almost all Serbo-Croat clitics have corresponding full forms (though se/ce in most uses, those not meaning '... self', has none). Clitic and full personal pronouns were given in table 7.6, of verb forms in tables 7.16 and 7.17. Serbo-Croat clitics are enclitic, forming an accentual group with a preceding word. Clitics display fixed order in a group (contributions to Filipović 1975: 105–34):

I li/ли.
II Auxiliary verbs and present of 'to be' (but not third person singular je/je):
   bih, bi, bi, bismo, biste, bi/бих, би, би, бисмо, бисте, би '(I, you, he/she/it, we, you, they) would'
   ću, ćeš, će, ćemo, ćete, ćē/ħy, ħеш, ħе, ħемо, ħете, ħē '(I, you, he/she/it, we, you, they) will'
   sam, si, _____, smo, ste, su/сам, си, _____, смо, сте, су '(I) have/did, (I) am' and so forth
III Dative pronouns:
   mi, ti, mu, joj, nam, vam, im/ми, ти, му, joj, нам, вам, им '(to) me, you, him/it, her, us, you, them'
IV Accusative/genitive pronouns:
   me, te, ga, je, nas, vas, ih/ме, тс, га, je, нас, вас, их 'me, you, him/it, her, us, you, them'
V se/ce, reflexive pronoun and particle.
VI je/je, third person singular auxiliary and present of 'to be'. Se + je/ce + je usually becomes just se/ce; je/je occasionally drops after me/ме and te/те as well. Je + je/je + je is replaced by ju je/jy je. Examples:

Slâvko će je vȉd(j)eti./Слâвко ħе је вȉд(j)ети.
'Slavko will see her.'
Slâvko ga se (je) bòjao./Слâвко га се (је) бòjao.
'Slavko feared it.'
Òlga mu ju je dála./Òлга му jу је дáла.
'Olga gave her to him.'
Vȋdȋ li je Slâvko?/Вȋдȋ ли је Слâвко?
'Does Slavko see her?'

The clitic group comes in second position in the simple sentence: after the first constituent, or after the first word of the first constituent.

(Mòja sèstra) će dóći u ùtorak./(Mòja cèстра) ħе дóħи у ỳторак.
Mòja će sèstra dóći u ùtorak./Mòja ħе cèстра дóħи у ỳторак.
'My sister will come on Tuesday.'

If the first constituent is comparatively long, as mòja mlȁđā sèstra/мòja млȁħā cèстра 'my younger sister', one can 'exclude it from the count', placing clitics after the (first word of the) next constituent:

Mòja mlȁđā sèstra dóći će u ùtorak./Mòja млȁħā cèстра дóħи ħе у ỳторак.

If the sentence begins with a clause introducer, clitics necessarily come immediately afterward, with no exclusions from the count:

... da će mòja mlȁđā sèstra dóći u ùtorak./... да ħе мòja млȁħā cèстра дóħи у ỳторак.
'... that my younger sister will come on Tuesday.'

Clause introducers are subordinating conjunctions like da/да 'that', relative or interrogative words and coordinating conjunctions (but i/и 'and', a/a 'and, but' do not count).

Ordering of elements within noun phrases is generally fixed (contributions to Filipović 1975: 87–96). Elements before the noun are totalizers ('all', 'every'), demonstratives, possessives, numerals and adjectives, in the order given:

svȉh òvȋh mòjȋh dȅsȇt cȓvenȋh rúžā/свȋх òвȋх мòjȋх дȅсȇт цȓвенȋх рýжā
'(Literally, 'all these my ten red roses.') All these ten red roses of mine.'

Any of these might follow the noun in poetic or expressive style: thus, rúža mòja/рýжа мòja might be a term of endearment. Postposing a numeral does not express approximation.

Elements normally appearing after the noun are genitives, prepositional phrases, relative clauses and complement clauses, in the order given.

knjȉga *Láva Tölstoja* u l(ij)épom ùvezu/књȕга *Лȁва Тȍлстоja* у л(иj)éпōм ỳвезу
'a book *of* (= *by*) *Leo Tolstoy* in a nice binding'

uv(j)erénje *nàprednīh ljúdī da je zèmlja òkrūgla*/ув(ј)ерéње нàпреднӣх љу́дӣ да je зѐмља òкрӯгла
'the belief *of progressive people that the world is round*'
uv(j)erénje *kòjē su ljúdi izražávali da je zèmlja òkrūgla*/ув(ј)ерéње кòjē су љу́ди изражáвали да je зѐмља òкрӯгла
'the belief *which people expressed that the world is round*'

Adjectives and participles with complements usually follow nouns:

knjȉga žúta od stàrosti/књѝга жу́та од стàрости
'a book yellow with age'

But they can precede if their own complements precede them: od stàrosti žúta knjȉga/од стàрости жу́та књѝга.

4.2 Non-declarative sentence types: interrogatives and imperatives

Yes–no questions are sometimes marked by intonation. A characteristic contour involves a drop before and during the accented syllable of the focused word, followed by high pitch on the remainder of the word (the 'reverse pattern': Lehiste and Ivić 1986: chapter 3; see also contributions to Filipović 1975: 172–9):

Slȁ^{vko} vȉdī Òlgu?/Слȁ^{вко} вӣдӣ О̀лгу?
'Does *Slavko* see Olga?'

If no word is especially focused, the reverse pattern goes on the main verb:

Slȁvko vȉ^{dī} Òlgu?/Слȁвко вӣ^{дӣ} О̀лгу?
'Does Slavko see Olga?'

More frequent yes–no question markers are clitic li/ли and sentence-initial dȁ li/дȁ ли. The finite verb (auxiliary if there is one, otherwise the main verb) precedes li/ли immediately and is thus sentence initial:

Vȉdī li Slȁvko Òlgu?/вӣдӣ ли Слȁвко О̀лгу?

A clitic finite verb is replaced in li/ли questions by its non-clitic (full) form:

Hòće li Slȁvko vȉd(j)eti Òlgu?/Хòће ли Слȁвко вӣд(ј)ети О̀лгу?
'Will Slavko see Olga?'

Dȁ li/дȁ ли, which may be regarded as the full form of li/ли, does not constrain the order of the remaining elements. The example above would be: dȁ li će Slȁvko vȉd(j)eti Òlgu?/дȁ ли ће Слȁвко вӣд(ј)ети О̀лгу?

Affirmative answers to yes–no questions of all types can be dȁ/дȁ 'yes', repetition of the finite verb (in full form) or both:

Q: Slâvko vȉ^{dȋ} Ȍlgu? Vȉdī li Slâvko Ȍlgu? Dȁ li Slâvko vȉdī Ȍlgu?/Слȃвко вȉ^{дȋ}
   Ȍлгу? Вȉдȋ ли Слȃвко Ȍлгу? Дȁ ли Слȃвко вȉдȋ Ȍлгу?
A: Dȁ./Дȁ. or Vȉdī./Вȉдȋ. or Dȁ, vȉdī./Дȁ, вȉдȋ.
   'Yes. He does. Yes, he does.'
Q: Hȍće li Slâvko vȉd(j)eti Ȍlgu?/Хȍће ли Слȃвко вȉд(j)ети Ȍлгу? Dȁ li će
   Slâvko vȉd(j)eti Ȍlgu?/Дȁ ли ће Слȃвко вȉд(j)ети Ȍлгу?
A: Dȁ./Дȁ. or Hȍće./Хȍће. or Dȁ, hȍće./Дȁ, хȍће.
   'Yes. He will. Yes, he will.'

Negative answers are given with nȅ/нȅ 'no', and/or repetition of the
negated finite verb (recall that paired clitic/full-form verbs have a single
negated form; sections 3.2.1 and 4.6):

Q: Slâvko vȉ^{dȋ} Ȍlgu? Vȉdī li Slâvko Ȍlgu? Dȁ li Slâvko vȉdī Ȍlgu?/Слȃвко вȉ^{дȋ}
   Ȍлгу? Вȉдȋ ли Слȃвко Ȍлгу? Дȁ ли Слȃвко вȉдȋ Ȍлгу?
A: Nȅ./Нȅ. or Nè vidī./Нȅ видȋ. or Nȅ, nè vidī./Нȅ, нȅ видȋ.
   'No. He doesn't. No, he doesn't.'
Q: Hȍće li Slâvko vȉd(j)eti Ȍlgu?/Хȍће ли Слȃвко вȉд(j)ети Ȍлгу? Dȁ li će
   Slâvko vȉd(j)eti Ȍlgu?/Дȁ ли ће Слȃвко вȉд(j)ети Ȍлгу?
A: Nȅ./Нȅ. or Nêće./Нȇће. or Nȅ, nêće./Нȅ, нȇће.

Yes–no questions can be formulated negatively by negating the verb.

Slâvko nè^{vidȋ} Ȍlgu?/Слȃвко нè^{видȋ} Ȍлгу? Nè vidī li Slâvko Ȍlgu?/Нȅ видȋ
li Slâvko Ȍlgu?
'Doesn't Slavko see Olga?'

Answers to such negative questions are

Nȅ, nè vidī./Нȅ, нȅ видȋ.
'No, he doesn't.'

or

dȁ, vȉdī/дȁ, вȉдȋ (probably not merely dȁ/дȁ).

Similar to English 'tag questions', zâr nȅ?/зȃр нȅ? or jè li?/jè ли? can
make yes–no questions from positive or negative statements:

Slâvko vȉdī Ȍlgu, zâr nȅ?/Слȃвко вȉдȋ Ȍлгу, зȃр нȅ?
'Slavko sees Olga, doesn't he?'

Alternative questions contain ili/или 'or' between two or more
elements in what is otherwise a yes–no question:

Vȉdī li Slâvko Ȍlgu ili Dóru?/Вȉдȋ ли Слȃвко Ȍлгу или Дóру?
'Does Slavko see Olga or Dora?'

An answer can be:

Nè vidī Ôlgu nego Dóru./Hè видӣ Ôлгу него Дóру.
'He doesn't see Olga but (rather) Dora.'

or simply: Dóru/Дóру.

WH questions are made with interrogatives such as (t)kô/(т)кô 'who',
čìjī/чѝjӣ 'whose', zâšto/зâшто 'why'. Such words front – come in first
position in the sentence – and can be preceded only by coordinating
conjunctions and prepositions:

Kòga vȉdī Màrija? Kòga Màrija vȉdī?/Kòга вѝдӣ Màрија? Kòга Màрија вѝдӣ?
'Whom does Marija see?'
S kim Màrija râdī?/С кѝм Màрија râдӣ?
'*With* whom does Marija work?'

A WH word (with preposition if any) counts as a sentence-introducer:
clitics follow it immediately.

Kòga je Màrija vȉd(j)ela?/Kòга je Màрија вѝд(j)ела?
'Whom did Marija see?'
S kim ga je vȉd(j)ela?/С кѝм га je вѝд(j)ела?
'With whom did she see him?'

Fronting can separate a WH word from the rest of its phrase:

Kȍliko Slâvko ìmā nȍvācā?/Kȍлико Слâвко ѝмā нȍвāцā?
'How much has Slavko money? (How much money has Slavko?)'

WH words can be conjoined. The resulting WH group fronts:

Kòga i gd(j)ȅ Màrija vȉdī?/Kòга и гд(j)ȅ Màрија вѝдӣ?
'Whom and where does Marija see? (Whom does Marija see and where does she
see him?)'

If there are clitics, their best position is after the first WH word:

Kòga je i gd(j)ȅ Màrija vȉd(j)ela?/Kòга je и гд(j)ȅ Màрија вѝд(j)ела?
'Whom did Marija see and where did she see him?'

They may also be after the group: kòga i gd(j)ȅ je Màrija vȉd(j)ela?/кòга и
гд(j)ȅ je Màрија вѝд(j)ела?
'Multiple' questions can be formed with non-conjoined WH words. In
general all are fronted. Clitics are best placed after the first WH word,
suggesting it differs in syntactic position from the others (Browne 1976):

(T)kô je gd(j)ȅ kòga vȉdio (vȉdeo)?/(Т)кô je гд(j)ȅ кòга вѝдио (вѝдео)?
'Who saw whom where?'

The order of WH words is not fixed; one can also ask, for instance: gd(j)ȅ je (t)kȍ kòga vȉdio (vȉdeo)?/гд(ј)ȅ је (т)кȍ кòга вȉдио (вȉдео)?

All types of direct questions, apart from the intonational yes–no type and the 'tags', can also function as indirect questions, as in the position of object to a predicate:

Nè znȃm dȁ li Slȃvko vȉdī Ȍlgu (vȉdī li Slȃvko Ȍlgu)./Нè знȃм дȁ ли Слȃвко вȉдӣ Ȍлгу (вȉдӣ ли Слȃвко Ȍлгу).
'I don't know whether Slavko sees Olga.'
Nísam sȉgūran (t)kȍ gd(j)ȅ kòga vȉdī./Нѝсам сȉгӯран (т)кȍ гд(ј)ȅ кòга вȉдӣ.
'I am not sure who sees whom where.'

If a question is to be object of a preposition, a form of the pronoun tȍ/тȏ 'it' in the required case is intercalated:

Govòrili smo *o tȍme* dȁ li Slȃvko vȉdī Ȍlgu./Говòрили смо *о тȍме* дȁ ли Слȃвко вȉдӣ Ȍлгу.
'We spoke about it whether Slavko sees Olga.'

In some instances the preposition and pronoun are omissible:

Pítānje *(o tȍme)* dȁ li Slȃvko vȉdī Ȍlgu jȍš nȉje r(ij)ȅšeno./Пȋтāње *(о тȍме)* дȁ ли Слȃвко вȉдӣ Ȍлгу jȍш нȉје р(иј)ȅшено.
'The question (about it) whether Slavko sees Olga is not yet resolved.'

Commands are given in the imperative:

Ȕzmi (plural or formal: Ȕzmite) krȕšku!/Ȳзми (plural or formal: Ȳзмите) крȳшку!
'Take a pear!'

A second-person subject may be omitted or (less commonly) expressed:

Ȕzmi *tî* krȕšku!/Ȳзми *тȋ* крȳшку!
'*You* take a pear!'

Negative imperatives require imperfective aspect:

Ne ùzimāj krȕšku!/Не ỳзимāj крȳшку!
'Don't take a pear.'

except for some verbs of involuntary psychological action:

Ne zabòravi!/Не забòрави!
'Don't forget (perfective)!'

Another, more polite, negative command is with nèmōj/нèмōj (1 PL nèmōjmo/нèмōjмо 'let's not'; 2 PL nèmōjte/нèмōjте) plus infinitive (either aspect):

Nèmōj ùzimati krùške!/Нѐмōj ỳзимати крȳшке!
'Don't take (imperfective) pears.'
Nèmōj ùzēti krùšku!/Нѐмōj ỳзȇти крȳшку!
'Don't take (perfective) a pear.'

Da/да₂ with present clauses can replace the infinitive, especially in the East: nèmōj da ùzimāš (da ùzmēš) krùšku/нѐмōj да ỳзимȃш (да ỳзмȇш) крȳшку! Da/да₂ clauses can also contain a verb not in the second person, as long as its subject is under the control or influence of the person addressed:

Nèmōj da se tô drùgī pût dògodī!/Нѐмōj да се тȏ дрȳгȋ пȗт дȍгодȋ!
Literally, 'Don't that this happens again! (Don't let this happen again!)'

Commands to be performed by another person are given as da/да₂-present or nèka/нѐка-present clauses:

Da Slâvko (ne) ùzimā krùške./Да Слȃвко (не) ỳзимȃ крȳшке.
Nèka Slâvko (ne) ùzimā krùške./Нѐка Слȃвко (не) ỳзимȃ крȳшке.
'Let (may) Slavko (not) take pears.'

Reported commands are formulated as da/да₂-present clauses, in the third person occasionally as nèka/нѐка-present:

Rèkla je da ùzmēm (ùzmēš) krùšku./Рѐкла је да ỳзмȇм (ỳзмȇш) крȳшку.
'She said I (you) should take a pear.'
Rèkla je da (or nèka) Slâvko ùzmē krùšku./Рѐкла је да (or нѐка) Слȃвко ỳзмȇ крȳшку.
'She said Slavko should take a pear.'

4.3 Copular sentences
The main copula is bȉti/бȉти 'to be', used with noun phrase, adjective phrase and adverbial phrase predicates:

Màrija je mòja sèstra./Мȁрија је мȍја сȅстра.
'Marija is my sister.'
Màrija je vr(ij)édna kao pčèla./Мȁрија је вр(иј)ѐдна као пчѐла.
'Marija is hard-working as a bee.'
Màrija je dòbro./Мȁрија је дȍбро.
'Marija is well.'
Kòncert je u ȍsam./Кȍнцерт је у ȍсам.
'The concert is at eight o'clock.'

In the genitive predicate construction, a noun mentions a property of the subject and an adjective specifies that property:

Šèšīr je odgovárajūćē velìčinē./Шȅшȋр је одговȃрајȳћē велȋчинē.
'The hat is (of) the right size.'

The normal case for noun phrase and adjective phrase copular predicates is nominative. The instrumental on these is archaic or literary, never obligatory:

Màrija je učitèljica (učitèljicōm)./Màрija je учитèљица (учитèљицōм).
'Marija is a teacher NOM (a teacher INST).'

Even if the sentence contains a subject in another case, the predicate is nominative:

Làko je Màriji bïti vr(ij)édna./Лȁко је Màрiji бȕти вр(иj)éдна.
'It is easy for Marija (DAT) to be hard-working (NOM).'

If the subject is unexpressed, the copular predicate adjective is nominative masculine singular for arbitrary human referents, otherwise nominative neuter singular.

Vážno je bïti vr(ij)édan./Вȁжно је бȕти вр(иj)éдан.
'It is important (for anyone) to be hard-working (NOM M).'

Bïti/бȕти and other copulas take only short-form adjectives as predicate:

Màrtin je vr(ij)édan./Màртин је вр(иj)éдан.
'Martin is hard-working (SHORT).'

But some adjectives lacking a short form (section 3.1.4) can use their long form:

Màrtin je mālī./Màртин је мȃлӣ.
'Martin is small.'
Ìvan je nàjmanjī./Ѝван је нȃjмањӣ.
'Ivan is the smallest.'

A zero copula is found only in proverbs, titles and other compressed styles:

Obećánje – lúdōm rȁdovānje./Обећáње – лýдōм рȁдовāње.
'A promise (is) joy for a fool. (Don't trust promises.)' (Proverb)

Bïti/бȕти has frequentative bívati/бȕвати 'be from time to time; become; happen':

Màrija je bívala (je pȍčēla bívati) sve vrèdnijā./Màрija је бȕвала (је пȍчēла бȕвати) све врèднийā.
'Marija was becoming (began to be) more and more hard-working.'

A specialized copula for adverbials of place is nàlaziti se/нàлазити се, perfective náći se/нáħи се 'be located, be'.

Škòla se nàlazī dalèko od sèla./Шкòла се нàлазй далèко од сèла.
'The school is located far from the village.'

Òstati/òстати, imperfective òstajati/òстајати 'to remain; to be left, find oneself', taking various predicate types, can mean a continuing state or a changed state:

Vláda je òstala ȕpōrna, ali stùdenti òstajū na tŕgu./Влáда је òстала ȳпōрна, али стỳденти òстајȳ на тŕгу.
'The government remained firm, but the students are staying in the square.'

Pòstati/пòстати, imperfective pòstajati/пòстајати 'to become' takes noun or adjective predicates, both of which can be nominative or instrumental without clear meaning distinctions:

Màrija je pòstala učitèljica (učitèljicōm)./Màрија је пòстала учитèљица (учитèљицōм).
'Marija became a teacher NOM (a teacher INST).'
Situácija pòstajē ȍzbīljna (ȍzbīljnōm)./Ситуáција пòстајē ȍзбйљна (ȍзбйљнōм).
'The situation is becoming serious NOM (serious INST).'

4.4 Coordination and comitativity
Two or more syntactic constituents can be joined by a conjunction to form a constituent of the same type. I/и 'and' joins nouns and noun phrases:

Ìvan i njègova žèna râdē./Ѝван и њègова жèна рâдē.
'Ivan and his wife are working.'

adjectives and adjective phrases:

Tô je plòdan i dòbro pòznāt slȉkār./Тô је плòдан и дòбро пòзнāт слȉкāр.
'He is a productive and well-known painter.'

verbs and verb phrases:

Žívī i stvárā u Ljubljàni./Жи́вӣ и ствâра у Љубљàни.
'He/she lives and works in Ljubljana.'

as well as entire clauses:

Zàuzēt sam i ne mògu vȉšē slȕšati./Зàузēт сам и не мògу вȉшē слȕшати.
'I am busy and I cannot listen any more.'

I/и appears before the last conjunct:

Ìvan, Màrija i Ȁna/Ѝван, Ма̀рија и Ȁна
'Ivan, Marija and Ana'

or can be repeated before all conjuncts after the first:

Ìvan i Màrija i Ȁna/Ѝван и Ма̀рија и Ȁна
'Ivan and Marija and Ana'

or before all, including the first:

I Ìvan i Màrija .../И Ѝван и Ма̀рија ...
'Both Ivan and Marija ...'

'And' taking scope over items grouped by i/и is te/те or kao i/као и:

Ìvan i Màrija, te (or: kao i) Jòsip i Ȁna/Ѝван и Ма̀рија, те (or: као и) Jо̀сип и Ȁна
'Ivan and Marija, and also (as well as) Josip and Ana'

Pa/па is 'and' for temporal succession: 'and then'.
Ȉli/ѝли 'either, or', ni/ни 'neither, nor' have the same distribution as i/и. A/a 'and (on the other hand)' for instances of contrast, joins predicates or clauses and is usually not repeated:

Ròmān je dèbeo, a zanìmljiv./Ро̀ма̄н je де̏бео, а зани̏мљив.
'The novel is thick, and (yet) interesting.'

A/a 'and' is combinable with i/и 'also, too':

Ìvan pùtujē, a i Màrija pùtujē./Ѝван пу̀туjе̄, а и Ма̀рија пу̀туjе̄.
'Ivan is travelling, and Marija is travelling too.'

Stronger contrasts are shown by ali/али 'but', which also appears just once in a series.

Ìvan pùtujē, ali Màrija òstajē kòd kućē./Ѝван пу̀туjе̄, али Ма̀рија о̀стаjе̄ ко̀д ку̏ће̄.
'Ivan is travelling, but Marija is staying home.'

An element of a negative statement is corrected by the conjunction nȅgo/не̏го or vȅć/вȅħ and a following statement:

Ne pùtujē Màrija, nȅgo (vȅć) Ìvan./Не пу̀туjе̄ Ма̀рија, не̏го (вȅħ) Ѝван.
'Marija isn't travelling; rather, Ivan is.'

Agreement with conjoined structures has been studied extensively by Corbett (1983 and other works); briefly summarized, modifiers within a conjoined noun phrase agree with the nearest noun:

Njên òtac i mâjka su dòšli./Његн о̀тац и ма̑jка су до̀шли.
'Her (M SG) father and mother have come (M PL).'

whereas predicates, relative pronouns and anaphoric pronouns are plural and follow gender-resolution rules (neuter plural if all conjuncts are neuter plural, feminine plural – but occasionally masculine plural – if all are feminine, otherwise masculine plural):

Njêna sèstra i mâjka su dòšle./Ње̑на сѐстра и ма̑jка су до̀шле.
'Her sister and mother have come (F PL).'
Njêno d(ij)éte i tèle su dòšli./Ње̑но д(иj)е́те и тѐле су до̀шли.
'Her child (N SG) and calf (N SG) have come (M PL).'

Agreement with the nearest conjunct is also observed, particularly in predicates preceding their subjects.

The comitative construction, 'mother with son' or 'we with son' in the sense 'mother and son', 'I and my son', is unknown. Examples like

Mȃjka sa sȋnom šȇtā./Ма̑jка са сȋном шȇта̄.
'Mother with son strolls.'

have only the nominative constituent as syntactic and semantic subject.

4.5   Subordination

Major types of subordinate clauses are complement (Browne 1987) and relative clauses.

Verbs and other predicates can lexically permit or require various types of complement clause as subjects or as one of their objects. Nouns, adjectives and prepositions can select a clause as object (= complement). Some examples will be given, followed by a classification of complement clause types.

Verb with [subject]:

Iz tòga *proìzlazī* [da je bȉtka ìzgubljena]./Из то̀га *прои̏злазӣ* [да je би̏тка и̏згубљена].
'From this (it) *follows* [that the battle is lost].'

Verb with [object]:

Znȃm [da je bȉtka ìzgubljena]./*Зна̑м* [да je би̏тка и̏згубљена].
'I *know* [that the battle is lost].'

Noun with [complement]:

Stìžū *v(ij)ȇsti* [da je bȉtka ìzgubljena]./Стѝжӯ *в(иј)ȇсти* [да је бȉтка
йзгубљена].
'Are-arriving *reports* [that the battle is lost].'

When a verb, adjective, preposition or noun requires a particular case or
preposition + case on its complement, the intercalated tȏ/тȏ strategy is
used. Ráditi se/ра́дити се 'to be a question/matter of' needs o/o with
locative, as in Rȃdī se o vlȃsti/Ра̑ди се о вла̑сти 'it is a question of
power', and its complement clause behaves accordingly:

Rȃdī se o tȏme [da li je bȉtka ìzgubljena ili ne]./Ра̑ди се о тȏме [да ли је бȉтка
йзгубљена или не].
'It is a question of [whether the battle is lost or not].'

The chief types of complement clause are those introduced by da/да$_1$,
by da/да$_2$, što/што and by question words (section 4.2). The two da/
да take different verb tenses within their clauses. A da/да$_1$ clause, as a
reported statement, can contain any tense usable in a declarative main
clause: any past tense, the future but not the bȕdēm/бу̏де̄м compound
tense (section 3.2.1) and the present but normally only from an imperfective verb.

Znȃm [da je Màrija napísala knjȉgu]./ *Зна̑м* [да је Ма̀рија напи́сала књи̏гу].
'I *know* [that Marija has written a book].'
Čȕo sam [da Màrija pȋšē knjȉgu]./ *Чу̏о сам* [да Ма̀рија пи̑ше̄ књи̏гу].
'I *heard* [that Marija is writing a book].'

Da/да$_2$ with the present of imperfective or perfective verbs expresses
hypothetical, unrealized actions – like the infinitive or subjunctive of other
languages. It has been termed the infinitive substitute.

Žèlīm [da Màrija pȋšē]./ *Жѐлӣм* [да Ма̀рија пи̑ше̄].
'I *want* that Marija write-imperfective (I want her to write).'
Žèlīm [da Màrija nàpīšē knjȉgu]./ *Жѐлӣм* [да Ма̀рија на̀пӣше̄ књи̏гу].
'I want Marija to write-perfective a book.'

Da/да$_2$ represents imperatives in indirect discourse (section 4.2).
Ambiguities can arise between the two da/да.

Rèkli su da Màrija pȋšē./Рѐкли су да Ма̀рија пи̑ше̄.
Da/да$_1$: 'They said that Marija is writing.'
Da/да$_2$: 'They told Marija to write.'

Što/што + statement clauses are factive, usually subordinated to items
expressing an emotional reaction:

Rȁdujēmo se [što smo vas pȍnovo vȉd(j)eli]./Рȁдујēмо се [што смо вас пȍново вȕд(j)ели].
'We are glad [that we have seen you again].'

The infinitive can be used in many of the same positions as the clause types above. It sometimes occurs as subject:

Žȋv(j)eti znȁčī rȁditi./Жȕв(j)ети знȁчȗ рȁдити.
'To live means to work.'

Here the two infinitives have their own understood subject which is unspecified but human.

The most frequent use of the infinitive is as complement to a verb.

Màrija žèlī písati./Мȁрија жèлȗ пȕсати.
'Marija wants to write.'

In almost all such instances the understood subject of the infinitive must be the same as the subject of the main verb. If it is identical to the main verb's object, or different from both, a da/да₂ complement is used instead.

Màrija žèlī da ȉvan pȋšē./Мȁрија жèлȗ да Ȉван пȕшē.
'Marija wants Ivan to write.'

Outside the Croat standard, da/да₂ clauses are frequent even when the same-subject condition holds:

Màrija žèlī da pȋšē./Мȁрија жèлȗ да пȕшē.
'Marija wants to write.'

See discussion of the future tense (cú/ħy + infinitive or da/да₂) in section 3.2.1 and of nèmōj/нèмōj + infinitive or da/да₂ in section 4.2.

Further means of subordination are two verbal adverbs, one verbal noun and a participle. The present adverb (from imperfectives) expresses an action simultaneous with that of the main verb. The past adverb (from perfectives), if preceding the main verb, states a prior action, otherwise the sequence of actions is indeterminate (M. Ivić 1983: 155–76). Both background one action *vis-à-vis* the other, and express accompanying circumstance, manner, means, cause or condition. Normally, the understood subject of a verbal adverb is identical with the subject of the main verb:

Ȏn se vrȁćā s pòsla p(j)ȅvajūći./Ȏн се врȁħā с пȍсла п(j)ȅвајȳħи.
'He returns from work singing' (*he* is singing).

The verbal noun in -(e)nje/-(e)ње, -će/-ħe from imperfective verbs participates in complement structures:

Màrija je pòčēla s písānjem knjȉgē./Мàрија je пȍчēла с пѝсāњем књѝгē.
'Marija has begun with (started) the writing of the book.'

where its subject is the same as that of the main verb. It is also used in nominalizations with either the subject or the object expressed by a genitive:

Písānje stùdenātā je zanìmljivo./Пѝсāње стỳденāтā je занѝмљиво.
'The students' writing is interesting.'
Písānje knjȉgē je bílo téško./Пѝсāње књѝгē je бѝло тéшко.
'The writing of the book was difficult.'

Subject and object can cooccur if the subject is expressed as a possessive adjective:

Màrijino písānje knjȉgē/Màријино пѝсāње књѝгē
'Marija's writing of the book'

or with the infrequent passive-agent phrase od stránē/од стрáнē and genitive:

(?)písānje knjȉgē od stránē Màrijē/пѝсāње књѝгē од стрáнē Màријē
'the writing of the book by Marija'

The verbal noun neutralizes the distinction of verbs with se/ce and verbs without: rȕšēnje kȕćē/рȳшēње кȳħē can be from rȕšiti/рȳшити, as in

Màrija rȕšī kȕću./Màрија рȳшӣ кȳħу.
'Marija destroys the house.'

and from rȕšiti se/рȳшити се:

Kȕća se rȕšī./Кȳħa се рȳшӣ.
'The house falls-down.'

The only participle is the 'passive' one with endings -(e)n/-(e)н, -t/-т. It is made primarily from perfective verbs, also from some imperfectives. It forms a passive construction:

Kȕća je srȕšena./Кȳħa je срȳшена.
'The house has been destroyed.'

An inanimate agent in a passive is expressed with the instrumental. An animate one is preferably omitted, but may be expressed with od/од 'from' or od stránē/од стрáнē 'from the side of' plus genitive:

Kȕća je srȕšena v(j)ȅtrom./Кȳħa je срȳшена в(j)ȅтром.
'The house has been destroyed by the wind.'
(?)Kȕća je srȕšena od (od stránē) nȅprijatelja./Кȳħa je срȳшена од (од стра́нē)
нȅпријатеља.
'The house has been destroyed by the enemy.'

The participle can be in attributive position:

srȕšenā kȕća/срȳшенā кȳħa
'the destroyed house'
kȕća srȕšenā v(j)ȅtrom, v(j)ȅtrom srȕšenā kȕća/кȳħa срȳшенā в(j)ȅтром,
в(j)ȅтром срȳшенā кȳħa
'the house destroyed by the wind' (section 4.1)

Relative clauses, unlike complements, can be attached to any noun phrase. In Serbo-Croat the head of the antecedent phrase determines the relativizers used. If the head is a noun or personal pronoun, the main relativizer is kòjī/кòjū 'which', which agrees with its antecedent in gender and number and takes case endings (section 3.1.4) according to function in the subordinate clause.

čòv(j)ek kòjeg vȉdīm/чòв(j)ек кòjeг вȉдūм
'man which-ACC (= whom) I-see'
čòv(j)ek s kòjīm sam rádio/чòв(j)ек с кòjūм сам рáдио
'man with which-INST I-have worked'

As we see, the relativizer is fronted; as a sentence introducer, clitics (sam/сам) follow it directly. An alternative relativizing strategy introduces the clause with an invariable word što/што 'that': the item agreeing with the antecedent in gender and number is a personal pronoun (in modern usage, always an enclitic, hence not the object of a preposition):

čòv(j)ek što ga vȉdīm/чòв(j)ек што га вȉдūм
'man that him I-see (man whom I see)'

If the antecedent's head is an interrogative, indefinite or demonstrative pronoun in the singular (expressed or dropped), the relativizer is (t)kȍ/(т)кȍ 'who' or declinable što, štȁ/штȍ, штȁ 'what' depending on the human/non-human distinction (Browne 1986: 112–19):

nȅšto što vȉdīm/нȅшто што вȉдūм
'something what I see (that I see)'
nȅšto o čèmu gòvorīm/нȅшто о чèму гòворūм
'something about what-LOC (about which) I speak'
svȁ(t)ko kòga vȉdīm/свȁ(т)ко кòга вȉдūм
'everyone whom I see'

Relative clauses also have (overt or dropped) time adverbials and place phrases as antecedents. A Serbo-Croat speciality is relative clauses on quality- and quantity-expression antecedents (Browne 1986: 102–7):

trȉ kònja, kȍliko ìmā i džokéjā/трȕ кòња, кȍлико ѝмā и џокéjā
'three horses, how-many there-are also of-jockeys (three horses, which is how many jockeys there are too)'
interesàntan ròmān, kàkav je 'Rȁt i mȋr'/интересȁнтан рòмāн, кàкав je 'Рȁт и мȕр'
'interesting novel, what-sort is 'War and Peace' (an interesting novel, which is the sort 'War and Peace' is)'

In Serbo-Croat constraints on extracting elements from subordinate clauses are not clear-cut in many instances. Examples exist with either subject or object of a subordinate clause fronted to the beginning of the upper clause in relativization and in questioning. Here '_____' shows the 'starting position' of the relativized element:

čòv(j)ek kòjī mȉslīm da vas je vȉdio (vȉdeo)/чòв(j)ек кòjȕ мȕслȕм да вас je вȕдио (вȕдео)
'the man who I think that _____ saw you'
čòv(j)ek kòjeg mȉslīm da ste vȉd(j)eli/чòв(j)ек кòjег мȕслȕм да сте вȕд(j)ели
'the man whom I think that you saw _____ '

Judgments are difficult because two alternative constructions are preferred. One is the za/за-topic strategy: the main clause contains a verb of saying or thinking, the preposition za/за 'for' + accusative and a noun phrase which recurs (in any syntactic role whatever) in the subordinate clause.

Za Ìvana gòvorē da ga svȉ pòštujū./За Ѝвана гòворē да га свȕ пòштуjȳ.
'For (about) Ivan₁ they say that him₁ everybody respects.'

(Za/за is not the usual preposition 'about', which is o/о + locative.) This strategy yields a relative clause in which the antecedent is followed by za kòjeg/за кòjег 'for whom, for which' and a lower clause without extraction:

čòv(j)ek za kòjeg mȉslīm da ste ga vȉd(j)eli/чòв(j)ек за кòjег мȕслȕм да сте га вȕд(j)ели
'the man for (about) whom I think that you saw him'
čòv(j)ek za kòjeg mȉslīm da vas je vȉdio (vȉdeo)/чòв(j)ек за кòjег мȕслȕм да вас je вȕдио (вȕдео)
'the man for (about) whom I think that he saw you.'

The same strategy is available for questions. Beside

(T)kò mìslīte da me je zam(ij)énio?/(Т)кò мѝслӣте да ме је зам(иј)е́нио?
'Who do you think that _____ replaced me?'

we can have:

Za kòga mìslīte da me je zam(ij)énio?/За кòга мѝслӣте да ме је зам(иј)е́нио?
'For (about) whom do you think that he replaced me?'

Another strategy formulates each clause as a separate question, with štò/
штò, štã/штã̀ 'what' as object of the main verb:

Štò mìslīte, (t)kò me je zam(ij)énio?/Штò мѝслӣте, (т)кò ме је зам(иј)е́нио?
'What do you think – who replaced me?'

4.6 Negation

Sentence negation is expressed with ne/не on the finite verb (the auxiliary,
if there is one):

Slâvko nè vidī Òlgu./Слâвко нѐ видӣ Òлгу.
'Slavko does not see Olga.'
Slâvko nêće vȉd(j)eti Òlgu./Слâвко нêħе вȉд(ј)ети Òлгу.
'Slavko will-not see Olga.'

Constituent negation is rare, and usually requires explicit statement of the
correct alternative.

Slâvko vȉdī ne *Òlgu* nego *Màriju*./Слâвко вȉдӣ не *Òлгу* него *Màрију*.
'Slavko sees not *Olga* but *Marija*.'

Even then, the normal formulation is as with sentence negation:

Slâvko nè vidī *Òlgu* (nego *Màriju*)./Слâвко нѐ видӣ *Òлгу* (него *Màрију*).
'Slavko doesn't see *Olga* (but *Marija*).'

One can also negate sentences with the negative conjunction nȉti/нѝти
'neither, nor':

Nȉti Slâvko vȉdī Òlgu, nȉti Ìvan vȉdī Màriju./Нѝти Слâвко вȉдӣ Òлгу, нѝти
Ìван вȉдӣ Màрију.
'Neither does Slavko see Olga, nor does Ivan see Marija.'

There is a negative-polarity phenomenon and, separate from it, a sort of
negative agreement. A sentence negated with preposed nȉti/нѝти can
contain indefinite forms made from interrogative pronouns and adverbs by
prefixing i-/и-: ȉ(t)ko/ӣ(т)ко 'anyone', ȉgd(j)e/ӣгд(ј)е 'anywhere' and
the like. (The same items occur in questions, conditional sentences and

second members of comparatives.) A positive sentence could not contain these:

Nȉti je Slȃvko vȉdī, nȉti ȉ(t)ko ȉšta znȃ ò njōj./Нȕти је Слȃвко вȕдȕ, нȕти ȕ(т)ко ȕшта знȃ ò њ̑ōj.
'Neither does Slavko see her, nor does anyone know anything about her.'

In sentences containing ne/не on the verb, i-/и- indefinites add initial n-/ н- to become negative forms: nȉ(t)ko/нȕ(т)ко 'nobody', nȉgd(j)e/ нȕгд(j)е 'nowhere' and so forth. So does the conjunction and particle i/и 'and; also, even': ni/ни 'neither, nor; not ... either, not even'. Several such items can appear together:

Nȉ(t)ko nȉgd(j)e nè vidī nȉkoga./Нȕ(т)ко нȕгд(j)е нè видȕ нȕкога.
'Nobody nowhere not sees nobody (Nobody sees anybody anywhere).'

Unlike the i-/и- set, ni-/ни- words can appear in isolation:

Nȉšta./Нȕшта.
'Nothing.' (Or 'Oh, that's all right.')

Prepositions other than bez/без 'without' split i/и and ni/ни from the rest of the word:

ȉ s kīm, nȉ s kīm; ȉ u čemu, nȉ u čemu/ȕ с кȕм, нȕ с кȕм; ȕ у чему, нȕ у чему
'with anybody, with nobody; in anything, in nothing'

although non-normative usage also has s nȉkīm, u nȉčemu/с нȕкȕм, у нȕчему.

Infinitive complements are occasionally negated:

Nísam mȍgao *ne mȉsliti* na tô./Нȕсам мȍгао *не мȕслити* на тô.
'I couldn't *not think* of it (I couldn't avoid thinking of it).'

but usually a special conjunction ȁ da₂ ne/ȁ да₂ не is used: Nísam mȍgao ȁ da nè mislīm na tô./Нȕсам мȍгао ȁ да нè мислȕм на тô. À da₁ ne/ȁ да₁ не expresses absence of concomitant action:

Ȕšla je ȁ da me nȉje pòzdravila./Ȕшла је ȁ да ме нȕје пòздравила.
'She entered without greeting me.'

When a verb is negated, its accusative object may appear in the genitive. In present-day Serbo-Croat such genitive objects are archaic and elevated in style except in fixed phrases and in two further circumstances: as object of némati/нȅмати (ne + ìmati/не + ȕмати) 'not to have' and when negation is strengthened by ni/ни, nijèdan/нијèдан, nȉkakav/нȕкакав 'not even, not a single, no' (Lj. Popović in Станојчић/Stanojčić et al. 1989: 219). Examples from Менац/Menac (1978):

Fixed phrases:

òbraćati pážnju – ne òbraćati pážnju *or* pážnjē/òбраħати пáжњу – не òбраħати пáжњу *or* пáжњē.
'to pay attention (ACC) – not to pay attention (ACC or GEN)'

Némati/нéмати:

Tàda se s(j)ètio da nēmā revolvéra./Tàда се с(j)ètиo да нēмā револвéра.
'Then he remembered that he didn't have a pistol (GEN).'

Negation strengthened:

ìgrati ȕlogu – ne ìgrati ȕlogu – ne ìgrati nȉkakvē ȕlogē/ѝграти ȳлогу – не ѝграти ȳлогу – не ѝграти нѝкаквē ȳлогē
'to play a role (ACC) – not to play a role (ACC) – to play no role whatever (GEN)'

The subject in negated sentences remains nominative, even in existential sentences (section 4.1):

Ne pòstojī r(j)ešénje./Не пòстojū p(j)ешéње.
'Not exists solution (NOM) (there is no solution).'

Only ne bȉti/не бȳти 'not to be' (present nēmā/нēмā) takes genitive subject:

U sòbi nēma Màrijē./У сòби нēмā Màрijē.
'Marija (GEN) is not in the room.'

4.7 Anaphora and pronouns
The simplest device for referring again to a noun phrase is a personal pronoun agreeing in gender and number: ȏn/ȏн 'he' for masculine gender, òna/òна 'she' for feminine, òno/òно 'it' for neuter, each with its plural. Such a pronoun is available for any antecedent noun phrase headed by a lexical noun, with the limitation that clitic forms (section 3.1.3) are favoured and full forms disfavoured for inanimate antecedents:

čòv(j)ek ... Nè znām ga. Njèga nè znām./чòв(j)ек ... Нè знāм га. Њèга нè знāм.
'man ... I don't know him. *Him* I don't know.'
grȃd ... Nè znām ga. ?Njèga nè znām./грȃд ... Нè знāм га. ?Њèга нè знāм.
'city ... I don't know it. *It* I don't know.'

The personal pronoun agrees with the antecedent, but incompletely. Antecedents can be either +animate or −animate, a distinction vital for choosing the accusative singular ending in the masculine *o*-declension and adjective/pronominal declension:

grâd [−animate]: Vîdīm *grâd òsāmljen.*/гра̏д [−animate]: Ви̏дӣм *гра̏д о̀са̄мљен.*
'city: I see *a city* (ACC) *alone* (ACC).'
čòv(j)ek [+animate]: Vîdīm *čòv(j)ek-a òsāmljen-ōg.*/чо̀в(ј)ек [+animate]: Ви̏дӣм *чо̀в(ј)ек-а о̀са̄мљен-о̄г.*
'man: I see *a man* (ACC) *alone* (ACC).'

Yet the personal pronoun has the feature [+animate] whether referring to grâd/гра̏д or to čòv(j)ek/чо̀в(ј)ек, as we see from its own shape and that of its modifier:

grâd ... Vîdīm *ga òsāmljen-ōg.*/град ... Ви̏дӣм *га о̀са̄мљен-о̄г.*
'city ... I see *it alone.*'
čòv(j)ek ... Vîdīm *ga òsāmljen-ōg.*/чо̀в(ј)ек ... Ви̏дӣм *га о̀са̄мљен-о̄г.*
'man .. I see *him alone.*'

A Serbo-Croat personal pronoun can show identity of sense without identity of reference, in instances like:

A: 'Nêmām àuto.' B: 'Zȁšto *ga* nè kūpīš?'/ A: 'Не̑ма̄м а̀уто.' B: 'За̏што *га* нè кӯпӣш?'
A: 'I haven't a car.' B: 'Why don't you buy *one* (literally *it*)?'

If the head of a noun phrase is not a noun but a demonstrative, interrogative or indefinite pronoun of neuter gender, or a clause or infinitive, it cannot antecede a personal pronoun (Browne 1986: 29). The neuter demonstrative tô/то̑ appears instead.

Òvō je za tèbe. Zadȑži tô!/О̀во̄ je за тѐбе. Задр̏жи то̑!
'This is for you. Keep it (literally *that*).'
Màrija vȍlī plésati. Ì jā tô vȍlīm./Ма̀рија во̏лӣ пле́сати. Ѝ ја̄ то̑ во̏лӣм.
'Marija likes to-dance. I too like it (literally *that*).'

Apart from this anaphoric function, demonstratives have situational and textual uses. The three demonstratives òvāj/о̀ва̄ј, tâj/та̑ј, ònāj/о̀на̄ј refer respectively to things near the speaker ('this'), near the hearer ('this, that') and further from both ('that over there'). Ònāj/о̀на̄ј is also for recalling something from a previous situation. Tâj/та̑ј is for things already under discussion, òvāj/о̀ва̄ј for things about to be mentioned and ònāj/о̀на̄ј for items to be made precise by a relative clause: tâ knjȉga/та̑ књи̏га 'the book we've been talking about', òvā knjȉga/о̀ва̄ књи̏га 'this book (which I now turn to)' and ònā knjȉga kòjā dȍbijē nàgradu na kòngresu/о̀на̄ књи̏га кòја̄ дȍбије̄ нàграду на кòнгресу 'the book that gets a prize at the congress'. Òvāj/о̀ва̄ј also serves to show a change in topical noun:

Ìvan je razgovárao s Pȇtrom, a òvāj s Màrijōm./Ѝван je разговáрао с Пȇтром, a о̀ва̄ј с Ма̀ријо̄м.
'Ivan talked with Petar, and he (Petar) with Marija.'

Where two items have recently been mentioned, òvāj/òвāj refers to the later and ònāj/òнāj to the earlier. Another equivalent to 'the former, the latter' is

pȓvī ròmān ... drȕgī ròmān/пȓви ròмāн ... дрȕгӣ ròмāн
'the first novel ... the second novel'

All these discourse devices function beyond the clause as well as within it. The personal pronoun is most frequently found outside the clause of its antecedent, since if the same entity is repeated within a clause, usually one of the references is in subject position and causes the other(s) to reflexivize (section 4.8).

Serbo-Croat is described as a pro-drop language, one in which a personal pronoun need not be used in subject position. Indeed, many clauses appear with no expressed subject; agreement markers on the verb enable recovery of the person, number and (if there is an *l*-participle in the verb form) gender.

Čȉtāmo./Чȉтāмо.
'We are reading.' (-mo/-мо, hence first person plural)
Mȉslila si./Мȉслила си.
'You (F SG) thought.' (si/си, hence second person singular; -l-a/-л-а, hence feminine)

In discourse, several criteria affect the (non-)use of subject pronouns. An individual being introduced as a topic is first mentioned as a full noun phrase or a first- or second-person pronoun. Thereafter subject pronouns referring to this topic may be omitted:

Mȃrko je dànas zàkasnio na rúčak. Ìmao je pȕno pòsla u grádu./Мȃрко je дànас зàкаснио на рýчак. Ѝмао je пȳно пòсла у грáду.
'Marko today came-late for dinner. (He) had a-lot-of work in town.'

But an overt subject pronoun need not change topics or introduce a non-coreferential subject. A frequent pattern is for the pronoun to be used on second mention, omitted thereafter:

Mȃrko je dànas zàkasnio na rúčak. Ȏn je ìmao pȕno pòsla u grádu. Zàtīm je zabòravio kljȕč od àuta i mórao se vrátiti p(j)èšicē./Мȃрко je дànас зàкаснио на рýчак. Ȏн je ѝмао пȳно пòсла у грáду. Зàтӣм je забòравио кљȳч од àута и мóрао се врáтити п(j)ȅшицē.
'Marko today came-late for dinner. He had a-lot-of work in town. Then (he) forgot the key to the car and (he) had to-return on-foot.'

Subjectꜱ are omitted when the referent does not figure in the narration:

Znâš, Mȁrko je dànas zàkasnio na rúčak. Mȉslȋm da je ȉmao pȕno pòsla u grádu./
Знȃш, Мȁрко је дȁнас зȁкаснио на рȳчак. Мȉслȋм да је ȉмао пȳно пȍсла
у грȃду.
'(Y') know, Marko today came-late for dinner. (I) think he had a-lot-of work in
town.'

They are included when rhematic or contrasted:

Rúčak sam sprémio *jà*./Рȳчак сам спрȅмио *jà*.
'Dinner prepared *I* (*I*'m the one who prepared dinner).'
Mȁrko je dànas zàkasnio, ali jȃ nísam./Мȁрко је дȁнас зȁкаснио, али jȃ нȉсам.
'Marko today came late, but *I* didn't.'

Their use can also indicate emphasis on the sentence as a whole:

Mȁrko? Jȃ njèga znȃm!/Мȁрко? Jȃ њȅга знȃм!
'Marko? *Certainly* I know him.'

Use of pronoun subjects within complex sentences is more grammaticalized. The subject in a complement clause is dropped when it is
obligatorily identical with an argument in the main clause. Thus 'have an
intention to ...' requires identity of subjects:

Slȁvko ìmȃ nám(j)eru da vȉdȋ Òlgu./Слȁвко ȉмȃ нȁм(j)еру да вȉдȋ Òлгу.
'Slavko has an intention that (he) see Olga.'

Without obligatory identity, as in 'be certain that ...', the pronoun will still
be dropped unless a contrast exists:

Slȁvko je sȉgūran da vȉdȋ Òlgu./Слȁвко је сȉгȳран да вȉдȋ Òлгу.
'Slavko is certain that (he) sees Olga.'
Slȁvko je sȉgūran da *ôn* vȉdȋ Òlgu a da je *jȃ* nè vidȋm./Слȁвко је сȉгȳран да *ôн*
вȉдȋ Òлгу а да је *jȃ* нȅ видȋм.
'Slavko is certain that *he* sees Olga and that *I* do not see her.'

A different phenomenon, involving omission of subjects as well as other
elements, is short answers consisting only of finite verb (section 4.2).

4.8   Reflexives and reciprocals
Repeated reference within a given domain is shown by the reflexive
pronoun sèbe/сȅбе. Like personal pronouns, sèbe/сȅбе has full and clitic
forms (section 3.1.3). It does not vary for person, gender or number:

Slȁvko gòvorȋ o sèbi. Mȋ gòvorȋmo o sèbi./Слȁвко гȍворȋ о сȅби. Мȋ
гȍворȋмо о сȅби.
'Slavko talks about himself. We talk about ourselves.'

but words modifying it show these features:

Slâvko gòvorī o sèbi *sámom*. Mî gòvorīmo o sèbi *sámima*./Слâвко гòворū о
сèби *сáмом*. Ми гòворūмо о сèби *сáмима*.
'Slavko talks about himself *alone* (M SG). We talk about ourselves *alone* (PL).'

The domain within which sèbe/cèбe occurs is the clause. Its antecedent
is the subject of the clause. The modifier sâm/câм permits objects as antecedents:

Jâ ću vas prepùstiti sèbi *sámim*./Jâ ħy вас препỳстити сèби *сáмим*.
'I will leave you₁ to yourselves₁ *alone*.'

The domain can also be a noun phrase if it contains a possessor interpretable as a subject. Mihaljević (1990: 151) discusses verbal nouns. A
possessive is antecedent to sèbe/cèбe:

njègovo zaljubljívanje u sèbe/њèгово заљубљúвање у cèбe
'his₁ infatuation with himself₁'

So is an unexpressed subject, whether arbitrary in reference or controlled
by a noun phrase in the clause:

zaljubljívanje u sèbe/заљубљúвање у cèбe
'one's₁ infatuation with oneself₁'
Òna se ográdila od zaljubljívanja u sèbe./Òна се огрáдила од заљубљúвања у
cèбe.
'She₁ disavowed (her₁) infatuation with herself₁.'

Reflexivization in Serbo-Croat does not extend into adjectival or participial constructions:

Ìvan je vŕšio pòv(j)erenū mu dúžnōst (not: pòv(j)erenū sèbi)./Ѝван је вŕшио
пòв(j)еренū му дýжнōст (not пòв(j)еренū сèби).
'Ivan₁ performed entrusted to-him₁ duty.'

Se/ce, the reflexive clitic, has many other uses: providing unspecified
human subject constructions, making verbs intransitive, being a component
of certain lexical items. The unspecified human subject can antecede
reflexives:

U Amèrici se mnògo gòvorī o sèbi./У Амèрици се мнòго гòворū о сèби.
'In America (one₁) speaks much about oneself₁.'

The reflexive possessive is svôj/cвôj. Its antecedent, as with sèbe/cèбe,
can be the subject of a clause or noun phrase.

Slâvko gòvorī o svòjem kònju./Слâвко гòворū̄ о свòјем кòњу.
'Slavko₁ talks about his₁ horse.'
òdnos īmenicē prema svôm glágolu/òднос ū̄менице̄ према свôм гла́голу
'relation of a noun₁ toward its₁ verb.'

If the subject of a clause is third person, svôj/свôj is normally obligatory; within noun phrases there is variation between it and the third-person possessives njègov/њѐгов 'his, its', njên, njézin/њên, њѐзин 'her', njīhov/њū̄хов 'their'.
    Exceptions to subject antecedency like

Pòstavi svè na svòje m(j)ȅsto!/Пòстави свè на свòје м(ј)ȅсто!
'Put everything₁ in its₁ place!'

are treated by Mihaljević (1990: 152ff.). The key factor is universal quantification of the non-subject antecedent. One could not have nȅšto/нȅшто 'something' or knjīgu/књū̄гу 'a book' in its stead.
    Alternatives to svôj/свôj for first- or second-person reference are the possessive pronouns môj/мôj 'my', nȁš/нȁш 'our', tvôj/твôj, vȁš/вȁш 'your'. The choice depends partly on empathy, svôj/свôj suggesting distance between the speaker and the possessed noun's referent. The teacher in

Jâ sam zȁhvālan svôm ùčitelju./Jâ сам зȁхвāлан свôм ỳчитељу.
'I am grateful to self's teacher.'

is one that I had, just as every student has some teacher.

Jâ sam zȁhvālan môm ùčitelju./Jâ сам зȁхвāлан мôм ỳчитељу.
'I am grateful to my teacher.'

speaks about a concrete teacher with his own name and personal qualities.
    Reciprocity is marked by a compound pronoun jèdan drȕgōg/jèдан дрȳ̀гōг 'one another'. Both parts inflect for gender, number and case:

Ôlga i Màrija vȉdē jèdna drȕgū./Ôлга и Мàрија вȉдē jèдна дрȳ̀гū̄.
'Olga and Marija see one (F NOM SG) another (F ACC SG).'

Prepositions go before the second member:

Gòvorīmo jèdan o drȕgōm./Гòворū̄мо jèдан о дрȳ̀гōм.
'We speak one about another (about each other).'

Unlike other pronouns, mixed-gender subjects take neuter singular jèdno drȕgō/jèдно дрȳ̀гō:

Slâvko i Òlga vȉdē jèdno drȕgō./Слâвко и Òлга вȉдē jèдно дрȳгō.
'Slavko and Olga see one another.'

The form of jèdan/jèдан has been nominative, agreeing with the clause subject, in these examples; it can also be genitive to go with the subject of a noun phrase. A newspaper story about the benefits resulting

... ȁko se òtvorīmo jèdni prema drȕgīma/... ȁko се òтворӣмо jèдни према дрȳгӣма
'... if we-open-up one (NOM PL) to another (DAT PL)'

is headlined

Kȍrīst od otvárānja jèdnih prema drȕgīma/Кȍрӣст од отвáрāња jèдних према дрȳгӣма. (*Полѝтика* 28 April 1989)
'Benefit from opening-up of-one (GEN PL) to another (DAT PL).'

Reciprocals, like reflexives, can occur in an infinitive phrase, but only where coreferential with the understood subject of the infinitive:

Slâvko i Òlga žèlē vȉd(j)eti jèdno drȕgō./Слâвко и Òлга жèлē вȉд(j)ети jèдно дрȳгō.
'Slavko and Olga wish to see one another.'

Jèdan drȕgōg/jèдан дрȳгōг with certain accusative-taking verbs (apparently lexically conditioned) is replaceable by se/ce, the clitic reflexive.

Òni bȉjū (vòlē, vȉdē) jèdan drȕgōg./Òни бȉjȳ (вȍлē, вȉдē) jèдан дрȳгōг. → Òni se bȉjū (vòlē, vȉdē)/Òни се бȉjȳ (вȍлē, вȉдē).
'They beat (love, see) one another.'

4.9 Possession

Possession can be expressed by a verb, a possessor constituent in a sentence or a possessor within a noun phrase. The normal verb used in a predication is ìmati/ѝмати 'to have' (or pòs(j)edovati/пȍс(j)едовати 'to possess'). The subject is the possessor, and the accusative object is the possessed item:

Màrija ìmā knjȉgu./Màрија ѝмā књѝгу.
'Marija has a book.'
Màrija ìmā sèstru./Màрија ѝмā сèстру.
'Marija has a sister.'

Prìpadati/прѝпадати 'to belong to' has the possessed item as nominative subject and the possessor as dative:

Kȕća prìpadā Màriji./Кȳћа прѝпадā Màриjи.
'The house belongs to Marija.'

With ìmati/ѝмати the use of genitive instead of accusative to express partitivity ('some') of plural or mass-noun objects is widespread, though otherwise the partitive genitive is restricted to perfective verbs:

Ìmām vòdē./Ѝмāм вòдē.
'I have some water (GEN).'

Compare:

Ìmām vȍdu./Ѝмāм вȍду.
'I have the water (ACC).'

The preposition u/y with genitive '(1) at the house of, *chez*, among; (2) in the possession of' is now rare. The first meaning is usually rendered as kod/код with genitive. The second meaning can form possessive sentences with the possessed as subject and a verb 'to be':

U lȁži su krȁtke nȍge./У лȁжи су крȁтке нȍге.
'A lie has short legs. (The truth eventually comes out.)' (proverb)
U Mȉlicē (su) dȕge trȅpavice./У Мȉлицē (су) дȕге трȅпавице.
'Milica has long eyelashes'. (folk poetry)

An u/y possessor phrase also occasionally appears in a sentence complete without it:

Òna je jedìnica (u mâjkē)./Òна je jедѝница (у mâjkē).
'She is the only daughter (her mother has).'

Dative constituents, particularly clitic pronouns, frequently express possessors.

Òtac mi je ȕmro prȍšlē gȍdinē./Òтац ми je ȕмро прȍшлē гȍдинē.
'Father to-me (my father) died last year.' (Mihailović 1971: 74)
Slȁvku je òtac ȕmro./Слȁвку je òтац ȕмро.
'Slavko-DAT father died.'

Kučanda (1985: 38) classifies nouns permitting dative possessors: 'parts of the body, kinship terms ... clothes, things the referent of the dative uses or possesses, nouns expressing part–whole relationship'. As his example shows:

Ràzbio mi je vázu./Pàзбио ми je вázу.
'He has broken my vase.'

this range goes beyond the traditional inalienably possessed nouns. The item with which the possessor phrase is interpreted is commonly a subject or direct object, but can have other functions:

Pȍštār mu se pojávio na vrátima./Пȍштāр му се појáвио на врáтима.
'The postman to-him appeared at door (at his door).'

The possessive dative can mark point of view (empathy): the event is told as if seen by the house owner. The transition to the dative of experiencer is gradual (the 'vase' sentence could be taken as 'He broke the vase "on" me, to my disadvantage').

In the above examples dative clitics, though associated with a noun phrase, occupy their usual position within the sentence. Such clitics can also appear within the possessed phrase.

Pozòvi Mȃrka i [sèstru mu]/Позòви Мȃрка и [сèстру му]. (now usually: i njègovu sèstru/и њèгову сèстру).
'Invite Marko and his sister.'

A possessor can be expressed as a genitive on the possessed phrase:

knjȉge Mȃrka Márkovića/књȉге Мȃрка Мáрковића
'books Marko-GEN Marković-GEN (Marko Marković's books)'

Genitive possessors are in almost complete complementary distribution with possessive adjectives in -ov/-ов, -ev/-ев, -in/-ин. If a possessor is definite, singular, human (or animal) and expressed by one word, it forms an adjective:

Mȃrkove knjȉge, Márkovićeve knjȉge/Мȃркове књȉге, Мáрковићеве књȉге
'Marko's books, Marković's books'
mȁčkin rȇp/мȁчкин рȇп
'the cat's tail'

Compare:

rȇp mȁčkē/рȇп мȁчкē
'the tail of a cat' (possessor not definite)
knjȉga stùdenātā/књȉга стùденāтā
'the book of the students' (not singular)
îme rúžē/ȉме рýшē
'the name of the rose' (not human/animal)
rȇp mòjē mȁčkē/рȇп мòjē мȁчкē
'the tail of my cat' (two words)

A departure from adjective/genitive complementarity occurs in instances like:

kȉp prȅds(j)ednȋka/кйп прѐдс(j)еднйка
'a statue of the president'

where a definite possessor is known only by reputation or professional role
(M. Ivić 1986).

The possessive adjective should be distinguished from adjectives showing various relationships, including possession, but not requiring singularity
or definiteness of the underlying noun:

Stùdentskī žȉvot je l(ij)ȇp./Стỳдентскй жѝвот je л(иj)ȇп.
'Student life is nice.' (song title)

paraphrasable as žȉvot stùdenātā/жѝвот стỳденāтā 'the life of students'
and not stùdentov žȉvot/стỳдентов жѝвот 'the life of the student'.

Finally possessors can be omitted, if identical with another constituent in
the sentence (Mihailović 1971: 75–7). One cannot have a possessive môj/
мôj 'my' in

Òtac mi je ȕmro./Òтац ми je ỳмро.
'My father died "on me".'

because it repeats the dative; nor in

Nòga me bòlī./Нòга ме бòлй.
'My leg hurts me.'

because it repeats the accusative object me/ме.

4.10 Quantification

Noun phrases can contain quantifiers telling the number of items expressed
by a count noun or the amount of substance expressed by a mass noun.
Two syntactic structures exist: adjectival (agreeing) and governmental (the
quantifier imposes a form on the noun). In adjectival quantification, the
noun bears the case of the noun phrase as a whole; the quantifier agrees
with it in case, number and gender, as is usual for adjectives.

brôjnē ùčesnīke/брôjнē ỳчеснйке
'numerous participants' (accusative masculine plural)

The numeral jèdan/jèдан 'one' appears in the adjectival pattern:

jèdan ùčesnīk/jèдан ỳчеснйк
'one participant' (nominative masculine singular)
jèdne nòvine/jèдне нòвине
'one newspaper' (nominative plural feminine on a plurale tantum)

Likewise adjectival in agreement are a set of numerals used with *pluralia tantum* heads: dvȍjī/двȍjӣ '2', trȍjī/трȍjӣ '3', up to '10':

dvȍjē nȍvine/двȍjē нȍвине
'two newspapers'

The usual numerals '2' to '4', as in governmental quantification, impose a specific form on the noun and other agreeing words, the 234 (paucal) form (sections 3.1.1–3.1.3); however, elements of agreeing quantification are seen in the fact that dvȃ/двȃ '2', ȍba/ȍба 'both' are used with masculine and neuter nouns, dvȋje (dvȇ)/двȉje (двȇ) and ȍb(j)e/ȍб(j)e with feminine nouns.

dvȃ dȍbra stùdenta/двȃ дȍбра стỳдента
'two good-234 students-234'.

The 234 form does not distinguish case. It can be used as nominative subject or predicate, accusative object, object of any preposition (whatever case the preposition governs) and genitive possessor:

Trȋ stùdenta su ȍdsutna./Трȋ стỳдента су ȍдсутна.
'Three students are absent.'
Pȍzvali smo ȍba stùdenta./Пȍзвали смо ȍба стỳдента.
'We invited both students.'
Stànujēm s čètiri stùdenta./Стàнуjēм с чèтири стỳдента.
'I live with four students.' (s/c otherwise demands instrumental)
Nè znām náslov tȇ trȋ knjȋge./Нè знȃм нáслов тȇ трȋ књȉге.
'I don't know the title of those three books.' (for genitive possessor)

It fills the role of an oblique case governed by a verb less successfully:

?S(j)ȅćām se tȃ čètiri stùdenta./С(j)ȅħȃм се тȃ чèтири стỳдента.
'I remember those four students.' (the verb demands genitive)
??Dȃjēm pȍklōn tȃ cetiri stùdenta./Дȃjēм пȍклȍн тȃ чèтйри стỳдента.
'I give a gift to those four students.' (indirect object needs dative)

The (rare) morphological oblique-case forms of these numerals (section 3.1.5), when used, accompany the desired case of head nouns according to the agreeing pattern.

The largest group of quantifiers governs genitive on the noun being quantified. These fall into two types. One has the shape of a noun or noun phrase (većìna/вeħȉна 'the majority of, most'; čȋtav nȋz/чȉтав нȉз 'a whole series of, a number of') and is declinable. It bears the case of the entire noun phrase. External attributive and predicative agreement is made with it rather than with the genitive complement.

Vèlikā većìna stùdenātā je stȉgla./Вѐликā веħѝна сту̀денāтā je стȉгла.
'Great-NOM SG majority-NOM SG of students-GEN PL has arrived-SG.'

Internal attributive agreement, that is, modifiers of the 'students', will, however, be genitive:

većìna dòbrīh stùdenātā/веħѝна до̀брȳх сту̀денāтā
'the majority of the good-GEN PL students-GEN PL'

The other type of genitive-governing quantifier is indeclinable. Besides items shaped like adverbs: mnȍgo/мнȍго 'much, many', pȕno/пу̏но 'a lot of', mȁlo/мȁло 'few, little; some, a few', it includes numerals from '5' up. Predicate agreement with it is usually the 'default' neuter singular, here -o/-o:

Mnȍgo vòdē je prolivèno./Мнȍго во̀дē je проливѐно.
'Much water-GEN is spilt.'
Mnȍgo stùdenātā je stȉglo./Мнȍго сту̀денāтā je стȉгло.
'Many students-GEN has arrived.'

Some indeclinable quantifiers have the shape of accusative nouns:

Stȍtinu stùdenātā je stȉglo./Стȍтину сту̀денāтā je стȉгло.
'One hundred students ...'

Similarly, tȉsuću/тȉсуħу, hȉljadu/хȉљаду '1,000', mȁsu/мȁсу 'a mass of'.

External modifiers of the quantifier-cum-genitive are themselves genitive:

Svȋh tȋh dȅsēt stùdenātā je stȉglo./Свȳх тих дȅсēт сту̀денāтā je стȉгло.
'All-GEN PL these-GEN PL ten students has arrived.'
Pròšlo je dòbrīh pȇt sátī./Про̀шло je до̀брȳх пȇт са́тȳ.
'Passed has good-GEN PL five hours-GEN PL (a good five hours passed).'

Like 234 forms, indeclinable quantifiers with genitive are usable in environments requiring various cases:

Stànujēm s mȁsu stùdenātā./Стàнујēм с мȁсу сту̀денāтā.
'I live with a lot of students.' (the preposition s/c calls for instrumental)
Nè znām náslov tīh dȅsēt knjȉgā./Нѐ знām на́слов тȳх дȅсēт књȳгā.
'I don't know the title of those ten books.' (genitive possessor)
S(j)ȅćām se tīh pȇt stùdenātā./С(j)ȅħām ce тȳх пȇт сту̀денāтā.
'I remember those five students.' (verb requires genitive)
??Dâjēm pòklōn òvīh četrdèsēt stùdenātā./Да̂jēm по̀клōн о̀вȳх четрдѐсēт сту̀денāтā.
'I give a gift to these forty students.' (dative indirect object)

Numerals can be compounded, as tri hìljade (tȋsuće) pȇtstō dvádesēt sèdam/три хѝљаде (тȋсуће) пȇтстō два́десēт сȅдам '3527'. The last word decides the construction used, so dvádesēt jèdan/два́десēт jèдан '21' has adjectival agreement between jèdan/jèдан and a singular head noun, pedèsēt dvȃ/педèсēт двȃ '52' demands 234 forms, whereas '3527' has genitive plural throughout the phrase and default neuter predicative agreement, like sèdam/сȅдам '7'.

The 'collective' numerals dvȍje/двȍje, trȍje/трȍje, čȅtvero (čȅtvoro)/чȅтверо (чȅтворо), pȇtero (pȇtoro)/пȇтеро (пȇторо), ... up to '9', are of the second genitive-taking type. (Grammars cite oblique case forms, but in practice they appear indeclinable.) They are used with mixed-sex groups of people and obligatorily with d(j)èca/д(j)èца 'children':

trȍje d(j)ècē/трȍje д(j)èцē
'three children'
trȍje stùdenātā/трȍje стỳденāтā; trȋ stùdenta/трȋ стỳдента
'three students (mixed sexes); three students (not necessarily mixed sexes)'

Another set of 'collectives' are numerals in -ica/-ица: dvòjica/двòjица, tròjica/трòjица, četvòrica/четвòрица, petòrica/петòрица (to '9') and nekolicìna/неколицѝна 'a few'. These signify groups of men, are feminine singular nouns in declension and behave like većìna/већѝна within the noun phrase:

svȃ petòrica dòbrīh stùdenātā/свȃ петòрица дòбрūх стỳденāтā
'all-F NOM SG five good-GEN PL students-GEN PL'

Predicate agreement with -ica/-ица phrases is plural on verbs; participles may take -a/-a or the semantically natural masculine plural -i/-и.

Genitive personal pronoun heads nȃs/нȃс 'us', vȃs/вȃс 'you', njȋh/њȋх 'them' combine with numerals above '1':

nȃs dvòjica/нȃс двòjица, nȃs dvȍje/нȃс двȍje, nȃs dvȋje (dvȇ)/нȃс двȋje (двȇ)
'we two' (male–male, male–female, female–female)
njȋh nekolicìna/њȋх неколицѝна, njȋh nèkoliko/њȋх нȅколико
'several men', 'several of them (mixed or female)'

5 Lexis

5.1 General composition of the word-stock
Fed by varied dialects, contacts (section 5.2) and more than one standard, the Serbo-Croat vocabulary is large. Academic dictionaries run to many volumes (*JAZU* 1880–1976, 1–23; *САНУ/SANU* 1959–, 1–14+; *MC-MX/MS-MH* 1967–76, 1–6). Unfortunately, we possess no full ety-

mological dictionary. Skok (1971–4), though abundant in rare and dialectal words, has many lacunae.

Statistical analyses of the vocabulary are also lacking. Word-origin figures might be computed for a dictionary or for running text. We have counted high-frequency vocabulary. Among the first hundred words of a lemmatized frequency count (Lukić 1983) of schoolchildren's writings in Serbia, one is foreign: škòla/шкòла 'school' (Italian from Greek). Two are nursery words of indeterminate origin (màma/мàма 'mummy', tàta/тàта 'daddy'); ninety-seven are inherited from Proto-Slavonic. The next hundred include two Church Slavonicisms: príčati/прȕчати 'to tell' from pritьča 'parable' and vàzdūh/вàздӯх 'air' from vъzduxъ; and a non-Slavonic item: sòba/сòба 'a room' (Turkish or Hungarian). In the top 500 lexemes, five (1.0 per cent) are from Church Slavonic, six or seven (1.2–1.4 per cent) have proximate sources in Turkish (one each originated in Persian, Arabic and Greek). Đâk/ђâк 'pupil' and lìvada/лѝвада 'meadow' are Greek, mâj/мâj 'May' and mìnūt/мѝнӯт 'a minute' Latin. French provides autóbus/аутóбус and partìzān/партѝзāн, English pàrk/пàрк, Hungarian lòpta/лòпта 'ball' and German pùška/пȳшка 'gun' (originally Ancient Greek). Some origins are less certain; príroda/прȕрода may be Czech or Church Slavonic. Our sample also contains škòlskī/шкòлскӣ, derived from škòla/шкòла, and ìzlēt/ѝзлēт 'excursion' and izglédati/изглéдати 'to appear', calques from German Ausflug, aussehen.

P. Ivić (Brozović and Ivić 1988: 43–4) enumerates words native in origin but restricted to South Slavonic or to Serbo-Croat. Of the first, our sample contains grána/грáна 'branch', šȕma/шȳма 'forest', kùća/кȳħа 'house', gòdina/гòдина meaning 'year'; the second group includes jȅr/jȅp 'for (conjunction)' < *ježe, pròl(j)eće/прòлеħе (прòљеħе) 'spring', ráditi/рáдити 'to work, do', râd/рâд 'labour, work', kȉša/кȉша 'rain', báciti/бáцити 'to throw', trážiti/трáжити 'to search for', dògađāj/дòгаħāj 'event'. Dòživljāj/дòживљāj 'an experience', a later coinage, is shared with Slovene. Some unexpected meanings have developed within Serbo-Croat: among our 500, we find vòl(j)eti/вòлети (вòљети) 'to love', older 'to prefer'; jâk/jâк 'strong' (Proto-Slavonic *jakъ 'what kind of'), pòsao/пòсао, genitive pòsla/пòсла 'work, task' (*posъlъ 'person who is sent'); čúvati/чȳвати 'keep' from the root *čuj- 'to perceive' seen in čȕti/чȳти 'to hear'; vȑlo/вȑло 'very' from 'virtuously'.

5.2 Patterns of borrowing

The best sketch is Brozović and Ivić (1988), followed closely here.

Greek loans attest the medieval Serbian state's Byzantine contacts. Some, as pàtos/пàтос 'floor', still characterize the Serbian standard; others like mìrīs/мѝрӣс 'smell' occur in all variants. Many religious terms entered Serbian Orthodox terminology through Church Slavonic: ìdol/

йдол 'idol', ѝguman/ѝгуман 'abbot'.

Orthodox religious and abstract vocabulary, if not Greek, is Church Slavonic, often calqued from Greek: prórok/пρόρок 'prophet' translating Greek *prophḗtēs*, ŭčenīk/ӯченйк 'disciple', later 'pupil', sáv(ij)ēst/ cáв(иj)ēст 'conscience', svĕštenīk/свѐштенйк 'priest'. As Ivić (Brozović and Ivić 1988: 44) observes, Croat vocabulary (presented here in Latinica) shares some of these religious Grecisms and Slavonicisms (*idol, prórok, ŭčenīk*), thanks to the Glagolitic writers' wide use of Church Slavonic, and also has many Latinisms (*brevijār* 'breviary') and domestic coinages (*svèćenīk* 'priest'). *Òpat* 'abbot', a Latin borrowing from Greek, probably came through Old Bavarian (German).

Romance words have been entering since medieval times, mostly near the coast. Some are Dalmatian Romance (dùpīn/дỳпйн 'dolphin'), many Italian (especially Venetian: sȉgūran/сѝгӯран 'sure').

Hungarian loans have entered Kajkavian, and some have spread further: kȉp/кйп 'statue', város/вáрош 'town'. Similarly with Germanisms: kȕhinja/кỳхиња 'kitchen', škòda/шкòда 'damage'.

Turkish influences on Serbo-Croat begin in the fourteenth century. Some words still mark Muslim milieus, as sèvdāh/сѐвдāх 'melancholy, love', sòkāk/còкāк 'alley', whereas others join the general vocabulary: bȁš/бȁш 'precisely', džèzva/џѐзва 'Turkish coffee pot', ćòrsokāk/ ħòрсокāк 'blind alley'. Škaljić's (1966) dictionary attests 8,742 Turkisms, many originally Arabic or Persian.

Turkisms and a later layer of Germanisms associated with the Hapsburg monarchy have frequently provoked searches for domestic replacements. Such purism, traditional among Croats, often generates stylistic distinctions: the loan (Turkish badàvā/бадàвā 'for free', German šnìcla/шнѝцла 'cutlet', paradàjz/парадàjз 'tomato', the last with exceptional placement of falling accent) is colloquial and its replacement (bèsplatno/ бѐсплатно, òdrezak/òдрезак, rȁjčica/рȁjчица based on rȁj/рȁj 'paradise') literary.

The nineteenth-century Illyrian movement Croatianized many words from Czech, which had had several decades of experience in finding equivalents for German and general European items: okólnōst 'circumstance', náslov 'title', prégled 'survey' (from Czech *přehled* by 'undoing' Czech palatalization of *r and spirantization of *g). Some then spread to Serbia: окόлнōст, нáслов, прéглед.

Numerous Greco-Latin words enter during the nineteenth and twentieth centuries: literatúra/литератýра, interesàntan/интересàнтан, etimològija/етимолòгиja, pòēzija/пòēзиja. All occur in French, German or other languages; we can speak of a common European 'pool' which various languages tapped. Native-based substitutes for these were sought, sometimes successfully: knjižévnōst/књижéвнōст for 'literature', p(j)èsnīštvo/п(j)ѐснйштво for 'poetry'. Other proposals failed:

korenoslovlje/коренословље for 'etymology'. Frequently substitutes are accepted in the Croat standard while internationalisms prevail elsewhere: br̄zojāv, tȅlegram/тȅлеграм; zȅmljopīs, geogràfija/геогрàфија.

English loan-words earlier trickled in through German or French, occasionally Russian. Since the Second World War contacts with Britain and America make English the leading source of loans. Filipović (1990) analyses the adaptation of over 5,500 items. Words with Greco-Latin elements behave as members of the European pool: *prohibition* › prohibīcija/прохибȋција, *infrastructure* › infrastruktúra/инфраструкту́ра. Other words take forms that accord with English spelling or pronunciation, in either event presenting consonant or vowel combinations untypical for Serbo-Croat: *pacemaker* › pejsmȅjker/пȅјсмȅјкер (also written pace-maker), *flower power* › flower power/flàuer pàuer/флàуер пàуер.

5.3 Incorporation of borrowings

Almost every borrowed noun declines in Serbo-Croat. Only nouns which end in sounds other than *a* and denote women remain indeclinable: Dolōres/Долȍрес (name), lédi/лéди 'lady' (our exposition follows P. Ivič/П. Ивич 1972 closely). Nouns in final -*a* join the *a*-declension and become feminine: korída/корȋда 'corrida', with stem as seen in genitive koríd-ē/корȋд-ē; Atlanta/Атлȁнта, Atlant-ē/Атлȁнт-ē (city). But -*a* nouns denoting human males or (sometimes) animals are *a*-declension masculines: Kaunda/Каунда (surname), gorȉla/горȉла 'gorilla'.

Nouns in final consonant, -*o* or -*e* join the masculine *o*-declension. Their -*o* or -*e* acts as an ending, not part of the stem: kùplung/ку̀плунг 'automobile clutch' (‹ German), genitive kùplung-a/ку̀плунг-а; àuto/àуто 'car', àut-a/àут-а; finále/финáле 'finale', finál-a/финáл-а. Nouns in final -*i*, -*u* or any long vowel include these segments in their stem: tábu/тáбу 'taboo', tábu-a/тáбу-а; bȉfē/бȉфē 'bar, snack bar', bifè-a/бифè-а; Màrā/Мàрā 'Marat (French revolutionary)', Marà-a/Мàрà-а. *J* is intercalated between -*i*/-и, -ī/-ȳ and endings: hȍbi/хȍби 'hobby', hȍbi-j-a/хȍби-ј-а; žȉrī/жȋрȳ 'jury', žirì-j-a/жирȋ-ј-а.

Sub-regularities characterize nouns of particular origins. Turkish forms in -*i*/*ü*/*ı*/*u* become *a*-declension nouns in -ija/-ија, masculine for human males, otherwise feminine: *sanatlı* › zanàtlija/занȁтлија (M) 'craftsman', *köprü* › ćùprija/ћу̀прија (F) 'bridge'. Europeanisms containing Latin -*tio* (English -*tion*) take the form -cija/-ција, *a*-declension (F): àmbīcija/àмбȋција, degradácija/деградáција.

Adjectives usually add a Serbo-Croat adjectival suffix: ȁbdomināl-nī/ȁбдоминāл-нȳ, *nostalgic* › nostàlgič-an/ностȁлгич-ан, or replace foreign suffixes with native ones: *atomic* › atȏm-skī/атȏм-скȳ. The resulting forms decline, and are compared if semantically justified: nostalgȉčnijī/ностáлгȉчнијȳ, najnostalgȉčnijī/нáјностáлгȉчнијȳ 'more, most nostalgic'. Some foreign adjectives however get no suffix, remaining indeclinable: bȇž hàljina/бȇж хàљина 'a beige dress', njȉhova ìgra je fȇr/ њȉхова ѝгра је фȇр 'their playing is sportsmanlike'. They compare periphrastically, if at all: vȉšē fȇr/вȉшē фȇр 'fairer', nâjvišē fer/нâjвишē фȇр 'fairest'.

Over 2,000 foreign verbs (Matešić 1965–7) add suffixes -íra-ti/-и́ра-ти, -ova-ti/-ова-ти or -isa-ti/-иса-ти (present stems -ira-/-ира-, -uj-e-/ -yj-e-, -iš-e-/-иш-е-): erodírati/ероди́рати 'to erode', paràlizovati/паràлизовати 'to paralyse', elimìnisati/елимѝнисати 'to eliminate'. Doublets exist, with -irati favoured in the Croat standard (*paralizírati, eliminírati*). Almost all such verbs are bi-aspectual; but pairs with prefixed perfectives appear: provocírati/провоци́рати, is-/ис- 'to provoke', komentírati/комент́ирати, pro-/про- 'to comment (on)'.

Loan verbs can also receive -a-ti/-а-ти (present -a-/-а-) and rarely -nu-ti/-ну-ти (present -ne-/-не-) without intervening suffix (Filipović 1990): stàrtati/стàртати 'to start (a race)' perfective; bildati/билдати 'to engage in body-building' imperfective; blefnuti/блефнути 'to bluff' perfective. Prefixed perfectives can be formed: mìksati/мѝксати 'to mix' imperfective, izmìksati/измѝксати perfective.

5.4 Lexical fields

5.4.1 Colour terms
These are adjectives, cited here in masculine singular nominative, with feminines added where necessary to show the stem.

1	white	ijekavski bȉjel/би̏jел, ekavski bȅo/бȅо, béla/бéла
2	black	cȓn/цȓн (but note cȓnō vínō/цȓнō ви́нō 'red wine')
3	red	cȑven/цȑвен, also rùmen/рỳмен 'ruddy, as of face (poetic)'
4	green	zèlen/зèлен
5	yellow	žût/жŷт
6	blue	plȃv/плȃв 'blue, also blond (of hair)', also mȍdar/мȍдар, mȍdra/мȍдра 'blue, dark blue (frequently poetic)'
7	brown	smȅđ/смȅђ, brȁon (brȁun)/брȁон (брȁун) indeclinable, mȓk/мȓк 'dark brown, dark'
8	purple	ljùbičast/љу̀бичаст 'violet'
9	pink	rùžičast/рỳжичаст, róza/рóза indeclinable
10	orange	nàrānčast, nàrāndžast/нàрāнчаст, нàрāнџаст
11	grey	sȋv/си̑в; s(ij)êd/с(иj)êд 'grey (of hair)'

The main entries under 1–6 and 11 are clearly basic (Berlin and Kay 1969: 6), being monolexemic, combinable with many objects, salient and not included under other terms. All occurred over a hundred times in V. Lukić's (1983) 1.5 million words. The choice of basic term for 'brown' is less obvious: mȑk/мр̏к has frequency 85 (some of which must have meant 'dark, gloomy'), smȅđ/смȅђ 42 and brȁon/бра̏он 32, but brȁon/бра̏он is probably least limited in combinability. Ljȕbičast/љу̏бичаст, rȕžičast/ру̏жичаст and nàrānčast/на̀ра̄нџаст, though derived from flowers and fruits (ljȕbi(či)ca/љу̏би(чи)ца 'a violet', rúža/ру́жа 'a rose', nàrānča/на̀ра̄нча, nàrāndža/на̀ра̄нџа 'an orange'), have no serious competition in the senses of colours 8 to 10. Ljȕbičast/љу̏бичаст and rȕžičast/ру̏жичаст are well established, occurring 21 and 20 times in Lukić. Nàrānčast/на̀ра̄нџаст is strikingly infrequent (6), appearing only after the fourth year of school. Even for adults its low perceived salience makes its basicness doubtful.

5.4.2   Body parts
Genitive singulars are given where needed; irregular plurals are also cited.

head	gláva/гла́ва
eye	ȍko/о̏ко
eyes	ȍči/о̏чи feminine *i*-declension, genitive ȍčijū/о̏чијӯ
nose	nôs/но̂с, plural nȍsovi (nȍsevi)/но̏сови (но̏севи)
ear	ȕho/ȳ̏хо; Serbian standard also ȕvo/ȳ̏во
ears	ȕši/ȳ̏ши feminine *i*-declension, genitive ȕšijū/ȳ̏шијӯ
mouth	ústa/у́ста neuter plurale tantum
hair	kòsa/ко̀са (all the hair on the head); dlȁka/дла̏ка 'a hair; hair(s) growing on the body'
neck	vrât/вра̂т, also šîja/ши̂ja
arm/hand	rúka/ру́ка
hand	šȁka/ша̏ка (considered part of rúka/ру́ка; also 'fist')
finger	pȑst/пр̏ст, plural pȑsti/пр̏сти, genitive pȑstī (pȑstijū)/ пр̏стӣ (пр̏стијӯ); pȑst na rúci/пр̏ст на ру́ци
thumb	pȁlac/па̏лац, pȁlca/па̏лца
leg/foot	nòga/но̀га
foot	stòpalo/сто̀пало (considered part of nòga/но̀га)
toe	pȑst/пр̏ст, pȑst na nòzi/пр̏ст на но̀зи, nȍžnī pȑst/ но̏жнӣ пр̏ст
big toe	pȁlac (na nòzi)/па̏лац (на но̀зи), nȍžnī pȁlac/но̏жнӣ па̏лац
chest	pȑsa/пр̏са neuter plural (also 'breast'); grȗdi/гру̂ди feminine *i*-declension plural (also 'breast'), singular rare
heart	sȑce/ср̏це

5.4.3   Kinship terms

mother	mȁjka/ма̏jка, mȁti/ма̏ти (see section 3.1.2)
father	òtac/о̀тац, genitive òca/о̀ца, plural òčevi/о̀чеви

sister	sèstra/сѐстра. Can include 'female cousin', but ròđenā/pòђенā ('born') sèstra/сѐстра is only 'sister'.
brother	brȁt/брȁт, plural brȁća/брȁħa (declined as feminine singular *a*-declension; attributive agreement accordingly; neuter plural predicative agreement). Can include 'male cousin', but ròđenī brat/pòђенū брȁт is only 'brother'.
aunt	tȅtka/тȅтка 'father's sister, mother's sister'; strȋna/стрȋна 'father's brother's wife'; ûjna/ŷjна 'mother's brother's wife'
uncle	strȋc/стрȋц, plural strȋčevi/стрȋчеви 'father's brother'; ûjāk/ŷjāк 'mother's brother'; tétak/тéтак, genitive tétka/тéтка, or téča/тéча 'husband of tȅtka/тȅтка'
niece	nèćakinja/нèħàкиња, nèćaka/нèħака, also sȅstrična/сȅстрична 'sister's daughter'; sinòvica/синòвица, brȁtič(i)na/брȁтич(и)на, nèćakinja/нèħàкиња 'brother's daughter'
nephew	nȅćāk/нȅħāк, also sȅstrić/сȅстрuħ 'sister's son'; sinóvac/синóвац, brȁtić/брȁтuħ, nȅćāk/нȅħāк 'brother's son'
cousin (female)	sèstra/сѐстра; ròđaka/pòђака, rođàkinja/poђàкиња 'relative'; sèstra od tȅtkē/сѐстра од тȅткē 'daughter of one's tȅtka/тȅтка'; sèstra od strȋca/сѐстра од стрȋца 'daughter of one's strȋc/стрȋц'; sèstra od ûjāka/сѐстра од ŷjāка 'daughter of one's ûjāk/ŷjāк'
cousin (male)	brȁt/брȁт; ròđāk/pòђāк 'relative'; brȁt od tȅtkē/брȁт од тȅткē 'son of one's tȅtka/тȅтка'; brȁt od strȋca/брȁт од стрȋца 'son of one's stric/стрȋц'; brȁt od ûjāka/брȁт од ŷjāка 'son of one's ûjāk/ŷjāк'

(Speakers disagree about subclassifications of nieces, nephews and cousins.)

grandmother	bȁba/бȁба, báka/бáка (diminutive, but frequent)
grandfather	d(j)ȅd/д(j)ȅд, ekavski also dȅda/дȅда
wife	žèna/жèна (also 'woman'); sùpruga/сỳпруга ('spouse')
husband	mûž/мŷж (not usually 'man'); sùprug/сỳпруг ('spouse')

daughter   (k)ćérka/(к)ћéрка, kći/кћи̏ (section 3.1.2)
son   sȋn/си̑н.

6 Dialects

Serbo-Croat speakers, conscious of dialect divisions, identify themselves as kájkavci/ка́jкавци, čákavci/ча́кавци or štókavci/што́кавци and according to their reflex of *jat'* (section 2.1) as ékavci/éкавци, (i)jékavci/(и)jéкавци or íkavci/и́кавци. The main divisions, Kajkavian, Čakavian and Štokavian, are named after their words for 'what': *kȁj* ‹ **kъjь* (dialect forms use Latin transcription), *čȁ* ‹ **čь* and *štȍ* or *štȁ* ‹ **čь-to* (*a* in *štȁ* is of later development). The Torlak (Prizren-Timok) group, sometimes termed transitional to Macedonian and Bulgarian (P. Ivić 1958), is generally, as here, included in Štokavian (Brozović and Ivić 1988). The *jat'* reflex is important for subdividing the three groups. The most recent survey, with detailed maps, is in Brozović and Ivić 1988; P. Ivić (1981) phonologically describes seventy-seven localities with historical summaries.

Kajkavian is spoken in north-west Croatia (see map 7.1). Features shared with adjacent Slovene, besides *kaj*, include reflexes *č, j* from Proto-Slavonic *tj, dj*: *noč* 'night', *meja* 'boundary' (in some places *medža*) and devoicing of final obstruents: *grat* from *grad* 'town'. Final and pre-consonantal *l* remains: *bil* 'was', Štokavian *bio*. Most vowel systems have more than five members and long–short contrasts. The reflex of **e* and **ę* is often low: *sælo* ‹ **selo* 'village', *zæt* ‹ **zętь* 'brother-in-law', unlike that of *jat'* as in *leto* ‹ **lěto* 'year', which is often joined by strong **ь/*ъ*: *pes* ‹ *рьsъ* 'dog'. **l̥* or **r̥* or both may give closed *ǫ* as in **vl̥kъ* › *vǫk* 'wolf', **mǫžь* › *mǫš* 'man'.

In morphology, nouns preserve old distinctions in the plural cases: nominative masculine *gradi*, feminine *žene*; genitive *gradof, žen*; dative *gradom, ženam*; instrumental *gradi, ženami*; locative *gradeh, ženah*. Genitive plural *-ā* and the Štokavian *-ov-/-ev-* long plural are lacking. The vocative is lost. Verbs have lost aorist and imperfect. The future, as in Slovene, consists of an auxiliary from **bǫdǫ* plus *l*-participle: *bom delal* (feminine *delala*) 'I'll work'.

Bases for subclassification are vocalism and accentuation. Kajkavian dialects started from a system with a single accent on short vowels but falling–rising (circumflex–neoacute) contrasts on longs. The dialects then undergo shifts and neutralizations (Brozović and Ivić 1988).

Kajkavian was a medium of literature until the Illyrian movement. Poets and songwriters continue using it to good effect. The Zagreb city sub-standard is a koinéized Kajkavian (five vowels, no length and accent contrasts).

Čakavian occurs on the north and central Croatian coast, Istria and the Adriatic islands. An island area south-west of Karlovac is separated from

Map 7.1   Serbo-Croat Dialects

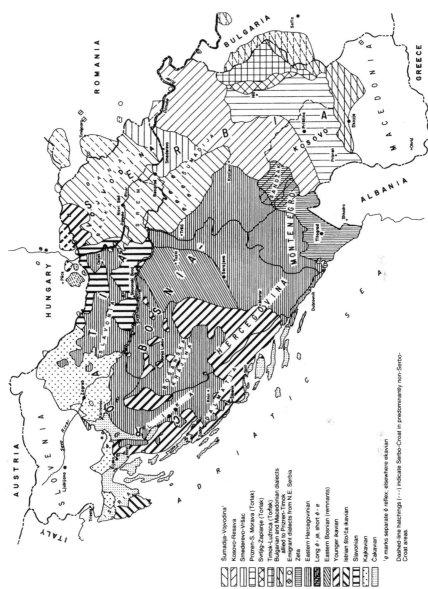

Šumadija-Vojvodina'

Kosovo-Resava

Smederevo-Vršac

Prizren-S. Morava (Torlak)

Svrljig-Zaplanje (Torlak)

Timok-Lužnica (Torlak)

Bulgarian and Macedonian dialects
allied to Prizren-Timok

Emigrant dialects from N.E. Serbia

Zeta

Eastern Hercegovinian

Long ě · je, short ě · e

Eastern Bosnian (remnants)

Younger ikavian

Istrian što/ča ikavian

Slavonian

Kajkavian

Cakavian

'ε marks separate ě reflex; elsewhere ekavian

Dashed-line hatchings (- - -) indicate Serbo-Croat in predominantly non-Serbo-
Croat areas.

the coast by later Štokavian settlements. The Burgenland Croats in eastern Austria speak Čakavian and use a Čakavian-based written form.

Defining characteristics include interrogative *ča*, genitive *česa* (some localities lose *ča*, but maintain compounds like *zač* ‹ *za čь). For Proto-Slavonic *tj* Čakavian has a variety of *ć* transcribed [t'], for *dj* it has *j*: *not'*, *meja*. In sporadic lexemes *ę, which otherwise becomes *e*, yields *a* after palatal: *językъ, *počęti › *jazik* (often metathesized: *zajik*) ‘tongue’, *počati* ‘to begin’. The auxiliary for the conditional is *bin*, *biš* ... from Proto-Slavonic *bimь, whereas Serbo-Croat generally has its auxiliary from *byxъ. Plural noun endings are mainly the old ones as in Kajkavian. The vocative is lost. Aorist and imperfect are mostly lost. The future has auxiliary verb *ću* and infinitive, as in Štokavian.

Vowel systems mostly have five short vowels and five long; diphthongizations and rounding of long *a* are frequent. Section 2.1 treats *jat'* reflexes. Word-final *l* may drop, remain or yield -*a*, but does not change to -*o*; *bi*, *bil*, *bija*.

A later feature, final *m* changing to *n* in endings: *govorim* › *govorin* ‘I speak’, *nogom* › *nogon* ‘foot (INST SG)’, covers coastal Čakavian and Štokavian areas. Root-final *m* is unaffected: *dim* ‘smoke’. Many localities are ‘cakavian’, merging *č* and *c*, *š* and *s*, *z* and *ž*. Many coastal dialects change *lj* to *j*: *jubav* ‘love’.

Čakavian dialects go back to either of two accentual systems, each having a single accent on short vowels and distinguishing rising neoacute from falling (neo)circumflex on longs. But the sources of the neoacute and neocircumflex are different. There was a rich Renaissance literature in Čakavian. Lyric poetry is still composed; popular song festivals flourish.

Štokavian, the most widespread group, covers Serbia, Bosnia-Hercegovina, Montenegro and much of Croatia. Since the 1400s refugees from Turkish rule have carried it north and west, into earlier Kajkavian and Čakavian territory. The pre-migration landscape presumably had smooth transitions to Čakavian and Kajkavian, but the present map shows abrupt boundaries and islands of older phenomena amid large homogeneous areas.

Features covering most or all of Štokavian include (closely following Brozović and Ivić 1988): interrogative *što* or *šta*, the long plural in *ov/ev*, preservation of the aorist, final *l* becoming *o*, the change of *jd* to *đ* (*dojьdešь › *dođeš* ‘you come’) and the new ending -*ā* for *o*-declension and *a*-declension genitive plurals. Most of the area has *št*, *žd* for older *šć*, *žđ* (section 2.2), but some ‘šćakavian’ western dialects preserve *šć*, *žđ*. Shared with part of Kajkavian is the change of *dj to an affricate *đ* (Kajkavian *dž*), opposed to Čakavian *j*. Shared with part of Čakavian are the changes *čr* › *cr* (*črn* › *crn* ‘black’), *vь/vъ* › *u* before consonant (prefix and preposition *u* ‘in’, *udovica* ‹ *vьdova ‘widow’) and metathesis *vs-* › *sv-* in the root ‘all’.

Two ‘neo-Štokavian’ innovations characterizing central Štokavian, as against the periphery, are neutralization of plural oblique cases (dative–instrumental–locative have endings *-ima*, *-ama* borrowed from the dual) and new (shifted) accentuation. The 'oldest' Štokavian systems resembled Čakavian, with one accent on short vowels (*ȍko, sestrȁ, glāvȁ*, also *bȁba* from Proto-Slavonic acute) but two, rising and falling, distinguished on longs (rising *sȗša* 'drought', falling *mȇso* 'meat'). A newer system neutralizes the long accents: *sȗša, mȇso*. Finally, the neo-Štokavian accent shift creates new rising accents on the syllable preceding non-initial accents: *sestrȁ* › *sèstra* with new short rising, *glāvȁ* › *gláva* with new rising on a long.

The *jat'* reflex splits Štokavian dialects into ekavian, (i)jekavian and ikavian. Combining these notions with central/peripheral distinctions permits the establishing of subdialects.

Eastern Hercegovinian, (i)jekavian with new accents and neutralized plurals, is the most widespread type, carried far from its home by migrations. As Karadžić's native dialect, it formed the basis for standard Serbo-Croat.

The Šumadija-Vojvodina type, as its name implies, occupies Serbia's northern province and part of central Serbia south-west of Beograd. It is ekavian (the standard of Serbia inherits ekavism from this type), except for part of Šumadija with [ẹ] (section 2.1). Its accents are new, its plural endings largely new. Unaccented syllables show a tendency to shorten long vowels which becomes stronger in east and south Serbia.

Younger Ikavian, lying between Eastern Hercegovinian and Čakavian, has mostly new accentuation and mostly neutralized plural cases. Parts of the area are šćakavian and share other features with Čakavian.

The Zeta-Lovćen (Zeta-South Sandžak) group occupies southern Montenegro and adjoining areas of Serbia. The accent neutralizes the oldest distinction on long vowels, but is largely unshifted. The plural syncretizes dative and insrumental, but joins locative with genitive. *Jat'* reflexes are mostly (i)jekavian, with the short version, *je*, causing extensive changes in preceding consonants. Some areas have *ə* or *ä* for strong *ъ/ь*.

East and north of it is the Kosovo-Resava type. Accents and plurals resemble Zeta-Lovćen. *Jat'* development is consistently ekavian, without *i* reflexes before *j* (section 2.1). Lengths in post-accentual syllables shorten.

Between Kosovo-Resava and Šumadija-Vojvodina lies the Smederevo-Vršac ekavian type. The accent is partly (and optionally) shifted. Plural case neutralization agrees with Šumadija-Vojvodina.

The Slavonian dialect in north-eastern Croatia shows a mixture of *jat'* reflexes. Plural cases neutralize only partially. Many localities preserve old place of accent and old rising and falling. The neo-Štokavian long rising is encroaching on Slavonian, yielding three long-vowel accent contours; Lehiste and Ivić (1986) provide measurements.

Eastern Bosnian, jekavian and šćakavian, has partly old accentuation with traces of falling–rising distinctions, but influence of neo-Štokavian-speaking migrants has been heavy. Plural cases neutralize.

South of Kosovo-Resava is Prizren-Timok. Ekavski, with unshifted accent position but neutralized length contrasts, these dialects have six-vowel systems, showing ə for strong *ъ/ь. Final *l* becomes *a* or remains: *bija, bil*. Of all Serbo-Croat dialects these are most affected by linguistic Balkanisms: apart from the vocative, the case system shrinks to nominative and a generalized oblique, sometimes with a separate dative. However, the aorist and imperfect tenses are vigorous. Clitic doubling of objects is widespread, as are postposed demonstratives used as definite articles; both are features shared with Macedonian.

References

Babić, Stjepan (1986) *Tvorba riječi u hrvatskom književnom jeziku: Nacrt za gramatiku*, Zagreb: Jugoslavenska akademija znanosti i umjetnosti, Globus.

Berlin, Brent and Paul Kay (1969) *Basic Color Terms: their Universality and Evolution*, Berkeley and Los Angeles: University of California Press.

Browne, Wayles (1976) 'Two Wh-fronting rules in Serbo-Croatian', *Južnoslovenski filolog* 32: 196–204.

—— (1986) *Relative Clauses in Serbo-Croatian in Comparison with English* (The Yugoslav Serbo-Croatian–English Contrastive Project, New Studies 4), Zagreb: Institute of Linguistics.

—— (1987) 'Classification of subordinate clauses in a grammar of Serbo-Croatian for foreign users', The Zagreb English–Serbo-Croatian Contrastive Project, *Contrastive Analysis of English and Serbo-Croatian* 3: 165–91, Zagreb: Institute of Linguistics.

Browne, Wayles and James D. McCawley (1965) 'Srpskohrvatski akcenat', *Zbornik za filologiju i lingvistiku* 8: 147–51, reprinted as 'Serbo-Croatian accent' in E.C. Fudge (ed.) (1973), *Phonology: Selected Readings*, Harmondsworth: Penguin, 330–5.

Brozović, Dalibor (1973) 'O ortoepskoj vrijednosti dugoga i produženog ijekavskog jata', *Jezik* 20: 65–74, 106–18, 142–9.

Brozović, Dalibor and Pavle Ivić (1988) *Jezik srpskohrvatski/hrvatskosrpski, hrvatski ili srpski. Izvadak iz II izdanja Enciklopedije Jugoslavije*, Zagreb: Jugoslavenski leksikografski zavod.

Corbett, Greville G. (1983) *Hierarchies, Targets and Controllers: Agreement Patterns in Slavic*, London: Croom Helm.

Filipović, Rudolf (ed.) (1975) The Zagreb English–Serbo-Croatian Contrastive Project, *Contrastive Analysis of English and Serbo-Croatian*, vol. 1, Zagreb: Institute of Linguistics.

—— (1990) *Anglicizmi u hrvatskom ili srpskom jeziku: porijeklo – razvoj – značenje*, Zagreb: JAZU, Školska knjiga.

Ivić, Milka (1983) *Lingvistički ogledi*, Belgrade: Prosveta.

—— (1986) 'On referential strategies: genitivization vs. adjectivization in Serbo-Croatian', *Linguistische Arbeitsberichte* (Leipzig) 54/5: 23–7.

Ivić, Pavle (1958) *Die serbokroatischen Dialekte: ihre Struktur und Entwicklung*, vol. 1: *Allgemeines und die štokavische Dialektgruppe*, The Hague: Mouton.

—— (ed.) (1981) *Fonološki opisi srpskohrvatskih/hrvatskosrpskih, slovenačkih i makedonskih govora obuhvaćenih opšteslovenskim lingvističkim atlasom* = Akademija nauka i umjetnosti Bosne i Hercegovine, *Posebna izdanja, knjiga LV*,

Odjeljenje društvenih nauka, knjiga 9, Sarajevo: ANUBIH.

JAZU (Jugoslavenska akademija znanosti i umjetnosti) (1880–1976) *Rječnik hrvatskoga ili srpskoga jezika* 1–23, Zagreb: JAZU.

Kučanda, Dubravko (1985) 'Some thoughts on the dative of possession', *Zbornik Pedagoškog fakulteta (humanističke i društvene znanosti)* 1: 37–54, Osijek.

Lehiste, Ilse and Pavle Ivić (1986) *Word and Sentence Prosody in Serbocroatian*, Cambridge, Mass.: MIT Press.

Lukić, Vera (1983) *Dečji frekvencijski rečnik*, Belgrade: Prosveta.

Matešić, Josip (1965–7) *Rückläufiges Wörterbuch des Serbokroatischen* (Lieferung 1–4 = Osteuropastudien der Hochschulen des Landes Hessen, V, Giessener Beiträge zur Slavistik, 1) Wiesbaden: Otto Harrassowitz.

Mihailović, Ljiljana (1971) 'Additional notes on noun phrases in the function of subject in English and Serbo-Croatian', The Yugoslav Serbo-Croatian–English Contrastive Project, *Reports* 4: 73–84, Zagreb: Institute of Linguistics.

Mihaljević, Milan (1990) 'Upotreba povratnoposvojne zamjenice *svoj* u hrvatskom ili srpskom jeziku', in Georg Holzer (ed.), *Croatica, Slavica, Indoeuropaea* (Wiener slavistisches Jahrbuch, Ergänzungsband VIII), 145–56, Vienna: Österreichische Akademie der Wissenschaften, Institut für Slavistik der Universität Wien.

Mrazović, Pavica, and Zora Vukadinović (1990) *Gramatika srpskohrvatskog jezika za strance*, Sremski Karlovci/Novi Sad: Izdavačka knjižara Zorana Stojanovića/Dobra vest.

Skok, Petar (1971–4) *Etimologijski rječnik hrvatskoga ili srpskoga jezika* 4 vols, Zagreb: Jugoslavenska akademija znanosti i umjetnosti.

Škaljić, Abdulah (1966) *Turcizmi u srpskohrvatskom jeziku*, Sarajevo: Svjetlost.

Ивич, П. (1972) «Система падежных окончаний существительных в сербохорватском литературном языке», *Русское и славянское языкознание*, Москва: Наука, 106–21. = Ивић, П. (1990) «Систем падежних наставака именица у српскохрватском књижевном језику», *О језику некадашњем и садашњем*, Београд: БИГС-Јединство, 286–309.

Менац, Антица (1978) *Падеж прямого дополнения с отрицанием в современном русском и хорватскосербском языках*, Petojezični kontrastivni projekt, *Hrvatskosrpsko-ruske kontrastivne studije* 1, Zagreb: Zavod za lingvistiku.

MC-MX (Матица Српска, Матица Хрватска) (1967–76) *Речник српскохрватскога књижевног језика* 1–6, Нови Сад-Загреб.

Реметић, Слободан (1981) «О незамењеном јату и икавизмима у говорима северозападне Србије», *Српски дијалектолошки зборник 27*, Београд: Српска академија наука и уметности, Институт за српскохрватски језик.

САНУ (Српска академија наука и уметности) (1959–) *Речник српскохрватског књижевног и народног језика* 1–14 (as of 1990), Београд.

Станојчић, Живојин, Љубомир Поповић и Стеван Мицић (1989) *Савремени српскохрватски језик и култура изражавања*, Београд: Завод за уџбенике и наставна средства.

8 Slovene

T.M.S. Priestly

1 Introduction

Standard Literary Slovene (*slovénski knjížni jézik*) is the official language of Slovenia; Slovene, in its various forms, is the native language of nearly 2 million speakers in Slovenia and in adjacent parts of Italy, Austria and Hungary, and of another 400,000 speakers in emigrant communities. For an overview of the demography, and a precise definition of the geographic area involved, see Lencek (1982: 15–22). The name 'Slovene' (ethnonym: *Slovénɔc*; language: *slovénščina* or *slovénski jézik*) has been used in this sense since the early nineteenth century.

Available descriptions and lexical compilations of Slovene (in, for instance, Lencek 1982, Toporišič 1984, the Academy Dictionary, the *Pravopis*) are of the prescribed, standardized *zbôrni jézik* (common language). The diversiform *splóšni pogôvorni jézik* (general colloquial language) remains to be adequately described. Contemporary varieties of Slovene display significant and interesting differences.

The earliest Slavonic settlements in this region were in the sixth century AD. At first, Slovene shared a number of developments with Kajkavian and Čakavian Serbo-Croat (see Lencek 1982: 59–74). From about the twelfth century in general, and prior to that in some localities, the Slovene lands were politically controlled by speakers of Romance and, especially, Germanic; this control restricted the use of Slovene to strictly localized (dialect) forms, and resulted in extensive but sporadic bilingualism. There are only a few extant texts from before the Reformation; among them, the *Freising Fragments* (about AD 1000) are especially noteworthy. In the sixteenth century a written form of the Slovene language was developed by Trubar, Dalmatin, Krelj, Bohorič and others, and some fifty books were printed in Slovene between 1550 and 1598. The Counter-Reformation decelerated the expansion and codification of this written language, but in the nineteenth century the literary forms were reinforced and adopted as the language of a creative intelligentsia. Since then, there has been much discussion (and some disagreement) about the form that the standard language should take; there is still a lively interest in the language question.

The nineteenth-century language planners were faced with many problems, including the results of bilingualism, the heterogeneity of the Slovene dialects, the attractions of competing contemporary theoretical approaches and practical considerations. In particular, there was, on the one hand, pressure for Slovene to surrender to varieties of Slavonic with wider application and, on the other, competition between geographic and historical varieties of Slovene itself; also, there were the puristic influences known elsewhere in Slavonic (see Lencek 1982: 257–78). Eventually, those with influence (re-)modelled the language on the Slovene of the sixteenth century, and adopted many of the archaic features which distinguish it from the colloquial variants in use today. The language of Reformation Slovene had (in the main) been based upon the 'dialect bases' of Gorenjsko, Dolenjsko and (to a lesser extent) Notranjsko (see section 6); the first two of these, being the most central, contributed much to the eventual development of Contemporary Standard Slovene. The standard language thus offers a mixture of both spatially diverse and temporally diverse features. The spatial compromise is well exemplified by the co-existence of two equally authorized phonological systems, one with tonemic distinctions and one without, the first typical of some dialects, the second of others. The diachronic compromise can be seen in, for example, the pervasiveness of the dual category, which without learned intervention would not have survived in its full contemporary use. A large number of features that occur in most or all Slovene dialects, such as 'vowel reduction', are absent from the standard.

In the former Yugoslavia, the official use of Slovene was supported more by the letter of the law than in practice: as a minority language in the country as a whole, it was exposed to the substantial pressure of a modern bilingual situation as well as the general effects of population movements, mass communications and the like. The subject is complex and unresolved: see Tollefson (1981), Lencek (1982: 278–93), Paternost (1984).

2 Phonology

2.1 Segmental phoneme inventory
The two phonological systems of standard Slovene differ only with respect to prosodic phenomena. The **tonemic system** is here described first, then the **non-tonemic system**. A comparative table shows the relationship between the two. Thereafter all forms are cited according to the tonemic system (with one modification). Non-tonemic transcriptional forms (including the contemporary orthography) may be derived from them by the algorithm provided.

Vowels and prosodic phenomena. Slovene (in both the tonemic and the non-tonemic systems) has eight **vowel phonemes**: /i e ɛ ə a ɔ o u/. Seven (all except /ə/) occur as long vowels, and six (all except /e o/) occur as short, namely [iː eː ɛː aː ɔː oː uː] and [i ɛ ə a ɔ u] respectively. Long vowels are always stressed; short vowels may be stressed and unstressed.

Phonetically, /eː oː/ are high-mid and /ɛː ɔː/ are low-mid; short /ɛ ɔ/ are normally low-mid, but are realized as mid before tautosyllabic /j v/ respectively. /eː oː/ do not occur before tautosyllabic /j v/ respectively. For further phonetic details see Toporišič (1984: 39–44).

The **tonemic system** has distinctive **stress**, **length** and **pitch**. A phonological word normally contains either one long vowel, or no long vowels; if it contains a long vowel, this is stressed; if it contains no long vowels, the final vowel is normally stressed; non-final short vowels also are stressed in a brief list of words (see Stankiewicz 1959: 74–5). The long vowels /iː eː ɛː aː ɔː oː uː/ are tonemically either low or high; tonemically high /ɛː ɔː/ are relatively uncommon. The short vowels /i ɛ a ɔ u/ are always tonemically high; the short vowel /ə/, however, shows the tonemic high versus low contrast on non-final syllables, especially before /r/, compare /pərstnica/ 'phalange' (with stressed tonemically high /ər/) and /pərstanəc/ 'ring finger' (with stressed tonemically low /ər/). Normally however, /ə/ has predictable tonemicity: high in final syllables and low in non-final syllables. The tonemically high and tonemically low syllables have traditionally (and in part misleadingly) been referred to, respectively, as 'falling' and 'rising'. Phonetic details are very complex: see Srebot-Rejec (1988) and Toporišič (1989).

The distinction between long and short vowels thus generally obtains in final syllables, and exceptionally elsewhere. The distinction between high and low tonemicity obtains on final and non-final syllables. The total number of possible phonetic combinations of vowel with length/brevity and high tonemicity/low tonemicity is as in table 8.1.

The standard transcription for the **tonemic system** cited in the Academy Dictionary (normally in parentheses after the headword) and also provided by Lencek (1982: 'phonemic tone system') and Toporišič (1984: 'tonemski naglas'), is as follows. First, as in Serbo-Croat, **superscript** diacritics are used to indicate differences in pitch on stressed vowels; in Slovene, the acute is marked on long low-pitch, the circumflex on long high-pitch, the grave on short low-pitch and the double grave on short high-pitch vowels. Second, the distinction between /eː/ and /ɛː/, and the distinction between /oː/ and /ɔː/, are shown with **subscript** marks, namely with a subscript dot marked beneath the more close vowel of each pair. In this system, therefore, í, ẹ́, é, á, ó, ọ́, ú represent long low-pitch (traditionally, 'rising') vowels; i, ệ, ê, â, ô, ộ, û represent long high-pitch ('falling') vowels; and ȉ, è, ȁ, ȍ, ȕ represent short stressed high-pitch ('falling') vowels. The shwa /ə/, represented orthographically as e, carries the double grave or the

Table 8.1   The tonemic vowel system

	Long	Short
Stressed		
High tonality	i　　　　　u 　e　　　o 　　ɛ　　ɔ 　　　a	i　　　　　u 　ɛ　ə　ɔ 　　a
Low tonality	i　　　　　u 　e　　　o 　　ɛ　　ɔ 　　　a	ə
Unstressed		i　　　　　u 　ɛ　ə　ɔ 　　a

single grave, if stressed. The combination /ər/ is represented as if it were a 'syllabic r': long low-pitch r̀, long high-pitch r̂. Vowels without diacritics are unstressed. Note also the use of the macron, for example ī in *njīhov* 'their', for long vowels which may be either tonemically high or low.

The famous dictionary of Pleteršnik (1894–5) used both subscript dots and subscript reversed-cedillas to mark both close /e/ and close /o/; this usage had comparative–historical relevance. Pleteršnik showed shwa with a special graphic variant of e. In this chapter, the 'tonemic' transcription (as just described) is used, except that 'shwa' is consistently represented as ə.

The **non-tonemic system** has distinctive stress and length but does not have distinctive pitch. A phonological word contains either one long vowel, or no long vowels; if it contains a long vowel, this is stressed; if it contains no long vowels, the final vowel is normally stressed (for exceptions, see Stankiewicz 1959: 74–5). The total number of possible phonetic combinations of vowel with length/brevity is thus as in table 8.2.

The normal contemporary transcription (non-tonemic), used – except in the citations in parentheses – in the Academy Dictionary, and used for most of the data in Lencek (1982: 'CSS norm system') and Toporišič (1984: 'jakostni naglas'), is as follows. Subscript diacritics are not used, and the superscript diacritics are used in two ways. The grave, as before, designates short stressed vowels. Long stressed vowels all bear the acute, except for /ɛ: ɔ:/, which are identified by the (now otherwise unused) circumflex. é, ó thus represent stressed /e: o:/, while ê, ô represent stressed /ɛ: ɔ:/. The schwa /ə/ is represented orthographically as e. Stressed /ər/ is represented by r̀.

The relationship between the tonemic and non-tonemic systems, for

Table 8.2   The non-tonemic vowel system

	Long				Short			
Stressed	i			u	i			u
		e	o					
		ɛ	ɔ			ɛ	ə	ɔ
			a				a	
Unstressed					i			u
						ɛ	ə	ɔ
							a	

stressed vowels, can be exemplified as in table 8.3. u and a follow the pattern exemplified here for i; o/ɔ follow that shown here for e/ɛ.

The Slovene forms presented in the modified tonemic transcription in this chapter can be rewritten according to the usual non-tonemic transcription (also modified to show shwa) by the following ordered rules:

1   rewrite é, ê as ê and ó, ô as ô;
2   rewrite ę́, ę̂ as é and ǫ́, ǫ̂ as ó;
3   rewrite à, ì, ù, r̀ as á, í, ú, ŕ;
4   rewrite ȉ, ȅ, ə̏, ȁ, ȍ, ȕ as ì, è, ə̀, à, ò, ù;
5   leave other vowel diacritics unchanged.

Let us now consider how these prosodic distinctions arose. Slovene inherited Proto-Slavonic phonemic length, phonemic pitch and phonemic stress, but – as the result of a number of changes in vocalic length and pitch, and also three major accent shifts with further concomitant changes in pitch – the incidence of prosodic phenomena became very different. In brief (see Lencek 1982: 81–117, *passim*) the following sequential changes occurred subsequent to the 'neoacute' accent shift (see chapter 3, section 2.26):

1   long rising vowels became short (rising);
2   short falling vowels became long (falling);
3   stress shifted from long falling non-final syllables one syllable to the right, producing new long falling vowels;
4   stress shifted from short final syllables one syllable to the left onto preceding long vowels, producing new long rising vowels;
5   old neoacute and all short rising vowels in non-final syllables were lengthened;
6   short rising vowels in final syllables became short falling;

Table 8.3   Comparison of the two systems

Tonemic	Transcription	Non-tonemic	Transcription
Long HT /i/ Long LT /i/	î⎫ í⎭	Long /i/	í
Short HT /i/	ì̂	Short /i/	ì
Long HT /e/ Long LT /e/	ê⎫ é⎭	Long /e/	é
Long HT /ɛ/ Long LT /ɛ/	ȩ̂⎫ ȩ́⎭	Long /ɛ/	ê
Short HT /ɛ/	è̂	Short /ɛ/	è
HT /ə/ LT /ə/	ə̂⎫ ə̀⎭	/ə/	ə́
HT /ər/ LT /ər/	r̂⎫ ŕ⎭	/ər/	ŕ

HT = High Tonality, LT = Low Tonality.

All the above changes occurred over the whole Slovene-speaking territory. The following accent shifts were localized:

7   stress shifted from short final syllables one syllable to the left onto preceding short /ɛ ɔ/, producing new long rising low-mid vowels;
8   stress shifted from short final syllables one syllable to the left onto preceding short /ə/, producing new stressed shwa.

Of these two developments, item 7 occurred in the dialects which formed the base of standard Slovene. Although item 8 did not generally occur in those dialects, it is now reflected in optional variants in the standard language, for example *məglà* ~ *mə̀gla* 'mist'.

Developments in the vowel system are extremely complex; in brief, the following changes occurred at different times but all at a relatively early date. In the dialects which were to form the base of standard Slovene, */ě/ results in /eː/, */ę ǫ/ change to /eː oː/, and the two strong *jers* (see chapter 3, section 2.25) change to /aː/ when long, and to /ə/ when short. Examples for the strong *jers*: *dân* ‹ **dьnь* 'day', *məglà* ~ *mə̀gla* 'mist' ‹ **mьgla*; for other examples, see below.

In addition, all mid vowels tended to be raised and/or diphthongized whenever they occurred both stressed and long, which (see above) was for historical periods of greatly varying duration, depending on their qualitative origin and the syllable in which they occurred. This is why the details of individual changes are so complex (see Rigler 1963, 1967; Lencek 1982: 92–121, *passim*). The distinction between /eː oː/ and /ɛː ɔː/ arose (in the Gorenjsko dialects, which contributed this feature to standard Slovene) because of the relatively recent date of prosodic change 7 above: by this time, all stressed mid vowels had been raised to mid-high [e o]; the newly lengthened mid vowels remained mid-low [ɛ ɔ]; hence words like *žéna* 'wife' ‹ **žená*, *góra* 'mountain' ‹ **gorá*, the stressed vowels of which contrast with those of words with original *jat'* and nasals, for example *cẹ́sta* 'road' ‹ **cěsta*, *mẹ́ta* 'mint' ‹ **měta*, *mọ́ka* 'flour' ‹ **mǫka*.

Further, unstressed and most short stressed vowels were 'reduced' (that is, many of their mutual oppositions were neutralized) and in some instances elided in most dialects, and especially the central ones. Although the standard pronunciation avoids reduced and elided vowels, these are very common in conversational styles, as in [kəp] 'heap' ‹ *kùp*, [prâu̯mo] 'we say' ‹ *právimo*.

Among other vocalic changes, vowel + liquid sequences (both initially before consonants and interconsonantally) were metathesized: **ōldi-* changed to *lādja* 'boat', **bērza* to *brẹ́za* 'birch' and **bōlto* to *bláto* 'mud'. Syllabic /r/ gave /ər/ and syllabic /l/ gave /ov/ (pronounced [ou]): **krt-* › *kȓt* 'mole', **dlg-* › *dȏlg* 'debt'.

Consonants. Slovene has twenty-one consonantal phonemes, as in table 8.4. Their distribution is as follows (here, C/ # = consonant or word-boundary and V = vowel):

/dž/ occurs in words of non-Slovene origin; it is not given phonemic status by some analysts.

/c x/ have voiced allophones [dz ɣ] occurring before voiced obstruents, for example *vzlíc gróžnji* [...dz gr...] 'in spite of the threat', *vȓh drevẹ́sa* [...rɣ dr...] '(at) the top of the tree'.

/n/ is realized as [ŋ] before /k g x/.

/v/ is realized as [u̯] between V and C/ #; [w] between C/ # and a resonant or voiced obstruent; [ʍ] between C/ # and voiceless ob-

Table 8.4   The consonant system

	Labials		*Dentals*		*Alveolar-palatals*		*Velars*	
Stops	p	b	t	d			k	g
Fricatives	f	v	s	z	š	ž	x	
Affricates			c		č	dž		
Nasals		m		n				
Glide					j			
Roll				r				
Lateral				l				

struent; [v] before V. Between V + /r/ and C/ #, /v/ is variously realized as [u] ~ [w] ~ [v].

/j/ is realized as [i̯] before C/ # and [i̯] ~ [j] before V.

The voiceless obstruents /p f t č s š k/ do not occur before a voiced obstruent; the voiced obstruents /b d dž z ž g/ do not occur before a voiceless obstruent, before a word boundary followed by a vowel or a resonant or in pre-pausal position.

/s z/ do not normally occur before /š č ž dž/.

In the standard consonantal orthography of Slovene the symbols used in table 8.4 are employed orthographically to represent their corresponding phonemes, except as follows:

When affected by the positional voicing and devoicing constraints just described; in these circumstances, the orthography is morphophonemic.

Orthographic v represents /v/, as above, except that the preposition *v* is optionally pronounced as [v], [u̯] or [u] before V.

Orthographic l is pronounced [u̯] or [u] (that is, it represents /v/) in many pre-consonantal and pre-pausal environments; there is some inconsistency in this (see Toporišič 1984: 73; and Lencek 1982: 168). It is always /v/ in the following circumstances: (a) in the masculine singular *l*-participle; (b) in masculine adjectives ending in el /əv/; and, normally, (c) in nouns ending in el /əv/ and in deverbal derivatives containing the sequence lc denoting inanimate agents, and in further derivatives therefrom containing the sequences lč, lk, lsk, lstv. Otherwise, its occurrence has to be specially listed.

Orthographic lj and nj represent respectively /l/ /n/ in pre-consonantal and pre-pausal position, and /lj/, /nj/ – that is, lateral + glide and nasal + glide – in pre-vocalic position.

Orthographic r represents the sequence /ər/ initially before a consonant and interconsonantally.

Orthographic h is used for the phoneme /x/.

When we consider the system from a diachronic perspective, we see that consonantal innovations in the dialects which form the base for the standard language were few in number, and in some cases changes that had occurred were excluded from it. The most important changes were as follows:

All palatal and potentially palatalized consonants were, earlier or later, resolved as non-palatal and non-palatalized. */ń ŕ ĺ/ changed to /nj rj lj/ pre-vocalically, /n r l/ elsewhere: *koń- › kònj /kòn/, kónja /kónja/ 'horse'; *čuvaŕ- › čuvár, čuvárja 'keeper'.

*/dl tl/ resulted in /l/, except in past verbal forms: *mydlo › mílo 'soap';

*pletla > plétla 'knit (l-PART F SG)'.

*/dj tj/ changed to /j č/: *medja > méja 'border', *svetja > svéča 'candle'; however, */zdj/ > /ž/ ~ /žj/: *dъzdj- > dɔ̄ž, dɔžjä 'rain'; */stj skj/ > /šč/: *isk-j- > iščem 'search (1 SG PRS)'.

*/v/ gave /v/ with allophonic distribution as described above.

*/l/ gave /v/ in the limited conditions described above.

*/ž/ changed to /r/ sporadically, for example, in */možete/ > mórete 'be able' (2 PL PRS)', */kъdo + že/ > kdɔ̣r 'who (REL)'.

Voiced obstruents were devoiced before voiceless obstruents, before a word boundary followed by a vowel or a resonant and in pre-pausal position, while voiceless obstruents were voiced before voiced obstruents.

2.2 Morphophonemic alternations inherited from Common Slavonic

Alternations in the **position of stress** (reflecting the Proto-Slavonic movable-stress pattern) are preserved in some nouns, for instance, gràdom (INST SG), gradɔ̣v (GEN PL) 'castle', and in some verbs, such as stopīti (INF), stópim (1 PRS) 'tread'.

Vowel–zero alternations, usually reflecting developments of jers, occur in the following environments: obstruent + obstruent, obstruent + sonorant, and sonorant + sonorant.

/ə/ ~ /Ø/ is very frequent, but is not automatic; compare in nouns: pɔ̄s (NOM SG), psä (GEN SG) 'dog' versus kɔs (NOM SG), kɔ̄sa (GEN SG) 'repentance'. Other examples in nouns: stəbɔ̄r (NOM SG), stəbrä (GEN SG) 'pillar'; kápəlj (GEN PL), káplja (NOM SG) 'drop'; in adjectives, təmɔ̄n (M NOM SG INDEF), tɔ̄mni (M NOM SG DEF) 'dark'; in preposition + clitic groups, third person singular masculine: nänj 'onto him' nâdɔnj 'above him'; and in l-participles, plę̄tɔl (M) plétla (F) 'knit'.

/i/ ~ /Ø/ occurs in nouns, before /j/: zârij (GEN PL), zárja (NOM SG) 'dawn'.

/a/ ~ /Ø/ occurs in a few nouns, like dân (NOM SG), dnę̄ (GEN SG) 'day'; ovāc (GEN PL), óvca (NOM SG) 'sheep'; and, as a variant of the /ə/ ~ /Ø/ alternation, in some adjectives, such as tɔmân ~ təmɔ̄n (M NOM SG INDEF), tɔ̄mni (M NOM SG DEF) 'dark'.

The /o/ ~ /e/ alternation – with the latter vowel occurring after /c č dž ž š j/ – is automatic in the context of what were, historically, 'hard' versus 'soft' stems. For examples in declension, see section 3.1.2 (prijâtelj 'friend', srcę̄ 'heart'), section 3.1.4 (vrɔ́če 'hot'). The alternation also occurs in derivative suffixes; see section 3.3.3 (prepisováti 'copy' versus izboljševáti 'improve').

The **first palatalization** and the **influence of following** *j are extensively preserved in verbal inflection and the formation of comparative adjectives, but are vestigial in nominal inflection. Together they give the following alternations, some of which show specific Slovene post-Proto-Slavonic developments:

/p ~ plj, b ~ blj, f ~ flj, v ~ vlj, m ~ mlj/;
/t ~ č, st ~ šč, d ~ j, zd ~ ž, z ~ ž, s ~ š, c ~ č/;
/n ~ nj, sn ~ šnj, l ~ lj, sl ~ šlj, r ~ rj/;
/k ~ č, sk ~ šč, g ~ ž, zg ~ ž, h ~ š/.

In verbs they are most apparent in two conjugation classes:

1   Class IIIb: in infinitive versus present forms: *gíbati, gíbljem* 'move', *rẹ́zati, rẹ́žem* 'cut', *klícati, klȋčem* 'call', *iskáti, íščem* 'search', *lagáti, lážem* 'tell lies';
2   Class IV: in infinitive versus past passive participial forms: *pozdráviti, pozdrávljen* 'greet', *branīti, bránjen* 'defend', *mísliti, mȋšljen* 'think', *udáriti, udárjen* 'strike'.

They also occur elsewhere, as in the present versus *l*-participle forms of *réčem, rékla* 'say', *lẹ́žem, légla* 'lie down'.

The alternation occurs in the inflection of only three nouns, see section 3.1.2 (*uhȏ* 'ear', *okȏ* 'eye', *igȏ* 'yoke'); it remains common in the comparison of adjectives (see section 3.1.4).

The **second palatalization** is preserved, but only barely, in verbal and nominal inflection. It comprises the following two alternations: /k ~ c, g ~ z/. The alternants /c z/ occur in derivatives; in the imperative forms of verbs with infinitive in *-či*, such as *réči, rékla, recîte* 'say', *striči, strigla, strízite* 'cut (hair)'; and in the plural of two masculine nouns: *vȏlk*, nominative plural *volcjȇ* 'wolf' (now considered archaic) and the standard *otrök* 'child, baby' (see section 3.1.2).

2.3   Morphophonemic alternations resulting from changes after Proto-Slavonic

Many of the numerous and complex changes listed in section 2.1, when added to an inherited system which already featured prosodic alternations, gave rise to even more of the same; none of these alternations are automatic, and very few are regular. Note should be taken especially of the following.

Of the **length alternations**, one is regular in nominal morphology: short vowels in final syllables alternate with long vowels when these syllables are non-final; for examples, see sections 3.1.2 (*hlëb* 'loaf', *deklë* 'girl', *mȉš* 'mouse') and 3.1.4 (*növ* 'new'). Length alternations also occur in verbs: *začnềm* (PRS 1 SG), *začnémo* (PRS 1 PL) 'begin'; *končǎl* (*l*-PART M SG), *končála* (*l*-PART F SG) 'finish'. **Alternations of position of stress** are common in nouns; for examples, see section 3.1.2 (*jézik* 'language', *srebrǫ* 'silver', *vréme* 'weather', *žéna* 'wife', *kǫst* 'bone'). Note also the stress retraction in prepositional phrases with some nouns, as in *primêr* 'example (ACC SG)' but *na prîmer* 'for example'; *vodǫ* 'water (ACC SG)' but *v vǫdo* 'into the water'. Stress alternations occur also in pronouns (see *jäz* in section 3.1.3) and in adjectives, see *mlâd* 'young' in section 3.1.4. They also occur in verbs: *vózi* (IMP 2 SG), *vozîte* (IMP 2 PL) 'drive'; *razvesêlil* (M PAST), *razveselíla* (F PAST) 'gladden'; *grešíl* (M PAST IMPFV), *pogrêšil* (M PAST PRFV) 'sin, err'. **Pitch alternations** occur frequently; see, for example, the nouns *grâd* 'castle', *mêsto* 'town', *žéna* 'wife', *kǫst* 'bone' in section 3.1.2; the pronoun *óna* 'she' in 3.1.3; and the adjective *médɔl* 'faint' in section 3.1.4. Examples in verbs include *umŕla* (PAST F), *umŕlo* (PAST N) 'die'; *víti* (INF), *vît* (supine) 'twist'; *dêlate* (PRES 2 PL), *dêlajte* (IMP 2 PL) 'work'. In numerals: *pêt* (NOM), *pétih* (GEN) 'five'.

Alternations between low-mid and high-mid vowels occur in nouns: *kǫst* (NOM SG), *kósti* (DAT SG) 'bone'; in adjectives: *vélik* (M NOM SG INDEF), *vêliki* (M NOM SG DEF) 'big'; and in verbs: *krêneš* (PRES 2 SG), *kréni* (IMP 2 SG) 'set out'; *prɔ̧siš* (PRES 2 SG), *prósi* (IMP 2 SG) 'ask'.

The regular consonantal alternation /l ~ v/ occurs in *l*-participial forms: *bîl* /biːv/ (M SG), *bilä* (F SG, M DU), *bilî* (F DU, M PL) 'be'; and in nominal morphology also: *mîsɔl* /miːsəv/ (NOM), *mîsli* (GEN) 'thought'. The sporadic change */ž/ › /r/ results in the unique alternation /g ~ r/ in the verb *móči* (INF): *mógla* (PAST F), *mɔ̧rem* (PRES 1 SG).

The neutralization of the voiced ~ voiceless opposition creates frequent automatic alternations: /d/ in *húdi brät* '(the) evil brother (DEF)', *hûd brät* '(an) evil brother (INDEF)' versus /t/ in *hûd stríc* '(an) evil uncle', *hûd óče* '(an) evil father', *hûd mɔ̧ž* '(an) evil husband'; /š/ in *izvršîti* 'to execute' versus /ž/ in *izvȓšba* 'execution'.

The alternation /k ~ x/ occurs in the preposition *k* 'towards', with /x/ occurring before /k g/: *h kováču* /xk-/ 'towards the smith', *h grâdu* /xg-/ [ɣg-] 'towards the town'; and occasionally elsewhere, as in *nikɔ̧gar* (GEN) ‹ **ni + koga + že* versus *nihčë* (NOM) ‹ **ni + kъto + že* 'nobody'.

3 Morphology

3.1 Nominal morphology

3.1.1 Nominal categories
Nouns, adjectives and pronouns are inflected for number, case and gender (including subgender); also, adjectives are inflected for definiteness and derive comparative and superlative degrees. For the relative frequency of the different subclasses within most of these categories, see Neweklowsky (1988).

Three **numbers** are distinguished: singular, dual and plural. There is
dual/plural syncretism in the genitive and locative cases in nouns and
adjectives, but no such syncretism obtains in pronouns. For limitations on
the use of the dual, see section 4.10.

There are six **cases**: nominative, accusative, genitive, dative, instrumental and locative. There is no separate vocative case. The locative (as in
other Slavonic languages), and also the instrumental, occur only in prepositional phrases. As compared with the other Slavonic languages that
have full declensions, there is relatively little case syncretism, but two
points may be mentioned: in the singular, most nouns and some pronouns
have dative–locative syncretism; and in the dual (which also shows number
syncretism, see above) there is nominative–accusative syncretism in nouns
and adjectives, and dative–instrumental syncretism in nouns, adjectives and
pronouns. A few nouns, adjectives and pronouns are indeclinable.

There are three **genders**: masculine, feminine and neuter. Nouns and
some pronouns have inherent gender. Gender is expressed by inflection in
other pronouns and in adjectives; it is also expressed in the nominative–
accusative of one numeral and in the nominative of two others. The gender
of nouns is partly predictable from their endings. A very few nouns may
have more than one gender; and a very few have gender varying according
to number. There is extensive gender syncretism, as in other Slavonic
languages, but note that adjectives do not fully neutralize gender oppositions in the nominative–accusative dual and plural. Unusually within
Slavonic, gender is expressed in personal pronouns other than the third
person singular, namely in all persons dual and plural. The neuter tends to
non-productivity: borrowed words normally become either masculine or
feminine. The opposition between the two animacy subgenders – animate
and inanimate – which is expressed in nouns and their co-referent adjectives and in some pronouns, occurs only in the singular. Only masculine
nouns are marked for animacy; animate nouns include, as well as human
and animal referents, also makes of car, kinds of illness, names of wines
and some other semantic categories (see Toporišič 1984: 212). Pronouns,
and also adjectives used pronominally, are marked as animate for masculine and neuter referents (see section 4.7).

The opposition between definite and indefinite is expressed in some
adjectives. Where it is expressed, it is generally very limited; in most
instances its overt marking is restricted to the masculine nominative singular. Nearly all adjectives (and adverbs derived from them) form analytic or
synthetic comparatives and superlatives.

3.1.2   Noun morphology
There are three major classes of declension, labelled here according to their
main Proto-Slavonic progenitor classes. The first continues the Proto-
Slavonic *o-stems, masculine and neuter; representatives of Proto-Slavonic

u-stems and *jo*-stems are in this class, the latter marked by automatic desinential alternations; nouns deriving from Proto-Slavonic consonantal stems are also subtypes of this class. The second continues Proto-Slavonic *a*-stems, *ja*-stems, *-y* stems and consonantal stems in *-er-*. The third is the continuation of the Proto-Slavonic *i*-stems. In addition to these classes, there are the following: (a) indeclinable nouns, for example acronyms such as *TÂM* (*Tovârna Avtomobilov Mâribor*) 'Maribor Auto Factory'; and (b) nouns with adjectival declensions (such as *dežúrni* 'male person on duty', *dežúrna* 'female person on duty' and many place names such as *Dolénjsko* (N) ~ *Dolénjska* (F) 'Lower Carniola').

Declensional type and gender are closely related: *o*-stem nouns are almost all masculine and neuter; *a*-stem nouns are typically feminine, but a few are masculine; all but one *i*-stem nouns are feminine. Neither gender nor declension class is predictable from the nominative singular form: nouns with nominative singular in a consonant are either masculine *o*-stems or feminine *i*-stems, whereby gender is largely predictable from derivative suffixes; nouns in *-a* are typically feminine and atypically masculine; and nouns in *-o*, *-e* are neuter (long-established words) or masculine (more recent borrowings). Some nouns have more than one gender and/or more than one declension, for instance *pót* 'path', which may be masculine (as *kót* 'corner') with a variant nominative plural, *póta*, or feminine (as *kóst* 'bone'). Indeclinable nouns may be masculine, feminine or neuter.

The most productive noun declensions are the masculine *o*-stems like *kót* 'corner' (table 8.5), the *a*-stems like *lipa* 'linden' (table 8.11), and the *i*-stems like *smŕt* 'death' (table 8.12). There is usually syncretism of the dative and locative singular (the exceptions being some *o*-stem nouns). Moreover the genitive dual is always identical to the genitive plural, while the locative dual has the same form as the locative plural and so the former are omitted in the paradigms given.

***O*-stem class.** The regular paradigm of ***o*-stem (masculine)** nouns is illustrated with *kót* 'corner' (table 8.5). Various nouns which might have been

Table 8.5   *o*-stems (masculine), inanimate

	SG	DU	PL
NOM	kót	kóta	kóti
ACC	kót	kóta	kóte
GEN	kóta	(= GEN PL)	kótov
DAT	kótu	kótoma	kótom
INST	kótom	kótoma	kọ̄ti
LOC	kótu	(= LOC PL)	kọ̄tih

Table 8.6   *o*-stems (masculine), animate

	SG	DU	PL
NOM	děd	dę́da	dę́di
ACC	dę́da	dę́da	dę́de
GEN	dę́da		dę̄dov

used for comparative purposes are irregular; some are illustrated below. Animate nouns have genitive desinences for the accusative *in the singular only*. The first half of the paradigm for *děd* 'grandfather' (which also occurs as *dę̄d, dę́da*) is thus as in table 8.6.

Variants (stem):
1 The /ə ~ Ø/ alternation is regular and frequent but not automatic, see section 2.2.
2 A few nouns in *-əlj* /əl/ have, instead of the /ə ~ Ø/ alternation, an extension of this suffix to /-əln-/ before all vocalic endings: thus *nágəlj, nágəljna* 'carnation'.
3 Most nouns in *-r* extend the stem to *-rj-* before all non-zero endings, as in *denár, denárja* 'money'. Also, most borrowings ending in vowels extend the final stem-vowel with /-j-/: *alíbi, alibíja* 'alibi'. *Dǝ̄ž* 'rain' extends its stem in the same way: *dəžjä*.
4 The /-ov-/ infix in the dual and plural, exemplified in *grȃd* 'castle' (table 8.7) occurs, often as a stylistic variant, with several nouns. Note that the infix **-ev-* does not occur. (*grȃd* has the optional variant genitive singular *gradȗ*, see item 9 below).
5 Many nouns show stress and/or pitch alternations; there are many different paradigmatic patterns. Note especially the alternation between short and long vowels (see section 2.3) in nouns like *hlěb, hlę́ba* 'loaf', *čěp čépa* 'bung'; these two examples show the neutralization, in the nominative singular, of the high-mid versus low-mid vocalic distinction. Note also stress shifts in, for instance, *jézik, jezíka* 'language', *trębuh trebúha* 'belly'.
6 *Člóvek* 'man, person' has a regular *o*-stem declension (*človę́ka* and so on) in the singular and dual (except where dual and plural show syncretism), but has the plural *ljudję̄, ljudȋ, ljudȋ, ljudę̄m, ljudmȋ, ljudę́h*, that is, it has endings much like those of *kǭst* 'bone' (see below).
7 *Otrǫ̀k, otrǫ́k/otrók-* 'child, baby' has plural *otróci, otróke, otrǫ̀k, otrókom, otrǫ́ki, otrōcih*.

Table 8.7   *o*-stems (masculine), with *-ov-* infix

	SG	DU	PL
NOM	grâd	gradôva	gradôvi
ACC	grâd	gradôva	gradôve
GEN	grâda		gradǫ́v
DAT	grâdu	gradôvoma	gradóvom
INST	grâdom	gradôvoma	gradôvi
LOC	grâdu		gradôvih

Variants (ending):

8   Stems ending in /j c č š ž dž/ automatically replace /-o-/ with /-e-/ in instrumental singular, dative–instrumental dual and genitive plural and dative plural; these stems represent (and pre-empt) the original *jo-stem class; for example, *prijâtelj* 'friend', respectively *prijâteljem, prijâteljema, prijâteljev, prijâteljem.*

9   Some nouns have genitive singular /-ū/ as a (usually, optional) variant of /-a/, for instance, *sîn* 'son', *sîna ~ sinû*; others have a (normally optional) stress shift in the genitive singular, as *mǫ̂ž* 'husband' below.

10 Some nouns have optional nominative plural in unstressed /-je/: thus *golǫ̂b, golǫ̂bi ~ golǫ̂bje* 'pigeon'; *fânt* 'boy' *fántje ~ fánti.*

11 The paradigm of *mǫ̂ž* 'husband' (table 8.8) illustrates a number of other common variant endings, especially those with stressed /-ę-/; genitive plural in -Ø; and instrumental plural in /-mi/.

For *o*-**stem (neuter)** the regular paradigm, *mę́sto* 'town' is given in table 8.9.

Variants (stem):

1   The zero ~ vowel alternation is regular and frequent. Two nouns have /-a-/: *dnö̀* 'ground', genitive plural *dán ~ dnȍv ~ dnóv*; *tlȁ* 'floor' (plurale tantum), genitive *tál*. Nouns with final /-j/ (except a list of nouns with /-nj/ /lj/) have /-i-/: *mȍrje* 'sea', genitive plural *mȍrij*. Otherwise, the alternating vowel is /-ə-/, as in *súkno* 'cloth' genitive plural *súkən.*

2   Many nouns show stress and/or pitch alternations: *blagǫ̂* 'goods', dative–locative singular *blâgu*; *srebrǫ̂* 'silver', dative–locative singular *srêbru ~ srȩbru.*

Variants (ending):

3   Stems ending in /j c č š ž/ automatically replace /-o-/ with /-e-/ in nominative–accusative and instrumental singular, dative–instrumental

Table 8.8   *o*-stems (masculine), irregular

	SG	DU	PL
NOM	mǫ̑ž	možȃ	možjȇ
ACC	moža	možȃ	možẹ̑
GEN	moža		mǫ́ž
DAT	mǫ̑žu	možẹ̑ma	možẹ̑m
INST	mǫ̑žem	možẹ̑ma	možmí
LOC	mǫ̑žu		možẹ̑h

Table 8.9   *o*-stems (neuter)

	SG	DU	PL
NOM	mẹ̑sto	mȇ̄sti	mẹ̑sta
ACC	mẹ̑sto	mȇ̄sti	mẹ̑sta
GEN	mẹ̑sta		mẹ̑st
DAT	mẹ̑stu	mȇ̄stoma	mẹ̑stom
INST	mẹ̑stom	mȇ̄stoma	mẹ̑sti
LOC	mẹ̑stu		mẹ̑stih

dual and dative plural; these represent the original *jo-stems (see section 2.2). Thus *srcẹ̑, sȓcem, sȓcema, sȓcem* 'heart'.

Three subtypes of *o*-**stem consonantal extensions** are firmly maintained in Slovene: those with /-n-/, those with /-s-/ and those with /-t-/. There are ten '*n*-nouns', fourteen '*s*-nouns' and the '*t*-noun' declension became productive and was extended so that not only young animals (*pīšče* 'chick') but various words for humans (*revšě* 'pitiable child') and men's names (*Tǫ̑ne* 'Tony') have been included; indeed, there are now one feminine and many masculine '*t*-nouns'. In all three instances, the endings are generally those of normal *o*-stem neuter nouns. A typical instance, the '*t*-noun' *jágnje* 'lamb', is given in table 8.10.

Variants (stem):
1 All three subtypes have truncated nominative–accusative singular and full stems in all other cases, as above. '*N*-nouns' have -*e* as the truncated stem, -*en*- elsewhere; '*s*-nouns' have -*o* and -*es*- respectively.
2 In each subgroup there are some nouns with no prosodic alternations, like *jágnje* 'lamb', for instance *imẹ̑ imẹ̑na* 'name', *drevǫ̑ drevẹ̑sa* 'tree'. Most nouns, however, have stress or pitch alternations: *deklȇ̌, deklẹ̑ta*

Table 8.10   *o*-stems (neuter), consonantal extension

	SG	DU	PL
NOM	jágnje	jágnjeti	jágnjeta
ACC	jágnje	jágnjeti	jágnjeta
GEN	jágnjeta		jágnjet
DAT	jágnjetu	jágnjetoma	jágnjetom
INST	jágnjetom	jágnjetoma	jágnjeti
LOC	jágnjetu		jágnjetih

genitive singular, *deklẹta* nominative plural 'girl'; *vréme, vremẹna* 'weather'; and see *uhọ* 'ear' below.

3   Three nouns have stem consonantal alternations: *uhọ ušẹsa* 'ear'; *okọ, očẹsa* 'eye'; *igọ, ižẹsa* 'yoke'.

Variants (ending):

4   The many masculine '*t*-nouns' – all of which have human referents – have accusative identical with genitive; *óče, očẹta* 'father'; *fantě, fantẹta* 'boy'; *Francě, Francẹta* 'Frank'. The feminine/neuter noun *deklě* 'girl' has accusative identical with nominative.

A-**stem class.** All nouns – both feminine (the vast majority) and masculine (like *slúga* 'man-servant') – have the same general declensional pattern. (The masculine nouns may also decline as animate *o*-stems; see above.) In table 8.11 are shown the regular paradigm, *lípa* 'linden', and the subtype *žéna* 'wife' (see item 4 below) which represents at most some twenty-five nouns. There are no morphophonemic alternations surviving from the **ja*-stems or **-ynji* nouns: for example, *dúša* 'soul' and *bogínja* 'goddess' decline like *lípa*.

Variants (stem):

1   The vowel ~ zero alternation is regular and generally predictable. /i ~ Ø/ occurs in nouns with stems ending in consonant + /j/: *lādja* 'boat', genitive plural *lādij*; *-nja, -lja* nouns must be listed. /ə ~ Ø/ occurs in stems ending in non-resonant + resonant (for instance, *séstra* 'sister', genitive plural *sêstər*), non-resonant + resonant + /j/ (*káplja* 'drop', genitive plural *kâpəlj*), some combinations of resonant + resonant, and (rarely and archaically) in other consonant clusters. Nouns like *cẹrkəv* 'church' and *britəv* 'razor' (see 5 below) are regular in this respect. /a ~ Ø/ is found in a few words, like *óvca* 'sheep', genitive plural *ovāc ~ óvc*.

2   Proto-Slavonic consonantal stems in /-r-/ survive in that two nouns have the extension /-er-/ in all cases except the nominative singular:

Table 8.11 *a*-stems

	SG	DU	PL
NOM	lípa	lípi	lípe
ACC	lípo	lípi	lípe
GEN	lípe		lip
DAT	lípi	lípama	lípam
INST	lipo	lípama	lípami
LOC	lípi		lípah
NOM	žéna	ženę̂	ženę̂
ACC	ženǫ̂	ženę̂	ženę̂
GEN	ženę́ ~ ženę̂		žên ~ ženā̄
DAT	žéni	ženâma	ženâm
INST	ženǫ́	ženâma	ženâmi
LOC	žéni		ženâh

máti 'mother' and *hčî* 'daughter', genitive singular *mátere hčę̂re*; see 5 below.

Variants (ending):

3   The nouns which decline like *žéna* 'wife', that is with stress shifts, such as *góra* 'mountain' and *gláva* 'head', have become largely regularized and usually now decline as *lípa*.

4   Nouns with stressed *-ǎ* as the nominative singular ending (all of which can also have regular stem stress) have a number of optional or obligatory long desinential vowels, for example, *stəzǎ* 'path', accusative singular *stəzę̂* ~ *stəzě̂*, instrumental plural *stəzâmi*.

5   The Proto-Slavonic *ý-stems, represented in Slovene by nouns in *-əv*, and the two '*r*-nouns' differ from the paradigms displayed here in two respects (in which cases these nouns follow the *i*-stem class): accusative singular in /-∅/ and instrumental singular in /-ijo ~ -jo/ (of which the former occurs after two consonants). Examples of accusative singular and instrumental singular: *máter*, *mâterjo*; *hčę̂r*, *hčę̂rjo*; *cę̂rkəv*, *cę̂rkvijo*; *brîtəv*, *brîtvijo*.

***I*-stem class.** All nouns in this class are feminine except *ljudję̂* 'people' (see above). The regular paradigm is that of *smr̂t* 'death'; also in table 8.12, *kǫ̂st* 'bone' exemplifies the stress, pitch and vocalic alternations that are very common in this class.

Variants (stem):

1   Four nouns have short vowels in the nominative–accusative singular which alternate with long vowels, for instance, *mȉš*, genitive singular

Table 8.12   *i*-stems

	SG	DU	PL
NOM	smr̂t	smr̂ti	smr̂ti
ACC	smr̂t	smr̂ti	smr̂ti
GEN	smr̂ti		smr̂ti
DAT	smr̂ti	smr̂tma	smr̂tim
INST	smr̂tjo	smr̂tma	smr̂tmi
LOC	smr̂ti		smr̂tih
NOM	kộst	kostî	kostî
ACC	kộst	kostî	kostî
GEN	kostí		kostī̃
DAT	kósti	kostę̄ma	kostę̃m
INST	kostjó	kostę̄ma	kostmí
LOC	kósti		kostę́h

míši 'mouse'. Very many monosyllabic and some polysyllabic nouns decline like *kộst* 'bone' above, with pitch and stress alternations. Some nouns have a pitch alternation but no stress alternation, thus *lúč* 'light', genitive singular *lúči*, instrumental singular *lũčjo*; some have qualitative alternations: *ộs* 'axle' dative–locative singular *ósi*.

2   The vowel ~ zero alternation occurs in this declension too: the normal vowel is /-ə-/, occurring when the stem ends in non-resonant + resonant: thus *mîsəl, mîsli* 'thought'; *povộdənj, povộdnji* 'flood'.

Variants (ending):

3   Stems in non-resonant + resonant, and non-resonant + resonant + /j/, have instrumental singular in *-ijo*, dative–instrumental dual in *-ima*, instrumental plural in *-imi*: *mîslijo, mîslima, mîslimi*.

3.1.3   Pronominal morphology

In the **personal pronouns**, Slovene has separate non-clitic forms for all three persons in all three numbers. All three persons show gender distinctions in the dual and plural, but in the nominative case only; the third person singular distinguishes all three genders in the nominative–accusative and makes a two-way distinction in all other cases. In the nominative a total of eighteen pronominal distinctions are made. There is also a reflexive personal pronoun, unmarked for number, gender and person, lacking a nominative.

The non-nominative dual person pronouns occur as exemplified below and also co-occur with the corresponding form of *dvâ* 'two' (3.1.5), for example, *nâju dvâ* 'us both (M ACC)', *nâju dvê* 'us both (F ACC)'.

Separate clitic forms obtain in accusative, genitive and dative for all singular persons, for the reflexive, and for the third dual and third plural; there is much syncretism. Note the separate bound clitic forms; see below for their use. First- and second-person pronouns, dual and plural, have clitic forms identical with their non-clitic forms except that they lack stress.

The forms of the first-person non-clitic pronouns *jäz* 'I', *midva*, *mędve/ midve* 'we both', *mî*, *mę̂* 'we (all)' are given in table 8.13. The second-person non-clitic pronouns *tî* 'you', *vîdva*, *vędve/vîdve* 'you both', *vî*, *vę̂* 'you (all)' can be found in table 8.14. Reflexive non-clitic pronouns are given in table 8.15. The third person singular non-clitic pronouns are *ŏn*,

Table 8.13 First-person pronouns

	SG		DU		PL	
		M		N/F	M	N/F
NOM	jàz	mîdva		mę̂dve/mîdve	mî	mę̂
ACC	méne		nâju		nàs	
GEN	méne		nâju		nàs	
DAT	méni		nâma		nàm	
INST	menój/mâno		nâma		nâmi	
LOC	méni		nâju/nâma		nàs	

Table 8.14 Second-person pronouns

	SG		DU		PL	
		M		N/F	M	N/F
NOM	tî	vîdva		vę̂dve/vîdve	vî	vę̂
ACC	tébe		vâju		vàs	
GEN	tébe		vâju		vàs	
DAT	tébi		vâma		vàm	
INST	tebój/tâbo		vâma		vâmi	
LOC	tébi		vâju/vâma		vàs	

Table 8.15 Reflexive pronoun

ACC	sébe
GEN	sébe
DAT	sébi
INST	sebój/sâbo
LOC	sébi

óno, óna 'he/it, it, she/it' (see table 8.16). The neuter nominative has a stylistic variant *onǫ̀*. There is gender syncretism between masculine and neuter in all non-nominative cases. The third person dual and plural non-clitic pronouns *ónadva, ónidve/onẹ̀dve* 'they both', *óni, óna, óne* 'they (all)' can be found in table 8.17. Four nominatives have stylistic variants: dual *onâdva*, plural *onî, onâ, onệ*. There is total gender syncretism in all non-nominative cases.

There are special **clitic** forms for first person singular, second person singular and third person singular, dual and plural. Note the distinction between free and bound clitics (table 8.18). The bound clitics are post-posed to most of the prepositions that take the accusative; in this context the prepositions receive a tonemically high pitch and, if containing a mid vowel, exhibit /ẹ/ or /ǫ/, for example, *nâme* 'on me', *čẹ̀zse* 'across oneself', *mệdnju* 'between the two of them', *nâdnje* 'over them'. With the third person singular masculine–neuter *-nj* the /ə ~ Ø/ alternation occurs: *nânj* 'on him/it', *nâdənj* 'over him/it'. In the pre-clitic context the preposition *v* occurs in the otherwise non-occurrent form *va-*: *vâme* 'into me', *vânj* 'into him/it'.

There are pronominal declensions (presented below) differing from adjectival declensions in many particulars, for *tâ* 'this' and *kdǭ* 'who', *kāj*

Table 8.16   Third person singular pronouns

	M		N	F
NOM	ȍn		óno	óna
ACC		njéga		njǫ̀/njǭ
GEN		njéga		njẹ́
DAT		njému		njéj/njȅj/njî̃
INST		njím		njǫ́
LOC		njém		njéj/njȅj/njî̃

Table 8.17   Third person dual and plural pronouns

		DU			PL		
	M		N/F	M	N	F	
NOM	ónadva		ónidve/onẹ̀dve	óni	óna	óne	
ACC		njĩju/njî̃h			njî̃h		
GEN		njĩju/njî̃h			njî̃h		
DAT		njíma			njî̃m		
INST		njíma			njími		
LOC		njĩju/njî̃h/njîma			njî̃h		

Table 8.18   Clitic pronouns

	1 SG	2 SG	REFL	3 SG M/N	F	3 DU	3 PL
Free clitics							
ACC	me	te	se	ga	jo	ju/jih	jih
GEN	me	te	se	ga	je	ju/jih	jih
DAT	mi	ti	si	mu	ji	jima	jim
Bound clitics							
ACC	-me	-te	-se	-nj	-njo	-nju	-nje

'what'. At least two pronouns are fully indeclinable, relative *kȉ* 'who' and *čigar* 'whose'; and *onę̄* 'whats'isname' is normally indeclinable. All other pronouns decline like regular adjectives, with nominative masculine singular either only short (ending in a consonant, like *tólik* 'so large'), or only long (ending in -*i*, like *tȋsti* 'that'). Pronouns are thus inherently definite or indefinite (see 3.1.4). Possessive pronouns decline like definite adjectives. Most pronouns may be used adjectivally as well as pronominally. The most common are as follows; for a fuller list see Toporišič (1984: 243–8, 271–5).

Demonstrative: *tȃ* 'this', *tȋsti* 'that', *ǫni* 'that (yonder)'; *onę̄* 'whats'isname', *tȃk, tȃkšən* 'such a'. The first three of these also occur, usually with emphatic meaning, with preposed *le-* or (more usually) with postposed -*le* affixed to fully declined forms: thus *letȩ̄ga* ~ *tȩ̄gale* 'this (EMPH, M GEN SG)'. In non-standard Slovene *tȃ* may function as a definite article (see 3.1.4).

Interrogative: *kdǭ* 'who?', *kȃj* 'what?', *kȃkšən* 'what sort of a?', *kǭlik* 'how large?', *čigáv* 'whose?', *katę̄ri* 'which?'.

Relative: *kdǭr* 'who', *kȁr* 'what', *katę̄ri, kȉ* 'which', *čigar* 'whose'.

Indefinite: (a) *kdǭ* 'any(one)', *kȁj* 'any(thing)', *katę̄ri* 'anyone/-thing'; (b) prefixed: *nekdǭ* 'someone' and *nę̄kaj* 'something'; *nekatę̄ri* 'some', *nę̄ki* 'a'.

Negative: *nihčȅ* ~ *nȋhče* ~ *nȋkdo* 'nobody', *nȉč* 'nothing', *nobȅn* 'no'.

Possessive: *mǫ́j, nȃjin, nȁš* 'my, our (DU), our (PL)'; *tvǫ́j, vȃjin, vȁš* 'your, your (DU), your (PL)'; *njegǫ́v* ~ *njegȍv, njȩ́n, njūn, njȋhov* 'his/its, her/its, their (DU), their (PL)'; *svǫ́j* 'own'. The above forms alternate with the following in all other cases, numbers and genders: *mǫ́j-, tvǫ́j-, svǫ́j-, nȃš-, vȃš-, njegǫ́v-*.

Other: *vȝs* 'all', *vsȃk* 'each', *sȃm* 'self, mere, the very'.

There are numerous other pronouns, most of them compounds of the preceding ones: *vsâkršɔn* 'every kind of', *málokatēri* 'few', *mãrsikdǭ* 'many a person', *kdǫ̂rkǫli* 'whoever'. Note that all these pronouns have masculine accusative singular forms identical to the nominative (for inanimate referents) and the same as the genitive (for animate referents); this is signalled by NOM/GEN. *Tâ* 'this' (table 8.19) has alternate forms: in the feminine dative–locative singular *téj* and the neuter/feminine nominative–accusative dual *tȩ̂*. In the dual, the relevant forms of *dvâ* usually co-occur. *Vɔ̂s* 'all' differs from *tâ* only in the nominative singular *vɔ̂s, vsḝ, vsǎ*, and in that the stem vowels are tonemically high and short. *Kdǭ* 'who?', *kdǫ̂r* 'who (REL)', *nihčḝ* 'nobody', *kāj* 'what?', *kãr* 'what (REL)' and *nĭč* 'nothing' decline as in table 8.20; further compounds of *kdǭ, kāj* follow the same pattern.

Table 8.19   Demonstrative pronoun *ta*

| | SG | | | DU | | | PL | | |
	M	N	F	M	N	F	M	N	F
NOM	tâ	tǫ̂	tâ	tâ	tî	tî	tî	tâ	tȩ̂
ACC	NOM/GEN	tǫ̂	tǫ̂	tâ	tî	tî	tȩ̂	tâ	tȩ̂
GEN		tȩ̂ga	tȩ̂		tȩ̂h			tȩ̂h	
DAT		tȩ̂mu	tèj		tȩ̂ma			tȩ̂m	
INST		tȩ̂m	tǫ́		tȩ̂ma			tȩ̂mi	
LOC		tȩ̂m	tèj		tȩ̂h			tȩ̂h	

Table 8.20   *kdǭ, kāj* and pronouns based on them

NOM	kdǭ	kdǫ̂r	nihčḝ	kāj	kãr	nĭč
ACC	kǭga	kǫ̂gar	nikǫ̂gar	kāj	kãr	nĭč
GEN	kǭga	kǫ̂gar	nikǫ̂gar	čȩ̂sa	čȩ̂sar	ničȩ̂sar
DAT	kǭmu	kǫ̂mur	nikǫ̂mur	čȩ̂mu	čȩ̂mur	ničȩ̂mur
INST	kǭm	kǫ̂mər	nikǫ̂mər	čȋm	čîmər	ničîmər
LOC	kǭm	kǫ̂mər	nikǫ̂mər	čȩ̂m	čȩ̂mər	ničȩ̂mər

Table 8.21   Use of long- and short-form adjectives

	Indefinite	*Definite*	
Adjective alone	nɔ̆v 'a new one'	ta nóvi 'the new one'	(1)
Noun alone	en pɔ̆s 'a dog'	pɔ̆s 'the dog'	(2)
Adjective + noun	{ nɔ̆v pɔ̆s 'a new dog' { en nɔ̆v pɔ̆s 'a new dog'	nóvi pɔ̆s 'the new dog' ta nóvi pɔ̆s 'the new dog'	(3a) (3b)

3.1.4   Adjectival morphology

In Slovene the Proto-Slavonic opposition between **short and long adjectives** survives in the opposition indefinite versus definite, but is formally very circumscribed. This opposition, in its most simple form, is expressed as in table 8.21.

The use of *en* and *ta*, which in many respects act as indefinite article and definite article respectively, is, however, not encouraged in the written literary norm, and is limited in spoken standard Slovene also; in these varieties, the normal adjective + noun phrase is (3a) in table 8.21 rather than (3b), and definite *nóvi* for (1) and indefinite *pɜs* for (2) are common. The indefinite versus definite opposition is, moreover, not expressed in all adjectives; and in those where it is expressed it obtains only in the masculine nominative (and accusative inanimate) singular, except in a very few where it extends to some more, or to all, of the declension. The indefinite versus definite opposition is not expressed in several types of adjectives, including the following (which can be used in either function). Denominal derivatives in *-v* and *-in* (like *brátov* 'brother's', *králjev* 'king's', *māterin* 'mother's') have indefinite forms only. Denominal and other derivatives in *-ji, -ski, -ški, -čki* (like *bóžji* 'God's', *slovénski* 'Slovene'), comparative and superlative forms and the words *ôbči* 'common', *prâvi* 'right, proper', *râjni* 'the late' have definite forms only.

In two adjectives the opposition is expressed in all forms. In one it is shown by a prosodic alternation: *vélik, veliko, velika* (INDEF) versus *vêliki, vêliko, vêlika* (DEF) 'large'. In the other it is expressed suppletively: *mâjhɔn, mâjhno, mâjhna* (INDEF) but *mâli, mâlo, mâla* (DEF) 'small'. In a few adjectives the opposition is expressed in more than just the masculine nominative singular, but not throughout the paradigm; in all other adjectives (except those listed above with only indefinite, and with only definite, forms) it is expressed in **only the masculine nominative singular**. In a few, the formal expression is by morphophonemic means. Examples (indefinite versus definite): with a qualitative alternation, masculine nominative singular *dóbɔr* versus *dóbri* 'good'; with a prosodic alternation, feminine nominative singular *bogáta* versus *bogâta* 'rich', *stára máti* 'an old mother' versus *stâra máti* 'grandmother'; with both qualitative and prosodic alternations, masculine/feminine nominative singular *débel, debéla* versus *debêli, debêla* 'fat'. In the great majority, the masculine nominative singular indefinite has a zero ending, and the definite ends in *-i*.

The adjective *nòv, nóv-* 'new' has regular declension; in the masculine (and, rarely, the neuter) accusative singular the choice of nominative versus genitive form depends on animacy (table 8.22).

Variants (stem):

1 The alternation of short vowel in the masculine nominative singular indefinite with long vowels elsewhere (see section 2.3), exemplified in *nòv*, is common.

Table 8.22   Regular adjective declension

	SG			DU			PL		
	M	N	F	M	N	F	M	N	F
NOM	{nòv / nóvi}	nóvo	nóva	nóva	nóvi	nóvi	nóvi	nóva	nóve
ACC	NOM/GEN	nóvo	nóva	nóvi	nóvi	nóve	nóva	nóve
GEN	nóvega	nóve					nóvih
DAT	nóvemu	nóvi		nóvima			nóvim
INST	nóvim	nóvo		nóvima			nóvimi
LOC	nóvem	nóvi					nóvih

2 Several adjectives optionally have mobile accent patterns. Of these, most belong to one type, exemplified by *mlad* (definite *mládi*) 'young': nominative singular *mlâd, mladǫ̂, mláda*, genitive singular *mládega, mláde*, instrumental singular *mládim, mladǫ̂*, etc.

3 The vowel ~ zero alternation is common: *otękəl, otékl-* 'swollen', *mirən, mīrn-* 'tranquil'; often, there is free qualitative/stress variation on the adjectives involved: *médəl ~ mə̀dəl ~ mədə̃l* 'faint'. Several adjectives have variants with /a/ as well as /ə/ occurring in the masculine nominative singular: *hládən ~ hladân, hládna* 'cool'. Those with stress on the ending in the masculine nominative singular definite tend to maintain this throughout the paradigm.

Variants (ending):
4 The /o ~ e/ alternation obtains in the nominative–accusative singular: compare *nóvo* 'new' and *vsakdánje* 'everyday', *vrǫ́če* 'hot'.

One adjective is used only predicatively and therefore declines for gender and number but has only nominative case, *räd, ráda* 'happy'. Fully indeclinable are the attributive adjective *pęš* 'by foot' in, for instance, *pę̂š hǫ́ja* 'walking tour'; and several attributive/predicative adjectives, as for instance, *pocę́ni* 'cheap': *pocę́ni pohištvo* 'cheap furniture', *pocę́ni knjiga* 'cheap book', *knjiga je pocę́ni* 'the book is cheap'; *tə̂šč* 'unbreakfasted': *s tə̂šč želǫ́dci* 'with empty stomachs', *óna je tə̂šč* 'she has not breakfasted'; and many relatively recent borrowings: *prima blagǫ̂* 'first-class goods', *prìma fîlm* 'first-class film'; *fâjn člóvek* 'fine person', *fâjn oblę̂ka* 'fine clothing'; *bę̂ž* 'beige', *fèr* 'fair'. See also section 4.3.

The **comparative** and **superlative** degrees of a given adjective are formed either analytically or synthetically. The analytic phrases use *bolj* 'more' and *nàjbolj* 'most'. Synthetic comparative forms utilize the suffixes *-ši, -ji* and *-ejši*, and their superlative degrees add the prefix *nàj-*. Adjectives which use analytic comparative or superlative forms include those which do not participate in the definite versus indefinite opposition, for example, *divji* 'wild' *bolj divji, nàjbolj divji*; adjectives derived participially from verbs, for example, *vròč* 'hot'; specific derivatives, for example, those in *-ast* such as *múhast* 'capricious'; words for colours; and others such as *mókər* 'wet' and *súh* 'dry'. In synthetic comparison, (a) *-ejši* is added to polysyllabic stems: *rodovītən* 'fertile' *rodovītnejši, nàjrodovītnejši*; to monosyllabic stems ending in more than one consonant: *čīst* 'clean' *čistêjši, nàjčistêjši*; and to a list of monosyllabic stems in single consonants, including *nòv* 'new', *novêjši, nàjnovêjši*; (b) *-ji* is, normally, added to stems which end in /ž/, /š/ or /č/ (deriving from the final velar of the positive degree): *drâg* 'dear' *drâžji, nàjdrâžji*; (c) *-ši* is added to other stems (after palatalization): *mlad* 'young', *mlâjši, nàjmlâjši*. If a polysyllabic adjective ends in vowel + /k/, this syllable is deleted, and rules (b) and (c) normally apply: *nízək* 'low' *nìžji, nàjnìžji*. There are several exceptional forms, such as *lêp* 'beautiful' *lêpši, nàjlêpši*, and suppletive forms like *dóbər* 'good' *bôljši* 'better' *nàjbôljši* 'best'.

Adverbs derived from adjectives form their comparative and superlative degrees according to the same subclasses (a), (b) and (c) above, but with the following differences: group (a) take *-eje*: *bogáto* 'richly' *bogatêje, nàjbogatêje*; group (b) replace *-ji* with *-(j)e*: *blizu* 'near' *blìž(j)e, nàjblìž(j)e*; and group (c) replace *-ši* with, normally, *-še*: *tənkô* 'thinly' *tânjše, nàjtânjše*.

3.1.5   Numeral morphology

Of the **cardinal numerals** '1' has a regular adjectival declension; except in the masculine nominative singular (where there are two forms: *édən*, used substantivally, and *èn*, adjectivally) the stem is invariant *én-*, hence masculine genitive singular *énega* and so on. The dual is not used. The plural is used with pluralia tantum words: *éna vráta* 'one door'. For the function of *èn* as an indefinite article see section 3.1.3. *Dvâ* '2', *tríje* '3' and *štírje* '4' decline similarly. All show the opposition masculine versus neuter/feminine in the nominative; '2' shows it in the accusative also (table 8.23). *Obâ, obê* 'both' declines exactly like *dvâ, dvê*.

All other numerals, except *tisôč, milijôn* and *milijarda* (see below) decline like '5' (table 8.24), but they may also not decline, as noted below. The same pattern is followed by, for example, *šêst* '6', *šêstnajst ~ šestnájst* '16', *šêstindvâjset* '26', *šêstdeset* '60' and so on. *Sédam, sédmih* '7' and *ôsəm, ósmih* '8' show the /ə ~ Ø/ alternation. '100' has a unique alternation: *stô, stótih*. Note that compounds between '21' and '99' have the morphemes reversed from their Arabic-numeral order: *énindvâjset* '21', *devêtindevêtdeset* '99'. Note also that in numerals over 100 terminating in non-compounds, only the final word declines: *tisôč dvâ/dvê* '1,002'.

The remaining numerals, *tisôč* (M) '1,000', *milijôn* (M) 'million' and *milijârda* (F) 'milliard/billion', decline like nouns.

Table 8.23   'Two', 'three', 'four'

	M	N/F	M	N/F	M	N/F
NOM	dvâ	dvệ	tríje	trí	štírje	štíri
ACC	dvâ	dvệ	trî		štíri	
GEN	dvẹ̄h		trẹh		štîrih	
DAT	dvẹ̄ma		trẹm		štîrim	
INST	dvẹ̄ma		trẹmi		štîrimi	
LOC	dvẹ̄h		trẹh		štîrih	

Table 8.24   'Five'

NOM	pệt
ACC	pệt
GEN	pétih
DAT	pétim
INST	pétimi
LOC	pétih

The loss of declinability, which is very noticeable in conversational Slovene, may be detected in the standard language in noun phrases headed by prepositions, where numerals above '4' are normally not declined.

Ordinal numerals decline like adjectives: *pr̂vi, pr̂va, pr̂vo* 'first'; *drùgi* 'second', *trẹ́tji* 'third', *četŕti* 'fourth', *péti* 'fifth', *šésti* 'sixth' and so on.

3.2   Verbal morphology

3.2.1   Verbal categories

Verbs are inflected for number, person and gender. Tense, voice and mood are expressed partly in inflection, partly in compound phrases. Aspect is inherent in verbal forms; normally, there is a derivational relationship between aspectual pairs. Finite verbal forms include the present, imperative, future, past pluperfect, present conditional and past conditional. There is also a series of optative forms. The verb 'be' is expressed in all appropriate numbers, persons and genders, and in three tenses. It has a special negative present-tense form.

The opposition in **number** singular : dual : plural is expressed in all finite verbal forms. There is no number syncretism. See section 4.10 for the use of the dual. In certain ('polite' or 'formal') circumstances, number is used conventionally rather than referentially. There are two conventions: (a) 'Vikanje': the second person plural (which is always masculine!) replaces the second person singular (but never the second person dual);

Table 8.25   Numerals

CARDINALS

édən, én- '1'	dvâjset '20'
dvâ, dvę̂ '2'	énindvâjset '21'
tríje, trî '3'	trídeset '30'
štírje, štíri '4'	štírideset '40'
pę̂t '5'	pę̂tdeset '50'
šę̂st '6'	šę̂stdeset '60'
sédəm '7'	sédəmdeset '70'
ósəm '8'	ósəmdeset '80'
devę̂t '9'	devę̂tdeset '90'
desę̂t '10'	stǫ̂ '100'
enájst '11'	dvę̂sto '200'
dvânajst ~ dvanájst '12'	trísto '300'
trînajst ~ trinájst '13'	štíristo '400'
štîrinajst ~ štirinájst '14'	pę̂tsto '500'
pę̂tnajst ~ petnájst '15'	šę̂ststo '600'
šę̂stnajst ~ šestnájst '16'	sédəmsto '700'
sę̄dəmnajst ~ sedəmnájst '17'	ósəmsto '800'
ǭsəmnajst ~ osəmnájst '18'	devę̂tsto '900'
devę̂tnajst ~ devetnájst '19'	tisǫ́č '1,000'

ORDINALS

pȓvi '1st'	dvâjseti '20th'
drũgi '2nd'	énindvâjseti '21st'
trę́tji '3rd'	trídeseti '30th'
četŕti '4th'	štírideseti '40th'
péti '5th'	pę̂tdeseti '50th'
šésti '6th'	šę̂stdeseti '60th'
sédmi '7th'	ϳédəmdeseti '70th'
ósmi '8th'	ósəmdeseti '80th'
devę̂ti '9th'	devę̂tdeseti '90th'
desę̂ti '10th'	stóti '100th'
enájsti '11th'	dvę̂stoti '200th'
dvânajsti ~ dvanájsti '12th'	tristóti '300th'
trînajsti ~ trinájsti '13th'	štiristóti '400th'
štîrinajsti ~ štirinájsti '14th'	petstóti '500th'
pę̂tnajsti ~ petnájsti '15th'	šeststóti '600th'
šę̂stnajsti ~ šestnájsti '16th'	sedəmstóti '700th'
sę̄dəmnajsti ~ sedəmnájsti '17th'	osəmstóti '800th'
ǭsəmnajsti ~ osəmnájsti '18th'	devetstóti '900th'
devę̂tnajsti ~ devetnájsti '19th'	tisǫ́či '1,000th'

(b) 'Onikanje': dialectally and archaically, the third person plural replaces the second person singular (but never the second person dual) in the same way. Slovene has three **persons** in finite verbal forms. The third person singular and third person plural are used impersonally. There is person syncretism in the dual, where the second and third persons have the same endings. The **gender** opposition masculine : feminine : neuter is expressed in participles, and hence in the past, future and so on. Unusually for Slavonic, a (now rare and archaic) gender distinction (masculine versus feminine/neuter) may be expressed by optional endings for the dual in the present and imperative: -*va* (M) versus -*ve* ~ -*vi* (F/N) and -*ta* (M) versus -*te* ~ -*ti* (F/N). Slovene distinguishes four **tenses**: future, present, past and pluperfect; past and pluperfect are opposed only in the indicative. The pluperfect seldom occurs. All except the present, the future of 'be' and one of two expressions of the future perfective are expressed by compounds. The four participles and three gerunds express time simultaneous with or anterior to that of the main verb. Tense is implicit in other categories, such as imperative, supine.

Normally, a given verb is inherently of imperfective or perfective **aspect**; and normally, aspectually correlative pairs have the same lexical meaning. The imperfective verb is semantically unmarked. The aspectual system is similar to that of the other Slavonic languages, except that the future perfective is expressed both (a) by the non-past form of the perfective, and (b) by the same compound formation that is used for the future imperfective (namely, the future of 'be' and the *l*-participle); the perfective with *verba dicendi* expresses the present tense; and perfective verbs with some temporal adverbs may denote repetition. All verbal categories occur with both aspects, except that both present gerunds and (with one lexical exception) the present active participle only occur in the imperfective. Some verbs are bi-aspectual. These include both native items like *rodīti* 'give birth to' and recent borrowings such as *protestīrati* 'protest'. A few perfective verbs, for instance *pogospǫditi se* 'put on airs', have no imperfective counterparts; and conversely, a few imperfective verbs, like *poslúšati* 'listen to', have no perfective ones. Some half-dozen pairs of imperfective verbs are limited semantically to determinate and indeterminate meaning respectively. These involve verbs of motion like *nosíti* versus *nésti* 'carry', *vozíti* versus *peljáti* 'convey'.

The following **moods** are expressed: indicative, imperative and conditional. All verbal categories except those listed in this subsection are indicative. A number of modal expressions are semantically close to the imperative and conditional moods. There is, normally, a partial imperative paradigm: the first person dual and plural, the second person singular, dual and plural and the third person singular. The conditional, expressed by compound forms using the invariable word *bi*, obtains in the present and past (with the meanings 'would' and 'would have' respectively). Semantically, the imperative is complemented (and partly overlapped) by present optative compounds (utilizing the particle *nàj*) with the meaning 'let ...'. In addition, there are compound past optatives: *nàj* + *bi* + (*bil*) + *l*-participle, normally equivalent to 'should'. Other modal expressions use invariable auxiliaries like *lahkǫ* and verbs such as *mǫrati*: *lahkǫ déla* 'he may work', *mǫra délati* 'he must work'.

Verbs are, inherently, either transitive or intransitive. For types of, and constructions using, reflexive verbs, see below and section 4.8. The **passive voice** is expressed with the following: (a) a reflexive verb; (b) a zero subject and the verb in the third person plural; (c) the past passive participle + 'be'.

There are five indeclinable **non-finite forms**: infinitive, supine, past gerund, present gerund in -(*j*)*e* and present gerund in -*č*. There are also four participles: present active, past active in -(*v*)*ši*, past active in -*l* (the '*l*-participle') and past passive. There is also a verbal substantive -*nje/-tje* (see section 3.3.1). The infinitive : supine opposition is expressed by a formal distinction which is largely neutralized in conversational Slovene. For usage see section 4.5. The two basic gerunds are the present gerund in -(*j*)*e* and the past gerund. Not all verbs form gerunds. The present gerund is supplemented semantically by the short-form present active participle in -*č*, which acts as a third gerund. Three participles are fully declinable: the present active participle, the (rarely used) past active participle in -*vši* and the past passive participle. The fourth participle, the past active participle in -*l*, is used only in the nominative; its use is restricted to compound verbal expressions, most importantly the past and the future.

There are as many as fifteen **compound-tense** constructions, some of them rare. The most common are here exemplified with the verb *hvalīti pohvalīti* 'praise' in the first person singular; where the perfective prefix *po-* is in parentheses, both aspects may occur. For the auxiliaries, present *səm* and future *bom*, see below.

1   Active: past (*səm* (*po*)*hválil* 'I praised'); pluperfect (*səm bil pohválil* 'I had praised'); future (*bǭm* (*po*)*hválil* 'I shall praise'); present conditional (*bi* (*po*)*hválil* 'I would praise'); past conditional (*bi bil* (*po*)*hválil* 'I would have praised'); present optative (*nàj* (*po*)*hválim* 'I should praise'); and past optatives (*nàj bi* (*po*)*hválil* and *nàj bi bil* (*po*)*hválil* 'I should have praised').

2   Passive: present (*səm* (*po*)*hváljen* 'I am praised'); past (*səm bil* (*po*)*hváljen* 'I was praised'); future (*bǭm* (*po*)*hváljen* 'I shall be praised'); present/past conditional (*bi bil* (*po*)*hváljen* 'I would be praised'); and imperative (*bǭdi* (*po*)*hváljen!* 'be praised!').

Three verbs have special present negative conjugations: (a) *ne bíti*: *nísəm* 'am not', *nísi ní, nísva* and then as the present of *bíti* (see below); (b) *ne iméti*: *nímam* 'haven't' and so on (see *imę̄ti* below); and (c) *ne hotę̄ti*: *nǫ́čem* ~ *nę́čem* 'don't want to' and so on (see *hotę̄ti* below).

3.2.2   Conjugation
Non-compound verbal categories are formed on the following: (a) the infinitive stem (infinitive, supine, past gerund, past active participle in

-(*v*)*ši*, *l*-participle, past passive participle); and (b) the present stem (present/simple future, imperative, present gerund in -(*j*)*e*, present gerund in -*č*, present active participle). To these stems are added various affixes.

The **infinitive** is normally formed by the addition of -*ti*; infinitives deriving from Proto-Slavonic forms in *-*kti*, *-*gti* have -*či*. In conversational Slovene, the final -*i* is elided and (in some verbs) the stress shifts. The **supine** is like the infinitive except that it lacks the final -*i*; hence, -*t* or -*č*. The **past gerund** is in -*ši* (most consonantal stems) or -*vši* (most vocalic stems). The **past active participle** is in -(*v*)*ši* and so is as the past gerund but with regular adjectival desinences. The **past passive participle** adds the normal adjectival endings to one of the affixes -*t*, -*n*, -*en*; these generally follow the normal Slavonic distribution among verbal classes. The **past active participle** in -*l*, the '*l*-participle', is used in compound forms and only in the nominative (see table 8.26).

Table 8.26   *l*-participle endings

	M	N	F
SG	-l	-lo	-la
DU	-la	-li	-li
PL	-li	-la	-le

The **present stem** cannot be predicted from the infinitive, except when certain derivative suffixes are involved (thus, -*niti* verbs have the present in -*ne*-, -*irati* verbs have -*ira*- and so on); there are, however, some regular and productive patterns, especially -*ati* : -*a*- and -*iti* : -*i*-. The present/ simple future endings are given in table 8.27.

In the third person plural, verbs in -*ijo* have the variant -*ę* and verbs in -*ejo* (plus a few in unstressed -*ejo*) have the variant -*ǫ*; most of these variants are stylistically very limited.

Most athematic verbs have different endings from the above only as follows: second–third person dual -*sta*, second person plural -*ste*, third person plural -*do*; there is variation between these and the regular endings

Table 8.27   Present-tense endings

	SG	DU	PL
1	-m	-va	-mo
2	-š	-ta	-te
3	-Ø	-ta	-jo

in the third person plural; for example, *bíti* future: *bǫ̂m, bǫ̂š, bǫ̂; bǫ̂va bǫ̂sta, bǫ̂sta; bǫ̂mo, bǫ̂ste, bǫ̂do ~ bǫ̂jo*. The verb *bíti* (present positive) is more irregular: *sɜ̀m, sì, jè; svà, stà, stà; smɔ̀, stè, sɔ̀*.

The endings of the **imperative** are as follows: second and third person singular *-i ~ -j*; first dual *-iva ~ -jva*; second dual *-iva ~ -jva*; first plural *-imo ~ -jmo*; second plural *-ite ~ jte*. The alternation *i ~ j* is regular (*-i-* with consonantal stems, *-j-* with vocalic stems); there are exceptions, such as *státi, stojím* 'stand' *stój!*

The **present active participle** endings are: 'class IV' verbs (see below): *-ěč, -éč-*; other classes with vocalic stems: *-jǫ̂č, -jǫ̂č-*; others with consonantal stems, *-ǫ̂č, -ǫ̂č-*; followed by the normal adjectival endings. The **present gerund** has: (a) generally *-e* after consonantal stems, *-je* after vocalic stems; also (b) as the present active participle with zero ending.

The classification of **conjugation classes** adopted here as suitable for comparative purposes is based on the thematic vowel of the present stem; it derives from a simplified version of Svane (1958: 89–117). This is not the optimal classification for non-comparative descriptions; such a classification would emphasize the productive classes (here, II, IIIc, IV and the *-ovati ~ -evati* verbs in IIIa) and categorize the more restricted verb types in fewer groupings; see also Toporišič (1987). The quoted thematic vowel occurs in all persons and numbers of the present/simple future conjugation (except alternant third person plural forms; see above). (Here, C = consonant, Cj = palatalized consonant, V = vowel):

Ia   (**infinitive -C-*ti***) **present -*e-***: The old 'consonantal infinitive class' is well maintained; note over ten 'velar' roots in *-či*, all showing the /*k ~ c*/ or /*g ~ z*/ alternation, including *móči, mórem, pomózi!, mǫ̂gɔl* 'be able'; and nine 'nasal' roots, including *vzẹ́ti, vzámem* 'take'. A total of over seventy roots can be classified in this group.

Ib   (**infinitive -*a-ti***) **present -*e-***: This class includes *bráti* and *zváti*, but only five other roots.

II   (**infinitive -*ni-ti***) **present -*ne-***: Slovene shows an idiosyncratic development of **-nǫ-* to *-ni-* in the infinitive stem. This class is still very well represented and is productive in native derivations.

IIIa   (**infinitive -V-*ti***) **present -*je-***: Slovene maintains ten roots in *-uti, -ujem* and fifteen in *-iti, -ijem*. Some *-eti* and *-ejati* verbs in this class have alternative conjugations, with present in *-ejem* and/or in *-em*; *-ajati* verbs usually have present in *-ajam*. There are some seven roots, like *kláti* and *mlẹ́ti*, that display the Proto-Slavonic metathesis. Verbs in *-ovati ~ -evati, -ujem* are numerous.

IIIb   (**infinitive -*a-ti***) **present -C*je-***: Many roots display the Proto-Slavonic consonantal palatalizations, for instance *písati* 'write', *kázati* 'show', *jemáti* 'take' below; see also section 2.2. Many conjugate also according to class IIIc, such as *škrípati* 'creak' present *škrípljem ~*

škrípam; *súkati* 'twist' present *súkam* ~ *súčem*.

IIIc **(infinitive -*a-ti*) present -*a*-:** Contraction of *-*aje*- to -*a*- resulted in the extremely productive class exemplified by *dẹlati* 'work'.

IV **(infinitive -V-*ti*) present -*i*-:** This class comprises the very numerous (and derivatively productive) verbs in -*iti* like *molīti* 'pray'; a relatively small group in -*eti* like *velẹti* 'command'; an even smaller group in -*ati* like *slišati* 'hear'; and four anomalous verbs like *spáti* 'sleep'.

V **Athematic and irregular:** Slovene has six verbs in the athematic class, namely *bīti* 'beat', *jẹsti* 'eat', *dáti* 'give', *dẹti* 'say; put' and *vẹdeti* 'know' below, and the present of *íti* 'go', namely *grẹm* ~ *grẽm*. There are a number of prefixed athematics, like *dobūti* 'obtain' *dobộm*, normally replaced by regularly conjugated forms such as *dobím*. Nearly all athematic verbs have variant forms, and some of the endings have been realigned with non-athematic ones. The originally athematic *ima- is now regularly conjugated, although its combination of infinitive in -*ẹti* and present in -*ām* (present conjugated as class IIIc) is unique. *Hotẹti, hộčem* 'want to' (present conjugated as class Ia) must also be treated as irregular.

Reflexes of Proto-Slavonic verb classes: Instances where the Modern Slovene reflex of the Proto-Slavonic example shows an atypical morphological shift are here enclosed in square brackets, followed by more regular representatives of the class or subclass in question, if available.

Theme in -*e*/-*o*

*nes-, nese-	nésti, nésem 'carry'
*ved-, vede-	vésti, védem 'lead'
[*čis-, čьte-	štẹti, štẽjem 'count']
	cvǝstī, cvǝtẽm 'blossom'
*i-/šьd-, id-	íti/šǝl [grẹm ~ grẽm] 'go'
	nájti, nájdem 'find'
[*ja(xa)-, jade-	jāhati, jāham ~ jāšem 'ride (horse)']
*gre-, grebe-	grébsti, grébem 'rake'
[*ži-, žive-	živẹti, živím 'live']
	plūti, plóvem 'sail'
*reč-, reče-	réči, réčem 'say'
*načę-, načьn-	začẹti, začnẽm 'begin'
*umrě-, umьr-	mrẹti, mrẽm 'die'
*sta-, stan-	státi, stânem 'cost'
[*sъsa-, sъse-	sǝsáti, sǝsâm 'suck']
*zъva-, zove-	zváti, zóvem 'call'
*bьra-, bere-	bráti, bérem 'read'

Theme in -ne
*dvign-, dvigne-   dvígniti, dvȋgnem 'lift'
*min-, mine-   mȋnīti, mīnem 'elapse'

Theme in -je
*ču-, čuje-   čúti, čȗjem 'hear, stay awake'
*pě-, poje-   pę́ti, pójem 'sing'
*kry-, krъje-   kríti, krȋjem 'conceal, cover'
*bi-, bьje-   bíti, bȋjem 'beat'
[*bra-, borje-   borȋti se, borím se 'fight']
                        kláti, kǫ́ljem 'slaughter'
*mle-, melje-   mlę́ti, mę́ljem 'mill'
[*děla-, dělaje-   dę́lati, dę́lâm 'work']
*umě-, uměje-   umę́ti, umêjem ~ umȩ̂m 'know how,
                        understand'
*kaza-, kaže-   kázati, kážem 'show'
*pъsa-, piše-   písati, píšem 'write'
*ima-, jemlje-   jemáti, jémljem 'take'
*darova-, daruje-   darováti, darȗjem 'present'
*sěja-, sěje-   sejáti, sêjem 'sow'

Theme in -i
*moli-, moli-   molȋti, mǫ́lim 'pray'
*xodi-, xodj-   hodȋti, hǫ́dim 'walk'
*velě-, veli-   velę́ti, velím 'command'
*slyša-, slyši-   slíšati, slȋšim 'hear'
*sъpa-, sъpi-   spáti, spím 'sleep'

Athematic and irregular
*by-, (je)s-   bíti, sǝm 'be'
*jas-, jas/d-   ję́sti, ję́m 'eat'
*da-, das/d-   dáti, dám 'give'
*dě-, dě-   dę́ti, dȩ̂m 'say; put'
*vě-, věs/d-   vę́deti, vę́m 'know'
*ima-, ima/e-   imę́ti, imâm 'have'
*xotě-, xotje-   hotę́ti, hǫ́čem 'want to'

Sample paradigms are given in table 8.28.

3.3 Derivational morphology
In this section, the patterns and forms cited exemplify only the most
productive derivations; many others exist.

Table 8.28   Illustrative verb paradigms

	Ia	IIIc	IV
INF	réči	délati	molíti
SUP	rèč	délat	mólit
PAST GER	rêkši	podélavši	pomolivši
l-PART M SG	rékəl	délal	mólil
l-PART F SG	rékla	dḗlala	molíla
PAST PASS PART	rečèn	dḗlan	móljen
PRS 1 SG	réčem	dḗlam	mólim
PRS 2 SG	réčeš	dḗlaš	móliš
PRS 3 SG	réče	dḗla	móli
PRS 1 DU	réčeva	dḗlava	móliva
PRS 2, 3 DU	réčeta	dḗlata	mólita
PRS 1 PL	réčemo	dḗlamo	mólimo
PRS 2 PL	réčete	dḗlate	mólite
PRS 3 PL	réčejo	dḗlajo	mólijo
IMP 2 SG	réci	dḗlaj	móli
IMP 2 PL	recîte	dḗlajte	molîte
PRS ACT PART	rekọ̄č¹	delajọ̄č	–³
PRS GER	–²	deláje	molę̄

Notes:
1 *rekọ̄č*, formally a participle, is used as a present gerund.
2 *réči*, like most class Ia verbs, has no formal present gerund (see note 1). The verb *iti* 'go' (which has an athematic present conjugation, see above) has a present gerund *gredę̄* which derives from a class Ia verb.
3 *molíti* has no present active participle; *nosíti* has the form *nosēč ~ nosĕč*.

3.3.1   Major patterns of noun derivation
Nouns are derived from other parts of speech, and from other nouns; chiefly by suffixation and by compounding, but also by other means.
Suffixation (Bajec 1950–2; Toporišič 1984: 124–47):

-e: denominal; offspring and other animate: *fantè* 'young boy' (*fànt* 'boy').
-ba: deverbal: *obrâmba* 'defence' (*obraníti* 'defend'), *glâsba* 'music' (*glasíti se* 'sound').
-oba: de-adjectival: *grenkóba* 'bitterness' (*grénək* 'bitter').
-təv: deverbal; alternate verbal nouns and/or with more concrete meanings: *molítəv* 'act of praying; prayer' (*molíti* 'pray').
-stvo: denominal and de-adjectival: *otrǭštvo* 'infancy' (*otròk* 'infant').
-ava: deverbal: *izgovarjâva* 'pronunciation' (*izgovârjati* 'pronounce').
-ota: mostly denominal and de-adjectival: *lepóta* 'beauty' (*lę̂p* 'beautiful').
-ost: the most common derivative: *lastnǭst* 'trait' (*lāstən* 'own').
-ica: *dę̑klica* 'young girl' (*deklè* 'girl'), *bīstrica* 'mountain brook' (*bístər*

'limpid'); especially productive in *-nica, -lnica*: *knjížnica* 'library' (*knjíga* 'book').

-ǝc: *lóvǝc* 'hunter' (*lovīti* 'hunt'); *brâtǝc* 'little brother' (*brȁt* 'brother'); especially productive in *-lǝc*: *igrâlǝc* 'player' (*igráti* 'play').

-nja: nomina actionis from verbs: *próšnja* 'request' (*prosīti* 'request').

-an, -jan: *nosȁn* 'large-nosed man' (*nộs* 'nose'); in compounds, for example, *-čan*: *Ljubljânčan* 'inhabitant of Ljubljana'.

-ina: *kovína* 'metal' (*kováti* 'forge'); especially productive in compounds: *-ovina*: *jeklovína* 'hardware' (*jéklo* 'steel'); *-ščina*: *slovénščina* 'Slovene language'.

-telj: borrowed, from Serbo-Croat and elsewhere: *odpošiljâtelj* 'sender' (*odpošíljati* 'dispatch').

-ar: however early this was first borrowed (from Old High German *-āri* and/or Latin *-arius*), its use was presumably reinforced by centuries of contact with Germanic (see Striedter-Temps 1963: 73–5). It remains in both early and later borrowings (*prídigar* 'preacher'); and became very productive: *kopìtar* 'cobbler' (*kopíto* 'last'), *harpunar* 'harpooner'.

-išče: location: *krompiríšče* 'potato-field' (*krompír* 'potato').

-je: de-adjectival abstracts: *mlādje* 'youth' (*mlâd* 'young'); phrasal derivatives: *meddộbje* 'interval' (*med* 'between' + *dóba* 'period'); and in compounds, regularly for verbal nouns in *-nje, -tje*: *gíbanje* 'movement' (*gíbati* 'move'), *pítje* 'drinking' (*píti* 'drink').

-ija: originally from Latin, this was nativized and remains productive. Alongside borrowings, *traparíja* 'stupidity', *filozofíja* 'philosophy', are many Slovene derivatives: *sleparíja* 'swindle' (*slệp* 'blind', *slepár* 'cheat').

-nik: replaced original (and now less productive) *-ik*: *črnílnik* 'inkwell' (*črnílo* 'ink').

-ǝk: *inter alia*, for diminutives: *gûmbǝk* 'small button' (*gûmb*), and deverbals: *izvlệčǝk* 'extract' (*izvléči* 'extract').

-ka; *inter alia*, in diminutives: *râčka* 'duckling' (*ráca* 'duck'); derivation of feminines: *cigânka* 'gypsy (F)' (*cigȁn* 'gypsy (M)'); common in compounds: *-lka*: *igrâlka* 'player (F)' (*igrâti* 'play').

Compound nouns (Vidovič-Muha 1988) are normally subordinating, that is, they consist of head plus modifier. The components are usually joined with *-o- ~ -e-*:

Noun + verb base: when the base comprises a noun and a verb, the compound normally places the noun first: *zemljevîd* ('land + see') 'map'.

Verb + noun base: more rarely, the verbal component precedes the nominal one: *smrdokâvra* ('stink + crow') 'hoopoe'.

Adjective + verb base: *brzojȁv* ('fast + communicate') 'telegraph'.

Adjective + noun base: *hudoûrnik* ('evil + hour/weather' + suffix) 'mountain torrent'.

Quantifier + noun base compounds are very common: *dvộbồj* ('two + fight') 'duel'; *malodûšje* ('little + spirit') 'faint-heartedness'.

Noun + noun base: *drevorẹd* ('tree + row') 'boulevard'.

Juxtaposition – where syntactic strings are combined with no modification other than some loss of stress – is uncommon: *dộlgčas* ('long + time') 'boredom'.

Most productive prefixes are recently borrowed (like *super-*) but many Slavonic prefixes are used productively in nominal derivation: *med-*, *ne-*, *pa-*, *pra-*, *proti-*, *raz-*, and so on: *pâkristâl* 'false crystal', *râzjezuît* 'former Jesuit'.

3.3.2   Major patterns of adjective derivation

Adjectives are derived from verbs and nouns, and from other adjectives; chiefly by suffixation and secondarily by compounding, but also by other means. Adjectives are also derived semantically from participles.

Suffixation (Bajec 1950–2; Toporišič 1984: 147–57):

-ljiv: deverbal: *prizanesljĩv* 'lenient' (*prizanésti* 'pardon'); denominal: *bojazljĩv* 'timorous' (*bojâzən* 'fear').

-ov ~ -ev: *inter alia*, masculine possessive: *brátova hiša* 'brother's house' (*brăt* 'brother'); animals: *lẽvov* 'lion's' (*lẽv* 'lion'); plants: *bâmbusov* 'bamboo' (*bâmbus* 'bamboo').

-in: especially for feminine possessive: *sẽstrina hiša* 'sister's house' (*séstra* 'sister'); animals: *levínjin* 'lioness's' (*levínja* 'lioness'); plants: *mírtin* 'myrtle' (*mírta* 'myrtle').

-ən: extremely productive, both alone and in compounds. Alone, especially for deverbals: *vidən* 'visible' (*vídeti* 'see'); denominals: *lẹ̃sən* 'wooden' (*lẹ̃s* 'wood'); de-adverbials: *hkrātən* 'simultaneous' (*hkrāti* 'at the same time'). It occurs in compounds with twenty or more nominal and adjectival suffixes.

-ji: very productive in animate denominals: *otrộčji* 'infantile' (*otrŏk* 'infant').

-nji: de-adverbial: *nekdānji* 'old-time' (*nẹ̃kdaj* 'once upon a time').

-ək: deverbal: *bridək* 'painful' (*bríti* 'shave'), *rézək* 'sharp' (*rẹ́zati* 'cut').

-ski: productive denominally, both simply: *stránski* 'lateral' (*străn* 'side'); and in compounds: *strânkarski* 'factional' (*strânka* '(political) party', *strânkar* 'party member').

Compound adjectives are both subordinate: *miroljúbən* 'peace-loving' (*mìr* 'peace', *ljubíti* 'love') and co-ordinate: *bẹ́lo-mộdro-rdẽč* 'white-blue-and-red (as of a flag)'. Juxtaposition is rare: *bojažéljən* 'bellicose'.

Many productive prefixes are of non-Slovene origin, like *anti-* and *ante-*; a few are native, such as *nad-*, *ne-*, *pa-*, *pra-*: *nădpolovičən* 'more-than-half' (*nad* 'over' + *polovičən* 'half'); *pre-* may be prefixed to very many adjectives: *prelệp* 'extremely beautiful'.

Adjectivalization of participles is frequent: both *l*-participle and past passive participle forms have become adjectivalized: *dorāsəl* 'fully grown' (*dorásti* 'grow up'); *poštĕn* 'honest' (*poštẹti* 'count').

In addition to those that are common in Slavonic, Slovene has some unusual patterns of **adverb derivation**. Note especially:

-oma ~ *-ema*, suffixed to stems deriving from: nouns (*oziroma* 'respectively', *stōpnjema* 'gradually'); adjectives (*rẹdkoma* 'rarely'); verbs (*nenệhoma* 'incessantly', compare *nệhati* 'cease'); and phrases (*natihoma* 'on the quiet'). The pattern is common: Mader (1981), which is based on a 40,000-word corpus, lists sixty-one of these adverbs.

3.3.3   Major patterns of verb derivation

Verbs are derived from other parts of speech, and (especially in the derivation of aspectual pairs) from other verbs; derivation is chiefly by prefixation and suffixation, but also by compounding. Conjugation classes (see section 3.2.2) are given in square brackets. One borrowed derivative suffix is listed here; see also section 5.3.

Normally, there is a derivative relationship between the two members of an aspectual pair. Slovene follows the general Slavonic system quite closely. Two patterns are generally employed: (a) suffixation, sometimes with alternation of the root and/or replacement of another suffix, and normally with change in conjugation; when the derivative suffix is -∅-, the root alternation and/or conjugation change become especially salient; (b) prefixation. The derivational patterns tend towards complementarity: imperfectives are most frequently derived from perfectives by suffixation and concomitant changes; perfectives are normally derived from imperfectives by prefixation. Suppletive aspectual pairs exist, but are uncommon, for instance, *govorīti* [IV] (or *práviti* [IV]) (IMPFV) / *réči* [Ia] (PRFV) 'speak', *dẹlati* [IIIc] (IMPFV) / *storīti* [IV] (PRFV) 'do'.

Only a few of the many suffixes are exemplified here; for brevity, neither root alternations nor suffixal alternations are noted:

-n-: *pihati* [IIIc] (IMPFV) / *píhniti* [II] (PRFV) 'blow'.
-j-: *začẹti* [Ia] (PRFV) / *začệnjati* [IIIc] (IMPFV) 'begin'.
-∅-: *pǫ́čiti* [IV] (PRFV) / *pǫ́kati* (IMPFV) [IIIc] (PRFV) 'explode'.
-ov- ~ *-ev-*: *izbǫljšati* [IIIc] (PRFV) / *izboljševáti* [IIIa] (IMPFV) 'improve'.
-av-: *zaznáti* [IIIc] (PRFV) / *zaznâvati* [IIIc] (IMPFV) 'perceive'.

Imperfective verbs, when prefixed, normally become perfective. Common prefixes are as follows (here, imperfective examples precede perfective ones; unless noted, both members of an aspectual pair have the same conjugation):

do-: *skočīti* [IV] 'jump' / *doskočīti* 'reach by jumping'; *trpẹti* [IV] 'suffer' / *dotrpẹti* 'die'.

iz-: *trẹsti* [Ia] 'shake' / *iztrẹsti* 'empty by shaking'.

na-: *lepīti* [IV] 'glue' / *nalepīti* 'affix by gluing'; *glọdati* [IIIb] 'gnaw' / *naglọdati* 'nibble'.

o-/ob-: *držáti* [IV] 'hold' / *obdržáti* 'keep'.

od-: *lomīti* [IV] 'break' / *odlomīti* 'break off'; *govorīti* [IV] 'speak' / *odgovorīti* 'reply'.

po-: *molčáti* [IV] 'be silent' / *pomolčáti* 'be silent for a short while'.

pod-: *písati* [IIIb] 'write' / *podpísati* 'sign'.

pre-: *peljáti* [IIIc] 'drive' / *prepeljáti* 'transport'.

pri-: *nésti* [Ia] 'carry' / *prinésti* 'bring'; *rẹzati* [IIIb] 'cut' / *prirẹzati* 'clip'.

raz-: *glasīti* [IV] 'sound' / *razglasīti* 'proclaim'.

u-: *pásti* [Ia] 'fall' / *upásti* 'subside'.

v-: *stopīti* [IV] 'tread' / *vstopīti* 'enter'.

vz-: *kipẹti* [IV] 'boil' / *vzkipẹti* 'fly into rage'.

z-/s-: *bráti* [Ib] 'pick' / *zbráti* 'collect'; *rásti* [Ia] 'grow' / *zrásti* 'grow up'.

za-: *īti* [Ia] 'go' / *zaíti* 'set (sun)'; *réči* [Ia] 'speak' / *zaréči se* 'make a slip of the tongue'.

Note that in some instances prefixation results in an aspectual change but a minimal change in meaning. The accumulation of prefixes occurs in examples like: *s* + *po-*: *spoprijateljīti se* [IV] 'make friends'; *pre* + *po* + *raz*: *preporazdelīti* [IV] 'redistribute'.

Verbs are derived from other parts of speech, and – apart from aspectual derivation – also from other verbs; chiefly by suffixation, but also by compounding and prefixation (Toporišič 1984: 158–61).

The following patterns exemplify the most common derivations, by suffixation.

-a-: *čenčáti* [IIIc] 'gossip' (*čẹnča* 'nonsense').

-e-: *belẹti* [IV] 'become white' (*bẹl* 'white'); *brzẹti* [IV] 'be in a hurry' (*bȓz* 'fast').

-i-: *belīti* [IV] 'make white' (*bẹl* 'white'); *človẹčiti* [IV] 'humanize' (*člóvek* 'person').

-ov- ~ *-ev-*: very productive in medieval Slovene, now much less so: *kraljeváti* [IIIa] 'rule as king' (*králj* 'king').

-ir-: marginally productive in the sixteenth century, now used for at least 90 per cent of verbs with borrowed stems (Priestly 1987): *rentgenizirati* [IIIc] 'X-ray'.

Compounding is very uncommon; the same formant (*-o-* ~ *-e-*) is used as in compound nouns and adjectives: *dolgočásiti* [IV] 'to be boring', compare the juxtapositionally derived noun *dôlgčas* 'boredom' in 3.3.1.

Prefixation, other than for aspectual derivation, is rare. Unprefixed imperfective versions of the verbs in the following examples are non-occurrent, and derivation from other sources is assumed:

o-/ob-: *obnemóči* ~ *onemóči* [Ia] 'lose vigour' (*nèmǫ̀č* 'weakness').
raz-: *razdevíčiti* [IV] 'deflower' (*devíca* 'virgin').
u-: *unóvčiti* [IV] 'realize as cash' (*nóvɔc* 'coin').

4 Syntax

4.1 Element order in declarative sentences

In sentences in which word order is the only device to mark the subject versus object opposition, the verb is normally in second position, preceded by the subject and followed by the object (Bennett 1987; Toporišič 1982: 161–81): *sosẹ́dovo téle glẹ́da náše žrebẹ̀* 'the neighbour's calf is looking at our foal' versus *náše žrebẹ̀ glẹ́da sosẹ́dovo téle* 'our foal is looking at the neighbour's calf'. Otherwise, Slovene word order is normally determined by functional sentence perspective: as elsewhere in Slavonic, the topic precedes and the comment follows. So, given the components *mója séstra* 'my sister (SUBJECT)', *obíšče* 'will visit', *jútri* 'tomorrow', *stáro učiteljico* 'old female teacher (OBJECT)', the word order reflects the old–new status of the components: *jutri obíšče stáro učiteljico mója séstra* 'the old teacher will be visited by my sister (not anyone else) tomorrow'; *mója séstra obíšče stáro učiteljico jùtri* 'my sister will visit the old teacher tomorrow (and not at any other time)', and so on.

Consider the following commonly cited text:

Bil je imenītən gròf. Tâ gròf je šə̀l v Gôrjance na lòv. Velíka drûžba prijâteljev in lōvcev ga je spremíla. Gròf uglẹ́da medvẹ́da in skǫ̀či za njím. Médved šíne v goščâvo ...
'There was an eminent count. This count went to Gorjance to hunt. A large company of friends and hunters accompanied him. The count catches sight of a bear and bounds after him. The bear darts into a thicket ...'

Here (*imenītən*) *gròf* is new information (and placed last) in the first sentence, and old information (and placed first) in the second and fourth. So also *médved* is new (and placed after the verb) in *gròf uglẹ́da medvẹ́da*, but old (and first) in *médved šíne v goščâvo*. The third sentence, however, has the comment *velíka drûžba prijâteljev in lōvcev* preceding the topical *ga*: this reflects an extra degree of emphasis attached to this particular noun phrase, as compared to the pronoun; unmarked word order would be *spremıla ga je velíka drúžba* with the topical pronoun preceding the comment noun phrase. As in the last example, emphasis is often marked by word order that conflicts with functional sentence perspective and/or with unmarked subject–verb–object order. Thus the sentence *Potrpljénje želęzne dūri prebīje*, with its subject–object–verb order, emphasizes the object: '(Even) iron gates are broken down by patience'.

The non-emphatic placement of adverbials depends, to a considerable extent, on functional sentence perspective. If more than one adverbial is topical, then adverbials of place and time tend to be placed earlier, and adverbials of manner and degree later (Davis 1989). Many non-focused adverbs are placed centrally in the sentence, and in this case they generally precede the verb they qualify: *fǎnt je mǫral trdǫ dęlati* 'the boy had to work hard'.

A clause normally contains only one group of clitics (for paradigms see section 3.1). If there is more than one element in the clitic group, the elements have fixed internal left-to-right order, whereby they fall into seven classes, as follows (Bennett 1986; Toporišič 1984: 535–40).

(I)   the particle *naj*;
(II)   any past auxiliary (or present copula) except *je* (namely, *sǝm, si, sva, sta, smo, ste, so*), or the conditional auxiliary (*bi*);
(III)   a reflexive pronoun (*se* or *si*);
(IV)   a dative pronoun (*mi, ti, ji* ...);
(V)   an accusative pronoun (*me, te, jo* ...);
(VI)   a genitive pronoun (*me, te, je* ...);
(VII)   the past auxiliary or present copula *je* or any future auxiliary (*bom, boš, bo,* ...).

The clitic group occurs in the 'second position' in the clause, whereby the 'first position' may be filled by one of the following: (a) a noun phrase, verb phrase, adjectival or adverbial phrase; (b) a subordinate clause; (c) a quotation; (d) a subordinating or (under certain conditions) a coordinating conjunction. The 'first position' may also consist of (e) one of a number of optionally deleted elements (ranging from particles to noun phrases); under such circumstances the clitic group actually occurs in 'first position'. Examples of (a) to (e) follow, with clitic slots identified by numbers used above:

1   *brǎt se bo ožénil* '(my) brother will marry' (*se* = III, *bo* = VII); *starêjši brǎt Tône se je ožénil* '(my) elder brother Tone has married' (*se* = III, *je* = VII); *starêjši brátje so se oženíli* '(my) elder brothers have married' (*so* = II, *se* = III); *učíl jo je je* 'he taught her it (F)' (*jo* 'her' = V, *je* 'it' = VI, *je* (AUX) = VII); *láni so se starši brátje oženíli* 'last year (my) elder brothers married' (*so* (AUX) = II, *se* = III).

2 *ko se vŕnem, se bo brȁt ožénil* 'when I return, (my) brother will marry.'

3 *'dä', mi je rẹ̑kɔl* ' "yes", he said to me' (*mi* = V, *je* = VII).

4 *vẹ̑m, da se bo brȁt ožénil* 'I know that my brother will marry'; but (with coordinating conjunction not occupying 'first position') *ostála bom nȅporočéna, tọ̑da brȁt se bo ožénil* 'I shall remain unmarried, but my brother will marry'.

5 *se bo brȁt ožénil?* = *ali se bo brȁt ožénil?* 'will the brother marry?' *se bo nadaljevál* = *ta člânɔk se bo nadaljevál* '(this article) will be continued'.

The unstressed negative particle *ne* succeeds all other clitics – it occupies position VIII: *prọ̑si, da naj bi se mu ne smejáli* 'he asks them not to laugh at him' (literally: 'he asks that / OPT-PTL (I)/COND-AUX (II)/REFL (III)/him-DAT (IV)/NEG (VIII)/laugh'). The combination *ne* + *je* is realized as stressed *nȋ*, that is, is non-clitic; the combinations *ne* + *bi*, *ne* + *bo* (and other future auxiliary forms) are stressed on the second element, which thus becomes non-clitic: *brȁt se ne bọ̑ ožénil* (se = III, ne = VIII) '(my) brother will not marry'.

If a verb phrase is reduced, concomitant clitics which remain will assume the stress:

Si že končȁl dẹ́lo? – Predvčẹ́rajšnjim še nȅ, včẹ́raj pa səm gȁ = Včẹ́raj səm ga končȁl

'Have you finished the work? – The day before yesterday I hadn't, but yesterday I did (finish it)'.

(Ali) se dóbro počúti? – Jā, sȅ = Jā, dóbro se počútim

'Do you feel well? – Yes, I do (feel well)'.

Compare *ali si si to izmíslil* 'did you think this up for yourself?' and (with deletion of particle) *si si izmíslil?*, and (with verb-phrase reduction) *Si sȋ?* Clitic placement is not affected by the preposing of an emphatic adverbial: *vsȁj krúha mi dájte* 'at least, give me some bread'. Clitics do not occur inside noun phrases, as they do in Serbo-Croat.

The question of clitics and phrase boundaries has not been investigated much; this is a tentative suggestion. If two or more verb phrases are combined, their several clitics may form a single clitic group (and the clitic-placement rules are followed), as long as the **same subject is 'understood'** for all the verb phrases involved. Hence 'yesterday he wanted to call them both' is normally *včẹ́raj ju je hótel poklícati*, where *je hótel* is one verb phrase and *ju poklícati* is another; and the reflexive clitic *se* and its infinitive *umíti* are separated by another verb in *včẹ́raj se je pozábil umíti* 'yesterday he forgot to wash' (*se* = III, *je* = VII). If, however, a **different subject is 'understood'**, a construction of this kind is not grammatical; thus **dánəs səm se slíšal séstro smejáti* (where *səm slíšal* is one verb phrase and *se smejáti* is another) is not acceptable for 'today I heard my sister laugh';

this idea can only be expressed otherwise, for instance, *dánəs səm slíšal séstro smejáti se* or *dánəs səm slíšal, kakǫ se séstra sméje.*

Within the noun phrase modifiers (adjectival pronouns, adjectives and so on) normally stand to the left of the head noun: *trúdna máti je imẹ̄la sūh* obrȁz, *globóke jáme so bilě v njẹ́nih lícih* 'the tired mother had a thin face, (and) there were deep hollows in her cheeks'. Within sequences of determiners, qualitative adjectives precede relational adjectives (*hládno jesẹ́nsko jútro* 'a cool autumn morning'), and adjectival pronouns precede all other determiners (*vsě tẹ̑ náše mȁjhne gǫ̑zdne žívȁli* 'all these small forest animals of ours'). Dependent prepositional phrases frequently precede adjectives: *življénje v za evrǫ̑pske pǫ́jme grozljívi rẹ̄vščini* 'life in poverty (that is) dreadful for European conceptions', *béžali so pred z nȅzadŕžno hitrǫ̑stjo približújočo se jim katastrǫ̑fo* 'they fled before the catastrophe (that was) approaching them with uncontrollable speed'. To the right of the head noun are placed other elements of the noun phrase, such as nouns in apposition (*dẹ́lavəc zdǫ̑məc* 'worker (who is) migrant' = 'migrant worker', *hlȃpəc Jérnej* 'Jernej the farmhand'; noun-phrase attributes in the genitive and other cases (*hȋša mójega očẹ́ta* 'the house of my father', *hímna domovíni* 'a hymn to the homeland'); prepositional phrases (*vójna z Nẹ̄mci* 'war with the Germans', *strȃh pred kȃznijo* 'fear of execution') and adverbials (*hȋša tȁm* 'the house over there'). Exceptions to these statements are stylistically marked (*prijȃtelj mǫ́j drȃgi* 'dear friend of mine').

4.2   Non-declarative sentence types
Yes–no questions are marked by: (1) word order; (2) a special particle; (3) a separate interrogative phrase; (4) interrogative intonation alone with unmarked word order. In both (1) and (2) the sentence bears interrogative intonation; in (3) the interrogative phrase bears this intonation. Corresponding to the positive *razumẹ́li ste* 'you understood' are thus:

1   Inversion: *ste razumẹ́li?* 'did you understand?'
2   The use of a particle. The normal particles are *ali* (in conversational Slovene, *a*) and *kaj*: *ali ste razumẹ́li?* 'did you understand?' The expressive variant *mar* adds a rhetorical and doubtful nuance: *mȁr tega rẹ̑s ne vẹ́ste?* 'don't you really know that?'
3   An interrogative phrase preposed or postposed to a positive or interrogative sentence. There are many: *kȃj, kajně, kajněda, kajně da ně, ne rẹ̑s, da, ali kȃj, mar ně* and so on. Examples: *razumẹ́li ste, kajně?* 'you understood, didn't you?', *ne rẹ̑s, da ste razumẹ́li?* 'isn't it true that you understood?', *ali je čȗdno, kȃj?* or *je čȗdno, ně?* 'it's odd, isn't it?'
4   The use of interrogative intonation: *razumẹ́li ste?*

Positive interrogative sentences may be answered with affirmative/negative particles, or by repetition of all or part of the verb phrase. Thus, in response to *ste razuméli?* we may find *dà/jā, razuméli, razuméli smo* 'yes'; *nĕ, nísmo, nísmo razuméli* 'no'. Of the two positive particles, *jä* is more common than *dä*. Other replies are, of course, possible, like *mordä* 'perhaps' and *sevẹda* 'of course'. Unambiguous responses to negative interrogative sentences are *pàč* and *nĕ*; and/or the verb is repeated (with negative marking, as necessary) for clarity: *ali nísi spàl?* 'haven't you slept?' - *pàč/sɜm* 'yes (I have)'; *nĕ/nisem* 'no (I haven't)'; *ali ne smrdí po petrolẹju? - pàč, smrdí/nĕ, ne smrdí* 'there isn't a stink of paraffin, is there? - yes, there is/no, there isn't'.

WH questions are introduced by interrogative pronouns (*kdọ?* 'who?', *kāj?* 'what?'), adjectives (*katẹri?* 'which?', *kākšɜn?* 'what sort of?', *čigáv?* 'whose?'), and adverbs (*kjẹ?* 'where?', *kdāj?* 'when?', *zakàj?* 'why?') and many more. The intonation differs from that of yes–no questions: normally, WH questions have falling, and yes–no questions rising, intonation. The verb may be indicative, optative or infinitive: *kāj bom storíl?* 'what shall I do?', *kāj naj storím?* 'what should I do?', *kāj storūti?* 'what is to be done?' These questions may be reinforced with the particle *pa*: compare *kām grĕš?* 'where are you going?' and *kām pa grĕš?* 'where is it that you're going?' If an interrogative sentence is repeated with one element changed, as a supplementary question, the unchanged elements in the sentence may be deleted and replaced by the particle *pa*: *kāj boš dẹlal dánɜs?* 'what are you doing today?' ... *pa drẹvi?* (= ... *kaj boš dẹlal drẹvi?*) 'and (what are you doing) this evening?'

Indirect yes–no questions are introduced by the conjunctions *ali, če*: *vprášal me je, ali / če sɜm vídel njegóvega bráta* 'he asked me if I had seen his brother'. The tense within the indirect question is the tense of the corresponding direct question. Indirect WH questions are introduced by interrogative conjunctions homophonous with those exemplified above: *vprášal me je, kdāj bodo šlì* 'he asked me when they would be going'.

Commands may be expressed with the imperative: both aspects are used in positive and in negative commands; the general meaning of the aspect, as relevant to the verb involved, is operative. Hence, positive: *odpīraj vráta!* (IMPFV) 'open the gate (as a general rule)' and *odprì vráta!* (PRFV) 'open the gate (at once)'; negative: *ne odpīraj vráta!* (IMPFV) 'don't open the gate (ever)' and *ne odprì vráta!* (PRFV) 'don't open the gate (right now)'.

Among other ways of expressing commands, note the following:

Infinitive, both imperfective: *nĕ me jezūti!* 'don't keep making me angry!' and perfective: *nĕ me razjezūti!* 'don't make me really angry!'
Da + conditional: *da bi se v žlíci vóde utọpil!* 'may you drown in a spoonful of water!'
Imperative, third person: *pa bọdi po tvójem* 'let it be the way you want'.
Present optative: *naj se zgodí tvója vólja* 'may your will be done'; *lĕ nàj plẹše!* 'just let her dance!'

4.3   Copular sentences

The unmarked copula is *bīti* 'be', expressed in all tenses, persons and numbers. Semantically marked copulas include *postáti* 'become', *imenováti se* 'be called', *zdẹ́ti se* 'appear (to be)': *že trẹ́tjič je postál óče* 'he became a father for the third time'. Predicate noun phrases are normally in the nominative. (For the loss of the predicative instrumental, see Štrekelj (1903).) Thus *Bârbara je poročéna (žéna)* 'Barbara is a married woman', *Bârbara je bilà dvẹ̀ lẹ́ti továrniška dẹ́lavka* 'Barbara was a factory worker for two years'; note *otròk se imenûje Jánez* 'the baby is called Janez', *Bârbara se mi zdí pošténa žẹ́nska* 'to me Barbara seems like an honest woman'.

A predicate following a reflexive *se* may be nominative, or accusative (and marked animate; see 4.7): *pokázal se je hvalẹ́žən/hvalẹ́žnega* 'he proved to be grateful'; *pokázal se je dóbər dẹ́lavəc/dọ́brega dẹ́lavca* 'he proved to be a good worker'.

Noun phrases in apposition to the objects of transitive verbs are accusative: *zapustíli so ga siromáka* 'they left him a pauper'; also when introduced by *kot* or *za*: *sosẹ́da smo doslệj smatrali za prijâtelja* 'until now we considered (our) neighbour a friend', *poznàl səm te kot otróka* 'I knew you as a child'.

For predicate noun phrases with the negative copula, see 4.6.

Adjectives in the predicate are in their historically 'long' or 'short' form (in so far as this opposition extends) depending on the semantic definite versus indefinite opposition (see 3.1.4).

Predicatives (Toporišič 1984: 347) are indeclinable words which occur as predicate modifiers; when the tense is past the copula is usually *bilȍ*, even when the predicative is homophonous with a non-neuter noun: thus *dộlgčas mi je po prijâtelju* 'I miss my friend', *dộlgčas mi je bilȍ po prijâtelju* 'I missed my friend'; *trẹ́ba ga je kaznováti* 'he must be punished', *trẹ́ba bi ga bilȍ kaznováti* 'he should have been punished'; *žàl mi je bilȍ zânj* 'I was sorry for him'; *ne bi bilȍ nâpak zâte, če bi to storíl* 'it wouldn't be a mistake for you to do that'; *sinộči je bil ~ bilȍ mràz* 'it was cold last night'. The last example shows a vacillation between substantival and predicative use. 'Impersonal' phrases which comprise neuter forms of adjectives are probably best analysed as predicatives: *oblâčno je / je bilȍ* 'it is / was cloudy'; *nocộj bo zanimívo* 'it will be interesting tonight'; *grôzno ga je bilȍ poslúšati* 'it was awful to listen to him'.

4.4   Coordination and comitativity

The conjunctions *in*, *pa* and *ter* are used as coordinators. Of the three, *pa* is more conversational than *in*; and *ter* 'and also; and so' does not often occur as first coordinator. Thus *zẹ́blo mi je in/pa láčən səm bil* 'I was cold and hungry': *ter* would suggest 'moreover' in this sentence, but not in *fânt je prišəl do kozolca, stǫ́pil mȋmo in/ter/pa je izginil za hlę̑vom* 'the boy came up to the hay-rack, walked past and disappeared behind the barn'.

Normally, as in the above examples, the last two coordinated elements have an explicit coordinator, whereas preceding coordination is with zero. Other options (such as *X in X in X*, or *X, X, X*) are common, but stylistically marked. 'Both X and Y' is normally *takǭ X kȁkor (tȕdi) Y*: *film je zbȗdil zanȋmanje takǭ pri občȋnstvu kȁkor (tȕdi) pri krȋtiki* 'the film aroused interest both with the public and with the critics'; another expression is *bōdisi X bǭdisi Y*. 'Either X or Y' is *ali X ali Y*: *ali dę́laj domȁ ali pa pǭjdi v svę̑t* 'either work at home or go into the world', *tjȁ bova šlȁ* (or *boš šə̀l*) *ali tȋ ali jȁz* 'either you or I will go there' (note the possible dual verb). 'Neither X nor Y' is *ne X ne Y* or, more emphatically, *nȋti X nȋti Y*: *nȋma ne brȃta ne sẹ́stre* 'he has neither brother nor sister'; *tę̑ga ne bǫ̑mo dočȃkali nȋti mȋ nȋti nȃši otrȏci* 'neither we nor our children will live to see that'.

The coordinating conjunctions are used to coordinate words, phrases and sentences. In phrases and sentences, deletion of repeated elements may occur. In verb phrases, normally, the auxiliary is deleted: *ozȓla sta se na mȃter in obstȃla sta srẹ́di sóbe* > *ozȓla sta se na mȃter in obstȃla srẹ́di sóbe* 'they both looked at (their) mother and came to a halt in the middle of the room'. Given clitic phrases, normally, the complete (but *not* the partial) deletion of a repeated clitic phrase may occur. Compare *vȋdim, da se mu vrtȋ in se mu blẹ́de* and *vȋdim, da se mu vrtȋ in blẹ́de* 'I see that he is giddy and delirious': here the clitic group *se mu* is either repeated, or deleted, as a whole.

When **verb agreement** in gender with conjoined noun phrases is required, usage varies. The following general rules apply: (a) if two feminine singular nouns are conjoined, the verb is feminine dual; (b) if two singular nouns of any other pairs of genders are conjoined, the verb is more commonly masculine dual: *Mȋlka* (F SG) *in nję́na mȃčka* (F SG) *sta bilȋ* (F DU) *zȗnaj* 'Milka and her cat were outside', but *Mȋlka* (F SG) *in nję́no tẹ́le* (N SG) *sta bilȁ* (M DU) *zȗnaj* 'Milka and her calf were outside'. So also in the plural: (a) with a conjoined noun phrase where the total is three or more and all the nouns are feminine, the verb is feminine plural; (b) in all other instances, the verb is normally masculine plural: *obẹ̑ dę́klici* (F DU) *in njūna mȃti* (F SG) *so bilë̏* (F PL) *zȗnaj* 'both the girls and their mother were outside', but *dvẹ̑ telẹ́ti* (N DU) *in éno žrebȅ* (N SG) *so bilȋ* (M PL) *zȗnaj* 'two foals and a calf were outside' (Corbett 1983: 183–6). If the subject of a verb is a conjoined noun phrase and one of the conjuncts is first person, the verb will be first person; if, under the same condition, one of the conjuncts is second person, the verb will be second person. Thus, *jȁz* (1) *in Tǫ́ne* (3) *sva* (1 DU) *prišlȁ* 'I and Tone have arrived'; *Tȋ* (2), *Tǫ́ne* (3) *in Tǫ́mo* (3) *ste* (2 PL) *prišlȋ* 'you, Tone and Tomo have arrived' (Corbett 1983: 207–8).

Comitative constructions and simple coordination both occur: thus, *s Tǫnetom sta prišlä* and *tɪ in Tǫne sta prišlä* are equally acceptable for 'you and Tone have arrived'. **Dual comitativity**, as in the above example, may be expressed by *X z Y* where X = dual pronoun and Y = singular noun or pronoun; so also: *midva z Lǫjzom sva sadïla* 'Lojz and I were planting'. Since the personal pronoun is normally deleted (see 4.7), the comitative phrase is normally reduced to *z Y*: *'hvála lępa!' sva rékla z Jánezom* '"many thanks!", said Janez and I'; *z gospodárjem sva šlä v vinǫgrad* 'the master and I went to the vineyard'. Simultaneous reciprocal comitativity and pronoun deletion may result in, for example, *vęm, da se imäta z Marjânco ráda* 'I know that he and Marjanca love each other' (= *ónadva z Marjânco* = *ǒn in Marjânca*). **Plural comitativity** is expressed in the same way; in this instance, the *Y* in *[X] z Y* may be dual or plural: *z njïma smo šlï na sprehǒd* 'we (including the two of them) went for a walk', *z njïmi smo šlï na sprehǒd* 'we (including them PL) went for a walk'; and similarly with the verb in the second person plural. This subject has not been investigated much; but note that because simple coordination also occurs there is much ambiguity: for instance, *z brátoma smo šlï* may mean 'I and my two brothers', 'we two and our two brothers' and 'we (three or more) and our two brothers ... went'.

4.5 Subordination

As generally in Slavonic, there are many types of subordinate clause. A few examples follow. Subject: *kdǫr je bolàn, mǫra ležáti* 'he who is sick must stay in bed'; *vsěm navzǫ́čim je znáno, da se ûčna ûra začně čez pęt minût* '(the fact) that the lesson begins in five minutes is known to everyone present'. Attribute: *obšlä me je slũtnja, da je domâ nękaj narǫbe* 'I was seized with the foreboding that something at home was wrong'; *govoríš o stvaręh, ki jih ne poznâš* 'you're talking about things that you don't know'. Predicate: *Marjânca je zdäj, kär sɘm bilä nekǫ́č jäz* 'Marjanca now is what I once was'. Object: *povędali so, da je milíčnik odšɘ̄l* 'they told (us) that the policeman had left'; *nímam räd, če se prepïrata* 'I don't like it if you two quarrel'. Adverb: *zverî živíjo, kjęr so gozdôvi* 'wild animals live where there are forests'; *čákal bom, doklēr se ne zmračí* 'I'll wait until it gets dark'; *ne grě vɘ̀n, ker se bojí mráza* 'he doesn't go outside, for he is afraid of the cold'; *če si láčɘn, ti dám krúha* 'if you're hungry, I'll give you some bread'; *vstǫpiš, ne da bi potr̄kal* 'you come in without knocking'.

There are two relative pronouns, *ki* and *katɘrɪ*. The latter is marked and is used (a) with a preposition: *ljudję, z katęrimi bom govǫril* 'the people with whom I shall talk' (here the use of *ki* is equally acceptable: *ljudję, ki bom z njïm govǫril*); (b) for possessives: *držâva, pod katęre zastâvo plúje tâ kitolôvka* 'the country under whose flag this whaleboat sails'; and (c) to avoid the ambiguity which is inherent in the indeclinable *ki*: compare *máti mójega prijâtelja, katęra* (F) *je zdäj na Blědu* 'my friend's mother, who is now in Bled' and *máti mójega prijatelja, katęri* (M) *je zdäj na Blędu* 'the mother of my friend, who is now in Bled'. Otherwise, unmarked *ki* is used as follows: alone if nominative: *po júhi smo dobili čŕno kávo, ki je bilä presládka* 'after the soup we got some black coffee which was too sweet'. In a non-nominative case *ki* is supported by a personal pronoun, normally third person: *fílmi, **ki jih** bomo glédali* 'the films (which them) we shall see'; *tộ je tîsti, **ki mu je** vsè zaûpala* 'that's the person to whom she confided everything'. The supporting pronoun may also be first or second person: *tîsti sɔm, **ki mi je** vsè zaûpala* 'I am the person to whom she confided everything'.

Extraction constraints have been little investigated. Note, however, that in spoken Slovene a clitic is not normally moved out of its main clause: 'the man whom I think you saw' is *člóvek, ki mîslim, da si ga vídel* and not **člóvek, ki ga mîslim, da si vídel*; while 'the man who I think saw you' is *člóvek, ki mîslim, da te je vídel*. In formal written Slovene extraction is avoided in a number of ways: for example, for 'the man I think you saw': *člóvek, o katệrem mislim, da si ga vídel*, literally: 'the man of whom I think that you saw him'.

Gerunds are normally used to express temporal relativity: the present gerund forms for actions simultaneous with, and the past gerund for actions anterior to, that in the superordinate clause: *vŕgla se je navpîk z visôkega prevîsa, hotèč* (PRS GER) *naredîti samomòr* 'she threw herself down from a high overhang, wishing to commit suicide'; *a ne umŕši* (PAST GER), *je po mnộgih dnệh zộpet ozdravệla* 'and, not having died, after many days she recovered'.

Participles are used instead of subordinate clauses relatively seldom. In the following, *že pred dvệma ūrama prispéle góste so kónčno pozdrāvili* (literally: 'they finally greeted the already before two hours having arrived guests') 'the guests – who had arrived two hours previously – were finally greeted', *prispéle* is used participially, without an auxiliary; a relative clause would be more usual: *góste, ki so pred dvệma ūrama prispéli, so kónčno pozdrāvili*.

The infinitive occurs as the complement of numerous verbs and verb phrases, for example, *nộčemo délati* 'we do not want to work', *ni mâral velíko govorîti* 'he did not care to say much', *dólžɔn sɔm vam tộ povédati* 'I am obliged to tell you that', *slišal sɔm ptîčko péti* 'I heard a small bird singing' and so on. In these respects Slovene differs from the other South Slavonic languages, and also in allowing the accumulation of infinitives, as in *môram začéti délati* 'I have to begin to work'.

In some contexts, an infinitive and a *da*-clause are interchangeable: *nása pŕva nalộga je, da se učímo = nása pŕva nalộga je učíti se* 'our first task is to learn'. A common conversational construction is X *za* + infinitive; in the standard norm other constructions are preferred, for instance, conversational *imâš kâj za jést?* 'do you have anything to eat?'; compare standard *imâš kâj jésti?* Similarly: conversational *kúpil si bom stròj za pomívat posǫdo* 'I shall buy a machine to wash the dishes'; compare standard *kúpil si bom stròj za pomívanje posǫde.*

The supine is used as the complement of verbs with meanings involving some kind of movement, both explicit: ***Spât hǫdim prèd deséto zvečr*** 'I go to bed before ten at night', ***šlà je krúha pèč*** 'she has gone to bake some bread', *poslála je sina **študirat*** 'she sent her son (away) to study'; and implicit: *mǫram **spât*** 'I must (go) to bed' (compare, with infinitive, *mǫram spáti* 'I must sleep'). The direct object of a supine, formerly in the genitive, is now in the accusative: *grȅm domǭv sežgȁt dnę̑vnik* has thus replaced earlier *grȅm domǭv sežgȁt dnę̑vnika* for 'I'm going home to burn (my) diary'.

4.6   Negation

Although both are possible, sentence negation (with the negative particle preposed to the verb) is normally preferred to constituent negation (with the negative particle preposed to another constituent), even if the semantically negated part of the sentence is that other constituent. Thus *tǫ̑ se ní zgodílo po mǫ́ji vǫ́lji* is more common than *tǫ̑ se je zgodílo nȅ po mǫ́ji vǫ́lji* for 'that happened not-according-to-my-will', that is, 'that did not happen according to my will'.

The unmarked negative particle is *ne*; there are special negative forms of the verbs 'want', 'have' and 'be' (see 3.2.1). Note that, since 'be' acts as the auxiliary in past tenses, *ni* replaces *je* as the auxiliary in the third singular: *Jánez je razbȉl ókno* 'Janez broke the window' versus *Jánez ni razbȉl ókna* 'Janez did not break the window'.

If the negative particle (*ne* or the *ni*-prefix on a negative verb) is repeated, the result is a positive sentence: *ne mǫ́rem vas ne poslúšati* 'I cannot not listen to you' = *mǫ́ram vas poslúšati* 'I must listen to you'. In the same way, if a negative particle co-occurs with a negative adjective, the result is positive: *nisəm nespámetən* 'I am not unreasonable' = *səm (dovǒlj) pámetən* 'I am (quite) reasonable'. Other negative elements require the co-occurrence of a negative particle: *nȉč nísəm vídel* 'I saw nothing', *z nikǫ́mər ne govorí* 'he talks to nobody', *nikjȅr jih nísi vídel* 'you saw them nowhere'. Many of these other negated elements may co-occur without rendering a sentence positive: *nihčȅ nam ni nikǫ́li ničę̑sar dȁl* 'nobody ever gave us anything'.

Normally, the direct object of a negative verb is genitive, as in the example *Jánez ní razbȉl ókna* above. If it is clear from the sentence structure and/or from prosodic features (stress, intonation) that it is a specific non-verbal constituent that is being negated, the accusative may replace the genitive.

If the copula expresses identity and is negated, subject and predicate are nominative: compare examples in 4.3 with *Bȁrbara ni poročéna (žéna)* 'Barbara is not a married woman', *Bȁrbara ní bilȁ dvȇ lę̑ti tovȁrniška dẹ́lavka* 'Barbara was not a factory-worker for two years'. If, however, the copula expresses existence, usually located spatially or temporally, then it has a single argument, its subject; when the copula is negated, the subject is genitive. Compare *óče je domâ* 'father is at home' and *očẹ́ta ni domâ* 'father is not at home'; *za njím so ostáli dolgȏvi* 'there were debts left behind him' and *za njím ní ostálo dolgóv* 'there were no debts left behind him'. In these instances it is, however, possible to negate a specific constituent, rather than the whole sentence, namely *óče ni domâ* 'father is not *at home* (but somewhere else)'; *za njím níso ostáli dolgȏvi* 'it was not *debts* that were left behind him (but something else)'.

4.7   Anaphora and pronouns

The nominative of the personal pronoun is omitted, not only when it is explicit in the verb ending (*kāj dẹ́laš?* 'what are you doing?' *bérem* 'I am reading') but also when it is not (*kāj bi stȯ́ril?* 'what would I/you/he do?'). Hence, the subject of the verb may not become explicit until later in the context: *Slovẹ́nci bi bilȋ mȯ́rali že zdávnaj spoznáti, da nam enakovrẹ́dno vključevánje v mednárodno družíno ... lahkȯ̀ samȯ̀ korísti* '(We) Slovenes should have long since realized that incorporation on equal terms in the international family may only be of benefit to us', where only in the subordinate *da*-clause does the pronoun *nam* identify the person of the subject of *bi bilȋ mȯ́rali.* So also: *otrȍk sǝm bȋl zmẹ́raj vesẹ̑l* '(I) as a child was always happy'; *popȯ́tnik, ki mᵎmo grȅš ...* '(you) traveller who pass by ...' The pronoun is expressed for contrastive emphasis: *kāj dẹ́laš? – jȁz bérem* 'what are you doing? – **I** am reading (but someone else perhaps not)'.

The most usual anaphoric pronoun, *ȍn, óno, óna,* is thus more frequently implicit than explicit, for example:

Ko je sẹ̄dǝmdesetlẹ̑tni óče umíral ..., je nenâdoma obȑnil ocȋ v strȍp, ... odpȓl ústa in kríknil: 'Vóda.' Natȯ̀ je omáhnil nazáj na zglávje ...
'As the seventy-year-old father was dying ..., (he) suddenly turned his gaze towards the ceiling, ... opened (his) mouth and cried, "Water." Then (he) collapsed back onto the pillow ...'

In non-nominative cases and when unstressed, the clitic third-person pronouns are used (see 4.1). Note the peculiarly Slovene use of the clitics in discourse contexts where the verb is implicit and the noun phrase or phrases is/are anaphorized: the verb phrase is expressed by repetition of the auxiliary, if any, on its own; and the noun phrase(s) is/are expressed by the clitic forms. Example with verb phrase lacking auxiliary:

Zdȁj razúmeš sosẹ́da? – Zdí se mi da **gȁ**
'Do you understand your neighbour now? I think that I (understand) him'.

With auxiliaries:

In zakāj je zabōdəl Klementíno věč kot énkrat? Da, zakāj **jo je?**
'And why did he stab Klementína more than once? Yes, why did he (stab) her?'
Žaríš, kot bi zadęl glâvni dobítək. – Sâj **səm gà**
'You're beaming as if you had won the jackpot. – But I have (won) it'.

In addition, the demonstrative pronouns *tâ*, *tísti*, *ǫ̂ni* are used ana-phorically:

Kākšna drevę̂sa so tǫ̂? – Tǫ̂le je bûkev, tístole tằm je jávor, ǫ̂nole ǫ̂nstran rę́ke pa je vŕba
'What sort of trees are they? – This one's a beech, that one there is a maple, and that one over on the other side of the river is a willow.'

'The former ... the latter' is expressed by *pŕvi ... slę́dnji*:

Kopîtar in Míklošič sta bilằ pomę̂mbna jezikoslôvca; pȓvi je bíl rójən v ǫ̂səmnajstem, slę́dnji pa v devę̂tnajstem stolę̂tju
'K. and M. were important linguists; the former was born in the eighteenth century and the latter in the nineteenth.'

Among other anaphoric expressions, *tǫ̂* corresponds to *kằr* 'what(ever)', as in *kằr je v sȓcu, to je tûdi na jezíku* 'whatever is in the heart is also on the tongue'; *tǫ̂* may also be elided in this context.

Slovene has a particularly interesting construction known as the **'Orphan Accusative'** (Perlmutter and Orešnik 1973). Any masculine or neuter adjective in direct-object position that is used pronominally (namely, in a noun phrase from which the noun is omitted) occurs with what is historically the genitive ending *-ega*: *katę́ri klobúk hǫ̂čete?* 'which hat do you want?' – *hǫ̂čem navádni klobúk* 'I want the ordinary hat'; but *hǫ̂čem navâdnega* 'I want (the) ordinary (one)'. The pronominal adjective is, in other words, marked as animate. There is thus overt case consistency between the use of pronouns and pronominally used adjectives in the singular: feminine: *dâjte mi čȓno oblę̂ko – dâjte mi jo – dâjte mi čȓno* 'give me the black dress' – 'give me it' – 'give me the black one'; neuter: *dâjte mi čȓno védro – dâjte mi ga – dâjte mi čȓnega* 'give me the black bucket' – 'give me it' – 'give me the black one'.

4.8 Reflexives and reciprocals
Reflexivity is expressed with reflexive pronouns which may be both clitic and – when emphatic – fully stressed, and both accusative and dative: *se/ sébe*: *umíti se = umíti sébe* 'wash oneself'; *si/sébi*: *pomágati si = pomágati sébi* 'help oneself'. Occasionally, the clitic–non-clitic distinction reflects something other than emphasis: compare *ubíti sébe* (literally: 'kill oneself') 'commit suicide', but *ubíti se*, which has an impersonal meaning, 'die by accident'.

Reflexivity may, but does not normally, extend across an infinitival phrase boundary. 'Yesterday he forced himself to wash himself' (with the same subject understood for both verbs) is more rarely *včęraj se je prisílil umíti sé ~ sébe*, and more usually, with the second reflexive pronoun omitted (compare 'he was afraid to laugh' below): *včęraj se je prisílil umíti.* If emphasis is needed, the stressed reflexive pronoun may occur, but reinforced with *sâm*: *včęraj se je prisílil umíti sámega sébe* 'yesterday he forced himself to wash *himself*'. If the (explicit or implicit) subject of the verbs in question is not the same, the reflexive pronoun is normally ambiguous: *Jǫ̂že je prisílil svója sinôva spoštováti sébe* can mean both 'Joe forced his two sons to respect themselves', and '. . . to respect him'.

Possible antecedents include not only nominative subjects, as in the above examples, but also implicit subjects in dative ('impersonal') phrases: *potrębno se mu je umíti (= potrębno mu je + se umíti*, literally: 'it is necessary for him' + 'to wash himself') 'he must wash'; *tébi se pa še ne mudí popráviti (= tébi pa še ne mudí + se popráviti*, literally: 'for you it is not yet urgent' + 'to reform yourself') 'you are not yet in a hurry to reform'.

Verbs with *se/si*, which are thus morphologically reflexive, are also used, without reflexive meaning, as follows:

1 Idiomatically: with *se* either obligatory: *smejáti se* 'laugh', *prizadęvati si* 'to endeavour'; or optional: *jǫ́kati se = jǫ́kati* 'weep', *mísliti si = mísliti* 'think'.

2 To express impersonal generalizations; with intransitive verbs: *v Slovęniji se veliko hǫ́di v hribe* 'in Slovenia people do a lot of mountain-walking'; and with transitive verbs, when the reflexive construction is equivalent to a third person plural non-reflexive with an unspecified agent, as in *íšče se mlâjša žęnska = iščejo mlâjšo žęnsko* 'a younger woman is sought'. The following alternative construction occurs: reflexive verb + object-ACC: *íšče se mlâjšo žęnsko*; here the verb is impersonal ('neutral'), compare *iskálo se bo mlâjše žęnske* 'younger women will be sought'. Also, an impersonal reflexive may complement a noun phrase in the dative: *Jánezu se hǫ́če denárja* 'Janez craves some money'. This usage is more limited than elsewhere in Slavonic.

If the usages in items 1 and 2 co-occur, one of the two instances of *se* is usually omitted: *pri njém se ne sméje nikǫ́li* (literally: 'at his house it does not laugh itself never') 'there is never any laughter in his house'. Similarly, if one morphologically reflexive verb has a second such verb dependent on it, the second *se* is usually omitted: *bál se je* 'he was afraid' + *smejáti se* 'to laugh' › *bál se je smejáti* 'he was afraid to laugh'.

Reciprocity is expressed (a) with reflexive verbs, both with accusative *se* and with dative *si*: *sręčati se* 'meet one another', *pomágati si* 'help each other'; and (b) with the explicit reciprocal *drûg- drûg-* or *én- drûg-*, thus (paralleling the above reflexives) accusative *srêčati drûg drûgega* 'meet one another', dative *pomágati drûg drûgemu* 'help one another', and with other cases also: genitive: *bojíta se drûg drûgega* 'they are afraid of each other'; instrumental: *umírajo drûg za drûgim* 'they are dying one after another'. The last example shows the intermediate position of the preposition. Note that if both persons concerned are female, this may be explicit: *bojíta se drûga drûge* 'the two (women) are afraid of each other'. A reciprocal can occur without a nominative subject antecedent: *trêba je drûg drûgemu pomágati* 'people should help each other'.

4.9   Possession

The verb *imêti* is used in a wide range of meanings with animate subjects: *imâm híšo* 'I have a house'; *imâš dósti gradíva* 'you have enough material'; *imâ bráta* 'he has a brother'; *imâva prijâtelja na obísku* 'we (DU) have a friend visiting'; *imâmo dôber spomín* 'we (PL) have a good memory'; *âvto imâte pokvârjen* 'you have (your) car wrecked' = 'your car is wrecked'; *imâjo zâjtrk ob ósmih* 'they have breakfast at eight'; *imêla bo otróka* 'she's going to have a baby' and so on. If the possessor is inanimate, also, *imêti* may be used: *têdən imâ sêdəm dní* 'the week has seven days'; *zákon nîma táke dolôčbe* 'the law does not have such a provision'; but in many instances a prepositional phrase is also possible: *vóda imâ prevêč kálcija = v vódi je prevêč kálcija* 'the water has too much calcium'; *plûg imâ ročíco = pri plûgu je ročíca* 'the plough has a handle'.

Possession may be shown by the genitive, but when the possessor is animate, a possessive adjective is very much more common. Thus 'mother's house' may be *híša mátere* or more likely *máterina híša*; 'the dictator's palace' may be *paláča diktâtorja* or more normally *diktâtorjeva paláča*. These phrases exemplify the normal word order: noun in genitive after head, possessive before head. In conversational Slovene possession is often expressed by *od*: *otróci od sosêde* 'the neighbour's children', '*Čigáv je tâ plášč?*' – '*Od méne*' '"Whose coat is that?" – "Mine"'. The use of the genitive/dative personal pronouns to express possession is considered stylistically marked and somewhat archaic.

4.10   Quantification

'One' is adjectival, and agrees with its head noun in number – singular or, for pluralia tantum, plural – gender, case and animacy. 'Two' agrees with its head in number (dual), gender and case; the predicate is dual; for example, nominative, *dvâ študénta sta prišlâ* 'two students have arrived'; instrumental, *med dvêma stóloma* 'between two stools'. Normally, dual forms are used in pronouns and in verbal forms whenever two actual referents are involved, be they explicitly mentioned or only implicit. However, in non-pronominal noun phrases with, for example, body parts that come in pairs like 'eyes' and 'feet', dual forms tend to be used only when the quantifiers 'two' or 'both' are explicitly stated in the context, and are replaced by the plural when this quantifier is unstated, even if a pair of referents are obviously implicit: so, *nóge me bolíjo* (PL) 'my feet hurt', but *obẹ̑ nógi me bolíta* (DU) 'both my feet hurt'. 'Three' and 'four' agree with their heads in number (plural), gender and case. The predicate is plural: nominative, *tríje (štírje) študénti so prišlì* 'three (four) students have arrived'; *mẹ́sto je trȋ (štíri) ūre hodá od tûkaj* 'the city is three (four) hours' walk from here'; instrumental, *s trẹ̑mi (štîrimi) stōli* 'with three (four) chairs'.

The syntax of higher numerals terminating in *édən, dvâ, tri, štíri* is determined by the last element: thus, *stȯ̑ ẹ̀n člóvek je prišə̀l* (singular) '101 people came'; *tisǫ̑č dvâ človẹ́ka sta prišlà* (DU) '1,002 people came'; *z dvẹ̑sto trẹ̑mi stōli* 'with 203 chairs'. 'Five' and higher numerals (other than those terminating in *édən, dvâ, tri, štíri*), in non-oblique cases, control the genitive plural; the predicate is neuter singular, for instance, *pẹ̑t študéntov je prišlȯ̑* 'five students have arrived', *srẹ̑čal sǝm pẹ̑tsto deklẹ̑t* 'I met 500 girls'. In the other cases, they agree with their referents in number (plural) and case, for instance, instrumental, *s pétimi (pẹ̑tstotimi) stōli* 'with five (500) chairs'. In these oblique cases the numerals are often not declined (see 3.1.5).

Indeterminates like *málo* 'little/few', *mǎnj* 'less/fewer', *veliko* 'much/ many', *vẹ̌č* 'more', *dósti* 'enough' behave syntactically like the numerals 'five and above', but do not decline: *tûkaj je bilȯ̀ mǎnj ljudi* (GEN PL) 'there were fewer people here'; *govǫ́ril sǝm z mǎnj ljudmí* (INST PL) 'I talked with fewer people'.

If the amount is unspecified, the genitive alone is sufficient: *narẹ́zal sem krúha in slaníne* 'I cut some bread and some bacon'. Similarly, any specified amount also requires the genitive: *stekleníca dóbrega čȑnega vína* 'a bottle of good red wine'.

5   Lexis

5.1   General composition of the word-stock

The Slovene word-stock is in many respects extremely idiosyncratic. On the one hand, it has not only retained much of the core of Proto-Slavonic lexis, but even maintained several items that were lost elsewhere; thus *ǫ̑l* 'beer' (cognate with English *ale*) survived as a simplex Slavonic word only in Slovene dialects. Other unusual survivals include *brésti* 'wade' and *dâvi* 'this morning'. Local semantic and phonological developments resulted in further unique items: *ampǎk* 'but', *besẹ́da* 'word', *dežéla* 'country', *grénǝk* 'bitter', *hudíč* 'devil', *in* 'and', *jẹ́ča* 'prison', *kljùb* 'in spite of', *mâjhən* 'small', *obljubīti* 'promise', *slẹ́herni* 'each'. In particular, Slovene managed to develop its native vocabulary in ways that mark it off as very different from its closest relative, Serbo-Croat (see Brozović 1988). The position of Slovene on the Slavonic periphery resulted in little medieval influence from other Slavonic languages, but the directly inherited lexicon was complemented both by extensive borrowing from contemporary Slavonic languages in the nineteenth and twentieth centuries and by the equally extensive coinage of new native derivations for referents in all areas of modern life.

On the other hand, its geography and history ensured that Slovene was subject to extensive non-Slavonic influence both spatially and temporally. Not only was it open to influences on three sides – from Romance, Germanic and Hungarian – but the thousand-year-long lack of political independence had its natural consequences. On the three geographical peripheries the degree of bilingualism, especially among certain classes of society, must at times have been very high: many rural Slovenes had to work for, or to trade with speakers of these other languages. In the urban areas, at least partial bilingualism – most important, Slovene–German bilingualism in Ljubljana – would have been normal for most of the Slovene populace. The relative proportions of lexical items from the three non-Slavonic sources vary greatly from dialect to dialect. In the standard language it is clear that direct influence from Germanic (specifically, Austrian German) far outweighs that from Romance (Venetian Italian, Friulian and so on), if (neo-)Latinisms are excluded. The penetration of items from Hungarian has been minor.

Since the Reformation the incorporation of non-native elements has received some deliberate attention, which developed over time into lesser or greater puristic tendencies; these came to a head in the eighteenth and nineteenth centuries and are still evident. The various nationalistic movements – Pan-Slavonic, Illyrian, Yugoslav and specifically Slovene aspirations, to mention just four – all had their effect, especially in attempts to replace Germanisms with borrowings from other Slavonic languages.

The coexistence of these concurrent influences has resulted in a standard language which is, potentially, extremely rich, in its wide range of coexisting items – directly inherited native words, modern native coinages, non-Slavonic borrowings and Slavonic borrowings. Thus alongside the international *migrácija, migrírati, imigrānt, emigrānt* there are the derivatives *preseljevânje, preseljeváti se, priséljenɔc, izséljenɔc*; and alongside the native *porǫ́ka* 'wedding' there is the Germanic borrowing *ǫ́hcet* 'wedding' (compare German *Hochzeit*). In instances of this kind, both semantic and stylistic differentiation have been extensively developed.

5.2   Patterns of borrowing

The **non-Slavonic** languages of the Balkans contributed a few items which Slovene shares with other South Slavs, such as *díple* 'musical instrument' and *gûmb* 'button' (originally from Greek); *bákər* 'copper' and *čížem* 'boot' (originally from Turkish). A few Hungarian words have penetrated to the standard language through the eastern dialects of Slovene and/or Serbo-Croat, like *búnda* 'warm coat', *cafúta* 'whore' and *hásniti* 'be of use'.

The contribution from and through Romance has been greater. Some items are shared with other South Slavonic (and in some instances other Slavonic) languages; some have extended only as far as Slovene. Examples: *bájta* 'shack', *bríga* 'care', *búča* 'pumpkin', *búrkle* 'fire-tongs', *čìk* 'cigarette end', *fȁnt* 'boy', *kmȅt* 'farmer', *kríž* 'cross'.

The influence of Germanic (as originating and mediating language) has been particularly strong on the non-standard forms of Slovene; its traces in the standard language are still quite evident (Striedter-Temps 1963). Examples: *u-bǫ̑gati* 'obey', *fára* 'parish', *gáre* 'hand-cart', *glíhati* 'haggle', *jā̀* 'yes', *kégǝlj* 'skittle', *krompȋr* 'potato', *ǫ̑pica* 'ape', *rȇgrat* 'dandelion', *rísati* 'draw', *úra* 'hour, clock', *žȅmlja* 'bread roll'. Many items were borrowed from Germanic long enough ago to have lost all transparent connection with German, thus *básati, bȃšem* 'fill' (from Old High German *faʒʒōn*). There has at times also been extensive calquing of German phrases: *izglȇdati* 'look' as in *bolȃn izglȇdaš* 'you look ill'; compare German *aussehen*, literally: 'out-see'. This example, like many others, has a contemporary native equivalent, *si vídeti*.

Since Slovene is in direct contact with European and North American culture, the influence of modern international vocabulary has been significant, and is much discussed. Sometimes native formations coexist with loans, as in *ptičeslǫ̑vje* = *ornitologíja* 'ornithology'; sometimes there is a native formation and no loan, as with *kljunáš* 'platypus'.

As if in recompense for the lack of medieval contacts, and for the borrowings from non-Slavonic sources, Slovene has found much of lexical benefit in the **Slavonic** languages, especially during and since the nineteenth century. Although often the geographic details are unclear, borrowings from nearly all the Slavonic languages can be found; three sources predominate: Czech, Serbo-Croat and Russian.

Czech made a large contribution to Slovene, especially in the nineteenth century, when there were cultural influences on Ljubljana from Prague: when reactions to non-Slavonic influence were strong, it was natural that the model of the puristic Czech should be followed. Examples: *bajeslǫ̑vje* 'mythology', *dopisováti* 'correspond', *géslo* 'slogan', *kislína* 'acid', *prispȇvek* 'contribution', *sklȃdba* 'musical composition', *slavospȇv* 'eulogy', *zlitína* 'alloy'.

Borrowings from Serbo-Croat, including items from other Slavonic languages and in particular Russian that came through Serbo-Croat (see Thomas 1987), were numerous before the creation of Yugoslavia and became even more so thereafter; it is too early to decide with certainty on the permanence of some items. Of particular note were the borrowings from this source that (on occasion, by design) replaced non-Slavonic loans;

thus *čáj* 'tea' and *káva* 'coffee' for *tę̂* and *kofě*, both of which are still extant but only in dialects and non-standard styles. *Čítati* was introduced as a replacement for *bráti* in its meaning 'read', since it was felt that this latter was calqued on German *lesen* 'gather; read'; there has been some dispute about this item.

The influence of Russian was also significant, at least from the mid-nineteenth century on; this influence was reinforced by politico-cultural parallels during the Communist period. Often, loans of non-recent date have resulted in useful semantic differentiation. Often, also, the borrowed word crowded out more native items: thus, for 'dictionary', the nineteenth-century *besednják*, *besednik* and *besedíšče* have all been replaced by *slovár*. Examples of politico-cultural loans: *udârnik* 'shock worker', *sòcrealîzəm* 'socialist realism', *otrǫ́ške jâsli* 'day-care'.

5.3   Incorporation of borrowings

There is vacillation in the spelling of borrowings. Thus the *Pravopis* of 1950 gave the spelling *jeep* and the *Pravopis* of 1962 *džip* for 'jeep'; the Academy Dictionary (1970–) has both *píca* and *pízza* for 'pizza'. Generally, however, modern borrowings are rapidly nativized, as shown by the spelling of *nylon* and *engineering* as *nâjlon* and *inženîring*. Aside from anomalies caused by influences from the orthography and intermediary languages, the closest equivalents of the sounds in the lending language are normally approximated. Exceptionally, the high-mid vowels /e o/ are normally preferred to the low-mid /ɛ ɔ/, for instance, *profêsor* /profêsor/ 'professor', *prǫ̂mptən* /prɔ̂mptən/ 'prompt'. As these words also exemplify, the tonemically high pitch is more common than the tonemically low pitch on borrowed words with long vowels.

Turning to morphology, we find that extremely few borrowed nouns are treated as indeclinables. Normally, if a borrowed noun ends in unstressed *-a*, it is feminine (declined as *lípa*) and otherwise the noun is masculine and declined as *kǫ̂t*. Note that nouns ending in *-r* or a vowel add *-j-* before non-zero endings, as in *abonmâ*, *abonmâja* 'subscription'; see also 3.1.2. Note also that virtually no recently borrowed nouns are neuter: hence *nòv kîno* 'new cinema', *nòv komitę̂* 'new committee', *nòv alîbi* 'new alibi', *nòv kanû* 'new canoe'. Adjectives, on the other hand, relatively often become indeclinable. Compare the borrowed adjectives in *pȓvi trîje âvti so olívni, drûgi trîje krę̂m ~ krę̂masti, in zâdnji trîje bę̂ž* 'the first three cars are olive, the next three cream, and the last three beige': the first is declined, the second is optionally declined and the third is not declined. In the sixteenth century many borrowed verbal roots incorporated the *-ov- ~ -ev-* suffix but this suffix was – in spite of a puristic attempt to reintroduce it in the nineteenth century – eventually replaced by the extremely productive suffix *-ir-* (which had been borrowed via German from French: see 3.3.3). Apart from *-irati* verbs (conjugation class IIIc), some modern borrowings are

Slovenized by adaptation into conjugation classes IIIc and IV, as *-ati* and *-iti* verbs respectively. As for aspectual differentiation, *-irati* verbs are usually bi-aspectual, the others not: so, for instance, for 'democratize', *demokratizírati* is imperfective/perfective, while *podemokrátiti* is perfective only.

5.4   Lexical fields

5.4.1   Colour terms

Nine colour terms seem to be 'basic' according to derivational criteria: *bẹ̑l* 'white', *siv* 'grey' and *čŕn* 'black'; *rdèč* 'red', *zelèn* 'green', *rumèn* 'yellow', *mọ́dǝr* 'blue (1)', *sīnji* 'blue (2)' and *rjä̀v* 'brown'. All nine have adjectival derivatives in *-(i)kast*; verbal 'inchoative' derivatives in *-eti*; and verbal 'factitive' derivatives in *-iti*: *bẹ̑lkast* 'whitish', *belẹ́ti* 'become white', *belíti* 'make (something) white'; *sīnjkast, sinjẹ́ti, sīnjiti* and so on. Three ('red', 'green', 'brown') may be derived from other 'basic' roots, namely *zèl* 'herb', *rdẹ́ti* 'redden', *rjä̀* 'rust'; this is not true of the remainder. Of the two standard words for blue, *mọ́dǝr* is darker ('the colour of cornflowers') and *sīnji* lighter. The Academy Dictionary defines *sīnji* in terms of *mọ́dǝr*, the more 'basic' of the two. Many speakers use *plä̀v* as an approximate synonym for *mọ́dǝr*.

The following, in contrast, are apparently not 'basic': they are derived from other simplex words; their adjectival derivatives are either non-existent or different from the above (namely, *-ast* rather than *-kast*); and they appear to lack the normal corresponding verbal derivatives: *orânžǝn* 'orange'; *rọ̑žnat* 'pink'; and numerous words for shades of purple/mauve/violet, the most common of which is *vijọ́ličǝn*.

One small curiosity: of the six spectrum colours, three begin with /ǝr/; and all three are at one end of the spectrum, opposed to the others.

5.4.2   Body parts

The following are straightforward correspondents of English lexical items: *glává* 'head'; *okọ̑, očẹ̑sa* 'eye'; *nọ̑s* 'nose'; *uhọ̑, ušẹ̑sa* 'ear'; *ústa* (N PL) 'mouth'; *lãs* (M SG) or (more commonly) *lasjẹ̑* (M PL) 'hair (on head)'; *vrãt* 'neck'; *srcẹ̑* 'heart'. The following involve more ambiguity. *Róka* is 'hand' or 'arm'; as necessary, a part may be specified, for instance, *lãket* (M *o*-stem or F *i*-stem) 'forearm', *dlân* (F *i*-stem) 'palm'. Similarly, *nóga* is 'foot' or 'leg'; specifically, *stopálo* 'foot'; *mẹ́ča* (N PL) 'calf', *bédro* = *stégno* 'thigh' and so on. The single word *pŕst* (M) is 'finger' or 'toe'; to specify one or the other, *pŕst na róki* and *pŕst na nógi* can be used. *Pŕsi* (F PL) is 'chest/breast' (male or female); a specifically female breast is *dọ̑jka*. For the use of dual versus plural forms of names for body parts that come in pairs, see 4.10.

5.4.3   Kinship terms

Many words are used for parents and grandparents. The most common (here, variants are given in the order: more ~ less formal) are *máti* ~ *máma* 'mother', *óče, očéta* ~ *áta* 'father'; *stâra máti* ~ *stâra máma* ~ *bábica* 'grandmother', *stâri óče* ~ *stâri áta* ~ *dèd* 'grandfather'. Note also *stârši* 'parents', *stâri stârsi* (PL) 'grandparents': these may also occur (see 4.10) as (*stâra*) *stârša* (DU) and even as (*stârɪ*) *stârš* (SG).

One set of terms is unspecified for sex: *otròk* / *dę́te dę́teta* 'child' – also used age-specifically, 'baby, small child'. Otherwise, terminology is exclusively sex-specific: *žéna* 'wife' and *mộž* 'husband' (formal *soprộga, soprộg* 'spouse (F, M)'); *hčî, hčę́re* 'daughter', *sɪn* 'son'; *séstra* 'sister', *brȁt* 'brother'; *téta* 'aunt' (mother's sister or father's sister); *stric* 'uncle' (mother's brother or father's brother) – note also *ûjɔc* and *ûjna* 'mother's brother/sister', now generally replaced by *stric, téta* – *nečákinja* 'niece', *nečák* 'nephew'; *sestrična* 'female cousin', *brátranɔc* 'male cousin'.

6   Dialects

It is generally acknowledged, although difficult to demonstrate, that Slovene is unique among the Slavonic languages in the heterogeneity of its dialects, especially in relation to the relatively small size of the Slovene-speaking area. This diversity, which exerted some influence on the evoluation of the standard language (see section 1), is reflected in some lack of mutual comprehension. It is also reflected in the analyses of dialectologists. Earlier authoritative analyses by Ramovš listed, respectively, thirty-six and forty-six different dialects and subdialects; the most recent map (Logar and Rigler 1986) shows fifty. More important, there has been inconclusiveness with respect to more general groupings. Nevertheless, it is usually accepted that the geographically differing varieties of Slovene can be categorized in eight major groups; this classification serves as a basis for the brief survey below (see Lencek 1982: 133–57).

The chief traditional criteria for distinguishing between dialects are two diachronic vocalic ones: the medieval reflexes (in stressed long syllables) of -*ě* (*jat'*) and the nasals, on the one hand, and of the *jers*, on the other (see Rigler 1963, 1967). By the first criterion the speech area is divided by a south-west/north-east line; by the second, it is divided by a line along the other diagonal. Other criteria result in important (if traditionally less usual) groupings: note in particular the differences in prosodic phonology, and especially the fact that tonemic distinctions have been lost in all but a longitudinally central band of dialects. Not only prosodic changes listed as items 7 and 8 in 2.1, but subsequent changes also, resulted in wide variations in patterns of stress, length and pitch. Other differences relate to specific vocalic systems, for example, inventories of from three to sixteen vowel phonemes; systems rich in diphthongs and those with no diphthongs;

Map 8.1   Slovene Dialects

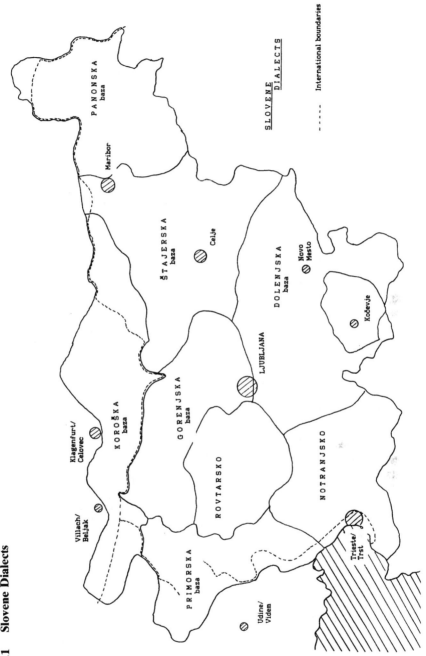

those with nasal vowels; those with more and those with less vowel reduction; differences in kinds of vowel reduction and so on. Major dialectal consonantal differences from standard Slovene include the following: the fricativization of */g/ › /ɣ/, /h/; */tj/ › /ć/; */ń/ › /j̃/, /n/, /jn/; */ĺ/ › /j/, /l/, /jl/; a (secondary) 'neopalatalization' of velars, namely /k g x/ › /č j̃ š/ (and other reflexes); various reflexes for */l/ and */v/, especially giving /w/ in some and/or all environments; */b/ › /β/, */t/ › /θ/, */k/ › /ʔ/, */f/ › /x/, */x/ › /j/.

Morphological differences have resulted from these phonological changes and from morphological developments. Most of the categories listed in 3.1.1 and 3.2.1 survive in most dialects, but note the following: the generally partial (but in one dialect the complete) loss of the neuter gender; the partial loss of the dual number; syncretism among case distinctions, especially in the oblique plural cases; extensive curtailment of the supine. There are also many dialect differences on the syntactic level, but these have as yet been little described. Depending on their geographical proximity to speakers of other languages – German, Friulian, Italian, Serbo-Croat, Hungarian – dialects show marked differences in lexical composition. Furthermore, dialects differ greatly in their development of the native lexicon.

The following eight groups comprise six '(pan-)dialect bases' and two large transitional areas. Omitted here are the smaller transitional dialects. Statements of vocalic reflexes relate to prototypical medieval stages, not always apparent in the contemporary reflexes.

Primorska baza (Littoral): nasals › low-mid, ě (*jat'*) › low-mid, *jers* › */a/. These dialects include the native dialects of Slovene-speakers in the Italian province of Friulia-Venezia Giulia (excluding those in the hinterland of Trst/Trieste); the pressure from Italian-speakers has in these areas at times been strong. Most of these dialects have lost phonemic length and pitch, but keep phonemic stress. Some of them share features with the Koroška dialect base, for instance, the fricativization of */g/ and the prefix */vy-/. Many show the results of Romance–Slovene bilingualism. Within this area are the highly idiosyncratic dialects of the Rezija valley, with their *zasopli* (centralized, formerly breathy (?)) vowels and where the aorist and imperfect tense forms have, in one form or another, survived.

Notranjsko (Inner Carniola): nasals › high-mid, *jat'* › high-mid, *jers* › */a/. This area is transitional between the Primorska and the Dolenjska dialect bases and covers dialects formerly classified as such. It includes the first language of the Slovene minority in Trst/Trieste and its hinterland; the pressure from Italian-speakers has been intense here also. All of these dialects have lost phonemic length and pitch, but keep phonemic stress.

Rovtarsko: These dialects (*róvte* means 'backwoods') represent innovative developments resulting from medieval colonization by both neighbouring Slovene-speakers and by speakers of Bavarian German dialects. In many respects, these dialects are transitional; in others, they are idiosyncratic.

Koroška baza (Carinthian): nasals › low-mid, *jat'* › low-mid, *jers* › */e/. These dialects, which generally maintain phonemic pitch and length, are very conservative: note, for instance, the preservation of nasal vowels in one small area; also, features apparently transitional to West Slavonic, such as the fricativization of */g/; */dl tl/ unchanged in nouns; derivational prefix */vy-/. In some respects they are innovative, as in the 'neopalatalization'. As well as areas in Italy and Slovenia, these dialects now comprise the mother tongues of the Slovene minority living in the Austrian province of Kärnten and survive despite heavy sociopolitical pressure from the German majority.

Gorenjska baza (Upper Carniolan): nasals › high-mid, *jat'* › high-mid, *jers* › */a/. This, one of the two central dialect areas, played a major role in the development of standard Slovene; in particular, the monophthongal long stressed vowels of the standard language have their origin here; also, these dialects helped to contribute the standard tonemic framework. Non-standard innovative features include the 'neopalatalization' and the partial loss of the neuter gender. The city of Ljubljana is, geographically, just inside the Gorenjska area, but has its own traditional speech styles.

Dolenjska baza (Lower Carniolan): nasals › high-mid, *jat'* › high-mid, *jers* › */a/. This was the other central dialect base which exerted a strong influence on the development of standard Slovene, especially on its tonemic system; its diphthongized vowels are, however, not reflected in the standard language. Within the Dolenjska area is a linguistic island that was for long inhabited mostly by German-speakers (Gottschee/Kočevje); its present population speaks a dialectal mixture. South of Kočevje the Belokranjsko dialects have some features transitional to Kajkavian Serbo-Croat (see chapter 7, section 6).

Štajerska baza (Styrian): nasals › high-mid, *jat'* › high-mid, *jers* › */e/. This extensive area includes dialects spoken close to the cities of Celje and Maribor. Most have lost phonemic pitch and length, but maintain phonemic stress. Some show features transitional to Kajkavian Serbo-Croat.

Panonska baza (North-east Styrian/Pannonian): nasals › high-mid, *jat'* › high-mid, *jers* › */e/. These dialects have lost distinctive pitch, but keep distinctive stress. Some show transitional Kajkavian Serbo-Croat features; those dialects closest to Hungarian show the influence of Hungarian–Slovene bilingualism, and many lexical innovations. A few speakers of these Slovene dialects live within the boundaries of Hungary.

Acknowledgement

The author acknowledges the extensive help and advice given by Velemir Gjurin (Ljubljana), without which this chapter could not have been written. Remaining mistakes are, of course, the author's.

References

Academy Dictionary = *Slovar slovenskega knjižnega jezika*, Ljubljana: Slovenska akademija znanosti in umetnosti. I: A–H, 1970; II, I–Na, 1975; III, Ne–Pren, 1979; IV, Preo–Š, 1985; V, T–Ž, 1991.

Bajec, Anton (1950–2) *Besedotvorje slovenskega jezika*, vol. I: *Izpeljava samostalnikov*, vol. II: *Izpeljava slovenskih pridevnikov*, vol. III: *Zloženke*, Ljubljana: Slovenska Akademija Znanosti in Umetnosti.

Bennett, David (1986) 'Towards an explanation of word-order differences between Slovene and Serbo-Croat', *Slavonic and East European Review* 64: 1–24.

—— (1987) 'Word-order change in progress: the case of Slovene and Serbo-Croat and its relevance for Germanic', *Journal of Linguistics* 23: 269–87.

Brozović, Dalibor (1988) 'Contemporary standard Slovene: a complex linguistic phenomenon', *Slovene Studies* 10, 2: 175–90.

Corbett, Greville (1983) *Hierarchies, Targets and Controllers: Agreement Patterns in Slavic*, London: Croom Helm.

Davis, Margaret G. (1989) *Aspects of Adverbial Placement in English and Slovene*, Munich: Sagner.

Lencek, Rado L. (1982) *The Structure and History of the Slovene Language*, Columbus, Ohio: Slavica.

Logar, Tine and Jakob Rigler (1986) *Karta slovenskih narečij*, Ljubljana: Geodetski zavod SRS.

Mader, Elfriede (1981) *Rückläufiges Wörterbuch des Slowenischen*, Klagenfurt: Klagenfurter Sprachwissenschaftliche Gesellschaft.

Neweklowsky, Gerhard (1988) 'Zur Häufigkeit morphologischer Kategorien in slowenischen Prosatexten', in B. Paternu and F. Jakopin (eds) *Sodobni slovenski jezik, književnost in kultura. Mednarodni simpozij v Ljubljani od 1. do 3. julija 1986*, Ljubljana: Univerza Edvarda Kardelja, 337–49.

Paternost, Joseph (1984) 'A sociolinguistic tug-of-war between Slovene and Serbo-Croatian in Slovenia today', *Slovene Studies* 6: 227–42.

Perlmutter, David M. and Janez Orešnik (1973) 'Language-particular rules and explanation in syntax', in S.R. Anderson and P. Kiparsky (eds) *A Festschrift for Morris Halle*, New York: Holt, 419–59.

Pleteršnik, Maks (1894–5) *Slovensko-nemški slovar*, Ljubljana: Knezoškofijstvo. (Reprint, Ljubljana: Cankarjeva založba, 1974).

Pravopis = Jože Toporišič *et al.*, (eds), (1962) *Slovenski pravopis*, Ljubljana: Državna založba Slovenije.

Priestly, Tom (1987) 'Verb-productivity: evidence from three varieties of Slovene', *Slovene Studies* 9: 195–203.

Rigler, Jakob (1963) 'Pregled osnovnih razvojnih etap v slovenskem vokalizmu', *Slavistična revija* 14: 25–78.

—— (1967) 'Pripombe k Pregledu osnovnih razvojnih etap v slovenskem vokalizmu', *Slavistična revija* 15: 129–52.

Srebot-Rejec, Tatjana (1988) *Word Accent and Vowel Duration in Standard Slovene. An Acoustic and Linguistic Investigation*, Munich: Sagner.

Stankiewicz, Edward (1959) 'The vocalic systems of Modern Standard Slovenian', *International Journal of Slavic Linguistics and Poetics* 1, 2: 70–6.

Štrekelj, Karl (1903) 'Die Ursache des Schwundes des prädikativen Instrumentals im Slovenischen und Sorbischen', *Archiv für slavische Philologie* 25: 564–9.

Striedter-Temps, Hildegard (1963) *Deutsche Lehnwörter im Slovenischen*, Wiesbaden: Harrassowitz.

Svane, Gunnar O. (1958) *Grammatik der slowenischen Schriftsprache*, Copenhagen: Rosenkilde und Bagger.

Thomas, George (1987) 'The slavization of the Slovene and Croatian lexicons: problems in their interrelationships in the nineteenth century', *Slovene Studies* 9: 217–25.

Tollefson, James W. (1981) *The Language Situation and Language Policy in Slovenia*, Washington DC: University Press of America.

Toporišič, Jože (1982) *Nova slovenska skladnja*, Ljubljana: Državna založba Slovenije.

—— (1984) *Slovenska slovnica. Pregledana in razširjena izdaja*, Maribor: Obzorja.

—— (1987) 'Grammatik der slowenischen Schriftsprache' (= review of Svane (1958)) in Jože Toporišič, *Portreti, pregledi, presoje*, Maribor: Obzorja, 421–40.

—— (1989) 'Slovenska knjižna tonemskost govora Jakoba Riglerja', *Slavistična revija* 37: 61–96.

Vidovič-Muha, Ada (1988) *Slovensko skladenjsko besedotvorje ob primerih zloženk*, Ljubljana: Partizanska knjiga.

WEST SLAVONIC LANGUAGES

9 Czech

David Short

1 Introduction

Czech is the official language of the Czech Republic, the western two-thirds of former Czechoslovakia. In its two provinces of Bohemia and Moravia, and the part of southern Silesia included in Moravia, it is spoken by about 9.5 million people. It is also widely understood by speakers of Slovak. There are isolated Czech-speaking communities in several nearby countries and some quite large communities overseas, especially in the Americas. Of whatever antiquity, they have arisen from a long tradition of economic or political emigration. Some cohesive communities with continuity of evolution since before the First World War are linguistically relatively undamaged, though with distinctive dialect features; younger communities are both less cohesive and less resistant to the effect of the host environment.

The standard language is based on Josef Dobrovský's early nineteenth-century codification, modelled on sixteenth-century Czech, but with some recognition of later developments. To Dobrovský Czech owes the revival of certain obsolete features, for example, the gerunds, which occur chiefly in higher registers.

The main distinguishing features of Czech date from the thirteenth century or earlier, but its modern form owes much to certain far-reaching changes in the fourteenth and fifteenth centuries, most strikingly the umlauts. The written language came to be based on the variant spoken at the main cultural centre, Prague (where the university was founded in 1348).

Standard Czech (*spisovná čeština*) is then a semi-artificial creation, archaic in many respects, while the vernacular has continued to evolve since the norms (whether of the sixteenth or the nineteenth century) were set. There is a consequent tension between the modern literary language and the spoken Czech, usually known as Common Czech (*obecná čeština*), in which natural development has culminated. This has its own distinctive morphology, relatively impoverished syntactic variation, and a lexicon, and in part syntax, that reveals the influence of German. Between these two

455

poles there are transitional strata, notably Colloquial Czech (*hovorová čeština*, an informal spoken version of the standard language, whose existence is often denied) and Commonly Spoken Czech (*běžně mluvená čeština*, basically the everyday speech of the big cities). For a discussion of this stratification see Townsend (1990). The transition forms are the channel by which 'upwardly mobile' features of Common Czech may penetrate the standard language. This century has seen, for instance, the acceptance of infinitives in -*t* as colloquial alternatives to the traditional forms in -*ti*, then as free variants with those in -*ti* and finally as the neutral norm. Similarly, the status of infinitives in -*ci* has altered, with alternatives in -*ct* being admitted into the standard language as recently as the late 1970s. The codification of words or forms is not a matter of common consent, but part of the job description of the national Academy's Institute for the Czech Language; once notoriously purist, it is increasingly tolerant of change. The tension between Standard and Common Czech and recent reductions in mother-tongue teaching in schools inform the perceived need for a body to weigh the changing norms in the balance and guide the standard accordingly. The Institute publishes, *inter alia*, the journals *Naše řeč* and *Slovo a slovesnost*.

2 Phonology

2.1 Segmental phoneme inventory

Czech has a simple **vowel system**: five vowels, /a/, /e/, /i/, /o/ and /u/, also occur in long syllables, hence the set of matching long vowels, /aː/, /eː/, /iː/, /oː/ and /uː/, written á, é, í, ó, ú, and, in the case of /uː/, also ů; /i/ and /iː/ are represented by both i, í (< PIE *ī*) and y and ý (< PIE *ū*). There is one native diphthong /ou/ and two that occur in loan-words, /eu/ and /au/. Length is phonemic, hence such minimal pairs as: *dal* 'he gave' and *dál* 'further', 'come in!'; *rychle* 'quickly' and *rychlé* 'quick' (N SG et al.); *ryby* 'fish' and *rybi* 'fish-'; *domu* 'house' (GEN SG) and *dómu* 'cathedral' (GEN SG); *dul* 'blew' and *důl* 'mine'.

The main distributional restrictions concern /oː/, and /uː/: /oː/ occurs only in loan-words, native /oː/ having developed within the Old Czech period into /uː/, now written ů; this occurs in monosyllabic roots, alternating with o (*stůl/stolu* 'table', *sůl/soli* 'salt', *můj/moje* 'my'), and in some genitive and dative plural noun endings (*hradů*, *hradům* 'castle'); elsewhere /uː/, written ú, features chiefly in noun prefixes, for example, *úraz* 'injury', but *urazit* 'injure'. Other long syllables containing /u/ have developed into the diphthong /ou/, hence such oppositions as *sud* 'barrel' and *soud* 'court'.

Initial *a-*, *e-* and *i-* only occur in loan-words, the conjunctions *a* and *i* 'and', *ale* 'but', and some interjections.

There are twenty-five **consonantal phonemes** (table 9.1), and several important allophones.

Occlusives: labial /p/, /b/, /m/; dental /t/, /d/, /n/; palatal /ť/, /ď/, /ň/; velar: /k/, /g/.
Semi-occlusives: alveolar /c/ (= [ts]); post-alveolar /č/ (= [tš]).
Fricatives: labio-dental /f/, /v/; alveolar /s/, /z/; post-alveolar (formerly palatal) /š/, /ž/; palatal /j/; velar /ch/ (= [x]); voiced (!) laryngeal /h/; lateral (almost frictionless) /l/; vibrants: an alveolar roll /r/, and post-alveolar /ř/ with considerable friction.

The 'missing' velar nasal occlusive [ŋ] occurs as an allophone of /n/ before a velar (*banka* [baŋka] 'bank'); the voiced affricates [dz] and [dž] occur as positional variants of /c/ and /č/ before voiced consonants that have voiceless counterparts in the system, as in *léčba* 'therapy', pronounced [le:džba]. Homorganic renderings of /d/ + /ž/ are to be heard in loan-words such as *džudo* 'judo', in the native words *džbán* 'jug' and *džber* 'tub' (Old Czech *čbán, čber*), and at some morpheme boundaries, for example *od ženy* 'from a woman', also /d/ + /z/ in, say, *podzemní* 'underground'. Similar homorganic renderings as /c/ and /č/ apply in the case of /t/ + /s/ and /t/ + /š/. Another non-phonemic sound is the glottal stop, which occurs usually before morpheme-initial vowels.

Most peripheral in the consonantal systems are /g/ and /f/. Original /g/ changed regularly into voiced /h/; /g/ is now therefore restricted to borrowings and in non-standard versions of the language it often replaces

Table 9.1   Czech consonantal sounds (non-phonemic in square brackets)

	Labial	Labio-dental	Alveo-dental	Post-alveolar	Palatal	Velar	Laryngeal
Occlusive							
oral	p b		t d		ť ď	k g	
nasal	m		n		ň	[ŋ]	
glottal							[ʔ]
Semi-occlusive			ts [dz]	tš [dž]			
Fricative		f v	s z	š ž	j	x [ɣ]	h
Lateral			l				
Roll			r				
Trill			[ř̩] ř				

Note: In terms of the IPA /ť/ = c, /ď/ = ɟ, /ň/ = ɲ, /š/ = ʃ, /ž/ = ʒ, /ts/ = tʃ, [dž] = dʒ, /ř/ = ɾ.

/k/ in other borrowings. /f/ is also largely confined to loans, acquired copiously since early medieval times; its first limited standing was in onomatopoeia, for example, *foukat* 'blow', and later from *pv*, for example, *upvati* › *upfati* › *úfati*, › modern *doufat* 'hope', *zoufat* 'despair'.

The treatment of the paired obstruents is important: before a pause or a glottal stop (that is, a morpheme-initial vowel), the opposition of voice is neutralized, hence *led* › [let] 'ice', *bez* › [bes] 'without', *páv* › [pa:f] 'peacock'; in these circumstances /h/ has as its voiceless counterpart /x/: *vrah* › [vrax] 'murderer'. A similar process appears as voice assimilation in consonantal clusters: in most cases where voiced and voiceless consonants meet, in either order, assimilation is regressive:

voiced + voiceless: *zpět* [spjet] 'back', *hádka* [ha:tka] 'argument';
voiceless + voiced: *sbor* [zbor] 'choir', *kde* [gde] 'where'.

In this pattern peripheral /g/ is integrated into the system. The pair /v/, /f/ is only partially integrated: /v/ is assimilated (it devoices before a voiceless consonant), but cannot itself cause voicing: *vtip* [ftip] 'joke', *vsadit* [fsadit] 'bet', but: *tvůj* [tvu:j] 'thy', *dvůr* [dvu:r] 'courtyard'. The reason is its relatively late development from bilabial /w/. On the other hand, /f/, although peripheral, is better integrated, though with few opportunities for demonstrating this: *podfuk* [potfuk] 'swindle'; *halvbek* ‹ *half-back*. /h/ and /ch/ are also deviant: while /h/ › /x/ before a voiceless consonant (*nehty* [nexti] 'nails'), it itself causes assimilation of a preceding voiceless consonant in the regional pronunciation of Moravia, for example, *shoda* [zhoda] 'agreement', while in Bohemia there is usually progressive assimilation, hence [sxoda]. In places where /x/ might assimilate – across word boundaries as in *kdybych byl* – it voices not to /h/, but to [ɣ]. The distribution of voiced and voiceless allophones of /ř/ is also anomalous: it assimilates both regressively: *řvát* [řva:t] 'rend', *vuřty* [vuřti] 'sausages'; and progressively: *dři* [dři] 'rub', *tři* [tři] 'three'.

Of the numerous Czech consonant clusters suffice it to say that two-consonant clusters are the most frequent syllable-initially (fricative + sonorant preferred) and word-finally (most frequent: *-st*), and that medially, at morpheme boundaries, clusters of four or more are quite common. Word-initially four consonants is the maximum, though rare (*pstruh* 'trout', *pštros* 'ostrich', [hřmňelo] spelled *hřmělo* 'thundered'), rising to five with the phonetic word (*s pštrosem* 'with an ostrich'). Word- and syllable-finally the limit is three, but only in borrowings like [tekst] (spelled *text*), *funkč-ni* 'functional'.

Combinations of velar + /e/ are rare; originally lost in the Proto-Slavonic palatalizations, they now occur only with /e/ ‹ /ъ/: *bukem* (INST SG) 'beech'. The fourteenth-century umlauts mean that combinations of 'soft' consonant + back vowel (especially *u* and *o*) are also rare outside 'expressive' items (*ďábel* 'devil', *ťuhýk* 'shrike', *ďobat* 'peck'), loans (*žumpa* 'cess-pit', *čokoláda* 'chocolate'), and derivationally and morphologically conditioned forms of verbs and adjectives (*vyloďovat* 'disembark', *poschoďový* 'double-decker', *mužův* 'the man's').

The Czech **alphabet** consists of: a, b, c, č, d, e, f, g, h, ch, i, j, k, l, m, n, o, p, q, r, ř, s, š, t, u, v, w, x, y, z, ž. Any additional graphemes (ť, ď, ň, ě, long vowels, including ů) are not alphabetized.

The relationship between phonemes and alphabet is close. A few rules govern representations of the palatal consonants (and the distribution of *ú* and *ů*, see above).

1 /ď/, /ť/ and /ň/ followed by /e/ are represented orthographically as dě, tě and ně, contrasting with /d/ + /e/ and so on as de, te, ne.

2 /ď/, /ť/ and /ň/ + /i/ are represented as di, ti, ni, contrasting with /d/ + /i/ and so on as dy, ty, ny.

3 /ď/, /ť/ or /ň/ + /a/, /o/, /u/, or word-finally are represented by ď, ť, ň; the handwriting and typing convention for ď and ť is to use the *háček*: ď, ť.

4 ě after b, p, f, v denotes not palatalized labials (lost in the fifteenth century), but a fully developed palatal element, [j], hence *oběd* /objet/ 'lunch', *pěna* /pjena/ 'foam', *věno* /vjeno/ 'dowry', *harfě* /harfje/ 'harp' (DAT/LOC SG); after bilabial /m/ nasal resonance extends over both segments, hence intervening /ň/ for /j/ in *město* 'town' = /mňesto/.

The letters *q*, *w* and *x* occur only in loan-words and are pronounced [kv], [v] and either [ks] or [gz]. German *ä*, *ö*, *ü* may occur in surnames, pronounced [eː], [eː], and [iː] respectively.

We now turn to the most interesting factors in the evolution of the Czech phonological system.

The **metathesis of the liquid consonants**. The chains C*or*C, C*ol*C, C*er*C, C*el*C (where C represents any consonant) developed into C*ra*C, C*la*C, C*rě*C, C*lě*C, hence *gordъ* › *hrad* 'castle', *golsъ* › *hlas* 'voice', *bergъ* › *břeh* 'bank', *melko* › *mléko* 'milk'. Vowel length reflects prehistoric intonation patterns: circumflex shows as short, acute as long. In initial *or*C, *ol*C groups intonation has also left its mark: where there was an acute accent the reflex is *ra*C, *la*C, while a circumflex generally produced *ro*C, *lo*C, as in *rádlo* 'plough', *laň* 'doe', *robota* 'corvée', *loď* 'boat'.

Czech has lost both the **nasal vowels** and the **jers** (ultra-short vowels; ъ = *ŭ*, ь = *ĭ*) of Proto-Slavonic.

The nasals survived to the first half of the tenth century, after which *ǫ* developed into *u*, still surviving unaltered in hard environments, and *ę* into *ä*. Before hard consonants this later developed, as a back variant, into *a*, while before soft consonants a front variant developed into *ě*; this change, and that of *u/ú* › *i/í* in a soft environment, coincides with those of the first two umlauts (see below). The change *ę* › *ä* › *ě* also occurred before *k*. Examples: *rǫka* › *ruka* 'hand'; *dušǫ* › *dušu* › *duši* 'soul' (ACC SG); *męso* › *mäso* › *maso* 'meat'; *svętiti* › *svätiti* › *světiti* 'consecrate'; *mękkъjь* › *mäkký* › *měkký* 'soft'.

In long syllables *ǫ* developed via *ú* into *ou*, or *i* in soft environments, while *ę* gave *ä*, thence *á* or the diphthong *ie* (equivalent to long *ě*), which like *ie* from other sources then produced *í*. Examples: *mǫka* › *múka* › *mouka* 'flour'; *dušejǫ* › *dušó* › *dušú* › *duši* 'soul' (INST SG); *pętъjь* › *pátý* › *pátý* 'fifth'; *zajęcь* › *zajäc* › *zajiec* › *zajíc* 'hare'; *dękъ* › *däk* › *diek* › *dik* 'thanks'.

In the treatment of the *jers* two basic patterns apply: the *jer*-like sounds that accompanied syllabic liquids were lost first, leaving pure syllabic *r* and *l*. Original CъrC and CьrC merged as CrC, hence *kъrkъ* › *krk* 'neck'; *tьrgъ* › *trh* 'market'; *žьrdь* › Old Czech *žrď* 'mast'; this situation survives, except that over the twelfth to fourteenth centuries syllabic *r* after *č* and *ž* acquired an accompanying -*e*-, hence *černý* 'black', *žerď* 'mast'. Original CъlC and CьlC also merged, as CluC, except after labials, where the CьlC variant survived with syllabic *l*, hence: (from CьlC) *žlutý* 'yellow', *dlouhý* 'long'; from (CъlC) *tlouci* 'beat', *slunce* 'sun'; (after labials) *mluvit* 'speak', but *mlčet* 'be silent', *vlk* 'wolf'.

The true *jers* disappeared or vocalized in the tenth century. The reflex for both *ъ* and *ь* is *e*: *dьnь* › *den* 'day'; *dъnъ* › *den* 'bottom' (GEN PL); *dьnьsь* › *dnes* 'today'; *sъ pьsъmь* › *se psem* 'with a dog'; *okъno* › *okno* 'window', *okъnъ* › *oken* (GEN PL); *sъbьra.i* (INF), *sъberǫ* (1 SG) › *sebrati*, *sberu* 'gather'. The last example is Old Czech and illustrates the Czech tendency to adjust forms in favour of morphemic consistency, hence modern *sebrat*, *seberu*. Some new nominatives have arisen in line with oblique cases: Modern Czech *domeček* 'little house' for Old Czech *domček* ‹ *domъčьkъ* from the general oblique stem *domeček*- ‹ *domъčьk*-.

Instances such as *oken* and *se psem* above probably gave rise to the use of *e* as a fill vowel in Czech, both in other genitive plurals (*sestrъ* › *sestr* › *sester* from *sestra* 'sister'; *mydlъ* › *mýdl* › *mýdel* from *mýdlo* 'soap'), and in vocalized prepositions which could not be of *jer* origin: before like consonants (*ke koni* 'towards the horse', *se synem* 'with his son'), and before many consonantal clusters (*ve škole* 'in school', *beze mě* = [mně] 'without me').

Loss of the *jers* produced a new set of syllabic liquids, as in *vítr* ‹ *vietrъ* 'wind', *vedl* ‹ *vedlъ* 'he led', *bratrský* ‹ *bratr-ьský* 'fraternal', *jablko* ‹ *jablьko* 'apple'; syllabification of the liquid was only one of a variety of solutions to the newly emerged consonantal clusters (compare *mýdel* above, and see Short 1988).

The **Czech umlauts** (*přehláska*). These changes contributed greatly to the split between hard and soft paradigms. They began early in the thirteenth century with the change *a* › *ě* in final position after soft consonants, and between soft consonants. The change affected not only original *a*, but also the front variant of *ä* ‹ *ę*, to which it must have been very close. The process was inhibited by a following hard consonant. Examples of original *a* › *ě*: *duša* › *dušě* › *duše*; *otca* › *otcě* › *otce* 'father' (GEN); *ležati* › *ležěti* › *ležet* 'lie'. In long syllables, as in the history of the nasals, the Old Czech reflex was *ie* (Modern Czech *í*): *přítel* 'friend', *číše* 'goblet', *znamení* 'sign' (GEN SG)'. About a century later a similar change affected *u/ú*, after any soft consonant, with *i/í* as the outcome: *jug* › *jih* 'south'; *zem'u* › *zemi* 'land' (F ACC SG); *oráču* › *oráči* 'plough-man' (M DAT SG); *kryju/kryjú* › *kryji/kryjí* 'cover' (1 SG/3 PL). A third umlaut affected the mid vowels *'o/ 'ó*. They too produced *ě/ie*, notably before certain inflections and suffixes; in almost every instance the effects have been reversed by analogy with hard stems: *ukřižovati* › *ukřižěvati* › *ukřižovat* 'crucify'; *zlodějóm* › *zlodějiem* › *zlodějům* 'thieves' (DAT PL). Survivals occur in soft neuter dative plural: *moř'óm* › *mořiem* › *mořím* 'sea', and the isolated *koním* ‹ *koniem* ‹ *koňóm* 'horse' (M DAT PL).

Prosodic phenomena. Czech has fixed stress on the first syllable. A preceding preposition, especially if it is an open monosyllable, attracts the stress, hence *ke stolu* 'to the table'. Several word categories are stressless, chiefly past and conditional auxiliaries and weak personal pronouns, which have fixed positions in the clause (see 4.1); sentence-initially, certain weakly stressed words may lose their stress, as in *Tak pòjďte!* 'Come on then!'

Czech has no tones, but their former presence is betrayed in the distribution of long and short syllables. Their history is complex, especially after the metatony which produced new acutes and new circumflexes; suffice it to note that Proto-Slavonic long syllables (those containing *i, y, ě, a, u, ę* or *ǫ*) survived in disyllables where they preceded the stress, for example, *tráva* ‹ *trāvà* 'grass'; from long acutes in the first syllable of disyllables, for example, *zdráv* ‹ *zdràvъ* 'healthy'; and from long syllables before medial stressed short syllables in trisyllabic words (*útroba* ‹ *ǫtròba* 'entrail'; *zákon* ‹ *zākónъ* 'law'). Most other long syllables in Czech are either the product of contraction (V*j*V › V̄, compare PSl. *dobraja*, Czech *dobrá* 'good' (NOM SG FEM), PSl. *bojati sę*, Czech *bát se* 'fear'), or from the new acute.

2.2 Morphophonemic alternations inherited from Proto-Slavonic or Proto-Czech

The palatalizations are reflected to varying degrees in the modern language. The **first palatalization of velars** involved the changes: *k* › *č*; *g* › *dž* › *ž*; *ch* › *š*. Prior to the de-affrication *dž* › *ž* there was symmetry between *k/g* and *č/dž*, with *ch* and *š* standing to the side. Afterwards, however, a voiced–voiceless relationship emerged between *ž* and *š*, not matched by *g:ch*. This provoked the change *g* › *h* (whence Czech *h* for all PSl. *g*), leav ing *h:ch* as a nearly matching pair of fricatives. Before and after de-affrication the picture was therefore:

Before: k:g   ch   After: k   h:ch
        č:dž š   č   ž:š

Examples: *k/č*: *peku/peče* 'bake' (1/3 SG), *pečivo* 'cakes'; *h/ž*: *mnoho* 'many', *množství* 'multitude' (*g* in recent imports undergoes the same alternation, hence: *Olga, Olžin* 'Olga's', *chirurg/chiruržka* 'surgeon' (M/F)); *ch/š*: *hřích* 'sin', *hříšný* 'sinful'.

   Second palatalization of velars: *k* › *c*; *h* › *z*; *ch* › *š* (NB not *s*). Here too the reflex of *g* has de-affricated from *dz* to *z*. Examples: *k/c*: *ruka/ruce* 'hand' (NOM/DAT-LOC SG); *h/z*: *neblahý* 'baneful', *neblaze* 'ill-' (also loans containing *g*: *geolog–geolozích* 'geologist' (NOM SG, LOC PL)); *ch/š*: *plachý, plaše* 'timid-ly'.

   The **third palatalization of velars** shared the outcome of the second, but its effects are confined to the alternation *c/č*, regular in words with the suffix *-ec* (‹ *-ьkъ*) and their derivatives, sporadic elsewhere. Examples: *chlapec/chlapče/chlapeček* 'boy' (NOM SG/VOC SG/DIMIN); *ovce* (‹ *ovcě* ‹ *ovc'a* ‹ *ovьka*) 'sheep', *ovčí* 'ovine'.

   Since *c* is also the reflex of *kt/gt* + front vowel, and of *t+j*, these provide additional conditions for the *c/č* alternation, for example, *noc/noční* 'night/nocturnal'. Analogously *d+j* › *dz* › *z* occurred, as in **med+ja* › *mezě* › *mez*, but with little scope for *z/ž* alternation. *c* and *z* from *tj* and *dj* do produce some regular alternations with *ť* and *ď*, notably in verbal morphology:

ť/c: *platit* 'pay', *placen* 'paid', *vyplácet* 'pay out'; a minority of verbs do not have this alternation, for example, *cítit/cítěn* 'feel/felt'.

ď/z: *hodit* 'throw' (PRFV), *vyhozen* 'ejected', *házet* (IMPFV), *vyhazovat* 'eject' (IMPFV); again a minority do not show the alternation, such as *zdědit/zděděn* 'inherit-ed'.

   Other ancient alternations:

s/š, *z/ž* (‹ *s/z* + *j*): *nosit, nošen, vynášet* (from 'carry'); *vozit, vožen, vyvážet* (from 'convey');

sl/šl (‹ *sl* + *j*): *poslat/pošlu* 'send/I send'; *myslet* 'think', *vymyšlený* 'fictitious' (but *kreslit/kreslen* 'draw-n').

Alternations caused by following back/front vowel:

d/ď, *t/ť*, *n/ň*: *mladý* 'young' (M SG), *mladí* (M PL AN), *mladě* (ADVERB), *mládí* 'youth' (ABSTRACT)', *mládě* 'youngling'; *krutý* 'cruel' (M SG), *krutí* (M PL AN), *krutě* (ADVERB); *plný* 'full', *plně* (ADVERB), *plnit/plněn* 'fill-ed'.

There are also various **vocalic alternations**. Most *regular* alternations are consequences of prehistoric developments in the distribution of tones; more recent items simply behave analogously.

diminutive formation (lengthening): *had–hádek* 'snake'; *poleva* 'sauce, icing', *polévka* 'soup'; (analogous) *telefon–telefónek*; (with shortening) *kráva–kravka* 'cow'; *lípa–lipka* 'linden';

past tense of most monosyllabic verbs (shortening, unless infinitive vowel is long by contraction): *dát–dal* 'give', *vést–vedl* 'lead' (but not *stát–stál* (‹ PSl. *stojati*) 'stand');

genitive plural of some disyllables (shortening): *chvíle/chvil* 'moment', *žába/žab* 'frog';

imperative formation (shortening of long present-tense stem syllables): *vrátí* › *vrať* 'return'; *rozpůlí* › *rozpul* 'halve';

infinitive formation of secondary imperfective verbs (usually lengthening): *utratit–utrácet* 'spend'.

For other related alternations entailing qualitative as well as quantitative differences see below.

Alternations between a vowel and Ø are widespread; they stem from the treatment of the *jers* and include the appearance of *e* as fill vowel. Some patterns are regular: (a) between the nominative singular (with *-e-*) and the oblique cases (with *-Ø-*) in nouns having the suffixes *-ek, -ec, -eň*: *domek/domku* 'small house', *chodec/chodce* 'walker', *píseň/písně* 'song'; and (b) between the genitive plural (with *-e-*) and other case forms of feminine and neuter nouns with stem-final consonant clusters: *her/hra* 'game', *skel/sklo* 'glass'; there are also some random survivals among monosyllables (*e/Ø* alternation between nominative singular and oblique cases): *pes/psa* 'dog' (also *psí* 'canine'), *den/dne* 'day', but not, for example, *led/ledu* 'ice'. In several verbal roots a Ø-degree alternates with full short and long vowels: *prát* 'wash' (loss of ь), *peru* 'I wash', *propírat* 'rinse' (stem vowel lengthened in secondary imperfective).

2.3   Morphophonemic alternations resulting from changes after Proto-Slavonic

Consonantal alternations due to:

1   assibilation of soft *r'* › *ř* in selected environments (thirteenth century):

   r/ř: *dobrý/dobří* 'good' (NOM SG and NOM PL AN), *dobře* 'well', *udobřit* 'reconcile';

2   dissimilation of *šč* (that is, *štš*) to *šť* (‹ *sk+j* or front vowel, or *st+j*), and of *ždž* to *žď* (‹ *zd+j*) (fourteenth to fifteenth centuries):

sk/šť: *nebeský/nebeští* 'heavenly' (M NOM SG and PL AN), *nebešťan*
'heavenly being';
st/sť/šť: *čistý* 'clean', *čistit/čištěn* 'clean-ed';
zd/zď/žď: *pozdní* 'late', *opozdit se* 'be late', *opožděn* 'delayed',
opožďovat se 'be running late'.

Vocalic alternations:

ě/a/á, reflexes of the nasal vowels after their evolution under the umlaut
conditions described above; there is one *regular* pattern, in the reflex of
the *-t-* declension: *děvče/děvčata/děvčátko* 'little girl' (NOM SG/NOM PL/
DIMIN); and some sporadic occurrences: *světit* 'consecrate', *svatý* 'holy',
svátek 'holiday'.

u/ou, where *ou* ‹ *ú* (late fourteenth and through the fifteenth centuries):
dub/doubek 'oak' and diminutive; *plul/plout* 'sail' (PAST/INF); in conditions where the umlauts applied, this alternation is now *i/í*. The diphthongization *ú* › *ou* was matched by a front-vowel change *ý* › *ej* in most
dialects, but the literary language retains spellings with *ý* and the
pronunciation /iː/; Common Czech has *ej* almost consistently, hence
there is an alternation *y/ej* as in *byl/bejt* 'be' (PAST/INF).

ě/i, where *i* ‹ *ie* ‹ long *ě* (fifteenth century): *květ/kvítek* 'flower' and
diminutive; *zajic* 'hare', *zaječí* 'hare's', *dílo/děl* 'work' (NOM SG/GEN
PL).

o/ů, where *ů* ‹ *uo* ‹ *ó* (fifteenth century): *potok/potůček* 'stream' and
diminutive; *stolu/stůl/stolek* 'table' (GEN SG/NOM SG/DIMIN).

e/i or *ý*, where /iː/ ‹ *é* (fifteenth to sixteenth centuries): *kámen/kaminek*
'stone' (NOM SG/DIMIN); *pohledět/pohlížet* 'look' (PRFV/IMPFV). This
alternation penetrated the literary language only partially; hence, for
example, *nést/nesl* 'carry' survives as a quantitative opposition, though
Common Czech has *nýst/nes(l)*; after *l* in particular the change *é* › *i/ý*
was inconsistent, leaving some variation in the alternants, for example,
letět–létat/litat 'fly'; *lepší–lépe/líp* 'better' (ADJECTIVE–ADVERB).

3 Morphology

3.1 Nominal morphology

Czech has a number of central declensional types among the nouns and
adjectives and a few mixed and peripheral types. Pronoun declension is a
hybrid between nouns and adjectives, while most numerals have only the
most rudimentary morphology. The umlauts have contributed to a broad
split between 'hard' and 'soft' versions of the main declensions. One major
factor is a redistribution of the case morphemes of original masculine *o-*

and *u*-stems, which has partially affected also the masculine *a*-stems.

Number is a two-member category – singular and plural – although Old Czech shows near-complete dual morphology, in both nouns and verbs. Vestiges of the old system survive in 'appropriate' items (body parts, 'two', 'both'), but are treated as anomalous plurals.

The full **seven cases** survive. About half the singular noun paradigms have a distinctive vocative form shared by no other case (see Short 1990); no adjectival, pronominal, numeral or plural noun paradigms have distinct vocative forms (vocative = nominative). A noteworthy development within the case system is the spread of dative–locative syncretism in singular noun classes.

There are **three genders**, the subcategory of **animacy** functioning within the masculine only. In the singular, animate accusative equals genitive, which itself, in the core (hard) masculine paradigm, differs from the inanimate genitive. Similarly, animate dative and locative usually differ from their inanimate equivalents. In the plural, the animacy opposition is expressed only in the existence of a distinctive nominative plural for animates. The morphological impact of animacy applies absolutely throughout the animal kingdom, from *prvok* 'protozoon' to *člověk* 'man', except in the masculine singular *a*-declension, which, like the feminine, has inherited unambiguous forms for nominative, genitive and accusative.

3.1.2   Noun morphology

Of the main declensional types Proto-Slavonic *o*- and **u-stems** have merged in Czech to form one class, subdivided according to animacy. Both nouns in table 9.2 are former *o*-stems, yet they employ several *u*-stem endings (DAT–LOC SG AN, GEN SG INAN, INST SG, GEN PL). The *u*-stem vocative ending also survives, chiefly as a means to avoid palatalization of velar stems, for example, *kluku* 'boy', *vrahu* 'murderer', and also as the 'true' vocative of the uniquely conservative former *u*-stem *syn* 'son'. Velar-stem vocatives in *-e* (*o*-stem) with palatalization preserved are the forms

Table 9.2   'Hard' masculine (former *o*- and *u*-stems)

	SG AN	SG INAN	PL
NOM	chlap 'fellow'	hrad 'castle'	chlapi, hrady
VOC	chlape	hrade	chlapi, hrady
ACC	chlapa	hrad	chlapy, hrady
GEN	chlapa	hradu	chlapů, hradů
DAT	chlapovi, /-u	hradu	chlapům, hradům
INST	chlapem	hradem	chlapy, hrady
LOC	chlapovi, /-u	hradě	chlapech, hradech

člověče 'man' and *bože* 'God', both used chiefly as interjections. Among non-velar stems only the case of stem-final *-r* is noteworthy: preceded by a vowel, *-r* is unchanged in the vocative, while a preceding consonant induces palatalization: *doktor–doktore*, but *Petr–Petře*. The *u*-stem locative singular ending is spreading in inanimates at the expense of (*o*-stem) *-ě*, most particularly to avoid velar stem-final palatalization: *na buku* 'in/on the beech-tree'. Both endings occasionally exist in free variation: *v potoce/ potoku* 'in the brook'; or contribute to lexical semi-independence: *v jazyce* 'in (a) language', but *na jazyku* 'on the (tip of one's) tongue'. Among inanimates there is also variation in the genitive singular: some 235 lexical items have the *o*-stem ending *-a* (predominantly the animate ending), while some 140 have *-a* or *-u* in free variation. The *-u/-ovi* variation in the dative–locative singular animate is now almost free, but *-ovi* is commoner in personal animates. Subclasses not recorded in the tables include many formally and semantically distinctive groups with nominative plural in *-é* or *-ové*, and some variation in the locative plural endings, including penetration of the *a*-stem ending.

In the masculine soft declension (table 9.3) the areas where animates differ from inanimates replicate those under the hard declension, though there is greater overall similarity between the animate/inanimate patterns. The *-ů(m)* endings in genitive and dative plural are not only *u*-declension in origin, but stand here after 'soft' consonants, an atypical environment for back vowels. A variant of the class, differing chiefly by having a case marker even in the nominative singular, are animates in *-ce* (VOC SG *-ce*; NOM PL *-i*, with decreasing frequency *-ové*, or both), originally the soft counterpart of masculine *a*-stems. Colloquially, they adopt the vocative ending *-če* of the *-ec* type.

The hard (former *o*-stem) neuters are among the most conservative paradigms (table 9.4). Stem-final consonantal clusters (often, but not only, suffixal), as in *družstvo* 'cooperative', *číslo* 'number', require a fill vowel in the genitive plural, hence *družstev*, *čísel*. Suffixed nouns ending in a velar contain the main deviation from the pattern, namely locative plural in

Table 9.3 'Soft' masculines (former *jo*-stems)

	SG AN	SG INAN	PL
NOM	muž 'man'	stroj 'machine'	muži, stroje
VOC	muži	stroji	muži, stroje
ACC	muže	stroj	muže, stroje
GEN	muže	stroje	mužů, strojů
DAT	muži/-ovi	stroji	mužům, strojům
INST	mužem	strojem	muži, stroji
LOC	muži/-ovi	stroji	mužích, strojích

Table 9.4   *o*-stems neuter

	o-stems	*jo*-stems	*ьjo*-stems
SG			
NOM/VOC	město 'town'	srdce 'heart'	učení 'study'
ACC	město	srdce	učení
GEN	města	srdce	učení
DAT	městu	srdci	učení
INST	městem	srdcem	učením
LOC	městě	srdci	učení
PL			
NOM/VOC	města	srdce	učení
ACC	města	srdce	učení
GEN	měst	srdcí	učení
DAT	městům	srdcím	učením
INST	městy	srdci	učeními
LOC	městech	srdcích	učeních

(usually) *-ách*, borrowed from the *a*-stems: *kolečko/kolečkách* 'small wheel'. As with the hard masculines, there is some variation in the locative singular between *-ě* (which pre-palatalizes) and the *u*-stem ending *-u* (*v mléku/mléce* 'in the milk'). Four *o*-stems denoting body parts have residual dual forms: *oko* 'eye' and *ucho* 'ear' have a plural declension based on *oči, uši* (GEN *očí/uší*, DAT *očím/ušim*, INST *očima/ušima*, LOC *očích/uších*); *koleno* 'knee' and *rameno* 'shoulder' have genitive/locative plural *kolenou/ramenou*. The *jo*-stems are few in number. A subset in *-iště* deviates morphologically in having *-Ø* in the genitive plural: *schodiště/schodišť* 'staircase'. The *ьjo*-stems have a high rate of case homonymy (due chiefly to the monophthongization of *ie* of various origins); the only overt case markers involve consonants.

Owing partly to sheer numbers (more than 18,000 items) the feminine **a-stems** (table 9.5) are another conservative paradigm, even retaining morphophonemic alternations in the dative–locative singular: *matka/matce* 'mother', *pata/patě* 'heel', *žába/žábě* 'frog' (/-bj-/), *dáma/dámě* (/-mň-/). The class includes *ruka* and *noha* ('arm' and 'leg'), whose plurals include some dual remnants: nominative–accusative plural *ruce* (*nohy* is regular), genitive–locative plural *rukou, nohou*, instrumental plural *rukama, nohama*. The masculine *a*-declension has assimilated somewhat to the central hard masculine class, especially in its plural forms (including alternation in velar stems: *sluha/sluzích* 'servant'), and in the dative–locative singular: *-ovi* is specifically associated with animates. Items with the suffixes *-ista* (*terorista* 'terrorist', *šachista* 'chess-player', *houslista* 'violinist') and *-ita* (*bandita* 'bandit', *jezuita* 'Jesuit') have nominative plurals in *-isté* and *-ité* respectively, with *-iti* beginning to replace the latter more rapidly than *-isti*

Table 9.5   *a*-stems

	SG	PL	SG	PL
Hard	F		M	
NOM	žena 'woman'	ženy	hrdina 'hero'	hrdinové
VOC	ženo	ženy	hrdino	hrdinové
ACC	ženu	ženy	hrdinu	hrdiny
GEN	ženy	žen	hrdiny	hrdinů
DAT	ženě	ženám	hrdinovi	hrdinům
INST	ženou	ženami	hrdinou	hrdiny
LOC	ženě	ženách	hrdinovi	hrdinech
Soft	*ja*-stems F		ьja-stem (one word only)	
NOM/VOC	duše 'soul'	duše	paní 'lady'	paní
ACC	duši	duše	paní	paní
GEN	duše	duší	paní	paní
DAT	duši	duším	paní	paním
INST	duší	dušemi	paní	paními
LOC	duši	duších	paní	paních

the former. The *duše* paradigm is marked chiefly by the effects of the umlauts. It includes a large subgroup in -(*n*)*ice*, with a genitive plural in -∅ (*ulice/ulic* 'street'), a feature shared by a few other items, for example, *ko-šile/košil* 'shirt', *lžice/lžic* 'spoon'. The paradigm is productive; many loans and neologisms based on Latin or Greek roots are assigned to it: *revoluce, agrese, eroze, absence, dyslexie, geologie*. Another *ja*-stem subclass includes nouns that lack an overt marker in the nominative–accusative singular and also differ by having vocative in -*i*. Most grammars give this type (*píseň* 'song') as a separate paradigm. Two additional factors make it worthy of mention: (a) it gives rise to alternating declensions of some forty or more nouns that may occur with or without final -*e*/-*ě*, such as *kuchyně/kuchyň* 'kitchen'; (b) it is the paradigm which is attracting more and more nouns out of the hotch-potch of subtypes that are neither fully like *píseň*, nor fully like *kost* 'bone' below (see *Mluvnice češtiny*, II:331).

Pani 'lady' is a unique item; former members of its class adapted fairly early to more central paradigms. Feminine neologisms in -*i*, like *průvodči* 'conductress', inflect adjectivally.

The *i*-stem declension (table 9.6) consists mostly of feminine abstract nouns in -*ost*, among which it is productive, a few other items in -*st* (such as *hrst* 'palm', *čelist* 'jaw') and *řeč* 'speech' and *věc* 'thing'. All other former feminine members of the class with an unmarked nominative singular show various degrees of overlap with the *píseň* type. The only masculine *i*-stem to survive is *lidé* 'people', plural of *člověk*. The *neuter* consonantal-stem *dítě* 'child' has a *feminine i*-stem plural *děti*.

Table 9.6   *i*-stems

	SG	PL
NOM	kost 'bone'	kosti
VOC	kosti	kosti
ACC	kost	kosti
GEN	kosti	kostí
DAT	kosti	kostem
INST	kostí	kostmi
LOC	kosti	kostech

Consonantal stems have left few traces in Modern Czech, with one exception. All others have adapted to more central types. Modern masculines like *den* 'day' and *kořen* 'root' generally follow *stroj* in the singular and *hrady* in the plural; those formerly marked by the infix *-in-* in the singular have lost it, producing a constant (hard) stem form, hence *křesťan* 'Christian' (NOM–VOC PL in *-é*); agent nouns in *-tel* all follow *muž* (NOM–VOC PL in *-é*). Feminine *r*-stems: an archaic declension of *máti* 'mother' survives, with support from derivates, but the neutral word is now *matka*; Proto-Czech *dci* has been replaced by (hard) *dcera* 'daughter', of which the consonantal-declension origin remains visible in the form *dceři* (DAT–LOC SG); former *ъv*-stems are now a subgroup, in final *-ev* (*mrkev* 'carrot'), of the feminine *ja*-stems (*píseň*), though there has been inter-action with hard feminines in *-va*. Neuters: a handful of *n*-stems survive in an archaic declension (*símě/semene* 'seed'), but in general a new nom-inative singular has emerged based on the oblique stem, hence *semeno* 'seed', *rameno* 'shoulder', *vemeno* 'udder', all now hard neuter *o*-stems; likewise former *s*-stems, but with some instances of historical or neo-logizing independent lexicalization of the two stems (*kolo* 'wheel', *koleso* 'big wheel (at fairground or on paddle steamer)', *slovo* 'word', *sloveso* 'verb'); *nebe*, plural *nebesa* 'sky, heaven', follows the *jo*-stems in the singular.

The great consonantal-stem survivor is the descendant of the *-nt-* type (table 9.7) now marked by suffixes containing *-t-*, consisting chiefly of nouns denoting animal young. Inflection is conservative, but the thematic infix changes form between singular and plural: only in the singular were conditions met for the umlaut version of the former nasal.

The class includes several human offspring (*dvojče* 'twin', *batole* 'toddler') as well as *štěně* 'puppy', *lvíče* 'lion-cub', also some adult animals (*zvíře* 'animal', *saranče* 'locust'), non-animates (*rajče* 'tomato', *koště* 'broom'), colloquial borrowings (*šuple* 'drawer', *paraple* 'brolly') and certain titles (*dóže* 'doge', *kníže* 'prince'). These last are anomalous in being masculine animate in the singular, but neuter in the plural.

Table 9.7   Neuter consonantal (-*t*-) stems

	SG	PL
NOM/VOC/ACC	jehně 'lamb'	jehňata
GEN	jehněte	jehňat
DAT	jehněti	jehňatům
INST	jehnětem	jehňaty
LOC	jehněti	jehňatech

3.1.3   Pronominal morphology

Genderless personal pronouns are shown in table 9.8. Of the second-person pronouns, *ty* is familiar, *vy* is polite singular (capitalized in writing) or plural.

The forms *mi, ti, si, tě* and *se* are enclitic only. Until recently the same applied to *mě*, which now also replaces (obsolescent, high-style) *mne*. The other 'long' forms are used only in emphasis or after prepositions, although dative *mně* is increasingly used enclitically in variation with *mi*. Where no choice of forms exists, the sole form occurs in all functions.

The stressed/unstressed opposition also applies in the nominative. Under emphasis the pronoun appears, without emphasis it will normally be absent: *udělám to* 'I'll do it', but *já to udělám* '*I'll* do it'. However, colloquial registers show an almost consistent tendency for subject personal pronouns to be inserted, at least in main clauses.

The distribution of nominative endings among the third-person pronouns (table 9.9) is to be found elsewhere, for example, in the hard noun declensions. Of the other forms, *ho* and *mu* are enclitic only, *jeho* and *jemu* emphatic. Other forms are used in all functions, but any third-person pronoun following a preposition attracts an initial *n*-, hence the spellings *něho, němu, ně. Jej*, once the 'long' accusative masculine, is now just one of the accusative/genitive shared forms – rare in speech, and of limited incidence even in written styles, especially as genitive. By contrast, the post-prepositional form *něj* is common as both accusative and genitive. Original accusative singular neuter *je* is also rare. An interesting obsolescent survival is the old masculine accusative *jь*, embedded in the post-prepositional form *-ň*, thus *naň, proň, oň* and *zaň* for *na něj/něho* and so on.

This paradigm is shared by the high-style relative pronoun *jenž*, which only has long forms in the oblique cases, and in the nominative has *jenž* (M SG), the rare *již* (M AN PL) and *jež* (F/N SG and all other plurals).

Pronominal declensions are represented (table 9.10) by the demonstrative *ten* (hard) and the possessive *náš* 'our' (soft). Again, the umlauts have enhanced the difference between them, with the extra consequence of

Table 9.8   The genderless pronouns

NOM	já 'I'	ty 'you (SG)'	– (REFL)	my 'we'	vy 'you (PL)'
ACC	mne/mě	tebe/tě	sebe/se	nás	vás
GEN	mne/mě	tebe/tě	sebe/se	nás	vás
DAT	mně/mi	tobě/ti	sobě/si	nám	vám
INST	mnou	tebou	sebou	námi	vámi
LOC	mně	tobě	sobě	nás	vás

Table 9.9   Third-person pronouns

	M AN	M INAN	N	F	PL
NOM	on	on	ono	ona	oni, ony, ona
ACC	jeho/jej/ho	jej/ho	je/jej/ho	ji	je
GEN		jeho/jej/ho		jí	jich
DAT		jemu/mu		jí	jim
INST		jím		jí	jimi
LOC		něm		ní	nich

Table 9.10   The demonstrative pronoun *ten* ‹ *tъ, and the possessive pronoun *náš* 'our'

	M	N	F	M	N	F
SG						
NOM	ten	to	ta	náš	naše	naše
ACC	ten/toho*	to	tu	náš/ našeho*	naše	naši
GEN		toho	té		našeho	naší
DAT		tomu	té		našemu	naší
INST		tím	tou		naším	naší
LOC		tom	té		našem	naší
PL						
NOM	ti*/ty	ta	ty	naši*/naše		naše
ACC	ty	ta	ty	naše		naše
GEN		těch			našich	
DAT		těm			našim	
INST		těmi			našimi	
LOC		těch			našich	

Note: * following words indicates animate forms.

even higher case syncretism in the feminine singular of the soft variety.

Ten is theoretically non-specific between 'this' and 'that', but in general equates to non-contrastive 'that', deictic in the context of situation and to realities outside the situation: *myslíš tu paní, kterou jsme potkali včera?* 'do you mean the/that woman we met yesterday?' Contrastive 'this' and 'that' are conveyed by addition of the suffix -*to* (more colloquially -*hle*) and the prefix *tam*- respectively. Neuter singular *to* (*toto, tamto*) is the general deictic pronoun 'it'/'they'/'this'/'these'/'that'/'those': *to je/jsou stůl/stoly* 'it/this/they/these is/are table-s'.

These paradigms are shared by the interrogatives *kdo* (M, hard; oblique-case stem *k*-) 'who' and *co* (N, soft; *č*-) 'what' and their many compounds (see table 9.13), but *kdo* has *kým* in the instrumental. The declension of *náš* is shared by *váš* 'your'.

The pronoun *všechen* 'all' (see table 9.11): the only non-oblique case survival of the short historic *vьsь* (except in *vesmír* 'universe') is the neuter general quantifier *vše* 'everything'; referential 'everyone' is the masculine plural animate form *všichni*. Non-referential 'everyone', 'all' is usually expressed by *každý* 'each; any'.

Other semi-anomalous prepositional types: *sám* '-self' (emphatic) or 'alone' has hard adjectival endings in the oblique cases, but short, pronominal forms in the nominative and accusative.

Můj 'my', also *tvůj* 'your' (familiar) and *svůj*, the reflexive possessive

Table 9.11   The pronoun 'all' (mixed hard–soft declension)

	M	N	F
SG			
NOM	všechen, všecek	všechno, všecko, vše	všechna, všecka
ACC	všechen, všecek	všechno, všecko, vše	všechnu, všecku
GEN	všeho		vší
DAT	všemu		vší
INST	vším		vší
LOC	všem		vší
PL			
NOM	{ všichni*, všicci* všechny, všecky	všechna, všecka	všechny, všecky
ACC	všechny, všecky	všechna, všecka	všechny, všecky
GEN	všech		
DAT	všem		
INST	všemi		
LOC	všech		

Note: * animate forms.

pronoun, decline as hard adjectives (*má, mého, mými,* etc.), but most nominative and accusative forms and the feminine singular throughout also have alternative non-contracted endings which comport with the soft pronominal declension, hence *moje* is nominative singular neuter and feminine, accusative singular neuter and nominative–accusative plural in all genders except nominative plural masculine animate, which is *moji*; also the forms *moji* (ACC SG F) and *moji* (F SG oblique cases).

Other possessive pronouns: *jeho* 'his' and *jejich* 'their' are uninflected, as are the equivalent relative possessive pronouns *jehož* and *jejichž*; *její* 'her' and its relative possessive counterpart *jejíž* decline like soft adjectives, that is, their origins in a genitive of the personal pronoun have been submerged by syntactic and morphological similarities to adjectives. *Čí?* 'whose?' follows the soft adjectival declension.

Týž/tentýž 'the same (*sensu stricto*)' (table 9.12) declines in its shorter form exactly like the hard adjectives, with the addition of the suffix -*ž*. The compound form follows, in cases where the reduplication has asserted itself, a hybrid pattern in which the second element sometimes inflects by gender and sometimes remains a genderless suffix -*též*. Reduplicated oblique-case forms are more recent variants. Existing variations in the declension of *týž* and widespread native-speaker uncertainty about the current standard have given rise to several non-standard forms which bring it closer to the pronominal declensions proper, for example *těchže* (GEN

Table 9.12   The pronoun 'the same'

	M	N	F
SG			
NOM	týž/tentýž	totéž	táž/tatáž
ACC	{ téhož* { týž/tentýž	totéž	touž/tutéž
GEN		téhož	téže
DAT		témuž	téže
INST		týmž/tímtéž	touž/toutéž
LOC		témž(e)/tomtéž	téže
PL			
NOM	{ tíž*/titíž* { tytéž	táž/tatáž	tytéž
ACC	tytéž	táž/tatáž	tytéž
GEN		týchž	
DAT		týmž	
INST		týmiž	
LOC		týchž	

Note: * animate forms.

PL), *těmže* (DAT PL), *těmiže* (INST PL) and *titéž* (NOM PL M AN). There is a gap in the paradigm where one would expect neuter nominative–accusative singular *též; the form exists, but as the adverb 'also' in stylistically higher registers. The sole neuter form *totéž* has both bound and free functions: *kluk rozbil totéž okno dvakrát* 'the boy broke the same window twice', and *ráno umyla podlahu a večer aby udělala totéž!* 'she washed the floor this morning, and now she'll have to do the same thing this evening!', or *Petr udělal totéž, co Pavel* 'Peter did the same (thing) as Paul'. *Týž* is often replaced by *stejný*, strictly meaning identity as to quality, or by *ten samý*, probably a colloquial calque on German.

Kdo 'who' and *co* 'what' lie at the heart of a complex range of **indefinite pronouns** and **pronoun adverbs**. Table 9.13 lists those that may claim to be

Table 9.13   Indefinite pronouns and pronoun adverbs

	1 *ně-*	2 *ni-*	3 *-si*	4 *-koli*	5 *málo-*	6 *mnoh-*	7 *lec-*
(a) kdo	někdo	nikdo	kdosi	kdokoli	málokdo	MNOHÝ	leckdo
(b) co	něco	nic	cosi	cokoli	máloco	MNOHO	lecco
(c) čí	něčí	ničí	čísi	číkoli	máločí		lecčí
(d) kdy	někdy	nikdy	(kdysi)	kdykoli	málokdy	mnohdy	leckdy
(e) kde	někde	nikde	kdesi	kdekoli	málokde	mnohde	leckde
(f) kam	někam	nikam	kamsi	kamkoli	málokam		leckam
(g) odkud	odněkud	odnikud	odkudsi	odkudkoli	máloodkud		lecodkud
(h) kudy	někudy	nikudy	kudysi	kudykoli			
(i) jak	nějak	nijak	(jaksi)	jakkoli			lecjak
(j) kolik	několik	ŽÁDNÝ					
(k) jaký	nějaký	nijaký	jakýsi	jakýkoli			lecjaký
(l) který	některý	ŽÁDNÝ	kterýsi	kterýkoli	málokterý		leckterý
(m) kolikerý	několikerý						

8 *leda-*	9 *kde-*	10 *vš-*	11 *všeli-*	12 *jin-*	13 *t-*	14 *s-*	15 *on-*
ledakdo	kdeko	VŠICHNI	všelikdo		ten	TENTO	onen
ledaco	kdeco	vše[chno]	všelico		to	TOTO	ono
ledačí							
ledakdy		vždy		jindy	tehdy	TEĎ	(onehdy)
ledakde		všude		jinde	TAM	zde	*onde
ledakam		VŠUDE		jinam	tam	sem	*onam
ledaodkud		odevšAd		odjinud	odtud	odsud	
				jinudy	tudy	TADYTUDY	
ledajak		(však)	všelijak	jinak	tak	TAKTO	*onak
					tolik	TOLIK	
ledajaký	kdejaký		všelijaký	jinačí	takový	TAKOVÝ	*onaký
ledakterý	kdekterý KAŽDÝ			JINÝ	ten	TENTO	onen
					tolikerý		

in regular use and together constitute the Czech system of reference, co-reference, quantification, etc., devices. The lines are based on the inter-rogatives: (a) 'who', (b) 'what', (c) 'whose', (d) 'when', (e) 'where', (f) 'whither', (g) 'whence', (h) 'which way', (i) 'how', (j) 'how many', (k) 'what (like)', (l) 'which', (m) 'of how many kinds'; the columns: (1) 'some-', or 'any-' in questions, (2) 'no-; not any-', (3) 'some- or other', (4) 'any-; -ever', (5) 'hardly any-', (6) 'many a', (7–8) 'all manner of' (often dis-paraging), '(not) just any' after negative, (9) 'all/every- (conceivable/ applicable)', (10) 'all; every-', (11) 'all sorts of; any old'. Thus, for example, (g/4) *odkudkoli* combines the meanings of 'from a place' and 'randomness' and hence translates 'from anywhere; from wherever'. Many suggested 'meanings' of the column headings are only approximate, since much depends on syntax or the availability of suitable English equivalents. Columns (12) 'else' and (13)–(15), deictic elements, are included since several of the entries relate well to items to their left; they are a residue of the ancient tripartite system of 'this–here–now–closer to *ego*', 'that–there–then–further from *ego*', and 'yon'; they are clearly defective and almost each item under (15) would merit its own discussion.

The conventions adopted in table 9.13 signify as follows: square brackets indicate potential alternative; parentheses, an expression fitting the slot formally exists, but not in the meaning predictable at the given line–column intersection, hence (a/3) *kdysi* does not mean 'at some time or other and I cannot (be bothered to) specify just when', but 'once, long ago', (a/15) *onehdy* does not mean 'on that earlier/earliest occasion', but 'the other day', (i/3) *jaksi* does not mean 'somehow or other and I'm not terribly sure how', but is more of a semi-apologetic, defensive particle like English *I mean, you see* or just *er*; (i/10) *však* is not 'in every manner', but an enclitic conjunction 'but, however, though'; small capitals, the meaning appropriate to the particular slot is expressible, but by a (part-)suppletive form from outside the system; an asterisk shows that the form is alive, but exists in solely idiomatic uses. Some of the blanks can be filled by analytic constructions (as in (a/12) *někdo jiný*, (b/12) *něco jiného*); the remaining blanks are accounted for by various constraints. Many of the items under *lec-* and *leda-* also occur with an additional suffixed or infixed *s*, such as *ledakam/ledaskam/ledakams*.

3.1.4   Adjectival morphology
Czech has three adjectival declensions: long hard, long soft and possessive, a 'short' type. The 'long' types arose out of contraction of original V*j*V chains in the endings. In most circumstances, the two vowels contracted, losing the *j*, to produce a single long vowel. As elsewhere in morphology (the *učení* and *paní* noun types) the umlauts have caused widespread case homonymy and syncretism in the soft declension, the only surface distinc-tions being those carried by consonantal elements. Table 9.14 shows the

Table 9.14   Long adjectival declension

| | | Hard | | | Soft | |
	M	N	F	M	N	F
SG						
NOM	nový	nové	nová 'new'	cizí	cizí	cizí 'alien'
ACC	{nový / nového*}	nové	novou	{cizí / cizího*}		cizí
GEN		nového	nové		cizího	cizí
DAT		novému	nové		cizímu	cizí
INST		novým	novou		cizím	cizí
LOC		novém	nové		cizím	cizí
PL						
NOM	{noví* / nové}	nová	nové		cizí	
ACC	nové	nová	nové		cizí	
GEN		nových			cizích	
DAT		novým			cizím	
INST		novými			cizími	
LOC		nových			cizích	

Note: * animate forms.

adjectival declensions. Before the *-i* (NOM PL M AN) ending the palatalizations of velars and dentals are observed: *jaký* › *jací* 'what', *mladý* › *mladi*
(= [mlaďí]) 'young', *dobrý* › *dobři* 'good', and the special case of stems in
-sk and *-ck*: *irský* › *iršti* 'Irish' and *anglický* › *angličti* 'English'. Common
Czech dispenses with all nominative–accusative plural oppositions, showing
both morphemic consistency and but one ending [-iː] for all genders.

Despite its morphological opacity, the soft class is very strong, for in
addition to a number of primary adjectives it includes, *inter alia*: all present
active participles in *-ouci* and *-ici*; verbal adjectives denoting purpose such
as *psaci* 'writing', *sklápěci* 'tipping, folding'; comparatives and superlatives;
the ordinals *prvni* 'first', *třeti* 'third' and *tisíci* 'thousandth'; adjectives
formed from animal names: *pavi* ‹ *páv* 'peacock', *žirafi* ‹ *žirafa*; and countless items with the suffix *-ni*, like *jarni* 'spring', *zubni* 'dental' and many
'internationalisms': *termálni* 'thermal', *obézni* 'obese'.

The adjectival declensions are shared by many noun types, denoting
callings (*krejči* 'tailor'), games (*schovávaná* 'hide-and-seek'), payments
(*výkupné* 'ransom'), meats (*vepřové* 'pork'), surnames (*Novotný/-á*,
Lepši/-i), the feminine form of other surnames, (*Nováková* ‹ *Novák*),
many toponyms (*Deštná* 'a mountain', *Deštné* 'the ski-resort nearby', *Teplá*
'a river'), and other Slav adjectival surnames (*Tolstoj*, genitive *Tolstého*;

Jaruzelski, genitive *Jaruzelského*; *Krupskaja,* genitive *Krupské*) and toponyms (*Mirnyj–Mirného, Černaja–Černé*).

The short declension is confined to the widely used possessive adjectives, formed from common or proper nouns. Two suffixes depend on the gender of the possessor, masculine possessors taking *-ův, -ova, -ovo,* feminines *-in, -ina, -ino,* which induces stem-final consonant alternations: *matka + -in* > *matčin* 'mother's', *Milada + -in* > *Miladin* (that is, milaďin), *dcera + -in* > *dceřin* 'daughter's'. Table 9.15 shows that this paradigm is 'short' only in part, since the instrumental singular and all plural oblique cases share the endings of the 'long' declension.

Table 9.15   Possessive adjectives

| | SG | | | PL | | |
	M	N	F	M	N	F
NOM	Petrův	Petrovo	Petrova	{Petrovi* {Petrovy	Petrova	Petrovy
ACC	{Petrův {Petrova*	Petrovo	Petrovu	Petrovy	Petrova	Petrovy
GEN	Petrova		Petrovy		Petrových	
DAT	Petrovu		Petrově		Petrovým	
INST	Petrovým		Petrovou		Petrovými	
LOC	Petrově/-u		Petrově		Petrových	

Note: * animate forms.

About a dozen short adjectives proper survive in active everyday use (see 4.3 below). (A systematic opposition between long and short forms occurs only in the passive participles; see 3.2.) Occurring in the predicate, they have nominative forms only, bearing the regular gender/number markers. Some disyllables show stem-vowel lengthening in the short form, for example, *zdravý* > *zdráv* 'healthy'. The 'adjective' *rád* exists only in short forms; unlike the others, it can occur with almost any verb: *být rád* 'be glad', *mít rád* 'love', *zpívat rád* 'like singing'; the negative is *nerad,* as in *nerad obtěžuji, ale...* 'I'm loth to disturb you, but...'. Some short neuters survive, but in new functions: thus *málo* 'few', *daleko* 'far', chiefly as adverbs, but also some abstract nouns: *nekonečno* 'infinity'.

Comparison of adjectives uses the basic suffix *-ejší/-ější,* or *-ší* or *-čí* in several smallish subclasses. The superlative is formed by prefixing *nej-* to the comparative:

rychlý – rychlejší – nejrychlejší 'quick'
pracovitý – pracovitější – nejpracovitější 'hard-working'
záviděníhodný – záviděníhodnější – nejzáviděníhodnější 'enviable'

drahý – dražší – nejdražší 'dear'
hezký – hezčí – nejhezčí 'good-looking'

There are just a few suppletive forms:

dobrý – lepší – nejlepší 'good'
špatný – horší – nejhorší 'bad'
velký – větší – největší 'bit, great'
malý – menší – nejmenší 'small'

Analytical constructions using *víc(e)* 'more', *nejvíc(e)* 'most' are rare, but necessary with items that are present participles in origin (*víc(e) vyhovující* 'more suitable'), or with the few indeclinables (*víc blond* 'blonder'); negative comparison uses only analytical forms, with *méně* 'less', *nejméně* 'least'.

The basic **adverbial** ending is *-ě/-e*: *nový* › *nově* 'new-ly', *rychlý* › *rychle* 'quick-ly'; as with *-ě* in the locative of nouns (these adverbs were originally locative singulars of short adjectives) dental and velar stem-final consonants palatalize: *tichý* › *tiše* 'quiet-ly', *těsný* › *těsně* 'tight-ly', *starý* › *staře* 'old'. The basic comparative adverbial suffix is *-ěji/-eji*, hence *těsněji, tišeji*, but items where the comparative adjective follows one of the minor patterns have a shorter comparative adverb: *dráž(e)*, *hůř(e)* 'worse'. Some monosyllabic forms entail a vowel change: *míň/méně* 'less', *líp/lépe* 'better'; they are used in less formal registers.

The few irregular adverbs include *pomalu* ‹ *pomalý* 'slow' and *hezky* ‹ *hezký* 'nice', and forms in *-sky* and *-cky* from adjectives in *-ský* and *-cký*, many denoting a language spoken or written: *mluvit anglicky* 'speak English'. Adverbs required to convey 'in an English manner' and so on are analytical: *zmizet po anglicku* 'take French leave'.

In competition with abstract adverbs in *-ě* are a set in *-o*, chiefly concerned with time and space, such as *mluvit dlouho* 'talk for a long time', *mluvit dlouze* 'talk at great length'; *ležet hluboko* 'lie deep (in water)', *být hluboce dojat* 'be deeply touched'; *stát blizko* 'stand nearby', *být blizce příbuzný* 'be closely related'.

3.1.5   Numeral morphology

Among the **cardinal numerals**, only '1', '2', '3' and '4' function adjectivally and retain the morphology of case. *Jeden/jedna* and so on '1' inflects like the demonstrative *ten*. *Dva* '2' (table 9.16) and *oba* 'both; the two' also retain some gender distinctions; these two words alone maintain almost intact the old dual declension. *Tři* and *čtyři* (see table 9.16) approximate closely to the plural *i*-stem substantival declension. The form *čtyřma* is used in agreement with nouns which retain dual forms in the instrumental plural: *mezi čtyřma očima* 'tête-à-tête'. Genitive *třech* and *čtyřech* are

Table 9.16   Declension of *dva* **'two',** *tři* **'three' and** *čtyři* **'four'**

	M			F/N
NOM–ACC	dva	dvě	NOM–ACC	tři	čtyři
GEN–LOC	dvou		GEN	tří/třech	čtyř/čtyřech
DAT–INS	dvěma		DAT	třem	čtyřem
			INST	třemi	čtyřmi/čtyřma
			LOC	třech	čtyřech

colloquial; their coincidence with the locative shows a shift by this declension towards pronominal and adjectival types, as well as being parallel to the case syncretism of *dva*.

The other cardinal numerals are given in table 9.17. Their inflection is limited to the oblique-case ending -*i*: *pěti, třiceti sedmi* and so on; '9' is further marked by an internal alternation *ě > i*: *devíti* (rarely also applying to '10', '20', etc., that is, *desíti* for the commoner *deseti*).

Numerals between '20' and '30' and similar are expressed analytically, for example *dvacet pět*, or as single words with the digits inverted, that is, *pětadvacet*. The old agreement patterns with numerals ending in '1' to '4', matching those with the single digits, as in *dvacet jeden student, dvacet jedna žena, dvacet dva studenti, dvacet dvě ženy*, are increasingly being replaced by 'genderless' forms in *jedna* and *dva*, followed by the genitive plural: *dvacet jedna studentů/žen, dvacet dva studentů/žen*. Similarly *dvacet tři studenti/ženy* is giving way to *dvacet tři studentů/žen*.

Sto is declined as a hard neuter noun (*bez sta* 'minus 100', *pět set* '500'; note the dual survival in *dvě stě*), though in many contexts it is left undeclined: *se sto lidmi* 'with 100 people-INST' has generally replaced *se stem lidí* 'with 100-INST people-GEN'. The reverse is true of the hard masculine *milión*: *s miliónem lidí* is the preferred form in non-colloquial usage. *Miliarda* is a hard feminine noun. *Tisíc* is declined as a soft masculine noun, but in compounds (after '5' and above) it shows a rare survival of a masculine genitive plural in -Ø, *pět tisíc* '5,000'.

Ordinal numerals are given in table 9.18. Those between tens or from multidigit numerals have all digits in the ordinal form: *dvacátý pátý, pětitisící sedmistý čtyřicátý třetí* '5,743rd', and fully declining: *bez pětitisícího sedmistého čtyřicátého třetího* and so on. Two-digit numerals between whole tens may have an inverted one-word form: *pětadvacátý* '25th', *v osmašedesátém* 'in (19)68'. In the formation of '200th' and similar forms, the first half is the genitive form of the relevant numeral, a pattern replicated in other compounds such as *dvounohý* 'two-legged', *čtyřkolý* 'four-wheeled'.

Table 9.17   Cardinal numerals

pět	'5'	třináct	'13'	třicet	'30'	sto	'100'
šest	'6'	čtrnáct	'14'	čtyřicet	'40'	dvě stě	'200'
sedm	'7'	patnáct	'15'	padesát	'50'	tři sta	'300'
osm	'8'	šestnáct	'16'	šedesát	'60'	tisíc	'1,000'
devět	'9'	sedmnáct	'17'	sedmdesát	'70'	milión	'1 million'
deset	'10'	osmnáct	'18'	osmdesát	'80'	miliarda	'1,000 million'
jedenáct	'11'	devatenáct	'19'	devadesát	'90'	nula	'zero'
dvanáct	'12'	dvacet	'20'				

Table 9.18   Ordinal numerals

první/prvý '1st'	jedenáctý '11th'	třístý '300th'
druhý '2nd'	dvanáctý '12th'	čtyřstý '400th'
třetí '3rd'	třináctý '13th'	pětistý '500th'
čtvrtý '4th'	...	tisící '1,000th'
pátý '5th'	dvacátý '20th'	milióntý 'millionth'
šestý '6th'	třicátý '30th'	*note also*:
sedmý '7th'	...	nultý 'zero'th'
osmý '8th'	devadesátý '90th'	n-tý, x-tý [enti:], [iksti:] 'n-th', 'x-th'
devátý '9th'	stý '100th'	
desátý '10th'	dvoustý '200th'	

3.2   Verbal morphology

3.2.1   Categories expressed

Person is expressed primarily in inflections and secondarily, for emphasis or in colloquial registers, by personal pronouns. Third persons are marked by vocalic endings; these differ between singular and plural, but coincide in most of the *i*-conjugation. Second persons carry universal markers in -*š* (SG, except in *být* below), and -*te* (PL), while first person plural is universally in -*me* (-*chom* in COND AUX). First person singular is marked in four different ways: -*m* (*i*- and *á*-conjugations), -*u* and/or -*i* (*e*-conjugations) and -*ch* (COND AUX). In the past tense and conditional only first and second persons are marked, by auxiliaries. The only finite forms marked for gender are in the past tense and conditional, namely the 'participles' that carry the lexical meaning. Explicit representation of gender, person and number in the past tense is maximally exploited in the second person, where the sex of an addressee, plurality of addressees and the familiar–polite distinction are all expressed: *byl jsi* (M SG familiar), *byla jsi* (F SG familiar), *byl jste* (M SG polite), *byla jste* (F SG polite), *byli jste* (M or mixed PL), *byly jste* (F PL); in speech the distinction between the last two is lost. Number and gender are rudimentarily expressed even in gerunds.

Three **tenses** are recognized, a superficially simple system refined by the Slavonic aspects. Present time meanings are expressed by the basic conjugated forms. The past consists, for both aspects, of the '*l*-participle' with auxiliaries (present-tense forms of *být* 'be'). The future perfective is expressed by present-tense forms of the perfective verb, and the imperfective by the future tense of *být* as auxiliary with the imperfective infinitive. Many tenses have been lost since Old Czech times.

The Slavonic **aspects** survive in the basic imperfective/perfective opposition. The perfective typically specifies completion of an act, which is usually relevant in terms of the (con-)sequentiality of acts. On the other hand, while the imperfective expresses the verbal action in general terms, as a process, it often highlights failure to achieve the goal, as in

Vnucovali jsme (IMPFV) mu předsednictví, ale on se nedal.
'We (tried to) thrust the chairmanship on him, but he wasn't having it.'

This is a type where duration is frequently explicit:

Celý den jsem kupoval (IMPFV) kravatu, ale nekoupil (PFV).
'I spent the whole day buying a tie but didn't get one.'

On the other hand, in certain context types a 'perfective' meaning may be expressed by an imperfective form, as in:

Tu knihu jsem četl dávno.
'I read that book ages ago.'

Aspectual pairs are of two main types:

1   Perfectives are formed from imperfectives by prefixation, for example, *u-/vařit* 'boil, cook', *pře-/číst* 'read', *o-/loupat* 'peal'; the semantic correspondence between the members of a pair is only approximate, but close enough for them to operate analogously to type 2 below. The reason is that each prefix which may act as a simple perfectivizer may be a lexical prefix elsewhere.
2   Imperfectives are formed from perfectives by suffixation, whether the motivating member is a primary verb (primary perfectives are rare), as in *dát* 'give' or *koupit* 'buy', or a prefixed verb, for example, *vymyslet* 'think up' or *slepit* 'stick/paste together'; many of the varied processes involved can be seen from the respective imperfectives: *dávat, kupovat, vymýšlet, slepovat.*

Two ranges of prefixes never act as purely perfectivizing:

1   Those with a concrete, especially local meaning, for example, *před-* 'pre-', *nad-* 'super-' *pod-* 'sub-', *v-* 'in-', *od-* 'away from'; they do perfectivize, but only to produce new lexical items (*vy-* 'ex-; out of; up' is, however, common as both a neutral and a lexical perfectivizer).
2   Those containing a long vowel; these never perfectivize at all and form only a very limited number of verbs: *závidět* 'envy', *nenávidět* 'hate', *příslušet* 'appertain'. Also the rare *pa-*, as in *padělat* 'counterfeit'.

Besides the main patterns of aspectual pairing, there are a few suppletive pairs, notably *brát/vzít* 'take', *klást/položit* 'lay', compounds of the latter, like *nakládat/naložit* 'load', and, ignoring a complex etymology, compounds of *jít* 'go on foot' such as *vycházet/vyjít* 'come out'.

Perfective-only verbs include: various prefixed reflexives (*rozpršet se* 'start to rain', *uběhat se* 'run one's feet off', *naplakat se* 'have cried and cried'); transitives with the prefix *na-* and the object–complement in the genitive (*navařit knedlíků* 'have done loads of dumplings', *nasekat dříví* 'have chopped heaps of firewood'); the verbs *uvidět* 'catch sight of' and *uslyšet* 'catch the sound of' (sometimes also true perfectives of *vidět* 'see' and *slyšet* 'hear'); and verbs marked by the modality of possibility, including *dokázat* and *dovést* 'be (cap-)able', 'know how', 'manage', *dát se* + infinitive 'can be -ed', *vydržet* '(with-)stand', *vejít se* 'fit (can go in)', *obejít se* 'do without'.

In addition to processual or stative verbs, **imperfective-only verbs** are: modal verbs: *muset* 'must', *moct* 'can', *smět* 'may', *mít* 'be (supposed) to', *chtít* 'want', 'will'; and frequentatives such as *dělávat* 'be wont to do', *chodívat* 'go quite often'.

A few native Czech verbs are **bi-aspectual**; they include *jmenovat* 'name', 'appoint', *zvěstovat* 'bring tidings; foretell', *věnovat* 'devote; dedicate', *obětovat* 'sacrifice', *žluknout* 'go rancid'. On the other hand, countless loan-neologisms in the most productive verb class, those in *-ovat*, like *absorbovat*, *havarovat* 'crash; break down', *informovat*, *kontejnerizovat*, *organizovat*, are bi-aspectual according to the most recent Czech dictionary (*SSČ*), though the position is by no means clear and many acquire explicit perfectives by prefixation.

Aspectually unique are the 'verbs of motion' (table 9.19). These determinate/non-determinate pairs are comparable to, but not quite co-extensive with, similar verbs in other Slavonic languages. The last three in the table are imperfect members of the system: there are various circum-stances where they can be interchanged, which never applies in the remainder, and the features given below for the determinates do not all hold with the same rigidity.

The determinate members are durative (linear, goal-oriented), the non-determinates either iterative and goal-oriented (for regularly repeated events) or lacking any goal. An irregularly repeated event, however, uses

Table 9.19   The 'verbs of motion'

jít	chodit	'go; walk'
jet	jezdit	'go; ride; drive'
běžet	běhat	'run'
letět	létat	'fly'
nést	nosit	'carry; bear'
vést	vodit	'lead'
vézt	vozit	'convey'
hnát	honit	'chase'
táhnout	tahat	'pull'
vléci/vléct	vláčet	'drag'
valit	válet	'roll'

the determinate, for example, *někdy tam jedu autem* 'I sometimes go there by car'. For the expression of a single round-trip Czech prefers 'be': *byl jsem loni v Praze* 'I went to Prague last year'.

Both sets are traditionally described as imperfective, though a case can be made for calling the determinates bi-aspectual. The morphology of the determinates presents a number of interesting features:

1   The future is formed by the prefix *po-* (*pů-* with *jít*), uniquely so in the case of *jít* and *jet*, and as the preferred form for the rest.
2   There is only one past-tense form, that is, forms such as **pojel* are absent; similarly there are no infinitives prefixed with *po-* (*pojít* exists, but means 'die', of animals).
3   There are two imperatives, with and without *po-*, those with *po-* bidding movement towards or with the speaker, as in *jdi!* 'go!', *pojď* (*sem*)*!* 'come (here)!', *pojď s námi* 'come with us'.
4   Reduplicated, the prefix *po-* produces full (perfective) paradigms of verbs meaning 'advance a short way', hence *popojít* 'take a few steps forward', *kufr poponesl* 'he carried the suitcase a few steps'.

Other prefixes produce new, perfective verbs, secondary imperfectives being formed from mutations of the stems of the non-determinates (table 9.20). Such pairings are entirely analogous to any other aspect pairs.

Morphologically and aspectually, the non-determinates are uncontroversial. As imperfectives they produce perfectives on prefixation. Relatively few verbs result from this process, and they are often unrelated in meaning to the similarly prefixed determinates and many have no imperfective; compare:

procházet/projít 'go through' (a gate, for example); *prochodit* 'go through' (the soles of one's shoes, perhaps);

obcházet/obejít 'go round (an obstacle); circumvent'; *obchodit* 'do the rounds';

donášet/donést 'bring', also 'tell tales'; *donosit* 'finish carrying; carry (a foetus) the full term'.

Table 9.20   Prefixed 'verbs of motion', illustrated by the prefix *vy-* 'out, up'

vycházet/vyjít	'go/come out/up'
vyjíždět/vyjet	'ride/drive/go/come out/up'
vybíhat/vyběhnout	'run out/up'
vylétat, vyletovat, vylítat/vyletět, vylétnout, vylítnout	'fly up/out'
vynášet/vynést	'bring/take out/up'
vyvádět/vyvést	'lead/take out/up'
vyvážet/vyvézt	'carry/convey/take out/up, export'
vyhánět/vyhnat	'drive out/into exile, outlaw'
vytahovat/vytáhnout	'pull/drag out/up'
vyvlékat, vyvlíkat/vyvléci, vyvléknout, vyvlíknout	'pull/draw out'
vyvalovat/vyvalit	'roll out/up'

Mood: The **imperative** is expressed morphologically in the second persons and first person plural, and analytically in others. The endings for the morphological imperative are, irrespective of conjugation, either -$^{(\cdot)}$-Ø, -$^{(\cdot)}$-*me*, -$^{(\cdot)}$-*te*, or -*i*, -$^{(\check{e})}$*me*, -$^{(\check{e})}$*te*; the choice depends on there being one or two consonants respectively in the third person plural after removal of the final vowel (not necessarily the whole ending): *nes, nesme, neste; veď, veďme, veďte; lež, ležme, ležte; choď, choďme, choďte; sázej, sázejme, sázejte; kupuj, kupujme, kupujte; mysli, mysleme, myslete; zajdi, zajděme, zajděte.* Two other factors apply in imperative formation: first, in the *á-*conjugation the change *a > e*, as in third person plural *dají,* stem *daj-,* imperative *dej/-me/-te*; and second, shortening of stem-final syllable, for example, *koupí, koup-,* imperative *kup/-me/-te; chválí, chvál-,* imperative *chval/-me/-te; navštíví, navštiv-,* imperative *navštiv; pospíší, pospíš-,* imperative *pospěš; rozpůlí, rozpůl-,* imperative *rozpul.* There are relatively few exceptions in imperative formation, and some formal variety in the *i-*conjugation (see *Mluvnice češtiny,* II: 471–3). Anomalous in the modern language are the endings -*c* and -*z* in *e-*conjugation verbs with velar stems (products of the second palatalization). The latter survives in *pomoz* 'help' (colloquial *pomož*), while the former, as in *pec* 'bake', is obsolescent and has been replaced by -*č: peč.* The former athematic verbs *vědět* (and *povědět* 'tell' and *odpovědět* 'reply') and *jíst* 'eat' also retain their ancient imperatives in -*z: od-po-věz/-me/-te, jez.* For non-morphological 'imperatives' see 4.2.2.

The **conditional** is expressed by a combination of the conjugated enclitic auxiliary *by,* derived from the aorist of *být* (see table 9.25, p. 491), and the *l*-participle: *řekl bych, že* ... 'I would say that ...', *Petr by nám pomohl* 'Peter would help us', *kdo by to řekl!?* 'who would say that?' (who would have guessed?). This unmarked version serves primarily for the present conditional, but may also occur in the past if appropriate time indicators are present: *Včera by nám Petr pomohl* 'yesterday Peter would have helped us'. The marked version of the past conditional requires the insertion of the *l*-participle of *být*, hence, adapting the previous examples: *byl bych řekl, že, ...*, *Petr by nám byl pomohl, kdo by to byl řekl!?*, *včera by nám byl Petr pomohl.*

Voice is a two-member verbal category, active and passive, though some types have led to periodic discussion of a possible middle voice in Czech.

There are two forms of passive:

1   using a passive participle (in the short form) of a transitive verb with *být* as auxiliary, hence from the active *hosté vypili všechen čaj* 'the guests drank all the tea', the passive *všechen čaj byl vypit* (*hosty*), where the agent may be suppressed but can be expressed if required;
2   using a reflexive transformation: *všechen čaj se vypil* (all tea-NOM REFL drank-PRFV); here the agent is suppressed completely.

With verbs complemented by an oblique case both a participial and a reflexive construction are possible, but best interpreted as impersonal constructions (based on the third person singular neuter); they retain the original case form of the complement, hence (*Petr*) *hnul stolem* (INST) 'Peter moved the table' has partial passive counterparts in *bylo hnuto stolem* and *hnulo se stolem*. The same considerations apply to prepositional complements: *výbor jednal o minulé schůzi* 'the committee discussed the previous meeting' again has versions *bylo jednáno o minulé schůzi* and *jednalo se o minulé schůzi*, in which no agent can be expressed. These are comparable to similar impersonal ('de-agentized' is the Czech term) constructions based on intransitive verbs proper, for example, active *celý večer jsme tancovali a domů jsme šli až po půlnoci* 'we danced all evening and didn't go home until after midnight' has as its counterpart with the agent suppressed: *celý večer se tancovalo a domů se šlo až po půlnoci*; however, these have no participial counterparts.

The participial passive can be used in all persons; both the subject and the agent may or may not be human, and the agent can be expressed, if known or required, in the instrumental. By contrast, the reflexive passive is confined to third-person forms. Also, while the anonymous agent will usually be marked 'human', the grammatical subject of a reflexive–passive sentence usually cannot be. A major limitation to reflexive passives is that they would clash with some of the countless other functions of formally reflexive verbal expressions. For example, *zabil se* (‹ *zabít* 'kill') cannot mean 'he was killed' by some anonymous agent, but merely 'he got killed, he perished' (besides meaning 'he killed himself'); *skupina se vrátila od hranic* cannot mean 'the group was turned back from the frontier', since *vrátit se* is the (formally reflexive) intransitive verb 'return'.

Reflexive passive and impersonal constructions are stylistically neutral, while participial passive constructions, though available for the entire paradigm of their main exponents (transitives with accusative object), are limited to more formal written registers.

Non-finite forms: The **basic infinitive** marker is *-t*, although throughout most of the century forms in *-ti* were the norm (including entries in *SSJČ*). The only exceptions have been *e*-conjugation verbs with velar stems (like **mog-ti* and **pek-ti*), the infinitives of which have until quite recently had *-ci* (*moci* 'can', *péci* 'bake') as the norm, with *-ct* evaluated as non-standard. Since the 1970s, the latter have been admitted to the standard language as informal alternatives to *-ci*. Thus *-t* is now universal. Well into the twentieth century grammars held a competing **supine** to be alive as well, though the only example widely quoted was *spat* from *spát* 'sleep', used after verbs of motion (*jít spat* 'go to bed').

Participles and gerunds: the imperfective ('present') gerund is formed from imperfective verbs only. Two sets of forms exist, derived from the third person plural of the present by removal of the final vowel (not necessarily the full personal ending) and addition of *-ě/e* (M), *-ic* (F/N) and *-ice* (PL) for the *i*-conjugation or wherever the stem-final consonant is 'soft', and *-a*, *-ouc* and *-ouce* for the remainder. Gender–number agreement is with the subject of the main clause. The far rarer perfective ('past') gerund is formed from perfective verbs; here two sets of endings depend on whether the past-tense stem ends in a vowel or consonant. For consonantal stems the endings are *-Ø*, *-ši*, *-še*; for vocalic stems *-v*, *-vši*, *-vše*. The same genders and agreement rules apply as above.

Use of the gerunds is confined to the higher styles, especially in official-ese and texts with an archaic flavour, but they are exploited to good effect as a condensing device by a number of modern writers. Examples of forms:

	Imperfective gerund	*Perfective gerund*
nést	nes-a/-ouc/-ouce	vynes/-ši/-še
brát	ber-a/-ouc/-ouce	vybra-v/-vši/-vše
plakat	pláč-e/-íc/-íce	zaplaka-v/vši/-vše
tisknout	tiskna/-ouc/-ouce	vytisk/-ši/-še
kupovat	kupuj-e/-íc/-íce	koupi-v/vši/-vše
vracet	vracej-e/-íc/íce	vráti-v/-vši/-vše

Adjectivalizations of the past gerund, ending in *-ší*, are an even rarer, artificial creation: *pominuvši nebezpečí* 'the danger that had passed', *vrátivší se emigrant* 'the returned émigré'.

The **present active participle** is formed from the feminine/neuter imperfective gerund by the addition of *-i* (or from the stem of the third person plural present by the addition of -*ící* for soft stems and -*oucí* for hard). It is formed only from imperfective verbs. Unremarkably, many have evolved into adjectives: *polehčující* 'mitigating', *vedoucí* 'leading', or even nouns: *cestující* 'passenger', *vedoucí* 'manager(ess)', but their main function is to condense relative clauses (see 4.5 below).

The '*l*-participle', used in forming the past tense, should perhaps not be called a participle now at all. However, it still retains gender–number markers, and, outside the third persons, requires auxiliary verbs. It is based on the infinitive stem (infinitive minus -*t*), with various patterns of stem-vowel shortening, hence, from vocalic stems: *být* › *byl*/-*a*/-*o*/-*i*/-*y*/-*a*; *bdít* 'keep vigil' › *bděl*/-*a* and so on; *zout* 'remove shoes' › *zul*; *chodit* 'go' › *chodil, kupovat* 'buy' › *kupoval*; from consonantal stems: *vést* 'lead' › *vedl*; *řici/říct* 'tell' › *řekl*; *tisknout* 'print' › *tiskl* (colloquial *tisknul*). Some *l*-participles may become lexical adjectives, but non-systematically. Most have meanings deducible from the underlying verb: *došlá* (*korespondence*) 'incoming (post)' ‹ *dojít* 'arrive', *zbylý* 'remaining' ‹ *zbýt* 'remain', but others are further removed from their source: *umělý* 'artificial' ‹ *umět* 'know how', *bdělý* 'vigilant' ‹ *bdít* 'keep vigil'.

Passive participles are based on -*n*- (the majority) or -*t*- (most monosyllabic verbs and many in -*nout*). The morphological variety is distributed as follows in short forms:

-*án, -ána, -áno*; -*áni, -ány, -ána* – from verbs whose infinitives end in -*at*;
-*en, -ena, -eno*; -*eni, -eny, -ena* – from verbs whose infinitives end in -*it, -ět,*
    -*et*, or consonantal stem;
-*t, -ta, -to*; -*ti, -ty, -ta* – from mostly monosyllabic verbs (+ their compounds).

Equivalent long forms, declined as long adjectives, end in *aný, -ený, -tý* and so on. Note the length difference between long and short forms in the *a*-theme type. Short forms are predicative only, typically in passive verb phrases; long forms may be predicative or attributive. Short forms, with or without *jsa* and so on (gerunds of *být*), function as passive gerunds: *postaven znova, dům vypadal lépe než předtím* 'rebuilt, the house looked better than before'. Short forms may still be found in the accusative as second complements: *mít knihu rozečtenu* (or *rozečtenou*) 'have a book half-read', *vidět se utopena* (or *utopeného*) 'see oneself drowned'. Passive participles are formed from both aspects, hence *přestavěný dům* 'a rebuilt house', *přestavovaný dům* 'a house under reconstruction'; *koupený chléb* 'the bread bought', *kupovaný chléb* 'shop bread'. Lexicalized forms are not uncommon, as shown by adjectives like *neslýchaný* 'unheard-of', *oblíbený* 'favourite', many even without a motivating verb: *pruhovaný* 'striped', *pihovaný* 'freckled'; or nouns: *představená* 'mother-superior', *obžalovaný* 'the accused'.

3.2.2   Conjugation
Five main conjugational types are recognized. They are discriminated on the basis of the third person singular, marked by the endings: (I) -*e*; (II) -*n-e*; (III) -*j-e*; (IV) -*i*; (V) -*á*. Class V is an historic innovation, born of the contraction of once disyllabic endings and assimilation to the athematic verb *dát*. Table 9.21 shows the relationships in contemporary Czech among the form or forms of the infinitive stem and the first and third persons singular present tense of verbs selected for reference throughout this volume. Some alternatives are supplied for those that have not survived. Some have relocated. The full extent of interference, merger and evolution among the conjugational types is revealed by table 9.22.

Most anomalies occur in former athematic verbs and *chtít* 'want' (table 9.23). Specimen conjugations are given in tables 9.24a–c. Table 9.25 gives the present and future tenses of *být* and the conjugation of the conditional auxiliary, a unique and little-changed survival of the aorist conjugation of the same verb.

3.3   Derivational morphology

3.3.1   Major patterns of noun derivation
All methods of word formation applicable in Czech apply *par excellence* to noun derivation, chief among them **suffixation**. Some suffixes have a near-constant function, like agentive -*tel* (M), -*telka* (F) (*uči-tel-ka* 'teach-er'); abstract -*ost* (F), or -*ství* (N) (*schopnost* ‹ *schopný* 'ability'); instrumental -*dlo* (N) (*měřidlo* 'gauge' ‹ *měřit* 'measure'), while others have an impressive range of functions, notably -*ek*, -(*n*)*ík*, (M), -*ka*, -(*n*)*ice* (F) and -*ko* (N), and the highly productive -*ák* (M AN and INAN) and -*ár*/-*ař* (M AN). The complete set of patterns of suffixation according to classes of source words, gender and other semantic considerations is described in *Mluvnice češtiny* (I: 235–312). A widespread concomitant feature of suffixation is quantitative and/or qualitative alternations in root syllables, with shortening far exceeding lengthening: *létat* › *letadlo* 'fly' › 'aeroplane', *vůl* › *volek* 'ox' › diminutive, *hrad* › *hrádek* 'castle' › diminutive. Many suffixes cause palatalization of stem-final consonants: *býk* 'bull' › *býček* (DIMIN), *chirurg* 'surgeon' (M) › *chiruržka* (F), *Persie* 'Persia' › *Peršan* 'Persian' (*peršan* 'Persian carpet or cat').

Prefixation is limited to (a) a half-dozen non-prepositional prefixes: *ne-smysl* 'non-sense', *pra-člověk* 'primeval man'; (b) a dozen prepositional prefixes used in calquing: *přes-čas* 'over-time', *místo-král* 'vice-roy'; and a dozen loan-prefixes: *arci-vévoda* 'arch-duke', *kvazi-věda* 'pseudo-science' (the hyphens here are not part of the orthography).

Combined **prefixation–suffixation** occurs in several types, usually reflecting an underlying prepositional phrase, hence *ná-den-ík* 'journey-man' is hired *na den* 'for a day', *bez-domov-ec* 'homeless person' is *bez*

Table 9.21   Key verbs, showing types of stem variations

Infinitive	Past tense	1 SG PRS	3 SG PRS
Theme in -e			
nést 'carry'	nesl	nesu	nese
vést 'lead'	vedl	vedu	vede
číst 'read'	četl	čtu	čte
jít 'go, walk'	šel[1]	jdu	jde
jet 'go, ride'	jel	jedu	jede
zábst[2] 'freeze'	zábl	zebu	zebe
péci 'bake'	pekl	peku/peču	peče
umřít 'die'	umřel	umřu[3]	umře
zvát 'invite'	zval	zvu[4]	zve[4]
brát 'take'	bral	beru	bere
mazat 'smear'	mazal	maži/-u	maže
mlet 'grind'	mlel	melu	mele
psát 'write'	psal	píši/-u	píše
Theme in -ne			
zdvihnout 'lift'	zdvihl[5]	zdvihnu	zdvihne
minout 'pass'	minul	minu	mine
za-čít[6] 'begin'	začal	začnu	začne
říci/říct 'tell'	řekl	řeknu	řekne
Theme in -je			
číti[7] 'sense'	čil[8]	čiji[8]	čije[8]
pět 'sing'	pěl	pěji[9]	pěje
krýt 'conceal'	kryl	kryji[9]	kryje
bít 'strike'	bil	biji[9]	bije
zout 'remove'[10]	zul	zuji[9]	zuje
hrát 'play'	hrál	hraji[9]	hraje
přát 'wish'[11]	přál	přeji[9]	přeje
darovat 'donate'	daroval	daruji[9]	daruje
set 'sow'	sel	seji[9]	seje
Theme in -i			
modlit se 'pray'	modlil se	modlím se	modlí se
chodit 'walk'	chodil	chodím	chodí
velet 'command'	velel	velím	velí
slyšet 'hear'	slyšel	slyším	slyší
trpět 'suffer'	trpěl	trpím	trpí
spát 'sleep'	spal	spím	spí
umět 'know how'	uměl	umím	umí
sázet 'plant'	sázel	sázím	sází[12]
Theme in -a			
dělat 'do, make'	dělal	dělám	dělá

Notes: [1]past gerund *šed*; [2]Old Czech *ziebsti*; [3]Old Czech *umru*; [4]Old Czech *zovu, zove*; [5]colloquial *zdvihnul*; [6]< *-čen-ti*; [7]obsolete form < *čúti*; [8]Common Czech *čul, čuju, čuje*; [9]Common Czech *pěju*, in so far as this verb ever penetrates that register; similarly the forms *kryju, biju, zuju, hraju, přeju, daruju, seju*; [10]shoes only; [11]Old Czech *přieti*; [12]It applies in general of this class that the third singular and plural are identical, but in the case of the two types the third plural is *uměji, sázeji.*

Table 9.22   Evolution of Czech verb classes and subclasses

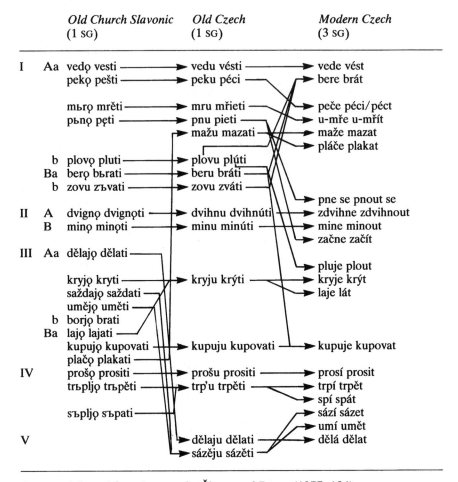

	Old Church Slavonic (1 SG)	Old Czech (1 SG)	Modern Czech (3 SG)

Source: Adapted from Lamprecht, Šlosar and Bauer (1977: 184).

Table 9.23   The former athematic verbs and *chtít*

být 'be'	byl	jsem	je	jsou
jíst 'eat'	jedl	jím	jí	jedí
dát 'give'	dal	dám	dá	dají
vědět 'know'	věděl	vím	ví	vědí
mít 'have'	měl	mám	má	mají
chtít 'want'	chtěl	chci	chce	chtějí

Note: *dát* and *mít* are entirely regular *á*-conjugation verbs; *jíst* and *vědět* are essentially *i*-conjugation and *chtít* is *e*-conjugation.

Table 9.24 Specimen conjugations

(a) *e*-theme	(b) *i*-theme	(c) *á*-theme
vedu 'lead'	prosím 'request'	dělám 'do, make'
vedeš	prosíš	děláš
vede	prosí	dělá
vedeme	prosíme	děláme
vedete	prosíte	děláte
vedou	prosí	dělají

Note: the *e*-theme paradigm is shared by the *-ne* and *-je* types; the main deviations are in most *-je* types, which have had, and in higher styles still retain, first person singular in *-i* and third plural in *-í* (a product of the *u* › *i* umlaut); conversely, in lower registers the endings *-u* and *-ou* have replaced them, borrowed from the hard-stem version of the paradigm. The *i*-theme paradigm has a large subgroup with the third person plural in *-ěji/-ejí*, chiefly soft-stem counterparts to the innovated *á*-conjugation, but altered beyond recognition by the *a* › *ě* and *á* › *ie* › *í* umlauts.

Table 9.25 *být*

Present	Future	Conditional auxiliary
jsem	budu	bych
jsi	budeš	bys
je	bude	by
jsme	budeme	bychom
jste	budete	byste
jsou	budou	by

domova 'without a home', and, a productive neuter type, *bez-větř-í* 'calm' is a state *bez větru* 'without wind'.

Affixless derivation is one of the simplest forms of conversion, chiefly from verbs: *plazit* 'crawl' › *plaz* 'reptile', *obvázat* 'bind' › *obvaz* 'bandage'; in combination with **composition** many technical terms are so produced: *teplo-měr* 'thermo-meter' (‹ *měřit* 'measure'), *perlo-rodka* 'pearl oyster' (‹ *rodit* 'give birth').

3.3.2 Major patterns of adjective formation

Adjectives formed from verbs chiefly express: (a) purpose, by the suffix *-cí*, attached to the infinitive stem, a type common in forming technical terms: *sací* (*bagr*) 'suction (dredger)' (‹ *sát* 'suck'), *holicí* (*strojek*) 'shaver' (‹ *holit* 'shave'); (b) passive potential, by *-telný* and non-productive *-ný*: *obyvatelný* 'habitable' (‹ *obývat* 'inhabit'), *pitný* 'drinkable' (‹ *pít* 'drink');

(c) propensity, by various suffixes ending in *-vý*: *hravý* 'playful' (< *hrát* 'play'), *citlivý* 'sensitive' (< *cítit* 'feel').

Relational adjectives are formed from nouns by four main suffixes: *-ový*, *-ní*, *-ný*, in descending order of productivity, and polyfunctional *-ský/-cký*. Source nouns are semantically too heterogeneous to provide a detailed survey; a few examples must suffice: *hrtanový* < *hrtan* 'larynx', *vínový* 'burgundy' (colour) < *víno* 'wine'; *výroční* < *výročí* 'anniversary' (*-ní* is strongly associated with times and places); *výzkumný* < *výzkum* 'research' – *-ný* is often used where there is an underlying verb (here *vyzkoumat* 'discover') or with material nouns: *senný* < *seno* 'hay'; *londýnský* < *Londýn* 'London', *vesnický* < *vesnice* 'village', *knihovnický* < *knihovník* 'librarian' or < *knihovnictví* 'librarianship', and in loans: *energický* 'energetic' (< *energie*), *energetický* < *energetika* 'energy (industry)', *luteránský*, *dogmatický*. A special class of relational adjectives from the names of animals uses the suffix *-í*: *pes* 'dog' > *psí*, *tygr* 'tiger' > *tygří*, *čáp* 'stork' > *čapí*.

Qualitative adjectives derived from abstracts usually take *-ný*, while those from concrete nouns have suffixes based on *-t-*: *obyčej-ný* 'customary', *nuda* > *nudný* 'boredom'–'boring'; *roh-atý* 'horn-ed', *vejce* > *vejčitý* 'ovoid'.

From existing adjectives suffixation produces augmentatives: *široký* > *širokánský* 'wide', and de-intensification of a quality: *bílý* > *bělavý* 'whitish', including cases of simultaneous prefixation from associated verbs: *nazelenalý* 'greenish' < *zelenat se* < *zelený* 'green'.

Adjectives are readily formed from adverbs (*dole* > *dolní* 'down'–'lower', *loni* > *loňský* 'last year-'s'), including numerous prepositional phrases: *mezi žebry* 'between the ribs' > *mezižeberní* 'intercostal'.

Many types of composition are represented: *tmavomodrý* 'dark blue', *barvoslepý* 'colour-blind', *motýlokvětý* 'papilionaceous' (< *motýl* 'butterfly', *květ* 'flower'), *dvounohý* 'two-legged', *samojízdný* 'self-propelled' (< *samo* + *jezdit* 'go'); there are also cases of syntactic juxtaposition: *chvályhodný* 'laudable' (= of-praise-worthy), *ohnivzdorný* 'fire-resistant' (= to-fire-resistant), *protijedoucí* 'oncoming' (= opposite going).

3.3.3   Major patterns of verb derivation

Verbs are derived by prefixation, prefixation + reflexivization, suffixation, suffixation + reflexivization, prefixation + suffixation, prefixation + suffixation + reflexivization and reflexivization. They are commonly derived from nouns, other verbs and adjectives. From nouns, of whatever semantic class, the suffixes *-ovat* and *-it* predominate, with immense variety in the semantics of the resultant verbs: *bláznit* 'go crazy' < *blázen* 'madman'; *papouškovat* 'repeat parrot-fashion' < *papoušek* 'parrot'; *vlnit* 'undulate' < *vlna* 'wave'; *formovat* 'shape' < *forma* 'shape, mould'; *bagrovat* 'dredge' < *bagr* 'dredger'; *brousit* 'whet' < *brus* 'whetstone'; *hřešit* 'sin' < *hřích* 'sin'.

The two main ranges of verbs from adjectives denote changes of state.

Intransitives have the suffixes *-ĕt/-et* or *-nout* (*šedivĕt* < *šedivý* 'grey'; *bled-nout* < *bledý* 'pale'), and usually perfectivize by the 'empty' prefix *z-*. Many exist solely as perfectives (*zpřísnĕt* 'become severe' < *přísný* 'strict', *otĕhotnĕt* 'become pregnant'). Transitives take the suffix *-it* and are perfectivized by a variety of often contributory prefixes (*vy-čistit* < *čistý* 'clean'; *za-hladit* < *hladký* 'smooth'). Spatial meanings tend to produce intransitive reflexives (*při-bližit se* 'approach' < *blizký* 'near'). Many items are derived only by simultaneous prefixation (*umožnit* 'facilitate' < *možný* 'possible'), are therefore perfective and regularly imperfectivize by means of *-ovat* (*umožňovat*).

The main source of verbs derived from verbs is prefixation (see the discussion of aspect above, pp. 481–4). Among the often polysemic prefixes in use the semantically most opaque is *z-*, rapidly becoming the neutral perfectivizer *par excellence*.

Secondary prefixation merely exploits one or other meaning of existing prefixes, tacked on to an already prefixed verb, as shown by distributive *po-* in *po-z-hasinat* 'put the lights out one by one' or additive *při-* in *při-ob-jednat* 'order extra'. Double prefixation is limited to *popo-* with verbs of motion (see above) and *vyna-* + reflexivization, usually in negative contexts (very few verbs can take this): *nemůže si ho vynachválit* 'he can't speak highly enough of him'.

Derivation by suffixation is preeminently the domain of secondary imperfectivization, the patterns of which are many and various, partially illustrated in section 3.2.1 above. Frequentatives are also formed by suffixation, namely by the suffix *-vat* with lengthening of a preceding vowel, hence *psát* > *psávat* 'write', *bolet* > *bolívat* 'ache', *chodit* > *chodívat* 'go'. Reduplication of the suffix, as in *chodívávat*, suggests repetition of the act either at a remoter time or over a longer period. The suffix *-nout* is used to form semelfactives: *padat/padnout* 'fall', *bouchat/bouchnout* 'bang', *pípat/pípnout* 'tweet'.

4 Syntax

4.1 Element order in declarative sentences

Czech is traditionally, if as an oversimplification, described as a language with free word order. This merely means that its inflectional system is so highly developed that there is little scope for ambiguity, and syntactic relations are practically always transparent. Many factors determine word order in real contexts, chief among them being the relative 'communicative dynamism' of constituents. In a neutral sentence the least communicatively dynamic element stands at the beginning and dynamism builds up from left to right until the final constituent, with the highest degree of communicative dynamism; 'subjectively' ordered sentences, with the order reversed completely, are also to be encountered. In consequence, any constituent may find itself anywhere in the sentence: 'pragmatic word order' takes precedence over syntax and is the main determinant of functional sentence perspective. To take a simple SVO sentence: *Petr zabil Pavla* 'Peter killed Paul' – traditionally regarded as the neutral order – has the subject *Petr* as theme and *zabil Pavla* as rheme. In fact, it is no more neutral than *Pavla zabil Petr* 'Paul was killed by Peter', with 'Paul's being killed' as theme and 'Peter' as rheme, or 'Paul' as theme and his 'being killed by Peter' as rheme. Both stand in opposition to *Petr Pavla zabil* and *Pavla Petr zabil*, which are less neutral, less likely to be unlinked contextually, and have the rhematic part occupied by the verb, that is 'Peter *killed* Paul', or 'Paul *was killed* by Peter'. (This flexibility of word order compensates for the relatively low incidence of passive constructions in Czech.)

The pressure of syntax may add to the stability of word order overall, but rarely to the extent that a given order is rigid. Relatively rigid is the position of adjectives before the nouns they qualify, or of dependent infinitives following the verbs on which they depend; reverse orderings are marked (and are due to convention – noun–adjective inversion in abuse or terminology: *husa pitomá* 'stupid cow', *kyselina octová* 'acetic acid' – or to the stronger pressure of functional sentence perspective). Most rigid is the postpositioning of attributes in the genitive (the type *žena středních let* 'a woman of middle age').

Another influence on word order is the placing of enclitics, elements lacking word stress, which generally follow the first stressed constituent in the clause. Czech enclitics are: the past and conditional auxiliaries, the atonic ('short', 'weak') forms of the personal pronouns (for example, *mi*, *se*, *ho* as opposed to *mně*, *sebe*, *jeho*), analogous uses of other personal pronouns lacking distinctive atonic forms, the conjunction *-li* (always hyphenated to the first word in the clause, usually the verb), and a small number of particles (*ale* 'though', *teda/tedy* 'so', *však* 'however, though', sometimes *asi* and *snad* – conjectural particles roughly denoting 'probably' and 'possibly'); the last have various other non-enclitic functions.

The rules for enclitic ordering are basically straightforward:

I   indirect question marker *-li* takes precedence overall; followed by
II   any past or conditional auxiliary;
III   any reflexive pronoun, even as particle;
IV   any non-reflexive dative pronoun;
V   other pronouns;
VI   and, finally, any particles present.

Example:

Ptali se,   nemělo-*li*   *by*   *se*   *mu*/*jim*   *to*   *tedy* říct.
asked-3.PL NEG-had-N.SG-if COND REFL he/they-DAT it-NOM so   tell-INF
'They asked whether he/they ought not then to be told.'

(The example is, frankly, cumbersome; the probability that all the sub-sidiary slots would be filled in reality is low.) In the example, *mu* and *se* are enclitic forms of the respective pronouns, while *to* and *jim* are enclitic uses of the single available forms. Compare for non-enclitic forms and uses in such sentences as

Dali jsme to *jemu*/*jim.*
'We gave it to *him*/*them.*'
Jemu/*jim* jsme to dali.
'It was him/them we gave it to.'
To jsme mu neřekli.
'That isn't what we told him.'

Just as pronouns with only one form are also used enclitically, so too in large measure are the 'prepositional cases' of pronouns, which also have only a single form, hence

Šli jsme *s nim* tam včera.
'We went there with him yesterday.'

although the pressure of the communicative dynamism of other elements may often leave such phrases with no other choice:

Tam by *bez něho* nešli.
'They wouldn't go there without him.'

Contrast: **bez něho** *by tam nešli,* which picks up the previously mentioned possibility of going without him, while *nešli by tam* **bez něho** emphasizes the (in)conceivability of going *without* him, or indeed without *him.* Rules are impossible to give in this area of considerable subtlety.

Since the fixed position of the enclitics after the first stressed constituent often leaves them at the end of a (short) sentence, rhythmical pressures clearly outweigh communicative dynamism: in a cross-referential function these pronouns represent 'old' information and 'ought' therefore to be closer to the beginning of the sentence. Particularly in subordinate clauses, enclitics, especially *se,* may slip into the third slot if preceded by a (relatively) stressed thematic element:

Jistě namítnete, ..., že[I] něco podobného[II] se[III] může stát jen v Americe. (press)
'You will certainly note that something similar can happen only in America.'

Such 'slippage' is increasingly common in spoken registers, even without the feature of stress. The language is clearly developing in this area.

4.2   Non-declarative sentence types

Interrogative expressions for WH **questions** are listed in table 9.13: they are supplemented by a number of others, chiefly relating to time and reason, such as *dokdy* 'until when'; *odkdy* 'since when'; *co...za* (+ ACC) 'what kind of'; *proč* 'why'. Intonation in WH questions is generally similar to that of declarative sentences. In marked variants the interrogative word may move away from the beginning of the sentence to the middle: *a do divadla kdy tedy půjdeš?* 'so *when* are you going to the theatre?', or to the end: *a do divadla půjdeš tedy kdy?* 'So when *are* you going to the theatre?'. Such variants have a rising–falling intonation contour, peaking on *kdy*.

Yes–no questions have distinctive cadences – rising or falling – to distinguish them unambiguously from statements, often as the only mark of the interrogative function, for example:

Přijde
'He's coming': ‾ _
Přijde?
'Is he coming?': _ – or ‾ –

In longer sentences the cadence extends over the rhematic element only: *Koupila sis ty hodinky?* 'Did you buy that watch?': ··· _‾ ‾ –

More visibly marked as interrogative are sentences with the subject preceding the verb:

Zabil Petr Pavla?
'Did Peter kill Paul?'   or:
Zabil Pavla Petr?
'Was it Peter who killed Paul?'

although SVO order and other permutations with interrogative intonation are equally possible.

Many yes–no questions may be formulated as negative or positive, that is, without any presupposition as to the likely answer; the difference may be neutralized, especially with the verb initially or finally:

Ne-/byli sousedé doma?
Sousedé doma ne-/byli?   'Were the neighbours in? (or not).'

In the medial position the choice of negative or positive tends to imply the particular presupposition:

Sousedé byli doma?
'The neighbours were in?' (I gather they were since you have obviously returned their screwdriver)
Sousedé nebyli doma?
'The neighbours weren't in?' (I thought they were).

That is the position as cautiously described in *Mluvnice češtiny* (III: 325), but informants' responses suggest that the permutations of negative and positive with various intonation contours may or need not produce neutralization practically irrespective of verb position.

The difference is not neutralized in questions conveying hope, fear or a desire for reassurance, confirmation and so on:

Vzala sis ten prášek?
'Have you taken that pill?' (I hope you have)
Nerozbije to takhle?
'Won't he break it like that?' (I'm afraid he might)
Neřekneš to na nás?
'You won't tell on us?' (Please don't)

Yes–no questions may open with the interrogative particles *zdalipak* or *jestlipak*, comparable to English sentences with 'I wonder if ...'. Their affinity with WH questions gives them the neutral falling intonation.

Presumptive yes–no questions may be introduced by the particle *že*, which also carries the intonation peak (*že přišla zase pozdě?* 'she came late again, didn't she?'), or terminated by tag questions having the forms: *že ano* after a positive statement, *že ne* after a negative statement, more colloquially just *že* for either, or *viď* or *viďte*, depending on whether the interlocutors are on *ty* or *vy* terms:

V Oxfordu jsme byli ve čtvrtek, že (ano)?
'We were in Oxford on Thursday, weren't we?'
Nerada by s námi mluvili beze svědků, že (ne)?
'She wouldn't like to speak to us without witnesses, would she?'
Půjdeš/půjde tam, viď?
'You (SG)/he will go there, won't you/he?'

Polite requests, cautious advice and so on can often be expressed in question form, in which case the positive–negative difference is again largely neutralized, as is that between indicative and conditional, hence:

Bude vám vadit, když otevřu okno?
Nebude vám vadit, když otevřu okno?
Vadilo by vám, kdybych otevřel okno?
Nevadilo by vám, kdybych otevřel okno?

all versions of 'Do/would you mind if I open/ed the window', sometimes described as ascending in order of relative politeness and/or uncertainty as to the response. Modal verbs figure to a huge extent in this type:

Můžeš/nemůžeš/mohl bys/nemohl bys mu to půjčit?
'Could you lend it to him?'

Neměli byste se mu omluvit? (NEG and COND only)
'Oughtn't you to apologize to him?' etc.

Responses to questions: *Ano* and *ne* ('yes' and 'no') are used according to the truth value of the reply, independently of that implied by the form of the question, hence both:

Máš pro mě moment?
Nemáš pro mě moment?   'Can you spare me a moment?'

will be answered *Ano* if a moment is available and *Ne* in the reverse case. It is, however, common for a positive answer to a negative question to be supported by *ale* 'but':

Neudělá to? Ale ano
'Won't he do it?' 'Yes, he will.'

Short answers requiring more than 'yes' or 'no' repeat the finite verb of the question, or any future or modal auxiliary present, adjusted for person. For the past and conditional the *l*-participles serve this function (the auxiliaries, as enclitics, are precluded):

Přijdeš v úterý? – Přijdu
'Are you coming on Tuesday?' 'Yes, I am.'
Nechce si ji vzít? – Nechce
'Doesn't he want to marry her?' 'No, he doesn't.'
Budeme malovat? – Budeme
'Are we going to paint the house?' 'Yes, we are.'
Udělal by nám to? – Udělal
'Would he do it for us?' 'Yes, he would.'

Similarly for a positive response to a negative question, in which *ale* is also fairly common:

Nešel by tam? – Ale šel
'Wouldn't he go there?' 'Yes ('But') he would'

Indirect WH questions use the same inventory as direct questions; **indirect yes–no questions** are introduced by *jestli* or, more formally, *zda*. *Zdali* in the same function is on the decline, while *-li*, if attached to the clause-initial verb, is stylistically neutral. Attachment of *-li* to other constituents is an archaic poetic device only.

The unmarked form for **commands** is the morphological imperative of the verb. Non-morphological 'imperatives', that is, desideratives and optatives, are formed by means of the particles *ať* or *nechť* 'let' combined with the indicative, or *kéž* 'would that' with the indicative or conditional. The former come closest to true imperatives in utterances such as *ať to* *koupí Petr* 'let Peter buy it', *nechť ABC je trojuhelník takový, že* ... 'let ABC be a triangle such that ...' (compare also *mějme trojuhelník ABC* ... 'let us take a triangle ABC ...'), while *ať mi už nechodí na oči* 'let him not come to my eyes any more' ('I don't want to see him again') is just one example of the many emotional shades which the construction may convey, in all persons, moreover: *pozor, ať ho tím žebříkem neprašti/š* 'look out, mind he doesn't/you don't bash him with that ladder'.

In the imperative, aspect operates as elsewhere in the verb system: a positive command seeking an outcome, a new state of affairs, will be perfective; a positive command enjoining a principle, or the continuance of an existing state of affairs, or the onset of an action, will be imperfective. A negative command proper will be imperfective, while one that embodies a warning will be perfective, hence:

Napiš dopisy a pošli je.
'Write the letters and post them.'
Piš!
'Carry on writing.' or 'Start writing.'
Dopisy nepiš v ruce, ale na stroji!
'Don't write (the) letters by hand, but type them.'
Nenapiš nějakou blbost!
'Mind you don't go and write anything stupid.'

Similarly in constructions with *ať*:

Ať jí o tom nenapíše/-š!
'Mind he doesn't/you don't write to her about it'

Commands with *ať* range from the gentle admonition:

Ať slušně poděkuje/š!
'Make sure he says/you say thankyou nicely'

to the categorical imperative:

Ať to tu máte/mají pěkně uklizeno, než přijde šéf!
'Make sure you/they have the place properly tidied up before the boss gets here!'.

Even the most categorical or aggressive type of imperative, the infinitive, as in *sednout!* 'siddown!', *snožit!* 'legs together!', may be used to formulate an ordinary request, as in the dentist's *pusu otevřít* 'mouth open, please'.

Optative sentences, when not expressed as questions (requests) or commands, or by lexical means, may be introduced by *kéž* with the conditional, or more rarely with the indicative:

Kéž přijde/by sem přišel včas.
'I hope he gets here in time.'

A more frequent construction in Modern Czech uses *jen aby* or *jen ať*:

Jen aby přišel včas.
'I hope he gets here in time.'
Jen ať přijde včas.
'I just hope/Just as long as he gets here in time!'

The past conditional *kéž* construction is used to convey wishes that are beyond fulfilment, that is, expressing regret:

Kéž bychom tam byli nešli!
'If only we hadn't gone there!'

while *jen aby* becomes in these contexts (*jen*) *kdyby*:

(Jen) kdyby toho tolik nenasliboval!
'If only he didn't make so many promises!'

Wishes may also be expressed by the infinitive:

Umět zpívat tak hezky jako Jana!
'If only I could sing as well as Jana!'

4.3   Copular sentences

The main copular verb is *být* and its frequentative *bývat*; it can never be omitted. It is in strong competition with *mít* 'have' as a semantically largely empty verb in several types of clause: *her eyes were blue* (preferred in English over the equally correct *she had blue eyes*) has as the preferred counterpart *oči měla modré*, as against the equally possible *její oči byly modré*.

Instrumental-case complementation after copular *stát se* 'become' is obligatory, for nouns or adjectives, but after *zdát se* 'seem' as a quasi-copula such complementation is obsolete; it may still be encountered in literature round the turn of the century (compare the example from Zeyer in *SSJČ*: *Vltava zdála se řekou z temného jantaru* 'the Moldau seemed (like) a river of dark amber'). Adjectival complements after *zdát se* are common in the nominative, but obsolescent in the instrumental.

After *být*, competition between instrumental and nominative in noun predicates is governed perhaps more by tendencies than rules. Uličný's extensive discussion of the topic (1984: 152–94) provides a complex sentence-semantic analysis of the opposition. However, 'In choosing between them [nominative and instrumental] the variation stems from semantic, period, stylistic and individual differences' (*Mluvnice češtiny*, III: 221). The prevailing distinction is for 'permanent attributes' to be expressed by nominative, transient, temporary, acquired (that is, professions and callings) or randomly distributed properties by instrumental; in less formal contexts nominative predominates:

Lev je kočkovitá šelma.
'The lion is a feline beast of prey.'
Tamta žena je moje sestra/Francouzka.
'That woman is my sister/French', but:
Náš nový soused je bankéřem/bankéř.
'Our new neighbour is a banker.' (Note here how one asks after a person's calling: *Čím je?* 'What (INST) is (he/she).')
Rozumné zacházení s penězi je jedinou zárukou/jediná záruka úspěchu.
'The wise handling of money is the only guarantee of success.'

With subject and predicate inverted, instrumental becomes obligatory (as in this version of the previous example):

Jedinou zárukou úspěchu je rozumné zacházení s penězi.

Expressions normally associated with permanency of the attribute tend to switch to instrumental in various unreal context types:

Kdybych byl tvým otcem já, ...
'If *I* were your father, ...'

Additional qualifiers may induce a (non-obligatory) switch from nominative to instrumental:

Praha je město v Čechách.
'Prague is a city in Bohemia', but:
Praha je hlavním městem/hlavní město České republiky.
'Prague is the capital of the Czech Republic', or
Petr byl jeho syn.
'Peter was his son', but:
Petr byl synem tehdy nejznámějšího českého houslisty.
'Peter was the son of the then best-known Czech violinist.'

In adjectival predicates there is no nominative–instrumental opposition equivalent to that in noun types (dictionary citations are marked 'obsolete'). As an equally peripheral alternative to the instrumental, contemporary standard Czech uses short forms of adjectives (Uličný 1984: 180). About a dozen 'short' adjectives proper are alive and in use after the copula, usually in meanings distinct from those of the long forms, for example, *být zvědavý* 'be inquisitive' (by nature), *být zvědav* 'wonder (whether)'; *být spokojený* 'be contented' (by nature), *být spokojen s* 'be satisfied with (something)'; *vědomý* 'conscious, deliberate', *být si vědom, že* 'be aware that'; *schopný* 'able', *schopen* + genitive 'capable of'. Many more short adjectives were used in nineteenth-century literature and still have a tenuous existence, exploited either for fun or as a conspicuous marker of the grander styles.

4.4   Coordination and comitativity

The simple coordinating conjunctions in Czech are: copulative: *a* 'and', *i* emphatic '*and*', *ani* 'neither, nor, and not, not even'; adversative: *ale* 'but', *avšak* 'however'; disjunctive: *nebo* 'or', *či* 'or'. Emphatic variants consist of more than one word:

Má psa, ba i kočku.
'He has a dog, and even a cat.'
Nemá psa, ba ani kočku.
'He doesn't have a dog, or even a cat.'

Yoked conjunctions use the pairs *i – i, jak – tak i, nejen – ale i/nýbrž i/nýbrž také* 'both – and; not only – but also', *jednak – jednak* 'on the one hand – on the other', *ani – ani* 'neither – nor', *buď – nebo* 'either – or'; of most interest is the often enclitic *sice* followed by *ale/avšak* 'while – nevertheless':

Má jak psa, tak i kočku.
'He has both a dog *and* a cat.'
Má sice psa, ale také kočku.
'He does have a dog, but a cat as well.'

Copulative coordination occurs at all levels of syntax, using the neutral conjunctions *a* (positive) and *ani* (negative). While *i* reinforces the link between items, its use between clauses may entail ambiguities which are overcome by resort to other devices (*a ještě, a dokonce*):

Petr řekl, že přijde, a přišel.
'Peter said he would come, and he did.'
Petr řekl, že přijde, i přišel.
'Peter said he would come, and indeed he came.'
Umyla nádobí i (a ještě) podlahu utřela.
'She washed the dishes and also wiped the floor.'

The conjunctions *a* and *i* provide a useful device for hierarchizing copulative constructions:

Slunce pozlacovalo bílou haciendu i zeleň trávníků a běl stromů i keřů.
'The sun gilded the white hacienda and the green of the lawns, and the white of the trees and shrubs.'

(*Mluvnice češtiny*, III: 339)

Of the other conjunctions mentioned above, the expression of 'not only – but also' with clauses takes the form *nejenže – nýbrž/ale*:

Nejenže přišel pozdě, nýbrž se také neomluvil.
'Not only did he arrive late, but he also didn't apologize.'   or:
Nejenže přišel pozdě, ale ani se neomluvil.
'Not only did he arrive late, but he didn't even apologize.'

When noun phrases are conjoined, the question of agreement arises. With noun phrases to the left of the verb, the latter will almost invariably be in the plural. Agreement with mixed-gender noun phrases (for past tenses and conditional) is dominated in turn by any masculine–animate, masculine–inanimate and feminine, for example:

Pes a kočka seděli (M AN PL) na rohožce.
'The dog and the cat were sitting on the mat.'
Dům/Domy (M INAN) i stáda (N PL) byly (M INAN PL) zničeny.
'The house/houses and flocks were destroyed.'
Kočka (F) a kotě (N) seděly (F PL) ... ,
'The cat and the kitten were sitting ...'

Anomalous agreement occurs with neuters: with a subject consisting solely of neuters, any one of which is singular, the verb agrees as for feminines:

Kotě (N SG) a štěňata (N PL) seděly (F PL) ...
'The kitten and puppies sat ...'

though with all elements neuter plural both feminine and neuter plural agreement are possible:

Koťata a štěňata seděly/seděla ...
'The kittens and puppies were sitting ...'

With the noun phrases following the verb, agreement is usually with the nearest conjunct:

Na rohožce seděl pes a kočka.
Na rohožce seděla kočka a pes.

However, the plurality of a complex subject can be anticipated:

Na rozhožce seděli pes a kočka.

We now turn to **comitativity**. The only common hypotactic device expressing coordination is the preposition *s* 'with'; it can only be used where there is close lexico-semantic equivalence between the joined constituents:

Marie s bratrem (rodiči, *psem) šli (M AN PL) za bývalou učitelkou.
'Mary and her brother (parents, *dog) went to see her former teacher.'

The construction is widely used where the left-hand member of the pairing is not expressed directly; given that a non-emphatic personal pronoun subject is represented by zero, a coordinated construction would be impossible, hence:

Kde je Petr? Jeli (PL) se s Marií podívat za její učitelkou.
'Where's Peter? He and Mary (with Mary they) have gone to see her teacher.'
S Marií půjdete (2 PL) do krámu a koupíš (2 SG) jí tužku.
'You and Mary will go to the shop and you'll buy her a pencil.'

If circumstances require insertion of the pronoun, it will be plural:

My s bratrem jsme to neviděli.
'My brother and I (we with brother) haven't seen it.'

Generally speaking, the chain $N+s+N$ forms a close unit and will be not interrupted by other constituents; thus in the last example it is not split by the enclitics, as in

My jsme to s bratrem neviděli.

which will usually mean 'We (others) did not see it with our brother', but, given the closeness between the two variants and the form lacking the subject pronoun:

S bratrem jsme to neviděli.

it is inevitably ambiguous.

Comitative constructions outside the subject are all potentially ambiguous and *and*-coordination is unquestionably preferred.

As follows from the examples, plural agreement in the verb ensures that the $N+s+N$ phrase is comitative, even if the subject has the form $(N=\emptyset)+s+N$; there is no need to interpret $s+N$ as an adverbial phrase. Were the verb in the singular, there is inevitable ambiguity, but a comitative interpretation may apply in some circumstances:

Marie s bratrem jela za bývalou učitelkou.
'Mary and her brother went to see her former teacher.'

Despite the potential ambiguities, comitative constructions are common in Czech and rarely genuinely ambiguous in context.

4.5 Subordination
Simple 'that'-subordination is expressed by the conjunction *že*, which, like all subordinating conjunctions, must be preceded by a comma:

Řekl, že přijde.
'He said he would come.'

The basic conjunction for **time-clauses** in *past and present* is *když*, in most senses of 'when':

Když hledal ponožky, našel pod postelí stovku.
'When/As he was looking for his sock he found a 100-crown note under the bed.'

In the present the main use is to express simultaneous and habitual events:

Když jde na nákup, bere s sebou čtyři tašky.
'When he goes shopping he takes four bags with him.'

A single event in the present requires the support of *teď* 'now':

Teď když o tom vím, mohu jim to říct.
'Now that I know, I can tell them.'

For future events *když* is replaced by *až*, in all types:

Až půjdeš kolem divadla, podívej se, co dávají.
'When you go past the theatre, have a look what's on.'

Simultaneity can be expressed explicitly by *zatímco*:

Já jsem opakoval dějepis, zatímco sestra dělala fyziku.
'I was revising my history, while my sister was doing her physics.'

However, the same conjunction may express a contrast between actions not necessarily simultaneous:

Já jsem studoval dějepis, zatímco sestra se dala na přírodovědu.
'I studied history, while my sister has gone in for science.'

Simultaneity with a conditional end-point to parallel states of affairs is expressed by *dokud*:

Dokud byl chudý, na auto ani nepomýšlel.
'While he was poor, he didn't even contemplate a car.'

Posteriority of the time clause is expressed by *než*:

Došli jsme tam, než přišel doktor.
'We got there before the doctor arrived.'

Recurrent events are introduced by *kdykoli* 'whenever' or *pokaždé když* 'each time that'; in present contexts such singularized repeated events are expressed by the 'perfective present':

Kdykoli ho potkala/potká, začala/začne na něj štěkat.
'Whenever she met/meets him she started/starts to snap at him.'
Pokaždé když ho potká, začne na něj štěkat.
'Whenever she meets him ...'

Other time conjunctions include *jakmile* 'as soon as', *dokud ... ne-* 'until' and *od té doby, co* 'since'.

The primary conjunction of **causality** is *protože*, which may also occur in correlative subordination as *proto, že*; compare:

Zemřel, protože ho špatně krmili.
'He died because they didn't feed him properly.'
Zemřel proto, že ho špatně krmili.
'The reason he died was that they didn't feed him properly.'

Other conjunctions include *poněvadž* and *jelikož* 'since', obsolescent *ježto* and numerous secondary conjunctions: *díky tomu, že* 'thanks to the fact that', *vzhledem k tomu, že* 'in view of the fact that', *v důsledku toho, že* 'in consequence of the fact that', *z toho, že* 'as a result of the fact that', *za to, že* 'on the grounds that'.

Explanation is introduced by *neboť* 'for'; the clause introduced by it, unlike all the foregoing, must follow the main clause.

Consequence is expressed paratactically by *a proto, a tedy, a tudíž, a z toho důvodu, a následkem toho*, and hypotactically by *takže*:

Nemá peníze, a proto si auto nekoupí.
'He hasn't any money, so he's not going to buy a car.'
Staniční rozhlas strašně chrastil, takže jsem hlášení pořádně neslyšel.
'The station loudspeaker was terribly crackly, so I didn't hear the announcement properly.'

Real conditions are introduced by *jestli* (informal), *jestliže, když, jak* or *-li*, all 'if', and *v případě, že* 'in the event that':

Už nikdy s tebou nebudu mluvit, jestliže hned neodejdeš.
'I'll never speak to you again if you don't go away at once.'
Když nevíš, o čem mluvíš, mlč!
'If you don't know what you're talking about, keep quiet!'

Counterfactual conditional clauses require the conjunction *kdyby*, which contains the conditional auxiliary and conjugates accordingly:

Kdybych věděl, že přijdeš, upekl bych dort.
'If I were to know you were coming, I would bake a cake.'

Similarly for a past unreal condition:

Kdybych byl věděl, že přijdeš, byl bych upekl dort.
'If I'd known you were coming I'd have baked a cake.'

In informal discourse the second part of the auxiliary (*byl*) may be deleted
from either clause, or, if the time-plane is obvious, from both.

For **concessive** clauses the main conjunctions are *ačkoli, třebaže* and *i
když*:

Ačkoli ví velmi dobře, co se od něho chce, dělá, že neví.
'Although he knows full well what is expected of him, he pretends not to know.'

A common device is the particle *sice*: translatable sometimes as a concessive conjunction, it actually anticipates an adversative clause:

Anglicky sice neuměl, ale dobře pochopil, o co jí jde.
'(While) He didn't speak English, but he well understood what was on her mind.'

Clauses denoting **purpose** are introduced primarily by the conjunction
aby, which conjugates like the conditional auxiliary from which it derives; it
is accompanied by the *l*-participle, never an infinitive. After main clauses
containing verbs of motion, *aby*-clauses are frequently replaced by an
infinitive. Some of the types below are more likely to be encountered in
colloquial registers only (while not being deemed non-standard):

1   Subjects of both clauses (or whole verb phrase) are identical:

Jel jsem k nim, abych se podíval na novou kočku.
Jel jsem se k nim podívat na novou kočku.   'I went to see their new cat.'

For a single round trip, provided no adverbs of direction are required,
an infinitive construction with *být* is used:

Byl jsem se podívat na jejich novou kočku.

2   Subjects of the two verbs differ; in many of these cases the infinitive
construction is preferred:

Nechal auto stát (aby stálo) před domem.
'He left his car standing outside the house.'
Pošleme Petra koupit (aby koupil) mléko.
'We'll send Peter to buy milk.'

3   A type that is colloquial only, and therefore not mentioned in the
Academy grammar, is the context-bound:

Kam chceš ten žebřík postavit?
'Where do you want the ladder put?'

Context-free, the meaning is unambiguously 'Where do you want to put the ladder?', but the same clause may imply a subject of *postavit* not even mentioned and is equivalent to the equally colloquial

Kam chceš, abych ten žebřík postavit?
'Where do you want me to put the ladder?'

a rare instance where (here) an adverb is extracted from the subordinate clause predicate (*postavit někam*).

Certain types of questions (direct or indirect) containing modality may also be replaced by an infinitive construction:

Nemá, komu by to řekl / Nemá to komu říct.
'He has nobody to tell it to.'
Neví, komu by to řekl / Neví komu to říct.
'He doesn't know who to tell.'
Není, komu by to řekl / Není komu to říct.
'There isn't anyone (for him) to tell.'

Where the agent need not be expressed, the infinitive construction is preferred.

The **relative** pronoun for a substantival antecedent is *který* (more formally *jenž*), which must be preceded by a comma. There is then no device for distinguishing restrictive and non-restrictive relative clauses. However, their participial counterparts can discriminate, by the same punctuation rules as in English, between the two types:

Nejstarší člen, který sedí/seděl v první řadě, je/byl můj strýc.
'The oldest member(,) who is/was sitting in the front row(,) is/was my uncle.'
Nejstarší člen sedící v první řadě je/byl můj strýc.
'The oldest member sitting in the front row is/was my uncle.' (there may be older members elsewhere)
Nejstarší člen, sedící v první řadě, je/byl můj strýc.
'The oldest member, sitting in the front row, is/was my uncle.' (the oldest member, my uncle, was sitting in the front row)

Other relative pronouns depend on the nature of the antecedent, with which they correlate: *to, co* 'that which', *cokoli, co* 'anything that', *tam, kde* 'the place where', *každý, kdo* 'anyone who', etc.

In addition to the infinitive and participial phrases, **gerundial phrases** may be used as a condensing device. They replace clauses of time or cause/reason expressing events simultaneous with (imperfective, 'present' gerund) or anterior to (perfective, 'past' gerund) those conveyed by the main clause, irrespective of the tense of the latter:

Proplýtvala celý den, nemajíc co dělat.
'She squandered the entire day, having nothing to do.'

Přišedši domů, hned zatopila, aby starý dům ožil.
'Having arrived home, she lit a fire at once so that the old house would come back
to life.'

Use of the gerunds is governed by several factors: (a) they are confined,
with the exception of a few idiomatic fossils (*chtě nechtě* 'willy-nilly'), to
higher, written styles; some writers exploit them to great effect; (b) they
can only be used where the subjects of the main clause and gerundial
phrase are identical; (c) they must agree with the main-clause subject in
gender and number, but, unlike morphological errors in, say, declension,
errors here are common and rarely provoke any corrective response in an
interlocutor – a side-effect of the retention of an obsolete feature only
imperfectly mastered at school; (d) the imperfective gerund is relatively
more widely used than the perfective.

Constraints on extraction out of subordinate clauses are very strong in
Czech, and it is difficult to gain clear evidence of actual extractions from
informants. Nor is it described in grammars, and mutations of such English
types as *the man that I think that you saw* or *the man who you said saw you*
produce uncertain responses and/or their blunt rejection as gross,
uneducated, colloquial or calquing distortions. There are always other
means to express the same ideas, namely adverbials or particles such as
podle mě, for 'I think', or *prý*, for 'you (or anyone else!) said', or full
clauses. Nevertheless, some types *are* to be heard, in one of the following
forms:

?muž,   kterého si   myslím,   žes   viděl
man-NOM who-ACC REFL.DAT think-1.SG that+AUX.2.SG saw-M.SG

?muž, co si   myslím,   žes   ho   viděl
man   what REFL.DAT think-1.SG that+AUX.2.SG him-ACC saw-M.SG

?muž, cos   řekl,   že tě   viděl
man   what+AUX.2.SG said-M.SG that thou-ACC saw-M.SG

None of these examples is authentic, but informants concede they could
occur. If clauses, rather than adverbials, were to be used to 'rectify' them,
the (variously acceptable) replacements could be, for example:

muž, o kterém si myslím, žes ho viděl 'the man of whom I think that you saw him'
muž, o kterém jsi řekl, že tě viděl   'the man of whom you said that he saw you'

or

muž, kterého jsi(,) myslím(,) viděl (with *myslím* as a weak parenthesis)
muž, který tě, jak říkáš, viděl (with parenthetic 'as you say')

4.6   Negation
Sentence negation is expressed by the prefix *ne-* attached to the verb:

Petr neplave.
'Peter doesn't swim.'

This produces a single word, so the negator attracts the stress. In the past tense and conditional it is attached to the *l*-participle:

Na Madagaskaru ještě nebyl.
'He hasn't been to Madagascar yet.'
Na Madagaskar bych nechtěl jet.
'I wouldn't like to go to Madagascar.'

Only in the past conditional is there a choice of position:

Nebyli byste jí to řekli. / Byli byste jí to neřekli.
'You wouldn't have told her.'

In the imperfective future, *ne-* is attached to the auxiliary:

Petr se nebude učit.
'Peter won't study.'

Similarly, it is attached to the modal auxiliaries, which are therefore what it negates; hence, for example:

Petr se musí učit.
'Peter must (has to) study.'
Petr se nemusí učit.
'Peter needn't (doesn't have to) study.'
Petr smí přijít.
'Peter may (is allowed to) come.'
Petr nesmí přijít.
'Peter must not (is not allowed to) come.'

The difference between subjective (deontic) and objective (epistemic) modality has no effect on the location of the negator, though out of context certain potential ambiguities arise:

Petr nemusí přijít.
'Peter needn't come.' / 'Peter may not turn up.'
Petr to nemohl vypít
'Peter couldn't drink it.' / 'Peter can't have drunk it.'

Constituent negation is expressed by the free negative particle *ne*, or, more emphatically, *nikoli*; when constituent negation is associated with adversativity, a common concomitant element is the particle *však*:

Byl jsem všude, nikoli však v Římě.
'I've been everywhere, but not to Rome.'

Quantifiers can be negated:

Ne všichni tomu věří.
'Not all of them believe it.'
Ne každý by si to koupil.
'Not everyone would buy that.'

but they are very commonly replaced by apparent sentence negation:

Všichni tomu nevěří   *or*   Každý by si to nekoupil

the literal meanings of which, 'They all (don't believe) it', that is, 'No one believes it', or 'Everyone would (not buy) it', that is, 'No one would buy it', are more theoretical than probable.

With total negation, negative elements accumulate; any negative subject or object pronoun or pronoun–adverb is reinforced by *ne-* in the verb:

Nikdo to nekoupil.
'No one bought it.'
Petr nekoupil nic.
'Peter didn't buy anything.'
Nemohli to koupit nikde.
'They couldn't buy it anywhere.'
Nikdy nikde nekupovali nic.
'They never ever bought anything anywhere.'

Two negatives with a (restricted) positive meaning are possible where one of them is lexical, or in verbal phrases containing infinitives:

On není nešikovný.
'He isn't useless.' (he's potentially quite handy)
Nechce kvůli tomu nespat.
'He doesn't want to lose sleep over it.' (he doesn't want because of that not to sleep)

The direct object after a negative is in the accusative. The negative genitive object survives as a feature of archaizing styles only. In Old Czech it was practically regular, and in the seventeenth century it was encouraged as a purist attack on the 'Latin' accusative that had begun to prevail; even in this century, however, some writers have still used it in free variation with the accusative. Survivals in modern standard Czech are semi-idiomatic phrases, mostly involving mass nouns or abstracts and the verb *mít* 'have' with the expression of quantity as the underlying motivating factor, for example, *nemít peněz/ani haléře/naděje/sil/nejmenší příčiny* 'not have

money/a single penny/hope/the strength/the slightest grounds'; in all
these the accusative is now preferred. Similarly *neznat mezí* 'know no
bounds' is yielding to *neznat meze.* In one (?) case only do both forms continue to compete, namely *nezamhouřit oka* 'not get a wink of sleep',
nezamhouřit oko 'not shut one's eye'.

The subject genitive is equally restricted; it occurs chiefly with *být*
(always neuter singular), but also *zůstat* 'remain' and *zbýt* 'be left':

Není důvodu si domnívat, že ...
'There is no reason to suppose that ...'
Po sněhu nezbylo/nezůstalo ani památky/stopy.
'There wasn't a hint/trace of the snow remaining.'

In most cases a nominative subject is now preferred, as also in the isolated
idiom, from *minout* 'pass':

nemine dne (GEN)/den (NOM) (, aby ... ne-).
'Not a day passes (without -ing)'.

Most surviving phrases containing subject genitive bear other marks of
their idiomatic quality, which helps to sustain them. The more complex an
idiomatic or phrasal unit, the greater the resistance to the switch from
genitive to nominative, hence in the rhyming proverb:

Není šprochu, aby na něm nebylo pravdy trochu.
'There's no smoke without fire.' (literally 'There's no rumour that doesn't have a bit
of truth in it.')

šprochu (GEN) is supported by the rhyme and cannot be replaced by *šproch*
(NOM).

4.7   Anaphora and pronouns
Czech normally requires subject personal pronouns only for emphasis,
contrast and so on:

Kdo by řekl, že to udělá?!
'Who would have thought (= 'said') he'd do it?'
Kdo by řekl, že to udělá on?!
'Who would have thought *he* would do it?'
On by to udělal, ale ona nechce.
'He would do it, but she doesn't want to.'
Kdo to udělá? On, nebo ona?
'Who'll do it? He or she?'

Identity of subjects in two successive clauses is typically expressed by
congruency between the finite verbs, the second subject being deleted:

V samoobsluze narazila Marie$_a$ na bývalou spolužačku$_b$. Deset let ji$_b$ neviděla, ale hned ji poznala.
'Mary bumped into an old classmate in the supermarket. She hadn't seen her for ten years, but she recognized her at once.'

However, a change of subject in the second clause produces ambiguity in the third, which need not be resolved even by insertion of an additional pronoun:

Marie$_a$ byla na nákupu. U pokladny na ni$_a$ narazila bývalá spolužačka$_b$ a hned ji$_a$ poznala.
'Mary was out shopping. Her former classmate bumped into her at the check-out and she recognized her at once.'

To ensure that *Marie* is the subject of *poznala, Marie* would have to be repeated in the third clause; there is no device, except a relative clause, to ensure that 'classmate' is the subject.

To achieve a change of subject Czech typically uses the demonstrative (not personal) pronoun:

V samoobsluze narazila Marie$_a$ na bývalou spolužačku$_b$. Ta$_b$ ji$_a$ deset let neviděla, ale hned ji$_a$ poznala.

Any theoretical ambiguity about the third clause is eliminated by semantic and pragmatic considerations. Obviously, with a gender difference between the two denotates no ambiguity can arise – where the predicate relies on past-tense forms. In other instances the scope for ambiguity is broader:

Marie s ním měla mluvit doma, ale nevěděla, kdy tam vlastně bude.
'She was to speak to him at home, but she didn't know when he/she would actually be there.'

The ambiguity, which would apply equally with *nevěděl* ('he didn't know'), can be eliminated by the use of various classes of pronoun:

... nevěděla, kdy tam vlastně sama bude
'when she would be there herself'
... nevěděla, kdy tam vlastně on bude
'when he would be there'

While a common subject in two successive clauses is not repeated, a common object is identified by means of a personal pronoun:

Jan potkal cizince a pozval ho k sobě domů.
'John met a foreigner and invited him home.'

Subsequent common objects may, however, be deleted:

Potkal cizince, pozval ho k sobě domů a představil rodičům.
'He met a foreigner, invited him home and introduced (him) to his parents.'

Cataphoric cross-reference is rare. The only standard occurrences are where the first member is in parenthesis:

Řekni to Pavlovi a, potkáš-li ho$_a$, taky Petrovi$_a$.
'Tell Paul, and, if you meet him, Peter as well.'

4.8   Reflexives and reciprocals
Reflexivity is expressed primarily by the free morpheme *se*. It is often described as a particle rather than a pronoun on the grounds of the many functions in which it is referentially empty (in passive and/or impersonal constructions, in the wide range of verbs that are *reflexiva tantum* and so on), and because under emphasis or where agreement might be required it behaves differently from other pronoun objects, even with such quintessentially reflexive verbs as *mýt se* 'wash':

Umyl ho. / Jeho umyl.
'He washed him.' / 'He washed *him*.'
Umyl se. / Sám se umyl.
'He washed.' / 'He washed *himself*.' (not *umyl sebe*)
Umyl ho(ACC) celého(ACC).
'He gave him a thorough wash', but
Umyl se celý(NOM).
'He had a thorough wash.'

Similarly, there is no accusative-to-genitive transformation with the verbal noun, in those instances where the reflexive morpheme is preserved, for example, *učení se cizím jazykům* 'learning foreign languages'; where there is no risk of ambiguity it is simply dropped; compare the following:

mýt auto 'wash the car' › *mytí auta* 'car-washing'
mýt se 'have a wash' › *mytí* 'ablutions', or
učit dítě 'teach a child' › *učení dítěte* 'the teaching of a child'
učit se 'study' › *učení* 'studying, apprenticeship, revision'

The morpheme *se* does express reflexivity to the extent that it may alternate paradigmatically with other nouns in analogous functions, irrespective of case, and guarantees that the action affects the subject:

hnout stolem 'move the table' / *hnout sebou* 'get a move on'
kupovat Petrovi aktovku 'buy Peter a briefcase' / *kupovat si aktovku*

Many uses of *si* (DAT) border closely on *reflexiva tantum* even as indirect objects; *kupovat* 'buy' is almost automatically accompanied by *si* in the absence of another intended recipient (*Petrovi* above); its omission signals that the purchaser is *not* the beneficiary. *Dát si* 'have', followed by names of food and drink, or, similarly, *vzít si* 'help oneself to', also 'marry', require explicit reference to the beneficiary (the grammatical subject) through the pronoun–particle *si*.

A reflexive verb can only denote actions affecting the subject; to the extent that embedding of various types occurs, any reflexive expression in an underlying clause (usually reduced to a dependent infinitive) will normally apply to the deleted subject of that clause, hence

doporučil   jim   se   umýt.   (‹ aby se umyli)
recommended-M them-DAT REFL wash-INF
'He recommended them to wash.' (themselves, not him)

Note the special case of the verbs *dávat/dát* and *nechávat/nechat* 'have' and 'let':

Dal   *si*   udělat   nový plot.   (‹ někdo *mu* udělal nový plot)
had-M REFL.DAT make-INF new fence-ACC
'He had a new fence made (for himself).'

Dává *se*   ostřihat v podniku   za   rohem.   (‹ někdo ho ostřihá)
has   REFL.ACC cut.INF in enterprise-LOC behind corner-INST
'He has his hair cut at the place round the corner.'

Nechává *sebou*   snadno manipulovat.   (‹ lidé *jim* snadno manipulují)
lets   self-INST easily   manipulate-INF
'He lets himself be manipulated easily.'

Another area in which the object of an underlying clause may become a reflexive complement of the main verb is after *slyšet* 'hear':

Slyšel o   sobě vykládat všelijaké hlouposti. (‹ x o něm vykládá hlouposti)
heard-M about self tell-INF sundry   nonsenses
'He heard a lot of nonsense talked about himself.'

But there are some rather opaque constraints; for example:

*Slyšel si připisovat různé nepravdy.
'He heard various untruths ascribed to him.'

ought to be from *x mu připisuje různé nepravdy*, yet it is not possible.

There are a few idioms where the morpheme *se* refers to an object, rather than subject. In one, *dát někomu něco na sebe* 'dress someone', *na sebe* 'onto self' is an adverbialization of its proper reflexive use in *mít něco na sebe* 'have something to wear' or *vzít si něco na sebe* 'put something on'. Similarly, *vzít něco s sebou* 'take something with one' may yield the transitive *dát někomu něco s sebou* 'give someone something (to take) with him'.

The **reflexive possessive pronoun** *svůj* is also restricted to cross-referring to a nominative subject as possessor. It is therefore possible to say:

Má rád svoje nové auto.
'He's fond of his (own) new car.'

but not

*Líbí se   mu   svoje   nové auto.
Like REFL him-DAT REFL.POSS new car-NOM
'He likes his (own) new car.'

since the grammatical subject is the car.

The precise co-referent of *svůj* may be undeterminable in certain infinitive phrases or phrases involving verbal nouns, as in:

Slyším   tě   zpívat svou píseň
hear-1.SG thou-ACC sing-INF POSS song-ACC
'I hear you singing your/my song.'

Such ambiguities are fairly common, and authoritative sources advise that person-specific possessives are preferable.

In isolated instances, as with *se* above, *svůj* may enter into adverbials in which cross-reference to the subject is precluded:

Dej   ten hrnec   na *své*   místo.
put-IMP DEM pot-ACC on REFL.POSS place-ACC
'Put that pan back in its place.'

Evidence of the idiomatic quality of this occurrence is the impossibility of replacing *své* here by the more colloquial *svoje*.

Reciprocity is also expressed primarily by *se/si*:

Mají se rádi.
'They love each other.'
Už dlouho si dopisují.
'They've been writing to one another for a long time.'

With verbs requiring complementation other than accusative or dative, the preferred expression of reciprocity is *jeden druhého* 'one-NOM another-ACC', the second element carrying relevant case markers; for example:

Opovrhují jeden druhým.
'They despise one another.'

Dívali se jeden na druhého.
'They looked at each other.'

A third device is *navzájem* 'mutually', often present semi-redundantly:

Rádi   si   navzájem pomáhají.
glad-PL REFL.DAT mutually help-3.PL
'They enjoy helping one another.'

or to eliminate ambiguity between reciprocity and reflexivity:

Kupují si navzájem dárky.
'They're buying each other presents.'

Reciprocity may be expressed from the perspective of both participants, that is, with a plural subject, or of one, with the subject in the singular and a 'with'-construction:

Slušně se pozdravili.
'They exchanged polite greetings.'
Slušně se s ním pozdravil.
'He exchanged a polite greeting with him.'
Dopisují si už léta.
'They've been corresponding for years.'
Dopisuje si s ní už léta.
'He's been corresponding with her for years.'

Adverbialized constructions where reciprocal *se* does not cross-refer to the subject may occur after verbs of putting:

Musíte cihly klást přes sebe.
'You must put the bricks across each other.'

A permutation of *jeden druhého* eliminates any ambiguity, as in:

Musíte cihly klást jednu na druhou

4.9   Possession
Possession, in all shades of appurtenance, is expressed primarily by *mít* 'have': *vůz má čtyři kola* 'a cart has four wheels', and other lexical items such as *vlastnit* 'possess' or, inversely, *patřit* + dative 'belong'.

The possessive dative (often close to *dativus* (*in-*)*commodi*) is almost obligatory in co-occurrence with the names of body parts:

Rozbil *si* nohu.
'He broke his (own, hence REFL) leg.'

Umyla *mu* vlasy.
'She washed his hair.'
Díval se *mu* do očí.
'He was looking into his eyes.'
Podlamovaly se *mu* nohy.
'His legs were giving way.'

but also with intimate possessions:

Strčil *ji* bonbony do kapsy kabátu.
'He popped the sweets in her coat pocket.'
vloupat se *někomu* do domu
'to burgle someone's house'
Rozpáraly se *ti* kalhoty.
'Your trousers have split.'
Unesli *mu* dceru.
'They kidnapped his daughter.'

In other contexts the usual means is the possessive pronoun: *můj, tvůj, jeho* (indeclinable), *její* (declined as a 'soft' adjective), *náš, váš, jejich* (indeclinable), or, when a (human) possessor is denoted by a one-word expression, the **possessive adjective**, formed from almost all masculine and feminine noun classes, for example, *synův, otcův, starostův, matčin, neteřin, Stěpánův, Milošův, Annin, Venušin, Shakespearův,* '(my/his) son's, father's, the mayor's, mother's, niece's, Stephen's, Miloš's, Anne's, Venus's, Shakespeare's'. Such adjectives cannot be formed from morphologically adjectival names, hence 'George's', 'Tolstoy's' are the (usually) antepositioned genitives *Jiřího, Tolstého,* or from feminine surnames, which usually use the postpositioned genitive: *rozhodnutí Thatcherové* '(Mrs) Thatcher's decision'.

If the possessor phrase consists of more than one word, possession is expressed by the genitive, which in the unmarked form follows the head:

syn starého pána
'the old gentleman's son'

though in context, inversion, the marked form, may be required and is not unusual.

4.10   Quantification
The main **indefinite quantifiers** are *málo* 'few, little', *mnoho* 'much, many', *nemálo* 'not a little/few', *nemnoho* 'not much/many', *trochu* 'a little', *několik* 'several', interrogative *kolik?* 'how much/many?' and anaphoric *tolik* 'so much/many'. (Secondary items include *pár* 'a few', *hrstka* 'a (mere) handful', *hromada* 'heaps', *spousta/spousty* 'lots', and others.)

In any nominative or accusative function a quantified noun is always in the genitive: *málo mouky* 'little flour', *trochu času* 'a little time', *mnoho lidí* 'many people', *několik dotazů* 'several questions'. Oblique-case functions are marked in the quantifiers (except *málo*, *nemálo* and *trochu*) by the general ending *-a*, unambiguous case markers being carried by the noun:

Šli jsme tam s několika cizinci (INST).
'We went there with several foreigners.'
Napsali mnoha bývalým žákům (DAT).
'They wrote to many former pupils.'

Málo and *nemálo* carry the *-a* marker only in genitive functions:

s málo žáky (INST) / jeden z mála žáků
'with few pupils / one of the few pupils'

Trochu, a fossilized accusative of *trocha*, usually reverts to its substantival status in oblique cases, the quantified expression remaining in the genitive:

Vystačili si s trochou (INST) mouky.
'They made do with a little flour.'
Udělali z trochy (GEN) mouky knedlíky.
'They made dumplings out of a little flour.'

Other substantival items generally retain their morphological attributes.

As the grammatical subject, a noun phrase containing a quantifier requires the verb in the third person singular, neuter in the past and conditional:

Přijde několik hostů.
'Several guests are coming.'
Zbylo mu trochu času.
'He had a little time left.'
Tu zkoušku udělá málo z nás/z kluků.
'Few of us/the boys will pass the exam.'

Note the preposition *z* used where the quantifier denotes a subset of the referent in the noun phrase.

The interrogative pronoun *co* and its compounds, including *nic*, constitute a separate set of quantifiers. Some may quantify substantival items in certain styles and contexts:

Ještě máme něco peněz.
'We still have a little money.' ('something of money')
Co tam bylo dnes cizinců!
'The number of foreigners there were there today!'

However, their important function is to quantify qualities, adjectival meanings. If the whole phrase is in a nominative or accusative slot the adjective is in the genitive, otherwise both constituents agree:

Co (je) nového?
'What's new?'
Ten se nezastaví před něčím takovým.
'He won't stop at something like that.'

Similar rules to the above also apply to the numerals '5' to '99'. Here the oblique case marker is -i:

přišlo (N.SG) pět studentů (GEN.PL)
'Five students came.'
s pěti studenty (INST)
'with five students'

The two key rules (noun and modifiers in the genitive and verb in the neuter singular) hold whatever word order may apply:

několik/deset dobrých jablek
'several/ten good apples'
dobrých deset jablek
'a good ten apples'
dobrých pár let
'a good few years'
dobrých jablek bylo několik/deset
'there were several/ten good apples'
z patnácti bylo dobrých jablek deset
'out of fifteen, ten apples were good'
pět jich bylo červivých
'five of them were maggotty'

The numerals '1' to '4' are 'adjectival', hence there is agreement in number, case and, where available, gender:

jedna studentka se ztratila
'one student has gone missing'
jedny nůžky se ztratily (PL)
'one pair of scissors has gone missing'

The numerals '21'–'24' and '31'–'34' may show agreement patterns based on the final digit:

dvacet jeden student (SG)
'twenty-one students (M)'
dvacet dvě studentky (PL)
'twenty-two students (F)'

but this is now obsolescent and the preferred forms are:

dvacet jedna (!) studentů
dvacet dva (!) studentek

or the non-problematic inversions:

jednadvacet/dvaadvacet studentů/studentek (GEN.PL)

The latter are preferred in oblique cases because of the simpler morphology, compare the now almost hypercorrect:

s dvaceti jedním studentem
'with twenty-one students (M)'
s dvaceti dvěma studentkami
'with twenty-two students (F)'

and the current

s jednadvaceti studenty/studentkami

Longer numerals may (but need not) decline in all their parts: *bez* (+ GEN) *dvou miliónů sedm(i) set padesát(i) osm(i) tisíc pět(i) set třiceti čtyř* 'minus 2,758,534'.

A special set of **collective numerals** is used with *pluralia tantum*: *jedny/ dvoje/troje/čtvery/patery dveře* '1/2/3/4/5 doors', *jedna/dvoje/troje/ čtvera/patera kamna* '... stoves', showing rudimentary gender agreement in the nominative and accusative and sharing their oblique-case forms with a set denoting the number of kinds of objects named, for example *dvojí/trojí/ čtveré*, etc. *kalhoty* '2/3/4 etc. kinds of trousers', which decline like adjectives. Another set denotes collectivities of like items: *čtvero* (*ročních dob*) '(the) four (seasons)', *desatero* 'the decalogue'; they decline like hard neuter nouns. These once clearly distinct types are prey to much morphological interference.

Of the **fractions**, the quantifier 'half' is expressed by indeclinable *půl*, followed by the genitive: *půl šesté* 'half past five' (half of the sixth hour), *půl pinty* 'half a pint', or the appropriate case if the entire phrase is in an oblique case: *před půl šestou* 'before five-thirty', *po půl roce* 'after six months'; *čtvrt* 'quarter', *tříčtvrtě* 'three-quarters', and *půldruha* 'one and a half' behave similarly, but the last declines more frequently these days as an adjective: *půldruha roku* › *půldruhý rok, před půldruha rokem* › *před půldruhým rokem* 'eighteen months ago'.

As nouns, fractions are derived from ordinals, hence *třetina* 'one-third', *čtvrtina* 'quarter', *tisícina* 'thousandth', *milióntina* 'millionth', or from the oblique-case stem of cardinals, hence *pětina* 'one-fifth', *sedmina* 'one-seventh', *devítina* 'one-ninth', *desetina* 'one-tenth', *devadesátina* 'one-ninetieth', *setina* 'one-hundredth'; 'half' is usually *polovina* and 'most (= majority)' is *většina*.

5 Lexis

5.1 General composition of the word-stock
The core of the word-stock is firmly Slavonic, with about 2,000 items shared with all or most of the other Slavonic languages. Borrowings are increasing rapidly, chiefly by adoption of Greco-Latin or English internationalisms. The relative share of Slavonic and non-Slavonic in the lexicon overall is hard to determine, but on average every seventh word in use is said to be a borrowing.

5.2 Patterns of borrowing
The first of many outside influences on Czech came from Old Church Slavonic, in the stabilization of religious terminology, as in *modlit se* 'pray', *mučedník* 'martyr'. (Forms and meanings quoted here and below apply to contemporary Czech; for the development of individual items see the standard reference works: Machek 1968; Holub and Lyer 1967; Gebauer 1970–; Klimeš 1981.) Some shared Czech/Old Church Slavonic items had already come from elsewhere: from German *půst* 'fast', Greek *pop* 'priest' (now 'Russian Orthodox priest' only), *sobota* 'sabbath, Saturday', from Latin, via other Romance languages, *koleda* 'carol', *kříž* 'cross', *papež* 'pope', *pohan* 'pagan'. Other early loans in this register include direct loans (from Latin *apoštol* 'apostle', *kostel* 'church', *anděl* 'angel'; from German *hřbitov* 'cemetery', *vánoce* 'Christmas'), Latin and Greek terms mediated by German (*almužna* 'alms', *biřmovat* 'confirm', *jeptiška* 'nun', *kalich* 'chalice') and calques (*svědomí* 'conscience', *prvorozenec* 'first-born son'). The strength of Latin is due to pre-Methodian missionary activity, and, from the eleventh century, to its role as the language of religion (replacing Old Church Slavonic) and administration.

From the twelfth century onwards, ecclesiastical and administrative functions were taken over by Czech, which was also widely used in literature. The fourteenth century saw the completion of the Old Czech Bible translation and the appearance of the first dictionaries. As society advanced new terminology was needed. Calquing (from Latin: *podstata* ‹ *substancia* 'essence', *jakost* (Old Czech still *kakost*) ‹ *qualitas*) and borrowing (from Latin: *majestát*, *figura*, *karta*, and again from German: *léno* 'feoff', *hrabě* 'count', *říše* 'realm, empire', *rytíř* 'knight', *škoda* 'shame; damage', *ortel* 'verdict', *děkovat* 'thank', *musit* 'must', *barva* 'colour', *klenot* 'gem', *halda* '(slag-)heap') were widespread and all the items quoted survive. Many others did not.

During the period of Humanism (mid-fifteenth to sixteenth centuries) more borrowings appeared, despite the efforts of some early grammarians who railed against German *and* Latin loans in Czech. Latin terminology was partly tolerated in education, medicine and the law, where the users would understand the terms. Survivals from this period include *puls, pilule, mutovat, proces.* Hapsburg military activities led to some early loans from French and Spanish (*armáda, kapitán, kurýr*; also the modern colloquial survivals *oficír, kvartýr*). German continued to penetrate, but permanently only in the jargons/terminologies of crafts; few items have become standard terms (*verpánek* ‹ *Werkbank* ‘(cobbler’s) bench’, *hoblík* ‘plane’).

The seventeenth and eighteenth centuries were the period of the major Baroque grammarians, who preferred neologizing from Czech roots; relatively few items survive, but Rosa’s *příslovce* ‹ *adverbium* is one calque that has stood the test first of inclusion in Jungmann’s dictionary, then of time. Most borrowings of the period merely reflected contemporary fashions and have largely disappeared, but *kavalír, lokaj* ‘footman’, *galán* ‘gallant’, *fraucimor* (‹ *Frauenzimmer*) ‘my lady’s chamber’, then ‘ladies-in-waiting’, later colloquial for one’s ‘woman’ or ‘women’ in general) survive.

The late eighteenth and early nineteenth centuries are marked by the National Revival, which for lexical development is almost synonymous with the work of Josef Jungmann, culminating in his five-volume Czech–German dictionary (1834–9), in which he sought to demonstrate the vast wealth of the Czech word-stock. The dictionary incorporates not only the living standard language, but countless archaisms, also some dialectisms and many new technical terms. He excluded contemporary and even well-established colloquial Germanisms (such as *hausmistr, rynk, pucovat* ‘clean’). Terminologies were hugely important in the Revival in order to render Czech serviceable in all domains. However, it has been suggested that the National Revival was so language-centred that scholarship was pursued for what it might contribute to the language, rather than the language’s being put at the service of learning. Jungmann created a literary terminology, while others worked on logic and semiotics, obstetrics, geometry and physics, psychology and the natural sciences. J.V.Presl, whose work in the last-named area has been studied the most widely, while drawing many new words from native resources, drew heavily on other Slavonic languages; these borrowings, together with some of his neologisms, have been the most durable. In a major study, Kolari (1981) shows that Presl’s botanical innovations included 107 items from Polish, 104 from Russian, 73 from South Slavonic and even two from Sorbian. Not all Presl’s terms have survived.

Early nineteenth-century borrowings were not solely from Slavonic, though the Slavonic languages were a preferred source. Latin, Greek and German input is concealed beneath another wave of calques: *zeměpis* ‘geography’, *krasopis* ‘calligraphy’; *jazykozpyt* ‘linguistics’ ‹ *Sprachkunde*; *přírodověda* ‘natural science’ have survived, but many other similar items were later ousted by the more recognizable internationalisms. The cosmo-politanization of European society of the day brought yet other borrowings into literature, like *cyklon, splín* (then written *spleen*), *nostalgie* and *non-šalantní.*

Inter-war terminological innovation was almost consistently based on Czech roots, but with many 'hidden Germanisms', as calques were fearfully described by the purists. Since the war, by contrast, resistance to internationalisms, at least, has gone, purism is dying out and a vast increase in technical loan-words, often, but not solely, from English continues. Names for many (sub-)cultural and other innovations are instant borrowings, again largely from English, for example, *mejkap* (or *make-up*), *lančmít* 'pork luncheon meat', *džínsy* 'jeans', to add to such earlier loans as *džez* 'jazz', *žokej* 'jockey', *buldok, mohér, ofsajd* 'off-side' (a noun), *sajdkar*.

The post-war period has led to a new influx of loans from or through Russian, such as *provĕrka* 'screening', *pĕtiletka* 'five-year plan', *stachanovec* 'Stakhanovite'; *kombajn* 'combine', *dispečer* 'despatcher'.

Perhaps the subtlest problem of other-Slavonic loans in Czech relates to Slovak. Such items as *zástava* 'banner', *znoj* 'great heat', *zbojnik* 'brigand', *výdobytek* 'gain, achievement', *namyšlený* 'conceited' and *nárokovat* 'claim, demand' are of mixed antiquity and frequency. *Namyšlený*, first recorded about 1945, had by the late 1980s almost replaced *domýšlivý* and *nafoukaný*, allegedly for its stylistic neutrality. On the whole, pressure from Slovak is slight, but insidious, as witness the recent ousting of informal *kafíčko* 'coffee', in the register of waiters, by Slovak *kávička*, isomorphic with what would have been the Czech diminutive of *káva* if it were used. Slovak–Czech interference is strongest among mobile social groups (such as the army, students, the pop-music world) and produces some magnificent hybrid slangs. Slovak is also the medium by which some Hungarian and Rumanian loans reached Czech, many of them exoticisms more than true loans.

5.3 Incorporation of borrowings

Borrowings generally adapt well to Czech morphological patterns. Difficulties arise chiefly out of conflict between gender and outward form, or, sometimes, because of pronunciation problems.

Nouns borrowed from the classical languages are adapted on the basis of the original stem, thus any final *-us, -um, -os, -on, -is* and so on is treated as an ending, alternating paradigmatically with Czech case morphemes: masculine *dinosaurus* has genitive *dinosaura*, nominative plural *dinosauři*; similarly *génius, génia, géniové*, accusative plural *génie* (the plural is adapted to the soft declension on account of the *-j-* glide in the ending); *papyros, papyru; diabetes, diabetu*; feminine *synopsis, synopse*; neuter *vízum, víza; kritérion, kritéria* (with 'soft' endings in the plural oblique cases). Many such items have entered the general word-stock, adapting so completely as to keep the full citation form of the word as the morphological base, hence *kaktus, kaktusu; epos, eposu; digitális, digitálisu*. Occasionally, a Ø-ending nominative singular is back-formed by analogy with the oblique cases, as with *tyfus, tyfu › tyf*. Instances of free variation also occur: *glóbus, glóbu/glóbusu, album, alba/albumu* (only *alba* sanctioned for the standard language), or separate lexicalization: *fikus, fíku* 'rubber-plant', *fík, fíku* 'fig'. Awareness of the form of an alien stem governs the treatment of other classical loan-words; a few examples will show the procedure: *panorama* (N), genitive (!), dative and locative singular *panoramatu; farao/Cicero, faraona/Cicerona; ion, iontu; falanx, falangy* (also back-formed nominative *falanga*); *larynx, laryngu* and so on.

Masculine animate borrowings ending in any short vowel adapt to declensional classes on the basis of the stem-final consonant, hence *gigolo, gigola; signore, signora; gaučo, gauča* (!), *gauče* (ACC PL). Those ending in [i] or [í] adapt in the singular to the declension of *ten*, hence *kuli, kuliho, mahdí, mahdiho*, and in the plural to *muž* (*kuliové, kuliů*, instrumental *kulii*, but *mahdími*). Similar treatments apply to many foreign surnames in *-i, -ey* and so on. Some nouns evolve new nominatives: *kolibri ⟩ kolibřík, pony ⟩ ponik*, which then present no declensional problems (similarly inanimate *taxi ⟩ taxik*). Nouns in *-u* either remain indeclinable (*zebu*) or add case morphemes to the entire word (*marabu, marabua*), but note the surname *Ceaușescu*, genitive *Ceaușeska*.

Among feminine and neuter borrowings problems arise with items which end in *-a* or *-o* preceded by another vowel. They produce various hybrid declensions; basically 'hard' *boa* or *rodeo* have genitive plural *boí* and *rodeí*. Nouns in *-ia* (*tibia*) decline as soft feminines, while those in *-yo* (*embryo*) and *-io* (*rádio*) decline as soft neuters in the plural oblique cases only. Nouns in *-ea* have parallel sets of hard and soft endings (*idea*, genitive *ideje/idey* and so on).

Other vocalic endings create their own problems, for example, *-é* in animates, which either produces indeclinables (*atašé* 'attaché') or, occasionally, words which borrow pronominal endings (*abbé-ho*); inanimates are usually indeclinable neuters (*dražé* 'dragée', *froté, pyré* 'purée'). Non-inflection and neuter gender is the most widespread solution for inanimates with phonetic/orthographic anomalies (*menu, interview, mini, ragby*), especially those items with an adaptive orthography (*angažmá, filé*), although non-adapted spellings can lead to a different gender and inflection (*interview* (M) genitive *interviewu*, pronounced [intervjúvu]). There are few indeclinable masculines (*buklé* 'bouclé', *para* 'Brasil nut') and feminines (*okapi, džentry*). Oddly, some neuters are indeclinable despite the ease with which they might have adapted: *faksimile, finale, konkláve, aloe, kánoe, skóre* 'score', *andante, purgans, reagens, copyright, jidiš, rekviem*.

With few exceptions, **adjectival loans** attract one of the productive Czech suffixes, especially *-ický, -ální, -ový*; unadapted words are peripheral or colloquial: colour terms: *khaki, béž* 'beige', *lila* 'lilac'; the well-established terms *brutto* and *netto*; one or two terms from mathematical theory and/or computerspeak like *fuzzy* (*množina*) 'fuzzy (set)';

and colloquial *fajn* 'great, okay', *prima* 'great', *fér* 'fair, sporting'.

Verbal borrowings appear almost daily and all adopt the suffix *-(iz)ovat*. If denoting acts subject to aspectual interpretations, they are bi-aspectual, that is, present-tense forms can acquire future meanings. Examples are *absorbovat, havarovat* 'crash; break down', *informovat, organizovat*. Some of these verbs acquire explicit perfectives by pre-fixation, most widely by the most nearly neutral prefix *z-*, as in *zkonfisko-vat, zorganizovat*, but also others, for example, *poinformovat, vydezinfikovat, okomentovat, nakoncipovat*, generally by analogy with native near-synonyms.

5.4   Lexical fields

5.4.1   Colour terms

white	*bílá*	(as a noun)	*běl*
black	*černá*		*čerň*
red	*červená* (politically *rudá*)		*červeň*
green	*zelená*		*zeleň* (also 'greenery')
yellow	*žlutá*		*žluť*
blue	*modrá*		*modř*
brown	*hnědá*		*hněď*
purple	*fialová* (‹ *fialka* 'violet')		
	purpurová is only for kings and cardinals		
pink	*růžová* (‹ *růže* 'rose')		
orange	*oranžová*		*oranž* (rare)
grey	*šedá, šedivá*		*šeď*

Note: colours are usually quoted as feminine adjectives, by association with *barva* 'colour'

All the above terms are 'felt' to be basic; *růžová* and *fialová* might be deemed non-basic by Berlin and Kay's (1969) criterion vi (name trans-ference from objects), and *oranžová* by their criterion vii (fairly recent loan). From the rest of the evidence we might conclude that a Czech colour term is basic if it exists separately as both adjective and noun; however, *oranž* as a rare item *and* recent loan lacks the strength to support the claim of *oranžová* to be 'basic' in the strict sense.

5.4.2   Body parts

head	*hlava*
eye	*oko* (anomalous plural *oči*)
nose	*nos*
ear	*ucho* (anomalous plural *uši*)
mouth	*ústa* (N pluralia tantum); informally also *rty* 'lips' or *pusa* 'kiss'

hair	*vlasy* (collective PL); single 'head-hair': *vlas*, otherwise *chlup*
neck	*krk* (also 'throat'), *šíje* (strictly: 'back of the neck')
arm/hand	*ruka* (anomalous plural *ruce*); explicit 'not-hand' *paže*
finger	*prst*
leg/foot	*noha*; *chodidlo* 'sole' occasionally used for 'foot'
toe	*prst na noze* ('thumb' and 'big toe' = *palec*)
chest	*hruď*, *prsa*
heart	*srdce*

hruď is formal and anatomical, but by no means as restricted as 'thorax'; *prsa* (pluralia tantum), 'chest' or 'breast' (non-countable) is the common word, despite partial overlap with *prs-y* 'breast-s' (countable, female). Strictly, *prsa* retains (like *oči, uši, ruce, nohy*) residues of the dual declension, while *prsy* declines as a regular plural.

5.4.3   Kinship terms

mother	*matka*, also *máti* (high style and low colloquial), *máma* (colloquial)
father	*otec*, also *táta* (general colloquial)
sister	*sestra*, also *ségra* (low colloquial)
brother	*bratr*, also *brácha* (colloquial)
aunt	*teta*
uncle	*strýc*
niece	*neteř*
nephew	*synovec*
cousin (F)	*sestřenice*
cousin (M)	*bratranec*
grandmother	*babička*
grandfather	*dědeček*
wife	*manželka, žena* (informal); *choť* (F) 'spouse'
husband	*manžel, muž* (informal); *choť* (M) 'spouse'; plural *manželé* 'Mr and Mrs'
daughter	*dcera*
son	*syn*

6   Dialects

The Czech dialects divide into four main groups: Bohemian, Haná, Lachian (Silesian) and Moravian–Slovak (south-east Moravia). In addition there is a belt of mixed Czech–Polish dialects in north-east Moravia. Each group is further subdivided, only the main divisions being identified on map 9.1.

The main features of the **Bohemian** dialects, not shared by the standard language, but including Common Czech, are:

Map 9.1 The main Czech dialect divisions

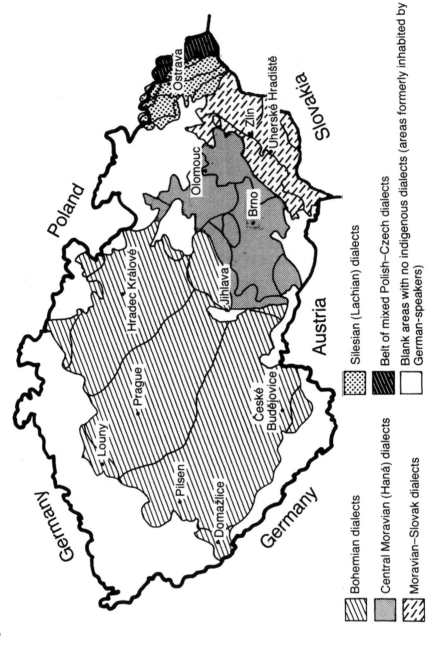

1   *ej* ‹ *ý* (and some *i*): *mlejn* 'mill', *dobrej* 'good', *cejtit* 'feel';
2   /í/ ‹ /é/: *dobrý mliko* 'good milk', *dobrý vody/vodě* 'good water' (GEN/DAT);
3   prothetic *v-* before *o-* (except in borrowings or words not occurring outside the standard literary language; also absent from the Doudleby subdialect): *vokno* 'window', *von* 'he', *vocet* 'vinegar' (but not *volovo 'lead', *votec 'father');
4   nominative–accusative plural in /í/ for all adjectives: *dobrí lidi/školy/jídla* 'good people/schools/meals';
5   instrumental plural universally in *-ma*: *těma našima dobrejma lidma/školama/jídlama/chlapcema* 'those our good people/schools/meals/boys'/ *šicíma strojema* 'sewing-machines'/*polema* 'fields'/ *telatama* 'calves' and so on;
6   *-aj*, *-ej* in the third person plural of *a-* and *i*-conjugation verbs: *dělaj/choďej/sázej* '(they) do, walk, plant';
7   loss of *-l* from the masculine past tense of consonantal stem verbs: *přines* 'brought', *vytisk* 'printed', *vypad* 'fell out', *upek* 'baked', *řek* 'said'.

The **Haná** dialects occupy much of central Moravia and share the following main features:

1   *é* ‹ *ý*: *bék* 'bull', *dobré* 'good (M NOM SG)'; also ‹ *i* after sibilants and certain other consonants: *nožék* 'knife' (DIMIN), *i*-conjugation verbs: *nosém* 'carry (1 SG)', and so on, *vešévat* (= *vyšívat* 'embroider'), *blésko* (= *blizko* 'near'); and ‹ *ej*: *dé* 'give (IMP)', *nélepší* 'best', even across morpheme boundary: *néde* (that is, *ne-jde* 'isn't going');
2   *ó* ‹ *ú* (standard Czech *ou*): *móka* 'flour', *ribó* 'fish (F INST SG)', including positions after soft consonants, since the umlauts were not effective here, hence: *dělajó* 'do', *pláčó* 'weep (3 PL)', *klóč* (= *klíč* 'key'), and in soft nouns: *ulicó* (= *ulicí* 'street (INST SG)');
3   *e* ‹ *a* by the first umlaut *internally*: *ležet* 'lie', but not in soft inflections: *duša* 'soul (NOM SG)', *otca* 'father (GEN SG)';
4   *i/í* ‹ *u/ú* by the second umlaut *internally*: *jih* 'south', *cizí* 'alien', but not in endings: *piju/pijo* 'drink (1 SG)', *ulicu/ulico* 'street (ACC SG)';
5   *ú/u* ‹ *ó*, *í/i* ‹ *ie*, *í/i* ‹ *é*: *kúň/kuň* 'horse', *písek/pisek* 'sand', *mlíko/mliko* 'milk' (that is to say, results similar to Bohemian, but with local tendency to vowel shortening);
6   short vowels in many types of disyllables (or former disyllables), where Bohemian (and standard Czech) has long vowels: *vrana* 'crow', *blato* 'mud', *mak* 'poppy', *pit* 'drink', *jest* 'eat';
7   divergent patterns of voice assimilation: [*zh*] ‹ *sh*: [nazhledanó] (= *na shledanou* 'good-bye'); across morpheme boundaries with non-paired consonants: [gmostu] (= *k mostu* 'towards bridge');

 8 *šč* preserved: *ščasný* (= *šťastný* 'happy');
 9 animacy marked in nominative plural adjectival endings: *dobří lidi*;
10 third person plural of *i*-conjugation verbs in *-ijó*: *chodijó*, even *vijó* (= *vědi* 'know');
11 imperatives in *-i/-ite* after stem-final consonantal cluster: *mesli, meslite* (that is, *mysli, myslete* 'think');
12 first person singular of *byt* (= *být*) is *su*.

The **Lachian** dialects share a number of features (numbers 3, 5, 7, 8) with the previous group. Feature 5 above applies in the short-vowel version, since of the two most conspicuous features of the Lachian dialects one is loss of vowel length. The other is the emergence of word stress on the penultimate. Additional features are as follows:

 1 *aj* is preserved in closed syllables: *daj, vajco* (= *dej* 'give', *vejce* 'egg');
 2 no syllabic liquids; accompanying vowels vary in quality and position: *pylny* (= *plný* 'full'), *mysel* (= *mysl* 'mind'), *vjeter* (= *vítr* 'wind'), *kryk* or *kyrk* (= *krk* 'neck');
 3 /d/, /t/, /n/ are palatalized before *e*, hence /veďeťe, ňešeťe/ for *vedete* 'lead', *nesete* 'carry (2 PL)';
 4 /ć, dź/ ‹ *ť, ď*: *ćicho* 'quiet'; *pić* 'drink', *chodźić* 'walk';
 5 palatal /ś/, /ź/ before front vowels and (historic) /j/: *śiň* 'hall', *prośić* 'request', *źima* 'winter', *vźać* 'take';
 6 *dz* ‹ *d+j*, chiefly in passive participles: *vysvobodzeny* 'liberated';
 7 non-merger of two original *l*-phonemes: *lipa / był* 'linden', 'was';
 8 non-merger of *i* and *y*: *lipa / był* (recall that in standard Czech the spellings *lípa* and *byl* and so on are historic; there is no qualitative difference in the sounds represented);
 9 absence of both prothetic *v-* (compare the Bohemian group) and prothetic *j-* before *i* (compare the standard language): *oko* 'eye', *oheň* 'fire'; *iskra* 'spark', *inačy* 'different';
10 genitive plural of masculine nouns in *-uv*;
11 the animate accusative plural is identical to the genitive: *ma dobrych suśeduv* (= *má dobré sousedy* 'has good neighbours').

Moravian–Slovak dialects – spoken largely in *Slovácko*, not to be confused with neighbouring Slovakia (*Slovensko*) – share some features with the Haná group, namely 7 and 8, and with the Lachian group, namely 7 (in the form *ľipa, był* (or *byw*)), 9 and 11 (in the form *má dobrych súsedú*). Other main features not shared with the standard language are as follows:

1 preservation of *ú*: *múka, nesú* (= *mouka* 'flour', *nesou* 'they carry');
2 preservation of *aj* in closed syllables (compare the Lachian dialects, point 1);

3   short vowels as in the Haná dialects, point 6;
4   few traces of the first umlaut: only medial ę > je: pjet 'five'; however, in
     long syllables á > ie > í: starší 'older' (FEM), and even smít sa (contrast
     standard smát se 'laugh');
5   no traces of the second umlaut, hence cuzí 'alien', piju 'drink (1 SG)',
     klúč 'key';
6   syllabic r even after ž, č: žrd (standard žerď 'mast'), ščrk (štěrk
     'gravel'); syllabic l > u: žutý 'yellow', but in final position also éł, eł, éw
     or ew, hence spadu/spadéł/spadéw 'fell' and védu/védeł/védew 'led';
7   preservation of é: řéct 'say', zelé 'cabbage';
8   dative and locative plural of masculine and neuter nouns in -om/och:
     chlapom/-och 'fellow', kolenom/-och 'knee'.

The Czech dialects have been well recorded and samples are available in
such collections as Lamprecht, Michálková, et al. (1976) or Bělič's
standard handbook (1972), incorporating detailed maps of isoglosses. Of
late, attention has turned to the speech of individual urban centres and
resulting studies show the extent to which Common Czech has spread out
from Central Bohemia, but also how it is coloured both by the original
local urban dialect and by the influence of incoming speakers of other
dialects. Common Czech itself, with its core in the speech of Prague,
reflects all the phonological features of Central Bohemian mentioned
above, and has a consequentially distinctive morphology. As an interdialect subject to local influences, it is now often divided into Common
Bohemian Czech and Common Moravian Czech. The urban speech of
Prague, with a discussion of Common Czech and the relation of both to
standard Czech, is described in Townsend (1990).

References

Auty, R. (1980) 'Czech', in A.M. Schenker and E. Stankiewicz (eds) The Slavic
    Literary Languages: Formation and Development, New Haven, Conn.: Yale
    Concilium on International and Area Studies, 163–82.
Bauer, E. (1983) Deutsche Entlehnungen im tschechischen Wortschatz des J.A.
    Comenius, Münster: Aschendorff.
Bělič, J. (1972) Nástin české dialektologie, Prague: SPN.
Berlin, Brent and Kay, Paul (1969) Basic Color Terms: their Universality and
    Evolution, Berkeley and Los Angeles: University of California Press.
Bílý, M. (1981) Intrasentential Pronominalisation and Functional Sentence Per-
    spective (in Czech, Russian and English), Lund: Slaviska institutionen vid Lunds
    Universitet.
Čermák, F. (1987) 'Relations of spoken and written Czech (with special reference to
    the varying degree of acceptability of spoken elements in written language)',
    Wiener Slawistischer Almanach 20: 133–50.
Cummins, G.M. (1983) 'On the aspect of motion verbs in Czech and Russian', Folia
    Slavica 6: 7–52.

Dvořák, E. (1983) *Přechodníkové konstrukce v nové češtině*, Prague: Universita Karlova.

Gebauer, J. (1970) *Slovník staročeský*, vols I–II, 2nd edn, Prague: Academia; later vols under various editorships: III (*na-obijěti sě*), 1977; IV (*obilé-ožžený*), 1984; the remaining volumes are in preparation at the Institute for the Czech Language.

Hausenblas, K. (1958) *Vývoj předmětového genitivu v češtině*, Prague: Nakl. ČSAV.

Holub, J. and Lyer, S. (1976) *Stručný etymologický slovník se zvláštním zřetelem k slovům kulturním a cizím*, Prague: SPN.

Jelínek, J., Bečka, J.V. and Těšitelová, M. (1961) *Frekvence slov, slovních druhů a tvarů v českém jazyce*, Prague: SPN.

Kavka, S. (1988) *An Outline of Modern Czech Grammar*, Uppsala: Slaviska Institutionen, Uppsala Universiteit.

Klimeš, L. (1981) *Slovník cizích slov*, Prague: SPN.

Kolari, V. (1981) *Jan Svatopluk Presl und die tschechischen botanische Nomenklatur*, Helsinki: Annales Academiae Scientiarum Fennicae.

Kučera, H. (1961) *The Phonology of Czech*, The Hague, Mouton.

Lamprecht, A., Michálková, V. *et al.* (eds and comps) (1976) *České nářecní texty*, Prague: SPN.

Lamprecht, A., Šlosar, D. and Bauer, J. (1977) *Historický vývoj češtiny*, Prague: SPN.

Machek, V. (1968) *Etymologický slovník jazyka českého*, Prague: Academia.

Mluvnice češtiny I: Dokulil, M., Horálek, K., Hůrková, J., Knappova, M. and Petr, J. (eds) *Fonetika, fonologie, morfonologie a morfemika, tvoření slov*, Prague: Academia, 1986.

—— II: Komárek, M., Kořenský, J., Petr, J. and Veselková, J. (eds) *Tvarosloví*, Prague: Academia, 1986.

—— III: Daneš, F., Grepl, M. and Hlavsa, Z. (eds) *Skladba*, Prague: Academia, 1987.

Orłoś, T.Z. (1987) *Polonizmy w czeskim języku literackim*, Kraków: Uniwersytet Jagielloński.

Rösel, H. (1983) *Wörterbuch zu den tschechischen Schriften des J.A. Comenius*, Münster: Aschendorff.

Short, D. (1988) 'Some notes on the distribution of /l/ in Czech – with special reference to butterflies', *Phonetica Pragensia VII*, Prague: Univerzita Karlova, 35–41.

—— (1990) 'The morphology of the vocative in Czech and Slovak', in Mojmír Grygar (ed.): *České studie*, Amsterdam and Atlanta: Rodopi, 31–45.

SSČ: Slovník spisovné češtiny pro školu a veřejnost, Prague: Academia, 1978.

SSJČ: Slovník spisovného jazyka českého, vols I–IV, Prague: Academia, 1958–71.

Townsend, C.E. (1990) *A Description of Spoken Prague Czech*, Columbus, Ohio: Slavica.

Uličný, O. (1984) *Instrumentál v struktuře české věty*, Prague: Ústřední knihovna – Oborové informační středisko Pedagogické fakulty Univerzity Karlovy (English summary).

10 Slovak

David Short

1 Introduction

Slovak is the official language of Slovakia, or the Slovak Republic, the eastern part of former Czechoslovakia. It is spoken by about 4.5 million people in Slovakia and by another half million still living in the new Czech Republic. Thus westwards the Slovak-speaking area meets Czech; northwards it meets Polish, south-westwards German (in Austria), southwards Hungarian and eastwards Ukrainian. There are considerable Hungarian and smaller Czech and Ukrainian (Ruthenian) minorities in Slovakia, and even fewer Poles, Russians and Germans, but a large Romany population (10 per cent of the population in East Slovakia). The Slovak-speaking area overspills into Poland, with a larger spread into Hungary and scattered pockets in Rumania and the former Yugoslavia (chiefly Vojvodina). Historical migrations gave rise to Slovak groups elsewhere in Europe and large colonies overseas (Canada, the United States and Argentina).

The basis of the contemporary standard language is Ľudovít Štúr's codification of the 1840s, based mainly on Central-Slovak dialects; the modern orthography and some other refinements are due to revisions by Michal Hodža and Martin Hattala; the language was effectively consolidated by the mid-1850s. Earlier there had been a codification based on Western Slovak (1790), by Antonín Bernolák, which, though relatively short-lived, did produce some literature and Bernolák's large posthumous dictionary (*Slowár slowenskí česko-laťinsko-ňemecko-uherskí*, 1825–7). In the east the Calvinists had also attempted to use consistently a Slovak based on the eastern dialect (the Lutherans used biblical Czech). Unlike these early local versions of a systematized written language (and even earlier, unsystematized, language patterns now known as 'cultured East/Central/West Slovak'), Štúr's codification eventually gained acceptance as the language of the newly consolidated Slovak nation. With the youth of the language go many problems in its development and stabilization – morphological variation, the evaluation of regionalisms, the insidious penetration of Czech forms and the morphological and orthographic treatment of borrowings. Research on both the standard language and the dialects is conducted at the Slovak Academy's Ľudovít Štúr Linguistics Institute in Bratislava, which publishes the periodicals *Slovenská reč* and *Kultúra slova*, and the foreign-language occasional papers *Recueil linguistique de Bratislava.*

2 Phonology

2.1 Segmental phoneme inventory

Practically speaking, Slovak has five **short vowels** organized triangularly:

$$/i/ \qquad\qquad\qquad /u/$$
$$/e/ \qquad\quad /o/$$
$$/a/$$

However, standard Slovak as codified has six short vowels organized in a plain front–back pattern:

/i/	/u/
/e/	/o/
/æ/	/a/

The anomaly is that /æ/ is observed only by about 5 per cent of speakers, and even when heard in formal contexts (high-style theatre, solemn proclamations) it is for the majority a quaint dialect feature, rather than a fine archaism. The substitute for /æ/, of which one informant working on its incidence says simply 'it has no future', is /e/.

The system of **long vowels** (vowels in long syllables) is much more complex. Five long vowels, /iː/, /eː/, /aː/, /oː/, /uː/, are supplemented by four (rising) **diphthongs**, /ie/, /ia/, /iu/, /uo/. The resulting pattern of short–long oppositions is asymmetrical: while /i/ and /æ/ have as their regular counterparts /iː/ and /ia/ respectively, /e/ has /aː/, but sometimes /ia/, /u/ has /uː/, but sometimes /iu/, and /o/ has /uo/, but sometimes (in borrowings only) /oː/. Orthographically, /æ/ is represented by ä (retained even when /æ/ is replaced by /e/, hence there are two symbols for /e/), /uo/ by ô, and long vowels by an acute accent. The retention of ä is historical, etymological, as is the distribution of i, y, í and ý as letters representing /i/ and /iː/. The sequence *ou* occurring in the instrumental case of feminine paradigms is not a true diphthong, but short /o/ + bilabial [w], indistinguishable from /o/ + post-vocalic /v/ (= [w]).

Restrictions on vowel distribution: /æ/ occurs only after labials, and /ia/, /ie/, /iu/ only after 'soft' consonants (/iu/ in just a few morphologically conditioned environments); /aː/, /eː/, /uː/ cannot occur after soft consonants, where they are replaced by the matching diphthongs; /aː/ may, however, occur after /j/ under certain morphological conditions (*jama* 'pit', genitive plural *jám*) and in derivation, notably before suffixes *-ár*, *-áreň* (*lejár-eň* 'foundryman–foundry'). /eː/ occurs only in borrowings, the native *dcéra* 'daughter' and adjective endings. There are twenty-seven **consonantal phonemes** (table 10.1). The letters ť, ď, ň, ľ (upper case Ť, Ď, Ň, Ľ/Ľ) are only used before back vowels or finally. Before front vowels, symbols without diacritics are used; thus before /i/, /iː/ spellings are ti, di etc.; by contrast non-palatal /t/, /d/ etc. before /i/, /iː/ appear as ty, dy etc. Exceptions to this spelling convention occur in borrowings and some morphologically conditioned environments (for example, nominative plural masculine animate endings of pronouns and adjectives). Exceptions where *te*, *de* and so on represent not /ťe/, /ďe/, but /te/, /de/ occur in similar conditions, and in forms of *ten* 'that' and *jeden* 'one'.

The main subclassification among consonants is the set of voiced–voiceless pairs: *b/p, d/t, ď/ť, dz/c, dž/č, z/s, ž/š, g/k, h/ch*, which are subject to patterns of assimilation – towards voicelessness before a voiceless consonant or pause, and voicedness before a voiced consonant, often even an unpaired one, or, at word boundaries, even a vowel. Examples:

stred = /stret/ 'middle', in which [t] represents the morphophoneme /d/, as distinct from the final /t/ in *stret* /stret/ 'encounter';
kde = /gďe/ 'where'; *hádka* = /hátka/ 'quarrel';
náš bol = /nážbol/ 'ours was', *had pil* = /hatpil/ 'snake drank'.

Before unpaired voiced: *vlak mešká* = /vlagmeška/ 'train's late'; *viac ráz* = /viadzrás/ 'several times'; similarly with transparent internal morpheme boundary: *takmer* = /tagmer/ 'almost'; *viacnásobný* /viadznásobný/

Table 10.1   Slovak consonantal sounds (non-phonemic in square brackets)

	Labial	Labio-dental	Alveo-dental	Post-alveolar	Palatal	Velar	Laryngeal
Occlusive							
Oral	p b		t d		ť ď	k g	
Nasal		m	n		ň	[ŋ]	
Semi-occlusive			ts	dz tš	dž		
Fricative	[w] f	v	s	z š	ž	j x	[ɣ] h
Lateral			l		ľ		
Roll			r				

Note: In IPA terms /ť/ = [c], /ď/ = [ɟ], /ň/ = [ɲ], /ľ/ = [ʎ], /š/ = [ʃ], /ž/ = [ʒ], /tš/ = [tʃ], [dž] = [dʒ].

'multiple'. Opaque boundaries reveal no assimilation: *vlákno* = /vlákno/ 'fibre'.

Inconsistencies occur with: (a) the prefix *s-*, which survives in spelling and pronunciation in some words (*sloh* 'composition', *svah* 'slope'), while in others voicing has led to orthographic revision (*zjednotiť* 'unite', *zmes* 'blend'); (b) the effect of *-m*, which sometimes causes regressive voicing: *nášmu, vášmu* = /nážmu, vážmu/ 'our, your (DAT SG M/N)', *nesme, kupme* = /nezme, kubme/ 'carry, buy (1 PL IMP)', and sometimes does not: *lesmi, vlakmi* 'forest, train (INST PL)', pronounced as written.

Regressive voice assimilation before vowels: *s otcom* = /zotsom/ 'with father'; *vlak ide* = /vlagiďe/ 'train's coming'; with prepositions *s* and *k* vocalized (that is *so, ku*), assimilation occurs in all circumstances: *ku koňu* = /gukoňu/ 'towards horse'; *so sestrou* = /zosestrou/ 'with sister'.

/v/–/f/ are an imperfect voiced–voiceless pair: while /v/ › [f] before a voiceless consonant (*vtip* = /fťip/ 'joke'), /v/ › [w] after a vowel (or equivalent), hence *pravda, krvný, polievka* = [prawda, krwni:, poliewka]; before unpaired voiced consonants there is free variation: *slávny* = [sla:wni] or [sla:vni]. This is all in part due to the historically peripheral nature of /f/ – once confined to loans and onomatopoeia, and to the late development of /v/ ‹ /w/.

Asymmetry also affects /h/ and /ch/: /h/ is devoiced before a voiceless consonant (*vrah pil* = /vrachpil/ 'murderer drank'), while if /ch/ occurs before a voiced consonant it voices to [ɣ] (*vzduch bol* = [vzduɣbol] 'air was'). Native /h/ arose from /g/, but a few items resisted the change, notably after /z/ (*miazga* 'sap'), and in onomatopoeia (*cengať* 'jangle'). For an appraisal of the phonological system with special regard to assimilation and neutralization see Sabol (1984).

Other factors: /l/ and /r/ can be syllabic and are fully integrated into patterns of syllable quantity and morpheme alternation, for example, *dlhý* 'long', *dĺžka* 'length'; *vrch* 'hill', *vŕšiť* 'pile up'.

The letters *q, w, x*, pronounced [kv], [v], and [ks] or [gz] occur only in loans, but are integrated into the above patterns of assimilation, for example, *prax* = /praks/, but *prax a teória* = /pragzateória/ 'practice and theory'.

Of the letters with diacritics, only *č, ô, š* and *ž* are subject to special alphabetical ordering, after *c, o, s* and *z*; *ch* follows *h*.

We shall now consider the most interesting factors in the history of the Slovak phonological system. The metathesis of liquids produced reflexes identical, *mutatis mutandis*, to those of Czech; hence for C*o*rC *hrad* 'castle', C*o*lC *hlas* 'voice', C*e*rC *breh* 'bank', C*e*lC *mlieko* (where C is any consonant). However, Central-Slovak developments differed from those in the west, hence many syllable-quantity contrasts between standard Slovak and both Czech and the West-Slovak dialects, for example, *vrana* 'crow' (Czech *vrána*), *slama* 'straw' (*sláma*), *breza* 'birch' (*bříza*) and others with short syllables for the old acute. In initial *or*C, *ol*C groups the Slovak reflexes, whatever the original intonation, are *ra*C, *la*C, for example, *rakyta* 'sallow', *lakeť* 'elbow', *lákať* 'lure', *ramä* 'shoulder'; many common exceptions (*robiť* 'do', *rozprávať* 'talk', *rovný* 'level') still await explanation.

Slovak has lost both **nasal vowels**. Original *ǫ* › *u*, hence *ruka* 'hand', *nesú* 'they carry', *dušu* 'soul (ACC SG)'; by contrast *ę* › *ä*, which has survived post-labially (but see the earlier discussion of vowels): *hovädo* 'beast', *päť* 'five', *žriebä* 'foal'; elsewhere *ę* › *a* in short syllables, *ia* in long: *často* 'often', *jazyk* 'tongue'; *chodia* 'they walk', *piaty* 'fifth'.

The *jers* were lost in general accordance with Havlík's rule: *dьnьsь* › *dnes* 'today', *sъbьrati* › *zobrať* 'take', *vъ tьme* › *vo tme* 'in the dark', *vъ pętъkъ* › *v piatok* 'on Friday'. A striking feature is the variety of reflexes for the strong *jer*: while *e* predominates for *ь*, there is also *a* (*ľan* 'flax'), *á* (*chrbát* 'back') and *o* (*ovos* 'oats'), and while *o* predominates for *ъ*, there is also *e* (*sen* 'dream'), *a* (*daska* 'board', also *doska*) and *á* (*dážď* 'rain'). Several explanations are offered for this, of which perhaps the most persuasive is regional variation within the central dialects.

The original distribution of lost and vocalized *jers*, that is Ø and *e*/*o*/*a* respectively, has been altered by later developments. The main trend has been towards morpheme consistency, hence *sъbьrati*/*sъberu* › *sebrati*/*sberu* › Modern Slovak *zobrať*/*zoberiem* ('take (INF/1 SG)'), a process most conspicuous in noun stems: the nominative form *domček* (‹ *domъčьkъ*) replaces the oblique stem *domeček-* (‹ *domъčьk-*) to overcome the alternation in strong and weak *jers* which the forms represent, hence modern *domček* (NOM), *domčeka* (GEN) 'little house'. Some monosyllables preserve the alternation (*pes*/*psa* 'dog', *deň*/*dňa* 'day'), others do not (*lev*/*leva* 'lion', *ľan*/*ľanu* 'flax'). Another innovation are the fill vowels in other clusters that arose after the loss of the weak *jers*. Here too there is great variety in the vowels so functioning, most striking in genitive plurals, for example, *poviedok* 'stories', *okien* 'windows', *vojen* 'wars', *sestier*/*sestár* 'sisters', *kvapiek*/*kvapák*/*kvapôk* 'drops' (currently, *-ie-* is preferred here, even in contravention of the rhythmical law (see below), for example, *čísel*/*čísiel* 'numbers'), and in vocalized non-syllabic prepositions, for example, *so synom* 'with his son', *ku mne* 'to me'. Other examples of fill vowels: *vietor* 'wind', *cukor* 'sugar', *viedol* 'he led', *pohol* 'he moved', *zmysel* 'sense', *myseľ* 'mind'.

Proto-Slavonic 'syllabic' liquids, that is, those accompanied by a *jer*-like element in the sequences *CъrC*, *CъlC*, *CьrC* and *CьlC*: in Central and standard Slovak that element has disappeared, the liquid consonants themselves becoming fully syllabic, and either long or short: *smrť* 'death', *mŕtvy* 'dead'. Another point here is the random development of items with *čr*C-, *žr*C-, for example, *čierny* 'black', *žarnov* 'grindstone', or unaltered *žrď* 'mast', and *červík* 'maggot', dialectal *črviak*.

Prosodic phenomena: standard Slovak has fixed stress on the first syllable. A preceding preposition, especially if monosyllabic and ending in a vowel, attracts the stress, hence ¹*kôň* 'horse', but ¹*na koni* 'on horseback'. Several stressless word categories, chiefly the past auxiliary, atonic personal pronouns and some particles, are enclitic, and have fixed positions in the clause (see 4.1).

Slovak has no **tones**, but former tones have affected the distribution of long and short syllables. Suffice it here to note: (a) in syllables before a weak final *jer* in the genitive plural a circumflex metatonized to a new acute, marked now by a long syllable: *rúk* 'hands', *hláv* 'heads', a pattern since generalized to all nouns of the class, hence *síl* (‹ **síl*) 'forces', *briez* (‹ **brez*) 'birches'; (b) other originally circumflex syllables became (usually) short: *dub* 'oak', *vlas* 'hair'; (c) original acute syllables also usually shortened: *krava* 'cow' and so on (see the metathesis of liquids above); (d) new acute syllables usually lengthened, that is, not only in the cases under (a) above: *stôl* 'table', *rúčka* 'hand (DIMIN)', *niesol, nesieš* 'carry (PAST, 3 SG)', *koniec* 'end'.

The most striking feature in standard Slovak and the central dialects is the **law of rhythmical shortening**, which states that quantity is neutralized in a morphophonemically long syllable after a preceding long syllable. Hence such instances as *krásny* 'beautiful', but regular *pekný* 'nice' (adjectival endings are long), *trávam* 'grasses', but *ženám* 'women (DAT PL)', *miesta* 'places', but *mestá* 'towns (NOM PL N)', *chválim* 'praise', but *myslím* 'think (1 SG)'. Significantly, it also accounts for the final short syllable in *čítavam* 'read (1 SG FREQ)', since while the preceding *a* is short, it is in a morphophonemically long syllable, shortened after the first syllable – compare *volávam* 'call'. In a few inflectionally and derivationally specifiable cases the rhythmical law is 'broken', owing to different patterns of tension between phonological and morphological processes. The main types are *chvália* 'praise (3 PL *i*-theme)', *čísiel* 'numbers (preferred GEN PL)', *páví* 'peacock's' (adjectives from animal names), *tisícnásobný* 'thousandfold' (composition), and others.

2.2   Morphophonemic alternations inherited from Proto-Slavonic

Effects of the first palatalization of velars survive in derivation: *k* › *č* (*žiak* 'pupil', diminutive *žiačik*), (*g* ›) *h* › *ž* (*noha, nožička* 'leg'), *ch* › *š* (*orech* › *oriešok* 'nut') and in minor conjugational patterns (*piekol/pečie* 'baked/ bakes'; *luhať/luže* 'lie/s'; *páchať/páše* 'commit/s'). Of the second palatalization, *k* › *c* survives mainly in the nominative plural of animate nouns (*vojak/vojaci* 'soldier/s'); *ch* › *s* is of low incidence (*valach* › *valasi* 'shepherd/s'), while *h* › *z* has been eliminated. The paucity of such alternations is due to a strong trend towards morphemic consistency. The sole effect of the third palatalization is its interaction with the first in the alternation *c/č*, regular in nouns with the suffix *-ec* and their derivates, sporadic elsewhere: *chlapec/chlapček* 'boy (and DIMIN)'; *ovca* ‹ **ovьka, ovčí* 'sheep, ovine'.

As a product of *kt/gt* + front vowel, and of *t + j, c* also alternates with *č* in, for example, *noc/nočni* 'night/nocturnal', *piecť/pečie* 'bake/s', *svieca/ sviečka* 'candle (and DIMIN)'.

Products of other ancient alternations (the spelling conventions as laid out on page 535 should be borne in mind):

t/c (‹ *tj*) *trestať/tresce* 'punish/es';
ť/c (‹ *tj*) *vrátiť/vracať* 'return (PRFV/IMPFV)';
ď/dz (‹ *dj*) *hodiť/hádzať* 'throw (PRFV/IMPFV)'; *hádže* (*dž* ‹ *dzj*) (3 SG);
s/š (‹ *sj*) *písať/píše* 'write/s'; *z/ž* (‹ *zj*) *mazať/maže* 'smear/s';
sl/šľ (‹ *slj*) *poslať/pošle* 'send/will send'; *sľ/šľ myslieť/myšlienka* 'think/ idea'.

In addition to these limited alternations there are numerous regular morphological and derivational environments in which members of the opposition '−/+ palatal' occur with *t/ť, d/ď, n/ň, l/ľ*: *Slovan/Slovania* 'Slav (NOM SG/PL M)'; *hrad/hrade* 'castle (NOM/LOC SG M)'; *mesto/meste* 'town (NOM/LOC SG N)'; *žena/žene* 'woman (NOM/DAT–LOC SG F)'; *dievčatá/dievčaťa* 'girl (NOM PL/GEN SG N)'; *šelma/šeliem* 'beast-of-prey (NOM SG/GEN PL F)'; *sokol/sokolik* 'falcon (NOM SG/DIMIN)'; and others.

Vocalic alternations: irregular alternations survive from ancient patterns of vowel gradation, for example, *nesie/niesť/nosiť/-nášať* 'carry (3 SG/DET INF/INDET INF/secondary IMPFV INF)', *kvet/kvitnúť* 'flower' (noun/verb), including cases of V/Ø: *berie/brať* 'take (3 SG/INF)' and others resulting from the loss of the *jers*, and from the fate of the front nasal:

e/Ø pes/psa 'dog';
á/Ø chrbát/chrbta 'back (NOM/GEN SG)';
o/Ø niesol/niesla 'carried (M/F)';
ie/Ø svetiel/svetlo 'light (GEN PL/NOM SG)';
ä/ia päť/piaty 'five/fifth'.

Quantitative oppositions stem chiefly from the loss of tones and some regular patterns in morphology, especially feminine and neuter genitive plurals as against the prevailing stem form (see 3.1.2). Other non-systematic alternations include such types as *stôl/stola* 'table (NOM/GEN SG)', *hviezda* 'star', *hvezdár* 'astronomer', *kúriť* 'heat', *kurič* 'stoker', and in diminutive formation: *hlas/hlások* 'voice'.

2.3 Morphophonemic alternations resulting from changes after Proto-Slavonic

Dissimilation of *šč* (that is, [štš] ‹ *sk* or *st+j* or front vowel) to *šť* has produced the following alternations:

sk/šť poľský/poľština 'Polish' (adjective/noun); *nebeský/nebešťan*
'heavenly/heavenly being';
st/šť mesto/mešťan 'town/burgher'.

More systematic is *sk/č* in the formation of nouns denoting languages:
latinský/latinčina 'Latin', *slovenský/slovenčina* 'Slovak'; compare
nemecký/nemčina 'German', but contrast *anglický/angličtina* 'English'.

The main development in the vowels has been the displacement for most
speakers of *ä* by *e*, producing an alternation *e/ia*: *päť* = [peť] 'five', *piaty*
'fifth'.

3   Morphology

3.1   Nominal morphology

In addition to the eventual merging of the *o*- and *u*-stems and considerable
attrition among minor paradigms, noun declension is marked by relatively
strong assertion of the gender principle (see masculine *a*-stems) and the
parallel sets brought about by the rhythmical law (see 2.1). Another feature
is the extent to which alternating stem forms have been eliminated in
favour of ᴎorphemic consistency. By contrast, there is considerable
morphological variety in numerous sub- and sub-subclasses, especially in
the nouns.

3.1.1   Nominal categories

The **number** category has two members only, singular and plural; there are
isolated traces of the dual in forms of *dva* 'two' and *oba* 'both'.

The **case** system has shrunk from seven members to six, the vocative
being replaced by the nominative. Some vocative forms survive, but are not
considered part of their respective paradigms. They occur in addressing
kin, close friends, the deity and high dignitaries and are essentially
formulaic, whether familiar, jocular or formal.

The three **genders** are well represented in several main paradigms each.
The subcategory of **animacy** operates within the masculine only. In general
terms, any animate noun in the accusative singular shares the form of the
genitive (but inanimate accusative and nominative are identical), and there
are distinctive forms for *human* animate nominative plural and accusative–
genitive plural (shared by just three or four animal names); inanimates and
most animal names have nominative plural and accusative plural identical
and different from the genitive plural. In all these instances animacy is
expressed secondarily in adjective agreement.

3.1.2   Noun morphology

We shall first consider the **main declensional types**. The hard masculine
declension (table 10.2) unites all former *o*- and *u*-stems, with a systematic

Table 10.2   'Hard' masculine former *o*- and *u*-stems

| | AN | | INAN | |
	SG	PL	SG	PL
NOM	chlap 'fellow'	chlapi	⎰dub 'oak'	duby⎱
ACC	chlapa⎱	⎰chlapov	⎱dub	duby⎰
GEN	chlapa⎰	⎱chlapov	duba	dubov
DAT	chlapovi	chlapom	dubu	dubom
INST	chlapom	chlapmi	dubom	dubmi
LOC	chlapovi	chlapoch	dube	duboch

redistribution of the two sets of available endings. The main factors are: (a) universalization of the *u*-declension dative singular marker *-ovi* for animate dative and locative, leaving the *o*-stem ending *-u* for inanimates; (b) the *o*-stem nominative plural ending *-i* reserved for human animates; a version of the *u*-stem ending, *-ovia*, occurring with some clearly defined subclasses (nouns in final *-ček*, *-čik*, *-h*, *-g*: *chlapčekovia* 'boys', *vrahovia* 'murderers', *filológovia* 'philologists', hence the disappearance of the alternation *g/h* > *z* which *-i* would induce, though analogous *k* > *c* and *ch* > *s* occur (see 2.2); some monosyllables also have *-ovia*: *členovia* 'members', *synovia* 'sons'); a third nominative plural animate ending is *-ia* (originally a singular collective marker as in *bratia* 'brothers', now also replacing *-é* in the consonantal declension), occurring with nouns in *-(č)an* and some isolates: *občania* 'citizens', *hostia* 'guests'); (c) *u*-stem locative ending *-u* for inanimate velar stems (*rohu* 'corner') as opposed to the preferred *o*-stem ending *-e*; (d) a loose distribution of the *o*- and *u*-stem genitive endings, *-a* and *-u*, between concrete and abstract nouns respectively (only native-speaker intuition or the dictionary can resolve the countless exceptions). A major innovation is the adoption of *i*- or *a*-stem instrumental plural endings; the former, *-mi*, is used after single stem-final consonants except *-m*, the latter, *-ami*, after *-m* or consonantal clusters (*domami* 'houses', *mostami* 'bridges'). A large subclass of mostly borrowed nouns with final *-r* and *-l* has *-i* in the locative singular and *-e* in the nominative–accusative plural (*mieri* 'peace', *hoteli/-e*, *revolveri/-e*); this irregularity is partly dependent on history (soft-declension endings surviving after depalatal-ization of the consonants), partly on the nature of the preceding vowel and partly on the native versus foreign origins of individual items. The nouns *raz* and *čas* show a rare survival of the *o*-stem genitive plural: *päť ráz* 'five times', *od tých čias* 'since those times'.

In the corresponding soft declension (table 10.3) the lack of the Czech umlauts and the strength of the animacy principle means that Slovak has no hard/soft split in the animates; in the inanimates the only difference is in the locative singular and nominative–accusative plural (in *-i* and *-e* respec-

Table 10.3   'Soft' masculines (former *jo*-stems)

	AN		INAN	
	SG	PL	SG	PL
NOM	muž 'man'	muži	⌠ stroj 'machine'	stroje ⌉
ACC	muža ⌉	mužov ⌉	⌡ stroj	stroje ⌡
GEN	muža ⌡	mužov ⌡	stroja	strojov
DAT	mužovi	mužom	stroju	strojom
INST	mužom	mužmi	strojom	strojmi
LOC	mužovi	mužoch	stroji	strojoch

tively). The main deviations are animates in *-teľ* with nominative plural in *-ia* (*učitelia* 'teachers'), a few abstract or mass nouns with genitive in *-u* (*čaj-u* 'tea', *bôľ-u* 'grief'), and some anomalous genitive plurals in nouns originally from other classes (*ľudia-ľudí* 'people', *kôň-koní* 'horse', *peniaze-peňazí* 'money', *deň-dni* 'day').

Neuter *o*-stems (table 10.4) are conservative in the singular. The endings in the *ъjo*-stem variant are the main source for occurrences of the three 'soft' diphthongs. In the plural of *o*- and *jo*-stems a crucial innovation is the penetration of oblique-case *a*-stem endings, the effects of which include transfer of length to the original *o*-stem nominative–accusative form. Where the rhythmical law applies, length is lost from all endings, for example, *číslo*, plural *čísla*, dative plural *číslam* and so on. As with masculine velar stems, the original *u*-stem locative ending is used; *mlieko-mlieku* 'milk', *sucho-suchu* 'dry(ness)'; it also appears in loans ending in *-Vum*: *múzeum-múzeu*, *individuum-individuu* (with paradigmatic alternation of Latin and native case morphemes). These loans, like a few native *jo*-stems, also have a divergent genitive plural in *-í*: *múzeí, more-morí* 'sea', *pole-polí* 'field'. The genitive plural is itself the most striking feature of this class, with the dominant ending *-Ø*, accompanied by lengthening of the stem-final syllable, whether in disyllables, as in table 10.4, even those containing a liquid (*zrno-zŕn* 'grain'), polysyllables (*kladivo-kladív* 'hammer', *letisko-letísk* 'airport', *jablko-jabĺk* 'apple'), or loans (*auto-áut* 'car'), but not where the crucial vowel is *-e* or *-o-* (*kvinteto-kvintet, konto-kont* 'account'). Lengthening is inhibited by length in the penultimate syllable of the genitive plural, in accordance with the rhythmical law: *zámeno-zámen* 'pronoun'. The principle of syllable lengthening before *-Ø* extends to the fill vowel, unless inhibited by a previous long syllable: *jadro-jadier* 'nucleus', but *drievko-drievok* 'bit of wood'; the preferred fill vowel is *-ie-*, occurring often in defiance of the rhythmical law, hence *číslo-čísel* or *čísiel* 'number'.

The feminine *a*- and *ja*-stems (table 10.5) are highly conservative and differ only in the dative and locative singular and nominative–accusative plural. Like the neuters, the *a*-stems also have lengthening in a syllable

Table 10.4   *o*-stems neuter

	o-stems	*jo*-stems	*ьjo*-stems
SG			
NOM	mesto 'town'	srdce 'heart'	poučenie 'instruction'
ACC	mesto	srdce	poučenie
GEN	mesta	srdca	poučenia
DAT	mestu	srdcu	poučeniu
INST	mestom	srdcom	poučením
LOC	meste	srdci	poučení
PL			
NOM	mestá	srdcia	poučenia
ACC	mestá	srdcia	poučenia
GEN	miest	sŕdc	poučení
DAT	mestám	srdciam	poučeniam
INST	mestami	srdcami	poučeniami
LOC	mestách	srdciach	poučeniach

Table 10.5   *a*-stems

	SG	PL	SG	PL
Hard	**F**		**M**	
NOM	žena	ženy 'woman'	sluha	sluhovia 'servant'
ACC	ženu	ženy	sluhu	sluhov
GEN	ženy	žien	sluhu	sluhov
DAT	žene	ženám	sluhovi	sluhom
INST	ženou	ženami	sluhom	sluhami
LOC	žene	ženách	sluhovi	sluhoch
Soft	*ja*-stems F		*ьja*-stems (one item only) F	
NOM	ulica	ulice 'street'	pani	panie 'lady, Mrs'
ACC	ulicu	ulice	paniu	panie
GEN	ulice	ulíc, duší*	panej	paní
DAT	ulici	uliciam	panej	paniam
INST	ulicou	ulicami	paňou	paniami
LOC	ulici	uliciach	panej	paniach

Note: *duši* (*duša* 'soul') represents the largish subclass with genitive plural in -*i*; they mostly end in -*ľa*, -*ča*, -*ňa*, -*ša*, though many with these same finals are regular.

before -Ø in the genitive plural: it may take the form of a diphthong (*stopa–stôp* 'trace', *žaba–žiab* 'frog'), it applies even to syllables with a liquid (*vlna–vĺn* 'wave'), and it is inhibited by length in the penultimate (*záhrada–záhrad* 'garden'). Also as with the neuters, a fill vowel will be long unless inhibited by a preceding long syllable (*hra–hier* 'game', *látka–*

látok 'material'); again, *-ie-* is increasingly preferred, irrespective of the rhythmical law (*výhra–výher/výhier* 'win'). The range of fill vowels is wide and can lead to much free variation (*kvapka–kvapôk/kvapiek/kvapák* 'drop'). Lengthening does not occur in many polysyllables with *-o-* in the penultimate (*budova–budov* 'building', *potvora-potvor* 'monster'), after *-j* (*spojka–spojok* 'conjunction', *vojna–vojen* 'war'), and in most borrowings with *-e-* or *-o-* in the critical syllable (*konzerva–konzerv* 'tin (of food)', *anekdota–anekdot*). The isolated ьja-stem noun *pani* 'lady' shares, in the singular oblique cases and nominative–accusative plural, forms of the soft adjectival declension, and its other plural forms with a variant soft declension (the *dlaň* 'palm' paradigm in Slovak grammars), except in the instrumental plural (*dlaňami*, but *paniami*); *pani* is uninflected in juxtaposition with another noun (*pani doktorka*, dative *pani doktorke 'Frau Doktorin'*). The *dlaň* type behaves generally like the *ja*-stems, but resembles *kosť* (table 10.6) in lacking a case marker in the nominative and accusative singular and in having *-i* in the genitive plural. There are many nouns that are hybrids between *dlaň* and *kosť*, though the set of items involved differs from the similar set in Czech.

Masculine *a*-stems are conspicuous for four features: (a) there is no difference between hard- and soft-stem versions of the class, hence *sudca* 'judge' declines exactly like *sluha* 'servant'; (b) the gender principle has overruled the theme-vowel principle almost completely, hence the many forms shared with the *o*-stems, except that (c) the animacy principle whereby accusative singular = genitive is inverted, the genitive having adopted the accusative form; (d) the declension is shared by native surnames ending in *-o* (*Botto*, genitive *Bottu*); non-native surnames in *-o* and native forenames and hypocoristics decline as *o*-stems (*Hugo*, genitive *Huga*, *Janko–Janka*, *ujo–uja* 'uncle'), a pattern now spreading as a progressive variant to native surnames (genitive *Botta*). A masculine *a*-stem subclass containing the suffixes *-ista*, *-ita* has nominative plurals in *-i*: *huslista–huslisti* 'violinist', *bandita–banditi*.

A minor feminine class has long adjectival endings in the singular and nominative–accusative plural and forms like *žena* in the plural oblique cases; it includes *gazdiná* 'mistress, farmer's wife', *švagriná* 'sister-in-law' and *kráľovná* 'queen'.

The *i*-declension (table 10.6) is well preserved in the singular, but has shifted in the plural towards other soft feminine types. Increasingly, it is the preserve of abstracts in *-osť*, but still contains several dozen other common items (*nemoc* 'sickness', *hus* 'goose'), including former ъv-stems (*krv–krvi* 'blood', *cirkev–cirkvi* 'church').

With one exception, Slovak preserves little trace of the **consonantal stems**, most types having switched to the central declensions: *kameň* 'stone' and others have joined *stroj*; *kresťan* 'Christian' and others formerly with the infix *-in-* now follow *chlap*, while agent nouns in *-teľ*

Table 10.6   *i*-stems

	SG	PL
NOM	kosť 'bone'	kosti
ACC	kosť	kosti
GEN	kosti	kostí
DAT	kosti	kostiam
INST	kosťou	kosťami
LOC	kosti	kostiach

follow *muž* (nominative plural in both types is in *-ia*). Feminine *mať* 'mother' has largely been replaced by *matka*, a regular *a*-stem, though the consonantal-stem declension survives with the stem *mater-* (also as back-formed nominative); feminine *ъv*-stems contain the thematic consonant in back-formed nominatives (see above), though there has been some inter-action with hard feminines in *-va*. Neuters: all the *n*-stems have passed in the extended-stem version to the hard *o*-stems (*bremeno–bremena* 'burden'), though short nominative–accusative forms (*bremä, semä* 'seed', etc.) survive as obsolescent high-style variants; *s*-stems have passed to the *o*-stems, with some neologizing separate lexicalization of alternative stems, shared with Czech (*slovo* 'word', *sloveso* 'verb'); only *nebo* 'heaven' retains the consonantal suffix, as the basis of its plural stem *nebes-*, which then has two declensions: like *srdce* (*nebesia* etc.) or, less often, like *mesto* (*nebesá* etc.). The great survivor among the consonantal types is the *nt*-class (table 10.7), which retains the consonantal suffix, as *-ať-* in the singular, *-at-* in the plural, and declines like *srdce* and *mestá* respectively. An alternative plural, with mostly soft masculine endings, is available with items denoting young living creatures. Non-living entities in the class include *dúpä* 'lair', *púpä* 'bud'; the main non-juvenile is *knieža* (M) 'prince'. Three items denoting animals (*prasa* 'pig', *teľa* 'calf', *šteňa* 'puppy') have short forms of the alternative plural, without the suffix *-en-*, hence *prase*, genitive singular *prasaťa*, nominative plural *prasatá/prasce*, genitive plural *prasiat/prasiec*.

Table 10.7   Neuter *nt*-stems (now *ť/t*-stems)

	SG	PL1	PL2
NOM	jahňa 'lamb'	jahňatá	jahnence
ACC	jahňa	jahňatá	jahnence
GEN	jahňaťa	jahňiat	jahneniec
DAT	jahňaťu	jahňatám	jahnencom
INST	jahňaťom	jahňatami	jahnencami
LOC	jahňati	jahňatách	jahnencoch

3.1.3   Pronominal morphology

Of the **genderless personal pronouns** (table 10.8) *ty* is familiar singular and *vy* polite singular or plural. The unstressed forms *ma, ťa, sa, mi, ti, si* are enclitic; at points in the table where no alternatives are indicated, the sole form may be enclitic or not according to functional sentence perspective. Prepositions may govern only non-enclitic forms. The stressed–unstressed opposition also applies in the nominative, in which the unstressed version is represented by zero, person being adequately expressed by the verb.

The third-person pronouns are fully marked for gender in the singular and partly so in the plural (table 10.9). Their declension exhibits several peculiarities: (a) the forms *ho* and *mu* are enclitic and contrast with *jeho* and *jemu*; other non-nominative forms, except those with a hyphen, may occur in enclitic or non-enclitic positions according to function; (b) after prepositions all third-person pronouns attract initial *n-*; the locative forms and the accusative plural *ne* occur only after prepositions; instrumental forms have initial *n-* in all functions; (c) the hyphenated forms occur only after prepositions, with which they are written as one word (*doň, doňho* 'into it', *zaň* 'for/behind it/him', *uňho* 'at his house', etc.); original accusative or genitive forms are used indiscriminately here.

Table 10.8   Genderless pronouns

NOM	ja 'I'	ty 'you (SG)'	(REFL)	my 'we'	vy 'you (PL)'
ACC	mňa/ma	teba/ťa	seba/sa	nás	vás
GEN	mňa/ma	teba/ťa	seba/sa	nás	vás
DAT	mne/mi	tebe/ti	sebe/si	nám	vám
INST	mnou	tebou	sebou	nami	vami
LOC	mne	tebe	sebe	nás	vás

Table 10.9   Third-person pronouns

| | SG | | | PL | |
	M	N	F	M AN	*Other*
NOM	on	ono	ona	oni	ony
ACC	¹jeho/²ho/-ň/¹-ňho	ho/-ň	ju	ich	ich/ne
GEN	¹jeho/ho/-ň/-ňho		jej	ich	
DAT	¹jemu/²mu		jej	im	
INST	ním		ňou	nimi	
LOC	ňom		nej	nich	

Notes: ¹animate stressed forms; ² inanimates use only these enclitic forms; if emphatic forms are required, these are generally taken from the demonstrative pronoun.

Demonstrative *ten* and possessive *náš* (table 10.10) represent other pronominal declensions. In its plural oblique cases and in the feminine singular *ten* overlaps with the adjectival declensions, and its declension is shared by *tento* 'this', *tamten* (and colloquial *henten*) 'that' and *tenže* 'the same' (the morphemes *-to, tam-, hen-* and *-že* remain constant), *kto* 'who' and *čo* 'what'. As with other non-substantival types the *t-* is not palatalized by any front-vowel case morphemes (hence, for example, nominative plural masculine animate [ti:]). The *náš* paradigm is shared by other possessives (*môj/moja/moje/moji* 'my', *tvoj* 'thy', *svoj* (REFL), *váš* 'your'), with long syllables in the same distribution, except in *tvoj* and *svoj*. Possessive *jeho* 'his', *jej* 'her' and *ich* 'their' are not declined.

Other pronouns: *sám/sama/samo/sami* '-self, the very' shares the mixed pronominal-adjectival declension of *jeden* (given in table 10.15 below); similarly *všetok/všetka/všetko/všetci*(!)/ *všetky* 'all'.

Interrogative *kto* and *čo* lie at the heart of a complex set of indefinite pronouns and pronoun–adverbs. Table 10.11 lists those that may claim reasonable frequency in the system of reference, co-reference, quantification, etc. The rows are based on interrogatives, the columns on the many modifying prefixes and suffixes: *kto* 'who', *čo* 'what', *či* 'whose', *kedy* 'when', *kde* 'where', *kam* 'whither' (a series increasingly replaced by the *kde* set), *odk(ad)iaľ, skadiaľ, odkade, skade* all 'whence', *kade* 'which way', *ako* 'how', *koľko* 'how much/many', *ktorý* 'which', *aký* 'what kind', *koľkoraký* 'how many kinds of', *koľký* 'how much/many/big' (see 4.10);

Table 10.10 The demonstrative pronoun *ten* ‹ **tъ*, and possessive pronoun *náš* 'our'

	M	N	F	M	N	F
SG						
OM	ten	to	tá	náš	naše	naša
ACC	ten/toho*	to	tú	náš/nášho*	naše	našu
GEN	toho		tej	nášho		našej
DAT	tomu		tej	nášmu		našej
INST	tým		tou	naším		našou
LOC	tom		tej	našom		našej
PL						
NOM	tí*/tie	tie		naši*/naše	naše	
ACC	tých*/tie	tie		našich*/naše	naše	
GEN	tých			našich		
DAT	tým			našim		
INST	tými			našimi		
LOC	tých			našich		

Note: * Following words indicates animate forms only.

Table 10.11

	nie-	voľa-	da-	-si	hoc(i)-	-koľvek	bár(s)-
kto	niekto	voľakto	dakto	ktosi	hoc(i)kto	ktotoľvek	bár(s)kto
čo	niečo	voľačo	dačo	čosi	hoc(i)čo	čokoľvek	bár(s)čo
čí	niečí	voľačí	dačí	čísi	hocičí	číkoľvek	bár(s)čí
kedy	niekedy	voľakedy	dakedy	kedysi	hoc(i)kedy	kedykoľvek	bár(s)kedy
kde	niekde	voľakde	dakde	kdesi	hoc(i)kde	kdekoľvek	bár(s)kde
kam/KDE	niekam/ -KDE	voľaKDE	daKDE	KDE-/kamsi	hocikam/ -KDE	kamkoľvek/ KDE-	bár(s)kam
odk(ad)iaľ	odniek(ad)iaľ			odkiaľsi		odkiaľkoľvek	
skadiaľ	zniekadiaľ						
odkade	odniekade						
skade	zniekade		zdakade				
kadiaľ						kadiaľkoľvek	
kade	niekade	voľakade	dakade	kadesi	hoc(i)kade	kadekoľvek/ KAM-	bár(s)kade
ako	NEJako	voľaJako/ voľáko	daJako/ dáko	akosi	hoc(iJ)ako	akokoľvek	bár(s)ako
koľko	niekoľko	voľakoľko	dakoľko	koľkosi	hoc(i)koľko		bár(s)koľko
ktorý	niektorý	voľaktorý	daktorý	ktorýsi	hoc(i)ktorý	ktorýkoľvek	bár(s)ktorý
aký	NEJaký	voľaJaký/ voľáky	daJaký/ dáky	akýsi	hoc(iJ)aký	akýkoľvek	bár(s)aký
koľkoraký	niekoľkoraký						
koľký	niekoľký				hoc(i)koľký		

nie-, voľa-, da- 'some-', *-si* 'some- or other', *hoc(i)-, -koľvek, bar(s)-voľa-*, 'any-; -ever', *poda-* 'some (DISTR)', *kade-, kde-, leda-* 'many a, all kinds of, sundry', *ni-* 'no-', *in(o)-* 'other, else', *všeli-* 'all manner of' (usually pejorative), *vš-* 'all, every-'. It is particularly difficult to specify exact English meanings of the various morphemes concerned since there is some overlapping (compare *voľa-*), much interference between sets denoting place, goal and direction, much idiolectal squabbling among native speakers on the relative stylistic markedness of quasi-synonyms (for example, between *nie-* and *da-*) and some genuine stylistic constraints.

3.1.4 Adjectival morphology

The three basic adjectival declensions are 'hard', 'soft' and possessive, a hybrid with elements of several non-substantival paradigms. The hard and soft types are historically 'long', but the long endings of many items shorten in consequence of the rhythmical law. Few true short (predicative) adjectives survive, except for *rád* (feminine *rada*, neuter *rado*, masculine animate plural *radi*, other plural *rady*) 'glad' and obsolescent *dlžen* (from *dlžný* 'owing'), *hoden* (*hodný* 'worthy') and *vinen* (*vinný* 'guilty').

The hard declension (table 10.12) conceals several systematic exceptions to the orthographic conventions involving dentals and front

poda-	kade-	kde-	leda-	ni-	in(o)-	všeli-	vš-
podakto	kadekto	kdekto	ledakto	nik(to)	NIEKTO inÝ	všelikto	VŠETCI
	kadečo	kdečo	ledačo	nič	NIEČO inÉ	všeličo	VŠETKO
	kadečí						
				nikdy	inokedy		vždycky
	kadekde		KDEKADE	nikde	inde	všelikde	všade
	KADEKDE			nikam/	inam/INDE	všelikam/	VŠADE
				-KDE		-KDE	
				odnikiaľ	odinAkiaľ		
					zinokadiaľ		
				odnikade			
				znikade	zinakade		
		kdekade		nikade	inokade		všade
	kadejako			niJako	inak(SIE)/		
					inÁĆ	všeliJako	
podaktorý		kdektorý		ŽIADEN	inÝ	všeliktorý	VŠETCI
	kadeJaký	kdeJaký	ledaJaký	nijaký/	inakŠÍ	všeliJaký	
				ŽIADEN			

Note: parentheses indicate optional morphemes; small capitals indicate morphological or lexical departures from the form predictable for the given field.

vowels: the feminine endings -*ej* and the masculine animate nominative plural -*i*, for example, *peknej* 'nice', *mladej* 'young' or *pekní, mladí* contain alveo-dental, not palatal, consonants; no change occurs in velar consonants either, hence *drahý, drahej, drahí* 'dear', *veľký, veľkej, veľkí* 'big' (here the trend towards stem-morpheme consistency has overruled palatalization). In rhythmically shortened items, for example, *krásny* 'beautiful', with short vowels throughout the endings, a deficiency of the orthography is seen in such forms as *krásne*, which as [krásne] is adjectival, but as [krásňe] is the adverb.

The 'soft' adjectival declension (table 10.13) is shared by a relatively small number of basic items; its strength lies in derived classes: comparatives and superlatives, adjectives based on the infinitive (*testovací* 'for testing'), on past participles (*porozumevší* 'having understood') and adverbs (*vtedajší* 'the then', ‹ *vtedy*). Present active participles follow the rhythmically shortened version of the paradigm (*volajúci* 'calling', compare *domáci* 'domestic'); if the stem vowel is long, however, the participial suffix does not undergo rhythmical shortening (*píšúci* 'writing'). Adjectives from animal names, while not necessarily having a 'soft' stem-final consonant, follow the soft paradigm and, again, if the stem vowel is long, the ending does not shorten (*páví* 'peacock's').

The possessive declension (table 10.14) is based on the suffix *-ov* for a male human possessor, *-in* for a female, whether expressed by a common noun or proper name. The feminine suffix does not pre-palatalize; nor do front-vowel endings in the declension affect the final *-n* of the feminine suffix, another exception to the spelling-pronunciation rule concerning the sequence *ne* and *ni.*

Table 10.12   'Hard' adjectival declension: *nový* 'new'

		SG			PL	
	M	N	F	M AN	*Other*	
NOM	nový	nové	nová	noví	nové	
ACC	nový/nového*	nové	novú	nových	nové	
GEN		nového		novej		nových
DAT		novému		novej		novým
INST		novým		novou		novými
LOC		novom		novej		nových

Note: * animate form only.

Table 10.13   Soft adjectival declension: *cudzí* 'alien', 'someone else's'

	M	N	F	M AN	*Other*
NOM	cudzí	cudzie	cudzia	cudzí	cudzie
ACC	cudzí/cudzieho*	cudzie	cudziu	cudzích	cudzie
GEN	cudzieho		cudzej		cudzích
DAT	cudziemu		cudzej		cudzím
INST	cudzím		cudzou		cudzími
LOC	cudzom		cudzej		cudzích

Note: * animate form only.

Table 10.14   Declension of possessive adjectives

		SG			PL	
	M	N	F	M AN	*Other*	
NOM	Petrov	Petrovo	Petrova	Petrovi	Petrove	
ACC	Petrov/Petrovho*	Petrovo	Petrovu	Petrových	Petrove	
GEN	Petrovho		Petrovej		Petrových	
DAT	Petrovmu		Petrovej		Petrovým	
INST	Petrovým		Petrovou		Petrovými	
LOC	Petrovom		Petrovej		Petrových	

Note: * animate form only.

The basic suffix in the **comparison of adjectives** is *-ejší* (*bežnejší* 'commoner', *cudzejší* 'more alien'), with *-ší* in several subclasses: (a) nonderived items ending in one stem-final consonant, except sibilants and some items in *-p*, *-m* or *-t* (*novší* 'newer', *bohatší* 'richer', but *krutejší* 'crueller'); (b) adjectives containing the suffixes *-k-*, *-ok-* or *-ek-*, which are deleted before the comparative suffix (*krátky–kratší* 'short–er', *hlboký–hlbší* 'deep-er'); (c) certain suppletive forms (*dobrý–lepší* 'good–better', *veľký–väčší* 'big–ger'). Points to note: pre-palatalization of velars before the basic suffix has been eliminated in favour of morphemic consistency (*mrzký–mrzkejší* 'base–r'), but it remains in the case of alveo-dentals (*hustý–hustejší*, pronounced [husťejší] 'dense–r'); the basic suffix *-ejší* can be attached to fully adjectivalized participles, including the present active (*prekvapujúci–prekvapujúcejší* 'surprising–more surprising').

The **superlative** is formed by prefixing *naj-* to the comparative. A subsidiary, analytical, method of forming comparatives and superlatives is based on the comparative and superlative of *veľa* 'much, very', namely *viac* or *väčšmi* 'more' and *najviac/najväčšmi* 'most' (*najviac vyvinutý* 'most developed' – also *najvyvinutejší*). Analytical forms based on *málo–menej–najmenej* 'little–less–least' are the only possibility for negative comparison. The conjunctions etc. of comparison are: *ako* 'as/like; than'; *než* 'than'; *z* 'from', *medzi* 'among', *spomedzi* 'from among': *starý ako ja* 'as old as I', *starší ako/než ja* 'older than I', *najstarší z/spomedzi nás/medzi nami* 'the oldest of us'.

Adverbs derived from adjectives are marked by largely morphophonologically conditioned suffixes *-e*, *-o*, *-y*. Adjectives in *-ský* form adverbs in *-sky*; for the rest there is considerable variation: *-e* is preferred for adjectives with the suffixes *-ovitý*, *-itý* and *-ný*, while *-o*, increasingly prevalent, is preferred with adjectives ending in *-tý*, *-lý* and velar, sibilant and labial stems. Exceptions abound on both sides and free variation is common.

Comparative and superlative adverbs coincide formally with the neuter singular forms of adjectives (*hustejšie–najhustejšie* 'more–most densely', *prekvapujúcejšie* 'more surprisingly'). Adjectives that have suppletive comparative–superlative forms, and some other minor types, also have distinctive comparative adverbs, for example:

dobre–lepšie–najlepšie 'well–better–best';
zle–horšie–najhoršie 'badly–worse–worst';
ďaleko–ďalej–najďalej 'far–further–furthest';
skoro–skôr/skorej–najskôr/najskorej 'soon–sooner–soonest' (here the shorter comparative and superlative also means 'rather' and 'more/most likely').

3.1.5 Numeral morphology

The numeral '1' (table 10.15) preserves the morphology of gender and case and functions adjectivally. The numeral '2' (table 10.16) retains a distinction between masculine and feminine–neuter in the nominative and accusative only, with the refinement of separate (human) animate masculine forms. The animacy distinction carries over as the sole gender category in '3' and '4', also optionally in '5' and above. In the latter (table 10.17)

Table 10.15   The numeral '1'

	SG			PL	
M	N	F	M AN	*Other*	
NOM	jeden	jedno	jedna	jedni	jedny
ACC	jeden/jedného*	jedno	jednu	jedných	jedny
GEN	jedného		jednej	jedných	
DAT	jednému		jednej	jedným	
INST	jedným		jednou	jednými	
LOC	jednom		jednej	jedných	

Note: * animate form only.

Table 10.16   The numeral '2'

	M AN	M INAN	F/N
NOM	dvaja	dva	dve
ACC	dvoch	dva	dve
GEN		dvoch	
DAT		dvom	
INST		dvoma	
LOC		dvoch	

Table 10.17   The numeral '5'

	M AN	*Other*
NOM	päť/piati*	päť
ACC	päť/piatich*	päť
GEN	piatich	
DAT	piatim	
INST	piatimi	
LOC	piatich	

Note: * optional explicitly animate forms.

Slovak has evolved a fully declining system relatable to the pronominal declensions. Thus all numerals potentially approximate to the status of adjectives.

Additional remarks on tables 10.15–10.17: the plural of '1' is used of each of two or more contrasted groups (*jedni . . . , jedni . . .* 'some . . . others . . .', or of *pluralia tantum*: *jedny nohavice* 'one pair of trousers', *jedny ústa* 'one mouth'. The declension of *dva* is shared by *oba* and *obidva* (*obidvaja, obidve, obidvoch* and so on) 'both', with similar forms of '3' (*traja, tri, troch,* instrumental *troma* or *tromi*) and '4' (masculine animate *štyria,* others *štyri, štyroch, štyrmi*). The forms *dvoma, oboma,* and through them *troma,* and the nominatives *dva, dve* are the sole remnants of the dual number. The declension of *päť* is shared by all numerals up to '99' (table 10.18), but in noun phrases after prepositions these numerals are often left undeclined. In the same circumstances *sto* '100' and the higher hundreds are also undeclined. *Sto* in isolation declines like *mesto*, but has suppletive genitive plural forms, *päť stoviek/stovák*, from the noun *stovka*. Similarly, *tisíc* '1,000' declines like *stroj*, but with variants *tisícami/tisícmi* (INST PL).

Table 10.18   Cardinal numerals

jeden	'1'	trinásť	'13'	šesťdesiat	'60'
dva	'2'	štrnásť	'14'	deväťdesiat	'90'
tri	'3'	pätnásť	'15'	sto	'100'
štyri	'4'	šestnásť	'16'	dvesto	'200'
päť	'5'	sedemnásť	'17'	tristo	'300'
šesť	'6'	osemnásť	'18'	päťsto	'500'
sedem	'7'	devätnásť	'19'	tisíc	'1,000'
osem	'8'	dvadsať	'20'	dvatisíc	'2,000'
deväť	'9'	dvadsaťjeden	'21'	päťtisíc	'5,000'
desať	'10'	tridsať	'30'	milión	'million'
jedenásť	'11'	štyridsať	'40'	dva milióny	'2 million'
dvanásť	'12'	päťdesiat	'50'	päť miliónov	'5 million'
				miliarda	'1000 million'

Table 10.19   Ordinal numerals

prvý	'1st'	jedenásty	'11th'	dvojtisíci	'2,000th'
druhý	'2nd'	pätnásty	'15th'	milióny	'millionth'
tretí	'3rd'	dvadsiaty	'20th'	päťmilióny	'5 millionth'
štvrtý	'4th'	dvadsiaty prvý	'21st'	stomilióny	'100 millionth'
piaty	'5th'	päťdesiaty	'50th'		
šiesty	'6th'	deväťdesiaty	'90th'	nultý ‹ nula	'zero'
siedmy	'7th'	stý	'100th'	n-tý	'n-th'
ôsmy	'8th'	dvojstý	'200th'		
deviaty	'9th'	deväťstý	'900th'		
desiaty	'10th'	tisíci	'1,000th'		

Milión and *miliarda* decline like *hrad* (but genitive singular *-a*) and *žena* respectively.

Ordinal numerals (table 10.18): 'third' and 'thousandth' follow the soft adjectival declension, the latter rhythmically shortened, like many of the hard-stems.

Other numerals: *dvoje, troje* 'two of a kind', etc. for use with *pluralia tantum*, decline like *piati*, that is, *dvojich* etc. *Jednaký, dvojaký, štvoraký* 'of one, two, four etc. kinds', also *mnohoraký* 'multifarious', decline as hard adjectives, as do *dvoj-, troj-, štvornásobný* and so on, 'double', 'triple', 'quadruple', and *viacnásobný* 'multiple'.

3.2   Verbal morphology

3.2.1   Verbal categories

Three **persons** are expressed primarily in inflections and secondarily, for emphasis and in colloquial registers, by insertion of subject pronouns. Third persons are marked by vocalic endings, different in singular and plural. The other persons always carry consistent markers, namely: *-m* (1 SG), *-š* (2 SG) (except for *byť* 'be', which has *si*), *-me* (1 PL), *-te* (2 PL). In the past tense and conditional only first and second persons are marked, on the auxiliaries. **Gender** is marked in all persons *singular* in the past and conditional, in contrast to non-gender-specific plural forms. The respective gender–number morphemes, carried by the *l*-participle, are *-Ø* (M), *-a* (F), *-o* (N), *-i* (PL).

Four **tenses** are recognized, a superficially simple system refined by the normal Slavonic aspects. Present-tense forms of the imperfective are used for all present, including generic, time reference and to express simultaneity in subordinate clauses after 'verbs of saying' and 'verbs of perception'. Futurity (and posteriority in analogous subordinate clauses) is expressed by present-tense forms of the perfective aspect and by the analytical imperfective future, consisting of the future of *byť* as auxiliary and the imperfective infinitive. Past-tense forms of either aspect, based on the *l*-participle, with auxiliaries (present-tense forms of *byť*) in first and second persons only, also express anteriority in subordinate clauses as above, that is, they express part of the range of west-European pluperfects; while not very frequent, the pluperfect, the fourth tense in Slovak, is still used in some contexts and is formed from the *l*-participle with the past tense of *byť* as auxiliary (*bol som prečítal* 'I had read'). Present-tense forms are widely used, even conversationally, in an 'historic present' function, and perfective present forms can also express habitual actions, with or without the support of explicit time expressions. Imminent events, that is, 'close future' in the present (and similar in the past) can be expressed by auxiliary *isť* 'go': *idem sa ženiť* 'I'm going to get married', *išlo mi srdce puknúť* 'my heart was about to burst'.

The normal Slavonic **aspects** survive in the standard imperfective–perfective opposition; the unmarked member is the imperfective. Aspectual pairs are of two main types: (a) the imperfective is formed from the perfective by suffixation, whether the source perfective is a primary verb (a minority pattern), thus *dať* 'give', *kúpiť* 'buy', or a prefixed verb such as *vymyslieť* 'think up' or *rozťať* 'cleave'; several of the individual patterns of suffixation are illustrated by the respective imperfectives of these verbs: *dávať, kupovať, vymýšľať, roztínať*. (b) The perfective member is formed from the imperfective (usually a primary item) by prefixation: *u-variť* 'cook', *na-písať* 'write', *vy-prať* 'wash (garments)'. A prefix which may perfectivize with one verb may be a lexical prefix elsewhere, compare *prať–vyprať* 'wash', but *dediť* 'inherit', *vydediť* 'disinherit'. Two sets of prefixes are used only lexically: (a) those with a concrete, often spatial meaning: *pred-* 'pre-', *nad-* 'super-', *pod-* 'sub-', *v-* 'in', *roz-* 'dis-', which perfectivize: *platiť* 'pay', *podplatiť* 'bribe', secondary imperfective *podplácať*; (b) prefixes containing a long vowel: *závidieť* 'envy', *nenávidieť* 'hate', *súvisieť* 'be connected', which do not perfectivize.

Suppletive aspectual pairings are rare: *brať*/*vziať* 'take', *hovoriť*/*povedať* 'tell', *klásť*/*položiť* 'put' and its compounds like *nakladať*/*naložiť*, 'load' and compounds of *isť* 'go' such as *prichádzať*/*prísť* 'arrive'.

Slovak has numerous *perfectiva tantum*: inchoatives of the type *rozpršať sa* 'start to rain'; verbs denoting an excessive measure of an action: *ubehať sa* 'be run off one's feet', *naplakať sa* 'have cried and cried' (and other prefixed reflexive types); transitive non-reflexives with *na-* with the 'object' in the genitive: *navariť* (*polievky*) 'have made (lots of soup)', *nasekať* (*dreva*) 'have chopped (lots of wood)'; some verbs having, or perhaps having once had, the modality of potentiality: *pristať* 'suit', *vydržať* '(with-) stand', *vmestiť sa* 'fit', *obísť sa* '(can/will have to) do without', *dokázať* 'be capable of, know how'.

Some items belonging semantically to the last-named are among the language's many *imperfectiva tantum*: *vládať* 'be able; can manage', *vedieť* 'know how', and the basic modal verbs: *môcť* 'can', *smieť* 'may', *musieť* 'must', *mať* 'be (supposed) to', *chcieť* 'want, will'. The interesting member of the group is the former perfective *dať sa*, denoting passive potential: *to sa dá*/*bude dať urobiť* 'that can be done', that is, '(he/we etc.) can/will be able to do it'. Frequentatives like *chodievať* 'go fairly regularly', *čítavať* 'read occasionally' are also *imperfectiva tantum*; they are quite widely used.

Few native verbs are bi-aspectual; they include *pomstiť* 'avenge', *počuť* 'hear', *venovať* 'donate, dedicate' and *obetovať* 'dedicate, sacrifice'. The last two, like their perfective close synonym *darovať*, have acquired imperfective counterparts: *venúvať, obetúvať* (*darúvať*). The two aspects of 'reply', with different conjugations (perfective *odpovedám*, perfective *odpoviem*), share the same infinitive, hence dictionaries misleadingly show *odpovedať* as bi-aspectual. Numerous loan-neologisms, all in *-ovať*, are also bi-aspectual.

A subcategory within the imperfective are the **verbs of motion**, which exist in determinate–indeterminate pairs (table 10.20). Original *honiť* has been replaced by a secondary formation *naháňať*. A former member of the group, *jazdiť*, now means 'drive' or 'ride', not simple 'go', and has no determinate partner; vehicles themselves and their passengers usually require *isť/chodiť*.

The determinate members express single, linear, goal-oriented actions, the non-determinates are frequentative and goal-oriented for regularly repeated events, for example, *chodí do školy* 'he goes to school', or lack any goal, as in *chodili sme po meste* 'we walked around the town'. An irregularly repeated event, however, will use the determinate, especially if supported by suitable adverbs: *niekedy ta ideme autom* 'sometimes we go there by car'. A single round trip is expressed using *byť*: *boli sme vlani v Bratislave* 'we went to Bratislava last year'.

The morphology of the determinates exhibits certain peculiarities:

1 The future – imperfective only, or aspectually neutral – is formed either by the prefix *po-*, *pobežim* 'I will run', or in some contexts with *byť* as auxiliary (*budem bežať*); *isť* has only one future paradigm, *pôjdem*.

2 There is only one past-tense form and only one infinitive, for example, *šiel* 'went' and *isť*, that is, there are no *po*-prefixed forms.

3 The imperatives reveal some disparities; for example, *iď* is practically confined to idioms, the everyday 'come–go' opposition being expressed by *poď–choď*. In other members the relations differ: *bež*, *nes* are imperative in any determinate sense, *behaj*, *nos* in indeterminate uses. In negation *isť* uses *nechoď*, while others generally negate either member of the pairs according to (in-)determinacy. On the evi-

Table 10.20   Verbs of motion

Determinate	Indeterminate	
isť	chodiť	'go'
bežať	behať	'run'
letieť	lietať	'fly'
niesť	nosiť	'carry'
viesť	vodiť	'lead'
viezť	voziť	'convey'
vliecť	vláčiť	'drag'
liezť	loziť (colloquial)	'crawl, climb'
hnať	naháňať	'chase, drive'

dence of informants, Slovak actually prefers directionally unambiguous prefixed imperatives (with *do-*, *pri-*, and *od-*) over the primary verbs.

Prefixation of the verbs of motion in Slovak produces perfective verbs from the determinates and imperfectives from the indeterminates, with a second, now dominant set of imperfectives derived from the latter (table 10.21). These pairings are analogous to other aspect pairs. Some gaps on the imperfective side (like *vyvodiť*, *vyvoziť*) cannot now be filled, since these forms have become new lexical perfectives: *vyvodiť* 'deduce' (imperfective *vyvodzovať*), distributive *vyvoziť* 'have conveyed up or out piecemeal' (*vyvoziť sneh z mesta* 'have removed all the snow from the town (by repeated journeys)'). Distributive meanings (*perfectiva tantum*) are more commonly expressed by secondary prefixation, for example, *povyvážať* to *vyvoziť*.

Table 10.21   Prefixed verbs of motion (specimens with *vy-*)

Perfective	*Imperfective*
výjsť	vychodiť, vychádzať
vybehnúť (!)	vybiehať (!), vybehávať, vybehovať, vybehúvať
vyletieť	vylietať, vylietávať, vyletovať, vyletúvať
vyniesť	vynosiť, vynášať
vyviesť	vyvádzať
vyviezť	vyvážať
vyvliecť	vyvliekať
vyliezť	vyliezať
vyhnať	vyháňať

Mood: the **imperative** is expressed morphologically in the second persons and first person plural, and analytically in others. For the morphological imperative the endings are *-∅*, *-me*, *-te* (with palatalization of stem-final *-d*, *-t*, *-n* or *-l*), or *-i*, *-ime*, *-ite*; the choice depends on whether there are one or two stem-final consonants in the third person plural after removal of the final vowel: *ber/-me/-te* 'take', *miň/-me/-te* 'pass', *chváľ/ -me/-te* 'praise', *dávaj/-me/-te* 'give'; *padn-i/-ime/-ite* 'fall', *mysl-i/-ime/ -ite* 'think', *zájd-i/-ime/-ite* 'go, pop in'. Exceptions are few, but note the athematic verbs *jesť* 'eat' and *vedieť* 'know' and their derivates: *jedz/-me/ -te*, *odpovedz/-me/-te* 'reply', and sporadic instances of free variation: *vrešti/vrešť* ‹ *vrešťať* 'shriek'.

The **conditional** is expressed by past-tense forms combined with the conditional particle *by*: *povedal by som, že* ... 'I would say that ...'. This, the unmarked 'present' conditional, may also express past conditionality if accompanied by appropriate adverbs: *včera by neprišiel, ale dnes* ... 'yesterday he wouldn't have come, but today ...'. However, the 'true' past conditional is extremely resilient; it is formed from the present conditional by the addition of the *l*-participle of *byť*: *bol by som povedal* 'I would have said'; it is often reinforced by the redundant addition of the *l*-participle of frequentative *bývať*; *boli by sme si to* (*bývali*) *kúpili* 'we would have bought it'. The conjunction which introduces counterfactual conditions is *keby*, incorporating the conditional particle: *ponúkol by som ti kávičku, keby som dáku mal* 'I'd offer you some coffee if I had some', *keby ste nás boli* (*bývali*) *poslúchli, neboli by ste teraz v takejto situácii* 'if you'd listened to us, you wouldn't be in this predicament now'.

Voice is a two-member category, active and passive. Passive is the marked member, with two means of expressing it:

1 the passive participle of any transitive verb with auxiliary *byť*; in this case the agent may, but need not be expressed: active *hostia vypili všetok čaj* 'the guests drank all the tea' transposes into *všetok čaj bol vypitý* (*hosťami*) 'all the tea was drunk (by the guests)'. Aspect operates as in other verb phrases: *nemčina nebola nikdy ohrozovaná iným jazykom* 'German has never been imperilled by another language' (IMPFV);

2 using a reflexive form: *všetok čaj sa vypil*, in which case the agent is completely suppressed (rare exceptions do occur: *pesnička sa zaspievala všetkými prítomnými* 'the song was sung by all present'). Effectively, the 'reflexive passive' is restricted to third persons and to contexts where the patient is inanimate; with an animate subject any other available interpretation will take precedence (reflexivity: *Peter sa zastrelil* 'Peter shot himself'; intransitivity: *Peter sa vrátil* 'Peter returned'). Verbs with non-accusative complementation generally permit only reflexive (that is, not participial) forms, but these are interpreted as impersonal, not passive, since the complement retains its case attributes: *nerozumeli tomu* 'they didn't understand it' › *nerozumelo sa tomu* 'it wasn't understood', *vedeli sme o vás* 'we knew about you' › *vedelo sa o vás* 'you were known about'. The principle extends to all intransitives, compare Hečko's

V povstaní   sa   bojovalo,   padalo a   umieralo spoločne.
in uprising-LOC.SG REFL fought-N.SG fell-N.SG and died-N.SG together
'In the Uprising people fought, fell and died together.' (note: one *sa* to all
   three verbs)

The verb is always third person singular and neuter in this stylistically neutral clause-type, widely used in all manner of generalizations, instructions, injunctions and as a device specifically to exclude agency, as in:

Išlo   sa   domov až   po polnoci.
went-3.SG.N REFL home   INTNS after midnight-LOC.SG
'We/they/one didn't go home until after midnight.'

By contrast, impersonal passive constructions using participles are rare and 'un-Slovak': *?*bolo zaklopané na dvere* 'there was a knock (it was knocked) on the door'.

Slovak also has an *active* impersonal construction based on the neuter third person singular of transitive verbs; semantically, the type is always connected with loss or natural disaster, with no responsibility imputed:

Odnieslo   nám   strechu.
carried away-N.SG us-DAT roof-ACC
'Our roof got blown away.'

Cez   vojnu   ho   ranilo   do hlavy.
during war-ACC him-ACC wounded-N.SG into head-GEN
'He was wounded in the head during the war.'

Non-finite forms: all **infinitives** are marked by *-ť*, both post-vocalically (*volať* 'call', *vypäť* 'switch off', *stáť* 'stand', *kliať* 'curse', *plieť* 'weed', *žiť* 'live', *vyť* 'howl', *žuť* 'chew', *hnúť* 'move'), and post-consonantally (*pásť* 'graze', *hrýzť* 'bite', *môcť* 'can'). Monosyllabic infinitives generally contain short vowels unless the vowel is the product of contraction (*stáť* < *stojati*), or *-ť* is preceded by a consonant, or the present-tense stem ends in *-aj-* or *-ej-*; the infinitive suffix *-núť* is also morphonologically long, that is, subject to rhythmical shortening, hence *lipnúť* 'cling', *kývnuť* 'nod'. In use the infinitive shares the typical European range of functions, but note its use in verbs of perception in copular sentences (see 4.3).

Active participial forms: the so-called *l*-participle, used in past-tense formation by the addition of *-l* to a version of the infinitive stem, should not be called a participle in the modern language. However, in the singular at least it betrays its participial origins through gender markers and the need for auxiliaries in the first and second persons. The final vowel of the infinitive usually shortens (*trieť–trel* 'rub-bed', *minúť–minul* 'pass-ed'), though not if produced by contraction (*kliať–klial* 'curse–d', *stáť–stál* 'stand-stood'). Consonantal stems require a fill vowel, always *-o-*, in the masculine (*niesť–niesol/niesla* 'carry', *padnúť–padol/padla* 'fall').

The **gerund** is formed from the third person plural by addition of *-c* (*nesú-c* 'carrying', *píšuc* 'writing', *chváliac* 'praising'), to verbs of either aspect (*na-píšuc* 'having written'); imperfectives denote actions/states simultaneous with those of the main clause, perfectives usually anteriority, rarely posteriority, of the subordinate action.

The (present) **active participle** is based on the present-tense stem of imperfective verbs only; the endings are those of the third person plural (morphologically *-ú*, *-ia*), with the addition of *-ci*, *-ca*, *-ce* and so on, that is adjectival endings rhythmically shortened. Unlike the *ú* version of the gerund, this vowel is *not* shortened in the participle, hence *píšuc*, but *píšúci*. Participles are a common substitute for relative clauses, many have become fully adjectivalized (*prekvapujúci* 'surprising'), and some even substantivized (*vedúci/-ca* 'manager/-ess').

Passive participles are based on the formants *-n-* or *-t-*, with long adjectival endings. The subclasses which use *-t-* are mainly monosyllables (and their prefixed derivates) without a stem marker in the past tense (*biť–bitý* 'strike', *najať–najatý* 'hire') and verbs in *-núť* (*spomenúť–spomenutý* 'mention', *zasiahnúť–zasiahnutý* 'hit (target)'). Forms in *-ený* occur in most verbs with present-tense themes in *-e*, *-ie* or *-i* (*viesť–vedený* 'lead', *prosiť–prosený* 'request', *rozumieť–porozumený* 'understand'), but those with infinitives in *-ať* have *-aný* (*drzať–držaný* 'hold'), like other classes with *-ať*, including *-ovať* (*zavolať–zavolaný* 'call', *háčkovať–háčkovaný* 'crochet'). Some free variation exists, in the *brať* subclass (*vybrať–vybraný/vybratý* 'select', *zodrať–zodraný/zodratý* 'scuff, skin'), and minimal lexical variation (*vydať–vydaný* 'publish', *vydať sa–vydatá* 'marry (of woman)').

Adjectivalized *l-*participles from intransitives in *-núť* (*zbohatnúť–zbohatlý* 'grow rich') are of limited incidence, having been replaced by forms reminiscent of *passive* participles (*spadnúť–spadnutý* 'fall–en', *zvyknúť si–zvyknutý* 'grow accustomed'); *-lý* types occur in other classes (*dôjsť–došlý* 'arrive–incoming', but *vyhladovieť–vyhladovený* 'starve–d').

3.2.2   Conjugation

The Slovak conjugations are illustrated in tables 10.22 to 10.26. Table 10.22 gives a breakdown of conjugational types and subtypes, organized so as to permit confrontation with their Old Slavonic antecedents. The layout on table 10.23 summarizes the routes by which most of the reorganization since early times has gone on. Table 10.24 stays with the synchronic theme, being a survey of the Slovak reflexes of the original 'athematic' verbs. Three core conjugations are set out in table 10.25, from which others can be deduced, while table 10.26 gives the full present, future and past conjugation of *byť* 'to be', which also serves to show in particular how any other verb behaves in the past tense.

Table 10.22   Survey of conjugations, including the various subclasses

INF	PAST	3 SG	3 PL
Themes in *-ie*, including *-Vnie*[1]			
niesť 'carry'	niesol	nesie	nesú
viesť 'lead'	viedol	vedie	vedú
piecť 'bake'	piekol	pečie	pečú
zomrieť 'die'	zomrel	zomrie	zomrú
brať 'take'	bral	berie	berú
mlieť 'grind'	mlel	melie	melú
minúť 'spend; pass'	minul	minie	minú

INF	PAST	3 SG	3 PL

Themes in -e, including -Cne[1]

íst 'go'	išiel	ide	idú
po-zvať 'invite'	-zval	-zve	-zvú
mazať 'smear'	mazal	maže	mažú
písať 'write'	písal	píše	píšu
zdvihnúť 'lift'	zdvihol	zdvihne	zdvihnú
ziabnuť 'freeze'	ziabol	ziabne	ziabnu
za-čať 'begin'	začal	začne	začnú
napäť/napnúť 'tense'	napäl/napol	napne	napnú

Theme in -je

po-čuť 'hear'	počul	počuje	počujú
kryť 'cover'	kryl	kryje	kryjú
biť 'strike'	bil	bije	bijú
vy-zuť 'remove shoes'	vyzul	vyzuje	vyzujú
priať 'wish'	prial	praje	prajú
siať 'sow'	sial	seje	sejú
sať 'suck, absorb'	sal	saje	sajú
chvieť sa 'tremble'	chvel sa	chveje sa	chvejú sa
darovať 'donate'	daroval	daruje	darujú

Theme in -i

modliť sa 'pray'	modlil sa	modlí sa	modlia sa
chodiť 'walk, go'	chodil	chodí	chodia
vidieť 'see'	videl	vidí	vidia
držať 'hold'	držal	drží	držia
trpieť 'suffer'	trpel	trpí	trpia
spať 'sleep'	spal	spí	spia
chváliť 'praise'	chválil	chváli	chvália[2]
báť sa 'fear'	bál sa	bojí sa	boja sa[3]

Theme in -á/-ie

volať 'call'	volal	volá	volajú
dávať 'give'	dával	dáva	dávajú[4]
roz-umieť 'understand'	rozumel	rozumie	rozumejú
vracať 'return'	vracal	vracia	vracajú[5]
sádzať '(type-)set'	sádzal	sádza	sádzajú[6]

Notes: [1]obviously missing from these groups are 'read', 'go by vehicle' and 'say'. The last-named, *riecť*, now conjugates like *piecť* (and is obsolescent), 'go by vehicle' has been lost to be replaced by *ísť* (or by *cestovať* 'travel' or *jazdiť* 'ride' (an animal) or 'drive'), while 'read' has been replaced by its frequentative *čítať* (*a*-theme);
[2]included to show effect of rhythmical law in 3rd singular;
[3]included to show effect of *j*-stem in 3rd plural;
[4] and [6] show the effect of the rhythmical law in 3rd singular; [5] and [6] show the *-ia*-alternant for *-á*- after a 'soft' consonant.

Table 10.23   Evolution of Slovak verb classes and subclasses

Old Church Slavonic (1 SG + INF)   *Modern Slovak* (3 SG + INF)*

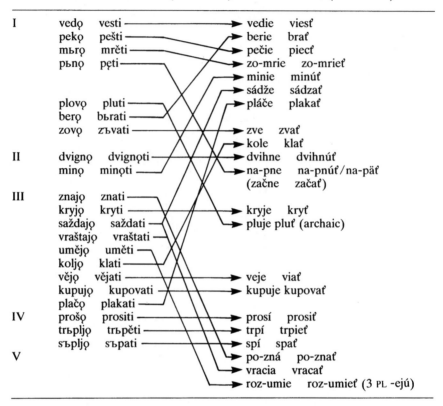

I		
vedǫ	vesti	vedie viesť
pekǫ	pešti	berie brať
mьrǫ	mrěti	pečie piecť
pьnǫ	pęti	zo-mrie zo-mrieť
		minie minúť
		sádže sádzať
plovǫ	pluti	pláče plakať
berǫ	bьrati	
zovǫ	zъvati	zve zvať
		kole klať
II	dvignǫ dvignǫti	dvihne dvihnúť
	minǫ minǫti	na-pne na-pnúť/na-päť
		(začne začať)
III	znajǫ znati	
	kryjǫ kryti	kryje kryť
	saždajǫ saždati	pluje pluť (archaic)
	vraštajǫ vraštati	
	umějǫ uměti	
	koljǫ klati	
	vějǫ vějati	veje viať
	kupujǫ kupovati	kupuje kupovať
	plačǫ plakati	
IV	prošǫ prositi	prosí prosiť
	trьpljǫ trьpěti	trpí trpieť
	sъpljǫ sъpati	spí spať
V		po-zná po-znať
		vracia vracať
		roz-umie roz-umieť (3 PL -ejú)

Note: * For reasons of space the Table does not record changes in meaning.

Table 10.24   The former athematic verbs and 'want'

INF	PAST	1 SG	3 SG	3 PL
byť 'be'	bol	som	je	sú
mať 'have'	mal	mám	má	majú
dať 'give'	dal	dám	dá	dajú
jesť 'eat'	jedol	jem	je	jedia
vedieť 'know'	vedel	viem	vie	vedia
chcieť 'want'	chcel	chcem	chce	chcú

Note: Apart from some anomalies in the relationship between infinitive and present-tense stem, and the anomalous third person plural of *jesť* and *vedieť*, all these verbs except *byť* have become fully integrated into the main conjugations. Compounds of *vedieť* take the form -*vedať*, past -*vedal*, with the above conjugation in the perfective, and as *á*-stems in the imperfective: *odpovedať* 'reply': third person plural imperfective *odpovedajú*, third person plural perfective *odpovedia*.

Table 10.25   Specimen conjugations

(a) *ie*-theme   (b) *i*-theme   (c) *á*-theme

vediem	prosím	volám
vedieš	prosíš	voláš
vedie	prosí	volá
vedieme	prosíme	voláme
vediete	prosíte	voláte
vedú	prosia	volajú

Note: Given the consistency of the person markers, all other conjugation variants can be inferred from the above and the items in table 10.22.

Table 10.26   *byť*

PRS	FUT	PAST
som	budem	bol/-a som
si	budeš	bol/-a si
je	bude	bol/-a/-o
sme	budeme	boli sme
ste	budete	boli ste
sú	budú	boli

3.3   Derivational morphology

Derivation by suffixation is still dominant in word formation, a lesser role being played by prefixation, and even lesser roles by other procedures, though composition is slowly increasing.

3.3.1   Major patterns of noun derivation

Twenty-three different suffixes occur in deriving nouns denoting male humans, of which *-teľ*, *-č*, *-ník*, *-ik*, *-ár* and *-ák* are highly productive, while others, often expressive, like *-áň*, *-oš*, *-áľ*, occur in relatively few items. Some suffixes are associated with one particular source, for example, *-teľ* or *-č* with verbal stems, as in *prekladateľ* 'translator', *nosič* 'porter'. Others, such as *-ník* or *-ár*, may be formed from a wide range of sources: *bojovník* 'warrior' (‹ *bojovať* 'fight'), *hudobník* 'musician' (‹ *hudba* 'music'), *fajčiar* 'smoker' (‹ *fajčiť* 'smoke'), *kvetinár* 'florist' (‹ *kvety* 'flowers'). A further group uses loan-suffixes, usually combined with other borrowings: *traktor/-ista* 'tractor/–driver', *huslista* 'violinist' (‹ *husle*), *historik* 'historian', *simulant* 'malingerer'. Prefixes used in masculine animate-noun derivation, mostly in calques, are confined to the items *pra-*, 'proto-': *praotec* 'progenitor'; *nad-* 'super-': *nadčlovek* 'superman'; *pod-* 'sub-': *podnájomník* 'sub-tenant'; *pred-* 'pre-': *predrečník* 'the previous speaker'; *proti-* 'counter-': *protikandidát* 'opposing candidate'; *ne-* 'un-':

nefajčiar 'non-smoker'; and *spolu-* 'co-': *spolumajiteľ* 'co-owner'.

Other, more limited, sources of masculine animate nouns are substantivization of adjectives, like *hlavný* '(head-)waiter', *predstavená* 'mother-superior', and compositions, consisting usually of a noun element, a verbal element and a suffix: *divotvorca* 'wonder-worker' (< *div* 'wonder' + *tvoriť* 'create'), *zverolekár* 'vet' (< *zviera* 'animal' + *liečiť* 'cure') – in both of these the second element is a noun in its own right; *rukojemník* 'hostage' (< *ruka* 'hand' + *jať* 'take'), *knihožrút* 'bookworm' (< *kniha* 'book' + *žrať* 'eat'). Productive in the technical sphere, and based on such borrowings as *rádiotechnik*, are compositions denoting modern professions: *zvukotechnik* 'sound technician', and, using native elements: *vodohospodár* 'water engineer or expert'.

Human feminine appelatives are derived by comparatively few suffixes, primarily *-ka*, but also *-ička*, *-yňa*, *-ica*, *-iná*, each associated with different ranges of masculines: *študent-ka*, *súdruh–súdružka* 'comrade', *Nemec–Nemka* 'German', *chirurg-ička* 'surgeon', *prorok-yňa* 'prophetess', *švagor–švagriná* 'brother-in-law/'s wife'.

Generally similar principles apply to the formation of names for inanimate objects, with twenty-one different suffixes in use across all three genders, some associated with particular semantic classes.

Diminutives, lexical or expressive, are extremely common, with a good repertoire of suffixes based on *-k-*, *-čk-* and *-nk-*.

3.3.2   Major patterns of adjective derivation

Here too suffixation predominates. Depending on the class of source word and particular choice of suffix there are some twenty-seven broadly distinctive types (Horecký 1971: 169–206). Many have counterparts in other Slavonic languages, but *-ní* is conspicuous by its absence. The most frequent suffixes are *-ný* (from verbal and substantival sources), *-ový* and *-ský*, while those in *-ací/-iaci* based on infinitives and denoting 'intended for -ing' or 'capable of being -ed' are a productive source of neologisms: *smerovacie číslo* 'post-code' (literally: directing number). Compounding is productive and frequent in calquing, and various types occur: from adverb + participle: *dlhotrvajúci* 'long-lasting', *znovuzrodený* 'born-again'; adjective + noun: *krátkozraký* 'short-sighted' (< *krátky* + *zrak*); numeral + noun: *dvojhrbý* 'two-humped' (< *dva/dvoje* + *hrb*); preposition + noun: *bezhlavý* 'headless' (< *bez* 'without' + *hlava*); noun + verb: *mäsožravý* 'carnivorous' (< *mäso* 'meat' + *žrať* 'eat'), and others. A third source is adjectivalization of participles (*rozčuľujúci* 'annoying', *nečakaný* 'unexpected'), while many neologisms look like participles of the most productive verb class, in *-ovať*, where no actual verb exists, for example, *zúbkovaný* 'serrated'.

A few adjectives are derived by prefixation of existing items. The distribution of the main prefixes (*polo-* 'semi-', *pre-* 'very', *pri-* 'too' and *ne-*

'un-') is restricted, but fairly predictable. In addition there are several minor types of simultaneous prefixation and suffixation of existing items: *podlhovastý* 'longish' (‹ *dlhý*), *nahluchlý* 'fairly deaf' (‹ *hluchý*, via *hluchnúť* 'go deaf').

3.3.3 Major patterns of verb derivation

'From the derivational point of view, the verb is a stable word-class' (Horecký 1971: 24), being poor in innovatory derivational processes. Verbs are readily formed from nouns and adjectives, with *-ovať* and *-iť* the main suffixes. Change-of-state verbs generally adopt the suffixes *-núť* and, more productively, *-ieť*, and many are formed, as perfectives in the first instance, by simultaneous prefixation–suffixation: *s-pohodln-ieť* 'become idle/lax', *o-ťarchav-ieť* 'become pregnant'. Many transitive *i*-conjugation verbs become intransitive by reflexivization: *po-nemč-iť* 'Germanize', *poněmčiť sa* 'become Germanized'.

Verbs are derived from other verbs by prefixation, each available prefix often having several distinct semantic possibilities. A prefix added to a basic imperfective verb produces a new perfective, to which a secondary imperfective is formed by suffixation – the general Slavonic pattern. Noteworthy Slovak factors include: (a) a measure of free variation among secondary imperfective forms: *vy-chládz-ať* or *vy-chladz-ovať* 'cool' (‹ *vychladiť* TR), *vy-chlád-ať* or *vy-chlad-úvať* 'cool' (‹ *vychladnúť* ITR); (b) vitality of stem-vowel alternation: *ponárať* ‹ *ponoriť* 'immerse', semi-colloquial *odbáčať* (for *odbočovať*) ‹ *odbočiť* 'turn off', a process which extends to secondary imperfectives of *-ovať* verbs: *prerokovať* › *prerokúvať* 'discuss', and to Ø/ý alternations before *-núť/-nať*: *nahnúť* › *nahýnať* 'bend', *odomknúť* › *odomkýnať* 'unlock', imitating the 'true' Ø/V gradation of, say, *vybrať/vyberať* 'select'.

Suffixation also produces the quite widely used frequentatives: *mávať* ‹ *mať* 'have', *chodievať* ‹ *chodiť* 'go often'.

Double prefixation is practically confined to the prefixes *s-/z-* and *po-*, which add a distributive dimension: *s-prehádzať* 'jumble up', *po-vyzliekať* 'undress one by one'; they may also have this function as sole prefix: *zhádzať* 'cast off piecemeal', *postrieľať* 'shoot one by one'.

4 Syntax

4.1 Element order in declarative sentences

Modern Slovak sources decline to refer to any unmarked order of constituents in terms of basic word order; this approach, which would indeed see Slovak as an SVO language, is viewed as an application of alien parameters. 'In Slovak the principle of functional sentence perspective (FSP, i.e., in a nutshell, the unfolding of a sentence from the 'known' or 'general' – the 'theme', to the 'new' or 'specific' – the 'rheme') is the basic word-order factor, other factors in an utterance being subordinated to it' (Mistrík 1966: 249). Thus, despite the attractive simplicity of exemplar sentences such as *pes pohrýzol poštára* (SVO) 'the dog bit the postman', they are deemed no more or less neutral than OVS versions: *poštára pohrýzol pes*, best translated as 'the postman was bitten by the dog'. Both are unmarked; the difference is merely occupancy of the thematic ('dog' and 'postman') and rhematic ('postman' and 'dog', respectively) parts of the clause. Mistrík goes on: 'The greater the resistance offered by such secondary factors, the more conspicuous is the change induced.' Such factors include spontaneity, expressiveness, deprecation or situations where the verb, generally regarded as a transit element between theme and rheme, needs to be incorporated within one or other of these two clause slots. Hence *poštára pes pohrýzol* 'the postman was *bitten* by the dog'. In *pes poštára pohrýzol*, with a marked high–low intonation contour between *pes* and *poš-*, 'it was a dog that bit the postman', rheme and theme are effectively inverted – a possibility common in speech. Freedom of word order centring on the verb and its arguments is the main instrument of 'dynamism, expressiveness and stylistic symptomatization' (Mistrík 1966: 249).

As clause constituents, the clitics have a fairly rigid position; adverbs, unless affecting the whole clause, or for FSP reasons being specifically thematic, or, especially, rhematic elements, tend to stand close to the item they qualify (usually before an adjective or other adverb, after a verb), and the position of adjectives and determiners within noun phrases is fairly rigid.

A basic rule places all enclitics in the second constituent slot in the clause, in the order: conditional particle, past auxiliary, reflexive pronoun–particle, dative pronoun, accusative pronoun:

¹Dnes ²by som sa   mu   to   ³bál   povedať.
today COND AUX REFL him-DAT it-ACC feared-M tell-INF
'I would be afraid to tell him (it) today.'

Dependent infinitives are commonly treated alternatively as embedded 'first slots' with their own enclitic complements attached after them:

¹Dnes ²by som sa ³bál (¹povedať ²mu to).

or, less artificially:

¹Bál ²by som sa ³(¹povedať ²mu to ³dnes).

The first constituent may vary in length and syntactic status; all sub-ordinating conjunctions qualify, as do disyllabic coordinating conjunctions.

This essentially disqualifies *a, i* and *aj* 'and', but, in spontaneous colloquial usage, at least *sa* may follow them immediately: *aj sa najem* 'and I *will* eat'; longer enclitic chains also occur: *a som sa ho spýtal* 'and I (duly) asked him'. Of all the clitics *sa* is most prone to movement, another common position being directly after the verb:

Z   iniciatívy Jozefa Kohúta   založil   sa   v Martine... hasičský zbor.
from initiative Jozef Kohút-GEN founded self in Martin...   fire   brigade
'A fire brigade was founded in Martin on the initiative of J.K.'

Within noun phrases the unmarked order is adjective–noun, with other attributes following:

veľký dom   na konci   ulice.
big   house at end-LOC street-GEN
'The big house at end of the street.'

Adjective–noun inversion occurs in a limited set of circumstances: (a) emphasis: *prvá hodina* 'first lesson' › *hodina prvá* '*first* (not second) lesson'; (b) affectionate address: *zlato moje!* 'my dear' (literally: gold my); (c) abuse: *líška prešibaná* 'crafty devil (= fox)'; (d) taxonomies, modelled on Latin: *drop veľký* 'great bustard', *kyselina octová* 'acetic acid'.

Strings of noun phrase determiners or qualifiers have a fairly fixed sequence:

toto/každé/prvé moje/dedkovo   dobré domáce   víno.
this/each/first   my/grandfather's good home-made wine
'This good home-made wine of mine/grandfather's.'
'Each good home-made wine of mine/grandfather's.'
'My/grandfather's first good home-made wine.'

where the first two positions (determiners and possessives) are fixed; aberrations further along are due to emotional colouring, afterthought or other more or less random influences. Cardinal numerals are mobile:

tie		naše		staré		parné	rušne
	↑		↑		↑		
	dva		dva		dva		
those		our		old		steam	engines
	↑		↑		↑		
	two		two		two		

4.2   Non-declarative sentence types
Yes–no questions are subject to the same 'freedom' of word order as applies to declarative sentences, for example, *poštára pohryzol pes?* 'was it a dog that bit the postman?', *poštára pes pohryzol?* 'did the dog *bite* the

postman?', and in speech by a distinctive anti-cadence (rising or rising–falling). Questions may be progressively toned down by being formulated in the negative, conditional, or negative conditional. Some yes–no questions may be introduced by the 'empty' particle *či*, or modal *azda*, *hádam* and others, largely 'untranslatable'. Deliberative and disjunctive questions have the second alternative introduced by *či* and *a či* respectively. Examples:

Počul Peter tú reláciu?
'Did Peter hear that programme?'
Pôjdete zajtra do divadla?
'Will you go to the theatre tomorrow?'
Nešli by ste zajtra s nami?
'Would you care to go with us tomorrow?'
Či ste tam?
'Are you there?'
Hádam to nemyslíš vážne?
'You don't mean that, do you?' (approximately 'Surely you don't think it seriously?')
Či mu mám napísať, či sa ho opýtať osobne?
'Should I write to him or ask him in person?'
Či sa mám na tú zkúšku prihlásiť, a či pôjdem s tebou do Viedne?
'Should I enter for the exam, or shall I go to Vienna with you?'

Answers to yes–no questions include *áno* (colloquial *hej*) 'yes' and its close equivalents (*pravdaže, veru, iste* 'indeed'), several particles indicating 'possibly' or 'probably' (*asi, hádam, azda, možno*) and *nie* 'no' or the more dogmatic *kdeže, čoby*. The use of *áno* and *nie* is not conditioned by the positive or negative formulation of the question, but by the truth-value of the reply, though contradiction may be supported by *ale*:

(Nie) ste chorý? 'Are(n't) you ill?'	Nie, som zdravý. 'No, I'm well.' Áno, som chorý. 'Yes, I am ill.'
(Ne-)volali ste ma? 'Did(n't) you ring me?'	Nie, nevolal. 'No, I didn't.' (Ále) áno, volal. 'Yes, I did.'
(Ne-)kúpia si to? 'Are(n't) they going to buy it?'	Nie, nekúpia. 'No, they aren't.' Áno, kúpia. 'Yes, they are.'

Áno and *nie* are often omitted, the positive or negative form of the relevant verb being an adequate response; this type is apparently preferred if the question was non-neutral (spoken in reproof or irony):

Naozaj si ma nevolal?	– *Nevolal*
'You really didn't call me?'	= 'not called'
Bude mu ešte pomáhať?	– *Bude*
'Will he still help him?'	= 'will'

In all responses consisting of just the verb, past (and conditional) auxiliaries and any dependent infinitives are dropped.

The main feature of WH **questions** is a falling cadence similar to that of declarative sentences. Most interrogative items are given in Table 10.11, to which may be added *dokedy* 'by/until when' and *prečo* 'why'. Types of answers are comparable to those in other languages.

Indirect WH questions are exact replicas of their direct counterparts, except for adjustments to person in noun phrases and verb phrases; tense forms need no adjustment, though word order may:

Direct: Kto nás bude zastupovať?
       'Who will represent us?'
Indirect: Opýtali sa, kto ich bude zastupovať.
       'They asked who would represent them.'

Similar adjustments apply to yes–no questions, introduced by *či* 'whether':

Direct: Vedia už o tom?
       'Do they know about it yet?'
Indirect: Zavolám, či o tom už vedia.
       'I'll phone (to ask) if they know about it yet.'

Clauses following a verb of speaking are introduced by *že* 'that'; this feature has spread redundantly to indirect questions, hence, in defiance of codification, such expressions as: *opýtali sa ho, že kto ich bude zastupovať* or *Zavolám, že či o tom už vedia.*

Commands are expressed primarily by the imperative, from a perfective verb for a positive and imperfective for a negative command. A perfective negative imperative generally contains a warning rather than an injunction (*neudri sa!* 'mind you don't bang yourself'), while an imperfective positive imperative implies a general principle, or that the addressee should commence and continue an action (*čítaj* 'read', *prac sa!* 'clear off!'), or adopt and/or sustain a given state – uses typical of the imperfective generally. Aspect-selection rules apply equally to uses of the non-morphological imperative, that is, the indicative introduced by the particle *nech* 'let': *nech príde* 'let him come', or of volitive constructions based on *aby*: *aby som ťa tu už nevidel!* 'don't let me see you here again!' (literally: that I not see you here anymore). Other imperative devices are shared with many languages, for example: indicative: *ten kľúč mi dáš!* 'you will give me that key!'; interrogative: *dáš mi ten kľúč?!* 'will you give me that key?'; conditional: *keby ste sa tak nerozčuľovali!* 'don't get so excited!' (literally: if you would not get so excited); infinitive: *stáť!* 'halt!'; sundry clause constituents with the verb deleted: *ten kľúč!* 'that key!'; *tu hore!* 'up here!'

4.3   Copular sentences

The main copula is *byť*: *naši študenti sú leniví* 'our students are lazy'; one difference between copular and existential *byť* is in the negative: copular and circumstantial sentences have the negative particle: *naši študenti nie sú leniví*, while existential sentences have an optional impersonal negative form *niet (-o)* (past *nebolo*, future *nebude*) with a genitive subject, hence *na to peniaze* (NOM) *sú/boli* 'there is/was the money for it', but *na to peňazi* (GEN) *niet/nebolo* 'there isn't/wasn't ...'. The construction may also apply to persons: *už ho* (GEN) *tu niet* 'he's no longer here'. Negation with *nie* is, however, increasingly preferred, hence *na to peniaze nie sú/ neboli, už nie je tu.*

In many registers the negative particle may follow the copula, a feature of folk speech, without implying negation of any following constituent: *už je nie tu* 'he/she/it is no longer there'.

Sentences having verbs of perception in the infinitive, and evaluated as copular, omit the copula in the present. Such verbs include: *badať* 'see, notice', *čuť* 'hear, smell', *počuť* 'hear', *vidieť* 'see', *zazrieť* 'see, spot', *citiť* 'feel, smell', *rozumieť* 'understand' and *poznať* 'know, see, tell':

Všade   (bolo/bude)   počuť,   že   vláda   odstúpi.
everywhere (was/will-3.SG.N) hear-INF that government resign-3.SG.PRFV
'Everywhere you (could/will) hear that the government will resign.'
Nevidieť   im   na tvári,   že   majú   strach.
not-see-INF them-DAT on face-LOC that have-3.PL fear
'You can't see from their faces that they're afraid.'

In the past and future the inserted copula attracts any negation:

Nebolo im vidieť na tvári, že majú strach.
'You couldn't see from their faces that they were afraid.'

The same construction also applies to *dostať* 'get': *zemiaky nedostať* 'you can't get potatoes'.

Several **modal adverbs** also dispense with the copula in the present, but attract the past and future auxiliaries as above: *(ne)treba* and *načim* (only positive) '(it is) (un-)necessary', *možno* 'possible (feasible)', *nemožné* 'impossible', *(ne-)slobodno* '(im-)possible (permissible), *vidno* 'apparent', *radno* 'advisable':

Treba   ísť   tam a   opýtať sa.
necessary go-INF there and ask
'You/we/one ought to go there and ask.'
Nebolo možno zohnať lístky. (*or* bolo nemožné ...)
wasn't possible get-INF tickets
'It was impossible to get tickets.'
Vidno, že   sa usiluje.
visible that try-3.SG

'You can tell he's trying.'
Štefan sedí   v chládku,   tak mu   načim.
Štefan sit-3.SG in cooler-LOC, so him-DAT necessary
'Stephen's in the cooler, serve him right.'

Modal copular constructions used only in the past and conditional also employ impersonal *byť* + infinitive:

Bolo mi   zájsť   na VB
was me-DAT go-INF to police
'I should have gone to the police.'
Máte   dlhé vlasy, bolo by   vám   ich   pristrihnúť.
have-2.PL long hair, was COND you-DAT them-ACC trim-INF
'Your hair's long, it ought to be trimmed.' (approximately: it would be desirable to trim it + possessive dative)

A noun predicate after the copula may be nominative or instrumental; the nominative dominates in the expression of general or permanent qualities: *byť Slovák* 'be a Slovak', while the instrumental is strongly preferred in more concrete, topical, relativized contexts and hence commonly expresses professions, titles and functions: *byť dôstojnikom/kniežaťom/ svedkom* 'be an officer/prince/witness'; blood and social relationships: *byť dcérou/vdovcom/cudzincom* 'be daughter/widower (of someone)/a foreigner'; various qualities expressed as nouns: *byť pätolizačom/silákom* 'be a sycophant/strongman', in which case the attribute may be expressed adjectivally with a generic noun: *byť dobrým človekom/váženým občanom* 'be a good man/respected citizen'. With inanimates the instrumental relativizes a particular quality to a given object or event, person or other abstract: *jeho obľúbeným nápojom je pivo* 'his favourite drink is beer', *pravidelná dochádzka je povinnosťou* 'regular attendance is a duty'. Specialized uses include such types as *keby som bol ja tebou* 'if I were you', *čaj nie je čajom, keď ...* 'tea isn't tea if ...'

The predicative instrumental is obligatory after copular *stať sa* 'become', *(z)ostať* 'remain': *stal sa učiteľom a do konca života ním ostal* 'he became a teacher and he remained one to the end of his life'.

4.4   Coordination and comitativity
The main coordinating conjunction is *a*, at all constituent levels. More than two conjoined items in unmarked sequences have *a* between the last two only; deletion of *a* or its insertion elsewhere in a list produces marked versions, almost individualizing the items. Only between clauses with strongly overlapping content is explicit coordination sometimes omitted; in such cases there is likely to be some other implicit element present, such as gradation or explanation:

Nemohol sa zbaviť dojmu blížiacej sa katastrofy, čoraz väčšmi ho tá predstava trápila.
'He couldn't rid himself of a sense of impending catastrophe, the thought worried him more and more.'

More emphatic coordination is by *aj* or *i* 'and (also/even)' '(emphatic) and', which unlike *a* are preceded by a comma when joining clauses:

To ho štvalo, i radovala sa v duchu.
'That riled him – and she rejoiced at heart.'

'Emphatic' coordination is particularly common between noun phrases, and is often hard to convey in translation without overemphasis:

z týchto i ďalších závažných dôvodov ... (press)
'for these and other important reasons ...'

Some hierarchization among conjoined noun phrases can be achieved by varying the conjunctions:

... český i zahraničný kapitál, ktorý nám priniesol biedu a vysťahovalectvo i súčasnú hrozbu (press)
'... Czech and foreign capital that brought us poverty and emigration and the current threat'

'Poverty and emigration' form a closer unit conjoined as a whole to the third woe. The *i* in the first phrase is the weakest rendering of 'both – and', but in a single member; stronger versions are reduplicated *i – i* or *aj – aj*:

Aj dom má od železnice, aj uhlie mu dáva železnica. (Šikula)
'He both has his house from the railway, and the railway gives him coal.'

Negative conjunction employs (*ani*) – *ani* 'neither – nor', omitting the first member for weaker variants:

(Ani) nič nemal, ani na nič neašpiroval.
'He neither had anything, nor did he aspire to anything.'

Conjoined subject noun phrases raise questions of agreement in the verb. Logical plurality is *supported* if: the verb follows the noun phrases; the latter are *concrete*; or the subjects are jointly, as opposed to individually, involved in the action or state. Logical plurality tends to be *overruled*, the verb being singular, if: the latter precedes the subject; the noun phrases are quasi-synonyms; the noun phrases are joined by *s* 'with'. These tendencies combine variously, though noun phrase–verb phrase as opposed to verb phrase–noun phrase ordering is the main factor. The following examples are drawn from Oravec and Bajzíková (1982: 88):

Hmla a dym *snovali* sa nad červenými strechami.
'Mist and smoke wove (PL) together above the red roofs.'
Štefan s Dorou ich *vyprevadili* až na dvor.
'Štefan and (with) Dora saw (PL) them all the way out to the yard.'
Bývajú v nej Paľo Stieranka, Jerguš a Zuzka Kosaľkuľa.
'(There) live (PL) in it P.S., J. and Z.K.'
Bola odvaha i úvaha.
'There was (SG) courage and deliberation.'
Radosť a veselosť *uletela* ako vtáča.
'Joy and gaiety flew off (SG) like a little bird.'

The *Štefan s Dorou* example illustrates the rare comitative construction. Most occurrences where the noun phrase precedes the verb phrase show plural agreement in the verb:

Veď vie, ako *mať s otcom* nažívali ...
'After all he knows how mother and (= with) father got on ... (PL)'

but singular agreement also occurs, suppressing the comitative function:

Keď sa *Joachim s Janom* vrátil k ohňu, starec sa modlil.
'When Joachim and (with) Jano returned (SG) to the fire, the old man was praying.'

Explicit reciprocity with comitativity, co-occurring with the order verb phrase–noun phrase may produce plural agreement:

'Len by sme sa obrobili, zájdeme si do kúpeľov!' potešovali jeden druhého *starý otec s materou.*
'"We'd just work ourselves to death, we'll go to a spa!" grandfather and (with) grandmother consoled (PL) each other.'

4.5 Subordination

Object clauses are introduced by the conjunction *že* 'that'; it never competes with the neuter interrogative or relative pronoun *čo.*

Purpose clauses, and many clause types denoting wishes, admonitions, etc., are introduced by *aby*, which includes the conditional particle *by*; it combines with past-tense forms and is equivalent to European subjunctives. Examples:

Pracoval rýchlo, aby mohol ísť domov skôr.
'He worked fast so that he could go home earlier.'
Chceme, aby si sa skoro uzdravil.
'We want you to get well soon.'

Many *aby*-clauses are anticipated by *preto* 'for that' (in various places in the preceding clause):

Preto   to urobil,   aby z   neho   mala   radosť.
for-that it did-M.SG that from him-GEN had-F.SG joy-ACC
'The reason he did it was to please her.'

Alternative expressions of purpose include (*nato* ...,) *žeby* and (*zato* ...,) *aby*.

The primary causal conjunction is *lebo* 'because':

Idem   neskoro, lebo   nechodili   trolejbusy.
come-1.SG late   because not-go-PAST.PL trolleybuses
'I'm late because the trolleybuses weren't running.'

The synonymous *pretože* is common in all, including spoken, registers (Czech influence?), though deemed acceptable only in non-literary written styles. A hybrid form has anticipatory *preto* as, to adapt the previous example, in:

Idem neskoro preto, lebo nechodili trolejbusy.
Zato   som   ti   to povedal, lebo   sa   to aj   tak dozvieš.
for-that AUX-1.SG you-DAT it told   because REFL it even so find out-2.SG
'The reason I told you is that you're bound to find out anyway.'

If the causal clause precedes the main clause the conjunction is *keďže*:

Keďže všetko už   vedel,   utiekol naspäť do redakcie.
since all   already knew-M.SG ran   back   to newspaper-office
'Since he now knew everything, he ran back to the office.'

Real conditions are introduced by *ak* 'if', but also by some conjunctions whose primary function lies elsewhere (*keď*, *až* 'when', *pokiaľ* 'in so far as'); it may have a coordinate in a following main clause, for example, (*ak/keď* ...,) *tak/potom/nuž/teda* '(if ...,) then', or, in a preceding main clause, usually (*len*) *vtedy*:

Ísť   ta   má len vtedy zmysel, ak vieš,   že tam bude.
go-INF thither has only then sense   if know-2.SG that there will be-3.SG
'It only makes sense to go there if you know he'll be there.'

Unreal conditions use *keby* + past-tense forms, that is, *keby* incorporates the conditional particle:

Keby sme   ich   mohli   zakúpiť, veľmi by   nám   uľahčili
if   AUX-1.PL them-ACC could-PL buy-INF very   COND us-DAT lightened-PL
                                                        robotu.
                                                        work-ACC
'If we could buy them they would make our work a lot easier.'

Alternatives include *ak by* and *čo by*.

Concessive clauses evince a great variety of devices, from basic *hoci* 'although', for clauses placed second in the sentence, to numerous alternatives including *akokoľvek, nech, a čo, hoc aj, čo aj/i, čo priam, čo hneď, čo ako*. If the concessive clause stands first, the conjunction is yoked to another (*predsa, jednako, aj tak, ešte, už* 'yet', 'however', etc.) at the head of the main clause. Examples:

Stále to ešte nevie, hoci sme mu to povedali už viac ráz.
'He still doesn't know it, though we have told him several times already.'
Akokoľvek sa   o dobrý výkon   usiloval, jednako sa   mu   to
however   REFL at good   performance tried-M.SG anyway REFL him-DAT it-NOM
                                                                 nepodarilo.
                                                                 not-succeeded-N.SG
'Although he tried to perform well, he failed none the less.'

Time clauses: 'when' is most frequently *keď*; consistent co-occurrence of two events is introduced by *kedykoľvek, čo raz*, or *čo* 'whenever', while parallel processes or states require *ako, ako tak, kým, medzitým čo* or *zatiaľ čo* 'while'. Anteriority of the main-clause event is indicated by *skôr ako, prv ako* or *kým* 'before', more immediate sequences of events by *ako, len čo, iba, len, len toľko čo, lenže, sotva, ledva, sotva čo* or *sotvaže* 'the moment, hardly'. 'Since' is expressed by *ako, od toho času/tých čias/tej doby, čo* or *odkedy ...*, (*odvtedy*), and 'until' by (*do-*)*kým, dokiaľ* or *pokiaľ*, followed by the verb in the negative, or *až* with a positive verb. *Pokiaľ, dokiaľ* and *dokedy* with a positive verb usually translate 'as long as'.

Relative clauses: the relative pronoun is *ktorý*, frequently replaced by the absolute *čo* in subject or object positions:

Stál pred chorým kráľom, ktorý/čo už bol len koža a kosť.
'He stood before the sick king, who now was just skin and bone.'

or, in colloquial usage, by *čo* and an appropriate oblique case of the personal pronoun:

Pomohol jej   sused,   čo   mu   bola vysvetlila   situáciu.
helped   her.DAT neighbour, what him.DAT was explained.F situation
'She was helped by the neighbour to whom she had explained the situation.'

Čo is required when the antecedent is an entire clause:

Nesmeli ísť von, čo sa im veľmi nepáčilo.
'They weren't allowed to go out, which didn't please them greatly.'

It is also required for any neuter pronominal antecedent (*niečo, čo* 'something that'); *kto* (or *čo*) serves for a referentially opaque or general animate antecedent (*ten, kto* 'he/anyone who'). For relative 'whose' Slovak uses only genitives of *ktorý* (*sused, ktorého pes sa stratil* 'the neighbour whose dog got lost').

Gerundial and participial clauses: participial clauses are practically confined to written registers. Unlike relative clauses proper, which they replace and which, as subordinate, must be separated by commas, participial relative clauses permit the distinction between non-defining (with commas) and defining types (without), a distinction widely ignored in practice. Short defining participial constructions may acquire the status of attributives and thus stand in front of their noun:

rozhodnutie, ktoré bolo prijaté včera › rozhodnutie prijaté včera › včera prijaté rozhodnutie
'the decision which was adopted yesterday › the decision adopted yesterday › (literally) the yesterday adopted decision'

Imperfective gerunds denote events simultaneous with those of the main clause, irrespective of tense; perfective gerunds usually denote anteriority:

'Dobrý deň,' povedal neodkladajúc noviny.
'"Good morning," he said, not putting down his newspaper.'
... antilopy, stratiac vodcov, podľahli ... panike
'the antelopes, having lost their leaders, gave in to panic'

As a condensing device, however, a perfective gerund may simply express perfectivity:

... povedal Jerguš, šklbnúc Rudka za šticu
'... said Jerguš, tugging (PRFV) Rudko by the forelock'

Passive gerundial phrases do not occur, being replaced by participial phrases:

Posmelený jeho stanoviskom, rozhodol som sa prehovoriť.
'Emboldened by his attitude, I decided to speak out.'

Constraints against extraction out of a subordinate clause are strong; sentences of the type 'the man that I think that you saw' are heard, but are viewed as nonce-forms and distortions; even the following grammatically almost tolerable occurrence still amounts to an anacoluthon:

muž, o   ktorom   si   myslím,   že ste   ho   videli
man about whom-LOC REFL.DAT think-1.SG that AUX-2.PL him-ACC saw-PL
'the man I thought you saw'

Occurrences of these types are rare in print, but:

... veršovaná tragédia Oulanen, ktorú   Marx považoval, že   sa
verse(-d)   tragedy Oulanen which-ACC Marx thought   that REFL

                   stane   Faustom   jeho doby
                   become-3.SG Faust-INST his   age-GEN
'... the verse tragedy O. which M. thought would become the Faust of his age'
                (*Večerník*, 3 April 1990, p. 3 – a translation from English!)

4.6 Negation

Sentence negation is expressed by simple negation of the verb (or equivalent), by means of the prefix *ne-*, which attracts word stress; in the past and conditional it attaches to the *l*-participle, and in the future to the auxiliary: *nemyslím, nemyslel som, nebudem myslieť* 'I do/did/will not think', *netreba* 'it is not necessary'. Exceptions: (a) present-tense forms of *byť* in all functions use the free-standing negator *nie*: *sekretárka už nie je chorá* 'the secretary is no longer ill', *nie sme odborníci* 'we aren't specialists', *jeho pracovňa nie je uprataná* 'his study hasn't been cleaned'. Future and past forms are regular: *nebol som, nebudem*. Increasingly rarely, cases are found where *nie* gravitates, irrespective of tense, away from its neutral position left of the copula to a position left of a nominal predicate: *tie hrušky sú/boli veru nie tvrdé* 'those pears are/were indeed not hard'; (b) in abbreviated repetition, in the negative, of a previous verb: *príde Peter, či nie?* 'is Peter coming or not?'; (c) as an alternative to existential *nie je, nie sú* there is a formal *niet(-o)* (matching *jest(-o)* in positive sentences): *celkom zlých ľudí niet* 'there are no totally bad people', *času niet* 'there's no time'; here the genitive subject is obligatory.

In clauses containing a negative item (pronoun subject, object, pronoun-adverb and so on) the verb carries secondary negation obligatorily: *nik neprišiel* 'no-one came', *nič si nekúpili* 'they bought nothing', *nikdy som nič také nevidel* 'I never saw anything like that anywhere'. Two negatives producing a positive occur with the separate parts of a complex verb: *nemôže neprísť* 'he cannot not come', or where one item is a lexical negative: *nie je to nepríjemné* 'it's not unpleasant'.

Constituent negation is rendered by the particle *nie*: *prídete dnes, nie inokedy* 'you'll come today, not some other time'; *nie alkohol, ale káva mu zničila zdravie* 'not alcohol, but coffee ruined his health'. In association with total quantifiers constituent negation may have the form of sentence negation: *oslava sa celkom nevydarila* = *oslava sa nie celkom vydarila* 'the celebration wasn't entirely successful'; *všetci ho nemajú radi* (all him NEG-have glad) = *nie všetci ho majú radi* (not all him have glad) 'they don't all like him', equivalent to *niektorí ho nemajú radi* 'some don't like him'.

4.7 Anaphora and pronouns

Zero anaphora applies in the case of common subjects of successive clauses:

Peter si išiel umyť ruky, ale nemohol nájsť mydlo.
'Peter went to wash his hands, but couldn't find the soap.'

However, comparable to the oblique-case opposition between emphatic (non-enclitic) and non-emphatic (enclitic) forms or uses of personal pronouns, in the subject there is an opposition between pronoun insertion and zero. Insertion is always marked, usually for contrast:

Ferko si tiež chcel umyť ruky a on mydlo našiel.
'Ferko also wanted to wash his hand and he did find the soap.'

Assertive emphasis likewise calls for insertion:

Ferko všetkým rozprával, že mydlo našiel iba on.
'Ferko kept telling everyone that only he found the soap.'

When an anaphoric relationship is to be established between the subject of one clause and a denotate other than the subject in the preceding clause, it is usual to insert not the personal pronoun, but demonstrative *ten*:

Ferko sa Petrovi$_i$ vysmial, ale ten$_i$ ostal pokojný.
'Ferko mocked Peter$_i$, but he$_i$ remained calm.'

The same applies if the new main-clause subject last appeared in subject position, but at subordinate-clause level:

Ferko čakal, či sa Peter$_i$ neohlási, ale ten$_i$ iba mlčal.
'Ferko waited (to see) whether Peter$_i$ would respond, but he$_i$ just kept silent.'

Such uses of the demonstrative are not confined to the nominative:

Ferko čakal, či sa Peter$_i$ neohlási, ale tomu$_i$ už bolo všetko jedno.
'F. waited (to see) whether P.$_i$ would respond, but it was all one to him$_i$ now.'

Similar conditions may apply even where no ambiguity as to denotate arises:

Vedľa chodníka ležal veľký kameň$_i$. Na ten$_i$ si sadol a ...
'Beside the path lay a large stone$_i$. He sat down on it$_i$ and ...'

Semantic constraints exclude the possibility that *kameň* (M) could be the subject of *sadol* (M). Here the anaphoric personal pronoun (-*ň*, in *naň* 'on it') could have been used instead of *ten* if a proper name or a common noun such as *pútnik* 'the pilgrim' or *náš hrdina* 'our hero' were inserted as subject, hence:

Vedľa chodníka ležal veľký kameň. Ferko si sadol naň a ...

However, even here, if for reasons of functional sentence perspective the stone had to be in the theme position proper at the head of the clause, one might find: ... *na ten si Ferko sadol a* ...

4.8   Reflexives and reciprocals

Reflexivity and reciprocity share the reflexive pronoun–particle *sa* as the main means of expression, normally only in co-reference ('reference' is problematical in many formally reflexive verbs) with the nominative subject of the same clause. Interpretation of *sa* as reflexive or reciprocal depends chiefly on the semantics of the predicate and the number of the subject. Oravec (1982) has observed that the position of *sa* as reflexive object is weakening, and that of reflexive indirect object *si* even more so, while reciprocal uses prosper, after verbs of volition and communication and transitive verbs with plural subjects. Thus while *má sa rád* has only one interpretation, 'he loves himself', the plural *majú sa radi* is almost guaranteed reciprocal, 'they love each other'. Disambiguating explicit reciprocal devices (*vzájomne* 'mutually', *jeden druhého* 'one another') are consequently rarer than expressions like *sám seba* ('self-EMPH.NOM self-REFL. ACC'), *sám sebe* (DAT) and so on, especially in the plural – *sami seba/sebe* etc. Thus *nerozumejú si* is adequate to convey 'they do not understand each other', any extra *jeden druhému* being possible, but redundant; the sense 'they do not understand themselves' requires explicit rendering of the reflexivity: *nerozumejú sami sebe.*

A reciprocal *sa* may refer to a grammatically singular subject only when a reciprocal act is portrayed from the perspective of one participant, whether or not the other party is equally involved in the action:

Pozdravila sa   s   profesorom.
greeted-F.SG REFL with professor-INST
'She greeted the professor.'
Stretne sa   s   ňou   na námestí.
meet-3.SG REFL with her-INST on square-LOC
'He'll meet her on the square.'

While reflexivity cannot extend beyond the clause, there are circumstances when it crosses infinitival phrase boundaries, most commonly with *dať* 'have, let':

Nedá sa podplatiť
'He can't (won't let himself) be bribed.'
Nedala sa chytiť.
'She didn't let herself get caught.'
Dala sa   ostrihať.
let-F REFL crop-INF
'She had her hair cut.'

That the reflexive pronoun–particle is an argument of the infinitives, not of *dať*, transpires from paradigmatic comparison with verbs complemented by other cases:

Dali si   predstaviť   nových zamestnancov.
let-PL REFL.DAT introduce-INF new   employees-ACC
'They had the new employees introduced to them.'
Prekvapenie nedalo   na seba   dlho čakať.
surprise   not-let-N.SG for self-ACC long wait-INF
'The surprise was not long in coming.' (that is, did not let itself be waited for too long)

Other, rarer, types of cross-infinitival reflexivization also occur, e.g.:

Žiadali   ste   sa   preložiť.
requested-PL AUX-2.PL REFL transfer-INF
'You applied to be transferred.'

a condensation of

Žiadali ste, aby *vás* preložili.
'You applied that they (IMPRS) transfer you.'

4.9   Possession

Possession is expressed primarily by *mať* 'to have'. It competes with more formal *vlastniť* 'possess', and with *byť* and a possessive pronoun. English 'her eyes were blue' and 'she had blue eyes' are both more likely to contain 'have': *oči mala modré, mala modré oči* respectively, than *jej oči boli modré*, with 'be'. Secondary expression of possession in *mať* sentences, by means of the reflexive possessive pronoun, applies only in emphasis, to exclude ambiguity, etc.: *má svoje auto* 'he has his own car' (for example, 'with him'). A different matter is *má vlastné auto* 'he has a car of his own', that is, not borrowed.

Otherwise, all the possessive pronouns are used where no predictions as to ownership could be made: *ich rozhodnutie ho rozčúlilo* 'their decision upset him'; *predáva náš dom* 'he's selling our house'; *môj pes má blchy* 'my dog has fleas'. Where high-probability ownership predictions can be made, possession need not be expressed overtly: *predáva dom* even out of context probably means he is selling his own house; similarly: *stratili sme psa* 'we've lost *our* dog'. With intimate possessions, clothing, body parts, etc. ownership is often expressed by the dative, though the borderline between plain possession and various *dativi (in-)commodi* is a fine one. Examples will suggest the range of possibilities:

Item possessed in nominative:

Vlasy mu vypadali.
hair-NOM him-DAT fell out-PL
'His hair fell out.'

where *mu* is in the enclitic slot, only coincidentally after the subject, compare *vypadali mu vlasy* with a different word order, or *Petrovi vypadali vlasy* 'Peter's hair fell out'.

Záhrada im/susedom pekne kvitne.
garden-NOM them/neighbours-DAT nicely blooms-3.SG
'Their/the neighbours' garden is flowering nicely.'
Stratili sa nám kľúče
lost-PL REFL us-DAT keys-NOM.PL
'Our keys have gone missing.'
Petruške zomrela matka
Petruška-DAT died-F mother-NOM
'Petruška's mother has died.'

Item possessed in non-nominative:

Chalani rozbili učiteľovi okno.
lads-NOM.PL broke-PL teacher-DAT window-ACC
'Some lads broke the teacher's window.'
Syn mu prerástol cez hlavu.
son-NOM him-DAT over-grew-SG over head-ACC
'His son has outgrown him.' (that is, 'over his head')
Umyl jej/mu/si vlasy
washed-M.SG$_a$ her/him$_b$/self$_a$ hair-ACC.PL
'He$_a$ washed her/his$_b$/his$_a$ hair.' (note: obligatory *si* in reflexive sense)

Possessive adjectives are widely used, based on any masculine or feminine one-word animate nouns except female surnames (in *-ová*) and other adjectival forms. The unmarked position is before the head noun: *otcov klobúk* 'father's hat', *s Verinou matkou* 'with Vera's mother'. If the possessor phrase consists of more than one word it will be in the genitive, usually post-positioned: *diela Františka Miku*, rarely *Františka Miku diela* 'the works of František Miko'. In the ante-position, an obsolete construction had the first constituent in the genitive and the second converted to the possessive adjective: *Františka Mikove diela*. A survival of this occurs in the press when the first constituent is an initial: *rozhodnutie G. Bushovho kabinetu* 'the decision of G. Bush's cabinet'.

4.10 Quantification
The adjectival syntax of numerals (see 3.1.5) is most marked in '1'–'4', and in the masculine animate forms of '5' upwards, hence the agreement in *jeden muž, dva stoly, dvaja muži, piati muži, dve ženy, dve okná, tri okná* 'one man, two tables, two men, five men, two women, two windows, three windows (all NOM)'; *jedným mužom, dvoma stolmi, dvoma mužmi, piatimi mužmi, dvoma ženami, dvoma oknami, tromi oknami* (all INST). With '5'

upwards there are three patterns to note: (a) in any nominative or accusative noun phrase the numeral is the head and the quantified entity is in the genitive plural – also possible with animates: *päť mužov/žien/okien*. Verb agreement is with the numeral, treated as neuter singular: *prišlo sedem cudzincov* 'seven foreigners came'. Genitive agreement usually extends into the predicate: *šesť stromov* (GEN) *bolo vyrubaných* (GEN) 'six trees were felled'. (b) In oblique cases there is usually agreement between both parts of the phrase: *piatim študentom* 'five students (DAT)', *siedmimi moriami* 'seven seas (INST)'. (c) The exception to (b) is prepositional phrases, when the numeral often does not inflect: *v sedem* (*siedmich*) *prípadoch* 'in seven instances', *s päťdesiat spolužiakmi* 'with fifty schoolfellows', *pred sto rokmi* 'a hundred years ago'. As quantifiers *sto* and *tisíc* and, often, inverted numerals from '21' to '99' (*jedenadvadsať* 'one-and-twenty', *päťatridsať* 'five-and-thirty') do not inflect, they have the dependent noun in the genitive plural in any nominative or accusative functions of the whole phrase and neuter third person singular agreement in the verb. Non-inverted numerals ending in '1' (*dvadsaťjeden*) behave similarly; those ending in other digits may be non-inflecting, or they may inflect in both parts: *pred dvadsaťdva rokmi* or *pred dvadsiatimi dvoma rokmi* 'twenty-two years ago'.

The above patterns are unaffected by expressions of approximation, namely the particles *zo* 'about' and *vyše* 'more than': *prišlo ich zo/vyše dvadsať* 'about/more than twenty of them came'.

Indefinite quantifiers behave much as the numerals. They include *niekoľko* (*dakoľko, voľakoľko*) 'several', *trocha* or *trochu* 'a little', *toľko* 'so much/many' and *koľko* 'how much/many', *mnoho* and *veľa* 'much, many', *priveľa* 'too much, many', *pár* and *zopár* 'a couple, a few' and *málo* 'little, few', and are generally uninflected. Inflecting, adjectival forms do exist, especially with animates and mass nouns: *niekoľkí/mnohí* (*ľudia*) *si myslia, že* ... 'several/many people think that ...', *keby mal toľký srd, koľký robí škrek* ... 'if he had the (that is, so much) guts to match the noise (that is, as much as the noise) he makes ...', *čo budeme robiť s toľkým časom?* 'what shall we do with so much time?'

Partitive expressions use primarily the preposition *z* 'out of': *traja/ niektorí/dakoľkí z nás* 'three/some/several of us', except for non-countables, when genitive alone suffices: *trocha/časť/polovica múky* 'a bit/some/half of the flour'. Neuter indefinite pronouns may also take a genitive, especially of adjectives: *čo (je) nového?* 'what's new?', *dačo modrého* 'something blue', but the standard codifies agreement in all cases, that is, not only *dačím modrým* (INST), but also *dačo modré* (NOM/ACC).

Collective numerals end in *-oro*: *pätoro, sedmoro* 'a fivesome, sevensome', and are uninflected even in conjunction with *pluralia tantum*: *pätoro šiat/detí* 'five dresses/children', *desatoro božích prikázaní* 'the ten commandments', *o pätoro dverách* 'concerning five doors' (*šaty* and *dvere* are *pluralia tantum*); the same applies to *dvoje* 'two', *troje* 'three', unless accompanying *pluralia tantum*, when they decline in full, like *piati.*

Fractions: 'half' is the non-inflected *pol*: *pol siedmej* (GEN) 'half past six', *o pol siedmej* (LOC) 'at six-thirty'. *Štvrť* 'quarter' is also non-inflecting. Both also exist as nouns, *polovica, štvrtina*, which like other fractional expressions, *tretina, dvadsatina, stotina* 'third, twentieth, hundredth' and so on, are followed in all circumstances by the noun in the genitive. *Väčšina* 'most' behaves likewise.

5 Lexis

5.1 General composition of the word-stock

Slovak is said to preserve the greatest number of Proto-Slavonic lexical items and to have built steadily on that core by derivation, expansion or reduction of original meanings; some of the wealth may survive in just one of the often quite distinctive dialects. Exact statistics cannot be given, owing to uneven tolerance of regionalisms even within the standard lexis, differing assessments of individual items among users and authoritative sources, the relative frequency of items, and the attrition in the native word-stock that accompanies developments in society. There are said to be some 500 new entrants to the word-stock annually, of which the highest proportion are 'international' loans. Currently, every sixth word in the press is a loan. In everyday speech the proportion is lower, while in literature, which draws freely on a vast stock of regionalisms, it is lower still, though pre-twentieth-century loans, and even more so those from before the seventeenth century, are ever-present; despite its 'Slavonic' strength, Slovak was always receptive to incomers, from Slavonic and non-Slavonic sources.

5.2 Patterns of borrowing

Slovak is not only hospitable to loans, but adapts them to native patterns with relative ease. The main sources of loans have been (Old High) German, Czech, Hungarian, Rumanian, Latin, Polish and Russian, French and English. The list is only approximately chronological, and says nothing quantitative.

Many of the first wave of borrowings from German were the early Christian internationalisms in Great Moravia, ultimately of Latin origin, for example, *krstiť* 'baptise' (‹ *kristenen*), *žehnať* 'bless' (‹ *seganen, signare*), but some secular items, like *chvíľa* 'moment', *ďakovať* 'thank' or *musieť* 'must', also date from then. The second wave of German loans came with the twelfth–fourteenth-century German colonization of the region. The colonists opened up mines, engaged in viticulture and crafts and in local commerce and administration, leaving in all these fields a permanent mark on all forms of the language. Examples: *garbiar* 'tanner', *šuster* 'cobbler', *handlovať sa* 'barter', *funt* 'pound', *pančucha* 'stocking'. Slovak retains more of the range (4,000 items in a recent analysis: see Rudolf 1991) than Czech, which confines many Germanisms to slangs and jargons.

Loans from Hungarian have entered Slovak ever since the twelfth century, but not with the same intensity as those from German. They also belong to more everyday life: *gazda* 'farmer', *gombik* 'button' (originally Slavonic loans in Hungarian), *ťarcha* 'burden', also *ťava* 'camel' (from further afield). Slovak and Hungarian opinion is sharply divided on the precise direction of borrowing within the shared stock; such arguments have concerned, for example, *driek* 'trunk', *guľáš* 'goulash' and *sihoť* 'island'.

The Rumanian input is in the terminology of upland sheep-farming, brought in by Wallachian migrants in the thirteenth to fifteenth centuries. Recognizably similar items occur in languages throughout the Carpathian and north Balkan area and include: *bača* 'head-shepherd', *bryndza* 'Liptauer cheese', *strunga* 'sheep-pen', *redikať sa* 'move to a new pasture'.

Latin has given not just the early, general European core of religious and some secular items (*diabol* 'devil', *omša* 'mass', *cintorín* 'cemetery', *kapusta* 'cabbage'), but also many words adopted at the height of Hungarian feudalism and later, when Latin was the language of the church, education, law and administration. The date of entry of individual items cannot be stated with certainty, but many were established by the seventeenth century: *dežma* 'tithe', *kúria* 'mansion', *protokol, kreditor, kalendár.*

Some items here are also disputed, Czech authors claiming the last example as mediated through Czech. Indeed, words from Czech are often impossible to date, or even identify, since they can be minimally modified to give an authentically Slovak appearance. Early borrowings whose Czech origins are not generally disputed include: *prozreteľnosť* 'providence', *otázka* 'question', *cisár* 'emperor', *Ježiš* 'Jesus' and *koleda* 'carol'. From the early fourteenth-century Czech–Slovak cultural contacts formed a strong tradition, associated with the founding of Prague University (1348), the Hussite campaigns (1423–31) and the spread in the use of the Kralice Bible (last quarter of the sixteenth century onwards); for many Slovaks a variously Slovakicized Czech was the literary language (see Ďurovič 1980). Undatable Czech loans include adjectives in -*itý* (*dôležitý* 'important', Czech *důležitý*) and -*teľný* (*znesiteľný* 'tolerable', Czech *snesitelný*), phonologically adapted. From the nineteenth century the picture is clearer: Czech was consciously modernized during the National Revival and many items passed rapidly into Slovak (*udalosť* 'event', *predmet* 'object', *totožný* 'identical' – again with Slovakicizing adjustments); indeed, large areas of terminology became common property, in grammar, the natural sciences and physical education. Twentieth-century purism expunged some Czech loans, but since the war neologizing has largely run parallel. Until quite recent times Czech influence remained strong in non-standard Slovak as spoken by conscripts or migrant workers, while informal speech in general contained, and may continue to contain, even conscious Czechisms, as part of a given register (*dik* 'thanks', for the stiffer native *vďaka*), or to supply a perceived gap (*všeho všudy* 'all told'). This merely extends the process whereby Czech terms are readily (re-)absorbed if there is no particularly strong motivation for the retention of a distinctive Slovak item (*diaľnica* ‹ *dálnice*, replacing *autostráda* 'motorway').

Czech was also the mediator of many Polish and Russian loans which penetrated various taxonomies and terminologies. Most Polish influence, however, affects only the East-Slovak dialects. Russian items unmediated by Czech include *iskrenný* 'sincere' and *jestvovať* 'exist', while many transparent Russianisms have to do with post-war sociopolitical developments.

The French and English input is in their largely international contribution in the arts (*žáner* 'genre', *rola* 'rôle'), sport (*bodiček, faul, derby*) and technology (*radar, laser, komputer*); computer jargon is one area that goes particularly far in its non-codified use of borrowings, hence such gems as /sejvnúť/ 'save' (on disk). For a good summary on borrowings see Ondruš, Horecký and Furdík (1980: 192–9).

5.3   Incorporation of borrowings

Borrowings are generally assigned to genders and paradigms according to their final sound. Very few fail to be assigned, because of their un-Slovak termination: uninflected *alibi, menu, defilé* (N), *revue, kanoe* (F). 'Classical' items ending in *-us, -um, -on*, etc. drop the alien case marker before native inflections: *komunizmus/-izmu, kozmos–kozmu, plénum–pléna,* though some are integrated whole: *cirkus–cirkusu, dátum–dátumu* (M!); even fewer exhibit variation: *týfus–týfusu/týfu*. Greek neuters in *-ma* become feminine *a*-stems, as do, with some morphological peculiarities, loans in *-ea*: *drama–dramy; idea–idey* (but *idei* (DAT/LOC.SG), *idei* (GEN.PL)).

Adjectival loans are adapted by addition of one or other productive suffix, especially *-ný, -ický* and *-ový*; *termálny, computerový, blonďavý*; few survive as non-inflecting: *khaki, gama* (*lúče*) 'gamma (rays)'.

Almost all verbal borrowings attract the *-ovať* suffix; every fourth verb now conjugates like this (Mistrík 1983: 72). They are frequently biaspectual, but the earlier they appeared, the greater the likelihood that a prefixed perfective will have emerged. Such 'new perfectivity' is a transparent feature of the dynamics of contemporary Slovak and affects many quite new arrivals. The prefixes used match those in semantically analogous native words: *za-protokolovať* 'put on record' as in *za-písať* 'note down', *o-xeroxovať* as in *o-písať* 'copy'. Borrowings may occur with an appropriate range of distinct prefixes: *montovať–zamontovať* 'instal', *zmontovať* 'assemble', *rozmontovať* 'dismantle', *primontovať* 'attach'.

5.4   Lexical fields

5.4.1   Colour terms

white	biela[1]	(primary noun) beľ (poetic)
black	čierna	čerň (bookish)
red	červená	červeň
green	zelená	zeleň (also 'greenery')
yellow	žltá	žlť
blue	modrá, belasá[2]; siná (pale blue)	
brown	hnedá, kávová (‹ *káva* 'coffee')[3]	hneď
purple	fialová (‹ *fialka* 'violet')[4]	
pink	ružová (‹ *ruža* 'rose')	
orange	oranžová (loan-word)	oranž (rare)
grey	sivá, popolavá (‹ *popol* 'ash'), šedivá, šedá[5]	

1   The adjectival forms here are feminine, by the normal association of colour terms with *farba* (F) 'colour'. The less widely used noun forms tend to be 'poetic' or 'bookish'; some appear in the names of paints or dyes (*tlačiarenská čerň* 'printing ink'), while others are replaced by adjectival forms (*berlínska modrá* 'Prussian blue').

2   *Modrá* and *belasá* are largely interchangeable and many dictionary examples are the same (sky, forget-me-not, lips in the cold, eyes). 'Blue stockings', 'blue foxes' and 'blue blood' can only be *modrá*.

3   *Hnedá* is the native word, but *kávová* is also widespread; in the standard Czech–Slovak dictionary the two share the load of Czech *hnědá*; *kávová* is fully integrated in the derivational system of colour terms, as in *maľovať na kávovo*, 'to paint something brown'.

4   *Fialová* covers 'purple', 'violet', 'lilac' (also *lilavá*), 'deep mauve' and so on. The colour term *purpurová* is more like crimson and is the colour of kings and cardinals. Another reddish-purple term is *nachová*.

5   The basic colour term here is *sivá*, the colour of, for example, pigeons, eyes, hair, grey cells and *éminences grises*; *šedá* is the grey of ash, dust, glaucoma and mediocrity, while *šedivá* is 'silvery grey', but also the grey of hair, an overcast sky, eyes, smoke and dust, an 'indefinite pale shade'. *Popolavá*, though descriptive in origin, is in wider use as a true colour term than Czech *popelavá*. Preference for any one 'grey' term in a given context type appears to be a matter of idiolect *par excellence*; all informants left it last, or omitted it, on being asked to list the main colour terms.

5.4.2   Body parts

head	hlava
eye	oko (anomalous plural, ex-dual, *oči*)
nose	nos

ear	ucho (anomalous plural, ex-dual *uši*)
mouth	ústa (N *plurale tantum*), pery (lips)
hair	vlasy (collective plural; SG *vlas* on head, otherwise *chlp* or *chĺpok* (DIMIN))
neck	krk (*šija* 'back of the neck'; *tylo, zátylok* 'back of the head', 'back of the neck')
arm/hand	ruka (*predlaktie* 'forearm'; *dlaň* 'palm'; *chrbát ruky* 'back of the hand')
finger	prst (*palec* 'thumb')
leg/foot	noha (*chodidlo* 'sole', rarely 'foot')
toe	prst na nohe (*palec* 'big toe')
chest/breast	prsia (*plurale tantum*, also 'breasts'); hruď 'chest, thorax'; prsník–y 'breast–s'
heart	srdce

Body terms are widely used in transferred senses, much as in other languages. However, the Slovak predilection for diminutives, lexical as well as expressive, is used widely to spread the metaphorical loading, hence, for example, a watch has *ručičky*, a pin has a *hlavička*, a jug has a *pyštek* (diminutive of *pysk* 'maw', colloquially also for 'mouth') 'spout', pigs' trotters as a comestible are *nôžky*, and delphinium is *stračia nôžka*.

5.4.3   Kinship terms

mother	mať, matka (plus *mama* and over a dozen other hypocoristic forms based on *mam-*)
father	otec (plus *tata* and about two dozen other hypocoristics based on *ot-*, *oc-* and *tat-*)
parents	rodičia (*rodič* 'sire'; *rodička* 'woman during or after parturition')
sister	sestra
brother	brat
aunt	teta (parent's sister)
	stryná (wife of paternal uncle)
	ujčiná (wife of maternal uncle; dial. also mother's sister)
uncle	strýko, strýc (father's brother)
	ujec, ujo (mother's brother; dialectal also mother's sister's husband)
	svák, sváko (parent's sister's husband)
niece	neter*
nephew	synovec

*While the distinctions between various uncles and aunts are still largely observed, attrition has greatly reduced the terms (often multiword expressions) for cousins and nieces/nephews (see Habovštiaková 1978).

cousin (female)	sesternica
cousin (male)	bratanec
grandmother	stará mama/mať, starká
grandfather	starý otec, dedko
wife	manželka (also *žena* 'woman' if accompanied by possessive pronoun)
husband	manžel (also *muž*, see above; *manželia* 'husband and wife', 'Mr and Mrs')
daughter	dcéra
son	syn

6 Dialects

The dialects of Slovak are remarkably well preserved in considerable variety, although the effects of a standard language and the pressure for uniformity it brings are strongly felt. The dialects themselves are so resilient that many regional features, especially lexical, are accorded the status of alternatives within the standard. The three main dialect groups are Central, the basis of the standard language, Western, which shares some features with adjacent Moravian dialects of Czech, and Eastern, the most striking both lexically and phonologically. In part because of physical geography, in part because of the relatively late start of major demographic changes, each area has many important surviving subdialects, too varied to describe here in detail, but regularly identified by the names of the old counties concerned.

The main distinctive features of **Western Slovak** are as follows (in broadly phonetic transcription):

1 *ort, *olt › *rot-*, *lot-* over much of the area, if not for every instance: for example, *rokita* 'sallow', (*v*)*loňi* 'last year';
2 almost all strong *jers* › *e*: *rež* 'rye', *len* 'flax', *déšč* 'rain';
3 front nasal *ę* › *a/á*: *maso* 'meat', *páti* 'fifth', *nosá* 'carry (3 PL *i*-conjugation)';
4 no rhythmical shortening;
5 no diphthongs, hence: *kóň/kúň* 'horse', *nésť/ňisť* 'carry', *vázať* 'tie';
6 *v/f* fully integrated into set of voiced–voiceless consonant pairs;
7 only one, middle, *l* phoneme;
8 gemination of certain consonants: *srcco, masso, kašša, stojjá* (for *srdce* 'heart', *maso* 'meat', *kaša* 'gruel', *stoja* 'they stand');
9 soft nouns nominative neuter singular in *-o*: *srcco, plecco* 'shoulder', *vajco* 'egg';
10 masculine animate neuter plural nouns in *-é* or *-ié* where standard has *-ia*: *luďé/ludé/ludié, sinovié* 'sons';

11 feminine instrumental singular in -*ú* or -*u*: *s tú dobrú ženú* 'with that good woman';

12 neuter nominative singular *ьjo*-stems in -*é* or -*í*: *znameňé/-i*;

13 soft adjectival declension closer to hard type: *cudzého*: *dobrého*;

14 certain infinitives and conjugations have short -*e*- to standard -*ie*-: *ňesem, veďeť*;

15 negative conjugation of *byť*: *ňeňi som, ňeňi si, ňeňi je ... ňeňi sú*, the parts quite mobile in the clause: *ešče sú tu ňeňi* 'they're not here yet'.

In addition to the **Central-Slovak** dialect area shown on map 10.1, the Slovak diaspora in Hungary and the Balkans also originated here. The main distinctive features of Central Slovak not present in the standard language include:

1 original -*tl*-, -*dl*- › -*l*-: *salo* 'lard', *omelo* 'flue-brush' (accepted in the standard language as alternative to *ometlo*);

2 bilabialization of final -*l* in *l*-participle masculine singular: *mislew* 'thought';

3 widespread incidence of *ä* of various origins in various environments; of particular interest is its appearance after softened velars (*kämeň* 'stone'), another local feature;

4 adjectives nominative singular neuter in -*uo* (or -*o* if rhythmical law applies): *nárečje slovenskuo* 'the Slovak language' (from a title by Štúr);

5 third person plural of *byť*: *sa* (standard *sú* is a western feature);

The main features distinguishing **Eastern Slovak** are:

1 loss of quantity;

2 penultimate word stress;

3 *orT, *olT › *roT*-, *loT*-: *rokita, loňi*;

4 nominative plural masculine animate in -*e* where standard has -*ia*: *ľudze, sinove*; this is one of many similarities to the western dialects, allowing for the loss of quantity. Others include the types *znameňe, ňešem* (1 SG), adjectival *cudze*: *dobre*, soft neuters *vajco, pľeco*, third person plural of *byť*: *su*;

5 *ie* › *i, uo* › *u* over most of the area, hence *mira* 'measure', *kuň* 'horse', with other monophthongizations elsewhere: *mera, koň*; in some parts the diphthongs survive;

6 original short nasal *ę* › *e*, but long › *ia* after labials and *a* elsewhere: *meso, piati, noša*;

7 *ť, ď* › *ts, dz*: *dzeci, isc* (for *deti* 'children', *ísť* 'go');

8 no syllabic liquids; solutions are many and various, including almost all available vowels as accompaniment, either preceding or following.

Map 10.1   The main Slovak dialects and county boundaries

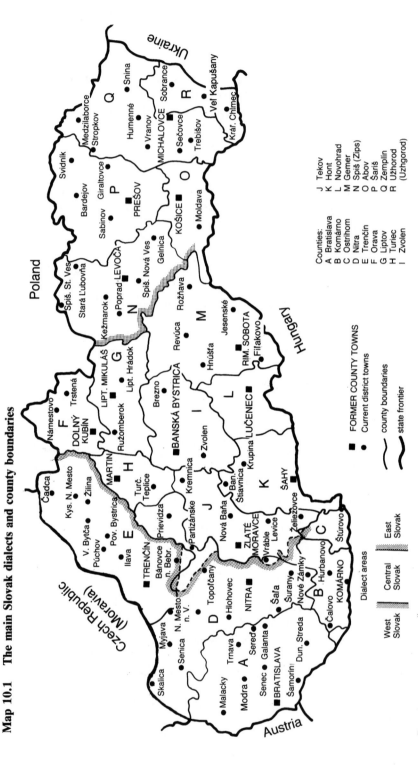

Based on a map by Jozef Štolc in J. Bělič *et al.*: 1980.

Almost as mixed are the various exceptions to the basic reflex of the *jers* as *e*;

9 genitive and locative plural of all genders in *-och* or *-of*, and all dative plural in *-om*;

10 instrumental singular feminine in *-u*: *s tu dobru ženu*;

11 possessive pronouns and adjectives in nominative plural end in *-o*, irrespective of gender: *mojo dzeci* 'my children', *bratovo chlapci* 'my brother's boys'; moreover, even a feminine possessor may use the suffix *-ovo* instead of *-in-*: *Haňkovo dzeci* 'Hana's children'.

Acknowledgement

The author gratefully acknowledges the sponsorship of the British Academy, which enabled him to spend two months at the Ľudovít Štúr Linguistics Institute in Bratislava, to many members of which he is also profoundly grateful for all their advice and guidance so freely given.

References

Bartoš, J. and Gagnaire, J. (1972) *Grammaire de la langue slovaque*, Bratislava: Matica slovenská, Paris: Institut d'Etudes Slaves.

Bělič, J., Jedlička, A., Jóna, E., Pauliny, E., Ružička, J. and Štolc, J. (1980) *Slovenština* (6th edn), Prague: Státní pedagogické nakladatelství, 159.

Ďurovič, Ľ. (1980) 'Slovak', in A.M. Schenker and E. Stankiewicz (eds) *The Slavic Literary Languages: Formation and Development*, New Haven, Conn.: Yale Concilium on International and Area Studies, 212–28, (bibliog.) 278–80.

Dvonč, L. (1968) 'On the formation of the passive participle in literary Slovak', *Recueil linguistique de Bratislava* 2: 124–7.

—— (1978) 'Words of English origin in Slovak', *Recueil linguistique de Bratislava* 5: 181–7.

—— (1989) 'Stability and dynamism in the declension of nouns in literary Slovak', *Recueil linguistique de Bratislava* 9: 97–106.

Habovštiaková, K. (1972) 'Le rôle de la langue tchèque dans la formation de la langue culturelle de la nationalité slovaque', *Recueil linquistique de Bratislava* 3: 127–34.

—— (1978) 'L'évolution de la microstructure sémantique des noms des membres de familles et des parents éloignés dans la langue slovaque', *Recueil linguistique de Bratislava* 5: 199–213.

Horecký, J. (1971) *Slovenská lexikológia*, vol. I: *Tvorenie slov*, Bratislava: SPN.

—— (1972) 'The phonological system of literary Slovak', *Recueil linguistique de Bratislava* 3: 37–49.

—— (1978) 'On semantic features of derivational meaning', *Recueil linguistique de Bratislava* 5: 93–7.

Horecký, J., Buzássyová, K. and Bosák, J. (1989) 'The dynamism of the word-stock of contemporary Slovak', in *Dynamika slovnej zásoby súčasnej slovenčiny*, Bratislava: Veda, 387–404.

Miko, F. (1972) 'Passive transformation in the Slovak language', *Recueil linguistique de Bratislava* 3: 73–7.

Mistrík, J. (1966) *Slovosled a vetosled v slovenčine*, Bratislava; Vydavateľstvo SAV, English résumé 245–50.

—— (1983) *A Grammar of Contemporary Slovak*, Bratislava, SPN.

—— (1985) 'The modernization of contemporary Slovak', in G. Stone and D. Worth (eds) *The Formation of the Slavonic Literary Languages*, Columbus, Ohio: Slavica, 72–6.

Ondruš, P., Horecký, J. and Furdík, J. (1980) *Súčasný slovenský spisovný jazyk: Lexikológia*, Bratislava: Slovenské pedagogické nakladateľstvo.

Oravec, J. (1982) 'The objective reflexive pronoun in Slovak', *Recueil linguistique de Bratislava* 6: 205–14.

—— (1984) 'Variant suffixes in Slovak genitive singular of pattern "dub"', *Recueil linguistique de Bratislava* 7: 97–102.

Oravec, J. and Bajzíková, E. (1982) *Súčasný slovenský spisovný jazyk: syntax*, Bratislava: SPN.

Oravec, J., Bajzíková, E. and Furdík, J. (1984) *Súčasný slovenský spisovný jazyk: morfológia*, Bratislava: SPN.

Rudolf, R. (1991) *Die deutschen Lehn- und Fremdwörter in der slowakischen Sprache*, Vienna: Verband der wissenschaftlichen Gesellschaften Österreichs.

Sabol, J. (1978) 'On the morphology of Slovak substantives', *Recueil linguistique de Bratislava* 5: 61–70.

—— (1984) 'A synthetic phonological theory', *Recueil linguistique de Bratislava* 8: 25–9.

11 Sorbian (Upper and Lower)

Gerald Stone

1 Introduction

The Sorbian speech area has no precisely defined boundaries, natural or otherwise. In the tenth century the Sorbian-speaking population was settled in an area between the rivers Saale (in the west) and Bober and Queis (in the east). In the north it extended to where Berlin and Frankfurt-an-der-Oder now stand. In the south it was bounded by the Erzgebirge and the Lausitzer Gebirge. The neighbouring languages were Polabian (to the north), Polish (to the east), Czech (to the south) and German (to the west). Sorbian was thus spoken in an area which extended east of the Neisse into what is today (1993) Polish territory and included, in the west, the land where the towns of Halle, Leipzig, Zwickau and Chemnitz were later to appear. In the course of the succeeding centuries it contracted steadily until by the nineteenth century it had become what is still regarded as the Sorbian speech area with its northern limits about 50 miles (80 km) to the south-east of Berlin (see map 11.1). It extends for about 57 miles (92 km) from north to south and is roughly 41 miles (66 km) wide at its widest point measured from east to west. The southern limits are less than 5 miles (8 km) north of the Czech frontier. Within this area until the early twentieth century the rural population was predominantly Sorbian-speaking, but the main towns (Cottbus, Spremberg and Bautzen) were always predominantly German-speaking from the time of their foundation in the Middle Ages.

The area inhabited by the Sorbs formerly constituted the margraviates (border provinces) of Upper Lusatia (on the upper reaches of the River Spree) and Lower Lusatia (on the lower reaches). For this reason the language is sometimes known in English as *Lusatian.* In German the most common term until the Second World War was *wendisch*, though *sorbisch* was also used. After the war *sorbisch* was given official support and is now (1993) dominant, though *wendisch* was revived in Lower Lusatia in 1991. In English *Sorbian* is standard, but *Wendish* also exists. The equivalent adjective in both Upper and Lower Sorbian is *serbski* (derived from *Serb* 'a Sorb'). The varieties spoken in Upper Lusatia are referred to in English as Upper Sorbian, those spoken in Lower Lusatia as Lower Sorbian. The

Map 11.1   The Sorbian speech area

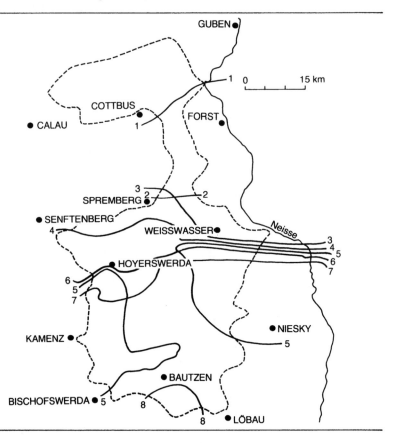

German and Sorbian equivalents are *Obersorbisch* (USo. *hornjoserbšćina*, LSo. *gornoserbšćina*) and *Niedersorbisch* (USo. *delnjoserbšćina*, LSo. *dolnoserbšćina*); for further information on the Sorbs generally see Stone (1972) and Urban (1980).

Long before the nineteenth century the Sorbian speech area had become an island surrounded by German-speakers and isolated from both Poles and Czechs. During and since the nineteenth century the Sorbian-speaking population has been steadily diluted by German immigration, by Sorbian emigration and by the tendency for Sorbs to transfer their allegiance from Sorbian to German. Today (1993) the area is overwhelmingly German-speaking, but Sorbian is far from being dead. In a cluster of about forty villages to the north-west of Bautzen which are both mainly Catholic and mainly Sorbian there is a fairly close-knit speech community. This is the nucleus of a larger loose-knit community scattered throughout Lusatia. A survey conducted in 1987 put the number of Sorbian-speakers at around

KEY:

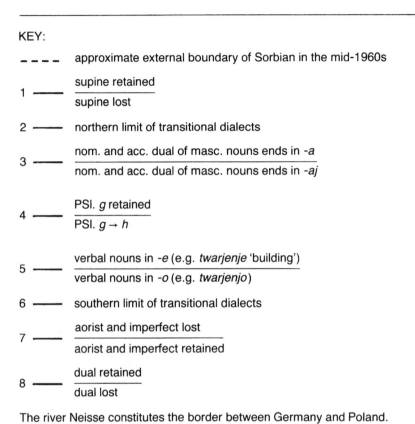

- - - -	approximate external boundary of Sorbian in the mid-1960s

1 —— $\dfrac{\text{supine retained}}{\text{supine lost}}$

2 ——   northern limit of transitional dialects

3 —— $\dfrac{\text{nom. and acc. dual of masc. nouns ends in } \textit{-a}}{\text{nom. and acc. dual of masc. nouns ends in } \textit{-aj}}$

4 —— $\dfrac{\text{PSl. } \textit{g} \text{ retained}}{\text{PSl. } \textit{g} \rightarrow \textit{h}}$

5 —— $\dfrac{\text{verbal nouns in } \textit{-e} \text{ (e.g. } \textit{twarjenje} \text{ 'building')}}{\text{verbal nouns in } \textit{-o} \text{ (e.g. } \textit{twarjenjo}\text{)}}$

6 ——   southern limit of transitional dialects

7 —— $\dfrac{\text{aorist and imperfect lost}}{\text{aorist and imperfect retained}}$

8 —— $\dfrac{\text{dual retained}}{\text{dual lost}}$

The river Neisse constitutes the border between Germany and Poland.

67,000. Of these more than half are Lutherans, about a quarter are Catholics and the rest have no denominational allegiance.

The Constitution of the German Democratic Republic from 1949 to 1990 guaranteed and supported the cultural rights of the Sorbs. These rights are also recognized in the treaty between the Federal Republic of Germany and the German Democratic Republic signed in September 1990. Provision is made in certain schools for most subjects to be taught through the medium of Sorbian or for Sorbian to be taught as a subject. Between 1948 and 1984 over 2,350 Sorbian titles were published by the state-supported Domowina publishing house. The Upper Sorbian daily newspaper *Serbske Nowiny* and the Lower Sorbian weekly *Nowy Casnik* are successful thanks to state subsidies. The German–Sorbian theatre in Bautzen presents plays in Sorbian from time to time. Sorbian has so far not managed to become a regular feature of German television, but there are daily radio broadcasts in Sorbian. The Sorbian Ethnological Institute

(*Institut za serbski ludospyt*) in Bautzen, founded in 1951, was replaced in 1992 by a new Sorbian Institute (*Serbski Institut*) in the same premises but with a Lower Sorbian branch in Cottbus. Its activities include research into the language, history and folklore of the Sorbs.

A central role in the maintenance of Sorbian is played by the Lutheran and Catholic Churches. Mass in Sorbian is said regularly in the Catholic parishes. Lutheran services are also held in Sorbian, but less regularly. The Churches publish the Upper Sorbian newspapers *Katolski Posoł* (twice monthly) and *Pomhaj Bóh* (monthly). The latter occasionally has a Lower Sorbian supplement.

The earliest surviving texts in Sorbian date from the sixteenth century, but fragmentary evidence from earlier centuries also exists in the form of Sorbian words, phrases or even short sentences scattered here and there in Latin and German documents. One of the main early sources of this kind is the Chronicle of Bishop Thietmar of Merseburg, written in 1012–18. The first Sorbian text is the Bautzen Burghers' Oath (1532), a formula by which citizens of Bautzen swore allegiance to the king and the town authorities. It is only forty-two years older than the first Sorbian printed book, Albin Moller's *Wendisches Gesangbuch* (Bautzen, 1574), which consists of a hymnal and catechism in Lower Sorbian. The first Upper Sorbian printed book is a catechism translated and published by Wenceslaus Warichius (Bautzen, 1595). The local features in these early texts are very clear and, in fact, things were to stay that way until the eighteenth century. A manuscript New Testament of 1548, translated from German by Mikławš Jakubica, is in the dialect once spoken to the east of the Neisse in the vicinity of Sorau (Żary in present-day Poland). Like the other translations of devotional works at this time it was intended solely for local use.

The seventeenth century saw the appearance of three Sorbian grammars, but only one of them was printed. This was the *Principia linguae wendicae quam aliqui wandalicam vocant* of Jacobus Xaverius Ticinus (Prague, 1679), based on the northern Catholic dialect of Wittichenau (Sorbian Kulow). Georgius Ludovici's manuscript 'Rudimenta grammaticae Sorabo-Vandalicae idiomatis Budissinatis', written before 1673, is based (as the title indicates) on the Bautzen dialect. The earliest of these three grammars, however, is Johannes Chojnanus's Lower Sorbian 'Linguae Vandalicae ad dialectum districtus Cotbusiani formandae aliqualis conatus', a manuscript dated 1650.

The main sphere of activity of the literary languages before the nineteenth century was the Churches. Therefore the translation of the Bible was of crucial importance in their development. The printing of the Upper Sorbian Bible for Lutherans began with the appearance in 1670 of Michał Frencel's translation of the gospels of St Matthew and St Mark. This was followed in 1706 (the year of his death) by his translation of the whole New Testament. Frencel wrote in the subdialect of the Bautzen dialect, spoken to the east and south of the town, known as the Hill Dialect (German *Gebirgsdialekt*, USo. *přihórska nareč*). In 1703, however, the Upper Lusatian States (Oberlausitzer Landstände) set up a committee to translate the whole Bible using a literary variety based broadly on the whole Bautzen region. The translation was published in 1728 and established this variety as the literary standard for Lutherans. Events of similar significance for Lower Sorbs were the publication of Gottlieb Fabricius's translation of the New Testament in Kahren in 1709 and of Johann Friedrich Fryco's Old Testament in Cottbus in 1796. They established the Cottbus dialect as the basis for the Lower Sorbian literary language.

The Upper Sorbian literary standard for Catholics in the seventeenth century was based on the dialect of Wittichenau (Sorbian Kulow). The special influence of this little town, situated about 7 kilometres south of Hoyerswerda (see map 11.1), was probably due to the fact that it had a grammar school and that consequently it was able to produce a number of influential clerics. Ticinus (see above) came from Wittichenau and chose to base his grammar on its dialect. It was also the birthplace of Jurij Hawštyn Swětlik (1650–1729), who between 1688 and 1707 translated the entire Vulgate into a literary language based on the same dialect. Swětlik's translation has never been printed, but a by-product of this work was his *Vocabularium Latino-Serbicum* (Bautzen, 1721), the first Sorbian dictionary. It served to confirm further the prestige of the Wittichenau dialect. In the mid-eighteenth century, however, Catholic Sorbs from the Crostwitz area (south-east of Kamenz) gained an increasingly influential position in the ruling circles of the Catholic hierarchy, and the literary language for Catholics may by about 1750 be said to be based on the Crostwitz dialect. A confusing custom emerged of calling the Crostwitz dialect the Catholic dialect despite the fact that the Sorbs of the Wittichenau parish are also Catholics. The Crostwitz-based literary variant was codified by Franz Schneider in his *Grammatik der wendischen Sprache katholischen Dialekts* (Bautzen, 1853).

Ticinus's orthography was based on that of Czech and, although a number of changes were made later, his influence on the Catholic spelling system remained perceptible until it ceased to exist as a separate entity. The orthography used in Protestant publications was mainly based on German. In 1841 Jan Ernst Smoler introduced a new orthographic system for Upper Sorbian, based on those already in use in some other Slavonic languages, notably Czech, and involving the use of Roman type. Hitherto, Sorbian had always been printed in the Black Letter typeface known as *Fraktur*, an example of which is reproduced in figure 11.1. In 1843 Smoler's system was used for the first time to print Lower Sorbian. In both Upper and Lower Sorbian, however, the new orthography was slow to acquire popularity.

In the 1840s secular matters began to be discussed with increasing

Figure 11.1 Lower Sorbian in Black Letter (*Fraktur*)

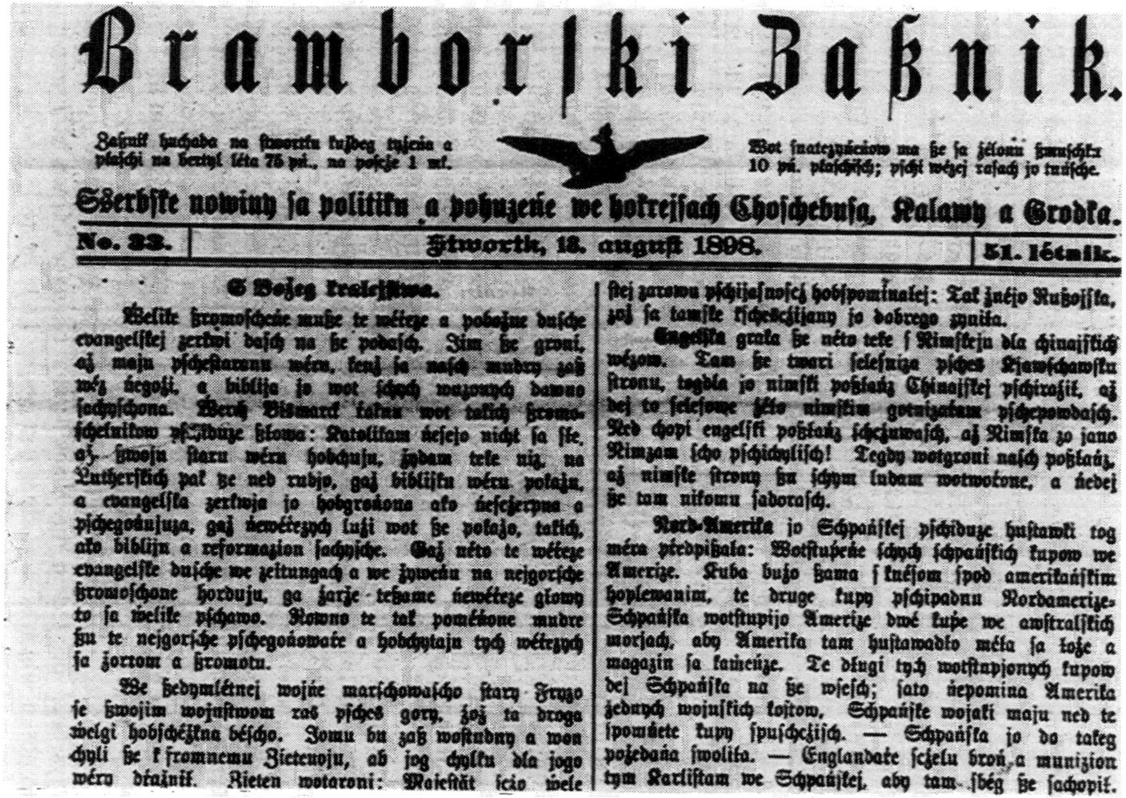

Bramborski Zaßnik.

Zaßnik huchada na ſtworth kuždeg tyźenja a płaśi na bertyl léta 75 pj., na pośće 1 mk. | Wot ſnatezyńćiow ma ße ſa źełonu ßmużkę 10 pj. płaśiśćh; pśśi wéśej raſach jo tuńśe.

Sserbſke nowiny ſa politiku a pohuzenie we hokrejſach Choſchebuſa, Kalawy a Grodka.

No. 33. | Stwortk, 18. auguſt 1898. | 51. létnik.

S Wojeg kralejſtwa.

Welike hromoſcheńe muže te wéteje a poboźne duśche evangelskej zerkwi daśch na ße podeśch. Zim ße groni, aź maju pśchestaranu wéru, kenż ja naśch mudry zaś wéz ńegoźi, a biblija jo wot ſchych wazonych dawno ſachyſchona. Werch Bismarck takne wot takich hromoſchelnikow pśidnże ßłowa: Katolikam ńeſejo nicht ſa ſke, aź ſwoju ſtaru wéru hobchuju, ſydam tele niz, na Lutherſkich pak ze ned rubjo, gaź biblijſku wéru polaju, a evangelſka zerkwja jo hobgrońona ako ńeſcherpna a pśchegońujuza, gaź ńewéteżych luźi wot ße polajo, takich, ako biblijn a reformazion ſachyſche. Gaź néto te wéteje evangelſke duśche we zeitungach a we ſywenu na nejgorſche hromoſchone horduju, ga zarje teſame ńewéteje głowy to ſa welike pśchawo. Rowno te tak pomékone mudre ßu te nejgorſche pśchegońowaŕe a hobchytaju tych wéteżych ſa zortom a hromotu.

We ßedymlétnej wojńe marśchowaśo ſtary Fryzo ſe ßwojim wojuſtwom raz pśches gory, źoź ta droga wjelgi hobſchéźkna béſcho. Jomu bu zaß woſtudny a won chyli ße k ſromnemu Zietenoju, ab jog chylku dla jogo wéry dráźnił. Zieten wotgroni: Majeſtät ſcio wele

ſtej zerowu pśchijeſnoſcj hobſpomnaſej: Tak znéjo Kuzoiſka, zaź ſa tamſke tſchekcijany jo dobrego zynika.

Engelſka graka ße néto teke ſ Nimſkeju dla chinajſkich wézow. Tam ße twari ſeleſniza pśches Sjawſchawſku ſtronu, togdla jo nimſki poßłańz Chinajſkej pśchirozit, aź dej to ſeleſnowe ßéto nimſkim gornizakam pśchepowdaśch. Ned chopi engelſki poßłańz ſchejuwaśch, aź Nimſka zo jano Nimzam ſcho pśchiwzliśch! Tegdy wotgroni naśch poßłańz, aź nimſke ſtrony ßu ſchym ludam wotwokone, a ńedej ße tam nikomu ſadoraśch.

Nord-Amerika jo Schpańſkej pśchiduze huſtawki tog méra pśedpiſała: Wotſtupeńe ſchych ſchpańſkich kupow we Amerize. Kuba bujo ßama ſ knéſom ſpod amerikańſkim hoplewanim, te druge kupy pśchipadnu Nordamerize. Schpańſka wotſtupijo Amerize dwé kupe we awſtralſkich morjach, aby Amerika tam huſtawadło méła ſa łoźe a magazin ſa kameńze. Te długi tych wotſtupjonych kupow dej Schpańſka na ße wześch; ſato ńepomina Amerika zedných wojuſkich koſtow. Schpańſke wojaki maju ned te ſpomńete kupy ſpuśchćiśch. — Schpańſka jo do takeg pożedańa ſwolila. — Englandaŕe ſchelu broń a munizion tym Karliſtam we Schpańſkej, aby tam ſbég ße ſachopił.

Source: Front page of the weekly *Bramborski Casnik* (18 August 1898).

frequency in Upper Sorbian publications and the vocabulary of the literary language underwent far-reaching changes. Words to denote new concepts were introduced from international terminology (though the immediate source for such words was naturally German): for example, *anthropologa* 'anthropologist', *grammatika* 'grammar', *musika* 'music', *werb* 'verb'. Simultaneously, there was a tendency to reject non-international German borrowings and to replace them with Slavonic words, usually based on Czech models.

Smoler was the main instigator of the foundation in 1847 of the *Maćica Serbska*, a scientific and cultural body, which published the *Časopis Maćicy Serbskeje*, a learned journal which influenced the development of the literary languages. It was printed in Smoler's new spelling system (known as the 'analogical' orthography), with Roman type, and in the new Upper Sorbian literary language, purged of many of the results of German interference. In the mid-nineteenth century there were five ways of writing and printing Sorbian. These were (a) that of the *Časopis Maćicy Serbskeje* (Upper Sorbian for secular purposes in the analogical orthography and in Roman type); (b) that of the Upper Sorbian Lutherans (based on the composite literary language of the 1728 Bible and in Black Letter); (c) that of the Upper Sorbian Catholics (based on the Crostwitz dialect, but vestigially Ticinian, and in Black Letter); (d) Lower Sorbian Black Letter (exemplified in figure 11.1); and (e) Lower Sorbian in the analogical orthography and in Roman (this was extremely rare).

From 1842 onwards there was a weekly newspaper for Upper Sorbs entitled *Tydźenska Nowina*, printed in the Protestant orthography and in Black Letter. The Lower Sorbian weekly *Bramborski serski casnik* (Black Letter) first appeared in 1848. A significant new departure was the monthly *Łužičan*, which from 1860 appeared under the joint auspices of Smoler (a Protestant) and Michał Hórnik (a Catholic priest) and printed in the analogical orthography in Roman type. Gradually a series of concessions were made by both Catholic and Protestant Upper Sorbian writers and editors. Nevertheless, even by the 1930s some Catholic publications were still reflecting certain peculiarities of the Crostwitz dialect and the daily *Serbske Nowiny* was still using Black Letter and the old orthography. Complete Upper Sorbian unification had still not been achieved when, in 1937, all printing in Sorbian was banned. Only the *Katolski Posoł*, protected from the ban by the Nazi Concordat with the Vatican, continued to appear until 1939, when it too was closed down. It was not until after the Second World War that a single set of norms for Upper Sorbian was adopted, using a slightly modified version of the analogical orthography and Roman type.

Lower Sorbian has only with great difficulty maintained its separate status as a literary language. A Lower Sorbian section of the *Maćica Serbska* was established in 1880, but the society's journal, the *Časopis*

Maćicy Serbskeje, only rarely published items in Lower Sorbian. It announced that it carried items 'in the Lower Sorbian dialect, when possible', but it also published articles by Lower Sorbian authors on Lower Sorbian topics, written in Upper Sorbian. Compared with Upper Sorbian, the number of books and periodicals published in Lower Sorbian has always been small. Until the 1930s most publications in Lower Sorbian were printed in Black Letter and in the old orthography, but since the revival of Sorbian activity after the Second World War it has been printed exclusively in the new spelling and in Roman type.

2 Phonology

2.1 Segmental phoneme inventory

The segmental vowel phonemes of both Upper and Lower Sorbian are as follows:

```
i                    u
  ě              ó
    e        o
       a
```

/u/, /ó/ and /o/ are labialized. The tongue position for /ě/ and /ó/ is higher than for /e/ and /o/, and in slow speech /ě/ and /ó/ are both subject to diphthongization ([ie] and [uo] respectively).

The segmental consonant phonemes of Upper Sorbian are shown in table 11.1.

Table 11.1   Consonant phonemes of Upper Sorbian

	Bilabial	Labio-dental	Dental	Alveolar	Pre-palatal	Post-palatal	Velar	Laryngeal
Plain	p	p̦	t				k	
stop	b	b̦	d				g	
Affricate			ts	ts̡	tʃ dʒ			
Fricative		f	s		ʃ		x	
	w	w̦ v	z		ʒ			h
Nasal	m	m̦		n ŋ				
Lateral				l				
Trill				r ŗ				
Semi-vowel						j		

Following the spelling reform of 1 December 1948 the Upper Sorbian alphabet consists of the following thirty-four symbols: A a, B b, C c, Č č, D d, Dź dź, E e, Ě ě, F f, G g, H h, Ch ch, I i, J j, K k, Ł ł, L l, M m, N n, Ń ń, O o, Ó ó, P p, R r, Ř ř, S s, Š š, T t, Ć ć, U u, W w, Y y, Z z, Ž ž. The reform substituted b for b́, m for ḿ, p for ṕ, r for ŕ, w for ẃ and ch for kh. The alphabetical order shown above is occasionally subject to variation. Normally (but not always) ó is not treated as a separate item from o. Therefore, for example, *hódny* 'worth, worthy' comes after *hober* 'giant' and before *hody* 'Christmas'. Only in the case of pairs of words that are in all other respects identical does o have precedence over ó (thus *ton* 'tone' precedes *tón* 'that'). But it is not unknown for o to have general precedence over ó, in which case *hódny* would follow *hody*. The unusual position occupied by ć is due to the fact that it results from the metaphony *t* (before front vowels) › *ć* (as in *ćěło* 'body' ‹ **tělo*). In some alphabetical lists it may follow not t but č, or it may even precede č.

In both Upper and Lower Sorbian the letters Q q, V v and X x are used only in foreign proper nouns, such as *Quebec, Voltaire, Marx*. In borrowings these letters are replaced by kw, w and ks: USo. and LSo. *kwalita* 'quality', USo. and LSo. *wila* 'villa', and USo. and LSo. *ekspedicija* 'expedition'.

The graphemes of present-day Upper Sorbian orthography correspond to the phonemes as follows:

Vowels

Grapheme	*Phoneme*	*Example*
a	a	*nan* /nan/ 'father'
e	e	*ćelo* /tɕelo/ 'calf'
ě	ě	*wěm* /w̭ěm/ 'I know'
	e (if unstressed; even then, only inconsistently)	*njewěm* /n̩ėw̭em/ or /n̩ėw̭ěm/ 'I don't know'
i (indicates that the preceding consonant is soft)	i	*bić* /bʲitʃ/ 'to beat'
y (indicates that the preceding consonant is hard)		*być* /bitʃ/ 'to be'
o	o	*pos* /pos/ 'dog'
ó	ó	*tón* /tón/ 'that'
	o (if unstressed; even then, only inconsistently)	*rozhłós* /rȯzwos/ or /rȯzwós/ 'radio'
u	u	*tu* /tu/ 'here'

Consonants

p	p	*kopor* /kopor/ 'copper'
p (before i or ě)	⎫	*pěc* /p̦ěts/ 'stove'
	⎬ p̦	*pjasć* /p̦astʃ/ 'fist'
pj	⎭	
b	b	*być* /bitʃ/ 'to be'
b (before i or ě)	⎫	*bić* /b̦itʃ/ 'to beat'
	⎬ b̦	*njebjo* /ɲeb̦o/ 'sky, heaven'
bj	⎭	
m	m	*štom* /ʃtom/ 'tree'
m (before i or ě)	⎫	*měć* /m̦ětʃ/ 'to have'
	⎬ m̦	*mjaso* /m̦aso/ 'meat, flesh'
mj	⎭	
ł	w	*hłós* /wós/ 'voice'
	⎧ w	*wóz* /wós/ 'cart, car'
w	⎨ Ø	(before initial consonants) *wzać* /zatʃ/ 'to take'
	⎩ v	(in foreign words) *kolektiwny* /kolektivni/ 'collective'
w (before i or ě)	⎫	*wić* /w̦itʃ/ 'to wind'
	⎬ w̦	*w rowje* /row̦e/ 'in the grave'
wj	⎭	
f ⎫		*foto* /foto/ 'photo'
hw ⎭ f	f	*hwězda* /fězda/ 'star'
n	n	*nan* /nan/ 'father'
n (before i or ě)	⎫	*ně* /ɲě/ 'no'
	⎬ ɲ	*njebjo* /ɲeb̦o/ 'sky, heaven'
nj	⎭	
ń	jn	*dźeń* /dʒejn/ 'day'
r	r	*raj* /raj/ 'paradise'
r (before i or ě)	⎫	*hrib* /ʀip/ 'mushroom'
	⎬ ʀ	*rjek* /ʀek/ 'hero'
rj	⎭	(both /r/ and /ʀ/ are normally uvular; lingual /r/ and /ɾ/ are archaic)
t	t	*tón* /tón/ 'that'
d	d	*do* /do/ 'to'
l	l	*lěto* /lěto/ 'year'
c	ts	*cuzy* /tsuzi/ 'foreign'
tř ⎫		*tři* /tʂi/ 'three'
tč ⎪		*wótčina* /wótʂina/ 'fatherland'
tš ⎬ tʂ	tʂ	*krótši* /krótʂi/ 'shorter'
dš ⎪		*młódši* /mwótʂi/ 'younger'
dč ⎭		*swědčić* /sw̦ětʂitʃ/ 'to witness'

tř	tʃ	(rarely: for example, *třasć* /tʃastʃ/ 'to shake')
č, ć	tʃ	*čin* /tʃin/ 'action'; *ćicho* /tʃixo/ 'quiet'
dź	dʒ	*dźeń* /dʒejn/ 'day'
s	s	*so* /so/ 'self'
z	z	*zo* /zo/ 'that'
š, ř	ʃ	*šat* /ʃat/ 'frock'; *křik* /kʃik/ 'cry' (*ř* occurs only in the combinations *tř* (see above), *kř* and *př*
ž	ʒ	*hižo* /hiʒo/ 'already'
j	j	*ja* /ja/ 'I' (also to soften certain consonants: *pj, bj, mj, wj, nj, rj*)
k	k	*kerk* /kerk/ 'bush'
g	g	*grat* /grat/ 'equipment'
ch	x	*ćicho* /tʃixo/ 'quiet'; /x/ is a velar spirant except at the beginning of a morpheme (where it is replaced by an aspirated plosive [kʰ] (for example, *chodźić* /kʰodʒitʃ/ 'to walk, go'))
	Ø	*chcu* /tsu/ 'I want' (initially before *c*)
h	h	*hat* /hat/ 'pond' (initially before a vowel)
	Ø	*hrěch* /ᶉěx/ 'sin' (initially before a consonant); *sněh* /sᶇě/ 'snow' (finally); *wuhlo* /wulo/ 'coal' (internally before a consonant), but in a few words *h* internally before a consonant may be [ɣ] (a voiced variant of /x/), for example, *nahły* /naɣwi/ 'steep'
	j	*kniha* /kᶇija/ 'book' (between vowels) (colloquial variant of /kᶇiha/)
	w	*noha* /nowa/ 'foot, leg' (between vowels) (colloquial variant of /noha/)

The paired hard/soft consonant phonemes are: /p/:/ᶈ/, /b/:/ᶀ/, /m/:/ᶆ/, /w/:/w̡/, /n/:/ᶇ/, /r/:/ᶉ/, /ts/:/tᶊ/. The phoneme /v/ is of extremely low frequency; its phonemic status is controversial. It occurs in oblique cases of certain foreign words (like *kolektiwa* /kolektiva/, genitive singular of *kolektiw* /kolektif/ 'collective') and in derivatives of the same words (*kolektiwny* /kolektivni/). The only Slavonic words in which it occurs are derivatives of *łhać* /fatʃ/ 'to lie', namely *zełharny* /zevarni/ 'deceitful' and *zełharnosć* /zevarnostʃ/ 'deceitfulness'. These words are typically used only by speakers of the Bautzen dialect. In the Catholic dialect they are replaced by *łžeć* /bʒetʃ/ and its derivatives. The phoneme /f/ occurs mainly in foreign and onomatopoeic words. The soft counterparts of /f/ and /v/ are extremely rare and not normally regarded as phonemes. The phonemic status of /ts̡/ is controversial.

The following are some of the main restrictions on phoneme distribution in Upper Sorbian:

1   Owing to the fact that in both Upper and Lower Sorbian Proto-Slavonic words and German borrowings acquired prothetic consonants (as in USo. *hić*/LSo. *hyś* ‹ *iti 'to go', USo. and LSo. *wokoło* ‹ *okolo 'around', USo. *wolbyrny* 'foolish' (compare German *albern* 'foolish')) hardly any Upper Sorbian words begin with a vowel. Initial /a/ occurs in *a* 'and', *ale* 'but', *abo* 'or' and *ani* 'nor'; otherwise it is restricted to recent borrowings, such as *algebra* 'algebra' and *awto* 'car'. The phonemes /ě/ and /ó/ never appear initially; /e/, /o/, /i/ and /u/ appear initially only in recent borrowings (such as *energija* 'energy', *idyl* 'idyll', *objekt* 'object', *uniwersita* 'university'). Initial vowels are normally preceded by a glottal stop (Михалк/Michalk 1974: 474): thus *ale* /ʔale/ 'but', *abo* /ʔabo/ 'or', *institut* /ʔinstitût/ 'institute'; but prothetic /h/ may also be heard: /hale/, /habo/ and so on.

2   The contrast between voiced and voiceless paired consonants (/d/ and /t/, /b/ and /p/, /z/ and /s/, /dʒ/ and /tʃ/, /g/ and /k/, /ʒ/ and /ʃ/) is neutralized in word-final position. The resultant sound is phonetically voiceless: *pad* /pat/ 'case', *snadź* /snatʃ/ 'perhaps', *nóž* /nóʃ/ 'knife'. The contrast is also neutralized in the position immediately before any one of these consonants owing to assimilation: *ličba* /lidʒba/ 'number', *susodka* /susotka/ '(female) neighbour'.

3   Post-vocalic soft consonants (including the historically soft *ń*) are preceded by epenthetic /j/, producing a diphthong: *kaž* /kajʃ/ 'as', *tež* /tejʃ/ 'also', *zemja* /zejma/ 'land', *dźeń* /dʒejn/ 'day'. If the vowel is /e/ or /ě/, the preceding consonant is often hard, notwithstanding the spelling, and /e/ is substituted for /ě/: *knjeni* /knejni/ 'lady', *běži* /bejʒi/ 'runs', *wječor* /wejtʃor/ 'evening' (Šewc 1968: 30–1).

4   The contrast between hard and soft paired consonants is, in the literary language, neutralized in word-final position. The sole phonetic function of the letter *ń* is to represent hard /n/ preceded by epenthetic /j/: *dźeń* /dʒejn/ 'day'.

The segmental consonant phonemes of Lower Sorbian are shown in table 11.2.

The Lower Sorbian orthography was last reformed in 1952. The alphabet now has the following thirty-five symbols: A a, B b, C c, Č č, Ć ć,

Table 11.2   Consonant phonemes of Lower Sorbian

	Bilabial	Labio-dental	Dental	Alveolar	Pre-palatal	Post-palatal	Velar	Laryngeal
Plain	p p̦		t				k	
stop	b b̦		d				g	
Affricate			ts	tʃ	tʃ			
Fricative		f	s	ʃ	ʃ		x	h
	w w̦	v	z	ʒ	ʒ			
Nasal								
	m m̦			n	ŋ			
Lateral				l				
Trill								
				r	r̦			
Semi-vowel						j		

D d, DŹ dź, E e, Ě ě, F f, G g, H h, Ch ch, I i, J j, K k, Ł ł, L l, M m, N n, Ń ń, O o, P p, R r, Ŕ ŕ, S s, Š š, Ś ś, T t, U u, W w, Y y, Z z, Ž ž, Ź ź.

The vocalic grapheme–phoneme correspondences of Lower Sorbian are identical with those of Upper Sorbian except in one respect. The letter ó, which before 1952 was used to represent /ó/, was abolished on the grounds that /ó/ is always substituted for /o/ when it occurs in a stressed syllable immediately following a velar or labial (but not ł) and is not itself immediately followed by a velar or labial: for example *gora* /góra/ 'hill'. According to this view /ó/ is merely a positional variant of /o/, not a phoneme, and its distribution is therefore predictable. In some dialects this is indeed the situation, but in the literary language *ł* and *w* have coalesced as /w/ and between /w/ (< *ł*) and a consonant that is neither a velar nor a labial /o/ is not replaced by /ó/ (for example *włose* /wose/ 'hair'). Therefore, the distribution of /o/ and /ó/ can be deduced only by taking the orthography into account. The grapheme o represents the two phonemes /o/ and /ó/.

The consonantal grapheme–phoneme correspondences of Lower Sorbian differ from those of Upper Sorbian in the following respects:

1   ń (written only finally and before consonants) is phonetically [ŋ].
2   dź represents not a phoneme, but a positional variant of /ʒ/ which occurs only immediately after /z/ or /ʒ/, as in *pozdźej* 'later', *droždźeje* 'yeast'.
3   ž /ʒ/, š /ʃ/ and tš /tʃ/ (rarely written č) are contrasted with soft ź /ʒ/, ś /ʃ/ and tś (or ć) /tʃ/: *žywy* 'alive' : *źiwy* 'wild'; *koše* 'baskets' : *kośe* 'kitten'; *tšmjeń* 'swamp' : *tśmjeń* 'stirrup'.

4   PSl. *č* has become *c* (for example, *cas* 'time'). Consequently, the
     grapheme *č* occurs only in loan-words like *čaj* 'tea'. However, the
     phoneme /tʃ/ is not rare owing to the fact that PSl. *tr* (before back
     vowels) has become *tš*, as in *tšach* 'fear' ‹ *straxъ.
5   The grapheme *ć* usually occurs after sibilants, for instance, *gosć* 'guest'.
     It is otherwise found only in the word *źowćo* 'girl' and its derivatives.
     However, the phoneme /tʃʲ/ is not uncommon, owing to the fact that
     PSl. *tr* (before front vowels) is represented by *tś* (thus *tri* 'three' › *tśi*).
6   There is no soft /tsʲ/ and no grapheme *ř*.
7   *ch* in all positions represents a voiceless velar spirant: *chojžiś* /xojʒʲiʃʲ/
     'to walk'.
8   Since /r̝/ can occur finally or immediately before consonants there is a
     separate grapheme to represent this: for example, *šlodaŕ* 'tailor'. The
     letters *b'*, *f'*, *ḿ*, *ṕ* and *ẃ* were abolished in the reform of 1952.

The following are some of the main restrictions on phoneme distribution
in Lower Sorbian:

1   /ě/ occurs only after soft consonants and *l*. The phonemes /ě/ and
     /ó/ never occur at the beginning of a word. A few conjunctions (such
     as *a* 'and', *ako* 'when', *ale* 'but', *až* 'that') can begin with *a*, but other-
     wise initial vowels are written only in recent loan-words, mainly from
     international terminology (for example, *awto* 'car', *ideja* 'idea').
     Slavonic words and old German loan-words are written with prothetic
     h or *w*: *hynak* ‹ *inakъ 'different', *hodlaŕ* 'eagle' (compare German
     Adler), *worjech* ‹ *orěxъ 'nut', *wuznaś* ‹ *uznati 'to recognize'. There
     is, however, much uncertainty about words which originally began with
     a vowel, and this uncertainty even affects the German spoken by
     Lower Sorbs. Their tendency to insert and delete initial /h/ (for
     example, *himmer* for German *immer* 'always'; *immel* for German
     Himmel 'sky, heaven') was noted as early as 1761 (Hauptmann). Until
     the Second World War pre-vocalic prothesis was most commonly
     written as *h-*: for example, *hucho* 'ear', *hokoło* 'around', but since
     1952 *h-* has been replaced by *w-* wherever this brought Lower Sorbian
     into line with Upper Sorbian: thus *wucho* and *wokoło* are the modern
     spellings in both Upper and Lower Sorbian. In fact, words with initial
     orthographic *w* are often pronounced without prothesis: /uxo/,
     /okowo/ and so on. The conjunctions *a, ale* and so on are in no way
     exceptional phonologically, for they too sometimes have prothetic /h/.
     Prothetic /w/ is, however, not lost where this would result in initial
     /ó/: for instance *woko* 'eye' may be realized as /hoko/ or /oko/, but
     the dual is only *wocy* /wótsi/ (Fasske 1964: 77 and 119). The
     phonemic status of /h/ is disputed.
2   As in Upper Sorbian (see p. 601) the distinction between /o/ and /ó/,

/e/ and /ě/ is weakened or lost in unstressed syllables (Janaš 1984: 36–8): *śpa* 'room' : *we jśpě* /wèjʃɲe/ 'in the room'; *dwor* /dwór/ 'yard' : *na dworje* /nàdwoṛe/ 'in the yard').

3   As in Upper Sorbian, the distinction between voiced and voiceless paired consonants is neutralized word-finally (Janaš 1984: 45): *lod* /lot/ 'ice', *woz* /wós/ 'cart, car'. The voiced member is replaced by its voiceless counterpart. However, this statement applies only to the literary language. In Lower Sorbian dialects and in the transitional dialect of Hoyerswerda final voicing (and thereby the distinction) is retained. Within the word, whether in dialects or in the literary language, the voiced/voiceless distinction is neutralized in the position before a consonant belonging to a voiced/voiceless pair: *glažk* /glaʃk/ 'glass', *pšosba* /pʃozba/ 'request', *roztajaś* /rostajaʃ/ 'to thaw', *rozdwojś* /rozdwojʃ/ 'to halve'.

4   Unlike Upper Sorbian, Lower Sorbian has two pairs of hard/soft consonants (/n/:/ɲ/ and /r/:/ṛ/) capable of preserving the hard/soft distinction word-finally and before a consonant, as in *goń* /góɲ/ 'drive!' : *gon* /gón/ 'field'; *měr* /měṛ/ 'measure!' : *měr* /měr/ 'peace'. Otherwise the hard/soft distinction is neutralized except before vowels.

5   /f/ only occurs in loan-words and onomatopoeic words; its voiced counterpart /v/ only occurs in loan-words.

The Proto-Slavonic nasal vowels have been replaced in Sorbian by oral vowels. The date of denasalization cannot be determined, but there may be some significance in the spelling of certain proper names in medieval German documents which appear to record nasal vowels. Thirteenth-century documents, for example, contain references to the village of *Welintin* or *Willentin* (now German *Wilthen*, USo. *Wjelećin*), which appear to reflect the front nasal *ę*. However, there are no nasal vowels in the first continuous texts (sixteenth century). In all parts of Sorbian territory and in both literary languages PSl. *ǫ > u* (for example, **rǫka* 'hand, arm' > USo. and LSo. *ruka*); but the developments of **ę* vary. Broadly speaking, in Lower Sorbian *ę > ě* (**męso* > LSo. *měso* 'meat, flesh') and in Upper Sorbian *ę > 'a* (USo. *mjaso*); but in Upper Sorbian the nominative and accusative of nouns of the type *ćelo* (< **telę*) 'calf' and undeclined present participles (gerunds), such as *stojo* < **stoję* 'standing', represent *ę > 'o* (Stieber 1934: 45–7).

Jers in weak positions disappeared (**dъno* > USo. and LSo. *dno* 'ground'), but the distribution of weak and strong was not always uniform (**dъska* > USo. *deska*, LSo. *cka* (only early sources) 'board') and the operation of analogy has produced some unusual results, such as USo. *són* (< **sъnъ*) 'dream', which has stem *son-* throughout (genitive *sona* and so on) except in the phrase *we snje* (or *wosnje*); but note *w słódkim sonje* 'in a sweet dream'. Analogy is also the cause of the loss of the vowel in the nominative and accusative singular of words of the type USo. and LSo. *kusk* 'piece' (‹ **kusъkъ*) and USo. *kónc*, LSo. *końc* 'end' (‹ **konьcь*), which has been re-formed to match the oblique cases (for instance genitive singular *kuska*, *kónca*). The Upper Sorbian toponyms *Moztech* (that is, **mostek* 'bridge (DIMIN)'), *Camenech* (**kamjenjec* (diminutive of *kamjeń* 'stone')), and *Winichopez* (including the word **kopjec* 'mound'), recorded in a Latin document of 1241, are said to attest the full vocalization of *jer* before the operation of analogy removed it.

In Upper Sorbian strong *ъ* › *o* (which in some cases in closed syllables › *ó*): *moch* 'moss' ‹ **mъxъ*, *woš* 'louse' ‹ **vъšь*, *són* 'dream' ‹ **sъnъ*, *bóz* 'elderberry' ‹ **bъzъ*. However, there are also cases of *e* ‹ *ъ*: *deska* 'board' ‹ **dъska*, *dešć* 'rain' ‹ **dъštь*, *ze wsy* 'from the country' ‹ **zъ vъsi*.

In Lower Sorbian strong *ъ* › *e*: *mech* 'moss', *weš* 'louse', *dešć* 'rain', *ze jsy* 'from the country'. Exceptions: *soń* 'dream' (sparsely attested; the normal Lower Sorbian word for 'dream' is *cowanje*), *baz* 'elderberry'.

In Upper Sorbian strong *ь* › '*e*: *wjes* 'village' ‹ **vьsь*, *dźeń* 'day' ‹ **dьnь*, *len* 'linen' ‹ **lьnъ*. Exceptions: *pos* 'dog' ‹ **pьsъ*.

In Lower Sorbian (before soft consonants) strong *ь* › '*e*: *cesć* 'honour' ‹ **čьstь*, *źeń* 'day' ‹ **dьnь*, but before hard (including depalatalized) consonants strong *ь* › '*a*: *wjas* 'village', *lan* 'flax', *pjas* 'dog'.

The development in Sorbian of the Proto-Slavonic syllabic liquids *r̥*, *r̥'*, *l̥* and *l̥'* is of crucial importance in establishing genetic relationships. The fact that before hard dentals (*t, d, s, z, n, r, l*) the soft vocalic liquids (*r̥'* and *l̥'*) were hardened and thus produced the same results as their hard counterparts *r̥* and *l̥* links Sorbian to the Lechitic languages (that is, to all the other West Slavonic languages except Czech and Slovak) where the same feature is observed, and distinguishes it from Czech and Slovak, where it is absent.

Proto-Slavonic syllabic *r̥* and *r̥'* are represented in Upper Sorbian as follows:

r̥ › *or*: *kormić* 'to feed' (‹ **kъrmiti*); *hordy* 'proud, magnificent' (‹ **gъrdъ*);
r̥' before a hard dental (*t, d, s, z, n, r* or *l*) also › *or*: *porst* 'finger' (‹ **pьrstъ*); *sorna* 'roe' (‹ **sьrna*);
r̥' otherwise › '*er*: *wjerch* 'top' (‹ **vьrxъ*); *pjeršćeń* 'ring' (‹ **pьrstenь*) (compare *porst* above).

Proto-Slavonic syllabic *l̥* and *l̥'* are represented in Upper Sorbian as follows:

l̥ › *ol*: *dołh* 'debt' (‹ **dъlgъ*); *tołsty* 'fat' (‹ **tъlstъ*);
l̥ before a hard dental also › *ol*: *połny* 'full' (‹ **pьlnъ*); *žołty* 'yellow' (‹ **žьltъ*);

l̦ otherwise › *'el*: *wjelk* 'wolf' (‹ *vьlkъ); *mjelčeć* 'to be silent' (‹ *mьlčati).

In Lower Sorbian:

r̦ › *ar*: *kjarmiś* 'to feed'; *marchwej* 'carrot' (‹ *mъrky) (*k* › *kj*, *g* › *gj* when preceding *r̦*);

r̦' before a hard dental also › *ar*: *sarna* 'roe'; *twardy* 'hard' (‹ *tvьrdъ);

r̦' otherwise › *'er*: *wjerch* 'top'; *serp* 'sickle' (‹ *sьrpъ);

l̦ › *łu*: *tłusty* 'fat', *dług* 'debt';

l̦ before a hard dental › *oł*: *połny* 'full'; *žołty* 'yellow';

l̦ otherwise › *'el*: *wjelk* 'wolf'; *mjelcaś* 'to be silent'.

That LSo. *l̦* becomes *łu* is significant. It links Lower Sorbian to Polish and Czech (for example, Polish *dług*, *tłusty*; Czech *dluh*, *tlustý*) and separates it from Polabian (for example, Polabian *dåug* 'debt'). Toponomastic evidence from areas Germanized before the sixteenth century (for example, *Dolgen*, the name of a lake to the north of Lübben) shows that the Polabian type began on the western and northern edges of Lower Sorbian territory.

The metathesis C*or*C › C*ro*C, C*ol*C › C*lo*C, C*er*C › C*re*C and C*el*C › C*le*C (C stands for any consonant) occurred consistently over the entire Sorbian area: USo. and LSo. *sroka* 'magpie' ‹ *sarka, USo. and LSo. *młody* 'young' ‹ *moldъ, USo. and LSo. *drjewo* 'wood' ‹ *dervo, USo. and LSo. *mloko* 'milk' ‹ *melko. The metathesized vowels were subject to lengthening (if bearing a rising tone) and to the metaphony *e* › *o* if before a hard consonant (*mloko* ‹ *mleko).

Sorbian has none of the phonemic distinctions of stress, pitch or length known to some of the other Slavonic languages. In Upper Sorbian the stress is always on the first syllable of polysyllabic words. It is a strong stress, sometimes causing vowels in unstressed syllables to be obscured or deleted, which has left its traces even in the literary language, as in USo. *rukajca* 'glove' ‹ *rǫkavica, *poskać* 'to listen' ‹ *posłuchać* (both forms of the latter are now used in the literary language). This weakening of unstressed syllables is less prominent in Lower Sorbian (compare USo. *pinca* 'cellar' ‹ *pivьnica, but LSo. *piwnica*). Prepositions in Upper Sorbian form a rhythmic group with a following noun or pronoun and bear the stress: *dó města* 'to the town', *wóte mšě* 'from mass', *zé mnu* 'with me'. Words containing more than three syllables may have a secondary, weaker stress on the third or fourth syllable: *dźiwadźélnik* 'actor', *Njebjelčicach* 'in Njebjelčicy (Nebelschütz)'. If the noun is preceded by an attribute and a preposition, the stress is not on the preposition but on the first syllable of the attribute: for example, *do wulkeho města* 'to the big town'. It may also be on the noun itself if this has more than two syllables: *do Budyšina* 'to

Bautzen'. Foreign words almost always have an anomalous stress: for example *problém* 'problem', *uniwérsita* 'university', but in dialects the transposition of accent onto the first syllable may be observed: *cúrik* 'back' (German *zurück*).

Lower Sorbian is described normatively as having an initial stress accent, but this accent is weaker than in Upper Sorbian and, as there is a strong secondary stress on the penultimate syllable, there is even controversy as to the primacy of initial and penultimate accents.

Vestiges of the Proto-Slavonic system of stress, length and pitch can in certain circumstances be detected in the contrast between *ó* (‹ *ō*) and *o*, and between *ě* (‹ *ē*) and *e*. For example, in Upper Sorbian words embodying the results of the metathesis of C*or*C, C*ol*C, C*er*C and C*el*C, *o* and *'e* represent Proto-Slavonic circumflex pitch, whereas *ó* and *ě* represent acute pitch or a pre-tonic long syllable: *złoto* 'gold' ‹ *zōlto* (compare Russian *zóloto*, Czech *zlato*, SCr. *zlâto*), *drjewo* 'wood' ‹ *dêrvo* (Russian *dérevo*, Czech *dřevo*, SCr. *drêvo*), *kłóda* 'stocks, pillory, prison' ‹ *kólda* (Russian *kolóda*, Czech *kláda*, SCr. *kläda*), *brěza* 'birch' ‹ *bérza* (Russian *berëza*, Czech *bříza*, SCr. *brèza*). Proto-Slavonic circumflex is represented in Russian by stress on the first syllable, in Czech by a short syllable and in Serbo-Croat by a long falling tone. Proto-Slavonic acute is represented in Russian by stress on the second syllable, in Czech by a long syllable and in Serbo-Croat by a short falling tone. In masculine nouns in Upper Sorbian the position has been obscured by the fact that *o* became *ó* in syllables closed by the loss of final *jer* (as in *golsъ* › *glosъ* › *hłós* 'voice'), but this only affects the nominative singular. Thus, for example, *hłós* (oblique cases: *hłos-*) represents the circumflex, but *mróz* 'frost' (oblique cases: *mróz-*) represents the acute (Дыбо/Dybo 1963).

2.2 Morphophonemic alternations inherited from Proto-Slavonic

Alternations resulting from the first palatalization may be seen in:

1 Conjugation:
   k–č: USo. *pjeku* 'I bake' : *pječe* 'bakes (3 SG)',
   g–ž: LSo. *gnaś* 'to drive' : *ženjo* 'drives (3 SG)',
   ch–š: USo. *běch* 'I was' : *běše* 'was (3 SG)';
2 the vocative:
   k–č: USo. *čłowjek* 'man' : *čłowječe* 'man!',
   g–ž: USo. *Bóh* 'God' : *Božo* 'God!';
3 Comparatives and superlatives:
   ch–š: LSo. *suchy* 'dry' : *sušej* 'drier';
4 Derivation:
   g–ž: USo. *noha* 'leg, foot' : *nóžka* 'leg, foot (DIMIN)',
   ch–š: LSo. *słuchaś* 'to listen' : *słušaś* 'to belong'.

Alternations resulting from the second palatalization occur in:

1   the nominative plural (masculine personal) (only Upper Sorbian):
     k–c: *wojak* 'soldier' : *wojacy* 'soldiers',
     h–z: *wbohi* 'poor (NOM SG)' : *wbozy* 'poor (NOM PL M personal)',
     ch–š: *paduch* 'thief' : *paduši* 'thieves';
2   the nominative/accusative dual (feminine and neuter):
     k–c: USo. and LSo. *jabłuko* 'apple' : *jabłuce* 'apples (DU)';
3   the locative singular (masculine and neuter):
     k–c: LSo. *bok* 'side' : *na boce* 'on the side',
     g–z: USo. *sněh* 'snow' : *w sněze* 'in the snow' (PSl. **g* › USo. *h*).

The number of masculines and neuters capable of forming locatives involving these alternations is limited. The predominant tendency is to avoid the alternation by means of the ending -*u* (for instance, USo. *kruh* 'circle' : *w kruhu* 'in the circle').

4   Dative and locative singular (feminine and masculine *a*-stems):
     k–c: USo. and LSo. *banka* : *w bance* 'in the bank',
     g–z: USo. *kniha* 'book' : *w knize* 'in the book',
     ch–š: USo. *třěcha* 'roof' : *na třěše* 'on the roof'.

In the dative and locative singular of *a*-stems (feminine and masculine) this alternation is fully systematic. It affects borrowings from German (compare *banka* above). USo. *kniha* 'book' is realized as /kņija/; the alternation is therefore capable of being perceived as -*ija*:-*ize* and may lead to such non-standard forms as /biologize/ 'in biology'.

In Upper Sorbian /g/ is of such low frequency (PSl. *g* having become *h*) that there is some doubt as to the correct alternation in such words as *figa* 'fig', *synagoga* 'synagogue' (borrowed from German). Both these words are attested with -*dz*- in the dative/locative singular, but the intuition of native speakers, unencumbered by philological complexes, always chooses -*z*-, and this is now recommended as the norm (Jenč 1976).

Vowel–zero alternations arising from the loss of the weak *jers* may be observed in:

1   conjugation:
     e–∅: USo. and LSo. *bjeru* 'I take' : USo. *brać*/LSo. *braś* 'to take',
     o–∅: USo. *přewozmje* 'will seize (3 SG)' : *přewzać* 'to seize';
2   declension:
     e–∅: LSo. *źeń* 'day' : *dnja* 'day (GEN SG)',
     o–∅: USo. *pos* 'dog' : *psa* 'dog (GEN SG)',
     a–∅: LSo. *pjas* 'dog' : *psa* 'dog (GEN SG)';
3   derivation:
     e–∅: LSo. *gerc* 'musician' : *graś* 'to play'.

Many vowel–zero alternations have been lost owing to the operation of analogy. For example, USo. *kozoł* 'goat', *kotoł* 'kettle', *posoł* 'messenger' and *wosoł* 'donkey' may retain the vowel throughout the paradigm (thus genitive singular *kozoła*, *kotoła* and so on). The zero forms (*kózła*, *kótła* and so on) are only optional variants. In the case of the common suffixes *-ъkъ* and *-ьcь* (‹ *-ьkъ*), however, even before the appearance of our first texts, analogy operated in the opposite direction (in favour of the zero form): for instance, USo. and LSo. *kusk* (‹ *kǫsъkъ*) 'piece', USo. *kónc*, LSo. *konc* (‹ *konьcь*) 'end'. This type is also found in Cassubian (see chapter 13).

A unique case (and not the result of the loss of a weak *jer*) is the *i–∅* alternation in *rić* (‹ *ritь*) 'arse' : *do rće* (*rće* occurs only with the preposition *do* 'to, into').

2.3 Morphophonemic alternations resulting from changes after Proto-Slavonic

PSl. *t* + front vowel › USo. *ć*/LSo. *ś*:
  USo. *čert* 'devil' : *čerći* 'devils',
  LSo. *stat* 'state' : *w staśe* 'in the state';
PSl. *d* + front vowel › USo. *dź*/LSo. *ź*:
  USo. *blido* 'table' : *na blidźe* 'on the table',
  LSo. *blido* 'table' : *na bliźe* 'on the table';
PSl. *zd* + front vowel › LSo. *zdź*: LSo. *gwězda* 'star' : *dwě gwězdźe* 'two stars';
PSl. *st* + front vowel › LSo. *sć*: LSo. *město* 'town' : *w měsće* 'in town';
PSl. *tr* + front vowel › USo. *tř* /tʂ/: USo. *sotra* 'sister' : *sotře* 'sister (DAT SG)';
PSl. *b* + front vowel › *bj* /bʲ/: LSo. *klěb* 'bread' : *w klěbje* 'in the bread';
PSl. *p* + front vowel › *pj* /pʲ/: USo. and LSo. *kupa* 'island' : *na kupje* 'on an island';
PSl. *r* + front vowel › *rj* /rʲ/: USo. *wučer* 'teacher' : *wučerja* 'teacher (GEN SG)';
PSl. *m* + front vowel › *mj* /mʲ/: LSo. *bom* 'tree' : *na bomje* 'on the tree';
PSl. *n* + front vowel › *nj* /nʲ/: USo. *kana* 'pot, vessel' : *w kanje* 'in the pot';
PSl. *w* + front vowel › *wj* /wʲ/: LSo. *głowa* 'head' : *dwě głowje* 'two heads';
PSl. *l* + back vowel › *ł* /w/: USo. and LSo. *doła* 'of the valley' : *w*
PSl. *l* + front vowel › *l* /l/: *dole* 'in the valley'.

(Since *ł* and *w* now represent a single phoneme /w/, there is sometimes confusion in non-standard Upper Sorbian between /w/ ‹ *l* and /w/ ‹ *w*, producing such forms as /dowe/ for /dole/.)

The alternations which might be expected as a result of PSl. *t* + *j* › *c*, *d* +

j › *z* are barely detectable, having been all but swept away by various kinds of morphological change. The *t*:*c* alternation may be seen in the contrast between the infinitive and present tense of a few verbs:

LSo. *šepotaś* 'to whisper' : *šepocu* 'I whisper';
USo. *mjetać* 'to throw' : *mjeceš* 'you throw'.

The *d*:*z* alternation is attested only in derivation:

USo. *howjado* 'cattle' : *howjazy* 'cattle' (adjective).

The first person present of USo. *widźeć* 'to see' (in which one might expect to find *z* ‹ *d* + *j*) is *widźu* (PAST PART PASS *widźany*). The Lower Sorbian equivalents are *wiźeś, wiźim, wiźony.*

PSl. *s* + *j* › *š* is reflected in, for example, USo. *prosyć* 'to ask' : *prošu* 'I ask';
PSl. *z* + *j* › *ž* is reflected in, for example, USo. *mazać* 'to smear' : *mažu* 'I smear'.

The main Upper Sorbian vowel alternations are as follows:

1   The change *o* › *ó* in syllables closed by the loss of final *jer* has produced the *ó/o* alternation: *hród* 'castle, palace (NOM and ACC SG)' : *hrod-* in all other cases and numbers, for instance, dative singular *hrodej.*
2   The corresponding change *e* › *ě* in syllables closed by the loss of final *jer* has produced a few cases of the *ě/'e* alternation: *pěc* 'stove (NOM and ACC SG)' : *pjec-* in all other cases and numbers, like genitive singular *pjecy.*
3   The change *a* (between soft consonants) › *e* has resulted in numerous cases of the *'a/'e* alternation: *rjad* 'row' : *w rjedźe* 'in the row', *pjata* 'heel' : *pjeće* 'heels (DU)', *Jendželčan* 'Englishman' : *Jendželčenjo* 'Englishmen'.
4   The change *w'* › *j* has resulted in the *-ej/-w'* alternation: *cyrkej* 'church' : *cyrkwje* 'church (GEN SG)'; *solotej* 'salad' : *solotwje* (GEN SG); *krej* 'blood' : *krwě* (GEN SG).

In Lower Sorbian vowel alternations are extremely rare: /o/:/ó/ can occur only in connection with consonant alternation, as, for example, in *woko* 'eye' /woko/ : *wocy* 'eyes (DU)' /wótsi/, *bok* 'side' /bok/ : *na boce* 'on the side' /na bótse/.

3   Morphology

3.1   Nominal morphology

3.1.1   Nominal categories

The three numbers, singular, dual and plural, are retained in both Upper and Lower Sorbian. The dual is still a systematic component of the category of number in both literary languages and nearly all dialects. However, in the dialects various dual forms are, with varying degrees of frequency, replaced by plural forms. The tendency to substitute plural forms for dual is greatest in the case of naturally paired referents (hands, feet, cheeks, shoes, and so on). However, in nearly all Lower Sorbian dialects and in the transitional zone (according to the *Sorbischer Sprachatlas* (hereafter *SS*) 11: 19–36) the dual, even in the case of natural pairs, is rarely replaced by the plural. The frequency with which dual forms are replaced by plural increases as one moves from north to south, but it is only in the extreme south of Upper Sorbian territory that the dual is no longer a systematic component of the category of number.

Upper Sorbian has seven cases (nominative, vocative, accusative, genitive, dative, instrumental and locative). Lower Sorbian, having lost the vocative, has only six cases. All the dialects have at least six cases (*SS* 11: 36). The vocative isogloss divides all Upper Sorbian dialects and the dialect of Nochten from the remaining transitional dialects and the whole of Lower Sorbian territory (*SS* 11: map 5). Even in Upper Sorbian it is only masculine nouns that have a separate vocative form (and only in the singular). There is one exception to this rule: USo. *mać* 'mother' has vocative singular *maći*. The Lower Sorbian vocative is attested only in Jakubica's New Testament (1548). Otherwise, even the earliest Lower Sorbian texts reveal only isolated fossilized vocatives (like *knĕzo* 'o Lord' in the Bible). However, some masculine nouns ending in -*o* (such as *wujko* 'uncle', *śĕsko* 'cousin' and certain Christian names, including *Hanzo*, *Hajno*) are believed to be vocatives by origin.

In both Upper and Lower Sorbian the independent, prepositionless function of the instrumental has been lost. It is always accompanied by a preposition and in paradigms is usually preceded by *z(e)* 'with'. The question whether Sorbian has a prepositionless locative is debatable. The preposition *w* 'in' is written before locatives, but is in fact silent: USo. *w Budyšinje* /budiʃiɲe/ 'in Bautzen'. This may seem to be a phonological matter, for there is a rule which prevents /w/ from standing immediately before another consonant (thus USo. *wzać* /zatʃ/ 'to take'). However, the orthographic preposition *w* is always silent even before vowels: USo. *w instituće* /institutʃe/ 'in the institute', *w awće* /awtʃe/ 'in the car'. There is a facultative variant *we* /we/ 'in', which does have a phonic realization.

The position is the same in both literary languages and all dialects. In paradigms the locative forms are usually preceded by *w(e)* 'in' or *wo* 'about'.

In addition to the three genders, masculine, feminine and neuter, Sorbian has a flexible subgender expressed in the separate status given, in certain circumstances, to masculine nouns denoting human beings and animals (the animate subgender), and, in other circumstances, only to those denoting human beings (the masculine-personal subgender). Feminines and neuters are unaffected.

The animate subgender is expressed primarily in the accusative and determines whether the accusative will have the same form as the genitive (animates) or the nominative (non-animates). Throughout the whole of Sorbian territory and in the literary languages in all three numbers (singular, dual and plural) masculine non-inanimates have the same form in the accusative as in the nominative (for instance, USo. *mam wóz* 'I have a cart'). Similarly, in all Sorbian dialects and in both literary languages mascuine animate nouns (other than *a*-stems, such as USo. *ćěsla* 'carpenter') in the accusative singular have the same form as in the genitive singular, and, in the singular at least, all such nouns (including the *ćěsla* type) take genitive-accusative agreement (USo. *mam dobreho konja*, LSo. *mam dobrego konja* 'I have a good horse', USo. *znam dobreho ćěslu* 'I know a good carpenter').

In the accusative dual, however, only Lower Sorbian (both literary language and dialects) has the same form as the genitive dual for all masculine nouns denoting animates (LSo. *mam dweju konjowu* 'I have two horses', *mam dweju wucabnikowu* 'I have two teachers'). In Upper Sorbian the subgender in the dual includes not all animate nouns, but only those denoting human beings (USo. *mam dweju wučerjow* 'I have two teachers', but *mam dwaj konjej* 'I have two horses').

In the accusative plural masculine nouns referring to animals (unless used with the numerals *tśi* '3' and *styri* '4' in the case of Lower Sorbian) have the nominative–accusative in all dialects and both literary languages (USo. and LSo. *mam konje* 'I have horses'). Nouns referring to male human beings in Upper Sorbian have the genitive–accusative in the plural (as in both other numbers). In Lower Sorbian, however, it is only if used with the numerals *tśi* or *styri*, or after the accusative plural pronouns *nas* 'us' and *was* 'you', that masculine plural animates (whether human beings or animals) take the genitive–accusative (LSo. *mam tśoch konjow* 'I have three horses', *mam tśoch wucabnikow* 'I have three teachers', *woni chwale was wucabnikow* 'they are praising you teachers'). Otherwise masculine plural animates in Lower Sorbian (even in the case of human beings) take the nominative–accusative (LSo. *mam dobre wucabniki* 'I have good teachers'). The rule to be found in some Lower Sorbian grammars ordaining that nouns denoting persons shall, in the plural, have a genitive–accusative is artificial and modelled on Upper Sorbian (Janaš 1984: 73–4).

The masculine-animate (not the masculine-personal) category is also manifested in Lower Sorbian in special forms of the numerals *tśi* and *styri* embodying the vowel -*o*-. In Upper Sorbian the masculine personal is expressed in the accusative dual, the accusative plural and in the nominative plural. Nouns, adjectives, pronouns and numerals all have separate nominative plural endings to distinguish masculine personals: thus *nanojo* 'fathers' (nominative plural of *nan*), but *borany* 'rams' (nominative plural of *boran*); *třo młodźi Serbja* 'three young Sorbs', but *tři młode jabłonje* 'three young apple trees'. In Lower Sorbian only numerals from '3' to '10' have separate forms in the nominative and their role is to distinguish masculine animates (persons and animals): *styrjo konje* 'four horses', but *styri jabłoni* 'four apple trees'.

3.1.2   Noun morphology
The basic declension pattern for Upper Sorbian masculine nouns is shown in table 11.3. The main variations are:

1   The *ó/o* alternation is characteristic of nouns with stem ending in a single consonant, whereas *ó* is usually retained throughout the paradigm of nouns whose stem ends in a double consonant (*chłódk/chłódka* 'shadow'), but there are exceptions to both types (*mróz/mróza* 'frost'; *móst/mosta* 'bridge').
2   Some nouns have an alternative vocative in -'*e* (*Jakubo* or *Jakubje*). This may involve consonant alternation (*člowjeko* or *člowječe* 'man!').
3   *Hród* is one of a number of monosyllabic, inanimate nouns that have an alternative genitive singular ending in -*u* (from the Proto-Slavonic *u*-stems). The *u*-ending is never obligatory.
4   The dative singular ending -*ej* comes from the Proto-Slavonic *u*-stems (*-evi* › -*ej*) (Mucke 1891: 311 n.). A few nouns may take the alternative ending -*u* (from the PSl. *o*-stems), when they follow the prepo-

Table 11.3   Declension of USo. *hród* 'palace, castle'

	SG	DU	PL
NOM	hród	hrodaj	hrody
VOC	hrodo	hrodaj	hrody
ACC	hród	hrodaj	hrody
GEN	hroda (hrodu)	hrodow	hrodow
DAT	hrodej	hrodomaj	hrodam
INST	z hrodom	z hrodomaj	z hrodami
LOC	w hrodźe (hrodu)	w hrodomaj	w hrodach

sition *k* 'to': *k wobjedu* 'to lunch'. The only noun which must have *-u*, even without *k*, is *bóh* 'god' (dative singular *bohu*).

5   The locative singular ending *-u* (inherited from the PSl. *u*-stems) must be used after sibilants (*na wozu* 'on the cart'), soft consonants (*wo mužu* 'about the man') and *k*, *g*, *h* and *ch* (*w běhu* 'in the course'); elsewhere it is optional. However, some nouns ending in *k*, *g* and *h* have alternative locatives involving consonant alternations (*w sněhu/w sněze* 'in the snow').

6   In the nominative plural nouns referring to human beings take the endings *-ojo* (*mužojo* 'men'), *-jo* (*Jendželčenjo* 'Englishmen'), *-'a* (*Serbja* 'Sorbs'), *-i* (which may cause consonant alternation as in *studenći* 'students', and may itself alternate with *-y*: *wojacy* 'soldiers' (nominative singular *wojak*)), or (after *-c*) *-y* (*hólcy* 'boys'). The ending *-ojo* (‹ **-ove*) comes from the *u*-stems. Its older variant *-owje* (*mužowje* 'men') was characteristic of the separate Catholic literary tradition. The choice of ending is partly morphologically and partly lexically determined.

7   The genitive dual is almost always the same as the genitive plural, which usually has the ending *-ow* for all genders. However, a few nouns, particularly *pluralia tantum*, take the Ø-ending: thus *Drježdžany* 'Dresden' has genitive *Drježdžan*, *pjenjezy* 'money' has *pjenjez*.

8   Masculine nouns with a soft stem vary from the hard-stem declension in: (a) the nominative/vocative/accusative dual, which has *-ej* (*mužej* 'men'); (b) the genitive plural, which has an alternative ending in *-i* (*muži* as well as *mužow*); inherited from the PSl. *i*-stems, this ending is prevalent in the Catholic dialect and popular with Catholic writers; (c) the nominative/vocative/accusative plural, which has *-e* (not human beings) (*koše* 'baskets'); this too comes from the *i*-stems; (d) the instrumental plural, which has *-emi* (*mužemi*); and (e) the locative singular (see item 5 above).

The basic declension pattern for Lower Sorbian masculine nouns is shown in table 11.4. The main variations are:

1   As in Upper Sorbian, some inanimate, monosyllabic nouns have an alternative genitive singular in *-u*.

2   The dative singular in *-oju* is made up of elements from both the *o*-stem (*-u*) and *u*-stem (*-ovi*) endings. Many nouns have an alternative dative in *-u*: *kóncoju/kóncu* (dative singular of *kónc* 'end').

3   There are no separate endings in the nominative plural for nouns denoting male persons (unlike Upper Sorbian): thus *nany* 'fathers' is comparable to *grody* 'castles'.

4   The alternative locative singular ending *-u* has a similar distribution to that in Upper Sorbian (for example, *wo mužu* 'about the man'), but it

Table 11.4   Declension of LSo. *grod* **'palace, castle'**

	SG	DU	PL
NOM	grod	groda	grody
ACC	grod	groda	grody
GEN	groda	grodowu	grodow
DAT	grodoju	grodoma	grodam
INST	z grodom	z grodoma	z grodami
LOC	wo groźe	wo grodoma	wo grodach

   may be used with nouns of any type (*na swětu* 'in the world' as well as *na swěše*).

5   Soft stems vary from hard stems in (a) the dative singular, which, in the case of stems ending in *-ar̆* and *-al,* has *-eju* (not *-oju*) (thus *murjarjeju* 'to the mason'); (b) the nominative plural (*konje* 'horses', *muže* 'men'); and (c) the genitive plural, which may have the alternative ending *-i* (*konjow* or *koni* 'of horses').

The basic declension pattern for Upper Sorbian neuter nouns is shown in table 11.5. The main variations are:

1   The dative singular, which in the literary standard ends in *-u,* has a colloquial variant in *-ej*: *městej* 'to the town'.
2   Soft-stem neuters (like *polo* 'field') usually have nominative singular in *-o*. The only category which regularly has *-e* is that of verbal nouns (like *wučenje* 'teaching'), but even these used to have *-o* in the Catholic literary language and may still retain it in the works of Catholic writers. There is also a number of words which vary between *-e* and *-o,* such as *zbože/zbožo* 'happiness, luck'.
3   Soft-stem neuters have endings varying from *město* in (a) the locative singular, which has *-u* (*na polu* 'in the field'); (b) the nominative/accusative dual, which has *-i* (*poli* '(two) fields'); (c) the instrumental plural, which has *-emi* (not *-ami*): *z polemi* 'with fields'.

The declension of Lower Sorbian *město* differs from that of Upper Sorbian *město* only in the following cases: (a) dative singular *městoju* or *městu*; (b) genitive dual *městowu*; (c) dative, instrumental, and locative dual *městoma*. LSo. *polo* 'field' differs from LSo. *město* in: (a) the locative singular (*na polu* 'in the field') and (b) the nominative/accusative dual (*poli* '(two) fields').

The basic declension pattern for Upper Sorbian feminine nouns is shown in table 11.6. The main variations are as follows:

Table 11.5   Declension of USo. *město* 'town'

	SG	DU	PL
NOM	město	mĕsće	mĕsta
ACC	město	mĕsće	mĕsta
GEN	mĕsta	mĕstow	mĕstow
DAT	mĕstu	mĕstomaj	mĕstam
INST	z mĕstom	z mĕstomaj	z mĕstami
LOC	w mĕsće	w mĕstomaj	w mĕstach

Table 11.6   Declension of USo. *žona* 'woman, wife'

	SG	DU	PL
NOM	žona	žonje	žony
ACC	žonu	žonje	žony
GEN	žony	žonow	žonow
DAT	žonje	žonomaj	žonam
INST	ze žonu	ze žonomaj	ze žonami
LOC	wo žonje	wo žonomaj	wo žonach

1 A few feminines have Ø in the genitive plural. This may involve vowel alternation *o/ó*: *do horow/ do hór* 'to the hills' (*hora* 'hill, mountain').

2 Soft feminines (like *duša* 'soul' (or 'shower')) vary from the *žona* paradigm as follows: (a) genitive singular *duše*; (b) dative and locative singular *duši*; (c) nominative and accusative dual *duši*; (d) nominative and accusative plural *duše*; and (e) instrumental plural *z dušemi*.

3 Some feminines (old *i*-stems) have a Ø-ending in the nominative/ accusative singular: for example, *kósć* 'bone'. They otherwise follow the soft feminine declension (like *duša*), unless they have a stem ending in *s* or *c*, in which case they follow the *žona* paradigm apart from the dative and locative singular and the nominative/accusative dual, which end in -*y*, thus *nóc* 'night' has *nocy*.

Lower Sorbian *žona* 'woman, wife' and *duša* 'soul' (or 'shower') differ from their Upper Sorbian counterparts only in details which are systematic, that is Lower Sorbian dual endings -*owu* and -*oma* correspond to USo. -*ow* and -*omaj*, Lower Sorbian has -*šy*, where Upper Sorbian has -*ši*, and Lower Sorbian has instrumental plural *z dušami* (USo. *z dušemi*). There is, however, a significant distinction between Upper and Lower Sorbian in the declensional type represented by LSo. *kosć* 'bone' (the old *i*-stems). Lower Sorbian, by preserving -*i* in those cases where Upper Sorbian has substituted -*e* (in the genitive singular and the nominative/accusative plural), has remained closer to the original paradigm (LSo. *kosći* (GEN SG and NOM/ACC PL).

Upper Sorbian masculine *a*-stems vary from the *žona* paradigm in (a) the accusative dual and plural (since they refer to male persons); these coincide with the genitive dual and plural: for instance, accusative dual and plural *herbow* (from *herba* 'heir'); (b) the nominative dual: *herbaj*; (c) the nominative and vocative plural: *herbojo* or *herbja*. Lower Sorbian masculine *a*-stems differ from their feminine counterparts only in so far as, being masculine animates, they have genitive–accusative in the dual and after the numerals *tśi* and *styri.*

Original consonant stems have been fully absorbed into the Upper and Lower Sorbian declensional systems, but vestiges of their former existence survive in:

1   the stem of such masculines as USo. and LSo. *kamjeń* 'stone' (genitive singular *kamjenja*; PSl. **kamy/*kamene*);
2   the extended stem of neuters in -*en* and USo. -*eć/-et* (LSo. -*eś/-et*): USo. *ramjo* 'shoulder' / *ramjenja* (GEN SG), USo. *ćelo* 'calf' (genitive singular *ćeleća*, nominative plural *ćelata*), LSo. *śele* 'calf' (genitive singular *śeleśa*, nominative plural *śeleta*);
3   the extended stem in -*er(j)* of USo. *mać* 'mother' (genitive singular *maćerje*), LSo. *maś* (genitive singular *maśerje*). USo *mać* is unique in that it has vocative singular *maći* (the only feminine vocative in Sorbian) and an optional accusative singular *maćer* (otherwise *mać*);
4   the USo. plural stem *njebjes-* (nominative plural *njebjesa*, genitive plural *njebjes*) of *njebjo* 'sky, heaven' (the plural occurs only in religious usage).

3.1.3   Pronominal morphology
The declension of Upper Sorbian personal pronouns is shown in table 11.7 and of Lower Sorbian personal pronouns in table 11.8.

Notes
1   The items shown in parentheses are used exclusively with prepositions.
2   Variation between the items divided by an oblique line (for example USo. *wo nas/wo nami*) has a regional basis, but in the literary language the choice is facultative.
3   In the case of items separated by a comma, the second is clitic or semi-clitic: it cannot appear in a prepositional phrase or bear stress and does not normally stand in the first position in the clause.
4   Where items are separated by a colon, the first is masculine animate.
5   When governed by a preposition, a pronoun beginning with *j-* (like *jeho*) acquires an initial *n-* (*bjez njeho* 'without him'). If followed by

Table 11.7   Declension of Upper Sorbian personal pronouns

1st person

	SG	DU	PL
	SG	DU	PL
NOM	ja	mój	my
ACC	mje (mnje)	naju	nas
GEN	mje (mnje)	naju	nas
DAT	mi (mni)	namaj	nam
INST	ze mnu	z namaj	z nami
LOC	wo mni	wo namaj	wo nas/wo nami

2nd person

NOM	ty	wój	wy
ACC	tebje, će	waju	was
GEN	tebje, će	waju	was
DAT	tebi, ći	wamaj	wam
INST	z tobu	z wamaj	z wami
LOC	wo tebi	wo wamaj	wo was/wo wami

3rd person singular

	M	N	F
	M	N	F
NOM	wón	wono/wone	wona
ACC	jeho : jón	jo/je	ju
GEN	jeho		jeje
DAT	jemu		jej, ji
INST	z nim		z njej
LOC	wo nim		wo njej

3rd person dual

	Masculine personal	*Non-masculine personal*
NOM	wonaj	wonej
ACC	jeju	jej
GEN	jeju	
DAT	jimaj	
INST	z nimaj	
LOC	wo nimaj	

3rd person plural

NOM	woni	wone
ACC	jich	je
GEN	jich	
DAT	jim	
INST	z nimi	
LOC	wo nich/wo nimi	

Reflexive

NOM	–
ACC	sebje, so
GEN	sebje, so
DAT	sebi, sej
INST	ze sobu
LOC	wo sebi

Table 11.8   Declension of Lower Sorbian personal pronouns

1st person

	SG	DU	PL
NOM	ja	mej	my
ACC	mě (mnjo)	naju	nas
GEN	mje (mnjo)	naju	nas
DAT	mě (mnjo)	nama	nam
INST	ze mnu	z nama	z nami
LOC	wo mnjo	wo nama	wo nas

2nd person

	SG	DU	PL
NOM	ty	wej	wy
ACC	tebje, śi	waju	was
GEN	tebje, śi	waju	was
DAT	tebje, śi	wama	wam
INST	z tobu	z wama	z wami
LOC	wo tebje	wo wama	wo was

3rd person singular

	M	N	F
NOM	won	wono	wona
ACC	jogo : jen	jo	ju
GEN	jogo		jeje
DAT	jomu		jej
INST	z nim		z njeju
LOC	wo njom		wo njej

3rd person dual

NOM		wonej	
ACC	jeju : jej		jej
GEN		jeju	
DAT		jima	
INST		z nima	
LOC		wo nima	

3rd person plural

NOM		woni	
ACC	jich : je		je
GEN		jich	
DAT		jim	
INST		z nimi	
LOC		wo nich	

Reflexive (all genders)

NOM	–
ACC	sebje, se
GEN	sebje, se
DAT	sebje, se
INST	ze sobu
LOC	wo sebje

-*i*- the *j*- is deleted (thus *jich*, but *wokoło nich* 'around them'), because the *n*- in the orthographic sequence *ni*- is always soft.

6 The second person plural pronoun *wy* may also be used as an honorific form to address one person (or two).

7 In both Upper and Lower Sorbian after prepositions taking the accusative or genitive it is (contrary to the normal rule governing clitics) the short form of the reflexive pronoun that is most commonly used: for instance, USo. *na so* 'onto (my etc.) self/selves', LSo. *na se.* In the dative after prepositions, however, the long form is obligatory, except in the case of LSo. *ku se* 'to (...)self/selves'.

The hard-stem pronominal declension in Upper Sorbian is exemplified by the demonstrative pronoun *tón* 'this, that' in table 11.9. Lower Sorbian pronominal declension is exemplified by the demonstrative pronoun *ten* 'this, that' in table 11.10. The soft-stem pronominal declension in Upper Sorbian is demonstrated by *naš* 'our' in table 11.11. The distinction between hard and soft stems does not exist in the declension of pronouns in Lower Sorbian.

Table 11.9   Declension of USo. *tón* 'this, that'

Singular			
	M	N	F
NOM	tón	to/te	ta
ACC	toho : tón	to/te	tu
GEN		toho	teje
DAT		tomu	tej
INST		z tym	z tej
LOC		wo tym/tom	wo tej

Dual		
	Masculine personal	*Non-masculine personal*
NOM	taj	tej
ACC	teju	tej
GEN		teju
DAT		tymaj
INST		z tymaj
LOC		wo tymaj

Plural		
NOM	ci	te
ACC	tych	te
GEN		tych
DAT		tym
INST		z tymi
LOC		wo tych

Table 11.10   Declension of LSo. *ten* 'this, that'

Singular

	M	N	F
NOM	ten	to	ta
ACC	togo : ten	to	tu
GEN	togo		teje
DAT	tomu		tej
INST	z tym		z teju
LOC	wo tom		wo tej

Dual

NOM	tej	
ACC	teju : tej	tej
GEN	teju	
DAT	tyma	
INST	z tyma	
LOC	wo tyma	

Plural

NOM	te	
ACC	tych : te	te
GEN	tych	
DAT	tym	
INST	z tymi	
LOC	wo tych	

Notes

1   Adjectival pronouns in Upper Sorbian with alternative forms in the neuter nominative singular are *to/te* 'this, that', *wšo/wšě* (from *wšón* 'all'), *wšitko/wšitke* (from *wšitkón* 'all'), *samo/same* (from *sam* 'self').

2   In Upper Sorbian texts dating from before the Second World War *teho* may be found as an alternative to *toho*, and *temu* as an alternative to *tomu*. In the old Protestant norm the only pronoun with *-oho* and *-omu* was *štó* 'who' (*koho, komu*). The present-day o-variants come from the Catholic norm. In the case of *što* 'what' the e-variants are still predominant (*čeho, čemu*), but *čoho* and *čomu* may be found in the work of Catholic writers.

3   The Upper Sorbian locative singular variant (*wo*) *tom* is archaic and rare.

4   Where items are separated by a colon, the first is masculine animate.

5   As in the case of other parts of speech in Upper Sorbian, the attempt to impose the personal/non-personal distinction in the masculine

Table 11.11   Declension of USo. naš 'our'

Singular

	M	N	F
NOM	naš	naše	naša
ACC	našeho : naš	naše	našu
GEN	našeho		našeje
DAT	našemu		našej
INST	z našim		z našej
LOC	wo našim		wo našej

Dual

	Masculine personal	*Non-masculine personal*
NOM	našej	
ACC	našeju	našej
GEN	našeju	
DAT	našimaj	
INST	z našimaj	
LOC	wo našimaj	

Plural

NOM	naši	naše
ACC	našich	naše
GEN	našich	
DAT	našim	
INST	z našimi	
LOC	wo našich	

nominative dual (*taj/tej*) has been only partly successful (Faßke 1981: 691).

The Proto-Slavonic pronoun **sь* 'this' has been lost in Sorbian apart from such sporadic vestiges as USo. *lětsa*, LSo. *lětos* (and *lětosa*) 'this year' ‹ **lěto se*. PSl. **vьхъ* is inherited in USo. *wšón*, whose paradigm is shown in table 11.12. A synonym of *wšón* is *wšitkón*, which is declined like an adjective apart from the masculine nominative singular. LSo. *wšen* 'all' follows the paradigm of *ten*. The question whether Sorbian words for 'all' can have a dual, tested by sentences of the type LSo. *Wobej mazańca stej wšej* (compare German *beide Kuchen sind alle*) 'both cakes are all gone', is reported on in *SS* 10 (map 100). It transpires that sentences of this type are acceptable in Lower Sorbian and the transitional dialects, but not in most Upper Sorbian dialects.

In Upper Sorbian PSl. **kъto* 'who' has been replaced by *štó* ([ʃtu] not [ʃtó]). The question of its etymological relationship to **kъto* and **čьto* has

Table 11.12   Declension of USo. *wšón* 'all'

Singular

	M	N	F
NOM	wšón	wšo/wšč	wša
ACC	wšeho : wšón	wšo/wšč	wšu
GEN	wšeho		wšeje
DAT	wšemu		wšej
INST	ze wšěm		ze wšej
LOC	we wšěm		we wšej

Plural

	Masculine personal	Non-masculine personal
NOM	wšitcy	wšě
ACC	wšěch	wšě
GEN	wšěch	
DAT	wšěm	
INST	ze wšěmi	
LOC	wo wšěch	

not been satisfactorily resolved (see Schuster-Šewc, *Wörterbuch*, under *štó*; *SS* 10: map 96). Its paradigm is as follows:

NOM	štó
ACC	koho
GEN	koho
DAT	komu
INST	z kim
LOC	wo kim

The Lower Sorbian equivalent is *chto*, which declines as follows:

NOM	chto
ACC	kogo
GEN	kogo
DAT	komu
INST	z kim
LOC	wo kim

Upper Sorbian *što* 'what' (‹ *čьto*) declines as follows:

NOM	što
ACC	što (but after prepositions *čo*)
GEN	čeho (rarely *čoho*)

DAT	čemu (rarely *čomu*)
INST	z čim
LOC	wo čim

Its Lower Sorbian equivalent is *co*:

NOM	co
ACC	co
GEN	cogo
DAT	comu
INST	z cym
LOC	wo com

In both Upper and Lower Sorbian indefinite pronouns are formed with the prefix *ně-*: USo. *něchtó* 'someone' follows the paradigm of *štó* (except in the nominative); LSo. *něchten* 'someone' follows the paradigm of *chto* (except in the nominative). Compare also USo. *něšto* 'something' and LSo. *něco* 'something'. Indefinite pronouns may be semantically adapted by the addition of the suffix *-žkuli* (in both Upper and Lower Sorbian): for instance, USo. *něštožkuli* 'many a thing'.

3.1.4   Adjectival morphology

Modern Sorbian has no separate short-form adjectives, but it is not possible to determine whether some of the nominative and accusative forms now in use are the results of contraction (for example, **dobra-ja* › *dobra* 'good (F NOM SG)') or original short forms. There is, however, textual evidence that a separate masculine nominative singular short form (ending in -∅, not -*y*) existed formerly: LSo. (sixteenth century) *ja som twojogo sluba wěst* 'I am sure of your promise' (*wěst* for *wěsty* 'sure') (Moller 1959: 91v.). There may be some significance in the fact that in the same sixteenth-century source the short masculine nominative singular is more frequently attested for past passive participles than for other adjectives:

Wjeźon njezbožnym' luźoju,
Fa[l]šnje wobskeržony,
Zapluwan a sromośon,
Ak to pismo groni.

'Led to a godless man, fasely accused, spat upon and shamed, as the scripture says.'
(Moller 1959: 35v)

The short-form masculine singular in the Upper Sorbian phrase *Bóh wjeršen* 'God the most high' survives to the present day (*wjeršen* for *wjeršny*) and in the unpublished 'Senftenberger Kirchenbuch' (1697) the adjective in this phrase is said to follow the short-form declension:

Bóhwjeršin, Bohawjeršna, and so on (Mucke 1891: 379). Vestiges of the short-form declension may also be seen in USo. *swjedźeń* 'feast' (< *swjat dźeń*) (first recorded in the seventeenth century as *swjadźen*), in undeclined Upper Sorbian adjectives of the type *naběł* 'whitish', *nakisał* 'sourish', undeclined adjectives of the type *zwulka* 'haughty, snobbish', *sćicha* 'quiet' and in adverbs such as *dočista* 'completely', *z daloka* 'from far off'. The genitive singular short form also survives (fossilized) in USo. *połdra* 'one and a half' (< *pol druga*), *połtřeća* 'two and a half' and so on (LSo. *połtera* 'one and a half', *połśeśa* 'two and a half' and so on). The dative singular short form lives on in phrases of the type *po němsku* 'in the German manner', and in *pomału* 'slowly'.

Upper Sorbian adjectival declension is demonstrated by *dobry* 'good' in table 11.13.

Table 11.13   Declension of USo. *dobry* 'good'

Singular

	M		N	F
	Animate	*Non-animate*		
NOM	dóbry		dobre	dobra
ACC	dobreho	dobry	dobre	dobru
GEN		dobreho		dobreje
DAT		dobremu		dobrej
INST		z dobrym		z dobrej
LOC		wo dobrym		wo dobrej

Dual

	Masculine personal	*Non-masculine personal*
NOM	dobraj	dobrej
ACC	dobreju	dobrej
GEN		dobreju
DAT		dobrymaj
INST		z dobrymaj
LOC		wo dobrymaj

Plural

NOM	dobri	dobre
ACC	dobrych	dobre
GEN		dobrych
DAT		dobrym
INST		z dobrymi
LOC		wo dobrych

Notes

1   In the endings containing -*y* the latter is replaced by -*i* after stems ending in velars (*h, k, ch*) and soft consonants (*š, ž, č, ć, l, ń*): *serbski* 'Sorbian (NOM SG)', *kušimaj* 'short (DAT/INST/LOC DU)'.

2   In the nominative plural before the ending -*i* the stem consonant *d* is replaced by *dź* (*młody* 'young' – *młodźi*), *t* by *ć* (*bohaty* 'rich' – *bohaći*) and *ł* by *l* (*mały* 'small' – *mali*). Before this ending too *h* alternates with *z*, *ch* with *š* and *k* with *c* (compare the discussion of the second palatalization in section 2.2); *z* and *c* are then followed by -*y* in accordance with the normal phonological rule (thus *nahi* (NOM SG) 'naked' – *nazy* (NOM PL M personal)).

3   The distinction in the nominative dual between masculine personal -*aj* and non-masculine personal -*ej* has no counterpart in the dialects. Until the twentieth century -*aj* was used in the nominative dual without distinction. Following the incursion of -*ej* into the literary language, however, there was a gradual tendency to restrict -*aj* to masculine personal referents. This was eventually made into a formal rule in normative grammars, but literary usage has remained only moderately consistent. In dialects -*aj* is attested only in the south of Upper Sorbian territory and its use is only facultative (Faßke 1981: 380).

Lower Sorbian adjectival declension is demonstrated in table 11.14.

Note

1   After stems ending in *g* or *k* the ending has -*i* not -*y* (for instance, *wjeliki* 'big (NOM SG)'), but in contrast to Upper Sorbian this rule does not apply to *ch* (thus *suchy* 'dry'; compare USo. *suchi*).

The Upper Sorbian comparative is formed synthetically by adding the suffix -*iš* or -*š* to the stem of the positive form: *nowy* 'new' – *nowiši* or *nowši* 'newer'. If the stem ends in a single consonant the suffix is usually -*š* (*stary* 'old' – *starši* 'older'); if it ends in more than one consonant the suffix is usually -*iš* (*spěšny* 'quick' – *spěšniši* 'quicker'). But there are several exceptions and a few adjectives are capable of forming comparatives in both ways. In these cases the longer form is stylistically elevated: thus *nowiši* is stylistically higher than *nowši* (Šewc 1968: 108). If the stem ends in -*c* or -*z* the comparative suffix is -*yš*: *horcy* 'hot' – *horcyši* 'hotter'. The stem often undergoes consonant alternation: *suchi* 'dry' – *sušiši* 'drier'. A syllable may be dropped (*daloki* 'far' – *dalši* 'further') and some comparatives are formally unrelated to their positives: *dobry* 'good' – *lěpši* 'better'.

The Upper Sorbian superlative is formed by prefixing *naj-* to the comparative: *stary* 'old' – *starši* 'older' – *najstarši* 'oldest'. A yet higher degree of comparison (the absolute superlative) is expressed by prefixing *na-* to the superlative: *nanajstarši* 'the oldest of all'.

Table 11.14   Declension of LSo. *dobry* 'good'

Singular

	M		N	F
	Animate	*Non-animate*		
NOM	dobry		dobre	dobra
ACC	dobrego	dobry	dobre	dobru
GEN		dobrego		dobreje
DAT		dobremu		dobrej
INST		z dobrym		z dobreju
LOC		wo dobrem		wo dobrej

Dual

	Masculine animate	*Non-masculine animate*
NOM	dobrej	
ACC	dobreju	dobrej
GEN	dobreju	
DAT	dobryma	
INST	z dobryma	
LOC	wo dobryma	

Plural

NOM	dobre	
ACC	*dobrych	dobre
GEN	dobrych	
DAT	dobrym	
INST	z dobrymi	
LOC	wo dobrych	

Note: * after numerals *tśi* or *styri*, or after pronouns *nas* 'us' or *was* 'you' (see section 3.1.1).

Analytic comparatives consist of the positive adjective preceded by the adverb *bóle* 'more': *bóle stary* 'older' (= *starši*). Not every adjective is capable of forming a synthetic comparative, but when both synthetic and analytic comparatives exist, they are semantically interchangeable. Analytic superlatives and absolute superlatives are formed with *najbóle* and *nanajbóle*: *najbóle stary* 'oldest', *nanajbóle stary* 'oldest of all'.

In Lower Sorbian the comparative suffixes are -*'ejš* and -*š*: *spěšny* 'quick' – *spěšnjejšy* 'quicker', *stary* 'old' – *staršy* 'older'. Consonant alternations include *d–ź* (*gjardy* 'proud' – *gjarźejšy* 'prouder'), *t–ś* (*kšuty* 'firm' – *kšuśejšy* 'firmer') and *ch–š* (*suchy* 'dry' – *sušejšy* 'drier'). The Lower Sorbian equivalent of USo. *naj-* is *nej-*: *nejstaršy* 'oldest'. There is also a variant form, *nejž-*: *nejžlěpšy* 'best'. Absolute superlatives are formed with *nanej-* and *nanejž-*: *nanejstaršy* 'oldest of all', *nanejžlěpšy* 'best of all'. The Lower Sorbian equivalents of USo. *bóle* are *wěcej* 'more' and *lěpjej* 'more'. They can be used to form analytic comparatives, such as *lěpjej kisały* 'sourer' (= *kisalšy*) from *kisały* 'sour'. *Nejwěcej, nejlěpjej* and *nanejwěcej* are used to form analytic superlatives and absolute superlatives.

Adverbs are derived from adjectives most commonly by means of the suffix *-'e*, which causes a change in the preceding consonant: *b–bj, p–pj, w–wj, m–mj, n–nj, r–rj*; for example, USo, and LSo. *słaby* 'weak' – *słabje* 'weakly'. The velars undergo the alternations resulting from the second palatalization: USo. *słódki* 'sweet' – *słódce* 'sweetly', LSo. *słodki* 'sweet' – *słodce* 'sweetly', but many adjectives can also form their corresponding adverbs by means of the suffix *-o* and this avoids palatalization. Thus USo. *słódko* and LSo. *słodko* 'sweetly' also exist. The dentals alternate with the results of palatalization before front vowels: USo. *twjerdy* 'hard' – *twjerdže* 'hard' (adverb) (LSo. *twardy* 'hard' – *twarźe/twardo* 'hard' (adverb)), USo. *kruty* 'firm' – *kruće* 'firmly' (LSo. *kšuty* 'firm' – *kšuśe* 'firmly').

Particularly interesting are Upper Sorbian adverbs derived from adjectives with the suffix *-sk* referring to languages: for instance, *serbsce* (from *serbski* 'Sorbian'), as in *rěčiće wy serbsce?* 'do you speak Sorbian?'. This type is unknown in Lower Sorbian, where it is replaced by the adverbial type derived from the instrumental plural of the short-form adjective: *powědaśo wy serbski?* 'do you speak Sorbian?'. In sentences of this kind in Lower Sorbian one may also hear the type *serbske* or *na serbske*. In Upper Sorbian the type *serbski* is dialectal or archaic. A further type formed with the preposition *po* and what is historically the dative singular of the short-form adjective (*po serbsku*) may also be encountered in both Upper and Lower Sorbian, but it is archaic.

Comparative and superlative adverbs in Upper Sorbian are in most cases derived from comparative and superlative adjectives, by substituting *-o* for the adjectival endings: *sylnišo* 'more strongly' (from *sylniši* 'stronger'). Some comparative adverbs, however, are derived from the adjectival stem (often with the loss of *-ok* or *-k*) by means of *-'e*: *hłuboki* 'deep' – *hłubje* 'deeper' (adverb), *bliski* 'near' – *bliže* 'nearer' (adverb). The prefixes *naj-* and *nanaj-* are used in the same way as with adjectives to form superlatives and absolute superlatives: *najsylnišo* 'most strongly'.

There is a marked contrast between Upper and Lower Sorbian in their methods of forming comparative adverbs. In Lower Sorbian they are formed with the suffix *-'ej*: *słabjej* 'more weakly' (from *słaby* 'weak'), *sušej* 'more drily' (from *suchy* 'dry'), *bližej* 'nearer' (adverb; from *bliski* 'near'). The prefixes *nej-, nejž-* and *na-* are used as with adjectives: *nanejždalej* 'furthest of all'.

3.1.5   Numeral morphology

The declension of the Upper Sorbian cardinal numeral *jedyn* '1' is shown in table 11.15. It has no dual and the plural exists mainly to modify *pluralia tantum* (thus *jedne durje* 'one door'). Masculine-personal forms are shown in the paradigm for the sake of completeness, but it is doubtful whether they have any real existence with numerical meaning. The indefinite pronoun *jedyn* 'certain, some', however, has a full paradigm, including masculine personal forms and the dual.

The declension of Lower Sorbian *jaden* '1' is shown in table 11.16. As in Upper Sorbian, it has no dual and its plural exists mainly to modify *pluralia*

Table 11.15   Declension of USo. *jedyn* '1'

Singular

	M Animate	Non-animate	N	F
NOM	jedyn		jedne	jedna
ACC	jednoho	jedyn	jedne	jednu
GEN		jednoho		jedneje
DAT		jednomu		jednej
INST		z jednym		z jednej
LOC		wo jednym		wo jednej

Plural

	Masculine personal	Non-masculine personal
NOM	jedni	jedne
ACC	jednych	jedne
GEN		jednych
DAT		jednym
INST		z jednymi
LOC		wo jednych

Table 11.16   Declension of LSo. *jaden* '1'

		SG			PL
	M Animate	Non-animate	N	F	
NOM	jaden		jadno	jadna	jadne
ACC	jadnogo	jaden	jadno	jadnu	jadne
GEN		jadnogo		jadneje	jadnych
DAT		jadnomu		jadnej	jadnym
INST		z jadnym		z jadneju	z jadnymi
LOC		wo jadnom		wo jadnej	wo jadnych

tantum. The Lower Sorbian indefinite pronoun *jaden* 'certain, some' has a full paradigm.

The declensions of Upper Sorbian *dwaj* '2' and Lower Sorbian *dwa* '2' are shown in table 11.17.

The numerals '3' and '4' (USo. *tři/štyri*, LSo. *tśi/styri*) are declined as shown in table 11.18. They have no singular and no dual. In Upper Sorbian *tři* and *štyri* in colloquial and dialectal speech, if used attributively, may be indifferent to gender and undeclined (for example, *před štyri lĕtami* 'four years ago' (literally: before four years)). If used absolutely they are inflected normally. This tendency to lose declinability has not been observed in Lower Sorbian dialects (*SS* 11: 58).

The declension of Upper Sorbian numerals from '5' upwards is exemplified by *pjeć* '5' in table 11.19. When used absolutely and referring to persons, numerals from five upwards are always declined in all varieties of Sorbian (LSo. *ze wšyknymi pĕśomi* 'with all five'). When used attributively, they tend not to be declined. This tendency is greater in Upper than in Lower Sorbian, and greatest when the attributive numeral does not refer to male persons. Until 1937 the situation in the Upper Sorbian literary language was different. With referents other than male persons the forms *pjećich* (GEN), *pjećim* (DAT), *z pjećimi* (INST) and *wo pjećich* (LOC) were predominant in both attributive and absolute use. Locative *pjećich* and the corresponding forms of other numerals from '5' to '12' survive as fossilized adverbial forms denoting the time of day (as in *w pjećich* 'at five o'clock') (Faßke 1981: 513–19, 533). Such forms are sometimes written without the *w*, which is, in any case, silent.

In Lower Sorbian the numerals from '5' (*pĕś*) to '99' (*źewjeśaźewjeśźaset*), when declined, follow the model provided by *tśi* '3'. With the exception of numerals from '11' (*jadnaśćo*) to '99' in the nominative (when they are indifferent to gender), they can take the *o*-forms agreeing with animates. If used absolutely, the numeral must be in the *o*-form (if appropriate) and declined. For example, *pĕś* '5' has the oblique cases (non-animate) *pĕśich* (GEN), *pĕśim* (DAT), *z pĕśimi* (INST), *wo pĕśich* (LOC), and (animate) *pĕśoch* (ACC and GEN), *pĕśom* (DAT), *z pĕśomi* (INST), *wo pĕśoch* (LOC).

3.2 Verbal morphology

3.2.1 Verbal categories

In almost all finite verbs in Upper and Lower Sorbian the categories of person (first, second and third) and number (singular, dual and plural) are expressed. A minor degree of ambiguity as to person occurs in the dual in all tenses (for example, USo. 2 DU and 3 DU *dźěłataj* 'you work' or 'they work') and in the singular in the aorist and imperfect (USo. 2 SG and 3 SG *dźěłaše* 'you were working' or 'he/she/it was working'). Ambiguity as to

Table 11.17   Declensions of USo. *dwaj* '2' and LSo. *dwa* '2'

	M	N and F

USo. *dwaj*

	Personal	*Non-personal*	
NOM	dwaj		dwě
ACC	dweju	dwaj	dwě
GEN		dweju	
DAT		dwěmaj	
INST		z dwěmaj	
LOC		wo dwěmaj	

LSo. *dwa*

	Animate	*Non-animate*	
NOM	dwa		dwě
ACC	dweju	dwa	dwě
GEN		dweju	
DAT		dwěma	
INST		z dwěma	
LOC		wo dwěma	

Table 11.18   Declension of the numerals '3' and '4'

USo. *tři* '3' and *štyri* '4'

	Masculine personal	*Non-masculine personal*
NOM	třo/štyrjo	tři/štyri
ACC	třoch/štyrjoch	tři/štyri
GEN	třoch/štyrjoch	
DAT	třom/štyrjom	
INST	z třomi/štyrjomi	
LOC	wo třoch/štyrjoch	

LSo. *tśi* '3' and *styri* '4'

	Masculine animate	*Non-masculine animate*
NOM	tśo/styrjo	tśi/styri
ACC	tśoch/styrjoch	tśi/styri
GEN	tśoch/styrjoch	tśich/styrich
DAT	tśom/styrjom	tśim/styrim
INST	z tśomi/styrjomi	z tśimi/styrimi
LOC	wo tśoch/styrjoch	wo tśich/styrich

Table 11.19   Declension of USo. *pjeć* **'5'**

	Masculine personal	*Non-masculine personal*
NOM	pjećo	pjeć
ACC	pjećoch	pjeć
GEN	pjećoch	pjeć
DAT	pjećom	pjeć
INST	z pjećomi	z pjeć
LOC	wo pjećoch	wo pjeć

number arises from the honorific use of ostensibly plural forms to address one person or two persons (thus USo. *što činiće?* 'what are you doing?' may be addressed to one, two or more persons). An attempt to reduce ambiguity is made by an artificial rule affecting both literary languages which says that if only one person is addressed the *l*-participle must be in its singular form, though the honorific meaning may still be expressed by the plural form of the auxiliary (USo. *što sće činiła?* 'what did you (F) do?'). The Upper Sorbian rule is that the plural form of the *l*-participle is to be used only if two or more persons are addressed (for instance, *što sće činili?* 'what did you do?' should be addressed only to two or more persons) (Faßke 1981: 551). Literary Lower Sorbian often follows the same practice, though the rule appears not to have been codified in Lower Sorbian grammars. In colloquial Sorbian, however, both Upper and Lower, the *l*-participle is in the plural even when only one person is addressed, if the utterance is honorific.

Gender is expressed in the singular of tenses involving the *l*-participle (for example, USo. *nan je dźěłał* 'father worked', *holca je dźěłała* 'the girl worked'). In Upper Sorbian the *l*-participle is capable of expressing the distinction between masculine personal and non-masculine personal (*mužojo su dźěłali* 'the men worked', *žony su dźěłałe* 'the women worked'); but this is not obligatory. The type *dźěłali* may be used whether the subject is masculine personal or not. Support for the distinction in dialects is found only to the south of Bautzen. The *dźěłałe* type agreeing with a third-person non-masculine personal subject is not unusual in present-day literature, but with the first and second persons such forms are bookish (Faßke 1981: 298). In Lower Sorbian gender is not expressed in the *l*-participle in the plural.

The following tenses are expressed synthetically: present, perfective future, aorist and imperfect. The perfect, pluperfect, and imperfective future are expressed analytically. The aorist is formed only from perfective verbs; the imperfect only from imperfective verbs. In some analyses the aorist and imperfect are treated as a single synthetic preterite. The endings are the same for both aorist and imperfect, except in the second and third person singular. The aorist and imperfect refer specifically to past historic events isolated in time from the time of speaking. They are used in both literary languages, but have disappeared from Lower Sorbian dialects (see map 11.1, p. 594). In Upper Sorbian dialects the possibility of their being replaced by the perfect is greater in the north than in the south (*SS* 11: 100). In all varieties of Sorbian the perfect tense is formed analytically from verbs of both aspects by means of the present tense of the verb 'to be' and the *l*-participle (USo. *ja sym dźěłała* 'I (F) worked'). The pluperfect is also formed with the *l*-participle, but in conjunction with the imperfect of the auxiliary (thus USo. *ja běch dźěłała* 'I (F) had worked'). The iterative perfect is formally identical with the conditional (USo. *ja bych dźěłała* 'I (F) would/used to work'). Another type of pluperfect, composed of the perfect tense of the auxiliary and the *l*-participle (USo. *ja sym była dźěłała* 'I (F) had worked') is occasionally found in dialects, but is not used in the literary languages (Šewc 1968: 179).

Verbs of motion exist in the following determinate/indeterminate pairs: USo. *hić/chodźić* 'to go (on foot)', *běžeć/běhać* 'to run/go (on foot)', *jěć/jězdźić* 'to travel/go (not on foot)', *wjesć/wodźić* 'to lead', *wjezć/wozyć* 'to convey', *lećeć/lětać* 'to fly', *lězć/łazyć* 'to crawl', *hnać (čěrić)/honić* 'to drive', *njesć/nosyć* 'to carry', *ćahnyć/ćahać* 'to move (ITR)', *hnać (čěrić)/hanjeć* 'to run'; LSo. *hyś/chojźiś* 'to go (on foot)', *běžaś/běgaś* 'to run/go (on foot)', *jěś/ jězdźiś* 'to travel/go (not on foot)', *wjasć/wozyś* 'to lead/convey', *leśeś/lětaś* 'to fly', *lězć/łazyś* 'to crawl', *gnaś/goniś* 'to drive', *njasć/nosyś* 'to carry', *śěgnuś/śěgaś* 'to move (ITR)', *gnaś/ganjaś* 'to run'.

The perfective future is expressed by the non-past tense of perfective verbs (USo. and LSo. *ja napišu* 'I shall write'). However, when the speech act is itself the action denoted by the verb, a perfective verb may have present meaning (USo. *přeprošu was* 'I invite you' (PRFV) is synonymous with *přeprošuju was* (IMPFV) (Faßke 1981: 183, 255; Šewc 1968: 182–3)). In colloquial Sorbian certain verbs of motion are particularly prone to German influence. For example, USo. *přinć* 'to come' (PRFV) is equated with German *kommen* 'to come' and the sense of its relationship with *hić* 'to go' (IMPFV) is lost, following the German model in which *gehen* 'to go' and *kommen* 'to come' are not formally related. Therefore *přinđźe* (PRFV 3SG) may mean either 'will come' or 'comes', although in the literary language it is expected to have future meaning. Nevertheless, by and large, the aspectual system of both Upper and Lower Sorbian (even of colloquial and dialectal varieties, where German influence is strongest) is intact.

The future tense of the Upper Sorbian verb *być* 'to be' is as follows:

	SG	DU	PL
1	budu	budźemoj	budźemy

2	budźeš ⎱		budźeće
		budźetaj/budźetej	
3	budźe ⎰		budźeja

It is used as an auxiliary to form the imperfective future by adding the imperfective infinitive (USo. *budu pisać* 'I shall write'). Lower Sorbian follows the same pattern (LSo. *budu pisaś*). Colloquially and in dialects a compound future may be formed with a perfective infinitive (USo. *ja budu napisać* 'I shall write', LSo. *ja budu napisaś*). Since the nineteenth century there have been attempts to exclude this type from the literary languages and to replace it with the perfective future. However, the latest authority on Upper Sorbian (Faßke 1981: 253) says that the analytic perfective future is permissible if the infinitive, for the sake of emphasis, is placed in first position in the clause (as in *přinjesć jemu nichtó ničo njebudźe* 'no one will bring him anything').

The determinate verbs of motion (see above) have only one future; this is formed with the prefix po- (USo. *ponjesu* 'I shall carry', LSo. *ponjasu*). Similarly, the verb 'to have' (USo. *měć*, LSo. *měś*) has only a synthetic future formed with z- (USo. and LSo. *změju* 'I shall have').

Despite German interference every Sorbian verb is either perfective or imperfective, but bi-aspectual verbs are not uncommon and are perfective or imperfective depending on their context. Perfectives are most commonly derived from simple imperfectives by prefixation (USo. *pisać* 'to write' (IMPFV) – *napisać* (PRFV)). Conversely, imperfectives can be derived from perfectives by suffixation (USo. *přepisać* 'to transcribe' (PRFV) – *přepisować* (IMPFV)). The aspectual distinction may be expressed solely by suffixation (neither aspect bearing a prefix) (USo. *kupować* 'to buy' (IMPFV) – *kupić* (PRFV)) or by verbs that are formally unrelated (LSo. *braś* 'to take' (IMPFV) – *wześ* (PRFV)). However, the proportion of unprefixed perfective verbs is small and there are very few imperfective verbs that have a prefix but no suffix. The latter category consists principally of verbs which have come into existence as loan-translations of German prefixed verbs (USo. *wobsedźeć* /LSo. *wobsejźeś* 'to possess' based on German *besitzen*). This process has been taken further in non-standard Sorbian, involving the use of adverbs as prefixes: for example, USo. *nutřćahnyć* 'to move in' (German *einziehen*); the standard Upper Sorbian form is *zaćahnyć*. In literary Upper Sorbian the adverb *nutř* 'in' can never be a verbal prefix.

The imperative in Upper Sorbian is formed from the short present stem to which is added the imperative morpheme -*j* or -*i* followed by the personal endings -*∅* (2 SG), -*moj* (1 DU), -*taj*/-*tej* (2 DU), -*my* (1 PL) or -*će* (2 PL) (*kopaj!* 'hack!' from *kopać*). If the stem ends in a consonant the morpheme -*j* may be represented in consonant alternation (*n–ń, d–dź, t–ć, k–č*), thus *stań!* 'stand up!' from *stanyć*, unless the consonant is already soft or incapable of being softened when in final position. If the short stem consists solely of consonants, the imperative morpheme is -*i* (*spi!* 'sleep!'). The morpheme -*i* may also be used after groups of consonants (*wotewri!* 'open!'). A few imperatives are simply irregular (*jěs!* or *jěz!* 'eat!' from *jěsć*). The third person (only singular) imperative is extremely rare and largely restricted to formulaic utterances, such as *přińdź k nam twoje kralestwo* 'thy kingdom come (to us)'. Clauses similar in meaning to imperatives may be created with the particle *njech* (*njech čita, štož chce* 'let him read what he likes') (Faßke 1981: 291). The Lower Sorbian imperative does not differ significantly as a verbal category from that of Upper Sorbian. The Lower Sorbian equivalent of *njech* is *daś* or *daśi* (*daś te luźe powědaju* 'let the people talk').

The Upper Sorbian conditional is formed with the *l*-participle in conjunction with a special set of forms of the verb *być* 'to be':

	SG	DU	PL
1	bych	bychmoj	bychmy
2	by	byštaj/-štej	byśće
3	by	byštaj/-štej	bychu

For example: *bych dźěłał* 'I (M) would work', *by dźěłała* 'you (F) or she would work', *bychu dźěłali* 'they would work'.

In the conditional of modal verbs the auxiliary is often omitted (Faßke 1981: 275), for instance, *to njesmělo so stać* 'that should not happen'. A type of conditional involving the *l*-participle of the verb *być* 'to be' is also found, but is regarded as both archaic and bookish (*bych był dźěłał* 'I would have worked'). It is thought to have been modelled on a similar form in Czech. On the other hand, a form of the conditional involving the following auxiliary was undoubtedly once a true vernacular feature of Upper Sorbian, but it is now archaic or defunct:

	SG	DU	PL
1	budźech/-ich	budźechmoj (budźichmoj)	budźechmy (budźichmy)
2	budźeše/-iše	budźeštaj/-štej	budźeśće (budźiśće)
3	budžeše/-iše	budźeštaj/-štej	budźechu (budźichu)

(The forms with -*i*- were characteristic of the old Protestant norm; Faßke 1981: 275.)

In Lower Sorbian all personal endings have been dropped from the auxiliary, leaving an invariable particle *by* (*ja by źěłał* 'I would work', *woni by źěłali* 'they would work', *wej by źěłałej* 'you (DU) would work').

The Upper Sorbian reflexive is formed with the particle *so* (*nan so truha* 'father is shaving' (*truhać so* 'to shave')). The Lower Sorbian equivalent is *se* (*nan se goli* 'father is shaving'). The passive may be formed in Upper

Sorbian and Lower Sorbian either with the verb 'to be' in conjunction with the past passive participle (USo. *wona je wuzamknjena* 'she is excluded', *wona budźe wuzamknjena* 'she will be excluded'; LSo. *wona bužo wuzamknjona* 'she will be excluded') or with a special part of the verb 'to be':

	SG	DU	PL
1	buch	buchmoj	buchmy
2	bu	buštaj/-štej	bušće
3	bu	buštaj/-štej	buchu

The Lower Sorbian equivalents vary from the above only in the dual (*buchmej, buštej*) and the second person plural (*bušćo*). The forms like *buch* are the Sorbian equivalents of German *werden* 'to become' and like *werden* are used both to form the passive and with the meaning 'to become' (USo. *buchmy wuzamknjeni* 'we were excluded' (masculine personal), *wón bu wučer* 'he became a teacher'; LSo. *buchmy wuzamknjone* 'we were excluded', *won bu wucabnik* 'he became a teacher'). These forms are exclusively past tense. In colloquial and dialectal Upper Sorbian the passive may be formed with the German loan-word *wordować* (USo. *wón je wonćisnjeny wordował* 'he was thrown out'). The Lower Sorbian equivalent *wordowaś* is used in the literary language (*ja worduju bity* 'I am being beaten').

The sense of the passive may also be expressed by means of the reflexive (USo. *a pon so zas posleni khěrluš spěwa* 'and then the last hymn is sung again' (T 9: 42), LSo. *wuknik se wot direktora chwali* 'the pupil is praised by the headmaster'). Reflexive verbs are also used in impersonal expressions, such as USo. *a tam so tež spěwa* 'and there is singing there too' (T 9: 42), but it is also possible to use an impersonal passive with *bu* (provided it is in the past tense) (USo. *pozdźišo bu spěwane* 'later there was singing'). When *wordować/wordowaś* is used there is no restriction on the tense (USo. *dyž předźene worduje* 'when there is spinning' (T 9: 14)). Impersonal passives are commonly formed from intransitive verbs (USo. *jemu bu pomhane* 'he was helped' (*pomhać* 'to help' takes the dative), *potom bu spane* 'then there was sleeping' (compare German *dann wurde geschlafen*).)

The Upper Sorbian infinitive nearly always ends in -*ć* (for example, *pisać* 'to write'), but a very small number of verbs belonging to the *e*-conjugation (those with velar stems) have an infinitive in -*c* (like *pjec* 'to bake'). A longer infinitive ending in -*ći* is attested in early texts, in folksongs and in dialects. In Lower Sorbian most infinitives end in -*ś* (*pisaś* 'to write'), but after sibilants -*ś* is replaced by -*ć* (*kłasć* 'to lay'). As in Upper Sorbian, verbs with velar stems have infinitives in -*c* (*pjac* 'to bake'). Longer infinitives in -*śi* and -*śći* are found in folk-songs and early texts.

They survived in dialects until the late nineteenth century (Mucke 1891: 533). Only Lower Sorbian has a supine. It is derived from the infinitive by replacing -*ś* or -*ć* with -*t*, for example *pisat* (from *pisaś*), *kłast* (from *kłasć*), but in the case of infinitives in -*c* the supine ending -*t* is added to the infinitive, as in *pjact* (from *pjac*). The supine is properly used only after verbs of motion (*źom spat* 'I am going to sleep'). It is a feature of literary Lower Sorbian and of Lower Sorbian dialects except those to the east and south-east of Cottbus (*SS* 12: map 41).

Both Upper and Lower Sorbian have a single active participle, formed only from imperfective verbs and ending, in the masculine nominative singular, in -*cy* (USo. *dźěłacy* 'working', LSo. *źěłajucy*). It declines like an adjective. The masculine nominative singular of the passive participle, which also declines like an adjective, ends in both Upper and Lower Sorbian in -*ny* or -*ty* (USo. and LSo. *zebrany* 'gathered', *bity* 'beaten'). Passive participles are used to form finite passive verbs (see above). The Upper Sorbian present gerund ends in -'*o*, -'*icy*, or -(*j*)*cy*. It is indeclinable. Some verbs can form more than one type (*stupajo/stupajcy* 'stepping', *so smějo/so smějicy* 'laughing'). The Lower Sorbian equivalent is identical in form with the masculine nominative singular of the active participle (*stojecy* 'standing'). Upper Sorbian in addition has a past gerund formed with the ending -*wši* (after a vowel) or -*ši* (after a consonant): *rozbiwši* 'having smashed', *priwjezši* 'having brought'. Lower Sorbian has no equivalent of this form.

The *l*-participle, used in both Upper and Lower Sorbian to form certain compound tenses, is composed of the infinitive stem and the affix -*ł*/-*l* (USo. *wón je pisał* 'he wrote').

3.2.2 Conjugation

On the basis of the thematic vowel used to form most or all parts of the present tense Upper Sorbian verbs fall into the following three conjugations:

1   *e*-conjugation (USo. *bić* 'to beat': *biju, biješ* and so on; *njesć* 'to carry': *njesu, njeseš*; *minyć so* 'to pass by': *minu so, minješ so*). This conjugation occasionally involves consonant alternations (as in USo. *wjesć* 'to lead': *wjedu, wjedźeš*; *pisać* 'to write': *pišu, pišeš*). Infinitive stems in -*owa*- regularly correspond to present stems in -*uje*- (*darować* 'to give': *daruju, daruješ*).

2   *i*-conjugation (*rozumjeć* 'to understand': *rozumju, rozumiš* and so on; *chodźić* 'to walk': *chodźu chodźiš*). The substitution of -*y*- for -*i*- occurs after *s* and *z* (*prosyć* 'to ask': *prošu, prosyš*; *kazyć* 'to spoil': *kažu, kazyš*). As shown by *prosyć* and *kazyć*, there are occasional consonant alternations.

3   *a*-conjugation (*dźěłać* 'to work': *dźěłam, dźěłaš* and so on; *třěleć* 'to shoot': *třělam, třěleš*). There are no consonant alternations, but

between soft consonants -*e*- is substituted for -*a*-. The infinitive stem always ends in -*a*, except after a soft consonant, when the *e*-substitution rule operates. The *a*-conjugation is distinguished also by its first person singular ending -*m* (as opposed to -*u* in other conjugations). Some verbs can be conjugated optionally according to either the *e*- or *a*-conjugation (for instance, *pisać* 'to write': *pišu, pišeš* and so on, or *pisam, pisaš*).

The present stem also forms the basis for the allocation of Lower Sorbian verbs into the following four conjugations:

1   *o*- or *jo*-conjugation (LSo. *njasć* 'to carry': *njasu/njasom, njasoš* and so on; *braś* 'to take': *bjerju/bjerjom, bjerjoš*). Consonant alternations occur (as in *wjasć* 'to lead'; *wjedu/wjeźom, wjeźoš*, third person plural *wjedu*; *pisaś* 'to write': *pišu/pišom, pišoš*). The infinitive stem in -*owa*-regularly corresponds to the present stem in -*ujo*- (*studowaś* 'to study': *studuju/studujom, studujoš*). The -*u* and -*om* forms in the first person singular are equally acceptable in the literary language. The ending -*u* is characteristic of western Lower Sorbian dialects (except the extreme west), whereas -*om* occurs in eastern dialects and the extreme western dialect of Vetschau (Wětošow).
2   *i*-conjugation (*spaś* 'to sleep': *spim, spiš* and so on; *chojźiś* 'to walk': *chojžim, chojžiš*). After *c, s, z, š* and *ž*, the substitution of -*y*- for -*i*-occurs (*słyšaś* 'to hear': *słyšym, słyšyš*). The first person singular always ends in -*m* and there are no consonant alternations.
3   *a*-conjugation (*źěłaś* 'to work': *źěłam, źěłaš* and so on). There are no consonant or vowel alternations. The infinitive stem always ends in -*a*.
4   *j*-conjugation (*stojaś* 'to stand'; *stojm, stojš* and so on). There are no consonant or vowel alternations.

The first person singular ending -*m* has spread much further in Lower than in Upper Sorbian. In Lower Sorbian, in fact, it is only in the *o*-/*jo*-conjugation that the vocalic ending -*u* is retained, and even here, in the literary language, there is a facultative variant in -*m*.

Upper Sorbian reflexes of Proto-Slavonic verb classes

Infinitive	Present	
Theme in -*e*/-*o*		
njes-	njese-	'carry'
wjes-	wjedźe-	'lead'
čita- (*čitać* is a nineteenth-century neologism)	čita-	'read'

Infinitive	*Present*	
†kćě-	kće- or kćěje-	'bloom'
hi-	dźe-	'go'
jěcha-	jěcha-	'ride'
jě-	jědźe-	'drive'
(*gre-* not attested)		
†hrjeba-	hrjeba-	'dig, bury'
ži-	žije-	'heal'

rjec 'say' has only infinitive and *l*-participle *rjekł*

†rěče-	rěči-	'speak'
nače-	načnje-	'cut the first slice' (the meaning 'begin', given in dictionaries, is artificial; see Schuster-Šewc, *Wörterbuch*, under 'načeć')
wumrě-	wumrje-	
	wumrěje-	'die'
sta- (only reflexive)	stanje-	'happen'
(*sъsa-* not attested)		
†cyca-	cyca-	'suck'
(*zъva-* not attested)		
†žwa-	žuje-	'chew'
bra-	bjerje-	'take'

Theme in *-ne*
(*dvignǫ-* not attested)

| †wukny- | wuknje- | 'learn' |
| miny- (only reflexive) | minje- | 'pass by, disappear' |

Theme in *-je*

| ču- | čuje- | 'feel' |

(*pě-* attested only in spěwać)

†spěwać	spěwa-	'sing'
kry-	kryje-	'cover'
bi-	bije-	'beat'

(*bor-* not attested)

†wobró-	woborje-	'restrain, defend'
mlě-	mjele-	
	mlěje-	'grind'
dźěła-	dzěła-	'work'

(*umě-* not attested)

Infinitive	*Present*	
†smě-	smě-	'make bold'
		(= German dürfen)
kaza-	kaza-	
	kaže-	'order'
pisa-	pisa-	
	piše-	'write'
jima-	jima-	'grasp'
darowa-	daruje-	'give'
sy-	syje-	'sow'

Theme in -*i*		
modli- (only reflexive)	modli-	'pray'
chodźi-	chodźi-	'walk, go'
(* velě- not attested)		
†woli-	woli-	'choose'
słyše- (słyša-)	slyši-	'hear'
spa-	spi-	'sleep'

Athematic		
by-	(1 SG sym, 2 SG sy,	
	3 SG je; 1 DU	
	smój, 2/3 DU	
	staj/stej, 1 PL	
	smy, 2 PL sće,	
	3 PL su)	'be'
jěs-	jě-	'eat'
da-	da-	'give'
wědźe-	wě-	'know'
mě-	ma-	'have'

Irregular		
chcy-	chce-	'want'

Note: †substituted for root/stem not attested in Upper Sorbian.

Lower Sorbian reflexes of Proto-Slavonic verb classes

Infinitive	*Present*	
Theme in -*e*/-*o*		
njas-	njaso-	'carry'
wjas-	wjeźo-	'drive, lead'
cyta- (nineteenth-century		
neologism)	cyta-	'read'

Infinitive	*Present*	
†plaś-	pleśo-	'plait'
hy-	źo-	'go'
jěcha-	jěcha-	'ride'
jě-	jěźo-	'drive'
†(*gre- not attested)		
grěba-	grěbjo-	'scratch, dig'
žy-	žyjo-	'heal'
rja-	rjaco-	'say'
nace-	nacejo-	'broach' (the meaning 'begin', given in dictionaries, is artificial; see Schuster-Šewc, *Wörterbuch*, under 'načeć')
wumrě-	wumrějo-	'die'
sta- (only reflexive)	stanjo-	'happen'
(*sъsa- not attested)		
†cyca-	cyca-	'suck'
(*zъva- not attested)		
†žu-	žujo-	'chew'
bra-	bjerjo-	'take'

Theme in *-ne*
(*dvignǫ- not attested)

†zwignu-	zwignjo-	'raise'
minu- (only reflexive)	minjo-	'pass by, disappear'

Theme in *-je*

cu-	cujo-	'feel'
(*pě- attested only in spěwaś)		
†spěwa-	spěwa-	'sing'
kšy-	kšyjo-	'cover'
bi-	bijo-	'beat'
(*bor- not attested)		
†proj-	proj-	'undo, separate'
mla-	mjelo-	
	mlejo-	'grind'
źěła-	źěła-	'work'
wumě-	wumějo-	'understand, be able'
kaza-	kažo-	'order'
pisa-	pišo-	'write'

Infinitive	*Present*	
(*jьma- imperfectly attested – sixteenth–seventeenth century)		
†łama-	łamjo-	'break'
(*darova- not attested)		
†kupowa-	kupujo-	'buy'
se-	sejo-	'sow'

Theme in -*i*

modli- (only reflexive)	modli-	'pray'
chojźi-	chojźi-	'go, walk'
(*velě- not attested)		
†woli-	woli-	'choose'
słyša-	słyšy-	'hear'
spa-	spi-	'sleep'

Athematic

by-	(1 SG som, 2 SG sy,	
	3 SG jo; 1 DU	
	smej, 2/3 DU	
	stej; 1 PL smy, 2	
	PL sćo, 3 PL su)	'be'
jěs-	jě-	'eat'
da-	da-	'let'
da-	dajo-	'give'
wěźe-	wě-	'know'
mě-	ma-	'have'

Irregular

kśě-	co-	'want'

Note: †substituted for root/stem not attested in Lower Sorbian.

Upper Sorbian illustrative paradigms

e-conjugation: *njesć* 'to carry'

Present

	SG	DU	PL
1	njesu	njesemoj	njesemy
2	njeseš		njeseće
3	njese	} njesetaj/njesetej	njesu (njeseja)

The 3 PL type *njeseja* is colloquial

Imperfect

	SG	DU	PL
1	njesech	njesechmoj	njesechmy
2	} njeseše	} njeseštaj/njeseštej	njesešće
3			njesechu

Aorist

1	nanjesech	nanjesechmoj	nanjesechmy
2	} nanjese	} nanjeseštaj/nanjeseštej	nanjesešće
3			nanjesechu

l-participle: SG *njesł, -o, -a*; DU *njesłoj/njesłej*; PL *njesli/njesłe*

Present gerund: *njeso* (some verbs have *-icy*: for instance, *bijo* or *bijicy* from *bić* 'to beat')

Past gerund: attested only for verbs whose infinitive stem ends in a vowel and for compounds of *hić* 'to go': for example, *napisawši* from *napisać* 'to write', *wušedši* from *wuńć* 'to go out'

Present participle: cannot be formed from verbs whose present stem ends in *s*, *z* or *r*; but from *bić* 'to beat', for example, we have *bijacy*

Past participle: *njeseny*

Imperative: *njes*

Verbal noun: *njesenje*

i-conjugation: *słyšeć* 'to hear'

Present

	SG	DU	PL
1	słyšu	słyšimoj	słyšimy
2	słyšiš	} słyšitaj/słyšitej	słyšiće
3	slyši		słyša

Imperfect

1	słysach	słysachmoj	słyšachmy
2	} słyšeše	} słyšeštaj/słyšeštej	słyšešće
3			słyšachu

Aorist

1	zasłyšach	zasłyšachmoj	zasłyšachmy
2	} zasłyša	} zasłyšeštaj/zasłyšeštej	zasłyšešće
3			zasłyšachu

l-participle: SG *słyšał, -o, -a*; DU *słyšałoj/-ej*; PL *słyšeli/słyšałe*

Present gerund: *słyšo* or *słyšicy*

Past gerund: *zasłyšawši*

Present participle: *słyšacy*

Past participle: *słyšany*

Imperative: *słyš*

Verbal noun: *słyšenje*

a-conjugation: *dźěłać* 'to work'

Present

	SG	DU	PL
1	dźěłam	dźěłamoj	dźěłamy
2	dźěłaš	} dźěłataj/dźěłatej	dźěłaće
3	dźěła		dźěłaju/dźěłaja

The third person plural ending -*u* is literary and archaic

Imperfect

1	dźěłach	dźěłachmoj	dźěłachmy
2	} dźěłaše	} dźěłaštaj/dźěłaštej	dźěłašće
3			dźěłachu

Aorist

1	nadźěłach	nadźěłachmoj	nadźěłachmy
2	} nadźěła	} nadźěłaštaj/nadźěłaštej	nadźěłašće
3			nadźěłachu

l-participle: SG *dźěłał, -o, -a*; DU *dźěłałoj/-ej*; PL *dźěłali/dźěłałe*
Present gerund: *dźěłajo* or *dźěłajcy*
Past gerund: *nadźěławši*
Present participle: *dźěłacy*
Past participle: *dźěłany*
Imperative: *dźěłaj*
Verbal noun: *dźěłanje*

Lower Sorbian illustrative paradigms

o-/jo-conjugation: *njasć* 'to carry'

Present

1	njasu/njasom	njasomej	njasomy
2	njasoš	} njasotej	njasośo
3	njaso		njasu

Imperfect

1	njasech	njasechmej	njasechmy
2	} njasešo	} njaseštej	njasešćo
3			njasechu

Aorist

1	donjasech	donjasechmej	donjasechmy
2	} donjase	} donjaseštej	donjasešćo
3			donjasechu

l-participle: SG *njasł, -o, -a*; DU *njasłej*; PL *njasli*

Present participle: *njasecy* (*njasucy*)
Past participle: *njasony*
Imperative: *njas*
Verbal noun: *njasenje*

i-conjugation: *słyšaś* 'to hear'

Present

	SG	DU	PL
1	słyšym	słyšymej	słyšymy
2	słyšyš	} słyšytej	słyšyśo
3	słyšy		słyše

Imperfect

	SG	DU	PL
1	słyšach	słyšachmej	słyšachmy
2	} słyšašo	} słyšaštej	słyšaśćo
3			słyšachu

Aorist

	SG	DU	PL
1	wusłyšach	wusłyšachmej	wusłyšachmy
2	} wusłyša	} wusłyšaštej	wusłyšaśćo
3			wusłyšachu

l-participle: SG *słyšał, -o, -a*; DU *słyšałej*; PL *słyšali*
Present participle: *słyšecy*
Past participle: *słyšany*
Imperative: *słyš*
Verbal noun: *słyšanje*

a-conjugation: *źěłaś* 'to work'

Present

	SG	DU	PL
1	źěłam	źěłamej	źěłamy
2	źěłaš	} źěłatej	źěłaśo
3	źěła		źěłaju

Imperfect

	SG	DU	PL
1	źěłach	źěłachmej	źěłachmy
2	} źěłašo	} źěłaštej	źěłaśćo
3			źěłachu

Aorist

	SG	DU	PL
1	naźěłach	naźěłachmej	naźěłachmy
2	} naźěła	} naźěłaštej	nazełaśćo
3			naźěłachu

l-participle: SG *źěłał, -o, -a*; DU *źěłałej*; PL *źěłali*

Present participle: *žěłajucy*
Past participle: *žěłany*
Imperative: *žěłaj*
Verbal noun: *žěłanje*

j-conjugation: *projś* 'to undo, disentangle'

Present

	SG	DU	PL
1	projm	projmej	projmy
2	projš	} projtej	projśo
3	proj		proje

Imperfect

	SG	DU	PL
1	projach	projachmej	projachmy
2	} projašo	} projaštej	projašćo
3			projachu

Aorist

	SG	DU	PL
1	rozprojch	rozprojchmej	rozprojchmy
2	} rozproj	} rozprojštej	rozprojšćo
3			rozprojchu

l-participle: SG *projł, -o, -a*; DU *projłej*; PL *projli*
Present participle: *projecy*
Past participle: *projty*
Imperative: *proj*
Verbal noun: *projenje*

3.3   Derivational morphology

3.3.1   Major patterns of noun derivation
Sorbian nouns are formed by the use of prefixes and suffixes or by composition. Suffixation is sometimes accompanied by vowel or consonant alternations in the stem. The following are some of the main types of noun
derivation by the use of suffixes:

Suffix	Semantic components	Examples
-ak	agent (pejorative)	U/LSo. *pisak* 'scribbler'
-an (Upper Sorbian only)	place of origin	USo. *měšćan* 'town-dweller' (compare LSo. *měsćanař*)
USo. -ar/LSo. -ař	USo. agent LSo. agent/place of origin	USo. *spěwar* 'singer' LSo. *spěwař* 'singer' LSo. *molař* 'painter' LSo. *Chośebuzař* 'Cottbuser'

Suffix	Semantic components	Examples
-c	agent/bearer of attribute	U/LSo. *kupc* 'merchant' U/LSo. *starc* 'old man'
-dło	instrument	U/LSo. *lětadło* 'aircraft'
USo. -ec(y)	family or members thereof	USo. *Nowakecy* 'the Nowaks' *Hanka Nowakec* 'Hanka Nowak' (unmarried)
USo. -er (allomorph of -ar)	agent	USo. *wučer* 'teacher'
-isko	augmentative	USo. *štomisko* 'a huge tree' LSo. *bomisko* 'a huge tree'
-išćo	place	USo. *mrowišćo* 'ant-hill' LSo. *mrojowišćo* 'ant-hill'
-k	diminutive	U/LSo. *kusk* (DIM of *kus* 'piece')
-ka	diminutive	USo. *nóžka* (DIM of USo. *noha* 'leg, foot') LSo. *nožka*
-ka	female	U/LSo. *Němka* 'German woman'
-ko	diminutive	USo. *kolesko* (DIM of *koleso* 'wheel'), LSo. *kolasko* (DIM of *kolaso*)
-nik	agent, bearer of attribute	U/LSo. *pomocnik* 'helper' USo. *dołžnik* 'debtor' LSo. *dłužnik* 'debtor'
-nja	place	USo. *kowarnja* 'smithy' LSo. *kowalnja* 'smithy'
LSo. -ojc	family or members thereof	LSo. *Nowakojc* 'the Nowaks' LSo. *Hanka Nowakojc* 'Hanka Nowak' (unmarried)
-osć	attribute	U/LSo. *młodosć* 'youth'
-stwo	place/collective	U/LSo. *sudnistwo* 'law court' U/LSo. *rybarstwo* 'fishery'

Suffix	*Semantic components*	*Examples*
USo. -ćel	agent	USo. *stworićel* 'creator'
LSo. -šel		LSo. *stworišel* 'creator'

Derivation by prefixation is demonstrated by the following examples:

Prefix	*Semantic components*	*Examples*
do-	continuation/ completion	U/LSo. *dosłowo* 'epilogue'
pa-	false	USo. *parod* 'miscarriage'
pra-	old, original	USo. *pradźěd* 'great-grandfather' U/LSo. *prapremjera* 'first performance'
roz-	separation	U/LSo. *rozdźěl* 'difference'
sobu-	with (English *co-*)	USo. *sobudźěłaćer* 'collaborator' LSo. *sobuźěłaśeŕ* 'collaborator'

(*sobu-* is widely used in German calques to translate *mit-*)

wu-	out	USo. *wuwzaće* 'exception' LSo. *wuwześe* 'exception'

In cases of composition (combination of two words or stems) the elements are commonly linked by means of the morpheme *-o-*: U/LSo. *wodopad* 'waterfall', USo. *časopis* 'journal'. USo. *runowaha*/LSo. *rownowaga* 'equilibrium'; but they may be joined directly to each other without any linking element: USo. *knihiwjazar*/LSo. *knigływězaŕ* 'bookbinder'. USo. *kołodźij*/LSo. *kołoźej* 'wheelwright'

3.3.2   Major patterns of adjective derivation
Possessive adjectives are derived from nouns by means of the suffixes *-ow-* (with masculines and neuters) and *-in-* (with feminines): U/LSo. *nanowy* 'father's' (from *nan* 'father'), USo. *sotřiny*/LSO. *sotśiny* 'sister's' (from *sotra/sotša* 'sister'). The suffix *-ow-*, however, has a wider derivational function in both Upper and Lower Sorbian: for example, USo. *dróhowy* (from *dróha* 'road'). Further common adjectival suffixes are:

USo. *-aty* (*brodaty* 'bearded' from *broda* 'beard'), *-acy* (*dźěćacy* 'childish, childlike' from *dźěćo* 'child'), *-liwy* (*pohibliwy* 'mobile' from *pohibać* 'to move'), *-ny* (*měrny* 'peaceful' from *měr* 'peace'), *-ojty* (*barbojty* 'coloured' from *barba* 'colour'), *-ski* (*přećelski* 'friendly' from *přećel* 'friend');

LSo. *-aty* (*brodaty* 'bearded' from *broda* 'beard'), *-jšny* (*žĕnsajšny* 'today's' from *žĕnsa* 'today'), *-ecy* (*žĕśecy* 'childish, childlike' from *žĕśe* 'child'), *-liwy* (*pogibliwy* 'mobile' from *pogibaś* 'to move'), *-ny* (*mĕrny* 'peaceful' from *mĕr* 'peace'), *-owaty* (*barwowaty* 'coloured' from *barwa* 'colour'), *-ojty* (*barwojty* 'coloured'), *-ski* (*pśijaśelski* 'friendly' from *pśijaśel* 'friend').

3.3.3   Major patterns of verb derivation

In both Upper and Lower Sorbian many verbs have been derived from nouns and adjectives by means of suffixes; thus by means of the suffix *-je* USo. *cĕmnjeć* 'to grow dark' has been derived from *cĕmny* 'dark'. Similarly, LSo. *chromjeś* 'to be/become lame' from *chromy* 'lame'. USo. *chwalić* and LSo. *chwaliś* 'to praise' are derived by means of the suffix *-i* from U/LSo. *chwała* 'praise' (also USo. *sušić* and LSo. *sušyś* 'to dry' from *suchy* 'dry'). By means of *-ny* USo. *twjerdnyć* 'to harden' is derived from *twjerdy* 'hard' (corresponding to LSo. *twardnuś* from *twardy* 'hard', using the Lower Sorbian suffix *-nu*). The Upper Sorbian suffix *-ować*, with which, for example, the verb *cĕslować* 'to carpenter' is derived from the noun *cĕsla* 'carpenter' (corresponding to LSo. *-owaś*) is still productive in the creation of borrowings from German and from international terminology, as in USo. *transformować*, LSo. *reklamĕrowaś*.

Verbs are derived from other verbs by means of the prefixes: *do-*, *na-*, *nad-*, *po-*, *pod-*, *pře-* (LSo. *pśe-*), *před-* (LSo. *pśed-*), *při-* (LSo. *pśi-*), *roz-*, *wo-*, *wob-*, *wot-*, *wu-*, *za-* and *z(e)-/s-*. The addition of a prefix to an imperfective verb normally produces a perfective verb (as in USo. *pisać* 'to write' (IMPFV) – *napisać* 'to write' (PRFV)), but the prefix may also introduce a new semantic component which is not only aspectual (USo. *předpisać*/LSo. *pśedpisaś* 'to prescribe', USo. *podpisać*/LSo. *podpisaś* 'to sign'). Imperfective verbs are derived from perfectives by suffixation: LSo. *podpisowaś* 'to sign' (IMPFV) from *podpisaś*. Other imperfectivizing suffixes are: *-je* (USo. *wotmołwjeć* 'to answer' (IMPFV) from *wotmołwić* (PRFV)) and *-wa* (USo. *rozbiwać* 'to smash' (IMPFV) from *rozbić* (PRFV)). Prefixes are often used to calque German prefixed verbs: USo. *wobsedźeć* 'to possess' calques German *besitzen* (*sedźeć* 'to sit' = German *sitzen*), LSo. *zacwiblowaś* 'to despair' calques German *verzweifeln* (*cwiblowaś* 'to doubt' = German *zweifeln*). Such calques, despite prefixation, are usually imperfective or bi-aspectual.

4   Syntax

4.1   Element order in declarative sentences

In Upper Sorbian, if the verb is simple (not compound), the unmarked order of main constituents in the clause is Subject + Object + Verb:

S   O   V
Nan trawu   syče.
father the grass is mowing

S   O   V
Awto Marju do chorownje dowjeze.
the car Marja to the hospital took

The unmarked position for the verb, whether in a main or a subordinate clause, is at the end:

S   V   [S not expressed] O
Hela měnješe, zo   swoje njepočinki wěsće
Hela thought that [he]   his   bad habits surely

V   [S not expressed] O   V
wostaji,   hdyž   ju za žonu změje.
will abandon, when [he]   her as wife will have

There is thus a partial similarity between Upper Sorbian and German in the order of elements in sentences containing a simple verb, for German too, in subordinate clauses, places the verb at the end. However, the similarity is indeed only partial, for German (unlike Sorbian) cannot have a finite verb standing at the end of a main clause. Even in subordinate clauses, in fact, there is a difference between the two languages, for in German final position is obligatory, whereas in Sorbian it is merely unmarked and can be avoided for reasons of emphasis.

If the verb is compound, the auxiliary or other finite component (including the parts of the verb *być* used to compose the conditional) stands in second position (Michałk 1956–7: 20–7; Jenč 1959: 7–12) and the participle or infinitive stands at the end of the clause:

S   V
Wona je (auxiliary) młoda była (participle)
she is/has   young been

S V
Ja sym (auxiliary) z   lěkarjom porěčała (participle).
I am/have   with the doctor spoken

This is the construction known in German grammar as the *Rahmenkonstruktion* (frame construction) and in main clauses the unmarked order of Upper Sorbian corresponds to the obligatory order in German:

Wona je młoda była.

Sie ist jung gewesen.

Ja sym z lěkarjom poŕečala.

Ich habe mit dem Artzt gesprochen.

As in German, the length of the frame may be substantial:

Naš reformator Měrćin Luther je nam hłowne tři artikule našeje křesćijanskeje wěry
wukładował.

                      (*Pomhaj Bóh*, čo. 5, May 1989, p. 1)

'Our reformer Martin Luther has for us the main three articles of our Christian faith
explained.'

However, the frame construction is normal in Upper Sorbian not only in
main but also in subordinate clauses:

Main clause: Wona je młoda była.
Subordinate clause: Hdyž je   wona młoda była ...
                   when is/has she   young been ...

In German, since in a subordinate clause the finite verb must go to the end,
this is impossible. In view of this important distinction between the two
languages it is uncertain whether the Upper Sorbian frame construction is
the result of German interference or not. Opinions vary (Michałk 1956–7:
23, 27; Jenč 1959: 32). The position is complicated by the fact that the
German spoken in Lusatia sometimes exhibits anomalous orderering of
constituents.

    In Upper Sorbian clitics are: (a) the short forms of personal and reflex-
ive pronouns (*mje, mi, će, ći, jón, je, ju, ji, so* and *sej*); (b) the present and
conditional parts of the auxiliary verb *być* 'to be' (and *bě* 'was'); and (c)
certain conjunctions and particles (such as *pak, drje, wšak*). Clitics
normally occupy the second position in the clause (*Bóh će žohnuj!* 'God
bless you!'). The rules for the position of the clitics relative to one another
are: (a) *so* always stands as the first pronoun; otherwise dative precedes
accusative; (b) a verb precedes a pronoun; (c) *pak* and *wšak* precede both
verb and pronoun:

Ja wšak   sym   ći   je   rjenje wumył.
I however am/have you (DAT) them (ACC) nicely washed
'but I washed them nicely for you'

Ja so će   prašam.
I self you (GEN) ask
'I ask you.'

                             (Михалк/Michalk 1974: 511)

As clitics, parts of the auxiliary *być* 'to be' cannot normally stand in first
position in the clause, but in literary works they are often found in this
position:

Sym z lěkarjom porěčala.
'I have spoken to the doctor.'

Je wšo wopušćić měl, swójbu a domiznu.
'He had to leave everything, family and homeland.'

In normal spontaneous speech this does not occur. The auxiliary is always preceded by a pronoun:

Ja sym z lěkarjom porěčala.
Wón je wšo wopušćić měl, swójbu a domiznu.

The fact that writers do not always write like this is explained as resulting from the overzealous application of the advice found in grammars to the effect that personal pronouns are unnecessary (Jenč 1959: 16–17, 39–40).

   The normal position for an Upper Sorbian adjective is immediately before the noun it modifies (*wulka wjes* 'a large village', *serbscy spiso-waćeljo* 'Sorbian writers' and so on). In the Bible, however, there are a number of well-known nominal phrases in which the adjective follows the noun (such as *duch swjaty* 'the Holy Ghost', *wótče naš* 'our father', *město Dawidowe* 'the city of David') and these phrases are also used in sermons and religious publications. Adverbs normally precede adjectives (*poměrnje wulka wjes* 'a relatively large village', *jara ćěžki nadawk* 'a very difficult task'). Prepositions stand obligatorily before their nouns or nominal phrases (*z mjechkim, chłódnym wětrom* 'with a soft, cool wind'), but *dla* 'for the sake of' or 'on account of', which takes the genitive, normally follows its noun or nominal phrase (*njedostatka bydlenjow dla* 'on account of the lack of housing').

   Element order in Lower Sorbian is a subject that has been little studied. Šwjela (1952: 103–4) devotes less than a page to it, but reveals certain essentials which appear to conform to the same pattern as Upper Sorbian. The verb has a preference for final position in the main clause:

Zmilny Bog, my tebje we takem swětem casu chwalimy a cesćimy.
'Merciful God, at such a sacred time we praise and honour thee.'

and the auxiliary in compound verbs prefers an early position even in a dependent clause:

Sused wulicowašo, až jo na wonem drogowanju wjele rědnego nazgonił.
'The neighbour related that on that journey he had experienced much that was
   pleasant.'

It as been observed, however, that the simple verb's preference for final position is less distinct than in Upper Sorbian and that it may therefore be found in second or middle position. The frame construction too, it is noted, operates less consistently than in Upper Sorbian (Waurick 1968: 126, as quoted in Michałk 1970: 1 n.). In Lower Sorbian dialects the predominant tendency is for the finite verb to appear in a later position than in Upper Sorbian, sometimes resulting in the disappearance of the frame construction altogether. Recalling the Upper Sorbian example *hdyž je wona młoda była* ... 'when she was young ...', we may use *ako wona jo była młoda* to exemplify the Lower Sorbian frameless type (Michałk 1970: 9–11). This loss of the frame may be connected with the tendency, following the loss of the synthetic preterite, to treat the auxiliary and its *l*-participle as a unit (Michałk 1970: 11–19).

4.2   Non-declarative sentence types
A statement may be converted into a 'yes–no' question by inverting the subject and the verb:

USo. Nan je doma.   (LSo. Nan jo doma)
    'Father is at home.'
USo. Je nan doma?   (LSo. Jo nan doma?)
    'Is father at home?'

But a question may equally well be marked solely by means of intonation (*nan je doma?*) and, since personal pronouns are often not expressed, the option of inversion does not always exist. The Upper Sorbian statement *maće sotru tež* '(you) have a sister too', for example, would normally become a question as *maće sotru tež?* The pronoun may naturally be added, but this is not normally felt to be necessary. Both *maće sotru tež?* and *maće wy sotru tež?* are well formed. Another possibility is to use the particles (USo. *hač*/LSo. *lěc*) which, as conjunctions, serve to introduce indirect questions (see below):

USo. Hač sy snadź chory?
    'Are (you) perhaps ill?'
LSo. Lěc su teke wšykno derje wugotowali?
    'Have (they) also prepared everything nicely?'

The use of the particle *-li* (as in U/LSo. *maš-li to?* 'have you got that?') is nowadays rare and limited to literary usage. Lower Sorbian also has the alternative form *-lic* with the same function (*maš-lic to?*).

The primary possible responses to 'yes–no' questions are USo. *haj* 'yes' and *ně* 'no' and LSo. *jo* 'yes' and *ně* 'no'. (The *haj/jo* isogloss is plotted in *SS* 10: map 130.) *Haj* and *jo* both confirm the underlying statement:

USo. A maće sotru tež?
    'And have you a sister too?'
    Haj, tři sotry mam hišćen.
    'Yes, I have three sisters too.'

                                  (Michalk and Protze 1967: 165)

LSo. Wumjeju te žěši něco na serbski se modliš?
       'Can the children say some prayers in Sorbian?'
       Jo, knjez doglědowaŕ.
       'Yes, inspector.'

In both Upper and Lower Sorbian *ně* negates the underlying positive statement:

LSo. Pśiźoš zasej raz sobu?
       'Will (you) come again with (us)?'
       Ně, žěnsa nic.
       'No, not today.'

A response may also involve repeating part of the question (usually a verb):

USo. Sy to hižo rozsudził?
       'Have (you) already decided that?'
       Sym.   or Njejsym
       '(I) have (= yes).'   '(I) haven't (= no).'
LSo. Njocoš teke pśiś?
       'Don't (you) want to come too?'
       Njok
       '(I) don't want (= no).'

Very commonly, the response repeats something from the question *in addition* to *haj, jo* or *ně*:

LSo. A maśo hyšći staśiwy?
       'And have (you) still got the loom?'
       Jo, staśiwy mamy ...
       'Yes, (we) have the loom ...'

(T 10: 42)

In Upper Sorbian an underlying negated statement is negated by *haj, ow haj, haj wšak, ju* or *tola*:

USo. Njepřińdźeš dźensa?
       'Aren't (you) coming today?'
       Ju, přińdu.
       'Yes, (I) am coming.'

In Lower Sorbian this is done by means of *jo wšak* or by repeating part of the question:

LSo. Njeźěła wěcej w Žylowje?
       'Isn't (he) working in Sielow any more?'
       Źěła.
       '(He) is working (= yes, he is).'

(Šwjela 1952: 107)

Negated questions in the second person are considered by Sorbs to be less direct and therefore more polite than non-negated questions. Sorbs can consequently be recognized, when speaking German, by the fact that they put questions in a negated form, whereas a German monoglot would not:

Können Sie mir nicht sagen, wie spät es ist?
'Can you not tell me what the time is?'
(compare USo. Njemóžeće mi prajić, kak na času je?)
(for Können Sie mir sagen, wie spät es ist?)

Indirect 'yes–no' questions are formed with USo. *hač* 'if, whether' and LSo. *lěc* 'if, whether':

USo. a wona praji, hač sym ja ta Serbowka ...
    'and she asked (literally: said) whether I was the Sorbian girl ...'
                                               (Michalk and Protze [1974]: 141)

Questions are also formed with interrogative pronouns, such as USo. *hdy* 'when', *hdźe* 'where', *što* 'what', *štó* 'who', and LSo. *ga* (or *gdy*) 'when', *žo* 'where', *co* 'what', *chto* 'who':

USo. Hdy so wróćiš?
    'When will (you) return?'
LSo. Chto jo to był?
    'Who was that?'

They also introduce indirect questions:

USo. Woprašach so jeho, hdy so wróći.
    '(I) asked him when (he) would return.'
LSo. Ja cu wěźeś, chto jo to był.
    'I want to know who that was.'

Commands are issued primarily by means of the imperative. An imperfective imperative is said to be less categorical than the corresponding perfective (for instance, USo. *sydajće so!* (IMPFV) 'sit down!' is less categorical than *sydńće so* (PRFV)). In negated imperatives, it is claimed, the same distinction exists, but in reverse. The negated perfective imperative (*njesydńće so!*) is less categorical than the corresponding imperfective (*njesydajće so!*). However, there is some uncertainty and controversy as to the aspectual values of imperatives (Faßke 1981: 289; Šewc-Schuster 1976: 13). Commands may also be issued in the form of infinitives (a highly categorical type), as in *změrom sedźeć!* 'sit quietly!', and by means of verbless phrases, for example, *won ze jstwy!* '(get) out of the room!'.

4.3   Copular sentences

The main copulas in Upper Sorbian are *być* 'to be' and *stać so* 'to become' (a special synthetic past tense of *być*, namely *buch, bu* and so on, also translates 'to become'). Nouns and nominal phrases in the complement linked to the subject by either of these verbs may stand in the nominative:

Jan je wučer.
'Jan is a teacher.'

Or they may stand in the instrumental preceded by the preposition *z* 'with' (there are no circumstances in which the instrumental may stand without a preposition):

Jan je z wučerjom.
'Jan is a teacher.'

The zero copula is unknown.

Since *stać so* is stylistically marked and characteristic of a professional and journalistic style it takes the instrumental more commonly than *być* (Faßke 1981: 83, 471):

Stachu so z prodrustwownikami.
'They became collective farmers.'

The instrumental with the copula is a distinctly literary device which does not normally occur in colloquial Sorbian (Upper or Lower). It is never obligatory and some writers avoid it. A wholly adjectival complement can never appear in the instrumental. Adjectives used in the complement are in no way distinct from those used attributively (there are no short forms).

The bookish nature of the instrumental complement suggests that it may result from the influence of other Slavonic languages in which it has a firmer base. However, it is attested in Upper Sorbian in the seventeenth and eighteenth centuries (when the influence of other Slavonic literary languages was weak or negligible) and it is found in Upper Sorbian folk-songs:

Hdyž mój wujk mi z krawcom běše ...
'When my cousin was a tailor ...'

(Haupt and Schmaler 1841: 212)

The fact that it had ceased to be systematic and tended to be associated with particular nouns (*z knjezom* 'lord, master', *z hrěchom* 'sin', *z wudowu* 'widow' and so on) is apparent from eighteenth-century sources.

The instrumental complement is only rarely used in Lower Sorbian, and only in the literary language. A Lower Sorbian variant of the folk-song noted above contains the nominative:

Ak moj foter šlodař běšo ...
'When my father was a tailor ...'

(Haupt and Schmaler 1843: 104)

Hauptmann (1761: 388) states unequivocally: 'The verb *ja som* "I am" has before and after it the nominative: *Krystus jo wěrny bog a cłowjek* "Christ is a true god and man".' The zero copula is unknown. There are no distinct adjectival forms for predicative use (there are no longer any short forms, but see section 3.1.4).

4.4   Coordination and comitativity

The main means of co-ordination in Upper Sorbian are the conjunctions *a* 'and', *abo* 'or' and *ale* 'but':

dźeń a nóc
'day and night'
dźensa abo jutře
'today or tomorrow'
dźěłamy, ale čakamy
'we are working, but waiting'

Not only individual words, but also whole phrases and clauses can be coordinated by means of these conjunctions:

Wčera sy přijěł a dźensa chceš so zaso wróćić.
'Yesterday you arrived and today you want to go back again.'

In a series of more than two items the conjunction *a* normally stands before the last component:

Wstań, wzmi swoje łožo, a dźi do swojeho domu.
'Arise, take up thy bed, and go unto thy house.'

(Mark 2.11)

Both the repeated use of the conjunction (polysyndeton) and the use of zero (asyndeton) are stylistically marked:

... ale su tam tež palmy wšěch družinow a cypresy a cedry a eukaliptusy a banany a draceny a pod nimi nic mjenje pyšne kerki ...

(M. Nowak; Šewc-Schuster 1976: 86)

'... but there are also all kinds of palms there and cypresses and cedars and eucalyptuses and bananas and dracaenas, and beneath them no less magnificent shrubs ...'

Štyri króć běch [...] přepućował Juhosłowjansku, jako moler, jako nowinar, jako Sokoł ...

(M. Nowak; Šewc-Schuster 1976: 87)

'Four times I had travelled through Yugoslavia, as a painter, as a journalist, as a Sokol [member of the Sokol gymnasts' organization].'

Normally the predicate agreeing with two or more conjoined nouns is in the dual or plural, as appropriate:

Haj, też knjeni a dźowka měještej tehdy čerwjenej, zapłakanej woči.
'Yes, then even the mistress and her daughter had (DU) eyes red from weeping.'

Jeničce młynk, kowar a korčmar su so z roboty wukupili.
'Only the miller, blacksmith and inn-keeper bought (PL) themselves out of serfdom.'

But, notwithstanding the real duality or plurality of the conjoined subject, the singular may occasionally occur (Faßke 1981: 296):

hatk a rěka mjerznje ...
'pond and river freeze (SG) ...'

Its likelihood is increased by inversion and the presence of attributes:

W nim so zwuraznjuje cyłe bohatstwo, rjanosć a móc našeje rěče.
'In it is/are (SG) expressed the entire richness, beauty and power of our language.'

In distributive expressions dual agreement is usual, notwithstanding arithmetic plurality:

A wón přińdźe zaso, a namaka jich spjacych; přetož jich woči běštej wobćeženej.
'And he came again and found them (PL) sleeping, for their (PL) eyes were heavy (DU).'

(Matthew 26.43)

Comitative subjects of the type *mój z maćerju* 'my mother and I' or *bratr ze sotru* 'brother and sister' normally take dual agreement:

Mój z bratrom wotjědźechmoj.
'My brother and I departed.'

The pronoun need not be expressed:

Z mandźelskej staj prawidłownje na serbske kemše chodźiłoj.
'(He) and (his) wife went regularly to Sorbian church services.'

(*Rozhlad* 1990, no. 9, p. 272)

The comitative subject (constituting a unit) and the predicative attribute linked to the subject by z may be distinguished either by verbal agreement (dual or singular) or by word order:

Tuž dźěše Jank z pućowarjom na hońtwu.
'So Jank went on the hunt with the traveller.'
Tuž Jank z pučowarjom na hońtwu dźěštaj.
'So Jank and the traveller went on the hunt.'

(Faßke 1981: 472-3)

In Lower Sorbian the main means of coordination are the same as in Upper Sorbian: *a* 'and', *abo* 'or' and *ale* 'but':

źeń a noc
'day and night'
źěnsa abo witśe
'today or tomorrow'
źěłamy, ale cakamy
'we are working, but waiting'

They can conjoin not only individual words, but also (as in Upper Sorbian) whole phrases and clauses. In a series of two or more items the conjunction normally stands only before the last component:

Stań gorej, wezmij twojo łožyśćo, a źij do twojogo domu.
'Arise, take up thy bed and go unto thy house.'

(Mark 2.11)

However, the repeated use of the conjunction (polysyndeton) and the use of zero (asyndeton) are also found:

Maśerina rěc, jatšowne spěwanje, ludna drastwa su radnje wobryte.
'The mother tongue, Easter singing, national costume are in a fairly poor state.'

The question of verb agreement with conjoined phrases is dealt with by Hauptmann (1761: 372) as follows:

> Two substantives, namely a dual, take the verb in the dual, three or several in the plural, e.g. *Mojzes a Aaron běštej bratša* "Moses and Aaron were brothers" ... *Ja moj foter a maś smy strowe* "I, my father and mother are well", *Ehebracharstwo, hurstwo, žraśe a žŕěśe, gněw a zawiść, su statki togo śěła* "Adultery, fornication, gluttony and drunkenness, anger and envy, are the works of the flesh".

Subsequent grammars of Lower Sorbian (none of which deals specifically with syntax) have not challenged this assertion; but occasional exceptions may be observed:

Zamrěł nama nan a moterka.
'Our father and mother have died.'

(Haupt and Schmaler 1843: 25)

(note ellipsis of the auxiliary)

Lěto a źeń se njebě minuło.
'A year and a day had not passed.'

First- and second-person comitative constructions of the type *mej z nanom* and *wej z nanom* may refer to either two or three persons in total, depending on the context. The pronoun need not be expressed. Janaš (1984: 171–2) gives the following examples:

Som nježelu doma była. Smej z nanom šach grałej.
'On Sunday I was at home. Father and I played chess.'
Som z pśijaśelku k nanoju woglědał. Smej z nanom w źiwadle byłej.
'Together with my girl friend I visited father. We and father went to the theatre.'

Third-person constructions of this type (*wonej z nanom*) always refer to three persons ('the two of them and father').

4.5   Subordination
The main types of subordinate clause in Sorbian (Upper and Lower) are noun clauses, relative clauses and adverbial clauses.

Noun clauses (declarative, interrogative, imperative/optative):

USo. Wěm, zo maš prawje.
'I know that you are right.'
LSo. Wěm, až maš pšawje.
'I know that you are right.' (literally: 'have right')

Relative clauses:

USo. Bě tam jedyn z prěnich, kiž nowe mašiny postaji.
'He was one of the first there who put in the new machines.'
LSo. Wšykne, kenž su pśišli, su nam derje znate.
'All those who have come are well known to us.'

(Janaš 1984: 187)

The relative pronouns introducing relative clauses are in most cases derived from interrogative pronouns by the addition of *-ž* (for instance, USo. *štóž* 'who', *štož* 'what', *kotryž* 'who, which', *hdžež* 'where', *hdyž* 'when, if'; LSo. *chtož* 'who', *což* 'what', *kotaryž* 'who, which', *žož* 'where', *gaž* 'when, if'). There are, however, no attested interrogative forms in Sorbian corresponding to USo. *kiž* 'who, which' and LSo. *kenž* 'who, which'. They are invariable and used only in the nominative and accusative (but not in conditions where the accusative coincides with the genitive). Their synonyms are USo. *kotryž* and LSo. *kotaryž*, both of which have full paradigms. In non-standard Upper Sorbian, however, it is possible to use *kiž* in cases other than the nominative and accusative by adding the anaphoric pronoun in the second or third position in the clause:

muž, kiž jeho znaju
'the man that I know' (literally: 'the man that him (I) know')

The corresponding construction in Lower Sorbian is formed with *ak(o)* 'who, which' and is not excluded from the literary language:

Tam sejźitej golca, ako som z nima grał.
'There sit the two boys with whom I was playing.'

If the cases in the main clause and subordinate clause coincide, it is not necessary to insert the anaphoric pronoun:

Won jěźo z tym awtom, ako cora jo jěł.
'He is going with the car with which he went yesterday.'

(Janaš 1984: 188)

Adverbial clauses: these are introduced by such conjunctions as USo. *zo* 'that', *dokelž* 'because', *jeli/jelizo* 'if', *hdy* 'if', *hačrunjež* 'although'; LSo. *až* 'that', *dokulaž* 'because', *joli až* 'if', *gaž* 'when, if', *lěcrownož/ rownož* 'although', *gaby* 'if'. In conditional sentences, if the condition is real, both main and subordinate clauses may be in the indicative:

USo. Jelizo budźeš strowy, móžeš hrać.
LSo. Joli až buźoš strowy, moźoš graš.
    'If you are fit, you can play.'

Sentences expressing hypothetical conditions have the conditional in both main and subordinate clauses:

USo. Mać by so wjeseliła, hdy by ju farar wopytał.
LSo. Mama by se wjaseliła, gaby k njej faraŕ woglědał.
    'Mother would be pleased if the priest visited her.'

(In Lower Sorbian the conditional particle *by* has become an inseparable part of the conjunction *gaby* 'if', which occurs only in clauses embodying hypothetical conditions.)
    The present gerund (verbal adverb) is formed only from imperfective verbs. It expresses action which is simultaneous with that of the main verb:

USo. Druzy trubku pachajo so   rozmołwjachu.
    others pipe   smoking were chatting
    'The others were chatting, while smoking a pipe.'
LSo. Wona jo tam hyšći chylku sejźecy wostała.
    'She remained sitting there for a while longer.'

It may refer to the subject (as in the above examples) or to the object:

USo. Ja sym jeho tam stejo widźał.
LSo. Ja som jogo tam stojecy wiźeł.
    'I saw him standing there.'

The past gerund (only Upper Sorbian) expresses an action which precedes that of the main verb. It is formed exclusively from perfective verbs:

USo. Tak ju hišće rano stanywši   z   łoža namakach.
    thus her still   early having risen   from bed (I) found
    'Thus I found her still, having risen from my bed in the morning.'

The gerunds are predominantly literary forms. The present gerund is, however, found in dialects, though here it is formed almost exclusively from USo. *stać*/LSo. *stojaś* 'to stand', USo. *ležeć*/LSo. *lažaś* 'to lie', USo. *sedźeć*/LSo. *sejźeś* 'to sit', USo. *wisać*/LSo. *wisaś* 'to hang' and USo. *tčeć* 'to be (located)', and is used mainly in conjunction with USo. *wostać*/LSo. *wostaś* 'to remain', USo. *wostajić*/LSo. *wostajiś* 'to leave', USo. *měć*/LSo. *měś* 'to have', USo. *widźeć*/LSo. *wiźeś* 'to see', USo. *namakać*/LSo. *namakaś* 'to find' and USo. *zetkać*/LSo. *trefiś* 'to meet' as main verb (*SS* 12: 309).

In both Upper and Lower Sorbian the infinitive is widely used in constructions which are synonymous with subordinate clauses:

USo. Prošu će so wróćić. = Prošu će, zo by so ty wróćił.
    '(I) ask you to return.' = (literally: '(I) ask you that you would return')

But infinitive constructions with modal and phasal verbs (and certain other verbs, including USo. *bojeć so*/LSo. *bojaś se* 'to be afraid', USo. *spytać*/LSo. *spytaś* 'to attempt', USo. *pomhać*/LSo. *pomagaś* 'to help', USo. *zabyć*/LSo. *zabyś* 'to forget') are not normally capable of conversion into subordinate clauses: thus USo. *bojach so nana prašeć* '(I) was afraid to ask father' cannot be converted (Faßke 1981: 329). There are also numerous nouns and adjectives in both Upper and Lower Sorbian which regularly form part of infinitive constructions: USo. *prawo*/LSo. *pšawo* 'right', USo. and LSo. *šansa* 'chance', USo. *móžno*/LSo. *možno* 'possible'. Among the verbs commonly followed in Upper Sorbian by infinitives are the verbs of motion (like USo. *hić*/*chodźić* 'to go (on foot)'), but in Lower Sorbian verbs of motion are followed by the supine:

Źensa wjacor pojźomy rejowat.
'This evening (we) shall go dancing.'

The infinitive construction with verbs of perceiving exemplified in USo. *město je widźeć* 'the town is visible' (literally: 'town is to see') is synonymous with a construction involving the verbal noun and the preposition *k* 'to' (USo. *město je k widźenju*, literally: 'town is to seeing').

The only natural way of translating the English sequences (1) *the man that I think that you saw* and (2) *the man that I think saw you* is to avoid the extraction:

1 USo. muž, kotrehož sy po zdaću widźał
       (non-standard: muž, kiž sy jeho po zdaću widźał)
   LSo. muž, kotaregož sy ako se zda wiźeł
       or: muž, ak sy jogo ako se zda wiźeł
2 USo. muž, kiž je će po zdaću widźał
   LSo. muž, kenž jo śe ako se zda wiźel

I think may also be translated as USo. *ja sej myslu* or *mi so zda*, LSo. *ja se myslim* or *mě se zda*.

4.6   Negation

Sentence negation in both Upper and Lower Sorbian is expressed by means of the negative particle *nje-*, which is written together with the verb to form a single word. The particle *nje-* thus bears the stress. For example, *piju* '(I) drink' : *njepiju* '(I) do not drink'. There are a few exceptions to this rule. In Upper Sorbian the modal verb *chcyć* 'to want' has two irregular negated forms: *nochcyć* and *njechać*, as in *nochcyśe swojimaj samsnymaj wočomaj wěrić* '(he) did not want to believe his own eyes', *wón njechaše ničo nowe słyšeć* 'he did not want to hear anything new'. *Nochcyć* is stylistically literary or bookish; *njechać* is stylistical neutral and preferred in colloquial speech. USo. *měć* 'to have' has negative *njeměć*, but in the present tense *nje-* → *ni-*: *nimam, nimaš, nima* and so on. In the present tense of USo. *njebyć* (the negated *być* 'to be') a *-j-* is inserted: *njejsym* '(I) am not', *njejsy* '(you) are not' and so on, (compare *njeńdu* '(I) shall not go', *njeńdźeš* '(you) will not go' and so on from the negated *hić* 'to go (on foot)').

In Lower Sorbian the negated form of *kśeś* 'to want' is *njekśěś*. Its present tense is as follows:

	SG	DU	PL
1	ja njok	mej njocomej	my njocomy
2	ty njocoš	wej njocotej	wy njocośo
3	won njoco	wonej njocotej	woni njekśě

In the present tense of *njeměš* (negated form of *měš*) and all tenses of *njamoc* (negated form of *moc* 'to be able') the negative particle takes the form *nja-*: *njamam* '(I) have not', *njamaš* '(you) have not' and so on, *njamogu* '(I) cannot', *njamožoš* '(you) cannot', *njamožach* '(I) could not'. As in USo., *-j-* is inserted in the present tense of *njebyś*: *ja njejsom, ty njejsy, won njejo* and so on, and also in the present tense of *njehyś* (negated form of *hyś* 'to go'): *ja njejdu, ty njejźoš*.

In analytical constructions it is to the auxiliary that the negative particle is usually attached:

USo. Njejsym na to myslił.
       '(I) did not think of that.'

LSo. Njejsy nic gronił.
'(You) have not said anything.'

In the case of conditional verbs the negative particle may be attached to either the auxiliary or the *l*-participle:

USo. either: zo by přesćěhany njebył
     or: zo njeby přesćěhany był   'so that (he) should not be persecuted'

In sentences containing negative adverbs or pronouns such as USo. *nihdy* 'never', *nihdźe* 'nowhere', *ničo* 'nothing', *nichtó* 'no one', *ženje* 'never'; LSo. *nigda/nigdy* 'never', *niźi* 'nowhere', *nic* 'nothing', *nichten* 'no one', *źednje* 'never', the verb must be negated:

USo. Jan njeje nikoho zetkał.
'Jan met nobody.'
LSo. Won how niźi njejo.
'He is nowhere here.'

It is possible to have several negative words in one sentence:

USo. Ty ženje nihdźe ničo nimaš.
'You never have anything anywhere.'
LSo. Njeźycym źednje nikomu nic złego.
'(I) never wish anyone anything bad.'

The pronouns *žadyn* (USo.) and *źeden* (LSo.) often occur in negated clauses with the meaning 'no, none, any' (USo. *nimam žadyn čas*, LSo. *njamam žeden cas* '(I) have no time'), but they may also appear in affirmative clauses with an indefinite meaning 'any, some, a few' (LSo. *něto źo won źedne kšoceńki dopředka* 'now he's walking a few steps ahead').

In constituent negation in both Upper and Lower Sorbian the particle *nic* stands before or after the constituent negated. It occurs frequently in adversative constructions, for example, USo. *nic ja, ale ty sy na tym wina* 'it is not my fault, but yours' (literally: 'not I but you are of that guilty'). The particle *nic* (in both Upper and Lower Sorbian) may also be substituted for a negated verb:

USo. Ja to wěm, ty nic
'I know that, not you.'

                                                (Faßke 1981: 769–70)

LSo. Styri punty možoš braś; ale wěcej nic.
'(You) can take four pounds, but no more.'

In both literary languages the direct object of a negated verb may appear in the genitive as a facultative variant of the accusative, but the genitive in these constructions is never obligatory:

USo. My nimamy žanoho chlěba wjac. (GEN)
    'We have no more bread.'
or: My nimamy žadyn chlěb wjac. (ACC)
LSo. My njamamy žednogo klěba wěcej. (GEN)
or: My njamamy žeden klěb wěcej. (ACC)

A survey of direct objects of negated verbs in Upper Sorbian literature (Faßke 1981: 458) found the genitive to be relatively rare and mainly associated with particular verbs. In the material examined 42 per cent of all cases of the genitive occurred with *měć* 'to have'. In colloquial and dialectal Sorbian the genitive is also rare, but more common in Lower than in Upper Sorbian. The likelihood of its occurring is greater with the emphatic negative particles *ani* and *nic* than with the simple negated verb:

LSo. Nic jadnogo zernka njejo tym kokošam dała.
    'She didn't give the chicken a single grain.'

The genitive may also occur with negated verbs as a facultative variant of the nominative:

USo. Jeho row běše nahi, ani kamjenja tam njebě.
    'His grave was bare, there wasn't even a stone (GEN) there.'

But this too is rare. In colloquial Upper Sorbian it can occur only with the particle *ani* (Faßke 1981: 459).

4.7   Anaphora and pronouns

The person and number of nearly all finite verbal forms are expressed by means of inflections: for example, in USo. *spěwam* 'I sing' the ending *-m* expresses the first person singular, in *přindźechu* 'they came' the ending *-chu* expresses the third person plural. Consequently, the nominative personal pronoun is frequently omitted:

USo. Dźěłam we Serbskim wučerskim wustawje.
    '(I) work in the Sorbian teachers' institute.' (omitting *ja* 'I')
LSo. Witśe maju šulsku ekskursiju.
    'Tomorrow (they) have a school excursion.' (omitting *woni* 'they')

Omission of the pronoun is, however, more common in the literary languages than in colloquial and dialectal Sorbian (compare 4.1 above). The expression of the nominative pronoun in cases where it is redundant is attributed to the influence of German. This influence may also be observed in the colloquial use of an indefinite pronoun in such sentences as:

USo. Wono było 'žon jary pozdźe.
    'It was already very late.'

                                  (Michalk and Protze 1967: 49)

USo. Wone je so sněh šow.
'It snowed.'

(Michalk and Protze [1974]: 107 and 119)

Wono and *wone* here translate German *es* (*es war schon sehr spät/ es hat geschneit*). In literary usage such constructions are usually avoided and the verb stands in first position:

USo. Běše patoržica.
'It was Christmas Eve.'
LSo. Jo se wopśestało dešćowaś.
'It stopped raining.'

In literary Upper Sorbian the nominative personal pronouns are supposed to be omitted unless there is a positive reason for their inclusion, such as: (a) to avoid leaving the auxiliary in first position; (b) for emphasis; (c) the existence of a noun in apposition (as in *my dźěći roboćanskeho luda znajachmy jenož chudobu* 'we, the children of menial workers, knew only poverty' (Šewc 1968: 115)); (d) with an imperative to soften the force of the command (*nano, dźi ty jónu k lěkarjej z twojej bolacej nohu* 'father, go to the doctor with your bad foot'); (e) in reported speech to impart a colloquial tone.

An anaphoric function similar to that of the personal pronoun is performed by the demonstrative pronoun *tón, ta, to* 'this/that'. For example:

Wróću so jutře zaso a to z ... prawiznikom. Tón budźe mje zastupować.
'(I)'ll come back tomorrow with ... a lawyer. He'll represent me.'

The Upper Sorbian equivalents of *dieser* 'the latter' are *tón, tutón* and *tónle*; the equivalents of *jener* 'the former' are *tamny* and *tamón*. The latter form is used only by writers from the Catholic dialect area (Šewc 1968: 125–6).

The position with regard to personal pronouns and their omission is similar, but not identical, in Lower Sorbian. In the literary language omission occurs slightly less frequently than in Upper Sorbian and grammars are less categorical about it: 'The nominative of the non-reflexive personal pronoun in the subject may be omitted' (Janaš 1984: 171). The anaphoric use of *ten* 'this/that' corresponds closely to that of *tón* in Upper Sorbian.

4.8 Reflexives and Reciprocals

Reflexivity is expressed by means of the reflexive personal pronoun (the forms of which were given in tables 11.7 and 11.8 above) and the reflexive possessive pronoun (USo. *swój*/LSo. *swoj*). Verbs are made reflexive by the addition of the accusative or dative reflexive personal pronoun (in Lower Sorbian there is no difference between them), the case corresponding to that of a non-reflexive noun phrase in the same position:

USo. *myć* 'to wash' → *myć so* 'to wash (oneself)', *dowolić* 'to permit' → *dowolić sej* 'to permit (oneself)';
LSo. *myś* 'to wash' → *myś se* 'to wash (oneself)', *dowoliś* 'to permit' → *dowoliś se* 'to permit (oneself)'.

Both Upper and Lower Sorbian also have a substantial number of *reflexiva tantum* (verbs which are reflexive in form but not in meaning and have no non-reflexive counterparts), such as: USo. *bojeć so*/LSo. *bojaś se* 'to fear', USo. *modlić so*/LSo. *modliś se* 'to pray', USo. *zdać so*/LSo. *zdaś se* 'to seem'.

The short forms of the reflexive personal pronouns are generally enclitic, but the rule prohibiting their use in the first position in the clause is not without exception. The long forms are used if stressed (USo. *kupich sebi nowu košlu* 'I bought *myself* a new shirt') or for contrast (USo. *njemóžach sebi, ani jemu pomhać* 'I could not help myself nor him'). With prepositions taking the accusative or genitive both long and short forms are found (USo. *wot so* or *wot sebje* 'from self'), but in the dative the long form is preferred, with the exception of *ku se* 'towards self' in Lower Sorbian (USo. *k sebi*).

As a rule, the antecedent of both reflexive and reflexive possessive pronouns is the subject of the clause (USo. *holca so česa* 'the girl is combing herself (that is, her hair)', LSo. *won pišo ze swojim wołojnikom* 'he is writing with his (own) pencil'). But the reflexive may refer to the logical rather than the grammatical subject, for instance the dative subject in such impersonal sentences as USo. *jemu bě swojeje dźowki žel* 'he was sorry for his daughter' (literally: 'him (DAT) was his daughter (GEN) sorry'). The subject may also be the understood subject of an infinitive, as in USo. *prošu was na so kedźbować* 'I ask you to take care of yourselves'. Here the antecedent is an unexpressed *wy* forming the subject of a finite verb underlying the infinitive *kedźbować* 'to take care'.

Sentences embodying reflexive pronouns are often ambiguous (as in USo. *Jan bě će prosył položić knihu na swoje městno* 'Jan had asked you to put the book in its/his/your place'). Therefore, a non-reflexive form is sometimes preferred in order to avoid even the possibility of ambiguity. There is, moreover, a tendency, even in sentences containing only one verb, to use the non-reflexive possessive pronouns, if the subject is the first or second person (USo. *smy našu chěžu předali* '(we) have sold our house' for *smy swoju chěžu předali*). This practice is now acceptable in both literary languages. However, in the third person the reflexive pronoun is an aid to avoiding ambiguity: for example, LSo. *won jo se swoje crjeje wzeł* 'he has taken his (own) shoes', but *won jo se jogo crjeje wzeł* 'he has taken his (own or someone else's) shoes'.

Reciprocity is expressed by means of reflexive personal pronouns, but many clauses formed in this way are ambiguous: for example, USo. *kedžbujemy na so* may mean 'we are looking after one another' or 'we are looking after ourselves'. Ambiguity may be removed by the context or by simple logic: for example, USo. *mój sebi napřećo sedžachmoj* means 'we (two) were sitting opposite each other'. The interpretation 'each of us was sitting opposite himself' is eliminated by its own absurdity. Ambiguity may also be eliminated by the addition of USo. *mjez sobu* and LSo. *mjazy sobu*:

USo. To wam přikazuju, zo byšće mjez sobu so lubowali.
LSo. Take pśikažu ja wam, aby se mjazy sobu lubowali.
    'These things I command you, that ye love one another.'

                                           (John 15.17)

The same meaning may be conveyed by USo. *jedyn druhi* and LSo. *jaden drugi* 'one another':

USo. Wonaj jedyn druhemu njedowěritaj.
    'They do not trust each other.'

4.9   Possession

Both Upper and Lower Sorbian have a strong inclination to express possession by means not of an adnominal genitive but of an adjectival construction. The simplest form of this construction is the possessive adjective, derived from a noun by means of the suffix *-owy* (for masculines, including *a*-stems) or *-iny* (*-yny*) (for feminines), for example, *nanowy dom* 'father's house'. The use of the adnominal genitive (*dom nana* 'father's house') is also possible, but rarer. It either imparts the stylistic connotation of formality or it puts emphasis on the noun in the genitive. If the modifier is composite, only the last element forms an adjective; the preceding elements are in the genitive singular: *Handrija Zejlerjowe basnje* 'Handrij Zejler's poems', *Karla Marxowa uniwersita* 'the Karl Marx University' (from the last example it can be seen that the meaning is not always strictly possessive).

If the noun underlying the possessive adjective itself has a modifier, the latter takes its gender from the underlying noun and is usually in the genitive singular: *našeho nanowy dom* 'our/my father's house' (*naš* is always substituted for *mój*, when speaking of older persons). The possessive adjective thus controls the gender and case of the modifier. It is also able to control relative pronouns:

Běchu słyšeć ... stupy Dietrichowe, kiž ... na konja skoči a wotjěcha.
'One could hear ... Dietrich's steps, who ... jumped on the horse and rode off.'

And personal pronouns:

To je našeho wučerjowa zahrodka. Wón wjele w njej dźěła.
'This is our (my) teacher's garden. He works a lot in it.'

The antecedent of *wón* is *naš wučer* 'our (my) teacher', which underlies the adjectival phrase *našeho wučerjowa*. However, in the last two examples the head noun is inanimate (*stupy* 'steps', *zahrodka* 'garden'). If the head noun is animate, the subject pronoun of the following clause will take this (and not the noun underlying the possessive adjective) as its antecedent. For example, in:

To je Janowy bratr. Wón je jemu knihu dał.
'This is Jan's brother. He's given him the book.'

the antecedent of *wón* is unambiguously *bratr*, not *Jan* (Corbett 1987: 338).

The possibilities in Lower Sorbian are similar to those in Upper Sorbian, but with one significant additional constraint. The unexpressed noun underlying the possessive adjective may (as in Upper Sorbian) be the antecedent of a personal or relative pronoun:

te dny mamineje smjerśi a jeje zakopowanje
'those days of mother's death and her burial'

(W. Bjero, *Na Kałpjeńcu*)

(example quoted by Corbett 1987: 317 from Richter 1980: 102–3). But the possessive adjective cannot control attributive modifiers. In other words, the type *našeho nanowy dom* does not exist. It is replaced by a type in which an adnominal genitive phrase *precedes* the head noun (LSo. *našogo nana dom* 'our (my) father's house'). In Upper Sorbian this type is virtually unknown.

4.10   Quantification
A noun or phrase quantified by a noun stands in the genitive, as in USo. *měch běrnow* 'a sack of potatoes', LSo. *strus rožow* 'a bunch of roses'. The case of the quantifier is determined by its syntactic function in the clause, but the element quantified remains in the genitive:

USo. Kupi sej trubu płata.
    'She bought herself a roll (ACC) of linen.'
LSo. Źowća rozwjaselichu mě z wjelikim strusom cerwjenych žywych rožow.
    'The girls gladdened me with a big bunch (INST) of red, bright roses.'

However, in colloquial and dialectal speech the phenomenon known to

Sorbian grammar as 'attraction' sometimes occurs, causing the quantified element to appear in the same case as the quantifier:

USo. z měchom (INST) běrnami (INST)
    'with a sack of potatoes'
USo. w karanje (LOC) piwje (LOC)
    'in a jug of beer'

A noun or phrase quantified by a pronominal quantifier (such as U/LSo. *mało* 'little, few', *wjele* 'much, many'; USo. *něšto*/LSo. *něco* 'some') is in the genitive only if the whole phrase of which it forms part is the subject or direct object of the clause:

USo. Na mužacych ławkach je dźensa wjele prózdnych městnow.
    'In the men's pews today there are many empty places.'
LSo. Mam mało casa.
    'I have little time.'

Otherwise the quantified element is in the case required by its syntactic function:

USo. W kak wjele eksemplarach daš dramatisku přiłohu ćišćeć?
    'In how many copies will you have the drama supplement published?'
                                    (Ćišinski, quoted in Faßke 1981: 612)

The numerals '1' to '4' are syntactically adjectives and agree in gender and case with the nouns they modify; '2' takes the dual, '3' and '4' the plural.

USo. Wón ma jednu dźowku.
    'He has one daughter.'
LSo. Turjańska šula měješo za moj cas 150–180 źěśi w tśich klasach.
    'The school in Tauer in my time had 150–180 children in three classes.'
USo. Tři traktory na polu woraju.
    'Three tractors are ploughing in the field.'

Numerals from '5' to '99' and pronominal quantifiers are syntactically neuter singular nouns. The noun quantified stands in the genitive plural, if the quantified phrase is in the nominative or accusative. The verb is singular and, in the perfect tense, neuter:

USo. Pjeć traktorow na polu wora (SG).
    'Five tractors are (literally: is) ploughing in the field.'
LSo. Pěš mužow jo pśišło (N SG).
    'Five men arrived.'

However, logical agreement may also be observed. It is particularly common in colloquial Sorbian, but rarer in the literary languages:

LSo. ... glja tog až wjele tych młodych du na žěło
'... because many young people go to work'

(T 10:14)

USo. Te sydom wsow podłu rěčki su čiste.
'Those seven villages along the stream are clean.'

(Faßke 1981: 296)

5   Lexis

5.1   General composition of word-stock

Sorbian has been in contact with German for about 1,000 years and during that time has absorbed and assimilated a large number of German lexical borrowings. Nevertheless, the Sorbian vocabulary remains overwhelmingly Slavonic. Bielfeldt's classic study of German loan-words in Upper Sorbian (1933), which was intentionally restricted to the most widespread and philologically most interesting borrowings, dealt with about 2,000 such words. If we estimate the total number of Upper Sorbian words at around 50,000, Bielfeldt's selection constitutes about 4 per cent of the total. In colloquial Upper Sorbian the percentage is higher, but it is not easy to say what is a fully integrated borrowing and what is merely the result of code-switching. However, excluding loan-translations and ignoring the distinction between true loan-words and substitutions resulting from code-switching, we find that the proportion of *nouns* of German origin in dialect texts may even exceed 50 per cent (Michalk and Protze 1967: 31). In literary varieties of Upper Sorbian, on the other hand, it seems likely that the proportion of German loan-words does not normally exceed 5 per cent, unless words from international terminology are included. The proportions in Lower Sorbian are probably similar, but the Lower Sorbian literary language is a little more tolerant of Germanisms than literary Upper Sorbian.

Borrowings from other Slavonic languages are mainly restricted to the literary languages. They are nearly all of Czech origin and in normal literary usage probably constitute about 1 per cent of the total. In dictionaries the proportion of Slavonic borrowings may be greater. The largest foreign element in both literary languages is supplied by international terminology (Europeanisms). In view of the contact situation these may, in a sense, be regarded as a subcategory of German borrowings.

5.2   Patterns of borrowing

So far as the spoken language is concerned (both Upper and Lower Sorbian) the main source of borrowings has always been and still is German. Loan-words still in common colloquial use include the following (the source-word is given in its New High German form except where specified): USo. *běrna* 'potato' (*Erdbirne*), *běrtl* 'quarter' (*Viertel*), *całta* 'roll (bread)' (Middle High German *zëlte*), *dyrbjeć* 'must' (*dürfen*), *faler* 'mistake' (*Fehler*), *krydnyć* 'to get' (*kriegen*); LSo. *bjatowaś* 'to pray' (*beten*), *głažk* 'glass' (*Glas*), *holowaś* 'to fetch' (*holen*), *šlodar* 'tailor' (Middle High German *schroder*), *wjazym* 'state, understanding' (*Wesen*).

Most early borrowings from other Slavonic languages are the subject of controversy. This applies in particular to much of the Christian terminology, which may or may not be of Czech or even Old Church Slavonic origin, such as: USo. *cyrkej*/LSo. *cerkwja* 'church' (perhaps from OCS *cirky* or Old Czech *cierkev*, but possibly direct from Old High German *kirihha*), USo. *žid*/LSo. *žyd* 'Jew' (compare Czech *žid*). However, the form of U/LSo. *kral* 'king' (attested since the sixteenth century) indicates its Czech origin unambiguously. The main flood of Slavonic borrowings came to Sorbian from Czech after 1841 as part of the national pro-Slavonic movement of that time. Among the common words from this source are: USo. *hudźba* 'music' (Czech *hudba*), U/LSo. *lětadło* 'aircraft' (Czech *letadlo*). USo. *železnica*, LSo. *zeleznica* 'railway' (Czech *železnice*). Writers have been at pains to exclude German borrowings from their works, but greater tolerance is normally shown to words with cognates in many European languages (even if the immediate source is German). The following are examples of this category: *administracija, aktiwny, biologija, centralny, demokratija, fabrika, idealny, objektiwny, telewizija*. (The form of all these examples is identical in Upper and Lower Sorbian.)

5.3 Incorporation of borrowings

It is not always possible to distinguish between integrated loan-words and substitutions resulting from code-switching. A word may be considered integrated, if it has been adapted in some way to the Sorbian phonological or morphological systems, but only certain parts of speech are capable of morphological adaptation. Adverbs, for example (such as *blows* 'only' (German *bloß*), *feste* 'firmly, thoroughly' (German *fest*), *fort* 'away' (German *fort*)) cannot be adapted morphologically, yet some of them are of such high frequency that they can only be regarded as integrated loan-words. Nouns and adjectives, on the other hand, are capable of morphological adaptation, but only in certain grammatical circumstances. When the word *brawtpor* 'bridal pair' (German *Brautpaar*), for example, occurs in the nominative or accusative singular, it is not possible to say whether it is integrated or not, but in the phrase *při toh' brawtpora* 'with the bridal pair (GEN SG)' integration has clearly taken place. The absence of integration is demonstrated when a word capable of acquiring a Sorbian morpheme in an oblique case fails to do so (for instance, *ze Serbien* 'from Serbia (GEN SG)'). Adjectives may remain unadapted (*tamle jo tón richtich ptačk* 'there is the right bird', German *richtig* 'right') or they may be adapted by derivation (*abnormalny* 'abnormal' (German *abnormal*), *wot tejele žony, tajkejele gajcneje žony* 'from this woman, such a mean woman'

(German *geizig* 'mean')) (Michalk and Protze [1974]: 141).

Verbs, however, are always adapted (except participles): for example, *hač sym ja ta holčka, kiž je so anonksěrowawa* 'whether I am the girl who announced herself' (German *sich annoncieren* 'to announce oneself'), *wječor potom zaso naše kofry zpakwachmy* 'then in the evening we packed our bags again' (German *packen* 'to pack') (Michalk and Protze [1974]: 201). Participles may be unadapted (*to su jich dobre ludźe, dobre, gebildet ludźe* 'they are good people, good educated people' (German *gebildet* 'educated'), but the attested examples indicate that they remain unadapted only when they are functionally adjectives. As part of a compound verb they are declined (*sem tež wjele, wjele wobšenk' wana boła* 'I also received many, many presents'; German *ich bin auch viel, viel beschenkt worden*; German *be-* is regularly translated as *wob-*) (T 6: 62). The only part of speech that is impervious to the borrowing process (so far as one can tell from published texts) is the preposition. German prepositions, it is true, may be found in Sorbian texts, but they always occur in phrases including other German words, like *zum Militär, in Leipzig, in Ordnung*. There is, however, no shortage of other grammatical words (such as *als* in *Salowčenjo su prjede přec znate po nas als bóle hłupo ludźe bóli* 'the people of Saalau were formerly always known among us as rather stupid people' (T 4: 16), *cu* (German *zu*) in *tam Nowom Poršicam cu* 'off to Neu-Purschwitz' (German *dort nach Neu-Purschwitz zu*) (T 5: 52)).

Many of the German loan-words in Sorbian are of great antiquity and, having undergone sound changes and semantic changes long since completed, are often not easily associated with the corresponding words in modern German. For example, some were borrowed before the German diphthongization *ī* > *aj* (usually written *ei*). We consequently have USo. *cwiblować*/LSo. *cwiblowaś* 'to doubt' (Middle High German *zwīvelen*, New High German *zweifeln*), USo. *šrybar* 'schoolmaster' (Middle High German *schrībære*, New High German *Schreiber* 'writer'), USo. *žida* 'silk' (Middle High German *sīde*, New High German *Seide*). Sorbian words borrowed before the German diphthongization *ū* → *au* include USo. *bruny* 'brown' (Middle High German *brūn*, New High German *braun*), USo. *rum* 'room' (Middle High German *rūm*, New High German *Raum*). In the case of the cognate words in Lower Sorbian (that is, *cwiblowaś, šrybaŕ, žyźe, bruny* and *rum*) the monophthongs are capable of a different explanation, for in the Low German dialects adjacent to Lower Sorbian diphthongization did not occur.

The metaphony of Middle High German *ě* to *a* in East Central German dialects is widely reflected in Sorbian borrowings (the source-words are given in their New High German form): U/LSo. *blach* 'tin' (*Blech*), USo. *blak*/LSo. *flak* 'spot, place' (*Fleck*), USo. *lazować*/LSo. *lazowaś* 'to read' (*lesen*), USo. *plahować*/LSo. *plagowaś* 'to raise, cultivate' (*pflegen*). Also reflected in Sorbian loan-words is the East Central German shift of *a* to *o*, as in: USo. *hodler*/LSo. *hodlař* 'eagle' (*Adler*), USo. *kofej* (but LSo. *kafej*) 'coffee' (*Kaffee*), USo. *lodować* 'to load' (*laden*). Loan-words with *a* corresponding to standard German *a* (like USo. *barba*/LSo. *barwa* 'colour, paint' (*Farbe*), USo. *hamt* 'office' (*Amt*)) are, however, not uncommon.

Verbs are most commonly borrowed by means of the suffix *-ować/ -owaś* (present stem in *-uj-*) and taken into Sorbian as imperfectives (thus USo. *pakować* 'to pack', compare German *packen*) which acquire a corresponding perfective by prefixation (*zapakować*; see section 3.3.3).

5.4 Lexical fields

5.4.1 Colour terms

white	USo./LSo. *běły*
black	USo. *čorny*/LSo. *carny*
red	USo. *čerwjeny*/LSo. *cerwjeny*. Hauptmann (1761: 21) has *zerwóni* (that is, *cerwjony*), but says some pronounce it as *zerwäni*. Also USo./LSo. *ryzy* 'fox-coloured'
green	U/LSo. *zeleny*
yellow	U/LSo. *žołty*
blue	USo. *módry*, LSo. *modry*. In some Lower Sorbian dialects *płowy* (*SS* 4: map 40)
brown	U/LSo. *bruny*. Also *ryzy* 'reddish-brown'
purple	U/LSo. *purpurowy* denotes several tones between red and a half-way point between red and blue. USo. *fijałkowy* 'violet' is probably close to purple in the spectrum.
pink	USo. *różowy, różojty, różowaty*/LSo. *rožany, rožowaty, rožowy*
orange	U/LSo. *oranžowy*; also USo. *pomorančojty*
grey	USo. *šěry*/LSo. *šery*, USo. *šědźiwy*/LSo. *šeźiwy*, USo. *sywy*. The distinction between *šěry/šery* and *šědźiwy/šeźiwy* is subtle. Both may be used of the hair of the head of human beings.

5.4.2 Body parts

head	USo. *hłowa*/LSo. *głowa*
eye	USo. *wóčko*/LSo. *woko*. The originally diminutive USo. *wóčko* has lost its diminutive meaning and is now the unmarked word for 'eye'. USo. *woko* means (a) 'drop of grease floating on broth' and (b) 'noose, loop' (*SS* 6: map 11).
nose	USo. *nós*/LSo. *nos*
ear	U/LSo. *wucho* (dual and plural USo. *wuši*/LSo. *wušy*). U/LSo. *wucho* also means 'handle, eye of a needle, eyelet', in which meaning it has plural *wucha*.

mouth

USo. *huba*/LSo. *guba.* In western Lower Sorbian dialects *prampa.* In western Lower Sorbian and transitional dialects *mula* (*SS* 6: map 15). In literary Upper Sorbian *ert* (the variants *ort, rt, ert, rót, hort* and *wort* are also recorded); *huba* is distinctly colloquial. Literary Lower Sorbian has *wusta* (*plurale tantum*). USo. *huba*/LSo. *guba* also has the meaning 'lip'.

hair

USo. *włós/włosy,* LSo. *włos/włose.* The collective meaning expressed by the plural *włosy/włose* occurs in all varieties, but the word for 'a hair' varies regionally: (a) *włos* (F) in almost all Lower Sorbian territory and eastern transitional dialects, but *włos* (M) in a few villages to the north and south of this area; (b) *włosa* in most Upper Sorbian dialects; (c) *włóska* in addition to *włos* (F) and *włosa* in both Upper and Lower territory; (d) *włosanka* in the Hoyerswerda dialect and some adjacent villages. Before the field-work for the *SS, włos* (F) had not been recorded, yet the signs are that *włos* (M) is secondary. This raises the question of a Proto-Slavonic **volsь* (F) (*SS* 6: map 7).

neck

Equivalents of German *Hals* (front of the neck) are USo. *šija*/LSo. *šyja.* Equivalents of German *Nacken/Genick* (nape of the neck) are in the literary languages USo. and LSo. *tył* and *tyło,* but *SS* 6 (map 32) shows a more complex picture. The main isogloss is that of the German loan-words *knyka* and *nyka,* which occur in the Lower Sorbian dialects and in the eastern part of the transitional zone. *Knyka* is to the north of *nyka. Tył* was found only here and there in both Upper and Lower Sorbian. *Tyło* was found in only one Lower and two Upper Sorbian villages. In many Upper Sorbian villages *šija* was noted in reply to a request for a translation of *Nacken.* It is possible that the *Nacken/Hals* distinction does not occur here.

arm/hand

U/LSo. *ruka*

finger

USo. *porst*/LSo. *palc.* The *porst/palc* isogloss coincides with the line dividing territory where the word for 'thumb' is *palc* (Upper Sorbian and Nochten dialect) from territory where it is *wjeliki palc* (the remainder) (*SS* 6: map 25).

leg/foot

USo. *noha*/LSo. *noga* has the general meaning 'leg and foot'. A question eliciting translations of German *Bein* 'leg' for the *SS* produced only *noha/noga.* However, a request for translations of German *Fuß* 'foot' (*SS* 6: map 42) produced *stopa* (variants *stowpa* and *stowpja*) for most dialects, *stop* (variant *stowp*) in the Wittichenau and

	Catholic dialects, and *noha/noga* in eleven scattered villages (mainly Upper Sorbian).
toe	In both standard languages the words for 'finger' and 'toe' are the same: USo. *porst*/LSo. *palc*. This is also true of most dialects, but in a group of villages to the east, south and west of Bautzen the word for 'toe' is the same as that for 'thumb' (*palc*) (*SS* 6: map 27). Some Upper Sorbian dictionaries give the meaning '*big* toe' for *palc*.
chest	USo. *hrudź* and LSo. *gruź* (F) (also LSo. *gruźa*) are literary words, dating from the nineteenth century and based on Czech *hrud'* 'chest'. The colloquial, older words for 'chest' (recorded since the sixteenth century) are USo. *bróst*/LSo. *brost*. It is, however, evident that there were other words, not loan-words, referring to this part of the body. Swětlik's dictionary (1721) under *pectus* has *hutrobno*. It is clear that USo. *wutroba*/LSo. *wutšoba* 'heart' formerly had the wider meaning 'heart and chest'. It was last recorded with this double meaning in the 1930s.
heart	USo. *wutroba*/LSo. *wutšoba*. PSl. **sьrdьce* 'heart' is attested only in sixteenth- and seventeenth-century sources from the east Lower Sorbian region. It seems that the disappearance of *serce*, the borrowing of *bróst* 'chest' and the narrowing of the meaning of *wutroba/wutšoba* until it meant only 'heart' were interdependent.

5.4.3   Kinship Terms

Writing in 1905, Šwjela (1952: 101) noted 'Several of these words [that is, kinship terms] have fallen into oblivion', and it is indeed a striking fact that Lower Sorbian, in particular, has replaced even such basic terms as these with loan-words from German. Kinship terms are mapped in *SS* 8 (maps 5–19 and 26).

mother	USo. *mać, maćer, mama*/LSo. *maś, mama*. Lower Sorbian dialects also have *muterka*, but the most common form in Lower Sorbian is *mama*; *maś* is now an exclusively literary word. Outside the literary languages PSl. **matь* is attested only in Upper Sorbian (*SS* 8: map 15). LSo. *muterka* is a loan-word (German *Mutter*).
father	USo./LSo. *nan*. Dictionaries also give the children's forms USo. *tata* and LSo. *tato*. *Nan* is attested in all Upper Sorbian dialects and the entire transitional area. It is also found in central Lower Sorbian dialects around Cottbus, but is bounded to the south, west and east by the loan-word *foter* (or *feter*) (German *Vater*). In the extreme

north *ato* is found. *Tato* has been found in two villages on the north-west periphery (*SS* 8: map 6). *Foter* is recorded as early as 1761 (Hauptmann). Early sources (sixteenth century) attest USo. *wótc*/LSo. *wośc* (< PSl. **otьcь*), but these are now only literary and mean 'ancestor'. They also survive in the Lord's Prayer: USo. *wótče naš*/LSo. *wośc naš* 'our father'.

sister | USo. *sotra*/LSo. *sotša*. The phonetic variants *sostra* and *šotša* exist in dialects. USo. *přirodna sotra*/LSo. *pśirodna sotša* 'step-sister' is distinguished from USo. *prawa sotra*/LSo. *pšawa sotša* 'full sister'.

brother | USo. *bratr* (colloquially *brat*)/LSo. *bratš*. USo. *přirodny bratr*/LSo. *pśirodny bratš* 'step-brother' is distinguished from USo. *prawy bratr*/LSo. *pšawy bratš* 'full brother'.

aunt | USo. *ćeta*/LSo. *śota*. These are also used as terms of respectful address to women older than the speaker who are not kin. USo. *wujowa* 'mother's sister' and *trykowa* 'father's sister' are known to have existed formerly, but are now no longer in use.

uncle | USo. *wuj*/LSo. *wujk* (*wujko*). These have a respectful function analogous to that of *ćeta/śota*. The *SS* (8: map 10) broadly confirms *wuj* as the only Upper Sorbian form and *wujk* as the main Lower Sorbian form with *wujko* in the extreme north. The latter was probably originally a vocative. USo. *tryk* 'father's brother' existed formerly, but has long since fallen out of use.

niece | USo. *bratrowka, sotrjenca*/LSo. *sotśine žowćo, bratšowa žowka*. In Lower Sorbian dialects *seśenica* sometimes has the meaning 'niece' in addition to the basic meaning 'female cousin'. Elsewhere (that is, in much of Lower Sorbian territory, the transitional dialects and the whole of Upper Sorbian) the meaning 'niece' is conveyed periphrastically (USo. *sotřina holca* and so on) or by means of the loan-word *nichta* (German *Nichte*) (*SS* 8: 54).

nephew | USo. *bratrowc, sotrjenc, sotrowc*/LSo. *bratšowy syn, sotśiny syn*. In Lower Sorbian dialects *seśko* and *seśenik* sometimes mean 'nephew' (in addition to 'male cousin'). Otherwise, throughout the whole Sorbian speech area the meaning 'nephew' is conveyed periphrastically (USo. *bratrowy hólc* and so on) or by means of the loan-word *nefa* (German *Neffe*) (*SS* 8: 54).

cousin (female) | USo. *wujowka, kuzina*/LSo. *seśenica*. The latter is found in almost all Lower Sorbian dialects. Upper Sorbian and

	transitional dialects have *kuzina* (*SS* 8: map 11). In older sources USo. *ćeta*/LSo. *śota* (now 'aunt') are found with the meaning 'female cousin'.
cousin (male)	USo. *wujowc, kuzenk*/LSo. *śeśko*. The latter is found in almost all Lower Sorbian dialects, but *śeśenik* 'male cousin' has been recorded once (*SS* 8: map 11). Upper Sorbian and transitional dialects have *kuzenk*. Older sources also attest USo. *bratrowski, trykowski, wuj* and *tryk* with this meaning.
grandmother	USo. *wowka*/LSo. *starka, stara mama*. Almost all Upper Sorbian dialects have *wowka*, but elsewhere the position is complex (*SS* 8: map 17). Transitional dialects have *baba, stara mać* and *wowa*. Lower Sorbian dialects have *starka, stara mama, tejka, dowda* and *grosa*.
grandfather	USo. *dźěd*/LSo. *stary nan*. Upper Sorbian and western transitional dialects have *dźěd*, but in the eastern transitional zone and Lower Sorbian *stary nan* predominates. Further terms found in Lower Sorbian dialects are *grosnan, nanstar, grosfeter* and *dowdan* (*SS* 8: map 8).
wife	USo. *žona, mandźelska, mandźelka*/LSo. *žona, žeńska, manželska*. The two words *žona* and *žónska* 'woman' occur in all Upper Sorbian dialects, but in most points only *žona* can have the additional meaning 'wife' (German *Ehefrau*) (*SS* 8: map 14). In Lower Sorbian dialects *baba* and *žeńska* generally mean both 'woman' and 'wife'. In the field-work for the *SS mandźelska* and *manželska* 'wife' were found to be widely attested, but they are nevertheless thought to be literary words which reach the dialects through church usage.
husband	USo. *muž, mandźel, mandźelski*/LSo. *muž, manželski, ćłowjek*. In Upper Sorbian dialects the most common word with this meaning is *muž*, but (like German *Mann*) it means both 'man' and 'husband' (*SS* 8: map 5). In Lower Sorbian dialects the predominant word for 'man' and 'husband' is *ćłowjek* (the meaning 'human being' is here expressed by *luź*), but *muž* is found sporadically. The position is complicated, not least by the fact that *žěd* (normally 'grandfather') is also widely attested in Lower Sorbian dialects with the meaning 'man/husband'.
daughter	USo. *dźowka*/LSo. *žowka*
son	USo./LSo. *syn*

6 Dialects

The same social conditions which enabled Sorbian to survive at all (isolation, economic self-sufficiency, stability, immobility) also resulted in an extraordinarily high degree of regional variation. In the early 1960s Sorbian dialectologists began a new project to describe this variation, and its results are now being published in the *Sorbischer Sprachatlas* (*SS*). Of a projected fifteen volumes, thirteen have already appeared. The atlas is a record not of the present state of the dialects, but of their condition in the early 1960s, as represented by the oldest inhabitants at that time. When the field-work began, it was still possible to gather information from 138 villages spread over an area measuring about 57 miles (92 km.) north to south and 41 miles (66 km.) east to west, but since then from some of them Sorbian has disappeared. Even today (1993), however, field-work continues, and in many villages (mainly Catholic) even the youngest generation still speaks Sorbian.

The concentrations of isoglosses mapped in the *Sorbischer Sprachatlas* confirm the previously postulated division of Sorbian into three zones: Upper Sorbian in the south, Lower Sorbian in the north, and a transitional zone between them (see map 11.1 on p. 594). The degree of internal variation is lowest in the Lower Sorbian zone, somewhat higher in Upper Sorbian and highest in the transitional zone. The eastern transitional dialects of Schleife (Slepo) and Muskau (Mužakow) have a pronounced individuality. They are separated by many isoglosses not only from Upper and Lower Sorbian, but also from the adjacent transitional dialects to the west. The individuality of the Catholic (or Kamenz) dialect spoken to the north and west of Bautzen, though clear, is not as pronounced as the former existence of a separate literary variant might lead one to suppose.

Some of the main isoglosses are as follows:

Phonological
1   In Lower Sorbian PSl. *g is retained (LSo. *gora* 'mountain, hill'), but in Upper Sorbian PSl. *g > h (USo. *hora*). Western transitional dialects have h; Schleife and Muskau have g.
2   In Lower Sorbian PSl. *$č$ > c (LSo. *cas* 'time'), whereas in Upper Sorbian $č$ is retained (USo. *čas*). Western transitional dialects have $č$; Schleife and Muskau have c.
3   In Lower Sorbian PSl. *t before front vowels > $ś$ (LSo. *swěśenje* 'lamp-oil' < *$světenje$). In Upper Sorbian *t before front vowels > $ć$ (USo. *swěćenje*). The affricate $ć$ is also found in almost the whole of the transitional zone.
4   In Lower Sorbian PSl. *d before front vowels > $ź$ (LSo. *źeń* 'day'). The corresponding reflex in Upper Sorbian is $dź$ (*dźeń* 'day'). The affricate $dź$ is also found throughout the entire transitional zone.

Morphological

1   The synthetic past tenses (aorist and imperfect) are not found in Lower
    Sorbian or transitional dialects, but are in common use in most Upper
    Sorbian dialects.

2   The masculine-personal category is present in Upper Sorbian, but
    missing from Lower Sorbian and transitional dialects (see 3.1.1).

3   In Lower Sorbian and the eastern transitional dialects the nominative
    dual of masculine nouns ends in -*a* (*Serba* '(two) Sorbs'); in the
    remaining transitional dialects and in Upper Sorbian the corresponding
    ending is -*aj* (*Serbaj*) (soft stems may optionally end in -*aj* or -*ej*).

4   In most dialects, Upper and Lower Sorbian, verbal nouns in the
    nominative singular end in -*e* (*twarjenje* 'building'), but there are two
    areas of Upper Sorbian where the ending is -*o* (*twarjenjo*). These are
    in the east (to the south of Weisswasser) and in the west (the Catholic
    dialect). Verbal nouns in -*o* were one of the characteristic features of
    the Catholic literary language.

Lexical

1   The verb 'to say' in Lower Sorbian dialects is *groniś*. In Upper Sorbian
    and the transitional zone it is *prajić*. (In some parts of Upper Sorbian
    territory the optional alternative *rjec* is also found.)

2   'Yes' in Lower Sorbian and in the Schleife and Muskau dialects is *jo*. In
    Upper Sorbian and some transitional dialects the equivalent is *haj*. In
    addition, in many parts of the *haj*-area an additional, more emphatic
    form *ju* or *jow* is attested.

3   'Wedding' in Upper Sorbian and some transitional dialects is *kwas*. In
    Lower Sorbian and some transitional dialects the equivalent is *swaźba*.
    In the dialects of Schleife and Muskau the form *swarba* or *swarba* is
    found.

4   'Who' in most Lower Sorbian dialects is *chto*, but in two villages in the
    extreme west *ko* is recorded. Upper Sorbian has *štu* (conventionally
    spelled *štó*). The corresponding form in the transitional dialect of
    Hoyerswerda and Spreewitz is *do* (recorded in the eighteenth century
    as *hdo*).

Acknowledgement

I am indebted to the late Dr Frido Michałk, of the Institut za serbski
ludospyt, Bautzen, for valuable comments on a draft of this chapter.

References

Bielfeldt, H.H. (1933) *Die deutschen Lehnwörter im Obersorbischen*, Berlin:
    Harrassowitz. (Kraus reprint, Nendeln, Liechtenstein, 1968.)

Corbett, G.G. (1987) 'The morphology/syntax interface: evidence from possessive adjectives in Slavonic', *Language*, 63(2): 299–345.

Faßke, H. (1964) *Die Vetschauer Mundart*, Bautzen: VEB Domowina.

—— (in collaboration with S. Michalk) (1981) *Grammatik der obersorbischen Schriftsprache der Gegenwart: Morphologie*, Bautzen: VEB Domowina.

Haupt, L., and Schmaler, J.E. (1841) *Volkslieder der Wenden in der Ober- und Nieder-Lausitz. Erster Teil*, Grimma: J.M. Gebhardt. (Reprinted Berlin: Akademie-Verlag, 1953.)

—— (1843) *Volkslieder der Wenden in der Ober- und Nieder-Lausitz. Zweiter Teil*, Grimma: J.M. Gebhardt. (Reprinted Berlin: Akademie-Verlag, 1953.)

Hauptmann, J.G. (1761) *Nieder-Lausitzsche Wendische Grammatica*, Lübben: J.M. Driemeln. (Reprinted Bautzen: Domowina, 1984.)

Janaš, P. (1984) *Niedersorbische Grammatik*, 2 edn, Bautzen: VEB Domowina.

Jenč, R. (1959) 'Městno finitnych formow pomocneho słowjesa a participa wuznamoweho słowjesa w hornjoserbskej sadźe', *Lětopis Instituta za serbski ludospyt*, Series A, 6: 3–47. (Bautzen: VEB Domowina.)

—— (1976) 'Alternacija g–z/dz w hornjoserbśćinje', *Lětopis Instituta za serbski ludospyt*, Series A, 23: 171–81. (Bautzen: VEB Domowina.)

Michałk, F. (1956-7) 'Słowosłěd w serbśćinje', *Lětopis Instituta za serbski ludospyt*, Series A, 4: 3–41. (Bautzen: VEB Domowina.)

—— (1970) 'K prašenjam słowosłěda w serbskich dialektach', *Lětopis Instituta za serbski ludospyt*, Series A, 17: 1–29. (Bautzen: VEB Domowina.)

Michalk, S., and Protze, H. (1967) *Studien zur sprachlichen Interferenz I. Deutsch-sorbische Dialekttexte aus Nochten, Kreis Weißwasser*, Bautzen: VEB Domowina.

—— [1974] *Studien zur sprachlichen Interferenz*, vol. II: *Deutsch–sorbische Dialekttexte aus Radibor, Kreis Bautzen*, Bautzen: VEB Domowina.

Moller, A. (1959) *Niedersorbisches Gesangbuch und Katechismus. Budissin 1574*, Berlin: Akademie-Verlag. (Facsimile reprint.)

Mucke, K.E. (1891) *Historische und vergleichende Laut- und Formenlehre der niedersorbischen (niederlausitzisch-wendischen) Sprache*, Leipzig: Fürstlich Jablonowski'sche Gesellschaft. (Reprinted Leipzig: Zentral-Antiquariat der Deutschen Demokratischen Republik, 1965.)

Richter, H. (1980) 'Die Possessivadjektive im Sorbischen unter Berücksichtigung der benachbarten slawischen Sprachen', Dissertation zur Promotion A, Karl-Marx-Universität, Leipzig.

Schuster-Šewc, H. (1978–89), *Historisch-etymologisches Wörterbuch der ober- und niedersorbischen Sprache*, 4 vols, Bautzen: VEB Domowina. (Abbreviated as *Wörterbuch*.)

SS = *Sorbischer Sprachatlas*, 1965– (in progress) ed. by H. Faßke, H. Jentsch and S. Michalk, Bautzen: VEB Domowina.

Stieber, Z. (1934) *Stosunki pokrewieństwa języków łużyckich*, Cracow: Gebethner i Wolff.

Stone, G.C. (1972) *The Smallest Slavonic Nation: the Sorbs of Lusatia*, London: Athlone Press.

Šewc, H. (1968) *Gramatika hornjoserbskeje rěče*, vol. 1: *Fonematika a morfologija*, Bautzen: VEB Domowina.

Šewc-Schuster, H. (1976) *Gramatika hornjoserbskeje rěče*, vol. 2: *Syntaksa*, Bautzen: VEB Domowina.

Šwjela, B. (1952) *Grammatik der niedersorbischen Sprache*, 2 edn, Bautzen: VEB Domowina.

T = *Sorbische Dialekttexte*, 1-10 (1963-72), Bautzen: VEB Domowina.

Urban, R. (1980) *Die sorbische Volksgruppe in der Lausitz 1949 bis 1977: ein dokumentarischer Bericht*, Marburg: J.G. Herder-Institut.

Waurick, I. (1968) 'Der Inhaltssatz im Niedersorbischen', in E. Eckert and E. Eichler (eds), *Zur grammatischen und lexikalischen Struktur der slawischen Gegenwartssprachen*, Halle (Saale): Niemeyer, 113–26.

Дыбо, В.А. (1963) 'Об отражении древних количественных и интонационных отношений в верхнелужицком языке', in Л.Е. Калнынь (ed.), Сербо-лужицкий лингвистический сборник, Москва: Академия Наук СССР.

Михалк, Ф. (1974) 'Краткий очерк грамматики современного верхнелужицкого литературного языка', in К.К. Трофимович, Верхнелужицко-русский словарь, 472–511. Москва-Бауцен: «Домовина» – «Русский язык».

12 Polish

Robert A. Rothstein

1 Introduction

Polish is the native language of most of the 38 million inhabitants of Poland and of some of the estimated 10 million Poles who live beyond the borders of Poland (including perhaps 1 million in the former Soviet Union).

Polish belongs to the Lechitic branch of the West Slavonic group, together with the extinct dialects of the Slavs who once inhabited the area between the lower and mid Oder and Elbe Rivers (see chapter 14). The recorded history of the Polish language is usually taken to begin with a papal bull to the Archbishop of Gniezno, dated 1136 but apparently forged some time between 1139 and 1146, the Latin text of which contains 410 Polish geographical and personal names. The oldest recorded Polish sentence dates from the thirteenth century and the oldest continuous text from the fourteenth century. By the beginning of the sixteenth century it is possible to speak of a more or less standardized literary language.

The literary language of the sixteenth century contained some features characteristic of the Wielkopolska dialect area of western Poland and others from the Małopolska area of south-eastern Poland, and the early history of the Polish state was connected with political–cultural–religious centres in both regions (Gniezno/Poznań and Cracow, respectively). Polish linguists therefore long argued about the dialect base of the literary language. Of late many have accepted the view, first fully articulated by Zdzisław Stieber in 1948, that both dialect areas contributed to the formation of the literary language, with conflicts between different variants resolved by the selection of that variant that was closer to Czech. The hypothesis of Czech as linguistic arbiter for Polish is connected with the strong influence of Czech language and culture starting in the tenth century, when Christianity came to Poland from Bohemia.

The Polish literary language has had a continuous development since its earliest period, although it had to compete with Latin in many functions until as late as the end of the eighteenth century. During the period of the partitions of Poland (1772–1918), the Poles resisted attempts at Russification and, in the Prussian zone, Germanization. The twentieth century, and especially the period since the Second World War, has brought about a

broadening of the social base of standard Polish with a concomitant decline
in regional dialects, a vast increase in technical and specialized terminology
(often internationalisms) and a loosening of many traditional norms, often
in the direction of 'regularization' of pronunciation or inflection.

2   Phonology

2.1   Segmental phoneme inventory

Polish has seven vowel phonemes and thirty-three consonantal phonemes,
which are given in table 12.1 in their usual orthographic representation
(with one exception discussed below). Palatals differ from the corresponding alveolars in having a longer constriction (which may extend from the
alveolar ridge to the mediopalatum) and one that is formed by the body of
the tongue rather than by its blade. Palatalized labials have a primary labial
constriction with a simultaneous raising of the tongue towards the hard
palate. The velar glide *ł* is actually labio-velar with two constrictions (IPA
[w]).

The inventory given here reflects a set of partly interrelated decisions
about some matters on which there is no firm consensus: (a) to treat the
semi-high, retracted front vowel represented by orthographic y as an allophone of /i/; (b) to treat the fronted (post-palatal) variants of the velars as
allophones of the latter; (c) to recognize the existence of palatalized labials
rather than treating them as sequences of (allophonically palatalized) labial
plus /j/ (a common realization); (d) to recognize the existence of nasal
vowel phonemes rather than treating them as sequences of oral vowel plus
some other segment.

The labio-velar glide /ł/ functions less like the palatal glide /j/ and
more like the dental lateral it once was (and still is for a small number of
speakers). Thus, unlike /j/, but like the alveolar lateral /l/, it can appear
as the first element of a word-initial cluster (*łza* 'tear', *lśni* 'shines') or as
the last element of a word-final cluster (*szedł* 'he was going', *myśl*
'thought'). It also alternates with /l/ while /j/ does not enter into any
alternations.

The palatals /ś, ź, ć, dź, ń/ are spelled with the acute accent when not
followed by vowels; before vowels they are spelled si, zi, ci, dzi, ni. If the
vowel is /i/, the letter i represents the vowel and simultaneously serves this
diacritic function. Thus nominative *koń* 'horse', instrumental plural *końmi*,
but genitive singular *konia* [końa] and genitive plural *koni* [końi]. The
palatalized labials occur only before vowels and are always spelled as
digraphs (*miasto* 'city' [m′asto] or [m′jasto]). The spellings ki, gi, chi
represent fronted (post-palatal) allophones of the corresponding velars,
and the spelling li represents a palatalized allophone of /l/ (which only
occurs before /i/).

Table 12.1 Polish segmental phonemes

Vowels

	Oral		Nasal	
High	i	u		
Lower-mid	e	o	ę	ǫ (orthographic ą)
Low	a			

Consonants

	Bilabial non-palatalized	Bilabial palatalized	Labio-dental non-palatalized	Labio-dental palatalized	Dental	Alveolar	Palatal	Velar
Voiceless stops	p	pi			t			k
Voiced stops	b	bi			d			g
Voiceless fricatives			f	fi	s	sz	ś	ch
Voiced fricatives			w	wi	z	ż	ź	
Voiceless affricates					c	cz	ć	
Voiced affricates					dz	dż	dź	
Nasals	m	mi			n		ń	
Laterals						l		
Trills						r		
Glides							j	ł

As a vowel symbol the letter i represents the basic variant of the phoneme /i/, which can occur everywhere but after hard (non-palatal and non-palatalized) consonants; after hard consonants the allophone spelled with the letter y appears. After a vowel it represents /ji/ (genitive singular *szyi* [šyji] ‹ *szyja* 'neck'). After a consonant in words of non-Polish origin it can represent /j/ (*Maria* 'Mary', spelled *Marja* until 1936) or even /ij/ (*biologia* [b'jolog'ja] or [b'ijolog'ja] 'biology'). In less assimilated foreign words the spelling consonant plus i can represent a palatalized dental or alveolar consonant followed by [i] (*sinus* [s'inus] 'sine' versus older *synteza* 'synthesis'; *Chile* (č'ile]).

Palatalized dentals and alveolars also occur allophonically in native words at word boundary before a word-initial /i/ or /j/ (*już idziemy* [juš'idźemy] 'we're leaving right now') and at prefix boundary before a root-initial /i/ or /j/ (*zirytować* (PRFV) [z'i-] 'annoy, irritate').

In words of native origin the velar stops are replaced by their fronted variants before the vowels /e/ and /i/, giving the spellings kie, gie, ki, gi instead of ke, ge, ky, gy (compare forms of the adjectives 'new' and 'Polish': *nowy, nowe* (M, N, NOM SG) versus *polski, polskie*). The velar fricative is not affected by following vowels (compare the parallel adjective forms *cichy, ciche* 'quiet') except in verbal derivation (*przepisywać* (IMPFV) 'rewrite' versus *podsłuchiwać* 'eavesdrop'). In non-native words all three velars are replaced by post-palatal variants before /i/ but are normally preserved as velars before /e/ (*gitara* 'guitar', *kelner* 'waiter').

Most speakers pronounce orthographic ch and h identically as a voiceless velar fricative, but some distinguish h as voiced.

The letters ę and ą represent the nasal vowel phonemes /ę/ and /ǫ/, respectively. Their phonetic realization depends on the following segment. Before /l/ and /ł/ they are pronounced without nasal resonance as [e] and [o]. (They do not occur before /r/ or /j/.) Before stops and affricates they are pronounced as a sequence of oral vowel plus homorganic nasal consonant (labial in *tępy* [tempy] 'dull', palatalized labial in *rąbie* [rom'b'e] 'chops', dental in *piąty* [p'onty] 'fifth', alveolar in *pączek* [poṇček] 'doughnut', pre-palatal in *pięć* [p'eńć] 'five', post-palatal in *węgiel* [veŋ'g'el] 'coal', velar in *ręka* [reŋka] 'hand'). It is only before a fricative (and for ą in word-final position) that ę and ą are pronounced as asynchronous nasal vowels, that is, [eũ] and [oũ]. Word-final ę is normally pronounced without nasal resonance [e] and there is a growing tendency to pronounce ę and ą before continuants and ą in word-final position as non-nasal diphthongs [eũ], [oũ].

In non-native words in position before a fricative the combination vowel plus nasal consonant can be pronounced as an asynchrous nasal vowel (*tramwaj* [traũvaj] 'tram, streetcar', *instytut* [iũstytut] 'institute'). In native words the palatal nasal is realized as a nasalized palatal glide before fricatives (*tańszy* [tajšy] 'cheaper') and as [jn] or [jṇ] before non-fricatives (*gońca* (GEN) [gojnca] 'courier', *kończyć* [koj̣n̦čyć] 'finish').

The digraphs au, eu represent diphthongs identical to *ał, eł* (*auto* [aŭto], *Europa* [eŭropa]). The combination rz represents the two consonants [r] plus [z] in some roots (*marznąć* 'freeze'); more frequently it spells the voiced alveolar fricative otherwise represented by ż. The spelling difference reflects the historical difference between a palatalization of /r/ (for rz) and of /g/ or /z/ (for ż). There is also a synchronic difference in behaviour with respect to assimilation (see below). The orthographic distinction of u and ó (both [u]) also reflects etymology: u < /u/ versus ó < /ō/. The spellings rz and ó have morphological motivation in some words but not in other. Compare *morze* 'sea' and *morski* 'maritime' or *ogród* (NOM), *ogrodu* (GEN) 'garden' versus *brzeg* 'shore' or *król* 'king' with no related forms containing /r/ or /o/, respectively.

The combinations dz, dź (or dzi) and dż can represent both unit phonemes and clusters (compare *nadzieja* [nadźeja] 'hope' and *nadziemny* [nad'źemny] or [nadźźemny] 'superterrestrial').

The letter n before /k/ and /g/ represents the velar nasal [ŋ] except in words in which the cluster /nk/ is broken up by an inserted vowel in some form. Compare *bank* [baŋk] but *szminka* [šm'inka] 'lipstick' (because of genitive plural *szminek*). The restriction does not apply in the Cracow variant of the standard language (compare Cracovian [šm'iŋka]).

Non-high vowels are raised when preceded or followed by soft (palatal or palatalized consonants), and consonants adjust their point of articulation to following consonants (dental to alveolar in *drzewo* [ḍževo] 'tree', dental to palatal in *zdziwić* [žḍźiv'ić] 'surprise'). The vowel assimilations are not reflected in spelling; the consonant assimilations, only partially (for example s > ś in *ściskać* 'squeeze'). See also the comments on voicing assimilation below.

In word-final position before pause neither palatalized consonants nor the post-palatal variants of velar consonants occur. Voiced obstruents are replaced by their voiceless counterparts. In other environments the voicing of obstruents can depend on the following segment(s). In an obstruent cluster (within a single word or not) regressive assimilation applies: *wódka* [vutka] 'vodka', *las brzozowy* [lazbžozovy] 'birch forest'. The two consonants spelled rz and w behave exceptionally by assimilating – within a morpheme – to a preceding voiceless obstruent: *przez* [pšes] 'through', *kwaśny* [kfaśny] 'sour'. In the case of /w/ the unassimilated version also occurs (as a normative variant in the Wielkopolska region, for example Poznań): [kvaśny]. Beyond the boundaries of a single morpheme rz and w cause normal regressive assimilation: *członek rządu* [čuonegžondu] 'government member', *jak wicher* [jagv'ixer] 'like a whirlwind'.

When a word ending in an obstruent is followed by a word beginning with a vowel or resonant, the result depends on geography. In Warsaw the obstruent is voiceless, while in Cracow and Poznań it is voiced: *brat/sąsiad ojca* (*Ryśka*) 'my father's (Rysiek's) brother/neighbour' is pronounced [brat]/[sǫśat] (Warsaw) or [brad]/[sǫśad] (Cracow/Poznań). A preposition is part of the same phonological word as the following noun, thus *bez ojca* 'without my father' or *bez Ryśka* 'without Rysiek' are pronounced as written in both areas. Various verbal clitics, including the imperative clitics and – in dialects – the personal clitics (see sections 3.2.1 and 4.1), are not part of the phonological word, so there is a geographic split, for example, between two versions of *chodźmy* 'let's go': [xoćmy] (Warsaw) and [xodźmy] (Cracow/Poznań).

The two short **nasal vowels** of Proto-Slavonic (front and back) coalesced in Old Polish into a single short nasal vowel, spelled ø; the two long nasal vowels similarly gave a single long nasal vowel, spelled øø. Old Polish also acquired new long vowels through contraction and compensation for lost syllables. In the contemporary standard language the reflex of the short nasal vowel is /ę/; the reflex of the long nasal vowel is /ǫ/ (orthographic ą). The Proto-Slavonic distinction of front versus back nasals is reflected in the character of the preceding consonant. Compare

OCS	mǫžь	bǫdǫ	vьzęti	pętь
Polish	mąż	będę	wziąć	pięć
	'husband'	'I will be'	'to take'	'five'

Proto-Slavonic reduced vowels (**jers**) in weak position were lost, while strong *jers* gave /e/; the character of the preceding consonant reflects the difference between a front *jer* (*pies* (NOM), *psa* (GEN) 'dog') and a back *jer* (*sen* (NOM), *sna* (GEN) 'sleep; dream'). The development of Proto-Slavonic syllabic liquids, on the other hand, was extremely complicated in Polish (together with Sorbian and Polabian) since the nature of the preceding and following consonant (designated C) affected the results:

1   CrC › CarC: *targ* 'market';
2   ClC and ClC › CłuC when C_1 is a dental: *tłusty* 'fat';
3   CŕC was affected by the second consonant, other ClC groups were affected by the first consonant, and other ClC groups were affected by both consonants.

   (a)   CŕC › CarC when C_2 is a hard dental: *martwy* 'dead';
   (b)   CŕC › CirC › CerC when C_2 is a soft dental: *śmierć* 'death';
   (c)   CŕC › CirzC › CerzC when C_2 is a non-dental: *wierzba* 'willow';
   (d)   ClC › CełC when C_1 is a velar: *kiełbasa* 'sausage';
   (e)   ClC › CełC, CułC or CołC when C_1 is a labial: *Świętopełk* (personal name), *pułk* 'regiment'; *mołwa* › *mowa* 'speech';
   (f)   ClC › CełC when C_1 is a labial, C_2 is a hard dental: *wełna*

'wool', C*k*C > C*il*C when C_1 is a labial, C_2 is some other consonant: *wilk* 'wolf';

(g)   C*k*C > Ce*ł*C > Co*ł*C (> Có*ł*C) when C_1 is *č* or *ž*: *żółty* 'yellow'.

The Proto-Slavonic **liquid diphthongs** simply metathesized in Polish: *droga* (‹ *dorga) 'road', *głowa* (‹ *golva) 'head', *drzewo* (‹ *dervo) 'tree', *mleko* (‹ *melko) 'milk'. Exceptions are due to later Polish developments, for example *ō* > *ó* in *wróg* (‹ *vorgŭ) 'enemy (poetic)', or to borrowings from Czech (*straż* 'guard' beside native *stróż* 'watchman') or from East Slavonic (*czereśnia* 'cherry' beside Old Polish *trześnia*). Word-initial liquid diphthongs with an acute intonation gave *ra-*, *ła-* (*radło* 'plow', *łabędź* 'swan'), while such diphthongs with a circumflex intonation gave *ro-*, *ło-* (*robota* 'work', *łokieć* 'elbow').

Polish does not make phonemic use of pitch accent, and word stress is normally fixed on the penultimate syllable. Secondary stress is initial in non-compounds (*stòwarzyszénie* 'society') but in compounds it falls on the penultimate syllable of the first half of the compound (*powièściopísarz* 'novelist'). Orthoepic norms recognize several categories of exceptions to the principle of penultimate main stress, including antepenultimate stress in some noun forms (*gramátyka* (NOM SG) but regular *gramatykámi* (INST PL) 'grammar') and plural past verb forms (*czytáliśmy* 'we were reading'), and ante-antepenultimate stress in plural conditional forms (*czytálibyśmy* 'we would have read').

Since at least the immediate post-war period, however, there has been an ever-growing tendency to eliminate these exceptions by generalizing penultimate stress. Pronunciations of the type *czytaliśmy* and *gramatýka* have become dominant among speakers born since the Second World War. At the same time a competing tendency to word-initial stress, first observed in emotional–rhetorical style in the 1930s, has made such inroads that for many speakers the penultimate stress has become a secondary stress.

The Old Polish phonemic opposition of **long and short vowels** persisted until about the first quarter of the sixteenth century. It survives in rudimentary form in northern Cassubian. Many other dialects, however, show qualitative oppositions as reflexes of the earlier quantitative opposition. In the literary language the opposition of back and front nasal vowels continues the Old Polish opposition of long and short nasals, respectively, and the grapheme ó for /u/ represents the reflex of an earlier /ō/. The nineteenth-century literary language also had a reflex of /ē/, spelled é and pronounced [y].

2.2   Morphophonemic alternations inherited from Proto-Slavonic
Table 12.2 shows Polish consonant alternations (represented in normal orthography). Column I shows the reflexes of the second velar palatalization; column II, the reflexes of consonant plus front vowel. The vowels

that caused the second velar palatalization had the same effect on non-velars as any other front vowel, so column II is identical to column I for non-velars (and for *ch*, since in West Slavonic the first and second palatalizations of *x* gave the same result). Column III shows the reflexes of consonant plus *j*, which differ from those of column II only for dentals. (Note the possible relics of an epenthetic *l* from labial plus *j* in such words as *kropla* 'drop'.)

The table defines alternations with respect to roots rather than in terms of 'surface' alternations. Thus, for example, the alternation *płacić* 'to pay' versus *płacę* 'I pay' represents the two alternations *t/ć* and *t/c* rather than *ć/c* (compare *płata* 'payment'). This is only a problem where the root form is absent from the contemporary language, as in a number of cases in which the surface alternation is *c/cz* or *dz/ż* and there is no extant form with a final velar (*chłopiec* 'boy' / *chłopczyk* (DIMIN)).

In what follows consonant alternations will be referred to in terms of 'hard' and 'soft' consonants, meaning the consonants that are found as left-hand or right-hand members, respectively, of pairs in table 12.2. This traditional terminology is convenient, but the reader should remember that the class of morphophonemically soft consonants includes both synchronically soft (palatal and palatalized) consonants and synchronically hard consonants that were once soft.

Hard consonants represent root consonants. Soft consonants from column I appear in noun declension (masculine and neuter locative singular, feminine dative/locative singular and masculine-personal nominative plural) as well as in adjective declension (masculine-personal nominative plural). The alternation *k/c* appears in the derivation of three adverbs; otherwise adverb derivation could be associated with column II.

Soft consonants from column II appear in masculine vocative forms and exceptionally in three locative plural forms: *we Włoszech* 'in Italy', *w Niemczech* 'in Germany' and *na Węgrzech* 'in Hungary'. They also appear in adjectival and adverbial comparison and in derivation. In conjugation they appear in the second and third person singular and first and second person plural non-past of the first and second conjugation (see section 3.2.2) and in the passive participle of the second conjugation.

Soft consonants from column III appear in derivation (including the derivation of imperfectives from first-conjugation perfectives) and in conjugation: in the entire non-past of the third conjugation, in the first person singular and third person plural non-past and the passive participle of the first conjugation, and in the masculine-personal form of the passive participle of the second conjugation (for some verbs).

Some alternations that are not listed in the table (*ch/ś*, *sz/ś* and the exceptional *ż/ź* and *dx/dź*) are the result of later analogies (see section 2.3). There are also some inherited alternations that are less general: *t/s*, *d/s*, *k/c*, *g/c* in forming infinitives (*plotę* 'I braid' / *pleść* 'to braid', *piekę* 'I

Table 12.2   Polish consonant alternations

I	II	III
t/ć		t/c
d/dź		d/dz
s/ś		s/sz
z/ż		z/ż
st/ść		st/szcz
zd/źdź		zd/żdż
	p/pi	
	b/bi	
	f/fi	
	w/wi	
	m/mi	
	n/ń	
	ł/l	
	r/rz	
	ch/sz	
k/c	k/cz	
g/dz	g/ż	
sk/sc	sk/szcz	
zg/zdz	zg/żdż	

bake'/*piec* 'to bake'); *h/ż* in declension and derivation involving three roots; and the alternation between nasal consonants and nasal vowels in conjugation (*zacznę* 'I will begin'/*zacząć* 'to begin').

Polish inherited **vowel–zero alternations** as the result of the loss of weak *jers* and the vocalization of strong *jers*. These alternations show up in noun declension: masculine nominative singular versus other cases (*pies* (NOM SG)/*psa* (GEN SG) 'dog'), feminine genitive plural versus other cases (*matek* (GEN PL)/*matka* (NOM SG) 'mother'), feminine *i*-stem nominative/accusative singular versus other cases (*marchew* (NOM SG)/*marchwi* (GEN SG) 'carrot'), neuter genitive plural versus other cases (*den* (GEN PL)/*dno* (NOM SG) 'bottom'); in some adjectival and numeral forms (masculine singular predicative form *godzien*/masculine nominative singular attributive form *godny* 'worthy', *jeden* (M NOM SG)/*jedna* (F NOM SG) 'one', non-masculine personal *osiem*/masculine personal *ośmiu* '8'); in verbal prefixes (*odesłać* (PRFV)/*odsyłać* (IMPFV) 'send away'); in prepositions (*ze szkła* 'from glass'/*z szeregu* 'from the line'); in past-tense forms of verbs (*byłem* (1 M) (*był* + (*e*)*m*)/*byłam* (1 F) (*była* + *m*)) 'I was', (*wysechł* (3 M)/*wyschła* (3 F) '(it) dried up'); and in derivation (diminutive *bluzeczka*/*bluzka* 'blouse', *jabłecznik* 'apple cake'/*jabłko* 'apple').

Historical reflexes have sometimes been modified by analogy: *szewc* (NOM)/*szewca* (GEN) 'shoemaker' for historically 'correct' **szwec/szewca* and, in the opposite direction, *szmer* (NOM)/*szmeru* (GEN) 'murmur' for *szmer*/**szemru*. In some forms an ahistorical vowel–zero alternation has been introduced, as in the following nominative/genitive singular pairs: *ogień*/*ognia* 'fire' for **ogń*/*ognia*, *Luter*/*Lutra* '(Martin) Luther'. Alternations of zero with /o/ and /i/ are a result of later changes (see section 2.3).

Another kind of vowel–zero alternation is the reflex of a Proto-Slavonic quantitative alternation in verbal derivation. Compare the following perfective and imperfective forms: *umrę* 'I will die'/*umieram* 'I am dying', *zapcham* 'I will fill'/*zapycham* 'I am filling', *przetnę* 'I will cut'/*przecinam* 'I am cutting'. The same quantitative alternation gave rise to the perfective/imperfective *o(ó)*/*a* alternation in *zarobić*/*zarabiać* 'earn' or *wrócić*/*wracać* 'return'.

2.3   Morphophonemic alternations resulting from changes after Proto-Slavonic

Some additional (but limited) **consonantal alternations** have been introduced into Polish as a result of analogy. Presumably on the basis of the *s*/*ś* alternation in masculine-personal nominative plural forms of nouns and adjectives, *sz* (whether original or from *ch*) was replaced in those forms by *ś*: *nasz* (M NOM SG)/*nasi* (M-PERS NOM PL) (‹ *naszy*) 'our', similarly *starszy* (and all other synthetic comparatives)/*starsi* (‹ *starszy*) 'older', *cichy*/*cisi* (‹ *ciszy*) 'quiet', *mnich* (NOM SG)/*mnisi* (NOM PL) (‹ *mniszy*) 'monk'. The new *sz*/*ś* alternation also occurs in derivation (*mysz* 'mouse'/*mysi* 'mouse's'), as does the *ch*/*ś* alternation, albeit inconsistently (*mnich*/*mnisi* or *mniszy* 'monk's'). The alternations *ż*/*ź*, *dz*/*dź* and *g*/*ź* occur in single words.

Certain vowel alternations characteristic of Polish appeared as a consequence of earlier quantitative alternations, as a result of the Lechitic backing of non-high front vowels before hard dentals, or as the effect of contractions. In standard Polish the **opposition of long and short vowels** was preserved only as a qualitative opposition and only in two pairs. The result is a potential alternation between closed syllables containing *ą* or *ó* (from the long nasal vowel and long *ō*, respectively) and open syllables containing *ę* or *o* (from the corresponding short vowels). This alternation shows up both in inflection *mąż* (NOM SG)/*męża* (GEN SG) 'husband', *rąk* (GEN PL)/*ręka* (NOM SG) 'hand', *zajął* (3 M PAST)/*zajęła* (3 F PAST) 'occupied') and in derivation (*rączka* (DIMIN) ‹ *ręka*, *dąb* 'oak' › *dębowy* 'made of oak'). Examples for *ó*/*o* include *nóż* (NOM SG)/*noża* (GEN SG) 'knife', *szkół* (GEN PL)/*szkoła* (NOM SG) 'school', *niósł* (3 M PAST)/*niosła* (3 F PAST) 'carried', *nóżka* (DIMIN) ‹ *noga* 'foot'. Both alternations are far from regular, with many examples of *ą* and *ó* in open syllables (*świątynia* 'shrine', *ogródek* 'garden') and of *ę* and *o* in closed syllables (*gęś* 'goose', *dozorca* 'caretaker').

The prehistoric Lechitic change of *e* to *o* and *ě* to *a* before what were then hard dentals has left Modern Polish with alternations of *o(ó)* or *a* before *t, d, s, z, n, r, ł* versus *e* before *ć, dź, ś, ź, ń, rz, l.* The alternations are present both in inflection *świat* ((NOM)/*świecie* (LOC) 'world', *kościół* (NOM)/*kościele* (LOC) 'church', *wiozę* (1 SG PRS)/*wieziesz* (2 SG PRS) 'transport', *siedziały* (3 NON-M-PERS PAST)/*siedzieli* (3 M-PERS PAST)) and in derivation (*miara* 'measure'/*mierzyć* 'measure', *zielony* 'green'/*zieleń* 'vegetation'). The alternations are fairly regular in verbal inflection and derivation, much less so elsewhere.

In some words the alternation occurs even though the historically soft dental that 'preserved' the front vowel was subsequently depalatalized: *wiatr* (NOM)/*wietrze* (LOC) 'wind'. The alternation was introduced by analogy in some cases (*wlokę* (1 SG PRS)/*wleczesz* (2 SG) 'drag') and lost in many more (*rozdział* (NOM)/*rozdziale* (LOC) 'chapter' but *rozdzielić* 'divide'). Sometimes alternative forms exist (*kwiaciarnia* (Warsaw)/*kwieciarnia* (Cracow) 'flower shop' ‹ *kwiat/kwiecie* (LOC) 'flower').

The historical development of a class of borrowed words in which a shift in stress led to the loss of a syllable ([marẏja] › [mȧryja] › current [mȧrja], orthographic *Maria*) introduced a new alternation between zero and *i/y*, which appears mostly in derivation: *Rosja* 'Russia'/*rosyjski* 'Russian', but also *lekcja* (NOM SG)/*lekcyj* (GEN PL) (more commonly: *lekcji*).

3 Morphology

3.1 Nominal morphology

3.1.1 Nominal categories

The modern **number system** distinguishes singular and plural, with relics of the Old Polish dual preserved in the declension of *ręka* 'hand', *ucho* 'ear', *oko* 'eye' and *dwa* '2'. A few dialects preserve dual forms with dual meaning (mostly in conjugation); much more common are remnants of dual endings with plural meaning.

Polish has preserved the full inherited **case system**, including the vocative, but there is a growing tendency to use the nominative instead of the vocative for personal names. The vocative is consistently used with titles and with personal names when they are used as part of a vocative phrase (*panie Janku* 'Janek (less familiar than first name alone)', *kochana Basiu* 'dear Basia').

The nominal **gender system** distinguishes as its primary categories masculine, feminine and neuter, with masculine nouns further divided on the basis of two semantically based categories into animate/inanimate and personal/non-personal. The basic three-way distinction is manifested primarily through syntactic means (agreement and anaphora), although particular declensional paradigms are associated with each gender. Animacy is manifested both paradigmatically and syntactically. The accusative singular of animate masculine nouns belonging to the 'typically masculine' paradigm is the same as the genitive. This is seconded by agreeing adjectives; this syncretism by agreement is the only manifestation of animacy for masculine nouns with nominative in -*a* (*znam tego psychiatrę.* 'I know that psychiatrist'). Animacy is relevant only in the singular, and the distinction of (masculine) personal and non-personal nouns is relevant only in the plural, where it has both syntactic (agreement, anaphora) and paradigmatic manifestations (accusative/genitive syncretism, special nominative plural endings). (Feminine and neuter nouns are grammatically non-personal.) Adjectives and third-person pronouns distinguish masculine, feminine and neuter paradigms in the singular and personal versus non-personal paradigms in the plural.

Although animacy is semantically based, there are several classes of semantically inanimate nouns (including units of money, names of dances and sports, brand names of cigarettes and automobiles) and some individual nouns that show the accusative/genitive syncretism in the singular (*grać w tenisa* 'play tennis', *kupić fiata* 'buy a Fiat', *zapalić giewonta* 'light up a Giewont'). This is a growing category; any masculine count noun with genitive singular in *a* is a potential member.

Within the class of masculine-personal nouns there are some pejorative terms (*łobuz* 'scoundrel', *cham* 'boor') that normally have non-personal endings and agreement but maintain accusative/genitive syncretism in the plural. Mixed agreement is also possible, with verbs and anaphoric pronouns showing personal forms but the noun itself and modifying determiners or adjectives showing non-personal forms:

Te łajdaki nie chcieli włączyć klimatyzacji.
Those good-for-nothings didn't want to turn the air conditioner on.

Most personal nouns can be 'depersonalized' for emotional effect, usually pejorative (*te inżyniery* 'those (lousy) engineers'), but occasionally positive (*te Warszawiaki* 'those (great) Warsaw guys').

Polish also has two types of common-gender nouns. The traditional type (*gaduła* 'chatterbox') takes agreement according to the sex of the person referred to (although emotionally marked feminine agreement is possible when the person is male). A newer type includes traditionally masculine nouns referring to professions (*profesor*). They can (but need not) show feminine agreement when referring to a woman. For the newer type referential agreement is more common for verbal forms and anaphoric pronouns, less common with adjectives. Nouns of this class become indeclinable when referring to women, regardless of agreement patterns.

Aside from *jeden* 'one', which displays adjective-like declension and agreement, and its compounds, which are indeclinable, numerals all distinguish masculine-personal and non-masculine-personal forms (*dziesięciu/ dziesięć* '10'). The numeral '2' and its compounds make more distinctions: *dwaj* or *dwóch* (M PERS), *dwie* (F), *dwa* (N and M NON-PERS).

3.1.2 Noun morphology

Masculine *o*-stems can be represented by *gród* 'medieval castle':

NOM	gród	grody
VOC	grodzie	grody
ACC	gród	grody
GEN	grodu	grodów
DAT	grodowi	grodom
INST	grodem	grodami
LOC	grodzie	grodach

The accusative singular of inanimate nouns is identical to the nominative; for animate nouns it is identical to the genitive. (But see section 3.1.1.) The genitive singular ending is *-a* for all animate nouns (except *wół* 'ox' and *bawół* 'buffalo', which take *-u*) and for many inanimate nouns. Most inanimate nouns take *-u*. There are some rules of thumb, for example Polish city names normally take *-a*, while abstract nouns and mass nouns take *-u*. The dative singular ending for almost all nouns is *-owi*; thirteen animate nouns (including *ojciec* 'father' and *pies* 'dog') take *-u*. The locative and vocative singular partially reflect the historical distinction of hard and soft stems: stems in hard consonants (except for velars) take the ending *-e*, which causes the column I alternation; stems in soft consonants and velars add *-u* (*mąż*, *mężu* 'husband'; *rok*, *roku* 'year'). A few nouns distinguish locative and vocative singular (*ojciec*, *ojcu* (LOC), *ojcze* (VOC)).

The nominative plural has the greatest variety of endings: *-e* for most nouns in soft consonants (*hotel*, *hotele*), masculine-personal nouns in *-anin* (*Rosjanin*, *Rosjanie* 'Russian' – note the loss of *-in* in such nouns throughout the plural) and a few non-native nouns in *-ans* (*awans*, *awanse* 'advance'); *-owie* for some masculine-personal nouns (*król*, *królowie* 'king'); *-a* for a few nouns (*cud*, *cuda* 'miracle'); and *-i/-y* for all the rest (*kruk*, *kruki*, 'raven'; *kot*, *koty* 'cat') with masculine-personal nouns replacing a hard consonant with the corresponding soft consonant from column I (*student*, *studenci*).

The accusative plural of masculine-personal nouns is identical to the genitive; for other nouns it is identical to the nominative. The genitive plural ending for nouns ending in hard consonants is *-ów*. Nouns ending in soft consonants take *-ów* or *-i/-y*, sometimes both (*król*, *królów*; *nauczyciel*, *nauczycieli* 'teacher'; *tłuszcz*, *tłuszczów/tłuszczy* 'fat'). Nouns in *-anin* drop *-in* and add *-ów* or zero (*Amerykanin*, *Amerykanów*;

Rosjanin, Rosjan – note hard stem-final *n* rather than *ń* in all plural forms but the nominative). The instrumental plural ending for almost all nouns, irrespective of declension class, is *-ami*; twelve nouns take *-mi* (*koń, końmi* 'horse').

This declension type also includes: (a) expressive personal names in *-ko* and *-cho* (*Jaśko, Zdzicho*); (b) some nouns that are semantically and syntactically pluralia tantum but follow the animate singular version of this paradigm (*państwo* 'couple', accusative (*tych*) *państwa*, but dative (*tym*) *państwu*, locative (*tych*) *państwu*); and (c) miscellaneous morphological and syntactic *pluralia tantum* (*nudy*, genitive *nudów* 'boredom').

Vowel–zero alternations in this paradigm and those below are mentioned in section 2.2 above; the *ę/ą* and *o/ó* alternations and the much less common *e/o* and *e/a* alternations, in section 2.3. One additional alternation involves labials: stems in a palatalized labial replace it with a plain labial in word-final position (*paw* (NOM), *pawia* (GEN) 'peacock') since palatalized labials occur only before vowels.

Neuter *o*-stems can be represented by *miasto* 'city':

NOM	miasto	miasta
VOC	miasto	miasta
ACC	miasto	miasta
GEN	miasta	miast
DAT	miastu	miastom
INST	miastem	miastami
LOC	mieście	miastach

The nominative, accusative and vocative singular partially reflect the historical distinction of hard and soft stems: stems in hard consonants end in *-o*; stems in soft consonants, in *-e* (*serce* 'heart'). Similarly in the locative singular: stems in hard consonants (except for velars) take the ending *-e*, which causes the column I alternation; stems in soft consonants and velars add *-u* (*serce, sercu; biurko, biurku* 'desk'). The genitive plural ending for nouns ending in hard consonants is zero. Nouns ending in soft consonants take zero or *-i/-y* (*serce, serc; narzędzie, narzędzi* 'tool'). The instrumental plural ending is *-ami* for all nouns but *dziecko* 'child' (*dziećmi*).

This paradigm also includes nouns in *-um* derived from Latin, which are indeclinable in the singular but follow the above paradigm (except for genitive plural in *-ów*) in the plural (*muzeum*, nominative plural *muzea*, genitive plural *muzeów*). Some *pluralia tantum* have the same *-ów* genitive (*cracoviana, cracovianów*); others have a zero ending (*usta, ust* 'mouth'). The two nouns *oko* 'eye' and *ucho* 'ear' have preserved their dual stems and some dual endings in their plural paradigm (nominative/accusative *oczy, uszy*; genitive *oczu, uszu*; instrumental *oczyma, uszyma* (beside instrumental *oczami* and more common *uszami*)). Nouns of the types *jagnię* 'lamb' and *imię* 'name' follow the paradigm above but have alternating stems (*jagnięć-, imień-* in oblique cases in the singular and *jagnięt-, imion-* in all cases in the plural).

   Feminine *a*-stems can be represented by *żona* 'wife':

NOM	żona	żony
VOC	żono	żony
ACC	żonę	żony
GEN	żony	żon
DAT	żonie	żonom
INST	żoną	żonami
LOC	żonie	żonach

   The dative and locative singular partially reflect the historical distinction of hard and soft stems: stems in hard consonants (including velars) take the ending *-e*, which causes the column I alternation; stems in soft consonants add *-i/-y* (*dusza, duszy* 'soul'). The vocative singular ending is *-o* for all nouns except hypocoristics with stem ending in a palatal, which take *-u* (*Kasia, Kasiu*) or (optionally for bisyllabic stems) zero (*mamusia, mamuś/ mamusiu* 'mum').

   The nominative plural ending for stems in hard consonants is *-i/-y*; for stems in soft consonants it is *e* (*dusze*). The accusative plural is identical to the nominative plural for both types of stems. The genitive plural ending for stems in hard consonants is zero; for stems in soft consonants it is *-i/-y* (*rzeźnia, rzeźni* 'slaughterhouse') or zero (*ciocia, cioć*) or both (*kawiarnia, kawiarni/kawiarń* 'cafe'); the ending *-i/-y* is expanding and zero is often felt to be archaic or bookish.

   The locative plural for almost all nouns is *-ach*. Three *pluralia tantum* – usually assigned along with some others to this paradigm because of their zero ending in the genitive plural – take *-ech* (*Niemcy, Niemczech* 'Germany').

   In addition to the vowel alternations mentioned previously, there is also a *ń/n* alternation in a few nouns that have optional zero-ending forms in the genitive plural (*suknia, sukien/sukni* 'dress').

   Masculine *a*-stems, which designate (at least potentially) human males, are declined like feminine *a*-stems, except that the nominative plural shows column I alternations (*poeta, poeci* 'poet') or, for family names and some common nouns, the ending *-owie*. Some stems in soft consonants, like the corresponding feminines, taking the ending *-e* (*cieśla, cieśle* 'carpenter'). The type is productive because of the productivity of suffixes like *-ista* (*baasista* 'member of the Arabic Ba'ath party'). Polish family names in *-o* (*Fredro*) belong to this class, although in contemporary practice they are often not declined.

A special subclass consists of pejorative terms like *oferma* 'schlemiel', which have accusative plural identical to genitive plural like all masculine-personal nouns but have non-personal agreement and nominative plural forms (*te ofermy*). They also behave like feminine *a*-stems when referring to women and can do so when referring to men.

Feminine *ja*-stems with nominative singular in *-i* can be represented by *bogini* 'goddess':

NOM	bogini	boginie
VOC	bogini	boginie
ACC	boginię	boginie
GEN	bogini	bogiń
DAT	bogini	boginiom
INST	boginią	boginiami
LOC	bogini	boginiach

Polish has no cognate for OCS *rabynji*. The most common word declined according to this paradigm, *pani* 'you; Ms; woman', has the anomalous accusative singular *panią*.

Feminine *i*-stems can be represented by *kość* 'bone':

NOM	kość	kości
VOC	kości	kości
ACC	kość	kości
GEN	kości	kości
DAT	kości	kościom
INST	kością	kośćmi (versus regular *nocami* 'nights')
LOC	kości	kościach

The only variations in this paradigm involve the nominative plural, where most nouns (except for those in *-ość*) take the ending *-e* (*noc, noce* 'night'), and the instrumental plural, where a few nouns replace the regular ending *-ami* with *-mi*. *Pluralia tantum* in this declension class include *drzwi* 'door' and *dzieci* 'children' (the plural of the otherwise regular neuter *dziecko*). A few stems in soft labials end in a plain labial in the nominative/accusative singular (*brew*, genitive *brwi* 'eyebrow').

As can be seen from the above paradigms, Polish masculine nouns are found in the declensions corresponding to those of the historical *o-*, *jo-*, *a-* and *ja*-stems. Feminine nouns are found in the declensions corresponding to those of the historical *a-*, *ja-* (with nominative singular in *-a* or *-i*) and *i*-stems. Neuter nouns are found in those corresponding to *o-* and *jo*-stems.

Nouns representing the Old Church Slavonic minor declension types have joined major types. Masculine *i*-stems and consonant-stems have become *o*-stems (*gość* 'guest', *kamy* › *kamień* 'stone'), as have *u*-stems (*syn* 'son'), which contributed endings to that declension (genitive singular -*u*, dative singular -*owi*, locative singular -*u*, nominative plural -*owie*, genitive plural -*ów*). Feminine consonant-stems have become *a*- or *i*-stems (*mati* › *mać* › *matka* 'mother', *kry* › *krew*, genitive *krwi* 'blood'). Neuter consonant-stems have become *o*-stems, leaving relics, however, in the form of the two types with nominative singular -*ę* and in derivation (*ciało* 'body' versus *cielesny* 'bodily').

3.1.3   Pronominal morphology

The **personal and reflexive/reciprocal pronouns** have the paradigms shown in table 12.3. Where more than one form is listed, the forms beginning with *n*- are used only after prepositions; the bisyllabic forms are the orthotonic variants (used only for contrast, emphasis and so forth); and the monosyllabic forms are the enclitic variants (used most frequently). The first person singular accusative/genitive *mię* is rare, being replaced by *mnie* even in enclitic use; the distinction between dative *mi* and *mnie* seems also to be breaking down, with both enclitic use of *mnie* and orthotonic use of *mi* being reported. The reflexive *se* is common in speech but is non-normative. The enclitic *się* is multifunctional; only rarely is it used in literal reflexive meaning, while its reciprocal meaning is less rare (see sections 3.2.1, 3.3.3 and 4.8).

The pronouns of non-familiar address follow noun paradigms: *pan*, plural *panowie* (to a man/men); *pani*, plural *panie* (to a woman/women); *państwo* (to a mixed group).

The **demonstrative** *tŭ › *ten* 'this, that' has joined the adjectival declension as one member of a small closed subset that includes some Proto-Slavonic pronominals as well as other elements. Its paradigm is as follows:

	S			PL	
	M	N	F	M-PERS	NON-M-PERS
NOM	ten	to	ta	ci	te
ACC	ten/tego	to	tę	tych	te
GEN	tego	tego	tej	tych	tych
DAT	temu	temu	tej	tym	tym
INST	tym	tym	tą	tymi	tymi
LOC	tym	tym	tej	tych	tych

In the masculine accusative singular inanimate nouns take *ten* and animate, *tego*. The subset of adjectives represented by *ten* is characterized by a zero ending in the masculine nominative singular: *tamten* and *ów* 'that', *sam* 'alone', *jeden* 'one', *niejeden* 'more than one', *wszystek* 'all' (in singular usually replaced by *cały* 'whole'), *pewien* 'a certain', *żaden* 'not a single', and the possessives *mój* 'my', *twój* 'your (SG)', *nasz* 'our', *wasz* 'your (PL)', *swój* (REFL), *czyj* 'whose' and *niczyj* 'no-one's'. The first six

Table 12.3 Personal and reflexive/reciprocal pronouns

	ja 'I'	ty 'you (SG)'	on 'he, it'	ono 'it'	ona 'she, it'
NOM	ja 'I'	ty 'you (SG)'	on 'he, it'	ono 'it'	ona 'she, it'
ACC	(mię)/mnie	cię/ciebie	go/jego/niego	je/nie	ją/nią
GEN	(mię)/mnie	cię/ciebie	go/jego/niego	go/jego/niego	jej/niej
DAT	mi/mnie	ci/tobie	mu/jemu/niemu	mu/jemu/niemu	jej/niej
INST	mną	tobą	nim	nim	nią
LOC	mnie	tobie	nim	nim	niej

	my 'we'	wy 'you (PL)'	oni 'they (M-PERS)'	one 'they (NON-M-PERS)'	(REFL)
NOM	my 'we'	wy 'you (PL)'	oni 'they (M-PERS)'	one 'they (NON-M-PERS)'	
ACC	nas	was	ich/nich	je/nie	się/siebie
GEN	nas	was	ich/nich	ich/nich	się/siebie
DAT	nam	wam	im/nim	im/nim	(se)/sobie
INST	nami	wami	nimi	nimi	sobą
LOC	nas	was	nich	nich	sobie

listed also have the ending -*o* for neuter nominative/accusative singular, while the rest have the usual adjectival ending -*e* (a remnant of the historical difference between hard- and soft-stem pronouns (OCS *to* versus *se*); see also section 3.1.4). Feminine accusative singular *tę* is anomalous; all other adjectives (including *tamten* and even *ten* in spoken Polish) have the normal adjectival ending -*ą*. The three possessives *mój*, *twój* and *swój*, which replace *ó* with *o* in all forms with endings, also have (bookish) shortened forms without the syllable -*oj*- in all cases but the nominative singular and masculine-personal nominative plural (*mej* (F LOC SG), *mych* (GEN PL)).

Three items from this subset also function syntactically as pronouns: *to* 'this, that' (with the neuter singular paradigm of *ten*), *wszystko* 'everything' (with the neuter singular paradigm of *wszystek*) and *wszyscy* 'everyone' (with the masculine-personal plural paradigm of *wszystek*).

The **interrogative and negative pronouns** *kto* 'who', *nikt* 'no-one', *co* 'what' and *nic* 'nothing' deviate from the adjectival declension in their non-oblique forms and in the preservation by *kto* and *nikt* of old hard-stem genitive and dative endings:

NOM	kto	nikt	co	nic
ACC	kogo	nikogo	co	nic
GEN	kogo	nikogo	czego	niczego/nic
DAT	komu	nikomu	czemu	niczemu
INST	kim	nikim	czym	niczym
LOC	kim	nikim	czym	niczym

The traditional use of *nic* as genitive of negation with verbs that govern the accusative versus *niczego* with verbs that govern the genitive has broken down and *niczego* is now often used in place of *nic*.

Other surviving Proto-Slavonic pronouns have simply become adjectives: *taki* 'such a', *inny* 'other', *cudzy* 'someone else's', *każdy* 'each'; *wszelki* 'all kinds of'.

Polish has three sets of **indefinite pronouns**. Adding -*ś* to an interrogative pronoun or other interrogative gives the meaning of lack of identification (through the speaker's ignorance or choice): *ktoś* 'someone', *gdzieś* 'somewhere'. Adding -*kolwiek*, *bądź* or -*kolwiek bądź* indicates that the speaker is indifferent – any X will do: *ktokolwiek* 'anyone at all', *gdzie bądź* 'anywhere at all'. Preposing *byle* or *lada* gives a meaning like the previous one but with a negative emotional connotation: *byle kto* 'any old person', *lada gdzie* 'in any old place'. (*Lada* is also used with time expressions: *lada chwila* 'any second now'.)

3.1.4 Adjectival morphology

Because of the contractions that took place in West Slavonic and the subsequent loss of length in Polish, reflexes of **long and short adjectival forms** are not always distinct in the modern language, for example feminine nominative singular *nowa* 'new' could be from either. Identifiable short forms were already rare in Old Polish and exist only as relics in the contemporary language. Masculine nominative singular forms are preserved in a few predicatives that have no corresponding long forms (*rad* 'glad', *wart* 'worth'); in some that alternate with more common long forms (*ciekaw* 'curious, inquisitive', *pewien* 'certain, convinced', and, as attributive with no long form, 'a certain'); and in some that are archaic or stylistically limited variants of long forms (*zdrów* 'healthy', *świadom* 'aware'). The two forms *winien* 'owe' and *powinien* 'ought' are part of verb-like paradigms: *winienem* or *jestem winien* 'I owe', *powinienem* 'I ought to', *powienien byłem* 'I should have' and so forth.

Neuter nominative singular forms are preserved as impersonal predicates: *warto* 'it's worth ...', *pełno* 'there are lots of ...' Relics of oblique cases can be found in adverbials: *po polsku* 'in Polish', *z lekka* 'slightly'. The two major adverb formations are also based on neuter short forms: *cicho* 'quietly', *źle* 'badly'. Many of these can be used as impersonal predicates: *zimno* 'it's cold'.

Polish comparatives and participles follow normal adjectival paradigms.

The historical distinction of **hard- and soft-stem adjectives** has been neutralized. The differences between the paradigms of *nowy* 'new' and *tani* 'cheap' involve only the allophonic (and orthographic) alternation of *y* and *i*:

	S		PL	
M	N	F	M-PERS	NON-M-PERS
NOM nowy/tani	nowe/tanie	nowa/tania	nowi/tani	nowe/tanie
ACC = NOM/GEN	nowe/tanie	nową/tanią	nowych/tanich	nowe/tanie
GEN	nowego/taniego	nowej/taniej	nowych/tanich	
DAT	nowemu/taniemu	nowej/taniej	nowym/tanim	
INST	nowym/tanim	nową/tanią	nowymi/tanimi	
LOC	nowym/tanim	nowej/taniej	nowych/tanich	

Stems in *k* and *g* have the fronted velar before endings beginning with *i* or *e* (*krótki* (M NOM SG), *krótkiego* (GEN) and so on 'short').

The masculine-personal nominative plural is characterized by the column I alternation; by analogy *sz/ś*, *ch/ś*, and – in one word – *ż/ź* also occur (see section 2.3). This may be accompanied by the *o/e* alternation (*wesoły, weseli* 'merry', but *zielony, zieloni* 'green'); it is regular in passive participles, which follow the adjectival paradigm (*gryziony, gryzieni* 'bitten').

Comparative forms of adjective are built with the suffix -(*ej*)*szy* or analytically with *bardziej*. The superlative is formed by adding the prefix *naj-* to either kind of comparative: *nowszy/najnowszy* 'newer/newest', *smutniejszy/najsmutniejszy* 'sadder/saddest', *bardziej chory/najbardziej chory* 'sicker/sickest'. The Analytic comparatives can be formed in principle from any adjective, but are normal with deverbal adjectives (*interesujący* 'interesting', *opalony* 'suntanned'), relational adjectives used qualitatively (*żelazny* 'iron(clad), firm'), and some others. The suffix *-szy* is normally used with stems in a single consonant (*nowy, nowszy*) or with the suffixes *-k-, -ek-, -ok-*, which drop in the comparative (*słodki, słodszy* 'sweet'); otherwise *-ejszy* is normally used (but note *prosty, protszy* 'simple; *twardy, twardszy* 'hard'). For some adjectives both forms exist (*czysty, czystszy/czyściejszy* 'clean'). The suffix *-ejszy* causes column II alternations; *-szy* causes only *g/ż, ł/l,* and *n/ń* plus potential vowel alternations (*wesoły, weselszy*). There are also isolated alternations (*lekki, lżejszy* 'light') and suppletive comparatives (*dobry, lepszy* 'good').

Analytic comparatives and superlatives of inferiority are formed with (*naj*)*mniej*: *mniej/najmniej zdolny* 'less/least talented'.

Those adjectives from which **adverbs** can be derived form them with the suffixes *-e* or *-o*. The suffix *-o* occurs with stems in soft consonants, with most unsuffixed stems, with stems in velars and with stems in certain suffixes (*-aty, -owaty, -owy*). The suffix *-e* is added to stems in *-ny* (whether a suffix or part of one), *-ły, -liwy*. It causes column I alternations. Variants in *-o* and *-e* sometimes coexist, often with different functions: *smutno* used as an impersonal predicate (*smutno mi* (DAT) 'I'm sad') versus *smutnie* as a verb modifier (*smutnie śpiewasz* 'you're singing sadly').

Some adjectives have related 'phraseological' adverbs consisting of a preposition plus the appropriate case form, often (historically speaking) of the short declension (*po staremu* 'in the old way', *z angielska* 'with an English accent').

Adverb comparatives and superlatives are formed analytically with (*naj*)*bardziej* or synthetically with the suffix *-ej* (and the prefix *naj-* for the superlative). The suffix causes column II alternations and causes the suffixes *-k-, -ek-* and *-ok-* to drop: *łatwo, łatwiej* 'easily'; *rzadko, rzadziej* 'rarely'. There are numerous irregular comparatives (*krótko, krócej* 'briefly') and some suppletive forms (*dobrze, lepiej* 'well').

In **comparative constructions**, with adjectives or adverbs, the terms of comparison can be joined by *niż* 'than':

Janek jest milszy niż Piotr.
'Janek is nicer than Piotr.'
Piotr pływa lepiej niż Janek.
'Piotr swims better than Janek.'

Such sentences, however, are more bookish than their equivalents with *od* plus genitive:

Janek jest milszy od Piotra.
Piotr pływa lepiej od Janka.

The construction with *od* is possible only when (a) the terms of comparison
are noun phrases and (b) the first term is either the grammatical subject of
the sentence or the logical subject of the comparative. Thus *niż* cannot be
replaced with *od* in

Bardziej lubię czytać niż rozmawiać.
'I like to read more than to talk.'
Basia jest lepszą tancerką niż śpiewaczką.
'Basia is a better dancer than a singer.'

In the former the terms of comparison are infinitives, while in the latter the
terms of comparison are *dancer* and *singer*, but *better* is predicated of
Basia (as a dancer). In the following sentence the terms of comparison are
city and *Cracow*, with *smaller* predicated of *city*:

Mieszkałem w mieście mniejszym od Krakowa.
'I lived in a city smaller than Cracow.'

The *niż* that alternates with *od* takes the nominative, while non-alternating
niż occurs in various syntactic contexts.

Superlative constructions use the preposition *z* or, less commonly,
spośród to specify the universe of discourse: *najpiękniejsza ze/spośród
wszystkich płyt gramofonowych* 'the most beautiful of all gramophone
records'. Both superlative and comparative forms can also be used absolutely: *bez większego powodzenia* 'without much success', *najwyższy czas*
'(it's) high time'. In such use the comparative form can refer to a point on
the scale between those occupied by the positive form and its antonym.
Starsza kobieta 'an older woman' is younger than *stara kobieta* 'old
woman' but older than *młoda kobieta* 'young woman'.

3.1.5 Numeral morphology

In addition to ordinal numerals, which follow the standard adjectival
paradigm, Polish has cardinal and collective numerals as well as some
miscellaneous types. The basic forms of the cardinal and ordinal numbers
are given in table 12.4. (see section 4.10 for the syntax of numerals).

The cardinal numeral *jeden* 'one' is declined like an adjective and shows
adjective-like agreement. When used as the last element of a compound
numeral, however, it becomes an invariable form which does not agree with
the noun in gender or case. The other cardinal numerals distinguish forms
for masculine personal and non-masculine personal in the nominative and
accusative. Only *dwa* '2' has a separate feminine form, *dwie*. The numerals
'2'–'4' have full paradigms:

Table 12.4   Polish numerals

	Cardinal numerals	Ordinal numerals
1	jeden/jedna/jedno	pierwszy
2	dwa/dwie	drugi
3	trzy	trzeci
4	cztery	czwarty
5	pięć	piąty
6	sześć	szósty
7	siedem	siódmy
8	osiem	ósmy
9	dziewięć	dziewiąty
10	dziesięć	dziesiąty
11	jedenaście	jedenasty
12	dwanaście	dwunasty
13	trzynaście	trzynasty
14	czternaście	czternasty
15	piętnaście	piętnasty
16	szesnaście	szesnasty
17	siedemnaście	siedemnasty
18	osiemnaście	osiemnasty
19	dziewiętnaście	dziewiętnasty
20	dwadzieścia	dwudziesty
21	dwadzieścia jeden	dwudziesty pierwszy
22	dwadzieścia dwa/dwie	dwudziesty drugi
23	dwadzieścia trzy	dwudziesty trzeci
30	trzydzieści	trzydziesty
40	czterdzieści	czterdziesty
50	pięćdziesiąt	pięćdziesiąty
60	sześćdziesiąt	sześćdziesiąty
70	siedemdziesiąt	siedemdziesiąty
80	osiemdziesiąt	osiemdziesiąty
90	dziewięćdziesiąt	dziewięćdziesiąty
100	sto	setny
200	dwieście	dwusetny (dwóchsetny)
300	trzysta	trzechsetny
400	czterysta	czterechsetny
500	pięćset	pięćsetny
600	sześćset	sześćsetny
700	siedemset	siedemsetny
800	osiemset	osiemsetny
900	dziewięćset	dziewięćsetny
1,000	tysiąc	tysięczny
2,000	dwa tysiące	dwutysięczny
5,000	pięć tysięcy	pięciotysięczny
10,000	dziesięć tysięcy	dziesięciotysięczny
100,000	sto tysięcy	stotysięczny
1,000,000	milion	milionowy
1,000,000,000	miliard	miliardowy
1,000,000,000,000	bilion	bilionowy

	M-PERS	N *and other* M	F
NOM	dwaj, dwu/dwóch	dwa	dwie
ACC	dwu/dwóch	dwa	dwie
GEN/LOC	dwu/dwóch	dwu/dwóch	dwu/dwóch
DAT	dwu/dwom	dwu/dwom	dwu/dwom
INST	dwoma	dwoma	dwiema/dwoma

	M-PERS	N, F *and other* M
NOM	trzej, trzech	trzy
ACC	trzech	trzy
GEN/LOC	trzech	trzech
DAT	trzem	trzem
INST	trzema	trzema

The forms *dwu* and *dwóch* are variants, as are *dwu* and *dwom.* Some speakers distinguish a feminine instrumental form *dwiema.* On the difference between *dwaj, trzej* and *dwu/dwóch, trzech* see section 4.10. The numeral *cztery* '4' is declined like *trzy* '3'. The two variants for 'both', *oba* and *obydwa*, are declined like *dwa*, except that their masculine-personal nominative forms are *obaj* and *obydwaj*, and *oba* has only the form *obu* in the genitive, dative and locative.

Numerals above '4' have a reduced paradigm, of which *pięć* 'five' is typical: *pięć* for non-masculine-personal nominative and accusative, *pięciu* for masculine-personal nominative and accusative and for all oblique cases of all genders, *pięcioma* as an alternative instrumental form for all genders. Some other miscellaneous numerals have a similar paradigm: *parę* 'a few' (*paru, paroma*); *kilka* 'several'; and so forth.

Collective numerals are rare except for '2'–'10' and *kilkoro* 'several'. (In compound numerals only the last element can be a collective numeral.) The numerals *dwoje* and *troje* follow one paradigm, *czworo* and all others follow another:

	dwoje	czworo
NOM	dwoje	czworo
ACC	dwoje	czworo
GEN	dwojga	czworga
DAT/LOC	dwojgu	czworgu
INST	dwojgiem	czworgiem

The numeral for 'one-and-a-half' has only two forms: *półtora* (M/N) and *półtorej* (F).

In contemporary Polish, especially in the spoken language, there are several tendencies towards simplification of the numeral system: (a) cardinal numerals are often used instead of collectives; (b) speakers sometimes do not decline numerals or – for compound numerals – decline only the last two digits; (c) cardinal numbers are sometimes used to replace ordinals, for example in dates.

One contrary tendency is that of using instrumental forms in *-oma* instead of the general oblique-case forms in *-u.*

3.2   Verbal morphology

3.2.1   Verbal categories

Most verbs distinguish all three persons in singular and plural in the present, past and future tenses and in the conditional mood. Gender is distinguished only in the past, the conditional and one variant of the imperfective future. Some verbs used without any subject (*wypada* 'it's appropriate') have only third person singular forms, and in general third person singular (neuter) is the default verb form if no nominative grammatical subject is present or understood.

Third-person forms are used in the meaning of second person in non-familiar address (with *pan, pani, państwo, panowie, panie* and occasionally with other words (*mamusia* 'mum')), although in non-familiar address to a group second person plural forms are also possible (*państwo wiedzą* or (*państwo*) *wiecie* 'you know').

Perfective verbs have finite forms for past and non-past. In independent clauses the latter normally express future, but can express modality as well or instead (*nie powiem* 'I can't say'). In subordinate clauses perfective verbs can express future, non-actual present

Kiedy pisklęta nauczą się (PRFV) fruwać, matka odlatuje.
'When the baby birds learn how to fly, the mother flies away.'

or modality

Koń ma cztery nogi, a potknie się (PRFV).
'A horse has four legs and can/will stumble.'

Imperfective verbs have finite forms for past, present and future. The future forms are analytic, consisting of a finite form of the future of *być* 'be' (the only verb that has synthetic forms for all three tenses) plus either the infinitive (*będę czytać* 'I will read') or a form of what was historically the *l*-participle (*będę czytał(a)*). Like perfective non-past forms, imperfective future forms can express modality rather than futurity:

Tacy ludzie będą pracowali przez całe życie.
'Such people will work their whole life long.'

The imperfective present and the perfective non-past follow the conjugations described in section 3.2.2. The past-tense forms of both aspects show traces of their origin as a compound tense consisting of auxiliary verb plus *l*-participle: the personal endings of the first and second person (singular and plural) are movable enclitics. The paradigm with unmoved endings is as follows:

	M	F	N	M-PERS	NON-M-PERS
1	byłem	byłam		byliśmy	byłyśmy
2	byłeś	byłaś		byliście	byłyście
3	był	była	było	byli	były

The enclitic appears in second position in

Gdzieście byli?
'Where have you (PL) been?'

The personal enclitics are obligatorily attached to any clause-initial word containing the element *by* and to the conjunction *byle*. Otherwise attachment is optional, being more likely with the plural forms, especially if the verb is polysyllabic.

Pluperfect forms are not mentioned in current grammatical descriptions of Polish, but they can be found in written texts as archaisms. They are formed by adding third-person forms of the past tense of *być* to normal past-tense forms (*pisałem był* 'I had been writing', *powiedzieliśmy byli* 'we had said').

Polish is more like Russian than like Slovak or Czech in its use of **perfective and imperfective verbs**, although it employs the perfective with greater freedom (in the context of repetition and in non-future meanings of non-past forms). Polish also lies between Russian and Czech and Slovak in its use of frequentatives (*jadać* 'eat (often)', *czytywać* 'read (often)'). Like Russian, Polish has few such verbs (about fourteen), but unlike Russian frequentatives, which are used only in the past tense, the Polish verbs have full paradigms. They are also used more often than their Russian counterparts, but are not regular formations as in Slovak and Czech.

Most unprefixed verbs are imperfective, although there are unprefixed perfectives (*paść* 'fall', *krzyknąć* 'yell'). Prefixed verbs with infinitives in *-ić/-yć, -eć, -nąć, -ować* and prefixed verbs formed from unsuffixed stems are normally perfective. Prefixed verbs with infinitives in *-iwać/-ywać* are normally imperfective. Prefixed verbs in *-ać* can be imperfective or perfective. Bi-aspectual verbs are mostly internationalisms (*abdykować* 'abdicate') but there are also some native examples (*kazać* 'order', *ranić* 'wound'). Concerning imperfective derivation see section 3.3.3.

The opposition of determinate and indeterminate **verbs of motion** is relatively well preserved in Polish. There are nine clear pairs: *iść/chodzić* 'go (on foot)'; *jechać/jeździć* 'go (not on foot)'; *biec/biegać* 'run'; *lecieć/*

latać 'fly'; *nieść/nosić* 'carry'; *wieźć/wozić* 'transport'; *płynąć/pływać* 'swim, float, sail'; *pełznąć/pełzać* 'crawl'; and *leźć/łazić* 'move slowly; climb'. Other pairs are mentioned in the literature, but are either rare in non-figurative use (*wieść/wodzić* 'lead', normally replaced in literal use by *prowadzić*, a simple imperfective) or participate only marginally in the opposition, having diverged semantically and/or stylistically.

The **imperative mood** expresses a command or request directed to a single addressee (*śpiewaj* 'sing!') or to a group (*śpiewajcie* '(you people) sing!'). The speaker may be included as a co-performer of the desired action (*śpiewajmy* 'let's sing'). Formal (non-familiar) address requires an analytic construction in place of the first two types above: *niech pan/pani śpiewa* in the singular and *niech państwo/panowie/panie śpiewają* in the plural. A similar analytic construction is used to express a command or request addressed to a third person or persons: *niech Basia śpiewa* 'have/ let Basia sing' and to express the 'deliberative' first person imperative: *niech zobaczę* 'let me see, why don't I see'.

Traces of an earlier synthetic third person imperative can be found in fixed phrases like *broń Boże*, 'God forbid'. Singular imperative forms are used as military commands even when addressed to a group (*spocznij* 'at ease' (literally 'rest')).

Polish traditionally distinguished 'present' and 'past' (or 'hypothetical' and 'counterfactual') **conditional** forms (*poszedłbym* 'I would go' versus *byłbym poszedł* 'I would have gone'). Speakers nowadays tend to employ the shorter form in both meanings.

The reflex of the Proto-Slavonic enclitic accusative reflexive pronoun (*się*) serves to form verbs and verbal constructions that are traditionally called '**reflexive**'. (The particle *się* can also occur with verbal nouns.) Many of the resulting meanings are shared with the other Slavonic languages, but one is peculiar to Polish (and to some Croatian and Slovene dialects): the use of *się* with a third person (neuter) verbal form to express a generalized human subject (like the French *on* or the German *man*) with the verb maintaining its normal (even accusative) government:

Tu się pije wódkę (ACC).
'One drinks vodka here.'

Like its French analogue, the Polish construction can imply the speaker or addressee as subject:

Miewało się różne przygody.
'One has (I have) had various adventures.'
Jak się spało?
'How did one (you) sleep?'

The subject position is also eliminated in a second construction, which

Polish shares only with Ukrainian. The construction is active (that is, a direct object or other governed case is possible) even though the verbal form is related to the passive participle and the most natural English translation is usually a passive construction:

Wypito całą butelkę (ACC).
'A whole bottle was drunk.'

Although not all verbs have this form, it occurs with many verbs that do not otherwise form a passive participle (for example, intransitive and 'reflexive' verbs). The construction has the value of past tense and the unspecified subject (singular or plural) is understood to be human and definite.

Passive constructions are formed with both perfective and imperfective transitive verbs by combining the passive participle with an auxiliary:

Dom był/jest/będzie budowany.
'The house was/is/will be (being) built.'
Dom został/zostanie zbudowany.
'The house was/will be built.'

The combination of a perfective passive participle with a present-tense auxiliary (*dom zostaje zbudowany*) occurs only in the historical or narrative present and in performative use:

Niniejszym zostaje pan zwolniony z pracy.
'You are herewith relieved of (your) job.'

The perfective participle is also used with all three tenses of *być* to form a passive of state:

Obraz był skradziony.
'The picture was stolen.' (that is, could not legally be sold)

A passive of state can also be formed from some verbs that do not form an ordinary passive (*jestem wypoczęty* 'I'm rested', from the intransitive verb *wypocząć*).

In ordinary passive sentences the agent can be expressed in a prepositional phrase (*przez* + accusative). No agent can be expressed, however, in the less common passive construction with *się*, which is limited to imperfective verbs with inanimate patients. Compare

Dom jest budowany przez spółdzielców.
'The building is being built by cooperative members.'
Dom się buduje pięć lat (*przez spółdzielców).
'The building has been under construction for five years.'

An instrumental phrase normally expresses means or material rather than agent. This is most common with an inanimate noun:

Przechodzień został potrącony samochodem.
'A pedestrian was hit by a car.' (that is, by someone using a car)

but is possible with animate or human nouns as well:

Wzgórza zostały obsadzone żołnierzami/przez żołnierzy.
'The hills were manned by soldiers.'

The version with *przez* presents the soldiers as agents; the instrumental version presents them as the instruments of someone's tactics (Saloni 1976: 101). Inanimate nouns can also get a more agentive interpretation when used with *przez* and a less agentive one when used in the instrumental:

Jego twórczość została przecięta przez śmierć/śmiercią.
'His output was cut short by death.'

All Polish verbs form an **infinitive** in *-ć* (or in *-c* if the stem ends in a velar or velar + *n*): *czytać* 'read', *robić* 'do', but *piec* (first person singular *piekę*) 'bake', *biec* (first person singular *biegnę*) 'run'; almost all form a verbal noun in *-nie* or *-cie* (see section 3.3.1).

Perfective verbs form a **verbal adverb** in *-wszy* or *-łszy* that expresses an action prior or subordinate to the action of the main verb. Imperfective verbs form a verbal adverb in *-ąc* that expresses an action simultaneous to the action of the main verb. (But see also section 4.5.1).

Imperfective verbs form a **verbal adjective** (participle) in *-ący* that expresses an action simultaneous to the action of the main verb. There is no regularly formed 'past' participle. Some perfective intransitive verbs, often expressing change of state, do form an adjective in *-ły* that can serve as a past participle (*zgniły* 'rotten'). Pseudo-passive participles from change-of-state verbs function in the same way (*wyschnięty* 'dried up').

Perfective and imperfective verbs form **passive participles** in *-ny* or *-ty*. (Traces of an older, distinct imperfective passive participle can be found in adjectives like *ruchomy* 'movable'.) Consonant alternations occur in two conjugations (section 3.2.2.): from column III in conjugation 1 (*zaprosić, zaproszony* 'invited') and from column II in conjugation 2 (*pryznieść, przyniesiony* 'brought'). Conjugation 2 verb stems in *t* and *d* unexpectedly introduce the soft consonant from column III into the masculine-personal participle form: *okradziony*, but *okradzeni* 'robbed'.

Colloquial Polish has long had a type of **perfect** involving forms of *mieć* 'have' and perfective passive participles. Unlike perfect constructions in other languages, the subject need not be identical to the agent. Compare

Mam już wszystkie egzaminy pozdawane.
'I've taken all my exams.' (subject identical to agent)
Ewa ma przyznane stypendium.
'Ewa has been awarded a scholarship' (subject not identical to agent)
Mam nos zatkany.
'My nose is stuffed up.' (no agent)

The subject is usually understood to be the beneficiary or, as in the last example, the anti-beneficiary of the action or state, but another beneficiary can be made explicit:

Pańskie podanie mamy rozpatrzone.
'We've reviewed your application.' (literally, 'We have your application reviewed')

There is now a tendency to generalize the neuter singular form of the participle, as in the following sentence, where the understood object is feminine accusative singular (*herbatę/kawę*):

Mam już posłodzone.
'I've already sweetened (my tea/coffee).'

3.2.2 Conjugation

The five Proto-Slavonic conjugation types have coalesced into four in Polish, distinguished on the basis of non-past forms. One of the four, continuing Proto-Slavonic themes in -*i*, has the theme vowel -*i*/-*y*. Two conjugations have theme vowel -*e*; the one with a consonant alternation in the non-past (first person singular and third person plural versus other forms) continues Proto-Slavonic themes in -*e*/-*o* and -*ne*, while the one with no consonant alternation continues themes in -*je* (except for the *děla*- and *umě*- types). The fourth conjugation, with theme vowel -*a* (or, for a few verbs, -*e*), is a West Slavonic innovation and continues Proto-Slavonic *je*- themes of the *děla*- and *umě*- types, as well as the athematic types (except for *by*-/*jes*-) that influenced them. The four contemporary conjugations can be represented by the following verbs (given in the infinitive and third person singular non-past, with first person singular added to show the presence or absence of consonant alternations):

1 modlić się 'pray'   modli się (modlę się)
   chodzić   'go'   chodzi (chodzę)
   woleć   'prefer'   woli (wolę) (not a reflex of *velě*-, which is not
                              continued in Polish)
   słyszeć   'hear'   słyszy (słyszę)
   spać   'sleep'   śpi (śpię)

2 nieść   'carry'   niesie (niosę)
   wieść   'lead'   wiedzie (wiodę)

pleść	'braid'	plecie (plotę) (compare Old Polish *czyść, cztę* 'read')
iść	'go'	idziesz (idę) (suppletive past: *szedł, szła* and so on)
jechać	'ride'	jedziesz (jadę) (irregular infinitive)

(Polish has no verbs of this type with roots in a labial; those that have survived have moved to other conjugations, for example *grzebać* (Old Polish *grześć*), *grzebie* 'dig'; *żyć, żyje* 'live'.)

| piec | 'bake' | piecze (piekę) (compare archaic *rzec, rzecze* › *rzeknie* 'say') |
| zacząć | 'begin' | zacznie (zacznę) |

(Note the regularization of the Proto-Slavonic athematic verb **jęti/ jĭme* 'take' in prefixed perfectives like *zająć, zajmie* 'occupy'. The only verb of this provenance that deviates from the pattern is *wziąć, weźmie* 'take'.)

umrzeć	'die'	umrze (umrę)
stać się	'become'	stanie się (stanę się)
ssać	'suck'	ssie (ssę)
nazwać	'name'	nazwie (nazwę) (compare archaic *zwać, zwie/ zowie* 'call')
brać	'take'	bierze (biorę)
dźwignąć	'lift'	dźwignie (dźwignę)
minąć	'pass'	minie (minę)

(A number of very common verbs shifted from the *nieść* type to the *dźwignąć* type, with or without change of infinitive, for example *kwitnąć, kwitnie* 'blossom'; *kraść, kradnie* 'steal'.)

3   czuć   'feel'   czuje (czuję)

(PSl. *pě-/poje-* › Polish *piać/pieje* 'crow' (compare *siać* below).)

| kryć | 'conceal' | kryje (kryję) |
| bić | 'beat' | bije (biję) |

(PSl. **bor-/borje-* › Old Polish and dialectal *bróć się* 'fight'. The parallel stems were reworked: **kol-/kolje-* › Old Polish *kłóć, kole* › *kłuć, kłuje* (but also *kole*) 'stab'; **por-/porje-* › Old Polish *próć, porze* › *pruć, pruje* 'rip'.)

mleć   'grind'   miele (mielę) (infinitive often *mielić*)

(The Proto-Slavonic type *děla-/dělaje-* shifted to a new conjugation, 4 below.)

niemieć	'grow mute'	niemieje (niemieję) (PSl. *umě-/uměje-* and its compounds shifted to a new conjugation, 4 below.)
kazać	'order'	każe (każę)
pisać	'write'	pisze (piszę)

(PSl. **jĭma-/jemlje* › Old Polish *jimać, jimie,* which then shifted to conjugation 4 (third person singular *jima*) and was later eliminated. Its role in deriving imperfectives from perfectives in *-jąć* was taken over by *-jmować.*)

	darować	'present'	daruje (daruję) (verbs in *-ywać* also belong here.)
	siać	'sow'	sieje (sieję) (‹ Old Polish *siejać*)
4	działać	'act'	działa (działam) (‹ PSl. *děla-/dělaje* by analogy to *dać* after contraction *aje › a*)
	dać	'give'	da (dam) (irregular third person plural *dadzą*)
	mieć	'have'	ma (mam) (irregular infinitive)
	umieć	'know how'	umie (umiem) (by analogy to *jeść, wiedzieć*)
	jeść	'eat'	je (jem) (irregular third person plural *jedzą*; compare *wiedzieć, wie* 'know' with irregular infinitive and third person plural *wiedzą*)

In addition to the four regular conjugations above Polish has both inherited and new irregular verbs. The most anomalous verb is *być* 'be' with its unique present: *jestem, jesteś, jest, jesteśmy, jesteście, są.* (Its future forms are regular according to conjugation 2: *będę, będziesz* and so on.) The present tense of *chcieć* 'want' (‹ PSl. **xotě-/xotje-*) would be regular in the third conjugation (*chcę, chcesz* and so on) if the infinitive were **chtać.* Other irregularities involve stem suppletion, as in *znaleźć, znajdzie* (*znajdę*) 'find'.

The four conjugations can be represented by the four paradigms in table 12.5, each for a verb with root ending in *s* (to show parallels and differences). All four verbs are imperfective. For the past verbal adverb, which is not formed from imperfective verbs, perfective forms are shown.

The infinitive stem for **conjugation 1** consists of the root plus *i/y* or *e.* The final root consonant appears as the soft consonant from column II (table 12.2, p. 694). The present shows an alternation of soft consonants from columns III (first person singular and third person plural) and II (all other forms). This represents a reworking of the third person plural to make it correspond to the first person singular (expected **prosią › proszą*), as it did in other conjugations.

Conjugation 2 is the most heterogeneous. The infinitive stem for unsuf-

Table 12.5   Polish conjugations

	1 'request'	2 'carry'	3 'write'	4 'hew'
Infinitive	prosić	nieść	pisać	ciosać
3 SG M PAST	prosił	niósł	pisał	ciosał
Past verbal adverb	(po)prosiwszy	(za)niósłszy	(na)pisawszy	(ob)ciosawszy
Passive participle	proszony	niesiony	pisany	ciosany
Present (non-past	proszę	niosę	piszę	ciosam
for perfectives)	prosisz	niesiesz	piszesz	ciosasz
	prosi	niesie	pisze	ciosa
	prosimy	niesiemy	piszemy	ciosamy
	prosicie	niesiecie	piszecie	ciosacie
	proszą	niosą	piszą	ciosają
Present verbal				
adverb	prosząc	niosąc	pisząc	ciosając
adjective	proszący	niosący	piszący	ciosający
Imperative	proś	nieś	pisz	ciosaj

fixed stems depends on the final root consonant: dentals give *ś* (spelled *ż* if from *z*), velars give *c* (which subsumes the infinitive ending), nasals give *ą* (except *stać się* ‹ *stanę się*), *r* gives *rze*. Some originally unsuffixed stems in dentals and velars have acquired the suffix *n* in the non-past, but their infinitive stem is formed as just specified (*padnę, paść* like *idę, iść*; *biegnę, biec* like *strzygę, strzyc*). Otherwise the infinitive stem consists of root plus *a* (four verbs: *ssać, zwać, brać, prać* 'launder') or root plus *ną*. The present shows an alternation of root consonant or *n* (first person singular, third person plural) versus the corresponding soft consonant from column II (all other forms).

The infinitive stem for **conjugation 3** consists of root plus *a, owa* or *ywa*. There are also some stems in which an original C*eja*- has contracted to C*a*- (*siać* ‹ *siejać*) or in which a root-final *j* has been truncated to form the infinitive stem (*czuj*- › *czuć*). Such stems keep *j* throughout the present (*sieję, siejesz* and so on) as do stems with the suffixes -*owa*-, -*ywa*-, -*iwa*-, which change to -*uj*- (*darować, daruje* – but note exceptional verbs like *przemyśliwać* 'think over', which has present-tense variants *przemyśliwa* and *przemyśliwuje*). Otherwise all forms of the present have a soft consonant from column III. (The verb *mleć* is an isolated phenomenon representing only itself and the even rarer *pleć* 'weed'.)

The infinitive stem for **conjugation 4** also consists of root plus *a*. The present stem consists of root plus *a(j)*, the *j* appearing only in the third person plural and the imperative.

All **past-tense** forms are built on the masculine third person singular. In conjugations 1, 3 and 4 the stem of this form is the same as the infinitive stem. This is also true in conjugation 2 for most verbs with vocalic infinitive stems. Conjugation 2 verbs with consonantal infinitive stems (including verbs like *piec* for stem *piek* plus the infinitive ending *-ć*) use the stem of the first person singular present (*piekę, piekł*). A suffixal *n* in the first person singular is dropped before the past ending *-ł* (*biec, biegnę, biegł*). Conjugation 2 verbs with roots in *-Cr* (infinitive stem *-Crze-*) have *-Carł* (*umrzeć, umrę, umarł*).

Conjugation 2 verbs with infinitive in *-nąć* follow one of two patterns in the past tense. Verbs of one class (mostly perfective even when unprefixed) keep the *-ną-* suffix throughout the past, changing it to *-nę-* in plural and feminine and neuter singular forms (*minąć, minął, minąłem, minęła, minęli*). Verbs of the other class (imperfective when unprefixed and generally denoting change of state) drop the suffix in all past-tense forms (*marznąć, marzł, marzła, marzli* 'freeze') or keep it as a variant in some or all forms (*brzydnąć, brzydł/brzydnął, brzydła, brzydli* 'grow ugly').

The *ą/ę* alternation in past forms like *minął* versus *minęła* is paralleled by the *ó/o* alternation in forms like *niósł* versus *niosła* (see section 2.3). The latter alternation, however, has been extended to first and second person masculine forms (*niosłem, niosłeś*), while such expansion of the *ą/ę* alternation is non-normative.

The singular **imperative** in conjugation 4 equals the third person plural non-past form minus the vocalic ending; in conjugations 1–3 it equals the third person singular form minus its stem vowel, except that *-ij/-yj* is added to prevent violations of syllable structure. This addition occurs with non-syllabic roots (*trzeć, trze, trzyj* 'rub'), with stems ending in an obstruent plus *n* (*biegnij*), and inconsistently with other clusters (with the zero form expanding: compare normative *zdejmij* from *zdjąć, zdejmie* 'take off' and frequent non-normative *zdejm*).

3.3   Derivational morphology

3.3.1   Major patterns of noun derivation
Nouns are derived primarily by suffixation (with explicit and zero suffixes, either of which may involve phonological changes), but prefixation, compounding and abbreviation also play a role.

Prefixation, especially with non-native prefixes, has become more common since the Second World War (*supergwiazda* 'superstar', *nadciśnienie* 'hypertension').

Compounding of various types has also increased in the same period. The most common type involves two noun stems (*oczodół* 'eye socket' ‹ *ocz-* 'eye' (plural stem), *dół* 'cavity'), but noun–verb and numeral–noun compounds are also common (*mrówkojad* 'anteater', *czworobok* 'rectangle'). Compounding may be combined with suffixation (*nosorożec* 'rhinoceros'). There are also increasing numbers of words whose first component is a non-native combining form (*telewidz* 'television viewer').

Other compounds are derived from prepositional phrases (*bezrobocie* 'unemployment' ‹ *bez roboty* 'without work').

Abbreviations include nouns formed by pronouncing the initial letters of a phrase (*PAN* ‹ *Polska Akademia Nauk* 'Polish Academy of Sciences') or by pronouncing the names of the initial letters (*rkm* or *erkaem* ‹ *ręczny karabin maszynowy* 'light machine-gun'). There are also abbreviation-based derivatives like *akowiec* 'member of the *Armia Krajowa* (Home Army)'.

Suffixation is used to derive nouns from nouns and from other parts of speech. The most productive types of derivation from nouns include the formation of diminutives (*kluczyk* ‹ *klucz* 'key'); of expressively marked terms (*psisko* or *psina* ‹ *pies* 'dog', *wóda* ‹ *wódka* 'vodka' – the last especially interesting because of the loss of a consonant but preservation of the phonological effect of that missing consonant (the *ó* for underlying *o* – see section 2.3); of feminine forms of titles and names of professions (*studentka* ‹ *student*, but also indeclinable feminine *profesor* ‹ declinable masculine *profesor*); of names of inhabitants of countries, cities and so forth (*Gabończyk* ‹ *Gabon*); of names of professions or jobs (*filmowiec* 'film-maker' ‹ *film*); of names of philosophies/ideologies and their adherents (*rasizm, rasista*).

Verbal nouns (nomina actionis) can be formed regularly from most Polish verbs (*czytanie* ‹ *czytać* 'read', *wyrzucenie* ‹ *wyrzucić* 'throw out'). In their primary meaning as names of states, activities or the like they preserve aspectual distinctions, can occur with *się*, and permit the expression of the subject and objects associated with the verb:

Pisanie przez Janka listu do żony trwało długo.
'John's writing of a letter to his wife took a long time.'

Many also have secondary meanings (*uzbrojenie* 'armament, armour', beside its primary meaning 'the arming of ...').

Other types of deverbal nouns show little regularity in choice of suffix or meaning(s) of the resulting noun. They do not occur with *się*, do not typically provide for the expression of subject or objects and do not consistently express aspect. For example *przebudowa* 'rebuilding' can correspond to *przebudowanie* (PRFV) or to *przebudowywanie* (IMPFV), but *budowa* 'construction' can correspond only to *budowanie* (IMPFV) and not to *zbudowanie* (PRFV). The most productive suffixes used to form the non-regular deverbal nouns are -∅ (*rozpad* 'disintegration') and -*acja* (*popularyzacja* 'popularization'). The suffix -*ka* is common in colloquial speech (*przesiadka* 'change (of trains or the like)'). Nouns are also derived from verbs to designate subjects (*badacz* 'investigator'), objects (*zguba* 'something lost'), products (*napis* 'inscription'), instruments (*obrabiarka* 'machine tool'), places (*pracownia* 'workshop') and so forth.

Nouns are derived from qualitative adjectives with great regularity by means of the suffix *-ość*. The primary meaning of such nouns is 'the state of being X' (*młodość* 'youth'); a common secondary meaning is 'something with the property X' (*piękność*, both 'beauty' and 'a beauty'). De-adjectival nouns of both meanings are also derived with other suffixes (*niechlujstwo* 'slovenliness' < *niechlujny*, *starzec* 'old man' < *stary*). Particularly common in colloquial Polish are nouns derived by condensation of an adjective–noun phrase (*zawodówka* 'trade school' < *szkoła zawodowa*, *pomidorowa* 'tomato soup' < *zupa pomidorowa*).

3.3.2   Major patterns of adjective derivation

Adjectives are derived from verbs by suffixation. Passive participles are regularly used as adjectives; often the imperfective participle is used where one might expect a perfective participle (*wędzona ryba* 'smoked fish'). Present verbal adjectives are also so used, sometimes in unpredictable meanings (*śpiący* 'sleepy' rather than 'sleeping'). Many intransitive verbs form adjectives with a resultative meaning based on their past-tense forms (*zbiegły* 'escaped') or use the form of an otherwise non-existent passive participle (*uśmiechnięty* 'smiling'). Productive suffixes in other formations include *-n-* (*podnośny* 'raisable'), *-liw-* (*łamliwy* 'breakable') and *-aln-*. The last of these regularly forms adjectives with the meaning 'X-able/-ible' (*jadalny* 'edible'). Negative deverbal adjectives can be created directly, for example *niezbadalny* 'unstudiable' does not necessarily imply the existence (other than potential) of ?*zbadalny*.

Adjectives are derived from nouns primarily by suffixation. The most productive suffixes include *-ow-* (*państwowy* 'state'); *-n-* and its compounds (*ręczny* 'manual' < *ręka* 'hand'); *-sk-* and its compounds (*rentgenowski* 'x-ray'); and *-owat-* (*gruszkowaty* 'pear-shaped'). Some formations with these suffixes involve simultaneous prefixation (*antyalkoholowy* 'anti-alcohol'). There are also prefixal–suffixal adjectives that imitate passive participles (*ugałęziony* 'ramified' – there is no verb **ugałęzić*). Zero suffixation (but with phonological change) is used to derive relational adjectives from the names of animals (*lisi* < *lis* 'fox').

Adjectives are derived from other adjectives both by prefixation (*nadgorliwy* 'over-eager') and by suffixation (*łysawy* 'baldish'). They can also be derived from adverbs (*tutejszy* 'local' < *tutaj* 'here') and from prepositional phrases (*przedrewolucyjny* 'pre-revolutionary'). Compound adjectives can combine the stem of an adjective, noun, quantifier or adverb with an adjective, noun or verb stem (*leworęczny* 'left-handed', *krótkotrwały* 'short-lived').

3.3.3   Major patterns of verb derivation

In contemporary Polish new **unprefixed verbs** can be formed from nouns by means of the suffixes *-owa-* and (less commonly) *-i-* and *-e(j)-*, and from adjectives by means of the suffix *-e(j)- (komputeryzować* 'computerize', *bezczelnieć* 'become arrogant'). Earlier formations made use of all verbal suffixes (see section 3.2.2). New prefixed verbs are derived from nouns and adjectives with the aid of the suffixes *-i-* and (less commonly) *-owa* (with derived imperfectives in *-aj-* and *-ywaj-*, respectively) and almost any verbal prefix (*przenaukowić* 'make too scholarly' ‹ *nauka* 'science').

Derivation of verbs from verbs can involve prefixation, suffixation, a combination of both or the addition or subtraction of *się*. Prefixation is used to create perfective counterparts to existing imperfective (*wydoktoryzować się* 'get one's doctorate') or bi-aspectual (*zaawansować* 'advance') verbs. The prefix *z-* is especially common in this function. It is not always clear whether a 'new' prefixed perfective is deverbal or denominal. Thus a supposed neologism of 1980 *zdekolonizować* 'decolonize' (PRFV) may have been derived from a non-attested *dekolonizować* 'decolonize' (IMPFV) or directly from the noun *dekolonizacja* 'decolonization', which was attested twenty years earlier. In the latter case the existence of perfective *zdekolonizować* implies a potential imperfective *dekolonizować*.

Prefixation is also used to create a wide variety of verbs (mostly perfective) with procedural (*Aktionsart*) meanings from old and new unprefixed verbs. Recent attestations include *pogłówkować* 'think something over a bit', *wypolitykować się* 'have one's fill of playing politics' (prefixation with addition of *się*). The prefixes can also carry more concrete meaning, as in *odrolować* 'taxi away (of an airplane)', *wyrejestrować* 'cancel the registration (of a car)' (with potential imperfectives in *-ywać*).

Suffixation is involved in the derivation of imperfectives, of semelfactives (*kichnąć* 'give a sneeze' ‹ *kichać* 'sneeze'), of frequentatives (*czytywać* 'read (repeatedly)' ‹ *czytać* 'read') and of some verbs of motion, but only the first two of these processes are still productive.

Imperfectives are derived by means of two main suffixes: *-aj-*, producing conjugation 4 verbs (see table 12.5, p. 718) from perfective verbs of conjugations 1 and 2 (*zaprosić/zapraszać* 'invite', *ostrzec/ostrzegać* 'warn'), and *-ywa-*, producing conjugation 3 verbs from perfective verbs of conjugations 3 and 4 (*zapisać/zapisywać* 'note', *wyciosać/wyciosywać* 'hew out'). A third suffix, *-waj-*, is used with most verbs with stems in *-j* (*nakryć, nakryje/nakrywać* (conjugation 4) 'cover', but *zabić, zabije/zabijać* 'kill'). The vowel and consonant alternations represented in the pair *zaprosić/ zapraszać* (as well as the vowel–zero alternations mentioned in section 2.2.2) are typical of derivation with *-aj-*. Imperfective derivation involves numerous other subregularities and irregularities.

The **'reflexive' particle** *się* has both clearly syntactic functions (see sections 3.2.1 and 4.8) and clearly derivational ones, the latter particularly in combination with prefixes, as in the recent *zdzwonić się* 'get in touch with one another by telephone' (‹ *dzwonić* 'call, telephone'). Other functions, such as that of making transitive verbs intransitive, could be treated as syntactic or derivational. Dropping *się* occasionally serves as a mechanism for deriving causative verbs: *wściekać* 'enrage' (‹ earlier *wściekać się* 'be/become enraged').

4   Syntax

4.1   Element order in declarative sentences

The unmarked order of the main constituents is Subject–Verb–Object, hence out of context the ambiguous sentence

Byt określa świadomość.

will more often be interpreted as 'existence determines consciousness' with *byt* read as nominative rather than accusative and *świadomość* read as accusative rather than nominative.

In context the principles of functional sentence perspective mandate theme followed by rheme in the unmarked case, with the inverse order being emphatic or otherwise emotionally marked. If the object is theme, or if there is no object and the subject and verb are both rhematic (for example, in discourse-initial position), the unmarked order is (Object)–Verb–Subject:

(Na przyjęciu spotkałem siostrę.) Basia przyprowadziła koleżankę.
'(At the party I met my sister.) Basia (my sister) had bought a friend.'
(Na przyjęciu spotkałem siostrę.) Basię przyprowadziła koleżanka.
'... Basia (my sister) had been brought by a friend.'

In the first example the theme is the subject *Basia*; in the second, the object *Basię*. If, however, both subject and object belong to the theme with the verb constituting the rheme, the order Subject–Verb–Object is common:

Sąd oczyścił go z tego zarzutu.
'The court cleared him of that accusation.'

An adverbial will occupy final position only if it constitutes the rheme:

Janek jedzie *jutro*.
'Janek is going *tomorrow*.'

If the adverbial constitutes the theme or is part of it, it will occupy initial position:

Dziś w Warszawie pada deszcz.
'Today in Warsaw is falling rain.' ('It's raining in Warsaw today.')

Most adverbials forming part of the rheme precede the verb:

Anna ładnie śpiewa.
'Anna sings nicely.'

but adverbials of means, of location and of direction normally follow the verb:

Basia jedzie samochodem do Poznania.
'Basia is going by car to Poznań.'

If a sentence contains both a direct object and a noun phrase in another case, the other phrase will normally follow the direct object, except for a dative phrase, which normally precedes:

Uczę Janka (ACC) angielskiego (GEN).
'I'm teaching Janek English.'
Piszę bratu (DAT) list (ACC).
'I'm writing a letter to my brother.'

Polish **enclitics** include the imperative enclitics (*-my, -cie*), which are affix-like in everything but their sandhi properties (see section 2.1); the particles *no* and *-że*; the verbal enclitics (the conditional particle *by* and the personal endings of the preterite *-(e)m, -(e)ś, -śmy, -ście*); and the atonic forms of the personal pronouns (including the 'reflexive' *się*).

The particles *no* (of entreaty) and *-że* (of impatience) are the most restricted in occurrence. They occupy second position following an imperative or its semantic equivalent:

Idźże do diabła!
'Go to the devil!'
Cicho no!
'Be quiet, now!'

The remaining enclitics can be divided as follows:

(I)   *by*
(II)   personal endings
(III)   dative pronouns
(IV)   *się*
(V)   accusative pronouns
(VI)   genitive pronouns
(VII)   instrumental pronouns

In a sentence enclitics generally follow the above order:

Nie chcę, żebyś (I + II) mi (III) ją (V) nim (VII) straszył.
'I don't want you to threaten her (on me) with him.'
Gdzieście (II) się (IV) go (VI) pozbyli?
'Where did you get rid of him?'

Besides their traditional position after the first stressed word or phrase in the clause, enclitics also occur after an element bearing sentence stress, or, more and more frequently, after the verb:

Ta kobieta mi przyniosła szczęście.
'That woman has brought me happiness.'
Ta kobieta *szczęście* mi przyniosła.
Ta kobieta przyniosła mi szczęście.

Pronominal enclitics (including *się*) can become proclitics (but not in sentence-initial position):

Cieszę się, że cię widzę.
'I'm glad to see you.'

Subject pronouns (first and second person in colloquial speech, third person in written style) are also used enclitically in post-verbal position, particularly when referring to someone other than the theme of the previous sentence:

Następnie wystąpił minister spraw zewnętrznych. Zaproponował on, żeby ...
'The next speaker was the foreign minister. He proposed that ...'

First- and second-person pronouns tend to precede other enclitics; third-person pronouns tend to follow them.

The non-familiar second-person pronouns normally occur as post-verbal or post-conjunction enclitics except when given contrastive stress or when serving to introduce or re-introduce a new theme:

Pan jest zmęczony. Powinien pan odpocząć.
'You're tired. You should rest.'
Ja nie jestem zmęczony, a pan jest.
'*I'm* not tired, but *you* are.'

Within the **noun phrase** the major question is the relative order of the adjective(s) and the head noun (Topolińska 1984: 367–83). The general ordering of pre-nominal elements (assuming non-emphatic, non-contrastive order) is fairly straightforward: (1) pronominal determiners (*ten* 'this/that'); followed by (2) numerals (cardinal and collective) and other quantifiers (*kilka* 'several'); followed by (3) 'modal' adjectives (*prawdopodobny* 'probable') and certain relational adjectives (possessives; ordinal numbers (including also adjectives like *ostatni* 'last'); certain temporal and spatial adjectives); followed by (4) qualitative adjectives; followed by (5) other relational adjectives (*te trzy moje ostatnie tutejsze nieprzyjemne wizyty*, literally: 'those three my last local unpleasant visits').

An adjective in group 5 can, however, occupy a post-nominal position. This is most likely to happen when the adjective–noun combination forms a particularly close collocation (often corresponding to a Germanic compound noun) and/or when there is more than one adjective from groups 4 and 5 modifying the noun: *włókno szklane* 'fibreglass' but *szklane drzwi* 'glass door'; *język polski* 'the Polish language, Polish' but *polski język literacki* 'literary Polish'. Qualitative adjectives can also be postposed when they lose their qualitative character by becoming terminologized: *panna młoda* 'the bride' (literally: 'young lady'). Conversely, a relational adjective used qualitatively is preposed: *attaché kulturalny* 'cultural attaché' versus *kulturalny attaché* 'cultured attaché'.

Groups 1 and 2 are normally represented by no more than one adjective each. Within group 3, possessives and ordinals (in that order) normally precede other adjectives. Ordering principles for adjectives within groups 4 and 5 have been proposed, but there is also the possibility of distinguishing constituent structure through ordering: *zakaźna* (*choroba tropikalna*) 'a tropical disease that is infectious' versus *tropikalna* (*choroba zakaźna*) 'an infectious disease from the tropics'.

Especially in written Polish a pronominal determiner (usually *ten*) may follow the noun when the phrase is used anaphorically:

Człowiek ten zawsze budził we mnie nieufność.
'That man always aroused distrust in me.'

4.2   Non-declarative sentence types

WH-questions are marked by the presence of an interrogative pronoun, adjective or adverb. Yes–no questions are marked by an initial *czy* 'is it the case that' or solely by intonation. Both kinds of questions (in neutral, non-emotional use) are marked by a rising intonation, but in WH questions it is preceded by a falling intonation, while in yes–no questions the initial intonation is high:

Która godzina?
'What time is it?'
Czy mogę zapalić?
'May I smoke (literally: 'light up')?

The fronting of a WH word does not affect the word order of remaining elements; the principles of functional sentence perspective still apply, thus:

Co Basia czyta? (neutral or contrastive stress on verb)
'What is Basia reading?'

versus

Co czyta Basia? (focus on Basia)
'What is *Basia* reading?'

An interrogative adjective often does not carry its noun along:

Jaki masz samochód?
'What kind of car do you have?'

versus

Jaką książkę czytasz?
'What kind/What book are you reading?'

(for the given verbs, *samochód* is 'more rhematic' than *książkę*).

Yes–no questions also preserve normal declarative word order, whether they are introduced by *czy* or not. The interrogative marker *czy* is also used to indicate alternatives:

Co wolisz, kawę czy herbatę?
'What do you prefer, coffee or tea?'
Nie wiem, czy iść czy zostać.
'I don't know whether to go or to stay.'

In response to a yes/no-question, *tak* 'yes' normally expresses agreement and *nie* 'no', disagreement, with the assertion questioned (Fisiak, Lipińska-Grzegorek and Zabrocki 1978: 193). Thus answers to a positive question are as in English:

–Czy Janek zdał egzamin?
'Did Janek pass the exam?'
–Tak, zdał. (Nie, nie zdał.)
'Yes, he did. (No, he didn't.)'

but answers to a negative question are not:

–Czy Janek nie zdał egzaminu?
'Didn't Janek pass the exam?'
–Nie, zdał. (Tak, nie zdał.)
(Literally) 'No, he did. (Yes, he didn't).'

Indirect questions are introduced by the same interrogative words as direct questions:

Nie wiem, czy/kiedy Janek przyjdzie.
'I don't know whether/when Janek will come.'

Commands are normally expressed by imperative forms (see section 3.2.1). Perfective imperatives occur most frequently with positive commands and imperfective imperatives, with negative ones, but imperfective imperatives are also used for positive commands when the focus is on process or repetition:

Jedz powoli!
'Eat slowly.'

and perfective imperatives can be used for negative commands when the focus is on avoiding the result:

Nie zgub tego klucza!
'Don't lose that key.'

Conditional forms can express an attenuated (normally positive) command:

Zadzwoniłbyś do niej.
'Why don't you call her?' (literally: 'you would call ...')

and infinitives – less commonly – can express a very categoric command (positive or negative):

Siedzieć! Nie ruszać się!
'Sit (there)! Don't move!'

An infinitive with *proszę* 'please' (literally: 'I request'), however, is a common substitute for an ordinary imperative, especially in non-familiar speech:

Proszę poczekać (for: Niech pan(i) poczeka).
'Please wait.'

(The imperative form is somewhat more polite.)
   The perfective present is used (a) in formulaic requests like:

Pani pozwoli, że się przedstawię.
'Permit me (literally: you will permit) to introduce myself.'

(b) in attenuated commands containing the modal *może*:

Może pan napisze parę słów.
'Perhaps you would (literally: will) write a few words.'

and (c) in stylistically marked, very categoric commands meant (and expected) to be carried out immediately:

Pan mi da paczkę papierosów!
'Give me (literally: you will give me) a package of cigarettes!'

4.3   Copular sentences

The main copulas are the verb *być* 'be' and the particle *to*. The verbal copula is used primarily to describe, while *to* is used primarily to identify and define. Thus

Ten wysoki blondyn jest pilotem.
'That tall blond man is a pilot.'
Ten wysoki blondyn to mój brat.
'That tall blond man is my brother.'
Morfologia to nauka o formach.
'Morphology is the study of forms.'

To may be combined with a form of *być* (normally third person, singular or plural) in the present tense and must be so combined in the past or the future. In identification sentences the verb follows *to*, while in definitions it precedes:

Te panie to są siostry.
'Those women are sisters.'
Morfologia jest to nauka o formach.

The *to* construction is not used with predicate adjectives. Predicate nouns or pronouns are in the nominative when used with *to* but in the instrumental when used with forms of *być*. In emotional speech the instrumental may be replaced by the nominative:

Jesteś idiota!
'You're an idiot!'

Predicate adjectives are normally in the nominative. They are in the instrumental, however, when *być* is in the form of a verbal adjective, adverb or noun:

Będąc jeszcze młodym, . . .
'While still (being) young, . . .'

in impersonal (nominativeless) clauses:

Gdy się jest młodym, . . .
'When one is young, . . .'

and potentially when *być* as an infinitive implies 'become':

Postanowił być oszczędnym.
'He decided to be frugal.'

Concerning short and long forms of adjectives (*zdrów/zdrowy*) see section 3.1.4.

Besides adjectives and nouns in the nominative or instrumental, other kinds of predicates that occur with the copula include genitive and prepositional phrases and, with an infinitive as subject, adverbs:

Posąg jest średnich rozmiarów/z brązu.
'The statue is of medium size/of bronze.'
Jeść lody w zimie jest niezdrowo.
'Eating (literally: to eat) ice cream in the winter is unhealthy.'

(Neuter forms – here *niezdrowe* – are possible for some adjectives.)

Other copulas include *bywać* 'be (from time to time)' and the verbs meaning 'become': *zostać* (PRFV)/ *zostawać* (IMPFV), *stać się/stawać się* and *zrobić się/robić się*. Zero as a copula is marked: it occurs in proverbs, slogans and so forth:

Starość nie radość (NOM).
'Old age is no pleasure.'
Przyjaźń przyjaźnią (INST), a interes interesem (INST).
'Friendship is one thing but business is another.' (literally: 'friendship is friendship ...')

4.4   Coordination and Comitativity

The main conjunctions used for **coordination** are *i* 'and', *a* 'and' (with an implication of logical connection between the conjoined elements), *albo* 'or' and *ale* 'but', as well as the negative conjunction *ani*: (*ani*) X *ani* Y 'neither X nor Y'. Clauses or smaller constituents can also be coordinated intonationally (in the meanings *i* or *a*) without a conjunction. The conjunctions *a* and *ale* are normally used in binary coordination, while *i*, *ani* and *albo* can conjoin more than two elements and can be repeated. A single *albo* is ambiguous as between the exclusive and inclusive readings of 'or'; multiple *albo* requires the exclusive reading. Similarly, X *i* Y can (but need not) mean 'first X and then Y', while *i* X, *i* Y tends to eliminate the sequential reading.

A differs from *i* in implying a logical connection (often contrast) between the conjuncts:

Janek śpiewa, a Ewa tańczy.
'Janek is singing and Ewa is dancing.'

The connection can simply be close association: the title *Niemcy a sprawa polska* 'Germany and the Polish question' announces the author's intention to treat the two topics in their interrelation.

The various conjunctions (including zero) can coordinate clauses, their constituents (noun phrases, verb phrases) or smaller elements (adverbials, prepositional phrases, adjectival and adverbial phrases, nouns, verbs).

Active and passive verbs can be conjoined:

Albo zostaniemy zatrudnieni na miejscu, albo nas poślą na inną budowę.
'Either we'll be hired on the spot or they'll send us to another construction site.'

Adjectives can be conjoined with simple adjectives or with adjectives modified by adverbs or even with extended participial modifiers:

Zawsze podziwiał sposób pakowania żony, typowo jego zdaniem {kobiecy}, a {polegający na tym, aby wszystko ... układać w różnych walizkach ...}.
(Misz 1981: 21)
'He always admired his wife's method of packing, (which was) in his opinion typically {feminine}, and {consisting in putting everything ... in various suitcases ...}.'

(In this rather literal translation the conjoined elements are marked by braces.) Post-nominal adjectives (in the predicate or in a reduced predication) can be conjoined with non-agreeing modifiers such as prepositional or genitive phrases:

Oni są złośliwi i bez serca.
'They are spiteful and heartless.' (literally: 'without a heart')

Different types of adjectives can be conjoined:

Odezwał się głos słaby, nie mój i drżący.
'A voice (that was) weak, not mine, and trembling spoke.'

The conjoining of a noun and an adjective is rare but possible: *wdowiec, ale bezdzietny* 'a widower but childless'.

Adverbials of different formal and semantic types can be conjoined:

Chodził elegancko, w meloniku i przy zegarku.
'He dressed (literally: walked around) elegantly, in a bowler, and with a (pocket) watch.'
Nagle a tuż przed sobą ...
'Suddenly and right in front of me ...'

Verb phrases can be conjoined without repeating a shared modal or anaphoric pronoun (unless a different case is required):

Powinnam ją (ACC) teraz ośmielić, ująć (∅) (ACC) jakoś, dać jej (DAT) zapomnieć dawnych uraz.
'I should encourage her now, win (her) over somehow, allow her to forget old resentments.'

Verbal agreement with conjoined noun phrases involves several variables. Agreement with respect to number depends on the conjunction, on the nature of the head nouns, and on the order of elements. With *albo* and its synonyms and negation (*ani ..., ani ...* 'neither ..., nor ...') the verb can be singular or plural; singular is more common if the verb precedes the subject.

Albo Janek, albo Basia przyjdzie (SG)/przyjdą (PL) po książkę.
'Either Janek or Basia will come for the book.'
Na obiad będzie (SG) albo ryba, albo kurczak.
'For dinner there will be either fish or chicken.'

With *i* and its synonyms the verb is normally plural, although it can be singular or plural with conjoined abstract nouns or when the verb precedes the subject:

Janek i Basia szli (PL) razem
'Janek i Basia were walking together.'
Nauka i technika ma (SG)/mają (PL) własne ministerstwo.
'Science and technology have their own ministry.'
Przy chorym czuwał (SG)/czuwali (PL) na zmianę lekarz i pielęgniarka.
'The doctor and the nurse took turns watching over the patient.'

The choice of a masculine-personal or non-masculine-personal verb form and/or predicate adjective is determined as follows, where X and Y designate the head nouns of the conjoined noun phrases:

1   If X or Y (or both) is masculine personal, the verb is normally masculine personal:

   Janek i Marysia przynieśli ciastka.
   'Janek and Marysia brought pastry.'

2   If X and Y are both masculine inanimate, or feminine, or neuter, the verb is non-masculine personal:

   Basia i Marysia przyniosły sałatę.
   'Basia and Marysia brought a salad.'

3   If X is masculine animate and Y is masculine or feminine animate or feminine personal, some speakers prefer masculine-personal agreement while others use non-masculine-personal forms:

   Pies i kot jedli/jadły w kuchni.
   'The dog and the cat were eating in the kitchen.'

Basia i pies bawili/bawiły się w ogrodzie.
'Basia and the dog were playing in the garden.'

Other combinations (including masculine personal plus inanimate) cause speakers difficulty; some choose masculine-personal forms, while others prefer to restructure the sentence. When one noun is plural or all are, the nearest one may influence the choice:

Panowie i psy szły/szli.
'The men and the dogs were walking.'

but only *szli* with the two nouns reversed.

When a noun or pronoun refers to a mixed group, neuter pronouns designate individuals of unspecified sex: *każde z rodziców* 'each of the parents', *jedno z was* 'one of you'.

When two or more adjectives specifying different types or instances of the noun that they modify are conjoined, the noun is normally singular but the verb and/or predicate adjective is plural (Topolińska 1984: 383):

Wczorajsza i dzisiejsza gazeta leżą na stole.
'Yesterday's and today's newspaper are on the table.'

Two nouns that are definite and human (or for some speakers, definite and animate) can be conjoined by the preposition *z* 'with'. In the resulting X *z* Y construction the *z* Y component can be subordinated to X, in which case it is movable, a verb will agree with X, and other syntactic properties show that X *z* Y is not a coordinated constituent:

Basia z Jankiem mieszka (SG) na Mokotowie.
'Basia and Janek live in Mokotów.'

The phrase *z Jankiem* 'with Janek' could occur after the verb or at the end of the sentence. Alternatively the X *z* Y construction can take plural agreement, in which case the construction is inseparable and it shows such properties of coordinated constituents as controlling reflexives:

Basia z Jankiem mieszkają (PL) na Mokotowie.
Basia z Jankiem kupili (M-PERS PL) sobie samochód.
'Basia and Janek bought themselves a car.'

A similar comitative construction is possible when X and/or Y are pronouns. One pronoun is subsumed in the verb, with the order of precedence being first person › second person › third person:

Pójdziemy z tobą (equals: ja/my + ty) do kina.
'You and I/we will go to the movies.'

Pójdą z Jankiem (equals: on/ona/oni/one + Janek) do kina.
'He/she/they and Janek will go to the movies.'

4.5   Subordination

Traditional taxonomies of subordinate clauses classify them in terms of their function as a constituent (or expansion of a constituent) of the main clause. Thus one distinguishes subordinate clauses functioning as subject or object noun phrases:

Dziwiło ją, skąd w tym prostym chłopie taka mądrość.
'(It) surprised her how there could be such wisdom in a simple peasant.'
Chcielibyście, aby już śnieg spadł?
'Would you like for snow to have fallen already?'

as modifiers of nouns, pronouns or adjective (relative clauses):

Zły to ptak, co własne gniazdo kala.
'It is an ill (literally: bad) bird that fouls its own nest.'

and as adverbials:

Niech idzie, dokąd chce.
'Let him/her go where he/she wants.'

An additional type functions as a 'sentential relative' and is in effect equivalent to a coordinate clause:

Powiedział mi szczerą prawdę, co mnie głęboko wzruszyło.
'He told me the plain truth, which (fact) moved me profoundly.'
Equivalent to: Powiedział ..., i to mnie ...
'He told me ..., and that (fact) moved me ...'

More detailed classifications distinguish subtypes in terms of their semantic functions, while formal taxonomies distinguish clauses subordinated by conjunctions; those subordinated by relative pronouns, adjectives or adverbs; and those without any segmental mark of subordination. The first two types are illustrated above; the third is exemplified by:

Lepiej wam na świecie niż mnie, macie choć dobre dzieci.
'Things are better for you in this world than for me (since) you at least have good children.'

Conditional clauses deserve special mention. They can contain verbs in the indicative or conditional mood and can combine with main clauses containing verbs in the indicative, conditional or imperative mood. The various possible combinations are distributed among four types as follows.

Type 1, which presents a statement of fact, combines indicative with indicative or with imperative:

Jeżeli się dowiem, to ci powiem.
'If I find out, I'll tell you.'
Jeżeli się dowiesz, to powiedz mi.
'If you find out, tell me.'

Type 2, which presents a statement of possibility, combines conditional with indicative, conditional or imperative:

Gdybym się dowiedział, to ci powiem/to bym ci powiedział.
'If I should find out, I'll tell you/I'd tell you.'
Gdybyś się dowiedział, to powiedz mi.
'If you should find out, tell me.'

Type 3, a counterfactual statement, uses conditional in both clauses:

Gdybym miał, to bym ci dał (ale nie mam).
'If I had (any), I'd give you (some) (but I don't).'
Gdyby ją zapytać, odpowiedziałaby ...
'If (you) were to ask her, she would answer ...'

In type 4, a much rarer combination of indicative (future) with conditional, the statement of fact is somewhat attenuated (in other words, if the condition obtains, the conclusion might):

Jeżeli dziś nie pójdziemy, to byśmy jutro poszli.
'If we don't (literally: won't) go today, then we could (literally: would) go
   tomorrow.'

Sentences expressing a condition can also be formed with neither a conditional conjunction nor *by*:

Łeb ci rozbiję, to będziesz cicho.
'I'll break your head; then you'll be quiet (If I ...).'

Clauses containing conditional forms occur as independent sentences:

Czy mógłbyś przyjść jutro o piątej?
'Could you come over tomorrow at five?'

and can be embedded in non-conditional constructions dominated by verbs of knowing and saying:

Zapytał, czy bym mógł (or: czy mógłbym) przyjść jutro o piątej.
'He asked whether I could come over tomorrow at five.'

A large group of verbs governs (obligatorily or optionally) a conditional-like clause, that is, a clause introduced by a conjunction containing the conditional particle *by* (*żeby, aby, by*) and including a verb in the past tense:

Chcę, żebyś przyszła jutro o piątej.
'I want you to come (literally: that you would come) tomorrow at five.'
Wątpię, żeby Janek zdążył.
'I doubt that Janek will (literally: would) make it in time.'

In sentences like the last two, as opposed to the previous two, the *by* (plus personal ending if present) cannot be separated from the conjunction, that is, both **że przyszłabyś* and **żeby przysłaś* are impossible, as is **że Janek zdążyłby*. Some verbs occur in such constructions only when negated:

Sądzę, że już wyjechał.
'I think he's already left.'

versus

Nie sądzę, żeby już wyjechał.
'I don't think he's left yet.'

Polish makes syntactic use of constructions headed by adjectival (inflected) and adverbial (uninflected) **participles**. The latter are reductions of subordinate clauses in various adverbial functions (temporal, conditional and so forth):

Szczęśliwie powróciwszy do Litwy, Kiejstut się rzucił w nowe boje. (Gdy powrócił
    ..., rzucił się ...)
'Having returned safely to Lithuania, Kiejstut threw himself into new battles.
    (When he returned ..., he threw himself ...)'

or of coordinate clauses:

Wpadł do izby ociekając wodę. (Wpadł ... i ociekał ...)
'He ran into the hut dripping water. (Ran ... and dripped ...)'

The former, which can involve active or passive participles can be interpreted as a reduced restrictive or non-restrictive relative:

Ksiądz(,) stojący po prawej stronie kardynała(,) dał mi znak, abym się nie odzywał.
'The priest(,) who was standing to the right of the cardinal(,) signalled to me
    (literally: gave me a sign) not to speak.'

In principle participles in -*ąc* and -*ący* refer to actions simultaneous with the action of the finite verb, and participles in -*szy*, to prior actions. In practice, participles in -*szy* can simply denote subordinate actions, including those subsequent to the finite-verb action:

Wyszedł z pokoju, zamknąwszy za sobą drzwi.
'He left the room, closing the door behind him.'

Although all active participles are much more common in written Polish than in the spoken language (except for phraseologisms like *szczerze mówiąc* 'speaking frankly'), this is especially true of the participle in -*szy*, which is becoming more and more 'literary' or even archaic. At the same time participles in -*ąc(y)* have expanded into contexts of non-simultaneity:

Zostawiając nie pogrzebane trupy, wojsko ruszyło do Torunia.
'Leaving corpses unburied, the army set off for Toruń.'

The traditional requirement that the (understood) subject of the participle be co-referential with the (nominative) subject of the main verb has also been weakened. Participial constructions are possible when the main verb occurs in a subjectless form that implies a (generalized or indefinite) human subject:

Dużo się mówi o tym, zapominając ...
'(People) talk about this a lot, forgetting ...'
Chcąc kupić bilet, trzeba stanąć w kolejce.
'If you want to (literally: wanting to) buy a ticket, you have to get in line/in the queue.'

Some speakers accept sentences with a dative subject ('experiencer'):

Słuchając dziewczyny, zrobiło mu (DAT) się żal.
'Listening to the girl, he began to feel sorry (for her).'

or even with an experiencer expressed in another case:

Słuchając zeznań świadków, ogarnia człowieka (ACC) przerażenie.
'Listening to the testimony of the witnesses, consternation overcomes one.'

or unspecified:

Patrząc z oddali, to danie wyglądało apetycznie.
'Looking from a distance, the dish appeared appetizing.'

Sentences in which the main verb is passive are accepted by many speakers:

Przechodząc jezdnię, został potrącony przez samochód.
'Crossing the street, he was struck by an automobile.'

The **infinitive** serves a wide variety of functions in main and subordinate clauses. It can serve as main verb in clauses with auxiliary verbs (*musieć* 'have to', *należy* 'one should') and in subjectless sentences of various types:

Co robić?
'What (can/should I) do?'
Wydać by (COND PTL) ją za mąż!
'(It would be nice to) marry her off!'
Tyle błędów zrobić!
'(How could you/he/they ...) make so many errors?'

An infinitive can serve as the equivalent of a simple noun-phrase subject or object:

Moim obowiązkiem jest prowadzić korespondencję.
'My responsibility is to conduct the correspondence.'

A **verbal noun** is often a possible equivalent for an infinitive in such sentences:

Moim obowiązkiem jest prowadzenie korespondencji.

and is the only possibility in some cases where other Slavonic languages might use an infinitive:

Zmuszasz mnie do ukrywania myśli przed tobą.
'You force me to hide my thoughts from you.'

Compare Slovak:

Nútiš ma skrývať myšlienki pred tebou.

A bare infinitive or infinitive clause can serve as the equivalent of a subordinate clause functioning as a noun phrase. The main verb may require subject–subject or object–subject co-reference:

Janek zamierza wyjechać.
'Janek intends to leave (town).'
Pozwoliłem Jankowi wyjechać.
'I allowed Janek to leave (town).'

(in both sentences only *Janek* can be the understood subject of *wyjechać*), or the choice of infinitive versus finite verb can depend on co-reference:

Chcę wyjechać.
'I want to leave.'

versus

Chcę, żeby Janek wyjechał.
'I want Janek to leave.'

When the subject of the subordinate verb is unspecified but different from the subject of the main verb, an infinitive can be used with a conjunction:

Prosił, żeby go odprowadzić.
'He asked that (someone) accompany him (home).'
Zgodziłem się, żeby postawić lampę na stole.
'I agreed that (someone) put the lamp on the table.'

Some speakers accept sentences like the last with a co-referential reading ('I agreed to put ...') and some accept sentences like

?Chcę, żeby wyjechać (for normative: Chcę, żebyśmy wyjechali).
'I want us to leave.'

(Topolińska 1984: 237)

Depending on the main verb, the infinitival construction may be paralleled by a clause with a finite verb or by a verbal noun:

Kazałem mu napalić (or: żeby napalił) w piecu.
'I told him to light the stove.'
Zabronił synowi wychodzić (or: wychodzenia) z domu.
'He forbade his son to leave the house.'

An infinitival clause introduced by a subordinating conjunction can appear in various adverbial functions, for example purpose:

Pan gubi tę dziewczynę, żeby ratować siebie!
'You are ruining that girl to save yourself!'

In principle there has to be identity of subjects or agents, although the agent can be generic or unspecified:

Robi się co nieco, żeby te nastroje poprawić.
'Some things are being done to improve the mood.'

For some speakers the subject of the infinitive can be co-referential with some other discourse participant:

(*)Wódkę stawia, żeby szefowi nic nie mówić.
'He buys (us) drinks so that (we) don't tell the boss anything.'

Bare infinitives or infinitive clauses can function as noun-phrase modifiers:

Ktoś rzucił myśl, aby świnkę hodować w piwnicy.
'Someone made the suggestion to raise the pig in the cellar.'

Extraction is generally impossible across clause boundaries, although there are some exceptions. Non-subject noun phrases can be moved from a subordinate clause introduced by *żeby* or its synonyms:

Co Janek chce, żeby Maria kupiła?
'What does Janek want Maria to buy?'

A subject noun phrase can normally not be extracted, although some speakers accept extraction when there is no intervening explicit subject of the main clause:

*Kto Janek chce, żeby kupił gazetę?
'Who does Janek want to buy the newspaper?'
?Kto chcesz, żeby kupił gazetę?
'Who do (you) want to buy the newspaper?'

Some speakers also accept extraction from *że*-clauses with particular matrix verbs:

Co Janek mówi, że Maria kupiła?
'What does Janek say that Maria bought?'

versus

*Co Janek myśli, że Maria kupiła?
'What does Janek think that Maria bought?'

(The last example is acceptable to some speakers.)
Relativization is possible from an infinitival WH clause:

Zadanie, które (którego) nie wiesz jak rozwiązać, jest bardzo trudne.
'The problem that you don't know how to solve is very difficult.'

4.6 Negation

The negative particle *nie* is used for sentence negation and for constituent negation, as well as in word formation (*niezależny* 'independent'):

Janek dziś nie rozmawiał z Basią.
'Janek didn't talk with Basia today.' (sentence negation)
Nie Janek rozmawiał dziś z Basią, tylko Rysiek.
'It wasn't Janek who talked with Basia today, but Rysiek.'
Janek nie rozmawiał dziś z Basią, tylko zostawił dla niej wiadomość.
'Janek didn't talk ..., but left a message for her.'

Multiple negative elements can occur together with sentence negation:

Janek nigdy z nikim nie rozmawia.
'Janek never talks with anyone (literally: no-one).'

The **direct object of a negated verb** is normally genitive, even if the negation is not directly on the transitive verb but rather on an auxiliary or other verb governing a transitive infinitive:

Nie czytałem tej książki.
'I haven't read that book.'
Nie mam ochoty czytać tej książki.
'I have no desire to read that book.'

and even the older, literary:

Stary nie ma gdzie głowy (GEN) położyć.
'The old man does not have (any)where to put his head.'

versus the contemporary colloquial

Nie mam co (ACC) robić.
'I don't have anything to do.'

The last example illustrates one of two opposed tendencies affecting the genitive of negation (Buttler, Kurkowska and Satkiewicz 1971: 306–10). On the one hand, the accusative is expanding, particularly in sentences in which the negation is rhetorical and not real:

Nie wstyd ci mówić takie rzeczy?
'Aren't you ashamed to say such things?'

and in sentences in which the direct object is far from the negated predicate:

Polak nie ma obowiązku znać język francuski (języka francuskiego).
'A Pole is not obliged to know French.'

On the other hand, the genitive is expanding (as a hypercorrect form) into sentences in which the traditional accusative is used in a meaning other than direct object (for example, experiencer or accusative of time or space):

Głowa już ją (ACC) (jej (GEN)) nie boli.
'(Her) head doesn't hurt her any more.'
To nie potrwa dwie godziny (ACC) (dwóch godzin (GEN)).
'It won't last two hours.'

The genitive case replaces the nominative when *być* is negated to deny existence or presence. The verb is used in the third person singular (in the form *nie ma* in the present tense):

Kiełbasy nie ma.
'There isn't any sausage.'
Janka nie było na wykładzie.
'Janek wasn't at the lecture.'

If the focus, however, is not on absence but on presence elsewhere or on failure to go, the nominative remains:

Janek nie był na wykładzie. On był u lekarza.
'Janek wasn't at the lecture. He was at the doctor's.'
Basia nigdy nie była w Krakowie.
'Basia has never been to Cracow.'

The nominative also remains with other verbs denying existence:

To nie istnieje.
'That doesn't exist.'
Nie zaszły żadne zmiany.
'No changes occurred.'

4.7   Anaphora and pronouns

The most common device for expressing anaphora is the use of third-person pronouns (including the reflexive/reciprocal pronoun – see section 4.8). Subject pronouns are normally omitted except under conditions of emphasis, contrast and so forth. Thus in subject position zero anaphora is common; in non-subject position it is much less common:

Naprzeciwko nas idzie wysoki mężczyzna. Poznajesz (go)?
'There's a tall man heading towards us. Do you recognize (him)?'

Third-person subject pronouns are sometimes needed to resolve potential ambiguity. They are also used to mark a change of theme; in this function they often follow the verb (especially in written style):

Zadanie odbiorcy jest znacznie trudniejsze: musi on rozpoznać konkretną wartość każdego słowa.
(Nilsson 1982: 41–2)
'The task of the addressee is much more difficult: he must recognize the concrete value of each word.'

An expressive colloquial variant of the third-person subject pronoun is provided by demonstrative adjectives (Topolińska 1984: 308, 329):

O Jurka się nie martw! Ten/Taki sobie zawsze poradzi.
'Don't worry about Jurek. That one/That kind can always take care of himself.'

A generic term that can serve as a definite description for the hearer or reader is often used to refer to previously mentioned items:

Chciałbym porozmawiać z panem o pańskim synu. Chłopiec źle się uczy.
'I'd like to talk with you about your son. (The) boy is not doing well in school (literally: is studying badly).'

as are noun phrases containing new information in a kind of quasi-anaphora (Topolińska 1984: 329):

Duszą towarzystwa był zięć Kowalskich. Młody architekt ...
'The Kowalskis' son-in-law was the life of the party. The young architect ...'

Special items used for noun-phrase anaphora include *powyższy* 'the above', *wymieniony/cytowany* 'the aforementioned', *tamten/pierwszy* 'the former', *ten/ostatni* 'the latter'. Note that a pronoun can serve as an anaphor for a non-referential noun phrase:

Chcę być prezydentem i będę nim.
'I want to be president and I will (be it).'

The deictic pronoun *to* and the relative pronoun *co* are used as sentence anaphors:

Janek nie zdał egzaminu, co mnie nie bardzo dziwi.
'Janek didn't pass the exam, which doesn't surprise me very much.'
Janek nie zdał egzaminu. To mnie nie bardzo dziwi.
'Janek didn't pass the exam. That doesn't surprise me ...'

An anaphoric element usually follows its controller (antecedent). The reverse order (cataphora) is subject to various restrictions. **Cataphora** (with explicit or zero cataphor) is possible within a single clause:

Po skończeniu studiów Tomek wyjechał do Ameryki.
'After graduating Tomek went to America.'

In coordinate clauses cataphora is impossible:

*Znam go$_i$, ale nie widzę Janka$_i$ tutaj.
'I know him$_i$ but I don't see Janek$_i$ here.'

In subordinate-clause constructions the cataphoric element must be in a clause subordinate to the one containing its controller:

Otkąd go$_i$ znam, nigdy Jurek$_i$ tu nie był.
'As long as I've known him$_i$, Jurek$_i$ has never been here.'
*Nigdy on$_i$ tu nie był, otkąd Jurka$_i$ znam.
'He$_i$ has never been here as long as I have known Jurek$_i$.'
Wydarzenie, którego (Ø$_i$) był świadkiem, wstrząsnęło Piotrem$_i$ do głębi.
'The event to which (he$_i$) had been a witness shook Peter$_i$ to his core.'

4.8 Reflexives and reciprocals

Reflexivity is expressed by forms of the reflexive pronoun (*siebie*), the reflexive possessive adjective (*swój*) and the emphatic pronoun (*sam*). The first two of these can also express reciprocity. What is historically the enclitic accusative form of the reflexive pronoun (*się*) only rarely has that function in the contemporary language; mostly it serves other syntactic and lexical functions. It does, however, serve as the enclitic accusative form when the reflexive pronoun is used in its reciprocal meaning (see below). Colloquial spoken Polish, but not the standard language, also has an enclitic dative form (*se*) of the reflexive/reciprocal pronoun.

In principle, reflexive elements refer back to a subject, which can be an explicit nominative subject, a zero anaphor or a generalized subject:

Janek$_i$ ciągle mówi o swoich$_i$ planach.
'Janek$_i$ is always talking about his$_i$ plans.'
Janek$_i$ się zapala, gdy (Ø$_i$) mówi o swoich$_i$ planach.
'Janek$_i$ gets excited when (he$_i$) talks about his$_i$ plans.'
Tak się nie mówi o swoich kolegach.
'One doesn't talk like that about one's friends.'

If the reflexive element is governed by a finite verb (or an infinitive in a subordinate clause), then the antecedent must be the subject of that verb:

Janek$_i$ kazał Piotrowi$_j$, żeby (Ø$_j$) przyniósł jego$_i$/swoją$_j$ książkę.
'Janek$_i$ told Piotr$_j$ (Ø$_j$) to bring his$_i$/his$_j$ book.'
Janek$_i$ rzucił myśl, żeby (Ø$_j$) wybrać go$_i$/*siebie$_i$ przewodniczącym.
'Janek$_i$ made the suggestion that (Ø$_j$) elect him$_i$ chairman.'

If, however, the reflexive element is governed by an infinitive not in a subordinate clause, by a verbal adjective or adverb or by a verbal noun, then the antecedent can be either the subject of that (de)verbal constituent or the subject of a higher verb:

Janek$_i$ kazał Piotrowi$_j$ (Ø$_j$) przynieść swoją$_{i/j}$ książkę.
'Janek$_i$ told Piotr$_j$ (Ø$_j$) to bring his$_{i/j}$ book.'
Syn$_i$ zmusza kolegów$_j$ do (Ø$_j$) sprzątania po sobie$_{i/j}$.
'(My) son$_i$ makes (his$_i$) friends$_j$ clean up after him$_i$/themselves$_j$.'

In fact, it seems that whenever a reflexive element is governed by something that can be interpreted as embodying a secondary predication, the (logical) subject of that predicate can serve as antecedent for the reflexive:

Janek$_i$ ocenia Ryśka$_j$ jako dobrego dla swojej$_{i/j}$ żony.
'Janek$_i$ views Rysiek$_j$ as kind to his$_{i/j}$ wife.'
Janek$_i$ pokłócił Basię$_j$ ze swoimi$_{i/j}$ kolegami.
'Janek$_i$ set Basia$_j$ at loggerheads with his$_i$/her$_j$ friends.'

In some sense these sentences are felt to contain the predication *Rysiek jest dobry* 'Rysiek is kind' and *Basia się kłóciła* 'Basia quarrelled'. (The verb *pokłócić* is a causative of *kłócić się*.) Compare a parallel sentence with possible reciprocal meaning:

Janek$_i$ pokłócił siostry$_j$ ze sobą$_{i/j}$.
'Janek$_i$ set the sisters$_j$ at loggerheads with him$_i$/each other$_j$.'

Anaphoric pronouns occasionally occur instead of, or as a variant to, reflexives:

(Ø$_i$) Dostał tak miły dla siebie/niego$_i$ list.
'(He$_i$) got such a nice (for him$_i$) letter.'

Some speakers accept as an antecedent for a reflexive or reciprocal a non-nominative noun or pronoun that serves as the logical subject of the governing verb:

?Markowi$_i$ (DAT) brakowało swoich$_i$ przyjaciół.
'Mark$_i$ missed his$_i$ friends.'
?Ciągnie ich$_i$ (ACC) do siebie$_i$.
'They$_i$ are attracted to one another$_i$.'

The **reciprocal** reading of a reflexive pronoun or (more rarely) a reflexive possessive adjective is usually clear from context:

Często dzwonimy do siebie.
'We often call each other.'
W swoim towarzystwie czujemy się skrępowani.
'We feel ill at ease in each other's company.'

If not, the adverbs *wzajemnie* or *nawzajem* 'mutually' are sometimes used, or the reflexive/reciprocal element is replaced by the appropriate form of *jeden drugiego* 'one another':

Ciągle myślą o sobie.
'They're always thinking about themselves/one another.'
Ciągle myślą jeden o drugim.
'They're always thinking about one another.'

The pronoun *się* regularly serves as the enclitic form of reciprocal *siebie* (accusative or genitive) although it is severely restricted as the enclitic of reflexive *siebie*:

Kochamy siebie.
'We love ourselves/each other.'
Kochamy się.
'We love each other.'

but

Pocałuj się w nos!
'Go to hell! (literally: kiss yourself in the nose!)'

The antecedent of a reciprocal element must be in the same clause, but it can be a zero anaphor:

(∅$_i$) Przekonałem ich$_j$, że (∅$_j$) nic nie wiedzą o sobie$_j$.
'(I$_i$) convinced them$_j$ that (they$_j$) don't know anything about each other$_j$/themselves$_j$.'

Reciprocals are even freer than reflexives in having non-subjects as antecedents:

(∅$_i$) Zapoznałem gości$_j$ ze sobą$_j$.
'(I$_i$) introduced the guests$_j$ one to another$_j$.'
Czas$_i$ spędzony razem pobudził w nich$_j$ miłość do siebie$_j$.
'The time$_i$ spent together awoke in them$_j$ love for one another$_j$.'

The **emphatic** element *sam* has both reflexive and non-reflexive functions. In its non-reflexive function it means 'X-self', 'by X-self' or 'alone' and shows normal adjectival agreement:

Napisałem do samego ministra.
'I wrote to the minister himself.'
Czy pani mieszka sama?
'Do you live alone?'

In its reflexive function it occurs in the nominative or (especially in non-finite constructions) dative, although the genitive plural is possible with a quantified antecedent and the dative (or even the masculine singular dative *samemu*) is sometimes generalized:

Zrobię to sam.
'I'll do it myself.'
Nie wypada iść tam samemu.
'One shouldn't go there oneself.'
Wielu studentów (GEN PL) idzie samych (GEN PL).
'Many students are going by themselves.'

4.9   Possession

Possession can be expressed with the verbs *mieć* 'have', *posiadać* 'possess' and *należeć* 'belong'.

The possessive adjectives of the first and second person (*mój, twój, nasz, wasz*) and the reflexive possessive *swój*, as well as *pański* (‹ *pan*) normally precede the noun they modify and agree with it in gender, number and case. Post-nominal use (*syn mój* 'my son') is expressive. The third-person possessives (*jego, jej, ich*) are indeclinable (and therefore non-agreeing) pre-nominal modifiers, as are the forms *pana* (‹ *pan*) and *pani* (‹ *pani*). These last five possessives are all identical to the genitive forms of the corresponding pronouns. The other non-familiar second-person possessives (*państwa* (for a mixed group), *panów* (for a group of men), *pań* (for a group of women)) are also genitive in origin, but they are used post-nominally like other genitive expressions of possession: *mój dom* 'my house', *pani dom* 'your (F non-familiar) house', *jego dom* 'his house' versus *dom państwa* 'your (PL non-familiar, mixed group) house', *dom naszego kolegi* 'our friend's house'. In spoken Polish genitive expressions of possession are sometimes preposed, especially when the noun refers to a person: *naszego kolegi siostra* 'our friend's sister'.

Possessive adjectives are normally omitted if the relationship is clear:

Jadę z mężem.
'I'm going with (my) husband.'

This is especially true of inalienable 'possessions' but is not limited to them:

Idę do biura.
'I'm going to (my/the) office.'

In some cases the possessive adjective is impossible. Compare

Basia złamała sobie nogę.
'Basia broke her leg.'
*Basia złamała swoją nogę.

The latter would be possible only if the leg in question were, say, a piece of sculpture (Wierzbicka 1988: 206–9).

Inalienable possessions (and some others) permit the use of a dative noun or pronoun to specify the possessor:

Józefowi (DAT) umarł ojciec.
'Józef's father died.'
Zajrzała mi (DAT) do gardła/do kieszeni.
'She looked into my throat/my pocket.'

Both possessive adjectives and genitive expressions of possession can be used as predicates with the copula, but only when describing alienable possessions:

Ta książka jest moja/Janka.
'That book is mine/Janek's.'

but not

*Matka/Ręka jest moja/Janka.
'The mother/The hand is mine/Janek's.'

4.10   Quantification

If a noun phrase containing a cardinal number is in a position requiring the **accusative or any oblique case**, then the entire phrase is in that case:

Znam [tych trzech studentów]$_{ACC}$.
'I know those three (male) students.'
Znam [te trzy studentki]$_{ACC}$.
'I know those three (female) students.'
Byłem we [wszystkich czterdziestu dziewięciu województwach]$_{LOC}$.
'I've been in all forty-nine Polish provinces.'

(See section 3.1.5 for the forms.)

In a position requiring the **nominative** case, however, case and number assignments depend on the gender of the head noun. If it is **not masculine personal**, then the situation is as follows:

1   The numerals '2', '3', '4' and their compounds ('22', '164' and so forth) govern the nominative plural of nouns and adjectives in the noun phrase, plural forms of the verb, and nominative plural forms of predicate adjectives or passive participles:

Te dwa duże konie są moje.
'Those two big horses are mine.'

2   The numerals '5'–'21', '25'–'31', '35'–'41' and so forth govern the genitive plural of nouns and adjectives in the noun phrase and of adjectives or passive participles in the predicate, and govern third person singular (neuter) verb forms:

Tych pięć nowych studentek było obecnych.
'Those five new (female) students were present.'

An adjective or, less commonly, a participle preceding the numeral can be in the nominative plural (*te pięć nowych studentek . . .*).

When a subject/nominative noun phrase has a **masculine personal** noun as head, the situation is as follows:

1 The numerals '2', '3' and '4' enter into two constructions. In one the forms *dwaj, trzej, czterej* govern the nominative plural of nouns and adjectives in the noun phrase, plural forms of the verb and nominative plural forms of predicate adjectives or participles:

Ci dwaj nowi studenci byli obecni.
'Those two new (male) students were present.'

In the other the forms *dwóch, trzech, czterech* govern the genitive plural of nouns and adjectives in the noun phrase, third person singular (neuter) forms of the verb and genitive plural forms of predicate adjectives or participles:

Dwóch nowych studentów zostało wybranych.
'Two new (male) students were elected.'

In compounds of '2', '3', '4', only the second set of forms is used. Use of the second set is expanding even for non-compound numerals, but there is also some evidence of a semantic distinction between the two sets, with a tendency to use *dwóch, trzech, czterech* simply to specify quantity ('two' or 'two of (them)' and so forth) and *dwaj, trzej czterej* to specify quantity and mark definiteness ('the two').

2 Starting with '5' the only forms available to use with masculine-personal nouns in subject noun phrases are forms that govern the genitive plural (*pięciu, dwudziestu* and so forth):

Wszystkich pięciu studentów przyszło.
'All five (male) students came.'

The quantifiers *ile* 'how many', *tyle* 'so many', *parę* 'a couple', *kilka* 'several' (and its compounds *kilkanaście* '10–20', *kilkadziesiąt* 'several dozen', *kilkaset* 'several hundred') and *wiele* 'many' behave syntactically like cardinal numbers '5' and above. *Dużo* is a synonym of *wiele* but is used only in contexts requiring nominative or accusative.

Collective numerals (*dwoje, troje* and so forth) are used with some pluralia tantum (*dwoje drzwi* 'two doors'); with some nouns designating paired objects (*dwoje oczu* 'two eyes'); with neuter nouns in *-ę/-ęta* (*kilkoro zwierząt* 'several animals'); with certain specific nouns (*dziecko* 'child'); and to indicate a human group of mixed sex (*sześcioro studentów* versus *sześciu studentów* (all male) versus *sześć studentek* (all female); *my dwoje* or *nas dwoje* 'the two of us'). If a noun phrase containing a collective numeral is in a context requiring dative or locative, then the whole phrase will be in that case:

Zadałem to dwojgu studentom.
'I assigned that to two (male + female) students.'

Otherwise (and optionally for locative) the collective numeral governs the genitive plural of the head noun and, in subject position, governs a verb in the third person singular (neuter). A predicate adjective or participle can be in the genitive plural or neuter singular:

Dwoje źrebiąt było uwiązane/uwiązanych u płotu.
'Two colts were tethered at the fence.'

The above statements describe the syntax of quantifiers from a normative point of view. Actual usage is more varied. A number of tendencies can be observed. (See also section 3.1.5 on changes in inflection.) (a) Collective numerals are often replaced by cardinal numerals, except where there is a difference in meaning. (b) Many speakers use third-person (neuter) verb forms even with subject noun phrases containing '2', '3', '4' and their compounds. (c) The use of genitive plural for predicate adjectives and participles is spreading. (d) Certain nouns used as quantifiers are tending to acquire numeral-like syntax:

Szereg osób wiedziało o tym.
'A number of people knew about that.'

or even *w szeregu* (LOC) *miastach* (LOC) 'in a number of cities' instead of the traditional *w szeregu miast* (GEN).

5 Lexis

5.1 General composition of the word-stock
In the mid-1930s Tadeusz Lehr-Spławiński compared data from the two existing Slavonic etymological dictionaries with his own vocabulary and concluded that the active vocabulary of the average educated speaker of Polish at that time (estimated at 8,000 words) preserved more than 1,700 Proto-Slavonic words. (He counted only words that had survived without basic changes in meaning or structure.) By comparison, the largest dictionary of Polish (Doroszewski 1958–69) contains some 125,000 words. Some of Lehr's words are no longer in active use (*świekier* 'father-in-law'); however, his list would have been much longer had he included Polish words built out of Proto-Slavonic elements.

Some forty years later Jiří Damborský analysed the 37,319 entires in the one-volume abridgement of Doroszewski's dictionary and concluded that these consisted of 28,532 'native' words and 8,787 'foreign' words. Of the foreign words, nearly 30 per cent were of Latin origin; French and Greek each provided over 14 per cent; German, over 10 per cent; and English and Italian, each around 3.5 per cent. Words of Slavonic (Russian, Ukrainian, Czech) origin constituted a little over 2 per cent. A somewhat different picture is provided by analyses of post-Second World War neologisms, which suggest English, Russian and international (often Greco-Latin) terminology as major sources of borrowings. It has been claimed that – at least for neologisms in the press in the late 1970s – some 90 per cent of neologisms are perceived by native speakers as foreign in origin.

5.2 Patterns of borrowing

The earliest borrowings into Polish were from Czech and German, with the former sometimes serving as a conduit for the latter and both so serving for Latin. Starting in the sixteenth century, Latin became a direct source as Czech became less influential. (After its early role as a source of borrowings in the thirteenth and fourteenth centuries, German lost its influence until the nineteenth century.) French and Italian both started to play a role in the sixteenth century, but Italian influence declined in the seventeenth century, while French remained important until the mid-nineteenth century. The sixteenth and seventeenth centuries also brought borrowings from Ukrainian and Belorussian and, through them or directly, from Turkic. In the nineteenth century Russian and English (the latter initially via French and German) appeared as source languages; their influence became especially strong in the period following the Second World War. Currently, English and international terminology are the major sources of neologisms.

Some examples of borrowings from Czech: the name *Władysław* (for Polish *Włodzisław*); from German via Czech: *żart* 'joke'; from Latin via Czech: *biskup* 'bishop'; from French: *parter* 'ground floor'; from Italian: *impreza* 'show; spectacle'; from Ukrainian: *hulać* 'make merry'; from Turkish via Ukrainian: *kaftan* 'caftan'; from German: *szwagier* 'brother-in-law'; from Russian: *nieudacznik* 'hapless person'; from English: *stres* 'stress'.

Foreign influence is also apparent in lexical, phraseological and semantic calques like *listonosz* 'letter carrier' (compare German *Briefträger*), *racja stanu* 'reason of state' (compare French *raison d'état*), *jastrzębie* '(military) hawks'.

5.3 Incorporation of borrowings

Borrowed nouns that end in a consonant or *-a* are declined regularly like the corresponding native masculine or feminine nouns. Since the category of non-suffixal native nouns ending in *-o* or *-e* is closed, borrowed nouns ending in these vowels – or in any others – are normally not declined: *dżudo, atelier* (pronounced as in French with final [e]), *alibi, menu, jury.* An indeclinable noun referring to a human being gets its gender referentially (for example, *attaché* is masculine or feminine depending on the person in question); other indeclinable nouns are normally neuter unless they take masculine or feminine gender from a generic term (*kiwi*, masculine because of *ptak* 'bird').

Borrowings may undergo adaptation to make them fit native declensional types or to make the declensional type fit referential gender, for example spelling pronunciation (*bufet* – inflected masculine – versus *foyer* – undeclined neuter pronounced [fwaje] as in French); depluralization (*fotos* 'publicity photo' – singular from English plural); gender adjustment (*girlsa* 'chorus girl').

Some borrowings in *-o* are used both with and without declension (*bistro*). This may be in keeping with the greater tendency of spoken Polish to regularize, which is also reflected in the declension of foreign geographical names not normally declined in written style: *do Tokia* 'to Tokyo'. Foreign family names in *-i, -y* or *-e* are declined like adjectives: *Kennedy*, genitive *Kennedy'ego*.

Polish has borrowed several adjectives that are not declined and are usually used post-nominally (*suknia bordo* 'bordeau dress'). Some have begun to function as combining forms (*spódniczka mini* or *mini-spódniczka* 'miniskirt').

Verbs based on borrowed material, usually with infinitives in *-ować*, may be bi-aspectual (*internować* 'intern'), but more often they are integrated into the Polish aspectual system through the creation of prefixed perfective form (*zaimportować* 'import'). Sometimes the verb is first attested in a prefixed perfective form, which implies the potential existence of an unprefixed imperfective (perfective *splagiatować* 'plagiarize' (TR) implies imperfective *?plagiatować*) or suffixal imperfective (perfective *przetestować* 'retest' implies imperfective *?przetestowywać*).

5.4   Lexical fields

5.4.1   Colour terms

white	biały
black	czarny
red	czerwony
green	zielony
yellow	żółty
blue	niebieski
brown	brązowy
purple	fioletowy
pink	różowy
orange	pomarańczowy
grey	szary

Eight of the above eleven names are basic; the possible exceptions are *fioletowy* (‹ *fiolet* '(the flower) violet'), *pomarańczowy* (‹ *pomarańcza* '(the fruit) orange') and *różowy* (‹ *róża* '(the flower) rose'). All three are of relatively low frequency and the first two are almost absent from phraseological combinations (but are supported by their 'official' position in the rainbow). *Różowy* is used slightly more frequently than the other two and plays a much greater role in phraseology. English *brown* more often corresponds to Polish *brunatny* than to Polish *brązowy* (with its initial meaning 'made of bronze'), but the latter is the more basic term, with *brunatny* defined as a dark shade of *brązowy*. A second translation of *blue* is *błękitny*, a more poetic synonym of the basic *niebieski* (‹ *niebo* 'sky'). Various shades of dark blue have their own names (*modry, granatowy* and regionally *siny* (more generally 'blue-violet')), but none are basic colours. *Purpurowy* for 'purple' is on the red side of *fioletowy*, being defined as 'dark red with a violet hue'. The alternative translations of *grey*, *popielaty* (‹ *popiół* 'ashes') and *siwy*, are on the light side, with the latter used primarily to describe hair colour.

5.4.2   Body parts

head	głowa
eye	oko
nose	nos
ear	ucho
mouth	usta
hair	włosy
neck	szyja, kark
arm/hand	ręka, ramię, dłoń
finger	palec (u ręki)
leg/foot	noga, stopa
toe	palec (u nogi)
chest	piersi
heart	serce

The neck as a solid body is *szyja*; *kark* refers to the nape (back) of the neck. The whole back from the *kark* to the small of the back (*krzyże*) is *grzbiet*. The back from the shoulders to the waist is *plecy* or *barki*. In the singular *bark* usually means 'shoulder'. 'Shoulder' is also one of the meanings of *ramię*, which can also refer to the upper arm and, loosely, to the whole arm. The whole arm can also be called *ręka*, the primary meaning of which is 'hand'. The word *dłoń* can mean both 'palm' and 'hand'. In parallel with *ręka*, the word *noga* can mean both 'leg' and 'foot'; for the latter there is an unambiguous term *stopa*.

The term for 'mouth', *usta*, belongs to the category of pluralia tantum. The word for 'hair', *włosy*, is also plural, but its singular *włos* exists and means 'one single hair'. In the meaning 'chest' the plural form *piersi* is normal; the singular *pierś* usually means 'a breast'.

5.4.3   Kinship terms

mother	matka
father	ojciec
sister	siostra
brother	brat
aunt	ciocia (ciotka)
uncle	wujek
niece	bratanica, siostrzenica
nephew	bratanek, siostrzeniec
cousin (female)	kuzynka
cousin (male)	kuzyn
grandmother	babcia
grandfather	dziadek
wife	żona
husband	mąż
daughter	córka
son	syn

There is no single term for 'niece' or for 'nephew'; in both cases Polish distinguishes a brother's child (*bratanica, bratanek*) from a sister's child (*siostrzenica, siostrzeniec*). The terms *babcia* and *wujek*, although historically hypocoristics, are more common as basic terms than *babka* and *wuj*. For 'aunt', however, *ciocia* and *ciotka* are equally frequent. The hypocoristics *mama* (for *matka*) and *tata* (for *ojciec*) are very common.

Although most speakers use only the listed terms for 'uncle' and 'aunt' (and children use them as a form of address and to refer to miscellaneous adults, related or not), many speakers have passive knowledge of a more traditional system of kinship terminology (still used actively by some speakers), in which *wuj* is 'mother's brother' or 'aunt's husband', while 'father's brother' is *stryj*. In this same system *ciotka* is only 'mother's (father's) sister'; an aunt by marriage is *wujna/wujenka* or *stryjna/ stryjenka*. The older system also involved a more complicated taxonomy of cousins – known passively to many speakers but normally simplified in active use to *kuzyn/kuzynka* – based on which blood relative the cousin is a child of: *wuj, stryj* or *ciotka*. Thus among male cousins one distinguishes *brat wujeczny, brat stryjeczny* and *brat cioteczny*, and similarly for female cousins.

6   Dialects

The Polish linguistic territory has traditionally been divided into five major dialect areas, corresponding to the historical–geographic regions of Małopolska, Wielkopolska, Mazowsze, Śląsk (Silesia) and Kaszuby (see map 12.1). This division does not include the territories in the west and

Map 12.1   The five major dialect areas of Polish

north (approximately 25 per cent of present-day Poland) that were
acquired from Germany at the end of the Second World War and which
are said to be populated by speakers of 'new mixed dialects' created as a
result of the population movements of the immediate post-war period.
(The territories in the east lost to the Soviet Union in 1939 were generally
not considered to represent a separate dialect area.)

Most present-day dialect speakers show diglossia: they speak both the
dialect and the standard language or some approximation thereto, that is,
an urban 'substandard' or a rural 'interdialect' (Topolińska and Vidoeski
1984: 35–53). The latter term refers to the best possible approximation of
the standard language given the local linguistic resources, for example the
use of a form like [košula] to represent standard [košula] (orthographic
koszula 'shirt') by a speaker whose native dialect has [kosula].

Two features have traditionally been used to define the five major
dialect areas. The voicing of word-final obstruents before word-initial

vowels and sonorants ([bradmuj] for orthographic *brat mój* 'my brother') is characteristic of Małopolska, Wielkopolska and Silesia, and distinguishes them from Mazowsze and Kaszuby, where obstruents are voiceless in that context ([vusmuj] for orthographic *wóz mój* 'my wagon' – see section 2.1). Secondly, the repertoire of central fricatives and affricates distinguishes Małopolska and Mazowsze (where the alveolar series collapsed with the dental series, leaving only /s/, /z/, /c/ and /dz/) both from Wielkopolska (where the dentals, alveolars and palatals are all distinct, that is, /s/ versus /sz/ versus /ś/ and so forth as in the standard language) and from Kaszuby (where there are no palatals). Northern Silesian dialects show the loss of the alveolar series (like Małopolska and Mazowsze; the phenomenon is known in the literature as *mazurzenie*), while southern Silesian dialects preserve the three-way distinction (like Wielkopolska).

Other dialect features include the treatment of the historical nasal vowels and long vowels, the results of secondary palatalization of velars before front vowels, the presence or absence of a category of masculine-personal nouns, relics of the dual in declension and conjugation, the mutual interference of declension paradigms, the presence or absence of personal clitics/endings in the past tense and patterns of nominal and verbal derivation.

Some dialect features also characterize regional variants of the standard language, for example voicing sandhi; the derivation of names of young animals in *-ę* versus *-ak* (southern *cielę* versus northern *cielak* 'calf'); lexical differences ('blueberries' are *borówki* in Cracow but *czarne jagody* or simply *jagody* in Warsaw).

What most Polish linguists view as the Polish dialects of the Kaszuby area are often viewed outside Poland as dialects of a separate Cassubian language. (See chapter 13.) The Polish view is motivated, among other things, by the apparent lack of a national identity among the Cassubians, who – it is claimed – view themselves rather as an ethnic group within the Polish nation. None the less, there have been recent attempts to create a literary standard for Cassubian.

Other Polish dialects have occasionally been used for literary purposes (particularly those of Silesia and of the Podhale area in the southern mountains), but without any systematic efforts at standardization. The attempt (beginning in the 1930s) to create a literary language based on Polish–Czech transitional dialects in the Ostrava area of Czechoslovakia – the so-called 'literary laština' or 'Lekhian' – has resulted in a literary idiolect used only by the poet Óndra Łysohorský.

Acknowledgements

Because of space limitations, the bibliography is restricted to general works. I cannot therefore acknowledge specifically the many authors whose ideas and examples have contributed greatly to this chapter. I am indebted to them and to my native-speaker consultants, Dorota Szlenk, Kazimierz Grześlak and Dr Halina Zuchowicz.

References

Buttler, D., Kurkowska, H. and Satkiewicz, H. (1971) *Kultura języka polskiego*, vol. 1: *Zagadnienia poprawności gramatycznej*, Warsaw: PWN.
Decaux, E. (1978) *Leçons de grammaire polonaise*, 4 vols, Paris: Institut d'Etudes Slaves.
Dejna, K. (1973) *Dialekty polskie*, Wrocław: Ossolineum.
Doroszewski, W. (ed.) (1958–69) *Słownik języka polskiego*, 11 vols, Warsaw: WP.
—— (ed.) (1973) *Słownik poprawnej polszczyzny PWN*, Warsaw: PWN.
Fisiak, J. and Puppel, S. (eds) (1992) *Phonological Investigations*, Amsterdam: J. Benjamins.
Fisiak, J., Lipińska-Grzegorek, M. and Zabrocki, T. (1978) *An Introductory English–Polish Contrastive Grammar*, Warsaw: PWN.
Grzegorczykowa, R., Laskowski, R. and Wróbel, H. (eds) (1984) *Gramatyka współczesnego języka polskiego: Morfologia*, Warsaw: PWN.
Gussman, E. (1978) *Contrastive Polish–English Consonantal Phonology*, Warsaw: PWN.
Jodłowski, S. (1976) *Podstawy polskiej składni*, Warsaw: PWN.
Karaś, M. and Madejowa, M. (eds) (1977) *Słownik wymowy polskiej PWN*, Warsaw and Cracow: PWN.
Klemensiewicz, Z. (1937) *Składnia opisowa współczesnej polszczyzny kulturalnej*, Cracow: PAU.
—— (1961–72) *Historia języka polskiego*, 3 vols, Warsaw: PWN.
Krasnowolski, A. (1909) *Systematyczna składnia języka polskiego*, 2nd edn, Warsaw: M. Arct.
Laskowski, R. (1972) *Polnische Grammatik*, Warsaw: WP, and Leipzig: Enzyklopädie.
Lehr-Spławiński, T. (1947) *Język polski: pochodzenie, powstanie, rozwój*, Warsaw: S. Arct. (Russian translation, Moscow: Izdatel'stvo innostrannoj literatury, 1954.)
Misz, H. (1981) *Studia nad składnią współczesnej polszczyzny pisanej*, Toruń: Uniwersytet Mikołaja Kopernika.
Nilsson, B. (1982) *Personal Pronouns in Russian and Polish*, Stockholm: Almquist & Wiksell.
Puppel, S., Nawrocka-Fisiak, J. and Krassowska, H. (1977) *A Handbook of Polish Pronunciation for English Learners*, Warsaw: PWN.
Rospond, S. (1971) *Gramatyka historyczna języka polskiego*, Warsaw: PWN.
Rubach, J. (1984) *Cyclic and Lexical Phonology: the Structure of Polish*, Dordrecht: Foris.
Saloni, Z. (1976) *Cechy składniowe polskiego czasownika*, Wrocław: Ossolineum.
Saloni, Z. and Świdziński, M. (1985) *Składnia współczesnego języka polskiego*, 2nd edn, Warsaw: PWN.
Schenker, A. (1964) *Polish Declension: a Descriptive Analysis*, The Hague: Mouton.
Stieber, Z. (1966) *Historyczna i współczesna fonologia języka polskiego*, Warsaw: PWN. (English translation of earlier version, Heidelberg: Carl Winter, 1973.)
Swan, O.E. (1983) *A Concise Grammar of Polish*, 2nd edn, Lanham, Md.: University Press of America.

Szymczak, M. (ed.) (1978–81) *Słownik języka polskiego*, 3 vols, Warsaw: PWN.
Tokarski, J. (1951) *Czasowniki polskie*, Warsaw: S. Arct.
Topolińska, Z. (ed.) (1984) *Gramatyka współczesnego języka polskiego: Składnia*, Warsaw: PWN.
Topolińska, Z. and Vidoeski, B. (1984) *Polski-macedoński: gramatyka konfronta- tywna (zarys problematyki)*, vol. 1: *Wprowadzenie*, Wrocław: Ossolineum.
Urbańczyk, S. (ed.) (1978) *Encyklopedia wiedzy o języku polskim*, Wrocław: Ossolineum.
Wierzchowska, B. (1980) *Fonetyka i fonologia języka polskiego*, Wrocław: Ossolineum.

13 Cassubian

Gerald Stone

1 Introduction

Cassubian (or Kashubian) is today spoken in an elongated band of territory to the west, north-west and south-west of Gdańsk (German Danzig) (see map 13.1). Since the Second World War the entire Cassubian speech area has been situated inside the Polish state. From the official point of view Cassubian is a Polish dialect; but its individuality is such that it is usually regarded by both laymen and linguists as an entity, separate from all other Polish dialects. Genetically, Cassubian is the last surviving link in a chain of dialects which once stretched across what is now north Poland and north Germany, linking Polabian to Polish. The Lechitic group consists of Polabian (west Lechitic), Polish (east Lechitic) and a chain of central Lechitic dialects (including Cassubian). The term Pomeranian is narrower: East Pomeranian is Cassubian; West Pomeranian refers to those extinct varieties of central Lechitic which were once spoken to the west of Cassubian. Toponymical evidence indicates that Cassubian was once spoken as far west as the River Parsęta (German Persante), which flows into the Baltic at Kołobrzeg (German Kolberg).

The question has been frequently asked whether Cassubian is not really a separate Slavonic language rather than just a dialect of Polish. If the answer to this is yes, it implies a further question as to the existence of a separate Cassubian nationality. There are no known linguistic criteria for the resolution of such questions, but it is, in any case, clear that the question is not purely linguistic. Poland's claim to access to the sea after the First World War was dependent on establishing that the coastal population was Polish. There is general agreement, however, that there is something special about Cassubian. Poles from other parts of Poland have difficulty in understanding it when they hear it spoken. The difficulties experienced by newly arrived teachers in understanding their Cassubian pupils even led in 1960 to the publication of a small Cassubian–Polish and Polish–Cassubian dictionary (Labuda 1960) intended to assist communication. Conditions were particularly favourable for the development of a separate linguistic identity in the period before 1918, when Cassubia (as the region is called) was part of the German Empire and standard Polish had no official status.

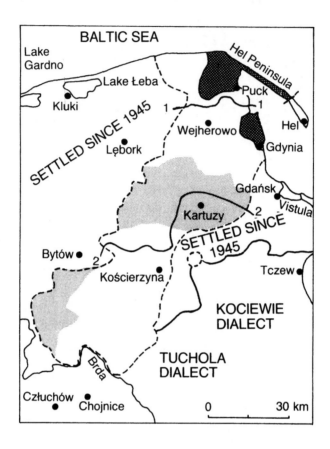

BALTIC SEA

Lake Gardno

Lake Łeba

Kluki

SETTLED SINCE 1945

Lębork

Wejherowo

Puck

Hel Peninsula

Hel

Gdynia

Gdańsk

Kartuzy

Vistula

SETTLED SINCE 1945

Bytów

Kościerzyna

Tczew

KOCIEWIE DIALECT

TUCHOLA DIALECT

Brda

Człuchów
Chojnice

0   30 km

Key:

| | /l/ and /w/ (ł) have merged as /l/ |

| | *sw* › *sj* (for example, *sjinia* 'pig'; compare Polish *świnia*) |

1 ——— southern limit of uncontracted present-tense forms of the type *jô szukaję* 'I seek' (compare *jô szukóm* and so on south of this line)

2 ——— boundary between final (north) and initial (south) stress in the words *żołądk* 'stomach' and *kôrwińc/krowińc* 'cow dung'

- - - - - - external limits of Cassubian, according to field-work for *AJK* in 1954–7

Note: 1 The tiny isolated Cassubian area 8 miles (12 km) to the north-east of Kościerzyna is the village of Grabówko, where even in the 1950s the number of Cassubian-speakers was small.
2 The tip of the Hel Peninsula was German-speaking before 1945.

Map 13.1   The Cassubian speech area

The rebirth of the Polish state, however, does not appear to have diminished consciousness of the Cassubian identity, even to the present day. The number of speakers is put at around 150,000 (Topolińska 1980: 183).

Attempts to create a Cassubian literary language have been neither a total success nor a total failure. Cassubian literature exists, but the language in which it is written has achieved only a moderate degree of standardization (Stone 1972). Written sources dating from before the nineteenth century (beginning in 1402) are written in a language which is not really Cassubian, but rather a kind of Polish containing a greater or lesser proportion of Cassubianisms. The first to write in undiluted Cassubian was Florian Ceynowa (1817–81), who between 1866 and 1868 published the periodical *Skôrb kaszébsko-słovjnskjè mòvé* ('A treasury of the Cassubo-Slovincian tongue'). He also published a grammar *Zarés do grammatikj kaŝébsko-słovjnskjè mòvé* ('An outline of the grammar of the Cassubo-Slovincian tongue') (Poznań 1879) and several literary works in Cassubian. The late nineteenth century also saw the appearance of a number of Cassubian literary compositions by Hieronim Derdowski (1852–1902). His masterpiece is a narrative poem entitled *O panu Czorlińscim co do Pucka po sece jachoł* ('About Mr Czarliński, who rode to Puck for nets'). The use of Cassubian in literature has tended to be restricted to short prose works and to verse. There is only one novel, *Żëcé i przigodë Remusa* ('The life and adventures of Remus') (Toruń 1938) by Aleksander Majkowski (1876–1938). Periodicals printed entirely in Cassubian, such as *Przyjaciel Ludu Kaszubskiego* ('The friend of the Cassubian people') (1928–9), *Bënë ë Buten* ('At home and abroad') (1930), and *Zrzesz Kaszëbskô* ('The Cassubian union') (1933–9), have existed from time to time. The monthly *Pomerania*, published in Gdańsk, regularly carries items on cultural matters, printed in Cassubian.

Efforts have been made to bring about unification and to standardize the written form of Cassubian. A grammar intended to set up 'a norm freed of the accidental features and peculiarities of the dialects, and thus standing above the dialects' was published by Friedrich Lorentz in 1919 (Lorentz 1919), but its influence has been limited. Some progress has been made, however, in the sphere of orthography by the orthographical committee of the Zrzeszenie Kaszubsko-Pomorskie (Cassubo-Pomeranian Association) (Breza and Treder 1984). Something approaching a standard grammar, but with systematic incorporation of local variation, is provided by *Gramatyka kaszubska* (Breza and Treder 1981). In the description given below emphasis is laid on salient points of diversion from Polish; this accounts for the absence of sections 3.1.5, 3.2.1, 3.2.2, 4.10, 5.1 and 5.3 from this chapter.

Around 1900 the territorial limits of Cassubian extended as far west as the southern shore of Lake Gardno (nearly 37 miles (60 km) west of the nearest point where Cassubian is spoken today) (see map 13.1 on p. 760).

In the villages between Lakes Łeba and Gardno and to the south of the latter the inhabitants applied the term *słowińsczi* 'Slovincian' to their dialect. It appears that previously (sixteenth century) this term had also been used further south, in the vicinity of Bytów (German Bütow or Budow) (Lorentz, Fischer and Lehr-Spławiński 1935: 4–5). It has never been argued that Slovincian was anything more than a Cassubian dialect, but the Slovincians were distinguished from other Cassubians not only linguistically but also by the fact that they were Lutherans, not Catholics. By the 1920s the Slovincian villages and those immediately to the east of them were linguistically German, but the people remained conscious of their non-German origin and after 1945, when this part of Germany was annexed by Poland and the German population was expelled, some Slovincians were permitted to remain. Others were expelled (Rogaczewski 1975: 49–61), but even in the 1950s, mainly in the village of Kluki (German Klucken), there were still a few old people who could remember fragments of the language of their ancestors (Stieber *et al.* 1961 *passim*; Sobierajski 1964: 109–27).

2   Phonology

2.1   Segmental phoneme inventory
There is no orthoepic standard and the degree of local variation is high. Nevertheless, it is possible to encompass the segmental phonemes of almost all Cassubian varieties in the scheme given in table 13.1. In comparison with Polish the vowel system is remarkable for its large number of items. The consonant system, on the other hand, contains a smaller number of items than that of Polish, owing to the almost complete absence of the soft:hard distinction. The only remaining soft:hard pair is /n/:/ŋ/, but this too is in decline as a result of hardening in many areas.

Initially or after a labial or a velar the phonemes /o/ and /u/ acquire a prothetic labial glide: *polé* [pwɛle] 'field', *koza* [kwɛza] 'goat', *mucha* [mwuxa] 'fly'. In the case of /o/, in most areas, this is accompanied by fronting of the second element to /ɛ/ or /e/; but in the south-east the [wo] type prevails: [pwole] 'field' (Breza and Treder 1981: 36–8; Breza and Treder 1984: 23; *AJK* XIV: 73, 76–7, 110–12, maps 7, 8, 9, 14, 15, 16). Some writers have, by various means, reflected this feature in their spelling, but since it is simply a matter of positional variants of /o/ and /u/ it is nowadays usual to retain the letters o and u (Breza and Treder 1984: 23).

The spelling system recommended by the Zrzeszenie Kaszubsko-Pomorskie is based on the Polish system with the following alterations and additions:

Table 13.1   Segmental phonemes of Cassubian

Vowels

	Oral			Nasal	
i			u		
			ɷ		
e			o		õ
		ə			
	ɛ		ɔ		
		a		ã	

Consonants

	Bilabial	Labio-dental	Dental	Alveolar	Palatal	Velar
Plain stop	p		t			k
	b		d			g
Affricate			ts	tʃ		
			dz	dʒ		
Fricative		f	s	ʃ		x
		v	z	ʒ		
Nasal						
	m		n		ŋ	
Lateral						
			l			
Trill						
			r		ɽ	
Semi-vowel	w				j	

1   To the Polish system of letters representing oral vowels the following
     changes have been made:
     (a) ô represents /ɔ/: *jô* 'I', *brzôd* 'fruit', *dôka* 'fog';
     (b) ó represents /ɷ/ (a vowel midway between /o/ and /u/): *żót*
         'stomach', *zwónk* 'bell';
     (c) é represents /e/ (a vowel between /i/ and /ɛ/): *grzéch* [gɽex]
         'sin', *chléb* [xlep] 'bread', *gazéta* [gazeta] 'newspaper';
     (d) ë represents /ə/: *bëlny* [bəlni] 'fine, sturdy', *cëchi* [tsəxi] 'quiet',
         bënë [bənə] 'inside'.
2   The Polish nasal letters ę and ą are used, but ę represents a nasalized
     /a/, that is, [ã] (not [ɛ̃]): *będze* [bãdzɛ] 'will be (3 SG)'. The letter ą
     represents /õ/: *ksądz* [ksõts] 'priest'.
3   The most distinctive feature of the consonant system is the appearance
     of *s*, *z*, *c* and *dz*, where Polish has *ś*, *ź*, *ć* and *dź* respectively (known as
     kaszubienie): *bëc* 'to be' (Polish *być*), *scana* 'wall' (Polish *ściana*),
     zëma 'winter' (Polish *zima*). Cassubian therefore does not make use of

the letters ś, ź, ć, dź. The opposition between the letters i and y, as found in Polish, occurs in Cassubian only after the letter n: *ni* represents /ɲi/, but *ny* represents /ni/ (as in *nisko* /ɲisko/ 'low', but *bëlny* /bəlni/ 'fine, sturdy'). Otherwise, i is written everywhere (as in *bik* 'bull', *dim* 'smoke') except after s, z, c and dz, where it is always replaced by y (as in *syn* 'son', *zymk* 'spring', *dzys* 'today') (Breza and Treder 1981: 39–40; Breza and Treder 1984: 24). The graphemes sz, ż, cz and dż represent phonemes (/ʃ/, /ʒ/, /ʧ/ and /ʤ/) which are phonetically soft, whereas in Polish they are hard (Breza and Treder 1981: 66).

Further phonological features not revealed in the orthography favoured by the Zrzeszenie Kaszubsko-Pomorskie are:

1   In many areas /o/ after hard dentals and /u/ are prone to fronting, producing vowels of the [ø] and [ʉ] types. Loss of rounding may lead to articulations similar to /ɛ/ (or /e/) and /i/ respectively (Breza and Treder 1981: 36–8).
2   /a/ before a nasal consonant is everywhere prone to nasalization: *scana* [stsãna] 'wall', *tam* [tãm] 'there'.
3   The grapheme rz represents [ɼ], a post-alveolar fricative trill, only in the speech of the older generation and mainly in the north. It is being replaced by Polish [ʒ] and [ʃ] (Breza and Treder 1981: 67).
4   The voiceless:voiced contrast of consonants (/p/:/b/, /t/:/d/ and so on) is neutralized at the end of the word. The consonants in question are phonetically voiceless. Inter-word assimilation is of the north-Polish (Warsaw) type (see chapter 12, pp. 690–1). Progressive assimilation by devoicing of /v/ in such words as *twój* 'your' and of /ɼ/ or /ʒ/ (orthographically rz) in such words as *trzeba* 'is necessary' does not normally occur.

Cassubian participated with Polish in the depalatalization of PSl. *ę to *ǫ before hard dentals, but was unaffected by the coalescence of non-depalatalized *ę and *ǫ in the early fourteenth century. On the contrary, the difference between the two nasal vowels increased in Cassubian as a result of a further fronting of the front nasal *ę to *į, which is first attested in 1198 (Stieber 1973: 137). It then underwent denasalization (*į became *i) and merged with original *i: thus Cassubian *jastrzib* 'hawk' (Polish *jastrząb*). Denasalization of *į is first attested in 1402. PSl. *ǫ remained, however, as short and long *ǫ.

The system of nine oral vowels has developed from an earlier ten-vowel system (*y* and *i* having already coalesced), embodying phonemic length:

ă   ĕ   ĭ   ŏ   ŭ
ā   ē   ī   ō   ū

The characteristic Cassubian phoneme *ë* is first attested at the end of the seventeenth century. It results from the metaphony: short *i* (including *i* from *y*) (except after palatalized consonants) became *ë*. For example, Cassubian *lëpa* 'lime' (Polish *lipa*), *rëba* 'fish' (Polish *ryba*). It included *i* from *i̯* (from *ę*): Cassubian *klëknąc* 'to kneel' (Polish *klęknąć*). A further metaphony, whereby short *u* (except after labials and velars) became *ë*, dates from the same period or, possibly, a little later (Stieber 1973: 138): Cassubian *lëdze* 'people' (Polish *ludzie*), *Kaszëbë* 'Cassubia' (Polish *Kaszuby*). The German loan-word *lëter* 'Lutheran' shows that the metaphony affected words borrowed after the Reformation.

The loss of phonemic vowel quantity and its replacement by qualitative distinctions occurred after the appearance of *ë* (which itself was never anything but short). The origin of the remaining eight oral vowels and the two nasals is as follows:

ă › *a* /a/	*ā* › *ô* /ɔ/
ĕ › *e* /ɛ/	*ē* › *é* /e/
ĭ (except *ĭ* which › *ë*) › *i* /i/	*ī* › *i* /i/
ŏ › *o* /o/	*ō* › *ó* /ʮ/
ŭ (except *ŭ* which › *ë*) › *u* /u/	*ū* › *u* /u/
ą̆ › *ę* /ã/	*ą̄* › *ą* /õ/

The *jers* are represented in Cassubian, as in Polish, by *e* in strong position and by Ø in weak position: *sen* 'sleep, dream' from PSl. *sъnъ, *dzéń* 'day' from PSl. *dьnь. The distribution of the reflexes of strong and weak *jers* is not always the same in Cassubian and Polish: Cassubian *dómk* 'house (DIMIN)', from PSl. *domъkъ, *kóńc* 'end' from PSl. *konьcь (Polish *domek, koniec*), but these nominatives are probably secondary formations which have arisen as a result of analogy with oblique cases (*w dómku* 'in the house (DIMIN)', *na kóńcu* 'at the end'). The vowelless variants of these suffixes were, in any case, once common in Polish too.

Syllabic *r̥* and *r̥'* developed in Cassubian as in Polish with the exception that whereas *r̥'* before a hard dental in Polish produced -*ar*- with hardening of the preceding consonant, in Cassubian hardening did not occur: Cassubian *czwiôrti* 'fourth' from PSl. **čvr̥tъjь*, *umiar* 'died (3 SG)' from PSl. **umr̥l* (Polish *czwarty, umarł*). Syllabic *l̥* and *l̥'* usually developed as in Polish (Cassubian and Polish *słup* 'pillar' from PSl. **stl̥pъ*), but there is vestigial evidence of the West Lechitic (and Upper Sorbian) type embodying -*oł*- both in toponyms (German *Stolp*, Polish *Słupsk*) and in appellatives (*dolzëna* 'tall person', *stolpa* 'post, prop', *tolsti* 'fat'; Polish *długi* 'long', *słup* 'pillar', *tłusty* 'fat'). However, the attestation of these Cassubian words is sporadic and only residual (Popowska-Taborska 1987: 237).

The Proto-Slavonic sequence C*ărC* (in which C stands for any consonant) is represented in Cassubian as both C*roC* and C*arC*: Cassubian *droga* 'way' from PSl. *dărga, but *bôrna* and *bróna* 'harrow' from PSl. *bărna, *bôrzda* and *brózda* 'furrow' from PSl. *barzda. The C*ar*C type is not unknown to Polish, but it is extremely rare. In Polabian, on the other hand, it is common. Its representation in Cassubian (particularly in view of the fact that C*ar*C forms were most common in Slovincian, its westernmost attested variety) is consistent with a transitional position between Polish and West Lechitic. The Cassubian developments of Proto-Slavonic C*er*C and C*el*C are identical with those in Polish, except for the fact that C*el*C produced C*ło*C more commonly in Cassubian than in Polish. Cassubian has, for example, not only *żłób* 'crib' (Polish *żłób*), but also *płoc* 'to weed' and *młoc* 'to grind' (Polish *pleć*, *mleć*). There were more of these forms in Slovincian (such as *młóko* 'milk'; Cassubian (non-Slovincian) *mléko*, Polish *mleko*) (Stieber 1973: 139–40).

Word stress in north Cassubian is free and mobile: *ro'lô* 'soil', *'niedzela* 'Sunday', *jô' budëję* 'I build', *të bu'dëjesz* 'you build (SG)'. In south Cassubian the stress is on the first syllable. Most of the word-stress isoglosses are in the central Cassubian region, but their location varies considerably both morphologically and lexically. The stress isogloss for *żołądk* 'stomach' and *kôrwińc/krowińc* 'cow dung' is shown on map 13.1 on page 760. It was once widely believed that the north Cassubian vowel system included the possibility of quantitative opposition, but field-work carried out in 1950 on and near the Hel Peninsula (where the likelihood of finding this opposition was thought to be greatest) revealed the absence of any phonological distinction based on vowel length. Moreover, the re-examination of the material recorded in north Cassubia (including Slovincian) at the end of the nineteenth century led to the conclusion that even then only the vowels /i/ and /u/ were capable of true quantitative distinction. The reason for the misunderstanding may have been the fact that stressed vowels are longer than unstressed (Stieber 1974: 417–22). Cassubian stress is stronger than in Polish and may lead to the loss of unstressed vowels.

2.2   Morphophonemic alternations inherited from Proto-Slavonic
First palatalization:

k:*č piekę* 'I bake' : *pieczesz* 'you bake (SG)'
g:*ž mogę* 'I can' : *móżesz* 'you can (SG)'
ch:*š miech* 'sack' : *miészk* 'sack (DIMIN), purse'

Second palatalization:

k:*c rëbôk* 'fisherman (NOM SG)' : *rëbôcë* 'fishermen (NOM PL)'
g:*dz słëga* 'servant' (NOM SG) : *słëdzë* 'servants (NOM PL)'
ch:*š strëch* 'beggar (NOM SG)' : *strëszë* 'beggars (NOM PL)'

Note: In Slovincian *dz* (whether resulting from the second or third palatalization or from *d + j*) is replaced by *z*: *na noze* 'on the foot'.

Vowel:zero alternations:

dzéń 'day (NOM SG)' : *dnia* 'day (GEN SG)'
pies 'dog (NOM SG)' : *psa* 'dog (GEN SG)'

Note: The number of vowel:zero alternations is reduced by the fact that the Proto-Slavonic suffixes **-ъkъ* and **-ьcь* are represented by -*k* and -*c* (Polish -*ek* and -*ec*): thus *dómk* 'house (DIMIN)'. (See also under 2.1 above.)

2.3 Morphophonemic alternations resulting from changes after Proto-Slavonic

Many consonant alternations coincide with those in Polish, but owing to *kaszubienie* (see above) the Polish alternations *s:ś* and *z:ź* are not found: *jô niosę* 'I carry': *të niesesz* 'you carry (SG)' (compare Polish *niosę:niesiesz*).

The Cassubian metaphony:

$$\left.\begin{matrix} k \\ g \end{matrix}\right\} \text{ (before } i \text{ or } e) \rightarrow \left\{\begin{matrix} cz \\ dż \end{matrix}\right.$$

(as in *dżibczi* 'pliant'; compare Polish *gibki*) results in frequent consonant alternations in the declension of nouns and adjectives:

rek 'crab (NOM SG)' : *reczi* (NOM PL)
rzeka 'river (NOM SG)' : *rzeczi* (GEN SG, NOM PL)
słëga 'servant (NOM SG)' : *słëdżi* (GEN SG)
mitczi 'soft (M NOM SG)' : *mitkô* (F NOM SG)
dłudżi 'long (M NOM SG)' : *długó* (F NOM SG)

The results of this metaphony are shown in the orthography recommended by the Zrzeszenie Kaszubsko-Pomorskie, but the corresponding *ch* (before *i* or *e*) to *sz*, which has a smaller territorial base, is not shown (thus the nominative plural of *mucha* 'fly' is written *muchi*, not *muszi*, even though it is thus pronounced in some northern regions) (Breza and Treder 1984: 24–5).

Owing to *kaszubienie*, *t* alternates with *c* (not *ć*) and *d* with *dz* (not *dź*):

post 'fast (NOM SG)' : *po posce* 'after the fast (LOC SG)'
sôd 'orchard (NOM SG)' : *w sadze* 'in the orchard (LOC SG)'

Vowel alternations are more numerous than in Polish owing to the fact that Polish (more precisely standard Polish) has eliminated some of the vocalic distinctions that remain in Cassubian:

a:*e miasto* 'town (NOM SG)' : *w miesce* 'in town (LOC SG)'
o:*e jô niosę* 'I carry' : *të niesesz* 'you carry (SG)'

Note: The *o*:*e* alternation is often eliminated owing to the operation of analogy (as *jô bierzę* 'I take' : *të bierzesz* 'you take (SG)'; compare Polish *biorę*:*bierzesz*). The following result from alternations between long and short vowels:

	NOM SG	GEN SG
ô:*a*	*brzôd* 'fruit'	*brzadu*
ó:*a*	*pón* 'master'	*pana*
é:*e*	*chléb* 'bread'	*chleba*
i(y):*ë*	*syn* 'son'	*sëna*
u:*ë*	*lud* 'people'	*lëdu*
ó:*o*	*dóm* 'house, shade'	*domu*
ą:*ę*	*ksądz* 'priest'	*ksędza*

3 Morphology

3.1 Nominal morphology

3.1.1   Nominal categories

Cassubian has two numbers, singular and plural, but vestiges of the dual are more prominent in Cassubian than in Polish. In the 1950s in some north Cassubian dialects certain forms of the first-person personal pronoun still retained a dual function (*AJK* XII: 164–5). At the beginning of the twentieth century the dual was a living category in Slovincian and the dialects immediately to its east (Główczyce and Cecenowo) (Lorentz 1958–62: 869).

The seven cases are the same as in Polish, but the tendency for the nominative to replace the vocative is greater than in Polish. The locative never occurs without a preposition, and there is a strong tendency for the instrumental to acquire the preposition *z* (*s*)/*ze* (*se*) 'with', when used with its basic function as an expression of instrument (but not in the complement of the copula).

The category of gender is very similar to that in Polish. In the singular the masculine, neuter and feminine genders are distinguished. Animacy is expressed in the accusative singular of masculine nouns (and adjectives agreeing with them) by the use of the same form as the genitive singular.

The use of a genitive–accusative in the singular may also extend to certain other semantic categories of masculine nouns, including coins, food and fruit, but in these cases the genitive–accusative is always a facultative alternative to the nominative–accusative (Lorentz 1958–62: 874). In the plural the only gender distinction is between masculine personal and non-masculine personal. In view of the relatively recent development of this distinction in both Cassubian and standard Polish (since the end of the seventeenth century) the degree of similarity between them is remarkable (Zieniukowa 1972: 96). There is a small discrepancy in that the otherwise characteristically masculine-personal nominative plural ending -*owie* is (or was until the 1950s) used in some north Cassubian villages not only with nouns denoting human beings, but also with some nouns denoting animals: thus *twórzowie* 'polecats', *zajcowie* 'hares' (*AJK* XII: 88–93, map 564). In M. Pontanus's translation of Luther's Little Catechism (1643) continuants of the Proto-Slavonic accusative plural are still in use (Lorentz 1958–62: 868).

3.1.2   Noun morphology
Masculine noun declension is demonstrated by *chłop* 'man' and *kóń* 'horse' in table 13.2.

Table 13.2   Declension of Cassubian *chłop* 'man' and *kóń* 'horse'

	SG	PL
NOM	chłop	chłopi/chłopë
VOC	chłopie	chłopi/chłopë
ACC	chłopa	chłopów
GEN	chłopa	chłopów
DAT	chłopu/chłopowi	chłopom
INST	chłopem	chłopami/chłopama
LOC	o chłopie	o chłopach
NOM	kóń	konie
VOC	koniu	konie
ACC	konia	konie
GEN	konia	koni/koniów
DAT	koniowi/koniewi/koniu	koniom
INST	koniem	koniami/koniama
LOC	o koniu	o koniach

Notes
1   Reflexes of PSl. **gordъ* have not been used as examples, owing to the fact that Cassubian *gard*, though given in some dictionaries, is of doubtful authenticity, and Cassubian *gród* is very rare.

2   In the genitive singular animates always take -*a*, but inanimates may take -*u* or -*a* and it is not possible to establish any pattern in which certain types of noun take one ending or the other. In fact, many masculine inanimates may take either -*u* or -*a*: *brzegu* or *brzega* (*brzég* 'bank, shore'), *lasu* or *lasa* (*las* 'forest'). In northern dialects the ending -*ë* (< *u*) occurs (*AJK* XI: 123–33, maps 525–7).

3   In the dative singular soft stems may have the ending -*ewi* (corresponding to -*owi* in hard stems). This is facultative. The distribution of -*owi* (-*ewi*) and -*u* does not correspond to that in standard Polish and is unpredictable. Many nouns may have -*owi* (-*ewi*) or -*u*. In northern dialects the dative singular ending -*ë* (< *u*) occurs (*AJK* XI: 125). In the north-east, nouns may acquire the adjectival endings -*omu* and -*emu*: *koniomu* or *koniemu* (*AJK* XI: 172–3, map 538). Various forms arising from the blending of -*owi* (-*ewi*) and -*u* are attested. The form -*ovu*, which Lorentz heard in the Kartuzy and Wejherowo regions early in the twentieth century (1958–62: 873), had almost disappeared by the 1950s (*AJK* XI: 171). In West Slovincian the forms -*owu* and -*ewu* were recorded; in East Slovincian their equivalents were -*oju* and -*eju* (*AJK* XI: 171). The latter are reminiscent of the dative endings -*oju* and -*eju* in Lower Sorbian (see chapter 11, section 3.1.2), which appear to have arisen from a similar blending of -*owi* (-*ewi*) and -*u*.

4   The instrumental singular is normally written -*em*, but -*ę* (reflecting northern pronunciation) also occurs (*AJK* XI: 179–86, maps 542–5). If the stem ends in *k* or *g* the alternations *k*/*cz* and *g*/*dż* may operate: thus *bocziem* (*bok* 'side'), *rodżiem* (*róg* 'horn'), but this is optional; one may also find *bokem, bokę, rogem, rogę*.

5   The locative singular, as in standard Polish, ends in -*e* (with possible consonant alternation) unless the stem is soft or a velar, when it ends in -*u*: *na brzegu* (*brzég* 'bank, shore'). There is a tendency for nouns ending in -*s* or -*z* to take -*u* too, but practice varies: thus *w lasu* (*las* 'forest'), *na wozu* (*wóz* 'cart') (Breza and Treder 1981: 114; *AJK* XI: 181–91, map 547).

Neuter noun declension is demonstrated by *miasto* 'town' and *sërce* 'heart' in table 13.3.

Notes

1   Soft neuter stems often substitute -*o* for -*e* in the nominative singular: thus *polo* 'field' (otherwise *pole*) (Breza and Treder 1981: 118). This reduces the number of features distinguishing hard from soft stems, leaving only the locative singular. However, certain soft neuter stems in -*e* may, in the singular, take a different set of endings, acquired from the adjectival paradigm. The two variants are demonstrated by means of the example *pole*/*polé* 'field' in table 13.4.

Table 13.3   Declension of Cassubian *miasto* **'town' and** *sërce* **'heart'
(the variants** *serce* **and** *sérce* **also exist)**

	SG	PL
NOM	miasto	miasta
VOC	miasto	miasta
ACC	miasto	miasta
GEN	miasta	miast/miastów
DAT	miastu/miastowi	miastom
INST	miastem/miastę	miastami/miastama
LOC	o miesce	o miastach
NOM	sërce	sërca
VOC	sërce	sërca
ACC	sërce	sërca
GEN	sërca	sërc/sërców
DAT	sërcu/sërcowi	sërcom
INST	sërcem/sërcę	sërcami/sërcama
LOC	o sërcu	o sërcach

Table 13.4   Alternative singular paradigms for Cassubian *pole/polé*
'field'

NOM	pole	polé
VOC	pole	polé
ACC	pole	polé
GEN	pola/polô	polégo
DAT	polu/polowi	polému
INST	polem/polę	polim
LOC	o polu	o polim

2   The neuters have acquired three endings which once belonged exclusively to the masculine *u*-stems: the dative singular in *-owi*; the locative
singular in *-u*; and the genitive plural in *-ów*. In the genitive plural the
zero ending is more common than *-ów* (Lorentz 1958–62: 905).

3   Consonant stems survive and are capable of having an extended stem
in the oblique cases: *remię* 'shoulder, arm', genitive singular *remienia*
and so on; but they may also have a shortened type *remio*, genitive
singular *remia*, and so on (Breza and Treder 1981: 118).

Feminine noun declension is demonstrated by *rzéka* 'river' in table 13.5.

Table 13.5   Declension of Cassubian *rzéka* 'river'

	SG	PL
NOM	rzéka	rzéczi
VOC	rzéko	rzéczi
ACC	rzékę	rzéczi
GEN	rzéczi	rzék/rzéków
DAT	rzéce	rzékom
INST	rzéką	rzékami/rzékama
LOC	o rzéce	o rzékach

Notes

1   *Żona* has not been used to illustrate the paradigm, owing to the fact that it is rare and believed to be a borrowing from literary Polish (*AJK* II: 88). The word for 'woman' and 'wife' is *białka* in north Cassubia and *kobiéta* in south Cassubia.

2   The genitive singular and nominative/vocative/accusative plural ending *-i* occurs primarily after affricated *k* and *g*. Elsewhere it is replaced by *-ë*: thus *węda* 'fishing rod' has genitive singular and nominative/vocative/accusative plural *wędë*.

3   Certain masculines denoting persons end in *-a* in the nominative singular (such as *słëga* 'servant') and have a paradigm similar to that shown in table 13.5. However, the vocative singular may be the same as the nominative (thus *słëga* as an alternative to *słëgo*), the dative singular may end in *-owi* (thus *słëgowi* as an alternative to *słëdze*), the nominative/vocative plural may end in *-owie* (thus *słëgowie* as an alternative to *słëdzë* or *słëdzi*), the accusative plural coincides with the genitive plural (as in *słëgów*), and the zero ending does not exist in the genitive plural (thus only *słëgów*).

4   In feminines vacillation between the originally masculine ending *-ów* and the zero ending occurs in all areas, but the zero ending is relatively rare in the south, whereas *-ów* is relatively rare in the north (Lorentz 1958–62: 895).

5   The soft stems vary in the nominative singular according to whether the ending was originally long or short: thus *swinia* 'pig', but *ceniô* 'shadow'. Otherwise, the soft stems differ from the hard only in the genitive singular (*swini* or *swinie*, *ceni* or *cenie*), the dative and locative singular (*o swini*, *o ceni*) and the nominative/vocative/accusative plural (*swinie*, *cenie*).

6   Feminine former *i*-stems also belong to this declension (as *jabłoń* 'apple-tree') and differ from other soft stems only in the nominative singular.

3.1.3   Pronominal morphology

The declension of personal pronouns is shown in table 13.6.

Table 13.6   Declension of Cassubian personal pronouns

First person

	SG	DU (may also have plural meaning)	PL
NOM	jô	ma	më
ACC	mnie, mie, mię	naju	nas, nôs
GEN	mnie, mie	naju	nas, nôs
DAT	mnie, mie	nama	nóm
INST	mną	nama	nami
LOC	o mnie, mie	o naju	o nas, nôs

Second person

	SG	PL	HON
NOM	të	wa	wë
ACC	cebie, ce, cę	waju	was, wôs
GEN	cebie, ce	waju	was, wôs
DAT	tobie, cë	wama	wóm
INST	tobą	wama	wami
LOC	o cebie, tobie	o waju	o was, wôs

Third person

	SG M	SG N	SG F	PL Masculine personal	PL Non-masculine personal
NOM	on	ono, no	ona, na	oni, ni	onë, në
ACC	jego, jen, go	je	ję	jich	je
GEN	jego		ji, jé	jich, jejich	
DAT	jemu, mu		ji	jim, jima	
INST	nim		nią	nimi, jima, nima	
LOC	o nim		o ni	o nich	

Notes

1   Until the 1950s (and possibly later) the first person dual forms *ma*, *naju* and *nama* in some north Cassubian dialects still had a dual function distinct from the plural. Elsewhere, however, they have acquired plural meaning and are thus not grammatically distinct from the original plural (Breza and Treder 1981: 125; *AJK* XII: 164, map 588).

2   As in Polish, third-person pronouns following prepositions substitute *ni-* (that is, /ŋ/) for initial *j-*: thus masculine accusative singular *jego* becomes *niego* (*na niego* 'at him').

3   The ending *-go* in the genitive singular of pronouns and adjectives is pronounced *-ųe* in north Cassubian and this feature is occasionally shown in writing by means of the letter *ł*: thus *jeło* for *jego* (Breza and

Treder 1984: 30). A further possible variant is *-ho* (as in *jeho*), which, though found in only two villages (Lorentz 1958–62: 924), has been used a good deal in Cassubian literature (Stone 1972: 527–8).

4   On the honorific second person, see section 3.2 below.

The reflexive pronoun is declined as follows:

NOM	–
ACC	sebie, sę, so
GEN	sebie, se
DAT	sobie, se, so
INST	sobą
LOC	o sebie, o sobie

3.1.4   Adjectival morphology

Short-form adjectives are better represented in Cassubian than in Polish, but, as in Polish, they are used only predicatively with the verb *bëc* 'to be' and only in the nominative. They are formally distinct from the long forms, as demonstrated by the example *zdrowi/zdrów* 'healthy':

	Long form	*Short form*
M	zdrowi	zdrów
F	zdrowô (‹ *-ā ‹ *-aja)	zdrowa (‹ *-ă)
N	zdrowé	zdrowo
PL	zdrowé	zdrowë

Among the adjectives which have short forms are *głodzén* 'hungry', *godzén* 'worthy', *gotów* 'ready', *nôłożén* 'accustomed', *pewién* 'certain', *pełén* 'full', *próżén* 'empty', *rôd* 'glad', *wôrt* 'worth', *winién* 'guilty', *zdrów* 'healthy', *żiw* 'alive' (Breza and Treder 1981: 119–20). In some areas the masculine form is used for all genders, singular and plural: thus *ona je zdrów* 'she is healthy', *oni są zdrów* 'they are healthy' (Breza and Treder 1981: 151–2).

The short type survives also in the nominative and accusative of possessive adjectives, which, however, unlike other short forms, are used attributively: for example, *bratów* 'brother's'. In the nominative plural and all oblique cases possessive adjectives take the same endings as other adjectives (Breza and Treder 1981: 121).

The adjectival paradigm is demonstrated by *młodi* 'young' in table 13.7.

Notes

1   The vocative always coincides with the nominative.

2   Soft-stem adjectives have the same endings as in the paradigm shown in table 13.7, except in the plural, where they lack the variants with *-ë-*.

3   In contrast to Polish, dentals are not palatalized before the masculine-

Table 13.7 Declension of *młodi* 'young'

| | SG | | | PL | |
	M	N	F	*Masculine personal*	*Non-masculine personal*
NOM	młodi	młodé	młodô	młodi	młodé
ACC	młodi (or młodégo)	młodé	młodą	młodich/-ëch	młodé
GEN		młodégo	młodi	młodich/-ëch	
DAT		młodému	młodi	młodim	
INST		młodim	młodą	młodimi/-ima/-ëmi/-ëma	
LOC		o młodim	o młodi	o młodich/-ëch	

personal nominative plural ending *-i* (compare Polish *młodzi*).

4 As in pronouns, the ending *-go* is pronounced in north Cassubian as *-ųe*, which in stylized literature may be written as *-łe*: thus *młodéłe* for *młodégo*.

3.2 Verbal morphology

In addition to first, second and third persons, singular and plural, the Cassubian verb has acquired an honorific second person singular or plural category expressed by means of the originally plural ending *-ce*: *wë môce* 'you have'. This is distinct from the non-honorific second person plural, which is expressed by means of the originally second person dual ending *-ta*: *wa môta* 'you have' (NON-HON PL).

On the basis of the present-tense endings (principally the vowel *-e-*, *-i-* or *-ô-* in the middle four members of the paradigm) the verbs fall into the four conjugations illustrated in table 13.8.

Notes

1 The uncontracted forms of the third conjugation are found in north Cassubia (see map 13.1 on p. 760). For most verbs of this conjugation the uncontracted form is attested only in the first person singular (thus, from *gadac* 'to speak': *jô gôdaję* 'I speak', but *të gôdôsz* 'you speak (SG)', and so forth) (*AJK* X: map 451). The verbs *grac* 'to play' and *znac* 'to know', however, have a complete present-tense uncontracted paradigm, in addition to the contracted type found in the south (Breza and Treder 1981: 130–1).

2 The only other verb belonging to the fourth conjugation is *wiedzec* 'to know' (*jô wiém*, *të wiész* (*wiés*) and so forth).

The present and future tenses of the verb *bëc* 'to be' are shown in table

Table 13.8   Examples of the four Cassubian conjugations

	SG	PL	HON
First conjugation: *niesc* 'to carry'			
1	jô niosę	më niesemë (-ma)	
2	të niesesz	wa nieseta	wë niesece
3	on/ono/ona niese	oni/onë niosą	
Second conjugation: *robic* 'to do, make, work'			
1	jô robię	më robimë (-ma)	
2	të robisz	wa robita	wë robice
3	on/ono/ona robi	oni/onë robią	
Third conjugation (contracted): *grac* 'to play'			
1	jô gróm	më grômë (-ma)	
2	të grôsz	wa grôta	wë grôce
3	on/ono/ona grô	oni/onë grają	
Third conjugation (uncontracted): *grac* 'to play'			
1	jô graję	më grajemë (-ma)	
2	të grajesz	wa grajeta	wë grajece
3	on/ono/ona graje	oni/onë grają	
Fourth conjugation: *jesc* 'to eat'			
1	jô jém	më jémë (-ma)	
2	të jész (jés)	wa jéta	wë jéce
3	on/ono/ona jé	oni/onë jédzą	

13.9. The future tense of other verbs is formed, as in Polish, with the non-past of perfective verbs or with the infinitive or *l*-participle of imperfective verbs in conjunction with the future of 'to be'. The past tense is capable of being formed in three different ways, none of which coincides with the Polish past tense:

1   The auxiliary *bëc* 'to be' is accompanied by the *l*-participle (for example, *robił* from *robic* 'to make, work'):

SG	PL	HON
1 jô jem robił(a)	më jesmë robilë/-łë	
2 të jes robił(a)	wa jesta robilë/-łë	wë jesce robilë
3 on/ono/ona je robił(o/a)	oni/onë są robilë/-łë	

Note: This type is widely used in literature, but in the spoken language it is characteristic of the older generation.

2   The *l*-participle is used without the auxiliary (the personal pronoun thus acquiring an added significance, as in Russian):

Table 13.9   Present and future tenses of *bëc* 'to be'

	SG	PL	HON
Present			
1	jô jem	më jesmë	
2	të jes	wa jesta	wë jesce
3	on/ono/ona je	oni/onë są	
Future			
1	jô będę/bądę/mdę/ bdę	më będzemë/ bądzemë/mdzemë/ bdzemë	
2	të będzesz/bądzesz/ mdzesz/bdzesz	wa będzeta/bądzeta/ mdzeta/bdzeta	we będzece/bądzece/ mdzece/bdzece
3	on/ono/ona będze/ bądze/mdze/bdze	oni/onë będą/bądą/ mdą/bdą	

	SG	PL	HON
1	jô robił(a)	më robilë/-łë	
2	të robił(a)	wa robilë/-łë	wë robilë
3	on/ono/ona robił(o/a)	oni robilë/onë robiłë	

Note: In north and central Cassubia the feminine ending *-ła*, if preceded by *-a-* or *-ę-*, is contracted: thus *pisała* 'wrote' → *pisa, wzęła* 'took' → *wzę* (Breza and Treder 1981: 133–4).

3   The auxiliary *miec* 'to have' is accompanied by the passive participle in its nominative singular neuter or masculine form, as in *on mô to wszëtko zrobioné/zrobiony* 'he has done it all' (Lorentz 1919: 45, 74; Breza and Treder 1981: 133). Passive participles are formed not only with *-n-* and *-t-* (*zrobiony* 'done', *zabiti* 'killed'), as in Polish, but also with *-ł-/-l-* (*zjadłi* 'eaten'):

Jô môm to widzałé.
'I have seen that.'

In the case of intransitive verbs of motion, this tense is formed with the auxiliary *bëc* 'to be' (instead of *miec* 'to have'). The participle then agrees in gender and number with the subject:

Ta białka je precz jidzonô.
'The (or that) woman has gone away.'

Pluperfect constructions are also possible (but rare):

Jô jem bél pisôł.
'I had written.'

Jak jô przëszëd, on ju wszëtko miôł zjadłé.
'When I arrived, he had already eaten everything.'

(Lorentz 1919: 74)

The conditional is formed by combining the particle *bë* (which may or may not acquire a personal ending) with the *l*-participle:

Jô bë ucekł   *or*   Jô bëm ucekł.
'I would run away.'
Të bë ucekł.   *or*   Të bës ucekł.
'You would run away.'

(Breza and Treder 1981: 134)

3.3 Derivational morphology

3.3.1   Major patterns of noun derivation
The following characteristically Cassubian suffixes are either not known in Polish or have a function which differs from that of their formal counterparts in Polish:

1   *-ëszcze/-iszcze* and derivatives *-czëszcze/-cziszcze*, *-owiszcze* and *-awiszcze*: *rżëszcze, rżanowiszcze, rżaniszcze* 'field of rye-stubble' (derived from *reż* 'rye') (compare Polish *rżysko* 'stubble'), *bulwiszcze* 'potato field' (derived from *bulwa* 'potato') (compare Polish *kartoflisko*), *mrowiszcze* 'ant-hill' (compare Polish *mrowisko*), *pastwiszcze* 'pasture' (compare Polish *pastwisko*). The equivalent of standard Polish *-isko*, this suffix often has the meaning 'place' (as in other Slavonic languages), but it is also capable of totally different functions, as in *grablëszcze/grabiszcze* 'handle of a rake', *kosëszcze* 'handle of a scythe', *szëplëszcze* 'handle of a spade'. It is found only in northern dialects and among speakers of the older generation. Among the young it is tending to be replaced by *-isko* (Breza and Treder 1981: 92–3).
2   *-'ô* (< *'-ā*) is used to form abstract nouns and often corresponds to Polish *-ość*: *grëbiô/grubiô* 'fatness', *wiżô* 'height', *szërzô* 'width'.
3   *-ota* is used to form abstract nouns and usually corresponds to Polish *-ość* (though Polish also has *-ota* for certain purposes): *bladota* 'pallor', *cëchota* 'quietness', *bëlnota* 'courage, virtue'.
4   *-iczé* is specifically Cassubian and is used to derive from the names of plants words denoting foliage, stalks or the place where the plant grows: *bobowiczé* 'bean leaves and stalks' (derived from *bób* '(broad) beans'), *bulwowiczé* 'leaves of the potato' (derived from *bulwa* 'potato'), *grochowiczé* 'pea stalks' (derived from *groch* 'peas'), *wrzosowiczé* 'heath' (derived from *wrzos* 'heather').

5   *-ajk* (M), *-ajka* (F) are used to derive nouns from verbs. They are often
pejorative, usually refer to human beings (but sometimes to animals
and objects), and are particularly characteristic of central Cassubian
dialects: *lizajk* 'lickspittle, flatterer' (from *lizac* 'to lick'), *nalinajk*
'importunate man' (from *nalënac* 'to insist'), *kopajka* 'cow that kicks
during milking' (from *kopac* 'to kick') (Popowska-Taborska 1987:
212–18).

3.3.2   Major patterns of adjective derivation
The following suffixes have different functions from their formal counterparts in Polish (which are given for comparison where appropriate):

1   *-'any*: *złocany* 'golden' (from *złoto* 'gold'; Polish *złoty* 'golden'),
ceniany 'shady' (from *céń* 'shade'; Polish *cienisty*), *krëwiany* 'bloody'
(from *krew* 'blood'; Polish *krwawy*), *deszczany* 'rainy' (from *deszcz*
'rain'; Polish *deszczowy*).

2   *-ny*: *bójny* 'fearful' (from *bojec sę* 'to fear'; Polish *bojaźliwy*), *dżibny*
'pliant' (from *dżibac* 'to bend'; Polish *gibki*).

3   *-i*: *chłopi* 'male' (from *chłop* 'man'), *knôpi* 'boyish' (from *knôp* 'boy'),
strëszi 'beggarly' (from *strëch* 'beggar'), *buczi* 'beech' (from *buk*
'beech'; Polish *bukowy*).

4   *-ati* in adjectives derived from adjectives denotes a weakening of the
attribute in question (English *-ish*): *długowati* 'longish' (from *dłudżi*
'long'), *sëwati* 'greyish' (from *sëwi* 'grey'; Polish *siwawy*), *głëchowati*
'hard of hearing' (from *głëchi* 'deaf'; Polish *głuchawy*) (Breza and
Treder 1981: 104–7).

4   Syntax

4.1   Element order in declarative sentences
To a considerable extent the unmarked order of constituents in the
Cassubian sentence coincides with that in Polish. The subject precedes the
predicate:

Subject   Predicate

Ubogô czôpka okriwô nierôz mądrą głowę.
'A poor cap often covers a wise head.'

Within the predicate the verb normally precedes the object:

Verb   Adverb   Object

... okriwô   nierôz   mądrą głowę

There is a tendency, however, for the verb to follow the object and thus to stand at the end of the clause. This is said to be an archaic feature, once present in Polish too, which Cassubian has retained (Breza and Treder 1981: 176). The difference between Cassubian and Polish in this respect may be seen from the following examples from Aleksander Majkowski's *Žëcé i przigodë Remusa* (1988) contrasted with the corresponding sentences from Lech Bądkowski's Polish translation *Życie i przygody Remusa* (1966):

Cassubian:	A tak jô umrzec muszę.	(p. 126)
Polish:	A tak muszę umrzeć.	(p. 78)
	'Otherwise, I must die.'	

Cassubian	Wkrąg zelenô dzarna jak diwan rozłożeła sę. (p. 265)
	around green turf like carpet spread self.

Polish	Naokoło rozłożyła się jak dywan zielona darń. (p. 161)
	around spread self like carpet green turf.
	'All around the green turf was spread out like a carpet.'

In analytic forms of the verb the auxiliary (or the particle *bë*) is often separated from the non-finite component, forming a 'bow', like that known from Sorbian (see chapter 11, section 4.1):

Nen parobk bél czekawi, co ona mdze (AUX) tam robiła (PART).
'That servant wondered what she would do there.'

(Sychta 1967–76, I: 157)

Cziej jem (AUX) tam pod trzema chojnami dôwôł (PART) bôczenié na moje bëdło, nico mie wiedno kuseło.

(Majkowski, p. 26)

(Polish translation: Gdy pod tymi trzema chojnami pilnowałem bydła, zawsze coś mnie kusiło.) (p. 21)
'When I was keeping watch on my cattle there under the three pines, something was always tempting me.'

4.2   Non-declarative sentence types

In a question seeking supplementary information the first position is taken by an interrogative pronoun or adverb (such as *chto(ż)* 'who', *co(ż)* 'what', *cziedy(ż)* 'when', *jak* 'how'):

Dzeż wa jidzeta?
'Where are you going?'

In these questions the order of elements following the interrogative word is the same as in the corresponding declarative sentence. Yes–no sentences, however, are derived from declarative sentences by moving the verb into first position:

Të możesz mie to powiedzec.
'You can tell me that.'

becomes a question as:

Możesz të mie to powiedzec?
'Can you tell me that?'

A negated verb is preceded by *nie*:

Nie zakôzôł jô tobie?
'Did I not forbid you?'

In a question presenting an alternative the second element is preceded by *czë* or *abo*:

Gôdôce wë po żartach, czë po prôwdze?
'Are you speaking in jest or in earnest?'
Znajesz të to, abo môm jo tobie to pokazac?
'Do you know it or have I got to show you it?'

Questions are frequently introduced by particles (*ë, a, i* or *ale*), which precede all other elements:

Ë béł të w Gduńsku, abo dze të béł?
'Were you in Gdańsk or where were you?'

It is possible for a yes–no question to be introduced by the particle *czë*:

Czë to je twoje?
'Is that yours?'

in which case the verb retains the same position as in the declarative sentence. But this type is rarer in Cassubian than in Polish.

The usual responses to a yes–no question (whether negated or not) are *jo* 'yes' and *nié* 'no':

Jedzeta wa?
'Are you going?'
Jo.
'Yes.'

These words are made more emphatic by the addition of the particle *le*: *jo le* 'yes indeed', *nié le* 'certainly not'.

Indirect yes–no questions are introduced by *czë*:

Jô sę pitôł, czë on je doma.
'I asked if he was at home.'

The order in indirect questions is the same as in the declarative sentence.

4.3   Copular sentences

The main copulas are *bëc* 'to be', *ostac* 'to remain' and *stawac sę* (perfective *stac sę*). The zero copula 'to be' is extremely rare and stylistically marked:

To ostatnô noc.
'That is the last night.'
To më nié, to ti sztërzej kole ognia.
'It's not us, it's those four by the fire.'
Co nowégo na swiecé?
'What's new in the world?'

(Lorentz 1919: 82)

The complement of any of the verbs named above may be in either the nominative or the instrumental. This applies both to nouns and noun phrases:

Nominative:

Ten karczmôrz je mój brat.
'The (or that) inn-keeper is my brother.'
Të ostôniesz mój syn.
'You will remain my son.'
Tak ten parobk sę stôł pón.
'So the servant became master.'

Instrumental:

Jan bêł dobrim rëbôczem.
'Jan was a good fisherman.'
On sę stôł królę.
'He became king.'

and to adjectives:

Nominative:

Wë jesce barzo łaskawi.
'You are very kind.'

Instrumental:

Jô nie jem taczim, jak të mëslisz.
'I am not such, as you think.'
On sę stôł barzo nieszczestlëwim.
'He became very unhappy.'

(Breza and Treder 1981: 151; Lorentz 1958–62: 1134)

The complement may also be formed with the preposition *za*, which may take the nominative, accusative or instrumental:

On bél w ti wsy za kowôl.
'He was the blacksmith in that village.'
Jô wice nie mdę za rëbôka.
'I shan't be a fisherman any more.'
On tam bél za królę.
'He was king there.'

(Lorentz 1925: 205, 214; 1958–62: 1134)

The use of the simple nominative is said to indicate a permanent characteristic (Lorentz 1919: 60; 1958–62: 1134), but with *stawac sę* (*stac sę*) the use of the nominative complement is rare (Lorentz 1925: 201–2).

4.4 Coordination and comitativity

Coordination, both of individual words and phrases and of clauses, is most commonly effected by means of coordinating conjunctions, such as *i* (varying locally with *ji* and *ë*) 'and', *a* 'and', *ale* 'but', *abo* 'or', *czë* 'or', *ani* 'neither/nor':

Bëlë brat a sostra.
'They were brother and sister.'

In contradistinction to Modern Polish (but as in Old Polish) the function of *a* is often connective (as in the above example), but it may also have a disconnective function (as in Modern Polish):

Nie wié, a gôdô.
'He does not know and (yet) he speaks.'

The process whereby *i* is replacing *a* in the connective function is less advanced than in Polish (Breza and Treder 1981: 163). The Slovincian conjunction *ôs* 'and' (also connective) was recorded extensively by Lorentz (as in *tata ôs mëma ju nie żëją* 'father and mother are no longer living'; 1958–72, I: 600).

Zero coordination also occurs:

W chałëpie, na polu, w lese, na jezerze jô muszíł robic.
'In the house, in the field, in the forest (and) on the lake I had to work.'

Zero may also be disconnective:

Do cebie on przëszed, mie on nie nawiedzył.
'He came to you, (but) he did not visit me.'

In a series each item may be preceded by a conjunction:

Chłopi ji białczi ji dzecë sę zbiegałë.
'Men and women and children gathered together.'

or the items may be in pairs:

Stołë ë stółczi, ławë ë szpinie oni wëniesłë.
'Tables and chairs, benches and cupboards they carried out.'

or only the last item may be preceded by a conjunction:

Jô môm troje dzecy, Jana, Môrcëna a Leoszę.
'I have three children, Jan, Môrcën and Leosza.'

(Lorentz 1925: 223; 1958–62: 1174)

Conjoined noun phrases in the subject generally take a plural verb:

Brat a sostra szlë w las.
'Brother and sister went into the wood.'

but occasionally singular verbs occur, in which case the verb agrees in gender with the noun standing closest to it:

Odraza (F) i strach (M) czierowôł (M SG) jego postępkama.
'Revulsion and fear directed his actions.'

(Lorentz 1925: 225; 1958–62: 1174; Breza and Treder 1981: 152)

Comitative constructions can consist only of nouns, not pronouns. They normally take singular agreement (an archaic feature):

Lesny z psem po lese chodzy.
'The forester and his dog are walking in the wood.'

But the innovatory use of the plural may also be observed:

Kawalér z brutką szlë szpacérę.
'The bridegroom and the bride went for a walk.'

Comitative phrases hardly ever occur in any case other than the nominative. (Lorentz 1925: 223, 225; 1958–62: 1175; Breza and Treder 1981: 152).

4.5   Subordination

The following are some of the main subordinating conjunctions: *bële* 'if', *bo* 'because', *choba* (*że*) 'unless', *choc* 'though', *chtëren* 'who, which', *chto* 'who', *cziedë* 'when', *cziej* 'when, if', *eż* 'that', (*g*)*dze* 'where', *jak* 'as', *jaż* 'until', *jeżle* 'whether, if', *ko* 'because, since', *że* 'that'. Quite distinct from standard Polish (though with parallels in Polish dialects) is the wide range of functions performed by *co* 'who, what, that'. As a relative pronoun it is undeclined:

ti lëdze, co na drodze bëlë
'the people who were in the road'

but the oblique cases are expressed by the insertion of the appropriate form of the anaphoric pronoun:

ta białka, co to dzecko ji (DAT SG) słëchało
the woman who the child   to her   belonged
'the woman to whom the child belonged'

(Lorentz 1919: 60)

As alternatives to subordinate clauses of certain types Cassubian has, as a result of German interference, evolved several constructions involving the use of non-finite parts of the verb:

1   Verbal noun:

Nakaż jemu te stëdnie do czëszczeniô.
'Order him to clean the well.' (only northern dialects)

2   Gerund/participle:

Ona obôczëła swojego chłopa na zemi leżącë.
'She saw her husband lying on the ground.'

3   Infinitive:

On czuł tego ptôcha spiewac.
'He heard the bird sing.'

(Lorentz 1958–62: 1064)

There are also many constructions in which (as in Polish and independently of German influence) infinitives are used, including those containing modal verbs and verbs of beginning, finishing, continuing, prohibiting, permitting, learning, teaching, fearing and so forth:

On sę zbojôł jic na wies.
'He was afraid to go to the village.'

In northern dialects the infinitive is subject to replacement by the verbal noun:

Mielë strach w karczmie do tańcowaniô.
'They were afraid to dance in the inn.'

Though amply attested by Lorentz (1958–62: 1098), this construction is now said to be rare (Breza and Treder 1981: 181), the influence of German having been replaced by the influence of Polish.

4.6   Negation

Sentence negation is expressed by the adverb *nie* 'not', which stands immediately before the main verb:

Jô to nie zrobiç.
'I shall not do that.'

In the case of intransitive verbs negation may be strengthened by the addition of *nic* before *nie*:

On sę nic nie smiôł.
'He did not laugh at all.'

(Lorentz 1958–72, I: 595)

Before parts of *miec* 'to have', *moc* 'to be able' and *muszëc* 'must' *nie* is replaced by the allomorph *ni*: *jô ni môm* 'I have not', *ona ni może* 'she cannot'.

Constituent negation is expressed by the adverb *nié* 'not', which stands immediately after the constituent negated:

Jô przińdę gwësno, ale mój brat nié.
'I shall come for certain, but not my brother.'

This is a homonym of the negative interjection *nié* 'no'. The form *nie* occurs only with verbs, the form *nié* only independently of verbs (Lorentz 1919: 72). Further negative adverbs are *nigdë* 'never', *nigdze* 'nowhere' and *nijak* 'in no way'. Negative pronouns are *nic* 'nothing' and *nicht* 'nobody'. There is no known limit to the number of negative elements that can be included in the clause:

Tu nicht nigdë nic nie przëniós.
'No one ever brought anything here.'

The direct object in a negated sentence may be in the genitive or the accusative:

Jô nie widzôł ti białczi.   'I did not see the woman.'
Jô nie widzôł tę białkę.

(Breza and Treder 1981: 153)

The question whether there are any lexical or other restraints on the choice of case has not been investigated, but according to Lorentz (1925: 202) any verb whose equivalent can be used with the accusative in German is also capable of taking the accusative in Cassubian.

The logical subject of certain negated sentences is also capable of appearing in the genitive:

Tam nie bëło nikogo.
'There was no one there.'

(Lorentz 1958–62: 1092)

But here too the genitive is not mandatory:

Tam nie bёł nicht.

(Lorentz 1958–72, I: 594)

4.7 Anaphora and pronouns

Anaphora is most commonly expressed by the personal pronouns *jô, të, on, ona, ono, më, va, oni, onë* and honorific *vë*:

Czim chudszô wesz, tim barżé ona grëze.
'The leaner the louse, the more it bites.'
Jedni rodzyce mieli jednégo syna, ale oni bёlё barzo ubodzy i oni nie moglё jemu
    nic dac.
'Some parents had a son, but they were very poor and could give him nothing.'

Forms of the originally demonstrative pronouns *ten, ta, to* and *nen, na, no* (commonly used as definite articles) also have an anaphoric function:

Jeden chłop a jedna białka, ti mieszkalё w lese.
'A man and a woman, they lived in a forest.'

It is possible to omit the subject pronoun, but this is rare:

Ni môm nikogo, cobё mie pomógł.
'(I) have no one to help me.'

(Breza and Treder 1981: 150; Lorentz 1958–62: 1164)

There are, however, cases in which the omission of the pronoun is a positive indication of the absence of anaphora (that is, with an indefinite subject interpretation, like English 'one'):

Cziej tak przez las jidze ...
'When one goes through the wood like that ...'
Jak organё nastroisz, tak grają.
'As the organ is tuned, so it will play.'

(Lorentz 1958–62: 1165)

The increasing omission of personal pronouns in certain types of modern Cassubian literature is a result of Polish influence. Their frequent and redundant use is a characteristic feature of the vernacular and of more traditional literature:

Jô sę ceszę, co jô to zrobił.
'I am glad that I did it.'

It is often the case that the pronoun is used *in addition* to a noun in the subject:

Jeden bogati a jeden biédny brat, oni sę ni moglë zgodzëc.
'A rich brother and a poor brother, they could not agree.'

In relative clauses anaphora is expressed by the relative pronouns *chtëren*, *jaczi*, *chto* and *co*. The most common of these is uninflected *co*, which can relate to nouns and pronouns of any gender or number. It acquires the equivalents of inflections in the form of parts of the personal pronouns:

ten chłop, co   jemu   jô to dôł
the man   who to him I   it gave
'the man to whom I gave it'
më wszëtcë, co   më tam   bëlë
we all   who we there were
'all of us who were there'

(Lorentz 1919: 29; 1925: 200)

4.8   Reflexives and reciprocals

Reflexivity is expressed by means of the reflexive pronoun (*sebie, sę, so* and so on) and of the reflexive possessive adjective *swój*:

On widzôł sebie w špéglu.
'He saw himself in the looking-glass.'
Jô weznę swoję palëcę.
'I shall take my stick.'

In the first and second persons the reflexive possessive adjective may be replaced by the personal possessive adjective:

Jô weznę moję palëcę.
'I shall take my stick.'

(Lorentz 1925: 199–200)

Reciprocity is expressed by means of the reflexive pronoun:

A wa sę znajeta?
'And do you know each other?'

or of *ten (jeden)* ... (*tego*) *drëdżiégo* '(the) one ... (the) other'

Ti bracë jeden tego drëdżiégo sę bilë.
'The brothers were fighting each other.'

(Lorentz 1958–62: 1076)

4.9   Possession

Possession is commonly expressed by means of the verb *miec* 'to have':

Jô môm dwie krowë ji jedno celę.
'I have two cows and one calf.'

In contrast to Polish a distinction is made between the normal negative third person singular *ni mô* 'has not' (*on ni mô nic* 'he has nothing') and *ni ma* 'there is not' (*ni ma nic* 'there is nothing') (Breza and Treder 1984: 20, 22). The possessive dative is extremely rare:

Jemu   bëło miono Karól.
to him was name Karól
'His name was Karól.'

(Lorentz 1958–62: 1114)

A possessive relationship may be expressed by means of an adnominal genitive, which normally follows its head noun, though it may also stand before it:

konie naszego pana
naszego pana konie   'our master's horses'

If the adnominal genitive is singular and consists only of a noun without a modifier it is normally replaced by a possessive adjective (Lorentz 1958–62: 1090–1): *panowé konie* '(the) master's horses' is normally preferred to *konie pana* '(the) horses of (the) master.' It is asserted by Breza and Treder (1981: 105) that the adjectival construction is obligatory; but in literature, at least, it is not difficult to find cases of singular unmodified adnominal genitives. In Cassubian (unlike Sorbian) possessive adjectives can control neither attributive modifiers nor relative pronouns, but, as in all other Slavonic languages (with the possible exception of Polish, in which the existence of the possessive adjective is marginal and its control ability doubtful – Corbett 1987: 314 and 319, table 1), control of the personal pronoun is normal:

Początk pisanjô Remusovégo. Jak on pôsôł dobëtk i jak sę dowiedzôł o Straszku ...
'The beginning of Remus's writing. How he tended cattle and learned about Straszk ...'

(Majkowski 1988: 18)

In the Polish translation of Majkowski's novel *Żëcé i przigodë Remusa* 'The life and adventures of Remus' (whose title, incidentally, demonstrates the adnominal genitive) the possessive adjectives are retained in most cases and impart a Cassubian ingredient to the Polish style (Majkowski 1966 *passim*).

5   Lexis

5.2   Patterns of borrowing

As a result of centuries of contact with German the Cassubian vocabulary has acquired a large number of German borrowings of various kinds. It has been estimated that about 5 per cent of the vocabulary is made up of German loan-words, as compared with 3 per cent in the case of the Polish vocabulary (Hinze 1965: 7–8). For example: Cassubian *brëkowac* 'to need, use' (Low German *brüken*), *brutka* 'bride, fiancée, spinster' (Low German *brüt*), *bôt* 'boat' (German *Boot*), *darvac* 'may, must' (Low German *darven*), *dënëga* 'wave' (German *Dünung*), *dërch* 'through' (German *durch*), *doch* 'yet, but' (German *doch*), *kanink(a)* 'rabbit' (Low German *kaninken*), *knôp* 'boy' (Low German *knäp*), *nara* 'fool' (Middle Low German *narre*), *twéla* 'twig, branch' (Low German *twelle*), *żoka* 'sock' (German *Socke*). The majority of the loan-words were borrowed from the Low German varieties spoken by the settlers with whom the Cassubians were in constant and prolonged contact. In many cases the form of the loan-word provides evidence that it is of Low German origin. The role of standard German was smaller, but not negligible. Central German is also represented (Hinze 1965: 12–15).

The likelihood of Latin, Prussian and Scandinavian influence on the vocabulary was mentioned in passing by Lorentz (Lorentz, Fischer and Lehr-Spławiński 1935: 12–13), but with few details (see also Lorentz 1925: 11–12). The question of Polish lexical influence is particularly difficult, for it depends on being able to say what is specifically Cassubian in the Cassubian vocabulary. Nevertheless, Cassubian words whose Polish equivalents are known to be Czech borrowings (such as *hardi* 'haughty', *wspaniałi* 'splendid') can scarcely be anything but Polish borrowings in Cassubian (Popowska-Taborska 1987: 18–26). The same is true of Cassubian words embodying the Polish dialectal (but not Cassubian) feature of *mazurzenie* (such as *cud* 'miracle') (Popowska-Taborska 1987: 43–8). In the twentieth century, of course, it is possible for linguists directly to observe the widespread replacement of traditional Cassubian words by Polonisms (such as substitution of Polish *narzeczona* 'fiancée' and *narzeczony* 'fiancé' for Cassubian *brutka* and *kawaler*; Popowska-Taborska 1980: 38).

5.4   Lexical fields

5.4.1   Colour terms
white	*biôłi*
black	*czôrni*
red	*czerwoni* (south and central dialects), *czerwioni* (north)
green	*zeloni*

yellow	*żôłti*
blue	*modri* (north, central, and part of south), *jasny* (south), *niebiesczi* (sporadically in north and central, but mainly south dialects) (*AJK* IV: 161–4, map 184).
brown	*bruny* (including horses)
purple	*lilewi*
pink	*różowi, różewi*
orange	*pomerańcowi*
grey	*sëwi* (of hair), *szari, popielati* 'light grey'

5.4.2 Body parts

head	*głowa* (human beings and animals), *łeb* (or *łep*) (animals)
eye	*oko* (plural *oczë*) (human beings and animals), *slépie* (animals)
nose	*nos*
ear	*ucho* (plural *uszë*)
mouth	*gęba* (human being), *pësk* (animals) (*usta* is not known – *AJK* I: 104), *flaba, munia, plapa*
hair	*włosë* (singular *włos*), *klat(ë), klësz(e), knisze*
neck	*kark, szëja* (human beings and animals); the meaning of *kark* (unlike Polish *kark*) is not restricted to 'nape' (*AJK* XV: 48)
arm/hand	*remię* (upper arm), *ręka* (from elbow to finger-tips)
finger	*pôlc*
leg/foot	*noga* 'leg and foot', *stopa* 'foot', *gajda* 'long leg'; *szpéra, szpéta* (animals)
toe	*pôlc kole nodżi*
chest	*piérs*
heart	*sërce*

5.4.3 Kinship terms

mother	varies regionally: northernmost dialects have *nëna, nënka,* and derivatives; further south *mëma, mëmka* and others. (*AJK* II: 115–17, map 80). Also *mata, matka, mac, nana.*
father	*ojc, tata, tatk, papa*
sister	*sostra, sostrzëca*
brother	*brat, bratin, bratk*
aunt	*cotka* (sister of mother or father), *wujna* (wife of mother's brother), *strijna* (wife of father's brother)
uncle	*wuja* (mainly north), *wuj* (mainly south) (both mean 'brother of mother'), *strij* (brother of father) (*AJK* VII: map 324)
niece	*bratinka* (brother's daughter), *sostrzëna, sostrzinia, sestrzónka* (sister's daughter)

nephew   *bratink, bratéwc, bratówc* (brother's son), *sostrzin, sestrzónk* (sister's son).

cousin (female)   *pólsostra* (also means 'half-sister') (Sychta 1967–76 IV: 128), *cotczëna córka* (aunt's daughter) (Sychta 1967–76, I: 140)

cousin (male)   *pólbrat* (also means 'half-brother') (Sychta 1967–76, IV: 125)

grandmother   varies regionally: *nënka, stara nënka, starka, staruszka, starucha, oma, omama* and others (*AJK* V: 182–7, map 235). Also *busz(k)a.*

grandfather   varies regionally: *stark, tatk, stary tatk, staruszk, opa, opapa* and others (*AJK* V: 175–82, map 234). Also *buszk, dada.*

wife   *białka* (north), *kobiéta* (south); both words mean both 'wife' and 'woman' (*AJK* II: 87–8, map 72). Also *czepnica, slëbnô, slëbnica.*

husband   *chłop* 'man, husband'; thus *woni żëlë jak chłop ë białka* 'they lived as man and wife' (Lorentz 1958–72, I: 277). Also *slëbny, slëbnik.*

daughter   *córka,* rarely *córa.* Also (archaic) *otroczëca.*
son   *syn.* Also (archaic) *otrok.*

6 Dialects

A comprehensive picture of territorial variation in Cassubian and the neighbouring Polish dialects is presented in *AJK* on the basis of field-work carried out in the period 1955–61. Material was collected from 186 villages, of which 104 are Cassubian. Particular weight was given to lexical isoglosses, as may be seen from the fact that of the 700 maps 300 deal with lexical questions, 150 with word-formation, 150 with inflection and 100 with phonetics and phonology. Before 1945 Cassubian came into contact with Polish dialects only in the south and south-east along a border about 16 miles (27 km) long. Here it met and still meets the Polish dialects of Kociewie and Tuchola. Otherwise it was surrounded by German and the sea. After 1945 the Germans were expelled and the areas they had left were filled with immigrants from other parts of Poland (see map 13.1 on p. 760).

The main isoglosses distinguishing Cassubian from its Polish neighbours are:

1   *Kaszubienie*: the substitution of *c* for *ć, s* for *ś, z* for *ź* and *dz* for *dź*;
2   South Cassubian initial stress accent (penultimate in the adjoining Polish dialect of Tuchola);
3   distinction between *ô* (‹ *ā̄*) and *a* (‹ *ă*) (in the neighbouring Polish

dialect of Kociewie *ā* and *ă* have merged as *a*);

4   loss of vowel in the suffixes *-k* (‹ *-ъkъ) and *-c* (‹ *-ьcь).

Internal isoglosses attest clearly the individuality of north Cassubian, particularly the far north:

1   The north-east, including the Hel Peninsula, has one phoneme /l/, where other dialects have two, /l/ and /w/ (*ł*): thus *głowa* 'head' is pronounced /glova/ (see map 13.1 on p. 760). The question as to whether this results from German influence remains unsolved (see Breza and Treder 1981: 31–2). In neighbouring Cassubian dialects this feature has motivated the nick-name *Bëlôk* 'one who substitutes /l/ for /w/' and the verb *bëlaczëc* 'to pronounce /l/ instead of /w/'.

2   In most of the north (but excluding the far north-west) /x/ before a front vowel › /ʃ/: as in /muʃi/, nominative plural of *mucha* 'fly'. The corresponding *k'* › *cz* and *g'* › *dż* extend over the whole of, and even beyond, Cassubian territory.

3   Northern first person singular *-aję* in certain verbs corresponds to *-am* further south: northern *szukaję* 'I seek': south and central *szukóm* (see map 13.1 on p. 760).

4   Examples of northern lexical isoglosses: *jiglëna* 'juniper' (Polish *jagłowiec*), *Jastrë* 'Easter' (Polish *Wielkanoc*), *naożeni* 'bridegroom' (Polish *pan młody*), *nogawica* 'stocking' (Polish *pończocha*), *okszô* 'axe' (Polish *siekiera*).

There are few specifically central or south Cassubian isoglosses. Features not shared with the north are often shared with adjacent Polish dialects. However, the following are at least typically, if not exclusively, south and central Cassubian:

1   *sj* ‹ *sw'*: *sjinia* 'pig' ‹ *swinia* (see map 13.1 on p. 760).

2   Neuter genitive singular in *-u* (sporadically in south): thus *żëcu* (genitive singular of *żëcé* 'life'), *ostrzu* (genitive singular of *ostrzé* 'blade'). This is only attested for soft stems (*AJK* XI: maps 536–7).

3   Lexical: *chałupnik* 'lodger' (south) (Polish *lokator*), *opi* 'vampire' (south and central) (Polish and North Cassubian *upiór*), *pozymk* 'spring (season)' (south) (Polish *wiosna*), *stępień* 'stirrup' (central) (Polish *strzemię*), *skrómka* 'first slice cut from a loaf' (south).

References

AJK = Atlas językowy kaszubszczyzny i dialektów sąsiednich (1964–78) 15 vols, ed. by Z. Stieber (vols I–VI) and H. Popowska-Taborska (vols VII–XV), Wrocław: Ossolineum.

Breza, E. and Treder, J. (1981) *Gramatyka kaszubska*, Gdańsk: Zrzeszenie Kaszubsko-Pomorskie.

—— (1984) *Zasady pisowni kaszubskiej*, 2 edn, Gdańsk: Zrzeszenie Kaszubsko-Pomorskie.

Corbett, G.G. (1987) 'The morphology/syntax interface: evidence from possessive adjectives in Slavonic', *Language* 63(2): 299–345.

Hinze, F. (1965) *Wörterbuch und Lautlehre der deutschen Lehnwörter im Pomoranischen (Kaschubischen)*, Berlin: Akademie-Verlag.

Labuda, A. (1960) *Słowniczek kaszubski*, Warsaw: Państwowe Zakłady Wydawnictw Szkolnych.

Lorentz, F. (1903) *Slovinzische Grammatik*, St Petersburg: Imperatorskaja Akademija Nauk.

—— (1905) *Slovinzische Texte*, St Petersburg: Imperatorskaja Akademija Nauk.

—— (1908–12) *Slovinzisches Wörterbuch*, 2 vols, St Petersburg: Imperatorskaja Akademija Nauk.

—— (1919) *Kaschubische Grammatik*, Danzig: Gedania.

—— (1958–62) *Gramatyka pomorska*, 2 vols (pages numbered continuously) (photographic reproduction of 1st edn, 1927–37, Poznań: Instytut Zachodnio-Słowiański), Wrocław: Ossolineum.

—— (1925) *Geschichte der pomoranischen (kaschubischen) Sprache*, Berlin and Leipzig: Walter de Gruyter.

—— (1958–72) *Pomoranisches Wörterbuch*, continued by F. Hinze, 3 vols, Berlin: Akademie-Verlag.

Lorentz, F., Fischer, A. and Lehr-Spławiński, T. (1935) *The Cassubian Civilization*, London: Faber & Faber.

Majkowski, A. (1988) *Das abenteuerliche Leben des Remus: ein kaschubischer Spiegel*, vol. II: *Kaschubische Ausgabe: Žёсё i Przigodё Remusa* (photographic reprint of 1st edn, Toruń: Stanica, 1938), Cologne and Vienna: Böhlau.

Majkowski, A. (1966) *Życie i przygody Remusa*, trans. by Lech Bądkowski, 2 edn, Gdynia: Wydawnictwo Morskie.

Popowska-Taborska, H. (1980) *Kaszubszczyzna. Zarys dziejów*, Warsaw: PWN.

—— (1987) *Szkice z kaszubszczyzny. Dzieje. Zabytki. Słownictwo*, Wejherowo: Muzeum Piśmiennictwa i Muzyki Kaszubsko-Pomorskiej.

Rogaczewski, F. (1975) *Wśród Słowińców*, Gdańsk: Zrzeszenie Kaszubsko-Pomorskie.

Sobierajski, Z. (1964) *Polskie teksty gwarowe z ilustracją dźwiękową*, vol. IV: *Lubawskie-Ostródzkie-Kaszuby*, Poznań: Poznańskie Towarzystwo Przyjaciół Nauk.

Stieber, Z. (1973) *A Historical Phonology of the Polish Language*, Heidelberg: Carl Winter.

—— (1974) *Świat językowy Słowian*, Warsaw: PWN.

Stieber, Z., Kamińska-Rzetelska, E., Taborska, H. and Topolińska, Z. (eds) (1961) *Słowińcy, ich język i folklor* (Zeszyty problemowe nauki polskiej XXII), Wrocław: Ossolineum.

Stone, G. (1972) 'The language of Cassubian literature and the question of a literary standard', *The Slavonic and East European Review* 50: 521–9.

Sychta, B. (1967–76) *Słownik gwar kaszubskich*, 7 vols, Wrocław: Ossolineum.

Topolińska, Z. (1974) *A Historical Phonology of the Kashubian Dialects of Polish*, The Hague and Paris: Mouton.

—— (1980) 'Kashubian', in A.M. Schenker and E. Stankiewicz (eds), *The Slavic Literary Languages: Formation and Development*, New Haven, Conn.: Yale Consilium.

Zieniukowa, J. (1972) 'Kategoria męskoosobowości w dialektach kaszubskich', *Studia z Filologii Polskiej i Słowiańskiej*, 12: 85–96.

14 Polabian

Kazimierz Polański

1 Introduction

Polabian belongs to the Lechitic subgroup of West Slavonic languages. Most of the dialects of West Lechitic were extinct by the late Middle Ages and are attested only by fragmentary, mainly toponomastic, evidence. Polabian was its westernmost variety, spoken by the Slavonic tribe living on the left bank of the Elbe river. It survived until the middle of the eighteenth century, when it was still spoken by a few people in the vicinity of the towns Lüchow, Wustrow and Dannenberg along the Jeetzel and Dumme rivers. In actual fact the Slavonic language spoken there was not called Polabian either by the Germans or by the people who used it. The Germans referred to it as *wendisch* and the people that spoke it called it *slüvenst'ĕ* (‹ *slovĕnьskъjь*) or *venst'ĕ* (‹ German *wend-* + *-ьskъjь*). (In order to help decode Polabian forms and compare them with their equivalents in the other Slavonic languages, each Polabian example will be provided with its Proto-Slavonic – or rather, pre-Polabian – reconstruction. Polabian forms will be cited in our transcription rather than in the way they were recorded by the compilers of the texts.)

The region is now called *Lüneburger Wendland* or *Hannover Wendland.* Formerly, it was called *Drawehn* or *Drawein*. The Slavonic tribe inhabiting this region was mentioned for the first time in 1004 in the form *Drewani* (‹ *dervjani*) 'inhabitants of forests'. There seems to be no doubt that the few people speaking Polabian at the beginning of the eighteenth century were descendants of the Drewani tribe. As far as the term *Polabian* is concerned it should rather refer to another Slavonic tribe whose name was also recorded as early as the eleventh century in the form *Polabi*. Yet the term has been used in this sense for a long time (for example, by Schleicher 1871; Lehr-Spławiński 1929; Trubetzkoy 1929) and there is no need to replace it by another one. Some authors make use of terms combining both constituents, such as *Draväno-Polaben* (Rost 1907), *Drzewianie Połabscy* (Lehr-Spławiński and Polański 1962), *lingua dravaenopolabica* (Olesch 1983–7).

At the turn of the seventeenth and eighteenth centuries the Polabian language was in the process of dying. Christian Hennig von Jessen, one of

795

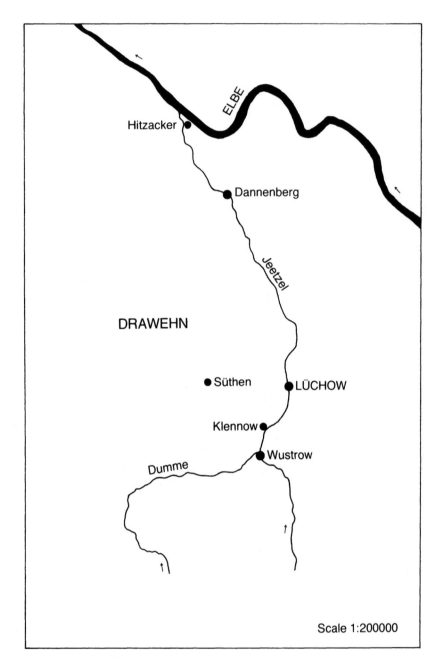

Map 14.1   The region of Drawehn

the recorders of Polabian, in the introduction to his *Vocabularium Venedicum*, states that only a few of the old people still spoke Polabian and goes on to predict that within twenty, or at most thirty, years, when the old people had died, the Polabian language would cease to exist. This was written about 1710.

The recorded Polabian material is highly fragmentary. It includes roughly 2,800 lexical items, the majority of which are registered in one grammatical form, not necessarily the basic one. Quite a number of words are cited misleadingly as basic units, for they must have been taken by the compilers out of a broader context, for example, *letă* (LOC SG) 'summer', *stărne* (DAT SG) 'side' from *vå letă* (‹ *vъ lětě*) 'in summer', *kå stărne* (‹ *kъ storně*) 'to the side, aside', respectively.

The paucity of the Polabian written records and all kinds of inconsistencies encountered in them invited some scholars to take liberties with the texts and speculate freely on the sounds and forms of Polabian. This generated a number of conflicting hypotheses concerning the phonology and almost all parts of Polabian grammar. However, a more careful examination of the Polabian records, carried out since the 1920s, shows that their notation was far more regular than previously assumed.

The most important sources of Polabian are: (a) Johann Parum Schultze's *Chronicle* with a German–Polabian glossary. Parum Schultze was the only Polabian among the compilers of the Polabian texts. (b) Hennig von Jessen's *Vocabularium Venedicum*, the most comprehensive and systematic of the Polabian texts; (c) Pfeffinger's *Vocabulaire Vandale*. These and practically all the rest were published by Rost (1907). All available Polabian material has been very carefully republished by Olesch (1959, 1962, 1967).

Polabian was exposed to the influence of the German language, in the first place to the Low German variety, from the Middle Ages to the final period of its existence. Most German loan-words can be traced to Middle Low German. German loan-words constitute about 20 per cent of the recorded lexicon. These were not only phonologically assimilated, but most of them were also morphologically adapted to the grammatical system of Polabian, being inflected according to the native paradigms as well as often provided with native prefixes or suffixes, for example, *brind'ojě* (‹ *(German *bring-*)-ajetъ*) 'brings', *krauckotě* (‹ *(Middle Low German *krüce-*)-katъjь*) 'crossed, cross'.

There were a number of German calques in Polabian, for example, *vå janü* (‹ *vъ jedьno*) 'together' (compare German *in eins* 'together'), *dirzol-să vit paivo* (‹ *dŕžalъ sę (v)otъ piva*) '(he) has abstained from beer' (compare German *sich enthalten vom Biere*), *jopt'ě-dǫb* (‹ *jablъko-dǫbъ*) 'apple-tree' (compare German *Apfelbaum*), *jisin-mond* (‹ *jesenь* (*mond* from Middle Low German *mand*)) 'September' (compare the German *Herbstmonat*).

In addition to the lexicon, German influence also affected Polabian grammar. Low German has been claimed as the source of the Polabian mixing of the dative and the accusative, as in *momĕ jim* (‹ *jьmamy jemu*) 'we have him' (instead of *momĕ jeg* ‹ *jьmamy jego*). One type of Polabian passive construction employed the Low German auxiliary verb *werden* (see 3.2.1). On the German model Polabian developed separable compound verbs using both German and Polabian prefixes–particles (see 3.3.3). The new perfect-tense forms with the auxiliary verbs *båit* (‹ *byti*) or *met* (‹ *jьmĕti*) are another example of German influence upon Polabian grammar, for instance, *ją våpodenĕ* (‹ *jestъ vъpadenъjь*) '(he) has fallen in', *vån mo nodenă* (‹ *(v)onъ jьmajetъ najьdenoje*) 'he has won'. Here we should mention forms with *så* (‹ *sъ*) plus the instrumental, which completely replaced the instrumental without preposition (see 3.1.2).

Polabian also borrowed from German such grammatical elements as the personal pronoun *jai* 'you (2 PL)' (from Middle Low German *jī*), the conjunction *un* 'and' (from Middle Low German *un*), the adverb *din* 'also' (from Middle Low German *den*).

Along with the Slavonic impersonal constructions of the type *gramĕ* (‹ *grьmitъ*) 'it thunders', *gramolü* (‹ *grьmĕlo*) 'it thundered' we also encounter *tü gramĕ, tü gramolü* (‹ *to grьmitъ, *to grьmĕlo*) on the German model *es donnert, es hat gedonnert*. Most probably, too, here belong the constructions of the typ *kå* plus the dative of the verbal substantive, which seem to have been formed on the model of German expressions *zu* plus the infinitive; compare *vån mo kå perdojĕ* (‹ *(v)onъ jьmajetъ kъ perdaji*) and German *er hat zu verkaufen* 'he has for sale', *nemăm nic kå våidoṅĕ* (‹ *ne jьmatь nečьso kъ vydanьju*) and German *ich habe nichts auszugeben* 'I have nothing to give away'.

2   Phonology

2.1   Segmental phoneme inventory

The segmental phonemes of Polabian are represented in table 14.1.

The letter *ė* stands for the closed *e*. The vowels *ü*, *ö* and *å* were the rounded counterparts of *i*, *e* and *a*, respectively, that is, *ü* was front, high, rounded, *ö* was front, mid, rounded and *å* was back, low, rounded.

The nasal vowels when followed by occlusive consonants tended to develop a homorganic nasal consonant before a stop, as can be seen from recordings of the type *Dûmb* (= *dǫb* ‹ *dǫbъ*) 'oak, tree', *Stumpó* (= *stǫpo* ‹ *stǫpa*) 'mortar' versus *Pûnt* (= *pǫt* ‹ *pǫtь*) 'road, way' *Selûnd* (= *zelǫd* ‹ *želǫdь*) 'acorn'.

In contradistinction to Polish, Polabian preserved the voiced/voiceless opposition at the end of a word: *laug* (‹ *lugъ*) 'meadow near a river' versus *lauk* (‹ *lukъ*) 'garlic'.

Table 14.1   Segmental phonemes

Vowels

Oral						Reduced		Nasal	
Non-reduced									
Monophthongs			*Diphthongs*						

i	ü	u	ai	åi	au	ĕ		ą	ǫ
ė									
e	ö	o							
a	å					ǻ			

Consonants

	Bilabial		Labio-dental	Dental		Alveolar	Palatal		Post-palatal	Velar	
Obstruents	p	b		t	d		t′	d′		k	g
	ṕ	ḃ									
Affricates				c	ʒ		ć	ʒ́			
Fricatives			f v	s	z	š	ś	ź	x́		x
			– ́v								
Nasals	m			n			ń				
	ḿ										
Laterals				l							
				ļ							
Trills				r							
				ŕ							
Semi-vowel							j				

The alveolar *š* listed in the consonantal part of table 14.1 represents the consonant occurring mainly in German loan-words, for example, *šopo* (Middle Low German *schape*) 'frying pan', *šopăt* (Middle Low German *schapen*) 'to create'. Polabian is said to have changed the original consonants *č, ž, š* into *c, z, s*, compare *coso* (‹ **čaša*) 'bowl', *zobo* (‹ **žaba*) 'frog', *cisĕ* (‹ **češetъ*) 'combs'. The phenomenon is referred to as 'Polabian mazurzenie' (after a similar phenomenon in some Polish dialects). In actual fact, however, one of the Polabian dialects had preserved remnants of the original distinction between *č, ž, š* and *c, z, s*. In Pfeffinger's glossary quite a few forms are noted with the letter combinations *tsch, dsch* for *č*, and *sch* for *š* or *ž*, compare *Tócatsch* = *tåkăč* (‹ **tъkačь*) 'weaver', *Dschela* = *čelă* (‹ **bъčela*) 'bee', *Deúscha* = *dåišă* (‹ **duša*) 'soul', *schribang* = *žribǫ* (‹ **žerbę*) 'colt, foal' (compare Małecki 1937: 32ff.; Trubetzkoy 1929: 83–8).

The Polabian consonantal system made ample use of the opposition of hard and soft (palatal or palatalized) consonants. Except for *f* and *š*, whose role in this system was marginal as they appeared only in German loan-words, all the other hard consonants had their soft counterparts. Several points, however, need explanation here. The soft consonants *t′* and *d′* served as the palatalized counterparts for both the dental *t*, *d* and velar *k*, *g*: compare, on the one hand, *tągnǫt* (‹ **tęgnǫti*) 'to pull' / *t′ǫg* (‹ **tęgъ*) 'ascent', *detą* (‹ **dětę*) 'child' / *d′otkă* (‹ **dětъka*) 'little child' and, on the other hand, *vilkă* (‹ **velikaja*) 'big' / *vilt′ă* (‹ **velikoje*) 'big', *daugă* (‹ **dĺgaja*) 'long' / *daud′ă* (‹ **dĺgoje*) 'long'. But the palatalized dental and velar fricatives differed in quality: compare, on the one hand, *disąt* (‹ **desętь*) '10' / *disǫtĕ* (‹ **desętъjь*) 'tenth' and, on the other hand, *blåxă* (‹ **blъxa*) 'flea' / *sauxĕ* (‹ **suxъjь*) 'dry'.

The Polabian language of the late seventeenth and early eighteenth centuries did not have quantity proper, that is, it did not distinguish between long and short vowels. On the other hand, apart from full vowels and diphthongs it possessed reduced vowels (marked *ă* and *ĕ*). The opposition between non-reduced and reduced vowels was conditioned by stress, which was on the final or on the penultimate syllable (see below). Vowels in stressed (= tonic) or immediately pre-tonic syllables did not undergo reduction, for example, *zobó* (‹ **žaba*) 'frog', *nidélă* (‹ **nedělja*) 'Sunday'. Such syllables are referred to as strong. Reduction regularly affected post-tonic syllables and, optionally, syllables occurring between the main and the secondary stress (the latter here marked `), compare *zĭnĕ* (‹ **ženetъ*) 'drives', *bledáiСă* (‹ **blĕdica*) 'paleness', *pàtărŭ* (‹ ** pętero*) '5'. The secondary stress most frequently fell on the antepenultimate syllable in polysyllabic words with final stress. Syllables in which reduction occurred are referred to as weak. Nasal vowels were usually non-reduced: *pöstilą* (‹ **posteljǫ* (ACC SG)) 'bed', *rǫ́kǫ* (‹ **rǫkǫ* (ACC SG)) 'hand'. However, *ą* could optionally undergo denasalization and reduction, compare *jó cą* or *jó că* (‹ **ja xъtjǫ*) 'I want', *så lüdă* (‹ **sъ oldъjejǫ*) 'by boat'. The reflexive particle **sę* always appears in the reduced form: *måit-să* (‹ **myti sę*) 'to wash onself', *büji-să* (‹ **bojitъ sę*) 'is afraid'.

It follows that the place of stress in Polabian can always be predicted from the distribution of non-reduced and reduced vowels in an accentual complex, that is, in a word with or without enclitics and proclitics: if the final syllable was non-reduced, it must have carried the stress, if it was reduced, the stress was on the penultimate syllable (see Trubetzkoy 1929: 77–84). Therefore, from now on the place of stress will not be marked.

The reduction of vowels resembles the Russian *akan'e* (see chapter 15, section 2.1) in that it neutralized most vowel oppositions (including the diphthongs) replacing them by the opposition between the high and low reduced vowels (*ĕ* and *ă*), compare *o/e* in *coso* (‹ **čaša*) 'bowl, cup' and *vå nüse* (‹ **vъ nosě*) 'in the nose' versus *zenă* (‹ **žena*) 'woman, wife' and *vå letă* (‹ **vъ lětě*) 'in summer'; *ü/i* in *nebü* (‹ **nebo*) 'sky, heaven' and *püli* (‹ **polje*) 'field' versus *risetĕ* (‹ **rešeto*) 'sieve, sifter' and *zilĕ* (‹ **zelje*) 'grass'; *ai/åi/au* in *bait* (‹ **biti*) 'to beat', *båit* (‹ **byti*) 'to be', *mauxo* (‹

*muxa) 'fly' versus åibĕt (‹ *ubiti) 'to kill', såmĕt (‹ *sъmyti) 'to wash off', klübĕk (‹ *klobukъ) 'hat'.

The Proto-Lechitic change of *ĕ › a and *ę › ǫ before the hard dentals (s, z, t, d, r, l) is evident also in Polabian. The new vowels a and ǫ developed in the same way as the original vowels *a and *ǫ (see below).

Initial *o- and *u- (except for the preposition–prefix *u) developed a prothetic u, which later changed into v, for example vågord (‹ *ogordъ) 'garden', våknü (‹ *okno) 'window', vaustă (‹ *usta) 'mouth'.

In early Polabian the hard syllabic ŗ changed into ar, the soft syllabic ŗ́ into 'ar (before hard dentals) or ir › er (elsewhere), the hard and soft syllabic ļ, ļ́ fell together and most probably yielded ul. The subsequent changes were ar › or, 'ar › 'or (softening the preceding consonant), er › ar, and ul › au/u (the latter variant in Parum Schultze's and Pfeffinger's dialects): *bŗže › borz 'sooner', *gŗnъkъ › gornăk 'milk pot', *bŗ́do › b́ordü 'flax swingle', *vŗ́ba › varbă 'willow', *tļstъjь › taustĕ/tustĕ 'thick', *vļ́kъ › vauk/vuk 'wolf'.

The Proto-Slavonic diphthongs orC, olC underwent metathesis and in early Polabian yielded raC (if long, or, in other terms, acute), roC (if short, or, in other terms, circumflex), laC (if long), loC (if short). Later, the vowels a, o evolved like a, o of non-diphthongal origin, for example, *ormę › råmą 'arm, shoulder', *ordlo › rådlü 'hookplough', *orsti › rüst 'to grow', *orkytьno › rüt' aitnĕ 'osier', *olbo › Lobü 'Elbe', *oldьjejǫ › lüdą 'by boat'.

The sequence CelC coalesced with ColC yielding ClåC; the combination CerC changed into CreC (e later developed like the same vowel of non-diphthongal origin); the CorC group gave the same result as the original hard syllabic ŗ, that is, or: *melti › mlåt 'to grind', *golva › glåvă 'head', *berza › breză 'birch', *na berzinĕ › no brizaină 'birchwood' (name of part of a village), *korva › korvo 'cow'.

The Proto-Slavonic jers were vocalized or lost, depending on whether they were in a strong or weak position. The treatment of the Polabian weak jers differed, however, from that of the weak jers in other Slavonic languages. The Proto-Slavonic weak jers in the initial syllable of a word were treated in Polabian as strong when originally stressed or immediately pre-tonic. This means that the jers in Polabian were vocalized in the initial syllable of all originally disyllabic words and of most polysyllabic ones.

The result of vocalization was not uniform and depended on the environment. The strong back jer (ъ), when after k, g, x and followed by an originally fronted consonant, developed into ė, elsewhere into å, for example, nüd'ėt (‹ *nogъtь) 'fingernail, toenail', lüt'ėt (‹ *olkъtь) 'elbow', vås (‹ *vъšь) 'louse', såpăt (‹ *sъpati) 'to sleep', kåtü (‹ *kъto) 'who'.

The strong front jer vocalized into 'å when followed by originally hard consonants and into a elsewhere: ḿåglă (‹ *mьgla) 'fog', ṕås (‹ *pьsъ) 'dog', pasai (‹ *pьsi) 'dogs', pan (‹ *pьnь) 'stump'. However, the initial *jь-sequence yielded *jai-* when originally stressed: *jaimą* (‹ *jьmę*) 'name', *jaid'ü* (‹ *jь'go*) 'yoke'. When unstressed and followed by hard consonants, it gave *ja-*, when unstressed elsewhere, *je-*, for example, *jåkră* (‹ *jьkrá*) 'roe', *jéver* (‹ *jьvérъ*) 'shaving, chip'. Examples of the loss of the weak *jers* in word-internal position are *janü* (‹ *jedьno*) 'one', *motkă* (‹ *matьka*) 'bitch'. Examples of the loss of the weak *jers* in the originally unstressed initial syllable: *celă* (‹ *bъčelá*) 'bee', *düjocě* (‹ *dъvojáčьjь*) 'twofold', *törě* (‹ *vъtorьjь*) 'other'.

The vowel *a* (both original and from *ě*) changed into *o* in strong positions and into *ă* in weak positions: *měra* › *mara* › *moro* 'measure', *na* › *no* 'on', *lěto* › *l'ato* › *l'otü* 'summer; year', *žena* › *zenă* 'woman; wife', *pekarь* › *pekăr* 'baker'. But the initial *ra-* sequence yielded *rå-*: *rana* › *råno* 'wound', *radostь* › *rådüst* 'wedding'.

The vowel *ě*, unless followed by originally hard dentals, evolved into *e* in strong positions and into *ă* in weak ones: *měšati* › *mesăt* 'to mix', *na světě* › *no svăte* 'in the world', *vъně* › *vănă* 'outside'.

The vowel *o* in strong positions evolved into *ö* when followed by originally hard dentals (*s, z, d, t, n, r, l*) or *ŕ*, and into *ü* elsewhere: *lono* › *lönü* 'bosom', *smola* › *smölă* 'resin; Hell', *vъ smolě* › *vå smüle* 'in Hell', *(v)ǫgorь* › *vǫd'ör* 'eel'. But in the sequence *vo* (whether with original or prothetic *v*) the vowel *o* in strong positions changed into *å* before originally hard consonants and into *i* elsewhere: *volъ* › *vål* 'ox', *voda* › *vådă* 'water', *onъ* › *vån* 'he', *oko* › *våt'ü* 'eye', *(v)ovьsъ* › *vivăs* 'oats', *(v)ovьca* › *vičă* 'sheep, ewe'. In the respective weak positions the results were: *ă* and *ě*, for example, *životъ* › *zaivăt* 'life; stomach', *vysokъ* › *våisěk* 'high', *rešeto* › *risetě* 'sieve'.

The vowel *e* in strong positions gave *e* when followed by hard consonants, and *i* elsewhere: *nebo* › *nebü* 'sky; Heaven', *polje* › *püli* 'field', *grebenь* › *gribin* 'comb; rooster's comb'. In weak positions it reduced to *ă* and *ě*, respectively: *na nebo* › *no năbü* 'to Heaven', *sъ nebeśa* (instead of *nebese*) › *să niběśo* 'from Heaven', *tęgnetь* › *tągně* 'pulls, stretches'. Yet, in the word-initial combination *je-* before hard dentals *e* yielded *a*, for example, *jedla* › *jadlă* 'fir tree', *jedъnъ* (instead of *jedьnъ*) › *jadån* 'one'.

The development of the vowels *e*, *o* in prefixes or prepositions departed from the regular processes irrespective of the following sounds, for example, *podъ* › *püd* 'under', *(v)obъ* › *vib* 'around, about', *perdъ* › *prid* 'in front of, before', *perzъ* › *priz* 'through; without'.

The nasal vowel *ę* (unless followed by hard dentals, see above) evolved into *ą*, for example, *pętь* › *pąt* 'five', *dětę* › *detą* 'child'. When preceded by a soft consonant, the nasal vowel *ǫ* changed into *ę* and then evolved in the same way as original *ę*, for example, *zьrjǫ* › *zarą* 'I look', *plęšǫtь* › *pląsą* '(they) dance'. Elsewhere, it remained a back nasal: *mǫka* › *mǫkă* 'flour, meal', *kapъkǫ* › *kopkǫ* 'drop (ACC SG)'.

The high vowels *i, *y, *u were diphthongized in strong positions: *i >
ai, *y > åi, *u > au or åi. The latter result obtained in the preposition or
prefix *u, in the position before labials and in all forms in the dialect represented by Parum Schultze and Pfeffinger. Examples: *biti > bait 'to beat',
*dymъ > dåim 'smoke', *korvy > korvåi 'cows', *u sebe > åi sibě 'on
oneself', *ulomiti > åilümět 'to break off', *gumьno > d'åimně 'farm,
homestead', *muxa > mauxo/måixo 'fly'. However, the sequences *ky, *gy,
*xy evolved into t'ai, d'ai, x́ai (most probably through the intermediate
stage *ki, *gi, *xi) and the vowels i, y changed into a when followed by r
and into å when followed by the hard l, compare cart'ai (< *cŕky) 'church',
t'enad'ainå (< *kъněgyńa instead of *kъněgyni) 'noblewoman', vrex́ai
(< *(v)orěxy) 'nuts', sarüt'ě (< *širokъjь) 'wide', sarötå (< *syrota) 'whey',
gnålå (< *gnilaja) 'rotten'. In weak positions all three high vowels reduced
to ě, for example, *ubiti > åibět 'to kill', *pokryti > pükrět 'to cover',
*klobukъ > klüběk 'hat'.

There is no general agreement as to the factors that caused the fronting
of the vowel *o (into ü, ö) and the diphthongization of *i, *y and *u in
Polabian.

Like some other Slavonic languages, Polabian tended to contract vowels
separated by j, for example, *bojěti > bet 'to be afraid', *sějati > śot 'to sow',
*vojevoda > våvådå 'prince', *stojati > stot 'to stand', *podъ zemjejǫ > püd
zimå 'under the earth'. But the contraction of vowels was not an absolute
rule: compare d'olå/d'olojě (< *dělajetъ) 'works', kǫsojě (< *kǫsajetъ)
'bites', svaitojě (< *svitajetъ) 'it dawns, day is breaking'.

In early Polabian, as in the other Lechitic dialects, consonants followed
by the front vowels (e, ě, ę, i, ь) were softened. This softness was a
redundant feature until the change *ě > a, *ę > ǫ, *ŕ > 'ar, that is, when soft
consonants could occur both before front and back vowels. Subsequently,
the soft consonants followed by front vowels underwent depalatalization,
for their palatalized character must have been perceived as positionally
conditioned. Examples: l'otü (< *lěto) 'summer, year' versus vå letå (< *vъ
lětě) 'in summer', ṕǫtě (< *pętъjь) 'fifth' versus pǫt (< *pętь) 'five', åiṁortě
(< *umŕtъjь) 'dead' versus såmart (< *sъmŕtь) 'disease of chicks or goslings'.

The changes in the Polabian consonantal system were considerably less
complex than the vocalic ones. The šč, žǯ sequences changed into st, zd,
compare stamil (< *ščьmelь) 'bumblebee', xrǫst (< *xręščь) 'beetle', dåzd
(< *dъžǯь) 'rain'. The stops of the clusters st, zd preserved their softness if
followed by originally back vowels: st'auko (< *ščuka) 'pike', pl'aust'å (<
*pljušča (GEN PTT)) 'ivy'. The consonants k, g became fricative if followed
by a stop, compare så lüxt'åm (< *sъ olkъtьmь) and lüt'ět (< *olkъtь)
'elbow', nüxte (< *nogъtě) 'finger- or toenails'. The clusters of the type
consonant + v were simplified, losing their second element if: (a) followed
by an original *o, as in: tüi (< *tvojь) 'your', x́öst (< *xvostъ) 'oven broom',
d'üzd (< *gvozdь) 'nail', dör (< *dvorъ) 'farm'; (b) preceded by a velar

consonant and followed by an original *a*, for example, *kos* (‹ *kvasъ*) 'yeast, leaven, barm', *xolĕ* (‹ *xvalitъ*) 'praises'. The clusters of this type changed into the sequence consonant + *j* if their second element was soft: *sjǫtü* (‹ *svęto*) 'holiday', *tjordă* (‹ *tvŕdoje*) 'hard', *kjot* (‹ *kvĕtъ*) 'flower', *gjozdă* (‹ *gvĕzda*) 'star'. In other cases post-consonantal *v* remained unchanged: *no svăte* (‹ *na svĕtĕ*), *dvarai* (‹ *dvьri*) 'door', *svorĕt* (‹ *svariti*) 'to quarrel'.

The consonants *k*, *g*, *x* were palatalized when followed by the original *o*, *u*, *y* as well as by the back *jer* (ъ) if that latter preceded an originally fronted consonant: *st'öt* (‹ *skotъ*) 'cattle', *våt'ü* (‹ *oko*) 'eye', *st'aibă* (‹ *skyba*) 'bread', *t'aurą* (‹ *kurę*) 'chick', *d'ölǫb* (‹ *golǫbь*) 'pigeon', *t'ed* (‹ *kъde*) 'where', *xüdĕt* (‹ *xoditi*) 'to go', *xaudĕ* (‹ *xudъjь*) 'bad, evil; thin', *xĕmil* (‹ *xъmelь*) 'hop'. This change was a result of the fronting of the vowels in question, which must have occurred before the diphthongization and contraction of vowels.

In word-final position or before another consonant, clusters consisting of a stop or an affricate followed by *r*, *l*, *m*, *n* were broken up by the insertion of a secondary *jer*-type vowel: *votĕr* (‹ *votr* ‹ *vĕtrъ*) 'wind', *visĕm* (‹ *vism* ‹ *(v)osmь*) 'eight', *vid'én* (‹ *(v)ognь*) 'fire', *sribarnĕ* (‹ *sribrnĕ* ‹ *serbrьnъjь*) 'silver'.

In several cases a *jer*-type vowel was inserted between a stop and *r* before a vowel: *kåråi* (‹ *kry*) 'blood', *påred* (‹ *pred* ‹ *perdъ*) 'formerly'. When used in the function of a preposition or prefix, the reflex of Proto-Slavonic *perdъ* sounded *prid*, as in *prid* 'before, in front of'.

2.2   Morphophonemic alternations inherited from Proto-Slavonic

Among the oldest alternations are those of the velar consonants *k*, *g*, *x* with *c*, *z*, *s* (‹ *č*, *ž*, *š*) and *c*, *ʒ* (‹ *c*, *ʒ*). They originated from the Proto-Slavonic first and second palatalizations (see chapter 3, sections 2.9 and 2.19). The result of the second palatalization of *x* must have been *s* (‹ *š*, as in the other Slavonic languages) but no example of it is attested.

The alternations resulting from the first palatalization were greatly reduced in Polabian and were chiefly limited to derivation: *rǫkă* (‹ *rǫka*) 'hand' versus *rǫcnĕk* (‹ *rǫčьnikъ*) 'towel', *büg* (‹ *bogъ*) 'God' versus *büzăc* (‹ *božьcь*) 'God (DIMIN)', *mex* (‹ *mĕxъ*) 'sack' versus *mesăk* (‹ *mĕšьkъ*) 'little sack'.

Residual instances of the first palatalization are encountered in inflection. In nominal declension we find it only in the nouns *våt'ü* (‹ *(v)oko*) 'eye' and *vauxü* (‹ *(u)xo*) 'ear', compare *vicai* (‹ *(v)oči* (NOM–ACC DU), *vausai* (‹ *(v)uši* (NOM–ACC DU)). In conjugation it could be used to oppose the present-tense forms to past tenses or the infinitive: *plocą* (‹ *plačǫ*) 'I cry' versus *plokol* (‹ *plakalъ*) '(he) cried', *plokăt* (‹ *plakati*) 'to cry', *påknĕ* (‹ *pъknetъ*) 'falls' versus *påci* (‹ *pъčetъ* (AOR)) 'fell', *müzĕs* (‹ *možešь* 'you can' versus *müg* (‹ *mogъ* (AOR)) 'I could'. For the most part, however, verbal stems tended to be levelled in the entire conjugation: *joz ricâl-mĕ* (‹ **jazъ rečlъ mu*) 'I told him', *ne-mĕzălo-jĕg noit* (‹ **ne možala jego najiti*) '(she) could not find him', *taucâl-să* (‹ **tļčlъ sę*) 'it was haunted' (instead of **reklъ*, **mogla*, **tļklъ sę* on the model of *ricĕ*, *müzĕ*, *tauci-să* (‹ **rečetъ*, **možetъ*, **tļčetъ sę*).

In general, however, both consonantal and vocalic alternations (with the exception of stress alternations and the related alternations between non-reduced and reduced vowels) were considerably limited within the Polabian conjugation. Present-tense forms abandoned consonantal alternations completely: *ricą* (instead of *rekǫ* ‹ **rekǫ*) '(I) say', *picą* (instead of *pekǫ* ‹ **pekǫtъ*) '(they) roast'.

The alternations *k/c*, *g/ʒ* occurred in the declension of nouns, where they reinforced morphological oppositions: *grauk* (‹ **grukъ*) 'pear tree' versus *graucai* (‹ **gruci*) 'pear trees', *krig* (from German *Krieg*) 'war' versus *vå kriʒe* (‹ **vъ (krig-)-ĕ*), *nügă* (‹ **noga*) 'foot, leg' versus *nüʒe* (‹ **noʒĕ* (NOM–ACC DU)) 'feet, legs'.

The opposition of hard and soft consonants, which originated from the depalatalization of consonants before front vowels, served as the most important consonantal alternation in Polabian morphology. It occurred in the declension of nouns where it replaced the opposition of originally front vowels to originally back ones: *büzăc* (‹ **božьcь*) 'God (DIMIN)' versus *büsćă* (‹ **božьca* (GEN–ACC SG)), *büsćĕ* (‹ **božьcu* (DAT SG)), *dan* (‹ **dьnь*) 'day' versus *dańo* (**dьńa* instead of **dьne* (GEN SG)), *pås* (‹ **pьsъ*) 'dog' versus *pasai* (‹ **pьsi*) 'dogs', *zimă* (‹ **zemja*) 'earth' versus *no zimą* (‹ **na zemjǫ*) 'to the earth', *staʒă* (‹ **stьʒa*) 'path' versus *staʒą* (‹ **stьʒǫ* (ACC SG)).

The declension of nouns also made use of the alternations *k/t'*, *g/d'*, *x/ẋ*, for example, *rǫkă* (‹ **rǫka*) 'hand' versus *priz rǫt'ĕ* (‹ **perzъ rǫky*) 'without a hand', *nügă* (‹ **noga*) 'foot, leg' versus *prit'ĕ nüd'ĕ* (‹ **perky nogy*) 'over the foot', *grex* (‹ **grĕxъ*) 'sin' versus *greẋĕ* (‹ **grĕxy*) 'sins'. But the role of this alternation is most noticeable in the inflection of adjectives, where it contributed, among other things, to the distinction of genders: *vilkă* (‹ **velikaja*) 'big' (F) but *vilt'ă* (‹ **velikoje*) 'big' (N), *draugă* (‹ **drugaja*) 'other' (F) but *draud'ă* (‹ **drugoje*) 'other' (N), **sauxă* (unattested, ‹ **suxaja*) 'dry' (F) but *sauẋă* (‹ **suxoje*) 'dry' (N).

The reduction of vowels brought about the most productive vocalic alternation in Polabian. This alternation was closely related to the alternation of stress and it affected both inflection and derivation as in the endings *-o/-ă* (*coso/zenă* ‹ **čaša* 'bowl', **žena* 'woman') or in the derivative *åibĕt* 'to kill' (‹ **ubiti*) versus *bait* 'to beat' (‹ **biti*).

It was, however, in conjugation that these alternations played the most essential role, thanks to the enclitic character of the reflexive particle *să* (‹ **sę*) and of the monosyllabic pronominal forms. Since the present-tense forms generalized the penultimate stress, the stress had to shift to the desinence when followed by an enclitic, given the Polabian limitation of stress to the penultimate syllable. In this way there arose the alternation of non-reduced and reduced vowels: *aidĕ* (‹ **idetъ*) 'goes', *bülĕ* (‹ **bolitъ*) 'it hurts' versus *kok aidi-să* (‹ **kako idetъ sę*) 'how are you doing', *büli-mĕ* (‹ **bolitъ mьne*) 'it hurts me'.

Other vowel alternations were due to various metaphonies. Some of them occurred in Lechitic or early Polabian, others took place in later periods. To the former belong vowel–zero, *e–'o, a–'ǫ and ar–'or* alternations (as well as their variants stemming from the reduction of vowels), to the latter *e–i, a–i, å–i, ö–ü, å–a, ai–å, åi–å* alternations.

Owing to the different treatment of the weak *jers* in Polabian from that of other Slavonic languages, the vowel–zero alternations were practically limited to final/penultimate syllables and occurred mainly in the declension of nouns: *d'ölǫbăk* (‹ **golǫbъkъ*) 'small pigeon' but *d'ölǫpt'ĕ* (PL) (‹ **golǫbъky*), *pican* (‹ **pečьnь*) 'loaf of bread' but *picne* (PL) (‹ **pečьnĕ*).

The *e–'o* alternation is attested mainly in the inflection of nouns: *l'otü* (‹ **lĕto*) 'summer, year' versus *vå letă* (‹ **vъ lĕtĕ*) 'in summer'. We find some examples of the *ar–'or* alternation in derivation: *såmart* (‹ **sъmŗtь*) 'disease of chicks' but *åimortĕ* (‹ **umŗtъjь*) 'dead', *cornĕ* (‹ **čŗnъjь*) 'black' but *carnaičă* (‹ **čŗnica*) 'blackberry'. The *ǫ–'ǫ* alternation is found in some individual forms: *plǫsǫ* (‹ **plęšǫ*) '(they) dance' versus *pl'ǫsät* (‹ **plęsati*) 'to dance', *disǫt* (‹ **desętь*) 'ten' versus *disǫtĕ* (‹ **desętъjь*) 'tenth'.

The vowel alternations due to later developments in Polabian were used in inflection: *cesăt* (‹ **česati*) 'to comb' but *cisĕ* (‹ **česetъ*) 'combs', *vådă* (‹ **voda*) 'water' but *vå vidă* (‹ **vъ vodĕ*) 'in water', *smölä* (‹ **smola*) 'Hell' but *vå smülä* (‹ **vъ smolĕ*) 'in Hell', *pås* (‹ **pьsъ*) 'dog' but *pasai* (‹ **pьsi*) 'dogs', *åipaustaix* (‹ **upustixъ*) 'I dropped (AOR)' but *åipaustål* (‹ **upustilъ*) '(he) has dropped (PRF)'.

3 Morphology

Polabian morphology cannot be fully described for several reasons. First, there is only a relatively small amount of source material. Second, most of it was given in glossaries, in which words were noted mainly as vocabulary items; no word is recorded in its complete paradigm. Third, the recorders did not know Polabian and may have made mistakes. Fourth, some of the informants might have had an imperfect knowledge of the language (since it was already dying). However, thanks to the fact that almost all the texts cite quite a number of sentences or expressions and that Hennig occasionally supplements some grammatical forms, it is possible to reconstruct the fundamentals of Polabian morphology and some aspects of syntax.

3.1 Nominal morphology

3.1.1 Nominal categories

From the viewpoint of morphology Polabian was very conservative, maintaining most of the categories of Proto-Slavonic. Like Sorbian and Slovene, it distinguished singular, plural and dual. The dual number was used in nouns which denoted paired objects, but was preserved only in the nominative–accusative and in the dative–instrumental: *rǫce* (‹ **rǫcě*) 'hands', *nüʒe* (‹ **noʒě*) 'legs', *vausai* (‹ **(v)uši*) 'ears', *vicai* (‹ **(v)oči*) 'eyes', *perisai* (‹ **peresi*) 'wings', *råměnai* (‹ **ormeni*) 'arms', *så vicaimă* (‹ **sъ (v)očima*) 'with the eyes', *rǫkomă* (‹ **rǫkama*) 'hands'. As in Sorbian, the genitive dual was replaced by the genitive plural: *åi dåvix grauk* (‹ **dъvoxъ grukъ*) 'at the two pear trees'.

Polabian had three genders: masculine, feminine and neuter. Within the masculine gender, Polabian made a distinction between animate and nonanimate nouns. In masculine nouns denoting human beings and most probably animals (although no such example is attested) the accusative coincided formally with the genitive, whereas the other genders distinguished the two forms: *bedě bügo* (*bedě* from Middle Low German *beden*) 'asks God (ACC = GEN)' and *vit bügo aipădeně* (‹ **(v)otъ boga upadenъjь*) 'fallen away from God (GEN)', *tåi ne-măs met drauʒex büd'üv likåm mane* (‹ **ty ne jьmašь jьměti druʒijixъ bogovъ* (*lik-* from Middle Low German *lik*)-*ъmь mьně*) 'you are not to have other gods (ACC = GEN) beside me' but *nügǫ* (ACC) *vibět* (‹ **nogǫ (v)obiti*) 'to trip somebody', *prit'ě nüd'ě* (GEN) (‹ **perky nogy*) 'over the foot'.

Polabian distinguished six case forms: nominative, accusative, genitive, dative, instrumental and locative, but had lost the original vocative. The function of the latter was taken over by the nominative: *zenă, pĕlüz detǫ vå zåipkǫ* (‹ **žena, položi dětę vъ zybъkǫ*) 'woman, put the child in the cradle', *defkă, aid, zåib* (‹ **děvъka, idi, zybi*) 'girl, go rock'. The instrumental was used only with prepositions (an example of German influence mentioned in section 1 above): *prid gårdåm* (‹ **perdъ gordъmь*) 'before the court', *virgně våisek så mǫcǫ* (‹ **vъgnetъ vysoko sъ męčejǫ*) 'throws the ball up'.

Polabian preserved some relics of the original short forms of adjectives. They were used mainly in the possessive function: *l'olěn brot* (‹ **ljalinъ bratъ*) 'father's brother', *Morajěn danăc* (‹ **Marijinъ dьnьcь*) 'St Mary's day'.

Several examples with short forms are attested in lexicalized expressions: *dausăn dan* (‹ **dušьnъ dьnь*) 'All Souls' Day', *nüvo laună* or simply *nüvo* (‹ **nova luna, *nova*) 'new moon', *storo launa* or simply *storo* (‹ **stara luna, *stara*) 'last-quarter moon'.

The short forms of the neuter acquired the function of adverbs and were always stressed word-finally: *püznü* (‹ **pozdьno*) 'late', *sauxü* (‹ **suxo*) 'dry', *daud'ü* (‹ **dļgo*) 'long'. Under German influence they could also function as predicative forms of adjectives: *tǫ kolai jǫ jist teplü* (‹ **tъnъ* (Middle Low German *kol-*)-*u jestъ ješče teplo*) 'this cabbage is still hot', compare German *es ist heiß* and *der Kohl ist heiß*.

The Polabian degrees of comparison were a clear continuation of the Proto-Slavonic forms: *zaimnesě* (‹ **zimьnějьšьjь*) 'colder', *lepsě* (‹ **lěpъšьjь*) 'better', *nastăresě* (‹ **najstarějьšьjь*) 'oldest'.

3.1.2 Noun morphology

The declension of nouns was closely related to the distinctions of gender. Two main declension types can be distinguished: (a) masculine and neuter nouns; (b) feminine nouns. Neither of them was uniform, but no further clear-cut classifications can be formulated. The attested endings are given in table 14.2.

The differences between individual paradigms reflected, to some extent, the Proto-Slavonic stem distinctions. The vast majority of masculine nouns ended in -Ø (= zero) in the nominative singular. Here belonged the reflexes of Proto-Slavonic **-o-*/**-jo-* stems (for example, *büg* (‹ **bogъ*) 'God', *dåzd* (‹ **dъžžь*) 'rain'), **-u-* stems (*med* (‹ **medъ*) 'honey'), **-i-* stems (*pǫt* (‹ **pǫtь*) 'road') and consonantal stems (*dan* (‹ **dьnь*) 'day', *jǫcmin* (‹ **jǫčьmenь*, instead of **jęčьmy*) 'barley'). The nominative ending of thirty or so attested masculine animate nouns was *-ă* (‹ **-a*), for example,

Table 14.2 The declension of nouns

Singular

	M		N	F
	AN	INAN		
NOM	-Ø, -ă ⎱	-Ø, -åi	-ü, -i/-ě, -a/-ă	-o/-ă, -åi, -Ø, -ai
ACC	= GEN ⎰			-ǫ, -ą/-ă, -Ø
GEN		-o/-ă, -au/-åi	-o/-ă	-åi/-ě, -ă, -i, -vě
DAT		-au/-ai/-ě		-e/-ă, -ai
INST		-åm		-ǫ, -ą/-ă
LOC		-e/-ă, -ai		-e/-ă, -ě

Plural

	M		N	F
NOM	-ai/-ě, -e, -üvě, -i ⎱		-ă	-åi/-ě, -ai/-ě, -e/-ă, -våi
ACC	-åi/-ě, -e ⎰			
GEN	üv/-ev, -Ø		-Ø	-Ø
DAT	üm		–	-åm
INST	ě(?)		–	-omě
LOC	–		-åx	–

Dual

	M	N	F
NOM–ACC	-ă	-ai/-ě	-e
DAT–INST	–	-aimå	-omå

vaujă (‹ **(v)uja*) 'uncle', *skocaikă* (‹ **skačika*) 'stallion'. One attested noun retained the ending *-ăi* (‹ **-y*) in this case: *komăi* (‹ **kamy*) 'stone'.

The neuter nouns in the nominative singular ended in *-ü* (‹ **-o*) / *-i* (‹ **-e*) / *-ĕ* (the reduced variant of the former two) or *-ǫ/-ă* (‹ **-ę*): *l'otü* (‹ **lĕto*) 'year, summer', *püli* (‹ **polje*) 'field', *gńozdĕ* (‹ **gnĕzdo*) 'nest', *zilĕ* (‹ **zelьje*) 'pasture', *jaimǫ/jaimă* (‹ **jьmę*) 'name', *t'aurǫ* (‹ **kurę*) 'chick'. Their accusative form in all numbers was identical with that of the nominative.

The endings reflecting the original **-o-/*-jo-* declension prevailed in the remaining declensional forms of the masculine and neuter nouns, but in some cases the influence of the original **-u-* stems can be observed. The ending *-au/-ăi* (‹ **-u*) alternated with *-o/-ă* (‹ **-a*) in the genitive singular masculine. The ending *-üv* (‹ **-ovъ*) and its secondary variant *-ev* almost completely replaced the original ending *-Ø* (‹ **-ъ*) in the genitive plural of masculine nouns. Under the influence of the **-u-* stems the ending of the instrumental singular **-otь* changed into **-ъtь*.

As far as the masculine nouns ending in *-ă* in the nominative singular are concerned, nothing can be said about the other forms of their paradigm because none of them is attested in the texts.

The feminine nouns in the nominative singular ended in *-o/-ă* (‹ **-a*), *-Ø* (‹ **-ь*), *-ăi* (‹ **-y*) or *-ai* (‹ **-y* (preceded by *k, g, x*) and **-i*), for example, *poro* (‹ **para*) 'swamp', *sredă* (‹ **serda*) 'Wednesday', *mail'o* (from Middle Low German *mile*) 'mile', *svećă* (‹ **svĕtja*) 'candle', *t'üst* (‹ **kostь*) 'bone, fishbone', *kărăi* (‹ **kry*) 'blood', *cart'ai* (‹ **cŕky*) 'church', *motai* (‹ **mati*) 'mother'. They continued the Proto-Slavonic declensions of the **-a-/*-ja-*, **-i-*, **-ū-*, and consonantal stems. The Proto-Slavonic **-ū-* declension was productive in Polabian. Some of its endings were used not only in original **-ū-* stems but also in others, especially German loan-words, compare not only *kărăi* 'blood', *cart'ai* 'church', but also *grausăi* (‹ **gruš-y*) 'pear tree', *sod'ai* (from Middle Low German *sage*) 'saw', *modăi* (from Middle Low German *made*) 'maggot'. As can be seen from the example *grausăi*, even originally soft stems could acquire the ending *-ăi* (‹ **-y*). Particularly productive was the ending of the nominative–accusative plural *-văi*, which came into being as a result of the contamination of the original **-ъvi* with the ending **-y* of the **-a-* stems. It could also occur in nouns ending in *-o/-ă* in the nominative singular, for example, *soko* (from Middle Low German *sake*) 'thing' and *sokvăi* (NOM–ACC PL).

In a number of nouns (originally belonging to consonantal stem paradigms) an alternation of stems occurs between the nominative singular and some other forms, for example, *komăi* (‹ **kamy*) 'stone', *kominĕ* (NOM–ACC PL) (‹ ** kamenьje*); *slüvi* (‹ **slovo*) 'word', *slüvesă* (NOM–ACC PL) (‹ **slovesa*); *răma* (‹ **ormę*) 'arm', *răminai* (NOM–ACC DU) (‹ **ormeni*); *pailǫ* (‹ **pilę*) 'duckling', *pailotă* (NOM–ACC PL) (‹ **pilęta*);

compare also *soko* 'thing' versus *sokvåi* 'things' (see above). Examples:

Singular

Accusative, feminine: *korvǫ* (‹ **korvǫ*) 'cow', *no zimą* (‹ **na zemjǫ*) 'to the earth', *zo nidelǎ* (‹ **za nedĕljǫ*) 'in a week'. As far as the accusative of masculine nouns is concerned, its form coincided either with the nominative or with the genitive (see 3.1.1).

Genitive, masculine–neuter: *bügo* (‹ **boga*) 'God', *daṅo* (‹ **dьṅa* instead of **dьne*) 'day', *gorxǎ/gorxåi* (‹ **gorxa, *gorxu*) 'pea', *l' oto* (‹ **lĕta*) 'summer', *vainǎ* (‹ **vina*) 'wine'; feminine: *slåmåi* (‹ **solmy*) 'straw', *pöl t' üpĕ* (‹ **polъ kopy*) 'half a threescore', *åi zimǎ* (‹ **u zemjĕ*) 'at the earth', *au jǎdai* (‹ **u jĕdi*) 'at a meal', *vėz doli* (‹ **jьz dale* instead of **dali*) 'from afar', *åi kokvĕ* (‹ **u* (Middle Low German *kâk-*)-*ъve*) 'at the pillory'.

Dative, masculine–neuter: *kå sjotau* (**kъ svĕtu*) 'to the world', *kå dånĕ* (‹ **kъ dьnu*) 'to the bottom', *kå våidoṅĕ* (‹ **kъ vydanьju*) 'to give away'; feminine: *kå stårne* (‹ **kъ stornĕ*) 'to the side', *kå maisǎ* (‹ **kъ* (Middle Low German *mis-*)-*ĕ*) 'to mass', *kå zimai* (‹ **kъ zemji*) 'to the earth'.

Instrumental, masculine–neuter: *prid gårdåm* (‹ **perdъ gordъmь*) 'before the court', *så lüxt'åm* (‹ **sъ olkъtьmь*) 'with the elbow', *prid lotåm* (‹ **perdъ lĕtъmь*) 'a year ago'; feminine: *püd zimą* (‹ **podъ zemjejǫ*) 'under the earth', *så lüdǎ* (‹ **sъ oldьjejǫ*) 'by boat', *mauckǫ* (‹ **mĺčьkojǫ*) 'in secret'.

Locative, masculine–neuter: *no svåte* (‹ **na svĕtĕ*) 'in the world', *vå letǎ* (‹ **vъ lĕtĕ*) 'in summer', *vå pülai* (‹ **vъ polji*) 'in the field'; feminine: *vå emerice* (‹ **vъ* (Middle Low German *hemmelrîk-*)-*ĕ*) 'in heaven', *vå smülǎ* (‹ **vъ smolĕ*) 'in Hell', *no zimĕ* (‹ **na zemji*) 'on the earth'.

Plural

Nominative masculine: *büʒai* (‹ **boʒi*) 'gods', *pasai* (‹ **pьsi*) 'dogs', *godaicĕ* (‹ **gadici*) 'worms', *nüze* (‹ **nožĕ*) 'knives', *vålüvĕ* (‹ **volove*) 'oxen', *t'agli* (‹ (*Middle Low German *kegel*)-*e*) 'skittles'.

Nominative–accusative, neuter: *våknǎ* (‹ **(v)okna*) 'windows', *jojǎ* (‹ **jaja*) 'eggs'; feminine: *sestråi* (‹ **sestry*) 'sisters', *gjozdĕ* (‹ **gvĕzdy*) 'stars', *vice* (‹ **(v)ovьcĕ*) 'sheep', *nidelǎ* (‹ **nedĕlĕ*) 'weeks', *t'üstai/ t'üstĕ* (‹ **kosti*) 'bones, fishbones', *grausvåi* (‹ **grušьvy*) 'pears'.

Accusative masculine: *grexai* (‹ **grĕxy*) 'sins', *påsĕ* (‹ **pьsy*) 'dogs', *daüste* (‹ **gostĕ*) 'guests'.

Genitive, masculine: *åi dåvix grauk* (‹ **u dъvoxъ grukъ*) 'by two pear trees', *büd'üv* (‹ **bogovъ*) 'gods', *danüv/danev* (‹ **dьnovъ, *dьnevъ*) 'days'; neuter: *dråv* (‹ **drъvъ*) 'wood'; feminine: *priz ṁor* (‹ **perzъ mĕrъ*) 'without measure'.

Dative, masculine: *gresnărüm* (‹ **grěšьnaromъ*) 'to sinners'; feminine: *kå vaikăm* (‹ **kъ* (Middle Low German *wik-*)-*amъ*) 'to the town'.

Instrumental, masculine: perhaps *să vilě vlåsě* (‹ **sъ velьje volsy*) (if not the nominative instead of the genitive) 'with lots of hair'; feminine: *sveckomě* (‹ **svěčьkami*) 'candles'.

Dual

Nominative–accusative, masculine: *rǫkovă* (‹ **rǫkava*) 'sleeves'; neuter: *vicai* (‹ **(v)oči*) 'eyes', *jojě* (‹ **jaji*) 'testicles'; feminine: *rǫce* (‹ **rǫcě*) 'hands'.

Dative–instrumental, neuter: *vicaimă* (‹ **(v)očima*) 'eyes'; feminine: *rǫkomă* (‹ **rǫkama*) 'hands'.

3.1.3 Pronominal morphology

The Polabian personal pronouns continued, with the exception of the second personal plural *jai* 'you' (see p. 798), the Proto-Slavonic forms: *joz/ jo* (‹ **jazъ, *ja*) 'I', *tăi/tě* (‹ **ty*) 'you, thou', *văn, vănă* (‹ **(v)onъ, (v)ona*) 'he, she', *măi* (‹ **my*) 'we', *vinai* (‹ **(v)oni*) 'they'. The attested forms of the oblique cases can be reconstructed as in table 14.3.

The mixing of the dative and the accusative (see p. 798) could also

Table 14.3

	1 SG	2 SG
ACC	mině/mane/mą/mě	tibě/těbe/tą/tě
GEN	mině/mane/maně	tibě/tibe
DAT	mine/mane/maně/mě	tibě/tibe/tě
INST	(să) manǫ (‹ *mъnojǫ)	(să) tăbǫ (‹ *sъ tebojǫ)

	1 PL	2 PL
ACC	nos/nås (‹ *nasъ)	–
DAT	nom/năm (‹ *namъ)	vom (‹ *vamъ)
INST	(så) nomě (‹ *sъ nami)	(så) vomě (‹ *sъ vami)

	3 SG	3 PL	3 DU
ACC	jig/jěg/něg (‹ *jego, njego)	–	
GEN	jig/jěg (‹ *jego)	–	–
DAT	jim/mě (‹ *jemu, *mu)	jaim (‹ *jimъ)	(kå) naimo (‹ *kъ njima)
INST	(så) něm (‹ *sъ njimь)	–	–

affect the genitive: *mině* ‹ **mene*, *mane* ‹ **mьně*, *maně* ‹ **mьne*; *tibě* ‹ **tebe*, *tibe* ‹ **tebě*, *těbe* ‹ **tebě*. The forms *mą*, *tą* occurred only after prepositions: *bed zo mą* (‹ (*bed* from Middle Low German *beden*) **za mę*) 'pray for me', *prid tą* (‹ **perdъ tę*) 'in front of you'. The forms *mě* (‹ **mi*), *tě* (‹ **ti*), *mě* (‹ **mu*) in the dative, *mě* (‹ **mьne?*) and *tě* (‹ **tebe?*) in the accusative are enclitic: *doj-mě* (‹ **daji mi*) 'give me', *kok aidi-tě?* (‹ **kako idetъ ti?*) 'how are you?' literally, 'how goes it to you (SG)?', *büli-mě* (‹ **bolitъ mьne*) 'it hurts me'. The form *tě* (‹ **ty*) in the nominative is attested only in the expression *cü tě t'autěs?* (‹ **čьso ty kutišь?*) 'what are you doing?' The accusative form *něg* (‹ **njego*) is attested in isolation but it must have occurred after prepositions as in the other Slavonic languages.

The reflexive pronoun is attested in the following forms: *są* (after prepositions)/*să* (as the reflexive particle after verbs) (‹ **sę*) (ACC), *sibě* (‹ **sebe*) (GEN), *sibe*/(*kå*) *sěbe* (‹ **(kъ) sebě*) (DAT), (*vå*) *sibe* (‹ **vъ sebě*) (LOC).

There were two demonstrative pronouns: *tǫ*, *to*, *tü* (‹ **tъnъ*, **ta*, **to*) 'that (over there'), and *sǫ*, *so*, *sü* (‹ **sъnъ*, **sa*, **so*) 'this (over here)'.

The possessive pronouns are attested in very few forms apart from the nominative: nominative singular, masculine: *müj* 'my', *tüj* 'your', *süj* 'one's own'; feminine: *müją*, *tüją*, *süjă*; plural, masculine: *nos* 'our', feminine: *vosă* 'your' (‹ **mojь*, **tvojь*, **svojь*, **moja*, **tvoja*, **svoja*, **našь*, **vaša*); accusative singular feminine: *müją*, *süją* (‹ **mojǫ*, **svojǫ*), locative singular masculine–neuter: (*vå*) *müjěm*, *tüjěm* (**vъ mojimь*, **tvojimь*); nominative plural masculine: *müjai*, *süjai* (‹ **moji*, **svoji*); dative plural masculine: *nosěm* (‹ **našimъ*).

The univeral pronouns are attested in the following forms: *ves* (M), *vesi* (N) (‹ **vьšь*, **vьše*) 'all, every' and *vesot'ă* (‹ **vьšakoje*) 'all, any'. Very few forms of the interrogative and negative pronouns are attested: *kåtü*, *t'ümau* (‹ **kъto*, **komu*) 'who', *cü*, *cig* (‹ **čьso*, **čego*) 'what', *kot'ě*, *kokă*, *kot'üg* (‹ **kakъjь*, **kakaja*, **kakogo*) 'which, which one'.

The negative ponouns were formed with the morpheme *ne*/*mi* (‹ **ne*, instead of **ni*): *nekåtü* (‹ **nekъto*) 'no one', *nic* (‹ **nečьso*) 'nothing', *nit'ed* (‹ **nekъde*) 'nowhere'.

3.1.4 Adjectival morphology

Polabian preserved some relics of the original short forms of adjectives. All of them represent the nominative singular (see 3.1.1). The long forms of adjectives are also quite well attested in the nominative. The remaining cases are much worse represented. On the basis of the recorded material the following endings can be reconstructed (table 14.4). Examples:

Singular

Nominative: *vilt'ě* (‹ **velikъjь*) (M), *vilt'ă* (‹ **velikoje*) (N), *vilkă*

Table 14.4   The declension of adjectives

| | SG | | | PL | | | DU |
	M	N	F	M	N	F	N
NOM	-ĕ ⎫	-å/-ĕ	-ă	-ĕ ⎫	-ă	-ă	-ă
ACC = NOM or GEN ⎭			-ǫ	-ă ⎭			
GEN	-åg/-ĕg		–	-ĕx	–	–	–
DAT	-ümĕ		-ĕ	–	–	–	–
LOC	–		-åj	–	–	–	–

(‹ *velikaja) (F) 'big, great', büžĕ (‹ *božьjь) (M), büžĕ (‹ *božьjeje)
(N), büză (‹ *božьjaja) (F) 'God's; pious';
Accusative feminine: dübrǫ (‹ *dobrǫjǫ) 'good';
Genitive masculine–neuter: våisükåg (‹ *vysokajego) 'high', tritĕg (‹
*tretьjego) 'third';
Dative: varxnümĕ (‹ *vŗxnomu) 'supreme';
Locative feminine: no provăj (‹ *na pravĕji) 'to the right'.

Plural

Nominative: vilcĕ (‹ *veliciji) (M) 'big', senenă (‹ *sĕnenaja) (N) 'hay', vil-
t'ă (‹ *velikyjĕ) (F) 'big';
Accusative masculine: lesnă vrexåi (‹ *lĕsьnyjĕ (v)orĕxy) 'hazelnuts' literally 'wood-nuts';
Genitive masculine: drauʒĕx büd'üv (‹ *druʒijixъ (instead of *drugyjixъ)
bogovъ) 'other gods''.

Dual

Nominative–accusative neuter: paună cilĕsai (‹ *pl'ǫnĕji čelesi) 'full
cheeks'.

3.1.5   Numeral morphology
The numerals are quite well attested in the texts. For the most part, they do
not depart from their counterparts in other Slavonic languages.
    Cardinals: jadån (‹ *jedъnъ instead of *jedьnъ), janü (‹ *jedьno) '1',
dåvo (‹ *dъva), dåve (‹ *dъvĕ) '2', tåri (‹ *trьje) '3', citĕr (‹ *četyre) '4',
pǫt (‹ *pętь) '5', sist (‹ *šestь) '6', sidĕm (‹ *sedmь) '7', visĕm
(‹ *(v)osmь) '8', divǫt (‹ *devętь) '9', disǫt (‹ *desętь) '10'. The cardinals
from '11' to '20' occur in two or more alternative forms: janădist/
jadånădist (‹ *jedьnъ na desęte), janünăcti (‹ *jedьno na desęte) '11',
dvenădist/dvenăcti/dvenăcte/dvenocte (‹ *dъvĕ na desęte) '12', trainădist/
trainăcte/trainocte/tårojnăcti (‹ *tri na desęte, *trajь na desęte) '13',

citĕrnădist/citĕrnocte/citĕrnocti (‹ **četyre na desęte*) '14', *pątnădist/ patnocti* (‹ **pętь na desęte*) '15', *sistnădist/sistnocti* (‹ **šestь na desęte*) '16', *sidĕmnădist/sidĕmnocti* (‹ **sedmь na desęte*) '17', *visĕmnădist/ visĕmnocti* (‹ **(v)osmь na desęte*) '18', *divątnădist/divątnocti* (‹ **devętь na desęte*) '19', *disątnocti* (‹ **desętь na desęte*) '20', *janü disątnocti/ disątnocti janü* '21' and so on. Apart from *disątnocti* the word *stig* (Middle Low German *stige* 'twenty sheaves') was used in this function. '30' was *pöl t'üpĕ* (‹ **polъ kopy*), '40' – *citĕrdiṣǫt* (‹ **četyre desętъ*), '50' – *pą(t)diṣǫt* (‹ **pętь desętъ*), '60' – *sis(t)diṣǫt* (‹ **šestь desętъ*), '70' – *sidĕmdiṣǫt* (‹ **sedmь desętъ*) '80' – *visĕmdiṣǫt* (‹ **(v)osmь desętъ*), '90' – *divą(t)diṣǫt* (‹ **devętь desętъ*. As can be seen from *pöl t'üpĕ* '30', alongside *sis(t)diṣǫt* Polabian must have also used **t'üpă* (‹ **kopa*, originally 'rick, stack, heap, pile', then in North Slavonic secondarily also 'sixty (sheaves), 60') in the sense of '60'. To express '100' the forms *disątdiṣǫt* (‹ **desętь desętъ*) or *pąt stid'ĕ* were used. '1,000' was *disąt pątstid'ĕ*.

Ordinals: *pară* (‹ **pŕvaja* or **pŕvoje*) 'first', *törĕ* (‹ **vъtorъjь*) 'second', *tritĕ* (‹ **tretьjьjь*) 'third', *cit'ortĕ* (‹ **četvŕtъjь*) 'fourth', * p̓ǫtĕ* (‹ **pętъjь*) 'fifth', *sestĕ* (‹ **šestъjь*) 'sixth', *våsmĕ* (‹ **(v)osmъjь*) 'eighth', *div̓ǫtĕ* (‹ **devętъjь*) 'ninth', *diṣǫtĕ* (‹ **desętъjь*) 'tenth'. 'First' was also *erstĕ* (from German *erste*) or *preńă* (‹ **perdьńaja*).

Collective numerals: *citvărü* (‹ **četvero*) '4', *pątărü* (‹ **pętero*) '5', *sistărü* (‹ **šestero*) '6', *sidmărü* (‹ **sidmărü*) '7', *vismărü* (‹ **(v)osmero*) '8', *divątărü* (‹ **devętero*) '9', *disątărü* (‹ **desętero*) '10'.

3.2 Verbal morphology

3.2.1 Verbal categories

Like other Slavonic languages, Polabian distinguished between the perfective and imperfective aspects. The distinction was implemented chiefly by prefixes, for example, the imperfectives *lümĕt* (‹ **lomiti*) 'to break', *mesăt* (‹ **měšati*) 'to mix', *aidĕ* (‹ **idetъ*) 'goes' had the perfectives *vézlümĕt* (‹ **jьzlomiti*) 'to break', *vézmesăt* (‹ **jьměšati*) 'to mix', *püdĕ* (‹ **pojьdetъ*) 'will go'.

Some aspectual pairs were marked by other morphological means, such as alternation or change of conjugation, compare the imperfectives *jaimojĕ* (‹ **jьmajetъ*) 'seizes', *dvaizĕ* (‹ **dvižetъ*) 'raises' with the perfectives *jémĕ* (‹ **jьmetъ*) 'seizes', *dvaignĕ* (‹ **dvignetъ*) 'raises'.

Polabian preserved all three past tenses of Proto-Slavonic, imperfect, aorist and perfect: compare the imperfects *tex* (‹ **xъtĕaxъ*) 'I wanted', *bejăs* (‹ **bьjaaše*) 'was beating', the aorists *våik* (‹ **vykъ*) 'I learned', *rici* (‹ **reče*) 'said', *åipaustaix* (‹ **upustixъ*) 'I dropped', *åităcix* (‹ **utъčexъ*) 'I met', *våzą* (‹ **vъzę*) 'took' and the perfects *rüdål-să* (‹ **rodilъ sę*) '(he) was born', *åiseklai* (‹ **usĕkli*) '(they) cut off'.

The present tense expressed the present when used in the imperfective and the future if in the perfective form: *pajǫ* (‹ *pijǫ*) 'I am drinking', *lǻzĕs* (‹ *lьžešь*) 'you are lying', but *praivǫzǫ* (‹ *privęžǫ*) 'I shall tie to', *püdǻpcĕ* (‹ *podъpъtjetъ*) 'will trample'.

The analytical future tense comprised the finite forms of the verb *cǫ* (‹ *xъtjǫ*) 'I want, I will' and the infinitive of the main verb: *jo cǫ pict st' aibǫ* (‹ *ja xъtjǫ pekti skybǫ*) 'I shall bake (some) bread', *ci dǻzd ait* (‹ *xъtjetъ dъžžъ iti*) 'it will rain'.

The imperative is well attested in the singular and only in two forms in the plural. It ended in *-∅/-ai* (‹ *-i*) in the singular and *-tĕ* (‹ *-te*) in the plural: *doj* (‹ *daji*) 'give', *ricai-mĕ* (‹ *reči mu*) 'tell him', *rüsplǎstaitĕ* (‹ *orzplaščite*) 'flatten out', *jectĕ* (‹ *jĕdjьte*) 'eat'. The verbs *dot* 'to give', *jest* 'to eat' and *vaiʒĕ* 'sees' preserved the original consonantal type of the imperative: *doʒ* (‹ *dadjь*), *jeʒ* (‹ *jĕdjь*), *jectĕ* (see above), *vaiʒ* (‹ *vidjь*). As a form of injunction, Polabian used the modal particle *nex* (‹ *nexaji*, the original imperative from *nexati* 'to let') with the third person present of the verb: *nex jǫ tok* (‹ *nexaji jestъ tako*) 'may it be so', *nex tibĕ tü smakojĕ* (‹ *nexaji tebe to* (Middle Low German *smak-*)-*ajetъ*) 'may it taste (good) to you.'

The Polabian verb had the following non-finite forms: the infinitive, the present active participle and the past passive participle. With few exceptions, they continued the Proto-Slavonic forms: *sǻpǎt* (‹ *sъpati*) 'to sleep', *zarǎt* (‹ *zьrěti*) 'to look', but *vǻst* (‹ *vъzti* instead of *vъzęti*) 'to take', *sedǫcĕ* (‹ *sĕdętjьjь*) 'sitting', *baitĕ* (‹ *bitъjь*) 'beaten', *ǻikǫsenĕ* (‹ *ukǫšenъjь*) 'bitten'.

The past passive participle served to form the passive voice in combination with the auxiliary verbs *bǻit* (‹ *byti*) 'to be' or *vǻrdot* (‹ (Middle Low German *werd-*)*-ati*) 'to become'. The texts seem to show that the two constructions differed in their function: the passive with *bǻit* most probably referred to the present, that with *vǻrdot* to the future, compare the following examples together with their German translations: *jǫ zazonĕ* (‹ *jestъ žьžanъjь*) 'er ist verbrandt' (= 'it is burned') versus *vǻrdǎ ǻirüdenĕ* (‹ (Middle Low German *werd-*)*-ajetъ urodenъjь* instead of *urodjenъjь*) 'er wird geboren werden' (= 'he will be born'). The past tense of the passive always contained the appropriate form of *vǻrdot*: *vǻrdol baitĕ* (‹ *(werd-)aľъ bitъjь*) '(he) was beaten', *v̌zv̌ǫzonĕ* (‹ *vъzvęzanзjь*) *vǻrdol* '(he) was tied up'.

3.2.2 Conjugation

In the present-tense forms, Polabian established stress on the penultimate syllable. Owing to the reduction of vowels the original *-e/o-* and *-i-* conjugations fell together, compare *aidĕ* (‹ *idetъ*) 'goes', *nüsĕ* (‹ *nositъ*) 'carries'. In disyllabic or polysyllabic forms, as well as before enclitics, the stress shifted one syllable towards he end of a form and the reduced ending

Table 14.5   The present tense

	SG		PL		DU	
	1	II	1	II	1	II
1	-ą	-m	-mĕ		–	
2		-s	-tĕ		–	
3		-∅	-ą		-tă/-to	

was replaced by the non-reduced one, compare *dojĕ* (‹ *dajetъ) ‘gives’ with *vitĕdojimĕ* (‹ *otъdajemy) ‘we forgive’ and *aidĕ* (‹ *idetъ) ‘goes’ with *aidi-să* (‹ *idetъ sę) ‘(am, are, etc.) getting along’, literally ‘goes (to me, to you, and so on)’. As a result of these processes Polabian distinguished between only two conjugation types: verbs with the -*ĕ*-/-*i*- stem and verbs with the -*ă*-/-*o*- stem. Let us refer to them as the first (I) and second (II) conjugations. The endings of the present-tense forms are given in table 14.5.

Examples: *plocą* (‹ *plačǫ) ‘I cry’, *ricą* (‹ *rečǫ) ‘I say’, *zarą* (‹ *zьrjǫ) ‘I look’, *nexăm* (‹ *nexamь) ‘I let’, *opăm* (‹ (Middle Low German *hop-*) *-*amь*) ‘I hope’; *cajĕs* (‹ *čuješь) ‘you feel’, *znojis-mĕ?* (‹ *znaješь mьne) ‘do you know me?’, *zarĕs* (‹ *zьrišь) ‘you look’, *mos* (‹ *jьmašь) ‘you have, you are to’, *ne-măs* ‘you are not to’, *ganăs* (‹ (Middle Low German *gönn-*) -*ašb*) ‘you are favourable to’, *ni ganos-mĕ* ‘you envy’; *plocĕ* (‹ *plačetъ) ‘cries’, *lümĕ* (‹ *lomitъ ‘breaks’, *pĕpădi-să* (‹ *popadetъ sę) ‘falls down’, *rüdi-să* (‹ *roditъ sę) ‘is born’, *zevă* (‹ *zĕva ‹ *zĕvajetъ) ‘yawns’, *strid'o-să* (‹ (Middle Low German *strid-*)*-*a sę*) ‘quarrels’; *cimĕ* (‹ *xъtjemy) ‘we want’, *vitĕdojimĕ* (‹ *(*v*)*otъdajemy*) ‘we forgive’, *momĕ* (‹ *jьmamy) ‘we have, we are to’; *citĕ* (‹ *xъtjete) ‘you want’, *motĕ* (‹ *jьmate) ‘you have’; *püją* (‹ *pojǫtъ) ‘(they) sing’, *vorą* (‹ *varętъ) ‘(they) cook’, *jaigroją* (‹ *jьgrajǫtъ) ‘(they) play’; *bĕjăto-să* (‹ *bьjeta sę) ‘(they two) beat each other’.

The perfect tense was formed by means of the morpheme -*l*/-*lă* (‹ *-*lъ*, *-*la*) in the singular and -*lai* (‹ *-*li*) in the plural, added to the original infinitive stem. The personal distinctions could be made either by the forms of the auxiliary verb *båit* (‹ *byti) ‘to be’ or by personal pronouns, compare *ją plokol* (‹ *jestъ plakalъ) ‘(he) cried’, *joz pl'ǫsăl* (‹ *jazъ plęsalъ) ‘I danced’ (M), *joz bålă* (‹ *jazъ byla) ‘I was’ (F), *tåi våipål* (‹ *ty

Table 14.6   The present tense of the verb *båit* ‘to be’

	SG	PL	DU
1	jis (‹ *jesmь)	jismåi/jismĕ (‹ *jesmy)	–
2	jis (‹ *jesь)	–	–
3	ją/jă	–	jistă (‹ *jesta)

vypiłъ) 'you drank' (M), *vån åirüdål-să* (‹ *(v)onъ urodiłъ sę*) 'he was born', *vinai bĕlai-să* (‹ *(v)oni bili sę*) 'they have beaten each other'.

Other tenses, the imperative and the non-finite forms of Polabian conjugation are much less well attested. They are presented in 3.2.1.

The only irregular verb in Polabian was *båit* (‹ *byti*) 'to be'. Its forms in the present tense are given in table 14.6. The form *jă* appears in reduced positions, for example, when preceded by the negative particle *ni* (‹ *ne*), compare *ni-jă*. The origin of the nasality of *ja* is not clear. Apart from the present tense, the following forms of the verb are attested: *ni-bäs* (‹ *ne bĕaše*) (IMPF) 'was not', *bǫdĕ* (‹ *bǫdetъ*) (FUT) 'will be', *bål* (‹ *byłъ*) (PRF M) and *bålă* (‹ *byla*) (PRF F) 'has been'.

3.3 Derivational morphology

In addition to Slavonic derivational patterns, Polabian also used some German elements in word formation (see 3.3.3).

3.3.1 Major patterns of noun derivation

The most clear categories of noun derivation include the following:

1 Diminutives formed by means of the suffixes *-ĕk* (‹ *-ikъ*) (M), *-ăk* (‹ *-ькъ, *-ъkъ*) (M), *-ăc* (‹ *-ьсь*) (M), *-kă* (‹ *-ъka*) (F), for example, *t'ütlĕk* (‹ *kotьlikъ*) from *t'üt'ål* (‹ *kotьłъ*) 'kettle', *varsăk* (‹ *vŗšькъ*) from *varx* (‹ *vŗxъ*) 'peak, top', *d'ölǫbăk* from *d'ölǫb* (‹ *golǫbь*) 'pigeon', *brotăc* from *brot* (‹ *bratъ*) 'brother', *t'öskă* from *t'öză* (‹ *koza*) 'goat', *t'üskă* (‹ *kožьks*) from *t'üză* (‹ *koža*) 'skin'. From some masculine nouns, diminutives were derived by means of the suffix *-kă*: *Ånskă* 'Johnny' from *Åns* 'John' (from Middle Low German *Hans*), *ramkă* (from Middle Low German *ram*) 'goat, ram', *Michelkă* 'Michael' (German *Michael*). The suffix seems to have been the contamination of the Low German suffix *-che/-ke* (compare German *-chen*) with the native *-kă*.

2 Nouns denoting females formed by means of the suffixes *-kă* (‹ *-ъka*), *-skă* (contamination of Middle Low German *-sche* with the native *-skă* ‹ *-ьska*): *erskă* 'mistress, lady' from *er* (Middle Low German *er*) 'master, gentleman', *toblårskă* 'witch' from *toblår* (Middle Low German *toverer*) 'sorcerer, wizard'.

3 Nomina agentis formed by means of the suffixes *-nĕk* (‹ *nikъ*), *-ăc* (‹ *-ačь*), *-aikă* (‹ *-ika*). The first one attached to nouns, the latter two to verbs: *crivnĕk* (‹ *červьnikъ*) 'shoemaker' from *criv* (‹ *červь*) 'shoe', *tåkăc* (‹ *tъkačь*) 'weaver' from *tåkăt* (‹ *tъkati*) 'to weave', *flåităc* 'lesser whitethroat (a song-bird)' from *flåitot* (Middle Low German *floiten*) 'to play the flute, the fife', *bezaikă* (‹ *bĕžika*) 'runner' from *bezăt* (‹ *bĕžati*) 'to run', *perdojaikă* (‹ *perdajika*) 'merchant' from *perdojĕ* (‹ *perdajetъ*) 'sells'.

4   Nomina actionis formed by means of the suffixes *-ně* (‹ *-ьje*), *-t'ě* (‹ *-tьju* (DAT) from verbs: *vobeně* (‹ *vabenьje*) 'baiting, alluring', *catině* (‹ *čьtenьje*) 'counting' from *catě* (‹ *čьtetъ*) 'counts', *kå pait'ě* (‹ *kъ pitьju*) 'to drink'.

Some of the suffixes mentioned above also fulfilled other functions, for example, *storěk* (‹ *starikъ*) 'leaven' from *storě* (‹ *starъjь*) 'old', *bolåk* (‹ *běĺъkъ*) 'the white of an egg'.

3.3.2   Major patterns of adjective derivation
The productive suffixes were *-n-* (‹ *-ьn-*), *-en-*(‹ *-en-*), *-ost-*(‹ *-'ast-*), *-üv-/-ev-* (‹ *-ov-/*-ev-*), *-ot-* (‹ *-at-*). With the exception of the suffixes *-n-* and *-en-*, which could form adjectives both from nouns and verbs, all the other suffixes mentioned attached to nouns: *xlådeně* (‹ *xoldenъjь*) 'cool' from *xlåd* (‹ *xoldъ*) 'shade, cool', *t'ülně* (‹ *kolьnъjь*) 'wagon' from *t'ölå* (‹ *kola*) 'wagon', *traivň* 'wedding' from *traivoje* (‹ *(Middle Low German *truw-*)-*ajetъ*) 'marries', *rüseně* (‹ *rošenъjь*) 'bleached' from *rüsě* (which is unattested, but compare *rüsi-så* ‹ *rositъ sę* 'is bleached'), *snörostě* 'fringed' from *snör* (Middle Low German *snôr*) 'string', *kolüvě* 'cabbage' from *kol* (Middle Low German *kôl*) 'cabbage', *šaprev* 'shepherd's' from *šapår* (Middle Low German *schaper*) 'shepherd', *krauckotě* 'crossed, cross' from *krauce* (Middle Low German *kruze*) 'Ascension'.

3.3.3   Major patterns of verb derivation
The main types of verb derivation are prefixation and separable compounding. The productive prefixes were: *åi-* (‹ *u-*), *prai-* (‹ *pri-*), *så-* (‹ *sъ-*), *vå-* (‹ *vъ-*), *våz-* (‹ *vъz-*), *vėz-* (‹ *jьz-*), *vi-* (‹ *(v)o-*), *våi-* (‹ *vy-*), *zo-* (‹ *za-*): *åibrükot* 'to wear out' from *brükot* (Middle Low German *brüken*) 'to use', *praibüvåt* 'to build onto' from *büvot* (Middle Low German *buwen*) 'to build', *såbrükoně* 'worn out' from *brükot* (see above), *våmarkojě* 'marks' from *markojě* (Middle Low German *marken*) 'draws, marks', *våzlodot* 'to load on' from *lodot* (Middle Low German *laden*) 'to load', *vėzlikål* '(he) has compared' from *likot* (Middle Low German *liken*) 'to make equal', *visåct* (‹ *(v)osěkti*) 'to cut apart' from *sect* (‹ *sěkti*) 'to cut', *våiråvåt* (‹ *vyrъvati*) 'to tear out' from *råvåt* (‹ *rъvati*) 'to pick, pull up', *zosüleně* 'dirtied, dirty' from the unattested verb borrowed from Middle Low German *solen*.

On the German model Polabian developed separable compound verbs using both German and Polabian prefixes–particles: compare, on the one hand, *to-vist* (‹ *(Low German *to*)-*vesti*) 'to ride to', *vizě-to* (‹ *vezetъ* (Low German *to*)) 'rides to', *to-zině* (*(Low German *to*)-*ženetъ*) also *zině-to* 'drives to', *derě-dal* (‹ *deretъ-*(Middle Low German *dal*)) 'pulls off, tears off', and on the other hand, *kĺają vånau* (‹ *kljujǫtъ vъnu*)

'(they) peck out, scratch out (of chickens)', *vånau dojĕ* (‹ *vъnu dajetъ)
'gives out', *aidĕ dånau* (‹ *idetъ dъnu) 'goes in', *dånau klodĕ* (‹ **dъnu
kladetъ*) 'puts in', *püslod t'autait* (‹ *poslĕdъ kutiti) 'to imitate' (compare
t'autait 'to make, to do' and German *nachmachen* 'to imitate', *machen* 'to
make'), *rǫbĕt våkorst* (‹ **rǫbiti (v)okrstь*) 'to hem around'. The native
elements *vånau, dånau, püslod, våkorst* were used to fulfil the function
corresponding to the German separable prefixes, such as *zu* (Low German
to), *heraus, hinein, nach, um, herum*, for example, *zufahren* (= Polabian
to-vist), *abziehen* (= Polabian *derĕ-dal*), *herausscharren* (= Polabian
kl'ają vånau), *herausgeben* (= Polabian *dojĕ vånau*).

4 Syntax

Given the relatively small amount of material available, it is not possible to
reconstruct all aspects of Polabian syntax. To facilitate comparison with
other chapters, the same subsection numbers are retained and there is no
subsection 4.7.

4.1 Element order in declarative sentences

Polabian had free word order in the sense that the major constituents could
in principle occur in any order. For example, the subject could precede or
follow the verb, and the verb could precede or follow its objects or any
adverbial modifiers: *dåzd aidĕ* (‹ **dъ̌ʒʒь idetъ*) 'rain goes' or *aidĕ dåzd*
'goes rain' (= 'it is raining'), *šapår posĕ vice* (‹ *(Middle Low German
schaper) *pasetъ (v)ovьcĕ*) 'the shepherd grazes the sheep' and *t'üskǫ derĕ
del* (‹ *kožькǫ deretъ (Middle Low German *del*)) 'takes off the skin',
virgnĕ dal no zimą (‹ *vŕgnetъ (Middle Low German *dal*) *na zemjǫ*)
'throws down to the ground' and *vå lönü våmĕ* (‹ *vъ lono vъjьmetъ)
'takes in one's arms'.

4.2 Non-declarative sentence types

Yes–no interrogative sentences seem to have been formed without any
particle: *cis-să kǫpăt ait?* (‹ **xъtješь sę kǫpati iti*) 'do you want to go and
take a bath?', *müzĕs venst'ĕ gornĕt?* (‹ *možešь (German *wend-*)-*ьsky
gorniti*) 'can you speak Wendish?', *znojis-jĕg?* (‹ **znaješь jego?*) 'do you
know him?'

Commands and negative commands are expressed by means of the
imperatives: *aid sąd kå mane* (‹ *idi sędi kъ mьnĕ) 'come and sit beside
me', *püd sem er* (‹ *pojьdi sĕmo (Low German *her*)) 'come here', *ni
brind'oj-năs kå farsükoňĕ* (‹ *ne (German *bring-*)-*aji nasъ kъ* (Middle
Low German *vorsak-*)-*anьju*) 'do not bring us into temptation'.

4.3 Copular sentences

The role of the copula was played by the verb *båit*: *nină joz mom tüjă brüt
båit* (‹ **nenĕ jazъ jьmatь tvoja* (Low German *brüt*) *byti*) 'now I am to be

your bride', *tåi jis vainĕk* (‹ **ty jesь vinьnikъ*) 'you are the guilty one'. Adjectives are used in long form with the copula: *ją glådüvnĕ* (‹ **jestъ goldovьnъjь*) '(he) is poor', *joz jis storĕ* (‹ **jazъ jesmь starъjь*) 'I am old' (M). Some examples are attested with the verb *vårdot* (‹ **(Middle Low German werd-)-ati*) in similar functions: *solix vårdås* (‹ **(Middle Low German sålich, werd-)-ašь*) 'you become happy', *śptä mo vårdot tüji jaimą* (‹ **svętoje jьmajetъ ... tvoje jimę*) 'thy name become holy'.

4.4–4.5 Complex sentences

Little can be said about the syntax of complex sentences as only twenty or so complex sentences are attested in the texts. The majority of them are asyndetic, coordinate structures, for example, *Morajä xüdi våkorst carkvaicĕ så tåraimä sveckomĕ, såikås büsćä, ne-mĕzälo-jĕg nit' ĕdĕ nojt* (‹ **Marija xodi (v)okŗstъ cŗkъvici sъ trima svĕčьkami* (Middle Low German *suk-)-aaše božьca, ne možala jego nekъde najiti*) 'Mary walked around the church with three candles, she was looking for the Lord, she could not find him anywhere'. Several comparative and relative clauses are attested: *kåtü ci sarăt, tǫ aid* (‹ **kъto xъtjetъ sьrati, tъnъ idi*) 'whoever wants to shit, may he go', *vitĕdoj-năm nos grex kăk måi vitĕdojimĕ nosĕm gresnärüm* (‹ **(v)otъdaji namь našь grĕxъ kako my (v)otъdajemy našimъ grĕšьnaromъ*) 'forgive us our sin as we forgive our sinners'.

4.6 Negation

The particle *ni/ne* was used in the function of negation: *ni ją mąt' ĕ* (‹ **ne jestъ mękъkъjь*) 'is not soft', *joz ne-müg zatĕk båit* (‹ **jazъ ne mogъ zętikъ byti*) 'I cannot be the groom'. As in other Slavonic languages, the negated transitive verb required its direct object to stand in the genitive: *ne-mä lüko* (‹ **ne jьmajetъ* (Middle Low German *lück-)-a*) 'has no luck' versus *vån mo vilt' ĕ moxt* (‹ **(v)onъ jьmajetъ velikъjь* (German *macht*)).

With negative pronouns double negation was used: *joz ni cają nic* (‹ **jacъ ne čujǫ nečьso*) 'I do not feel anything', *ni vaid'äl nit'üg?* (‹ **ne vidĕlъ nikogo?*) 'didn't you see anybody?'.

4.8 Reflexives and reciprocals

The Polabian reflexive verbs were formally distinguished by the particle *să* (‹ **sę*) and were used in several functions, among others: (a) to denote that the subject acts upon itself: *joz mål-să* (‹ **jazъ mylъ sę*) 'I have washed myself', *våzdälai-să* (‹ **vьzdĕli sę*) 'they have got dressed'; (b) to signal impersonal constructions: *kok aidi-să vom?* (‹ **kako idetъ sę vamъ?*) 'how are you doing?'; (c) to refer to uncontrolled actions: *pĕpådål-să* (‹ **popadlъ sę*) '(he) has fallen', *åitüpål-să* (‹ **utopilъ sę*) '(he) has drowned'; (d) to denote reciprocity: *krigălai-să* (‹ **(German krig-)-ali sę*) 'they have fought'. In some cases the use of reflexives was close to that of the passive: *beli-să* (‹ **bĕlitъ sę*) 'is bleached'. Reciprocity was also expressed by means of *jadån ... draug* or *draug ... draug*: *jadån sl'od* *draugăg* (‹ **jedьnъ slědъ drugajego*) 'one after the other', *draug draugau drauzĕt* (‹ **drugъ drugu družiti*) 'to help one another'.

Some verbs could occur only as morphological reflexives: *büji-să* (‹ **bojitъ sę*) 'is afraid', *strid'o-să* (‹ **(Middle Low German strid-)-ajetъ sę*) 'quarrels'.

4.9 Possession

Possession was expressed by means of the verb *met* (‹ **jьmĕti*) 'to have', possessive pronouns, and perhaps also possessive adjectives: *mos pǫ̆ză?* (‹ **jьmašь pǫza?*) 'do you have money?', *ne-năm pǫ̆ză* 'I have no money', *müjă soko* (‹ **moja (Middle Low German sake))* 'my thing', *süj düm* (‹ **svojь domъ*) 'one's own house', *šaprev stok* (‹ **(Middle Low German schaper-)-evь (Middle Low German stok))* 'shepherd's crook', *malnait'üv knext* (‹ **malnik-ovъ*; *mal-*, *knext* from Middle Low German) 'miller's hand'. Examples of the latter type are very few and are not certain, for they can also be interpreted as representing qualitative adjectives (that is, 'the type of crook a shepherd uses; mill hand'). No examples of the genitive case in this function are attested.

4.10 The partitive genitive

The partitive genitive was employed in Polabian to a much greater extent than in other Slavonic languages. A noun in the partitive genitive could serve not only as the object of a verb but also as the subject of a sentence: *tü paivo ją dübră* (‹ **to piva jestъ dobroje*) 'this beer is good', *tǫ kolai ją jist teplü* (‹ **tъnъ (Middle Low German kol-)-u jestъ ješče teplo*) 'this cabbage is still hot', *to zenă mo dübră mlåkå* (‹ **ta žena jьmatь dobroje melka*) 'the woman has good milk'. A noun used in the partitive genitive seems to have been qualified by adjectives in the nominative no matter what role the noun played in a sentence.

4.11 Impersonal and passive constructions

In addition to the personal (active, passive and reflexive) constructions characterized by the presence of the subject, Polabian had impersonal constructions which were either intransitive or reflexive: *svaitojĕ* (‹ **svitajetъ*) 'day is breaking', *svetĕ* (‹ **svĕtitъ*) 'lightning flashes', *kok aidi-să vom* (see 4.8).

The use of the passive was quite frequent in Polabian. The texts seem to show that the passive started to supersede typically Slavonic reflexive constructions in some of their functions: *plåtnĕ ją rüsenă* (‹ **poltьno jestъ rošenoje*) alongside with *plåtnĕ rüsi-să* (‹ **poltьno rositъ se*) 'the linen is bleached', *vårdă airüdenĕ* (‹ **(Middle Low German werd-)-ajetъ urodenъjь* instead of *urodjenъjь*) '(he) will be born' alongside *airüdăl-să* (‹ **urodilъ sę*) '(he) was born'.

5   Lexis

5.1–5.2   General composition and borrowings
The recorded material includes roughly 2,800 words, predominantly (about 2,000 words) of Slavonic origin. But a considerable proportion of them (more than 600) are German loan-words. Most of the latter can be traced to Middle Low German. Some lexical items were mixed forms, which comprised both native and borrowed elements: *jisin-mond* 'September' (< native **jesenь* 'autumn' and Middle Low German *mand* 'month'), *vρsĕpuc* 'barber' (from native *vρs* 'beard' and Low German *putzen* 'to shave').

In view of the incompleteness of the recorded material it would be unjustified to draw any conclusions concerning the general composition of the Polabian word-stock.

5.3   Incorporation of borrowings
German loan-words were not only phonologically assimilated, most of them were also morphologically adapted to the grammatical system of Polabian; they were inflected according to the native paradigms as well as often gaining native prefixes or suffixes, for example, *lük/glük* (Middle Low German *(g)lück* 'luck', genitive singular *lüko/glüko* (< **((g)lük-)-a*), *t'arl* 'man, husband, fellow' (Middle Low German *kerle*), dative singular *t'arlau* (< **(kerl-)-u*), *praibüvăt* (< **pri-*(Middle Low German *buw-*)-*ati*) 'to build onto', *snŏrostĕ* (< ***(Middle Low German *snôr-*) *-'astьjь*) 'fringed'.

5.4   Lexical fields

5.4.1   Colour terms
The only colour terms which are attested are *bŏlĕ* (< **bĕlьjь*) 'white', *cornĕ* (< **čŕnьjь*) 'black', *carvenĕ* (< **čŕvenьjь*) 'red', *saivĕ* (< **sivьjь*) 'grey'.

5.4.2   Body parts
Glåvă (< **golva*) 'head', *våt'ü* (< **(v)oko*) 'eye', *nös* (< **nosь*) 'nose', *vauẋü/väiẋü* (< **(v)uxo*) 'ear', *vaustă/våistă* (< *(v)usta*) 'mouth', *vlås*, plural *vlåsåi* (< **volsъ*, **volsy*) 'hair', *våjo/våjă* (< **vyja*) 'neck', *råmạ* (< **ormę*) 'arm', *rρkă* (< **rρka*) 'hand', *polăc* (< **palьcь*) 'finger, toe', *nügă* (< **noga*) 'leg', *stüpă* (< **stopa*) 'foot', *borst'ä* (Middle Low German *borst*) 'chest'. The word for 'heart' is not attested.

5.4.3   Kinship terms
Motai (< **mati*) 'mother', *ĺolă* (< **ljalja*), also *fader* (Middle Low German *vader*), *aită* (Germanic, compare Old Frisian *heitha*) 'father', *sestră* (< **sestra*) 'sister', *brot* (< **bratъ*) 'brother', *stråjefkă* (< **stryjevъka*) 'aunt,

father's sister', *vaujefkă* (‹ **(v)ujevъka*) 'aunt, mother's sister', *strǻjǎ* (‹ **stryja*) 'uncle, father's brother', *vaujǎ*(‹ *(v)uja*) 'uncle, mother's brother', *tetanǫ* (origin unclear, but compare LSo. *śeśeńe* 'great nephew') 'cousin's child', *grotkǎ* (Middle Low German *groteke*) 'grandmother', *storě lolǎ* (‹ **starъjь ljalja*) or *grotefor* (Low German *grōtevåd′r*) 'grandfather', *zenǎ* (‹ **žena*) 'woman, wife', *t′arl* (Middle Low German *kerle*) 'man, fellow, husband', *defkǎ* (‹ **děvъka*) 'girl, daughter', *våtrük* (‹ **(v)otrokъ*), also *sǻinkǎ* (‹ **synъka*) 'son'.

6 Dialects

Owing to the paucity of the written records, little can be said about the dialects of Polabian. A close scrutiny of the notation used in the records shows that part of what has been considered to be spelling inconsistencies is due to the dialectal differentiation of the language. Three dialects have been distinguished in Polabian: the Süthen dialect (represented by Parum Schultze), the Lüchow dialect (represented by Pfeffinger) and the Klennow dialect (represented by Hennig; see section 1). The most evident differences among them related to the results of certain sound changes. The original syllabic *ļ* changed into *u* in Schultze's and Pfeffinger's dialects, but into *au* in Hennig's dialect; the original vowel **u* in strong positions was diphthongized (depending on the environment, see 2.1.2) into *au* or *ǻi* in the dialect represented by Hennig, but only into *ǻi* in Schultze's and Pfeffinger's dialects; Pfeffinger's dialect had preserved some remnants of original *č, ž, š*, whereas the two other dialects had completely changed the original *č, ž, š* into *c, z, s* (see 2.1, 2.1.2).

Acknowledgement

I am most grateful for the comments I have received on earlier versions of this paper from my friends Alexander M. Schenker and Edward Stankiewicz.

References

Lehr-Spławiński, T. (1929) *Gramatyka połabska*, Lwów: K.S. Jakubowski.

Lehr-Spławiński, T. and Polański, K. (1962) *Słownik etymologiczny języka Drzewian Połabskich*, vol. 1, *a-d′üzd*, Wrocław: Ossolineum. (Continued as Polański (1971–6).)

Małecki, M. (1937) 'Przyczynki do cakawizmu cakawizm pd.-słowiański, grecki, polski i połabski', *Sprawozdania z czynności i posiedzeń Polskiej Akademii Umiejętności*, vol. 42, Nr 1, Cracow: 32–33.

Olesch, R. (1959) *Vocabularium Venedicum von Christian Hennig von Jessen, Nachdruck besorgt von R. Olesch*, Cologne and Graz: Böhlau.

—— (1962) *Juglers lüneburgisch–wendisches Wörterbuch*, Cologne and Graz: Böhlau.

—— (1967) *Fontes lingvae dravaeno-polabicae minores*, Cologne and Graz: Böhlau.

—— (1968) *Bibliographie zum Dravaeno-Polabischen*, Cologne and Graz: Böhlau.

—— (1975) 'Die mundartliche Gliederung des Dravänopolabischen', *Wiener Slavistisches Jahrbuch* 21: 182–201.

—— (1983–7) *Thesaurus linguae dravaeno-polabicae*, 4 vols, Cologne and Vienna: Böhlau.

Polański, K. (1962) *Morfologia zapożyczeń niemieckich w języku połabskim*, Wrocław: Ossolineum.

—— (1965) 'Problem różnic gwarowych w języku połabskim', *Studia z Filologii Polskiej i Słowiańskiej* 5: 365–9.

—— (1971–6) *Słownik etymologiczny języka Drzewian Połabskich*, vols 2–4, *d'üzd-ŕott'ě*, Wrocław: Ossolineum.

Polański, K. and Sehnert, J.A. (1967) *Polabian–English Dictionary*, The Hague and Paris: Mouton.

Rost, P. (1907) *Die Sprachreste der Dravæno-Polaben im Hannöverschen*, Leipzig: J.C. Hinrichs'sche Buchhandlung.

Schleicher, A. (1871) *Laut- und Formenlehre der polabischen Sprache*, St Petersburg: Commissionäre der Kaiserlichen Akademie der Wissenschaften, Eggers und Co., H. Schmitzdorff, J. Issakoff and A. Tscherkessoff.

Szydłowska-Ceglowa, B. (1963) 'Materialna kultura ludowa Drzewian Połabskich w świetle poszukiwań językowych', *Lud* 48: 19–256.

Trubetzkoy, N. (1929) *Polabische Studien* (Sitzungsberichte der Akademie der Wissenschaften in Wien, Philosophisch-historische Klasse, 211, 4. Abhandlung), Vienna and Leipzig.

Супрун, А.Е. (1987) Полабский язык, Минск: Издательство "Университетское".

EAST SLAVONIC
LANGUAGES

15 Russian

Alan Timberlake

1 Introduction

Russian is the native language of virtually all of the 137 million (in the 1979 census) ethnic Russians in the former Soviet Union. Of the 125 million people of other ethnic groups, 16 million claimed Russian as their first language, putting the number of people whose first language is Russian at 153 million. An additional 61 million declared themselves to be functional in Russian.

Russian in its modern form, especially its codified written form, results from an extended and by no means linear evolution. What is now the Russian language area began as northern outposts of the Kievan confederation (first Novgorod, Smolensk and Pskov, then Rostov and Suzdal'), dating from before the official Christianization of Rus' in 988. The dissolution of the Kievan confederation by the Mongol period (1240 to the final liberation of Moscow in 1480) indirectly allowed Moscow to develop from a minor крéмль/kréml' 'fortress' into a medieval imperial power which, by the end of the fifteenth century, had brought the older principalities of the north under its control.

Writing during the Kievan period was predominantly Church Slavonic. In the Muscovite period, use of the secular chancery language, broadly understood, expanded from administrative to other functions; it served eventually as the vehicle for cultural and linguistic borrowing from Poland in the seventeenth century and directly from western Europe starting with the reign of Peter the Great (1696–1725). The Muscovite koine, as some have termed the complex of the written chancery language and the oral Muscovite dialect (a mixed dialect of southern and northern features), was responsible for the development of implicit norms of usage and for their national propagation; these became the norms of Modern Russian (on Muscovite language, see Виноградов/Vinogradov 1949: ch. I, 10–13; II, 1–7; Левин/Levin 1964: 71–112). The development culminates in Puškin (1799–1837), whose 'poetic language was admired as a manifestation of the pentecostal miracle combining the humble speech of the "people of God" with both the prophetic gift of the Biblical fathers and the wisdom of the Classical philosophers' (Picchio in Picchio and Goldblatt 1984, I: 18). The subsequent history of the literary language is characterized by continuing tensions between nativism and Europeanism and between populism and elitism (see the studies by Uspenskij and Gasparov in Picchio and Goldblatt 1984, II).

Modern Russian varies along many axes – regional, social, written versus oral mode and register. The literature on variation takes the literary form of Russian as central and defines a typology of deviations from this standard: colloquial (разговóрная рéчь/razgovórnaja réč′ 'colloquial speech', understood both as oral and less than standard), dialect and urban non-standard (просторéчие/prostoréčie 'simple speech', a catch-all for unacceptable speech variants, including violations of linguistic taboos). Recent investigations (Земская/Zemskaja 1973 and related studies) have documented a gulf between разговóрная рéчь/razgovórnaja réč′ and literary Russian; the difference, however, may be no greater than in other contemporary societies. Along the social axis, measured by profession or education (see Крысин/Krysin 1974 or Comrie and Stone 1978), the speech of workers, as a rule of thumb, is more innovative than that of professionals. Change usually proceeds in a unidirectional fashion across age groups, as measured by decades of years of birth.

2 Phonology

2.1 Segmental phoneme inventory
Russian phonology (see Аванесов/Avanesov 1968; Jones and Ward 1969; Матусевич/Matusevič 1976; Бондарко/Bondarko 1977) revolves around two phenomena, stress in vowels and palatalization in consonants.

It is common to recognize five stressed vowel phonemes, /a, e, o, i, u/, which vary depending on palatalization in adjacent consonants, as discussed below. Fewer distinctions are made in unstressed position. Throughout, stress will be indicated by a vertical mark, except with the grapheme ё, which implies stress. Where orthography as such is discussed, graphemes are marked in bold type.

Palatalized consonants (informally, 'soft' – notationally often C′, here Ç) are articulated with the middle portion of the tongue raised towards the soft palate in a convex shape. Non-palatalized consonants (informally, 'hard' – notationally simply C) are to some or another extent velarized, with the middle of the tongue depressed in a concave shape. Dentals and labials are phonemically 'paired' for palatalization, in that contrasts occur before vowels (other than /e/, which automatically palatalizes a preceding paired consonant) and word-finally. Compare /va/ in вáл/vál 'rampart' versus /γa/ in вял/vjál 'listless' or /to/ in тóмный/tómnyj 'languid'

verus /t̯o/ in тёмный/tëmnyj 'dark', and final /p/ in окóп/okóp 'trench'
versus /p̯/ in кóпь/kóp̯' 'mine' or final /t/ in вы́пит/vы́pit 'drunk' versus
/t̯/ in вы́пить/vы́pit̯' 'drink'. Palatalization is restricted before other
consonants. Labials make no distinction (тёмный/tëmnyj 'dark' has /m/
but masculine short-form тёмен/tëmen has /m̯/) and dentals do so only
before consonants other than dentals (тьма́/t̯'má 'darkness', гоньба́/
gon̯'bá 'chase', хорóшенький/xoróšen̯'kij 'pretty' but пусты́нный/
pustы́nnyj 'pertaining to a desert', from пусты́ня/pustы́nja 'desert'); /l̯/ is
maintained in all positions (льсти́вый/l̯'stívyj 'flattering').

Velars /k, g, x/ are unpaired for palatalization, but vary depending on
environment. The palatalized variant occurs before /i/ and /e/, the
unpalatalized variant elsewhere. Palatals and the dental affricate /c/ are
unpaired for palatalization, and are invariantly either hard (/c/, /š/, /ž/)
or soft (/č/ > [č̣], [ṣ̌:], [ẓ̌:] and /j/). One of the uncertainties of synchronic
Russian phonology is what analysis to assign to the phones [ṣ̌:], associated
with the letter щ, and [ẓ̌:], associated with зж and жж in a diminishing
number of lexical items like дрóжжи/dróžži 'yeast' but not пóзже/pózže
'later'. Historically, [ṣ̌:] derives from the cluster [ṣ̌č̣] when [č̣] lost closure.
This process still operates on combinations of dental fricative plus /č/
depending on the strength of the boundary – hence in the order of
рассказчик/rasskázčik 'story-teller' > [ṣ̌:] ≥ исчи́слить/isčíslit̯' 'cal-
culate' > [ṣ̌:] ~ [ṣ̌č̣] ≥ с чéстью/s čést̯'ju 'with honour' > [ṣ̌č̣] ~ ?[ṣ̌:].
(Hierarchical statements of the type 'x ≥ y' are to be read as 'the process is
at least as likely to occur in the context x as in y'.) The phone [ẓ̌:] results
from the incomplete hardening of /ž/ in clusters.

A list of consonantal phonemes and prominent phones is given in table
15.1, in which hard consonants are given before soft; /c/, [ʒ], /č/, and [ǯ]
are affricates rather than stops in the strict sense.

The once regular tendency to palatalize a consonant preceding a palatal-

Table 15.1 Consonantal phonemes and allophones

	Labial		*Dental*			*Palatal*		*Velar*	
Voiceless stop	p	p̯	t	t̯	c		č̣	k	[k̡]
Voiced stop	b	b̯	d	d̯	[ʒ]		[ǯ]	g	[g]
Voiceless fricative	f	f̯	s	s̯		š	[ṣ̌:]	x	[x̣]
Voiced fricative	v	ɣ̯	z	z̯		ž	[ẓ̌:]	[ɣ]	
Nasal	m	m̯	n	n̯					
Lateral liquid			l	l̯					
Non-lateral liquid			r	r̯					
Glide							j		

Note: [ ] = allophone or phone with uncertain phonemic status.

ized consonant has been losing ground. Usage depends on measures of cohesion between the consonants, such as syllable structure and the place and manner of articulation. With prefixes, to take one context, combinations of labial (P) and dental (T) assimilate according to the hierarchy TŢ (раздѐл/razdèl 'division' › [ʒd̦]) ≥ TP (сбѝть/sbit́ 'knock off' › [ʒb̦ ~ zb̦]) ≥ PP (вбѝть/vbit́ 'beat into' › [vb̦ ~ γb̦]) ≥ PŢ (вдѐлать/vdèlat́ 'fix into' › [vd̦]); thus dental targets assimilate better than labials, and same place of articulation in trigger and target favours assimilation. Analogously for manner of articulation, SŞ (иссякнуть/issjáknut́ 'dry up' › [şş]) ≥ SŢ (раздѐл/razdèl 'division' › [ʒd̦]) ≥ TŢ (поддержа́ть/podderžát́ 'support' › [d̦d̦ ~ dd̦]) ≥ TŞ (отсѐчь/otsèč́ 'hack off' › [tş]); thus fricative (S) targets and same manner of articulation in trigger and target favour assimilation.

Most obstruents are phonemically paired for voicing: for example, для/dlja 'for, on behalf of' and тля/tljá 'beetle' differ by initial /d/ and /t/, бить/bit́ 'beat' and пить/pit́ 'drink' by initial /b̦/ and /p/. Obstruents participate in two rules of voicing. They devoice at the end of words: поро́г/poróg 'threshold' › [k], го́лубь/gólub́ 'dove' › [p]. And they assimilate to a following obstruent: сдѐлать/sdèlat́ 'do' › [ʒd̦], подписа́ть/podpisát́ 'sign' › [tp], and, with both rules, гво́здь/gvózd́ 'nail' › [şt]. Unpaired and normally unvoiced /c, x, č/ develop voiced allophones through assimilation: отѐц бы́л/otèc býl 'father was' › [ʒb], тка́ч бы́л/tkáč býl 'the weaver was' › [ǯb], мо́х бы́л /móx býl 'the moss was' › [γb]. Voicing assimilation applies regularly within a word, and between prefix or preposition and head word; it may apply between words within a phrase: тру́дность заключа́лась/trúdnost́ zaključálaś 'the difficulty consisted of' › [ʒ(d̦)z].

Sonorants (nasals, liquids and glide /j/) and the labio-dental approximates /v, γ/ participate in voicing rules only to a limited extent. They normally do not cause voicing assimilation: твой/tvój 'your' › [tv], тьма́/t́má 'shade' › [țm], тлѐть/tlèt́ 'rot' › [țl̦], пью́/p´jú 'I drink' › [pj]. But before obstruents /v, γ/ assimilate in voicing, and cause voicing assimilation in a preceding obstruent: от вдовы́/ot vdový 'from the widow' › [dvd], под вторы́м/pod vtorým 'under the second' › [tft]. (Sonorants in comparable positions tend to become syllabic.) Word-finally after vowels, /v, γ/ devoice: кро́в/króv 'cover' › [f], кровь/króv́ 'blood' › [f]. At the end of words sonorants do not devoice after a vowel (ко́л/kól 'stake' › [l], до́м/dóm 'house' › [m], but ко́рь/kóŕ 'measles' › [r̝ ~ r̝̂]), usually remain unaffected after a voiced obstruent (as in рубль/rúbĺ › [bl̦] 'rouble' and жизнь/žizń 'life' › [ʒn̦] or, occasionally, [pl̦], [şn̦]), but not uncommonly devoice after a voiceless obstruent (теа́тр/teátr 'theatre' › [tr̝̂]). Overall with respect to voicing – phonemic pairing, final devoicing and voicing assimilation – vowels are completely inert, sonorants largely so, while /v, γ/ are transitional between sonorants and obstruents.

Russian spells morphophonemic alternations in place or manner of consonants, but not alternations in voicing. The exception is prefixes ending in /z/, which are spelled to reflect devoicing, as in развиться/razvit´sja 'develop' but раскаяться/raskajat´sja 'repent'. Pairs of palatalized and non-palatalized consonants are spelled by a single Cyrillic letter, the distinction being indicated by the next grapheme. (The Russian alphabet, with transliteration systems, is given in table 15.2.) At the end of words, a paired consonant is palatalized if the letter is followed by the 'soft sign' ь. Before a vowel, palatalization is indicated by the following vowel letter. The five vowels can each be spelled by two letters: /a/ by a or я, /u/ by y or ю, /i/ by ы or и, /e/ by э or e and /o/ by o or either ё (if stress is marked) or, more usually, plain e (since stress is rarely marked). In general terms, a following 'hard vowel letter' – a, y, ы, э or o – indicates that the preceding consonant is not palatalized, a following 'soft vowel letter' – я, ю, и, e or ё – that it is.

There are various restrictions, exceptions and asymmetries. In practice, there is little call for э after consonants. Plain e is more usual than ё. In most texts ё is used only to disambiguate (singular всё/vsë 'everything' but plural все/vse 'all'); it is used systematically only in instructional texts (encyclopedias, cook-books) or in metalinguistic texts which mark all stresses (such as the current discussion) and is sometimes avoided in borrowings (синьор/sin´or 'señor'). After ц, ч, ш, ж and щ, which represent unpaired consonants, a mixed set of vowel letters is used: a (never я), y (exceptionally ю), и (generally not ы, except after ц in a few roots and regularly in endings) and o or, more usually, ё or plain e. After ч, ш, ж and щ, ь marks the noun as a member of declension IIIa (рожь/rož´ 'rye'); чь occurs in velar-stem infinitives; and шь marks the second singular of the present tense.

Soft vowel letters, additionally, have the function of indicating that /j/ precedes a vowel when there is no consonant letter immediately preceding. Thus, я implies /ja/ word-initially in ясно/jasno 'clearly', after a vowel in делая/delaja 'doing', after ь in пьяный/p´janyj 'drunk' (in which ь marks п as /p/), and after ъ in объявить/ob˝javit´ 'make a declaration'. This rule does not hold for и, since /i/ tends to absorb /j/: искать/iskat´ 'search' and поискать/poiskat´ 'search a bit' have no /j/, but чьи/č´i 'whose' does. The glide /j/, then, is spelled by a soft vowel letter before a vowel and by й after a vowel letter.

Allophones of stressed /i, e, a, o, u/ are determined by phonetic palatalization in adjacent consonants. Basic /a, o, u/ are articulated with front transitions adjacent to soft consonants. In the extreme case, between soft consonants, they may be fronted throughout: люлька/ljul´ka 'cradle' is phonemically /ļuļka/, phonetically [ļüļkə]. Phonemes /i, e/ are retracted after hard consonants, /i/ to [ɨ] (выл/vyl '(he) howled' › [vɨ̈l], c именем/s imenem 'with the name' › [sɨ̈]), and /e/ to [ɛ] (целый/celyj 'whole' › [sċ], в э́том/v ètom 'in that' › [vċ]).

When not under stress, vowels are 'reduced'. They are shorter in duration, qualitatively reduced and tend to merge. High vowels /i/ ([ɨ] after hard consonants) and /u/ are lowered slightly to [ɪ (ɨ) ʊ]. After hard consonants, /a/ and /o/ are subject to **а́канье/ákan´e**, or merge as a low back unrounded vowel; the result is [ʌ] in first pre-tonic position (сара́й/saráj 'barn' › [sʌrái], соро́чка/soróčka 'shirt' › [sʌro̝čkə]) and [ə] else-where. After soft consonants, all non-high vowels merge and approach /i/ or, in the current norm, merge with /i/ as [ɪ]: часо́к/časо́k 'hour (DIMIN)' › [čɪsо́k], чесно́к/česnók 'garlic' › [čɪsnók], число́/čisló 'number' › [čɪsló].

Table 15.2   Orthography and transliteration

Cyrillic	Library of Congress transliteration	Linguistic transliteration
а	a	a
б	b	b
в	v	v
г	g	g
д	d	d
е	e	e
(ё)	e	ë
ж	zh	ž
з	z	z
и	i	i
й	ĭ	j
к	k	k
л	l	l
м	m	m
н	n	n
о	o	o
п	p	p
р	r	r
с	s	s
т	t	t
у	u	u
ф	f	f
х	kh	x
ц	t͡s	c
ч	ch	č
ш	sh	š
щ	shch	šč
ъ	″	″
ы	y	y
ь	′	′
э	ė	è (~ ė)
ю	i͡u	ju
я	i͡a	ja

Two transliteration systems, recorded in table 15.2, map automatically from Russian to a Latin, or modified Latin, alphabet. The 'linguistic' system used here avoids digraphs for consonant letters; ч is č, ц is c, though щ is šč. It renders the soft vowel letters я and ю as ja and ju, both after consonants and in other positions. Cyrillic э is marked with a diacritic, as è or ė (continental); Cyrillic й is j. The Library of Congress system, in its traditional form, employs a ligature sign and diacritics, which are sometimes omitted in informal practice and definitively lost in computerized bibliographies. For consonants, this system uses digraphs: ч is ch, щ is shch, and ц is t͡s (or ts). In general, where the technical system uses j, this system uses i. The letter й is ĭ (or i). The soft vowel letters я and ю are i͡a and i͡u (informally without the ligature); pre-revolutionary ѣ is ie. Cyrillic э (if not simply e) may be specified as ė and thereby distinguished from e; ё, normally not written in Russian, is just e. To illustrate, the author **Фёдор Михайлович Достоевский** is cited as **Fedor Mikhaĭlovich Dostoevskiĭ**, his daughter **Любовь Фёдоровна Достоевская** as **Liubov′ Fedorovna Dostoevskaia**. In neither system is the /j/ that precedes /e/ (after vowels and word-initially) reflected in transliteration. In both systems, ь is rendered as ′ and ъ as ″.

Russian words are sometimes informally anglicized as a guide to pronunciation. Consonants follow the Library of Congress system, though ь is lost; **Гоголь** is **Gogol** in literary studies and **гласность** is **glasnost** in journalism. This practice uses y where the other systems use i or j, and this y may be used for the automatic /j/ before /e/; in two recent translations **Фёдор Достоевский** is once **Fyodor Dostoevsky**, once **Fyodor Dostoyevsky**; y also renders the -[ск]ий of proper names. (See further chapter 2, B2 and B3.)

The contemporary Russian phonological system can be derived transparently from one of the variant Late Proto-Slavonic systems with relatively few changes (see Kiparsky 1963–75, I; Vlasto 1986).

Front nasal *ę denasalized to ä and back nasal *ǫ to u: *žętva › жа́тва/ žátva 'harvest', *pǫtь › пу́ть/pút′ 'road'. At this time (into the eleventh century), one can assume for East Slavonic the following vowel system: high i, y (= [ɨ]) and u; front jer ь and back jer ъ; closed mid vowel ě (possibly diphthongal [ie]); open mid vowels e and o; and low vowels ä (from *ę) and a. The jers, from Proto-Slavonic *ĭ and *ŭ, were probably open high vowels, approximately /ь/ › [ɪ], /ъ/ › [ʊ].

As elsewhere in Slavonic, the watershed event in the history of Russian is the set of processes known as the fall of the *jers* (narrowly, from the middle of the twelfth to the middle of the thirteenth centuries). *Jers* were shortened in duration (that is, became 'weak') and eventually eliminated in most positions – word-finally and internally before a vowel other than a *jer*. In the bargain they compensated preceding vowels, including preceding (that is, 'strong') *jers*; strong *jers* were identified with mid vowels, strong *ь as /e/, strong *ъ as /o/. Marking weak and strong *jers* by minus and plus, respectively, we have: nominative singular *dь⁺nь⁻ › де́нь/dén' 'day' but genitive plural *dь⁻nь⁺jь⁻ › дне́й/dnéj 'days', *sъ⁻tereti › стере́ть/sterét 'wipe off' but first person singular *sъ⁺tь⁻ru › сотру́/sotrú 'I wipe off'.

Proto-Slavonic liquid diphthongs with *e or *o were subject to **полногла́сие/polnoglásie**, whereby the same vowel appeared on both sides of the liquid: *bérgъ › бе́рег/béreg 'shore', *korva › коро́ва/koróva 'cow'. As here, circumflex accent becomes stress on the first of the two vowels and original acute becomes stress on the second (see chapter 3, section 2.22). Adjacent to liquids, *jers* have overt reflexes: genitive singular *krъvi › кро́ви/króvi 'blood', *pъlnъjь (from earlier *piln-) › по́лный/pólnyj 'full'.

Proto-Slavonic accent has another reflex in the opposition of two back mid vowels, attested in some medieval texts (with varying graphemic strategies) and some modern dialects, though not in the standard language. Open /o/ (= [ɔ]) reflects unaccented *o and *o under circumflex accent in initial syllables: nominative singular *bŏkъ 'side' › бо́к/bȯk, genitive singular *bŏka › бо́ка/bȯka. Closed /ô/ (= [o] or diphthongal [ᵘo]) developed from original accent in non-initial syllables (гото́во/gotȏvo 'ready', рабо́та/rabȏta 'work') and when accent was retracted from *jers* (nominative singular *stolь › сто́л/stȏl 'table', genitive plural *golvь › голо́в/golȏv 'head') or from other vowels (*moltiši › моло́тишь/molȏtiš' 'you thresh'). Initial /ô/ is resolved to /vo/, as in *osьmь › во́семь/vȯsem' '8'. In the central dialect zone, the /v/ from *g in pronominal evo ~ ovo, as in сего́дня/segȯdnja 'today', probably results from re-evaluation of intervocalic [ɣ] before the typically accented *o (therefore /ô/) of the following syllable.

Prior to the loss of *jers*, front vowels palatalized preceding consonants. When the *jers* were eliminated, palatalization became distinctive in consonants; *i and *y merged as /i/ and *ä and *a as /a/. This gives maximally a seven-vowel system of /i, u, ě, ô, e, o, a/ after the loss of *jers*.

From the period around the fall of the *jers*, Russian phonology has been relatively stable. Unpaired consonants (first š, ž, later c, but not č) hardened. Velars palatalized before /i/ ‹ *y and before /ě/ (after the morphophonemic alternations from the second palatalization were eliminated). Palatalization has been restricted before other consonants. The most important change is that of stressed *e (including the reflex of strong *ь) to o before hard consonant and word-finally: genitive plural *ženъ › жён/žen 'women', *pьsъ › пёс/pës 'dog', *lice › лицо́/licȯ, but *ženьskъjь › же́нский/žénskij 'female'. Jer–liquid diphthongs participated, though before hard dentals only: *četvьrtъjь › четвёртый/četvërtyj 'fourth' but *pьrvъjь › пе́рвый/pérvyj 'first' and *vьrxъ › ве́рх/vérx 'top'. Closed mid vowels ě and ô have been eliminated except dialectally, although ѣ was used for etymological ě until the Revolution.

2.2   Morphophonemic alternations inherited from Proto-Slavonic

The earlier phonological processes dating from Proto-Slavonic through the fall of the *jers* have left behind a residue of **alternations of consonants**, which can be stated synchronically as relations between the columns of overlapping grades in table 15.3. An alternation of C^J, reflecting first palatalization of velars before $*j$ and jotation of dentals and labials, with etymological C^0 occurs in verbs with suffix {-a-} and their present stems: писа́ть/pisát′ 'write', пишу́/pišú (1 SG), пи́шешь/píšeš′ (2 SG) and пла́кать/plákat′ 'cry', пла́чу/pláču (1 SG), пла́чешь/pláčeš′ (2 SG). C^0 alternates with C^1, which reflects first palatalization of velars and 'bare' palatalization of other consonants before front vowels, within the present of obstruent stems: несу́/nesú (1 SG) 'I carry', несёшь/nesёš′ (2 SG) and пеку́/pekú (1 SG) 'I bake', печёшь/pečёš′ (2 SG). In *I*-conjugation verbs, C^J in the first person singular and past passive participle alternates with C^1 elsewhere: молочу́/moločú (1 SG) 'I thresh', -моло́чен/-moločen (PASS PART) versus молоти́ть/molotít′, моло́тишь/molótiš′ (2 SG). There are additional, minor, patterns. C^J has a variant with *šč* and *žd* for the Russian interpretation of the Church Slavonic reflexes of $*tj$ and $*dj$. $C^{1\alpha}$ is the reflex of C^1 that developed when consonants (except /l/) lost palatalization before a dental; thus $C^{1\alpha}$ occurs before the reflexes of suffixes *-ьsk-* and *-ьn-*: ры́бный/rýbnyj 'fish (adjective)', ме́стный/méstnyj 'local', убы́точный/ubýtočnyj 'unprofitable', дверно́й/dvernój 'pertaining to a door', but разде́льный/razdél′nyj 'separate'.

The **alternation of vowels** deriving from the fall of the *jers* is most visible in nominal declension. The null grade appears in most case forms, the full grade in specific environments: nominative singular of declension Ia (ножо́к/nožók 'knife (DIMIN)', otherwise ножк-/nožk-); nominative singular and instrumental singular of declension IIIa (во́шь/vóš′ 'louse', во́шью/vóš′ju, stem вш-/vš-); and genitive plural of declension Ib and II (окно́/oknó 'window', о́кон/ókon; коро́бка/koróbka 'box', коро́бок/koróbok).

Table 15.3   Consonant alternations

C^0	C^J	C^1	$C^{1\alpha}$
P = {p, b, f, v, m}	Pḷ	P̦	P
T = {t, d, s, z}	{č, ž, š, ž}	Ț	T
K = {k, g, x}	{č, ž, š}	{č, ž, š}	{č, ž, š}
R = {n, r, l}	Ṛ	Ṛ	{n, r, ḷ}

2.3 Morphophonemic alternations resulting from changes after Proto-Slavonic

Few morphophonemic alternations date from after the fall of the *jers*. The alternation derived from **e* > *o* to some extent follows the original distribution of *e* before soft consonant, *o* before hard – ель/él' 'fir tree' versus diminutive ёлка/ëlka or ёлкич/ëlkič 'wood sprite' – but the alternation has been obscured by subsequent changes. Some formerly palatalized consonants have hardened, and **ě*, which was exempt from **e* > *o*, has merged with *e*: **tělo* > тéло/télo 'body'. Analogically, /o/ has replaced /e/ from **ě* in certain morphological contexts – in the plurals звёзды/zvëzdy 'stars' and гнёзда/gnëzda 'nests' and in the masculine past tense of obstruent-stem verbs (пренебрёг/prenebrëg '(he) neglected').

3 Morphology

3.1 Nominal morphology

3.1.1 Nominal categories

Nominal parts of speech express distinctions of case, number and gender, but not always by the same morphological means, and with different degrees of consistency.

Number is expressed in all nominal parts of speech except numerals themselves. Because it is difficult to formulate principles that would determine algorithmically how many cases Russian has (see Comrie in Brecht and Levine 1985), it seems sensible to assume that Russian has six primary cases and two secondary cases (second genitive and second locative), the secondary cases being available for a decreasing number of masculines. If the six primary cases are arranged in the order nominative, accusative, genitive, locative, dative and instrumental, then all instances of syncretism within a paradigm select continuous intervals. The historical vocative is moribund, with the isolated exception of Бóже/Bóže 'oh God', and Гóсподи/Góspodi 'oh Lord', now usually just expletives. Colloquial Russian has developed a new vocative, the bare stem of the noun: Мáш/Máš! 'oh Maša!'.

Nouns can be grouped into equivalence classes according to various criteria. One such grouping is declension class; another is (syntactic) gender, expressed through agreement in other parts of speech – attributive adjectives, predicative adjectives, the past tense of verbs and ultimately pronouns. Declension type and gender are largely isomorphic – the members of a given declension or subdeclension condition the same agreement, and belong to the same gender.

The exceptions mostly involve animate nouns. Declension II, otherwise composed of feminines, includes many nouns whose reference is male (or conventionally assumed to be so) and whose syntactic gender is masculine, such as дядя/djádja 'uncle' or судья/sud'já 'judge'. Declension II also includes 'common-gender' nouns which may be used with either feminine or masculine agreement (usually in both adjective and verb), depending on reference (for example, masculine это был страшный непосе́да/èto býl strášnyj neposéda 'that was a terrible fidget' in reference to a male, feminine это была́ стра́шная непосе́да/èto bylá strášnaja neposéda in reference to a female). Declension I names for occupations, in reference to women, can still be used with masculine agreement in both attributive adjective and verb, but there is a tendency to use referential feminine agreement, in the verb alone, or, non-standardly but increasingly (up to 25 per cent in the generation born in the decade of 1940), in both attributive modifier and verb; feminine agreement in adjectives, however, has so far been restricted to the nominative. Thus, although the vast majority of nouns have a unique and stable gender which can be predicted from declension type, nouns referring to human beings show some variation between conventional, grammatical gender and gender based on reference.

Another equivalence class of nouns is defined by the **animate accusative**, the use of the genitive for a syntactic accusative (see Klenin 1983: ch. 1, ch. 3). Among singular nouns, this substitution occurs only with masculines of declension I, including the rare masculine animate with neuter-like morphology (подмасте́рье/podmastér'e 'apprentice') but excluding the occasional neuter animate (дитя́тко/ditjatko) and declension III animates (ма́ть/mát' 'mother'). In the plural, animacy is expressed by nouns of all genders. Anaphoric pronouns invoke the animate accusative regardless of gender or referential animacy, as in его́/egó (N ACC SG) or и́х/íx (ACC PL). Under agreement, masculine singular and all plural adjectives agree with the animacy of their head noun. Any attributive modifier agrees with the referential animacy of a declension II masculine noun, even though the noun itself does not invoke the syncretism: хорошо́ зна́ли моего́ де́душку/xorošó ználi moegó dédušku '(they) knew my grandfather well'. The boundaries of what counts as animate and what as inanimate are mostly fixed, down to certain nouns of variable reference, such as у́никум/únikum 'unique item, person' or чле́н/člén 'member'. Face cards are animate.

3.1.2 Noun morphology

Nouns in Russian make use of relatively few case–number morphemes, and the three declensional patterns into which they are organized are also limited and relatively uniform, though there are some recognizable sub-declensions. A partition of nouns into declension types is less easy to motivate in the plural. Aside from the residual instrumental plural in -ьми/-'mi, which ranges from less preferred with две́рь/dvér' 'door' to preferred with ло́шадь/lóšad' 'horse' and до́чь/dóč' 'daughter' to obligatory with лю́ди/ljúdi 'people' and де́ти/déti 'children', plural morphemes are otherwise uniform for dative, locative and instrumental for all nouns; further, the morphemes used for the two remaining positions – nominative (and accusative of inanimates) and genitive (and accusative of animates) – cross class boundaries. For these two case forms, each sub-declension has preferences, recorded in the tables; deviations are discussed in the text (see Stankiewicz 1968; Зализня́к/Zaliznjak 1977).

Declension I includes two recognizable subdeclensions, which differ primarily in the nominative singular and less consistently in the plural. Declension Ia, all masculine or basically masculine with incipient common gender, has nominative singular {-∅}, and prefers {-i} for the nominative plural and an overt ending in the genitive, {-ov/-ev} with stems ending in hard, non-palatal consonants (and also in /j/ or /c/), {-ej} with stems ending in paired palatalized consonants and palatals (see table 15.4, with citation forms чи́н/čin 'rank' and ко́нь/kon' 'horse'). Soft stems, listed separately here, differ from hard stems only in superficial details of ortho-graphy (except for genitive plural). Here and in other paradigms, morpho-phonemic *e* substitutes for *o* in soft stems. In this and other declensions, the locative singular of nouns in {-ij-} is **ии** rather than **ие** (сцена́рий/scenárij (NOM SG) 'script', сцена́рии/scenárii (LOC SG)).

Certain masculine nouns as a matter of course use the second locative {-ú} with в/v 'in' and на/na 'in, on', but not with о/o 'about' (в снегу́/v snegú 'in snow' but о сне́ге/o snége 'about snow'). A number of mass and some abstract nouns use {-u} for the genitive with a partitive meaning, more emphatic than the ordinary genitive in this function: я́ не вы́пил ча́ю/já ne výpil čáju 'I didn't drink any tea at all' versus я́ не вы́пил ча́я/já ne výpil čája 'I failed to drink tea'. The second genitive in {-u}, however, is fading; it occurs with ever fewer nouns, and often is equivalent to the primary genitive in {-a}.

Variation in the stem of the singular and plural is usually confined to recognizable groups, which also have deviations from the unmarked plural endings. Nationality terms, which alternate a singular suffix {-in} with no suffix in the plural, use an otherwise unique nominative plural ending {-e} and genitive plural {-∅}: армяни́н/armjanín (NOM SG) 'Armenian', армя́не/armjáne (NOM PL), армя́н/armján (GEN PL). Names for young, whose singular and plural stems differ, exhibit the doubly unusual com-bination of nominative plural {-a} and genitive plural {-∅} (телёнок/telёnok 'calf', nominative plural теля́та/teljáta, genitive plural теля́т/telját). The thirty-odd collectives with plural stem augment in *-j-* have nominative plural {-a}, usually with the unmarked genitive plural {-ov/-ev} (ко́лос/kólos 'ear', nominative plural коло́сья/kolós'ja, genitive plural коло́сьев/kolós'ev).

There are some other deviations from the unmarked plural endings. The combination of nominative plural {-á}, implying end stress throughout the

Table 15.4   Declension Ia

(a)	*Hard stem*	*Soft stem*
Singular		
NOM	чѝн 'rank'	кѡнь 'horse'
ACC	= NOM	= GEN
GEN	чѝна	коня̀
DAT	чѝну	коню̀
INST	чѝном	конём
LOC	чѝне	конѐ
Plural		
NOM	чины̀	кѡни
ACC	= NOM	= GEN
GEN	чинѡв	конѐй
DAT	чина̀м	коня̀м
INST	чина̀ми	коня̀ми
LOC	чина̀х	коня̀х

(b)	*Hard stem*	*Soft stem*
Singular		
NOM	čín 'rank'	kón' 'horse'
ACC	= NOM	= GEN
GEN	čína	konjá
DAT	čínu	konjú
INST	čínom	konëm
LOC	číne	koné
Plural		
NOM	činý	kóni
ACC	= NOM	= GEN
GEN	činóv	konéj
DAT	činám	konjám
INST	čínami	konjámi
LOC	čináx	konjáx

plural, and the usual genitive plural ending occurs with a substantial number of nouns, including borrowings: инспѐктор/inspéktor (NOM SG) 'inspector', инспектора̀/inspektorá (NOM PL). The combination of usual nominative plural {-i} with uncharacteristic genitive {-∅} is found with lexical items that tend to be used in quantified collocations; for example, ра̀з/ráz (NOM SG = GEN PL) 'time', солда̀т/soldát (NOM SG = GEN PL) 'soldier'.

Declension Ib (see table 15.5, with citation forms болѡто/bolóto 'swamp' and ущѐлье/uščél'e 'gorge') differs from declension Ia by having an overt ending {-o ~ -e} in the nominative singular, and by a preference

Table 15.5   Declension Ib

(a)	Hard stem	Soft stem
Singular		
NOM	болóто 'swamp'	ущéлье 'gorge'
ACC	= NOM	= NOM
GEN	болóта	ущéлья
DAT	болóту	ущéлью
INST	болóтом	ущéльем
LOC	болóте	ущéлье
Plural		
NOM	болóта	ущéлья
ACC	= NOM	= NOM
GEN	болóт	ущéлий
DAT	болóтам	ущéльям
INST	болóтами	ущéльями
LOC	болóтах	ущéльях

(b)	Hard stem	Soft stem
Singular		
NOM	bolóto 'swamp'	uščél´e 'gorge'
ACC	= NOM	= NOM
GEN	bolóta	uščél´ja
DAT	bolótu	uščél´ju
INST	bolótom	uščél´em
LOC	bolóte	uščél´e
Plural		
NOM	bolóta	uščél´ja
ACC	= NOM	= NOM
GEN	bolót	uščélij
DAT	bolótam	uščél´jam
INST	bolótami	uščél´jami
LOC	bolótax	uščél´jax

for nominative plural {-a} and genitive plural {-Ø}. It is almost exclusively neuter, except for derivatives of masculines (городúшко/gorodíško 'town', ножúще/nožíšče 'knife') and a few isolated masculines (подмастéрье/podmastér´e 'apprentice'). Soft stems are restricted: there are nouns in {-Ç-j-}, whose genitive plural is {-Ç-Vj-Ø}, spelled **ий** or **ей**, such as ущéлье/uščél´e, genitive plural ущéлий/uščélij or питьé/pit´ë 'drinking', genitive plural питéй/pitéj; nouns in {-Ç-ij-}, whose locative singular is spelled **ии** and whose genitive plural is {-ij-Ø}, spelled **ий**, such as здáние/zdánie 'building', locative singular здáнии/zdánii, genitive plural зда́ний/zdánij; and a minuscule number with paired soft consonant (по́ле/póle 'field', мо́ре/móre 'sea', го́ре/góre 'woe'), with overt genitive plural (поле́й/poléj).

An overt genitive plural {-ov/-ev} occurs with nouns with -j- augment, such as перо́/peró 'feather', nominative plural пе́рья/pér'ja, genitive plural пе́рьев/pér'ev, and also with пла́тье/plát'e 'dress' (genitive plural пла́тьев/plát'ev) and о́блако/óblako 'cloud' (nominative plural облака́/oblaká, genitive plural облако́в/oblakóv). The opposite combination of genitive {-Ø} with nominative {-i}, more characteristic of declension Ia, occurs as a rule with (pejorative) diminutives, both masculines (доми́шко/domíško 'house', nominative plural доми́шки/domíški, genitive plural доми́шек/domíšek) and neuters (око́шко/okóško 'window', nominative plural око́шки/okóški, genitive plural око́шек/okóšek).

Declension II is composed primarily of feminines, though it includes some masculine and common-gender human nouns as well (see table 15.6, with гора́/gorá 'mountain' and неде́ля/nedélja 'week'). Alone of the declensions, declension II avoids syncretism of the accusative singular; the accusative plural syncretizes with the nominative or genitive, by animacy, as in all paradigms. Again, hard and soft stems do not differ other than orthographically; locative singular (and syncretically, dative singular) is again **ии** for stems in {-ij-}, such as ли́ния/línija 'line', dative–locative singular ли́нии/línii. In the plural, the nominative is universally {-i}, and the genitive is preferentially {-Ø} for stems in {-Vj-}, spelled with **й**. The overt genitive plural {-ej} is possible for certain miscellaneous soft-stem nouns (дя́дя/djádja 'uncle', genitive plural дядей/djádej; до́ля/dólja 'portion', genitive plural доле́й/doléj) and some nouns with a stem-final cluster; still, the latter group preferentially uses {-Ø} and an inserted vowel (ка́пля/káplja 'drop', genitive plural ка́пель/kápel'). Nouns in {-Cn̦-} have {-Ø} and usually harden the consonant (пе́сня/pésnja 'song', genitive plural пе́сен/pésen).

Declension III, characterized by the syncretic ending {-i} in genitive, dative, locative singular, includes two subparadigms (see table 15.7, with citation forms ко́сть/kóst' 'bone' and пле́мя/plémja 'tribe'). Feminine IIIa has nominative singular {-Ø}, instrumental {-ju} (with possible vowel alternation in the stem, as in во́шь/vóš' 'louse', вши́/vši, во́шью/vóš'ju), nominative plural {-i} and genitive plural {-ej}. The near-dozen IIIb neuters have nominative singular {-a}, when a diminished stem without {-Vn-} is used, an instrumental {-em}, nominative plural {-a} and genitive {-Ø}. IIIb stems alternate stem-final /n̦/ (singular) with /n/ (plural). Lone masculine пу́ть/pút' 'road' follows IIIa except in the instrumental singular.

3.1.3 Pronominal morphology

The declension of pronouns is idiosyncratic in various respects (see table 15.8). The reflexive pronoun, except for the impossibility of a nominative,

Table 15.6   Declension II

(a)	Hard stem	Soft stem
Singular		
NOM	горá 'mountain'	недéля 'week'
ACC	гóру	недéлю
GEN	горы́	недéли
DAT	горé	недéле
INST	горóй	недéлей
LOC	горé	недéле
Plural		
NOM	гóры	недéли
ACC	= NOM	= NOM
GEN	гóр	недéль
DAT	горáм	недéлям
INST	горáми	недéлями
LOC	горáх	недéлях

(b)	Hard stem	Soft stem
Singular		
NOM	gorá 'mountain'	nedélja 'week'
ACC	góru	nedélju
GEN	gorý	nedéli
DAT	goré	nedéle
INST	gorój	nedélej
LOC	goré	nedéle
Plural		
NOM	góry	nedéli
ACC	= NOM	= NOM
GEN	gór	nedél′
DAT	gorám	nedéljam
INST	gorámi	nedéljami
LOC	goráx	nedéljax

declines like the second person singular pronoun: genitive себя́/sebjá and so on; the second person plural declines like first person plural (вы́/vý, genitive вác/vás and so on). The inanimate interrogative 'what' declines like 'who', with an obvious difference in stem and animacy (чтó/čtó, genitive чегó/čegó and so on). Third-person pronouns occur with a preceding н when they are governed by a preposition. The instrumentals мнóй/mnój, тобóй/tobój, собóй/sobój, (н)éй/(n)éj, allow variants with ю (for example, мнóю/mnóju) to the extent the pronoun is prosodically independent.

Table 15.7   Declension III

(a)	*IIIa*	*IIIb*
Singular		
NOM	кость 'bone'	пле́мя 'tribe'
ACC	= NOM	= NOM
GEN	ко́сти	пле́мени
DAT	ко́сти	пле́мени
INST	ко́стью	пле́менем
LOC	ко́сти	пле́мени
Plural		
NOM	ко́сти	племена́
ACC	= NOM	= NOM
GEN	косте́й	племён
DAT	костя́м	племена́м
INST	костя́ми	племена́ми
LOC	костя́х	племена́х

(b)	*IIIa*	*IIIb*
Singular		
NOM	kóst´ 'bone'	plémja 'tribe'
ACC	= NOM	= NOM
GEN	kósti	plémeni
DAT	kósti	plémeni
INST	kóst´ju	plémenem
LOC	kósti	plémeni
Plural		
NOM	kósti	plemená
ACC	= NOM	= NOM
GEN	kostéj	plemën
DAT	kostjám	plemenám
INST	kostjámi	plemenámi
LOC	kostjáx	plemenáx

Кто́/któ and что́/čtó (and other interrogatives) can be combined with post-positive particles to form indefinites; кто́-то/któ-to 'someone' and что́-то/čtó-to 'something' are specific (the speaker has in mind a unique entity), кто́-нибудь/któ-nibud´ 'someone or other', что́-нибудь/čtó-nibud´ 'something or other' are truly indefinite. These pronouns can also be combined with pre-positive particles (не́кто/nékto 'a certain someone', не́что/néčto 'a certain something', никто́/niktó 'no one', ничто́/ničtó 'nothing', ко́е-кто́/kóe-któ 'somebody or another') or ultimately with whole phrases (кто́ бы то ни ста́ло/któ by to ni stálo 'whoever it might

Table 15.8   Pronominal declensions

(a)	1 SG	2 SG	1 PL	INT
NOM	я́	ты́	мы́	кто́
ACC	= GEN	= GEN	= GEN	= GEN
GEN	меня́	тебя́	на́с	кого́
DAT	мне́	тебе́	на́м	кому́
INST	мно́й	тобо́й	на́ми	ке́м
LOC	мне́	тебе́	на́с	ко́м

	3 M–N	3 F	3 PL	
NOM	о́н ~ оно́	она́	они́	
ACC	= GEN	= GEN	= GEN	
GEN	(н)его́	(н)её	(н)и́х	
DAT	(н)ему́	(н)е́й	(н)и́м	
INST	(н)и́м	(н)е́й	(н)и́ми	
LOC	нём	не́й	ни́х	

(b)	1 SG	2 SG	1 PL	INT
NOM	já	tý	mý	któ
ACC	= GEN	= GEN	= GEN	= GEN
GEN	menjá	tebjá	nás	kogó
DAT	mné	tebé	nám	komú
INST	mnój	tobój	námi	kém
LOC	mné	tebé	nás	kóm

	3 M–N	3 F	3 PL	
NOM	ón ~ onó	oná	oní	
ACC	= GEN	= GEN	= GEN	
GEN	(n)egó	(n)eë	(n)íx	
DAT	(n)emú	(n)éj	(n)ím	
INST	(n)ím	(n)éj	(n)ími	
LOC	nëm	néj	nix	

turn out to be'). Morphologically the compounds behave identically to the pronominal bases, but pre-positive particles move left of prepositions: ни о чём/ni o čëm 'about nothing', ко́е с ке́м/kóe s kém 'with somebody or another'.

The declension of demonstratives, proximate э́тот/ètot and distal то́т/tót (see table 15.9), is reminiscent of that of third-person anaphoric pronouns.

Table 15.9   Demonstrative paradigms

(a)	M–N		F	PL	
NOM	тóт ~ тó		тá	тé ~ э́ти	
ACC	= NOM ~ = GEN		тý	= NOM ~ = GEN	
GEN	тогó		тóй	тéх ~ э́тих	
DAT	томý		тóй	тéм ~ э́тим	
INST	тéм ~ э́тим		тóй	тéми ~ э́тими	
LOC	тóм		тóй	тéх ~ э́тих	

(b)	M–N		F	PL	
NOM	tót ~ tó		tá	té ~ èti	
ACC	= NOM ~ = GEN		tú	= NOM ~ = GEN	
GEN	togó		tój	téx ~ ètix	
DAT	tomú		tój	tém ~ ètim	
INST	tém ~ ètim		tój	témi ~ ètimi	
LOC	tóm		tój	téx ~ ètix	

3.1.4   Adjectival morphology

Short-form adjectives, whose syntactic distribution is restricted, preserve
only the nominal endings of the nominative case: masculine крáсен/
krásen 'red', feminine краснá/krasná, neuter крáсно/krásno, plural
крáсны/krásny ~ красны́/krasný. Long-form adjectives decline like
demonstratives (see table 15.10, with citation forms крáсный/krásnyj
'red' and дáльний/dál'nij 'far'). Soft-stem adjectives differ from hard-
stem adjectives only in adjustments in the spelling of vowel letters. Under
stress, the masculine nominative singular form is -óй/-ój (молодóй/
molodój 'young').

The synthetic comparative ends residually in {-e} (basically with C^J
mutation, but in addition the stem may be modified and -š- may creep in)
for a number of common adjectives, such as дорогóй/dorogój 'dear,
expensive', дорóже/doróže; корóткий/korótkij 'short', корóче/
koróče; дóлгий/dólgij 'long', дóльше/dól'še; the productive ending is
{-eje}, as in мúлый/mílyj 'kind', милée/milée. The synthetic comparative
cannot be used attributively, but only as a predicative (сначáла онá былá
недóбрая, потóм {былá ~ стáла ~ казáлась} живéе/snačála oná
bylá nedóbraja, potóm {bylá ~ stála ~ kazálas'} živée 'at first she was
unkind, then she {was ~ became ~ seemed} livelier') or as a post-positive
reduced relative clause (пóмнит óн зáмкнутого арестáнта стáрше
себя́ годáми/pómnit ón zámknutogo arestánta stárše sebjá godámi 'he
recalls a withdrawn prisoner (who was) years older than him'). The analytic

Table 15.10   Adjectival declension

Hard stem   M–N   F   PL

(a)

		F	PL
NOM	красный ~ красное 'red'	красная	красные
ACC	= NOM ~ = GEN	красную	= NOM ~ = GEN
GEN	красного	красной	красных
DAT	красному	красной	красным
INST	красным	красной	красными
LOC	красном	красной	красных

Soft stem   M–N   F   PL

		F	PL
NOM	дальний ~ дальнее 'far'	дальняя	дальние
ACC	= NOM ~ = GEN	дальнюю	= NOM ~ = GEN
GEN	дальнего	дальней	дальних
DAT	дальнему	дальней	дальним
INST	дальним	дальней	дальними
LOC	дальнем	дальней	дальних

Hard stem   M–N   F   PL

(b)

		F	PL
NOM	krásnyj ~ krásnoe 'red'	krásnaja	krásnye
ACC	= NOM ~ = GEN	krásnuju	= NOM ~ = GEN
GEN	krásnogo	krásnoj	krásnyx
DAT	krásnomu	krásnoj	krásnym
INST	krásnym	krásnoj	krásnymi
LOC	krásnom	krásnoj	krásnyx

Soft stem   M–N   F   PL

		F	PL
NOM	dál′nij ~ dál′nee 'far'	dál′njaja	dál′nie
ACC	= NOM ~ = GEN	dál′njuju	= NOM ~ = GEN
GEN	dál′nego	dál′nej	dál′nix
DAT	dál′nemu	dál′nej	dál′nim
INST	dál′nim	dál′nej	dál′nimi
LOC	dál′nem	dál′nej	dál′nix

comparative, which can be used in all contexts, is formed by modifying the adjective by the adverb бо́лее/bólee.

The neuter singular short form of adjectives (including of comparatives) functions as an adverb: я́рко/járko 'brightly', проница́тельно/pronicátel′no 'incisively', доро́же/doróže 'more expensively'.

3.1.5   Numeral morphology

Numerals use declensional strategies (see table 15.11) which range from near indeclinability to demonstrative-like declension.

Certain cardinal numerals expressing large round units of counting (ordinals will be given in parentheses) have minimal declension, with one form for the nominative and accusative, another for the remaining cases;

Table 15.11   Numeral paradigms

(a)	Round	Ordinary	Paucal	Collective
NOM	сто́	пя́ть	три́	дво́е
ACC	= NOM	= NOM	= NOM ~ = GEN	= NOM ~ = GEN
GEN	ста́	пяти́	трёх	двои́х
DAT	ста́	пяти́	трём	двои́м
INST	ста́	пятью́	тремя́	двои́ми
LOC	ста́	пяти́	трёх	двои́х

	Compound decade	Compound hundred
NOM	пятьдеся́т	три́ста
ACC	= NOM	= NOM
GEN	пяти́десяти	трёхсо́т
DAT	пяти́десяти	трёмста́м
INST	пятью́десятью	тремяста́ми
LOC	пяти́десяти	трёхста́х

(b)	Round	Ordinary	Paucal	Collective
NOM	stó	pjat´	tri	dvóe
ACC	= NOM	= NOM	= NOM ~ = GEN	= NOM ~ = GEN
GEN	stá	pjati	trëx	dvoix
DAT	stá	pjati	trëm	dvoim
INST	stá	pjat´jú	tremjá	dvoimi
LOC	stá	pjati	trëx	dvoix

	Compound decade	Compound hundred
NOM	pjat´desját	trista
ACC	= NOM	= NOM
GEN	pjatidesjati	trëxsót
DAT	pjatidesjati	trëmstám
INST	pjat´júdesjat´ju	tremjastámi
LOC	pjatidesjati	trëxstáx

such are стό/stó ~ стά/stá (сότый/sótyj) '100', сόрок/sórok ~ сорокά/soroká (сороковόй/sorokovój) '40', девянόсто/devjanósto ~ девянόста/devjanósta (девянόстый/devjanóstyj) '90' and полторáста/poltorásta ~ полýтораста/polútorasta ~ 'a hundred and a half', the last two etymologically derived from стό/stó. 'One and a half' has the same pattern, but additionally the nominative distinguishes gender, like the paucal '2' (полторá/poltorá (M–N), полторы́/poltorý (F)). Multiples of 'hundred' – двéсти/dvésti '200', три́ста/trista, четы́реста/četýresta, пятьсόт/pjat'sót, шестьсόт/šest'sót, семьсόт/sem'sót, восемьсόт/vosem'sót, девятьсόт/devjat'sót – are compounds which decline both parts. Their ordinals are built from the genitive forms: трёхсόтый/trëxsótyj, шестисόтый/šestisótyj.

The majority of numerals decline as declension III nouns. 'Five' to '9' stress the ending in the oblique cases: пять/pjat' (пя́тый/pjátyj), шесть/šest' (шестόй/šestój), céмь/sém' (седьмόй/sed'mój), вόсемь/vósem' (восьмόй/vos'mój) and дéвять/dévjat' (девя́тый/devjátyj). 'Eleven' to '19', though historically compounds, have this declension with fixed stem stress: оди́ннадцать/odinnadcat' (оди́ннадцатый/odinnadcatyj), двенáдцать/dvenádcat' (двенáдцатый/dvenádcatyj), тринáдцать/trinádcat' (тринáдцатый/trinádcatyj), четы́рнадцать/četýrnadcat' (четы́рнадцатый/četýrnadcatyj), пятнáдцать/pjatnádcat' (пятнáдцатый/pjatnádcatyj), шестнáдцать/šestnádcat' (шестнáдцатый/šestnádcatyj), семнáдцать/semnádcat' (семнáдцатый/semnádcatyj), восемнáдцать/vosemnádcat' (восемнáдцатый/vosemnádcatyj), девятнáдцать/devjatnádcat' (девятнáдцатый/devjatnádcatyj). The first three decades have the pattern of пять/pjat': дéсять/désjat' (деся́тый/desjátyj), двáдцать/dvádcat' (двадцáтый/dvadcátyj), три́дцать/tridcat' (тридцáтый/tridcátyj). The decades from '50' to '80' (recall that сόрок/sórok '40' and девянόсто/devjanósto '90' have minimal declension) are declensionally still compounds; the second component ends in a hard consonant in the nominative: пятьдеся́т/pjat'desját (пятидеся́тый/pjatidesjátyj), шестьдеся́т/šest'desját (шестидеся́тый/šestidesjátyj), céмьдесят/sém'desjat (семидеся́тый/semidesjátyj), вόсемьдесят/vósem'desjat (восьмидеся́тый/vos'midesjátyj).

Paucal numerals – двá/dvá (M–N) ~ двé/dvé (F) '2', три́/tri '3' and четы́ре/četýre '4' – use the case morphemes of plural adjectives, merging genitive and locative, but have idiosyncratic stems (дву-/dvu-, трё-/trë-, четырё-/četyrë- but instrumental четырьмя́/četyr'mjá).

Collectives (двόе/dvóe 'twosome', трόе/tróe 'threesome', чéтверо/čétvero 'foursome' and so on) likewise have a plural adjectival declension in oblique cases. Indefinites like скόлько/skól'ko 'how many' (genitive скόльких/skól'kix) follow this strategy. 'Both', which distinguishes gender throughout, declines in this fashion (όба/óba (M–N NOM), обόих/obóix (GEN); όбе/óbe (F NOM), обéих/obéix (GEN) and so on).

Finally, 'one' (plural 'some') declines like the demonstrative э́тот/ètot: оди́н/odín (M NOM SG) (with an exceptional full vowel), одно́/odnó (N NOM SG), одному́/odnomú (M–N DAT SG) and so on. Ты́сяча/týsjača 'thousand' and миллио́н/millión 'million' decline like ordinary nouns, although ты́сяча/týsjača archaically allows instrumental ты́сячью/ týsjačʹju.

3.2 Verbal morphology

3.2.1 Verbal categories

Verbs generally distinguish finite forms, infinitives, verbal adjectives (or participles) and verbal adverbs (or gerunds). Verbal adverbs and active participles are formally past or non-past, but there is a tendency, especially with verbal adverbs, to align the tense with aspect – past with perfective, present with imperfective; a tense distinction is still viable only with imperfective participles. The past passive participle is formed unproblematically from transitive perfectives. Present passive participles from imperfectives, limited to written Russian, tend to acquire a modal meaning.

Russian forms a subjunctive mood by combining the past tense with the particle бы/by. The combination is less of an inflectional category than, say, tense. The particle can occur in various positions in a clause, and it can co-occur with non-verbal modal predicatives without the past tense of 'be' (лу́чше бы/lúčše by 'would be better'). The subjunctive is used most naturally in counterfactual conditionals.

The imperative is usually built from the present-tense stem; an overt suffix {-i-} occurs after consonant clusters or under stress, otherwise there is no suffix. The singular has no further marker, the plural uses {-te}. With the intonation of polarity questions, indicative first person plural forms can be used hortatively to express requests.

Imperfectives distinguish past, present and future, the latter a periphrastic combination of auxiliary (бу́ду/búdu (1 SG) and so on) and imperfective infinitive. Perfectives distinguish past and a morphological present, which reports true future or singularized habitual situations. For example, the perfective present in отка́жут – ми́гом утеша́лся/otkážut – mígom utešálsja 'if they [= belles] should refuse, he was consoled in a moment' (Puškin, *Evgenij Onegin*, ch. 4.X) establishes the protasis of a condition whose apodosis is stated in the imperfective past.

The present inflects for person and number. The aorist and imperfect continued in written Russian (in the Church Slavonic register) into the seventeenth century, but in the vernacular the *l*-participle, which inflects for gender and number, had centuries before become the universal verbal form for reporting events prior to the speech situation.

Most verb forms can be assigned to the macro-categories of imperfective and perfective aspect. This partition is evidently a generalization over some recognizably distinct lexical subsystems. Semantically, in contrast to the long-standing attempt to define aspect as non-temporal (in order to distinguish it from tense), recent investigations from various perspectives cluster around the notion that aspect deals with how an event proceeds over time. An event reported by a perfective presumes a delimited temporal interval in which there is change in the state of the world and, further, all change is confined to this interval. An event expressed by an imperfective fails this definition, and indicates that the states or changes of state are extended over time in one way or another.

3.2.2   Conjugation

If nouns have relatively uniform stem shape with transparent internal structure but heterogeneous endings, the situation is reversed in verbs. Endings are largely uniform, but stems have internal structure and vary. Verbs commonly display two major stem alternants, the present allostem, used for the present tense, imperative and present participles, and the past/ infinitive allostem, used for past, infinitive, past (active) participle and (past) passive participle. Stem allomorphy revolves primarily around the classificatory suffix, a recurrent derivational morpheme that occurs after the root. The suffix, for verbs which have one, is present in the past/ infinitive allostem; it may be longer, shorter, modified or absent in the present, following a general principle of complementarity: since past/ infinitive markers start with a consonant, the stem of a suffixed verb will end in a vowel; and since the present conjugational markers begin with a vowel, the present allostem ends in a consonant. A minority of verbs do not have a classificatory suffix, and these suffixless verbs divide into a number of classes. Although at a higher level of abstraction it is possible to posit a single basic stem from which allostems can be derived by process rules (Jakobson 1984: ch. 3), it is convenient to refer to verbs by their two basic allostems.

Verbs fall into two conjugations, depending on the **thematic ligature** (enclosed here by uprights) in the second and third persons singular and first and second persons plural forms of the present: |i| (or *I*-conjugation, traditionally the second conjugation) and |e| (or *E*-conjugation, traditionally the first conjugation; under stress, the vowel is /o/). The thematic ligature is absent before the first singular {-u}; the third person plural forms differ according to the conjugation class: ligature |i| implies third person plural {-at}, |e| implies third person plural {-ut}.

The *I*-conjugation has limited groups. The verbal suffix may be {-i-}, {-e-} (from *ě) or {-a-} (also from *ě, after palatals and *j). The classificatory suffix is overt in the past/infinitive stem, absent in the present. Consonants were palatalized before the classificatory suffix (whether *i or *ě) and before the thematic ligature, implying C' (as discussed in section 2.2 above): просить/prosit' 'request', second person singular просишь/

prósiš'; обидеть/obidet' 'insult', second person singular обидишь/obidiš'. Consonants were jotated in the first person singular, implying C^J (прошу/prošu, обижу/obižu) and in the past passive participle of {-i-} verbs (-прошен/-prošen); the resulting C^J has been extended to verbs in *ě (обижен/obižen but residual увиден/uviden 'seen'). If the two allostems are written in an abstract morphophonemic form in braces separated by the sign of variation, with the past/infinitive first (and the thematic ligature after the present allostem), I-conjugation verbs fit the formula {CVC-V- ~ CVC-li|}, the suffixal V being /i/, /e/ or /a/. The conjugation of one representative verb, грабить/grábit' 'rob', is given in table 15.12.

Suffixed E-conjugation verbs tend to maintain the suffix in both stem allomorphs, but not in a consistent form. Three groups are characterized by a suffix ending in a vowel in the past/infinitive (complementarily before the consonantal endings) and a suffix ending in /j/ in the present (complementarily before the vocalic thematic ligature). A common type (for example делать/délat' 'do', whose conjugation is given in table 15.13) has stem shapes {CVC-a- ~ CVC-aj-|e|}. A similar type with suffixal {-e-} ({CVC-e- ~ CVC-ej-|e|}) names inchoative processes derived from adjectives (угрюметь/ugrjúmet' 'become gloomy', угрюмею/ugrjúmeju (1 SG); пьянеть/p'janét' 'become drunk', пьянею/p'janéju (1 SG)). In a third, very productive, group of verbs, past/infinitive {CVC-ova-} alternates with present {CVC-uj-|e|}: требовать/trébovat' 'demand', требую/trébuju (1 SG); колдовать/koldovát' 'practise sorcery', колдую/koldúju (1 SG).

In the other types of suffixed E-conjugation, the suffix is reduced in the present. The type {CVC-nu- ~ CVC-n-} productively makes semelfactive perfectives of intrinsically repetitive or undifferentiated processes: брызнуть/brýznut' 'splash', брызну/brýznu (1 SG), толкнуть/tolknút' 'shove', толкну/tolknú (1 SG). Another class has a minimal suffix {-a-} in the past/infinitive and no suffix but C^J in the present, notationally {CVC⁰-a- ~ CVC^J-|e|}: плакать/plákat' 'cry', плачу/pláču (1 SG), плачешь/pláčeš' (2 SG); писать/pisát' 'write', пишу/pišú (1 SG), пишешь/pišeš' (2 SG). No doubt because of the identity of the past/infinitive allomorph {CVC-a-}, this type is being absorbed into the {CVC-a- ~ CVC-aj-|e|} verbs (see Крысин/Krysin 1974).

A small group of verbs has suffixed {CVC-a} in the past/infinitive but a bare {CVC-|e|} in the present: сосать/sosát' 'suck', сосу/sosú (1 SG), сосёшь/sosëš' (2 SG); similarly, жаждать/žáždat' 'thirst', стонать/stonát' 'moan'. Related are verbs whose root-final consonant is /j/: сеять/séjat' 'sow', сею/séju (1 SG); смеяться/smeját'sja 'laugh', смеюсь/smejús' (1 SG).

Suffixless verbs are heterogeneous. A small group has a stem {CCa-} which is less than a full closed syllable in the past/infinitive; in the present, the stem is either the bare consonant cluster (that is, {CC-|e|}), such as

Table 15.12   I-conjugation: гра́бить/grábit′ 'rob'

(a) *Conjugation*	{CVC-i- ~ CVC-lil}
PRS 1 SG	гра́блю
PRS 2 SG	гра́бишь
PRS 3 SG	гра́бит
PRS 1 PL	гра́бим
PRS 2 PL	гра́бите
PRS 3 PL	гра́бят
PRS ACT PART	гра́бящий
PRS VERBAL ADVERB	гра́бя
IMP 2 SG	гра́бь
IMP 2 PL	гра́бьте
INF	гра́бить
PRT M	гра́бил
PRT F	гра́била
PRT N	гра́било
PRT PL	гра́били
PRT ACT PART	гра́бивший
PRT VERBAL ADVERB	-гра́бив(ши)
PRT PASS PART	-гра́блен

(b) *Conjugation*	{CVC-i- ~ CVC-lil}
PRS 1 SG	gráblju
PRS 2 SG	grábiš′
PRS 3 SG	grábit
PRS 1 PL	grábim
PRS 2 PL	grábite
PRS 3 PL	grábjat
PRS ACT PART	grábjaščij
PRS VERBAL ADVERB	grábja
IMP 2 SG	gráb′
IMP 2 PL	gráb′te
INF	grábit′
PRT M	grábil
PRT F	grábila
PRT N	grábilo
PRT PL	grábili
PRT ACT PART	grábivšij
PRT VERBAL ADVERB	-grábiv(ši)
PRT PASS PART	-gráblen

Table 15.13   E-conjugation: де́лать/délat´ 'do' and нести́/nesti 'carry'

(a) *Conjugation*   {CVC-a- ~ CVC-aj-|e|} {CVC- ~ CVC-|e|}

PRS 1 SG	де́лаю	несу́
PRS 2 SG	де́лаешь	несёшь
PRS 3 SG	де́лает	несёт
PRS 1 PL	де́лаем	несём
PRS 2 PL	де́лаете	несёте
PRS 3 PL	де́лают	несу́т
PRS ACT PART	де́лающий	несу́щий
PRS VERBAL ADVERB	де́лая	неся́
IMP 2 SG	де́лай	неси́
IMP 2 PL	де́лайте	неси́те
INF	де́лать	нести́
PRT M	де́лал	нёс
PRT F	де́лала	несла́
PRT N	де́лало	несло́
PRT PL	де́лали	несли́
PRT ACT PART	де́лавший	нёсший
PRT VERBAL ADVERB	-де́лав(ши)	-нёсши
PRT PASS PART	-де́лан	-несён

(b) *Congugation*   {CVC-a- ~ CVC-aj-|e|} {CVC- ~ CVC-|e|}

PRS 1 SG	délaju	nesú
PRS 2 SG	délaeš´	nesëš´
PRS 3 SG	délaet	nesët
PRS 1 PL	délaem	nesëm
PRS 2 PL	délaete	nesëte
PRS 3 PL	délajut	nesút
PRS ACT PART	délajuščij	nesúščij
PRS VERBAL ADVERB	délaja	nesjá
IMP 2 SG	délaj	nesi
IMP 2 PL	délajte	nesite
INF	délat´	nesti
PRT M	délal	nës
PRT F	délala	neslá
PRT N	délalo	nesló
PRT PL	délali	nesli
PRT ACT PART	délavšij	nësšij
PRT VERBAL ADVERB	-délav(ši)	-nësši
PRT PASS PART	-délan	-nesën

ждáть/ždát´ 'wait', жду́/ždú (1 SG); врáть/vrát´ 'lie', вру́/vrú (1 SG), or the cluster with an inserted vowel (that is, {CVR-|e|}), such as брáть/brát´ 'take', беру́/berú (1 SG).

Another subgroup has a past/infinitive stem which is an open monosyllable (that is, {C(R)V-}) and either {C(R)VJ-} or {CJ-} in the present. The consonantal augment J in the present can be /j/ (мы́ть/mýt´ 'wash', мóю/móju (1 SG); пéть/pét´ 'sing', пою́/pojú (1 SG); пи́ть/pít´ 'drink', пью́/p´jú (1 SG); бри́ть/brít´ 'shave', брéю/bréju (1 SG); знáть/znát´ 'know', знáю/znáju (1 SG); грéть/grét´ 'warm', грéю/gréju (1 SG)) or /v/ (жи́ть/žít´ 'live', живу́/živú (1 SG); плы́ть/plýt´ 'swim', плыву́/plyvú (1 SG)). In another subgroup the consonantal augment is a nasal: жáть/žát´ 'reap', жну́/žnú (1 SG); (на)-чáть/(na)-čát´ 'begin', (на)-чну́/(na)-čnú (1 SG); дéть/dét´ 'put', дéну/dénu (1 SG); стáть/stát´ 'stand, become', стáну/stánu (1 SG).

The largest and most homogeneous class of suffixless verbs is that of the type нести́/nestí 'carry', несу́/nesú (1 SG), несёшь/nesëš´ (2 SG), which generally maintains a fully syllabic stem; a general formula for this type, whose conjugation is illustrated in table 15.13 above, would be {CVC- ~ CVC-|e|}. Some idiosyncratic consonant alternation occurs in the past and infinitive, in the root or (exceptionally for Russian conjugation) the grammatical marker.

Consonant alternations within the present of suffixless verbs are uniform: C^0 in the first person singular and third person plural forms alternates with C^1 elsewhere.

Irregularity in Russian verbs takes limited forms. As noted, suffixless verbs are often heterogeneous in their stems, and in this sense are 'irregular'. Few verbs have an irregular conjugation as such. Хотéть/xotét´ 'want' switches between E-conjugation with C^J in the singular (хочу́/xoču̇, хóчешь/xóčeš´, хóчет/xóčet) and I-conjugation in the plural (хоти́м/xotím, хоти́те/xotíte, хотя́т/xotját). Дáть/dát´ 'give' and éсть/ést´ 'eat' preserve reflexes of the athematic conjugation in the singular, in which endings were added directly to a consonantal stem: дáм/dám, дáшь/dáš´, дáст/dást (from reduplicated *dad-), and éм/ém, éшь/éš´, éст/ést (from *ĕd-). Their plurals look like conventional I-conjugation: дади́м/dadím, дади́те/dadíte, даду́т/dadút (with a switch to the E-conjugation in the third person plural) and еди́м/edím, еди́те/edíte, едя́т/edját. The forms бýду/búdu, бýдешь/búdeš´ and so on, used as the future of бы́ть/být´ and in its perfective compounds (прибы́ть/pribýt´ 'arrive', прибýду/pribúdu (1 SG)), are regular if the allostem is taken to be {bud-}.

3.3 Derivational morphology

Derivation in Russian involves the same strategies as elsewhere in Slavonic: basically, affixation with some vocalic and consonantal alternations.

Suffixes have shown a tendency to accrete additional segments, resulting in a system (in adjectives and noun gradation) of overlapping suffixes. All parts of speech, but more frequently nouns, could be formed by compounding independent lexical units, with a ligature vowel if necessary. In recent times nouns are formed by compounding lexical partials (or 'stumps'), or acronymically just the first segments, of an extended phrase (Comrie and Stone 1978: 99–101).

3.3.1   Major patterns of noun derivation

Masculine agentive nouns and corresponding feminines are formed with -тель/-tel´ (feminine -тельница/-tel´nica) and suffixes built on the morph -ик/-ik, such as -ник/-nik, -чик/-čik, -щик/ščik, -овщик/ -ovščik (feminine -ница/-nica, -чица/-čica, -щица/-ščica, -овщица/ -ovščica). Borrowings often contain -тор/-tor or -тёр/-tër (feminine -торша/-torša or -тёрша/-tërša): редáктор/redáktor 'editor' (feminine редáкторша/redáktorša). The stylistic value of feminine derivates is delicate (see Comrie and Stone 1978: 159–66). For classificatory (nationality) and descriptive nouns, such as кошáтник/košátnik 'cat-fancier' and кошáтница/košátnica, use of the feminine is normal in reference to a woman. With names for professions, the masculine characterizes someone who practises the profession generally, while the feminine allows for the inference that the practice of the profession is not completely general, so that in the extreme instance some feminine derivatives (поэтéсса/poètéssa 'poetess', врачúха/vračíxa 'lady doctor') may be effectively slurs.

Abstract nouns are derived in various ways. Declension Ib deverbals are from the past passive participle stem, such as утаéние/utaénie 'concealing' (утаúть/utaít´) or присыпáние/prisypánie 'dusting (with powder)' (присы́пать/prisýpat´). Some declension II deverbals are formed with -ка/-ka: утáйка/utájka 'concealment', присы́пка/prisýpka 'dusting'. Adjectives form abstracts productively with the declension III suffix -ость/-ost´: педантúчность/pedantíčnost´ 'pedantry'. The sufix -ство/ -stvo makes abstracts describing a condition or behaviour or associated institutions: педáнтство/pedántstvo 'pedantry'. The suffix -изм/-izm makes nouns denoting an ideology or adherence to one: педантúзм/ pedantízm 'pedantry'. With various roots, including proper names, -щина/-ščina describs a characteristic syndrome (эмигрáнтщина/ èmigrántščina 'emigration syndrome', ноздрёвщина/nozdrëvščina 'behaviour of (Gogol's hero) Nozdrëv´).

The system of nominal gradation – diminutives and augmentatives – remains productive in nouns (Unbegaun 1957; Stankiewicz 1968). First-degree diminutives are formed with masculine -к/-k, -ик/-ik, -чик/-čik, feminine -ка/-ka, neuter -цó/-có (~ це/-ce). Second-degree diminutives are formed by expanded suffixes, the series in -чк-/-čk- or the series in

-шк-/-šk-, the latter often pejorative. Augmentatives (typically pejorative) are formed by masculine -ище/-išče, feminine -ища/-išča, neuter -ище/ -išče. A single root can form numerous derivatives: for example, masculine нóс/nós 'nose' gives носо́к/nosók, но́сик/nósik, носо́чек/nosóček, носи́шко/nosiško, носи́ще/nosišče; feminine нога́/nogá 'leg, foot' gives но́жка/nóžka, но́жечка/nóžečka, ножо́нка/nožónka, ножи́ща/ nožišča; neuter окно́/oknó 'window' gives око́нце/okónce, око́шко/ osóško, окни́ще/oknišče. Semantically, gradated forms are the speaker's assessment that the entity deviates from the norms for the type of entity, most tangibly in size. Personal names have rich and idiosyncratic patterns of gradation.

3.3.2   Major patterns of adjective derivation

Adjectives can be derived from nouns by means of various suffixes, most frequent of which is the 'all-purpose' (Unbegaun 1957) morph -н-/-n- and its various expansions: рюкза́чный/rjukzáčnyj 'pertaining to a knapsack', анке́тный/ankétnyj 'pertaining to a form'. The suffix -ск-/-sk- makes adjectives describing the characteristics of individuals or groups thereof. Expansions of these suffixes are productive in the adaptation of foreign words and technical vocabulary (эллинисти́ческий/èllinistíčeskij 'Hellenistic', амфибрахи́ческий/amfibraxíčeskij 'amphibrachic'). Nouns of mass and essence yield relational adjectives by suffixation of -ист-/-ist- (abundance) or -оват-/-ovat- (attenuation): щели́стый/ščelístyj 'having slits', стеклова́тый/steklovátyj 'glassy'. Adjectives can be gradated with -еньк-/-en'k- (сла́вненький/slávnen'kij 'rather wonderful') and its expansions (худёхонький/xudëxon'kij 'thinnish', чернёшенький/ černëšen'kij 'blackish') or with -оват-/-ovat- (хитрова́тый/xitrovátyj 'a bit clever').

3.3.3   Major patterns of verb derivation

Verbs are derived from other parts of speech by characteristic morphological operations. Assigning the verb the shape {CVC-i- ~ CVC-li|} makes a causative ((o)суши́ть/(o)sušit' 'dry'), the shape {CVC-e- ~ CVC-ej-lel} an inchoative ((o)стервене́ть/(o)stervenét' 'become frenzied'). The suffixes -нича-/-niča- and -ствова-/-stvova- yield simplexes with the sense of engaging in a characteristic activity (церемо́нничать/ceremónničat' 'act ceremoniously', филосо́ф-ствовать/filosófstvovat' 'philosophize'). The suffix -ова-/-ova- and its expansions are widely used in adapting foreign roots (классифици́ровать/klassificírovat' 'classify'). The etymological reflexive affix derives verbs from verbs, the most productive subprocess being detransitivization, whereby the subject of the reflexive corresponds roughly to the object of the transitive (суши́ться/sušit'sja 'dry' (ITR)).

The basic and productive aspectual system, viewed as a set of derivational relations among lexical units, is tripartite. Simplex (unprefixed) verbs describe states or undelimited activities and are typically imperfective: мота́ть/motát' 'wind, shake'. To simplexes are added prefixes, making perfectives that impute a limit to the state or activity: вы́-мотать/vý-motat' 'wind out', у-мота́ть/u-motát' 'wind up', с-мота́ть/s-motát' 'wind off', от-мота́ть/ot-motát' 'wind off', на-мота́ть/na-motát' 'wind onto'. Prefixed perfectives then form secondary imperfectives by the addition of a suffix while retaining the sense of an imputed limit: вы-ма́тывать/vy-mátyvat', с-ма́тывать/s-mátyvat', от-ма́тывать/ot-mátyvat', на-ма́тывать/na-mátyvat'. Prefixed perfectives and their corresponding imperfectives clearly constitute 'aspectual pairs'. For certain prefixal meanings – beginning or end phases of an activity or quantification of an activity – a prefixed perfective normally does not form a secondary imperfective, or forms one only in an iterative sense; such a perfective may be the closest thing to a perfective partner that a simplex has. Even на-мота́ть/na-motát' 'wind onto', which forms a regular secondary imperfective на-ма́тывать/na-mátyvat', may function as the perfective of мота́ть/motát'. Simplexes suffixed with {-nu-} yield semelfactive perfectives, reporting a single token of undifferentiated activity: мо́тнуть/mótnut' 'make a shaking motion'. The 'verbs of motion' distinguish two imperfectives, one a directed, or determinate, process (идти́/idti 'walk'), the other an undirected, or indeterminate, process (ходи́ть/xodit' 'walk'). The distinction is available for a dozen or so verbs, the number depending on where one draws the line. Reasonably certain as pairs of determinate and indeterminate verbs are бежа́ть/bežát' ~ бе́гать/bégat' 'run', везти́/vezti ~ вози́ть/vozit' 'take (by conveyance)', вести́/vesti ~ води́ть/vodit' 'lead', гна́ть/gnát' ~ гоня́ть/gonját' 'chase', е́хать/éxat' ~ е́здить/ézdit' 'ride', идти́/idti ~ ходи́ть/xodit' 'walk', лете́ть/letét' ~ лета́ть/letát' 'fly', нести́/nesti ~ носи́ть/nosit' 'carry', плы́ть/plýt' ~ пла́вать/plávat' 'swim', ползти́/polzti ~ по́лзать/pólzat' 'crawl', тащи́ть/taščit' ~ таска́ть/taskát' 'drag'. Less certain are брести́/bresti ~ броди́ть/brodit' 'wander', кати́ть/katit' ~ ката́ть/katát' 'roll', ле́зть/lézt' ~ ла́зить/lázit' 'climb'.

The mechanics of imperfectivization depend on the type of verb formation. The older strategy puts verbs directly in the {CVC-a- ~ CVC-aj-lel} class (-пе́чь/-péč' ~ -пека́ть/-pekát' 'bake'), sometimes with C^J (-пра́вить/-právit' ~ -правля́ть/-pravlját' 'direct'). The productive strategy yields a derived verb of the shape {CVC-iva- ~ CVC-ivaj-lel}, with C^J mutation (-винти́ть/-vintit' 'screw' ~ -ви́нчивать/-vinčivat') or without (-писа́ть/-pisát' ~ -пи́сывать/-pisyvat' 'write').

4 Syntax

4.1 Element order in declarative sentences

As is often observed, the word order of the predicate and its major noun phrases (subject and objects) is relatively free in Russian, but its freedom is not without consequences. The naturalness and frequency of various orders depends on the role of the noun phrase and the semantics of the verb (see the classic Адамец/Adamec 1966 or, more recently, Yokoyama 1986), and different orders have different stylistic consequences.

In describing word order, one may take the view that the predicate is central, and work outwards from it. If X and Y are major constituents, the order X|Verb implies that the current text is a statement about an individual (the referent of X) which is assumed to be known independently of the verb. Conversely, the order Verb|Y implies that Y is relevant as part of the information reported by the verb. Positions next to the verb are less prominent than those distant from the verb; thus initial position X in X|Y|Verb is an emphatic topic imposed on the addressee, and conversely, Y in Verb|X|Y is the position for elaborated comment. In examples below, it will be convenient to identify constituents in the Russian examples by self-evident superscripted abbreviations.

For subjects, Subject|Verb order is unmarked. This order is used when the subject is known in context, as are the speaker and his companion in:

Он^S кре́пко сжа́л^V мне́ ру́ку. Мы^S поцелова́лись^V. Он^S се́л^V в теле́жку./On^S krėpko sžál^V mnė rúku. Mý^S pocelovális$^{'V}$. On^S sėl^V v telėžku.
'He firmly squeezed my hand. We kissed. He sat down in the cart.'

This order can be used even if the subject has not been specificially mentioned, provided it is implied by the prior text, as horses would be in the continuation of the foregoing:

Мы^S прости́лись^V ещё ра́з, и ло́шади^S поскака́ли^V./Mý^S prostilis$^{'V}$ eščė ráz, i lôšadi^S poskakáli^V.
'We took leave once more, and the horses galloped off.'

Verb|Subject order, marked in relation to Subject|Verb, has different functions depending on whether the subject is known in context. If the subject is not known, Verb|Subject order may be used to describe a scene:

В отдале́нье темне́ют^V леса́^{S}, сверка́ют^V пруды́^{S}, желте́ют^V дере́вни^S./V otdalėn'e temnėjut^V lesá^S, sverkájut^V prudý^S, želtėjut^V derėvni^S.
'In the distance forests look dark, there glisten ponds, villages look yellow.'

Verb|Subject order may establish the existence (and subsequent relevance) of a new individual:

Лѐт вѐсемь томý назѝд проживѐл^V у неё мѝльчик^S лѐт двенѝдцати, сы́н её покѐйного брѝта./Lĕt vȯsem′ tomȕ nazȧd proživȧl^V u neë mȧl′čik^S lĕt dvenȧdcati, sýn eë pokȯjnogo brȧta.
'Eight years ago there lived with her a lad of about twelve, the son of her late brother.'

Verb|Subject order in these functions is common with existential predicates (in the order of 68 per cent), not infrequent with other intransitives (approximately 42 per cent) and rare but not impossible (less than 10 per cent) with transitives. If the subject is in fact known in context, Verb|Subject order is a stylistic device which affects an epic or folkloric style of narrative:

Принялсѐ^V ѐ^S бы́ло за неподслащённую налѝвку; признаѐсь, побоѐлся^V ѐ^S сдѐлаться пьѐницею с гѐря./Prinjalsjȧ^V jȧ^S býlo za nepodslaščȅnnuju nalivku; priznajȕs′, pobojȧlsjȧ^V jȧ^S sdĕlat′sja p′jȧniceju s gȯrja.
'I started to take to unsweetened liqueur; but I became frightened of the prospect of becoming a drunkard from grief.'

For objects, Verb|Object order is usual. This order may introduce new entities, as in:

Онѝ^S принимѐет^V какѐе-то лекѝрство^O, котѐрое ѐй привезлѝ из Итѝлии./Onȧ^S prinimȧet^V kakȯe-to lekȧrstvo^O, kotȯroe ȅj privezli iz Itȧlii.
'She is taking some medicine which she was brought from Italy.'

Or it may subordinate a previously mentioned object to the current verb, as in:

Её рассердѝла однѝ странѝца, посвящённая смѐрти. Онѝ^S прочитѝла^V мнѐ^O ѐту странѝцу^O вслѝх^{ADV} – тѝхим, рѐвным гѐлосом./Eë rasserdila odnȧ stranica, posvjaščȅnnaja smȅrti. Onȧ^S pročitȧla^V mnȅ^O ȅtu stranicu^O vslȕx^{ADV} – tixim, rȯvnym gȯlosom.
'She was angered by one page devoted to death. She read me this page aloud – in a quiet, even voice.'

Object|Verb order emphatically makes the object the topic when, for example, it is contrasted with other entities:

Онѝ сказѝла по телефѐну, что в вѐсемь к нѐй придёт Ѐксман, а менѐ^O онѝ^S прѐсит^V придтѝ в сѐмь./Onȧ skazȧla po telefȯnu, čto v vȯsem′ k nȅj pridȅt Ȯksman, a menjȧ^O onȧ^S prȯsit^V pridti v sȅm′.
'She said over the phone that at eight Oksman would come, and me she was asking to come at seven.'

Pronouns, like ѐй^O привезлѝ^V/ȅj^O privezli^V 'to her (they) brought' or прочитѝла^V мнѐ^O/pročitȧla^V mnȅ^O 'read to me' above, tend to attach to the verb on one side or the other as quasi-enclitics, consistent with the observation that positions close to the verb are unprominent. In most narrative, since a general calendrical and geographical orientation can be presumed, temporal and locative phrases naturally occur pre-verbally, like в во́семь/v vósem´ 'at eight' above. Other adverbs – evaluative, degree, modal and manner – gravitate to the verb. Position on one or the other margin is emphatic; thus, вслу́х/vslúx 'aloud' above is an elaborated comment, answering the implied question of how the subject read.

Within noun phrases, adjectives are ordinarily pre-nominal; participial phrases are either, relative clauses and complement noun phrases (including genitives) usually post-nominal: давно́ не прове́тривавшиеся ба́рхатные альбо́мы фотогра́фий/davnó ne provétrivavšiesja bárxatnye al´bómy fotográfij 'the long unventilated velvet albums of photographs'. Moving a quantified noun locally in front of the quantifier (and across a preposition) makes the quantification more tentative, as in the example above ле́т во́семь тому́ наза́д/lét vósem´ tomú nazád, or in ра́з в деся́тый/ráz v desjátyj 'for the tenth time or so'. Putting the adjective after the noun is a stylistic device suggesting lyric poetry or folklore:

Змий лю́тый о семи голо́в ужа́сных меня́ всю цара́пал кочеры́жкой о́строй./Zmij ljútyj o semi golóv užásnyx menjá vsjú carápal kočerýžkoj óstroj.
'A dragon ferocious with seven heads horrible scratched me all over with a cabbage stalk sharp.'

One expects constituents of noun phrases to be contiguous, but discontinuity of quantifier and noun is frequent: corresponding to the neutral order тогда́ бы́ло мно́го таки́х ме́ст/togdá býlo mnógo takíx mést 'at that time there were many such places', one can also have таки́х ме́ст тогда́ бы́ло мно́го/takíx mést togdá býlo mnógo 'of such places at that time there were many' and, colloquially, мно́го тогда́ бы́ло таки́х ме́ст/ mnógo togdá býlo takíx mést 'many there were of such places at that time'. Discontinuity is less frequent and more marked stylistically with attributive adjectives: шелести́нные смея́лись голосо́чки во все́х уголо́чках/šelestínnye smejális´ golosóčki vo vséx ugolóčkax 'rustling laughed the voices in all corners'.

4.2   Non-declarative sentence types
Content questions are formed with the appropriate question word, usually in sentence-initial position: что́ случи́лось? како́й до́ктор пи́шет?/ čtó slučílos´? kakój dóktor píšet? 'what has happened? what sort of doctor is writing?'. General polarity questions are formed with question intonation (нра́вится?/nrávitsja? 'do you like (it)?'); localizing the intonation contour to some constituent makes a narrow polarity question that questions a specific entity or property against alternatives (со смета́нки начнём?/so smetánki načném? 'is it with the sour cream we should

start?'). The particle ли/li after any constituent in sentence-initial position has the same function: не здесь ли совершён поворот истории?/ne zdes' li soveršën povorot istorii? 'was it not here that the turning point in history occurred?' After a verb, the structure with ли/li is similar to a general polarity question ('is it the case that …') and is used regularly in indirect questions:

(Я осмелилась спросить её,) была ли Цветаева первой женщиной в его жизни./(Ja osmelilas' sprosit' ee,) byla li Cvetaeva pervoj ženščinoj v ego žizni.
'(I made so bold as to ask her) was Tsvetaeva the first woman in his life.'

The minimal response to a positive polarity question (such as –а вы и вчера стояли?/–a vy i včera stojali? '–and did you stand (in the queue) yesterday as well?') would be simply the appropriate particle (да/da 'yes' or нет/net 'no') or, frequently, the verb alone (–стояла/stojala '(I) stood'). Responses to negative polarity questions, such as –не дозвонилась?/–ne dozvonilas'? '–you didn't get through?', depend elusively on presuppositions. The most neutral response would be the particle нет/net 'no'; the doubly negative response would emphasize the failure: –нет, не дозвонилась/–net, ne dozvonilas' 'no, (obviously) I didn't get through'. Mixed responses address the presupposition of failure, –нет, дозвонилась/–net, dozvonilas' countering the expectation ('on the contrary, I did get through') and –да, не дозвонилась/–da, ne dozvonilas' confirming the expectation ('as you thought, I didn't get through').

The imperative issues commands; other modal constructions can be used with a comparable illocutionary force. As a rule of thumb, positive imperatives are simplex imperfective (да держи за ручку!/da derži za ručku! 'just hold it by the handle!') or perfective (Серёж, возьми!/Serëž, voz'mi! 'Sereža, take it!'), negative imperatives imperfective (не напираете!/ne napiraete! 'don't push!'). But there are conventionalized exceptions. A negative perfective is a warning not to proceed with an action that is imminent (смотри, не подгадь!/smotri, ne podgad'! 'watch you don't mess up!'), while, conversely, an imperfective in a positive imperative is less categorical (возьмите ещё, берите, берите!/voz'mite ešče, berite, berite! 'take some more, go ahead, take some, take some!').

4.3 Copular sentences

Sentences stating copular relations – equations, descriptions, class membership – consist of a (nominative) subject, a predicative noun or adjective and, sometimes, a copular verb. In the present tense, there is normally no overt copular verb, the conjugated forms of 'be' having been eliminated in all functions. The particle есть/est', etymologically the third person singular, can be inserted in emphatic or tautological definitions, and in scientific style the plural суть/sut' can be used. Outside of the present, the appropriate forms of 'be' are used (был/byl (PAST M SG), буду/budu

(FUT 1 SG) and so on). It is sometimes said that Russian lacks a verb 'be', an observation which may then lead to speculation about the Russian world-view. It should be emphasized that Russian has the syntactic means to express copular and existential relations, even though it fails to employ a verb in the present tense.

A predicative noun can appear in the nominative or instrumental. The instrumental, impossible in the present but usual (in the order of 80 per cent) in the past or future, is used when there is the slightest hint of restriction on the predicative relation. Thus, the instrumental is used if the subject acts in a certain capacity:

Они всё сознательно и по своей воле были творцами и соучастниками всего этого./Oni vsė soznatel'no i po svoėj vole byli tvorcami i součastnikami vsegò ėtogo.
'They all were consciously and by their own choice creators and collaborators in all that.'

or if there is contrast of one time to another:

Но тогда я был мальчишкой, а теперь у меня полно седины в бороде./No togda jà byl mal'čiškoj, a teperʹ u menja polno sediny v borodė.
'But at that time I was just a lad, whereas now I have a beard full of grey.'

Nominative is a pure unrestricted description:

Я был несмышлёныш, потеря родителей для меня ничего не представляла./Jà byl nesmyšlёnyš, potėrja roditelej dlja menja ničegò ne predstavljàla.
'I was a dunce, the loss of my parents didn't mean anything to me.'

Predicative adjectives have three morphological options. The instrumental, which occurs less frequently with adjectives than with nouns, indicates a restriction on the property; thus она была счастливой/ona bylà sčastlivoj 'she was happy' suggests that happiness was limited to some time. The opposition of long form and short form has a noticeably lexical character (though, as a syntactic constraint, two different forms are not normally conjoined). Occasionally, the two are semantically differentiated, as in the textbook opposition of short-form болен/bolen 'sick, ailing' versus long-form больной/bol'nój 'invalid'. Moreover, many lexical items exhibit a strong preference for one or the other form (see Gustavsson 1976). The long form is required of adjectives characterizing a property derived from a noun: деревянный/derevjannyj 'wooden', шведский/švedskij 'Swedish', буржуазный/buržuaznyj 'bourgeois', белокожий/belokòžij 'white-skinned', морщинистый/morščinistyj 'wrinkled' and двухкомнатный/dvuxkòmnatnyj 'two-roomed'. As an extension of this lexical rule, one can suggest that the long form signals that the subject, viewed as a type of individual, instantiates an essence, a quality. In:

"свой" дедушка добрый, он привозит подарки всем детям и иногда
катает их на собственных лошадях./"svój" děduška dòbryj, on privózit
podárki vsěm dětjam i inogdà katáet ix na sòbstvennyx lošadjàx.
'their own grandfather is kind, he brings presents to all the children and sometimes
takes them for a ride with his horses.'

the long form describes one individual, implicitly in contrast to another, as
a token of a type, as someone who instantiates the quality of goodness.

The short form is required for adjectives that characteristically take a
complement stating the circumstances under which, or with respect to what
standard, the property holds: возможен/vozmóžen 'possible',
необходим/neobxodim 'necessary', обязан/objázan 'obligated',
убеждён/ubeždën 'convinced', уверен/uvéren 'certain', виден/víden
'visible', ощутим/oščutím 'perceptible', презираем/preziráem
'despicable', велик/velík 'big', далёк/dalëk 'far', полон/pólon 'full',
доволен/dovólen 'satisfied', согласен/soglásen 'agreed', присущ/
prisúšč 'intrinsic', похож/poxòž 'similar', готов/gotóv 'ready' and
способен/sposóben 'capable'; for some adjectives, such as рад/ràd
'pleased', no long form is said to exist at all. The short form is usual even
when the complement is not overt, but imputed; thus она была
счастлива/oná bylà sčástliva suggests that there was something which was
responsible for the happiness of the subject. Further, with an adjective that
otherwise prefers the long form, a complement forces the short form (normally беременная/berèmennaja 'pregnant' but беременна от него/
berèmenna ot negó 'pregnant by him'). The short form indicates that the
subject, viewed as a unique individual rather than as a type, manifests the
property in potentially variable ways under different circumstances. Thus, in

Отец был добр, спокоен и мягок, он сглаживал страстную нетерпимость
матери./Otèc byl dòbr, spokóen i mjágok, on sglážival stràstnuju neterpímost'
màteri.
'Their father was kind, calm, and mild, he smoothed out the passionate impatience
of their mother.'

the three short forms describe how the father behaved – how he manifested
properties.

Over the long history of Slavonic languages and, specifically, Russian,
long forms have been gradually displacing short forms, first from attributive function (starting with cases other than the nominative), and more
recently in predicative function as well. Thus it would no longer be appropriate to use a short form in some contexts where Puškin did: Нашёл он
полон двор услуги/Našël on pólon dvòr uslúgi 'he found the house full
of servants' (Puškin, *Evgenij Onegin*, ch. 1.LIII) or В привычный час
пробуждена/V privýčnyj čàs probuždenà // Вставала при свечах
она/Vstavàla pri svečàx onà 'awakened at the usual time // she arose to
candlelight' (Puškin, *Evgenij Onegin*, ch. 2.XVIII). The development in

contemporary Russian has reached the point where, at least in the colloquial register, long forms (most readily neuter) can be used anywhere one might expect short forms.

Predicative nouns and adjectives occur with predicates other than 'be' (see Nichols 1981). Most closely related to 'be' are **aspectual** predicates like остаться/ostát'sja 'remain' and оказаться/okazát'sja 'turn out', which superimpose the notion of change of state on the copular relation, and **epistemological** predicates like казаться/kazát'sja 'appear' or явиться/javít'sja 'appear', which attenuate the certainty of the copular relation. (The imperfective являться/javlját'sja has become a functional synonym of 'be' in scientific and journalistic style.) Since these predicates limit the property, they demand the instrumental or residually allow the short form:

Они встречались, даже слышали стихи друг друга – и остались
{равнодушными ~ равнодушны ~ *равнодушные}./Oni vstrečális', dáže
slýšali stixi drug drúga – i ostális' {ravnodúšnymi ~ ravnodúšny ~ *ravnodúšnye}.
'They met, even heard each other's poems – but remained indifferent.'

At the opposite extreme from copular 'be', predicatives may report a circumstantial property of the subject, commonly the subject of a verb of motion or transfer. **Circumstantials** require the instrumental of nouns and nominalized adjectives, such as взрослая/vzróslaja 'adult' in:

Уже взрослой Цветаева часто видела умершего Александра Блока
живым./Užé vzrósloj Cvetáeva části videla uméršego Aleksándra Blóka živým.
'Even as an adult Cvetaeva often saw the deceased Aleksandr Blok alive.'

Circumstantials prefer but do not require the nominative long form with adjectives: он вернулся возмущённый/on vernúlsja vozmuščénnyj 'he returned agitated'.

The possibilities for predicatives referring to a nominative subject of a finite verb are summarized in table 15.14.

Predicatives can be predicated of an object, usually in the instrumental, as in живым/živým 'alive' above, though adjectives occasionally allow accusative: мужчин погоняли голодных/mužčin pogonjáli golódnyx '(they) drove the men off hungry'.

4.4   Coordination and comitativity
Coordination is effected by a conjunction – conjunctive и/i 'and' (or folkloric да/da), adversative но/no 'but', adversative а/a 'but (rather)', disjunctive или/ili 'or', negative ни/ni 'not (even)' – placed before the last conjunct. When и/i, или/ili or ни/ni are repeated before two or more conjuncts, the effect is emphatic, approximately 'both x and y', 'either x or y', 'neither x nor y', respectively, as in я не хотел ни есть, ни пить, ни

Table 15.14   Morphological options for predicatives

	Noun NOM	Noun INST	Adjective NOM	Adjective INST	Adjective short
Copula (present tense)	+	*	+	*	+
Copula (other tense)	±	+	+	+	+
Epistemological	*	+	?	+	±
Aspectual	*	+	?	+	±
Circumstantial	*	+	+	±	*

спать/ja ne xotėl ni ėst´, ni pit´, ni spat´ 'I did not want to eat nor drink nor sleep'. With a single conjunct, и/i and ни/ni compare the given entity with other, virtual ones: трéтьего мáрта отрёкся от престóла и егó брáт/trėt´ego márta otrëksja ot prestóla i egó brát 'on the third of March his brother also renounced the throne'.

Under coordination of predicates with a shared subject, there are no particular constraints other than semantic compatibility. When two predicates share an object as well as subject, they must govern the same case. Hence conjunction of two predicates governing the accusative is possible: онá не переставáла любить и уважáть егó/oná ne perestavála ljubit´ i uvažát´ egó 'she never ceased to love and respect him'. Predicates governing dative (благоволить/blagovolit´ 'be favourably inclined to') and accusative (уважáть/uvažát´ 'respect') cannot be conjoined with a single object pronoun, regardless of whether dative емý/emú or accusative егó/egó is used: онá не переставáла благоволить и уважáть {*емý ~ *егó}/oná ne perestavála blagovolit´ i uvažát´ {*emú ~ *egó} 'she never ceased being favourably inclined to and respecting him'.

Coordination is one context with variation in agreement. Conjoined subject arguments usually occur with plural predicates but singular agreement with the conjunct closest to the predicate is possible, if the conjoined elements form a collective unit:

Егó поразило величие архитектýры и красотá внýтреннего убрáнства собóра./Egó porazilo veličie arxitektúry i krasotá vnútrennego ubránstva sobóra.
'He was astounded by the grandeur of the architecture and the beauty of the decoration of the cathedral.'

As in this example, singular agreement is more common with abstract nouns and more common with Verb|Subject order.

The comitative expression – preposition c/s plus instrumental – achieves an effect similar to coordination of nouns. It is usual when one element is a pronoun, which then is almost obligatorily plural with first and second persons and preferably plural with third. Thus, the plural pronoun in the following may have a single referent: они с Парнок живут в это время на даче/oni s Parnok živut v èto vremja na dače 'she and Parnok are living at the dacha then' or герой нашей первой любви с Мариной/ geroj našej pervoj ljubvi s Marinoj 'the hero of the first love of mine and Marina'; as in the latter instance, the comitative can detach from the pronoun. When the head of a subject comitative phrase is a singular noun, the predicate can be plural, indicating the parallel participation of two individuals, as in Ася со своим возлюбленным уезжали в тот же день/ Asja so svoim vozljublennym uezžali v tot že den´ 'Asja with her beloved left the same day'; the singular (уезжала/uezžala in this example) focuses on the activities of the head noun alone. Agreement is correlated with parameters elsewhere applicable to contexts of optional agreement: Subject|Verb order, animacy, individuation of conjuncts and individuating predicates favour plural agreement over the opposite values of these parameters (Corbett 1983).

4.5 Subordination

Subordinate clauses fulfil the same syntactic roles as lexical units; often a role can be filled by a finite clause or a non-finite one.

Finite clauses functioning as circumstantial modifiers of the predicate are introduced by one of a number of subordinating conjunctions, which encode a mixed temporal–modal meaning; thus когда/kogda 'when' is 'on certain occasions' and/or 'under certain circumstances'.

Finite attributive modifiers of nouns – that is, relative clauses – are formed usually with the interrogative pronoun который/kotoryj, originally 'which of two', at the front of the relative clause, which normally follows the modified noun: всё сказки, которые могла запомнить ключница/vsе skazki, kotorye mogla zapomnit´ ključnica, 'all the stories which the maid could recall'. Restrictive and non-restrictive senses are not distinguished, even by punctuation. Other interrogative pronouns (чей/čej 'whose', что/čto 'what', какой/kakoj 'what kind of', кто/kto 'who') can be pressed into service for specific purposes. For example, кто/kto 'who', which can only be used with personal masculine (or mixed-gender) antecedents, defines a non-referential possible individual, and is usual with pronominal adjectives as heads: кто были те, к кому она ушла?/kto byli te, k komu ona ušla? 'who were those to whom she went?'

Finite subordinate clauses, as arguments of predicates, can occur in positions where one would expect a subject, object or (with a place-marking demonstrative) oblique argument:

[Было неясно ~ Надо было решить ~ Она не интересовалась тем], что и кому оставить, какие рукописи взять с собой./[Bylo nejasno ~ Nado bylo

rešit' ~ Oná ne interesoválas' tém}, čtó i komú ostávit', kakíe rúkopisi vzját' s
sobój.
'{It was unclear ~ It was necessary to decide ~ She was not interested in} what to
leave with whom, which manuscripts to take with her.'

With such clauses, tense is normally internal – that is, determined relative
to the time of the matrix event, not the speech event – there being no
sequence of tense rule in Russian. In particular, an imperfective present is
used when the embedded event is simultaneous with the matrix event: сын
говори́л, что не хо́чет уезжа́ть/sýn govoril, čto ne xóčet uezžát' 'her
son said he did not want to leave'.

There are four types of governed infinitives, distinguished by the way
the infinitival clause is linked to the matrix predicate. Infinitives occur:

(a) as the central noun phrase of 'impersonal' modals, when the implicit
subject of the infinitive is linked to the dative domain of the matrix predicate; note the first embedding in:

Мне́ иногда́ удава́лось умоли́ть её восстана́вливать стро́ки,
искале́ченные е́ю в уго́ду цензу́ре./Mné inogdá udaválos' umolit' eë
vosstanávlivat' stróki, iskaléčennye éju v ugódu cenzúre.
'It was sometimes successful for me to beseech her to restore lines mangled by her
for the benefit of censorship.'

(b) As object of intentional predicates, when the implicit subject of the
infinitive is linked to the matrix subject:

Я изо все́х сил пыта́лась поня́ть её мысль, но та́к и не поняла́./Já izo vséx
sil pytálas' ponját' eë mýsl', no ták i ne ponjalá.
'I tried with all my might to understand her idea, but even so did not understand.'

(c) As object of predicates reporting imposition of modality (obligation,
possibility or prohibition), with the implicit subject linked to the dative
object of the matrix predicate:

А́нна Андре́евна дава́ла ка́ждой го́стье проч́есть «После́днюю
любо́вь»./Anna Andréevna davála káždoj góst'e pročést' «Poslédnjuju ljubóv'».
'Anna Andreevna let each guest read "Last Love"'.

(d) Or as object of a predicate of request, where the implicit subject is
linked to a matrix accusative object; an example is the middle portion of
the sentence in (a) above (умоли́ть её восстана́вливать/umolit' eë
vosstanávlivat' 'beseech her to restore').

Clauses introduced by the conjunction что́бы/čtóby have the functions
both of adverbs and of noun phrases. Purpose что́бы/čtóby clauses occur
with infinitives or past finite verbs: ка́к сде́лать, что́бы ухо́д не
заме́тили?/kák sdélat', čtóby uxód ne zamétili? 'what could be done so

that the departure would not be noticed?' Чтобы/čtóby clauses occur as arguments in variation with infinitives with certain matrix verbs: она попросила меня передать часики дяде/oná poprosíla menjá peredát' čásiki djáde 'she asked me to deliver the watch to her uncle' ~ она попросила меня, чтобы я передал часики дяде/oná poprosíla menjá, čtóby já peredál čásiki djáde 'she asked of me that I deliver the watch to her uncle'. They are used when infinitives are not available, as they are not with хотеть/xotét' when its subject is not the same as that of the desired event (thus only она хотела, чтобы я передал часики дяде/oná xotéla, čtóby já peredál čásiki djáde 'she wanted that I should deliver the watch to her uncle' but not *она хотела меня передать часкик дяде/*oná xotéla menjá peredát' čásiki djáde 'she wanted me to deliver ...'). They can occur in place of что/čto clauses if the matrix context is heavily modalized or negated, indicating the speaker's lack of credence in the truth of a normally factive complement: невероятно, чтобы Цветаева не читала ахматовских стихов/neverojátno, čtóby Cvetáeva ne čitála axmátovskix stixóv 'it's unlikely that Cvetaeva would not have read Axmatova's poetry'.

Extraction, as the linkage between interrogative or relative pronouns and their source predicates has come to be known, is quite restricted in Russian. Although relativization is possible into the argument of an infinitive, such as строки, которые мне иногда удавалось умолить её восстанавливать .../stróki, kotórye mné inogdá udaválos' umolít' eë vosstanávlivat' ... 'lines, which I sometimes managed to persuade her to restore ...', it is not possible into any finite clause; thus, constructed examples such as *строки, которые я хотела, чтобы она восстанавливала .../*stróki, kotórye já xotéla, čtóby oná vosstanávlivala ... 'lines, which I wanted that she restore ...' are regarded by speakers as metalinguistic puzzles at best.

4.6 Negation

The negative particle не/ne can attach to any major constituent, with local scope. Thus Лизу не очень радовала перспектива переезда/Lizu ne óčen' radovála perspektíva pereézda and Лизу очень не радовала перспектива переезда/Lizu óčen' ne radovála perspektíva pereézda differ in the strength of displeasure ('Liza was not particularly pleased' versus 'very displeased by the prospect of moving').

Negation shows an affinity with genitive case marking in place of nominative for subjects of intransitives or accusative for objects of transitives (see Timberlake 1975 or the numerous other studies of the 'genitive of negation' listed in the bibliography of Corbett in Brecht and Levine 1985). Corresponding to the nominative subject of the positive intransitive подлинник письма сохранился/pódlinnik pis'má soxranílsja 'the original of the letter was preserved', under negation one can have, with different interpretations, either nominative or genitive. The nominative (подлинник письма не сохранился/pódlinnik pis'má ne soxranílsja 'as for the original of the letter, it wasn't preserved') individuates the predicate and its subject – given a certain referent, the predicate states a negative property of it. The genitive, which implies default neuter singular in the predicate (подлинника письма не сохранилось/pódlinnika pis'má ne soxranílos'), denies the existence of a kind of individual (accordingly, 'no original was preserved' or 'there was not preserved any original'). What case is selected under negation depends in part on the predicate. 'Be' sharply distinguishes the two options (see Chvany 1975). With predicative nouns and adjectives, which necessarily individuate the subject, only nominative is possible: я не был каким-нибудь необыкновенным ребёнком/já ne byl kakim-nibud' neobyknovénnym rebënkom 'I was not an unusual child', *меня не было каким-нибудь необыкновенным ребёнком/*menjá ne bylo kakim-nibud' neobyknovénnym rebënkom being inconceivable. With domain phrases the interpretation is usually existential, so that genitive case occurs under negation almost obligatorily (as high as 99 per cent) with nouns, though less frequently with pronouns (70 per cent). Then the verb is neuter singular (in the past or future tenses); in the present tense, the synthetic form нет/nét expresses both negation and 'be' in its existential sense: его {не было ~ нет} в конторе/ego {ne bylo ~ nét} v kontóre 'there was none of him in the office (= He was not ...)'. Aspectualized copulas like 'remain' and 'become' are similar. Other intransitives normally invoke the individuated reading, but can be existentialized with emphatic negation. Subjects of transitives are never put in the genitive.

In parallel fashion, when one negates a transitive predicate normally taking an accusative object, such as он сохранил подлинник письма/ on soxranil pódlinnik pis'má 'he preserved the original of the letter', one can have either accusative or genitive: он не сохранил {подлинник ~ подлинника} письма/ón ne soxranil {pódlinnik ~ pódlinnika} pis'má 'he didn't preserve the original of the letter'. Though the accusative has been gaining ground, it still occurs less frequently than the genitive (in the order of one-fifth to one-third of examples in texts.)

A genitive object negates the existence of the event involving the object or its result – он не сохранил подлинника письма/ón ne soxranil pódlinnika pis'má 'he did not preserve the original of the letter (and the original does not exist)'. As a consequence, under emphatic negation, which proposes that a positive state of affairs might be entertained and then categorically dismisses it, the genitive is almost always used, even with personal nouns: во все те дни я не помню ни папы, ни Лёры/vo vsé té dni já ne pómnju ni pápy, ni Lëry 'throughout all those days I remember neither Papa nor Laura'. Among predicates, иметь/imét' 'have', as a transitive existential, strongly prefers genitive. At the level of the object argument, genitive is appropriate with non-individuated entities, such as with plural nouns and abstracts.

The accusative is appropriate to the extent that the negated event is only one property which might be reported of an individual; it activates the possibility of other events. Thus in он не сохранил подлинник письма́/ón ne soxranil pódlinnik pis'ma 'he failed to preserve the original of the letter', accusative suggests that non-preservation is merely one of the relevant properties of the entity, or that the event might easily have taken place. Accusative is required when the negated verb is contrasted with another verb, as in она не строила свою жизнь, она её выполняла/ oná ne stróila svojú žizn', oná eë vypolnjála 'she didn't construct her life, she performed it'; and accusative is usual when the force of negation is attenuated by particles (чуть не/čút' ne 'almost not' or едва не/edvá ne 'almost not') or in rhetorical questions, which presuppose the reality of the positive state of affairs:

Джек Потрошитель! Кто не помнит это страшное имя!/Džěk Potrošitel'! Kto ne pómnit èto strášnoe imja!
'Jack the Ripper! Who does not remember this terrible name!'

At the predicate level, the accusative is required when the predicate governs an instrumental predicative. At the level of the noun phrase, proper and/or animate nouns usually appear in the accusative: в эти дни я совсем не помню Андрюшу/v èti dni já sovsém ne pómnju Andrjúšu 'during those days I do not remember Andrjuša at all'.

In some instances the context may not decide case choice, and instead the choice of case may impose a reading on the context:

Помню поездку в театр. Самой пьесы я не помню. Память сохранила только впечатление от театра./Pómnju poézdku v teátr. Samój p'ésy já ne pómnju. Pámjat' soxranila tól'ko vpečatlénie ot teátra.
'I recall a visit to the theatre. The play itself I do not remember. Memory has preserved only the impression of the theatre.'

The genitive here denies the existence of any memory of a possible entity (the something that would be the essence of the play). Compare:

Я не помню канву описанных Мариной событий, но жива в памяти юная романтика отношений./Já ne pómnju kanvú opisannyx Marinoj sobýtij, no živá v pámjati júnaja romántika otnošénij.
'I do not recall the thread of the events Marina described, but still alive in my memory is the youthful romanticism of the story.'

The accusative in this virtually identical context denies memory specifically of one entity ('the canvas', the thread of events), which is contrasted with another related entity which is in fact remembered.

4.7   Anaphora and pronouns

Naming devices differ in the way in which they invite one to locate or construct a referent, from selecting a unique individual with multiple properties known independently to defining a possible individual by means of some contextually relevant property.

Demonstratives (proximate э́тот/ètot and distal то́т/tót) differentiate the intended referent from other members of some class of possible entities; this process involves first establishing that class. Thus in

Музе́й, наконе́ц, открыва́лся. Из всех дете́й э́то де́тище оказа́лось еди́нственной неомрачённой ра́достью его́ ста́рости./Muzéj, nakonéc, otkryválsja. Iz vsex egó detéj èto détišče okazálos´ edinstvennoj neomračënnoj rádost´ju egó stárosti.
'The museum, finally, was about to open. Of all his children this child was the only untainted joy of his old age.'

э́тот/ètot establishes that a certain entity is to be reclassified as a member of the class of 'children', which is different from other members of that class. То́т/Tót is used, anaphorically, to identify the most recently mentioned member of a class (Ли́за Мари́ну Ива́новну не зна́ла, та́ е́й представилась/Liza Marinu Ivánovnu ne znála, tá éj predstávilas´ 'Liza did not know Marina Ivanovna, that one (= M.I.) introduced herself to her (= L.)') and, cataphorically, to introduce an entity defined by a relative clause (в те́х города́х, куда́ эвакуи́ровали населе́ние/v tèx gorodáx, kudá èvakuirovali naselénie 'in those cities, to which the population was evacuated').

In anaphora, the most interesting question concerns the use of implicit pronouns, or zero anaphora, in contrast to overt pronouns. In indirect speech, zero anaphora is usual when the embedded subject is the same as the secondary speaker. With zero, the speech is reported from the perspective of the secondary speaker: она́ сказа́ла, что разде́нется сама́/oná skazála, čto razdénetsja samá 'she said that (she) would undress by herself'. When, occasionally, the overt pronoun is used, as in

О́н уверя́л, что о́н зна́ет гора́здо бо́лее, не́жели мо́жно бы́ло е́й предполага́ть./Ón uverjál, čto ón znáet gorázdo bólee, néželi móžno býlo éj predpolagát´.
'He assured (her) that he knew more than she might suppose.'

the indirect speech becomes a looser paraphrase of the sense of the gentleman's banter.

Zero anaphora also occurs in connected texts:

... О́льга Ива́новна не люби́ла ду́мать о неприя́тном и почти́ никогда́ не ду́мала. Избега́ла разгово́ров о боле́знях, а когда́ му́жу или до́чери случа́лось хвора́ть, говори́ла с ни́ми та́к, то́чно они́ всё выду́мывают.

Разумéется, при э́том окружáла и́х сáмым забóтливым ухóдом.
   Онá недýрно игрáла на пианофóрте.
... Ol'ga Ivánovna ne ljubíla dùmat' o neprijátnom i po̧či nikogdá ne dùmala.
Izbegála razgovórov o boléznjax, a kogdá mùžu ili dóčeri slučálos' xvorát', govorila
s nimi ták, tóčno oni vsë vydùmyvaet. Razumèetsja, pri èetom okružála ix sámym
zabótlivym uxódom.
   Onà nedùrno igrála na pianofórte.
'... Ol'ga Ivanovna did not like to think about anything unpleasant and almost
never thought. (She) avoided conversations about illness, and when her husband or
daughter should happen to be under the weather, (she) talked with them as if they
were making it all up. Of course at the same time (she) surrounded them with the
most attentive care.
   'She played tolerably on the pianoforte.'

In this extended description, zero pronouns are used consistently so long as
the referent remains uniquely identifiable and the text continues in the
same thematic vein – here, the protagonist's attitude towards uncontrollable events; the overt pronoun in the final sentence announces a shift to
the new theme of her accomplishments.

4.8   Reflexives and reciprocals

Russian has two reflexive pronouns, an independent pronoun (there being
no nominative, the citation form is себя́/sebjá (GEN)) and a possessive
adjective (свóй/svój (M NOM SG)). In the vast majority of sentences, the
antecedent of a reflexive is the subject of that clause; thus the mother
recognizes herself and her attributes in Мáть угáдывала в Мари́не
себя́ со свои́ми слóжностями/Mát' ugádyvala v Marine sebjá so
svoími slóžnostjami 'Mother recognized in Marina herself with her own
complications'. Complementarily, a non-reflexive cannot refer to the
subject; non-reflexives above (... угáдывала её с её слóжностями/...
ugádyvala eë s eë slóžnostjami) would mean that the mother recognized
some other person in her daughter. This complementarity holds in finite
clauses with third-person subjects, and for first- and second-person antecedents with the independent pronoun. Almost all syntactic relations are
accessible to reflexives, including various obliques; linear order is irrelevant, in that the reflexive can occur before its antecedent (see in general
Падучева/Padučeva 1985: 180–208).
   Complications arise when the syntactic relations between pronoun and
antecedent fall short of this ideal. Then, generally, both reflexive and non-
reflexive can be used with the same denotation, but with an additional
nuance. A non-reflexive specifies a unique individual defined outside the
current text. (The non-reflexive can still refer to some other individual.) A
reflexive describes a procedure for selecting a referent in terms of the antecedent. Thus, in the example below, with first- (or second-) person antecedent, a non-reflexive possessive adjective is appropriate because the
speaker's reckoning with his charges is independently defined:

Я заме́тил и положи́тельные после́дствия мое́й распра́вы с двумя́ колони́стами./Ja zamétil i položitel′nye poslédstvija moéj rasprávy s dvumjá kolonístami.
'I noticed also positive consequences of my dealing with the two members of the colony.'

A reflexive invokes a distributive situation, in which a set of possessed objects is defined in relation to a set of possessors including the speaker: Я горжу́сь до́лей своего́ уча́стия в украше́нии земли́/Ja goržús′ dólej svoegó učástija v ukrašénii zemlí 'I take pride in the fraction of my own participation in the beautification of the land'.

While the subject is the natural antecedent for reflexives within finite clauses, certain predicate–argument relations differ. In passives, reflexives can be anteceded by the passive agent as well as by the surface subject. In ordinary transitives, when the domain (source or goal) is the same as the direct object, a possessive adjective is normally non-reflexive, but an independent pronoun is reflexive:

Цвета́ева противопоставля́ет Казано́ву не то́лько его́ ничто́жному окруже́нию в за́мке, но и его́ – самому́ себе́./Cvetáeva protivopostavljáet Kazanóvu ne tól′ko egó ničtóžnomu okruženiju v zámke, no i egó – samomú sebé.
'Cvetaeva opposes Casanova not only to his insignificant surroundings in the castle, but also (opposes) him to himself.'

But the possessive adjective can be reflexive in a distributive situation:

Нача́льство тепе́рь беспоко́илось лишь об одно́м – скоре́е развести́ пья́ных по свои́м суда́м./Načál′stvo tepér′ bespokóilos′ liš′ ob odnóm – skorée razvesti p′jányx po svoim sudám.
'The authorities were concerned now with just one thing – how to get the drunken men back to their (own) ships as soon as possible.'

With quantifying, existential and modal predicates, the natural antecedent is the domain, expressed by dative or y/u plus genitive. Reflexive for the independent pronoun is usual: у него́ не остава́лось вре́мени для себя́/u negó ne ostaválos′ vrémeni dlja sebjá 'for him there remained no time for himself'. Possessive adjectives are also typically reflexive, inasmuch as what exists, or is required, or occurs in sufficient quantity, is a type of thing defined by virtue of its relation to the antecedent: А́се хвата́ло свои́х бе́д и забо́т/Áse xvatálo svoix béd i zabót 'for Asja there was enough of her own cares and troubles'.

In non-finite clauses (verbal adverbs, infinitives, participles), the implicit subject is the antecedent for a reflexive:

Поручи́в себя́ и свою́ поэ́зию Ге́нию, Цвета́ева утверди́ла созна́ние себя́ поэ́том, не поэте́ссой./Poručiv sebjá i svojú poéziju Géniju, Cvetáeva utverdila osoznánie sebjá poétom, ne poétéssoj.

'Having commended herself and her poetry to the Muse, Cvetaeva confirmed the conception of herself as a poet, not just as a poetess.'

As the third reflexive above shows, the implicit agent of deverbal nouns antecedes reflexives. Infinitives whose implicit subject is an object of the matrix clause allow the subject of the matrix clause to antecede a reflexive (as well as the implicit subject of the infinitive). To illustrate, consider the following frame:

Она _____ передать золотые часики {своему ~ её} дяде./Onà _____ peredàt' zolotýe čàsiki {svoemù ~ eë} djàde.
'She _____ to deliver the gold watch to {her own ~ her} uncle.'

With an auxiliary-like verb such as дала мне́/dalà mnè 'let me', the reflexive своему́/svoemù would be normal. At the other extreme, with a matrix verb which makes a request of an accusative object, such as попроси́ла меня́/poprosìla menjà 'asked me', the non-reflexive её/eë would be the preferred (but not exclusive) possibility. In between, with a verb which imposes an action on a dative object, such as веле́ла мне́/velèla mnè 'ordered me', either would be possible. The non-reflexive means the uncle is already known; the reflexive defines the destination for the watch ('to deliver the watch to that person defined as her uncle').

Reciprocal друг дру́г-/drug drùg- (whose first component is an indeclinable that moves to the left of prepositions) has a distribution similar to себя́/sebjà. It occurs in any argument position with a subject antecedent: они́ дари́ли друг дру́гу свои́ жи́зни до встре́чи/onì darìli drug drùgu svoì žìzni do vstrèči 'they gave each other their own lives before they met'. And it can occur with certain non-subject antecedents: что́ привлекло́ их друг к дру́гу?/čtò privleklò ix drug k drùgu? 'what was it that attracted them to each other?'

4.9   Possession

At the sentence level, possession is normally expressed by the existential construction. The possessed entity is the subject whose existence is asserted relative to the domain of some individual – the possessor, approximately – expressed by the preposition у/u plus genitive (when the possessor is animate): у неё бы́ло всё, о чём мо́жно мечта́ть/u neë bỳlo vsë, o čëm mòžno mečtàt' 'by her there was (= she had) everything one could dream of'. As a kind of existential construction, the word order Domain|Verb|Subject is usual. No overt verb is necessary in the present tense, though the relic form е́сть/èst' can be added to emphasize existence of the entity against the contrary presupposition. The possessed entity appears in the genitive under negation: тако́й жи́зненной шко́лы у неё ещё не́ бы́ло/takòj žìznennoj škòly u neë eščë nè bylo 'by her there still had not been any such experience in the school of life (= she still had not had ...)'.

Transitive име́ть/imét' 'have' is used in idioms in which the possessed entity is an abstract quality, possession of which is a property of the possessor, such as име́ть {че́сть ~ возмо́жность ~ влия́ние ~ авторите́т}/imét' {čest' ~ vozmóžnost' ~ vlijánie ~ avtoritét} 'to have the {honour ~ possibility ~ influence ~ authority}'. Deviations occur in both directions. The existential construction individuates an abstract quality: и бы́л у него́ ещё оди́н тала́нт: тала́нт превраще́ния/i býl u negó eščё odin talánt: talánt prevraščénija 'and there was by him (= he had) yet another talent: the talent of transformation'. Conversely, with a noun for which the existential construction is usual, име́ть/imét' can be used if the syntax demands it, such as under coordination: жи́л о́н в бе́дности, де́лал перево́ды, не име́л бы́та/žil ón v bédnosti, délal perevódy, ne imél býta 'he lived in poverty, did translations, didn't have a home'.

At the level of the argument, two formal devices are available, possessive adjective and adnominal genitive. (A third option – no overt marker of the possessor – is often invoked with inalienable (body-part) possession, under conditions similar to the use of zero for subjects.) For first and second persons and the reflexive, the possessive adjectives agree in case, gender and number with the head (which normally follows): на́шего ше́ствия/nášego šéstvija 'our (N GEN SG) procession (N GEN SG)', свою́ карти́ну/svojú kartínu 'one's own (F ACC SG) picture (F ACC SG)'. The third-person forms are invariant and identical to the genitive: и́х ше́ствия/ix šéstvija 'their procession', и́х карти́ну/ix kartínu 'their picture'.

When the possessor is a noun, it is usual to use the genitive (after the possessed noun): от и́мени Мандельшта́ма/ot imeni Mandel'štáma 'in the name of Mandel'štam'. Possessive adjectives can be formed from some nouns, most readily with declension II diminutives. In она́ понима́ла, что окружа́ющие осужда́ют и виня́т её в сме́рти Ири́ны/oná ponimála, čto okružájuščie osuždájut i vinját eё v smérti Iriny 'she understood that people around her condemned her and blamed her for the death of Irina', the genitive reflects the opinion of others. Possessive adjectives suggest the speaker's familiarity with the possessor, as in: Ири́нина сме́рть сыгра́ла огро́мную ро́ль в ма́мином отъе́зде за грани́цу/Irinina smért' sygrála ogrómnuju ról' v máminom ot"ézde za granicu 'Irina's death played an enormous role in Mama's emigration'.

Like predicates, nouns govern noun phrases. Obvious deverbals govern the same oblique cases as their source predicates (for example, стремле́ние к по́лному облада́нию че́м-нибудь/stremlénie k pólnomu obladániju čém-nibud' 'the striving for complete possession of something', from стреми́ться к чему́/stremit'sja k čemú 'to strive for something' and обладать чем/obladát' čem 'to possess something'). In the deverbal of an intransitive, a genitive corresponds to the subject (увлечение Марины/uvlečénie Mariny 'the infatuation of Marina', from reflexive intransitive увлечься/uvlèč'sja 'to be carried away'). Deverbals of transitives with two nominal arguments look passive – agent in the instrumental, patient in the genitive (окончание им гимназии/ okončánie im gimnázii 'completion of the gymnasium by him').

4.10   Quantification

Syntactically, quantifiers are neither fish nor fowl; in some respects they behave like nouns, in others like modifiers of the quantified noun (see in general Мельчук/Mel'čuk 1985). It is useful to distinguish four groups: approximates (несколько/néskol'ko 'some', много/mnógo 'many', мало/málo 'few'); paucal numerals (четыре/četýre '4', три/tri '3', два/ dvá ~ две/dvé '2', also óба/óba ~ óбе/óbe 'both'); ordinary numerals (пять/pjat' '5', девятнадцать/devjatnádcat' '19', семьдесят/ sém'desjat '70' and the like); and collectives (двое/dvóe 'twosome, pair', трое/tróe 'threesome, triplet' and so on). At the margins of quantifiers in the narrow sense are один/odin 'one' (plural 'some'), некоторый/ nékotoryj 'certain' or многие/mnógie 'many (individual)', which agree in case, gender and number with their head. The large numerals миллион/ millión 'million' and тысяча/týsjača 'thousand' normally have the syntax of nouns, so they take genitive plural of the quantified noun in all cases (though тысяча/týsjača residually allows quantifier syntax).

True quantifiers are defined primarily by their sensitivity to case. When the quantifier phrase occurs where one expects oblique case – genitive, dative, locative or instrumental – the quantifier, like any modifier, adopts the same oblique case as the quantified noun: (строение о двух окнах/ stroénie o dvúx óknax 'a building with two windows', с пятью сидевшими офицерами/s pjat'jú sidévšimi oficérami 'with five seated officers', больше шести лет/ból'še šesti lèt 'for more than six years'). When the quantifier phrase is in a direct case – nominative or accusative – the quantifier itself is nominative(–accusative), the quantified noun genitive and usually plural. With paucals, however, the noun is singularized (четыре солдата работали/četýre soldáta rabótali 'four soldiers were working'); this is the reflex of an older construction in which the numeral '2' and noun were nominative dual, a form which was often formally identical with the genitive singular.

Agreement of modifiers in direct cases is largely consistent across quantifiers. Pronominal adjectives preceding the quantifier are nominative-accusative plural. Adjectives between quantifier and quantified noun are genitive plural: эти пять последних писем/èti pjat' poslédnix písem 'those five last letters', эти два последних письма/èti dvá poslédnix pis'má 'those two last letters'; with the combination of paucals and feminine nouns, however, nominative plural is preferred; эти две первые и три последние строки/èti dvė pėrvye i tri poslėdnie stroki 'those two first and the three last lines'.

Only masculine два/dva versus feminine две/dvė '2' in direct cases and masculine оба/óba versus feminine обе/óbe 'both' in all cases reflect the gender of the quantified noun. Animacy differentiates quantifiers. In the accusative, paucals and collectives obligatorily adopt the genitive, in which instance the noun is genitive plural rather than singular, while higher numerals like пять/pjàt' retain the nominative–accusative: он держит {двух ~ пять} соловьёв у себя в комнате/òn dėržit {dvúx ~ pjàt'} solov'ëv u sebjà v kómnate 'he keeps {two ~ five} nightingales in his room'. With approximates (сколько/skól'ko 'how many') the animate accusative applies optionally.

Quantifiers allow in principle two agreement patterns in the predicate. Default neuter singular agreement merely establishes the existence of a certain quantity: по дороге ехало два экипажа/po doróge èxalo dvà èkipàža 'there were two conveyances travelling on the road'. Plural agreement reports participation of differentiated entities:

По дороге ехали два экипажа. В передней карете сидели две женщины. Одна была госпожа, другая – горничная./Po doróge èxali dvà èkipàža. V perèdnej karète sidèli dvė žènščiny. Odnà bylà gospožà, drugàja – górničnaja. 'On the road two conveyances were travelling. In the front carriage two women were sitting. One was a lady, the other – a maidservant.'

Quantifiers differ in preference, depending on how natural an individuated reading is; the smaller and more precise the quantifier, the more likely plural agreement is. Predicates also show different preferences. Existentials and modals strongly prefer singular (92 per cent in count); other intransitives vary (52 per cent singular). Transitives almost always take plural (only 9 per cent singular), as do copular predicates with predicative nouns or adjectives. Agreement further correlates with word order: Verb|Subject order, usually existential, favours default agreement, while Subject|Verb is more tolerant of plural (see Corbett 1983).

The use of collectives in opposition to ordinary cardinals is possible only for masculine (or mixed) referents, and is encouraged by: small quantities; direct (as opposed to oblique) case; animacy; low stylistic status; adjectival declension; and, within masculines, declension II (Зализняк/Zaliznjak 1977: 66–7). A collective imputes the sense that the grouping is natural and organic, and not merely a random collection of entities.

The behaviour of complex numerals is determined largely by the last member. Thus the noun is genitive singular with a paucal (двадцать три соседа молчат за дверьми/dvàdcat' tri sosèda molčàt za dver'mi 'twenty-three neighbours were silent behind doors') but plural with an ordinary numeral (двадцать пять соседей/dvàdcat' pjàt' sosèdej

Table 15.15   Quantifier matrix

	Oblique agreement	Animate accusative	Plural agreement	Singularized noun	Gender agreement
большинство́/ bol´šinstvó	*	*	?	*	*
пя́ть/pjàt´	+	*	±	*	*
не́сколько/ néskol´ko	+	±	±	*	*
дво́е/dvóe	+	+	±	*	*
три́/trí	+	+	±	+	*
два́/dvá ~ две́/dvé	+	+	±	+	+
оди́н/odín	+	+	—	*	+

'twenty-five neighbours'). They are supposed to decline all parts in oblique cases, but there is a tendency to restrict declension to the last member (Comrie and Stone 1978: 95–6).

The properties of quantifiers are summarized in table 15.15, which is approximately a cline with the diagonal from top left to bottom right reflecting decreasing nominality and increasing adjectivity.

5   Lexis

5.1   General composition of the word-stock
The lexicon of Modern Russian is to a large extent constructed from roots of Proto-Slavonic provenance, though much of it may have been formed by productive processes in the history of Russian. On the general history of the lexicon, see Kiparsky (1963–75, III), Vlasto (1986: ch. 5) and, for the recent history, Comrie and Stone (1978: ch. 5).

5.2   Patterns of borrowing
There are multiple layers and sources of borrowings. Church Slavonicisms, whether genuine or neologistic, occupy a special layer in the lexicon of Modern Russian. A recognizable Church Slavonicism still has the function of making the stylistic register more formal or pompous. After Church Slavonicisms, the most important layer is the last three centuries of European borrowings, in some instances from specific languages, often from a generalized European vocabulary. Direct borrowings from other Slavonic languages are insignificant, except seventeenth-century borrowings from Polish, which in turn often have their source in Czech, German or Latin.

Contiguous languages (such as Finnic) have contributed some etyma, usually on a regional level. The most salient derive from Turkic languages during the Mongol period; familiar examples include деньга́/den′gȧ 'coin', чума́/čumȧ 'plague' and изю́м/izjȕm 'raisins'.

5.3   Incorporation of borrowings

Borrowings assimilate reasonably well to Russian phonology, although vowel reduction and palatalization before /e/ may be held in abeyance and geminate consonants maintained. Morphologically, verbs and adjectives are borrowed in suffixed form, and so are regular. Nouns are declined if their structure allows them to be assigned to declension Ia or II. Thus, фио́рд/fiȯrd 'fiord' and фло́ра/flȯra 'flora' decline but хо́бби/xȯbbi 'hobby', табу́/tabȕ 'taboo' and протеже́/protežȇ 'protégé' do not. Nouns which could fit declension Ib, like дина́мо/dinȧmo 'dynamo' and кино́/kinȯ 'cinema', are not declined except in non-standard speech. Indeclinables are neuter except animates, which use referential gender.

5.4   Lexical fields

5.4.1   Colour terms

Colour terms differ in abstractness, connotations, frequency, morphological productivity and psychological accessibility (see Corbett and Morgan 1988, with references). Unrestricted are бе́лый/bȇlyj 'white', чёрный/čërnyj 'black', кра́сный/krȧsnyj 'red', си́ний/sinij 'blue', зелёный/zelёnyj 'green' and жёлтый/žëltyj 'yellow'. Two additional, typologically surprising, terms belong in this group of basic terms: се́рый/sȇryj 'grey' and голубо́й/golubȯj 'sky-blue', a lighter and paler colour than си́ний/sinij. These eight rank at the top of operational tests of frequency, derivational productivity (only these eight form attenuatives like черновáтый/černovȧtyj 'blackish', чёрненький/čërnen′kij 'a little black') and psychological accessibility to speakers (except for се́рый/sȇryj 'grey', which connotes indistinctness of light).

After this, some uncertainty, and some interesting complexity, sets in. In the brown range, кори́чневый/koričnevyj, originally a reddish brown derived from 'cinnamon', is expanding, in part at the expense of бу́рый/bȕryj, which characterizes not so much a specific hue as a dull or mottled appearance. Terms translating English *purple* are not completely abstract: пурпу́рный/purpȕrnyj retains imperial connotations; багро́вый/bagrȯvyj, a purplish red glossed as 'crimson', is the colour of flushed cheeks and hands, blood or dawn; лило́вый/lilȯvyj 'lilac' and фиоле́товый/fiolȇtovyj 'violet' are still associated with florae. The last, however, is becoming more general. Ора́нжевый/orȧnževyj 'orange' still seems a compromise between yellow and red. Certain entities that are orange in English (jaguars, carrots, apricots, oranges themselves) were described in pre-revolutionary encyclopedias as кра́сно-жёлтый/krȧsno-žëltyj 'red-yellow' or the like; some, but not all, of these have become 'orange' in the most recent encyclopedia. 'Pink' (ро́зовый/rózovyj) belongs to this transitional group as well.

Evidently, after the eight basic colour terms, four additional terms – кори́чневый/koričnevyj, ро́зовый/rózovyj, фиоле́товый/fiolétovyj and ора́нжевый/oránževyj – are less-than-basic terms which are moving towards greater integration.

5.4.2 Kinship terms

Russian kinship is rich in lexical variants (diminutives) whose usage varies in different contexts – in address, definition and ordinary reference, and in domestic and public situations. Оте́ц/otéc 'father' and ма́ть/mát' 'mother' are neutral, but па́па/pápa and ма́ма/máma (and their diminutives) would be more usual in a domestic context. Children are сы́н/sýn 'son' and до́чь/dóč' 'daughter' (or diminutives). For collective plural reference, де́ти/déti 'children' and роди́тели/roditeli 'parents' are usual. Grandparents are normally referred to by the diminutives де́душка/déduška 'grandfather' and ба́бушка/bábuška 'grandmother'. Grandchildren are вну́к/vnúk 'grandson' and вну́чка/vnúčka 'granddaughter'. Marital partners are individually му́ж/múž 'husband' and жена́/žená 'wife', collectively супру́ги/suprúgi 'spouses'. Siblings are бра́т/brát 'brother' and сестра́/sestrá 'sister'. Дя́дя/djádja 'uncle' and тётя/tëtja 'aunt' are either mother's or father's siblings; their children are племя́нник/plemjánnik 'nephew' and племя́нница/plemjánnica 'niece'.

The modifier двою́родный/dvojúrodnyj 'second-degree' characterizes relationships with an additional generation up and down between *ego* and the relative. With бра́т/brát or сестра́/sestrá, it identifies first cousins; with племя́нник/plemjánnik or племя́нница/plemjánnica, child of first cousin (first cousin once removed). The modifier, used to define a relationship, is not essential in ordinary reference or address. Thus, in the chapter of *Family Chronicle* relating the unfortunate marriage of the female cousin of his grandfather, Aksakov first uses двою́родный бра́т/dvojúrodnyj brát and двою́родная сестра́/dvojúrodnaja sestrá, but once the relationship has been established, he omits the modifier. Aksakov also states that his grandfather addressed his cousin with diminutives like сестри́ца/sestrica.

5.4.3 Body parts

Much of Russian's terminology for body parts corresponds to English reference: голова́/golová 'head', но́с/nós 'nose', у́хо/úxo 'ear' (with an archaic remnant of dual morphology in the nominative plural у́ши/úši), ро́т/rót 'mouth', ше́я/šéja 'neck' and се́рдце/sérdce 'heart'. Гру́дь/grúd' covers English 'chest' as well as 'breast'. Во́лос/vólos 'hair', more strictly a count noun than in English, is normally used in the plural (for example, in describing hair colour), the singular being reserved for 'a strand of hair'. Глаз/gláz 'eye' (nominative plural глаза/glazá), originally the eyeball, has long since displaced око/óko (nominative plural óчи/óči). The two were still in variation into the nineteenth century. In Puškin's *Evgenij Onegin*, глаза/glazá refers to eyes as instruments of physical perception, with which one reads or merely looks. With óчи/óči one gazes actively or reflects a sad thought. In an identical collocation, the insensitive general does not take his глаза/glazá from Tat'jana, but this perceptive heroine does not take her óчи/óči from Onegin.

As is well known, Russian uses a single word рука/ruká to refer to what English would differentiate as 'arm' and 'hand' and нога/nogá for 'leg' and 'foot'. (Палец/pálec is the digit indifferently of hand or foot.) Though the extremities can be specified as кисть/kist' and ступня/stupnjá, respectively, the terms are infrequent. When one hears Russians say in English 'I twisted the hands of my colleagues', one suspects that they think of the limbs and extremities without differentiation. Thus Turgenev writes of an acquaintance that he exuded Russianness down 'to his puffy short-fingered ручки/rúčki and his nimble ножки/nóžki with thick calves'. The modifiers force an English translation with 'hands' and 'legs', obscuring what Turgenev evidently saw as a parallelism between the upper and lower limbs.

6 Dialects

Several layers of innovations can be distinguished in Russian dialects, reflecting shifting political affiliations and demographic movement (see Орлова/Orlova 1970: 223–37; Vlasto 1986: ch. 6). The oldest changes in East Slavonic spread from the south-west to the north-east, leaving behind isoglosses that bifurcate the Russian language area laterally in the middle. As the northern outposts of Kievan civilization become autonomous, they become centres for linguistic innovation. The next layer of changes, accordingly, are either eastern (extending north and south from Rostov, Suzdal' and Vladimir) or western (distributed in an arc from the south-west through Pskov and Novgorod and on into the north and even into the north-east, following the path of colonization in the thirteenth to mid-fifteenth centuries). A third layer of innovation is due to the spread of Muscovite norms, which often eroded earlier dialect features. As a consequence, eastern changes are often discontinuous around Moscow, and western features are better preserved in the south-western lands affiliated with the Grand Duchy of Lithuania and in the remote north-east than in their original centre around Pskov and Novgorod.

Of the early changes, southernmost is the change of $*g > \gamma$, a general East Slavonic innovation that reached a line that starts south of Pskov (56°N) and continues east-southeastwards passing just below Moscow. Next comes the northern limit for **аканье/ákan'e** – merger of /a/ and /o/

after hard consonants in first pre-tonic position; the isogloss, parallel to *g > γ, starts between Pskov and Novgorod in the west and runs above Moscow.

Well within the *akan´e* area is the northern limit of dissimilation in unstressed vocalism, similar but not identical for position after hard and position after soft consonant. The most archaic (Obojansk) type uses a low vowel in positions before non-low /i, u, ê, ô/, a high vowel before non-high /a, e, o/: пятно̂/pjatnồ 'spot' and неси́/nesí 'carry!' have [ă] for the first pre-tonic vowel, marked here in bold, but взяла́/vzjalá '(she) took' and глядя́т/gljadját '(they) look' have [ĭ]. The notoriously variegated types of dissimilative vocalism can be derived by adjusting the classes of conditioning vowels. To the north of the dissimilative region, unstressed vocalism is non-dissimilative: western central dialects (Pskov) have strong **яканье/jákan´e** (пятно̂/pjatnồ, неси́/nesí, взяла́/vzjalá, глядя́т/gljadját, with consistent [ă]), the mid central dialects (Moscow) **иканье/íkan´e** (consistent [ĭ]) and intermediate dialects transitional types, such as the 'moderate' principle ([ă] before hard consonant in пятно̂/pjatnồ, взяла́/vzjalá, [ĭ] before soft in неси́/nesí, глядя́т/gljadját).

Synchronically, Russian dialects are classified first into two macro-dialects, or dialect complexes (наре́чие/naréčie), which are separated by a narrow intermediate zone, and then further into regional dialects (го́воры/góvory) (see Аванесов and Орлова/Avanesov and Orlova 1965). The southern macro-dialect, defined positively by the change of *g > γ and unrestricted *akan´e*, divides into three south-western dialects (western; Upper Dnepr; Upper Desna), one mid (Kursk–Orel) and one eastern dialect (Rjazan´), with additional transitional dialects. The northern macro-dialect, defined negatively by the absence of both *g > γ and *akan´e* (hence **о́канье/ókan´e**, the distinction of atonic /o/ and /a/ after hard consonants), divides into north-western (Ladoga–Tixvin), Vologda and Kostroma dialects, with additional transitional regions. In between the two macro-dialects is the central zone (центра́льные го́воры/centrál´nye góvory), which is defined by the absence of *g > γ and by partial *akan´e*; it divides into eastern (Vladimir; the eastern *akan´e* dialect) and western (Novgorod; Pskov; Gdov; historical Tver´) dialects. This classification, shown in map 15.1, applies only to older, European, Russia, a funnel-shaped area bounded in the south-west and west by the political boundaries with the Ukraine and Belorussia, in the north by 62°N, and in the east by a line which, starting at 46°E, angles first south by eastwards and then southwestwards to Voronež. The far north continues features from adjacent areas to the south. The areas to the south-east and east (and ultimately Siberia) are dialectally mixed, since they have been settled from the sixteenth century on by heterogeneous populations.

Some innovations correlate approximately with the division into northern and southern macro-dialects. The south neutralizes the oblique

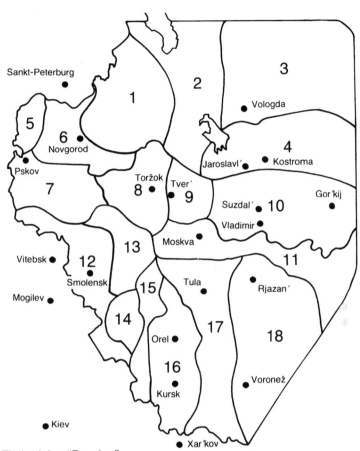

Key: Timberlake, "Russian"

Source: Avanesov and Orlova/Аванесов and Орлова 1965

Northern dialects
1   Ladoga-Tixvin
2   northern transitional zone
3   Vologda
4   Kostroma

Central dialects
5   Gdov
6   Novgorod
7   Pskov
8   Seliger-Toržok
9   Tver´
10 Vladimir
11 eastern *akan´e*

Southern dialects
12 western
13 Upper Dnepr
14 Upper Desna
15 southwestern transitional zone
16 Kursk-Orel
17 southeastern transitional zone
18 Rjazan´

Map 15.1   Russian Dialects

cases (except the instrumental) of first and second persons singular and reflexive pronouns, while the north distinguishes two forms, approximately following the *g > γ isogloss. Some dialects fail to distinguish the reflex of the first palatalization and *tj (both normally *č*) from the reflex of the second palatalization (normally *c*); western central dialects have [c] and the north-east [ç] for both. Given the geography, this цо́канье/cókan'e is probably a north-western archaism reflecting the incomplete development of the second palatalization. Only northern *okan'e* dialects have experienced loss of intervocalic /j/ and vowel contraction (ду́мает/dúmaet '(he/she) thinks' > [maiet > maet > maat > mat]); this is evidently an eastern (Rostov–Suzdal'–Vladimir) innovation. Northern dialects merge dative and instrumental plural in adjectives and often nouns (maximally к ~ с но́вым дома́м/k ~ s nóvym domám 'to ~ with the new houses'). This feature, not attested in the extreme north-east, is a late western innovation. In general, northern features that are not archaisms are either eastern or western innovations.

Differences in consonantism (other than *g > γ) are typically western or eastern innovations. The progressive palatalization of velars after soft consonants (Ва́нька/Ván'kja 'Vanja (DIMIN)', ча́йкя/čájkja 'seagull', with [ḱ]) is an eastern innovation found in an elongated north–south swath from the southern border of Russian as far north as Vologda. This swath, however, is discontinuous around Moscow. Most widely distributed of the western innovations shared with Belorussian is the loss of palatalized labials word-finally, attested in a continuous arc from the south-west through the western central dialects on into the north-east. In the south-west and in significant pockets in the north-east, hard /l/ became /w/ syllable-finally: во́лк/vólk 'wolf' > [vouk]. This feature may once have been distributed continuously from the south-west to the north-east but interrupted in the central western dialects by Muscovite influence.

In syntax, of greatest curiosity value is the use of the nominative case of declension II nouns for objects of impersonal infinitives, as in на́до земля́ паха́ть/nádo zemljá pahát' 'it is necessary to plough the land'. The construction is now found only in north-eastern dialects, but it was earlier attested in Novgorodian chancery documents. This construction may be a calque of a Finnic construction; the contexts in which the nominative occurs are comparable, and in both the nominative is not used with pronouns.

Another syntactic peculiarity, centred in the west around Novgorod and extending throughout the far north, is the impersonal passive. It is formed regularly from transitives with accusative objects, as in у меня́ телёнка заре́зано/u menjá telënka zarézano 'by me there was slaughtered a calf', and less pervasively from intransitives, as in у него́ зале́зено на ёлку/u negó zalézeno na ëlku 'by him it was climbed on the fir tree'. The participle is morphologically neuter singular; the sentential possessive phrase (у/u plus genitive) optionally expresses the agent.

Throughout the western half of Russia, along a north–south line at 36°E (but most regularly in the central Novgorod area), the morphologically invariant verbal adverb is used as a perfect, or with auxiliaries, as pluperfect or future perfect: кот с обеда до вечера не был и проснувши/ kót s obéda do véčera né byl i prosnúvši 'the cat had not woken up from dinner till evening'. These western syntactic features have not been codified in the national language.

References

Brecht, R. and Levine, J. (eds) (1985) *Case in Slavic*, Columbus, Ohio: Slavica.

Chvany, C. (1975) *On the Syntax of BE-Sentences in Russian*, Cambridge, Mass.: Slavica.

Comrie, B. and Stone, G. (1978) *The Russian Language since the Revolution*, Oxford: Clarendon Press.

Corbett, G.G. (1983) *Hierarchies, Targets and Controllers: Agreement Patterns in Slavic*, London and Canberra: Croom Helm.

Corbett, G.G. and Morgan, G. (1988) 'Colour terms in Russian: reflections of typological constraints in a single language', *Journal of Linguistics* 24: 31–64.

Gustavsson, S. (1976) *Predicative Adjectives with the Copula BYT' in Modern Russian* (Acta Universitatis Stockholmiensis, 10), Stockholm: Almqvist and Wiksell.

Jakobson, R. (1984) *Russian and Slavic Grammar Studies 1931–1981*, ed. Linda R. Waugh and Morris Halle (Janua Linguarum, Series Maior, 106), Berlin, New York and Amsterdam: Mouton.

Jones, D. and Ward, D. (1969) *The Phonetics of Russian*, Cambridge: Cambridge University Press.

Kiparsky, V. (1963–75) *Russische historische Grammatik*, vol. I: *Die Entwicklung des Lautsystems*; vol. II: *Die Entwicklung des Formensystems*; vol. III: *Entwicklung des Wortschatzes*, Heidelberg: Carl Winter.

Klenin, E. (1983) *Animacy in Russian: a New Interpretation* (UCLA Slavic Studies, 6), Columbus, Ohio: Slavica.

Nichols, J. (1981) *Predicate Nominals: a Partial Surface Syntax of Russian* (University of California Publications in Linguistics, 97), Berkeley and Los Angeles: University of California Press.

Picchio, R. and Goldblatt, H. (eds) (1984) *Aspects of the Slavic Language Question*, vol. I: *Church Slavonic – South Slavic – West Slavic*; vol. II: *East Slavic* (Yale Russian and East European Publications, 4a; 4b), Columbus, Ohio: Slavica.

Stankiewicz, E. (1968) *Declension and Gradation of Russian Substantives in Contemporary Standard Russian* (Description and Analysis of Contemporary Standard Russian, 4), The Hague and Paris: Mouton.

Timberlake, A. (1975) 'Hierarchies in the genitive of negation', *Slavic and East European Journal* 19: 123–38.

Unbegaun, B.O. (1957) *Russian Grammar*, Oxford: Clarendon Press.

Vlasto, A.P. (1986) *A Linguistic History of Russia to the End of the Eighteenth Century*, Oxford: Clarendon Press.

Yokoyama, O. (1986) *Discourse and Word Order* (Pragmatics and Beyond Companion Series, 6), Amsterdam and Philadelphia: John Benjamins.

Аванесов, Р.И. (1968) *Русское литературное произношение* (изд. 4-е), Москва: Просвещение.

Аванесов, Р.И. и Орлова, В.Г. (1965) *Русская диалектология* (изд. 2-е), Москва: Наука.

Адамец, Прж. [= Adamec, Př.] (1966) *Порядок слов в современном русском языке* (Rozpravy Československé Akademie Věd, Řada společenských věd, 76.15), Prague.

Виноградов, В.В. (1949) *Очерки по истории русского литературного языка XVII–XIX вв.*, Leiden: E.J. Brill.

Бондарко, Л.В. (1977) *Звуковой строй современного русского языка*, Москва: Просвещение.

Зализняк, А.А. (1977) *Грамматический словарь русского языка. Словоизменение*, Москва: Русский язык.

Земская, Е.А. (ред.) (1973) *Русская разговорная речь*, Москва: Наука.

Крысин, Л.П. (ред.) (1974) *Русский язык по данным массового обследования. Опыт социально-лингвистического изучения*, Москва: Наука.

Левин, В.Д. (1964) *Краткий очерк истории русского литературного языка* (изд. 2-е), Москва: Просвещение.

Матусевич, М.И. (1976) *Современный русский язык. Фонетика. Учебное пособие для студентов педагогических институтов по специальности «Русский язык и литература»*, Москва: Просвещение.

Мельчук, И.А. (1985) *Поверхностный синтаксис русских числовых выражений* (Wiener Slawistischer Almanach, Sonderband 16), Vienna: Institut für Slawistik der Universität Wien.

Орлова, В.Г. (ред.) (1970) *Образование севернорусского наречия и среднерусских говоров (по материалам лингвистической географии)*, Москва: Наука.

Падучева, Е.В. (1985) *Высказывание и его соотнесенность с действительностью*, Москва: Наука.

16 Belorussian

Peter Mayo

1 Introduction

Ethnically the Belorussians are the descendants of those ancient East Slavonic tribes – the Dregoviči, Radimiči and Kriviči – which inhabited the territory between the rivers Pripjat´ (Pripyat) and Western Dvina in the upper reaches of the Dnepr (Dnieper) and along the Sož (Sozh). When, in the middle of the thirteenth century, Russia fell under the Tatar yoke, there began a long period of political separation of what is now Belarus, until recently known as Belorussia, and the Ukraine. Between then and the end of the first quarter of the fourteenth century the principalities which lay on the territory of present-day Belarus were incorporated into the Grand Duchy of Lithuania; later, following the Union of Lublin (1569), they became part of the Polish–Lithuanian Commonwealth until re-unification with Russia in 1795. It was this period of separation that saw the break-up of Old Russian into three distinct East Slavonic languages: Belorussian, Ukrainian and Russian.

A written language developed on Belorussian territory at an early stage. In the twelfth and thirteenth centuries the tradition of copying manuscripts was carried out in such centres as Polack (Polotsk) and Turaŭ (Turov), but the language of these was Church Slavonic. It was only from the fourteenth century that vernacular elements began to appear in texts of Belorussian provenance, while the establishment of Belorussian as a literary language belongs to the fifteenth and sixteenth centuries, when its status was greatly enhanced by its adoption as the official language of the Grand Duchy. During this period the orthographical and grammatical norms of Old Belorussian were established, despite a tendency to preserve traditional Church Slavonic-influenced forms, both in spelling and morphology. Thus already in the orthography of fourteenth-century documents we can discern such characteristic features of Belorussian pronunciation as the change of initial pre-consonantal [v] to [u]; the use of fricative [ɣ] (plosive [g] was represented by the digraph гк); the depalatalization of [ž'], [č'], [š'], [c'] and [r']; and the clusters [rɨ], [lɨ] in place of Proto-Slavonic liquid + ъ. However, the most salient feature of Belorussian vowel phonology, *ákanne* (the pronunciation of unstressed [o] as [a]), was reflected in the orthography only sporadically at this time and even two centuries later its reflection remained inconsistent. The fifteenth and sixteenth centuries also saw much innovation in Belorussian lexis. The principal source of loan-words was Polish, which, since it also served as the medium for the intro-duction into Belorussian of loan-words from Latin and the western European languages, played an important role in the expansion of the vocabulary of Belorussian at this period in its history.

The end of the sixteenth century, however, saw the beginning of a gradual decline in the use of written Belorussian, initially in favour of Latin after the Union of Brest (1596) which was intended to unite the Orthodox and Catholic churches, but increasingly as the seventeenth century wore on in favour of Polish. This decline culminated in 1697 in the banning of Belorussian from use in all state documents and court proceedings, a ban which ushered in perhaps the bleakest century in the whole history of the language. During the eighteenth century written Belorussian was kept alive almost entirely through 'interludes' to school dramas which were performed at religious festivals and on other public holidays (the plays themselves were written in Church Slavonic, Latin or Polish).

With the partitions of the Polish–Lithuanian Commonwealth (1772–95) Belorussia became part of the Russian Empire, but the shift of political power from Warsaw to St Petersburg provided no greater opportunities for the country to develop cultural and linguistic independence. On the contrary, the tsarist authorities treated it simply as the north-western province of Russia and its language as a dialect of Great Russian, banning it as a medium of instruction in schools and placing an embargo on the publication of works in Belorussian in Russian journals which was lifted only in 1905.

Thus, at the beginning of the twentieth century Belorussian still had no codified alphabetical, orthographical or grammatical norms. Work was begun on these in the period of the newspaper Náша нíва/Náša níva 'Our cornfield' (1906–14), which succeeded in establishing standard alphabets, both Cyrillic and Latin (see Mayo 1977). It was continued in particular by Branislaŭ Taraškevič, whose *Belorussian Grammar for Schools* (Тарашкевіч/Taraškevič 1918) quickly became the standard against which other proposals for orthographical and grammatical norms were measured.

The period from 1918–30 was one of intense activity on the part of Belorussian linguists: in an atmosphere of optimism and linguistic freedom work was begun on the first dictionaries of Modern Belorussian and in addition to Taraškevič's *Grammar* a number of others made their appear-ance. All this came to an end with the rise of Stalin and the publication in 1933 of a decree entitled 'On the changes and simplification of the Belo-russian orthography'. The introduction to the decree (which, incidentally, also prescribed certain morphological changes) left no doubt as to its politi-

Table 16.1   Belorussian alphabet

Cyrillic		Transliteration	Cyrillic		Transliteration
А	а	a	О	о	o
Б	б	b	П	п	p
В	в	v	Р	р	r
Г	г	h	С	с	s
Д	д	d	Т	т	t
(Дж	дж)[a]	dž	У	у	u
(Дз	дз)[a]	dz	Ў	ў	ŭ
Е	е	e	Ф	ф	f
Ё	ё[b]	ë	Х	х	x
Ж	ж	ž	Ц	ц	c
З	з	z	Ч	ч	č
І	і	i	Ш	ш	š
Й	й	j	Ы	ы	y
К	к	k	Ь	ь	'
Л	л	l	Э	э	è
М	м	m	Ю	ю	ju
Н	н	n	Я	я	ja

Notes:The apostrophe ('), representing /j/ after a consonant and before a vowel, is conventionally regarded as not being a letter of the alphabet.

[a]The digraphs дж and дз represent the affricates /dž/ and /dz/, but for the purposes of alphabetical ordering (for example, in dictionaries) each is treated as a sequence of two letters. They may not, however, be separated when hyphenating a word at the end of a line.

[b]In alphabetical ordering ë is treated as distinct from e and merits a separate section (following e) in dictionaries.

cal nature nor as to its aim of bringing Belorussian closer to Russian (see Mayo 1978). There followed a period of intensive Russification of the language in all its aspects. Something of a revival in the fortunes of written Belorussian at least began in the 1960s with a resurgence of scholarly interest in the language, the appearance of a 90,000-word *Belorussian–Russian Dictionary* and of the first edition of the Academy of Sciences *Grammar of Belorussian.* In the ensuing quarter of a century much more has appeared: grammars, textbooks and a wide range of dictionaries, including a long-awaited comprehensive monolingual dictionary of Belorussian (Атраховіч/Atraxovič 1977–84).

Against this must be set the spread of Russian as the primary means of public communication and an increasing, if imperfect, bilingualism, particularly among the educated urban population. According to the 1979 census, there were just under 9.5 million ethnic Belorussians in the former Soviet Union, of whom just over 7.5 million (about 80 per cent) were resident in the Belorussian Soviet Socialist Republic (BSSR); disturbingly, the same census found that only 74.2 per cent (83.5 per cent of those living in the BSSR, but only 36.8 per cent of those outside) considered Belorussian their native language. This compares with figures of 84.2 per cent in 1959 and 80.6 per cent in 1970 and is the lowest figure for any of the titular nationalities of the Union Republics (for all the others, with the exception of the Ukrainians at 82.8 per cent, the figure was above 90 per cent). Since it is a reasonable assumption that most of the remaining 25.8 per cent regarded Russian as their native language, and given that the census also revealed that 57 per cent of all Belorussians claimed fluent command of Russian as a second language, the status of Belorussian within the Soviet Union remained somewhat problematical. Nevertheless, the most recent signs are rather more encouraging. There is clear evidence of a national revival, predominantly political and cultural but also linguistic: for example, one hears far more Belorussian spoken on the streets of the capital, Minsk, than even five years ago; there is growing concern at the contamination of the language by Russian and a corresponding resistance to the adoption of Russisms where adequate native resources exist; the Таварыства беларускай мовы/Tavarýstva belaruskaj móvy 'Society for the Belorussian Language' publishes its own journal and has set up a terminological commission to revive and continue work begun in the 1920s.

Outside the territory of the former Soviet Union there is a sizeable national minority living in the Białystok region of eastern Poland and the language is also kept alive by émigré communities in western Europe, North America and Australia.

2 Phonology

2.1 Segmental phoneme inventory
The inventory of segmental phonemes in Belorussian is set out in table 16.2. In the discussion which follows, unless otherwise indicated, the orthography (through the transliteration given) matches the phoneme inventory. The vowel sounds [i] and [ɨ] (orthographically ы/y) do not represent separate phonemes in Belorussian, since the two are found entirely in complementary distribution: [i] occurs in word-initial position or following a palatalized consonant; [ɨ] is restricted to following a non-palatalized consonant, for example, сіты/síty 'sieves' [s'ítɨ] versus сыты/sýty 'satisfied' [sɨtɨ]. On the role of the semi-vowel [w] (spelt ў/ŭ), see below.

Looking at the table, one is immediately struck by the high incidence of opposition between palatalized consonants (indicated by ') and non-palatalized consonants, illustrated in such contrasts as стол/stol 'table' /stol/versus столь/stol' 'ceiling' /stol'/. Belorussian has only seven non-palatalized consonant phonemes which lack palatalized counterparts: /t/,

Table 16.2 Segmental phonemes of Belorussian

Vowels

    i (i) u
   e   o
     a

Consonants	Bilabial		Labio-dental		Dental		Alveolar		Palato-alveolar	Velar	
Plain stop	p	p′			t					k	k′
	b	b′			d					g	g′
Affricate					c	c′			č		
					dz	dz′			dž		
Fricative			f	f′			s	s′	š	x	x′
			v	v′			z	z′	ž	ɣ	ɣ′
Nasal	m	m′			n	n′					
Lateral					l	l′					
Trill							r				
Semi-vowel	(w)								j		

/d/, /r/, /č/, /dž/, /š/, /ž/; and just /j/ without a non-palatalized counterpart. It should be noted, however, that the functional yield of palatalization with the velars is minimal and that the dental affricate /dz/ is a marginal segment.

In Belorussian no single accentual pattern is used throughout the language. The stress can, in principle, occur on any syllable of a word and is mobile. (It is not usually marked in writing, but is shown in this chapter by an upright accent, ′). It may thus be the sole means of distinguishing between different lexical items, for example, музы́ка/muzýka 'musician' and му́зыка/múzyka 'music', сталы́/stalý 'tables' and ста́лы/stály 'grown-up'; and between morphological forms of the same item, for example, пілы́/pilý (GEN SG), пі́лы/píly (NOM–ACC PL) from піла́/pilá 'saw'.

Linked to the mobility of the stress and a major restriction on the distribution of vowel phonemes in Belorussian is the phenomenon of ákanne, whereby in unstressed syllables the opposition between /o/ and /a/ and, in certain contexts, between /e/ and /a/, is neutralized. The details and orthographic representation of this phenomenon are different from those of Russian ákan'e. Belorussian – at least in the Central dialects upon which the standard language is based – is characterized by 'strong' or 'full' ákanne, that is, a type which requires a fully fledged [a] in *all* unaccented syllables, pre- or post-stress. Furthermore, it is highly visible since, with few exceptions, it is reflected in the orthography, as the following examples will show: вада́/vadá 'water' – во́ды/vódy (NOM–ACC PL); малады́/maladý 'young' – мо́ладзь/móladz′ 'youth'; вы́насіць/výnasic′ 'to wear out' – выно́сіць/vynósic′ 'to carry out'; рака́/raká 'river' – рэ́кі/rèki (NOM–ACC PL); чарапы́/čarapý nominative–accusative plural of чэ́рап/čèrap 'skull'. Standard Belorussian is also characterized by strong *jákanne*, in which the opposition between /e/ and /a/ and between /o/ and /a/ after palatalized consonants is neutralized in unaccented syllables. Here the orthography is less consistent: *jákanne* is mirrored only in the pre-tonic syllable of native words and a small number of loan-words long assimilated into the language, for example, нядо́ля/njadólja 'bad luck', калянда́р/kaljandár 'calendar'. Elsewhere historical spelling prevails, thus нежана́ты/nežanáti 'unmarried' [n′ažanáti], секу́нда/ sekúnda 'second' [s′akúnda].

A further constraint on the phoneme /o/ is that in native words, with a very small number of exceptions, it does not occur word-initially. (Атрахо́віч/Atraxovič 1977–84 lists only seventy entries under the letter *o*, of which fifty-three are of foreign origin, and of the remainder eight are interjections.) Before initial stressed /o/ prothetic /v/ develops, for example, во́ка/vóka 'eye'. A similar development is found with initial stressed /u/, as in ву́гал/vúhal 'angle'. In the case of unstressed /u/ there is normally no prothesis, for example, ура́д/urád 'government', but occasionally, by analogy, prothetic /v/ is found here also, as in вуса́ты/vusáty 'bewhiskered' by analogy with вус/vus 'moustache'. Another important restriction on /u/ is that, except at the beginning of a sentence, after a pause or at the beginning of a proper noun, it cannot occur after a vowel. In such a position it is replaced by the semi-vowel /w/: compare the form of the preposition in ён прые́хаў у го́рад/ën pryéxaŭ u hórad 'he arrived in town' and яна́ прые́хала ў го́рад/janá pryéxala ŭ hórad 'she arrived in town'. (For other origins of /w/, including that in прые́хаў/pryéxaŭ, see below.)

The orthographical representation of palatalization in Belorussian is achieved not by having distinct symbols for palatalized and non-palatalized consonants which, given the number of such oppositions, would have resulted in a rather cumbersome alphabet, but by the following expedient. Word-finally or medially before another consonant, palatalization is shown by the use of the letter ь (the so-called 'soft sign') after the palatalized consonant, as in дзень/dzen′ 'day' or пісьмо́/pis′mó 'letter'. Before a vowel, palatalized and non-palatalized consonants are distinguished by the use of different vowel symbols: after a non-palatalized consonant the letters а, э, ы, о, у are used; after a palatalized consonant – я, е, і, ё, ю: compare быць/byc′ 'to be' /bic′/ and біць/bic′ 'to beat' /b′ic′/. After the formerly palatalized consonants /c/, /č/, /š/, /ž/, Belorussian consistently uses the vowel symbols а, э, ы, о, у, as in цэ́лы/cèly 'whole', жыць/žyc´ 'to live'. Representation of the semi-vowel phoneme /j/ in Belorussian is complex: syllable-finally the letter й is used, for example, чай/čaj 'tea', бойкі/bójki 'bold'; after a consonant /j/ is represented by the apostrophe (') followed by an iotated vowel, for example, аб'ёM/ab´ëm 'volume' /abjóm/; word-initially or following a vowel the symbols я, е, i, ё, ю represent the sequence of /j/ plus vowel, for example, яго/jahó 'his' /jaɣó/, вёяць/vějac´ 'to blow' /v´ějac´/.

There are a number of major restrictions on the distribution of consonant phonemes, not all of which are reflected in the orthography. Word-final obstruents are always voiceless; orthographically, however, Belorussian maintains a distinction between, for example, лёт/lët 'flight' and лёд/lëd 'ice', both of which are pronounced /l´ot/. The same is true medially where clusters of obstruents assimilate to the final one, for example, казка/kázka 'tale' /káska/, просьба/prós´ba 'request' /próz´ba/. This assimilation is reflected orthographically only at the prefix–stem boundary in the case of prefixes ending in з/z and с/s, for example, раздаць/razdác´ 'to distribute' versus раскінуць/raskinuc´ 'to scatter'. Although the voiced labio-dental fricatives /v/, /v´/ have voiceless counterparts in /f/, /f´/, the relationship between them is not the same as that between, say, /z/, /z´/ and /s/, /s´/. The sole source of the phonemes /f/, /f´/ in Belorussian is loan-words, in which they are encountered in the same environments as other voiceless obstruents, for example, фасоля/fasólja 'kidney beans', феномен/fenómen 'phenomenon'. The restriction on /v/, /v´/ is wider: they cannot occur before *any* consonant, whether voiced or voiceless, or word-finally; in such positions we find instead the semi-vowel /w/, for example, праўда/práwda 'truth' /práwda/, кроў/kroŭ 'blood' /krow/. A similar restriction applies to the lateral /l/, but only to the non-palatalized version and, word-finally, only in the past tense masculine singular, for example, поўны/póŭny 'full' /pówni/, чытаў/čytaŭ 'was reading' /čitáw/, but вол/vol 'ox' /vol/. Characteristic of Belorussian is the depalatalization of labials (including non-native /f´/) in pre-consonantal and word-final positions, as in сем/sem '7' /s´em/ but genitive сямі/sjami /s´am´i/. The opposition of palatalized and non-palatalized labials is thus confined to pre-vocalic position, for example, мёта/měta 'mark' /m´éta/ versus мэта/měta 'aim' /méta/. Pre-consonantal word-initial /m/, /l/ and /r/ are restricted to an environment in which the preceding word, not separated by a pause, ends in a vowel; otherwise prothetic /i/ develops; compare яна лгала/jana lhála 'she lied' and ён ілгаў/ën ilhaŭ 'he lied'.

We shall now turn our attention to those important phonological processes not already referred to that have characterized the development of Belorussian from Proto-Slavonic via Old Russian. The earliest of these was the treatment of the groups *orC, *olC and *CorC, *ColC, *CerC, *CelC. Belorussian shares the treatment of *orC, *olC with Russian,

Ukrainian and the West Slavonic languages except Czech and Slovak: under falling pitch it shows metathesis, under rising pitch metathesis with lengthening; thus, PSl. *orstъ, *orlo, Bel. рост/rost 'growth', ра́ла/ра́la 'plough'. In word-medial position these groups underwent, in East Slavonic only, what is traditionally known as pleophony, that is the diphthong developed a vowel either side of the sonant, for example, *CorC › CoroC. The Proto-Slavonic pitch pattern is directly reflected in the position of the stress in Belorussian pleophonic groups: rising pitch = stress on second syllable, falling pitch = stress on first, for example, бало́та/balóta 'bog', бе́раг/bérah 'bank'. Another early change, shared with Ukrainian and some Southern Russian dialects, is the spirantization of [g] to [ɣ] (orthographically г/h), as in год/hod 'year' /ɣot/, which Wexler (1977: 98) associates with phonological developments resulting from the third palatalization of the velars. A plosive [g] (also spelt г/h) is now heard in only a few words, chiefly borrowings from Polish such as гу́зік/húzik 'button' /gúzʲik/. Still in the pre-literary period, the Proto-Slavonic nasal vowels were lost: *ǫ became [u], while *ę gave [a] with palatalization of the preceding consonant (though later depalatalization may obscure this), for example, PSl. *mǫžь, *rędъ, Bel. муж/muž 'husband', рад/rad 'row'. In Belorussian the East Slavonic innovatory shift of [e] to [o] before non-palatalized consonants (but with retention of palatalization in the preceding consonant) is limited to stressed syllables, for example, сёлы/sёly (NOM–ACC PL) from сяло́/sjaló 'village' (‹ [sʲeló]), спёка/spёka 'heat' but яго́/jahó 'his' (‹ [jʲeɣó]). This shift must have taken place in the pre-Belorussian dialects before the depalatalization of [šʲ] and [žʲ], since nowhere are these consonants preceded by /ʲo/ – compare Belorussian нясе́ш/njaséš 'you (SG) carry', грабе́ж/hrabéž 'robbery' with Russian несёшь/nesёšʲ [nʲisʲóš] and грабёж/grabёž [grʌbʲóš]. By approximately the thirteenth century, however, the depalatalization of [rʲ] and all palatalized fricatives and affricates was complete in Belorussian. New palatalized dental affricates /cʲ/ and /dzʲ/ arose later (see below).

The loss of the jers in East Slavonic (see chapter 2, section 2.25) produced in Belorussian very much the same developments as in Russian and Ukrainian. Strong ъ and ь gave /o/ and /e/ respectively, with these vowels subject to the same modifications as PSl. *o and *e (/e/ › /o/, ákanne, jákanne). The weak jers were lost, though palatalization of the consonant preceding a weak ь remained in most circumstances, for example, Old Russian сънъ/sъnъ, dative singular съну/sъnu 'sleep', Belorussian сон/son, сну/snu; Old Russian пьнь/рьnь, dative singular пьню/рьnju 'stump', Belorussian пень/penʲ, пню/pnju. An exception to this rule was found in the reflexes of PSl. *СъrC, *СъlC, *СьrC, *СьlC and *СrъC, *СlъC, *СrьC, *СlьC. Here, instead of disappearing and leaving syllabic sonants, weak jers followed the development of strong jers and vocalized. The two types of group – those in which the jer preceded the sonant and those in which it followed it – must be distinguished. In the former the development was uniformly CъrC › CorC, СъlC and СьlC › CowC, СьrC › CerC, hence Belorussian горб/horb 'hump', доўг/douh 'debt', воўк/vouk 'wolf', смерць/smerc´ 'death'. Where the *jers* followed the sonant, strong ones developed as elsewhere, that is, CrъC and CrьC › CroC ([r´] became depalatalized around the same time), ClъC › CloC, ClьC › CleC, giving Belorussian кроў/krou 'blood', плот/plot 'fence', сляза́/sljazá 'tear'. Weak *jers*, however, developed differently: in place of CrъC and CrьC, ClъC, ClьC (mostly in unaccented syllables) Belorussian has /rɨ/, /lɨ/, /li/, this last being only poorly attested, thus крыва́вы/kryvávy 'bloody', трыво́га/tryvóha 'alarm', глыта́ць/hlytác´ 'to swallow'.

The loss of the *jers* brought a number of other changes in its wake. Word-finally, and medially before non-palatalized consonants, Belorussian acquired six new phonemically palatalized consonants (/p´/, /b´/, /m´/, /w´/, /t´/, /d´/) to add to its existing ones (/l´/, /n´/, /r´/, /s´/, /z´/), the frequency of which increased. Of these /r´/ was soon lost completely, the labials became depalatalized pre-consonantally and word-finally and, somewhat later, the dentals /t´/, /d´/ underwent affrication. For the remainder, though word-final palatalization was preserved, in medial position it tended to be lost before the dentals /n/, /s/, /c/, for example, ледзь/ledz´ 'scarcely', рэ́дзька/rèdz´ka 'radish' (‹ *rьdьka), but бе́дны/bédny 'poor' (‹ *bědьnyj). Many new consonant clusters arose through the loss of a *jer* which had previously separated their components. Some of these, including ones which earlier had not been admitted, were now tolerated, for example, /tl/, /dl/ – PSl. *gъrdlo › Belorussian го́рла/hórla 'throat', but *sědъlo › сядло́/sjadló 'saddle'; others were subject to further change. We have already described above the restriction on word-final obstruents and the assimilation of voiced and voiceless obstruents in mixed clusters. Like these developments, many others affecting consonant clusters are not reflected orthographically. Exceptions are the medial triconsonantal clusters /stb/, /stl/, /stn/, /zdn/, /rdn/, /rdc/, which were simplified by the elimination of the middle dental, for example, пасьба́/pas´bá 'pasture' /paz´bá/, по́зні/pózni 'late', сэ́рца/sèrca 'heart'; and a few other sequences in which dissimilation or simplification occurs, for example, што/što 'what' (‹ *čьto), хто/xto 'who' (‹ *kъto), мно́ства/mnóstva 'great number' (‹ *množьstvo). Belorussian shares with Ukrainian its treatment of new clusters of palatalized consonant + /j/ arising from the loss of the *jers*. There was no qualitative change in the consonant preceding /j/ (compare the Proto-Slavonic simplification of these groups); instead, provided the cluster was not itself preceded by another consonant, gemination occurred in dentals and post-dentals, most frequently across a morpheme boundary, for example, пыта́нне/pytánne 'question' (‹ *pytanьje), збо́жжа/zbóžža 'grain' (‹ *zbožьje).

A change in the Belorussian vowel system which followed the loss of the
jers, but was not directly related to it, was the coalescence of /ě/ with /e/,
a consequence of which was the elimination of the Proto-Slavonic morphophonemic alternation between them. At the same time the merger restored
stressed /e/ to a position before a non-palatalized consonant, since /e/
from /ě/ did not in principle participate in the change of /e/ to /o/, for
example, лета/léta 'summer' (‹ *lěta) versus лёт/lët 'flight' (‹ *letъ).
There are, however, exceptions resulting from morphological analogy:
гнёзды/hnëzdy (NOM–ACC PL) from гняздо/hnjazdó 'nest' by analogy
with, say, сёлы/sëly from сяло/sjaló 'village'. As the preceding examples
make clear, /e/ from /ě/ did become subject to *jákanne*.

One of the last changes to occur in the history of Belorussian phonology,
dated by Wexler (1977: 169) to between the fourteenth and sixteenth
centuries, was also one of the most significant for the consonant system:
the affrication of /t'/, /d'/ to /c'/, /dz'/, known in Belorussian as
cékanne and *dzékanne*. Examples are цixi/cixi 'quiet', дзéцi/dzéci
'children'; compare Russian тихий/tixij, дети/déti. Phonetically, this
development created palatalized counterparts for the recently depalatalized
/c/ and the marginal non-palatalized segment /dz/; there are, however, no
minimal pairs involving /dz/ and /dz'/ and very few involving /c/ and
/c'/, such as цэлы/cèly 'whole' and цéлы/cély (NOM–ACC PL) from
цéла/céla 'body'. Much more significant for the shape of Belorussian
phonology was the fact that functionally /c'/ and /dz'/ made pairs with
/t/ and /d/, as in вéцер/vécer 'wind', дзень/dzen' 'day', versus genitive
singular вéтру/vétru, дня/dnja. *Cékanne* and *dzékanne* thus had an effect
on the morphophonemic alternation of consonants in Belorussian comparable to that of *ákanne* and *jákanne* in the vowel system.

2.2   Morphophonemic alternations inherited from Proto-Slavonic

These are mainly morphophonemic alternations which arose through the
successive Proto-Slavonic palatalizations of velar consonants and palatalization processes in /j/ clusters. The first regressive palatalization of velars
has given rise to the Modern Belorussian alternations к–ч/k–č, г–ж/h–ž,
х–ш/x–š as in пяку/pjakú 'I bake', пячэш/pjačéš 'you (SG) bake'; бог/
boh 'god', бажаствó/bažastvó 'deity'; страх/strax 'fear', стрáшны/
strášny 'terrible'. The second regressive palatalization of velars, the earliest
known Proto-Slavonic change to produce different results in different parts
of the Slavonic speech territory, led to the Belorussian alternations к–ц/k–
c, г–з/h–z, х–с/x–s and is particularly in evidence in the noun declension
system in the locative singular of *o*-stem nouns and the dative/locative
singular of *a*-stems, for example, парóг/paróh 'threshold', парóзе/
paróze (LOC SG); рукá/ruká 'hand', руцэ/rucé (DAT–LOC SG); мýха/
múxa 'fly', мýсе/múse (DAT–LOC SG). Prior to the seventeenth century
this alternation was also found in the nominative plural of *o*-stem nouns,

but morphological levelling has eliminated this, for example, Modern Belorussian парогі/paróhi. In the imperative of certain verbs, too, the second palatalization has been eliminated, but in this instance replaced by the first: пячы́/pjačý 'bake', памажы́/pamažý 'help'. Except in the noun suffixes -ец/-ec, -ца/-ca and -іца/-ica, the third (progressive) palatalization of velars is sparsely represented, with just a few alternations of the type княгіня/knjahinja 'princess', князь/knjaz' 'prince'.

The elimination of the /j/ element from Proto-Slavonic clusters of dental, labial or velar + /j/ produced palatalized segments in morphophonemic alternation with non-palatalized ones, most of which have survived into Modern Belorussian. This alternation was particularly productive in verbal morphology: in verbs with a theme in -*i* the Proto-Slavonic palatalization is evident in the form of the stem found in the first person singular non-past tense (also past passive participle and derived imperfective) in contrast with all other forms of the non-past tense; in verbs with a theme in -*je* the palatalized segment characterizes the non-past-tense stem versus the non-palatalized infinitive stem. Another area in which this morphophonemic alternation is common is derivation, since the segment /j/ formed the initial element of a number of suffixes. For the velar consonants the results are identical to those of the first palatalization, thus Belorussian плакаць/plákac' 'to cry', плачу/pláču 'I cry', плачаш/pláčaš 'you (SG) cry' and so on; дух/dux 'spirit', душа/dušá 'soul' (‹ *duxja*). PSl. *sj*, *zj*, *tj*, *dj* shifted to palatalized fricatives, though all have since become depalatalized in Belorussian. This has resulted in the alternations с–ш/s–š, з–ж/z–ž, т–ч/t–č, for example, пісаць/pisác' 'to write', пішу́/pišú 'I write'; мазаць/mázac' 'to grease', мажу/mážu 'I grease'; лапатаць/lapatác' 'to beat', лапачу/lapačú 'I beat'. One would have expected also д–ж/d–ž from *dj*, but in fact, although ж/ž is found as the outcome in, for example, мяжа/mjažá 'boundary' (‹ *medja*), morphophonemically the alternation is д–дж/d–dž, for example, ход/xod 'motion', хаджу/xadžú 'I go'. It is not clear whether дж/dž is an original reflex of *dj* or, as Wexler (1977: 73–4) prefers to interpret it, a later morphologically conditioned development following the affrication of /d'/ to /dz'/ in the infinitive хадзіць/xadzic' and other forms; compare also the alternation зд–здз–здж/zd–zdz–zdž in язда/jazdá 'journey', ездзіць/ézdzic' 'to travel', езджу/ézdžu 'I travel'. The development of the Proto-Slavonic clusters of labial + /j/ has led to the alternations п–пл, б–бл, м–мл, в–ўл/p–pl, b–bl, m–ml, v–ŭl in Belorussian, for example, цярпець/cjarpéc' 'to suffer', цярплю́/cjarpljú 'I suffer'; лавіць/lavic' 'to hunt', лаўлю́/laŭljú 'I hunt'. By the time that foreign words with /f/ were taken into Belorussian, this alternation had become regular in that it was extended to, for example, графіць/hrafic' 'to draw lines', графлю́/hrafljú 'I draw lines'.

Other morphophonemic alternations inherited by Belorussian from

Proto-Slavonic include those resulting from the monophthongization of diphthongs and the simplification of certain consonant clusters. Thus, the creation of nasal vowels (later denasalized) from diphthongs whose second element was *n or *m has led to the alternation of я/ja or a/a with н/n or м/m (sometimes preceded by a vowel), for example, жаць/žac' 'to reap', жну/žnu 'I reap'; узяць/uzjàc' 'to take', вазьму/vaz'mú 'I shall take'; імя/imjà 'name', genitive singular імені/imeni. The monophthongization of Proto-Slavonic *ou to *u has given rise (via *ákanne*) to the characteristic alternation ав–y/av–u between the infinitive and non-past-tense stems of verbs of the type каваць/kavàc' 'to forge', кую/kujù 'I forge'. Changes in the consonant clusters *tt, *dt produced the alternations т–c/t–s and д–с/ d–s, for example, пляту/pljatú 'I weave', плесці/plèsci 'to weave' (‹ *$pletti$); вяду/vjadú 'I lead', весці/vèsci 'to lead' (‹ *$vedti$). Simplification of the groups *dl, *tl, *dn, *pn by the elimination in each case of the initial consonant resulted in alternations of that consonant with zero, for example, упаду/upadú 'I shall fall', упаў/upàŭ 'fell (M SG)' (‹ *$upadlъ$); завядаць/zavjadàc' (IMPFV), завянуць/zavjànuc' (PRFV) 'to fade'. Finally, the elimination of the middle consonant from the cluster *skn has produced the alternation ск–c/sk–s, as in плёскаць/plëskac' (IMPFV), плёснуць/plësnuc' (PRFV) 'to plop'.

2.3 Morphophonemic alternations resulting from changes after Proto-Slavonic

To the morphophonemic alternations inherited from Proto-Slavonic Belorussian has added a considerable number of its own. The loss of the *jers* gave rise to vowel–zero alternations, since in some morphological forms of a word the *jer* was strong and vocalized, while in others it was weak and disappeared, thus ражок/ražók 'horn', genitive singular ражка/ražkà; канец/kanèc 'end', genitive singular канца/kancà. To these two alternations (o–∅ and e–∅) *ákanne* has added a third (a–∅), as in лапак/ làpak (GEN PL) from лапка/làpka 'paw'. The distinctive Belorussian treatment of weak *jers* in the combinations CrъC, ClъC has resulted in the vowel alternation o–ы/o–y, for example, глотка/hlòtka 'gullet', глытаць/hlytàc' 'to swallow'. Other developments consequent on the loss of the *jers* have also given rise to morphophonemic alternations. Thus the change of /e/ to /o/ has produced the alternation e–ё/e–ë, for instance, нясеш/njasèš 'you (SG) carry', нясём/njasëm 'we carry', to which, courtesy of *jákanne*, one may add я–ё/ja–ë, as in ярша/jaršà (GEN SG) from ёрш/ёrš 'ruff' (fish). The depalatalization of [r'], [č'],]dž'], [š'] and [ž'] created a third variant: э–o/è–o, as in шэсць/šèsc' '6', шосты/šósty 'sixth'. Final devoicing has given rise to alternations because in different forms of a given word a consonant may appear now word-finally, now before a vowel, for example, нож/nož 'knife' /noš/, genitive singular нажа/nažà /nažà/. Similar alternations of voiced and unvoiced consonants occur medially where there is a vowel–zero alternation resulting from the loss of a *jer*, as in гарадо́к/haradók 'small town' /ɣaradók/, genitive singular гарадка́/haradká that is, /ɣaratká/. The elimination of the middle dental from certain triconsonantal clusters (see 2.1 above) has led to consonant–zero alternations, as in чэсць/čèsc′ 'honour', чэсны/čèsny 'honest'; сардэ́чны/sardèčny 'cordial', сэ́рца/sèrca 'heart'.

Particularly striking in Belorussian are the vowel alternations which have arisen from the combination of *ákanne* and *jákanne* with mobile stress. They occur widely in both the stems and morphological endings of all inflected categories, thereby endowing Belorussian inflectional morphology with a high degree of surface complexity. The alternations concerned are the following: stressed ó/ó with unstressed a/a, for example, го́рад/hórad 'town', nominative–accusative plural гарады́/haradý; stressed э́/è with unstressed a/a, for example, трэ́сці/trèsci 'to shake', трасу́/trasú 'I shake'; stressed е́/è with unstressed я/ja, for example, сме́ла/smèla 'boldly', смяле́й/smjalèj 'more boldly'; and stressed ё/ё with unstressed я/ja, for example, нясём/njasëm 'we carry', несяце́/nesjacè 'you (PL) carry'. A particular variant of the stressed ó/ó – unstressed a/a alternation is found where the stressed vowel historically occurred word-initially: /v/-prothesis has produced the alternation во́-a/vó-a, as in во́зера/vózera 'lake', nominative–accusative plural азёры/azëry.

In the consonant system, equally striking are the alternations produced by *cékanne* and *dzékanne*: т–ц/t–c and д–дз/d–dz, for example, indeterminate imperfective лята́ць/ljatác′, determinate imperfective ляце́ць/ljacèc′ 'to fly'; наро́д/naród 'people, nation', locative singular наро́дзе/naródze; and, with /v/ intervening between dental and vowel, два/dva 'two (NON-ACC M N–N)', дзве/dzve (F). The restriction of /v/ to a pre-vocalic position has produced the alternation в–ў/v–ŭ, as in плыве́ц/plyvèc 'swimmer', accusative–genitive singular плыўца́/plyŭcá. A similar alternation between л/l and ў/ŭ is morphophonemically restricted to the past tense of verbs: быў/byŭ (M SG) 'was' versus была́/bylá (F), было́/byló (N), былі́/bylí (PL).

3   Morphology

As mentioned in section 2.3, the morphophonemic alternations brought about by *ákanne* and, to a lesser extent, *jákanne* have given the Belorussian declension and conjugation systems a considerable degree of complexity, at least on the surface. Accordingly, in the tables accompanying this section we have, where appropriate, subdivided declension and conjugation types into ending-stressed and stem-stressed.

3.1 Nominal morphology

3.1.1 Nominal categories

Modern standard Belorussian has two numbers, six cases and three genders. As in all the Slavonic languages except Slovene and Sorbian, the dual number has been lost. Remnants survive only in the numerals два/dva, дзве/dzve '2' and дзвесце/dzvésce '200' and the anomalous plurals вочы/vóču from вока/vóka 'eye', вушы/vúšy from вуха/vúxa 'ear' and плечы/pléču from плячо/pljačó 'shoulder', though this last would be the expected plural in any case (see 3.1.2). More interestingly, an instrumental plural in -ыма/-yma, derived from the old dual, has recently become accepted as a stylistically neutral alternative to -амі/-ami for these three nouns plus the *pluralia tantum* грошы/hróšy 'money' and дзверы/dzvéry 'door': thus вачыма/vačýma, грашыма/hrašýma, дзвярыма/dzvjarýma and so on. The vocative case can no longer be regarded as a living category in the standard language, which has only the remnants божа/bóža from бог/boh 'god' (as an exclamation) and браце/bráce from брат/brat 'brother', дружа/drúža from друг/druh 'friend' and сынку/sýnku (with stress shift) from сынок/synók 'son' (as modes of address). The category of animacy (accusative = genitive) in Belorussian embraces all genders in the plural, but in the singular only the masculine (in the noun declension *o*-stem only). It is extended to the figurative usage of such nouns, for example, узяць слана/uzjác' slaná 'to take a bishop' (chess), as well as the figurative usage of normally inanimate nouns, as in узяць языка/uzjác' jazyká 'to take a prisoner' (literally: 'to take a tongue'). Finally, it should be noted that the unreduced instrumental singular endings shown in parentheses in tables 16.3–16.6 are rarely encountered in the standard language.

3.1.2 Noun morphology

In table 16.3 we show the main noun declension types. A unique Belorussian innovation is the extension of the nominative–accusative plural ending -ы/-y to *o*-stem neuter nouns, as shown in the table by сёлы/sóly and дрэвы/drévy. A further innovation, brought about by the effects of *ákanne*, is the coincidence of the nominative singular ending of non-palatalized *a*-stem nouns and *o*-stem neuter nouns with stem stress, as illustrated in the table by бяроза/bjaróza and дрэва/dréva. From the form alone it is therefore impossible to predict the declension type of such nouns. The same is not true of palatalized variants of the two types since, in accordance with the general rules governing the orthographical reflection of *jákanne*, e/e remains in post-stress position, thus *a*-stem песня/pésnja 'song' but *o*-stem поле/póle 'field'. Note, however, anomalous 'morphological' post-stress *jákanne* in the *a*-stem instrumental singular, for example, песняй/pésnjaj, and in the variant -яў/-jaŭ of the genitive plural

Table 16.3   Belorussian noun declension

(a)   *Masculine o-stem*   *Neuter o-stem*

Singular

NOM	стол 'table'	горад 'town'	сялó 'village'	дрэ́ва 'tree'*
ACC	стол	горад	сялó	дрэ́ва
GEN	сталá	горада	сялá	дрэ́ва
DAT	сталý	гораду	сялý	дрэ́ву
INST	сталóм	горадам	сялóм	дрэ́вам
LOC	сталé	горадзе	сялé	дрэ́ве

Plural

NOM	сталы́	гарады́	сёлы	дрэ́вы
ACC	сталы́	гарады́	сёлы	дрэ́вы
GEN	сталóў	гарадóў	сёл	дрэў
DAT	сталáм	гарадáм	сёлам	дрэ́вам
INST	сталáмі	гарадáмі	сёламі	дрэ́вамі
LOC	сталáх	гарадáх	сёлах	дрэ́вах

	a-stem		*i-stem*

Singular

NOM	галавá 'head'*	бяро́за 'birch'	косць 'bone'
ACC	галавý	бяро́зу	косць
GEN	галавы́	бяро́зы	ко́сці
DAT	галавé	бяро́зе	ко́сці
INST	галавóй (-óю)	бяро́зай (-аю)	ко́сцю
LOC	галавé	бяро́зе	ко́сці

Plural

NOM	гало́вы	бяро́зы	ко́сці
ACC	гало́вы	бяро́зы	ко́сці
GEN	гало́ў	бяро́з	касце́й
DAT	галавáм	бяро́зам	касця́м
INST	галавáмі	бяро́замі	касця́мі
LOC	галавáх	бяро́зах	касця́х

Note: *Reflexes of *město and *žena are not available in Belorussian.

(b)   *Masculine o-stem*   *Neuter o-stem*

Singular

NOM	stol 'table'	hórad 'town'	sjaló 'village'	drèva 'tree'*
ACC	stol	hórad	sjaló	drèva
GEN	stalá	hórada	sjalá	drèva
DAT	stalú	hóradu	sjalú	drèvu
INST	stalóm	hóradam	sjalóm	drèvam
LOC	stalé	hóradze	sjalé	drève

Table 16.3 continued

	Masculine o-stem		Neuter o-stem	
Plural				
NOM	stalẏ	haradẏ	s̈ely	drẹ̀vy
ACC	stalẏ	haradẏ	s̈ely	drèvy
GEN	stalòu̇	haradòu̇	s̈el	drèu̇
DAT	stalàm	haradàm	s̈elam	drèvam
INST	stalàmi	haradàmi	s̈elami	drẹ̀vami
LOC	stalàx	haradàx	s̈elax	drèvax

	a-stem		i-stem
Singular			
NOM	halavà 'head'*	bjaròza 'birch'	kosc' 'bone'
ACC	halavù	bjaròzu	kosc'
GEN	halavẏ	bjaròzy	kòsci
DAT	halavè	bjaròze	kòsci
INST	halavòj (-òju)	bjaròzaj (-aju)	kòscju
LOC	halavè	bjaròze	kòsci
Plural			
NOM	halòvy	bjaròzy	kòsci
ACC	halòvy	bjaròzy	kòsci
GEN	halòu̇	bjaròz	kascèj
DAT	halavàm	bjaròzam	kascjàm
INST	halavàmi	bjaròzami	kascjàmi
LOC	halavàx	bjaròzax	kascjàx

Note: *Reflexes of *město and *žena are not available in Belorussian.

of all declensions (for examples see below).

Apart from the animate category mentioned above, important variants of the basic types illustrated occur mainly in the o-stem and a-stem declensions, especially in the locative singular of the former and the dative/locative singular of the latter. Here nouns with a stem ending in a palatalized consonant, which otherwise share the same endings as their non-palatalized counterparts (albeit differently spelled), retain a reflex of the old Proto-Slavonic jo-stem and ja-stem ending, for example, агнì/ahni from агóнь/ahòn' 'fire'; зямлì/zjamli from зямля́/zjamljà 'land'. Those with stems ending in the formerly palatalized consonants ч, ж, ш, ц, р/č, ž, š, c, r have the same ending in the morphophonemic variant -ы/-y, thus на нажы́/na nažẏ 'on the knife'; пра́цы/pràcy from пра́ца/pràca 'work'. Also well preserved in these cases is the second palatalization of velars: рука́/rukà 'hand, arm', нага́/nahà 'leg, foot', dative–locative singular руцэ́/rucè, назе́/nazè; у гарóце/u haròse 'in the peas', from гарóх/haròx. In the o-stem locative singular, however, the second palatalization is obviated by the use of the old *ŭ*-stem locative ending -y/-u for all nouns with a stem in к/k and for those with a stem in г, х/h, x denoting abstract concepts, thus у во́ку/u vóku 'in the eye', аб по́дзвігу/ab pódzvihu 'about the feat'. Semantic criteria determine the use of this same ending in nouns with a stem in a palatalized or formerly palatalized consonant which denote human beings, for example, аб ву́чню, песняру́/ab vúčnju, pesnjarú 'about the pupil, poet', from ву́чань/vúčan´ and пясня́р/pjasnjár respectively. *Cékanne* and *dzékanne* cause mutation of stem-final т, д/t, d, as illustrated in the table by го́радзе/hóradze and similarly in nouns like плане́та/planéta 'planet', dative–locative singular плане́це/planéce. A feature of the masculine *o*-stem declension not revealed by the table is the regularity of the former *ŭ*-stem genitive singular ending -y/-u in abstract nouns and those denoting materials and substances or collectives; thus лёс/lës 'fate', тыту́нь/tytún´ 'tobacco', нато́уп/natóŭp 'crowd' have genitive singular лёсу/lësu, тытуню́/tytunjú, нато́упу/natóŭpu.

Variants within the *i*-stem declension are few, but two are worthy of mention. Firstly, the depalatalization of ч, ж, ш, ц, р/č, ž, š, c, r has resulted in a non-palatalized subtype with appropriately different spelling of the case endings: мыш/myš 'mouse', шыр/šyr 'expanse', genitive singular мы́шы/mýšu, шы́ры/šýry and so on. Secondly, the instrumental singular exhibits a doubling of (single) stem-final consonants except labials and р/r, thus дало́нню/dalónnju from дало́нь/dalón´ 'palm', пе́ччу/péčču from печ/peč 'stove', but глы́б'ю/hlýb´ju from глыб/hlyb 'depth'.

A strong tendency towards generalization is observable in the genitive plural of Belorussian nouns, with the extension of the characteristic masculine *o*-stem ending (morphophonemically {-ow}, appearing in four variants -о́ў, -аў, -ёў, -яў/-óŭ, -aŭ, -ëŭ, -jaŭ depending on stress and the nature of the preceding consonant) not only, as might perhaps be expected, to neuter nouns within the same declension, but also to other declension types. This is very much a live tendency in Modern Belorussian, with a wide dialect base. Consistent predictive criteria for it are, however, difficult to identify, since in identical morphophonemic environments it may or may not occur or, more accurately, may or may not be recognized as standard. For the moment, too, it is most frequently acknowledged as an alternative; thus among *o*-stem neuter nouns we find such generally accepted pairs as ако́н/akón and во́кнаў/vóknaŭ from акно́/aknó 'window', вёсел/vësel and вёслаў/vëslaŭ from вясло́/vjasló 'oar'; among *a*-stem nouns зяме́ль/zjamél´ and зе́мляў/zémljaŭ from зямля́/zjamljá 'land', бомб/bomb and бо́мбаў/bómbaŭ from бо́мба/bómba 'bomb'; among *i*-stem nouns дро́бязей/dróbjazej and дро́бязяў/dróbjazjaŭ from дро́бязь/dróbjaz´ 'trifle'. Nouns of the *a*-stem and *i*-stem declensions in which the ending {-ow} is the sole recognized form, for example, ро́ляў/róljaŭ from ро́ля/rólja 'role', рэ́чаў/rèčaŭ from рэч/rèč 'thing', remain few, with the exception of *a*-stem nouns whose stem ends in a cluster of consonants, for example, бі́тваў/bítvaŭ from бі́тва/bítva 'battle', го́сцяў/hóscjaŭ from го́сця/hóscja '(female) guest', where it is widespread though not (yet?) universal. Among neuter *o*-stem nouns only those with a palatalized stem-final consonant consistently show it: палёў/palёŭ from по́ле/póle 'field', пыта́нняў/pytánnjaŭ from пыта́нне/pytánne 'question'.

Belorussian has a high, but not exclusive, correlation between gender and declension type. The *i*-stem declension is the most exclusive since, with a single masculine exception, *i*-stem nouns are all feminine. The exception is the traditional Slavonic one пуць/puc′, semantically limited in Belorussian to the sense '(railway) track'. The *o*-stem declension is divided, as we have seen, between masculine and neuter nouns. While most *a*-stem nouns are feminine, this declension type also includes masculine nouns – all, apart from сабáка/sabáka 'dog', with clear male reference – and a significant number of nouns of common gender, that is, masculine or feminine according to sense. Moreover, in both groups male reference has resulted in variants on the basic declensional endings in the dative, instrumental and locative singular. These variants reflect the close correlation between gender and declension type in that they consist in the adoption of masculine *o*-stem endings as in, for example, бáцьку/bác′ku (DAT–LOC SG), бáцькам/bác′kam (INST SG) from бáцька/bác′ka 'father'; калéку/kaléku (DAT–LOC SG), калéкам/kalékam (INST SG) from калéка/kaléka '(male) cripple'. Masculine *a*-stem nouns with stress on the ending, however, decline like feminines, as do, naturally enough, those of common gender when feminine, thus суддзі́/suddzí (DAT–LOC SG), суддзёй/suddzёj (INST SG) from суддзя́/suddzjá 'judge'; калéцы/kalécy (DAT–LOC SG), калéкай/kalékaj (INST SG) from калéка/kaléka '(female) cripple'.

The interaction of declensional types illustrated in several of the features discussed above is part of a general process of merger of declension in the evolution of Belorussian from Proto-Slavonic which has included the absorption of almost all minor declension types by the three main ones. The *ŭ*-stem declension has merged with the *o*-stem though, as we have seen, it has left its mark in the genitive and locative singular and in the genitive plural where the infix *-ov-*, after the loss of the following *jer*, was re-interpreted as an ending. Former masculine *i*-stem nouns, with the exception of пуць/puc′ mentioned above, have adapted to the palatalized variant of the *o*-stem declension, for example, госць/hosc′ 'guest', genitive singular го́сця/hóscja. The few former *u*-stem nouns that have survived into Modern Belorussian have assimilated fully to one of the two feminine declension types, for example, смо́ква/smókva 'fig' (*a*-stem) from PSl. *smoky*, свякро́ў/svjakróŭ 'mother-in-law', genitive singular свекрыві́/svekryví (*i*-stem) from PSl. *svekry*. Only among consonant-stems is there some evidence of the continuation of earlier declension patterns, mainly in the form of stem alternation. Thus *t*-stems – neuter nouns denoting the young of animals, including дзіця/dzicjá 'child' in the singular only – have the stem formant -яц-(-ят-)/-jac-(-jat-) in all cases other than the nominative–accusative and (a Belorussian innovation) instrumental singular, for example, цяля (цялё)/cjaljá (cjalë) 'calf' has genitive singular цяляці/cjaljáci, instrumental singular цялём/cjalëm, nominative plural цаляты/cjaljáty. In terms of declension, however, these nouns have adapted in the singular to the *i*-stem type (neuter *o*-stem in the instrumental) and in the plural to the *o*-stem. With *n*-stems there is even greater evidence of adaptation, since alongside, for example, імя/imjá 'name', імені/imeni (GEN SG), іменем/imenem (INST SG), імёны/iměny (NOM–ACC PL), there is an alternative declension, without stem alternation, according to the neuter *o*-stem type (palatalized variant): імя/imjá (GEN SG), імем/imem (INST SG), імі/imi (NOM–ACC PL) and so on. Indeed, of this group of nouns only імя/imjá, племя/plémja 'tribe' and стрэмя/strèmja 'stirrup' retain the longer forms; the rest have adapted fully to the *o*-stem declension. The *r*-stem noun маці/máci 'mother' may either decline (with stem formant -ep-/-er-) in the singular according to the *a*-stem and in the plural according to the *i*-stem type, or – another Belorussian innovation – be indeclinable.

3.1.3   Pronominal morphology

The declension of the personal pronouns is shown in full in table 16.4, from which it will be evident that Belorussian has no clitics. The reflexive pronoun сябе/sjabé, which has no nominative form, is otherwise declined like ты/ty. The distribution of the Proto-Slavonic ablaut variants of the stem in these two pronouns though somewhat obscured by *cékanne* and *jákanne*, is: accusative–genitive *teb-, *seb-; dative–instrumental–locative *tob-, *sob-. In Belorussian, personal pronouns distinguish gender only in the third person singular, all three forms of which thus have the anaphoric function of English *it*, depending on the gender of the antecedent. Two uniquely Belorussian innovations in the third-person pronoun are the extension of the initial /j/ element of the other cases to the nominative, and the total absence of prothetic /n/, thus ад яго/ad jahó 'from him, from it', з ёй/z ëj 'with her, with it' and so on. Not unique, since shared with Polish and Sorbian, is the syncretism of the instrumental and locative singular forms of the masculine and neuter third-person pronoun, which is carried over into the declension of other pronouns and adjectives.

First- and second-person possessive pronouns (see the example мой/ moj in table 16.4) are fully declined, distinguishing case, number and – in the singular – gender. Third-person possessive pronouns, on the other hand, are usually invariable forms identical with the genitive case of the personal pronoun: яго/jahó 'his, its', яе/jae 'her, its', іх/ix 'their'. Note,

Table 16.4   Belorussian pronominal declension

(a)   Personal

	1st	2nd	3rd M	N	F	1st	2nd	3rd all genders
		Singular					*Plural*	
NOM	я	ты	ён	яно́	яна́	мы	вы	яны́
ACC	мяне́	цябе́	яго́	яго́	яе́	нас	вас	іх
GEN	мяне́	цябе́	яго́	яго́	яе́	нас	вас	іх
DAT	мне	табе́	яму́	яму́	ёй	нам	вам	ім
INST	мной (-о́ю)	табо́й (-о́ю)	ім	ім	ёй, ёю	на́мі	ва́мі	імі
LOC	мне	табе́	ім	ім	ёй	нас	вас	іх

Possessive   Interrogative

	M	N	F	All genders		
NOM	мой 'my'	мае́	мая́	мае́	хто 'who'	што 'what'
ACC	= NOM/GEN	мае́	маю́	= NOM/GEN	каго́	што
GEN	майго́	майго́	мае́й	маіх	каго́	чаго́
DAT	майму́	майму́	мае́й	маім	каму́	чаму́
INST	маім	маім	мае́й (-ёю)	маімі	кім	чым
LOC	маім	маім	мае́й	маіх	кім	чым

увесь 'all'

	M	N	F	Plural all genders
		Singular		
NOM	уве́сь	усё	уся́	усе́
ACC	= NOM/GEN	усё	усю́	= NOM/GEN
GEN	усяго́	усяго́	усе́й, усяе́	усіх
DAT	усяму́	усяму́	усе́й	усім
INST	усім	усім	усе́й (-ёю)	усімі
LOC	усім	усім	усе́й	усіх

(b)   Personal

	1st	2nd	3rd M	N	F	1st	2nd	3rd all genders
		Singular					*Plural*	
NOM	ja	ty	ën	janó	janá	my	vy	janý
ACC	mjané	cjabé	jahó	jahó	jaé	nas	vas	ix
GEN	mjané	cjabé	jahó	jahó	jaé	nas	vas	ix
DAT	mne	tabé	jamú	jamú	ëj	nam	vam	im
INST	mnoj (-óju)	tabój (-óju)	im	im	ëj, ëju	námi	vámi	imi
LOC	mne	tabé	im	im	ëj	nas	vas	ix

| Possessive | | | | Interrogative | |
| | *Singular* | | *Plural* | | |
M	N	F	*all genders*		
NOM	moj 'my'	maë	majá	maë	xto 'who'	što 'what'
ACC	= NOM/GEN	maë	majú	= NOM/GEN	kahó	što
GEN	majhó	majhó	maëj	maix	kahó	čahó
DAT	majmú	majmú	maëj	maim	kamú	čamú
INST	maim	maim	maëj (-ëju)	maimi	kim	čym
LOC	maim	maim	maëj	maix	kim	čym

uvës´ 'all'

| | *Singular* | | | *Plural* |
M	N	F	*all genders*
NOM	uvës´	usë	usjá	usë
ACC	= NOM/GEN	usë	usjú	= NOM/GEN
GEN	usjahó	usjahó	usëj, usjaë	usix
DAT	usjamú	usjamú	usëj	usim
INST	usim	usim	usëj (-ëju)	usimi
LOC	usim	usim	usëj	usix

however, the recently acquired stylistic neutrality (Атраховіч/Atraxovič 1977–84 *sub verbo*) of іхні/ixni 'their' which is declined as an adjective with a palatalized stem. Ягоны/jahóny 'his, its' and ейны/éjny 'her, its', both declined as stem-stressed adjectives with a non-palatalized stem, are common in works of literature but, for the moment at least, retain in dictionaries the usage label 'colloquial'. Like мой/moj are declined твой/ tvoj 'your (SG)' and the reflexive possessive свой/svoj 'one's own'; наш/ naš 'our' and ваш/vaš 'your (PL or polite SG)' are declined as stem-stressed adjectives with non-palatalized stem, except in the nominative and inanimate accusative, where they have noun endings; thus ваш сын/vaš syn 'your son', ваша кніга/váša kniha 'your book', accusative вашу кнігу/vášu knihu, ваша пісьмо/váša pis´mó 'your letter', вашы ідэі/vášy idèi 'your ideas'.

Also shown in table 16.4 is the declension of the interrogative (and relative) pronouns хто/xto 'who' and што/što 'what', and of the pronoun увесь/uvës´ 'all'. (The demonstrative той/toj 'that' is not illustrated since it has adapted fully to the adjectival declension.) Of other pronouns чый/ čyj 'whose' declines like мой/moj, while the remainder broadly follow the adjectival declension, albeit with certain idiosyncrasies. Perhaps most idiosyncratic of all is the emphatic pronoun сам/sam 'oneself', which everywhere substitutes i/i for ы/y in its endings, thus masculine–neuter genitive singular самога/samóha, but instrumental–locative самім/ samim.

Indefinite pronouns in Belorussian are formed from other pronouns both by prefixation and by suffixation. Thus from хто/xto 'who', for example, are derived нѐхта/nѐxta and хтóсьці/xtós′ci. абы-хтó/aby-xtó and хто-нѐбудзь/xto-nѐbudz′, and this pattern is repeated with other pronouns. There is a broad semantic distinction between those formed with нѐ-/nѐ- and -сьці/-s′ci, on the one hand, and those formed with абы-/ aby- and -нѐбудзь/-nѐbudz′, on the other: the first pair denote 'someone, etc.' specific, but unidentified; while the second carry the implication of choice – 'anyone, etc. (at all)'. Using our examples based on хто/xto we may contrast нѐхта (хтóсьці) пастýкаў у акнó/nѐxta (xtós′ci) pastú-kaŭ u aknó 'someone knocked at the window' with ці пры̀йдзе хто-нѐ-будзь?/ci prýjdze xto-nѐbudz′? 'will anyone come?'.

3.1.4 Adjectival morphology

Table 16.5 illustrates the pronominal adjectival declension of Belorussian. For adjectives with a non-palatalized stem both stem-stressed (showing *ákanne*) and ending-stressed variants are exemplified, by нóвы/nóvy and малады̀/maladý respectively. The only other variant on this type are adjectives with a velar stem, such as дарагí/darahi 'dear', which, because of the rule that к, г, х/k, h, x cannot be followed by ы/y, have i/i instead in the appropriate endings. There are no ending-stressed adjectives with a palatalized stem, but note the consistent presence of 'morphological' post-stress *jákanne* in the stem-stressed type асѐнні/asѐnni. The higher degree of syncretism relative to Old Russian or Proto-Slavonic is seen in the singu-lar in the coincidence of the masculine and neuter instrumental and loca-tive forms, and in the plural with the loss of gender distinction. The variant endings of the feminine genitive singular both derive from the Old Russian ending -оѣ/-oě: -oe/-oe is a direct continuation of the earlier ending following the merger of [ě] and [e], while -ой/-oj has arisen through elision of the final vowel.

An unproductive category in Modern Belorussian is the short (nominal) form derived from a relatively small number of qualitative adjectives. Where found, it is used solely in the predicate and does not decline, though gender and number are distinguished, for example, from гатóвы/hatóvy 'ready, prepared' we have masculine singular гатóў/hatóŭ, feminine–neuter singular гатóва/hatóva, plural (all genders) гатóвы/hatóvy. More characteristic of Belorussian, however, is the use of the long (pronominal) form in predicative as well as attributive functions, compare маладáя жанчы̀на/maladája žančýna 'young woman' and жанчы̀на былá зусім маладáя/žančýna bylá zusim maladája 'the woman was very young'. Even those few short-form adjectives in regular use will often be merely alter-natives to the long forms, for example, ён бýдзе таксáма рад (рáды)/ën búdze taksáma rad (rády) 'he too will be glad'. Only in the nominative and inanimate accusative of possessive adjectives does the short form survive

Table 16.5 Belorussian adjectival declension

(a)

	Singular			Plural
	M	N	F	all genders

Non-palatalized stem

NOM	но́вы 'new'	но́вае	но́вая	но́выя
ACC	= NOM/GEN	но́вае	но́вую	= NOM/GEN
GEN	но́вага	но́вага	но́вай, но́вае	но́вых
DAT	но́ваму	но́ваму	но́вай	но́вым
INST	но́вым	но́вым	но́вай (-аю)	но́вымі
LOC	но́вым	но́вым	но́вай	но́вых

NOM	малады́ 'young'	маладо́е	маладая́	малады́я
ACC	= NOM/GEN	маладо́е	маладу́ю	= NOM/GEN
GEN	маладо́га	маладо́га	маладо́й, маладо́е	малады́х
DAT	маладо́му	маладо́му	маладо́й	малады́м
INST	малады́м	малады́м	маладо́й (-о́ю)	малады́мі
LOC	малады́м	малады́м	маладо́й	малады́х

Palatalized stem

NOM	асе́нні 'autumn'	асе́нняе	асе́нняя	асе́ннія
ACC	= NOM/GEN	асе́нняе	асе́ннюю	= NOM/GEN
GEN	асе́нняга	асе́нняга	асе́нняй, асе́нняе	асе́нніх
DAT	асе́нняму	асе́нняму	асе́нняй	асе́ннім
INST	асе́ннім	асе́ннім	асе́нняй (-яю)	асе́ннімі
LOC	асе́ннім	асе́ннім	асе́нняй	асе́нніх

(b)

	Singular			Plural
	M	N	F	all genders

Non-palatalized stem

NOM	no´vy 'new'	no´vae	no´vaja	no´vyja
ACC	= NOM/GEN	no´vae	no´vuju	= NOM/GEN
GEN	no´vaha	no´vaha	no´vaj, no´vae	no´vyx
DAT	no´vamu	no´vamu	no´vaj	no´vym
INST	no´vym	no´vym	no´vaj (-aju)	no´vymi
LOC	no´vym	no´vym	no´vaj	no´vyx

NOM	malady´ 'young'	malado´e	malada´ja	malady´ja
ACC	= NOM/GEN	malado´e	maladu´ju	= NOM/GEN
GEN	malado´ha	malado´ha	malado´j, malado´e	malady´x
DAT	malado´mu	malado´mu	malado´j	malady´m
INST	malady´m	malady´m	malado´j (-o´ju)	malady´mi
LOC	malady´m	malady´m	malado´j	malady´x

Palatalized stem

NOM	ase´nni 'autumn'	ase´nnjae	ase´nnjaja	ase´nnija
ACC	= NOM/GEN	ase´nnjae	ase´nnjuju	= NOM/GEN
GEN	ase´nnjaha	ase´nnjaha	ase´nnjaj, ase´nnjae	ase´nnix
DAT	ase´nnjamu	ase´nnjamu	ase´nnjaj	ase´nnim
INST	ase´nnim	ase´nnim	ase´nnjaj (-jaju)	ase´nnimi
LOC	ase´nnim	ase´nnim	ase´nnjaj	ase´nnix

with an attributive function: дзе́даў брат/dzèdaŭ brat 'grandfather's brother', краўцо́ва ме́рка/kraŭcòva mèrka 'tailor's measure'.

To form the comparative and superlative degrees of adjectives Belorussian employs both synthetic and analytic methods. The synthetic comparative is formed by means of the suffix -е́йш-(-э́йш-)/-ėjš-(-ėjš-) plus pronominal adjectival endings, thus навейшы/navèjšy, маладзейшы/maladzėjšy, старэйшы/starèjšy, from но́вы/nòvy 'new', малады́/maladý 'young', стары́/starý 'old' respectively. The fact that the suffix is invariably stressed leads to *ákanne* and *jákanne* in the stem of the adjective, as exemplified by навейшы/navèjšy above and, for example, бялейшы/bjalèjšy from бе́лы/bèly 'white', зелянейшы/zeljanèjšy from зялёны/zjalëny 'green'. With some lexical items the stem suffixes -ок-(-ёк-, -к-)/-ok-(-ëk-, -k-) are dropped in this process, thus in глыбейшы/hlybèjšy from глыбо́кі/hlybòki 'deep', далейшы/dalèjšy from далёкі/dalëki 'far', вузейшы/vuzèjšy from ву́зкі/vùzki 'narrow'. This may also entail a change in the final consonant of the stem, as in вышэйшы/vyšèjšy from высо́кі/vysòki 'high'. Where the stem suffix -к-/-k- is preserved and also where the stem ends in г/h or х/x, the synthetic comparative exhibits the first palatalization of velars, for example, крапчэйшы/krapčèjšy, цішэйшы/cišèjšy from крэ́пкі/krèpki 'strong' and ці́хі/cìxi 'quiet'. The synthetic superlative is formed by the addition of the prefix най-/naj- to the comparative.

The analytic comparative is formed by combining the adverb больш/bol´š with the positive degree of the adjective, for example, больш гра́зкі/bol´š hràzki 'muddier'. Similarly, an analytic superlative may be formed with the aid of the adverb найбо́льш/najbòl´š: найбо́льш гра́зкі/najbòl´š hràzki 'muddiest'. An alternative analytic superlative is created by combining the (declinable) emphatic pronoun са́мы/sàmy with the positive – or, for particular emphasis, synthetic comparative – degree of the adjective, thus са́мы мо́цны/sàmy mòcny or са́мы мацнейшы/sàmy macnèjšy 'most powerful'.

Suppletive formations in Belorussian are as follows: до́бры/dòbry 'good' – ле́пшы/lèpšy 'better'; дрэ́нны/drènny or благі́/blahi 'bad' – го́ршы/hòršy 'worse'; вялікі/vjaliki 'big' – бо́льшы/bòl´šy 'bigger'; малы́/malý 'small' – ме́ншы/mènšy 'smaller'. In each case the superlative is formed by the addition of the prefix най-/naj-.

Adverbs derived from adjectives have the ending -а/-a (under stress, -о́/-ò) after a hard consonant, -е/-e following a soft consonant, for example, бага́та/bahàta 'richly', даўно́/daŭnò 'long ago', лішне/lišne 'too, excessively'. The comparative and superlative are formed in the same way as for adjectives: analytically by combining больш/bol´š and найбо́льш/najbòl´š with the positive degree; synthetically by means of the suffix -ей(-эй)/-ėj(-èj) and, for the superlative, of the prefix най-/naj-, with the same consonant mutations and other changes to the stem:

глыбе́й/hlybéj 'more deeply', вышэ́й/vyšéj 'more highly', найглыбе́й/najhlybéj 'most deeply' and so on.

3.1.5   Numeral morphology

The declension types for cardinal numerals are shown in table 16.6. Except in the nominative and inanimate accusative, the numeral '1' declines like an ending-stressed adjective with a non-palatalized stem. Note, however, that in the genitive singular and in the masculine and neuter dative singular it is the *final* syllable of the ending which is stressed. The plural form of '1' is used with *pluralia tantum* such as вíлкi/vílki 'pitchfork', са́нi/sáni 'sledge'. For the numeral '2' Belorussian has a distinct feminine form for all cases; або́два (абе́дзве)/abódva (abédzve) 'both' follows the same pattern. The instrumental endings of '2, 3, 4' are a relic of the dual number. Like the numeral '5' (*i*-stem type) decline '6'–'20' and '30'; like '50' (also *i*-stem type, but with both elements changing) are declined '60', '70', '80'. The hundreds ('200'–'900') also have both elements changing, the second on the pattern of *o*-stem nouns in the plural. The numerals '40' со́рак/sórak and '100' сто/sto have a single form for all cases except the nominative–accusative: сарака́/saraká, ста/sta.   Дзевяно́ста/dzevjanósta '90', though originally following the same pattern, is now indeclinable as a result of *ákanne* in the final vowel of the nominative–accusative. Ты́сяча/týsjača 'thousand' declines as an *a*-stem noun with an alternative instrumental singular ты́сяччу/týsjačču; мiльён/mil'én 'million' is a masculine *o*-stem noun. In compound cardinal numerals each word declines, for example, genitive трохсо́т пяцiдзесяцi шасцi/troxsót pjacidzesjaci šasci from тры́ста пяцьдзесят шэсць/trýsta pjac'dzesját šesc' '356'. Colloquially, however, there is a tendency towards non-declension of all but the final element of such forms.

Special collective numerals дво́е/dvóe '2', тро́е/tróe '3', чацвёра/čacvéra '4' up to дзеся́цера/dzesjácera '10' are used with pluralia tantum, nouns denoting the young of animals, collectives such as лю́дзi/ljúdzi 'people', and – optionally – nouns denoting male human beings. Дво́е/dvóe and трое/tróe decline like the plural of мой/moj (see table 16.4), чацвёра/čacvéra and so on like the plural of адзíн/adzin.

Ordinal numerals in Belorussian are, with three exceptions, stem-stressed adjectives with a non-palatalized stem: пе́ршы/péršy 'first', сёмы/sémy 'seventh', пяцiдзеся́ты/pjacidzesjáty 'fiftieth'. The exceptions are: другí/druhi 'second' (ending-stressed velar stem), трэ́цi/tréci 'third' (palatalized stem) and саракавы́/sarakavý 'fortieth' (ending-stressed non-palatalized stem). Only the final element of compound ordinal numerals is ordinal and declines; the other elements are cardinal and remain unchanged: тры́ста пяцьдзесят шо́сты/trýsta pjac'dzesját šósty 'three hundred and fifty-sixth', masculine–neuter genitive singular тры́ста пяцьдзесят шо́стага/trýsta pjac'dzesját šóstaha and so on.

Table 16.6 Belorussian numeral declension

(a)

	M	Singular N	F	Plural all genders
NOM	адзі́н '1'	адно́	адна́	адны́
ACC	= NOM/GEN	адно́	адньу́	= NOM/GEN
GEN	аднаго́	аднаго́	адно́й, аднае́	адны́х
DAT	аднаму́	аднаму́	адно́й	адны́м
INST	адны́м	адны́м	адно́й (-о́ю)	адны́мі
LOC	адны́м	адны́м	адно́й	адны́х

	M/N	F		
NOM	два '2'	дзве	тры '3'	чаты́ры '4'
ACC	= NOM/GEN	= NOM/GEN	= NOM/GEN	= NOM/GEN
GEN	двух	дзвюх	трох	чатыро́х
DAT	двум	дзвюм	тром	чатыро́м
INST	двума́	дзвюма́	трыма́	чатырма́
LOC	двух	дзвюх	трох	чатыро́х

NOM	пяць '5'	пацьдзеся́т '50'	дзве́сце '200'	пяцьсо́т '500'
ACC	пяць	пяцьдзеся́т	= NOM/GEN	= NOM/GEN
GEN	пяці́	пяцідзеся́ці	двухсо́т	пяцісо́т
DAT	пяці́	пяцідзеся́ці	двумста́м	пяціста́м
INST	пяццю́	пяццю́дзесяццю	двумаста́мі	пяццюста́мі
LOC	пяці́	пяцідзеся́ці	двухста́х	пяціста́х

(b)

	M	Singular N	F	Plural all genders
NOM	adzin '1'	adnȯ	adnȧ	adný
ACC	= NOM/GEN	adnȯ	adnu̇	= NOM/GEN
GEN	adnahȯ	adnahȯ	adnȯj, adnaė	adnẏx
DAT	adnamu̇	adnamu̇	adnȯj	adnẏm
INST	adnẏm	adnẏm	adnȯj (-ȯju)	adnẏmi
LOC	adnẏm	adnẏm	adnȯj	adnẏx

	M/N	F		
NOM	dva '2'	dzve	try '3'	čatẏry '4'
ACC	= NOM/GEN	= NOM/GEN	= NOM/GEN	= NOM/GEN
GEN	dvux	dzvjux	trox	čatyrȯx
DAT	dvum	dzvjum	trom	čatyrȯm
INST	dvumȧ	dzvjumȧ	trymȧ	čatyrmȧ
LOC	dvux	dzvjux	trox	čatyrȯx

NOM	pjac' '5'	pjac'dzesjȧt '50'	dzvėṡce '200'	pjac'sȯt '500'
ACC	pjac'	pjac'dzesjȧt	= NOM/GEN	= NOM/GEN
GEN	pjaci	pjacidzesjaci	dvuxsȯt	pjacisȯt
DAT	pjaci	pjacidzesjaci	dvumstȧm	pjacistȧm
INST	pjaccju̇	pjaccju̇dzesjaccju	dvumastȧmi	pjaccjustȧmi
LOC	pjaci	pjacidzesjaci	dvuxstȧx	pjacistȧx

3.2 Verbal morphology

3.2.1 Verbal categories

In comparison with Proto-Slavonic and Old Russian, the inflectional morphology of the Belorussian verb distinguishes only a small number of categories, as illustrated in the chart of conjugation types (table 16.7). Some other categories are expressed periphrastically (see below). In the verb form itself person is distinguished only in the non-past (present/future), gender only in the (singular) past, whilst there is number agreement between subject and verb in both instances. The tense system has been much simplified: gone completely are the aorist, imperfect and original pluperfect, and the perfect has evolved, through the loss of the copula 'be', from an original participial form into a simple verb form which covers all past meaning. Thus, in appropriate contexts, я чытаў/ja čytaŭ may correspond to 'I read/was reading/have read/had read/had been reading'. The only survival of a compound past tense in Belorussian is the pluperfect derived from the Old Russian 'second pluperfect' of the type язъ есмь былъ читалъ/jazъ esmь bylъ čitalъ 'I had read', again through the loss of the copula. Essentially confined to colloquial speech and the language of literature, this form is encountered almost entirely in the perfective aspect, denoting an action in the past anterior to another past action, for example,

Ён прыехаў быў з Мінска і ўладкаваўся на кватэру каля ўніверсітэта./Ën pryéxaŭ byŭ z Minska i ŭladkavaŭsja na kvatèru kalja ŭniversitèta.
'He had arrived from Minsk and settled into a flat near the university.'

Only the verb быць/byc′ 'to be' has a morphological future (first conjugation): буду, будзеш/budu, budzeš and so on. This acts as the auxiliary in forming, in combination with the infinitive, the periphrastic future of imperfective verbs: я буду чытаць/ja budu čytac′ 'I shall read/be reading'. Future meaning in perfective verbs is carried by the non-past form: я прачытаю/ja pračytaju 'I shall read', in contrast to the present meaning of the imperfective non-past.

It will be clear from the foregoing that Belorussian has moved from a tense-based verb system to one based on aspect. As in Slavonic generally, the imperfective–perfective opposition is a privative one: the perfective, the marked member of the pair, is used for a single action in which the focus is on the total performance of that action, on the result produced and potential consequences; the imperfective is used whenever this focus is lacking. Compare, for example, калі я прыйшоў, ён ужо згатаваў (PRFV) вячэру/kali ja pryjšoŭ, ën užo zhatavaŭ vjačèru 'when I arrived, he had already prepared supper' with: калі я прыйшоў, ён гатаваў (IMPFV) вячэру/kali ja pryjšoŭ, ën hatavaŭ vjačèru 'when I arrived, he was preparing supper' (action in progress); калі ён быў дома, ён заўсёды

Table 16.7 Belorussian conjugation types

(a) *First conjugation*

Infinitive			чытаць 'to read'	несці 'to carry'	пісаць 'to write'	браць 'to take'
Non-past:	SG	1	чытаю	нясу́	пішу́	бяру́
		2	чытаеш	нясёш	пішаш	бярэш
		3	чытае	нясе́	піша	бярэ́
	PL	1	чытаем	нясём	пішам	бяро́м
		2	чытаеце	несяце́	пішаце	бераце́
		3	чытаюць	нясу́ць	пішуць	бяру́ць
Past:	SG	M	чытаў	нёс	пісаў	браў
		F	чытала	несла	пісала	брала
		N	чытала	несла	пісала	брала
	PL		чыталі	неслі	пісалі	бралі
Imperative:	SG	2	чытай	нясі	пішы́	бяры́
	PL	1	чытаем	нясе́м	пішэм	бярэм
		2	чытайце	нясіце	пішы́це	бяры́це

			Second conjugation			*Athematic*
Infinitive			маліць 'to beg'	ляце́ць 'to fly'	гаварыць 'to say'	е́сці 'to eat'
Non-past:	SG	1	малю́	лячу́	гавару́	ем
		2	мо́ліш	ляціш	гаво́рыш	ясі
		3	мо́ліць	ляціць	гаво́рыць	есць
	PL	1	мо́лім	ляцім	гаво́рым	ядзім
		2	мо́ліце	леціце́	гаво́рыце	ясце́, ясцё
		3	мо́ляць	ляцяць	гаво́раць	яду́ць
Past:	SG	M	маліў	ляцеў	гаварыў	еў
		F	маліла	ляцела	гаварыла	е́ла
		N	маліла	ляцела	гаварыла	е́ла
	PL		малілі	ляцелі	гаварылі	е́лі
Imperative:	SG	2	малі	ляці	гаверы́	еш
	PL	1	мале́м	ляце́м	гаварэм	ядзім
		2	маліце	ляціце	гаварыце	е́шце

(b) *First conjugation*

Infinitive			čytác´ 'to read'	nésci 'to carry'	pisác´ 'to write'	brac´ 'to take'
Non-past:	SG	1	čytáju	njasú	pišú	bjarú
		2	čytáeš	njaséš	pišaš	bjarèš
		3	čytáe	njasé	piša	bjarè
	PL	1	čytáem	njasém	pišam	bjaróm
		2	čytáece	nesjacé	pišace	beracé
		3	čytájuc´	njasúc´	pišuc´	bjarúc´
Past:	SG	M	čytáů	nës	pisáů	braů
		F	čytála	nésla	pisála	brála

		N	čytála	nésla	pisála	brála
		PL	čytáli	nésli	pisáli	bráli
Imperative:	SG	2	čytáj	njasi	pišý	bjarý
	PL	1	čytáem	njasèm	pišèm	bjarèm
		2	čytájce	njasice	pišýce	bjarýce

	Second conjugation			Athematic

			malic′	ljacèc′	havarýc′	ésci 'to eat'
Infinitive			'to beg'	'to fly'	'to say'	
Non-past:	SG	1	maljù	ljačù	havarù	em
		2	móliš	ljaciš	havóryš	jasi
		3	mólic′	ljacic′	havóryc′	esc′
	PL	1	mólim	ljacim	havórym	jadzim
		2	mólice	lecicè	havóryce	jascè, jascè
		3	móljac′	ljacjàc′	havórac′	jadùc′
Past:	SG	M	maliù	ljacèù	havarýù	eù
		F	malila	ljacèla	havarýla	èla
		N	malila	ljacèla	havarýla	èla
	PL		malili	ljacèli	havarýli	èli
Imperative:	SG	2	mali	ljaci	havarý	eš
	PL	1	malèm	ljacèm	havarèm	jadzim
		2	malice	ljacice	havarýce	éšce

гатавáў (IMPFV) вячэ́ру/kali ën byŭ dóma, ën zaŭsédy hataváŭ vjačèru 'when he was at home, he always prepared supper' (repetition); учóра ўвéчар ëн гатавáў (IMPFV) вячэ́ру/učóra ŭvéčar ën hataváŭ vjačèru 'yesterday evening he prepared supper' (simple naming of the action). Compare also прыйшóў (PRFV) Кандрáт. Ëн чакáе ўнíзе/pryjšóŭ Kandrát. Ën čakáe ŭnize 'Kandrat has come. He is waiting downstairs' with калí ты былá на прáцы, прыхóдзіў (IMPFV) Кандрáт. Ëн пайшóў на пасяджэ́нне/kali ty bylá na prácy, pryxódziŭ Kandrát. Ën pajšóŭ na pasjadžènne 'while you were at work, Kandrat came. He has gone to the meeting' (result of action no longer in force).

The most common morphological markers of aspect in Belorussian are prefixation and suffixation. Typically, simple verbs are imperfective and a corresponding perfective is created with the aid of a (largely unpredictable) prefix which, apart from adding perfectivity, is semantically empty, as in the pair гатавáць – згатавáць/hatavác′ – zhatavác′ in the examples above, or пісáць – напісáць/pisác′ – napisác′ 'to write', вітáць – прывітáць/vitác′ – pryvitác′ 'to greet'. Most prefixes are capable of fulfilling this function in conjunction with particular verbs, but the three in most common use are (in descending order of frequency): па-/pa-, for example, звані́ць – пазвані́ць/zvanic′ – pazvanic′ 'to ring'; з-(с-, са-)/z-(s-, sa-), for example, рабі́ць – зрабі́ць/rabic′ – zrabic′ 'to do, make'; a-(аб-)/a-(ab-), for example, слéпнуць – аслéпнуць/slépnuc′ –

aslėpnuc´ 'to go blind'. The only suffix which is used to create perfective verbs from simple imperfectives is -ну-/-nu-, as in свістаць – свіснуць/ svistác´ – svisnuc´ 'to whistle'. There is a very small number of suppletive pairs, including (imperfective first) гаварыць – сказаць/havaryc´ – skazác´ 'to say' and класціся – легчы/kláscisja – lėhčy 'to lie down'. Where a prefix, when added to a simple imperfective verb, modifies it semantically in addition to making it perfective, an imperfective counterpart is usually created by suffixation. Thus, from пісаць/pisác´ 'to write' is created the pair запіаць – запісваць/zapisác´ – zapisvac´, with imperfective suffix -ва-/-va-. Other suffixes with an imperfectivizing function are: -я-/-ja-, for example, замяніць – замяняць/zamjanic´ – zamjanjác´ 'to replace'; -оўва-/-oŭva-, for example, уз'яднаць – уз'ядноўваць/ uz'jadnác´ – uz'jadnoŭvac´ 'to re-unite'; and, rarely and unproductively, -a-/-a-, for example, абнемагчы – абнемагаць/abnemahčў – abnemahác´ 'to become weak'. In this process both -ва-/-va- and -я-/-ja- entail the morphophonemic alternations associated with the Proto-Slavonic /j/ element described in 2.2, thus абрасіць – аброшваць/abrasic´ – abrošvac´ 'to sprinkle', аслабіць – аслабляць/aslábic´ – aslabljác´ 'to weaken' and so on. Among the few native verbs in Belorussian which are bi-aspectual are абяцаць/abjacác´ 'to promise' and раніць/ranic´ 'to wound', but note also the perfectives паабяцаць/paabjacác´ and параніць/paranic´. Much more typically it is loan-words with the suffix -аба-/-ava- which display this characteristic: адрасаваць/adrasavác´ 'to address', рэстаўрыраваць/rèstaŭrýravac´ 'to restore'.

A subaspectual distinction within the imperfective aspect which – morphologically, at least – continues the Indo-European indeterminate-determinate opposition is found in the category of the so-called 'verbs of motion'. Conventionally, Belorussian grammars have recognized fifteen such pairs of simple verbs: (indeterminate first) хадзіць – ісці/xadzic´ – isci 'to go (on foot)'; ездзіць – ехаць/ezdzic´ – exac´ 'to travel'; бегаць – бегчы/bėhac´ – bėhčy 'to run'; брадзіць – брысці/bradzic´ – brysci (see below); насіць – несці/nasic´ – nesci 'to carry'; вадзіць – весці/vadzic´ – vesci 'to lead'; вазіць – везці/vazic´ – vezci 'to convey'; плаваць – плыць/plávac´ – plyc´ 'to swim, sail'; лятаць – ляцець/ljatác´ – ljacéc´ 'to fly'; лазіць – лезці/lázic´ – lezci 'to climb'; поўзаць – паўзці/ poŭzac´ – paŭzci 'to crawl'; ганяць – гнаць/hanjác´ – hnac´ 'to chase'; катаць – каціць/katác´ – kacic´ 'to roll'; цягаць – цягнуць/cjahác´ – cjahnúc´ 'to drag, pull'; саджаць – садзіць/sadžác´ – sadzic´ 'to plant'. The entries in Атраховіч/Atraxovič (1977–84), however, deny this status to two of them: брадзіць/bradzic´ and брысці/brysci are defined in terms which distinguish them semantically, the former as 'to wander, amble, stroll', the latter as 'to drag oneself along', while the entry for саджаць/sadžác´ merely cross-refers it as a synonym to садзіць/sadzic´.

Of the non-indicative moods the imperative is morphological in the first person plural and second person (see table 16.7 and 3.2.2) but uses the periphrasis хай (няхай)/xaj (njaxáj) plus non-past tense for the third person, thus хай (няхай) адкажа на ліст сам/xaj (njaxáj) adkáža na list sam 'let him answer the letter himself', хай (няхай) éдуць, калі хóчуць/ xaj (njaxáj) éduc´, kali xóčuc´ 'let them go if they want to'. A more categorical imperative meaning may be expressed using the infinitive: не адставаць!/ne adstavác´! 'don't lag behind!' The conditional mood is also periphrastic in form, consisting of the past tense (of either aspect) plus the invariable clitic бы/by (after a consonant), б/b (after a vowel): ён сказаў бы/ën skazáŭ by 'he would say', яна сказала б/janá skazála b 'she would say'.

'Reflexive' verbs in Belorussian are formed by the agglutination of the particle -ся/-sja, derived from the clitic *sę, with a non-reflexive verb. The only variants of it are to be found in the infinitive and the third person of the non-past tense, where in conjunction with final -ць/-c´ it becomes -цца/-cca after a vowel or -ца/-ca after a consonant, for example, купаюся/kupájusja 'I bathe', but купацца/kupácca 'to bathe', купаюцца/kupájucca 'they bathe', здасца/zdásca 'he/she will surrender'. In addition to expressing reflexive voice proper, as in мыцца/ mýcca 'to wash (oneself)', reflexive verbs fulfil a number of functions associated with the middle voice, for example, яны пацалаваліся/janý pacalaválisja 'they kissed (each other)' (reciprocal action) or як мы хваляваліся!/jak my xvaljaválisja! 'how we worried!' (action concentrated within the subject). A major function is the expression of the passive voice, which in Belorussian divides almost completely along aspectual lines: reflexive–passive for imperfective verbs, auxiliary 'to be' plus past passive participle for perfectives. Compare рукапіс перапрацóўваецца (IMPFV) аўтарам/rúkapis perapracóŭvaecca áŭtaram 'the manuscript is being revised by the author' with рукапіс перапрацаваны (PRFV) аўтарам/ rúkapis perapracavány áŭtaram 'the manuscript has been revised by the author'.

Of the participles, only the past passive, formed with the aid of the suffixes -н-/-n- (never doubled) or -т-/-t-, is regarded as standard in Modern Belorussian. By far the more widely used of the two suffixes is -н-/-n-, with -т-/-t- confined to verbs with an infinitive stem in -ну-/-nu-, for example, кінуты/kínuty from кінуць/kínuc´ 'to throw', and first-conjugation 'irregular' verbs with a monosyllabic stem in a vowel, for example, разбіты/razbíty from разбіць/razbíc´ 'to smash'. Variants occur with some verbs in -ну-/-nu- and a few (unproductive) verbs with a stem in р/r or л/l, thus замкнуць/zamknúc´ 'to close' has past passive participle замкнуты/zamknúty or замкнёны/zamknëny, пакалóць/pakalóc´ 'to prick' has паколаты/pakólaty or паколаны/pakólany. The use of the short form of the past passive participle in the predicate is limited: it is not found in the masculine singular and is an alternative to the long form in the feminine, thus тэа́тр пабудава́ны з адбо́рнага матэрыя́лу/tèа̀tr pabudavány z adbórnaha matèryjálu 'the theatre has been built with choice materials', шко́ла пабудава́ная (пабудава́на) ... /škóla pabudavánaja (pabudavána) ... 'the school has been built ...'. A recent innovation is a marked increase in the attributive use of the *l*-participle (of intransitive verbs only), for example, раста́лы снег/rastály sneh, вы́мерлыя жывёлы/výmerlyja žvëly, which literally mean 'having melted snow' and 'having become extinct animals'. On the other hand, invariable gerunds – etymologically the feminine nominative singular short forms of the active participles – *are* a feature of the standard language, though they no longer carry any tense meaning, only that of aspect, thus ро́бячы/róbjačy (IMPFV GER) from рабі́ць/rabic´, зрабіу́шы/zrabiùšy (PRFV GER) from зрабі́ць/zrabic´ 'to do'.

3.2.2   Conjugation

Leaving aside for the moment a handful of anomalous verbs, Belorussian has two conjugations, though within each, as illustrated in table 16.7, we may distinguish a number of subtypes occasioned by the effects of *ákanne* and *jákanne* and the hardening of formerly palatalized consonants. Thus, for example, the endings of the non-past tense of the first-conjugation verbs in the table show the following morphophonemic alternations: in the second and third persons singular e–a–э/e–a–è, in the first person plural e–ё–a–o/e–ë–a–o, in the second person plural e–я–a/e–ja–a. In the neuter singular past tense stressed -о́/-ó, as in вяло́/vjaló from ве́сці/ vésci 'to lead', alternates with unstressed -a/-a, as in не́сла/nésla and all the other examples in table 16.7, with the result that where the neuter form is stem-stressed it coincides with the feminine. The infinitive ending shows alternation between -ць/-c´ after vowels, -ці/-ci after consonants other than velars (irrespective of the stress position), and -чы/-čy where the stem ends in a velar, with /k/ (only) being assimilated into the ending, thus чыта́ць/čytác´, не́сці/nésci, магчы́/mahčý 'to be able', пячы́/pjačý 'to bake' (stem {pek-}). Stress shifts within the paradigm may give rise to morphophonemic alternations in the stem of the verb, as demonstrated by all the verbs in the table except чыта́ць/čytác´.

Belorussian has only partial retention of final /t´/ in the third person singular non-past, namely in the second conjugation, thus мо́ліць/mólic´ but чыта́е/čytáe. It is, however, re-instated in first-conjugation verbs if they are reflexive, for example, смяе́цца/smjaéssa from смяя́цца/ smjajácca 'to laugh'. In the second person plural non-past of ending-stressed verbs it is the *final* syllable which is stressed, as illustrated in table 16.7 by несяце́, бераце́, леціце́/nesjacé, beracé, lecicé. For most verbs the first person plural imperative is distinct from the indicative. It is formed with the ending -ем/-em, a continuation of Old Russian -ѣмъ/-ěmъ, and has the variant -эм/-èm after formerly palatalized consonants. (In verbs with a velar stem the original second palatalization has been replaced by the first, for example, памажэ́м/pamažèm 'let us help'.) However, where the non-past is stem-stressed the indicative may also be used with imperative meaning: по́йдзем/pójdzem 'let us go', спы́нім/spýnim 'let us stop', and in the case of first-conjugation verbs with a stem in /j/, such as чыта́ць/čytác' in the table, this is now the only form of the first person plural imperative accepted as standard, forms in -ма/-ma being considered dialectal.

Table 16.8 shows the Belorussian reflexes of the five Proto-Slavonic verb classes. They divide between the two conjugations as follows: themes in -e/-o, -ne, -je – first conjugation; theme in -i – second conjugation. As may readily be seen from the table, the characteristic Belorussian morphophonemic innovations (see 2.3) frequently obscure the underlying stem, so that in the non-past of verbs with a theme in -e/-o, for example, we find вядз-(вяд-), цвіц-, граб-, пяч-(пяк-), бяр-/vjadz-(vjad-), cvic-, hrab-, pjač-(pjak-), bjar- as realizations of the stems {ved-, cvit-, hrèb-, pek-, ber-} respectively. Depalatalization and/or *ákanne* may also affect the theme vowel, as in бяр-э-/bjar-è- ‹ *ber-e-, пор-а-/por-a- ‹ *por-j-e and ляж-ы-/ljaž-y- ‹ *lež-i-. A further innovation is the restoration in the infinitive stem of the labials б, п/b, p and the velar г/h, earlier assimilated to the ending, thus грэ́бці/hrèbci 'to rake', храпці/hrapci 'to snore', ле́гчы/lèhčy 'to lie down'. Among verbs with a theme in -je we may note the extension of the stem пе-/pe- of the infinitive пець/pec' 'to sing' to the non-past tense, albeit in the *jákanne*-produced realization пя-/pja-.

Of the five athematic verbs of Proto-Slavonic, Belorussian retains only three. The present tense of быць/byc' 'to be' is usually not formally expressed; thus ён ура́ч/ën uráč, literally 'he doctor'. The sole surviving form is ёсць/ësc', etymologically the third person singular but now generalized for all persons and both numbers; it is used for emphasis or, principally in scientific and technical styles, in definitions. The conjugation of the other two surviving athematic verbs, éсці/ésci 'to eat' (see table 16.7) and даць/dac' 'to give' (which follows the same pattern), more closely continues that of Proto-Slavonic than is the case in any of the other Slavonic languages except Ukrainian. Only the first and third person plural have adapted to thematic conjugation (second and first respectively). An innovation in Belorussian is the complete adaptation of the Proto-Slavonic irregular verb *xotěti to the first conjugation. The one truly irregular (as opposed to athematic) verb in Modern Belorussian is бе́гчы/bèhčy 'to run', which has first-conjugation endings in the first person singular and third person plural, but second-conjugation endings in all other forms of the non-past, thus бягу́, бягу́ць/bjahú, bjahúc' but бяжы́ш, бяжы́ць, бяжы́м, бежыцé/bjažýš, bjažýc', bjažym, bežycè.

Table 16.8   Belorussian reflexes of Proto-Slavonic verb classes

(a) *Infinitive stem*   *Non-past stem*

Theme in -*e/-o*
нес-   няс-е-
   вес- (‹ *ved-)   вядз-е- (S1, P3 вяд-)
     цвіс- (‹ *cvit-)   цвіц-е- (S1, P3 цвіт-)
     іс- (‹ *id-)   ідз-е- (S1, P3 ід-)
     еха-   едз-е- (S1, P3 ед-)
   грэб-   граб-е-
     жы-   жыв-е-
   пяч- (‹ *pek-t-)   пяч-э- (Sl, P3 пяк-)
   па-ча- (‹ *-čen-)   па-чн-е-
   па-мер-   па-мр-э-
   ста-   стан-е-
сса-   сс-е-
   зв-а-   зав-е-
   бр-а-   бяр-э-

Theme in -*ne*
цяг-ну- (‹ *tęg-nǫ-)   цяг-н-е-
   мі-ну- (‹ *mi-nǫ-)   мі-н-е-

Theme in -*je*
чу-   чу-е-
   пе-   пя-е-
   кры-   кры-е-
   бі-   б'-е-
   паро- (‹ *por-)   пор-а- (S1 пар-)
   мало- (‹ *mel-)   мел-е- (S1 мял-)
ігр-а-   ігр-а-е-
   ум-е- (‹ *um-ě-)   ум-е-е-
каз-а-   каж-а- (‹ *kaz-j-e-)
   піс-а-   піш-а- (‹ *pis-j-e-)
   дарав-а- (‹ *darov-a-)   дару-е-
   се-я-   се-е-

Theme in -*i*
мал-і- (‹ *mol-i-)   мол-і- (Sl мал-)
   хадз-і- (‹ *xod-i-)   ходз-і- (S1 хадж- ‹ *xod-j-)
   сядз-е- (‹ *sěd-ě-)   сядз-і- (S1 сядж- ‹ *sěd-j-)
   ляж-а- (‹ *lež-a-)   ляж-ы-
   сп-а-   сп-і- (S1 спл- ‹ *sp-j-)

Athematic
бы-   ёс-
ес- (‹ *ěd-)   е(с/д/дз)-
да-   да(с/д/дз)-

Irregular
хац-е-   хоч-а- (S1 хач- ‹ *xot-j-)

(b) *Infinitive stem*   *Non-past stem*

Theme in *-e/-o*
nes-   njas-e-
  ves- (‹ *ved-)   vjadz-e- (S1, P3 vjad-)
    cvis- (‹ *cvit-)   cvic-e- (S1, P3 cvit-)
    is- (‹ *id-)   idz-e- (S1, P3 id-)
    exa-   edz-e- (S1, P3 ed-)
    hrèb-   hrab-e-
    žy-   žyv-e-
  pjač- (‹ *pek-t-)   pjač-è- (S1, P3 pjak-)
  pa-ča- (‹ *-čen-)   pa-čn-e-
  pa-mer-   pa-mr-è-
  sta-   stan-e-
ssa-   ss-e-
  zv-a-   zav-e-
  br-a-   bjar-è-

Theme in *-ne*
cjah-nu- (‹ *tęg-nǫ-)   cjah-n-e-
  mi-nu- (‹ *mi-nǫ-)   mi-n-e-

Theme in *-je*
ču-   ču-e-
  pe-   pja-e-
  kry-   kry-e-
  bi-   b′-e-
  paro- (‹ *por-)   por-a- (S1 par-)
  malo- (‹ *mel-)   mel-e- (S1 mjal-)
ihr-a-   ihr-a-e-
  um-e- (‹ *um-ě-)   um-e-e-
kaz-a-   kaž-a- (‹ *kaz-j-e-)
  pis-a-   piš-a- (‹ *pis-j-e-)
  darav-a- (‹ *darov-a-)   daru-e-
  se-ja-   se-e-

Theme in *-i*
mal-i- (‹ *mol-i-)   mol-i- (S1 mal-)
  xadz-i- (‹ *xod-i-)   xodz-i- (S1 xadž- ‹ *xod-j-)
  sjadz-e- (‹ *sěd-ě-)   sjadz-i- (S1 sjadž- ‹ *sěd-j-)
  ljaž-a- (‹ *lež-a-)   ljaž-y-
  sp-a-   sp-i- (S1 spl- ‹ *sp-j-))

Athematic
by-   ës-
es- (‹ *ěd-)   e(s/d/dz)-
da-   da(s/d/dz)-

Irregular
xac-e-   xoč-a- (S1 xač- ‹ *xot-j-)

3.3   Derivational morphology

3.3.1   Major patterns of noun derivation

Most productive is suffixation, principally from underlying verb, adjective (including participle) and noun stems. The suffixes which combine with the greatest number of parts of speech are -ак/-ak, -iк/-ik, -нiк/-nik and -к- /-k-. Thus, for example, рыбак/rybàk 'fisherman', юнак/junàk 'young man', сваяк/svajàk 'relation', пятак/pjatàk 'five-kopeck coin' and спявак/spjavàk 'singer' are derived from the stems of, respectively, a noun, adjective, pronoun, numeral and verb. Among the most productive suffixes are: -нiк/-nik, -чык/-čyk and -ец(-эц)/-ec(-èc), which create predominantly animate nouns, for example, жартаўнiк/žartaùnik 'joker' from жартаваць/žartavàc' 'to joke', грузчык/hrùzčyk 'docker' from грузiць/hruzic' 'to load', навучэнец/navučènec 'pupil' from навучэнне/navučènne 'study'. The suffixes -ств-/-stv-, -анн-(-енн-, -энн-)/-ann-(-enn-, -ènn-) and -асць/-asc' all create abstract nouns, thus знаёмства/znaëmstva 'acquaintance', аблягчэнне/abljahčènne 'alleviation', мудрасць/mùdrasc' 'wisdom', motivated by знаём-ы/znaëm-y 'familiar', аблягч-ыць/abljahč-ỳc' 'to alleviate' and мудр-ы/mùdr-y 'wise'.

Within the noun category suffixation is also used for modificatory purposes. Highly productive in the derivation of masculine diminutives are, again, -iк(-ык)/-ik(-yk), -чык/-čyk and -ок(-ак)/-ok(-ak), giving rise to such forms as столiк/stòlik, пакойчык/pakòjčyk and, with consonant mutation, унучак/unùčak, from стол/stol 'table', пакой/pakòj 'room' and унук/unùk 'grandson' respectively. Most productive where feminine diminutives are concerned is -ачк-/-ačk-, for example, лямпачка/ ljàmpačka from лямпа/ljàmpa 'lamp', followed by -к-/-k-, as in бярозка/bjaròzka from бяроза/bjaròza 'birch'. The latter suffix is also, though less productively, used to derive neuter diminutives: слоўка/ slòùka from слова/slòva 'word', and plays a major role in the derivation of female nouns from their male equivalents, for example, касiрка/ kasirka from касiр/kasir 'cashier'. Other suffixes with a modificatory function include -ан-(-ян-)/-an-(-jan-), which creates nouns denoting the young of animals: ваўчаня (ваўчанё)/vaučanjà (vaučanè) 'wolf cub' from воўк/voùk 'wolf'; and -/j/-, used to form neuter collectives and in the process, except after labials and /r/, assimilated by the preceding consonant: сук/suk 'branch' gives сучча/sùčča 'branches', дуб/dub 'oak' gives дуб'ё/dub'ё 'oaks'.

Prefixation plays a much lesser role in the derivation of nouns, though the negative prefix не-(ня-)/ne-(nja-) is highly productive in the creation of antonyms, such as неспакой/nespakòj 'anxiety' from спакой/spakòj 'calm', няшчасце/njaščàsce 'unhappiness' from шчасце/ščàsce 'happiness'. Compounding, on the other hand, is a fruitful source of noun derivation, whether it be appositional, as in вагóн-рэстарáн/vahón-rèstarán 'restaurant car'; by interfix, as in законапраéкт/zakonapraékt = закóн+a+праéкт/zakón+a+praékt '(legal) bill'; or with truncation of the first element, as in бензасхóвішча/benzasxóvišča 'petrol tank' ‹ бензíн+схóвішча/benzín+sxóvišča.

3.3.2 Major patterns of adjective derivation

In deriving adjectives from nouns the most productive suffixes are -н-/-n-, -óв-(-ёв-, -ав-, -ев-)/-óv-(-ёv-, -av-, -ev-) and -ск-/-sk-, for example, кóнны/kónny 'horse', клянóвы/kljanóvy 'maple', акіянскі/akijánski 'ocean', motivated by конь/kon´, клён/klën and акіян/akiján respectively. The process of suffixation may be accompanied by truncation of the motivating stem, as in птýшка/ptúška › птушы́ны/ptušýny 'bird's'; by contraction at the morpheme boundary, as in маладзéц+ск-i/maladzéc+sk-i › маладзéцкі/maladzécki 'dashing'; or by mutation of the stem-final consonant, as in пясóк/pjasók › пясчáны/pjasčány 'sandy'. Possessive adjectives are derived from animate nouns and personal names with the aid of the suffixes -óў(-ёў, -аў, -еў)/-óǔ(-ёǔ, -aǔ, -eǔ) and -iн(-ын)/-in(-yn), for example, Лукашóў/Lukašóǔ 'Lukaš's', мýжаў/múžaǔ 'husband's', бáбін/bábin 'grandmother's'. Adjectives motivated by adjectives themselves almost invariably modify the meaning of the underlying form in some way; thus, the suffix -ават-/-avat- limits the quality: халаднавáты/xaladnaváty 'rather cold' by comparison with халóдны/xalódny 'cold', while -енн-/-enn- augments it: здаравéнны/zdaravénny 'robust' compared with здарóвы/zdaróvy 'healthy'. Derivation of adjectives from other parts of speech is more limited. Most commonly, the motivating stem is verbal, as in адкідны́/adkidný 'collapsible' or забы́ўчывы/zabýǔčyvy 'forgetful'.

Prefixation is a productive method of intra-adjectival derivation in two areas: the creation of antonyms or adjectives that negate the quality expressed by the motivating adjective: здáтны/zdátny 'able' › няздáтны/njazdátny 'not able', закóнны/zakónny 'legal' › беззакóнны/bezzakónny 'illegal'; and of superlatives and other forms expressing a heightened degree of that quality: высóкі/vysóki 'tall' › завысóкі/zavysóki 'too tall', рэакцы́йны/rèakcýjny 'reactionary' › архірэакцы́йны/arxirèakcýjny 'arch-reactionary'. In the compounding of two adjectives the first element appears always in the short neuter form, as in кісла-салóдкі/kisla-salódki 'bitter-sweet' (coordinative) and блéдна-жóўты/blédna-žóǔty 'pale yellow' (subordinative).

3.3.3 Major patterns of verb derivation

Prefixes have a dual role in intraverbal derivation. In acting as a morphological marker of aspect (see 3.2.1) they are semantically empty of all but the component 'perfectivity'. More often, however, they make other semantic modifications to the simple verb to which they are attached. Furthermore, while in the former role many prefixes are only weakly productive, in the latter the reverse is true. Many are also polysemantic: thus, for example, the prefix вы-/vy- may add to the simple verb the meaning 'outwards' as in выйсці/vyjsci 'to go out'; 'completion' as in выслужыць/vyslužyc´ 'to serve out'; or, in conjunction with the reflexive particle, 'exhaustiveness' as in выспацца/vyspacca 'to have a good sleep'. Indeed, this polysemy is frequently to be found within a single derived verb; thus the prefix за-/za- may add to весці/vesci 'to take' both the meaning 'action beyond a given point' and 'commencement of action', so that завесці/zavesci means both 'to take too far' and 'to set up, start'.

Aside from aspectual derivation, suffixation is used almost exclusively to derive verbs from other parts of speech. An exception to this is the suffix -ану-/-anu-, which adds the nuance of intensity or unexpectedness to the meaning of the motivating verb; thus from сказаць/skazac´ 'to say' is derived сказануць/skazanuc´ 'to rap out'. Such forms are characteristic of colloquial style. Among the suffixes deriving verbs from nouns and adjectives two are particularly productive: -i-(-ы-)/-i-(-y-), as in бяліць/bjalic´ 'to whiten' from белы/bely 'white' or рыбачыць/rybačyc´ 'to fish' from рыбак/rybak 'fisherman'; and -ава-(-ява-)/-ava-(-java-), which occurs mainly, though not exclusively, in loan-words, as in друкаваць/drukavac´ 'to print', лютаваць/ljutavac´ 'to rage'. The suffix -i-(-ы-)/-i-(-y-) is also the most productive second element in the confixal derivation of verbs, for example, in узаконіць/uzakonic´ 'to legalize', derived from закон/zakon 'law' with the aid of у-/u-. Occasionally, the prefixal element in such derived verbs may be one not encountered where prefixation alone is involved, for example, абез-/abez- in абезнадзеіць/abeznadzeic´ 'to dishearten', motivated by надзея/nadzeja 'hope'.

4   Syntax

4.1   Element order in declarative sentences

In Belorussian, since syntactic relations are generally explicit in the morphology, the order of the major constituents of a sentence (or clause) is relatively free, though this should not be interpreted to mean random. What determines which of the six possible permutations of subject, verb and object is employed in a given instance is communicative dynamism. The given information precedes those elements which communicate the new information or bear the greatest emphasis. Morphologically identical sentences conveying the same factual information will therefore show variation in the order of their constituents. Thus, depending on what question (or potential question) is being answered, the sentence 'Ryhor hit Mikola' might appear in any of the following forms: Рыгор ударыў Міколу/

Ryhór udáryŭ Mikólu (Subject–Verb–Object, answering '*whom* did Ryhor hit?'); удáрыŭ Рыгóр Мікóлу/udáryŭ Ryhór Mikólu (VSO: 'whom did Ryhor *hit?*'); Рыгóр Мікóлу ŭдáрыŭ/Ryhór Mikólu ŭdáryŭ (SOV: '*what* did Ryhor do to Mikola?'); Мікóлу Рыгóр удáрыŭ/Mikólu Ryhór udáryŭ (OSV: 'what did Ryhor do to *Mikola?*'); Мікóлу ŭдáрыŭ Рыгóр/Mikólu ŭdáryŭ Ryhór (OSV: '*who* hit Mikola?'); удáрыŭ Мікóлу Рыгóр/udáryŭ Mikólu Ryhór (VOS: 'who *hit* Mikola?'). As to which of these represents unmarked order, one might reasonably argue that, in their appropriate context, they all do. Support is lent to this argument by the fact that in the spoken language the topic–focus order may be varied so that, for example, unmarked Мікóлу ŭдáрыŭ Рыгóр/Mikólu ŭdáryŭ Ryhór becomes stylistically marked Рыгóр удáрыŭ Мікóлу/Ryhór udáryŭ Mikólu '*Ryhor* hit Mikola'. However, there is some evidence to suggest that the basic order in Belorussian, as in English, at least for the written language, is SVO. In sentences in which subject and object are not morphologically unambiguous (both nouns have nominative = accusative and are of the same person and number) the most likely interpretation is that the first element is the subject, for example, град змяніў дождж/hrad zmjaniŭ doždž 'hail replaced the rain'. In speech, though, sentence intonation would allow the order OVS, giving the meaning 'rain replaced the hail'.

Adverbials relating to the clause as a whole, rather than a particular constituent, are placed in clause-initial position; where they qualify a particular constituent they are also generally preposed to that constituent. Immediate pre-verbal position is the norm for adverbials of time, place or degree, thus ён дóўга расказваў пра сваé прыгóды/ën dóŭha raskázvaŭ pra svaé pryhódy (literally: 'he long talked about his adventures') 'he talked for a long time about his adventures'; да слёз кранўў мянé ягó расказ/da slëz kranúŭ mjané jahó raskáz (literally: 'to tears moved me his story') 'his story moved me to tears'. Postposition of such adverbials is stylistically marked (emphatic, expressive). For adverbials of manner there is a division between pre-position and postposition: qualitative adverbs precede the verb: яны вéсела смяялíся/janý vésela smjajálisja (literally: 'they merrily laughed') 'they laughed merrily'; if, however, the adverbial is derived from a noun, it follows: ён ішóў вóбмацкам каля сцяны/ën išóŭ vóbmackam kaljá scjaný (literally: 'he went by groping along the wall') 'he groped his way along the wall'; those derived from gerunds are regularly found in both pre- and postposition to the verb, thus ён сумéўшыся стаяў пéрад éй/ën suméŭšysja stajáŭ pérad ëj or ён стаяў пéрад éй сумéўшыся/ën stajáŭ pérad ëj suméŭšysja (literally: 'he having become embarrassed stood before her' or 'he stood before her having become embarrassed') 'he stood before her in embarrassment'. If the adverbial is one of cause or purpose, expressed by an adverb or a noun in an oblique case, then again both preposition and postposition are possible: ён застаўся дома знарок/ën zastaŭsja doma znarok or ён знарок застаўся дома/ën znarok zastaŭsja doma (literally: 'he stayed at home on purpose' or 'he on purpose stayed at home') 'he stayed at home on purpose'. Where more than one adverbial occurs in a clause, the order is time > place > cause > manner and others.

There are no pronominal clitics in Belorussian. Within the noun phrase unmarked order is for determiners and adjectives (if both are present, in that order) to precede the head noun, thus гэтыя маладыя людзі/hètyja maladyja ljudzi 'these young people', усё новыя кнігі/usè novyja knihi 'all (the) new books'. Any inversion, such as зубы крывыя/zuby kryvyja for крывыя зубы/kryvyja zuby 'crooked teeth', is emotionally expressive. Genitives and relative clauses, on the other hand, follow the head noun.

4.2   Non-declarative sentence types

Interrogative sentences in Belorussian are marked by the use of inter-rogative words (pronouns, adverbs, particles) and/or a special inter-rogative intonation, with word order playing only a secondary role. Interrogative intonation consists in a sharp rise in pitch (less marked if an interrogative word is used) on the word requiring an answer. The intonation of the sentence as a whole will be falling if the word is at the beginning, rising–falling if it is in the middle and rising if it is at the end. Any declarative sentence can be turned into an interrogative one in this way, without alteration to the word order, thus declarative вы хадзілі ў кіно/vy xadzili ŭ kino 'you went to the cinema' may become interrogative **вы** хадзілі ў кіно? 'did **you** go to the cinema?', вы **хадзілі** ў кіно? 'did you **go** to the cinema?', вы хадзілі ў **кіно**? 'did you go to the **cinema**?' Among the particles used to mark interrogative sentences is ці/ci, which takes first position in the sentence and requires inversion of subject and verb: ці ведае ён гэта?/ci vedae ën hèta? 'does he know that?', ці не холадна табе?/ci ne xoladna tabè? 'aren't you cold?'. It is also the means of marking indirect questions: ён не помніць, ці бачыў яго/ën ne pomnic', ci baĉyŭ jaho 'he doesn't remember whether he saw him'.

An affirmative answer to a general interrogative is usually in the form так/tak, алé/alè or ага/ahà, all meaning 'yes'. The negative response is не/ne 'no', for example, ці вярнулася маці? – Не/ci vjarnulasja maci? – Ne 'has mother returned? – No'; this is also used, however, to confirm the truth of a negative interrogative, as in ці не вярнулася маці? – Не/ci ne vjarnulasja maci? – Ne 'hasn't mother returned? – No'. Question-word questions are usually answered with incomplete sentences: хто застанецца дома? – Мікола/xto zastanecca doma? – Mikola 'who will stay at home? – Mikola'.

Commands, including prohibitions, may be issued not only by means of the imperative and infinitive (see 3.2.1) but also with the aid of the conditional, which has more the intonation of request or advice, for example, адпачы́ў бы ты тро́хі/adpačýŭ by ty tróxi 'you should rest a little'. Exceptionally, other parts of speech may also have imperative meaning: comparative adverb, for example, хутчэ́й!/xutčéj! (literally: 'more quickly') 'hurry up!'; past tense of certain verbs of motion, as in паехалі!/ paéxali! (literally: 'went') 'let's go!'; impersonal predicate, for example, не́льга!/nél'ha! (literally: 'it is not allowed') 'don't!'.

4.3 Copular sentences

The grammatical role of pure copula in compound nominal predicates is fulfilled by the various tense and mood forms of быць/byc' 'to be'. An exception is the present tense, where there is a zero copula unless subject and complement are expressed by the same noun, when the copula ёсць/ ёsc' is obligatory. The main semi-abstract copulas (verbs which have partially lost their lexical meaning) are з'яўля́цца – з'яві́цца/z'jaŭljàcca – z'javicca, in its copular function synonymous with быць/byc' and much used in the written language in definitions; рабі́цца – зрабі́цца/rabicca – zrabicca, станаві́цца – стаць/stanavicca – stac', both meaning 'to become'; and здава́цца – зда́цца/zdavàcca – zdàcca 'to seem'. Material copulas in Belorussian are chiefly verbs of movement or state, such as вярта́цца – вярну́цца/vjartàcca – vjarnùcca 'to return', стая́ць/stajàc' 'to stand' and so on.

There is no detailed study of the distribution between nominative and instrumental case for predicative nouns and adjectives in copular sentences. Where the pure copula is concerned, the one absolute constraint applies to the present tense: here, both with zero copula and with ёсць/ёsc', only the nominative may be used. Otherwise the rules are not rigid, though it is rare for the nominative case to be used in conjunction with the future tense or imperative mood of быць/byc'. With the past tense some scholars have suggested a broad division between permanent attribute (nominative) and temporary one (instrumental). However, the facts of usage do not appear to bear this out; compare the following two examples, both drawn from twentieth-century literature: ён сам быў яшчэ́ дзіця́/ën sam byŭ jaščè dzicjà 'he himself was still a child' (nominative) and я яго́ тры гады́ ве́даю, яшчэ́ калі́ ён студэ́нтам быў/ja jahó try hadý vèdaju, jaščè kali ën studèntam byŭ 'I have known him since three years ago, when he was still a student' (instrumental). The nominative seems also to be particularly common where the complement is an adjective, as in яна́ была́ яшчэ́ зусі́м малада́я/janà bylà jaščè zusim maladàja 'she was still very young'. The instrumental case is invariably used with з'яўля́цца – з'яві́цца/ z'jaŭljàcca – z'javicca, for example, Адэ́са з'яўля́ецца буйне́йшым по́ртам на Чо́рным мо́ры/Adèsa z'jaŭljàecca bujnèjšym pòrtam na Čòrnym mòry 'Odessa is the largest port on the Black Sea'. It is generally described as 'the norm' for other semi-abstract copulas, though the nominative may be found with no obvious sense difference, thus дні сталі кароткія (кароткімі)/dni stáli karótkija (karótkimi) 'the days became short'.

4.4   Coordination and comitativity

The principal means of coordination in Belorussian are conjunctions (copulative, adversative and disjunctive) and zero coordination. Except in the case of цi/ci (in the sense 'or'), disjunctive coordination requires each coordinated element to have a coordinator, thus баліць у вас галава цi перастала?/balíc' u vas halavá ci perastála? 'does your head (still) ache or has it stopped (aching)?', but або сёння, або заўтра, або паслязаўтра/abó sённja, abó záŭtra, abó pasljazáŭtra 'either today or tomorrow or the day after'. Adversative conjunctions, on the other hand, show only the pattern 'X but X' and are invariably preceded by a comma: стомлены, але вясёлы/stómleny, alé vjasёly 'tired but happy'; ён пайшоў, а мы засталіся/ën pajšóŭ, a my zastálisja 'he left, but we remained'. The most flexible of the coordinating conjunctions in terms of its occurrence (or non-occurrence) alongside each coordinated element is the copulative i/i 'and', which may be found in the patterns 'X and X', 'and X and X' or 'X, X and X', thus на дварэ было холадна i сыра/na dvarè byló xóladna i sýra 'outside it was cold and damp'; i ў полі, i ў лесе чуецца вясна/i ŭ póli, i ŭ lése čúecca vjasná '(both) in the fields and in the woods one can feel the spring'; ён устаў, падышоў да акна i паглядзеў на неба/ën ustáŭ, padyšóŭ da akná i pahljadzéŭ na néba 'he stood up, went over to the window and looked at the sky'.

On the whole, Belorussian prefers plural verb agreement with conjoined nouns or noun phrases if the coordination is copulative. However, singular agreement is possible if a singular noun stands immediately before or after the verb, for example, побач з iм стаіць меншы сын i ўсе астатнія партызаны/póbač z im staíc' ménšy syn i ŭse astátnija partyzány 'along-side him stands (his) youngest son and all the other partisans'. If such singular agreement is used in the past tense, gender agreement is also with the nearest noun. Where two or more singular nouns are conjoined by то ... то/to ... to 'now ... now', verb agreement may be either singular or plural, but in the past tense must be plural if the nouns are of different gender, thus то сын, то дачка прыязджае (прыязджаюць) да маці/ to syn, to dačká pryjazdžáe (pryjazdžájuc') da máci 'sometimes the son, sometimes the daughter comes (come) (to visit) the mother', but only то сын, то дачка прыязджалі да маці/to syn, to dačká pryjazdžáli da máci 'sometimes the son, sometimes the daughter came (PL) (to visit) the mother'.

Comitative noun phrases in Belorussian may be of two types: those in which the element in the instrumental case is also included in the nomin-ative pronoun, for example, мы з табой/my z tabój 'you and I' (literally:

'we with you'), and those in which it is not, for example, янá з сястрóй/ janá z sjastrój 'she and her sister' (literally: 'she with sister'). Verb agreement with both is usually plural, though singular agreement is possible in the case of the second type, for example:

Кóсця з малéнькай сястрóй Сóняй ганяýся па лéсе за матылькáмі./Kóscja z malén'kaj sjastrój Sónjaj hanjáŭsja pa lése za matyl'kámi.
'Koscja chased through the woods after butterflies with his little sister Sonja.'
(literally: 'Koscja with little sister Sonja chased (M SG) . . .')

4.5   Subordination

Examination of samples of Belorussian text quickly reveals that the language makes far greater use of coordination than of subordination and that it is much given to asyndeton. Nevertheless, all the major types of subordinate clause, whether classified in syntactic terms (subjective, predicative, completive) or in semantic terms (temporal, conditional, relative and so on), are present. A detailed analysis of such clauses is beyond the scope of the present work, but one or two points are of particular interest. Thus, in relative clauses, whilst Belorussian has the relative pronoun які/ jaki 'which' to act as a conjunctive, and in doing so to show agreement in number and gender with its antecedent head, it also makes substantial use of што/što 'that' with an antecedent of any gender or either number. Since што/što used in this way is neutral as to number and gender, it is found only as subject or direct object in the subordinate clause; verbal agreement is according to the features of the antecedent head. Compare, for instance:

Ён падступіў да кампáніі, якáя (што) вялá гарáчую дыскýсію./Ën padstupiŭ da kampánii, jakája (što) vjalá haráčuju dyskúsiju
'He joined a group which was having a heated discussion.'

but only

кампáнія, да якóй ён падступіў, вялá гарáчую дыскýсію./kampánija, da jakój ën padstupiŭ, vjalá haráčuju dyskúsiju.
'The group he joined was having a heated discussion.'

Хто/xto 'who', in the nominative only and always with masculine singular verbal agreement, may similarly replace які/jaki, for example, старшыня́, які (хто) вёў дыскýсію/staršynjá, jaki (xto) vëŭ dyskúsiju 'the chairman, who was leading the discussion'.

Another characteristic of Belorussian is the frequent balancing of the conjunction introducing a subordinate clause by a pronoun or pronominal adverb in the main clause. Where the main clause precedes the subordinate, this antecedent effectively signals the upcoming subordinate clause; thus in the sentence яны́ кінуліся туды́, адкýль чýўся крык/ janý kinulisja tudý, adkúl' čúŭsja kryk 'they rushed to where the cry had been heard from', туды́/tudý 'to there' points to the clause introduced by адку́ль/adkúl´ 'from where'. In цяпе́р я хачу́ пракаменці́раваць ты́я зме́ны, які́я мы прапану́ем/cjapér ja xačú prakamencíravac´ týja zmény, jakija my prapanúem 'now I want to comment on the changes which we are proposing', ты́я/týja 'those (ACC PL)' points to the ensuing relative clause.

In addition to subordinate clauses a widely used subordinate element, at least in written Belorussian, is the gerundial phrase. In principle, it is possible to take either of two coordinated sentences and substitute a synonymous gerundial phrase, for example, in place of ён сядзе́ў за стало́м і чыта́ў кні́гу/ën sjadzéŭ za stalóm i čytáŭ kníhu 'he sat at the table and read a book', one may say ён сядзе́ў за стало́м, чыта́ючы кні́гу/ën sjadzéŭ za stalóm, čytájучy kníhu 'he sat at the table, reading a book' or се́дзячы за стало́м, ён чыта́ў кні́гу/sédzjačy za stalóm, ën čytáŭ kníhu 'sitting at the table, he was reading a book'. In practice, however, both from a sense and syntactic point of view the first variant is preferable, since it is the second coordinated element which is subordinated to express a secondary action, manner or purpose. Conversely, the first element is subordinated where the construction is temporal, causal, conditional or concessive: compare ён сабра́ў усе́ сі́лы і ўзня́ўся на гару́/ën sabráŭ usé síly i úznjáŭsja na harú 'he summoned all his strength and climbed the hill' and сабра́ўшы ўсе сі́лы, ён узня́ўся на гару́/sabráŭšy úse síly, ën uznjáŭsja na harú 'summoning all his strength, he climbed the hill'. A restriction on the use of the gerundial phrase is that the subject of the action expressed by the gerund must be the same as the subject of the main-clause verb; thus one may say:

Любу́ючыся го́радам, ён успаміна́ў аб міну́лым./Ljubújučysja hóradam, ën uspamináŭ ab minúlym.
'Gazing at the city, he remembered the past'

but not:

*Любу́ючыся го́радам, у яго́ ўзніка́лі ўспамі́ны аб міну́лым./*Ljubújučysja hóradam, u jahó úznikáli úspamíny ab minúlym.
'Gazing at the city, memories of the past arose in him.'

In general, this requirement precludes the use of a gerundial phrase with impersonal constructions, but an exception occurs with certain modal words, for example, мо́жна/móžna 'it is possible, one may', трэ́ба/tréba 'it is necessary', не́льга/nél´ha 'it is impossible, one may not', лёгка/lëhka 'it is easy', as in, for example:

Гаво́рачы з дзяўчы́най, лёгка было́ заўва́жыць яе́ ўсхвалява́насць./

Havóračy z dzjaŭčýnaj, lёhka byló zaŭvážyc' jać ŭsxvaljavánasc'.
'Talking to the girl, it was easy to notice her anxiety.'

Participial phrases play only a minor role as subordinate elements since, as was pointed out in 3.2.1, participles are very restricted both in formation and use. The past passive participle is an exception and in certain circumstances is an important syntactic means of avoiding ambiguity. In the sentence

Вяршы́ні хвóяў, якія былі асвéтленыя цéплымі прамéнямі блізкага да захóду сóнца, я́рка вылучáліся на фóне цёмнай хмáры./Vjaršýni xvójaŭ, jakija byli asvétlenyja cёplymi praménjami blizkaha da zaxódu sónca, járka vylučálisja na fóne cёmnaj xmáry.
'The tops of the pines, which were lit up by the warm rays of the sun that was close to setting, stood out clearly against the background of the dark cloud.'

it is not clear whether the clause introduced by якія/jakija refers to вяршы́ні/vjaršýni or хвóяў/xvójaŭ. If, however, one substitutes for the relative clause a participial phrase, all ambiguity is removed as the participle agrees in case as well as number with the noun to which it refers. Thus вяршы́ні хвóяў, асвéтленыя/vjaršýni xvójaŭ, asvétlenyja means that it is the tops of the trees which are illuminated; вяршы́ні хвóяў, асвéтленых/vjaršýni xvójaŭ, asvétlenyx means that it is the whole trees.

The use of a subordinated infinitive as opposed to a subordinate clause in Belorussian is restricted essentially to constructions in which the finite verb belongs to one of three semantic groups: modal, phasal or verb of motion. With modal verbs, if the subject of both finite verb and infinitive is the same, the infinitive is synonymous with completive што/što + finite verb, thus ён паабяцáў маўчáць/ёn paabjacáŭ maŭčác' 'he promised to keep quiet' = ён паабяцáў, што бýдзе маўчáць/ёn paabjacáŭ, što búdze maŭčác' 'he promised that he would keep quiet'. Where the subject of the infinitive is expressed as the accusative or dative object of the finite verb the subordinated infinitive is synonymous with final каб/kab + finite verb, thus я папрасíў ягó прынéсці кнíгу/ja paprasíu jahó prynésci knihu 'I asked him to bring the book' = я папрасíў ягó, каб ён прынёс кнíгу/ja paprasiú jahó, kab ёn prynёs knihu, literally 'I asked him that he bring the book'. With phasal verbs the subordinated infinitive is opposed not to a subordinate clause but to an object noun, compare ён пачáў вуяы́цца/ёn пačáŭ vučýcca 'he began to study' and ён паяáуђ вуяóбу/ ёn pačáŭ vučóbu 'he began (his) studies'. With verbs of motion the construction is synonymous with 'verb of motion + final каб/kab + infinitive'; thus ён пайшóў паглядзéць/ёn pajšóŭ pahljadzéc' 'he went to have a look' = ён пайшóў, каб паглядзéць/ёn pajšóŭ, kab pahljadzéc' 'he went in order to have a look'.

4.6   Negation

Sentence negation is expressed by the negative particle не/ne, placed directly before the verb. Other negative elements (pronouns, adverbs) must also be accompanied by не/ne, for example, яна ніколі не была ў Мінску/janá nikóli ne bylá ŭ Minsku 'she has never been to Minsk' (literally: 'she never not was in Minsk'), ён ніколі нікому нічога не расказваў аб гэтым/ën nikóli nikómu ničóha ne raskázvaŭ ab hètym 'he never told anyone anything about this' (literally: 'he never to no-one nothing not told about this'). If it is a particular constituent which is being negated, then не/ne immediately precedes that constituent, thus дні былі не сонечныя, а пахмурныя/dni byli ne sónečnyja, a paxmúrnyja 'the days were not sunny, but dull'.

The direct object of a negated verb may be in either the accusative or the genitive case. In some circumstances there is no grammatical distinction between the two cases, for example, for 'I have not read this novel' one may say either я не чытаў гэты раман/ja ne čytaŭ hèty ramán or я не чытаў гэтага рамана/ja ne čytaŭ hètaha ramána. In many situations, however, there are factors which cause a choice to be made. Broadly, the accusative case focuses attention on the object, while the use of the genitive case heightens the negation of the process. Thus, the genitive is usual where the negative particle не/ne is accompanied by ні/ni or another negative element which has ні-/ni- as a prefix: ён ні слова не сказаў/ën ni slóva ne skazáŭ 'he didn't say a (single) word'; я ніколі не пісаў ёй пісьма/ja nikóli ne pisáŭ ëj pis′má 'I have never written her a letter'. The genitive is also the choice for the direct object of negated verbs of thinking, perception, desire: яна як бы не заўважыла яго слоў/janá jak by ne zaŭvážyla jahó sloŭ 'she appeared not to notice his words'; and is used in many set expressions in which the direct object is an abstract noun, for example, не траціць часу/ne trácic′ času 'not to waste time'. Conversely, the accusative case is used if the direct object of a negated verb is a person's name: ён не асуджаў Валю/ën ne asudžáŭ Válju 'he did not condemn Valja'; if the construction is 'negated modal verb + infinitive + direct object', for example, яна не магла змяніць тон/janá ne mahlá zmjanic′ ton 'she could not change her tone'; and, usually, where the direct object is preposed to the negated verb, especially if it stands at the very beginning of the sentence: Маскву мы яшчэ не навёдалі/Maskvú my jaščè ne navédali 'Moscow we haven't yet visited'.

In the expression of absence, non-existence or non-possession, the negative of the present tense of 'to be' is няма/njamá and of the past tense не было/ne bylò; in both instances the sentence is an impersonal one, with the subject in the genitive case, for example, у мяне няма часу/u mjané njamá čásu 'I haven't got (the) time' (literally: 'at me is not of time'), мяне не было дома/mjané ne bylò dóma 'I wasn't in' (literally: 'of me not was at home'). In the future tense, however, a personal construction is usual, that is, one says я не бу́ду до́ма/ja ne bùdu dòma 'I shall not be in' rather than *мяне́ не бу́дзе до́ма/*mjanè ne bùdze dòma. The same is true of the frequentative быва́ць/byvàc' 'to be/happen', though one may note the fixed expression чаго́ не быва́е/čahò ne byvàe 'anything's possible' (literally: 'of what not happens').

4.7 Anaphora and pronouns

Most anaphora in Belorussian is pronominal and, in addition to the obvious case of the relative, most other types of pronoun may be involved in its expression: **personal**, as in

Я каха́ю Мікі́ту, і Аню́та такса́ма каха́е яго́./Ja kaxàju Mikìtu, i Anjùta taksàma kaxàe jahò.
'I love Mikita and Anjuta loves him too.'

possessive, as in

У вас ёсць запа́лкі? Сваё́ я згубі́ў./U vas ёsc' zapàlki? Svaè ja zhubìù.
'Have you any matches? I've lost mine.'

demonstrative, as in

Тацця́на ўва́чыла на адны́м во́зе Лю́бу. Та́я сядзе́ла каля́ куляме́та./
Taccjàna ùbàčyla na adnỳm vòze Ljùbu. Tàja sjadzèla kaljà kuljamëta.
'Tatiana caught sight of Ljuba on one of the carts. She (literally 'That') was sitting by a machine-gun.'

negative, for example,

Мы сядзе́лі мо́ўчкі. Ніхто́ не хаце́ў пача́ць./My sjadzèli mòùčki. Nixtò ne xasèй pačàc'.
'We sat in silence. Nobody wanted to begin.'

Pro-phrase anaphora in Belorussian is conveyed by the relative conjunction што/što, thus я зно́ў хво́ры, што мяне́ непако́іць/ja znoù xvòry, što mjanè nepakòic' 'I am ill again, which worries me'. There is no pro-verb anaphora of the type found in English sentences such as *she came early and so did he*. Instead there is zero anaphora, which in writing may be represented by the dash:

Яны́ прые́халі з адпачы́нку ў субо́ту, а мы – у нядзе́лю./Janỳ pryèxali z adpačỳnku ù subòtu, a my – u njadzèlju.
'They arrived back from their holidays on Saturday and we (arrived back) on Sunday.'

A further type of zero anaphora occurs with the omission of the subject pronoun. In standard Belorussian this normally occurs only in coordinated clauses (with or without an expressed coordinator) or in subordinate clauses with a clear subject–nominative antecedent, for example, ён упэ́унены, што спра́віцца/ën upèŭneny, što správicca 'he is convinced (that) he will manage' (literally: 'he convinced that will manage'). In more colloquial style, however, it may be extended to other types of sentence, including one-word sentences, provided there is no contextual ambiguity.

4.8   Reflexives and reciprocals

One means of expressing reflexivity is the reflexive verb: compare the two sentences ён памы́у дзіця́/ën pamýŭ dzicjá 'he washed the child' and ён памы́уся/ën pamýŭsja 'he washed (himself)'. Reflexive verbs in Belorussian (and East Slavonic as a whole) are really a refinement of the construction 'verb + accusative reflexive pronoun', brought about by the agglutination of the clitic form of that pronoun with the verb. For emphasis, though, one may still use the unagglutinated structure 'verb + (non-clitic) accusative reflexive pronoun'. Thus, parallel to the example just given, we have ён памы́у сябе́/ën pamýŭ sjabė, and it is this structure which is used to express reflexivity across an infinitival phrase boundary, for example, ён прыму́сіу чака́ць сябе́/ën prymúsiŭ čakác´ sjabė 'he made (us) wait for him' (literally: 'he made to wait himself'). With both the above the antecedent is a subject–nominative. In reflexive 'have' constructions it is 'у/u + genitive of noun/personal pronoun' and the reflexivity is expressed by the reflexive possessive свой/svoj: у яго́ сва́я машы́на/u jahó svajá mašýna 'he has his own car'. Finally, the antecedent may be a dative phrase in an impersonal construction, as in яму́ немагчы́ма трыма́ць сябе́ у рука́х/jamú nemahčýma trymác´ sjabė ŭ rukáx 'it is impossible for him to control himself'.

Reflexive verbs are also used to express reciprocity, for example, яны́ пацалава́ліся/janý pacalaválisja 'they kissed (one another)'. Alternatively, 'one another, each other' is адзі́н адна́го/adzín adnahó, with the second element changing according to case. Thus, яны́ пацалава́лі адзі́н адна́го (ACC)/janý pacalaváli adzín adnahó 'they kissed one another', яны́ падары́лі адзі́н адна́му (DAT) кве́ткі/janý padarýli adzín adnamú kvétki 'they gave one another flowers' and so on. Antecedents in reciprocal constructions are either, as here, subject–nominative or the understood subject of a subordinated infinitive, as in ім не хаце́лася пакры́удзіць адзі́н адна́го/im ne xacélasja pakrýŭdzic´ adzín adnahó 'they did not want to hurt one another'.

4.9   Possession

Of the means of expressing possession Belorussian makes full use of both the verb мець/mec´ 'to have' and the construction 'у/u + genitive case of the possessor + verb "to be" + nominative case for the thing possessed'. In both instances what is possessed may be a concrete object, an animate being or an abstract quality, thus ён ма́е гро́шы (каня́, та́лент)/ën ma̋e hrőšy (kanja̋, ta̋lent) 'he has money (a horse, talent)' and у яго́ машы́на (сын, магчы́масць)/u jahő mašy̋na (syn, mahčy̋masc´) 'he has a car (a son, the opportunity)'. Much less use is made of the dative case, but it is found in certain verb phrases involving parts of the body, for example, ён сціснуў мне руку́/ën scisnuŭ mne rukű 'he squeezed my hand' (literally: 'he squeezed to me hand'); and also in noun phrases where both possessor and possessed are personal forms, for example, ты во́раг мне/ty vőrah mne 'you are my enemy' (literally: 'you enemy to me').

Within the noun phrase, possession is most typically expressed by the genitive case of a noun or by a possessive pronoun or adjective. The former is postposed to its head: го́нар брыга́ды/hőnar bryha̋dy 'honour of the brigade', во́чы жанчы́ны/vőčy žančy̋ny 'the woman's eyes' (literally: 'eyes of woman'); the latter, in unmarked usage at least, are preposed: ма́е дзе́ці/ma̋e dze̋ci 'my children', дзе́дава ква́тэра/dze̋dava kvate̋ra 'grandfather's flat'. In Modern Belorussian noun phrases with possessive adjectives remain live forms and are synonymous with those involving a noun in the genitive case, thus сын рыбака́/syn rybaka̋ or рыбако́ў сын/rybakőŭ syn 'fisherman's son'. Possessive adjectives cannot, however, be used where it is a question of belonging to a group, since they cannot differentiate individual and collective possession; thus рыбако́вы сыны́/rybakővy syny̋ can only mean '(the) fisherman's sons', not *'fishermen's sons', which would have to be expressed as сыны́ рыбако́ў/syny̋ rybakőŭ, literally 'sons of fishermen'. Belorussian also makes some use, within the noun phrase, of 'у/u + genitive' postposed to the head noun, for example, кабіне́т у дырэ́ктара/kabine̋t u dyre̋ktara 'director's office' (literally: 'office at director').

4.10 Quantification

In noun phrases involving the numerals '1–4' (and compound numerals with '1–4' as their last element) there is concord, irrespective of case: nominative адзі́н вялі́кі стол/adzi̋n vjali̋ki stol 'one large table', два вялі́кія сталы́/dva vjali̋kija staly̋ 'two large tables', адна́ но́вая кні́га/adna̋ nővaja kniha 'one new book', дзве но́выя кні́гі/dzve nővyja knihi 'two new books' and so on. It will be observed from these examples that, in contrast to Russian, '2', '3', '4' do not govern the genitive singular of nouns when they themselves stand in the nominative or accusative case. An interesting feature, however, is that feminine and neuter nouns with mobile stress, whilst having the *ending* of the nominative–accusative plural, show the *stress* of the singular, thus вядро́/vjadrő 'bucket', nominative plural вёдры/ve̋dry, but тры вядры́/try vjadry̋ 'three buckets'; труба́/truba̋ 'pipe', nominative plural тру́бы/trűby, but чаты́ры трубы́/čaty̋ry truby̋ 'four pipes'. In the case of feminine nouns, of course, such plural forms are homonymous with the genitive singular.

The numerals '5' and above, when in the nominative or accusative, govern nouns (and adjectives) in the genitive plural, but show full concord in all other cases, thus nominative–accusative пяць вялікіх сталоў/pjac' vjalikix stalóŭ 'five large tables', genitive пяці вялікіх сталоў/pjaci vjalikix stalóŭ, dative пяці вялікім сталам/pjaci vjalikim stalám and so on. The same applies to collective numerals (see 3.1.5) and indefinite numeral-words such as столькі/stól'ki 'so many' and нéкалькі/nékal'ki 'some, a few'. Мнóга/mnóha, шмат/šmat and, more colloquially, багáта/baháta, all meaning 'much, many, lots of', are indeclinable forms which govern the genitive singular or plural as appropriate: мнóга лéсу/ mnóha lésu 'a lot of forest', шмат разóў/šmat razóŭ 'many times'. In the plural only, declinable мнóгія/mnóhija 'many' is used in concord with its head noun.

The general principles underlying verb agreement with a quantitative noun phrase in Belorussian are the following: a singular verb (showing appropriate gender in the past tense) for '1', and also for '21' and so on: вярнуўся адзін (двáццаць адзін) салдáт/vjarnúŭsja adzin (dváccac' adzin) saldát 'one soldier (twenty-one soldiers) returned'; singular also (past tense neuter) with other numerals when the subject is non-human, for example, пяць гадóў прайшлó з тагó чáсу/pjac' hadóŭ prajšló z tahó čásu 'five years had passed since that time', or, if human, where large or approximate quantity is involved, thus за дóўгім сталóм сядзéла чалавéк з двáццаць/za dóŭhim stalóm sjadzéla čalavék z dváccac' 'at a long table sat about twenty people'. A plural verb is used if the subject is human, the numeral is small and the active nature of the verbal action is stressed, for example, пéрад ягó пóзіркам прамільгнýлі дзве пóстаці/pérad jahó pózirkam pramil'hnúli dzve póstaci 'two figures flashed before his gaze'. The distribution between singular and plural is thus heavily loaded in favour of the former. Plural verb agreement with a non-human subject may, however, be found if the dependent noun is feminine, for example, дзве машыны стаялі крыху напéрадзе іншых/dzve mašýny stajáli krýxu napéradze inšyx 'two vehicles stood slightly in front of the others'; or if the noun phrase as a whole or the noun within it is modified, particularly if the modification serves to emphasize the individuality of the units making up the whole, for example:

Шаснáццаць стрáшных, нясцéрпных год штогадзінным бóлем адмéралі свой лік мáтчыным сэрцы./Šasnáccac' strášnyx, njascérpnyx hod štohadzinnym bólem admérali svoj lik u mátčynym sércu.
'Sixteen terrible, unbearable years marked themselves off in hourly pain in the mother's heart.'

5 Lexis

5.1 General composition of the word-stock

For Belorussian no statistical data have yet been produced which would allow us to state with any degree of precision the proportion of items within the word-stock of the language which can be traced directly back to Proto-Slavonic. The nearest one may get to such a calculation is to extrapolate from a generally accepted figure of about 2,000 for lexical items of Indo-European and Proto-Slavonic origin in the modern Slavonic languages as a whole, and from the approximately 95,000 words recorded in Атраховіч/Atraxovič (1977–84), that it is of the order of 2 per cent. Small though this figure may be, the words themselves are, of course, among the most frequently encountered in everyday linguistic situations, since they denote the most fundamental objects, phenomena, characteristics and activities: kinship terms, such as брат/brat 'brother', кум/kum 'godfather'; body parts, like вёка/vёka 'eyelid', горла/hórla 'throat'; food terms: блін/blin 'pancake', сала/sála 'fat, lard'; flora and fauna: клён/klën 'maple', арол/aról 'eagle'; natural phenomena: град/hrad 'hail', дождж/doždž 'rain'; temporal concepts: зіма/zimá 'winter', мёсяц/mёsjac 'month'; basic activities in man's physical and mental existence: варыць/varýc' 'to cook', вёдаць/vёdac' 'to know'; as well as numerals, pronouns and basic prepositions, conjunctions and adverbs.

A significantly greater (though again unquantified) proportion of Belorussian vocabulary is what is conventionally termed East Slavonic, that is, lexical items which can be traced back to the eight centuries between the break-up of Proto-Slavonic and the beginnings of the formation of the individual East Slavonic languages at the end of the thirteenth/beginning of the fourteenth century. Much of this stratum, held in common by Belorussian, Russian and Ukrainian, belongs to the same lexical fields as those mentioned above, thus бацька/bác'ka 'father', клык/klyk 'fang, tusk', сабака/sabáka 'dog', пёрац/pérac 'pepper', радуга/ráduha 'rainbow', прывыкаць/pryvykác' 'to become accustomed', сорак/sórak '40'. In addition, however, it illustrates in particular the socio-economic changes which occurred in the life of the Eastern Slavs during that period and includes items in such fields as agriculture (сенажаць/senažác' 'hayfield', ярына/jaryná 'spring crops'), implements (аброць/abróc' 'bridle', каромысел/karómysel 'yoke'), clothing (сарочка/saróčka 'shirt').

From the fourteenth century onwards one may speak of the creation of Belorussian lexis proper. Some of this vocabulary has in time replaced earlier lexical units, for example, бачыць/báčus' 'to see' and будаваць/budavác' 'to build' for Old Russian видѣти/viděti and строити/stroiti; сход/sxod 'meeting' for earlier сабранне/sabránne; and the grammatical terms дзёйнік/dzёjnik 'subject' and дзеяслоў/dzejaslóǔ 'verb', neologisms of the Soviet period. The vast majority of it, however, is accounted for by derived lexical units, based on Indo-European, Proto-Slavonic or East Slavonic roots but given a distinctive Belorussian form by the choice of prefix and/or suffix. Included here are such items as авечка/avečka 'sheep', вучань/vučan´ 'pupil', слухач/sluxač 'listener', красамоўнасць/krasamóŭnasc´ 'eloquence' and пранізаць/pranizác´ 'to pierce'. It would also seem appropriate, for historical reasons, to regard as Belorussian lexis proper certain words common to Belorussian and Ukrainian and to Belorussian and Polish. Examples of the former are звычай/zvýčaj 'custom' and лічба/ličba 'figure', created at a time when, within the Grand Duchy of Lithuania, Belorussians and Ukrainians shared a written language; examples of the latter are згода/zhóda 'agreement' and смутак/smútak 'sadness', dating from the period between 1569 and 1795, when much of Belorussia was part of the Polish–Lithuanian Commonwealth.

5.2   Patterns of borrowing

Among the Slavonic languages the main sources of loan-words in Belorussian have been Polish and Russian, which have also served as a medium for the introduction of loan-words from other, non-Slavonic, languages. The earliest borrowings from Polish, such as моц/moc 'strength' and скарб/skarb 'treasure', date from the end of the fourteenth century, but the greatest influx of Polonisms into Belorussian took place during the period of the Polish–Lithuanian Commonwealth, when the use of the Belorussian literary language was banned. They cover a wide range of lexical fields from the everyday to sociopolitical, military and cultural terminology and abstract concepts; examples are вяндліна/vjandlína 'ham', відэлец/vidèlec 'fork', маёнтак/maëntak 'estate', зброя/zbrója 'weapons', ксёндз/ksëndz 'priest' and сродак/sródak 'means'. Since that time Polish has exerted little influence on Belorussian and only a small number of borrowings have entered the language in the nineteenth and twentieth centuries, for example, д'ябал/d'jábal 'devil', апанаваць/ apanavác´ 'to seize'.

Active Russian influence on the vocabulary of Belorussian began at the end of the eighteenth century following re-unification, and the oppression of Belorussia by the tsars during the nineteenth century is well reflected in Russisms from that period such as пераварот/peravarót 'revolution' and ссылка/ssýlka 'exile'. In the Soviet period this influence continued strong, embracing a large number of lexical fields but especially the sociopolitical (савет/savét 'soviet'), the scientific (кукалка/kúkalka 'chrysalis'), and the technical (абкатка/abkátka 'running in'). For the historical reasons referred to in 5.1, it is notoriously difficult to identify Belorussian borrowings from Ukrainian (as opposed to words held in common by the two languages in contrast to Russian), but among the relatively small number that can be so identified we may cite жупан/župán 'župan' (kind of jerkin) and прыкме́та/prykméta 'sign'. Like Ukrainian, Belorussian has very few Church Slavonicisms: дрэ́ва/drèva 'tree' and глава́/hlavá 'chapter' are rare examples of non-pleophonic forms.

Outside the Slavonic languages the main sources of borrowings in Belorussians are, among Indo-European languages, Latin, German, French and increasingly, English, with smaller numbers of words coming from Greek (mainly religious, philosophical and scientific terminology), Italian (music, the theatre, finance and economics) and Dutch (predominantly maritime and shipbuilding terms). Many Latin words came into Belorussian in the sixteenth and seventeenth centuries via Polish; examples are аргуме́нт/ arhumént 'argument', го́нар/hónar 'honour', лі́тара/lítara 'letter'. Many more have arrived (and continue to arrive) in the twentieth century via Russian. These are almost exclusively terminological, from a wide variety of fields: а́фікс/áfiks 'affix', вакцы́на/vakcýna 'vaccine', абера́цыя/ aberácyja 'aberration', арбі́та/arbíta 'orbit' and so on. Belorussian has borrowed from German since the thirteenth century, occasionally directly, for example, вага́/vahá 'weight', дах/dah 'roof', but more often via Polish and, in modern times, Russian. The main lexical fields concerned are trade, crafts and building (га́ндаль/hándal' 'trade', цэ́гла/cèhla 'brick'), military terms (афіцэ́р/aficèr 'officer', ла́гер/láher 'camp') and the arts (мальбе́рт/mal'bèrt 'easel', камерто́н/kamertón 'tuning-fork'). Some loan-words from French, such as банке́т/bankét 'banquet', сержа́нт/ seržánt 'sergeant', entered Belorussian as early as the sixteenth or seventeenth century; most, however, are more recent, for example, гара́ж/haráž 'garage', шала́нда/šalánda 'barge'. Almost all English loan-words in Belorussian date from the nineteenth and twentieth centuries and have entered the language via Russian. They include many terms in the sporting, military, political and economic, and technical spheres, such as бокс/boks 'boxing', сна́йпер/snájper 'sniper', парла́мент/parláment 'parliament', імпарт/impart 'import' and грэ́йдэр/hrèdèr 'grader'.

The major non-Indo-European source has been the Turkic languages, principally Tatar and Turkish. However, few Turkic borrowings are recent; most go back either to the period of a common East Slavonic language, for example, арда́/ardá 'horde', бара́н/barán 'ram', or to the fourteenth to sixteenth centuries when Tatar settlements appeared on Belorussian territory, like апанча́/apančá 'cloak', кута́с/kutás 'tassel'.

5.3 Incorporation of borrowings

Both formal and semantic criteria play a role in the adaptation of borrowed nouns to the Belorussian morphological system. In the case of animate nouns gender is determined by sex. Following from this, such nouns do not decline unless masculine and ending in a consonant (*o*-stem) or feminine and ending in -a(-я)/-a(-ja) (*a*-stem). Thus дэ́ндзі/dèndzi (M) 'dandy' and мада́м/madám (F) 'madame' are indeclinable. Inanimate nouns, on the other hand, are assigned declensional type and gender on purely formal criteria, irrespective of gender (or lack thereof) in the source language. Thus, both *lampe* and *pension* are feminine in French, but in Belorussian, while лямпа/ljámpa 'lamp' declines as a feminine *a*-stem noun, пансіён/ pansiën 'boarding house' is masculine *o*-stem. Nouns with the nominative singular ending in a soft consonant may be assigned to either the masculine *o*-stem (біль/bil' 'bill') or feminine *i*-stem declension (спіраль/spiral' 'spiral'). Inanimate nouns ending in a vowel other than -a/-a, and also those in -a/-a from /o/ by *ákanne*, are treated as indeclinable and neuter: арго́/arhó 'slang', кліше́/klišè 'cliché', джэ́рсі/džèrsi 'jersey', эмба́рга/ èmbárha 'embargo'. Occasionally, number is also assigned purely on formal grounds, thus the English plural *beams* becomes singular бімс/ bims 'beam'.

Foreign verbs are borrowed almost exclusively with the aid of the suffix -ава-/-ava-. A count of such (non-prefixal) verbs in the first three volumes of Атрахові́ч/Atraxovič (1977–84) produces a total of 492, of which 305 (62 per cent) are bi-aspectual, 181 (36.8 per cent) imperfective and only six (1.2 per cent) perfective. Some of the imperfective verbs are non-paired, for example, артыкуляваць/artykuljavác' 'to articulate', but most have corresponding perfectives formed by prefixation, as in the case of гіпнатызава́ць – загіпнатызава́ць/hipnatyzavác' – zahipnatyzavác' 'to hypnotize'. That this is a living feature of Belorussian is shown by the co-existence of some bi-aspectual verbs with derived perfectives, thus along-side bi-aspectual дэмаралізава́ць/dèmaralizavác' 'to demoralize' we find perfective здэмаралізава́ць/zdèmaralizavác'. Of the six non-prefixal perfectives only адукава́ць/adukavác' 'to educate' is unpaired; the others derive imperfectives by means of the suffix -о́ўва-/-óuva-, for example арганізава́ць – арганізо́ўваць/arhanizavác' – arhanizóuvac' 'to organize'.

5.4   Lexical fields

5.4.1   Colour terms

'White' бе́лы/bély; 'black' чо́рны/čórny; 'red' чырво́ны/čyrvóny; 'green' зяле́ны/zjalëny; 'yellow' жо́ўты/žóuty; 'blue' сіні/sini and блакітны/blakitny; 'brown' кары́чневы/karyčnevy, бу́ры/búry and руды́/rudý; 'purple' ? барво́вы/barvóvy, пурпу́рны (пурпуро́вы)/ purpúrny (purpuróvy), фіяле́тавы/fijalétavy, ліло́вы/lilóvy; 'pink' ружо́вы/ružóvy; 'orange' ара́нжавы/aránžavy; 'grey' шэ́ры/šéry and сівы́/sivý.

Questions raised by Corbett and Morgan (1988) concerning which colour terms are basic in Russian are equally relevant to Belorussian. Thus, all the evidence points to there being no purple term fully established as basic: барво́вы/barvóvy suggests 'crimson', пурпу́рны (пурпуро́вы)/

purpúrny (purpuróvy) also tends in that direction, whilst фіялётавы/ fijalétavy and лілóвы/lilóvy have only a restricted application. Of the three terms for 'brown' бýры/búry would appear to have the strongest claim to being basic, since it covers the range from 'greyish-brown' to 'dark brown', while карычневы/karýčnevy is at the paler end of the range (the colour of an acorn or cinnamon), and рудьі/rudý suggests 'ginger, reddish-brown', compare рудáя вавёрка/rudája vavërka 'red squirrel'.

Worth further investigation in Belorussian are the terms for 'blue' and 'grey'. Are both terms for 'blue' basic, given that сіні/sini appears to cover both 'dark blue' and 'light blue' and блакітны/blakitny is suspect (see Berlin and Kay 1969: 6) on the grounds of being derived from the name of an object блакіт/blakit 'clear sky' and, possibly, as a borrowing (from Czech)? Conversely, does Belorussian perhaps have two basic terms for 'grey'? Сівьі/sivý, though predicated of hair, has a much wider range of application, being associated with nouns as diverse as хмáра/xmára 'cloud', каракуль/karákul´ 'astrakhan (fur)' and халáт/xalát 'dressing-gown'; while both grey terms may be applied as epithets to твар/tvar 'face'.

5.4.2 Body parts

'Head' галавá/halavá; 'eye' вóка/vóka; 'nose' нос/nos; 'ear' вýха/ vúxa; 'mouth' рот/rot; 'hair' валасьі/valasý; 'neck' шьія/šýja; 'arm/ hand' рукá/ruká; 'finger' пáлец/pálec; 'leg/foot' нагá/nahá; 'toe' пáлец/pálec; 'chest' грýдзі/hrúdzi; 'heart' сэрца/sèrca.

In Belorussian 'hand' and 'arm', 'leg' and 'foot' are not normally differentiated. Where it is important to be more specific кісць/kisc´ denotes the area from wrist to fingertips, ступня/stupnjá that from ankle to toes. Note, incidentally, a single word for 'finger' and 'toe'. Грýдзі/hrúdzi 'chest' is a pluralia tantum noun. Валасьі/valasý 'hair' (as a mass) is the plural of вóлас/vólas '(single) hair'.

5.4.3 Kinship terms

'Mother' мáці/máci or мáтка/mátka; 'father' бáцька/bác´ka; 'sister' сястрá/sjastrá; 'brother' брат/brat; 'aunt' цётка/cëtka; 'uncle' дзядзька/dzjádz´ka; 'niece' плямéнніца/pljaménnica; 'nephew' плямéннік/pljaménnik; 'cousin (female)' дваюрадная (стрыéчная) сястрá/dvajúradnaja (stryéčnaja) sjastrá; 'cousin (male)' дваюрадны (стрыéчны) брат/dvajúradny (stryéčny) brat; 'grandmother' бáба/bába or бáбка/bábka; 'grandfather' дзед/dzed; 'wife' жóнка/žónka; 'husband' муж/muž; 'daughter' дачкá/dačká; 'son' сын/syn.

For the peculiarities of мáці/máci, see 3.1.2. Айцéц/ajcéc is archaic as a kinship term and now means 'father' only in the religious sense. Amongst the terms for immediate family, note the preponderance on the female side of derived forms with the suffix -к-/-k-, the underlying forms (except in the case of 'grandmother') having ceased to be current. The alternatives for 'cousin' are free variants and do not differentiate between the male and female line.

6 Dialects

The dialects of Modern Belorussian are conventionally divided into either two or three major groups. Both classifications recognize a north-eastern and a south-western group; the difference between them lies merely in whether the band of central subdialects which runs approximately north-west–south-east across the country (see map 16.1) is regarded as a group in its own right or whether, since it combines features of both the other major groups, it is regarded as transitional. Since the publication in 1963 of the Dialect Atlas of the Belorussian Language (Аванесаў/Avanesaŭ *et al.* 1963), it is the latter approach which has been favoured. As illustrated on map 16.1, the two main dialect groups may be further subdivided: the north-eastern into the Polack group and the Vicebsk–Mahilëŭ group; the south-western into the Sluck–Babrujsk–Mazyr, western and Brèst–Pinsk (Palessian) groups.

The north-eastern dialect group is distinguished by dissimilative *ákanne* and *jákanne*, that is, in words where the stressed vowel is /a/, pre-tonic /o/, /e/, /a/ become not [a] but [ɨ] or [ʌ], while pre-tonic /e/ after a palatalized consonant becomes [i]. Only where the tonic vowel is other than /a/ do pre-tonic /o/, /e/, /a/ coalesce in [a]. Thus, nominative singular вадà/vadà 'water', ракà/rakà 'river' and вясн à/vjasnà 'spring' are pronounced [vɨdà] or [vʌdà], [rɨkà] or [rʌkà], [v'isnà] respectively, whilst, for example, genitive singular вады́/vadý, ракі/raki and вясны́/ vjasný are pronounced, as in the standard language, [vadɨ], [rak'i], [v'asnɨ]. Other characteristic phonetic features of the north-eastern dialects are prothetic [v] before initial stressed /o/, /u/, for example, вóсень/vòsen' 'autumn' [vòs'en'], вуж/vuž 'grass snake' [vuš]; gemination of dentals and post-dentals in clusters of palatalized consonant + /j/ arising from the loss of the *jers*, for example, вясéлле/vjasèlle 'wedding' [v'as'èl'l'e] (both features adopted by the standard language); assimilation in the cluster /dn/, thus [xalònna] for standard [xalòdna] халóдна/ xalòdna 'cold'; some elements of *còkanne*, for example, [p'ec] for standard [p'eč] печ/peč 'stove', [dʌckà] for standard [dačkà] дачкà/dačkà 'daughter'. In the Vicebsk–Mahilëŭ group only, we find palatal [r'].

Morphological features of the north-eastern dialect group which distin- guish it from the standard language include the ending of the masculine nominative singular adjective – compare [dòbrɨj], [s'l'apèj] with standard [dòbrɨ] добры/dòbry 'good' and [s'l'apɨ] сляпы́/sljapý 'blind'; the presence of [c'] ‹ [t'] in the third person singular non-past of first- conjugation verbs as well as second, as in [n'as'èc'] for standard нясé/

Map 16.1   Belorussian dialects

North-eastern dialect

≡ Polack group

|||| Vicebsk–Mahilëŭ group

South-western dialect

▨ Sluck–Babrujsk–Mazyr group

▨ Western group

▨ Brèst–Pinsk (Palessian) group

Central dialects

▢

njasé 'carries'; a reduced infinitive suffix for verbs with a stem ending in a consonant, for example, [n'es'c'], [klas'c'] for standard нéсці/nésci 'to carry' and клáсці/klásci 'to put'; and a first-conjugation ending in the first person plural non-past of the two athematic verbs, thus [jadz'óm], [dadz'óm].

In contrast to the north-eastern group, the dialects of the south-western group are characterized, like standard Belorussian, by non-dissimilative *ákanne* and, for the most part, *jákanne*, that is, unstressed /a/, /o/, /e/ coalesce in [a] irrespective of the quality of the stressed vowel, thus [vadá] вадá/vadá 'water', [marós] марóз/maróz 'frost', [pšan'íca] пшаніца/

pšanica 'wheat', [ɣlʹadzʹécʹ] глядзе́ць/hljadzéc' 'to look'. In the Minsk and Homel' regions, however, there is widespread *ékanne* in place of *jákanne*, for example, сястра́/sjastrá 'sister' is pronounced [sʹestrá]. The south-western dialects share with the northern dialects of Ukrainian the diphthongization of stressed /e/ and /o/ to [i͡e] and [u͡o], as in the pronunciations [mʹiéra]. [mu͡ost] of ме́ра/méra 'measure' and мост/most 'bridge'; alternatively, a closed [ê] or [ô] is heard, thus [mʹêra], [môst]. Other characteristic phonetic features of the south-western group are prothetic /ɣ/ before initial /a/, /o/, /u/, /i/, as in [ɣarác'], [ɣósʹenʹ] for standard ара́ць/arác' 'to plough', во́сень/vósenʹ 'autumn'; contraction of the geminated dentals and post-dentals that arose in clusters of palatalized consonant + /j/ after the loss of the *jers* to single, unlengthened consonants, thus вясе́лле/vjasélle 'wedding' is pronounced [vʹasʹélʹa]; hard [r], as in the standard language.

The nominal morphology of the south-western dialect group has a number of characteristic features distinguishing it from the standard language. In the noun declension system several older features are retained: the full ending -о́ю(-аю, -е́ю, -яю)/-óju(-aju, -éju, -jaju) in the instrumental singular of *a*-stem nouns (гаро́ю/haróju from гара́/hará 'mountain'); neuter nominative plural in -a/-a (гнёзда/hnëzda 'nests' for standard гнёзды/hnëzdy); stressed -о́м/-óm and -о́х/-óx in the dative and locative plural respectively of masculine *o*-stem nouns (у гарадо́х/u haradóx 'in the towns'); dual forms of feminine and neuter nouns (дзве ха́це/dzve xáce 'two houses' – compare standard дзве ха́ты/dzve xáty). Innovations include a masculine nominative plural in stressed -э́(-é)/-è(-é), for example, гарадэ́/haradè, бураке́/burakè for standard гарады́/harady 'towns' and буракі́/burakí 'beets'; and the spread of the animate accusative singular to inanimate nouns, as in ён знайшо́ў гры́ба/ën znajšóŭ hrýba 'he found a mushroom'. In adjectival morphology we encounter a feature characteristic also of Ukrainian: the loss of intervocalic /j/ and fusion of the two vowels in the feminine and neuter nominative and accusative singular endings, thus малада́/maladá, маладу́/maladú, маладо́/maladó from малады́/malady 'young' – compare the standard forms in table 16.5. In some dialects of the south-western group adjectives retain the old ending -о́м/-óm in the masculine and neuter locative singular. In verbal morphology, characteristic of the south-western dialects is the first person plural imperative ending -ма/-ma referred to in 3.2.2: чыта́йма/čytájma 'let us read', кі́ньма/kínʹma 'let us throw'. Also found is a synthetic form of the future tense created by combining the infinitive with appropriate forms of the Old Russian auxiliary имати/imati: рабі́цьму/rabícʹmu 'I shall do', рабі́цьмеш/rabícʹmeš 'you will do' and so on. Finally, the reflexive particle occurs in a non-palatalized form -ca/-sa, for example, яны́ смяя́ліса/janý smjajálisa 'they laughed' for standard смяя́ліся/smjajálisja.

Acknowledgements

I am indebted to Tamara Suša, Alena Ščuka and Alena Tabolič of the Minsk State Pedagogical Institute of Foreign Languages for checking the accuracy of the Belorussian examples; and to Nigel Gotteri for helpful comments on an earlier draft of the phonology, syntax and dialects sections.

Bibliography

Berlin, B. and Kay, P. (1969) *Basic Color Terms: their Universality and Evolution*, Berkeley: University of California Press.

Corbett, G. and Morgan, G. (1988) 'Colour terms in Russian: reflections of typological constraints in a single language', *Journal of Linguistics* 24: 31–64.

McMillin, A.B. (1973) *The Vocabulary of the Byelorussian Literary Language in the Nineteenth Century*, London: The Anglo-Byelorussian Society.

Mayo, P.J. (1976) *A Grammar of Byelorussian*, Sheffield: The Anglo-Byelorussian Society in association with the Department of Russian and Slavonic Studies, University of Sheffield.

—— (1977) 'The alphabet and orthography of Byelorussian in the twentieth century', *The Journal of Byelorussian Studies* 4, 1: 28–48.

—— (1978) 'Byelorussian orthography: from the 1933 reform to the present day', *The Journal of Byelorussian Studies* 4, 2: 25–47.

—— (1982) 'The Byelorussian language: its rise and fall and rise and ...', in F.E. Knowles and J.I. Press (eds) *Papers in Slavonic Linguistics* vol. 1, Birmingham; University of Aston in Birmingham, 163–84.

Wexler, P. (1977) *A Historical Phonology of the Belorussian Language*, Heidelberg: Carl Winter, Universitätsverlag.

Аванесаў, Р.І., Крапіва, К.К., Мацкевіч, Ю.Ф. (1963) *Дыялекталагічны атлас беларускай мовы*, ч. 1–2, Мінск: Інстытут мовазнаўства АН БССР.

Атраховіч, К.К. (рэд.) (1977–84) *Тлумачальны слоўнік беларускай мовы*, т. 1–5, Мінск: Беларуская Савецкая Энцыклапедыя.

—— (рэд.) (1982) *Руска-беларускі слоўнік*, т. 1. А–О, т. 2. П–Я, 2-е выд., дап. і перапрац., Мінск: Беларуская Савецкая Энцыклапедыя.

—— (рэд.) (1988–9) *Беларуска-рускі слоўнік*, т. 1. А–О, т. 2. П–Я, 2-е выд., перапрац. і дап., Мінск: Беларуская Савецкая Энцыклапедыя.

Бірыла, М.В., Шуба, П.П. (1985–6) *Беларуская граматыка. 1. Фаналогія. Арфаэпія. Марфалогія. Словаўтварэнне. Націск* (1985); *2. Сінтаксіс* (1986), Мінск: Інстытут мовазнаўства АН БССР.

Бурак, Л.І. (1987) *Сучасная беларуская мова. Сінтаксіс. Пунктуацыя*, Мінск: Універсітэцкае.

Жураўскі, А.І. (1967) *Гісторыя беларускай літаратурнай мовы*. т.1, Мінск: Навука і тэхніка.

Крамко, І.І., Юрэвіч, А.К., Яновіч, А.І. (1968) *Гісторыя беларускай мовы*. т.2, Мінск: Навука і тэхніка.

Крывіцкі, А.А., Падлужны, А.І. (1984) *Фанетыка беларускай мовы*, Мінск: Вышэйшая школа.

Суша, Т.М., Шчука, А.К. (1989) *Англа-беларуска-рускі слоўнік*, Мінск: Беларуская Савецкая Энцыклапедыя.

Тарашкевіч, Б. (1918) *Беларуская граматыка для школ*, Вільня.

Шуба, П.П. (1987) *Сучасная беларуская мова. Марфаналогія. Марфалогія*, Мінск: Універсітэцкае.

Янкоўскі, Ф.М. (1989) *Гістарычная граматыка беларускай мовы*, 3-е выд., выпраўленае. Мінск: Вышэйшая школа.

17 Ukrainian

George Y. Shevelov

1 Introduction

Present-day standard Ukrainian is based primarily on the south-eastern group of dialects, more precisely those spoken in the south Kievan, Čerkasy and Poltava regions. But it has also been significantly influenced by the south-western dialects where Lviv (Lvov) was an important cultural centre. This influence has been exerted, especially in lexis, but also in phonology, since the Middle Ages; in modern times it was quite strong in the nineteenth and early twentieth centuries. As a result one may with some justification speak of a bidialectal basis of standard Ukrainian, even though the eastern contribution is certainly more important. The direct impact of the northern group of dialects in modern times has been negligible. But it was substantial indirectly through the participation of Northern Ukrainian in the very formation of the south-eastern dialects, the mainstay of standard Ukrainian. This was caused by the country's historical circumstances. Beginning in the thirteenth century, under the pressure of Turkic-speaking nomadic tribes the south-eastern part of the country was lost, so that Kiev became an outpost of the realm. Both northern and south-western Ukrainians participated in the later reconquest of the lost territories in the south and east. This new settlement took about two centuries, ending in the eighteenth century, and the south-eastern dialects arose from the dialectal mixture of the underlying dialects. For more details see section 6.

The history of the literary language was less complicated. The oldest literary language of the Ukraine was imported from other Slavonic countries, primarily from Bulgaria and Macedonia, as a linguistic tool of the newly introduced Christianity, from the tenth century. It was common to all Christianized Slavs of the Byzantine rite; only individual slips into the colloquial local languages appear in these texts, Old Ukrainian in the texts

Editorial note: Following Professor Shevelov's preference, the term 'Common Slavonic' is used in this chapter where other chapters have 'Proto-Slavonic'.

written in the Ukraine. With the incorporation of the country into the Grand Duchy of Lithuania (and partly into Poland) in the fourteenth century, there evolved, especially in the chanceries of the time, a new literary language which united Belorussians and Ukrainians. All these components – Church Slavonic, Ukrainian, Belorussian and Polish – participated in various proportions in the literary languages of the sixteenth to the eighteenth centuries. But in the late eighteenth and early nineteenth centuries the literary language underwent a radical revolution: many of the non-native components were eliminated and the literary language was restructured on the Ukrainian dialectal basis as outlined above. Consequently, literary (standard) Ukrainian is a language that has gone through certain interruptions in its tradition and several new starts.

A further complication was created, especially in 1863–1905, for the bulk of Ukrainians, namely those who lived in the Russian Empire, when St Petersburg prohibited the use of Ukrainian in public life and, in particular, in schools (until 1917): even the name 'Ukrainian' was forbidden and replaced by the politically more suitable term 'Little Russian'. After the Revolution of 1917 the development and standardization of Ukrainian had their ups and downs, sometimes rather drastic. All the above have left an imprint on the status of the language and on its use. Specifically, Ukrainian was to a great extent crowded out in many big cities, especially among the upper classes.

The long-lasting division of Ukrainian territory among various states, changing at different times, such as Poland, Russia, Austro-Hungary, Czechoslovakia, Rumania and others, has also left its trace in the history of both the standard and the spoken languages. Particularly in the nineteenth and twentieth centuries, the language standard in Galicia and in the (greater) central-eastern part of the country reflected some differences in language habits and norms. To some extent this state of affairs survives today in the differences between the language standard of the former Soviet-governed or influenced areas and that of the emigrants to other countries. The most important of these differences will be referred to at the relevant points below.

2 Phonology

2.1 Segmental phoneme inventory

Modern standard Ukrainian has six vowels, four unrounded and two rounded. See table 17.1. The phoneme /o/ is usually open [ɔ], but is close [o], by assimilation, if unstressed, before a stressed syllable with *u* or *i*. Such an [o] is allophonic and is not reflected in spelling: голубка/ h[o]lùbka, feminine of голуб/h[ɔ́]lub 'dove, pigeon'. A peculiar sound in the Ukrainian vocalism is [y]. Although in the Latin transliteration it is

Table 17.1   Vowels of modern standard Ukrainian

denoted by the same letter as Russian and Belorussian ы, phonetically it is not a central back high vowel (as in Russian сын/syn 'son'), but a central front mid vowel. Historically, this vowel is the result of a merger of the older и/i and ы/y, which took place in the late thirteenth century in most dialects of the west of the country and was completed in the east by the mid-fifteenth century. In modern standard Ukrainian this vowel is articulated in the zone of *e*. Accordingly, in unstressed non-word-final position it is as a rule not distinguished from *e*, that is, unstressed *e* and *y* are merged phonologically, the phonetic realization depending on the quality of the stressed vowel in the next syllable. Thus мене́/mené 'I (GEN)' and мине́/myné 'pass (3 SG)' have identical realizations. Hence typically the unstressed vowels in standard Ukrainian are five and not six.

Like Belorussian and Russian, Ukrainian developed *polnoglasie* in the place of Common Slavonic sequences **or*, **er*, **el*/**ol* between consonants (моро́з/moró z 'frost', бе́рег/béreh 'shore', хо́лод/xólod 'cold'). Word-initially, a metathesis took place in these sequences, the results of which depended on the pitch: under rising pitch they were *ra-*, *la-*, under falling pitch *ro-*, *lo-*: рамено́/ramenó 'arm of cross', but робо́та/robóta 'work'. (Reliable examples with *e* are lacking.) These changes occurred about AD 800.

The Common Slavonic nasal vowels *ę*, *ǫ* generally developed in Ukrainian by the mid-tenth century in the same way as in Belorussian and Russian into, respectively, *'a* and *u*: п'ять/pjat′ 'five', суд/sud 'court'. There is, though, some evidence that in North Ukrainian, *ę* became *e* if unstressed: *pjat′*, genitive singular *petý*, versus standard Ukrainian п'ять/pjat′, п'яти́/pjatý.

The vowels denoted in Old Church Slavonic by the letters ъ and ь (the so-called *jers*), originating from Common Slavonic *ŭ* and *ĭ*, respectively, were lost in Old Ukrainian. In the weak position (including word-finally), that is, if not followed in the next syllable by a weak *jer*, they were dropped; if followed in the next syllable by a weak *jer* they yielded *o* and *e* respectively: *kъto* › *kto* (now хто/xto) 'who', *pьsъ* › пес/pes 'dog', *bъzъ* › боз/boz 'lilac'. These changes developed about 1150, spreading from certain phonetic environments to others. In sequences of consonant + *jer* + *r* or *l* + consonant, ъ always yielded *o*, while ь split: it gave *e* before *r* but *o* before *l*: *tъrgovlja* › торгівля/torhivlja 'commerce', *vьrxu* › ве́рху/vérxu 'top (GEN SG)', *vьlky (original root *vilk-) › вовки́/vovký 'wolves'. The reflexes of *jers* in the configuration consonant + *r* or *l* + *jer* + consonant depended on the position. In the strong position there were the usual reflexes of strong *jers*, in the weak position we find *y*: *krъvь* › кров/krov 'blood', but *krъvavъ* › крива́в[ий]/kryvа́v[yj] 'bloody'. There is no evidence that Ukrainian ever had syllabic sonants *r* and *l* except possibly in word-final position after a consonant.

In addition to the coalescence of *y* and *i* in the specifically Ukrainian *y*, discussed above, and the overall change of *ě* into *i* (*děti* › ді́ти/díty 'children'), the most peculiar development in Ukrainian vocalism, one which is unique among the Slavonic languages as spoken nowadays, was the evolution of *o* and *e* in the position before a lost weak *jer*. For *o* in that position the following stages may be uncovered: *o* › *ô* (that is, close [o], since, at the latest, the thirteenth–fourteenth centuries; in some texts denoted by the Greek letter omega, ω) › *u* (attested since the fourteenth century) › *ü* (attested since 1600, spelled ю) › *i* (attested since 1653): *kotъ* › *kωt* › *kut* › *küt* (spelled кют/kjut) › кіт/kit 'cat'. For *e* the development was twofold, before a lost ь and before a lost ъ. Before the lost ь it was: *e* › *ě* (attested since 1161, the so-called 'new' *ě'*) › *i* (along with the original *ě*, in the fourteenth–fifteenth centuries): *pečь* › *pěč* › піч/pič 'stove'. Before lost ъ, except in some western dialects, *e* did not undergo any changes, except possibly under retracted stress: *medъ* › мед/med 'honey', but *uteklъ* › утік/utik 'fled (M)', contrast утекло́/uteklо́ 'fled (N)'.

All these developments of *e* and *o* occurred in southern dialects. In northern dialects, instead, *o* and *e* before the syllable which lost a *jer* developed into diphthongs. This diphthongization affected only stressed syllables.

Modern standard Ukrainian as well as all Ukrainian dialects does not have phonemically relevant length and pitch in vowels. It only preserves free dynamic stress (with concomitant lengthening), which can fall on any syllable and which can shift within a paradigm. The distribution of paradigms with fixed and with shifting stress is unpredictable unless morphological rules interfere. The chronology of the loss of phonemic pitch and length in Ukrainian is uncertain. But since no phonetic changes have depended on them in the time since the tenth century, nothing precludes the assumption that they were lost at that time or soon after, that is still in the Proto-Ukrainian period.

The consonant system of Ukrainian is set out in table 17.2. Several of these consonants have limited distribution. /r'/ never occurs syllable-finally. The consonants /f/ and /g/ occur only in foreign (and onomato-poetic) words. The former was introduced in loan-words which entered Old Ukrainian with Christianization, mostly from Greek. In the spoken language it was replaced by *p*, *v* or *x*, as in the Christian names Stepan, Vekla, Oxrim, but later, with the growing influx of loan-words from Greek,

Table 17.2   Consonants of modern standard Ukrainian

| | Labial | | Dental | | Palatal | Velar | Laryngeal |
			Plain	Palatalized			
Plosive	p b		t d	t′ d′		k g	
Fricative	f v/w		s z	s′ z′	š ž	x	h
Affricate			c ʒ	c′ ʒ′	č ǯ		
Nasal	m		n	n′			
Lateral			l	l′			
Trill			r	r′			
Glide					j		

western European and other sources a new sound and phoneme was introduced, namely the labialized fricative x^w, which is still widely used in non-standard language. However, in the language of the educated, x^w was considered vulgar and f was accepted, probably on the Russian and Polish pattern. Common Slavonic /g/ changed in Old Ukrainian into h (or [ɣ]) in the late twelfth or early thirteenth century. /g/ was introduced anew, mostly in loan-words of western origin as well as from other sources, and is attested since 1388. In writing it was rendered by a digraph кг and in other ways, until a special letter г was introduced in 1619. This special letter was, however, abolished in 1933 in the Soviet Ukraine (in favour of plain г), so that now it is only used outside the country. The affricates ʒ, ʒ′ and ǯ do not have special letters either and are denoted by digraphs дз/dz and дж/dž. These affricates also have limited distribution, primarily in onomatopoetic words and in words of foreign origin; only ǯ is better adopted in that it participates in alternation with d in verbal and verb-derived forms, as in водúти/vodýty 'to lead', воджý/vodžú (1 SG), вóджений/vódženyj (PAST PART).

As a rule voiced consonants preserve their voicing in all positions, except in the preposition and prefix з/z, which is prone to devoice before voiceless consonants. This may be accounted for historically by its origin: it continues two original prepositions/prefixes: *sъ* and *iz(ъ)*. On the other hand, voiceless consonants become voiced before voiced obstruents: боротьбá/borot′bá 'struggle' is pronounced with [d′]. The consonant presented in table 17.2 as *v/w* is realized in syllable-final position as [w], in other positions its realization varies between [v] and [w], more often [w].

There are also long consonants. Usually they appear at morpheme boundaries and, consequently, are phonemically double and not long consonants: віддáти/vi[d̄]áty 'to give away' from від/vid 'from' and дáти/dáty 'to give'; вúнна/vý[n̄]a 'guilty (F)', with the adjective-forming suffix -*n*, compare винá/vyná 'guilt'. Palatalized long consonants occur in some morphological categories, most usually in deverbal nouns of the type знання/znannjà 'knowledge' and in the instrumental singular of feminine nouns ending in a consonant: тінь/tin´ 'shadow', instrumental singular тінню/tinnju. Historically, this length arose from the consonantal cluster palatalized consonant + *j*. Its phonemic status is debatable: /C̄´/ or /C´j/.

Common Slavonic palatalized /r´/, /l´/, /n´/ were preserved in Old Ukrainian longer than in Old Russian, but their palatalization was lost by the late twelfth century. The question of whether Old Ukrainian automatically palatalized all consonants before front vowels is to be answered in the affirmative for *ě* and for *'a* from *ę*; for the position before *e* and *i* (> *y*) the situation is not so obvious, but there seem to be more arguments in favour of the negative answer.

For the relation between Ukrainian orthography and the phonological system, reference should be made to table 17.3 and to the following notes. There are no special letters for the affricates ʒ, ʒ´ and ǯ, the digraphs дз and дж being used, respectively; in the former Soviet Ukraine, г was used for both *h* and *g*. The phoneme /j/ is indicated by й only if syllable-final or before the vowel *o*; word-initially or after a vowel, *ja*, *je*, *ji*, *ju* are indicated by the special letters я, є, ї, ю; after labials and *r*, the same symbols are used, though separated from the labial by an apostrophe (not represented in the transliteration). A sequence of palatalized consonant plus vowel is indicated by using the letter for the equivalent plain consonant plus the following letter or letter combination: я, є, i, ьо, ю; syllable-finally, palatalization is indicated by adding ь after the letter for the corresponding plain consonant.

2.2   Morphophonemic alternations inherited from Common Slavonic

The best-preserved Common Slavonic alternations of consonants are those of velars (including the laryngeal) with dental and palatals (table 17.4). They originate in the first and second palatalizations of velars. Today, however, they are devoid of phonetic motivation and, mostly, are morphologized. The alternations of velars with (palatalized) dentals is basically limited to the pre-desinential position (that is, the position before the inflectional ending) before word-final -*i* in the dative and locative singular: рука/rukà 'hand', dative/locative singular руці/rucì; круг/kruh 'circle', locative singular крузі/krùzi. The only survival of this alternation in the nominative plural is друг/druh 'friend', plural друзі/drùzi, although the alternation is extended to the other plural cases, as in genitive plural друзів/drùziv. The alternation of velars with palatals encompasses more instances, namely: vocative singular in -*e* of masculine nouns: чоловік/čolovik 'man', vocative singular чоловіче/čoloviče; the present, imperative and past participle passive in verbs of the first conjugational class: пекти/pektý 'to bake', печу/pečù (1 SG PRS), печи/pečý (2 SG IMP), печений/pečenyj (PAST PART PASS); and finally, before suffixes which begin in -(*o*)*k*, -(*e*)*c´*, *e* and *y* (except the suffix -*yn*(*ja*) to denote female

Table 17.3 Ukrainian alphabet

Ukrainian		*Transliteration*
А	а	a
Б	б	b
В	в	v
Г	г	h
(Ґ	ґ	g)
Д	д	d
Е	е	e
Є	є	je
Ж	ж	ž
З	з	z
И	и	y
І	і	i
Ї	ї	ji
Й	й	j
К	к	k
Л	л	l
М	м	m
Н	н	n
О	о	o
П	п	p
Р	р	r
С	с	s
Т	т	t
У	у	u
Ф	ф	f
Х	х	x
Ц	ц	c
Ч	ч	č
Ш	ш	š
Щ	щ	šč
Ю	ю	ju
Я	я	ja
	ь	′

Table 17.4 Alternations from Common Slavonic palatalizations

k	:	c′	:	č
x	:	s′	:	š
h/g	:	z′	:	ž

persons, of the type княгѝня/knjahýnja 'princess'), as in рукá/ruká 'hand', diminutive рýчка/rúčka, affective рýченька/rúčen´ka.

Other alternations of consonants (labials and dentals) of Common Slavonic origin historically originated in clusters of consonants followed by *j*. These alternations typically characterize verbs of the second conjugation when they occur in the first person singular present and the past participle passive, as shown in table 17.5. Examples are: молотѝти/molotýty 'to thresh', молочý/moločú (1 SG) молóчений/moločenyj (PAST PART PASS); любѝти/ljubýty 'to love', люблю̀/ljubljú (1 SG), лю̀блений/ljúblenyj (PAST PART PASS).

Table 17.5 Alternations from Common Slavonic *j

t	:	č	d	:	ǯ	s	:	š	z	:	ž	labial	:	labial + l′

Alternations of vowels going back to Common Slavonic and even Indo-European times appear now unsystematically and only in a limited number of roots. They are typical relics. They are relatively better preserved in verbal roots where they may be utilized to mark aspectual changes. They are of three types (table 17.6). Examples are: пожéрти/požérty 'to devour (PRFV)', imperfective пожирáти/požyráty; заместѝ/zamestý 'to sweep (PRFV)', imperfective замітáти/zamitáty; допомогтѝ/dopomohtý 'to help (PRFV)', imperfective допомагáти/dopomaháty. Particularly eroded is the type *o* : *a*, limited to three verbal roots.

Table 17.6 Vowel alternations inherited from Common Slavonic

e (as a rule fugitive)	:	y
e	:	i
o	:	a

2.3 Morphophonemic alternations resulting from changes after Common Slavonic

There are no alternations of consonants that arose in Ukrainian after the completion of its formation as a separate language.

A number of vowel alternations arose specifically in Ukrainian, but, as with those of Common Slavonic origin, motivation of the alternation and by the same token its productivity is lost in most instances. These alternations are the following:

e, *o* : *y* грóми/hrómy 'thunderstrokes', гримíти/hrymíty 'to thunder'; хрест/xrest 'cross', христѝти/xrystýty 'to baptize' (about five roots with active alternation); this alternation derives from the different developments of *jers* adjacent to liquids depending on stress and openness/closeness of the syllable.

e : o after palatals: четве́ртий/četvértyj 'fourth', чоти́ри/čotýry 'four' (about nine roots with the active alternation, and also the suffix *-ev-/-ov-* in adjectives). Originally, *e* was preserved before syllables with a front vowel, but after Old Ukrainian *i* and *y* merged as *y* this motivation was lost, as in шести́/šestý 'six (GEN)', шо́стий/šóstyj 'sixth', from older *šesti, šestъ*, respectively, now both with *y* in the next syllable.

e, o : Ø (the so-called 'fugitive' or 'fleeting' vowels, with historically *e* from ь, *o* from ъ or ь), as in ві́тер/víter 'wind', genitive singular ві́тру/vítru. This alternation is totally unproductive even though it has been partly morphologized: for the most part *e, o* are typical of the nominative singular of masculine nouns, the genitive plural of feminine and neuter nouns, and the residual short forms of adjectives with the suffix *-n-*.

The most widespread alternation of vowels is that of *o, e : i* (on its origin, see section 2.1), but its phonetic motivation has been lost entirely and the alternation has been morphologized. The main forms in which *i* occurs instead of *o, e* are:

nominative singular of masculine nouns, versus oblique cases: лід/lid 'ice', genitive singular льо́ду/l'ódu (but as a rule not in *polnoglasie* groups);

nominative and instrumental singular of feminine nouns ending in a consonant: ніч/nič 'night', instrumental singular ні́ччю/níččju, genitive singular но́чі/nóči;

pre-suffixal syllables in feminine and neuter diminutives: сирі́тка/syrítka, diminutive of сирота́/syrotá 'orphan';

neuter nouns of the type весі́лля/vesíllja 'wedding', compare весе́лий/vesélyj 'joyful';

adjectives whose root ends in a consonant followed by a suffix beginning with a consonant: потрі́бний/potríbnyj 'needed', compare потре́ба/potréba 'need';

past tense masculine and past gerund of verbs with a stem in a consonant: ніс/nis 'carried (M), нісши/nisšy 'having carried', compare нести́/nestý 'to carry'.

Besides these cases there are many isolated instances of the alternation, so that there cannot be any absolute predictability in the choice between *o, e* on the one hand and *i* on the other.

In summary, the alternations discussed in sections 2.2 and 2.3 are either merely traditional (not motivated synchronically) or partially motivated morphologically. Of phonetically conditioned vowel alternations in modern standard Ukrainian there is only one, namely e, y : y^e, conditioned by stress placement (section 2.1).

3 Morphology

3.1 Nominal morphology

3.1.1 Nominal categories

Nominals in modern standard Ukrainian are declined for case and number. There are two numbers, singular and plural. The dual was lost as a productive category in the sixteenth to seventeenth centuries; individual case forms of the dual survive as irregularities in the plural, for example о́чи/ о́či, plural of о́ко/о́ko 'eye', instead of the regular neuter plural in -*a*. The most important and consistent trace of the dual is found in the stress of the nominative of nouns with movable stress in sequences with the numerals '2' to '4'. While their normal stress in the nominative plural is word-final, in phrases with the above numerals stress is on the preceding syllable: брати́/bratý 'brothers', жінки́/žinký 'women', but два бра́ти/dva bráty 'two brothers', дві жі́нки/dvi žínky 'two women'.

Ukrainian preserves the original set of cases: nominative, accusative, genitive, dative, instrumental and locative. In addition, the vocative is preserved even though the vocative singular in colloquial speech is occasionally replaced by the nominative and in the plural the vocative has no forms of its own, except in the word пано́ве/panóve 'gentlemen' (nominative plural пани́/paný).

There are three genders, masculine, feminine and neuter, in the singular; these genders are not distinguished in the plural.

3.1.2 Noun morphology

The Common Slavonic distribution of nouns according to their (Indo-European) stem, a system which started decaying in late Common Slavonic, lost its motivation completely in Old Ukrainian. A new basis for the distribution of declensional types was found in genders and, within a gender, in the types of endings. Modern standard Ukrainian has the following fully fledged declensional types: masculine, feminine in a vowel, feminine in a consonant, neuter. Within each of these types (except the third) there is a division into the 'hard' and the 'soft' subtypes; their interrelation is manifest basically in the choice of the vowel in the endings. The set of correspondences between the two subtypes is the following: when the hard subtype has o or y the soft subtype substitutes e (in neuters also $'e$) and i respectively. (But the opposite is not true: e and i do appear in the hard paradigm.)

The basic declensional types are set out in table 17.7. The soft subtype is

Table 17.7 Declensional patterns of nouns

(a)

	Masculine 'kitchen garden'	Neuter 'city'	Feminine in vowel 'sister'	Feminine in consonant 'night'
Singular				
NOM	горóд	мíсто	сестрá	нíч
VOC	горóде	мíсто	сéстро	нóче
ACC	горóд	мíсто	сестрý	нíч
GEN	горóда	мíста	сестрú	нóчі
DAT	горóдові	мíсту	сестрí	нóчі
INST	горóдом	мíстом	сестрóю	нíччю
LOC	горóді	мíсті	сестрí	нóчі
Plural				
NOM/VOC	горóди	містá	сéстри	нóчі
ACC	горóди	містá	сестéр	нóчі
GEN	горóдів	міст	сестéр	ночéй
DAT	горóдам	містáм	сéстрам	ночáм
INST	горóдами	містáми	сéстрами	ночáми
LOC	горóдах	містáх	сéстрах	ночáх

(b)

	Masculine 'kitchen garden'	Neuter 'city'	Feminine in vowel 'sister'	Feminine in consonant 'night'
Singular				
NOM	horód	místo	sestrá	nič
VOC	horóde	místo	séstro	nóče
ACC	horód	místo	sestrú	nič
GEN	horódu	místa	sestrý	nóči
DAT	horódovi	místu	sestrí	nóči
INST	horódom	místom	sestróju	níččju
LOC	horódi	místi	sestrí	nóči
Plural				
NOM/VOC	horódy	místá	séstry	nóči
ACC	horódy	místá	sestér	nóči
GEN	horódiv	mist	sestér	nočéj
DAT	horódam	místàm	séstram	nočám
INST	horódamy	místámy	séstramy	nočámy
LOC	horódax	místáx	séstrax	nočáx

not represented in this table because, generally, it derives from the hard subtype by the above-mentioned substitutions; examples would be князь/ knjaz´ 'prince' for masculines, пóле/póle 'field' for neuters, будíвля/ budívlja 'edifice' for feminines in a vowel.

This relatively simple structure of noun declension might be further simplified by regarding masculine and neuter as one paradigm, for they are very close to each other. But on the other hand, it is complicated by the presence of desinential doublets in some instances and of some remnants of basically lost declensional types.

Desinential doublets exist in the following instances. Among masculines in the nominative singular there are also nouns ending in -*o*, such as Павло́/Pavló 'Paul', Дніпро́/Dnipró 'Dnieper'. In the vocative singular, some isolated masculine hard nouns take the ending -*u*: ба́тько/bát'ko 'father', vocative ба́тьку/bát'ku; син/syn 'son', vocative си́ну/sýnu. Neuters have no special vocative form. In masculine nouns of the soft subtype, the normal ending -*e* appears only after the suffix -(*e*)*c*′; otherwise the ending -*u* is used: хло́пець/xló pec′ 'lad', vocative хло́пче/xló pče, but кова́ль/kovál′ 'smith', vocative кова́лю/koválju.

The accusative singular in neuters is identical to the nominative. In masculines the basic factor is animacy versus inanimacy. Animate nouns take a form identical to the genitive. In the singular this is obligatory for nouns denoting persons and animals; in the plural the form of the nominative may still be used in the names of animals: ба́чив бра́та, коня́, брати́в, ко́ней (ко́ні)/bá čyv bráta, konjá, brativ, kónej (kóni) 'he saw the brother, the horse, the brothers, the horses'. In the masculine singular the ending of the genitive singular may also be used, with a certain amount of affectivity, for names of well-shaped concrete objects other than persons and animals, as in посла́в листа́/posláv lystá 'he sent a letter', дав карбо́ванця/dav karbóvancja 'he gave a rouble'. Here, then, the category of animacy tends to be broadened into that of being (well) shaped. In feminines and neuters the category of animacy applies only in the plural.

In the genitive singular beside the ending -*u* the ending -*a* is also widespread. The distinction between them is based partly on tradition but more often on semantic criteria. Generally, -*a* is taken by nouns which denote clearly outlined or shaped objects, including persons, while -*u* characterizes names of objects seen as collective, abstract, shapeless; this ending easily conveys also a partitive meaning. Examples are лист/lyst 'letter', genitive листа́/lystá; брат/brat 'brother', genitive бра́та/bráta; but колекти́в/kolektýv 'collective', genitive колекти́ву/kolektývu; ро́зум/rózum 'mind', genitive ро́зуму/rózumu. In neuters only the ending -*a* is used. In the dative singular masculine nouns have -*ovi* alongside -*u*. In neuters, only -*u* is used.

In the locative singular (the locative is always used with a preposition), beside the ending -*i* there are in the masculine and neuter the endings -*u* and -*ovi*. The choice among them is governed by both morphophonemic and semantic criteria. The ending -*u* is taken by those nouns that end in a suffixal velar, usually -*k*, as in га́нок/gánok 'porch', locative га́нку/gánku, ли́чко/lýčko 'face', locative ли́чку/lýčku, versus о́ко/óko 'eye', locative о́ці/óci (where *k* belongs to the root; velars before the locative ending -*i* alternate with palatalized dentals: see section 2.2). The semantic factor is visible in that nouns denoting persons may take the ending -*ovi* (transferred from the dative): селянин/seljanýn 'peasant', locative селянинові/seljanýnovi. Finally, masculine monosyllabic nouns with root stress in the singular oblique cases may take the ending -*u* but with stress on the ending in the locative, as in степ/step 'steppe', genitive стéпу/stépu, locative степý/stepú.

In the nominative and instrumental plural there are a few deviations from the general pattern due to the incorporation of isolated forms of the dual: in the nominative plural masculine вýса/vúsa 'moustache' and рукáва/rukáva 'sleeves', in the neuter nouns óчi/óči 'eyes', вýши/vúši (also вýха/vúxa) 'ears' and плéчi/pléči 'shoulders', and in the instrumental plural очима/ošýma, вушима/vušýma, but also грошима/hrošýma 'money'.

In the two feminine declensions there are very few doublet endings. Of greater significance is only the competition between the endings -*ej* and -*iv* in the genitive plural of the consonantal declension (подорож/pódorož 'trip', genitive plural подорожей/pódorožej or подорожів/pódoroživ; the standard language gives clear priority to -*ej*) and the transfer of the ending -*ej* from the consonantal declension to several nouns of other declensional types such as feminines свиня/svynjá 'pig', миша/mýša 'mouse', вóша/vóša 'louse', стаття/stattjá 'article', genitive plural свинéй/svynéj, мишéй/myšéj, вошей/vóšej, стат(т)éй/stat(t)éj; masculines кінь/kin´ 'horse', гість/hist´ 'guest', genitive plural кóней/kónej, гостéй /hostéj; and neuters óко/óko 'eye', плечé/plečé 'shoulder', genitive plural очéй/očéj, плешей/plečéj.

The present-day noun declension of Ukrainian is the result of many mergers of Old Ukrainian declensional types inherited from Common Slavonic. Common Slavonic *o*-, *jo*- and *u*-stems supplied most endings in the Modern Ukrainian masculine and neuter declension; *a*- and *ja*-stems were most substantial in the shaping of the Modern Ukrainian feminine vocalic declension, while *i*-stems and consonant stems were decisive in the formation of the feminine consonantal declension. Most nouns are now declined according to these productive types.

There are, however, a few noun declensional types which so far have not been engulfed by the productive types. They survive in a limited number of nouns, as words of long-lasting tradition, as a rule. Genetically, these types go back to various consonant stems: *t*-stems (which is the only type that may still absorb newly arising nouns, albeit rarely), *n*-stems and *r*-stems. Nowadays, the main characteristic of these declensional types is that they take in the oblique cases an 'insertion' (-*at*-, -*en*-, -*er*-) between the root (stem) and the ending: дівчá/divčá 'girl', genitive дівчáти/divčáty (*t*-stem) ім'я/imjá 'name', genitive iмeнi/imeni (but usually pronounced as if *imeny*) (*n*-stem), мáти/máty 'mother', genitive мáтерi/máteri (*r*-stem). Nowadays *r*-stems are limited to the one noun just quoted; only *t*-

stems are a relatively open group, owing to their semantic unity: as a rule they denote young or small beings.

3.1.3   Pronominal morphology

The inflectional endings of some pronouns are like those of nouns, of others like those of adjectives, but with some peculiarities, the crucial ones being suppletion of the root in some pronouns and in some the use in certain cases of peculiar case forms. For the forms, see table 17.8, noting that adjective-based patterns which have a plural do not differ in their declension from adjectives (table 17.9), and that the reflexive pronoun себе́/sebé is declined like ти/ty, apart from the lack of a nominative.

Suppletion takes place in the personal pronouns of the first person singular (я/ja (NOM); мене́/mené (ACC–GEN), мені́/mení (DAT–LOC); мно́ю/mnóju (INST)), of the second person singular (ти/ty (NOM); тебе́/tebé (ACC–GEN); тобі́/tobí (DAT–LOC), тобо́ю/tobóju (INST)), of the first person plural (ми/my (NOM); нас/nas (ACC–GEN–LOC), нам/nam (DAT), на́ми/námy (INST)), of the third person (nominative він/vin (M), вона́/voná (F), воно́/vonó (N); oblique cases with the stem *j*-, in the instrumental and after prepositions *n*- or *n'*-, as in його́/johó (ACC–GEN– M–N) but до ньо́го/do n'óho 'to him'), and in two interrogative pronouns хто/xto (NOM) 'who', oblique stem *k*-; що/ščo (NOM–ACC) 'what', oblique stem *č*-).

The peculiar pronominal endings, that is, those that do not occur in the declension of nouns and adjectives, are those in the personal pronouns mentioned above (-*e* in accusative–genitive мене́/mené, тебе́/tebé and -*s* in accusative–genitive–locative нас/nas, вас/vas) and the following in demonstrative pronouns: -*oj*, -*ej*, in the nominative–accusative singular masculine (той/toj 'that', цей/cej 'this'), -*ijeji* in the genitive singular feminine (тіє́ї/tijéji, ціє́ї/cijéji) and -*ijeju* in the instrumental singular feminine (тіє́ю/tijéju, ціє́ю/cijéju). In many pronouns the root consists of only one consonant, which is not typical of nouns and adjectives.

Clitic forms of personal and anaphoric pronouns, which were used in Old and Middle Ukrainian and are still current in south-western dialects (such as accusative *mja*, *tja*, *sja*, *ho*, dative *my*, *ty*, *sy*, *mu*), have been lost in standard Ukrainian. The reflexive clitic *sja* (after vowels and sonants optionally *s'*) has become a verbal postfix (that is, an element inseparable from the verb and occurring after all other endings). It is placed after verbal endings, with the final consonant of which it merges by assimilation: сміє́шся/smijéšsja 'you laugh', pronounced -[s':a], сміє́ться/smijét'sja 'he laughs', pronounced -[c':a].

An accentual peculiarity of pronouns in their disyllabic forms is that after governing prepositions the stress is retracted by one syllable: мене́ /mené, кого́/kohó, but до ме́не/do méne, до ко́го/do kóho; contrast trisyllabic ціє́ї/cijéji, до ціє́ї/do cijéji. This stress shift does not occur if

Table 17.8 Declensional patterns of pronouns

(a)

| | Noun-based patterns | | | Adjective-based patterns | | | | Gender-free | |
| | 'I' | 'thou' | 'we' | 'he, she, it' | | 'that' | | 'who' | 'what' |
				M/N	F	M/N	F		
NOM	я	ти	ми	він/воно́	вона́	той/те	та	хто	що
ACC	мене́	тебе́	нас	його́	ї́	= NOM/GEN	ту	кого́	чого́
GEN	мене́	тебе́	нас	його́	ї́	того́	тіє́ї	кого́	чого́
DAT	мені́	тобі́	нам	йому́	їй	тому́	тій	кому́	чому́
INST	мно́ю	тобо́ю	на́ми	ним	не́ю	тим	тіє́ю	ким	чим
LOC	мені́	тобі́	нас	ньо́му/нім	ній	то́му/тім	тій	ко́му/ким	чо́му/чім

(b)

| | Noun-based patterns | | | Adjective-based patterns | | | | Gender-free | |
| | 'I' | 'thou' | 'we' | 'he, she, it' | | 'that' | | 'who' | 'what' |
				M/N	F	M/N	F		
NOM	ja	ty	my	vin/vonó	vonà	toj/te	ta	xto	ščo
ACC	mené	tebé	nas	johó	jijí	= NOM/GEN	tu	kohó	ščo
GEN	mené	tebé	nas	johó	jijí	tohó	tijéji	kohó	čohó
DAT	mení	tobí	nam	jomu	jij	tomú	tij	komu	čomú
INST	mnóju	tobóju	námy	nym	néju	tym	tijéju	kym	čym
LOC	mení	tobi	nas	n'ómu/nim	nij	tómu/tim	tij	kómu/kim	čomu/čim

the preposition governs the following noun: contrast до ньо́го/do n'óho but до його́ до́му/do johó dómu 'to his house'.

Indefinite and negative pronouns are formed by adding a pre- or post-positive particle to an interrogative pronoun. Thus, on the basis of хто/xto 'who', we have абихто/abýxto 'whoever', будьхто́/bud'xtó or хто-бу́дь/xto-bud' 'anybody', де́хто/déxto 'someone', хтось/xtos' 'someone (unidentified or irrelevant)', ніхто́/nixtó 'nobody'. In prepositional phrases with the negative pronouns the preposition is usually placed immediately after the particle, cutting the word in two: ні на ко́го/ni na koḍ ho 'onto nobody'.

3.1.4   Adjectival morphology

Of the two Common Slavonic adjectival paradigms, short (like nouns) and long (like pronouns), Ukrainian has preserved the long forms; see table 17.9. Short forms exist only residually and only in the nominative singular masculine. Such short forms are obligatory in possessive adjectives (ба́тьків дім/bát'kiv dim 'father's house', сестри́н дім/sestrýn dim 'sister's house'); in recent years there has appeared a tendency to use the long form, ба́тьковий дім/bát'kóvyj dim, although this is considered non-standard. The choice of form is optional in ко́жний/kóžnyj, ко́жен/kóžen 'each' and, though with the short form only in predicative function, in up to a dozen or so adjectives including the following: ва́ртий/vártyj or варт/vart 'worth', ви́нний/výnnyj or ви́нен/výnen 'guilty', зго́дний/zhódnyj or зго́ден/zhóden 'agreeing', ла́дний/ládnyj or ладе́н/ladén 'apt, ready', пе́вний/pévnyj or пе́вен/péven 'sure', пови́нний/povýnnyj

Table 17.9   Adjective declension

(a)

	Masculine	Singular Neuter	Feminine	Plural
NOM	нови́й	нове́	нова́	нові́
ACC	= NOM/GEN	нове́	нову́	= NOM/GEN
GEN	ново́го		ново́ї	нови́х
DAT	ново́му		нові́й	нови́м
INST	нови́м		ново́ю	нови́ми
LOC	ново́му/нові́м		нові́й	нови́х

(b)

	Masculine	Singular Neuter	Feminine	Plural
NOM	novýj	nove	nova	novi
ACC	= NOM/GEN	nove	novu	= NOM/GEN
GEN	novoho		novoji	novýx
DAT	novomu		novij	novým
INST	novým		novoju	novýmy
LOC	novomu/novim		novij	novýx

or повйнен/povýnen 'most'. Even in these adjectives all forms but the nominative singular masculine follow the regular adjectival declension. The present-day adjectival declension has undergone many simplifications. Genders are no longer distinguished in the plural. The stress undergoes no shifts. There are no doublet endings, except for the two options in the locative singular masculine–neuter. There is no soft subtype: stems ending in palatalized consonants take the same endings as those ending in non-palatalized consonants.

Participles (the widely used past participles passive in *-nyj* and *-tyj* and the extremely rare present participles active in *-čyj*) decline following the pattern of adjectives.

Beside the normal adjectival forms of the nominative–accusative feminine, neuter and plural there are, in poetic language only, the so-called 'non-contracted' forms: новая/novája, новую/novúju, новеє/novéje, новії/novíji. The term is misleading. Actually, they are petrified forms of the full long-form adjectives before these underwent truncation under the influence of the pronominal declension, with its monosyllabic endings. Historically, thus, there were three stages in the development of Ukrainian adjectival declension. Exemplified by the form of the nominative singular feminine they were: (1) noun-like *nova*; (2) pronominalized by addition of the Common Slavonic pronoun *ja* 'she' into *novaja*; (3) truncated to *nova* with a monosyllabic ending as in pronouns of the type *ta* 'that', formally identical with the oldest of the three forms.

Ukrainian adjectives, wherever their semantics allows, may have comparative and superlative degrees. The comparative degree is usually formed by the suffixes *-š-* and *-iš-*: молодйй/molodýj 'young', comparative молодший/molódšyj or молодіший/molodíšyj. The suffix *-š-* is non-productive and is used with a fixed set of about twenty-five adjectives. It entails some consonant alternations: *h* or *z* plus *š* gives *žč*, as in дорогйй/dorohýj 'dear', comparative дорожчий/doróžčyj, вузькйй/vuzʹkýj 'narrow', comparative вужчий/vúžčyj; *s* plus *š* gives *šč*, as in висóкий/vysókyj 'tall', comparative вйщий/výščyj; after *ž* the suffix changes into *č*, as in дужий/dúžyj 'strong', comparative дужчий/dúžčyj; the suffix *-(o)k* (see the forms just given for 'tall') and the consonant *h* after another consonant are lost before the suffix *-š-*, as in дóвгий/dóvhyj 'long', comparative дóвший/dóvšyj.

The suffix *-iš-* entails no phonetic changes. It is productive and subject to no limitations, except that it is not applied to adjectives with the suffix *-sʹk-*, to participles and to some adjectives with affective suffixes.

The superlative is derived from the comparative by adding the prefix *naj-*: вйщий/výščyj 'taller', найвйщий/najvýščyj 'tallest'.

Alongside these synthetic forms, but much less frequently used, there are analytical comparative and superlative forms, the basic form of the adjective preceded by the word бíльш(e)/bílʹš(e) 'more' for the comparative and найбільш(е)/najbíl′š(e) 'most' for the superlative. Typically, these constructions are used in chains of comparatives or superlatives and in the opposition ме́нш(е)/ménš(e) 'less', бі́льш(е)/bíl′š(e) 'more', but also occasionally in competition with the synthetic forms. There are a few suppletive comparatives: мали́й/malýj 'small', comparative ме́нший/ménšyj; вели́кий/velýkyj 'big', comparative бі́льший/bíl′šyj; пога́ний/pohányj 'bad', comparative гі́рший/híršyj; до́брий/dóbryj and га́рний/hárnyj 'good', comparative кра́щий/kráščyj. All comparatives and superlatives decline like other adjectives and stand in agreement with their nouns.

Adverbs derived from adjectives follow the same pattern in forming degrees of comparison: то́нко/tónko 'thinly', comparative то́нше/tónše.

3.1.5 Numeral morphology

All numerals decline, except masculine–neuter півтора́/pivtorá, feminine півтори́/pivtorý 'one and a half', but their declension types are varied.

'One', masculine оди́н/odýn, feminine одна́/odná, neuter одне́/odné (less commonly одно́/odnó) declines like the pronoun той/toj 'that' (see table 17.8). In the function of an indefinite article оди́н/odýn is also used in the plural, as it is with pluralia tantum as in одні грабли́/odní hrabli 'one rake'.

The numerals '2' (masculine–neuter два/dva, feminine дві/dvi), '3' (три/try), '4' (чоти́ри/čotýry) have a declension of their own (see table 17.11).

The numerals п'ять/pjat′ '5' to вісімдеся́т/visimdesját '80' (as well as the regional, South-western Ukrainian дев'ятдеся́т/devjatdesját '90'), with the exception of со́рок/sórok '40', decline in two ways, either on the pattern of чоти́ри/čotýry or, maintaining this pattern only in the instrumental, they have the ending -ý in all other oblique cases.

The numerals со́рок/sórok '40', дев'яно́сто/devjanósto '90' and сто/sto 'hundred' have the ending -a in all oblique cases except the accusative: genitive–dative–instrumental–locative сорока́/soroká, дев'яно́ста/devjanósta, ста/sta (though also instrumental стома́/stomá). In the higher hundreds, both parts of the numeral are declined, with the following oblique plural forms of the second part: genitive -сот/-sot, dative -стам/-stam, instrumental -стами/-stamy, locative -стах/-stax.

The numerals ти́сяча/týsjača 'thousand' and above follow the declension of nouns with the same ending (ти́сяча/týsjača like кру́ча/krúča 'precipice').

In a broad historical overview Ukrainian numerals preserved their ability to decline with just one exception, but regrouped fairly radically the types of declension inherited from Common Slavonic. On the syntax of quantifiers, see section 4.10.

Table 17.10 Numerals

	Cardinal	*Ordinal*
1	один/odýn	пе́рший/péršyj
2	два/dva	дру́гий/drúhyj
3	три/try	тре́тій/trétij
4	чоти́ри/čotýry	четве́ртий/četvértyj
5	п'ять/pjat'	п'я́тий/pjátyj
6	шість/šist'	шо́стий/šóstyj
7	сім/sim	сьо́мий/s'ómyj
8	вісім/visim	во́сьмий/vós'myj
9	де́в'ять/dévjat'	дев'я́тий/devjátyj
10	де́сять/désjat'	деся́тий/desjátyj
11	одина́дцять/odynádcjat'	одина́дцятий/odynádcjatyj
12	двана́дцять/dvanádcjat'	двана́дцятий/dvanádcjatyj
13	трина́дцять/trynádcjat'	трина́дцятий/trynádcjatyj
14	чотирна́дцять/čotyrnádcjat'	чотирна́дцятий/čotyrnádcjatyj
15	п'ятна́дцять/pjatnádcjat'	п'ятна́дцятий/pjatnádcjatyj
16	шістна́дцять/šistnádcjat'	шістна́дцятий/šistnádcjatyj
17	сімна́дцять/simnádcjat'	сімна́дцятий/simnádcjatyj
18	вісімна́дцять/visimnádcjat'	вісімна́дцятий/visimnádcjatyj
19	дев'ятна́дцять/devjatnádcjat'	дев'тна́дцятий/devjatnádcjatyj
20	два́дцять/dvádcjat'	двадця́тий/dvadcjátyj
30	три́дцять/trýdcjat'	тридця́тий/tryadcjátyj
40	со́рок/sórok	сороко́вий/sorokóvyj
50	п'ятдеся́т/pjatdesját	п'ятдеся́тий/pjatdesjátyj
60	шістдеся́т/šistdesját	шістдеся́тий/šistdesját yj
70	сімдеся́т/simdesját	сімдеся́тий/simdesjátyj
80	вісімдеся́т/visimdesját	вісімдеся́тий/visimdesjátyj
90	дев'яно́сто/devjanósto	дев'яно́стий/devjanóstyj
100	сто/sto	со́тий/sótyj
200	дві́сті/dvisti	двосо́тий/dvosótyj
300	три́ста/trýsta	трисо́тий/trysótyj
400	чоти́риста/čotýrysta	чотирисо́тий/čotyrysótyj
500	п'ятсо́т/pjatsót	п'ятисо́тий/pjatysótyj
600	шістсо́т/šistsót	шестисо́тий/šestysótyj
700	сімсо́т/simsót	семисо́тий/semysótyj
800	вісімсо́т/visimsót	восьмисо́тий/vos'mysótyj
900	дев'ятсо́т/devjatsót	дев'ятисо́тий/devjatysótyj
1,000	ти́сяча/týsjača	ти́сячний/týsjačnyj
1,000,000	мільйо́н/mil'jón	мільйо́нний/mil'jónnyj
1,000,000,000	мілья́рд/mil'járd	мілья́рдний/mil'járdnyj

Table 17.11 Declension of numerals

(a)	'two'	'three'	'four'	'five'
NOM	два (F двí)	три	чотúри	п'ять
ACC	= NOM/GEN	= NOM/GEN	= NOM/GEN	= NOM/GEN
GEN	двох	трьох	чотирьóх	п'ятьóх ~ п'ятú
DAT	двом	трьом	чотирьóм	п'ятьóм ~ п'ятú
INST	двомá	трьомá	чотирмá	п'ятьмá
LOC	двох	трьох	чотирьóх	п'ятьóх ~ п'ятú

(b)	'two'	'three'	'four'	'five'
NOM	dva (F dvi)	try	čotýry	pjat′
ACC	= NOM/GEN	= NOM/GEN	= NOM/GEN	= NOM/GEN
GEN	dvox	tr′ox	čotyr′óx	pjat′óx ~ pjatý
DAT	dvom	tr′om	čotyr′óm	pjat′óm ~ pjatý
INST	dvomá	tr′omá	čotyrmá	pjat′má
LOC	dvox	tr′ox	čotyr′óx	pjat′óx ~ pjatý

3.2 Verbal morphology

3.2.1 Verbal categories

Ukrainian verbs in their finite forms inflect for person, number, tense and mood. However, in the past tense and the conditional, verbs do not inflect for person, but do inflect for gender in the singular. In addition, each verb belongs to an aspect, but the change of aspect does not proceed by inflection (see below). There are three moods, the indicative, the imperative and the conditional. In one of them, the indicative, three tenses are distinguished, not counting the optional pluperfect; the present, the past and the future (verbs of perfective aspect have a syncretic present–future form), as in читáє/čytáje 'read (3 SG PRS)', читáв/čytáv (M PAST), читáтиме/ čytátyme (3 SG FUT), читáв би/čytáv by (M COND), читáй/čytáj (2 SG IMP). Two numbers (singular and plural) are distinguished in all moods and tenses, and within each number three persons (except in the past tense of the indicative and in the conditional). The three persons are: the first, that of the speaker; the second, that of the addressee; and the third, that of the non-speaker and non-addressee, as in the present-tense forms читáю/ čytáju (1 SG), читáєш/čytáješ (2 SG), читáє/čytáje (3 SG). Yet the imperative only has three person–number forms as in читáй/čytáj (2 SG), читáймо/čytájmo (1 PL), читáйте/čytájte (2 PL). The verb бýти/búty 'to be' has one form for all persons and numbers in the present, є/je (which may be extended to єсть/jest′). The past indicative and the conditional have no personal forms, instead, as mentioned above, they inflect for gender in the singular, as in past читав/čytáv (M), читала/čytála (F), читало/čytálo (N) and the corresponding conditional forms (читав би/ čytáv by, читала б/čytála b, читало б/čytálo b) and pluperfect forms (читав був/čytáv buv, читала була/čytála bulá, читало було/čytálo búlo).

The Common Slavonic system of past tenses (the aorist, imperfect and perfect) underwent a thorough revamping in Old Ukrainian. The perfect lost its auxiliary verb 'to be', giving rise to the modern past tense, and the aorist and imperfect were lost entirely. The chronology of these changes is difficult to pin down (it was different in different regions), but it is safe to assume that in the Central Ukrainian area the imperfect was lost at the latest in the twelfth century, the aorist in the fourteenth century and the use of the auxiliary verb in the perfect by the seventeenth century.

Of non-finite forms the Ukrainian verb has the (atemporal) infinitive читати/čytáty), the uninflected gerund (with two forms, traditionally called present and past, respectively читаючи/čytájučy and читавши/ čytávšy), the declined past participle passive (читаний/čýtanyj) and the rarely used and bookish present participle active (читаючий/čytájučyj). Actually, tense in the gerund is relative to the time reference of the finite verb in the sentence. The so-called present gerund, but also the past gerund of imperfective verbs, usually expresses simultaneity, as in читаючи (читавши) листа він плакав/čytájučy (čytávšy) lystá, vin plákav 'while he was reading the letter he cried', whereas the so-called past gerund of perfective verbs expresses an action which precedes that of the finite verb of the sentence, as in прошитавши листа, він заплакав/pročytávšy lystá, vin zaplákav 'after having read the letter he cried'.

Voice in the Ukrainian verb hardly exists as a fully fledged grammatical category. One may only speak of an opposition of verbs with the postfix -sja versus verbs without it. One of the functions of this postfix is to build passive forms: фабрика виробляє комп'ютери/fábryka vyrobljáje kompjútery 'the factory produces computers', комп'ютери виробляються фабрикою/kompjútery vyrobljájut'sja fábrykoju 'computers are being produced by the factory' (usually with imperfective verbs; the passive with perfective verbs is formed with the past participle passive: комп'ютери вироблені фабрикою/kompjútery výrobleni fábrykoju 'computers have been produced by the factory', but such constructions are very bookish and atypical of the spoken language). Yet passivization is by no means the only function of the postfix -sja (see section 4.8); the only common feature in the uses of the postfix -sja is that they exclude a direct object, but even this restriction is nowadays not quite absolute, as shown by phrases like дивитися телебачення/dyvýtysja telebáčennja 'to watch television'.

The category omnipresent in all verbal forms, both finite and non-finite, is aspect. Change of aspect is effected by derivational suffixes or prefixes, never by inflections, the latter being shared by both aspects. With a given root there can be two or three levels in aspect formation. The basic form is prefixless and suffixless, or prefixless but having a suffix -*a*-, -*y*- or -*i*- (if the root is adjectival also -*nu*-), such as нести/nestý 'carry', рı́зати/rı́zaty 'cut', ходи́ти/xodýty 'go', тремтı́ти/tremtı́ty 'tremble', ки́снути/kýsnuty 'go sour'. Such verbs are usually imperfective, but a small group of them are perfective, such as да́ти/dáty 'give', cı́сти/sı́sty 'sit down'. Second-level verbs, which are all perfective, are formed from those of the first level by adding a prefix or by replacing a suffix, namely using -*nu*- instead of -*a*- or -*i*- (such as торка́ти/torkáty, perfective торкну́ти/ torknúty 'touch', свистı́ти/svystı́ty, perfective сви́снути/svýsnuty 'whistle'), less frequently -*y*- instead of -*a*- (such as кінча́ти/kinčáty, perfective кінчи́ти/kinčýty 'finish'). The prefixes used to form second-level verbs are twofold. Some change only the aspect, such as роби́ти/ robýty, perfective зроби́ти/zrobýty 'do'; other prefixes both change the aspect and introduce semantic changes, such as зна́ти/znáty 'know (IMPFV)', пізна́ти/piznáty 'learn (PRFV)'. In the second case one and the same first-level verb may, and in most cases does, take various prefixes for various new (additional) meanings, as in пізна́ти/piznáty 'learn', зізна́ти/ziznáty 'testify', ви́знати/význaty 'admit'. It is these semantically modified verbs which need a new, third level, an imperfective aspect which would preserve the shade of meaning developed on the second level but cancel its perfectivity. The third-level verbs are formed with the suffixes -*a*- (after a vowel -*va*-) or -*uva*-, as in пізна́ти/piznáty, imperfective пізнава́ти/piznaváty, заспіва́ти/zaspiváty 'start singing', imperfective заспı́вувати/zaspı́vuvaty.

In addition, there are mono-aspectual verbs used only in the imperfective aspect (such as ко́штувати/kóštuvaty 'cost') or only in the perfective aspect (such as збагну́ти/zbahnúty 'grasp'); finally, there are a few bi-aspectual verbs with identical imperfective and perfective forms, such as велı́ти/velíty 'order', обіця́ти/obicjáty 'promise'. The number of mono- and, especially, bi-aspectual verbs has tended to decrease with the development of the language, so that in the above examples велı́ти/velíty and обіця́ти/obicjáty are more and more often assigned imperfective aspect only while the forms звелı́ти/zvelíty and пообіця́ти/poobicjáty have, in recent decades, have been derived as corresponding perfectives. On the other hand, the number of bi-aspectual verbs is constantly replenished in newly borrowed foreign words, such as фінансува́ти/finansuváty 'finance', until they have developed prefixed perfective verbs, as with арештува́ти/areštuváty 'arrest', bi-aspectual and, newer, perfective заарештува́ти/zaareštuváty, thus relegating the basic form to imperfective aspect (which, in turn, can be made unambiguous by forming a third-level imperfective: заарешто́вувати/zaareštóvuvaty, the newest form).

An additional means of changing verbal aspect is vowel alternation in the root, namely *e* (fugitive) : *y*, as in умéрти/umérty 'die (PRFV)', imperfective умирáти/umyráty; *e* (non-fugitive) : *i*, as in заместú/zamestý 'sweep (PRFV)', imperfective замітáти/zamitáty; and *o* : *a*, as in перемогтú/peremohtý 'conquer (PRFV)', imperfective перемагáти/peremaháty. Stress shift is also occasionally used as a means of changing aspect, as in розсúпати/rozsýpaty 'spill (PRFV)', imperfective розсипáти/rozsypáty, although the present stems differ in terms of suffixation, respectively (third person singular) розсúпле/rozsýple and розсипáє/rozsypáje. These devices are marginal, occasionally redundant; the root vowel alternations are unproductive and used in a limited number of roots (see section 2.3 above).

The most common nuances in meaning introduced by prefixes in perfective (perfectivized) verbs are the following:

beginning of an action, with the prefixes *za-* or *po-* (говорúти/hovorýty 'talk', заговорúти/zahovorýty 'begin talking');

limitation of an action in time, 'from ... to ...', typically with *po-* or *pro-* (сидíти/sydity 'sit', посидíти/posýdity 'sit for a while');

exhaustion of an action by reaching the maximum result, with the prefixes *za-* and *vy-* (кусáти/kusáty 'bite', закусáти/zakusáty 'bite all over, bite to death');

saturation of the action, with the prefix *na-* (наговорúти/nahovorýty 'tell as much as possible');

distribution in time or space, with the prefix *po-* (розставляти/rozstavljáty 'place', порозставляти/porozstavljáty 'place here and there');

intensive and lasting action, with the doubled prefix *po-po-* (працювáти/pracjuváty 'work', попопрацювáти/popopracjuváty 'work hard and long').

In the nineteenth century use was still made of frequentative forms of verbs with the suffix *-va-* (жúти/žýty 'live', frequentative живáти/žyváty) and with the prefixes *po-* and *pro-* and secondary imperfectivization (ходúти/xodýty 'go', frequentative походжáти/poxodžáty). The former type of verb is now completely out of use, the latter is rare. Frequentativity as a morphological category has been virtually lost in Ukrainian.

In up to twenty verbs of motion there are two forms. The basic form refers to a one-time action and/or action in one direction (нестú/nestý 'carry', летíти/letíty 'fly'), the secondary form denotes repetition of action and/or indefiniteness of direction (носúти/nosýty, літáти/litáty). This opposition occurs in verbs of high frequency and is therefore well rooted in the language, but it is totally unproductive and does not apply to neologisms.

3.2.2 Conjugation

With the exception of three verbs, да́ти/dа́ty 'give', ïсти/jísty 'eat' and -вíсти/-vísty (as in оповíсти/opovísty 'tell') which have a conjugation apart (see table 17.12), the set of verbal endings is uniform for all verbs, with the sole exception of the third person singular. In the present tense they are: -*u* (1 SG), -*š* (2 SG), -*mo* (1 PL), -*te* (2 PL), -*t'* (3 PL). In the third person singular some verbs have a zero ending, while others have -*t'*. The vowel before the endings (used in all persons except the first person singular) is -*e*- (in the third person plural, -*u*-) in some verbs but -*y*- (third person plural -*a*-) in others. It is the *y/a* verbs that take the above-mentioned ending -*t'* in the third person singular (see table 17.12). In the vernacular, particularly in the eastern Ukraine, however, the third person singular of *y/a* verbs preserves the ending -(*y*)*t'* only under stress; if unstressed it is replaced by -*e*: кричи́ть/kryčýt' 'shout' versus но́се/nóse (standard но́сить/nósyt') 'carry'.

The *y/a* verbs have alternation of consonants in the first person singular: *t* : *č*, *d* : *dž*, *s* : *š*, and *z* : *ž*, as in молочу́/moločú 'thresh (1 SG)', compare моло́тиш/molótyš (2 SG). If the stem ends in a labial it takes *l'* in both first person singular and third person plural, as in люблю́/ljubljú 'love (1 SG)', лю́блять/ljúbljat' (3 PL), compare лю́биш/ljúbyš (2 SG).

The system of endings in the past tense is even simpler than that of the present tense. There are only four endings: masculine -*v*, feminine -*la*,

Table 17.12 Present tense

(a)	*e/u* verbs 'carry'	*y/a* verbs 'shout'	Irregular verbs 'give'	'eat'
1 SG	несу́	кричу́	дам	ïм
2 SG	несе́ш	кричи́ш	даси́	ïси́
3 SG	несе́	кричи́ть	дасть	ïсть
1 PL	несемо́	кричимо́	дамо́	ïмо́
2 PL	несете́	кричите́	дасте́	ïсте́
3 PL	несу́ть	крича́ть	даду́ть	ïдя́ть

(b)	*e/u* verbs 'carry'	*y/a* verbs 'shout'	Irregular verbs 'give'	'eat'
1 SG	nesú	kryčú	dam	jim
2 SG	neséš	kryčýš	dasý	jisý
3 SG	nesé	kryčýt'	dast'	jist'
1 PL	nesemó	kryčymó	damó	jimó
2 PL	neseté	kryčyté	dasté	jisté
3 PL	nesút'	kryčát'	dadút'	jidjat'

neuter *-lo* and plural *-ly*: кричáв/kryčáv, кричáла/kryčála, кричáло/ kryčálo, кричáли/kryčály 'shout'. Two rules are to be added dealing with consonant clusters. If the verb stem ends in *-t-* or *-d-*, these consonants are lost before all past-tense endings: метý/metú 'I sweep', past мів/miv, мелá/melá. If the stem ends in some other consonant the ending *-v* is lost in the masculine: повзý/povzú 'I creep', past повз/povz, but повзлá/ povzlá; трясý/trjasú 'I shake', past тряс/trjas, but тряслá/trjaslá.

Some verbal categories are expressed analytically based on the above forms. The pluperfect (which actually expresses an action frustrated by the following one, as in він пішóв був, алé повернýвся/vin pišóv buv, alé povernúvsja 'he had gone, but then came back', and is anyway used optionally) is formed by the past tense of the lexical verb and the same past-tense form of the verb бýти/búty 'be', as in пішóв був/pišóv buv, пішла булá/pišlá bulá. The imperfective future tense has two forms: either the conjugated auxiliary verb бýду/búdu '(I) shall be' plus the infinitive of the lexical verb, as in бýду просѝти/búdu prosýty 'I shall ask', or the infinitive of the lexical verb followed by the otherwise no longer used auxiliary of the *e/u* type in the present tense, *mu* (spelled as one word with the lexical verb), as in просѝтиму/prosýtymu 'I shall ask', просѝтимеш/ prosýtymeš 'you will ask'. The conditional is based morphologically on the past tense by adding the particle би/by (б/b after a vowel): просѝв би/ prosýv by, просѝла б/prosýla b 'would ask'.

The only synthetic form of the finite verb beside the present tense with its own set of endings is the imperative with its three persons, second singular, first plural and second plural. The basic set of imperative endings is *-y* (2 SG), *-im* (1 PL), *-it'* (2 PL), added to the present-tense stem as found, for instance, in the second person singular; thus from нес-éш/nes-éš 'you carry' the imperative forms are: несѝ/nesý, несíм/nesim, несíть/nesit'. However, the ending *-y* in the second person singular is lost if stress does not fall on it (with the exception of certain stem-final consonant clusters, illustrated below, and when stress is transferred onto the prefix *vy-*, as in вѝнеси/výnesy 'carry out'). In such cases word-final dentals capable of palatalization do so: кинь/kyn' 'throw', сядь/sjad' 'sit down'. The plural imperatives of such verbs are formed by adding the endings *-mo*, *-te* to the singular forms: кѝньмо/kýn'mo, кѝньте/kýn'te. Hence the second set of endings, with an agglutinative plural: *-'*, *-'mo*, *-'te*. The first set is also used even though unstressed if the stem ends in a consonant plus *r, l, m, n*, as in стýкни/stúkny 'knock', стýкнім/stúknim, стýкніть/stúknit'. If the verb root contains no vowel and ends in *-j*, the vowel *y* is inserted into the root: б'єш/bješ 'you beat', imperative бий/byj.

Of the non-finite forms, the infinitive uniformly has the ending *-ty*, before which root-final *t* and *d* change into *s*: кладé/kladé 'he puts', infinitive клáсти/klásty, метé/metе́ 'he sweeps', infinitive местѝ/mestý; *č* and *ž* before the infinitive ending *-ty* are replaced by *k* and *h* respectively:

пече́/pečé 'he bakes', infinitive пекти́/pektý, мо́же/móže 'he can', infinitive могти́/mohtý. In non-standard Eastern Ukrainian and as a poetic licence, -*ty* may be replaced by -*t'* after a vowel.

The present gerund ends uniformly in -*čy*. Before this ending the vowel is that of the third person plural present, namely *u* or *a*; but in actual speech there is a strong tendency to replace the unstressed *a* in the gerund by *u*: пи́шуть/pýšut' 'they write', gerund пи́шучи/pýšučy, ба́чать/báčat' 'they see', gerund ба́чачи/báčačy, actually more often ба́чучи/báčučy. The past gerund ends in -*šy*, with the masculine past-tense form used as a stem: брав/brav 'take (PAST)', gerund бра́вши/brávšy, ніс/nis 'carry (PAST)', gerund ні́сши/níššy.

Participles have adjectival endings (see section 3.1.4). In the past participle passive there are two suffixes, -*n*- and -*t*-, as in сі́яний/síjanyj 'sown', ши́тий/šýtyj 'sewn'. The suffix -*t*- is used after suffixless stems ending in -*y*-, -*i*-, -*u*-, -*r*- and -*a*- (the latter alternating with a nasal consonant, and deriving from Common Slavonic *ę*): ми́тий/mýtyj 'washed', грі́тий/hrítyj 'warmed', ду́тий/dútyj 'blown', де́ртий/dértyj 'torn', жа́тий/žátyj 'reaped' (compare жну/žnu 'I reap'). After the suffix -*n(u)*- the choice between -*n*- and -*t*- is free: ки́нути/kýnuty 'to throw', past participle passive ки́нутий/kýnutyj, ки́нений/kýnenyj. There are a few other cases of vacillation, such as моло́ти/molóty 'to grind', past participle passive мо́лотий/mólotyj, ме́лений/mélenyj.

As a rule the Ukrainian verb has two stems, one in the present tense (and the forms based on it: imperative and present gerund) and the other which is found in the past tense, the infinitive, the past gerund and the past participle passive. Traditionally, they are called the present stem and the infinitive stem. The two stems are represented below by the infinitive and by the third person singular present. In some verbs the two stems are identical, for example нес-ти́/nes-tý, нес-е́/nes-é 'carry', греб-ти́/hreb-tý, греб-е́/hreb-é 'row', but this is exceptional. The present stem always ends in a consonant, the infinitive stem may end in a consonant but typically ends in a vowel (see examples below). Because of this, infinitive stems ending in a vowel either undergo truncation of their final vowel or add a consonant, typically *j*, when converted to present stems.

Truncation takes place mainly in the *y/a* conjugation with the suffixes -*y*-, -*i*- and -*a*-, as in носи́-ти/nosý-ty, но́с-ить/nós-yt' 'carry', блища́-ти/blyščá-ty, блищ-и́ть/blyšč-ýt' 'shine', горі́-ти/horí-ty, гор-и́ть/hor-ýt' 'burn'. In some cases this same procedure is followed in the case of the suffix -*a*- in the *e/u* conjugation, as in жда́-ти/ždá-ty, жд-е/žd-e 'wait', сса́ти/ssá-ty, сс-е/ss-e 'suck'.

The opposite procedure, namely preserving the vowel of the infinitive and inserting *j* in the present stem, is seen in such verbs as ви́ти/vý-ty, ви́є/výj-e 'howl'; it is also applied in many verbs with the suffix -*a*-, such as хапа́ти/xapá-ty, хапа́є/xapáj-e 'catch', гаса́ти/hasá-ty, гаса́є/

hasáj-e 'run about'. Some verbs with infinitive stems in -a- have doublets, one with truncation, one with insertion, of *j*, as in дихати/dýxa-ty, дихає/ dýxaj-e or дише/dýš-e 'breathe', колихати/kolyxá-ty, колихає/ kolyxáj-e or колише/kolýš-e 'rock', and there are rather many cases of vacillation. In the case of verbs with the suffix -(*u*)*va*- in the infinitive stem both techniques are applied in the same verbs: -*a*- is dropped and *j* inserted, as in купувати/kupuvá-ty, купує/kupúj-e 'buy', давати/davá- ty, дає/daj-é 'give'.

Besides these basic procedures in deriving one verbal stem from the other there are several less widespread and more irregular supplemental changes such as alternation of consonants (as in стригти/strýh-ty, стриже/stryž-é 'cut (hair)', кликати/klýka-ty, кличе/klýč-e 'call'), alternation of vowels with Ø (as in мерти/mér-ty, мре/mr-e 'die') and many more in individual verbs with some odd alternations (for instance, alternation of a vowel with a nasal consonant, as in дути/dú-ty, дме/dm-e 'blow'), which in some cases go so far and are so irregular and so isolated that one may be tempted to speak of suppletion (as in гнати/hná-ty, жене/žen-e 'drive', сісти/sis-ty, сяде/sjád-e 'sit down').

For a comparison between Common Slavonic and Ukrainian present and infinitive stems, see table 17.13.

3.3 Derivational morphology

3.3.1 Major patterns of noun derivation
The derivation of nouns typically operates with suffixes. Prefixes most frequently are transferred from verbs from which the noun is derived, as in вибір/výbir 'choice', from вибирати/vybyráty 'choose'. The most important noun prefixes proper are:

pá- with feminines ending in a consonant to show collectivity, as in памолодь/pámolod´ 'undergrowth';
pra- to show remoteness in time, great age, as in прабатько/prabát´ko 'forefather';
uz- shows adjacency, neighbourhood, as in узлісся/uzlissja 'edge of forest'.

The most productive suffixes are:

to denote a man by his activity or profession: -*nyk* (робітник/robitnýk 'worker'), -*ač* (читач/čytáč 'reader'), -*ar* (друкар/drukár 'printer'), -*ec´* (виборець/výborec´ 'voter'), -*ist* (a western European borrowing, україніст/ukrajinist 'Ukrainianist');
to denote a man by his features: -*ak* (дивак/dyvák 'crank'), -*ec´* (мудрець/mudréc´ 'wise man');

Table 17.13   Correspondences between Old Church Slavonic and Ukrainian verb classes

Old Church Slavonic Present	Infinitive	Ukrainian Present	Infinitive	Gloss
nesetъ	nesti	несе́/nesé	не́сти́/nésty̆	'carry'
vedetъ	vesti	веде́/vedé	ве́сти́/vésty̆	'lead'
idetъ	iti	іде́/idé	іти́/ity̆	'go'
jĕdetъ	jĕxati	їде/jĭde	їхати/jĭxaty	'travel'
grebetъ	greti	гребе́/hrebé	гребти́/hrebty̆	'row'
pečetъ	pešti	пече́/pečé	пекти́/pekty̆	'bake'
načьnetъ	načęti	почне́/počné	почати́/počaty	'begin'
mьretъ	mrěti	мре́/mré	ме́рти/mérty	'die'
stanetъ	stati	ста́не/stáne	ста́ти/státy	'stand'
beretъ	bьrati	бере́/beré	бра́ти/bráty	'take'
zovetъ	zъvati	зве/zve	зва́ти/zváty	'call'
minetъ	minǫti	мине́/myné	мину́ти/mynúty	'pass'
čujetъ	čuti	чу́є/čúje	чу́ти/čúty	'hear'
kryjetъ	kryti	кри́є/kry̆je	крити/kry̆ty	'cover'
bijetъ	biti	б'є/bje	би́ти/by̆ty	'beat'
borjetъ	brati	бо́ре/bóre	боро́ти/boróty	'fight'
meljetъ	mlěti	ме́ле/méle	моло́ти/molóty	'grind'
igrajetъ	igrati	игра́є/ihráje	ігра́ти/ihráty	'play'
umějetъ	uměti	уміє/umije	умі́ти/umity	'be able'
kažetъ	kazati	ка́же/káže	каза́ти/kazáty	'say'
imetъ	ęti	(при́)йме/(pry̆)jme	(прийн)я́ти/(pryjn)játy	'accept'
darujetъ	darovati	дару́є/darúje	дарува́ти/daruváty	'donate'
sějetъ	sějati	сіє/sije	сі́яти/sijaty	'sow'
molitъ	moliti	мо́лить/mólyt'	моли́ти/molýty	'pray'
xoditъ	xoditi	хо́дить/xódyt'	ходи́ти/xodýty	'go'
velitъ	velěti	вели́ть/vely̆t'	велі́ти/velity	'order'
ležitъ	ležati	лежи́ть/ležĭt'	лежа́ти/ležáty	'lie'
sъpitъ	sъpati	спить/spyt'	спа́ти/spáty	'sleep'

to denote a man by his origin: *-anyn* (киянин/kyjányn 'inhabitant of Kiev'), *-ec'* (чужи́нець/čužĭnec' 'stranger');

to denote a woman by her occupation or profession: *-k-a* (переклада́чка/perekladáčka 'translator', учи́телька/učýtel'ka 'teacher'), *-nycj-a* (перемо́жниця/peremóžnycja 'victor');

to denote tools: *-al-o/-yl-o, -ylk-a/-ilk-a* (точи́ло/točýlo 'whetstone', сопі́лка/sopilka 'pipe') and also those suffixes that also denote men by their activity (лічи́льник/ličýl'nyk 'meter', вими́кач/vymýkač 'switch').

Ukrainian makes broad use of the category of collectivity. The most widespread suffix for persons is *-stv-o* (селя́нство/seljánstvo 'peasantry') and for non-persons the emotionally neutral type are neuters in *-ja* preceded (except in the case of labials and *r*) by a long consonant (зілля/ zillja 'herbs', пір'я/pirja 'feathers'). The suffixes *-v-a* and *-nj-a* combine the meaning of collectivity with a pejorative nuance (мишва/myšvá 'mice', босячня/bosjačnjá 'vagabonds'). The broad use of collective nouns is balanced by the possibility of deriving singulatives from them. The most typical singulative suffix is *-yn* (which in masculines is used only in the singular and dropped in the plural): селянин/seljanýn (plural селяни/seljány) 'peasant', зернина/zernýna '(one) grain'.

Nouns that denote processes and actions most often use the following suffixes: Ø in masculines and (with the feminine inflection *-a*) in feminines (запит/zápyt 'question', онова/onóva 'renovation') and especially *-ennj-a* or *-uvannj-a,* both neuter (дихання/dýxannja 'breathing', групування/hrupuvánnja 'grouping'). The most typical suffix to denote qualities is *-ist',* feminine (молодість/mólodist' 'youth').

A typical feature of Ukrainian is its wide use of affective suffixes. Some of them are predominantly pejorative and/or augmentative, others, more frequently used, are endearing and/or diminutive (бабище/babýšče 'big and unpleasant woman', ручка/rúčka 'nice little hand' and, with reduplication of the same suffix, ручечка/rúčečka).

3.3.2   Major patterns of adjective derivation

Adjectives may be derived by means of suffixes from nouns, adverbs, verbs and other adjectives.

The main types of adjectival derivation from nouns are:

with possessive meaning (always referring to one person as possessor) with the suffixes *-iv* (alternating with *-ov-* when followed by a vowel) and *-yn* (батьків/bát'kiv 'father's', сестрин/sestrýn 'sister's');
relational, with the suffixes *-n-, -ov/ev-, -s'k-, -'ač-* (державний/ deržávnyj 'concerning the state', тижневий/tyžnévyj 'weekly', господарський/hospodárs'kyj 'concerning the economy', свинячий/ svynjáčyj 'concerning pigs');
referring to material composition, with the suffixes *-n-* or *-ov/ev-* (залізний/zaliznyj 'of iron', паперовий/paperóvyj 'of paper');
pointing to similarity, with the suffixes *-ast-, -yst-, -uvat-* (кулястий/ kuljástyj 'similar to a ball', драглистий/drahlýstyj 'similar to head-cheese', вовкуватий/vovkuvátyj 'behaving like a wolf'). Similarity can also be conveyed by compound adjectives with the second component -подібний/-podibnyj, less frequently -видний/-výdnyj (павукоподібний/pavukopodíbnyj 'similar to a spider').

The main types of adjectival derivation from verbs include those with the suffixes *-al'n-* (with the meaning of property or peculiarity:

відповідальний/vidpovidál'nyj 'responsible'), -uč- and -ušč- (with the meaning of a prominent feature: балакучий/balakúčyj 'talkative'), -lyv- and -k- (with the meaning of a disposition towards or an ability to perform an action: зрадливий/zradlyvyj 'treacherous', липкий/lypkyj 'sticky'), -enn- or -ann- (with the meaning of feasibility: здійсненний/zdijsnénnyj 'feasible'), -č- (with the meaning of a relation: виборчий/vyborčyj 'electoral').

Adjectives are occasionally derived from adverbs, by means of the suffix -n'- or -šn'-: торік/torik 'last year', adjective торішній/torišnij, вчора/ včóra 'yesterday', adjective вчорашній/včorášnij.

The derivation of adjectives from adjectives usually marks gradation in the presence and/or intensity of a feature and introduces a certain affectivity. The weakening or incompleteness of a feature if shown by the suffixes -av- or -'av- (жовтавий/žovtávyj 'yellowish'), while intensification of a feature is expressed by the suffixes, -enn-, -ann-, -ezn-, -'ašč- (здоровенний/zdorovénnyj 'quite big', старезний/staréznyj 'very old', добрящий/dobrjáščyj 'very good'). The suffix -isin'k- is specialized in the meaning of an undiluted manifestation of a feature (білісінький/ bilisin'kyj 'absolutely white'), as opposed to -esen'k- (and -en'k-), in which affectivity is predominant (багатесенький/bahatésen'kyj or багатенький/baháten'kyj, roughly 'nicely rich').

3.3.3 Major patterns of verb derivation

The most important device in the derivation of verbs is prefixation. The primary meaning of verbal prefixes is spatial; on this primary meaning are then deposited secondary meanings of a more abstract character. To limit the discussion to one example, roz- has as its basic meaning motion in various directions (розбігтися/rozbíhtysja 'scatter by running'), from which the meaning of comprehensiveness of an action developed (розіспатися/rozispátysja 'sleep one's fill'), on the one hand, and, on the other, that of losing ability to do something (розучитися/rozučýtysja 'unlearn, forget how to'). The number of verbal prefixes hardly exceeds fifteen; therefore nearly every one of them covers a large range of meanings, sometimes mutually exclusive. Only zne- is devoid of spatial meaning: it shows the loss of a feature expressed in the root (знесиліти/znesýlity 'lose strength, grow weak').

Verbal suffixes are few and mostly their function is to oppose transitivity to intransitivity or perfectivity to imperfectivity: білити/bilýty 'make white', біліти/bilíty 'be white'; кінчати/kinčáty (IMPFV), кінчити/ kinčýty (PRFV) 'finish'. Simultaneously, they serve to derive a verb from a noun or adjective. As a result, their main function (if there is one) is often blurred. The most productive among them are -uva- (in alternation with -u- and -ova-), which is productive in the adaptation of foreign verbs (телефонувати/telefonuváty 'make a telephone call'), and -n/nu- in its double function: to show the transition into a state (if the basic word is an adjective: сліпий/slipýj 'blind', сліпнути/slipnuty 'go blind') and to perfectivize an imperfective verb, usually with a shade of meaning of rapidity (стукати/stúkaty (IMPFV), стукнути/stúknuty (PRFV 'knock'). The nuance of rapidity and intensivity is particularly emphasized if -nu- is replaced by -onu-.

4 Syntax

4.1 Element order in declarative sentences

Word order in a Ukrainian sentence can be standard (unmarked, basic) or deviating (marked). Within standard word order there are cases of obligatory (fixed) word order as opposed to non-obligatory ones. Obligatory word order encompasses the following cases:

Prepositions are placed before the noun phrase (except a few prepositions, usually longer than disyllabic and developing from adverbs, which also admit postposition): на столі/na stolí 'on (the) table', на письмóвому столі/na pys′móvomu stolí 'on (the) writing table', but заради нього/zarády n′óho or його заради/johó zarády 'for his sake'.

Coordinating conjunctions are placed between the elements they link, subordinating conjunctions at the beginning of the subordinate clause: вулиці й майдани/vúlyci j majdány 'streets and squares', не прийшов через те, що захворів/ne pryjšóv čerez te, ščo zaxvoriv or через те, що захворів, не прийшов/čerez te, ščo zaxvoriv, ne pryjšóv 'he did not come because he had fallen sick'.

Particles (as a rule, clitics) also have a fixed place. Some of them are placed clause-initially, such as (не)хай/(ne)xáj 'let', чи/čy 'if, whether', while others, such as же/že 'indeed', are placed after the first phrase of the clause: хай він прийде/xaj vin prýjde 'let him come', він же знав це/vin že znav ce 'he certainly knew that'. If же/že appears in addition to another clitic particle, it is же/že which comes first (usually in exclamatory sentences): іди ж бо/idý ž bo 'now then go'. As can be seen from the above, fixed word order prevails in the case of syntactic words only.

Standard word order is regulated by the following rules:

The subject precedes the verb.
The verb precedes its object(s), with the dative or instrumental object
    preceding the accusative: дав йому слово/dav jomú slóvo '(he) gave
    him the floor (literally: word)'.
The attributive adjective precedes its head noun.
The adnominal genitive follows its head noun.
An adverb derived from an adjective precedes the word it modifies; an
    adverb of other origin follows the word it modifies: він прийязно

дивився/vin prýjazno dyvývsja 'he looked in a friendly manner', but він дивився вперед/vin dyvývsja vpered 'he looked forward'.

However, statistically, sentences with consistent standard word order by no means prevail. Much more often one phrase (or more) is displaced for the reason of emphasis, either to make its contextual ties more obvious (topicalization) or to make it prominent logically and/or emotionally (focus). Every shift from the standard word order emphasizes the shifted phrase, especially if placing it in the first or last place in the sentence. Promoting a phrase to initial position leads to what may be called impulsive word order as if stressing the impulse which prompted the speaker to utter the sentence. Pushing a word or phrase into sentence-final position creates an enhanced tension in the listener due to the postponement in revealing that word or phrase: cumulative word order.

It is because of such departures from standard word order that one can hardly expect too many sentences in which all components are unshifted from their standard position. Shifts in word order make sense against the background of the standard word order; if such a standard were lost entirely the shifts would have no effect. Paradoxically as it may sound, the standard word order is omnipresent, but more through departures from it than through straight adherence to it.

4.2   Non-declarative sentence types

Interrogative sentences are marked first of all by interrogative intonation (a sharp rise over the last word of the sentence or over any word that is supposed to be the nucleus of the addressee's answer). In addition, they may have interrogative particles (чи/čy for a simple question, хіба/xibá or невже/nevžé with a shade of doubt or surprise) or an interrogative pronoun or adverb (such as хто/xto 'who', де/de 'where') which are placed at the beginning of the sentence, except that in questions with an alternative чи/čy is placed between the two (or more) alternatives among which the addressee is supposed to select: чи ти там був?/čy ty tam buv? 'were you there?' ти був у театрі чи в музеї?/ty buv u teátri čy v muzéji? 'were you at the theatre or in the museum?'. In either case, with or without a particle (or interrogative pronoun or adverb), the speaker may also change the word order, placing the predicate or the central word of the interrogative sentence at the beginning, but this shift is by no means obligatory. Hence the three possibilities are: чи ти там був?/čy ty tam buv?, ти був там?/ty buv tam?, був ти там?/buv ty tam (or, with a different central word: там ти був?/tam ty buv?). The third type is the least frequent. The interrogative intonation usually becomes less prominent when the interrogative particle (or pronoun or adverb) is present.

Indirect questions have only one of the above possibilities, being introduced by чи/čy or an interrogative pronoun or adverb: я спитав, чи він там був/ja spytáv, čy vin tam buv 'I asked if he was there', я спитáв, де він був/ja spytáv, de vin buv 'I asked where he was'.

The possible types of answers to a yes–no question are threefold: (a) the word так/tak 'yes' or ні/ni 'no'; (b) repetition of the central phrase or one of the alternatives; (c) combining (a) and (b). Thus, to the question чи ти був там?/čy ty buv tam? 'were you there?' an affirmative answer may be так/tak, or був/buv, or так, був/tak, buv. To questions with interrogative pronouns or adverbs the answer would be the phrase substituting for and having the same syntactic function as that interrogative: де ти був?/de ty buv? 'where were you?', answer: у теáтрі/u teátri.

In answering negative questions, such as чи ти не був там?/čy ty ne buv tam? 'weren't you there?', the answer так implies agreement with the corresponding positive proposition, that is 'no, I wasn't there', while ні/ni implies disagreement with this proposition, that is 'yes, I was there'.

Commands usually have no subject expressed and their verb tends to stand in initial position: іди сюди!/idý sjudý! 'come here!' The same applies to negative commands; their peculiarity is that typically the verb in them is used in the imperfective aspect; contrast скажи йому́ пра́вду!/ skažý jomú právdu! 'tell him the truth!' and не кажи йому́ пра́вди!/ne kažý jomú právdy! 'don't tell him the truth!' If a subject pronoun is inserted into the imperative construction, usually enclitic to the verb, the sentence may acquire the character of advice rather than a command. The use of perfective aspect in negative commands adduces the meaning of a warning.

Since the imperative does not have third-person forms, commands addressed to a third person use the indicative preceded by the particle (не)ха́й/(ne)xáj 'let': неха́й він прийде!/nexáj vin prýjde! 'let him come!' The basic meaning of such constructions is, however, not a command in the strict sense, but rather a wish.

4.3   Copular sentences

The most typical copular verbs are бу́ти/búty 'be', лиши́тися/lyšýtysja, (з)оста́тися/(z)ostátysja 'remain', ста́ти/státy, зроби́тися/zrobýtysja, опини́тися/opynýtysja 'become', зва́тися/zvátysja, назива́тися/ nazyvátysja 'be called'. The verb бу́ти/búty as copula is normally replaced by zero in the present tense: він відо́мий науко́вець/vin vidómyj naukóvec′ 'he is a renowned scholar'; potentially, there may appear in such cases a specific intonation: a sharp rise in pitch followed by a pause in the place where the copula would stand. If the predicate proper is a noun phrase, then between it and the preceding noun phrase the neuter demonstrative pronoun то/to 'that' or це/ce 'this' may be inserted: рома́н це літерату́рний жанр/román ce literatúrnyj žanr 'the novel is a literary genre'. (Note that in other functions the neuter of 'that' is те/te, not то/ to; this shows that one is dealing here with a mere indication of predicativity.) The presence of the indicator то/to or це/ce often emphasizes completeness in the identification of the subject with the predicate noun phrase.

The predicate noun phrase stands in the nominative or the instrumental or takes the preposition за/za plus the accusative: він був пастух, пастухом, за пастуха/vin buv pastúx, pastuxóm, za pastuxá 'he was a shepherd'. The main factor in this choice is the copula itself. With the copulas опинитися/orynýtysja 'become', здаватися/zdavátysja 'seem' the instrumental is nearly obligatory. With стати/státy, зробитися/ zrobýtysja, лишитися/lyšýtysja, (на)зватися/(na)zvátysja the instrumental is predominant but the nominative can occur. With the copula бути/búty in forms other than the present tense the choice is very much free, though the instrumental is more frequent. In the present tense, with the zero form of the copula, the nominative is normal; if the copula є/je is used, the decisive factor is word order: if the predicate noun phrase stands before the subject it tends to be in the instrumental, otherwise the nominative prevails. Examples are: він здається мені зрадником (INST)/vin zdajét′sja mení zrádnykom (INST) 'he seems to me a traitor', він став зрадником (INST)/vin stav zrádnykom (INST) 'he became a traitor', він був зрадник (NOM), зрадником (INST)/vin buv zrádnyk (NOM), zrádnykom (INST) 'he was a traitor', він зрадник (NOM), він є зрадник (NOM), зрадником (INST)/vin zrádnyk (NOM), vin je zrádnyk (NOM), zrádnykom 'he is a traitor'.

The accusative with за/za differs semantically. It conveys the meaning of substitution, not of complete identity: він мені був за брата/vin mení buv za bráta 'he was like a brother to me'.

If the predicate is an adjective the nominative is more typical than the instrumental, except with the copulas здаватися/zdavátysja 'seem', вважатися/vvažátysja 'be reputed', уявлятися/ujavljátysja 'appear': місто здається мертвим (INST)/misto zdajét′sja mértvym (INST) 'the city seems dead'. If the copula is zero the nominative is the only form used: він уже здоровий (NOM)/vin užé zdoróvyj (NOM) 'he is already healthy'.

4.4   Coordination and comitativity

Coordination in a sentence in most cases encompasses morphologically identical elements (such as adverbs: тут і там/tut i tam 'here and there'), but this is not obligatory. The decisive factor is the identity of syntactic function, which in most cases is revealed by the identity of the interrogative pronoun or adverb to which the two (or more) coordinated elements would be an answer, as in дома і в школі/dóma i v školi 'home and in school', where an adverb and a prepositional phrase function as coordinated, the corresponding question being де?/de? 'where?' In the case of adjectives, a would-be coordinated chain is actually present under the condition of semantic homogeneity; compare білі, блакитні, зелені будинки/bili, blakýtni, zeléni budýnky 'white, blue, green houses', a coordinated chain

based on the feature of colour, with високі білі житлові будинки/
vysóki bíli žytloví budýnky 'high white residential houses', a chain in which
each adjective refers not directly to the noun but rather to the following
noun phrase as a whole. Schematically, the two cases may be presented as
follows: білі будинки + блакитні будинки + зелені будинки/bíli
budýnky + blakýtni budýnky + zeléni budýnky, versus високі + білі
житлові будинки, білі + житлові будинки, житлові + будинки/
vysóki + bíli žytloví budýnky, bíli + žytloví budýnky, žytloví + budýnky.

Coordinated chains may be signalled by parallel intonation alone. In
addition, and more explicitly, they are signalled as such by the presence of
one or more conjunctions as coordinators. These conjunctions are threefold: copulative, disjunctive or adversative. Typical copulative conjunctions
are i/i (after a vowel also й/j), та/ta 'and', in negative sentences (a)ні/
(a)ni 'nor'; disjunctive conjunctions are або/abó, чи/čy 'or', то/to 'now';
adversative conjunctions are але (ж)/alé (ž), проте/proté, та/ta 'but':
люди і тварини/ljúdy i tварýny 'men and animals', люди або
тварини/ljúdy abó tварýny 'people or animals', розумний, але
недотепний/rozúmnyj, ale nedotépnyj 'intelligent but awkward'.

Adversative conjunctions do not admit of more than two-member
chains; the same is true, with rare exceptions, of the copulative та/ta.
Other conjunctions introduce open chains. In such series if there are in fact
two members the conjunction may be placed between them or before each
of them: люди і тварини/ljúdy i tварýny or і люди і тварини/i ljúdy i
tварýny. Double conjunction is obligatory in the case of то/to: то люди,
то тварини/to ljúdy, to tварýny 'now people, now animals'. In chains
which contain more than two elements the conjunction may be placed
either only before the last element (which implies closing of the chain):
люди, тварини, комахи і бактерії/ljúdy, tварýny, komáxy i baktériji
'people, animals, insects and bacteria', or before each member of the chain,
or the elements may be grouped in pairs: люди і тварини, комахи і
бактерії/ljúdy i tварýny, komáxy i baktériji.

If members of a coordinated chain are nouns in the nominative singular
the predicate (verbal or adjectival) may be in the singular or plural. The
plural is typically chosen if the predicate is placed after the subject; if it is
placed before the predicate, in non-formal speech the singular is more
frequent while in formal or written usage the plural is preferred: жінка й
чоловік плакали/žínka j čolovík plákaly 'the woman and the man cried',
плакала ~ плакали жінка й чоловік/plákala ~ plákaly žínka j
čolovík. The same tendency in agreement (or lack of agreement) is manifested if in such conjoined nominative cases the non-initial noun phrase (or
phrases) is placed in the instrumental preceded by the preposition з/z
'with', the so-called comitative construction: жінка з чоловіком
плакали/žínka z čolovíkom plákaly, with verb–subject order плакала ~
плакали жінка з чоловіком/plákala ~ plákaly žínka z čolovíkom.

Such comitative constructions are limited to nouns which denote living beings or personified notions. In these constructions, the noun phrase in the nominative is understood as the main actor while that in the instrumental is secondary, an accessory. If the main actor corresponds to a pronoun, that pronoun is used in the plural even though it denotes a single person, as in ми з ним пішли геть/my z nym pišlý het´ 'he and I (literally: we with him) went away', вони з ним пішли геть/vony z nym pišlý 'het´ 'he (or she) and he (literally: they with him) went away'.

4.5   Subordination

The main means of subordination is the use of conjunctions, although asyndeton (the mere juxtaposition of clauses) is by no means rare. Of the rather numerous subordinating conjunctions the most frequent are the following:

objective (noun clause): що/ščo 'that', also ніби/niby (after verbs of speech, with the nuance of uncertainty or mistrust), чи/ču 'if, whether' (and other interrogative pronouns and adverbs);
relative: який/jakýj 'who, which', що/ščo 'that';
of place: де/de 'where', куди/kudý 'whither', звідки/zvidky/ 'whence';
of time: коли/koly 'when', як/jak 'as', поки/póky 'while', як тільки/ jak til´ky 'as soon as';
causal: бо/bo 'for', тому що/tomú ščo 'because';
of purpose: щоб/ščob 'in order that';
conditional: якби/jakbý, якщо/jakščó/ 'if';
of manner and comparative: як/jak 'as', наче/náče, ніби/niby, (не)мов/(ne)móv 'as if';
consecutive: так що/tak ščo, (що) аж/(ščo) až 'so that';
concessive: хоч/хоč, дарма що/darmá ščo 'although';
explanatory: то/to, тобто/tóbto, себто/sébto 'that is'.

Most subordinating conjunctions admit (some even require, especially if the main clause comes first) a demonstrative pronoun in the main clause, such as той/toj 'that' in its various forms, так/tak 'thus', тоді/todi 'then', whose function is to point to the subordinate clause to follow: людина, що знає правду/ljudýna, ščo znáje právdu or та людина, що знає правду/ta ljudýna, ščo znáje právdu 'the (that) man who knows the truth'. In recent decades, the habit of placing the word факт/fakt 'fact' after той/ toj has spread in objective clauses, possibly in imitation of the corresponding English construction: усім відомо те/usim vidómo te or усім відомий той факт, що «Гамлета» написав Шекспір/usim vidómyj toj fakt, ščo "Hámleta" napysáv Šekspir 'everyone knows that *Hamlet* was written by Shakespeare'. In the case of causal тому що/tomú ščo and consecutive так що/tak ščo, the first element, now an integral part of the subordinating conjunction in the subordinate clause, is etymologically just such a demonstrative. Concessive хоч/хоč, less often дармá що/darmá ščo, when in a subordinate clause before the main clause takes as its (optional) counterpart in the main clause алé/alé 'but', and not a demonstrative: хоч iдé снiг, (алé) надвóрi тéпло/хоč idé snih, (alé) nadvóri téplo 'although it is snowing, (yet) it is warm outside'. A few conjunctions do not allow an antecedent counterpart in the main clause: objective нíби/niby, temporal як тiльки/jak tíl´ky, causal бо/bo, consecutive аж/až and all the explanatory conjunctions.

The relative position of the two clauses, main and subordinate, is interchangeable in most types of composite sentences, even though in some types the subordinate clause tends to precede (temporal clauses) and in other types it tends to follow (objective clauses, causal clauses with томý що/tomú ščo). Placing the subordinate clause after the main clause is obligatory in the case of temporal clauses with the conjunction аж/až, causal clauses with the conjunction бо/bo, consecutive and explanatory clauses. Finally, relative clauses must stand after the noun to which they refer.

In Ukrainian, it is not possible to extract interrogative and relative pronouns out of finite subordinate clauses, to give literal translations of English sentences like *who do you think that I saw?* or *the man that I think that you saw.*

Subordinate clauses of time, sometimes with additional nuances of cause, condition, concession or consequence may be replaced by gerundial constructions, provided the two clauses have the same subject, as in утомúвся бiгавши/utomývsja bihavšy 'he got tired while running (or: because he had been running)'.

Perfective verbs have gerunds in -šy, imperfective ones in both -šy and -čy: добiгши/dobihšy 'having run to', бiгаючи/bihajučy, бiгавши/bihavšy 'running'. As a rule, gerunds of perfective aspect refer to the preceding action, as in добiгши, вiн упáв/dobihšy, vin upáv 'having run up, he fell', in which he first reached his goal, then fell down; occasionally, if such a gerund is placed after the main clause, it denotes a subsequent action, as in вонá сiдáє, вúтягнувши нóги/voná sidáje, výtjahnuvšy nóhy 'she sits down and stretches her legs'. Gerunds of imperfective aspect, both those in -čy and those in -šy, as a rule refer to simultaneous actions or conditions, as in сúдячи, вонá витягáє нóги/sýdjačy, voná vytjaháje nóhy 'while sitting she stretches her legs'. The imperfective gerunds in -šy are more typical if the verb in the main clause is imperfective and in the past tense, but the present gerund is also possible here (сидíвши ~ сúдячи, вонá витягáла нóги/sydívšy ~ sýdjačy, voná vytjahála nóhy 'while sitting she stretched her legs'). The stronger the subsidiary nuances of cause, concession and so on, the weaker the temporal identity of the gerund, which then tends to become an adverb.

Subordinate clauses of purpose with the conjunction щоб/ščob 'in order that' and its synonyms usually have the verb in the infinitive if their subject is identical with that of the main clause, as in приїхав, щоб оглянути місто/pryjixav, ščob ohljánuty misto 'he came in order to look around the city'. In such constructions the conjunction is optional, though statistically constructions with щоб/ščob prevail. The щоб/ščob construction is, however, inadmissible with modal verbs such as могти/mohtý 'be able', хотіти/xotity 'want', мусіти/músity 'must', дозволяти/dozvoljáty 'permit', наказувати/nakázuvaty 'order' in the main clause, and these require a following plain infinitive.

In addition to such cases, the infinitive is also used as a subject (співати – високе мистецтво/spiváty – vysóke mystéctvo 'singing is a high art') and as an expression of a wish or order (іти швидко!/ity švýdko! 'go quickly!'). The use of the infinitive with nouns to denote their function is obsolete (казан варити куліш/kazán varýty kuliš 'cauldron to cook kulish (a kind of soup)').

4.6   Negation

Sentence negation is expressed by putting the particle не/ne before the predicate: він був там/vin buv tam 'he was there', він не був там/vin ne buv tam 'he was not there'. Constituent negation, if it does not refer to a pronoun, is expressed by putting не/ne before the negated constituent: бачив комедію в театрі/báčyv komédiju v teatri 'he saw the comedy in the theater', бачив не комедію в театрі(, а трагедію)/báčyv ne komédiju v teátri(, a trahédiju) 'he didn't see the comedy in the theatre(, but the tragedy)', бачив комедію не в театрі(, а в телебаченні)/báčyv komédiju ne v teátri(, a v telebáčenni) 'he didn't see the comedy in the theatre(, but on television)'. In the case of a negated pronoun multiple negation with the particles не/ne and ні/ni is used:

Ніхто не бачив (цієї) комедії в театрі./Nixtó ne báčyv (cijéji) komédiji v teátri.
'No one saw the (this) comedy in the theatre.'
Ніхто не бачив у театрі ні комедії, ні трагедії./Nixtó ne báčyv u teátri ni komédiji, ni trahédiji.
'No one saw either the comedy or the tragedy in the theatre.'
Ніхто не бачив ні комедії, ні трагедії ні в театрі, ні в телебаченні./Nixtó ne báčyv ni komédiji, ni trahédiji ni v teátri, ni v telebáčenni.
'No one saw either the comedy or the tragedy either in the theatre or on television.'

There are certain other differences between sentences with and without sentence negation. These concern the direct object and the subject. The direct object which in the positive sentence would be accusative may appear in the genitive: курить люльку/kúryt′ ljúl′ku '(he) smokes a pipe (ACC)', не курить люльки/ne kúryt′ ljúl′ky 'he does not smoke a pipe

(GEN)'. However, this case shift is not obligatory and the accusative may remain unchanged. Statistically speaking, the genitive is a little more frequent than the accusative of the object in negative sentences. Semantically, the genitive in such sentences is more general, not concentrating on a specific object, so that не читав газети (GEN)/ne čytáv hazéty (GEN) may mean 'he did not read any newspaper' while не читав газету (ACC)/ ne čytáv hazétu (ACC) may easily refer to a specific newspaper, that is 'he did not read the newspaper'. Moreover, the use of the genitive for the negated object is more typical of formal speech.

Given sentences with the general meaning of presence, under negation the nominative is replaced by the genitive. The verb бути/búty 'be' in the past tense is placed in the neuter singular form, in the future in the third person singular, and in the present tense it is replaced by the word нема/ nemá 'there is not': були хліби (NOM)/bulý xlibý (GEN) 'there were loaves', не було хлібів (GEN)/ne buló xlibiv (GEN) 'there were no loaves', не буде хлібів (GEN)/ne búde xlibiv (GEN) 'there will be no loaves', нема хлібів (GEN)/nemá xlibiv (GEN) 'there are no loaves'. The sentence becomes impersonal in all such cases. While in 'be'-sentences such a shift is obligatory, it is optional in application to other verbs with a more concrete meaning that contain the notion of presence or possession: сьогодні газет (GEN) не виходило/s'ohódni hazét (GEN) ne vyxódylo or сьогодні газети (NOM) не виходили/s'ohódni hazéty (NOM) ne vyxódyly 'today no newspapers came out'.

4.7 Anaphora and pronouns

The type of sentence that is, statistically, the most frequent and, stylistically, the most neutral has, if there is no other subject, a personal pronoun (including anaphoric pronouns) as subject alongside the verb, except in the imperative: я червонію/ja červoniju 'I blush', він червоніє/vin červonije 'he blushes', я червонів/ja červoniv 'I blushed', він червонів/ vin červoniv 'he blushed'. However, in informal speech, sentences without personal pronouns in the indicative and conditional are quite frequent and serve as a means of emphasizing the informality of the utterance. The absence of personal pronouns is nearly obligatory in answers to yes–no questions: ти там був?/ty tam buv? 'were you there?', був/buv 'I was' (and not я був/ja buv). The same applies to non-initial clauses provided a co-referential pronoun is used in the initial clause: він знав, що туди не піде/vin znav, ščo tudý ne píde 'he knew that he would not go there' (and not він знав, що він туди не піде/vin znav, ščo vin tudý ne píde). In the imperative personal pronouns appear only under strong stress: ти іди!/ty idý! 'you go (not me)!' instead of the more normal іди!/idý!.

In formal usage if there are two nouns of the same gender (person) and number the ensuing ambiguity in the use of pronouns may be resolved by using перший/péršyj (literally: 'first') 'the former' and другий/drúhyj (literally: 'second') or останній/ostánnij, (literally: 'last') 'the latter': ýчень і вчи́тель розмовля́ли ... пе́рший спита́в ..., дру́гий відпові́в/účen′ i včýtel′ rozmovljály ... péršyj spytáv ..., drúhyj vidpovív ... 'the pupil and the teacher were conversing ... the former asked ... the latter answered ...'

4.8 Reflexives and reciprocals

Most typically, reflexivity is expressed by the verbal postfix -*sja* (after a vowel or a resonant, optionally -*s′*): умива́юся/umyvájusja 'I wash myself', умива́вся/umyvávsja 'I washed myself', also умива́юсь/umyvájus′ and (rarely) умива́всь/umyvávs′. But the functions of this postfix are manifold:

passive voice (збро́я кува́лася в ку́зні/zbrója kuválasja v kúzni 'weaponry was forged in the smithy');
reciprocity (вони́ поцілува́лися/vоný pociluválysja 'they kissed each other');
fulfilment of an action (наївся/najivsja 'he ate his fill');
impersonalization (хо́четься/xóčet′sja 'one feels like (doing something)');
exclusion of the object (ки́дає/kýdaje 'he throws (something, expressed in the accusative)', but ки́дається/kýdajet′sja 'he throws (with no possibility of an accusative object)'; see also section 3.2.6 above).

Many verbs are not used at all without the postfix, such as намага́ється/namahájet′sja 'he endeavours', in some others the use of the postfix is optional, as in обіця́в(ся)/obicjáv(sja) 'he promised'.

As a result of this accumulation of meanings the meaning of the postfix became vague, in some cases rather stylistic, with a lesser degree of formality. As a result, there appeared a tendency to replace here and there, in cases of true reflexivity, the postfix -*sja* by the apparently less ambiguous pronoun себе́/sebé, as in він лю́бить (само́го) себе́/vin ljúbyt′ (samóho) sebé 'he loves himself', or, in cases of reciprocity, the phrase оди́н одного́/odýn odnohó (also stressed о́дного/ódnoho), as in вони́ люби́ли оди́н одного́/vоný ljubýly odýn odnohó 'they loved each other' instead of люби́лися/ljubýlysja. The expansion of these types is relatively recent; traditionally used reflexive and reciprocal verbs are still used (as in the examples above), the new type of construction is spreading gradually, filling the gaps and eliminating ambiguities, so that it is impossible to give an exact delimitation of new constructions from traditional postfixal verbs. One of the differences between the traditional -*sja* forms and their phrasal replacements is that in the case of conjoined chains the postfix is repeated in each member, which is not the case with the phrasal equivalents: він голи́вся й умива́вся/vin holývsja j umyvávsja 'he shaved and washed himself', but вони́ обійма́ли й цілува́ли оди́н о́дного/vоný obijmály j ciluvály odýn ódnoho 'they embraced and kissed one another'.

Postfixed impersonal verbs like хо́четься/xóčet´sja 'one feels like (doing something)' exclude the possibility of a subject in the nominative case; instead, they require a noun phrase in the dative, as can be seen in the contrast between я хо́чу/ja xóču 'I want' and мені хо́четься/menı xóčet´sja 'I feel like'. Traditionally, sentences of this type are called impersonal sentences. Impersonal sentences of several types are widespread in Ukrainian. The chief types are:

Absolutely impersonal sentences in which no subject or its substitute may appear: світа́є/svitáje 'it dawns'.

Relatively impersonal sentences, in which a subject in the nominative case is possible but is left unnamed or unidentified: у ву́хах стогна́ло/u vúxax stohnálo 'it (something) moaned in his ears'.

Impersonal sentences consisting of a genitive noun phrase preceded by не до/ne do, literally 'not to', with zero copula in the present tense and appropriate forms of бу́ти/búty in other tenses: мені́ було́ не до смі́ху/meni bulo ne do smíxu 'I was not up to laughing'.

Adverbial sentences specializing in depicting situations independent of the will of persons, with forms of бу́ти/búty (including zero in the present tense) and a dative noun phrase: мені́ було́ су́мно/meni buló súmno 'I felt sad'. A subtype here are sentences with negative pronouns in the dative: ніко́му було́ співа́ти/nikomu buló spiváty 'there was nobody to sing'.

Infinitive sentences of various modal meanings with a present or potential noun phrase in the dative, as in вам не поневóлити нарóд/vam ne ponevólyty naród 'you will be unable to enslave the people'.

Participial sentences with a petrified form of the head word in what used to be the neuter singular in -no or -to (contrast the current neuter singular in -ne or -te): стра́ву зва́рено/strávu zváreno 'the meal is cooked', люди́ну вби́то/ljudýnu vbýto 'the man is killed'. As seen in these examples, these sentences admit a noun in the accusative.

Negative existential sentences (see section 4.6).

4.9 Possession

Predicative constructions in possessive sentences are of three kinds:

The preposition y/u plus the genitive case of the noun phrase denoting the possessor plus the nominative case (under negation, the genitive case) of the thing possessed; the predicate proper is a non-omissible form of the verb 'be' ('existential' 'be', thus the negative present is не́ма/néma): у ньо́го є гро́ші/u n´óho je hróši 'he has money'.

A noun phrase in the nominative denoting the possessor and the appropriate form of the verb ма́ти/máty 'have' with the accusative of the noun phrase denoting the thing possessed (or, under negation, also the genitive of the thing possessed): він ма́є гро́ші/vin máje hróši 'he has money'.

A noun in the nominative denoting the thing possessed, the copula (which may be zero in the present tense) and a possessive pronoun or adjective denoting the possessor: (ці) гро́ші мої́/(ci) hróši mojí 'this money is mine'.

All three constructions are well rooted in the language.

Attributive means of expressing possession are primarily possessive adjectives (with the suffixes -iv or -yn) or possessive pronouns (usually before the head noun) as well as the genitive of nouns (usually after the head noun): ба́тьків, ма́терин руко́пис/bát′kiv, máteryn rukópys 'father's, mother's manuscript' or руко́пис ба́тька, ма́тері/rukópys bát′ka, máteri. With nouns as possessors, the adjectival construction prevails when the possessor is singular, the genitive is used when it is non-singular; compare руко́пис батькі́в/rukópys bat′kiv 'parents' manuscript', where батькі́в/bat′kiv is genitive plural.

4.10 Quantification

Numerals in their syntactic behaviour are not uniform (for their declension, see section 3.1.5). They fall into the divisions set out below.

Оди́н/odýn '1' functions as an adjective in full agreement with its noun, that is, it agrees in case and number in the plural and also in gender in the singular: оди́н буди́нок (M)/odýn budýnok (M) 'one house', одна́ ха́та (F)/odná xáta (F) 'one cottage', одне́ теля́ (N)/odné teljá (N) 'one calf', одні́ теля́та/odni teljáta 'some calves', одного́ буди́нка/odnohó budýnka 'one house (GEN SG)'.

Два/dva '2', три/try '3', чоти́ри/čotýry '4' agree with the noun to which they refer in case (два/dva also in gender), but require the noun in the plural. However, if the phrase is nominative (or the nominative-like accusative), then the noun is used in a form identical to the nominative plural but with the stress of the genitive singular, as in два бра́ти/dva bráty 'two brothers', in contrast to брати́/bratý 'brothers'. This stress rule does not apply to other cases. In this combination, an accompanying adjective can be either nominative plural or genitive plural: два нові́ буди́нки/dva noví budýnky or два нови́х буди́нки/dva novýx budýnky 'two new houses'; the genitive forms are particularly frequent with feminine nouns.

П'ять/pjat′ '5' to дев'ятсо́т/devjatsót '900' govern the genitive plural when the phrase is nominative (including the nominative-like accusative), but in other cases agree with the noun: сім днів/sim dniv 'seven days', but genitive семи́, сімо́х днів/semý, simóx dniv, dative семи́, сімо́м дням/semý, simóm dnjam.

Ти́сяча/týsjača 'thousand', мільйо́н/mil′jón 'million' and higher numerals require the noun in the genitive plural: тисяча осіб/týsjača osib 'a thousand persons', instrumental тисячею осіб/týsjačeju osib.

Compound numerals such as сорок шість/sórok šist' '46', require the noun in the form as dictated by their last component, that is сорок один зошит/sórok odýn zóšyt 'forty-one writing-books', сорок два зошити/ sórok dva zóšyty 'forty-two writing-books', сорок п'ять зошитів/sórok pjat' zóšytiv 'forty-five writing-books'.

Alongside the above numerals, quantities from '2' to '80' may be represented by the numerals traditionally called collective: двоє/dvóje, троє/ tróje, четверо/čétvero, ... вісімдесятеро/visimdesjátero. They are used with *pluralia tantum* (двоє саней/dvóje sanéj 'two sledges'), with nouns whose plural stem differs from that of the singular (such as око/óko 'eye', plural очі/óči, двоє очей/dvóje očéj 'two eyes') and optionally with neuter nouns (двоє вікон/dvóje vikon 'two windows'). In oblique cases collective numerals are not distinguished from the ordinary numerals, so that the genitive of двоє саней/dvóje sanéj is двох саней/dvox sanéj. Syntactically, they follow the pattern of п'ять/pjat' '5'.

Non-numeral quantifiers are represented primarily by such words as багато/baháto (rarely багацько/bahác'ko) 'much, many', мало/málo and трохи/tróxy 'a little, few', (де)кілька/(de)kil'ka 'a number (of)'. In affective language there are, particularly for the notions of large number, quite a few nouns of the type сила/sýla (literally: 'strength'), безліч/ bézlič (literally: 'numberless'). They all require a noun in the genitive when they stand in the nominative (or the accusative identical with the nominative): багато, мало, кілька, сила людей/baháto, málo, kil'ka, sýla ljudéj 'many, few, several, lots of people'. Some of them are declinable on the pattern of три/try or п'ять/pjat', as in genitive багатьох/bahat'óx, кількох/kil'kóx, and follow the syntactic pattern of п'ять/pjat'; those that are nouns, like сила/sýla, retain their declension as nouns and govern the genitive case throughout; the remainder are indeclinable (мало/málo, трохи/tróxy).

5 Lexis

5.1 General composition of the word-stock

The general idea of the share of Common Slavonic vocabulary in modern standard Ukrainian can be drawn from the following observation. In a randomly taken page of a work of fiction (text 1: 300 words) 216 words have Common Slavonic roots; in a randomly taken page of non-fiction (text 2: 300 words, from a linguistics journal), this number falls to about 150. Among the remaining word-stock, borrowings play an important part. In text 1 there are 8 borrowings from Polish (mostly made in the sixteenth or seventeenth centuries), 16 from Russian (mostly of relatively recent date) and 8 of common European word-stock (so-called 'international' words). Corresponding numbers in text 2 are 23, 9 and 72, respectively. The words of Polish or Russian origin in certain cases appear as loan trans- lations in which all components are apparently Ukrainian but the word as a whole is entirely based on the pattern of the other Slavonic language, such as, in our texts, кількість/kil'kist' 'quantity', copied from Polish ilość (Ukrainian кілька/kil'ka corresponds to Polish ile 'several, how many', the Ukrainian suffix -ist' corresponds to Polish -ość) and спілкування/ spilkuvánnja 'communication', patterned on Russian общéние/obščénie (Ukrainian спільний/spil'nyj 'common' corresponds to Russian óбщий/ óbščij, with in both languages a suffix which derives nouns denoting a process from verbs).

5.2 Patterns of borrowing
During the Old Ukrainian period (the tenth to thirteen centuries) the main source of loan-words were Church Slavonic in its Bulgarian and Mace- donian recensions, Greek and Turkic languages. The first two operated primarily on the level of the ecclesiastical and literary languages, Turkic languages on the level of the spoken language. A few examples are Church Slavonic дух/dux 'spirit', блажéнство/blažénstvo 'bliss', Greek áнгел/ ánhel 'angel', грáмота/hrámota 'charter'. In many cases Greek words entered Old Ukrainian via Church Slavonic. The main sources of Turkic borrowings were the languages of the nomadic Turkic tribes of the steppes south and east of the then Ukrainian frontier. Such are words like богатúр/bohatýr 'hero', товáр/továr 'field-camp' (now 'goods'). Borrowing from Old Scandinavian was of limited import. These words concerned mostly military and commercial activities, such as варяг/varjáh 'man-at-arms', щóгла/ščóhla 'mast'. (Here and below loan-words are quoted as a rule in their modern form.)

The crucial influence in the Middle Ukrainian period (the fourteenth to the eighteenth centuries), especially after the Union of Lublin of 1569, which created the Polish commonwealth (Poland, Lithuania, Ukraine) until about 1720, was Polish. It shaped much of the administrative language of the time, mediated in the expansion of the western word-stock concerning culture, technology, abstract thinking and so on: words from Latin, Czech, German (there were also direct borrowings into Ukrainian from German), Italian, French and other languages. Moreover, under the conditions of the general bilingualism of the nobility, educated and urban classes, a situation arose in which, time and again, it was irrelevant whether a native or a Polish word was used, so that gradually not only were new words intro- duced for new notions but quite a few native words were crowded out by Polonisms. This influx abated after 1720 when most of the Ukraine became a Russian province, but it resumed in the nineteenth century, although on a narrower scale, because the intellectuals occasionally saw in Polonisms and/or loan translations from Polish a means to counteract expansion of Russianisms. Of the almost innumerable Polonisms adopted in the Middle Ukrainian period a part (about 50 per cent) were lost subsequently, but Modern Ukrainian is still closer in its word-stock to Polish than to any other Slavonic language. This was, of course, a result of Polish political domination but not less so of cultural seduction.

Another strong influence in the Middle Ukrainian period, though by no means as powerful as that of Polish, was the Turkic languages. It was particularly strong in the military terminology of Ukrainian Cossacks but also in sheep-breeding, gardening, clothing, music and other areas.

After the defeat of Ukrainian autonomism in 1709 the Ukrainian language stood under the growing and eventually overpowering (especially since 1930) influence of Russian, which resulted in numerous borrowings, loan translations and syntactic calques from Russian. Even loans from western languages are made most often through Russian mediation. Virtually universal bilingualism causes frequent mixing of the two languages. The expansion of Russian elements was until recently supported by the administrative establishment, which went so far as to reject one or another Ukrainian word and prescribe its replacement by another which was closer to Russian or was straight Russian.

5.3   Incorporation of borrowings

In modern standard Ukrainian the general rule is to adopt foreign words to the morphological system of Ukrainian. Thus, nouns ending in a consonant or in -*a* decline like native nouns with such an ending independent of their gender in the original language. For example, болíд/bolíd 'fireball' declines like слíд/slid 'trace', терáса/terása 'terrace' declines like прикрáса/prykrása 'adornment', флот/flot 'navy' declines like рот/rot 'mouth' in disregard of the fact that in French it is feminine: *la flotte.* Exceptions like адрéса/adrésa 'address', patterned ultimately on the French feminine (*une adresse*), are extremely rare.

Those nouns which end in a vowel or combination of vowels that do not occur in native nouns are indeclinable: какадý/kakadú 'cockatoo', жюрí/ žjurí 'jury', амплуá/ampluá 'line (of business)'. Foreign substantives in -*e* do not decline because native substantives of that type have in some cases palatalized stem-final consonants, which is not the case in foreign words: contrast native мóре/móre 'sea', genitive singular мóря/mórja and borrowed пюрé/pjuré 'purée'. Foreign nouns in -*o* tended to be treated like native neuters in -*o* until, in 1934, this treatment was declared non-standard and eliminated from the standard language: thus, кінó/kinó 'cinema' had genitive singular кінá/kiná, but now кінó/kinó is supposed to be retained as such in all cases.

Adjectives as a rule are adopted by taking in the nominative singular masculine the ending -*yj* with its set of gender, number and case endings, usually preceded by a native suffix, as in суповий/supovýj from суп/sup 'soup'.

All foreign verbs take a native suffix, most typically -uva(-ty) : -uj(-u) and are conjugated as native verbs, such as монтувати/montuváty : монтую/montúju 'to mount'. The German-origin suffix -yr- is normally omitted (contrast German *montieren*), except in cases of possible ambiguity, such as командувати/kománduvaty 'to give orders', командирувати/komandyruváty 'to send on business', both *kommandieren* in German. Verbs of foreign origin enter Ukrainian without aspect differentiation; when they are naturalized, however, they tend to mark perfective aspect by adding a prefix. For instance, арештувати/areštuváty 'to arrrest', attested in Ukrainian since 1583, was first used in this form without aspect differentiation; but later (at the latest in the mid-nineteenth century) заарештувати/zaareštuváty was introduced as a perfective verb, and by the same token the original form took the function of imperfective.

5.4 Lexical fields

5.4.1 Colour terms

Білий/bílyj 'white'; чорний/čórnyj 'black'; червоний/červónyj 'red'; зелений/zelényj 'green'; жовтий/žóvtyj 'yellow'; синій/sýnij 'blue' and блакитний/blakýtnyj and голубий/holubýj 'light blue'; сірий/síryj 'grey'.

For 'brown' there is no generally accepted term; possible equivalents are брунатний/brunátnyj, коричнявий/korýčnjavyj (variant: коричневий/korýčnevyj), less often цинамоновий/cynamónovyj. The most authoritative Academy dictionary of 1929 placed first цинамоновий/cynamónovyj, marked коричнявий/korýčnjavyj as dialectal (without quotations), then placed брунатний/brunátnyj (with quotations from the early nineteenth century); the Hrinčenko dictionary of 1908 has брунатний/brunátnyj, without quotations, and no коричневий/korýčnevyj at all. The post-war Soviet dictionaries place emphasis on коричневий/korýčnevyj for the obvious reason that it is current in Russian.

For 'purple' there is again no basic generally accepted term, червоний/červónyj 'red' being used to cover this colour range. The following are all typical of poetic language and atypical of colloquial language: пурпурний/purpúrnyj (variant: пурпуровий/purpúróvyj), багровий/bahróvyj and archaic шарлатовий/šarlátovyj.

For 'orange', жовтогарячий/žovtoharjáčyj, literally 'yellow hot', is known in the vernacular but is understood rather as a poetic denotation of a shade of yellow; оранжевий/oránževyj, from Russian, is being introduced and promoted by language legislators.

5.4.2 Body parts

Головá/holová 'head'; óко/óko 'eye'; нíc/nis 'nose'; вýхо/vúxo 'ear'; рот/rot and вустá/vustá (PL) 'mouth'; волóсся/volóssja 'hair'; шѝя/ šýja 'neck'; рукá/ruká 'arm, hand'; пáлець/pálec′ 'finger'; ногá/nohá 'leg, foot'; пáлець (ногѝ)/pálec′ (nohý) 'toe'; грýди/hrúdy (PL) 'chest'; сéрце/sérce 'heart'.

5.4.3 Kinship terms

бáтько/bát′ko, тáто/táto 'father'; мáти/máty, less commonly нéнька/ nén′ka 'mother'; брат/brat 'brother'; сестрá/sestrá 'sister'; дядько/ djád′ko 'uncle' (regional western стрѝй(ко)/strýj(ko) 'father's brother', вýй(ко)/vúj(ko) 'mother's brother'), тíтка/títka 'aunt'; племíнник/ pleminnyk, нéбіж/nébiž 'nephew' (regional western братáн(ич)/ bratán(yč), братáнець/bratánec′ 'brother's son', сестрíнок/sestrínok 'sister's son'); племíнниця/pleminnycja, небóга/nebóha 'niece' (regional western братáниця/bratánycja 'brother's daughter', сестрѝниця/sestrýnycja, сестрíнка/sestrinka 'sister's daughter'; кузéн/ kuzén, брат у дрýгих/brat u drúhyx, двоюрíдний брат/dvojúridnyj brat '(male) cousin' (regional western кузѝнок/kuzýnok); кузѝна/ kuzýna, сестрá в дрýгих/sestrá v drúhyx, двоюрíдна сестрá/ dvojúridna sestrá '(female) cousin' (regional western кузѝнка/kuzýnka); дід(ýсь)/did(ús′) 'grandfather' (regional western дíдо/dido); бáб(к)а/ báb(k)a, бабýня/babúnja, бабýся/babúsja 'grandmother'; чоловíк/ čolovík, дружѝна/družýna, подрýжжя/podrúžžja 'husband'; жíнка/žinka, дружѝна/družýna, подрýжжя/podrúžžja 'wife'; син/syn 'son'; дочкá/dočká, дóня/dónja, дóнька/dón′ka 'daughter'.

6 Dialects

Ukrainian dialects are traditionally divided into three groups (see map 17.1). Northern dialects are spoken north of the approximate line Luc′k–Kiev–Sumy. South of that line one finds the area of southern dialects which, in turn, are divided into south-western (west of the approximate line Xvastiv–Balta) and south-eastern ones, east of that approximate line. The main criterion on which the delineation south versus north is based is (as suggested by Ганцов/Hancov 1923) the part played by the accent in the development of the vocalism. In the north the most important changes of vowels took place under stress, in the south they ran identically in stressed and unstressed syllables. This basic difference is supplemented by some other distinctions in phonology, morphology and lexicon.

The northern and the south-western dialects are more archaic than the south-eastern ones. The former two groups already began to take shape in prehistoric times, while the formation of the south-eastern dialects falls into the sixteenth to eighteenth centuries. It was at that time that the present-

Map 17.1 Ukrainian dialects (after Zilyns'kyj (1979) and Жилко/Żyłko (1966))

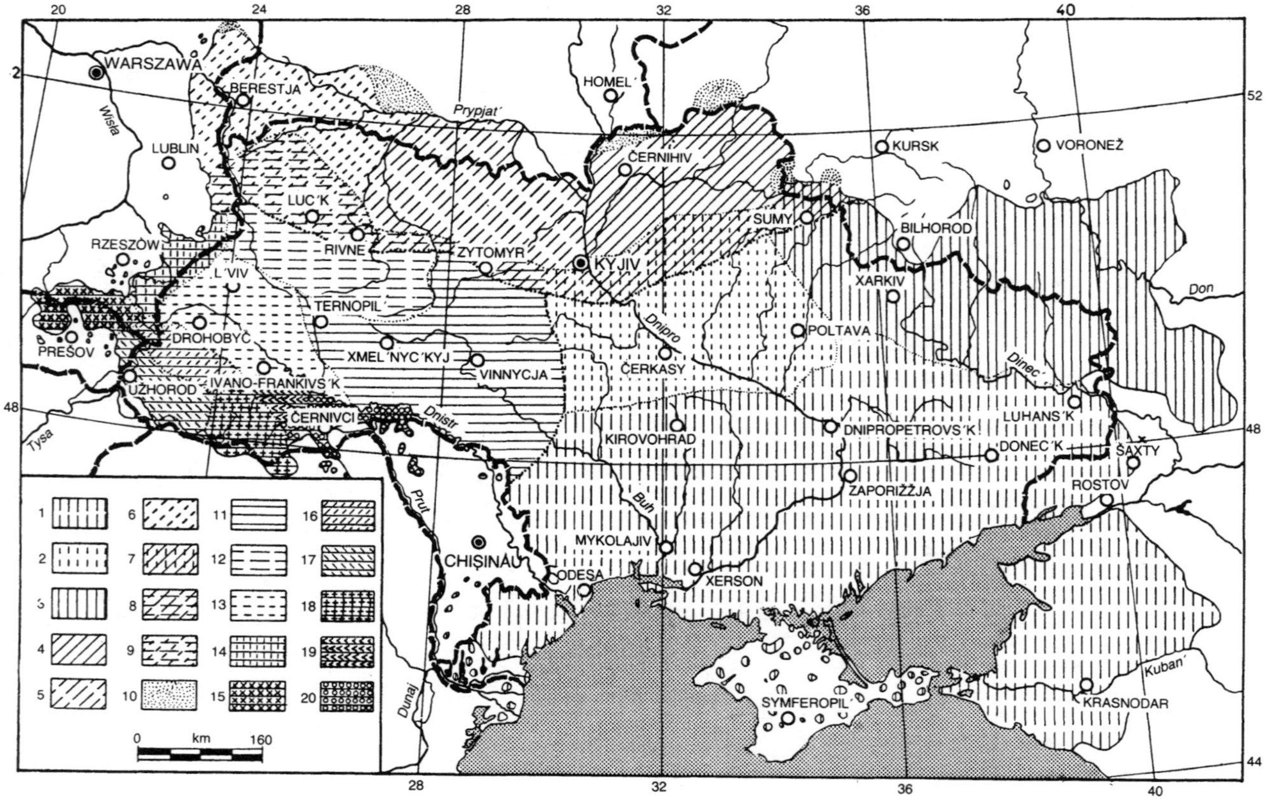

KEY
1–3 South-eastern dialects
    1   Steppe dialects
    2   Čerkasy–Poltava dialects
    3   Slobožanščyna dialects
4–10 Northern dialects
    4   Eastern Polissian dialects
    5   Central Polissian dialects
    6   Western Polissian and Pidljašian dialects
    7–9   Transitional dialects (from northern to southern)
    10   Transitional Ukrainian–Belorussian and Ukrainian–Russian dialects
11–20 South-western dialects
    11   Podillja dialects
    12   South Volhynian dialects
    13   Dnister dialects
    14   Sjan dialects
    15   Lemkian dialects
    16   Bojkian dialects
    17   Central Transcarpathian dialects
    18   Hucul dialects
    19   Pokuttia dialects
    20   Bukovyna dialects

day south-eastern Ukraine was, after its reconquest from the Tatars by the Cossacks, resettled or settled by people from south-western and northern regions. The unity of the south-eastern dialects was created by the dynamic migrational processes and the mixing of population from territories of the two more archaic dialects (see section 1).

The south-eastern dialects are relatively uniform. The northern dialects fall into three chief groups, Western, Central and Eastern Polissian. The south-western dialects are strongly differentiated, into eight groups, or more.

The most striking distinctive features of the principal dialects are the following:

1   In the north *o* and *e* (the latter from *e* and *ě*) under certain conditions (see section 2.1) alternate, under stress, with diphthongs (which, phonetically, vary from place to place); by now they have monophthongized into *u*, *y*, *ü* or *i* in some places, but these are secondary developments. In the south there never were any diphthongs of that origin. The main line of development in the south of, for example, *o* in the newly closed syllables (after the loss of weak *jers*) was *o* › *u* › *ü* › *i*. In some local dialects, especially in Transcarpathia, the stages *u* and *ü* are still retained.

2   In the north *r´* was depalatalized by the mid-twelfth century; in the

south this happened only in some local dialects and much later.

3   Some local south-western dialects depalatalized word-final c', preserve the distinction of y and i and developed dorsal palatalization of s', z', c' (which became $ś$, $ź$, $ć$).

4   In declension, the south-west has preserved the word-final y in the soft declension (as in locative singular на земли́/na zemlÿ 'on earth') versus south-eastern i: на землі/na zemli). In the dative singular of masculine nouns the south-west has the ending -*ovy* while the north has -*u* and the south-east both -*u* and -*ovi*. The south-west in most local varieties preserves clitic forms of personal pronouns (such as dative singular ми/my 'to me', versus south-eastern only мені/meni).

5   In conjugation, the south-west preserves enclitic forms of the auxiliary verb in the past tense but in the north and the south-east these are lost, as in south-western спа́вем/spávjem versus northern and south-eastern я спав/ja spav 'I slept'.

A special problem is that of the so-called Rusyn (Ruthenian) language. The term has various meanings depending on when and where it is/was used. In the Transcarpathian region of the Ukraine and in the adjacent East Slovak region around Prešov it was the name of one of the three orientations in shaping the standard language before 1945 (when the bulk of the area became part of the Soviet Ukraine): Ukrainian, Russian and the regional one based on some local 'Rusyn' dialects, the latter orientation supported by Hungary. Nowadays this is a historical and dated use. In a sense, however, it is applied to the language of immigrants from the area (Carpatho-Rusyn) in the United States, but with much stronger admixture of the Russian Church Slavonic traditional in Transcarpathia. It is basically a written language cultivated by the Greek Catholic church with its centre in Pittsburgh. Thirdly, the term is used by immigrants from western Transcarpathia who settled in the mid-eighteenth century in the former Yugoslavia, with their centre in Kerestur. This is an independent standard micro-language for a population of up to 20,000 people. This language is essentially based on Eastern Slovak dialects with some Western Ukrainian admixture. The speakers are inclined to call it Ukrainian under the influence of the Ukrainian Greek Catholic clergy of Byzantine rite who were active in shaping this language.

References

Birnbaum, Henrik (1985) 'What is Ukrainian in the multilayered speech of the Jugoslav Rusini?', in Jacob P. Hursky (ed.), *Studies in Linguistics in Honor of George Y. Shevelov* (= *Annals of the Ukrainian Academy of Arts and Sciences in the United States* 15), 39–47.

Kolessa, A[lexander] (1896) 'Dialektologische Merkmale des südrussischen Denk-males "Žitije sv. Savy"', *Archiv für slavische Philologie* 18: 203–28, 473–523.

Shevelov, George Y. (1966) *Die ukrainische Schriftsprache 1798–1965*, Wiesbaden: Otto Harrassowitz.

—— (1979) *A Historical Phonology of the Ukrainian Language*, Heidelberg: Carl Winter.

—— (1986) 'Das Ukrainische', in Peter Rehder (ed.), *Einführung in die slavischen Sprachen*, Darmstadt: Wissenschaftliche Buchgesellschaft.

—— (1989) *The Ukrainian Language in the First Half of the Twentieth Century (1900–1941), its State and Status*, Cambridge, Mass.: Harvard Ukrainian Research Institute.

Smal-Stockyj, Stephan and Gartner, Theodor (1913) *Grammatik der ruthenischen (ukrainischen) Sprache*, Vienna: Ševčenko Gesellschaft der Wissenschaften.

Stankiewicz, Edward (1960) 'Stress alternations in the Ukrainian substantive declension: types and role', *Annals of the Ukrainian Academy of Arts and Sciences in the United States* 8: 25–6.

Ukraine: a Concise Encyclopaedia, vol. I, ed. Volodymyr Kubijovyč (1963), Toronto: University of Toronto Press. (The chapter 'Language'.)

Zilyns′kyj, Ivan (1979) *A Phonetic Description of the Ukrainian Language*, Cambridge, Mass., Harvard Ukrainian Research Institute.

Академія наук Української РСР, Інститут мовознавства ім. О.О. Потебні, Інститут суспільних наук (1984–8) *Атлас української мови, I: Полісся, Середня Наддніпрянщина і суміжні землі; II: Волинь, Наддністрянщина, Закарпаття і суміжні землі*, Київ: "Наукова думка".

Академія наук Української РСР, Інститут мовознавства ім О.О. Потебні (1978–83) *Історія української мови: Фонетика* (1979); *Морфологія* (1978); *Синтаксис* (1983); *Лексика і фразеологія* (1983), Київ: "Наукова думка".

Білодід, I[ван] (ed.) (1969–73) *Сучасна українська літературна мова: Вступ, Фонетика* (1969); *Морфологія* (1969); *Синтаксис* (1972); *Лексика і фразеологія* (1973), *Стилістика* (1973), Київ: "Наукова думка".

Бузук, П[етро] (1927) *Нарис історії української мови: Вступ, фонетика і морфологія*, Київ. (Reprinted Munich: Український вільний університет, 1985.)

Булаховський, Л[еонід] (ed.) (1931) *Підвищений курс української мови*, Харків: "Радянська школа".

Булаховський, Л[еонід] (ed.) (1951) *Курс сучасної української літературної мови, I: Вступ, Лексика, Морфологія, Наголос; II: Синтаксис*, Київ: "Радянська школа".

Булаховський, Л[еонід] (1956) *Питання походження української мови*, Київ: Академія наук Української РСР. (Reprinted in Л[еонід] Булаховський, *Вибрані праці в п'яти томах, II: Українська мова*, Київ: "Наукова думка" (1977) 9–216.)

Булаховський, Л[еонід] (1977) 'Історичний коментарій до української літературної мови', in Л[еонід] Булаховський, *Вибрані праці в п'яти томах, II: Українська мова*, Київ: "Наукова думка", 217–569.

Ганцов, Всеволод (1923) *Діялектологічна класифікація українських говорів*, Київ: Українська академія наук. (Reprinted Cologne: Universität Köln, 1974.)

Жилко, Ф[едот] (1966) *Нариси з діалектології української мови*, Second edition, Київ: "Наукова думка".

Мельничук, О[лександер] (1982–) *Етимологічний словник української мови в семи томах*, Київ: "Наукова думка" (vols 1–3 published by 1993).

Михальчук, К[онстантин] (1877) 'Наречия, поднаречия и говоры Южной России в связи с наречиями Галичины', in П. Чубинский (ed.), *Труды этнографическо-статистической экспедиции в Западно-русский край*, VII, С. Петербург: Имп. географическое общество.

Огієнко, Іван (1930) *Українська літературна мова XVI ст.*, I, Варшава: Друкарня синодальна.

Синявський, Олекса (1931) *Норми української літературної мови*, Київ: Література і мистецтво. (Reprinted Львів: Українське видавництво, 1941.)

Сімович, Василь (1921) *Граматика української мови*, Second edition, Київ-Ляйпціг: Українська накладня. (Reprinted Munich: Український вільний університет, 1986.)

Сулима, Микола (1928) *Українська фраза*, Харків: "Рух". (Reprinted Munich: Український вільний університет, 1988.)

Тимошенко, П[етро] (1959–61) *Хрестоматія матеріалів з історії української літературної мови*, 2 vols, Київ: "Радянська школа".

Шерех, Юрій (= George Y. Shevelov) (1951) *Нарис сучасної української літературної мови*, Мюнхен: "Молоде життя".

18 Slavonic languages in emigration

Roland Sussex

1 Introduction: homeland and emigration

If they were not great seafarers, the Slavs have been among the most constant migrants to lands which others own or have captured. According to Davies (1981), for instance, almost a third of all ethnic Poles live outside Poland, and the 6.5 million Americans of Polish descent constitute not only the largest Polish population outside the homeland, but also one of America's largest ethnic groups. As a result of wars and redrawn geo-political boundaries, the Slavs have formed minority communities in others' countries, including those of other Slavs.

We shall be concerned principally with the Slavs who have undertaken migrations for political, economic or ethnic reasons. This excludes what Stephens (1976) calls the linguistic minorities of western Europe (see also Straka 1970; Décsy 1973). These minorities fall into two groups. The first may form significantly numerous speech communities, but do not possess a language which is recognized as a national language. To this category belong the Sorbs, who inhabit what used to be part of East Germany, but with a density nowhere greater than 25 per cent of the total population. This group also contains the Basques of Spain and France, the Welsh, and the Bretons of France. A second group of minority languages are those which are used as national or official languages in the homeland, but which are used outside the homeland by linguistic minorities who have been stranded by voluntary or involuntary migration, or by the redrawing of national boundaries after cataclysms like world wars. In this category are the Slovenes of Carinthia in Austria (Neweklowsky 1984) and Trieste, and the Croats of Mezzogiorno in Italy. Outside western Europe we find settlements of Macedonians in Albania, Greece and Bulgaria (Hill 1991). All these peoples inhabit what are their traditional homelands, but which have been isolated from the rest of their nation, and oriented towards other nations, by geo-political events. As a result of national language movements, these Slavonic minorities have been marginalized, and sometimes linguistically persecuted: Prussia and Russia prohibited Polish from public use in their areas of partitioned Poland after 1860; the Hungarians imposed Magyar uniformity on the Slavs of the Austro–Hungarian Empire after Hungarian replaced Latin as the official national language in 1844; and socialist Rumania has been less than welcoming to the many nationalities, including numbers of Slavs, which inhabit its territories (Gilberg 1978).

Nor do we deal here with the Slavs displaced by the Second World War within, or close to, the boundaries of the Slavonic homelands. One such group were the many Slavs among the 5 million Soviet citizens repatriated to the Soviet Union under the Yalta Agreement of 1945. Many of those who were not shot were deported to labour camps in Siberia. The records of this migration are scarce. While very large numbers of European Slavs died in Siberia, we do not have enough evidence of their linguistic survival. Another such group are the Aegean Macedonians. In the north of Greece, close to the border of what used to be Yugoslavia, lies a group of villages where Macedonian is still spoken. The social history of these villages has not been conducive to language maintenance. They were under Ottoman control until the early years of this century. They passed into Greek control after the formation of the Greek state in 1913, and with the military losses in Asia Minor in 1923 the area was partially repopulated by Greeks from Asia Minor and what was becoming the Soviet Union. The Macedonian language of these villages has suffered considerable attrition from the Hellenizing policies of the Greek government (Hill 1991). There are few chances for the language to be used in education or administration, and the cultural level of the inhabitants has not enabled them to benefit from the presence of standard Macedonian across the border. None the less, this variety of Macedonian is still maintained by the inhabitants of these villages, centred on Lerin (Greek: Flórina), and by a number of speakers who have settled in Australia and Canada. The Lerin Macedonians identify to varying degrees with Macedonian and Greek national consciousness.

A different, and special, case concerns the Russians in the former Soviet Union. Since the times of Stalin there was an intermittent, but broadly cohesive, policy of resettlement: of non-Russians into other homelands, including the Russian Republic; and of Russians into non-Russian homelands. The goal of this policy was the ethnic dilution of potential points of unrest, and the promotion of Russian as a national language, together with the weakening of local language nationalist movements (Lewis 1972). Russians everywhere in the Soviet Union had access to Russian-language schooling and language support. But – in spite of Lenin's insistence in the formulation of the first Soviet Constitution – the rights of ethnic minorities to access to their languages and cultures have not always been upheld: what motivation is there to support Estonian language and culture for the family of an engineer relocated to Georgia or Tadzhikistan? With Russian as a sole common language between the relocated Estonians and the resident Georgians or Tadzhiks, the transplanted Estonian language and culture will need strong family resources to be self-sustaining. Since Russian populations in parts of the Baltic states reach 50 per cent, and since Russian was a national language in the USSR and was obligatorily taught in schools, even the homeland languages found it difficult to maintain full cultural activity.

The plebiscite results in the disintegrating Soviet Union in the first months of 1991 showed some voting patterns which did not run on ethnic lines. The expectation was that the ethnic Russians would everywhere vote for the maintenance of the Soviet Union; but the strong anti-Union vote in the Baltic states, and in Georgia, Armenia and Moldavia, showed that many Russians were voting for independence in their new homelands. These Russians may therefore become, in time, part of Stephens' second category of linguistic minorities, speaking a language which is a national language, but in another country.

These Slavs, however, are not the primary focus of the present study. We shall concentrate instead on Slavs who do not live close to the homeland, whatever the political boundaries; on Slavs who do not live in Slavonic countries with other host languages; and on those Slavs who have found new homes further afield, predominantly in western Europe, North America and Australasia. The numbers are indeed substantial. Census figures are often not comparable between countries, where they are available at all, but the following sample figures will give some idea of the size of the émigré Slavonic populations in three key countries of Slavonic immigration. The figures are in thousands:

	Poles	Ukrainians	Russians	Yugoslavs	Czechs+ Slovaks
Australia	63	18	18	159	8
Canada	135	310	32	74	45
USA	2,185	253	461	251	477

The title 'Yugoslavs' to cover Croats, Serbs, Slovenes and Macedonians is for demographic purposes only. The Australian data, from the 1976 Census (Clyne 1982), are for 'regular speakers of languages other than English'. The Canadian data from the 1971 census show mother-tongue users; the actual number of ethnic Ukrainian–Canadians was 580,000 (Kubijovyč 1971). The US figures are for 'estimates for three generations of claimants of non-English mother tongues' from the 1960 census (Fishman and Hofman 1966: 42).

2   Issues of language maintenance

The effort for language maintenance has been a central feature of émigré Slavonic communities (section 2.1). Language maintenance has been determined by, and linked to, a number of key factors: social and core values, which drive the notion of ethnic identity (section 2.2); policies and rights, which embody the host nation's view of its attitude towards the émigré nationalities (section 2.3); the question of standard languages, which define the goals of language maintenance (section 2.4); and the abstand (distinctiveness) and elaboration of the language and culture, which define their domain of operation (section 2.5). All these factors can be summarized in the concept of language ecology (section 2.6), which brings together the overall viability of the émigré language in its foreign context.

2.1   Language maintenance at home and abroad

The agencies which contribute to language maintenance in émigré communities have been studied by scholars like Haugen (1953), Weinreich (1957) and Fishman (1966). These factors include the numbers and concentration of émigrés; cohesive institutions, including churches, schools, clubs and friendly societies; old people's homes; cultural activities, including theatre, reviews and literature; media, including newspapers, radio and television; self-esteem and the valuing of the émigré language and culture for their own sake, either in opposition to, or as complementary to, the language and culture of the host nation; the elaboration ('vitality') of the émigré language (Stewart 1968), or the range of roles which the language fulfils; motivation and desire to maintain autonomy and distinctiveness (abstand) from the host culture; in-marriage and the preservation of two-parent language and culture support, rather than outmarriage and integration with the surrounding community; folklore and culture maintenance, notably on national feast-days; and the ability of the community to sustain a fully articulated social, economic and cultural existence and identity. All these factors are wholly or largely within the control of the community itself. Other factors are not within the community's control, and yet can still have a decisive influence on the depth and effectiveness of language maintenance. These include ongoing immigration from the homeland, and good access for tourist, personal, cultural and economic return visits by the émigrés to the homeland. There is also the complex issue of the perception of the émigré community by the host community. There have been times when host nations have been apprehensive that the proliferation of émigré communities would weaken their own fabric. There was a fear in Canada during the early part of this century, for instance, that continued immigration would 'balkanize' Canada and turn it into a mosaic, rather than a country in its own right. That this has not happened has a lot to do with Canadian language policies, as well as with the inherently less separatist and confrontationist attitudes of the émigré communities themselves, including large groups of Russians, Ukrainians, Poles, Czechs, Slovaks and peoples of the former Yugoslavia. The other key factor, and one linked to the perception of the émigré communities by the host country, has to do with educational and cultural support. If educational policies encourage and value ethnic diversity and language maintenance, and make official provision for these in educational policies and curricula, the standing and self-esteem of the émigré cultures can be enormously enhanced. If they are not, the responsibility for education and maintenance falls on the émigré community itself. The tendency is for the language and culture to be ghettoized, either physically, or culturally, or both. After-hours schools are only a partial success, though educational immersion programmes on the Canadian model are more successful. Without at least a benevolent attitude on the part of the host country, émigré communities are forced to draw heavily on their own resources. In a hostile environment children of school age will tend to be drawn to the majority peer group. The coherence and motivation of the émigré group can be lost in less than a generation.

A typical example is the Ukrainian community in the United States, where the mechanisms for language maintenance have been described in detail by Nahirny and Fishman (1966). The nineteenth-century Ukrainian immigrants to the United States were predominantly of peasant origins. They had folklore and ethnic traditions, but less 'high' culture, since many were illiterate. On reaching the United States they had to change their underlying social pattern from one of a communal society (fairly homogeneous, kinship-based) to an 'associational society' based rather on mobility and external relations, often linked to employment:

> The major consequence of this transition from communal to associational society was that newly established ethnic communities had to be constituted on a network of voluntary associations and organizations. This consideration suggests at once that the vitality of ethnic organizations and associations – membership growth, organizational strength – represents one of the most meaningful criteria for gauging the generational continuity of ethnic groups in the United States.
>
> (Nahirny and Fishman 1966: 340–1)

In such a group the Orthodox and Catholic churches, as well as mutual-aid societies like the Ukrainian National Association, played a pivotal role, not only in the organizing and cohesion of the Ukrainian communities, but also in their relations with the non-Ukrainian communities of America. The Ukrainian Catholic and Orthodox churches in the United States counted 450,000 adherents in the 1960 census, while only 107,000 claimed the Ukraine as their birth-place. In the Ukrainian National Association, however, 65 per cent of members were foreign-born. The twin forces of American ideological nationalism and English ethnic dominance clearly have a major influence on the continuing membership of such societies. As Nahirny and Fishman observe, ethnic heritage among the Ukrainians has dwindled virtually to zero by the third generation, and Ukrainian-ness is then seen more in terms of religious and economic affiliations. The Canadian Ukrainians, who are concentrated more in rural areas, have fared scarcely better (von Raffler Engel 1979).

The broad-scale picture of Ukrainian migration to the United States is repeated in a number of large émigré communities, including the following: the Ukrainians in Britain and Canada; the Czechs and Slovaks in America and Australia; the Russians in America, Australia and Canada; the Sorbs, Kashubians and Slovenes in America; the other Yugoslavs in America, Australia, Canada, Germany, New Zealand and Sweden; the Macedonians in America and Australia; and the Poles in America, Australia, Britain and France. What is less expected is the way in which some quite small, and theoretically perilous, communities of Slavs in emigration have managed to preserve their language and culture against inroads from the host culture.

The Czechs of the Banat in Rumania present such a profile (Salzmann 1984). They migrated from Bohemia in the 1820s, seeking new opportunities in agriculture. Though now small in number (in the 1966 census a total of 9,978 for the whole of Rumania claimed Czech nationality, but only 6,116 claimed Czech as their mother tongue), they have survived a century of life in emigration with a good proportion of their language still intact. The village of Ravensca, with a population of only 240, shows very strong in-group allegiance. The Czechs there have engaged in less out-marriage than most émigré groups in the New World, and have identified their ethnic, cultural, linguistic and economic space as closely as possible with the village. Although their opportunities for schooling in Czech are restricted, and their employment prospects limited by the kinds of jobs which are available in and near Ravensca, they have compensated for a potentially precarious linguistic situation with strong internal solidarity. The area is fairly isolated, and there is not a great deal of traffic into or out of Ravensca. The Rumanian government seems to have left the Czechs fairly much to their own devices. As a result of geographical concentration, in-marriage, lack of physical mobility (many of the Banat Czechs seldom travel far from their home village), and internal cohesion, these Czechs have preserved a variety of Central Bohemian Czech which is distinct from both the Modern Czech standard and dialect varieties. In addition, their language shows some influences from Rumanian, although the nature and extent of these influences is constrained by the limited interactions of the Banat Czechs with the Rumanian speakers of the region. The women of Ravensca speak Rumanian distinctly less well than the men, who are the ones who travel outside Ravensca for employment.

The Doukhobors of Canada left their homeland in 1898–9 (Vanek and Darnell 1971). The Doukhobors (the name means 'spirit wrestlers') were one of the dissident splinter groups which left the Russian Orthodox Church in the seventeenth century. With the help of the novelist Tolstoj and the British Quakers, major groups of Doukhobors were resettled in Canada. Here they have formed a number of small, cohesive and inwardly directed communities, now numbering about 20,000 believers, mainly in Saskatchewan and British Columbia. Their social strength comes from shared values, including a rejection of civil and religious authority (including the authority of the Bible), and sometimes an antagonism to laws concerning property. Their language has been well maintained within the Doukhobor community, though with some innovative features which have found commonality with the communalistic ideology of the Soviet Union, and thus with homeland Russian.

A small Slavonic émigré community with strong cohesion but less favourable prospects are the Dalmatians of New Zealand (Stoffel 1982). The Dalmatians, who speak a variety of Serbo-Croat, came to New Zealand during the latter years of the nineteenth century to escape from the depressed economic conditions of their homeland. In New Zealand they formed one of the few trilingual Slavonic émigré communities (the others are principally Jewish), since their language now contains admixtures not only from New Zealand English, but also from the Polynesian Maori language. The New Zealand Dalmatians were few in number, and the immigration was sexually out of balance: of the original 5,468 settlers between 1897 and 1919, only 177 were women, with the result that outmarriage with English- and Maori-speaking women was a major factor from very early in their residence in New Zealand.

The recent Russian Jewish exodus from the former Soviet Union promises to be the last of the great Slav migrations, at least for the time being. Many have already reached Israel, bringing with them expectations and high qualifications. They are also experiencing considerable problems of settlement and resettlement. They will tend to gravitate towards the émigré Jewish communities in the countries where they settle, enriching the pool of especially Russian language expertise.

2.2 Social and core values

Language among the English-speaking peoples is not so much a part of their cultural identity and ethnic values, as a presumption. It is difficult for Anglophones to imagine conditions where the use of their native language is prohibited or restricted by a foreign occupying power. And yet this is what happened to most of the Slavonic nations at some point in their history. Poles in partitioned Poland could be expelled from school for using Polish, and parents organizing Polish classes in the Russian partition of Poland could be exiled to Siberia (Smolicz 1979: 59). If the Slavs had not had a fervent, and often desperate, loyalty to their language and their country, more Slavonic languages like Polabian would probably have perished, and émigré Slavonic languages would have vanished much more rapidly.

The close link between nation and language has its roots in the linguistic nationalistic movements of German Romanticism of the early nineteenth century. Herder (1744–1803), Fichte (1762–1814) and especially von Humboldt (1767–1835) were responsible for developing the idea of the

identity of language, state and homeland. This concept, powerfully reinforced by the revolutions of 1848 and the pan-Slavonic movement, contributed to the belief that a nation's boundaries should be set by its
linguistic limits, and that foreign domination by speakers of other
languages was contrary to natural law. These sentiments, and the ways in
which they were identified with national aspirations, have been one of the
most powerful forces acting for the maintenance and support of Slavonic
languages, both in the homeland and in the diaspora. Religious sentiment
has also been a major factor, since the Polish and Croatian Catholics, the
Ukrainian, Russian, Serbian and Bulgarian Orthodox believers and the
Czech Protestants, have all found support in the identification of language
with religion and country. Only Russian has been virtually free from threat
or repression, largely because of Russia's size and its political strength. All
the other languages have suffered at some time from linguistic repression
from foreign masters in the homeland: the Bulgarians, Macedonians and
Serbs from the Turks during the Ottoman Empire; the Croats, Slovenes,
Czechs, Slovaks and Poles from the Austro-Hungarian Empire; the Poles,
Cassubians and Sorbs from Prussia; the Poles, Belorussians and Ukrainians
from tsarist Russia; and the Belorussians and Ukrainians from Soviet
Russian hegemony. During these periods the Slavonic languages have
been, to different degrees, suppressed or hampered in their natural social
and cultural use. At the end of the First World War, indeed, 30 million
Europeans were left under foreign domination (excluding the Soviet
Union). The Charter of the United Nations, while affirming 'self-
determination of peoples', failed to define 'peoples'. This tacit acceptance
only served to compound existing linguistic problems: by 1939, for
instance, almost 40 per cent of the populations of Poland and Czechoslovakia consisted of ethnic minorities, including major groups of other
Slavs.

Survival in linguistic minorities under foreign domination is a skill which
the Slavs have practised over long periods. They learnt many mechanisms
to overcome linguistic repression. One was a strong culture of language in
the home and the cultivation of folklore and ethnic traditions, in the spirit
of the Romantic language movements of the nineteenth century. There
were also official organizations, such as the *matice*, established (where
permitted by the occupying powers, and as long as they were tolerated) as
centres of language and culture maintenance and enrichment. The very
issue of establishing the bona fides of a national language, and developing
it in the face of official discouragement, were major achievements. This is
particularly true of tiny groups like the Sorbs, the smallest modern Slavonic
language group, who number now probably less than 70,000 in their homeland within the former German Democratic Republic.

One answer to the problem of cultural and linguistic repression at home
was to take both culture and language elsewhere, to cultural centres in

Europe. During the nineteenth century there were many eminent cultural refugees, on a more or less temporary basis, in Europe's cultural capitals. There were colonies of Polish and Russian writers and musicians in Paris – the Russians, while linguistically secure in their homeland, were by no means secure from the tsarist police. Vienna was a gathering point for the Slavs of the Austro-Hungarian Empire. Political refugees from communism in the twentieth century have formed cultural and linguistic enclaves in many major centres in western Europe and North America.

The Slavs, then, have had experience in maintaining both their language and their culture within a strongly felt identity, but not necessarily in their homeland. Small wonder that this linguistic resilience should translate itself to the Slavs in emigration, or that they should stubbornly maintain their languages and cultures in the midst of host communities which were at best passive, and at worst antagonistic, to the presence of new and different ethnic groups.

2.3 Issues of language maintenance: policies and rights
The countries where the Slavonic languages are now used, both homeland and outland, seem on the surface to have common policies to preserve the rights of citizens to use their native languages. The Mexico Declaration on Cultural Policies, which was passed by the 1982 Second UNESCO Conference on Cultural Policies, explicitly underlines the role of cultural identity, cultural policies and cultural interrelations. The Helsinki Accords were designed to assure human rights among the European signatory nations. And the European Community has put in place policies which are formulated to safeguard access to national languages and cultures in its member nations. None of this is new. It was a feature of the first Soviet Constitution, and should have been one of the foundations of a Union-wide policy of human rights in the Soviet Union. Alas, ethnic rights sit ill with centralized autocracies, and tend to provide a focus for separatist movements and local dissent. So while Isaev (1977) presents the official picture of multilingual rights in the former Soviet Union, the reality has been less flattering. Even within the Soviet Union, Russian had a disproportionate percentage of media and publishing resources, and the rights of linguistic minorities included in the Soviet Union after 1945 were not safeguarded.

A policy which permits language use and cultivation is a start; but it is not the same as one which explicitly supports and facilitates ethnic languages and cultures. While the Slavonic languages – particularly behind the Iron Curtain – have nominally had the right to exist and be used, in many cases the speakers have had to provide the resources themselves, with little support from the state. Multicultural policies and policies which explicitly support bilingualism and national minorities, like those in Australia and Canada, are not the norm (Cobarrubias 1985). Attitudes in the host countries have sometimes been blatantly assimilationist. At other times they have been characterized more by neglect and lack of active support:

Forget your native land, forget your mother tongue, do away in a day with your inherited customs, put from you as a cloak all that inheritance and early environment made you and become in a day an American par excellence. This was precisely the talk I used to hear when I first came to this country. There was then as now, I regret to say, a spirit of compulsion in the air.

(Panuncio 1926: 194)

The field of education is probably the area where the lack of organizational support in language culture and maintenance has been most acutely felt. The recognition of émigré languages for the purposes of school and university entry and certification is a major factor in establishing and maintaining the self-respect of the émigré language among school-age speakers. The inclusion of émigré languages in regular school curricula, as opposed to after-hours or Saturday morning schools, is an even stronger step. National policies which officially affirm bilingualism, like those resulting from the Canadian Royal Commission on Bilingualism and Biculturalism, or the Australian National Policy on Languages (Lo Bianco 1987), provide a necessary framework for the maintenance of émigré languages as viable components of a multicultural society.

2.4   Standard languages

For Slavonic émigré communities there have been two principal models for language maintenance: the language originally brought by the first émigrés, and the modern standard. With the exception of intellectually motivated emigrations like the nineteenth-century colonies of Russians and Poles in Paris, or of the Slavs of the Hapsburg Empire in Vienna, or of the Russian Jews in contemporary Israel, the language of the original settlements was often based on dialects. Not infrequently, this was the dialect of an individual town or region, since émigrés from coherent regions in the homeland often settled together in the outland. While this situation provided a stable language base for about a generation, a number of factors tended to erode the coherence of the language model over time: the presence of speakers of various dialects in the outland community, the influence and intrusion of the outland's language, natural attrition of the émigré language through contact with other languages, and contact with the standard variety of the homeland language through written and media materials, newly arriving speakers and visits home.

All the Slavonic countries have strong, centralized organizational structures which are charged with the regulation and propagation of the language. This is usually in the hands of the institute of the national language, which forms part of the Academy of Sciences. There are often agencies in the homeland to provide newspapers, radio and television programmes for émigrés, as well as institutes which mount courses, notably for second-generation émigré children. The goal of these institutes, particularly before the fall of Communism, was partly the maintenance of language and culture; and partly, in the opinion of many older émigrés, for the purposes of what they regard as 'cultural imperialism' and the ideological, and well as the cultural, nurturing of subsequent émigré generations. Be that as it may, the national standard language is the basis of the overwhelming majority of published and recorded materials available to the émigrés. In long-established emigrations there have been systematic attempts to avoid changes taking place in the national standard. Emigré Russians, for instance, have tried to limit the number of neologisms which tended to flow naturally from Soviet Russian publishing. And there is no doubt that within half a generation there are clear stylistic differences between the homeland and the émigré press. None the less, the homeland standard is such a potent force that it tends to impinge, more or less directly, on patterns of language maintenance in emigration.

There has been a strong tendency to view émigré language variants as deviations from the norm, particularly when the émigré variant was not originally based on the standard variant. Only in more isolated communities, like the Czechs of the Banat (Salzmann 1984), has there been a tendency to preserve the local variant in the conscious awareness that 'this is not the way it is said in Bohemia'. The result of the homeland standard's influence has sometimes been a conflict of standards, particularly when the émigré press is fostering a variety and a style of language which may be based on norms already several decades old. Younger speakers find themselves uncertain of which model to follow: the variety spoken at home, which may well be dialectal; the standard propagated by the émigré media and publishing houses; or the standard emanating from the homeland. The result has often been a perception, particularly among the émigré youth, that whatever variety they speak, it will inevitably be a deviation from the standard.

This perception has also guided a large proportion of research on émigré languages, which has tended, explicitly, to use the national standard as a reference point. A welcome alternative is the approach of an informal group of linguists at several universities in the state of New York and at the Adam Mickiewicz University in Poznań. They take the view that contemporary American Polish is forming a norm of its own. Although this norm may differ from the Polish standard, it is none the less sufficiently regular, and sufficiently widely used across a variety of speech communities, to constitute a viable local variant. From this point of view American Polish can be considered on the same basis as regional variants in Poland. As Preston and Turner argue (1984), American Polish in western New York shows a systematic organization which makes it more than merely a deformed and debased variety of standard Polish. The principal factor against this analysis is the inherent instability of many émigré languages. Not only do they exhibit widespread variation; they also allow variation which, in frequency and distribution, is not comparable to the phenomena which we find in standard languages. The better established émigré Slavonic languages can, in certain functional respects, be almost as stable as dialects, at least over the time span of the first generation.

2.5 Abstand and elaboration

Studies of dialectology and multilingualism (Stewart 1968) have shown how abstand – the degree to which a language variety is distinct from contiguous variants – and elaboration – the extent to which the language fulfils a full range of communicative and social functions – are among the key factors affecting the interaction of languages in contact. Abstand and elaboration are also central to the formation, maintenance and functionality of the Slavonic languages at home and abroad (Sussex 1985).

For those Slavonic languages which have found themselves in other-Slavonic enclaves, like the Ukrainians and Belorussians in Poland between the world wars, abstand has indeed been an issue. Here the closeness of the languages has been able to threaten the maintenance and vitality of the émigré language, to the point where major interference and interpenetration have taken place. For the Slavonic languages further abroad, however, the issue of abstand is less critical. Most Slavonic variants abroad have been represented by small numbers of speakers, so that dialects have survived, if at all, on a very local basis. The principal question of abstand is therefore one of the regional variant versus the national standard, the variety championed by the ethnic press, media and authoritative organizations. As a result many émigré Slavs are functionally diglossic, speaking a regional variant but writing more or less correctly in the national standard. With the regional variant being threatened from two sides – the standard variant and the non-Slavonic host language – it can become more unstable and the level of interference can rise. In the written form of the language, however, writers tend to be more careful. This reflects the strongly authoritarian and purist view of the language taught in the Slavonic homelands and in emigration, with its strong bias against foreign expressions and non-standard usage. Among émigré Slavs, and particularly educated émigré Slavs, it is not uncommon to find correct, if slightly old-fashioned, written language, contrasting with major interference from the host language on the phonological, morphological, syntactic and especially lexical systems in their spoken language.

Elaboration is another matter. There is no doubt, as Clyne, Fishman, Haugen and others have shown for a variety of émigré languages, that the range, variety and depth of functions performed by the émigré language are major determinants of its continued vitality and integrity. Languages with restricted social and communicative functions, and particularly languages restricted to the home, will fail to develop a range of roles and functions which will sustain them in full vitality. The most successfully maintained Slavonic languages in emigration have been those which either concentrated their range of elaboration, like the Texas Poles or the Rumanian Czechs; or those which, by force of numbers and social outreach, have been able to place some constraints on their speakers from going outside the ethnic circle for employment and social advancement. Analyses like those of Nahirny and Fishman (1966) show how social institutions can provide an index to elaboration, and the ways in which it is implemented in émigré communities. The range of elaboration in émigré languages also has a major influence on their overall ecology.

2.6 Language ecology

The Slavonic languages overseas have shown, on the whole, typical ecological (Haugen 1953) features of languages in diaspora. There has been widespread interference from the host language, which has been more contained among adult, and especially educated adult, immigrants from the Slavonic lands. This interference has been much stronger with the second and succeeding generations.

There have also been some more specific studies of interference in émigré Slavonic languages. These have tended to concentrate on inflectional morphology and lexis, both areas where the traditional European pattern of schooling in the Slavonic homelands has been most obviously violated in the diaspora. Although few examples are as extreme as the (apocryphal, I hope) *nasi boysi runnuja po stryce* ('our boys are running around the street'), which is supposed to be Chicago Polish, the influence of host languages has been pervasive, intrusive and in some cases so extensive that the grammar of the émigré Slavonic language is no longer that of the mother tongue, but becomes a kind of interlanguage.

Parallel to the progressive interference from the host to the émigré language is the tendency for the émigré language to lose its powers of self-regeneration. Languages tend to freeze at the point of departure from the homeland, particularly when this departure is caused by political or military factors against the émigrés' will. Emigré Slavonic communities have tended to stand still linguistically, or to go into reverse, except in the largest émigré communities with sufficient numbers of speakers and a group of intellectuals, writers, journalists and other creative talents to develop further the language's response to its new environment. Emigré languages tend to be lexically passive: they fail to generate new words and expressions from indigenous stock. Since in the past they have usually been committed to political goals in conflict with those of the Slavonic homeland, they assiduously try to avoid sounding like the homeland standard. This in turn cuts them off from innovations in the homeland language. And émigré languages also tend to be formally conservative and prescriptive, with a very traditional approach to language learning and language maintenance, based on grammatical and translation models of language pedagogy. All of these factors tend to reduce the vitality and variety of the émigré languages, and to make them easier prey to incursions from the host language and culture.

Most modern Slavonic émigré groups find themselves in societies which are less actively antagonistic to the maintenance and preservation of other languages and cultures. But it is still far from easy for Slavs in emigration to ensure the preservation of language and culture in their children. Educational syllabuses, especially in the Anglophone world, are not notably open to initiatives for language study. And maintaining language through after-hours or Saturday morning schools is at best a second best. The biggest of the Slavonic émigré groups – in large cities like London, New York and Chicago – have had sufficient internal energy to maintain a minimal critical cultural and linguistic mass, together with the social and workplace conditions which this requires. On the whole, however, the host communities, even where they have been neutral or favourably disposed to the maintenance of émigré languages, have not been able to provide sufficient stimulus and enrichment. The current opening up of eastern Europe, and the increased interchange in people and expertise which it will engender, offer much better prospects for the émigrés and the fate of their languages.

3 Linguistic features

We now turn to the linguistic features of the émigré Slavonic languages. These follow the general order of sections in Chapters 3–17; but we do not present a full parallel structure, since many of the features which distinguish the Slavonic languages in emigration do not map directly on to the standard descriptive categories of these preceding chapters.

3.1 Orthography

The émigré Slavonic orthographies have been consistently more conservative than the homeland languages, particularly as regards spelling reform. The Soviet Russian spelling reform of 1917, which removed duplicated letters (the three forms of /i/, the vowel *jat'* and the redundant use of the hard sign after word-final hard consonants) was energetically opposed by émigré Russians, whose media and publishing houses continued to use the old spelling conventions, including *jat'*, long after these had disappeared from Soviet Russian usage. This conservatism was linked to the usage of Russian Church Slavonic, since the Soviet reforms marked a move away from more liturgical-like orthography.

3.2 Phonetics and phonology

(In this chapter only standard language forms, or forms which I have collected, are given with tones (Slovene, Serbo-Croat) or Cyrillic equivalents where appropriate. Most of the data are from the spoken language, and most were reported without stress or tone marks, so that the émigré Slavonic forms may or may not have been pronounced correctly.)

Although the phonetic systems of native-born adult Slavs tend to withstand interference moderately well, adolescent and younger children show systematic and regular interference from the host language. This is particularly true of children born outside the Slavonic homeland, whose pronunciation seldom achieves full native competence, and whose language often deteriorates after they start school, when the contact with the Slavonic-rich home is broken, and – with relatively few exceptions like Saturday morning language school – the educational environment is not oriented towards the Slavonic language, and in some cases is actively inimical to it.

Particularly prominent in these patterns of interference are near-identical families of sounds, where the articulatory settings of the host language impinge on those of Slavonic. Dental stops readily become post-dental/alveolar: Russian вот/vot 'here is': Australian Russian [vot], standard Russian [vot̪]. In English host contexts, voiceless initial stops before vowels are regularly aspirated as well: Polish *tam* 'there' Australian Polish [tʰam], standard Polish [t̪am]. Palatal fricatives are often assimilated to the host language's pattern, so that the less strident and rounded Russian /š/ is replaced by a more strident English-like [š]: Russian шум/šum 'noise': Australian Russian [šum], standard Russian [s̨um]. Similarly, the low-strident Czech /v/ ([ʋ]) is regularly replaced by the more strident English [v]: Czech *veselý* 'cheerful': British Czech [v-], standard Czech [ʋ-]. Velarized /ł/ in Bulgarian or Russian is replaced by a lighter, less velar [l]: Russian лук/luk 'onion': Australian Russian [l-], standard Russian [ł-]. There is a partial exception of word-final position, where the English tendency to use a more velar pronunciation, as in 'feel' [fiːł], helps to maintain the Russian norm.

Few sounds are safe from the tendency to assimilate to the host language pattern: there are cases where trilled /r/ is replaced by a flapped or English-like [ɹ] even among adolescent speakers within five years of their leaving the Slavonic homeland. Indeed, virtually the only sounds to remain untouched by interference in the consonant systems are the nasals /m n/, the fricatives /s z f/ and the glide /j/.

Most at risk are sounds which are difficult to pronounce. Czech /ř/ is regularly replaced by /r/, (phonetically [ɹ]), [ž], [dž] or [š]. Henzl (1982) presents these examples from American Czech:

Czech *pořád říkala* 'she kept saying': American Czech [poɹaːdɹekla], standard Czech [pořaːtřiːkala]; note the non-standard American Czech use of the perfective where standard Czech has an imperfective;

Czech *přáli* 'they wished': American Czech [pšijali], standard Czech [přa:li];

Czech *neřekl* 'he didn't say': American Czech [nežek], standard Czech [neřekl];

Czech *dobře* 'well'; American Czech [dobrže], [dobdže], standard Czech [dobře].

Stankovski, Ďurovič and Tomašević (1983) report a loss of palatals in the Serbo-Croat spoken in Sweden. Poles in English-speaking communities regularly lose the contrasts /sz ~ ś/, /rz ~ ź/, /ż ~ ź/, /cz ~ ć/, and normalize on a sound close to English /š ž č/. Palatals are lost, and palatalized series, as in East Slavonic, tend to merge with the unpalatalized series, so that Russian ýгол/úgol 'corner' and ýголь/úgol' 'coal' are both pronounced [ugəł]. The influence of English operates to remove word-final devoicing of voiced obstruents, according to which вот/vot 'here is' and вод/vod 'of waters' are pronounced identically in standard Russian. Assimilation of voice and place/manner of articulation in consonant clusters is progressively lost.

On the other hand, native Slavonic articulatory patterns are strong enough, at least in the first generation, to influence the pronunciation of borrowed words. For instance, Slavonic final devoicing of voiced obstruents is commonly carried over to English borrowings by those speakers whose native language has this characteristic (that is, not Ukrainian or Serbo-Croat). Observe also the tendency to follow English spelling in some cases, and English pronunciation in others: American Russian *džap* 'job', *beč* 'badge', *gut* 'good', *vikent* 'weekend', *najtklup* 'night club'. There is also a fairly systematic retrogressive assimilation of voice in consonant clusters: American Croatian *drukstor* 'drugstore' (Gasiński 1986: 37).

In the vocalic system there is frequent, and often radical, interference from the host language. Most of the research done in this area has involved interference of English on Slavonic. English patterns of stress and vowel-quality reduction in unstressed syllables can have a significant effect on fixed-stress languages like Polish and Czech, which have relatively less difference of energy between stressed and unstressed syllables, and relatively better retention of unstressed vowel quality, than in English. Slavonic pure vowels are often diphthongized and nasalized in those English dialects where such pronunciations are standard. And in the area of tone and stress, languages like the East Slavonic ones, with mobile and free stress, begin early to show major errors of stress placement. Mobile stress tends to normalize on the citation form, so that Russian рука́/ruká 'hand (NOM SG)', ру́ку/rúku (ACC SG), руки́/ruki (GEN SG) tend to standardize on the ending-stress of the nominative singular.

Interference phenomena are also clear in borrowed words and

expressions. Vowels like English [æ], which occur only marginally in Slavonic (for example between palatal(-ized) consonants in Russian) are represented by [e], [ɛ] in Slavonic émigré languages: *badge* – American Russian [bɛdž], [bɛtč]. English patterns of vowel quantity are not preserved in borrowed words: long (stressed) English vowels before voiced consonants are shortened: *room* [ɹuːm] – American Russian [rum].

The influence of regional dialects is strong in a number of areas, especially when both parents come from the same dialect area. This produces a clash with the national standard, which is the variety heavily promoted through the educational system and Saturday morning schools. Such is the Doukhobor treatment of Russian /g/, which in standard Russian is pronounced [g], or [k] in devoicing environments. In the genitive singular of masculine–neuter adjectives and pronouns, however, a written g, formerly the phoneme /g/, is pronounced [v]:

добрый/dòbryj	'good'	(MASC NOM SG)
доброго/dòbrogo	[-v-]	(MASC GEN SG)

In Doukhobor Russian /g/ is usually pronounced [ɦ], as in South Russian dialects. But unlike South Russian dialects this change takes place in *all* positions, including the genitive singular of masculine–neuter adjectives and pronouns. Some Doukhobor speakers, however, in an attempt to imitate what they imagine Modern Soviet Russian to be, overcorrect this written g to pronounce it as [g] instead of Modern Standard Russian [v]: thus Doukhobor доброго/dòbrogo [-g-] (Vanek and Darnell 1971).

In some communities speakers from a particular area have settled together in the same location overseas, which results in relatively better maintenance for non-standard variants. This is what has happened with the Czechs of the Banat in Rumania, and in Panna Maria in Texas, a Silesian Polish settlement now 130 years old (Rappaport 1990). Here the well-known features of mazurzenie, or Masurian pronunciation (see chapter 12, section 6), have been preserved from the homeland:

Standard Polish	*Panna Maria Polish*
z zeszłego roku 'from last year'	z zesłego roku (/š/ > /s/)
z mężem 'with my husband'	z męzem (/ž/ > /z/)
czytam 'I read'	cytam (/č/ > /c/)
jeszcze 'still'	jescc (/šč/ > /sc/)

The general effect of these changes on the sound systems of the émigré Slavonic languages is to decrease phonetic distinctiveness. As with Russian рука/rukà 'hand' (above), there is an increase in homophones. Phonologically contrasting pairs like Russian угол/ùgol 'corner' – уголь/ùgol′ 'coal' are increasingly poorly distinguished. It is not yet clear which of these types of interference might also have something to do with the inherent instability of the phonological systems of the émigré Slavonic languages.

Nor is it clear which features of – say – English are most intrusive, and in what order, in the phonology of émigré Slavonic.

3.3   Morphology

The general pattern in the inflectional morphology of émigré Slavonic languages has been predictable. Since the highly inflected Slavonic nominal morphological systems have been in contact with host languages with poorer noun morphology, especially West Germanic and Scandinavian languages, the case systems have suffered major reduction. This has not, of course, affected Bulgarian and Macedonian, which already show only the remains of their original case systems. And since the verb paradigms of Slavonic, particularly in the area of aspect, have not matched the patterns of the host languages, there has been decline in the range of verb paradigms, and in the variety of conjugational forms.

One of the most comprehensive studies of morphological decline has been carried out at the University of Lund by the JUBA group ('jugos-laviska barn', that is, 'Yugoslav children') led by D'urovič. Their focus was the Yugoslav immigrants to Sweden. During the 1960s and 1970s approximately 60,000 Yugoslavs made an economic migration to Sweden, and 81 per cent of these were speakers of Serbo-Croat. About 40,000 still remain in Sweden, and arrangements were made for the children to receive some instruction in Serbo-Croat from native-speaker teachers as part of their regular schooling. By 1983, the publication date of *Lingua in Diaspora*, nearly 550 children had been recorded in a longitudinal study of their spoken language. The transcription of the recordings has so far concentrated on the strictly segmental features of the informants' Serbo-Croat, and has not attempted to tackle the difficult issue of the interference of Swedish in the Serbo-Croat tone and quantity systems.

The data from inflection, however, are convincing. D'urovič (1983: 24) shows that children aged seven show a breakdown of remaining case forms; the numbers refer to the number of informants showing each repertoire of cases:

NOM, ACC:	3
NOM, ACC, GEN:	5
NOM, ACC, GEN, LOC:	2
NOM, ACC, LOC, INST:	8
NOM, ACC, GEN, INST:	4
NOM, ACC, GEN, LOC, INST, DAT:	4
NOM, ACC, GEN, INST, DAT:	1
NOM, ACC, GEN, LOC, INST, DAT, VOC:	2
NOM, ACC, GEN, INST, DAT, VOC:	not found

The locative is often replaced by the accusative. Preston and Turner (1984) find a very similar display of cases in American Polish, as does Gasiński (1986) for American Croatian. The order of maintenance of the cases shows a striking resemblance to Jakobson's 1936 analysis of markedness in the Russian case system (Jakobson 1984). There are also intriguing implicational universals: as Ďurovič notes, with the exception of the locative, the cases in his list predict the case forms to the *left*, so that (for instance) an informant with a genitive will always show a nominative and accusative as well.

The decline of case morphology is reported by a number of studies on émigré Slavonic languages: Albijanić and Jutronić-Tihomirović for American Croatian, Henzl for American Czech, Paternost for American Slovene, and Kouzmin for Australian Russian, to name but a few. Preston and Turner (1984) took this analysis a step further in comparing case usage in Polish-born and American-born Poles from Dunkirk, in western New York. Their results show some of the predicted degeneration of the case system when compared to standard Polish ('Polish' = Polish Poles; the figures are percentages of total case usage):

Nouns

	NOM	VOC	ACC	GEN	DAT	INST	LOC
Polish-born	28	0	27	27	0	4	14
American-born	28	1	31	24	1	4	12
Polish	34	0	19	27	3	5	12

Adjectives

	NOM	ACC	GEN	DAT	INST	LOC
Polish-born	47	23	22	1	1	5
American-born	48	28	16	1	1	7
Polish	49	19	20	1	4	7

The informants were four Polish-born, one German-born and twelve American-born Poles. Their performance is not radically different from the average Polish norm, with the exception of increased use of the accusative, and decreased use of the nominative. These figures, however, do not show correct or incorrect usages. A sample of the case used for negated direct objects, however, gives a more divergent picture (percentages of total case usage):

	ACC	GEN
Polish-born	6	94
American-born	28	72

where standard Polish would have an obligatory genitive. Here the Polish-born inhabitants of Dunkirk, N.Y. are already 6 per cent short of a perfect score, and the American-born clearly show the progressive loss of the use of the genitive in one generation. None the less, the overall results are surprisingly close to the standard Polish norms, though data from other studies suggest a much more radical degeneration in many other speech communities, particularly in the second generation.

Case systems degenerate not only in verbal government and in noun phrases. Meyerstein (1969) has found widespread simplification of noun case systems after prepositions in American Slovak, which goes as far as making nouns indeclinable. The normal proportion of indeclinable nouns in standard Slovak is about 3 per cent. First-generation immigrants made 6 per cent of nouns indeclinable, and second-generation immigrants scored 20 per cent.

No preposition in standard Slovak is followed by a noun in the nominative. In American Slovak, however, the nominative (the citation form) is used instead of various cases:

Standard Slovak	*American Slovak*
od jedného dňa (GEN) 'from one day'	od jeden deň (NOM)
okolo krku (GEN) 'around the neck'	okolo krk (NOM)
pri mori (LOC) 'by the sea'	pri more (NOM)
v lete (LOC) 'in summer'	v leto (NOM/ACC)

In émigré Slovak some complex noun phrases show mixtures of morphology, suggesting an uncertain mastery of the required forms:

Standard Slovak: od môjho tatu a manželky
                 'from my dad and wife'
American Slovak: od moju (F ACC) tata (M NOM) a manželku (F ACC)

The issue of how much case loss is found in émigré Slavonic, and how it is to be modelled, remain open questions. Henzl's (1982) data from Czech, for instance, show some informants who have collapsed all the cases into the nominative. Such analogical levelling is also common in case forms for child language learners. It remains to be seen whether language loss among Slavonic émigrés is recapitulating, in reverse, the natural language-acquisition chronology of native Slavs in the homeland.

These examples show the internal breakdown of grammatically distinct categories. This process, combined with false analogies within the émigré Slavonic language, can occur with numerals: Stankovski, Ďurovič and Tomašević (1983) report a new number *dvi*, on the model of *trî* and *čètiri*, in Swedish Serbo-Croat, replacing the original *dvâ/dvê/dvòje/dvòja* forms.

Internal simplification is also at work in the verbal paradigms. In West and South Slavonic the personal pronouns are optional in verb conjugations: Polish *czytam* '(I) read', *czytasz* '(you) read' and so on. In many émigré Slavonic languages the weakening of the verbal inflections – even to the extent of erasing the distinction between singular and plural in the Serbo-Croat spoken in Sweden (Stankovski, D'urovič and Tomašević, 1983: 19), presumably under the influence of Swedish – results in paradigms where the pronouns are now the only means of marking the person–number distinction. In Panna Maria Polish (Rappaport 1990) verb paradigms have been re-analysed and simplified, so that standard Polish *umieją* '(they) know (how to)' is now *umią*, the result of a normalization between two conjugational patterns. And gravestones at Panna Maria show variable morphophonology, so that standard Polish *urodził się* '(he) was born', *urodziła się* '(she) was born' emerge as *urodzioł się, urodzieła się*.

Tense/aspect systems also suffer: under the influence of English, Australian Russian has adopted a strong preference for the future imperfective with the auxiliary 'be', with the result that the future perfective (though not the past perfective) is largely lost in speakers below a certain level of competence:

Я бу́ду одева́ться./Ja bùdu odevàt´sja.
'I shall get dressed.'
(not я оде́нусь/ja odènus´: Kouzmin 1982: 83)

Knowledge of both aspect use and aspect forms is affected. Incompetent speakers will use verb forms indiscriminately, and will not use, and will not know at the meta-level, that Russian, for instance, tends to use the imperfective with negative commands.

3.4   Syntax

Interference in émigré Slavonic syntax comes from two principal directions: imitation of the syntax of the host language, and the decline in the inflectional system of the Slavonic languages, which reduces the means for marking grammatical relations, and makes the émigré Slavonic languages less synthetic and more analytic. Not surprisingly, émigré Slavonic languages show considerable simplification in syntax. The less common and more complex constructions of the standard languages, like expanded participal constructions:

Russian:
эта ещё не все́ми студе́нтами прочи́танная кни́га/èta eščё ne vsèmi studèntami pročitannaja knìga
(literally: this yet not by-all-students having-been-read book)
'this book, not yet read by all students'

are either simplified into relative clauses, or divided into conjoined clauses, or avoided: insecure speakers simplify the content of what they are willing to risk saying. Participles and gerunds are less common than in the standard language. Subordinate clauses and hypotactic constructions in general are proportionately less common and are often re-analysed into paratactic constructions. And utterances of weak speakers are often interrupted by exclamations and markers of indecision, taken from either language:

Russian:
Воло́дя, зна́чит, не предпочита́л, um, sort of, y'know, .../Volódja, znáčit, ne predpočitàl, um, sort of, y'know, ...
'Volodja, that is, didn't prefer ...'

A striking feature of the syntax of the émigré Slavonic languages is the decline in variety of word order. The well-developed inflectional systems of case making in Slavonic (excluding Bulgarian and Macedonian) allow wide variation in word order for information marking, pragmatics and stylistic purposes. To some extent the loss of word-order variation in émigré Slavonic is a consequence of the decline of the case inflections (above), with a resultant loss of means to distinguish grammatical relations. The languages then revert, as has been noted with examples like Jakobson's мать лю́бит дочь/mat´ ljùbit doč´ 'the mother loves the daughter' to Subject–Verb–Object order. This order is already more common in first-generation Slavonic émigré adults than in the homeland. And it is over-whelmingly dominant in the speech and written language of children who either emigrated before adulthood, or who were born outside the Slavonic homeland. One also finds copies of English word order in structures like preposed possessives in émigré Polish: *mojej siostry tata* 'my sister's father' (standard Polish: *tata mojej siostry*). Constructions like the passive present special problems. This construction is the regular way of marking the patient as the topic (known information) of a sentence in English, and is a regular alternative for inverted Object–Verb–Subject order in Slavonic:

Russian:
SVO: Ива́н купи́л кни́гу./Ivàn kupil knigu.
      'Ivan bought a book.'
OVS: Кни́гу купи́л Ива́н./knigu kupil Ivàn.
      'The book was bought by Ivan.'

Weaker speakers are not in full command of the passive. And since their case systems can lose the distinction between nominative and accusative, their syntax is often unable to express coherent sequences of old and new information.

In extreme cases émigré Slavonic languages can be partially pidginized, with almost no inflection, simplified constructions, an avoidance of all but the simplest verbs, and, in English-speaking contexts, SVO word order (Henzl 1982: 43):

American Czech:	telefon číslo
	'telephone number'
Standard Czech:	číslo telefonu, telefonní číslo
American Czech:	Slečna má pejseček.
	'The young lady has a little dog.'
Standard Czech:	Slečna má psíčka/pejsečka.

3.5   Lexis

The lexis of émigré Slavonic languages is the area most susceptible to inter-ference from the host language, and to degeneration from within.

3.5.1   Internal degeneration

The lexical degeneration of the Slavonic languages in émigré communities operates partly in conjunction with interference phenomena, and partly through the internal dynamics of the linguistic systems. We have seen how phonological and morphological categories and distinctions tend to break down, resulting in simpler formal systems and more lexical homophones, as well as more indeclinable nouns, or at least nouns which are not declined after prepositions. These processes can result in re-analyses of whole subsystems of linguistic structure.

The Lund group working on the language of Serbo-Croat-speaking children in Sweden, for instance, tested the knowledge of their subjects, aged from 6 to 14, on 50 common words like 'key', 'reads', 'elephant' in Serbo-Croat and Swedish. The researchers then ranked the words in order of response for both languages (Friberg 1983). The first 13 best-known words received a higher percentage for Serbo-Croat than for Swedish, and the remaining 37, with some major differences in rank-ordering, higher scores for Swedish than for Serbo-Croat. The researchers did not test 'core vocabulary' words like 'brother', but the results do pattern roughly with frequency of use, moderated by considerations of the kinds of words with which 6–14-year-old children would come into contact: the least successful were words like 'weight' and 'left-handed person'.

If the émigré Slavs' vocabulary is prone to erosion in this way, it is also subject to simplification as a result of the removal of too-close similarities. A case in point concerns prepositions in American Slovak (Meyerstein 1969). The preposition system itself is also undergoing simplification. Standard Slovak *od* 'from' and *z* 'from', both governing the genitive case, contrast semantically and grammatically with each other and with *s* 'with' which governs the instrumental. In the 'from' sense second-generation immigrants show a preference for *od*, which in the standard language is used principally with persons: *od matki* 'from mother', but *z kraju* 'from the homeland'. For these immigrants the choice between the two prepo-sitions for 'from' is not clear, and *z* and *s* are confused because they have almost identical pronunciations, depending on the first segment of the following word: [z] before voiced segments except /s/, /š/ and /z/, where it has the form [zo]; and [s] before voiceless segments; *s* also has an alter-nant [so]:

Standard Slovak: z kraju [sk-] 'from the homeland'
                      z krajom [sk-] 'with the homeland'

This overlap appears to contribute to the incorrect form: American Slovak *od kraju* 'from the homeland', with *od* taking over as the exclusive representative of 'from', leaving *z* for 'with'. The picture is further complicated by what is presumably a phonetically motivated confusion of *od* 'from' and *o* 'about', with the abandonment of the prepositional case form:

Standard Slovak:	o mašinách 'about machines'
American Slovak:	od mašini 'about machines'

A confusion similar to that created by *od* and *z* 'from' occurs with *u* 'near, by, at' with the genitive, and *v* 'in, at, on' with the locative. The problem is how to represent the spatial 'at' and 'in'. In general terms, standard Slovak uses *u* for people and *v* for places:

Standard Slovak:	u Johnsona 'at Johnson's'
	v našom meste 'in our town'

Meyerstein's informants never used *v* in place of *u*, but they did use *u* where standard Slovak has *v*: American Slovak *u našom meste* 'in our town'. There are possible phonetic explanations for this change, since Slovak, like Czech, has a low-strident /v/ which can sound like a weak [w] or short [u]. In this instance, unlike the *od/z/s* example, the system maintains the same number of items, but their functions fail to be properly distinguished.

A different phenomenon concerns the decay of lexical systems. The Doukhobors of Canada have been substantially separated from Soviet Russian for several generations, and there has been a corresponding lack of input from the homeland language. Doukhobor Russian shows, over three generations, a progressive decay of the system of kinship terms. It also shows a decay in the variety and use of diminutives, which are a characteristic feature of Slavonic nominal morphological systems, particularly kinship terms and proper names. While standard Russian often has more than six forms of Christian names, each with its appropriate level of intimacy and implications in terms of age and social status, the Doukhobors have collapsed the system to two or three terms, which are used without regard for their former capacity to define social levels of the speaker and hearer. A similar decay of interpersonal language is found in the use of the Russian pronouns ты/ty 'you (SG)' and вы/vy 'you (PL and/or polite SG)'. Doukhobors who came to Canada three generations ago used only ты/ty for singular address, with no form for polite address. The youngest generation does use the polite singular вы/vy in imitation of modern homeland Russian, but includes in the scope of вы/vy some affective functions, like 'being nice to someone', which are not part of homeland Russian (Vanek and Darnell 1971).

3.5.2   Interference

It is in the area of lexis that the émigré Slavonic languages have shown the greatest interference. There is nothing strange in the borrowing and grammatical assimilation of words for realia in the new homeland – *wimpy, kangaroo, boomerang, joint* are all borrowed freely. Very common are borrowings for currency, weights and measures, particularly imperial measures in the undecimalized United States. There is, however, greater importance in the borrowing of vocabulary items and idioms to replace existing expressions of the native Slavonic language. Haugen (1953) provided a taxonomy of borrowing which is still very useful: transfers, or direct lexical borrowings; extensions, where the meaning of a word is broadened from its original sense; loan translations (also known as calques), where the individual words in a phrase, or parts of a word, are translated without reference to the meaning of the whole; and hybrid compounds, involving a combination of one or more of the above. To these we add shifts, where words are borrowed *in toto* and with donor language phonology and morphology.

3.5.3   Transfers

Transfers, or the borrowing of a word into the Slavonic language, are endemic in émigré Slavonic languages. Transfers are one of the first signs of linguistic interference from the host language, and tend to progress in advance of the growing interference in phonology, morphology and syntax. They also penetrate the written language earlier than morphological or syntactic interference, and, once established in the émigré language, can form a stable and expanding core.

Some words are borrowed with phonological adaptation, and often with morphological adaptation as well to the norms of the recipient language. The less competent the speaker, the greater the proportion of unassimilated transfers. Kess (1970: 101) lists from American Slovene:

aker 'acre':
ki je doslej uničil 119,000 akrov grmovja in suhe trave
'which up to this time has destroyed 119,000 acres of bush and dry grass'
kontraktor 'contractor':
in kontraktorji gradijo vojaške instalacije
'and contractors are building military installations'

Sometimes word-building suffixes of the recipient language are added, as a further means of consolidating the status of the new word in the Slavonic language:

gerilec 'guerilla':
med ameriškimi četami in vietnamskimi gerilci
'between the American troops and the Vietnamese guerillas'

aplavdiranje 'applause':
so bili dclcžni vcliko navdušcncga aplavdiranja
'participated in much spirited applause'

Some loan-words are reborrowed: although Slovene had already borrowed *strike* as *štrajk*, American Slovene reborrowed it as *strajk*.

Adjectives, adverbs and verbs are less common as transfers in American Slovene. Some adjectives are taken over as loan-words without suffixation or agreement:

beig(e) 'beige':
Na razpolage so beige, plave, zlate, zelene in bele.
'Available are beige-, blue-, gold-, green- and white (coloured) ones.'

Some adjectives show both suffixation and agreement:

slumski 'slum':
da zatira revščino povsod v deželi, zlasti v slumskih distriktih velikih mest
'that poverty be eradicated throughout the country, especially in the slum districts of the large cities'

Verbs are almost always adapted with Slavonic morphology, usually with the productive verbal suffixes:

devaluirati 'to devaluate'
Funt sterling devaluiran za 14.3%.
'The pound Sterling was devalued by 14.3%.'

In émigré Polish, however, there is a common use of *misnąć* 'to miss', following non-productive Polish verb morphology patterns:

Misnąłem mój ulubiony program telewizyjny.
'I missed my favourite television progamme.'

Transfers are not an all-or-nothing phenomenon. Competent native speakers will adapt a transfer to the phonological and grammatical patterns of the Slavonic language. Less competent speakers will assimilate the borrowings less, and in extreme cases will switch (section 3.5.8; Clyne 1967) into the host language for whole phrases or clauses.

3.5.4 Transfers by part of speech
Lexical transfers in émigré Slavonic languages have been widely studied. They can be categorized by part of speech: function words (prepositions, conjunctions) are relatively seldom borrowed, verbs somewhat more frequently and adjectives more frequently still; but the most common class of borrowings is nouns.

The gender assigned to the nouns is subject to some variation. Benson (1957) reports that the phonological *form* of the noun was decisive in determining the gender assigned to it as a transfer: nouns ending in a consonant were assimilated into émigré Russian as masculine and so on. Dudek (1925: 205), however, finds that transfers into American Czech are influenced by the gender of the word they are replacing, a result also reported by Mencken for American Ukrainian (1936: 664). American Russian *strit* 'street', for instance, is parallel to American Ukrainian *strita* (standard Russian у́лица/úlica, standard Ukrainian ву́лиця/vúlicja). More recently Jutronić-Tihomirović (1985: 35) reports a number of such instances in Steelton (Pennsylvania) Croatian (the Croatian word being replaced is given in parentheses; all are feminine):

buka	'book'	(*knjïga*)
broša	'brush'	(*čëtka*)
blanketa	'blanket'	(*kùvērta*, from the Čakavian variant)
bolza	'bowl'	(*zdjëla*: note the formation from the English plural)
genka	'gang'	(*grüpa*)

All five English nouns end in a consonant, and would normally be interpreted on formal grounds as masculines on borrowing into Croatian. But the residual gender of the replaced word affects both the morphophonological form of the new borrowing, in the addition of the suffix *-a*, and its treatment in terms of declensional paradigms. Benson (1957) has parallel data from American Russian:

kara	'car'	(Russian маши́на/mašina)
farma	'farm'	(Russian фе́рма/férma)
korna	'corn' (on the foot)	(Russian мозо́ль/mozól')

He also records *rumsy* 'rooms', which echoes the American Slovene *bolza* 'bowl', but goes further in providing both an English (*-s*) and a Russian (*-y*) plural morpheme. *Rumsy* (singular *rum*) has a full range of case forms in the plural, like a regular Russian noun.

Many Slavonic languages contain lexical doublets, with one term of Slavonic origin, or of ancient borrowing into Slavonic, and one more recently borrowed. In émigré contexts the clear preference is for the non-Slavonic word over the established Slavonic one, as Benson (1957) reports from his study of Americanisms in the language of the American Russian press. The overwhelming majority of such words are either English borrowings, or are cognate with English words:

American Russian favours		*Standard Russian also has*
имити́ровать/imitirovat'	'to imitate'	подража́ть/podražát'

персонáл/personál	'personnel'	лúчный состáв/ličnyj sostáv
нуклеáрный/nukleárnyj	'nuclear'	я́дерный/jádernyj
пóмпа/pómpa	'pump'	насóс/nasós

It is necessary, in considering such lexical transfers, to take into account Anglicisms or other borrowings which have entered the homeland language's lexicon, or which have established themselves in preference to the Slavonic word. In Russian, while both языкознáние/jazykoznánie and лингвúстика/lingvistika 'linguistics' are regularly used, лингвистúческий/lingvističeskij is the only possible choice for an adjective (языковóй/jazykovój relates to язы́к/jazýk 'language', not to языкознáние/jazykoznánie), and this in turn exerts pressure in favour of лингвúстика/lingvistika over языкознáние/jazykoznánie. More recent examples from Soviet Russian cited by Benson (1957) include *boss, broker, dollar, donor, gengster, klerk, mimeograf, pikap* (pickup), *poker, polismen, prodjuser, reketir, tred-junion.* If such processes occur in the émigré Slavonic language, it is often impossible to say whether this merely emulates a development in the homeland language, or is influenced by it, or is an instance of transfer in its own right.

The phenomenon of lexical doublets is less common in Croatian and Czech, where there is a strong tendency to prefer Slavonic to non-Slavonic roots (Croatian *knjižnica*, Czech *knihovna* 'library'; compare Russian библиотéка/bibliotéka, Serbian *bibliotéka*). As a result, lexical borrowings have a more disruptive effect on the lexical identity of the language, since instead of reinforcing a preference for the non-Slavonic member of the pair, it involves transfer. Czech *klokan* 'kangaroo', for instance, is very often replaced by the borrowing (= transfer) *kenguru.*

The clearly less dominant tendency to borrow verbs appears to be linked to the problems of morphological adaptation: while it is possible to dispense with a large portion of case marking and still produce interpretable utterances, verbs require all or most of their conjugational properties to make sense. There are, for instance, quite a few indeclinable nouns in Slavonic, but very few verbs, usually onomatopoetic, as in Russian:

Russian:
а он хлоп в вóду/a on xlop v vódu
'and he goes/went splash into the water'

The forms in which verbs are borrowed often reflect simplified paradigms, sometimes using verb phrases with deverbal nouns in *-ing*: Australian Russian *ja budu delat' šopink* 'I'm going to do the shopping.' Verbs which are borrowed are assimilated directly into major regular paradigms (Albijanić 1982: 16):

American Croatian:
Oni su muvali.
'They moved.'
Nisu mu nika bilivili:
'They never believed him.'

The Slavonic tendency to code in preposition + verb sequences concepts which in English are represented as verb + adverb shows itself in a preference for the latter structure (Albijanić 1982: 16):

American Croatian:
Kad je otišao u Jugoslaviju natrag.
'When he went back to Yugoslavia.' (standard: *vrátio*)

3.5.5   Extensions

Extensions commonly involve a widening of the semantic coverage of the original term. American Russian systematically widens the meaning of a number of words which, though already present in standard Russian, have a more restricted meaning there. The new semantic scope is comparable to the scope of the cognate word in English:

	Standard Russian
бизнес/biznes 'business'	affair, business (often pejorative or disreputable)
картóн/kartón 'carton'	cardboard
клуб/klub 'club'	sporting club
митинг/miting 'meeting'	political meeting
сóда/sóda (US 'soda', 'soft drink')	various chemical salts

3.5.6   Loan translations

Loan translations occur in American Slovene as words or phrases, and often occur as part of word-for-word translations of phrases in the donor language. The word order tends to follow the order of the donor language. Kess's examples from American Slovene, which cover both partial and full loan translations, as in the Russian examples, include:

kolonialna hiša	'colonial house'
mehke pijače	'soft drinks'
sončna porč	'sun porch'
vroča zveza	'hot line'
zamrzniti	'to freeze' (in the sense of freezing financial deposits)

3.5.7   Hybrid compounds

Under 'hybrid compounds' we can also classify the common errors of collocation, which are often the result of generalizing the phrasal combinations of verbs in the host language to the Slavonic language. American Russian (Benson 1957), for instance, shows the following, all with clear interference from English:

делать деньги/délat' dén'gi 'to make money'
(Russian зарабатывать деньги/zarabátyvat' dén'gi)
брать поезд/brat' póezd 'to take the train'
(Russian ездить поездом/ézdit' póezdom)
брать русский язык/brat' rússkij jazýk 'to take Russian'
(Russian учить русскому языку/učit' rússkomu jazyků
поймать простуду/pojmát' prostúdu 'to catch a cold'
(Russian простудиться/prostudit'sja)
спрашивать вопрос/sprášivat' voprós 'to ask a question'
(Russian задавать вопрос/zadavát' voprós)

Particularly common and typical is the overuse of иметь/imét' 'to have'.
Russian does not usually use иметь/imét' for non-metaphorical meanings
of 'have', and instead has a construction based on 'at me is ...'. Phrases like

Мы будем там иметь ужин./My búdem tam imét' úžin.
'We shall have supper there'
(Russian Мы будем там ужинать./My búdem tam úžinat')

are common in émigré Russian, particularly in not fully competent
speakers.

3.5.8   Switching

Switching involves the importation of words and phrases unchanged into
the recipient language, as in Californian Croatian (Albijanić 1982: 13):

Ja sam rabotala ovde for nothing.
'I worked here for nothing.'
To su naš only expenses, only luxuries.
'Those are our only expenses, only luxuries.'

Switching is less interesting in terms of linguistic content, since it involves
the importation of unassimilated words and phrases. Its significance lies
rather in the sociolinguistic factors which accompany it, and the cognitive
issues which it raises in terms of processing and the capacity of the
speaker's native language competence.

3.5.9   Overview: lexicon

In terms of the functional efficiency of the lexicon as a whole, the lexical
innovations in the émigré Slavonic languages fall into four broad groups.

First, and most vilified by the purists, is gratuitous replacement, where a
native Slavonic word or expression has been replaced or otherwise changed
by the innovation.

Second are words for new realia and predicates (verbs, adjectives),
which are semantically and lexically justifiable, and offend native speakers
mainly by the avoidance of the possibility of using the resources of the
native Slavonic language. Sneakers are referred to in Poland as *adidasy*,

from the trade name Adidas, but émigré Poles will usually use *snikerz* (plural), even though 'Adidas' is more than familiar to them. Another key example is AIDS, which is very widely used by émigré Slavs as *ejdz*, in spite of the existence of well-known acronyms in the homelands (Russian СПИД/SPID, though many Slavonic countries use *ejdz* anyhow. Colloquial Polish, with wry humour, also uses *adidas* for AIDS).

Third is a group of near-replacements, often corresponding to Haugen's 'extensions', where native Slavonic words have been re-adapted to fit the new conditions and realia. In North America and Australasia many people live in self-contained houses. But *dom* is not necessarily an accurate translation, since in Slavonic languages *dom* very often refers to a whole block of flats. Is Russian да́ча/dáča a viable designation for what is called variously in English a *bungalow, weekender, weekend house/cottage, crib, holiday house* or *batch*? Even 'school' (in North America covering primary, secondary and post-secondary, and in Britain and Australasia only the former two levels) does not match with *škola* in the Slavonic education systems: consider Russian вы́сшая шко́ла/výsšaja škóla (*not* 'high school' but closer to 'university' or North American 'college'). A *professor* in the Slavonic homeland is fairly close to a (university) professor in Britain or Australasia, but not at all like the North American professor. And there is the problem of the ideological and evaluative meaning of political and economic words like *east, west, socialist, communist, bourgeois*, which until 1990 had different rhetorical and connotative systems. Such words become tantamount to lexical *faux amis*: their apparent portability conceals differences of culture, economic or social function. And the traditional lexical *faux amis*, in émigré speakers, are often and catastrophically misused: Polish *karawan* 'funeral cortege' for 'caravan', *bękart* 'bastard', used for 'bank card' and so on.

And fourth is a group where tendencies of the homeland language towards lexical innovation, change and borrowing are mirrored in the émigré language, but without clear proof of cause and effect. This last category is particularly evident with English, which is the major current source of internationalisms. The Swedish-speaking Yugoslavs studied in the Lund experiments could find virtually no Swedish words in the Serbo-Croat spoken in the homeland, although some of the English-derived internationalisms which are also part of Modern Swedish also find a place in contemporary homeland Serbo-Croat.

It is also possible to make some comparisons between different émigré groups. Albijanić (1982) contrasts the treatment of loan-words in Pennsylvania Croatian, as reported by Jutronić, with his own data for California. He finds that the Pennsylvania Croats' language has lost more than the Californian. In Pennsylvania there is a stronger preference to neutralize all cases to the nominative, and for invariant adjectives to replace inflected ones. Furthermore, the proportion of loan-words differs:

	First generation (%)	Second generation (%)
Pennsylvania	8.1	19
California	5.4	8.9

And assimilated loan-words are markedly more common in second-generation Californians than in second-generation Pennsylvania Croats:

	First generation (%)	Second generation (%)
Pennsylvania	99	11
California	99	50

which indicates a higher degree of retention of the grammatical system, even with words which, from an outside source, would otherwise be more susceptible to morphological loss.

4   Conclusion

The émigré Slavonic communities have striven long to maintain their languages and cultures in the diaspora. Some communities have been remarkably successful over a number of generations, like the Poles of Panna Maria, Texas. Many communities have been revitalized by a sporadic but ongoing migration from, and interchange with, the homeland. But what will be the ultimate fate of these communities, and their longer-term identity in the midst of non-Slavonic cultures?

Saint-Jacques (1979), in reviewing the immigrant language communities of Canada, has an overall pessimistic view of their longer-term survival as entities distinct from the English, and to a lesser degree French, macro-groups. As he argues, language and culture are largely dead in fourth-generation migrants, and are at best passive in third-generation migrants. And this in a country where 30 per cent of the population is not of English, French or Canadian Indian stock, and where a quarter of all the incoming migrants settle in Ontario, creating groups of more than minimal critical mass. In Saint-Jacques's view, the rural areas have been more successful in language and culture maintenance than the urban (the Doukhobors, though rural and an apparent confirmation for this generalization, are probably too atypical as an immigrant group to be considered under average parameters of culture maintenance). Some ethnic groups, notably the Germans and the Dutch, achieve a switch to English for children–parent communication within five to six years of arrival in Canada, so that the survival of these communities as linguistically viable entities depends almost entirely on immigration. The Italians and Chinese, and several small groupings of Japanese, on the other hand, have established and maintained a higher level of language and culture retention. Nevertheless, third-generation children are showing the same rate of language and culture loss as that found in other groups, which include large settlements of Ukrainians (the fifth largest ethnic group in Canada) and Poles, of whom more than 100,000 arrived in Canada between 1946 and 1970. Data reported in Kubijovyč (1971) show that in 1941, 5.1 per cent of persons of Ukrainian origin reported that their mother tongue was English. The figure was 10.6 per cent in 1951 (in spite of the large influx of post-war Ukrainian immigrants), and 23.6 per cent in 1961.

The central factor in the decline of émigré languages and cultures, in Saint-Jacques's view, has to do with perceptions of prestige models:

The most powerful and most universal factor of integration and assimilation remains the desire for *identification with the majority group, the prestige group: the Anglophone community of Canada.* This is particularly evident with the youth of the various ethnic groups. The desire for identification includes all aspects of human behavior: plays, ways of dressing, recreation, food, the set of values, and finally the language. Linguistic identification means to speak English perfectly and without accent. It means therefore the possibility to be recognized and accepted as one of the prestige group. The desire to identify with the peers, the prestige group, is so powerful that it implies the rejection of everything which could delay this identification. This includes one's mother-tongue.... After a while, when the youth has lost even the comprehension of the mother tongue, parents have to shift to English to be understood by their children.

(1979: 212)

Saint-Jacques's own research into language maintenance in Canada supports this interpretation. But for the Slavs the context is changing, and with it some of the prospects for language maintenance. Major changes in the former Soviet Union, the break-up of Comecon and the Warsaw Pact and the return of countries like Poland, the Czech Republic, Slovakia, East Germany, Hungary and Bulgaria to self-rule are having some major consequences for language maintenance, language policy and educational implementations in these countries. The new regimes in eastern Europe, and their more open policies, will certainly result in the return to the homeland of some émigrés. But it will also result in more emigration from the Slavonic homelands. These movements of peoples will potentially enrich and sustain language and culture more effectively than has been possible in the past, where the émigré communities have had to assert their identity, abstand and elaboration not only from the surrounding communities of the host countries, but also from the potentially threatening models of their homelands.

The full effect of these changes is hard to foresee. In the first place, the removal of the Soviet Union as the dominating partner in economic, cultural and military life in eastern Europe will inevitably lead to a radical lessening in the importance of Russian as an international, and indeed as a national, language. Throughout eastern Europe the predominance of the Soviet military and the use of Russian as a means of international communication in military service will be removed with the departure of the

Soviet troops. The economic weakness of the former Soviet Union will reduce the imperative for learning Russian throughout eastern Europe, while the new markets of western Europe, Asia and the Americas will provide a major incentive for the learning of those languages.

Parallel to the weakening of the role and function of Russian in international affairs – it will still remain an official language of the United Nations – is a major resurgence of national spirit, and pride in the national language, in the homelands. We find here the logical conclusion to Herder's concept of the unity of language and homeland: throughout eastern Europe and the former Soviet Union, nations are pressing for varying degrees of autonomy. The traditional identification of nationalist sentiment with language, and the view of language as something between the carrier of the national pride and a holy grail, are leading to political disintegration. The former Yugoslavia is an archetypal example. While 87 per cent of its population consisted of Serbs, Croats, Slovenes and Macedonians, there was a vigorous 13 per cent comprising Albanians, Bulgarians, Czechs, Italians, Hungarians, Poles, Rumanians, Slovaks, Turks and Ukrainians. The decentralized nature of Yugoslavia's political structure helped it to make some accommodations to the needs of its major linguistic groups, as did the decentralized, and well-tried, model of Switzerland.

The émigré Slavonic communities in Europe, the Americas and Australia are already feeling some effects of the changes in eastern Europe. The Hungarians have returned the crown of St Stephen to Hungary, and the Polish government in exile in London has returned the Polish Constitution to the new government of Poland. With the passing of émigré governments in exile, the communities who have struggled so long, and so effectively, to maintain their language and culture will find some loss of identity and purpose. The émigré Poles, who found such stimulus during the period of Solidarity in Poland, are already finding that the sentiments which sustained a feeling of ethnic and linguistic identity outside the homeland are significantly less potent.

This tendency will be offset, to some extent, by migration from the Slavonic homelands to the west. This is already happening in major quantities with Russian Jews, who are leaving the former Soviet Union for Israel at an increasing rate. If they gravitate to the émigré communities in the diaspora, the future of émigré Russian is more secure, at least for the next generation. There is also, however, a growing tendency for émigré Slavs to consider returning home, particularly with western currency. One can predict that the influx of such revenants, bringing with them significant quantities of westernized vocabulary, may well have an internationalizing, and also denationalizing, effect on the lexicons of the Slavonic languages in the homelands.

References

The sources relating to the Slavonic languages in emigration are widely dispersed. We have drawn particularly on the materials listed in Magner (1982), who includes a number of citations which, though not devoted purely to linguistic topics, are relevant to research in the fields of sociolinguistics, bilingualism and languages in contact. In addition, there are bibliographic resources and research centres, mentioned in Magner (1982), which are relevant to the researcher in the area of Slavonic languages in emigration:

1   Immigration History Research Center, University of Minnesota, 826 Berry St, St Paul, Minnesota 55114, USA.
2   Ethnic Studies Research Project (Professor Andrei Simić), Department of Anthropology, University of Southern California, Los Angeles, CA 90089–0032, USA. Simić's description of his bibliography, quoted from Magner (1982: 94), is as follows:

An archive of over 8,000 annotated entries regarding East European ethnic groups outside their homelands, principally in the United States and Canada but including Latin America and Australia. The file includes entries for forty nationalities (Slavic and non-Slavic), and covers such topical areas as: archives, bibliographies, journals and periodicals, newspapers, academic programs, scholars engaged in research on these groups, voluntary associations, media (radio and T.V.), religious institutions, and other foci of ethnic articulation.

Albijanić A. (1982) 'San Pedro revisited: language maintenance in the San Pedro Yugoslav community', in Roland Sussex (ed.) *The Slavic Languages in Emigre Communities*, Carbondale and Edmonton: Linguistic Research Inc., 11–22.
Albin, A. and Alexander, R. (1972) *The Speech of Yugoslav Immigrants in San Pedro, California* (Research Group for European Migration Problems 17), The Hague: Nijhoff.
Benson, Morton (1957) 'American influence on the immigrant Russian press', *American Speech* 32: 257–63.
—— (1960) 'American Russian speech', *American Speech* 35: 163–74.
Canada. Royal Commission on Bilingualism and Biculturalism (1969), *The Cultural Contribution of the Other Ethnic Groups*, Ottawa: Queen's Printer.
Cigler, M. (1983) *The Czechs in Australia*, Melbourne: A.E. Press.
Clyne, Michael G. (1967) *Transference and Triggering*, The Hague: Martinus Nijhoff.
—— (1982) *Multilingual Australia*, Melbourne: River Seine.
Cobarrubias, J. (ed.) (1985) *Language Policy in Canada: Current Issues*, Quebec: CIRB.
Darnell, Regna (ed.) (1973) *Canadian Languages in their Social Context*, Edmonton and Champaign: Linguistic Research Inc.
Davies, N. (1981) *God's Playground: a History of Poland*, London: Oxford University Press.
Décsy, G. (1973) *Die linguistische Struktur Europas*, Wiesbaden: Otto Harrassowitz.
Doroszewski, W. (1938) *Język polski w Stanach Zjednoczonych*, Wydział 1, Nr. 15, Warsaw: Prace Towarzystwa Naukowego Warszawskiego.
Dudek, J.B. (1925) 'The Czech language in America', *The American Mercury* 5: 202–7.
Ďurovič, Ľ. (1983) 'The case systems in the language of diaspora children', in *Lingua in Diaspora: Studies in the Language of the Second Generation of*

Yugoslav Immigrant Children in Sweden = Slavica Lundensia 9: 21–94.

Fishman, Joshua A. (1966) *Language Loyalty in the United States*, London, The Hague and Paris: Mouton.

Fishman, Joshua A. and Hofman, John E. (1966) 'Mother tongue and nativity in the American population', in Joshua A. Fishman, *Language Loyalty in the United States*, London, The Hague and Paris: Mouton, 34–50.

Friberg, Ann-Christin (1983) 'The vocabulary test', in *Lingua in Diaspora: Studies in the Language of the Second Generation of Yugoslav Immigrant Children in Sweden = Slavica Lundensia* 9: 95–9.

Gasiński, T.Z. (1986) 'English elements in the speech of the Croatian immigrant community of Santa Clara Valley, California', *Zborik matice srpske za filologiju i lingvistiku* (Novi Sad) 29 (2): 31–45.

Gilberg, Trond (1978) 'Multilingualism, ethnic separatism and political decision-making in Socialist Romania', in William R. Schmalstieg and Thomas F. Magner (eds) *Sociolinguistic Problems in Czechoslovakia, Hungary, Romania and Yugoslavia*, Columbus, Ohio: Slavica, 353–87.

Haugen, E. (1953) *The Norwegian Language in America*, Philadelphia: University of Pennsylvania Press.

Henzl, V.M. (1982) 'American Czech: a comparative study of linguistic modifications in immigrant and young children speech', in Roland Sussex (ed.) *The Slavic Languages in Emigre Communities*, Carbondale and Edmonton: Linguistic Research Inc., 33–46.

Hill, P. (1991) *The Dialect of Gorno Kalenik*, Columbus, Ohio: Slavica.

Isaev, M.I. (1977) *National Languages in the USSR: Problems and Solutions*, Moscow: Progress.

Jakobson, R. (1984) 'Contribution to the general theory of case: general meanings of the Russian cases', in Roman Jakobson, *Russian and Slavic Grammar: Studies 1931–1981*, The Hague: Mouton, 59–103. (Originally published in 1936.)

Jutronić-Tihomirović, D. (1976) 'Language maintenance and language shift of the Serbo-Croatian language in Steelton, Pennsylvania', *General Linguistics* 16: 166–86.

—— (1985) *Hrvatski jezik u SAD*, Split: Logos.

Kess, J. (1970) 'Some English borrowings in the American Slovenian press', *General Linguistics* 10: 96–110.

Kouzmin, L. (1982) 'Grammatical interference in Australian Russian', in Roland Sussex (ed.) *The Slavic Languages in Emigre Communities*, Carbondale and Edmonton: Linguistic Research Inc., 73–87.

Kubijovyč, V. (ed.) (1971) *Ukraine: a Concise Encyclopedia*, Toronto: University of Toronto Press.

Lencek, R.L. and Magner, T.F. (eds) (1976) *The Dilemma of the Melting Pot = General Linguistics* 16 (2–3).

Lewis, E. Glyn (1972) *Multilingualism in the Soviet Union*, The Hague: Mouton.

Lingua in Diaspora (1983) *Studies in the Language of the Second Generation of Yugoslav Immigrant Children in Sweden = Slavica Lundensia* 9.

Lo Bianco, J. (1987) *National Policy on Languages*, Canberra: Department of Education.

Lyra, F. (1966) 'Integration of English loans in U.S. Polish', *The Slavic and East European Journal* 10 (3): 303–12.

Magner, T. (1976) 'The melting pot and language maintenance in South Slavic immigrant groups', *General Linguistics* 16: 59–67.

—— (1982) 'Bibliography of publications on immigrant Slavic languages in the United States', in Roland Sussex (ed.) *The Slavic Languages in Emigre Com-*

munities, Carbondale and Edmonton: Linguistic Research Inc., 89–95.

Mencken, H.L. (1936) *The American Language*, New York: Knopf.

Meyerstein, G.P. (1969) 'Interference in prepositional phrases: immigrant Slovak in America', *Lingua* 22: 63–80.

Nahirny, Vladimir C. and Fishman, Joshua A. (1966) 'Ukrainian language maintenance efforts in the United States', in Joshua A. Fishman, *Language Loyalty in the United States*, London, The Hague and Paris: Mouton, 318–57.

Neweklowsky, Gerhard (1984) 'Investigating Burgenland-Croatian dialects', in Roland Sussex (ed.) *The Maintenance of the Slavonic Languages Abroad = Melbourne Slavonic Studies* 18: 1–14.

Panuncio, C.M. (1926) *The Soul of a Migrant*, New York: Macmillan.

Paternost, J. (1976) 'Slovenian language in Minnesota's Iron Range: some sociolinguistic aspects of language maintenance and language shift', *General Linguistics* 16: 95–150.

Perkowski, Jan L. (1969) *A Kashubian Idiolect in the United States*, Bloomington, Ind.: Indiana University, and The Hague: Mouton.

Preston, Dennis R. and Turner, Michael (1984) 'The Polish of Western New York: case', in Roland Sussex (ed.) *The Maintenance of the Slavonic Languages Abroad = Melbourne Slavonic Studies* 18: 135–54.

Rappaport, G. (1990) 'Sytuacja językowa Amerykanów polskiego pochodzenia w Teksasie' in W. Miodunka (ed.) *Język polski w świecie*, Kraków: PAN, 159–78.

Saint-Jacques, B. (1979) 'The languages of immigrants: sociolinguistic aspects of immigration in Canada', in J.K. Chambers (ed.) *The Languages of Canada*, Ottawa: Didier, 207–25.

Salzmann, Zd. (1984) 'Some observations on the Czech spoken by the villagers of Ravensca in the Southern Romanian Banat', in Roland Sussex (ed.) *The Maintenance of the Slavonic Languages Abroad = Melbourne Slavonic Studies* 18: 65–118.

Smolicz, J.J. (1979) *Culture and Education in a Plural Society*, Canberra: Curriculum Development Centre.

Stankovski, M., Ď'urovič, Ľ, and Tomašević, M. (1983) 'Development structures in the family language of Yugoslav immigrant children in a Swedish language environment', in *Lingua in Diaspora: Studies in the Language of the Second Generation of Yugoslav Immigrant Children in Sweden = Slavica Lundensia* 9: 11–20.

Stephens, Meic (1976) *Linguistic Minorities in Western Europe*, Llandysul: Gomer Press.

Stewart, W.A. (1968) 'A sociolinguistic typology for describing national multilingualism', in Joshua Fishman (ed.) *Readings in the Sociology of Language*, The Hague: Mouton, 531–45.

Stoffel, H.-P. (1982) 'Language maintenance and language shift of the Serbo-Croatian language in a New Zealand Dalmatian community', in Roland Sussex (ed.), *The Slavic Languages in Emigre Communities*, Carbondale and Edmonton: Linguistic Research Inc., 121–39.

Stölting, W. (1984) 'Serbo-Croatian in the Federal Republic of Germany', in Roland Sussex (ed.) *The Maintenance of the Slavonic Languages Abroad = Melbourne Slavonic Studies* 18: 26–45.

Straka, Manfred (ed.) (1970) *Handbuch der Europäischen Volksgruppen*, Vienna: Braumüller.

Sussex, Roland. (ed.) (1982a) *The Slavic Languages in Emigre Communities*, Carbondale and Edmonton: Linguistic Research Inc.

—— (1982b) 'The phonetic influence of Australian English on Australian Polish', in Roland Sussex (ed.) *The Slavic Languages in Emigre Communities*,

Carbondale and Edmonton: Linguistic Research Inc., 141–53.
—— (ed.) (1984) *The Maintenance of the Slavonic Languages Abroad* = *Melbourne Slavonic Studies* 18.
—— (1985) 'Lingua nostra: the nineteenth-century Slavonic language revivals', in Roland Sussex and J.C. Eade (eds) *Culture and Nationalism in Nineteenth-Century Eastern Europe*, Colombus, Ohio: Slavica, and Australian National University, Canberra: Humanities Research Centre, 111–27.
Sussex, Roland and Zubrzycki, Jerzy (eds) (1985) *Polish People and Culture in Australia*, Canberra: The Australian National University.
Vanek, Anthony L. and Darnell, Regna (1971) 'Canadian Doukhobor Russian in Grand Forks, B.C.: some social aspects', in Regna Darnell (ed.) *Linguistic Diversity in Canadian Society*, Edmonton and Champaign: Linguistic Research Inc., 267–90.
von Raffler Engel, W. (1979) 'The language of immigrant children', in J.K. Chambers (ed.) *The Languages of Canada*, Ottawa: Didier, 226–59.
Weinreich, Uriel (1957) *Languages in Contact*, The Hague: Mouton.
Wierzbicka, Anna (1985) 'Different cultures, different languages, different speech acts: Polish vs. English', *Journal of Pragmatics* 9: 145–78.

Index

Note: Page references in italics indicate tables.